Lecture Notes in Artificial Intelligence   7637

Subseries of Lecture Notes in Computer Science

Juan Pavón
Néstor D. Duque-Méndez
Rubén Fuentes-Fernández (Eds.)

Advances
in Artificial Intelligence –
IBERAMIA 2012

13th Ibero-American Conference on AI
Cartagena de Indias, Colombia, November 13-16, 2012
Proceedings

 Springer

Series Editors

Randy Goebel, University of Alberta, Edmonton, Canada
Jörg Siekmann, University of Saarland, Saarbrücken, Germany
Wolfgang Wahlster, DFKI and University of Saarland, Saarbrücken, Germany

Volume Editors

Juan Pavón
Rubén Fuentes-Fernández
Universidad Complutense de Madrid
Facultad de Informática
c\ Profesor José García Santesmases, 28040 Madrid, Spain
E-mail: {jpavon, ruben}@fdi.ucm.es

Néstor D. Duque-Méndez
Universidad Nacional de Colombia
Carrera 30 No 45-03, Edificio 477, Bogotá DC, Colombia
E-mail: ndduqueme@unal.edu.co

ISSN 0302-9743   e-ISSN 1611-3349
ISBN 978-3-642-34653-8   e-ISBN 978-3-642-34654-5
DOI 10.1007/978-3-642-34654-5
Springer Heidelberg Dordrecht London New York

Library of Congress Control Number: 2012950602

CR Subject Classification (1998): I.2.6-9, H.3-5, I.4, I.2.3, I.2.11, F.1

LNCS Sublibrary: SL 7 – Artificial Intelligence

Typesetting: Camera-ready by author, data conversion by Scientific Publishing Services, Chennai, India

Printed on acid-free paper

Springer is part of Springer Science+Business Media (www.springer.com)

Preface

IBERAMIA is the biennial Ibero-American Conference on Artificial Intelligence. This volume presents the proceedings of the 13th edition in this series, IBERAMIA 2012, held during November 13–16, 2012, in Cartagena de Indias (Colombia). The conference is supported by the main Ibero-American societies of artificial intelligence (AI), and provides researchers from Portugal, Spain, and Latin America the opportunity to meet with AI researchers from all over the world. Since its inception (Barcelona, 1988), IBERAMIA has expanded its scope to become a well-recognized international conference in the AI field. Its papers have been published in English by Springer in the LNCS/LNAI series since the sixth edition in Lisbon (1998).

The organizational structure of IBERAMIA 2012 was similar to other international scientific conferences. The backbone of the conference was the scientific program, which is complemented by tutorials, workshops, and open debates on the principal topics of AI.

The scientific program of the conference was organized along several areas, co-ordinated by Area Chairs. Each submitted paper was reviewed by three members of the Program Committee (PC), coordinated by the corresponding Area Chair. In certain cases, extra reviewers were recruited to write additional reviews. The PC consisted of 220 researchers from 29 different countries. The statistics of the PC members are shown in Table 1; the full list of Area Chairs, PC members, and reviewers can be found in the pages after this preface.

Table 1. PC members by country

Country	PC Members	Country	PC Members
Argentina	16	Korea	1
Australia	1	Malaysia	1
Austria	1	Mexico	25
Belgium	3	The Netherlands	1
Brazil	46	Norway	1
Canada	2	Poland	2
Chile	5	Portugal	32
Cuba	3	Slovenia	1
Cyprus	1	Spain	45
Czech Republic	1	Turkey	1
France	6	UK	5
Germany	4	USA	5
Greece	1	Uruguay	1
Ireland	1	Venezuela	3
Italy	5	Total:	220

IBERAMIA 2012 received 170 papers from 23 different countries, 11 from Ibero-America, and 12 from other regions of the world, attesting to the truly international nature of the conference. After review by the international PC, 75 papers were accepted for presentation and publication in this volume. The number of submissions to IBERAMIA is similar to the last edition, but it seems that the quality has considerably improved, according to the reviews that papers received. The Program Chair together with the Area Chairs considered whether to maintain a lower rate of acceptance, as in previous editions at around 30%, but this would imply rejecting papers that did not receive any negative review or relevant points against them. Because of this, the acceptance rate is around 44% this time. By areas, the distribution of submissions and accepted papers is the following:

Table 2. Contributions for each area

Area	Submitted	Accepted
AI in Education	14	7
Bioninspired computing	17	7
Information and Knowledge Processing	3	1
Knowledge Discovery and Data Mining	19	10
Knowledge Engineering and Applications	12	5
Knowledge Representation and Reasoning	4	4
Machine Learning and Data Mining	26	10
Multi-Agent Systems	15	4
Natural Language Processing	9	4
Planning and Scheduling	10	4
Computer Vision and Robotics	20	10
Uncertainty and Fuzzy Systems	4	4
Modelling and Simulation	9	3
Human-Computer Interface	5	1
Ambient Intelligence	3	1
Total:	170	75

We would like to express our sincere gratitude to all the people who helped to bring about IBERAMIA 2012. First of all, thanks to the contributing authors, for ensuring the richness of the conference and for their cooperation in the preparation of this volume. Special thanks are due to the members of the PC and reviewers for their professionalism and their dedication in selecting the best papers for the conference. Thanks also to the IBERAMIA Executive Committee for its guidance and continuous support.

We owe particular gratitude to the invited speakers, Ajith Abraham, the director of MIR Labs (USA), Hector Geffner, research professor at the ICREA and University Pompeu Fabra in Barcelona (Spain), María Manez, senior researcher at the Climate Service Center in Hamburg (Germany), and Jaime Simão

Sichman, professor at Universidade de São Paulo (Brazil), for sharing with us their experiences and their most recent research results.

Nothing would have been possible without the initiative and dedication of the Organizing Committee from the Universidad Nacional de Colombia. We are very grateful to all the people who helped in the large variety of organizing tasks.

Also, we thank IBERAMIA's Secretariat for their continuous support in administrative matters, as well as Federico Barber and his team from Universidad Politécnica de Valencia (Spain) for supporting the website of the conference. We also want to acknowledge EasyChair for the facilities provided to support the submission and review of the papers, as well as for the preparation of the proceedings.

Finally, we would like to acknowledge the role of the IBERAMIA 2012 sponsors: Universidad Nacional de Colombia, Sociedad Colombiana de Computación (SCo2), Universidad Tecnológica de Bolívar en Cartagena, Universidad de Caldas, and Universidad Tecnológica de Pereira. All of them provided constant support for both the conference organization and the proceedings publication.

November 2012

Juan Pavón
Néstor Darío Duque Méndez
Rubén Fuentes-Fernández

Organization

IBERAMIA 2012 was organized by the Universidad Nacional de Colombia, Colombia. The conference was sponsored by the main Ibero-American artificial intelligence and computer science societies: Sociedade Brasileira de Computação (SBC), Asociación Española para la Inteligencia Artificial (AEPIA), Sociedad Mexicana de Inteligencia Artificial (SMIA), Associação Portuguesa Para a Inteligência Artificial (APPIA), Sociedad Cubana de Matemática y Computación (SCMC), Sociedad Peruana de Inteligencia Artificial (SPIA), Asociación Argentina de Inteligencia Artificial (AAIA), Sociedad Colombiana de Computación (SCo2), and Sociedade Brasileira de Inteligência Computacional (SBIC).

Organizing Committee

Program Chair

Juan Pavón   Universidad Complutense de Madrid, Spain

Organizing Chair

Nestor Darío Duque Méndez   Universidad Nacional de Colombia, Colombia

Publications Chair

Rubén Fuentes-Fernández   Universidad Complutense de Madrid, Spain

Area Chairs

Luis Antunes	Universidade de Lisboa, Portugal
Elisa Boff	Universidade de Caxias do Sul, Brazil
Rafael H. Bordini	Universidade Federal do Rio Grande do Sul, Brazil
Juan Botía	Universidade de Murcia, Spain
Rui Camacho	Universidade do Porto, Portugal
Valérie Camps	IRIT, France
Amílcar Cardoso	Universidade de Coimbra, Portugal
Luís Carriço	Universidade de Lisboa, Portugal
Luis Correia	Universidade de Lisboa, Portugal
Paulo Cortez	Universidade do Minho, Portugal
José Alfredo F. Costa	Universidade Federal do Rio Grande do Norte, Brazil

Fabio Cozman   Universidade de São Paulo, Brazil
Erik Cuevas Jiménez   Universidad de Guadalajara, Mexico
Eduardo Fermé   Universidade da Madeira, Portugal
Cristina García Bicharra   Universidade Federal Fluminense, Brazil
Alejandro Guerra-Hernández   Universidad Veracruzana, Mexico
María Guijarro   Universidad Complutense de Madrid, Spain
Enrique Herrera-Viedma   Universidad de Granada, Spain
Ana Gabriela Maguitman   Universidad Nacional del Sur, Argentina
Manuel Montes   Instituto Nacional de Astrofísica, Óptica y
                                   Electrónica, Mexico
Paulo Novais   Universidade do Minho, Portugal
Eva Onaindia   Universidad Politécnica de Valencia, Spain
Jose M. Peña   Linköping University, Sweden
Rafael Pérez y Pérez   Universidad Autónoma Metropolitana, Mexico
André Ponce De Leon   Universidade de São Paulo, Brazil
Eliseo Reategui   Universidade Federal do Rio Grande do Sul,
                                   Brazil
Paolo Rosso   Universidad Politécnica de Valencia, Spain
Silvia Schiaffino   Universidad Nacional del Centro de la
                                   Provincia de Buenos Aires, Argentina
Jaime Sichman   Universidade de São Paulo, Brazil
Sara Silva   Instituto de Engenharia de Sistemas e
                                   Computadores Investigação e
                                   Desenvolvimento em Lisboa, Portugal
Guillermo Simari   Universidad Nacional del Sur, Argentina
Andrés Soto   Universidad Autónoma del Carmen, Mexico
Luis Enrique Sucar   Instituto Nacional de Astrofísica, Óptica y
                                   Electrónica, Mexico

Program Committee

Silvana Aciar   Instituto de Informática, Universidad Nacional
                                   de San Juan, Argentina
Diana Francisca Adamatti   Universidade Federal do Rio Grande, Brazil
José Júlio Alferes   Universidade Nova de Lisboa, Portugal
Yudivian Almeida   Universidad de la Habana, Cuba
Laura Alonso Alemany   InCO, Universidad de la República, Uruguay /
                                   FaMAF, Universidad Nacional de Córdoba,
                                   Argentina
Tayseer Alshanableh   Near East University, Cyprus
Matias Alvarado   Centro de Investigación y de Estudios
                                   Avanzados del IPN, Mexico
Alexessander Couto Alves   Imperial College London, UK
Karina Anaya   Universidad Politécnica de Querétaro, Mexico
Urrutia Angelica   Universidad Católica del Maule, Chile

Luis Antunes — Universidade de Lisboa, Portugal

Marcelo Gabriel Armentano — ISISTAN, Fac. Cs. Exactas, Universidad Central / Consejo Nacional de Investigaciones Científicas y Técnicas, Argentina

John Atkinson — Universidad de Concepción, Chile

Juan Carlos Augusto — University of Ulster, UK

Jorge Baier — Pontificia Universidad Católica de Chile, Chile

Javier Bajo — Universidad Pontificia de Salamanca, Spain

João Balsa — GUESS, Universidade de Lisboa, Portugal

Guilherme Barreto — Universidade Federal do Ceará, Brazil

Carmelo J. A. Bastos Filho — Universidade de Pernambuco, Brazil

Agnes Baud — University Robert Schuman - Strasbourg, France

Flavia Bernardini — Universidade Federal Fluminense, Brazil

Albert Bifet — University of Waikato, New Zealand

Marco Block-Berlitz — Mediadesign Hochschule in Berlin, Germany

Elisa Boff — Universidade de Caxias do Sul, Brazil

Olivier Boissier — ENS Mines Saint-Etienne, France

Blai Bonet — Universidad Simón Bolívar, Venezuela

Rafael H. Bordini — FACIN / Pontifícia Universidade do Rio Grande do Sul, Brazil

Juan Botía — Universidad de Murcia, Spain

Antonio Braga — Universidade Federal de Minas Gerais, Brazil

Ivan Bratko — University of Ljubljana, Slovenia

Jose Bravo — MAmI Research Lab, Universidad de Castilla-La Mancha, Spain

Ramon Brena — Tecnológico de Monterrey, Mexico

Sofía Brenes

Stefano Cagnoni — University of Parma, Italy

Rui Camacho — Universidade do Porto, Portugal

Valérie Camps — IRIT, France

Javier Carbó — Universidad Carlos III de Madrid, Spain

Jaime S. Cardoso — Universidade do Porto, Portugal

Luís Carriço — Universidade de Lisboa, Portugal

Andre Carvalho — Universidade de São Paulo, Brazil

Oscar Castillo — Instituto Tecnológico de Tijuana, Mexico

Pedro A. Castillo — Universidad de Granada, Spain

Luis Cavique — Universidade Aberta, Portugal

Silvio César Cazella — Universidade do Vale do Rio dos Sinos, Brazil

Eva Cerezo — Universidad de Zaragoza, Spain

Carlos Iván Chesñevar — Universidad Nacional del Sur, Argentina

Sung-Bae Cho — Yonsei University, South Korea

Helder Coelho — Universidade de Lisboa, Portugal

Chris Cornelis — Ghent University, Belgium

Luis Correia	Universidade de Lisboa, Portugal
Ulises Cortés	Universitat Politècnica de Catalunya, Spain
Paulo Cortez	Universidade do Minho, Portugal
José Alfredo F. Costa	Universidade Federal do Rio Grande do Norte, Brazil
Ruben Crespo	Universidad Pontificia de Salamanca, Madrid, Spain
Juan Manuel Cueva	Universidad de Oviedo, Spain
Erik Cuevas Jiménez	Universidad de Guadalajara, Mexico
Agostinho Da Rosa	Institute for Systems and Robotics, Instituto Superior Técnico, Portugal
Walter Daelemans	University of Antwerp, Belgium
Nuno David	Instituto Universitário de Lisboa, Portugal
Pablo De La Fuente	GRINBD, Universidad de Valladolid, Spain
Flavia Delicato	Universidade Federal do Rio de Janeiro, Brazil
Yves Demazeau	Laboratoire LIG, CNRS, France
Cecilia Dias Flores	Universidade Federal de Ciências da Saúde de Porto Alegre, Brazil
Alicia Diaz	LIFIA, Universidad Nacional de La Plata, Argentina
Graçaliz Dimuro	Universidade Federal do Rio Grande, Brazil
Juan Peralta Donate	Universidad Carlos III de Madrid, Spain
Carlos Duarte	LaSIGE, Faculdade de Ciências da Universidade de Lisboa, Portugal
Amal El Fallah Seghrouchni	LIP6 - University of Pierre and Marie Curie, France
Marcelo Errecalde	Universidad Nacional de San Luis, Argentina
Victoria Eyharabide	ISISTAN Research Institute - UNICEN / CONICET, Consejo Nacional de Investigaciones Científicas y Técnicas, Argentina
Marcelo Falappa	Universidad Nacional del Sur, Argentina
Florentino Fdez-Riverola	Universidade de Vigo, Spain
Eduardo Fermé	Universidade da Madeira, Portugal
Antonio Fernández-Caballero	Universidad Castilla-La Mancha, Spain
Inhauma Ferraz	Universidade Federal Fluminense, Brazil
Nuno Fonseca	European Bioinformatics Institute, UK
Mohamed Gaber	University of Portsmouth, UK
João Gama	Universidade do Porto, Portugal
Ana Cristina Bicharra García	Universidade Federal Fluminense, Brazil
Antonio Garrido	Universitat Politècnica de València, Spain
Leonardo Garrido	Centro de Computación Inteligente y Robótica, Tecnológico de Monterrey, Mexico
Hector Geffner	ICREA / Universitat Pompeu Fabra, Spain

Anselmo Peñas   NLP & IR Group, Universidad Nacional de
                                  Educación a Distancia, Spain
Marcelo Pimenta   Universidade Federal do Rio Grande do Sul,
                                  Brazil
Ramón Pino Pérez   Universidad de Los Andes, Venezuela
Alexandre Plastino   Universidade Federal Fluminense, Brazil
André Ponce De Leon   Universidade de São Paulo, Brazil
Aurora Pozo   Universidade Federal do Paraná, Brazil
Davy Preuveneers   Department of Computer Science, K.U. Leuven,
                                  Belgium
Marte Ramirez-Ortegon   Freie Universität Berlin, Germany
Eliseo Berni Reategui   Universidade Federal do Rio Grande do Sul,
                                  Brazil
Kate Revoredo   Universidade Federal do Estado do Rio de
                                  Janeiro, Brazil
Alberto Reyes   Instituto de Investigaciones Eléctricas, Mexico
Solange Rezende   Universidade de São Paulo, Brazil
Rita Ribeiro   Universidade de Lisboa, Portugal
Luis M. Rocha   Indiana University, USA
Ricardo Oscar Rodríguez   Universidad de Buenos Aires, Argentina
Camino Rodríguez-Vela   Universidad de Oviedo, Spain
Raul Rojas   Freie Universität Berlin, Germany
Francisco P. Romero   Universidad de Castilla-La Mancha, Spain
Paolo Rosso   Universidad Politécnica de Valencia, Spain
Miguel A. Salido   Universidad Politécnica de Valencia, Spain
Nayat Sanchez-Pi   Universidad Carlos III de Madrid, Spain
Eugene Santos   Dartmouth College, UK
Jorge M. Santos   Instituto Superior de Engenharia do Porto,
                                  Portugal
David Sanz   Universidad Politécnica de Madrid, Spain
Sebastian Sardina   RMIT University, Australia
Silvia Schiaffino   Universidad Nacional del Centro de la
                                  Provincia de Buenos Aires, Argentina
Laura Sebastia   Universitat Politecnica de Valencia, Spain
Chan Chee Seng   University of Malaya, Malaysia
Ivan Serina   University of Brescia, Italy
Jesús Serrano-Guerrero   Universidad de Castilla-La Mancha, Spain
Jaime Sichman   Universidade de São Paulo, Brazil
Sara Silva   Instituto de Engenharia de Sistemas e
                                  Computadores Investigação e
                                  Desenvolvimento em Lisboa, Portugal
Viviane Silva   Universidade Federal Fluminense, Brazil
Ricardo Azambuja Silveira   Universidade Federal de Santa Catarina, Brazil
Guillermo Simari   Universidad Nacional del Sur, Argentina

Vaclav Snasel	Technical University of Ostrava, Czech Republic
Carlos Soares	Universidade do Porto, Portugal
Alejandro Sobrino Cerdeiriña	Universidad de Santiago de Compostela, Spain
Thamar Solorio	University of Alabama at Birmingham, USA
Humberto Sossa	CIC, Instituto Politécnico Nacional, Mexico
Alvaro Soto	Pontificia Universidad Católica de Chile, Chile
Andres Soto	Universidad Autónoma del Carmen, Mexico
Marc Strickert	University of Siegen, Germany
Vera Strube	Pontifícia Universidade Católica do Rio Grande do Sul, Brazil
Luis Enrique Sucar	Instituto Nacional de Astrofísica, Óptica y Electrónica, Mexico
João Luis Tavares	Universidade de Caxias do Sul, Brazil
Oswaldo Terán	Universidad de Los Andes, Venezuela
Murat Caner Testik	Hacettepe University, Turkey
Luz Abril Torres	CINVESTAV Unidad Saltillo, Mexico
Leonardo Trujillo	Instituto Tecnológico de Tijuana, Mexico
Paulo Urbano	Universidade de Lisboa, Portugal
M. Birna Van Riemsdijk	TU Delft, The Netherlands
Tiago Vaquero	University of Toronto, Canada
Juan Velasco	Universidad de Alcalá de Henares, Spain
Juan Velasquez	Universidad de Chile, Chile
Renata Vieira	Pontifícia Universidade Católica do Rio Grande do Sul, Brazil
Adriana Vivacqua	DCC-IM, Universidade Federal do Rio de Janeiro, Brazil
Dimitris Vrakas	Aristotle University of Thessaloniki, Greece
Renata Wassermann	Universidade de São Paulo, Brazil
Carine Webber	Universidade de Caxias do Sul, Brazil
Marco Winckler	ICS-IRIT, Université Paul Sabatier, France
Leandro Krug Wives	Universidade Federal do Rio Grande do Sul, Brazil
Dina Wonsever	Instituto de Computación, Universidad de la República, Uruguay
Michal Wozniak	Wroclaw University of Technology, Poland
Bianca Zadrozny	Universidade Federal Fluminense, Brazil
Daniel Zaldivar	Universidad de Guadalajara, Mexico

Additional Reviewers

Luís A. Alexandre	Igor Braga
Carmelo J. A. Bastos Filho	Marcos Cintra
Marta Rosecler Bez	Ines Domingues

Leonardo Emmendorfer
Carlos Ferreira
Marcelo Finger
Antonio Juárez-González
Jorge Kanda
Bartosz Krawczyk
Thibault Langlois
Orestes Llanes-Santiago
Pedro Lopes
Rigoberto Lopez
Sérgio Matos
João Mendes-Moreira
Silvia Moraes
Tatiane Nogueira
Davide Nunes

John Osborne
Fernando Osorio
Fábio Paiva
Leandro Pasa
Marco Perez-Cisneros
Mauro Roisenberg
Anna Roubickova
Ubaldo Ruiz
Alynne Saraiva
Leonardo Silva
Ricardo Sousa
Jackson Souza
Luis Valentin
Adenauer Yamin

Table of Contents

Machine Learning

Bio-inspired Computing

Fuzzy Systems

Modelling and Simulation

Ambient Intelligence

Multi-Agent Systems

Human-Computer Interaction

Natural Language Processing

Computer Vision & Robotics

Planning and Scheduling

AI in Education

Knowledge Engineering and Applications

Contradiction Detection and Ontology Extension in a Never-Ending Learning System[*]

Vinicius Oliverio and Estevam R. Hruschka Jr.

Federal University of Sao Carlos, UFSCar Sao Carlos, Brazil

Abstract. The notion of *Contradiction* is present in many aspects of the world and human information processing. As a consequence, more and more computer systems have been pushed into dealing with the contradiction detection task. Contradiction Detection (CD) is not a simple task, thus, it is subject to many discussions and approaches in different areas of human knowledge, such as Philosophy, Ethics, Linguistics, Computer Science, etc. and, as such, approached under different perspectives and goals. In this paper we focus on CD in a never-ending learning system called NELL (Never-ending Language Learner). Considering that NELL is intended to be self-supervised, as well as, self-reflective, it takes advantage of every new acquired knowledge (and stored its Knowledge Base - KB) to learn better and better each day. In this sense, NELL uses its own knowledge to achieve better performance in every new learning task. Therefore, the presence of contradictions in the KB of a never-ending learning system, like NELL, can result in the exponential propagation of incorrect knowledge that can lead to concept-drift. Following along these lines, in this work we proposed an approach to detect and eliminate contradictions from NELL's KB. The results obtained from the performed experiments shows that the proposed approach can detect contradictions, as well as, eliminating them by deletion or by extending the KB hierarchy structure.

Keywords: contradiction detection and elimination, knowledge based system, machine learning, never-ending learning system.

1 Introduction

The notion of Contradiction is present in many aspects of the world and human information processing. As a consequence, more and more computer systems have been pushed into dealing with the contradiction detection task. Contradiction Detection (CD) is not a simple task, thus, it is subject to many discussions and approaches in different areas of human knowledge, such as Philosophy, Ethics, Linguistics, Computer Science, etc. and, as such, approached under different perspectives and goals. Computational knowledge-based systems can take advantage of CD in order to enhance their performance on knowledge representation, knowledge acquisition and inference tasks. The many proposals for dealing and representing the notion contradiction found in the

---

[*] Authors thank the Brazilian research agency FAPESP.

J. Pavón et al. (Eds.): IBERAMIA 2012, LNAI 7637, pp. 1–10, 2012.

literature can be seen as evidence of its importance. NELL[1] (Never-Ending Language Learner) is a computer system that runs 24 hours per day, 7 days per week. It was started up on January, 12th, 2010 and should be running forever, gathering more and more facts from the web to grow and populate its own knowledge base. In a nutshell, NELL's initial knowledge base (KB) is an ontology defining hundreds of categories (e.g., **person**, **sportsTeam**, **fruit**, **emotion**) and relations (e.g., ***athletePlaysForTeam***(**athlete**, **sportsTeam**), ***musicianPlaysInstrument***(**musician**, **instrument**)) and a handful of examples (instances) for each one of the categories (e.g. **person**(*Angelina Jolie*), **fruit**(*strawberry*), etc.) and the relations (e.g. ***athletePlaysForTeam***(*Kobe Bryant, LA Lakers*), ***musicianPlaysInstrument***(*Eric Clapton, guitar*), etc.). The system is based on a number of different learning components (or subsystems). These learning subsystem are coupled in a way they can cooperate and continuously grow the initial KB [5] in the number of instances (number of facts) and, also, in the number of categories and relations. The creation of new relations might be seen as an ontology extension procedure as proposed in [1] [14] and can provide NELL the ability to automatically decide on new knowledge that is relevant to be learned, but was not previously defined as target in its initial ontology.

Considering that NELL is intended to be self-supervised, as well as, self-reflective, it takes advantage of every new acquired knowledge (and stored in its KB) to learn better and better each day. In this sense, NELL uses its own knowledge to achieve better performance in every new learning task. Therefore, the presence of contradictions in the KB of a never-ending learning system, such as NELL, can result in the exponential propagation of incorrect knowledge that can lead to concept-drift as addressed in [6]. Therefore, when a contradiction is present in NELL's KB and it is used as input to NELL's learning algorithms, the contradiction is propagated generating new contradictions (and mistakes), which will be used to feed again the never-ending learning process in a *snowball* effect. Thus, it is easy to see why contradiction detection and removal is key for a good performance in a never-ending learning system like NELL.

One example of contradictions, in NELL's knowledge base, are facts that are correctly learned independently, but become contradictory when put together. Consider, for instance, the following three predicates representing three independent facts:

- ***athlethePlaysSport***(*Joe Smith, basketball*): representing the fact: *Joe Smith is an athlete who plays basketball*;
- ***athletePlaysForTeam***(*Joe Smith, Mets*): representing the fact: *Joe Smith is an athlete who plays for the Mets*;
- ***teamPlaysSport***(*Mets, baseball*): representing the fact: *Mets is a sports team that plays baseball*;

The three facts above, are not, by themselves, contradictory. But, when putting them all together, they represent a contradiction. In other words, if *Joe Smith*

---

[1] http://rtw.ml.cmu.edu

plays basketball and plays for *Mets*, then, *Mets* should play *basketball*, but not *baseball*. This contradiction is observed in Nell's KB because there are two homonyms *Joe Smiths* in the KB, the first one who plays basketball and second one who plays baseball.

The main goal of this paper is to describe an approach prosed to identify and eliminate contradictions present in NELL's KB. The approach is based on a method that takes advantage of NELL's knowledge about every item stored in its own KB. The proposed method (presented in Sect. 3) is based on first order rules automatically induced (by NELL) from its own KB (as described in [5] as the "Rule Learner").

2 Related Work

In this section, an overview on related work that has been done in the contradiction detection field is presented. Considering the broadness of the area, we divided the related works in 3 subgroups, namely Contradiction Detection in General, Contradiction Detection Based on Dictionaries and Contradiction Detection in Text Reading tasks.

2.1 Contradiction Detection in General

Among some of the most relevant work in Contradiction Detection (CD), such as [9,11,13,17,18,19] , the paper [11] has an interesting contradiction definition, that fits the most with the contradiction definition used in this paper. In its paper Lembo brings two important concepts created by [2], the TBox and the ABox and differentiates contradictions based on those two TBox and ABox ideas. The TBox contradiction includes axioms sanctioning properties of concepts and relations (such as *Cat is_a Mammal*), whereas the ABox contains axioms asserting properties of instances of concepts and relations (such as *Felix is an instance of Cat*). Taking these two concepts into account, the author shows that the contradictions can be in both components (TBox and ABox). The TBox alone might be consistent but the ABox might contradict the axioms in the TBox. In addition, they both can be inconsistent. These ideas are present in the method described in Sect. 3 of this paper and also presented in the examples shown in Sect. 1, but as will be seen the focus of the proposed method is to detect contradicitions in the TBox.

2.2 Contradiction Detection Based on Dictionaries

When focusing our attention to Contradiction Detection based on dictionaries, some of the most relevant works are [3,4,12,17]. Among them, the work presented in [17] brings a complete idea of application of this type of contradiction detection incorporating some ideas from the other authors. Ritter describes in this paper, a system for contradiction detection based in functional relations (i.e. born_in(Person) = Place) called *AuContraire*, that automatically discovers phrases that denotes functional relations with high precision. The system proposed in [17] statistically identifies *functional phrases* after creating a large corpus of apparent contradictions. Then, the system filters this corpus to find genuine contradictions using knowledge about synonymy, meronymy, argument types, and ambiguity using information from dictionaries such as WordNet and Gazetteer.

2.3 Contradiction Detection in Text Reading

There are some interesting works base on Contradiction Detection in Text Reading. Among various works such as [3,4,8,9,10], the work described in [9] presents a framework for contradiction detection using multiple text sources by relying on three forms of linguistic information, namely: (a) *negation*; (b) *antonymy*; and (c) *semantic and pragmatic information* associated with the discourse relations. The paper considers two views of contradictions, in which a method of recognizing contrast and of finding antonyms is described. These two views are:

- **View 1**: Contradictions are recognized by identifying and removing negations of propositions and then testing for textual entailment;
- **View 2**: Contradictions are recognized by deriving linguistic information from the text inputs, including information that identifies (a) negation, (b) contrasts, or (c) oppositions (antonyms) and by training a classifier based on examples, similarly the way a classifier for entailment is trained.

The authors claim that in some cases their systems achieved a precision of 75.63% in identifying contradictions in Question Answering (Q/A) tasks, where the system have to detect contradicting answers for a common question.

3 Detecting and Eliminating Contradictions in NELL's Knowledge Base

NELL's Rule Learner (RL) component [5] induces first order rules from NELL's KB using a FOIL-based [16] probabilistic algorithm. These rules are are used to inform the system how different categories can interact with each other (semantic relations inference). When the induced rules are applied to the system, NELL's beliefs on the categories (covered by the rules) are updated.

An example of a rule created by RL can be:

Rule1: *athletePlaysSport*(x,*Basketball*) :- *athletePlaysInLeague*(x,*NBA*)

where *athletePlaysSport*(**athlete**, **sport**) as well as *athletePlaysInLeague*(**athlete**, **sportsLeague**) are binary predicates, x is a variable, *Basketball* and *NBA* are constants, and finally, **athlete, sport** and **sportsLeague** are NELL's categories.

If "Rule1" is introduced as knowledge into NELL's KB, the system will raise its belief that all athlete who plays in the NBA plays Basketball. Nevertheless, some of the rules learned by RL might be wrong. Thus, before being introduced into the system as knowledge, these rules are, currently, validated by human inspection. Following along these lines, the first CD method, herein presented, is called Rule-Based Contradiction Detection (RBCD) and is intended to work with NELL allowing an automated way for identifying contradictions in rules induced by RL. Therefore, RBCD first step is to detect the contradictions by testing RL's rules against NELL's KB to find negative examples. To do so, based on a *Prolog*-like syntax, a modified form (called R') of every rule R is automatically created in order to extract (from the KB) all the negative examples. The modified form (Rule1') of "Rule1" shown above would be:

Rule1':

$$\textbf{athletePlaysSport(x,Basketball):-athletePlaysInLeague(x,y),}$$
$$\textbf{y/==NBA}$$

where *athletePlaysSport(athlete, sport)* and *athletePlaysInLeague(athlete, sportsLeague)* are binary predicates, x and y are variables, *Basketball* and *NBA* are constants, and *athlete, sport* and *sportsLeague* are NELL's categories.

Then, using the original rule (R), as well as, the modified version of it (R'), is possible to extract (from the KB) all the positive examples, as well as all the negative examples for each rule, thus, generating a dataset D^2 .

The main idea of this method is to use, for each rule R, the same dataset D to find out whether its negative examples form a homogeneous group or not. In the case they do form a homogeneous group, a new subcategory should be added to the KB and the contradiction will be eliminated. The process creates new *subcategories* in NELL's KB whenever it can help to eliminate contradictions. RBCD can be summarized as follows:

Consider a rule R1:

$$\textbf{\textit{predicate1}}\,(x,A)\textbf{:-emphpredicate2}(x,B)$$

and its modified version R1':

$$\textbf{\textit{predicate1}}\,(x,A)\textbf{:-\textit{predicate2}}(x,y),\ y/{==}B$$

where **predicate1** (**C1,C2**) and **predicate2** (**C1,C3**) are predicates, x and y are variables, A and B are constants, and *C1, C2* and *C3* are NELL's categories. Also, consider that the set of positive examples (all **C1** possible values that satisfy R) are given by $\mathcal{P}$, and the set of negative examples (all **C1** possible values that satisfy R') are given by $\mathcal{N}$. Thus, in this case $D = \mathcal{P} + \mathcal{N}$. If we can cluster D in M groups and find a single group G (where $G \subset D$) and $G = \mathcal{N}$, then we can suggest the creation of two new categories (**C4** and **C5**) in NELL's KB. In addition, **C4** and **C5** will be subcategories of **C1** (in the KB hierarchy), and $\forall x,\ x \in \mathcal{N} \Rightarrow x \in \textbf{C5}$, as well as, $\forall x,\ x \in \mathcal{P} \Rightarrow x \in \textbf{C4}$.

---

[2] In order to automate the process of dataset D creation, an algorithm was implemented to, having a rule R as input, generate R' as output.

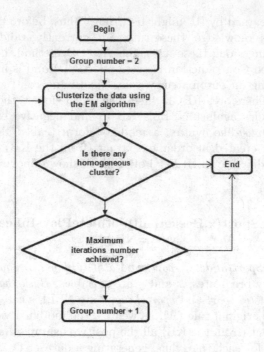

Fig. 1. EM-based clustering process

Having these modifications in the KB will impose some different patterns to be learned, and the results obtained by RL (when *trying* to induce the same rule R1) based on the modified KB will be different, generating R1". The new rule (R") to be induced by RL (free of contradictions) will be:

$$predicate3\,(x,A)\text{:-}predicate4\,(x,B)$$

where **predicate3**(**C4**,**C2**) and **predicate3**(**C4**,**C3**) are predicates, x is a variable, A, B are constants, and **C2**, **C3** and **C4** are NELL's categories. In addition, **C4** is a subcategory of category **C1**.

One of the key issues in this method is to define the optimal number M of clusters to be found when applying the clustering algorithm in D (in our experiments we have used the EM [7] clustering algorithm). Thus, the process shown in Fig. 1 was used to invoke the EM clustering algorithm until the right number of clusters have been found. Notice that in spite of using an unsupervised method (EM clustering algorithm) we guide identification of the correct number of clusters using the *labeled* instances (positive or negative examples) given by the instances which satisfy (or not) the rules induced by RL. Thus, the definition of the number of clusters to be used follows a supervised approach.

4 Experiments and Discussion

For all the experiments, however, the 140th iteration NELL's KB was used. It is worth mentioning that, as can be seen in NELL's website (http://rtw.ml.cmu.edu/), this version of the KB have received "shallow" human supervision to correct inconsistencies and mistakes, thus, we do not expect to find a great number of contradictions in these experiments. What we do intend, however, is to show that our method can help finding contradictions that were not found by the "shallow" human supervision periodically performed on NELL's KB. In the proposed experiments, NELL's KB was retrieved with all information and all the rules generated by the rule learner RL. This information was used to feed the proposed method and contradictions were found in 6 rules:

1. R1: *citylocatedinstate*(x, y) :- *citycapitalofstate*(x, y), *statelocatedincountry*$(y,\ united\ states)$.
2. R2: *athleteplayssport*(x,y):-*athleteplaysforteam*(x,z), *teamplayssport* $(z,\ y)$
3. R3: *athleteplaysforteam*(x,y):-*teammate*$(x,\ z)$, *athleteplaysforteam*$(z,\ y)$
4. R4: *athleteplaysinleague*(x,y):-*athleteplaysforteam*$(x,\ z)$, *teamplaysinleague*$(z,\ y)$
5. R5: *teamplaysincity*$(x,\ y)$:- *teamhomestadium*(x,z), *stadiumlocatedincity* (z,y)
6. R6: *teamplaysinleague*(x,y):- *teamplaysagainstteam*(x,z), *teamplaysinleague*(z,y)

After identifying the rules having contradictions, RBCD started the contradiction elimination step. For rule R1, RBCD created two new subcategories (**City1** and **City2**) for the category **City**. Thus, the predicate *citylocatedinstate*(**City**,**State**) was substituted by *citylocatedinstate*(**City1**,**State**) in the new induced rule R1". And all instances in the new subcategory **City1** (grouped by RBCD clustering method) are cities inside the US. After this KB modification no contradiction was detected in the new induced rule. It is interesting noticing that the name of a new subcategory is used only internally (by NELL), thus, there is no need to generate a meaningful name.

As for rule R2, after creating two new subcategories (**Athlete1** and **Athlete2**) for the category **Athlete**, RBCD did not converged and created, again, two new subcategories (**Athlete3** and **Athlete4**) as subcategories of **Athlete1**. Analyzing the clustering results, all instances in **Athele1** are *NHL* and *MBL* players. All instances in subcategory **Athlete2** are from sports different from baseball and hockey. All instances clustered together in subcategory **Athlete3** are *NHL* players, while the instances in subcategory **Athlete4** are *MBL* players. After the KB modifications, the new induced rules presented 85% less negative examples (contradictions) than R2.

When concerning rule R4 the same new subcategories (created when dealing with rule R2: **Athlete1** and **Athlete2** as subcategories of **Athlete**, and **Athlete3** and **Athlete4** as subcategories of **Athlete1**) were suggested by

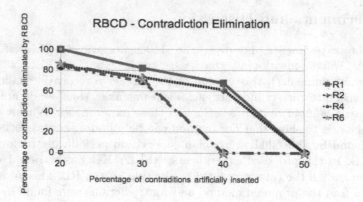

Fig. 2. Average

RBCD. The new subcategories reduced in 75.3% the number of contradictions for this rule. For rule R6, RBCD created subcategories **SpotsTeam1** and **SportsTeam2** as subcategories for **SportsTeam**, and **AportsTeam3** and **SportsTeam4** as subcategories for **SportsTeam1** following the same pattern identified for rules R2 and R4. After the insertion of the new subcategories in the KB, the number of contradictions was reduced in 75% for this rule.

When considering rules R3 and R5, RBCD could not find homogeneous clusters, thus no new subcategory was created and no contradiction could be eliminated based on these rules. The most probable explanation for such RBCD behavior is that NELL's KB did not have many instances learned for the predicates involved in the rules and/or there are too many mistakes (wrong instances) in these predicates instances. Based on this behavior, and, aiming at having a better idea on how robust RBCD is, another experiment was conducted as described in the sequel.

Based on rules R1, R2, R4 and R6, artificial contradictions were inserted in the KB to simulate a situation where RBCD have to cope with very noisy KBs. Therefore, for each rule were inserted 20%, 30% and 50% of contradictions in the KB and then, RBCD was used to try to eliminate the artificially inserted mistakes. Figure 2 summarizes the obtained results.

From the chart depicted in Fig. 2 is possible to see that when 50% of contradiction were inserted in the KB, RBCD was not able to solve any contradiction. It means that for a very noise KB (where 50% of the facts are wrong) RBCD can not find any pattern among the instances and cannot help in eliminating contradictions. On the other hand, when the KB is not so noisy (20% or 30% of contradictions), RBCD could help eliminating around 80% of the contradictions from the KB for all 4 rules.

5   Conclusions

NELL (Never-Ending Language Learning) is a system that seeks to learn how to learn better and better in an continuous way, extracting structured information from unstructured web pages and uses a set of learning algorithms and components. As the result of this system a continuously growing knowledge base is being built. Currently, however, NELL's knowledge base in not free from contradictions. Considering that the current KB content is continuously used to feed NELL's never-ending learning process, contradiction detection, as well as, contradiction elimination both play a critical role in NELL's ability to keep learning and avoiding the concept-drift problem. Based on the contradiction detection and contradiction elimination in the never-ending learning scenario, this paper proposes an approach based on the idea of identifying contradictions using first order logic rules automatically generated by NELL. This method makes use of a clustering algorithm and a specific way of identifying the suitable number of clusters to be found in the KB. After finding how instances can be arranged in groups, the method proposes new subcategories to be added to the KB (automatically extending the KB hierarchical structure) so that the found contractions can be corrected without having to delete information from the KB.

The performed experiments revealed that the proposed approach achieved good results, finding and solving the contradictions that it was supposed to solve. Based on the experiments it was possible to observe that the proposed addition of new subcategories (done by RBCD) can eliminate contradictions without the need of deleting information from the KB. The experiments also revealed that for a very noisy KB RBCD can face difficulties in eliminating contradictions. Considering however that NELL's KB has on average 75% of precision (correct facts), RBCD seems to be a suitable method to be used with NELL.

As future work, we intend to report on some collaboration among other NELL's components, i.e., the system could ask in the Internet (Twitter, Yahoo Answer, etc.) if the information that it has found in steps two and three is really contradictory, so depending on the answers it could take an action [15]. Another possibility is to implement a method to name the created subcategories in a human readable way. Also, we intend to show in a long term experiment how other two proposed methods for solving contradictions can benefit the method shown in this paper and help NELL to keep its KB free from contradictions in the long term run.

References

1. Appel, A.P., Hruschka Jr., E.R.: Prophet – A Link-Predictor to Learn New Rules on NELL. In: 11th IEEE International Conference on Data Mining Workshops (ICDMW 2011), pp. 917–924. IEEE (2011)
2. Baader, F., Calvanese, D., McGuinness, D.L., Nardi, D., Patel-Schneider, P.F. (eds.): The Description Logic Handbook – Theory, Implementation, and Applications. Cambridge University Press, New York (2003)
3. Banko, M., Cafarella, M.J., Soderland, S., Broadhead, M., Etzioni, O.: Open Information Extraction from the Web. In: 20th International Joint Conference on Artificial Intelligence (IJCAI 2007), pp. 2670–2676 (2007)
4. Banko, M., Etzioni, O.: The Tradeoffs Between Open and Traditional Relation Extraction. In: 46th Annual Meeting of the Association for Computational Linguistics: Human Language Technologies (ACL 2008: HLT), pp. 28–36. ACL (2008)

5. Carlson, A., Betteridge, J., Kisiel, B., Settles, B., Hruschka Jr., E.R., Mitchell, T.M.: Toward an Architecture for Never-Ending Language Learning. In: 24th Conference on Artificial Intelligence (AAAI 2010), pp. 1306–1313. AAAI (2010)
6. Carlson, A., Betteridge, J., Wang, R.C., Hruschka Jr., E.R., Mitchell, T.M.: Coupled Semi-Supervised Learning for Information Extraction. In: 3rd ACM Intl. Conference on Web Search and Data Mining (WSDM 2010), pp. 101–110. ACM (2010)
7. Duda, R., Hart, P., Stork, D.: Pattern classification. Wiley-Interscience (2001)
8. Ennals, R., Trushkowsky, B., Agosta, J.M.: Highlighting Disputed Claims on the Web. In: 19th International Conference on World Wide Web (WWW 2010), pp. 341–350. ACM (2010)
9. Harabagiu, S., Hickl, A., Lacatusu, F.: Negation, Contrast and Contradiction in Text Processing. In: 21st National Conference on Artificial Intelligence (AAAI 2006), vol. 1, pp. 755–762. AAAI Press (2006)
10. Kawahara, D., Inui, K., Kurohashi, S.: Identifying Contradictory and Contrastive Relations between Statements to Outline Web Information on a Given Topic. In: 23rd International Conference on Computational Linguistics (COLING 2010), Posters, pp. 534–542. ACL (2010)
11. Lembo, D., Lenzerini, M., Rosati, R., Ruzzi, M., Savo, D.F.: Inconsistency-Tolerant Semantics for Description Logics. In: Hitzler, P., Lukasiewicz, T. (eds.) RR 2010. LNCS, vol. 6333, pp. 103–117. Springer, Heidelberg (2010)
12. Lin, Y.: A New Approach to Improve CD Based on the Context. In: 1st International Workshop on Education Technology and Computer Science (ETCS 2009), vol. 3, pp. 76–78. IEEE (2009)
13. de Marneffe, M.C., Rafferty, A.N., Manning, C.D.: Finding Contradictions in Text. In: 46th Annual Meeting of the Association for Computational Linguistics: Human Language Technologies (ACL 2008: HLT), pp. 1039–1047. ACL (2008)
14. Mohamed, T.P., Hruschka Jr., E.R., Mitchell, T.M.: Discovering Relations between Noun Categories. In: 2011 Conference on Empirical Methods in Natural Language Processing (EMNLP 2011), pp. 1447–1455. ACL (2011)
15. Pedro, S.D.S., Hruschka Jr., E.R.: Collective Intelligence as a Source for Machine Learning Self-Supervision. In: 4th International Workshop on Web Intelligence and Communities (WIC 2012), pp. 5:1–5:9. ACM (2012)
16. Quinlan, J.R., Cameron-Jones, R.M.: FOIL – A Midterm Report. In: Brazdil, P.B. (ed.) ECML 1993. LNCS, vol. 667, pp. 1–20. Springer, Heidelberg (1993)
17. Ritter, A., Downey, D., Soderland, S., Etzioni, O.: It's a Contradiction — No, It's not – A Case Study Using Functional Relations. In: 2008 Conference on Empirical Methods in Natural Language Processing (EMNLP 2008), pp. 11–20. ACL (2008)
18. Sanchez-Graillet, O., Poesio, M.: Discovering Contradicting Protein-Protein Interactions in Text. In: 2007 Biological, Translational, and Clinical Language Processing Workshop (BioNLP 2007), pp. 195–196. ACL (2007)
19. Voorhees, E.M.: Contradictions and Justifications – Extensions to the Textual Entailment Task. In: 46th Annual Meeting of the Association for Computational Linguistics: Human Language Technologies (ACL 2008: HLT), pp. 63–71. ACL (2008)

Pattern Recognition and Monte-CarloTree Search for Go Gaming Better Automation

Arturo Yee[*] and Matías Alvarado

Computer Sciences Department, Center of Research and Advances Studies, México D.F.
ayee@computacion.cs.cinvestav.mx, matias@cs.cinvestav.mx

Abstract. Go gaming automation is AI relevant because during a match the search space is enormous and the game tree size is around 10^{360}, versus the 10^{123} for Chess. Thus, finding out methods providing efficient solutions to, is truly relevant. The Monte-Carlo-based approaches have leading Go gaming automation but efficiency is distant: to strengthen on efficiency, a hybrid automated Go player Neural-Networks-based for learning and recognition on tactics/strategic patterns, in average, during the first $^2/_3$ parts of a match is introduced; by the remaining match's part it uses RAVE Monte-Carlo Tree Search (MCTS). Results on the precision of pattern recognition and a comparison against competitive automated Go players are presented.

Keywords: Go tactics patterns recognition, MCTS, neural network learning and recognition, Go gaming and game theory.

1   Introduction

The two-player Go game is a zero-sum, deterministic and perfect information game [1] being one of the most complex board games. Go has a growing interest on Artificial Intelligence (AI) community because the huge search space. Complexity in computer gaming is measured by the game tree size and the state space size; in Go is around 10^{360} for game tree size, 10^{172} for state space and up to 361 legal moves [2]. Nowadays, computer Go is considered as the *new drosophila of AI*[1] and the new grand challenge task [3]. Go board official size is shaped 19 x19 horizontal-vertical lines, taking turn, each player places one black/white stone on a board's empty intersection, the black playing first [4]; *connection* of two or more same color single stones form a *chain*. From now on, the term stone is used to refer to both, single and *chain*, but if required the explicit difference is made; black player takes the white stones and conversely. The aim of Go players is to control as much territory as possible, so the player who controls the largest territory when game ends is the winner, see **Fig 1**. The control is done by constructing *eyes*, *nets* and *ladders* as the basic tactics, see examples in **Fig 3**; as well by *invasion*, *reduction*, *connection*, *capture*, among others [5]. An enclosed liberty is called *eyes*; a *ladder* is a sequence of connection moves that

---

[*] Corresponding author.
[1] Drosophila is the fruit fly.

J. Pavón et al. (Eds.): IBERAMIA 2012, LNAI 7637, pp. 11–20, 2012.

forces the enemy into a capture circumstance; a *net* is a sequence of connection moves that surrounds the enemy's stones avoiding it escape in any direction and capturing in successive moves. Placing a live-stone into enemy's area is *invasion*; put a stone far enough into enemy's area but not so far from a friend-stone is reduction. *Capture* is by removing of enemy's stones.

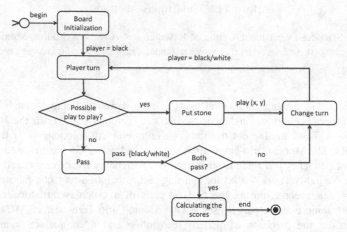

Fig. 1. Go game process flow

Once a stone is placed on the board it cannot be moved unless is captured. A stone's *liberty* is an empty adjacent intersection, vertical or horizontal, to the stone. If a black stone is surrounded by a white stones and direct adjacent intersection is not empty the black stone is *dead*, and conversely. A *dead* stone is removed from the board. The game ends when both players pass and the score is calculated. White player receives a compensation *komi* because black player plays first.

Go's **tactics** correspond to local situations where there exist confrontation between stones to dominate an area locally or life-threatening conditions *e.g.*, *nets*, *ladders* [5]. The **strategies** correspond to global situations [5], and are developed from tactics.

The playing level of the best current Go automated simulator versus human being is still modest compared to the great successes achieved in other games of skill such as chess [6]. Currently, the best Go automated players mostly use MCTS and Artificial Neural Networks. The main focus for Go automation is on evaluating non-final positions for estimating potential territory [4, 7, 8]. Prospective methods for programming Go gaming are being deployed in AI related domains like evaluation functions, heuristic search, machine learning and automatic knowledge generation [9].

The SANE (Symbiotic, Adaptive Neuro-Evolution) is used to evolve networks capable of playing Go on small boards with no pre-programmed go knowledge [7]. The *Honte* go-playing program uses neural nets together with alpha-beta search [10], and Go AI program based on BP-Neural Network [11].

Monte-Carlo (MC) methods root in statistical physics [12] used to obtain approximations to intractable integrals, in numerical algorithms being successful in various AI game. MCTS is a best-first search technique uses stochastic simulations, see **Fig. 2**. It uses that the true value of an action may be approximated using random simulations;

and that value may be used efficiently to adjust the policy towards a best-first strategy [12]. The algorithm progressively builds a partial game tree, guided by the results of previous exploration of that tree; the tree is built to more accurate estimate the values of moves; the algorithm builds a tree according to the following mechanisms [13]:*selection, expansion, simulation* and *back-propagation*.

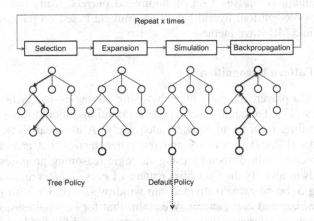

Fig. 2. MCTS Approach

Gelly and *Silver* present two extensions to the MCTS algorithm. The *Rapid Action Value Estimation* (RAVE) shares the value of actions across each sub-tree of the tree search and the *heuristic MCTS* uses a heuristic function to initializes the value of the new positions in the tree search [14]. Go programs based on MCTS now play at human-master level [15], Rave MCTS is a relevant Go gaming work and the one our proposal advantages as is shown in Section 3.

A Go match can be represented as a tree, where each node corresponds to a particular board configuration. The root node is for game beginning. The children of each node are the positions reachable in one move. A complete strategy for Go, even on the 9 x 9 board is astronomically large. Even the disarming simplicity of the rules of Go, it conceals a formidable combinatorial complexity [16], being measured by the **state space complexity** and the **game tree size** [2]. **Table 1** shows a comparative analysis of complexity of games.

The rest of this paper follows by Section 2 being devoted to our Go game automation. Section 3 is for experiments and the analytical comparison and conclusion.

Table 1. Complexity of Go, Chess and Checkers games

Game	Board size	State space	Game tree size
Go	19 x 19	10^{172}	10^{360}
Chess	8 x 8	10^{50}	10^{123}
Checkers	8 x 8	10^{18}	10^{54}

2   Hybrid Automated Go Player

The Go game simulator is formal based on a regular grammar [17]; the Go game diagram flow is in **Fig.1**, that indicates the states/moves. The simulator is implemented in Java, is a heuristic method having running variability, sometimes giving an optimal result. The simulator comprises a set of automated players, using random, strategic based on pattern recognition, hybrid based on strategic based on pattern recognition with MC-Rave and MC-Rave method.

2.1   Tactics Pattern Recognition

The automated Go player rationally plays by using strategies and tactics in order to reach the victory [17]. To identify the opponent intentions, should recognize the tactics it is performing, in order to respond adequately. A classical Back-Propagation Neural Networks (BPNN) to identify and recognize tactics that are being applied during a Go match is trained; then by using strategic reasoning proposes gaming actions. The idea is to identify the Go tactics pattern of *eyes*, *ladders* and *nets*, see some examples in **Fig 3**: board game is divided into window size of 3 x 3 for *eyes* patterns and 5 x 5 for *ladders* and *nets* patterns. We claim that for *eyes* patterns, window size of 3 x 3 is enough to determine these kinds of patterns and for *ladders* and *nets* patterns, window size of 5 x 5 is enough too.

The architecture of the BPNN is as follows, for the input layer, the number of neurons is fixed according to the window size, *e.g.*, for *eyes* is 9 and for *ladders* and *nets* 25, the input layer receives a set of positions from the board. The number of neurons in the hidden layer is obtained experimentally and for output layer, the number of neurons is 2 which define if a pattern is recognized.

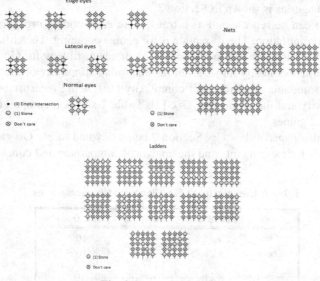

Fig. 3. Patterns examples

For the training stage, we identified some general patterns, in which includes don´t care symbols, which roughly speaking does not matter what things are on these positions. The only matter is the positions in where appear symbols of 1s or 0s; some examples are illustrated in **Fig. 3**.

To create a robust reliable network, in some cases, some noise or other randomness is added to the training data [5]. We added noise and randomness replacing don not care symbols by 1s or 0s and through this way, we create a robust training set.

2.2 Strategic Reasoning by Pattern Recognition and MCTS

The strategic Go player additional to use BPNNs is capable to perform strategies through use of a strategic reasoning. Analyzing the Go game stages, we identified that, in the beginning and middle stages, there are more opportunities to apply pattern recognition method along with a strategic reasoning to form strategies because there exist more probabilities to develop a desirable strategy, *e.g.*, capture, form *eyes*, *ladders*, *nets*, *invasion*, among other. In the final stage, the space on the board is small, reducing the opportunities to develop a desired strategy; under this circumstance one way is to evaluate the set of free positions on the board to determine which one is the best position to play.

Hybrid Go player uses a pattern recognition to identify tactics such as *ladders*, *nets*, *eyes*, a strategic reasoning to form strategies and MCTS to evaluate some positions in the final stage of Go match, we developed MCTS(Rave) following the ideas from Gelly and Silver [14], see hybrid player in **Fig.4**.

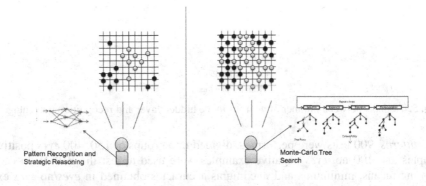

Fig. 4. Hybrid Go player

The pattern recognition and the strategic reasoning are applied in the game's beginning and middle stages: reason is that the board is few occupied and it allows the deployment of *a priori* Go-knowledge-based strategies. On the opposite when a match is ending the thin board spaces make difficult to deploy these kinds of methods, and the usage of MCTS is helpful to assess the next play to occupy empty board positions. In our Go automated player the stages are roughly determined by the number of moves played, *e.g.*, to 9 x 9 board size the number of moves is around 40 per player so each stage is around 13 moves.

Pattern recognition and strategic reasoning work as follows: once the BPNNs have identified a pattern that looks like a Go tactic on the board, previously encoded Go game actions, *eyes*, *nets*, *ladders, invasion, reduction, connection, capture*, among others, are used to perform an offensive/defensive gaming. Thus, the hybrid approach allows the automation of Go player by recognizing well known Go's tactics patterns to first and middle game actions in a match, then use MCTS for closing.

3   Experiments and the Results Analytical Comparison

The recognizing of *eyes*, *ladders* and *nets* patterns on the Go board is highly complex. The BPNNs were trained and tested as described below. A correct design of multi-layers NN is needed that implies the right number of hidden neurons so the NN be able for recognizing and learning the expected (complex) patterns; as well, the training time should not be large to avoid over-learn producing noise and/or redundancy. For present proposal the best recognition performance is fixing to five the number of neurons of the hidden layer. The average recognition performances got by different number of hidden neurons are shown in **Fig. 5**.

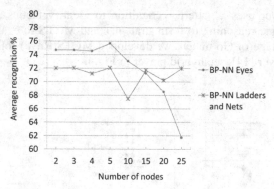

Fig. 5. Tradeoff between number of neurons in the hidden layer and recognition percentage

Eyes patterns. 900 tests were performed, divided into groups of 150. 400 *eyes* positive examples and 100 not-*eyes* negative examples were used to test the BPNN. In each group the means, minimums and maximums accuracies obtained in *eyes*/no-*eyes* examples, and the mean accuracy of BPNN are calculated. The average accuracy is above 70% as shown in **Table 2**.

Ladders and Nets patterns. A similar analysis was done for *ladders* and *nets*, applying 900 tests. Each test uses 100 hundred *ladders-nets* positive examples and one 100 no-*ladders-nets* negative examples; 70% accuracy is obtained, see **Table 3**.

Major difficulty to identify Go tactics patterns is to characterize a wide variety of shapes and sizes that in the Go match can appear. Obtained results prove certain improving on the BPNNs effectiveness to recognize complex patterns for Go gaming. In [18] focus on find Go patterns in game records *e.g.*, edge and corner patterns but few represent proper Go play patterns. In our approach, the recognized patterns are through a wide variety of shapes, not obvious (too complex) sometimes, but representing true

Go's tactics. See results in **Tables 2** and **3** that show only the accuracy of nets. Even the around 70% of efficiency recognition, results are good due to the complexity of these kinds of patterns.

Table 2. Results of BPNN *eyes*

Number of tests	Eyes positive examples			No-eyes negative examples			Total classification Eyes + No-eyes
	(Correct classification cases %)						
	Mean	Min.	Max.	Mean	Min.	Max	Mean
1 -150	83.68	80	90	67.58	58	74	75.77
151-300	83.24	80	88	68.04	60	74	75.64
301-450	83.58	80	91	67.72	56	74	75.65
451-600	83.78	80	91	67.45	60	74	75.62
601-750	83.62	80	90	67.69	60	74	75.65
751-900	83.32	81	88	67.96	60	74	75.64

Table 3. Results of BPNN *Ladders* and *nets*

Number of tests	Ladders-nets positive examples			No-ladders-nets negative examples			Total classification Ladders-net + No-ladders-nets
	(Correct classification cases %)						
	Mean	Min.	Max.	Mean	Min.	Max.	Mean
1 -150	86.96	60	100	56.06	21	75	71.51
151-300	87.19	61	100	56.16	30	75	71.67
301-450	86.7	48	100	56.89	26	90	71.79
451-600	85.88	29	100	57.58	25	100	71.73
601-750	86.34	43	100	56.83	25	90	71.58
751-900	87.78	63	100	55.09	22	80	71.44

3.1   Performance Comparison among Go Automated Players

Hybrid player uses recognition patterns, strategic reasoning along with MCTS (MC-Rave) [14]. **Strategic player** uses recognition patterns and strategic reasoning. **MC-Rave player** [14]. 30 tests on board size of 9 x 9 of the following combination were performed to make a comparison among them; with this amount of simulations we obtain a certain degree of confidence but do not rule out a larger set. 1). Hybrid vs. Hybrid, 2). Hybrid vs. Strategic player, 3). Strategic player vs. Hybrid, 4). Hybrid vs. MC-Rave, 5). MC-Rave vs. MC-Rave.

In **Fig. 6** is shown the performing of automated players based on 30 simulations. Result on black (hybrid) player vs. white (hybrid) player is 14/16 wins see **Fig. 6 (A)**. Result on: black (hybrid) player vs. white (strategic) player is 16/14 wins see **Fig. 6 (B)**. Black (strategic) player vs. white (hybrid) player is 19/11 wins see **Fig. 6 (C)**. In **Fig. 6**

(D) black (hybrid) player vs. white (MC-Rave) player is 22/8 wins and **Fig. 6 (E)** black (MC-Rave) player vs. white (MC-Rave) player is 13/17 wins.

The main idea to hybridize is to use techniques that have proven to be good in automating Go game. Our approach combine a learning technique along with a strategic reasoning in early and middle stages to improve the development of tactics and strategies that serves as the basis for the game progress and also with a simulation-based search algorithm MCTS to help to estimate the best positions in the final stage. As shown in the results, there is an advantage to the hybrid automated player vs. the other automated players: the hybrid method improves the performing of automated player with the use of different techniques depending on the evolution of Go match, i.e., in the Go game stages.

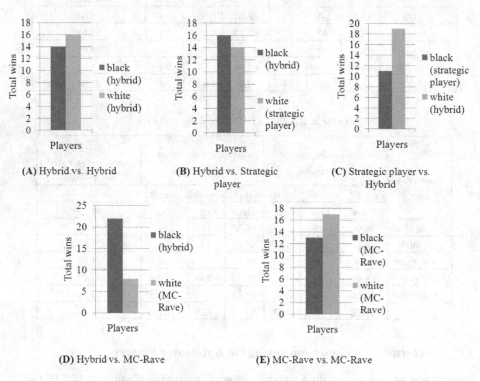

(A) Hybrid vs. Hybrid   **(B)** Hybrid vs. Strategic player   **(C)** Strategic player vs. Hybrid

(D) Hybrid vs. MC-Rave   **(E)** MC-Rave vs. MC-Rave

Fig. 6. Results of performing of automated players

3.2 Discussion

Learning methods help identify potential Go patterns. In some way, be aware of what the enemy is doing is good to propose game actions that inhibit enemy. The way human being think is varied and complex, and by *observing* people make decisions. In Go gaming, observed patterns in the Go board could be attractive to do something by offensive/defensive role, so being critical to decide the action to do. BPNNs identify forms that could be Go tactics patterns and provide information for a strategic reasoning method to make decisions.

Methods focused on simulation-based search algorithm such as Rave MCTS [12, 14, 15] tend to be very random in the beginning of any Go match. However, due to the large set of free positions the search is too complex for selecting a position; in contrast, by using strategic method makes efficiently the selection of a position. The Go game *is the long-term influence moves* [15], that means that moves made in the beginning affect the outcome of the later moves.

Our approach, from the beginning tries to make the best moves through the constructions of standard but previously known effective tactics and strategies; but when this method performance is coming down MCTS opportunely takes place.

The results show that the combination of pattern recognition, strategic reasoning and MCTS improves the performing of the player, according to results in Section 3.2. In the beginning and middle of match the use of a strategic reasoning is appropriated because allows the formations of the strategies and in the end of the game MCTS helps to evaluate the remainder free positions on the board.

4   Conclusions

Go automation is a complex task due to the enormous search space despite the simplicity of its rules. The automated Go player presented in this paper combines learning methods to enrich the automated player for recognizing Go tactics patterns, a strategic reasoning to make decisions with the aim of forming strategies and MCTS to choose free positions in the end of the game. The automated Go player is a work in progress, so open to be improved. Our approach combines some techniques to overcome a few the highly complex Go gaming decision making. The combination of these techniques merit further investigations since it shows results potentially can be applied to huge search space problem.

Acknowledgments. Thanks to the National Council of Science and Technology (CONACyT) from Mexico by the Arturo Yee Rendón PhD degree grant 261089.

References

1. Chen, K., Chen, Z.: Static Analysis of Life and Death in the Game of Go. Information Sciences 121(1), 113–134 (1999)
2. Allis, L.V.: Searching for Solutions in Games and Artificial Intelligence. PhD Thesis. University of Limburg, The Netherlands (1994)
3. McCarthy, J.: AI as sport. Science 276(5318), 1518–1519 (1997)
4. Benson, D.B.: Life in the game of Go. Information Sciences 10(2), 17–29 (1976)
5. Yoshiaki, N.: Strategic Concepts of Go. Ishi Press (1972)
6. Müller, M.: Computer Go. Artificial Intelligence 134(1), 145–179 (2002)
7. Richards, N., Moriarty, D.E., Miikkulainen, R.: Evolving Neural Networks to Play Go. Applied Intelligence 8(1), 85–96 (1998)
8. van der Werf, E.C.D., van den Herik, H.J., Uiterwijk, J.W.H.M.: Learning to Estimate Potential Territory in the Game of Go. In: van den Herik, H.J., Björnsson, Y., Netanyahu, N.S. (eds.) CG 2004. LNCS, vol. 3846, pp. 81–96. Springer, Heidelberg (2006)

9. Bouzy, B., Cazenave, T.: Computer Go(An AI Oriented Survey. Artificial Intelligence 132(1), 39–103 (2001)
10. Dahl, F.A.: Honte, a Go-Playing Program Using Neural Nets. Machines that Learn to Play Games, pp. 205–223. Nova Science Publishers, Inc. (2001)
11. Jianming, L., Difei, Z., Rui, L.: Improve Go AI based on BP-Neural Network. In: 2008 IEEE Conference on Cybernetics and Intelligent Systems (CIS 2008), pp. 487–490. IEEE (2008)
12. Browne, C.B., Powley, E., Whitehouse, D., Lucas, S.M., Cowling, P.I., Rohlfshagen, P., Tavener, S., Perez, D., Samothrakis, S., Colton, S.: A Survey of Monte Carlo Tree Search Methods. IEEE Transactions on Computational Intelligence and AI in Games 4(1), 1–49 (2012)
13. Chaslot, G., Bakkes, S., Szita, I., Spronck, P.: Monte-Carlo Tree Search A New Framework for Game AI. In: 4th Artificial Intelligence Interactive Digital Entertainment Conference (AIIDE 2008), pp. 216–217. AAAI (2008)
14. Gelly, S., Silver, D.: Monte-Carlo Tree Search and Rapid Action Value Estimation in Computer Go. Artificial Intelligence 175(11), 1856–1875 (2011)
15. Gelly, S., Kocsis, L., Schoenauer, M., Sebag, M., Silver, D., Szepesvari, C., Teytaud, O.: The Grand Challenge of Computer Go Monte Carlo Tree Search and Extensions. Communication of the ACM 55(3), 106–113 (2012)
16. Berlekamp, E.R., Wolfe, D.: Mathematical Go Chilling Gets the Last Point. A K Peters Ltd. (1997)
17. Yee, A., Alvarado, M.: Formal Language and Reasoning for Playing Go. In: 7th Latin American Workshop on Logic / Languages, Algorithms and New Methods of Reasoning (LANMR 2011). CEUR Workshop Proceedings, pp. 125–132 (2011)
18. Shi-Jim, Y., Tai-Ning, Y., Chang, C., Shun-Chin, H.: Pattern Matching in Go Game Records. In: 2nd International Conference on Innovative Computing, Information and Control (ICICIC 2007), pp. 297:14. IEEE (2007)

Exploring the Rationality of Some Syntactic Merging Operators

José Luis Chacón and Ramón Pino Pérez

Departamento de Matemáticas
Facultad de Ciencias
Universidad de Los Andes
Mérida, Venezuela
{jlchacon,pino}@ula.ve

Abstract. Most merging operators are defined by semantics methods which have very high computational complexity. In order to have operators with a lower computational complexity, some merging operators defined in a syntactical way have been proposed. In this work we define some syntactical merging operators and explore its rationality properties. To do that we constrain the belief bases to be sets of formulas very close to logic programs and the underlying logic is defined through forward chaining rule (Modus Ponens). We propose two types of operators: arbitration operators when the inputs are only two bases and fusion with integrity constraints operators. We introduce a set of postulates inspired on postulates LS, proposed by Liberatore and Shaerf and then we analyze the first class of operators through these postulates. We also introduce a set of postulates inspired on postulates KP, proposed by Konieczny and Pino Pérez and then we analyze the second class of operators through these postulates.

Keywords: belief revision, information fusion, merging operators, syntactic logic based belief change, postulates of rationality.

1 Introduction

Belief merging [2, 18, 24–27, 30] aims at combining several pieces of information when there is no strict precedence between them, unlike belief revision [1, 12, 17] where one combines two pieces of information one of which has higher priority. The agent faces several conflicting pieces of information coming from several sources of equal reliability[1], and he has to build a coherent description of the world from them. One important aspect of belief merging, differentiating this theory from belief revision -even from non-prioritized belief revision (see [13])- is the fact that n sources of information (with $n \geq 2$) are considered.

This work is about belief merging in the framework of logic-based representation of beliefs. In this framework beliefs are sets of propositional formulas.

---

[1] More generally the sources can have different reliability, but we will focus on the case where all the sources have the same reliability. There is already a lot to say in this case.

J. Pavón et al. (Eds.): IBERAMIA 2012, LNAI 7637, pp. 21–30, 2012.

Many merging operators have been defined in that setting (a complete survey of logic-based merging is [19]). Most merging operators are based in semantical representations and the computational complexity of the entailment problem is at least in the second level of the polynomial hierarchy. Precisely, the problem of deciding if a formula is entailed by the revised base is in the class Π_2^P [9, 28] and the fact that belief revision operators are a particular case of belief merging operators [18] tells us that the last operators are complex at least concerning the entailment problem.

In recent years there has been a growing interest in studying belief revision and merging in some particular fragments of propositional logic. In particular Horn clauses [5, 6, 8, 22], logic programs [7, 14] and other more general definable fragments [4].

Some works have been done to define change operators in a syntactic way [3, 10, 11, 15]. One interesting feature of some operators defined in [3] is that the computational complexity is polynomial. In that work some revision operators and update operators are syntactically defined with a restriction of the language and the logic. Therein the only inference rule is Modus Ponens and the formulas are very close to clauses in Logic Programming. But the semantics is classical and very simple and natural. Our representation of beliefs will be close to Logic Programs but with the natural and classical semantics. In the present work we study some operators of merging for which the beliefs have this simple representation.

The first idea we explore is the use of a revision operator $*$ to define binary merging operator $\triangle$. The key point is trying to emulate the following equation[2]

$$\varphi \triangle \psi = (\varphi * \psi) \vee (\psi * \varphi) \tag{1}$$

Notice that this kind of operators have been called arbitration operators by Liberatore and Schaerf [23, 24]. Actually they characterized these operators by a set of postulates of rationality. Here we adapt the postulates to the simple logic we use, we define syntactic arbitration operators and we study them in light of Liberatore and Shaerf postulates modified.

We explore afterwards the idea of defining merging operators with integrity constraints using the following equation as a guide:

$$\Delta_\mu(\varphi_1, \ldots, \varphi_n) = \begin{cases} \varphi_1 \wedge \cdots \wedge \varphi_n \wedge \mu, & \text{if consistent;} \\ \bigvee(\varphi_i * \mu), & \text{otherwise.} \end{cases} \tag{2}$$

We shall define syntactic merging operators with integrity constraints adapting the previous equation to the logic of forward chaining we use; we shall define the postulates characterizing merging operators (the natural adaptation of KP postulates [18]) in this simple setting and then we shall analyze the satisfaction of these postulates by our syntactic integrity constraint merging operators.

For the two kinds of operators we will see, on one hand, that the computational complexity is polynomial. This is a considerable gain with respect to the

---

[2] The symbols φ, ψ and μ (with subscripts if necessary) denote propositional formulas which are usually used to represent beliefs.

more classical merging operators; on the other hand, some postulates are not satisfied. That is the compromise in order to have tractable operators: you gain in computational complexity but you lose some properties.

The rest of the paper is organized as follows: Section 2 contains the basic definitions and the syntactic revision operators (first defined in [3]) used later. Section 3 is devoted to study a syntactic arbitrage operator following the lines of Equation 1. Section 4 is devoted to analyzing the syntactic merging operators defined following the lines of Equation 2. We finish with a section containing some concluding remarks. Due to space limitations, we have omitted the proofs and some examples. All this can be found in an extended version of this work at arXiv.org.

2 Preliminaries

Let $\mathcal{V}$ be a finite set of propositional variables. The elements of $\mathcal{V}$ are called atoms. A literal (or fact) is an atom or the negation of an atom. The set of literals will be denoted Lit. A rule is a formula of the shape $l_1 \wedge l_2 \cdots \wedge l_n \to l_{n+1}$ where l_i is a literal for $i = 1, \ldots, n+1$. Such a rule will be denoted $l_1, l_2, \cdots, l_n \to l_{n+1}$; the part $l_1, l_2, \cdots, l_n$ is called the body of the rule and l_{n+1} is called the head of the rule. A fact l can be seen as a rule $\to l$ with empty body.

Let R and L be a finite set of rules with non empty body and a finite set of facts respectively. A program P is a set of the form $R \cup L$. In such a case we will say that the elements of R are the rules of P and the elements of L are the facts of P. The set of programs will be denoted $Prog$. Let $P = R \cup L$ be a program. We define the consequences by forward chaining of P, denoted $C_{fc}(P)$, as the smallest set of literals (with respect to inclusion) L' such that:

(i) $L \subseteq L'$.
(ii) If $l_1, l_2, \ldots, l_n \to l$ is in R and $l_i \in L'$ for $i = 1, \ldots, n$ then $l \in L'$.
(iii) If L' contains two opposed literals (an atom and its negation) then $L' = Lit$.

A program P is consistent if $C_{fc}(P)$ does not contain two opposed literals (or alternatively $C_{fc}(P) \neq Lit$), otherwise we say that P is inconsistent and it will be denoted $P \vdash \bot$. Let R, L and L' be a finite set of rules and two finite sets of facts respectively. L is said to be R-consistent if $R \cup L$ is consistent. L is said to be $R \cup L'$ consistent if $L \cup (R \cup L')$ is consistent. Thus, if P is a program, L is P-consistent if $L \cup P$ is consistent. Let L and P be a set of literals and a program respectively. L is said to be fc-consequence of P if $L \subseteq C_{fc}(P)$.

It is important to note that in this setting the problem of the consistency is polynomial and the problem of a literal entailment is also polynomial.

We can define a very natural hierarchy over $C_{fc}(P)$ for a program P. Let L be $C_{fc}(P)$. We define a partition of L, $L = L_0 \cup L_1 \cdots \cup L_r$, inductively in the following way: L_0 is the set of facts of program P; L_i are the literals $l \in L \setminus \{L_0 \cup L_1 \cdots \cup L_{i-1}\}$ such that there is a rule $l_1, l_2, \ldots, l_k \to l \in P$ satisfying $\{l_1, \ldots, l_k\} \subset L_0 \cup L_1 \cdots \cup L_{i-1}$. Thus, in L_1 we find the literals not in L_0 and obtained by the rules of P using the literals of L_0. In L_i we find the literals not in L_j with $0 \le j < i$ obtained by the rules of P using the literals of $L_0 \cup \cdots \cup L_{i-1}$. Since $P = R \cup L_0$, where R is a finite set of rules and L_0 is a finite set of facts, it follows that $|L| \le |L_0| + |R|$, so each L_i is a finite set.

Now we shall recall some definitions of operators in [3].

Definition 1 (Exceptional sets of literals and rules). *Let P be a program. A set of literals L is said to be exceptional for P if L is not P-consistent. A rule $L \to l$ in P is exceptional for P if L is exceptional for P.*

The point that makes all computations simple is the fact that, given the definition of entailment and consistency we have, to know if a set of literals is P-consistent is polynomial.

Notice that if P is not consistent all its rules are exceptional. The following hierarchy of a program appears in [29]. It has been very useful (e.g. [21]).

Definition 2 (Base). *Let P be a program. We define $(P_i)_{i \in w}$ a decreasing sequence of programs in the following way: P_0 is P and P_{i+1} is the set of exceptional rules of P_i. Since P is finite, there is a first integer n_0 such that for all $m > n_0$, $P_m = P_{n_0}$. If $P_{n_0} \ne \varnothing$ we say that $\langle P_0, \ldots, P_{n_0}, \varnothing \rangle$ is the base of P. If $P_{n_0} = \varnothing$, then $\langle P_0, \ldots, P_{n_0} \rangle$ will be the base of P.*

Definition 3 (Rank function). *Let P be a program and let $\langle P_0, \ldots, P_n \rangle$ be its base. We define $\rho(P, \cdot) : Prog \to \mathbb{N}$, the rank function, as follows: $\rho(P, Q) = min\{i \in \mathbb{N} : Q \text{ is } P_i - consistent\}$ if P and Q are consistent, otherwise $\rho(P, Q) = n$. Notice that if $Q_1 \subseteq Q_2$ then $\rho(P, Q_1) \le \rho(P, Q_2)$.*

Definition 4 (Rank revision). *Let P and P' be two programs. We define the rank revision operator of P by P', denoted $P \circ_{rk} P'$, as follows:*

$$P \circ_{rk} P' = P_{\rho(P,P')} \cup P'$$

That is, we take the new piece of information P' together with the first program in the base (the least exceptional) which is consistent with P'.

In order to generalize this operator we need to define the hull of a program P with respect to another program P'. Let $I_P(P')$ be the set of subsets of P which are consistent with P', contain $P_{\rho(P,P')}$ and maximal with these properties. We define $h_P : Prog \to \mathcal{P}(P)$ by letting $h_P(P') = \bigcap I_P(P')$. The computation of $I_P(P')$ is exponential.

Definition 5 (Hull revision). *Let P and P' be two programs. We define the hull revision operator of P by P', denoted $P \circ_h P'$, as follows:*

$$P \circ_h P' = h_P(P') \cup P'$$

Observation 1. *It is easy to see, by the definitions, that $C_{fc}(P \circ_{rk} P') \subseteq C_{fc}(P \circ_h P')$. In such a case we say that $\circ_h$ is a conservative extension of $\circ_{rk}$. Actually, there are examples in which the inclusion is strict.*

In order to define the extended hull revision we define first what is a flock of programs. This is simply a vector $\langle Q_0, \ldots, Q_n \rangle$ where each Q_i is a program. We use the letters $\mathcal{A}$, $\mathcal{F}$ (with subscripts if necessary) to denote flocks. We define the concatenation of flocks in the natural way: $\langle P_1, \ldots, P_n \rangle \cdot \langle Q_1, \ldots, Q_m \rangle \overset{def}{=}$ $\langle P_1, \ldots, P_n, Q_1, \ldots, Q_m \rangle$. Suppose that $\mathcal{A}$ is a flock, say $\mathcal{A} = \langle Q_1, \ldots, Q_n \rangle$, we define $C_{fc}(\mathcal{A}) = \bigcap_{i=1}^{n} C_{fc}(Q_i)$. We identify a program P with the flock $\langle P \rangle$. With this identification flocks are more general objects than programs. We are going to define revision operators of flocks by programs in which the output will be a flock. First we consider $I_P(Q)$ as a flock and we give the following definition:

Definition 6. *Let P, P' be two programs. Let $I_P(P')$ be as before. We put*

$$P \circ_{eh} P' = \begin{cases} \langle H_1 \cup P', \ldots, H_n \cup P' \rangle & \text{if } I_P(P') = \{H_1, \ldots, H_n\} \\ P' & \text{if } I_P(P') = \varnothing \end{cases}$$

More generally, if $\mathcal{A} = \langle Q_1, \ldots, Q_n \rangle$, we define

$$\mathcal{A} \circ_{eh} P = (Q_1 \circ_{eh} P) \cdot (Q_2 \circ_{eh} P) \cdots (Q_n \circ_{eh} P)$$

where the symbol $\cdot$ denotes the concatenation of flocks.

Observation 2. *With the previous definition $\circ_{eh}$ is a conservative extension of $\circ_h$, that is, $C_{fc}(P \circ_h P') \subseteq C_{fc}(P \circ_{eh} P')$. To see that, it is enough to notice that $h_P(P') \subseteq H_i$ for all $H_i \in I_P(P')$. For this reason the operator $\circ_{eh}$ is called extended hull revision.*

For a study of AGM postulates satisfied by the previous operators we suggest the reader see the work in [3].

3 Syntactic Arbitrage Operators

Liberatore and Schaerf [23, 24] define a kind of merging operators called arbitrage operators (or commutative revision operators). They consider beliefs that are represented by propositional formulas built in a finite propositional language. Their operators, denoted $\diamond$, map two belief bases in a new belief base and they are characterized by a set of postulates of rationality. Actually, Liberatore and Schaerf [24] prove that if $\circ$ is a revision operator (see [16]) then $\diamond$ defined by letting $\varphi \diamond \mu = (\varphi \circ \mu) \vee (\mu \circ \varphi)$ is an arbitrage operator.

Inspired by the previous ideas and having syntactic revision operators we are going to define syntactic arbitrage operators. We shall redefine the postulates of arbitrage in the syntactical framework and we shall analyze the relationships between our operators and these new postulates.

In order to define the syntactic operators and state the new postulates, we must provide operators simulating over programs the conjunction and the disjunction over formulas respectively. Thus, the operator $\odot : Prog^2 \to \mathcal{P}(Lit)$ (simulating the conjunction) is defined by:

$$P_1 \odot P_2 = C_{fc}(P_1 \cup P_2)$$

and the operator $\oplus : Prog^2 \to \mathcal{P}(Lit)$ (simulating the disjunction) is defined by:

$$P_1 \oplus P_2 = C_{fc}(P_1) \cap C_{fc}(P_2)$$

The operator $\odot$ over programs corresponds to operator $\wedge$ over formulas and the operator $\oplus$ over programs corresponds to operator $\vee$.

Now we define three syntactic arbitrage operators of the shape $\diamond : Prog^2 \to \mathcal{P}(Lit)$ in the following way:

$$P_1 \diamond P_2 = (P_1 \star P_2) \oplus (P_2 \star P_1) \tag{3}$$

where $\star \in \{\circ_{rk}, \circ_h, \circ_{eh}\}$ with $\circ_{rk}, \circ_h, \circ_{eh}$ the rank revision, the hull revision and the extended hull revision respectively. Thus we dispose of three syntactic operators: $\diamond_{rk}, \diamond_h, \diamond_{eh}$ called rank arbitration operator, hull arbitration operator and extended hull arbitration operator respectively.

The following postulates are the natural translation of the postulates of Liberatore and Shaerf [24] for arbitration operators to our framework (SA states Syntactic Arbitration):

(SA1) $P \diamond Q = Q \diamond P$
(SA2) $P \diamond Q \subseteq P \odot Q$
(SA3)   If $P \odot Q \nvdash \bot$ then $P \odot Q \subseteq P \diamond Q$
(SA4) $P \diamond Q \vdash \bot$ if and only if $P \vdash \bot$ and $Q \vdash \bot$
(SA5)   If $C_{fc}(P_1) = C_{fc}(P_2)$ and $C_{fc}(Q_1) = C_{fc}(Q_2)$ then $P_1 \diamond Q_1 = P_2 \diamond Q_2$
(SA6) $P \diamond (Q_1 \oplus Q_2) = \begin{cases} P \diamond Q_1 & \text{or} \\ P \diamond Q_2 & \text{or} \\ (P \diamond Q_1) \oplus (P \diamond Q_2) \end{cases}$
(SA7) $P \oplus Q \subseteq P \diamond Q$
(SA8)   If $P \nvdash \bot$ then $P \odot (P \diamond Q) \nvdash \bot$

Postulate SA1 states that the two pieces of information have equal priority. Postulate SA2 says that "conjunction" is stronger than arbitration. Postulate SA3, together with SA2, say that under the consistency of the "conjunction" of programs, such a "conjunction" is the result of arbitration of programs. Postulate SA4 says that the only possibility for the inconsistency of arbitration is the inconsistency of each input. Postulate SA5 is the equivalence of the syntax in our context. Postulate SA6 is the trichotomy postulate in our context. Postulate SA7 says that arbitration is stronger than "disjunction". Postulate SA8 says that the output of arbitration will be consistent with any consistent input.

The following result summarizes the behavior of our arbitration operators with respect to the postulates above defined.

Theorem 1. *The operators $\diamond_{rk}, \diamond_h, \diamond_{eh}$ satisfy the postulates SA1, SA2, SA3, SA4, SA7 and SA8. They don't satisfy SA5 nor SA6.*

Next example will illustrate the behavior of our three syntactic operators. In particular we shall see that they have behaviors well differentiated.

Example 1. *Let P and Q be two programs defined as follows: $P = \{a, b \to \neg c; b \to d; b \to \neg c; \neg c \to e; a, \neg c \to f; a\}$ and $Q = \{a, b \to c; a \to e; a, e \to c; a, e \to d; c \to d; c \to f; b\}$. Then $C_{fc}(P) = \{a\}$ and $C_{fc}(Q) = \{b\}$. It is easy to verify that the bases of P and Q have two levels. No rule is exceptional, thus*

$P_1 = Q_1 = \varnothing$. *Since $P \cup Q$ is not consistent, we have $P_{\rho(P,Q)} = Q_{\rho(Q,P)} = \varnothing$. Therefore $I_Q(P)$ is the set of maximal subsets of Q which are P-consistent. With a simple computation, we can verify that $I_Q(P) = \{T_1, T_2\}$ where $T_1 = \{a \to e; a, e \to d; c \to d; c \to f; b\}$ and $T_2 = \{a, b \to c; a \to e; a, e \to c; a, e \to d; c \to d; c \to f\}$. Moreover $C_{fc}(T_1 \cup P) = \{a, b, \neg c, d, e, f\}$ and $C_{fc}(T_2 \cup P) = \{a, d, e\}$. For the same reasons as before, $I_P(Q)$ is the set of maximal subsets of P which are Q-consistent. This can be easily computed: $I_P(Q) = \{H_1, H_2\}$ where $H_1 = \{b \to d; \neg c \to e; a, \neg c \to f; a\}$ and $H_2 = \{a, b \to \neg c; b \to d; b \to \neg c; \neg c \to e; a, \neg c \to f\}$. Then, $C_{fc}(H_1 \cup Q) = \{a, b, c, d, e, f\}$ and $C_{fc}(H_2 \cup Q) = \{b, \neg c, d, e\}$. Thus, $\cap I_Q(P) = \{a \to e; c \to d; c \to f\}$ and $\cap I_P(Q) = \{b \to d; \neg c \to e; a, \neg c \to f\}$. Therefore, $C_{fc}(\cap I_Q(P) \cup P) = \{a, e, d\}$ and $C_{fc}(\cap I_P(Q) \cup Q) = \{b, d\}\}$. Finally we can compute the outputs for the three operators. $P \diamond_h Q = (P \circ_h Q) \oplus (Q \circ_h P) = C_{fc}(P \circ_h Q) \cap C_{fc}(Q \circ_h P) = \{d\}$. Since $P_{\rho(P,Q)} \cup Q = Q$ and $Q_{\rho(Q,P)} \cup P = P$, we have $P \diamond_{rk} Q = C_{fc}(P) \cap C_{fc}(Q) = \varnothing$. For the last operator we have $P \diamond_{eh} Q = (P \circ_{eh} Q) \oplus (Q \circ_{eh} P) = C_{fc}(P \circ_{eh} Q) \cap C_{fc}(Q \circ_{eh} P)$ where $C_{fc}(P \circ_{eh} Q) = C_{fc}(H_1 \cup Q) \cap C_{fc}(H_2 \cup Q) = \{b, d, e\}$ and $C_{fc}(Q \circ_{eh} P) = C_{fc}(T_1 \cup P) \cap C_{fc}(T_2 \cup P) = \{a, d, e\}$. Therefore $P \diamond_{eh} Q = \{d, e\}$. Summarizing, we have:*

$$P \diamond_{rk} Q = \varnothing \subset \{d\} = P \diamond_h Q \subset \{d, e\} = P \diamond_{eh} Q$$

4   Merging Programs

Merging operators with integrity constraints were defined in [18]. Therein we can find a characterization in terms of postulates. The aim of this section will be to define merging operators for the representation of beliefs as programs, as those presented in Sect. 2 with the logic of forward chaining defined therein. We shall also define the merging postulates in this syntactical framework and we shall study the relationships between our new operators and the postulates.

We denote by *Prog* the set of all the programs; $\mathcal{M}(Prog)$ will denote the set of finite and nonempty multisets of nonempty programs. The merging operators Δ we are interested in, are operators from $\mathcal{M}(Prog) \times Prog$ into subsets of *Lit*. The multisets of programs are called profiles and we shall use the letters Φ and Ψ (with subscripts if necessary) to denote them. If $\Phi = \{P_1, \ldots, P_n\}$ is a profile and P is a program, $\Delta(\Phi, P)$ must be understood as the result of merging the programs in Φ under the constraint P. We shall write $\Delta_P(\Phi)$ or $\Delta_P(P_1, \ldots, P_n)$ instead of $\Delta(\Phi, P)$. For a profile Φ we denote by $\cup \Phi$ the union of all programs in Φ. If Φ_1 and Φ_2 are profiles we denote by $\Phi_1 \sqcup \Phi_2$ the new profile resulting of the union of multisets (e.g. $\{P\} \sqcup \{P\} = \{P, P\}$).

Guided by Equation 2, and the interpretation of "disjunction" already defined, we set the following definition for $* \in \{rk, h, eh\}$:

$$\Delta_P^*(P_1, \ldots, P_n) = \begin{cases} C_{fc}(P \cup P_1 \ldots \cup P_n), & \text{if this is consistent;} \\ \cap C_{fc}(P_i \circ_* P), & \text{otherwise.} \end{cases} \tag{4}$$

where the profile is $\{P_1, \ldots, P_n\}$ (the programs to merge), under the integrity constraint P and $\circ_*$ is the rank revision, hull revision or extended hull revision if $*$ is rk, h or eh respectively. We adopt the following definition of entailment for programs P and Q: we put $P \vdash Q$ whenever $C_{fc}(Q) \subset C_{fc}(P)$.

The following postulates are the adaptation of postulates characterizing merging operators with integrity constraints (see [18]):

Let $\Phi = \{P_1, \ldots, P_n\}$.

(FP0) $\Delta_P(\Phi) \vdash P$

(FP1) If P is consistent, then $\Delta_P(\Phi)$ is consistent.

(FP2) If $C_{fc}(\cup\Phi \cup P)$ is consistent, then $\Delta_P(\Phi) = C_{fc}(\cup\Phi \cup P)$.

(FP3) If $\Phi_1 = \{P_1, \ldots P_n\}$, $\Phi_2 = \{Q_1, \ldots, Q_n\}$, $C_{fc}(P_i) = C_{fc}(Q_i)$, $C_{fc}(P) = C_{fc}(Q)$, then $\Delta_P(\Phi_1) = \Delta_Q(\Phi_2)$

(FP4) If $P_1 \vdash P$, $P_2 \vdash P$ and P_1 and P_2 are consistent, then

$$C_{fc}(\Delta_P(P_1, P_2) \cup P_1) \neq Lit \Rightarrow C_{fc}(\Delta_P(P_1, P_2) \cup P_2) \neq Lit$$

(FP5) $\Delta_P(\Phi_1) \cup \Delta_P(\Phi_2) \vdash \Delta_P(\Phi_1 \sqcup \Phi_2)$

(FP6) If $\Delta_P(\Phi_1) \cup \Delta_P(\Phi_2)$ is consistent, then $\Delta_P(\Phi_1 \sqcup \Phi_2) \vdash \Delta_P(\Phi_1) \cup \Delta_P(\Phi_2)$

(FP7) $\Delta_P(\Phi) \cup Q \vdash \Delta_{P \cup Q}(\Phi)$

(FP8) If $\Delta_P(\Phi) \cup Q$ is consistent, then $\Delta_{P \cup Q}(\Phi) \vdash \Delta_P(\Phi) \cup Q$

Postulate FP0 means that the integrity constraint is respected. Postulate FP1 establishes the consistency of the merging whenever the integrity constraints are consistent. Postulate FP2 establishes that in the case where there is no conflict between the pieces of information, the output is the consequence of putting all pieces together. Postulate FP3 is the independence of the syntax in our framework. Postulate FP4 is the postulate of fairness. Postulates FP5 and FP6 refer to a good behavior of the merging of subgroups: if the merging of subgroups agree on some facts and it is consistent, the result of the merging on the whole group is the set of facts on which the subgroups agree. Postulates FP7 and FP8 concern the iteration of the process (see [18] for more detailed explanations about the postulates).

The following theorem shows the behavior of the operator defined by Equation (4) with respect to the postulates in the case of ranked revision.

Theorem 2. *The operator Δ^{rk} satisfies the postulates* FP0, FP1, FP2 *and* FP4. *It doesn't satisfy* FP3 *nor* FP5-FP8

The following theorem shows the behavior of the merging operators defined by Equation (4) with respect to hull revision and extended hull revision.

Theorem 3. *The operators Δ^h and Δ^{eh} satisfy the postulates* FP0, FP1 *and* FP4. *They don't satisfy* FP3-FP8

5 Conclusions

We have defined three syntactic arbitration operators. They satisfy Postulates (SA1)−(SA4) and (SA7)−(SA8) but they fail to satisfy Postulates (SA5)−(SA6). These operators seem to be a good compromise between rationality and computation, good properties and tractability. The operator $\diamond_{rk}$ is polynomial because

$\circ_{rk}$ is clearly polynomial. The other operators have a higher computational complexity inherent to computation of maximal consistent sets.

Concerning merging with integrity constraints, we have also three syntactic operators. The operator defined using rank revision satisfies Postulates (FP0), (FP1), (FP2) and (FP4), whereas the merging operators defined using hull revision and extended hull revision satisfy only Postulates (FP0), (FP1) and (FP2). Thus in the case of merging with integrity constraints the operator Δ defined with rank revision is better than the two other operators both from the point of view of rational behavior as from the point of view of computational complexity.

In order to satisfy more rational properties, it will be interesting to explore other alternatives to definition given by Equation (4), in particular, the use of some kinds of aggregation functions (like majority) to produce the resulting facts(see for instance [20]) could lead to operators having a better behavior. It remains also to explore the exact relationships between properties of arbitration and merging operators defined in Equations (3), (4) and the properties of revision operators used in those definitions.

References

1. Alchourrón, C.E., Gärdenfors, P., Makinson, D.: On the Logic of Theory Change – Partial Meet Contraction and Revision Functions. Journal of Symbolic Logic 50, 510–530 (1985)
2. Baral, C., Kraus, S., Minker, J.: Combining Multiple Knowledge Bases. IEEE Transactions on Knowledge and Data Engineering 3(2), 208–220 (1991)
3. Bezzazi, H., Janot, S., Konieczny, S., Pino Pérez, R.: Analysing Rational Properties of Change Operators Based on Forward Chaining. In: Freitag, B , Decker, H., Kifer, M., Voronkov, A. (eds.) Dagstuhl Seminar 1997, DYNAMICS 1997, and ILPS-WS 1997. LNCS, vol. 1472, pp. 317–339. Springer, Heidelberg (1998)
4. Creignou, N., Papini, O., Pichler, R., Woltran, S.: Belief Revision within Fragments of Propositional Logic. In: Brewka, G., Eiter, T., McIlraith, S.A. (eds.) 13th International Conference on the Principles of Knowledge Representation and Reasoning (KR 2012), pp. 126–136. AAAI Press (2012)
5. Delgrande, J.P.: Horn Clause Belief Change – Contraction Functions. In: Brewka, G., Lang, J. (eds.) 11th International Conference on the Principles of Knowledge Representation and Reasoning (KR 2008), pp. 156–165. AAAI Press (2008)
6. Delgrande, J.P., Peppas, P.: Revising Horn Theories. In: Walsh, T. (ed.) 22nd International Joint Conference on Artificial Intelligence (IJCAI 2011), pp. 839–844. IJCAI/AAAI (2011)
7. Delgrande, J.P., Schaub, T., Tompits, H., Woltran, S.: Merging Logic Programs under Answer Set Semantics. In: Hill, P.M., Warren, D.S. (eds.) ICLP 2009. LNCS, vol. 5649, pp. 160–174. Springer, Heidelberg (2009)
8. Delgrande, J.P., Wassermann, R.: Horn Clause Contraction Functions: Belief Set and Belief Base Approaches. In: 12th International Conference on the Principles of Knowledge Representation and Reasoning (KR 2010), pp. 143–152 (2010)
9. Eiter, T., Gottlob, G.: On the Complexity of Propositional Knowledge Base Revision, Updates, and Counterfactuals. Artificial Intelligence 57(2-3), 227–270 (1992)
10. Falappa, M.A., Kern-Isberner, G., Reis, M., Simari, G.R.: Prioritized and Non-prioritized Multiple Change on Belief Bases. Journal of Philosophical Logic 41, 77–113 (2012)

11. Fuhrmann, A.: An Essay on Contraction. Studies in logic, language and information. CSLI Publications (1997)
12. Gärdenfors, P.: Knowledge in flux. MIT Press (1988)
13. Hansson, S.O.: What's New Isn't Always Best. Theoria 63, 1–13 (1998)
14. Hué, J., Papini, O., Würbel, E.: Merging Belief Bases Represented by Logic Programs. In: Sossai, C., Chemello, G. (eds.) ECSQARU 2009. LNCS, vol. 5590, pp. 371–382. Springer, Heidelberg (2009)
15. Hué, J., Würbel, E., Papini, O.: Removed Sets Fusion – Performing Off the Shelf. In: 18th European Conf. on Artificial Intelligence (ECAI 2008), pp. 94–98 (2008)
16. Katsuno, H., Mendelzon, A.O.: On the Difference Between Updating a Knowledge Base and Revising It. In: 2nd International Conference on Principles of Knowledge Representation and Reasoning (KR 1991), pp. 387–394. Morgan Kaufmann (1991)
17. Katsuno, H., Mendelzon, A.O.: Propositional Knowledge Base Revision and Minimal Change. Artificial Intelligence 52, 263–294 (1991)
18. Konieczny, S., Pino Pérez, R.: Merging Information Under Constraints – A Logical Framework. Journal of Logic and Computation 12(5), 773–808 (2002)
19. Konieczny, S., Pino Pérez, R.: Logic Based Merging. Journal of Philosophical Logic 40(2), 239–270 (2011)
20. Konieczny, S.: On the Difference Between Merging Knowledge Bases and Combining Them. In: 7th International Conference on Principles of Knowledge Representation and Reasoning (KR 2000), pp. 135–144. Morgan Kaufmann (2000)
21. Lang, J., Marquis, P.: Resolving Inconsistencies by Variable Forgetting. In: 8th International Conference on Principles of Knowledge Representation and Reasoning (KR 2002), pp. 239–250. Morgan Kaufmann (2002)
22. Langlois, M., Sloan, R.H., Szörényi, B., Turán, G.: Horn Complements – Towards Horn-to-Horn Belief Revision. In: 23rd AAAI Conference on Artificial Intelligence (AAAI 2008), pp. 466–471 (2008)
23. Liberatore, P., Schaerf, M.: A Commutative Operator for Belief Revision. In: 2nd World Conference on the Fundamentals of Artificial Intelligence (WOCFAI 1995), pp. 217–228. Angkor (1995)
24. Liberatore, P., Schaerf, M.: Arbitration or How to Merge Knowledge Bases. IEEE Transactions on Knowledge and Data Engineering 10(1), 76–90 (1998)
25. Lin, J.: Integration of Weighted Knowledge Bases. Artificial Intelligence 83(2), 363–378 (1996)
26. Lin, J., Mendelzon, A.O.: Merging Databases Under Constraints. International Journal of Cooperative Information System 7(1), 55–76 (1998)
27. Lin, J., Mendelzon, A.O.: Knowledge Base Merging by Majority. In: Pareschi, R., Fronhofer, B. (eds.) Dynamic Worlds: From the Frame Problem to Knowledge Management. Kluwer (1999)
28. Nebel, B.: Belief Revision and Default Resoning – Syntax-Based Approaches. In: 2nd International Conference on Principles of Knowledge Representation and Reasoning (KR 1991), pp. 417–428. Morgan Kaufmann (1991)
29. Pearl, J.: System Z – A Natural Ordering of Defaults with Tractable Applications to Nonmonotonic Reasoning. In: 3rd Conference on Theoretical Aspects of Reasoning About Knowledge (TARK 1990), pp. 121–135. Morgan Kaufmann (1990)
30. Revesz, P.Z.: On the Semantics of Arbitration. International Journal of Algebra and Computation 7(2), 133–160 (1997)

Fuzzy Cognitive Maps for Modelling, Predicting and Interpreting HIV Drug Resistance

Isel Grau, Gonzalo Nápoles, Maikel León, and Ricardo Grau

Centro de Estudios de Informática
Universidad Central "Marta Abreu" de Las Villas, Santa Clara, Cuba
{igrau,gnapoles,mle,rgrau}@uclv.edu.cu

Abstract. The high mutability of Human Immunodeficiency Virus (HIV) leads to serious problems on designing efficient antiviral drugs. In fact, in last years the study of drug resistance prediction for HIV mutations has become an open problem for researchers. Several machine learning techniques have been proposed for modelling this sequence classification problem, but most of them are difficult to interpret. This paper presents a modelling of the protease protein as a dynamic system through Fuzzy Cognitive Maps, using the amino acid contact energies for the sequence description. In addition, a Particle Swarm Optimization based learning scheme called PSO-RSVN is used to estimate the causal weight matrix that characterize these structures. Finally, a study with statistical techniques for knowledge discovery is conducted, for determining patterns in the causal influences of each sequence position on the resistance to five well-known inhibitor drugs.

Keywords: HIV, drug resistance, fuzzy cognitive maps, particle swarm optimization, clustering, knowledge discovery.

1 Introduction

The Human Immunodeficiency Virus is a complex and dynamical *Lentivirus* plaguing humanity harshly causing millions of deaths yearly. Although antiviral drugs are not able to eradicate the HIV, they are designed to inhibit the function of three essential proteins in the virus replication process: protease, reverse transcriptase and integrase. For example, protease inhibitors avoid the maturation of released viral particles by cleaving precursor proteins. However, due to a high mutation rate, this virus is capable to develop resistance to existing drugs, eventually causing the treatment failure. Thus, modelling of resistance mechanism requires the study of viral genome for designing more effective therapies using existing drugs [1].

Resistance testing can be performed either by measuring viral activity in the presence and absence of a drug (phenotypic resistance testing), or by sequencing the viral genes coding for the drug targets (genotypic resistance testing). Genotypic assays are much faster and cheaper, but sequence data provide only indirect evidence of resistance [2], giving a limited knowledge of the HIV behaviour. Therefore, in order to discover more relevant and consistent information, other biological, mathematical or computational approaches are required.

J. Pavón et al. (Eds.): IBERAMIA 2012, LNAI 7637, pp. 31–40, 2012.

Several machine learning techniques have been proposed to predict phenotypic resistance using genotypic information including Neural Networks [3], Recurrent Neural Networks [4], Support Vector Machine regression [5] and Decision Tree classification [6]. These models have achieved good performance in terms of prediction accuracy, but only a few can be interpreted in order to explain the effect of mutational patterns on the resistance phenotype, that is, the relationships among the amino acids and its influence on the resistance.

In this work, Fuzzy Cognitive Maps (FCMs) are used for modelling the protease protein as a dynamic system. These neural structures are useful to create models that emulate the behaviour of complex processes using fuzzy causal relationships. For this reason, this technique allows us to predict drug resistance from a given mutation sequence and to interpret the effect of a punctual mutation on the resistance.

The rest of the paper is organized as follows: in next Sect. 2 the theoretical background of FCMs is described, and also the proposal for the modelling problem. In Sect. 3 we introduce a learning scheme to estimate the FCMs weight matrixes or causal relation values. Section 4 gives the experimental settings, while Sect. 4.1 provides details about the knowledge discovery process. Finally, conclusions and further research aspects are discussed in Sect. 5.

2 Fuzzy Cognitive Maps

Fuzzy Cognitive Maps [7] are an effective Soft Computing technique for modelling and simulation of dynamic systems that combine some aspects of Fuzzy Logic and Neural Networks in their representation schemes: the heuristic and common sense rules of Fuzzy Logic with the learning heuristics of the Neural Networks. They are directed graphs with feedback, consisting of nodes and weighted arcs (see Fig. 1). Nodes of the graph stand for the concepts that are used to describe the behaviour of the system and they are connected by signed and weighted arcs representing the causal relationships that exist among the concepts.

It must be mentioned that the values in the graph are fuzzy, so concepts take values in the range between [0,1] and also the weights of the arcs are in the interval [-1,1]. The weights of the arcs between concept C_i and concept C_j could be positive which means that an augment in the value of concept C_i leads to the increase of the C_j value, whereas a decrease in the value of concept C_i leads to a reduce of the C_j value; or there is negative causality which means that an increase in the value of concept C_i leads to the decrease of the C_j value and vice versa [8].

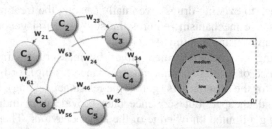

Fig. 1. Simple Fuzzy Cognitive Map. Concept activation level

The FCMs inference process involves a mathematical model. It consists of a state vector $A_{1 \times n}$ which includes the values of the n concepts and a weight matrix $W_{n \times n}$ which gathers the weights w_{ij} of the interconnections among the n concepts. For each concept, its value is influenced by the values of the connected concepts with the appropriate weights and by its previous value. The activation value for each concept is iteratively calculated by the following rule (1):

$$A_i^{(t+1)} = f\left(\sum_{j=1}^{n} w_{ij} A_j^{(t)}\right), i \neq j. \tag{1}$$

where t indexes the current time, A_i is the activation level of concept C_i, A_j is the activation level of concept C_j, and w_{ij} is the weight of the interconnection between C_i and C_j, whereas f is a threshold or normalization function. The new vector shows the effect of the change in the value of one concept in the whole map.

In order to build a single FCM, the knowledge and experience of one expert on the system operations must be used. The expert determines the concepts that best illustrate the system; where a concept can be a feature of the system, a state or a system variable; identifying which factors are central for the system modelling and representing a concept for each one. Moreover, the expert has observed which elements influences other elements, and for corresponding concepts the experts could be determine the negative or positive effect of one concept on the others.

2.1   Modelling Protease Proteins through Fuzzy Cognitive Maps

The main proposition in this work is to model the protease protein as a dynamic system using FCMs theory. This modelling is able to support the prediction of the drug resistance from a given protease mutation sequence and to interpret the causal relations among the amino acids and its influence on the resistance.

Protease sequence is defined by 99 amino acids where each one is characterized by the contact energy. The contact energy [9] of an amino acid is a numerical descriptor that corresponds to the tridimensional structure of proteins and it is calculated statistically from a large number of diverse sequences. So, for modelling this, each sequence position (amino acid) is taken as a map concept, and another extra concept for the resistance is also defined. Moreover we establish causal relations among all amino acids, and between each one of them and the resistance concept. This proposal is supported by the fact that exist relations among not necessarily adjacent positions of the sequence; where a change in the contact energy of a specific amino acid (to be considered as a mutation) could be relevant in the drug resistance.

To predict the resistance concept (phenotype) from predictor concepts (genotype) means to solve, for each drug, the related sequence classification problem; where the activation value for each predictor is taken as its normalized contact energy (in the range [0,1]). Following this idea, the resistance concept should be considered as a binary concept (1-resistent, 0-susceptible) defined by a drug-specified cut-off. The causal relations among concepts are defined by a causal weight matrix ($W_{n \times n+1}$). This augmented matrix defines, for each amino acid AA_i, the interaction with the others (AA_j), and additionally characterizes the causal interaction between each descriptor

AA$_i$ and the resistance concept (denoted as R). In this model we assume that self-connections are not allowed in the graph, which means that i ≠ j. Figure 2 shows the general scheme for the modelling process.

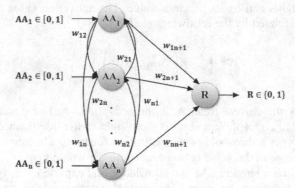

Fig. 2. General scheme for modelling protease through FCMs theory

Although developing an FCM using automatic approaches is relevant, could be complex to find the causal weight matrix W, since the knowledge from experts is not enough and it is difficult to handle knowledge from different sources of information. For this reason, in the next Sect. 3, a Particle Swarm Optimization based learning method to estimate this matrix using historical data is also proposed.

3   Weight Matrix Estimation Using Particle Swarm Optimization

Problems associated with automatic (or manual) modelling of an FCM encourage researchers to work on automated or semi-automated computational methods for learning FCMs structures using historical data. Semi-automated methods still require a relatively limited human intervention, whereas fully automated approaches are able to compute an FCM model solely based on historical data [10]. In this section is proposed an automated learning scheme to estimate the causal weight matrix using an evolutionary meta-heuristic: Particle Swarm Optimization (PSO).

The PSO algorithm is a stochastic technique that simulates the social behaviour observed in groups or swarms of biological individuals [11]. This meta-heuristic is based on the principle that intelligence does not lie in individuals but in the collective, allowing for the solution of complex optimization problems from a distributed point of view, without centralized control in a specific individual. Each organism (particle) adjusts its position by using a combination of an attraction to the best solution that they individually have found, and an attraction to the best solutions that any particle has found [12], imitating those who have a better performance.

The particles are interpreted as possible solutions for the optimization problem and are represented as points in n-dimensional search space. In the case of standard PSO, each particle (X_i) has its own velocity (V_i) bounded by a maximum value (V_{max}), a memory of the best position it has obtained (Xp_i) and knowledge of the best or global solution found in its neighbourhood (Xg). In the search process each particle adjusts it position and velocity according to the following equations (2) and (3):

$$V_i^{(k+1)} = \chi \left(V_i^{(k)} + c_1 r_1 \left(Xp_i - X_i^{(k)} \right) + c_2 r_2 \left(Xg - X_i^{(k)} \right) \right). \tag{2}$$

$$X_i^{(k+1)} = X_i^{(k)} + V_i^{(k+1)}. \tag{3}$$

where k indexes the current generation, c_1 and c_2 are positive constants, r_1 and r_2 are random numbers with uniform distribution on the interval [0, 1], whereas χ represents the constriction coefficient introduced by Clerc et al. [13] and it can be expressed in terms of c_1 and c_2 as shown in (4):

$$\chi = \frac{2}{\left| 2 - \varphi - \sqrt{\varphi^2 - 4\varphi} \right|} \text{ and } \varphi = c_1 + c_2, \varphi > 4. \tag{4}$$

In this model, the swarm is often attracted by sub-optimal solutions when solving complex multimodal problems, causing premature convergence of the algorithm and swarm stagnation [14]. Once the particles have converged prematurely, they continue converging to within extremely close proximity of one another so that the global best and all personal bests are within one minuscule region of the search space, limiting the algorithm exploration. For this reason, we use in this paper a variant of constricted PSO called PSO-RSVN [15] that uses random samples in variable neighbourhoods for dispersing the particle swarm whenever a premature convergence state is detected, offering an escaping alternative from local optima.

The causal weight matrix estimation could be modelled as an optimization problem where each agent of the swarm represents a possible weight matrix; in this design the particles will encoded as vectors; following equation (5) shows this idea:

$$\vec{x} = (w_{11}, ..., w_{1n}, w_{1n+1}, w_{21}, ..., w_{2n}, w_{2n+1} ..., w_{n1}, ... w_{nn}, w_{nn+1}). \tag{5}$$

As mentioned, PSO-RSVN can be used to learn FCMs structures based on historical data, consisting of a sequence of state vectors that leads to a desired fixed-point attractor state. In the optimization process the search space is explored, trying to find the best configuration that guarantees a convergence or expected results [16], [17]. This scheme improves the quality of resulting FCMs models by minimizing the following objective or heuristic function (6) characterized as:

$$f(\vec{x}, \Phi) = \sum_{i=1}^{|\Phi|} |I(\vec{x}, \Phi_i) - R(\Phi_i)|. \tag{6}$$

where Φ represents the set of protease mutations or train-cases, whereas I is a binary function that calculates the map inference for the i-th mutation using the $\vec{x}$ as weight matrix. Moreover, another binary function R is used for compute the drug resistance (or objective attribute) for the current train-case Φ_i.

4   Results and Discussion

In this section we evaluate the proposed model using historical data of five protease inhibitors[1]: Atazanavir (ATV), Indinavir (IDV), Lopinavir (LPV), Nelfinavir (NFV) and Saquinavir (SQV). As mentioned, a stored case represents a protease mutation having 99 attributes or descriptors and a binary class for the resistance.

From previous studies of HIV proteins, it is known that not all the amino acids that characterize the sequence are determinant in predicting resistance, since only a subset of them are in the active centre of the protein. In fact, the action of the existing drugs is targeted to these amino acids; inhibiting the protein function. Thus, we use a feature selection based on positions that are previously associated with resistance, from both experimental and numerical perspective [19].

So, for each drug we get 100 maps (trials), where the causal weight matrix is estimated using the learning scheme described in Sect. 3. Table 1 shows the average prediction accuracy obtained by several machine learning techniques implemented in WEKA toolkit [20]: a Decision Tree (J48), a Bayesian Network (BN) with K2 as learning algorithm, a Support Vector Machine (SVM) with linear kernel function and a Multilayer Perceptron (MLP). Also a Recurrent Neural Network (RNN) model from [21] was considered. FCM accuracy values were achieved using as parameter settings of the learning scheme: 100 particles, 500 generations, five variable neighbourhoods (M = 5), and a tolerance (threshold) for the maximum radius of the swarm $\alpha = 1.0E\text{-}5$.

Table 1. Comparison of the performance of FCM against other machine learning techniques in terms of classification accuracy (the best performing algorithm is emphasized in boldface)

Drug	J48	BN	SVM	MLP	RNN	FCM
ATV	0.653	0.678	0.752	0.760	0.744	**0.837**
IDV	0.899	0.894	0.897	0.881	0.875	**0.914**
LPV	0.891	0.897	0.874	0.897	0.897	**0.904**
NFV	0.901	0.859	0.881	0.881	**0.916**	0.859
SQV	**0.928**	0.905	0.905	0.905	0.915	0.848

Although the average prediction accuracies are promising, this work is more focused on identifying the effect of mutational patterns on the resistance phenotype, i.e. the causal influences of each sequence position on resistance concept. However, we first need to justify if the further study is reasonable. So, the accuracy is used as a quality measure of the knowledge expressed in the causal relationships. The obtained accuracies are best ranked at ATV, IDV, and LPV; and only differ about 5% to the other techniques at NFV and SQV. Therefore, in the next section a qualitative study with statistical techniques for knowledge discovery to determine these patterns is conducted, using the knowledge of the causal weight matrix.

---

[1] The five knowledge bases were extracted from Stanford HIV Drug Resistance Database [18].

4.1   Knowledge Discovery and Interpretation

In order to find patterns in the causal relationships between each amino acid and the resistance concept (direct relations), five new knowledge bases are designed by extracting these relations from the 100 weight matrixes obtained before for each drug. Following this idea, an instance of a new base is a vector V_i that represents all direct relations from the i-th weight matrix, as shown in (7):

$$V_i = \left(w_{1n+1}^i, w_{2n+1}^i, \dots, w_{nn+1}^i \right). \tag{7}$$

Next, a cluster analysis takes place in order to gather similar vectors; i.e., weight vectors with similar behaviour for analogue relationships. Clustering is a common technique for statistical data analysis used in many fields, including machine learning, pattern recognition, image analysis, information retrieval, and bioinformatics. We choose the SPSS Two Step Cluster algorithm [22] since it performs well with continuous data and the priori estimation of the number of clusters is not required. In addition, the Akaike's Information Criterion (AIC) was used as clustering criterion, whereas Log-likelihood was taken as distance measurement.

In the experimental results a stable behaviour is observed: for all drugs the causal vectors were grouped in two clusters (C_i). Using the charts of the simultaneous 95% confidence intervals for means we found the signs for each direct relation. Following Tables 2, 3, 4, 5 and 6 show the discovered patterns; where (+) means that a positive causality is detected, (-) means that there is a negative causality and (?) means that there is no causal pattern between the amino acid and the resistance. Occasionally, no causal patterns are observed, due to the confidence intervals for means are too large and include both negative and positive causality.

Table 2. Amino acid causal influences over resistance for ATV

C_i	AA_{10}	AA_{20}	AA_{24}	AA_{32}	AA_{33}	AA_{36}	AA_{46}	AA_{47}	AA_{48}	AA_{50}
C_1	-	+	-	?	?	?	?	?	+	+
C_2	-	+	-	?	-	?	?	?	+	+

C_i	AA_{53}	AA_{54}	AA_{63}	AA_{71}	AA_{73}	AA_{82}	AA_{84}	AA_{88}	AA_{90}	AA_{93}
C_1	?	+	-	+	+	-	-	?	-	+
C_2	?	+	-	+	?	-	-	?	-	+

Table 3. Amino acid causal influences over resistance for LPV

C_i	AA_{10}	AA_{20}	AA_{24}	AA_{32}	AA_{33}	AA_{36}	AA_{46}	AA_{47}	AA_{48}	AA_{50}
C_1	-	?	?	?	?	+	+	?	+	-
C_2	-	+	?	+	?	+	+	+	?	+

C_i	AA_{53}	AA_{54}	AA_{63}	AA_{71}	AA_{73}	AA_{82}	AA_{84}	AA_{88}	AA_{90}	AA_{93}
C_1	+	-	+	+	?	-	-	+	?	?
C_2	?	?	+	+	?	?	?	?	?	+

Table 4. Amino acid causal influences over resistance for IDV

C_i	AA_{10}	AA_{20}	AA_{24}	AA_{32}	AA_{33}	AA_{36}	AA_{46}	AA_{47}	AA_{48}	AA_{50}
C_1	-	+	?	+	+	-	+	+	+	+
C_2	-	+	?	+	+	-	+	+	+	+

C_i	AA_{53}	AA_{54}	AA_{63}	AA_{71}	AA_{73}	AA_{82}	AA_{84}	AA_{88}	AA_{90}	AA_{93}
C_1	+	-	-	+	+	-	-	+	-	+
C_2	+	-	-	+	+	-	-	+	-	+

Table 5. Amino acid causal influences over resistance for NFV

C_i	AA_{10}	AA_{20}	AA_{30}	AA_{36}	AA_{46}	AA_{48}	AA_{50}	AA_{53}	AA_{54}	AA_{63}
C_1	-	+	+	+	+	+	+	+	-	?
C_2	-	+	+	+	+	+	+	+	-	-

C_i	AA_{71}	AA_{73}	AA_{77}	AA_{82}	AA_{84}	AA_{88}	AA_{90}	AA_{93}
C_1	+	?	+	-	-	?	-	?
C_2	+	+	+	-	-	?	-	?

Table 6. Amino acid causal influences over resistance for SQV

C_i	AA_{10}	AA_{20}	AA_{36}	AA_{46}	AA_{48}	AA_{50}	AA_{53}	AA_{54}	AA_{63}	AA_{71}
C_1	+	-	?	-	-	-	-	+	+	-
C_2	+	-	-	-	-	-	-	+	+	-

C_i	AA_{73}	AA_{82}	AA_{84}	AA_{90}	AA_{93}
C_1	-	-	+	+	?
C_2	-	-	+	+	?

For example, analysing the causal patterns for IDV described in Table 4, some conclusions came out. (i) In both clusters a positive causality for the direct relations from AA_{20}, AA_{32}, AA_{33}, AA_{46}, AA_{47}, AA_{48}, AA_{50}, AA_{53}, AA_{71}, AA_{73}, AA_{88} and AA_{93} exists; which means that when a mutation in one of these amino acids takes place, the resistance value is proportionally affected. More specifically, if one of these amino acids mutes to another one with higher (lower) contact energy then the resistance value increases (decreases). (ii) In both clusters a negative causality for the direct relations from AA_{10}, AA_{36}, AA_{54}, AA_{63}, AA_{82}, AA_{84} and AA_{90} is observed; this behaviour means that when a mutation in one of these amino acids occurs, the resistance value is reverse-proportionally affected. More specifically, if one of these amino acids mutes to another one with higher (lower) contact energy, then the resistance value decreases (increases). (iii) For the direct relation from AA_{24} there is an unstable causal behaviour over the resistance concept, i.e. the confidence interval for this direct relation include negative and positive causality. Likewise can be drawn conclusions about causal patterns in the direct relations of the other four modelled drugs. In fact, following this logic, the knowledge extraction process also could be applied to other protease inhibitors that are often used in the treatments.

These patterns characterize the direct effect of a mutation on the resistance value, allowing to the drugs designer a more competent compression of this complex biological system. For example, this knowledge could be useful to reconstruct the chemical reactions that occur in the active centre of the protein between the enzyme and its substrate, which is relevant information for creating inhibitor drugs for specific enzymes. We know that the proposed study of the direct relations is not yet enough for designing more effective drugs; due to the effect of a position mutation in other amino acids and consequently on the drugs resistance is omitted. However, the proposed methodology provides a strong scheme for representing and discovering knowledge that describe the dynamics of HIV proteins. Future work will be focused on extending the knowledge discovery process to all relations on the map (using the whole protein), for studying how all the amino acids influence to each other and the resistance, after multiple mutations take place.

5   Conclusions

In this paper was proposed a novel FCMs based scheme for modelling the dynamic of the protease protein; the behaviour of this complex system is very difficult to be described by a precise mathematical model, due to its high mutation rate. Although several machine learning techniques have been proposed for predicting the drug resistance, most of them are difficult to interpret. However, through FCMs theory it is easier and more practical to represent it in a graphical way, showing the causal relationships between all the protein positions and the resistance.

We showed the benefits of the application of a learning method inspired in the PSO meta-heuristic to fine-tune the causal relationships of a modelled FCM. This supervised weight adaptation methodology adjusts the maps parameters based only on historical data, without human intervention. Experimental results showed that the FCMs based model and the learning method proposed get promising classification accuracies against other approaches reported in the literature.

The cluster analysis was used as a knowledge discovery tool for finding patterns in the causal influences of each sequence position on resistance to five inhibitor drugs. The knowledge about how the modelled system behaves when mutation takes place is helpful for characterizing the chemical processes that occurs in active centre of the protease, making more understandable the behaviour of this protein. So, the proposal is a first approximation to modelling and studying the dynamics of the HIV proteins on the drug resistance problems, through FCMs. As future work, the knowledge discovery process will be extended and deeper assessed by modelling and interpreting all the relations on the maps. Moreover this methodology will be applied to reverse transcriptase and integrase inhibitors, also other descriptors must be used in order to characterize the amino acids sequence.

Acknowledgments. We would like to thank Prof. Yovani Marrero-Ponce, PhD, from Unit of Computer-Aided Molecular Biosilico Discovery and Bioinformatics Research, UCLV, for fruitful discussions and critical reading of the manuscript.

References

1. Prosperi, M., Ulivi, G.: Evolutionary Fuzzy Modelling for Drug Resistant HIV-1 Treatment Optimization. In: Abraham, A., Grosan, C., Pedrycz, W. (eds.) Engineering Evolutionary Intelligent Systems. SCI, vol. 82, pp. 251–287. Springer, Heidelberg (2008)

2. Beerenwinkel, N., et al.: Computational Methods for the Design of Effective Therapies Against Drug Resistant HIV Strains. Bioinformatics 21(21), 3943–3950 (2005)
3. Drăghici, S., Potter, R.: Predicting HIV Drug Resistance with Neural Networks. Bioinformatics 19(1), 98–107 (2003)
4. Bonet, I., et al.: Predicting Human Immunodeficiency Virus (HIV) Drug Resistance Using Recurrent Neural Networks. In: Mira, J., Álvarez, J.R., et al. (eds.) IWINAC 2007. LNCS, vol. 4527, pp. 234–243. Springer, Heidelberg (2007)
5. Beerenwinkel, N., et al.: Geno2pheno: Interpreting Genotypic HIV Drug Resistance Tests. IEEE Intelligent Systems 16(6), 35–41 (2001)
6. Beerenwinkel, N., et al.: Diversity and Complexity of HIV-1 Drug Resistance A Bioinformatics Approach to Predicting Phenotype from Genotype. Proceedings of the National Academy of USA 99, 8271–8276 (2002)
7. Kosko, B.: Fuzzy Cognitive Maps. Intl. Journal of Man-Machine Studies 24, 65–75 (1986)
8. Kosko, B.: Neural Networks and Fuzzy Systems, a Dynamic System Approach to Machine Intelligence. Prentice-Hall, Englewood Cliffs (1992)
9. Miyazawa, S., Jernigan, R.L.: Contacts Energies Self-Consistent Estimation of Inter-Residue Protein Contact Energies Based on an Equilibrium Mixture Approximation of Residues. PROTEINS: Structure, Function, and Genetics 34, 49–68 (1999)
10. McMichael, J.M., et al.: Optimizing Fuzzy Cognitive Maps with a Genetic Algorithm. In: AIAA 1st Intelligent Systems Technical Conference, Chicago, Illinois, pp. 1–11 (2004)
11. Kennedy, J., Eberhart, R.: Particle Swarm Optimization. In: 1995 IEEE International Conference on Neural Networks (ICNN 1995), vol. 4, pp. 1942–1948. IEEE (1995)
12. Bratton, D., Kennedy, J.: Defining a Standard for Particle Swarm Optimization. In: 2007 IEEE Swarm Intelligence Symposium (SIS 2007), pp. 120–127. IEEE (2007)
13. Clerc, M., Kennedy, J.: The Particle Swarm (Explosion, Stability, and Convergence in a Multidimensional Complex Space. IEEE Trans. on Evolutionary Comp. 6(1), 58–73 (2002)
14. Kennedy, J., Russell, C.E.: Swarm Intelligence. Morgan Kaufmann Publishers (2001)
15. Nápoles, G., Grau, I., Bello, R.: Particle Swarm Optimization with Random Sampling in Variable Neighbourhoods for Solving Global Minimization Problems. In: Dorigo, M., Birattari, M., Blum, C., Christensen, A.L., Engelbrecht, A.P., Groß, R., Stützle, T. (eds.) ANTS 2012. LNCS, vol. 7461, pp. 352–353. Springer, Heidelberg (2012)
16. León, M., Nápoles, G., et al.: Two Steps Individuals Travel Behavior Modeling through Fuzzy Cognitive Maps Pre-definition and Learning. In: Batyrshin, I., Sidorov, G. (eds.) MICAI 2011, Part II. LNCS, vol. 7095, pp. 82–94. Springer, Heidelberg (2011)
17. León, M., Nápoles, G., et al.: A Fuzzy Cognitive Maps Modeling, Learning and Simulation Framework for Studying Complex System. In: Ferrández, J.M., Álvarez Sánchez, J.R., de la Paz, F., Toledo, F.J. (eds.) IWINAC 2011, Part II. LNCS, vol. 6687, pp. 243–256. Springer, Heidelberg (2011)
18. Stanford HIV Drug Resistance Database, http://hivdb.stanford.edu
19. Woods, M., Carpenter, G.A.: Neural Network and Bioinformatic Methods for Predicting HIV-1 Protease Inhibitor Resistance. CAS/CNS Technical Report 2007-004 (2007)
20. Witten, I.H., Frank, E., Hall, M.A.: Data Mining: Practical Machine Learning Tools and Techniques, 3rd edn. Morgan Kaufmann Publishers (2011)
21. Bonet, I.: Modelo para la Clasificación de Secuencias, en Problemas de la Bioinformática, Usando Técnicas de Inteligencia Artificial. PhD Thesis, UCLV (2008)
22. SPSS Inc.: The SPSS TwoStep Cluster Component. TSCWP-101 Technical Report (2001)

An Unsupervised Method for Ontology Population
from the Web

Hilário Tomaz, Rinaldo Lima, João Emanoel, and Fred Freitas

Informatics Center, Federal University of Pernambuco, Recife, Brazil
{htao,rjl4,jeag,fred}@cin.ufpe.br

Abstract. Knowledge engineers have had difficulty in automatically construct-ing and populating domain ontologies, mainly due to the well-known know-ledge acquisition bottleneck. In this paper, we attempt to alleviate this problem by proposing an iterative unsupervised approach to identifying and extracting ontological class instances from the Web. The proposed approach considers the Web as a big corpus and relies on a confidence-weighted metric based on se-mantic measures and web-scale statistics as types of evidence. Moreover, our iterative method is able to learn, to some extent, domain-specific linguistic pat-terns for extracting ontological class instances. We obtained encouraging results for the final ranking of candidate instances as well as an accuracy performance up to 97% for the patterns found by our method.

Keywords: ontology population, ontology-based information extraction, confidence metric, pattern learning, similarity measure.

1 Introduction

In recent years, there has been an increasing interest in ontologies, mainly because they have become very popular as a means for representing and sharing machine-readable semantic knowledge. From the computer science point of view, ontologies are also defined as logical theories able to encode knowledge about a certain domain in a declarative way. Also, ontologies are extensively used in the Semantic Web [1].

Although domain ontologies are recognized as essential resources for the Semantic Web, it turns out that the manual development of ontologies is very time-consuming and error-prone [2]. Thus, an automated or semi-automated mechanism able to con-vert the information contained in existing web pages into ontologies is highly desired. In this scenario, Ontology-Based Information Extraction (OBIE) [3] seems as a prom-ising candidate of such a mechanism. The main reason is that an OBIE system can process natural language text through a mechanism guided by ontologies in order to extract certain types of information, and present the output using ontologies [3].

This paper describes our method for extracting class instances from the Web. The proposed method integrates: (i) linguistic patterns to identify text realizations of onto-logical classes; (ii) shallow syntactic information for disambiguation purposes; and, iii) a component able to learn new specific surface text patterns in order to expand the initial set of patterns. Additionally, we use a confidence-weighted metric based on the

J. Pavón et al. (Eds.): IBERAMIA 2012, LNAI 7637, pp. 41–50, 2012.

Pointwise Mutual Information (PMI) metric [4], WordNet similarity measures, and simple heuristics in order to calculate the final confidence score for a given candidate instance. The PMI metric is a web-scale statistics to assess the degree of relationship between two terms that is estimated from the hit count given by a web search engine.

Moreover, this work proposes an iterative unsupervised method that considers the Web as an enormous corpus, overcoming in this manner the data sparseness problem. The method relies on the basic idea of splitting up the entire learning process into several simpler steps. These steps are integrated in a cyclic process in which a step takes profit of the knowledge previously acquired, and that might be useful in posterior iterations of the method.

The rest of this paper is organized as follows: Section 2 is dedicated to related work. Section 3 presents the assumptions and a detailed description of our method for ontology population. We report experimental results in Sect. 4. Finally, Sect. 5 concludes this paper and outlines future work.

2   Related Work

Much research work has already followed the central idea of using the Web as a big corpus and applying Hearst´s patterns for the ontology population task. In the following, we present some representative systems that adopted a similar approach to ours.

The KnowItAll system [4] extracts instances of classes and relations from the Web using domain-independent patterns. For assessing candidate instances, KnowItAll uses the PMI metric to compute features, and a Naive Bayes classifier to combine such features for achieving a rough estimate of the probability that each candidate instance is correct.

The OntoSyphon approach [5] focuses on learning instances of ontological classes from two representative corpora: a local one, containing 60 million web pages, and the whole Web. In [5], the authors have performed many experiments for evaluating normalized confidence metrics based on hit counts for instance ranking.

In [6] it was proposed a domain-independent method to learn effective surface text patterns representing relations (taxonomic or non-taxonomic) using a web search engine. The proposed method uses three criteria to identify the most effective patterns among the candidates found. The authors reported precision results up to 95% for learned patterns.

The learning patterns algorithm proposed by [7] is based on the idea of learning patterns and uses them as extractors and discriminators in an ontology population task. They extract patterns and assess them using both estimated precision and recall, and some heuristics. The authors evaluated the impact of using the learned patterns along with an initial set of baseline patterns.

The current work focuses on the evaluation of a confidence-weighted metric that, besides PMI information, also considers semantic features, and some simple heuristics for improving the classification performance. That constitutes the main difference between the method presented in this paper and previous work. Moreover, this paper introduces a component in our functional architecture responsible for learning domain-specific linguistic pattern. This component allows the expansion of the initial set of pattern used for retrieving candidate instances from the Web. In [6,7] they followed the same idea of our learning process, but they differ from ours w.r.t the steps of pattern classification. Our research hypothesis is that using web-scale statistics along with other type of evidences (heuristics), we should improve the set of learned patterns and, consequently, the overall extraction process of class instances.

3   The Proposed Method

The Unsupervised Method for Ontology Population from the Web (UMOPOW) takes profit of the high redundancy present in the web content, considering it as a big corpus. Sharing the same idea, several authors pointed it out as an important feature because the amount of redundant information can represent a measure of its relevance [4,5,8]. Moreover, we take into account the portability issue, i.e., the method should be able to perform independently of the domain ontology.

Basically the UMOPOW relies on an initial set of domain-independent linguistic patterns [8] that are used as both discriminators and extractors of candidate instances for domain ontologies. These patterns have been successfully used in many previous works [4, 5, 8]. However, a problem with this initial set of patterns is that they do not produce a reasonable recall, due to different ways that class instances can be expressed in natural language texts. Aiming to address this problem, we integrated a module for learning domain-specific linguistics patterns for each class in domain ontology in order to increase the number of different patterns that our prototype recognizes.

The whole process of the UMOPOW is composed in 4 main steps as shown in Fig. 1. It essentially consists of an iterative cycle that is executed for each class of the input ontology. It is quite reasonable to accept that is not possible to acquire all possible instances for a class in just one big iteration, instead, we split up the entire learning process into several simpler steps. Each iteration of the UMOPOW receives acquired knowledge information from the previous one.

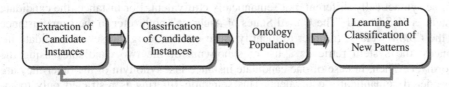

Fig. 1. Steps of the UMOPOW

The prototype system implemented for validating the UMOPOW uses the OpenNLP[1] shallow syntactic parser for English, which performs the preprocessing task of identifying Noun Phrases (NP) containing instances of ontological classes. In order to assess and rank candidate instances, we proposed, in a previous work [9], a combination of different semantic measures and web-scale statistics that explores various levels of evidence. The following subsections further describe the main steps presented in Fig. 1.

---

[1] http://opennlp.apache.org

3.1   Extracting Candidate Instances

Firstly, we select a class C of the input ontology and them, by using a set of domain-independent linguistic patterns P and a web search engine, we formulate queries that are performed for collecting relevant documents. We use seven patterns adapted from [6,8]:

P1: <CANDIDATE> *is a/an* <CLASS>
P2: <CLASS>(s) *such as* <CANDIDATES> <u>*and*</u>
P3: *such* <CLASS>(s) *as* <CANDIDATES> <u>*and*</u>
P4 and P5: <CLASS>(s) *(especially/including)* <CANDIDATES> <u>*and*</u>
P6 and P7: <u>*and*</u> <CANDIDATE> *(and/or) other* <CLASS>(s)

The above patterns would match sentences in natural language such as *"is a city"*, *"cities such as"*, *"such cities as"*, *"cities especially"*, *"cities including"*, *"and other cities"*, *"or other cities"*. These phrases likely indicate instances of C in the <CANDIDATE(s)> part [8].

Next, the first N web documents fetched by each pattern are processed for matching occurrences of the patterns into the document content. We are interested in sentences like "such cities as CANDIDATES" or "CANDIDATE is a city", in which CANDIDATE(S) denotes a single noun phrase or a list of noun phrases. For instance, in the sentence: "Why did cities such as Pittsburgh, Cincinnati grow rapidly in the 1830's", the "Pittsburgh" and "Cincinnati" words are extracted as candidate instances of the *City* class. In addition, each candidate instance keeps a list containing the patterns that extracted it.

In order to avoid invalid and repeated candidate instances, the method performs some filtering actions: (1) removing all candidate instances found in a StopList; (2) deleting a candidate instance that either represents a class in the ontology or already is an instance of the class; (3) by using a stemming algorithm, the method identifies syntactic variations of candidate instances. In this case, if two candidate instances are syntactically equivalent, just one of the syntactic forms is maintained and the lists of extraction patterns of both forms are merged; and finally, (4) two candidate instances can be syntactically different, but semantically equivalent. For instance, the candidate instances "USA" and "The United States of America" both refer to the same instance of the *Country* class. In order to identify these cases among the set of candidate instances, the system retrieves a list of synonyms of the two candidates using the WordNet[2]. Then, in case of one candidate instance is a synonym of the other they are considered semantically equivalent. This semantic filtering is restricted only to instance candidates having an entry in the WordNet. The list of extraction patterns are merged in analogous way as in the previous action.

3.2   Classifying Candidate Instances

The above step produces a list of candidate instances. Next, it is necessary to decide which candidate instance is an actual instance for a given class in the input ontology. Thus, the UMOPOW uses several web-scale statistics, semantic metrics, and heuristics

---

[2] http://wordnet.princeton.edu

for evaluating confidence scores to be applied on each candidate instance. Such a combined confidence metric should estimate the likelihood that a candidate instance is an actual instance of the related class. In the following, we explain how the aforementioned elements are used in order to calculate the final confidence score.

Pointwise Mutual Information (PMI)[4]. The PMI metric gives the number of hits for a pair (ci, c), corresponding to a candidate instance ci and a class c, for each pattern p belonging to the set of extraction patterns P listed in Sect. 3.1. There exist some variants of PMI in the literature [4] [5]. We chose the variant in Formula 1 because it achieved better performance in experiments carried out in our previous work [9]. In this formula, the sum of the *hits* (ci, c, p) is normalized by a value determined by sorting the set of candidate instances by *hits* (ci) and then selecting the hit count that appears at the 25th percentile ($Count_{25}$). We refer the reader to [5] for details about this formula.

$$\text{Str-INorm-Thresh}(ci,c) = \frac{\sum_{p \in P} hits(ci, c, p)}{\max(hits(ci), Count_{25})} \tag{1}$$

This processing step will use the patterns listed in Section 3.1 to calculate the PMI value by formulating queries like "cities such as Barcelona and". In this step, it is very important the presence of the word "and", either *after* or *before* a candidate instance using the patterns P2 to P7. As pointed out by [6], the use of this word should avoid some misclassifications. For instance, if we had extracted the candidate instance "Las" instead of "Las Vegas", and since this candidate has a high PMI value because of the query hits for "cities such as Las" include the hit count for the correct phrases like "cities such as Las Vegas", this would lead to a misclassification. Hence, the presence of the word "and" would alleviate this kind of problem.

WordNet Similarity. Semantic similarity measures based on WordNet have been widely used in NLP applications [10], and they typically take into account the WordNet structure to produce a numerical value for assessing the degree of the semantic similarity between two concepts. In this work we will use two well-known similarity measures based on WordNet proposed by Lin [11], and Wu and Palmer [12]. In our method, these similarity measures provide the degree of similarity between the class c and the candidate instance ci. The two above-mentioned measures range from 0 to 1. We use the sum of them (WNS) as our semantic similarity score. Therefore, the maximum similarity score (MaxWNS) assigned to each candidate instance is 2.

Number of Extra Patterns. This heuristic is based on the main idea that if a candidate instance is extracted by many extraction patterns, this gives strong evidence that this candidate instance is a valid instance for the selected class. Based on this assumption, we defined the *Extra Pattern Score* (EPS) as the number of extraction patterns that extracted a particular candidate instance. In this manner, the maximum score (MaxEPS) assigned to a candidate instance is equal to the size of the initial list of extractions patterns, i. e., MaxEPS = 7.

Direct Matching. This last heuristic is based on the idea of finding the label of the class within the instance candidate [13]. To this end, we employ a classical stemming algorithm on both labels of the class and the candidate instance. If they match, 1 is assigned to the *Direct Matching Score* (DMS), or 0 otherwise. For example, given the *University* class and the candidate instance *"University of London"*, then the DMS for this candidate instance is 1.

We can finally define the confidence-weighted score (*ConfScore*) of a candidate instance as the weighted sum of all constituent scores shown above, i.e., PMI combined with WordNet similarity measures, number of extra patterns utilized, and direct matching of candidate instances. Formula 2 shows how to calculate the final score *ConfScore* for a candidate instance ci of a class c.

$$ConfScore(ci, c) = \frac{EPS + WNS + DMS + 1}{MaxEPS + MaxWNS + MaxDMS + 1} \times PMI(ci, c) \qquad (2)$$

The idea behind Formula 2 is to give more weight to heuristics that we believe are more reliable for the task at hand. More information about our approach to the classification of candidate instances can be found in [9]. By the end of this step, a list of candidate instances sorted in decreasing order of their confidence values is built.

3.3   Population of the Input Ontology

Typical noisy information found on the Web can produce incorrect candidate instances. Such spurious candidate instances may also take place for other reasons, such as incorrect parsing of noun phrases, misspelled instance names, etc. We argue that it is imperative to provide reliable estimation of the quality of the extracted instances. Accordingly, the UMOPOW removes candidate instances having a confidence value below a given threshold. Finally, the promoted candidate instances selected by the UMOPOW are used as input for the learning pattern module described in next section.

3.4   Learning and Classifying New Patterns

The objective of this step is to expand the initial set of domain-independent patterns by learning specific patterns for each class. Therefore, in further iterations of the method, besides the initial set of patterns, all the specific patterns learned in this step will be used by the step of candidate instance extraction. For doing that, the learning pattern step proceeds as follows:

1. For each instance i of the set of instance I learned by the previous step do:
   (a) formulate two queries using the pairs $(i \in I, class)$: (1) *"class * i"* and (2) *"i * class"*. The * is a regular expression operator that indicates zero or more words between i and *class*. Perform the queries to a web search engine and fetch the first D retrieved documents for each query;
   (b) for each occurrence of i in the set of documents retrieved by query (1), extract w words *before i;* analogously, extract w words *after i* from the documents returned by query (2). The obtained text fragment is a candidate for a new pattern p;

(c) using a stemming algorithm, remove patterns that do not have an occurrence of the class in its content;

(d) before inserting a pattern p in the list of candidate patterns P, verify if this pattern was already extracted. Otherwise, insert the instance I used for extracting p in its list of instances L.

2. Classify the best patterns according to the confidence metric described below.

The last step of the cited algorithm is in charge of ranking the patterns based on a confidence score. Formula 3 shows how to calculate the confidence score for each new learned pattern.

$$Conf(p) = \frac{\sum_{i \in I} hits(p,i)}{hits(p)} \times L_{size} \qquad (3)$$

Where p is a pattern in P; i is each instance in I; and L_{size} is the size of distinct instances i of L. A candidate pattern is eliminated if one of the hit count of a pair (p, i) is zero. Our underlying idea of this constraint is to remove patterns that are too specific for just one instance.

By the end of this ranking step, a list of new extraction patterns, sorted by the confidence score, is produced. In order to keep control of the extractions, just patterns with a confidence score higher than a given threshold will be promoted as actual extraction patterns. These patterns are specific for one class and will be used in further iterations of the UMOPOW for this class in the domain ontology.

4 Experimental Evaluation

Dataset Description. The dataset used for the experiments reported in this section was created using the seven initial extraction patterns listed in Sect. 3.1. We used an ontology containing 15 classes[3], most of them used in related work. For each extraction pattern, we gathered 700 web pages snippets, totalizing 4,900 snippets for each class. The snippets were gathered using the Bing Search Engine API[4].

After the first iteration of the UMOPOW on this dataset, for each class, we selected the first 100 candidate instances sorted by confidence score in descending order. Finally, a considerable annotation effort was necessary in which two humans evaluators were in charge of manually confirming the system predictions.

Evaluation Measures and Preliminary Results. Aiming at evaluating the effectiveness of the UMOPOW, firstly we report the classification results at a given cut-off rank, considering only the n topmost candidate instances returned by the method. In our experimental setup, we determined four cut-off points corresponding to the top 10, 25, 50, and 100 in the list of candidate results. Thus, the Accuracy at the top n candidate instances, $A(n)$, is defined as follows:

---

[3] Mammal, Amphibian, Reptile, Bird, Fish, Insect, City, Country, River, Disease, Symptom, Movie, Sport, TV Series, and University.

[4] http://www.bing.com/developers/s/APIBasics.html

$$A(n) = \frac{number\ of\ correct\ system\ predictions}{n} \qquad (4)$$

Figure 2 presents the results of our experiments using the 15 aforementioned classes. We can observe in Fig. 2 four grouped bar graphs representing the variations (top 10, 25, 50, and 100) for each class.

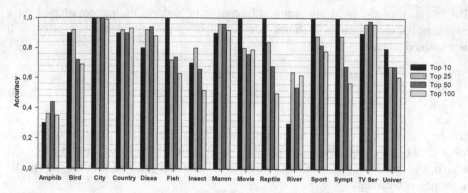

Fig. 2. Classification results in Top N

The results shown in Fig. 2 are encouraging, since our proposed method showed to be able to successfully extract a considerable amount of positive instances for several classes. In the first iteration, we only used domain-independent linguistic patterns, and we can see that some classes yielded better results than others did.

In general, the best score results were obtained by the classes City, Country, Mammal, and TV Series. One possible reason is that the above classes have a higher frequency of using with the initial patterns, i. e., it is very likely to find the surface text pattern "cities such as" followed by positive instances of the *City* class. On the other hand, other classes like *Amphibian* and *River* did not seem to have the same behavior. For instance, considering the *River* class some wrong classifications happen because of the false facts found on the Web. We can cite the wrong instance "Life" taken as a positive instance for the *River* class, mainly due to the high PMI value calculated for the pattern in some sentences like "Life is a River". Of course, to tackle this problem would be necessary to have a more sophisticated treatment of some semantic aspects of the natural language.

Secondly, we wanted to evaluate the pattern learning task in our method. For that, we selected the 10 best candidate instances, according to the ConfScore metric (marked as CS in table below), and fetched 100 snippets for each candidate instance, totalizing 1,000 web snippets. We defined $w = 5$ as the window size, the number of words extracted before and after a given instance i. Table 1 shows the performance results of the 10 best patterns that we have extracted in terms of *accuracy* (*A*).

Table 1. Extraction results of the learned patterns

Pattern	CS	A	Pattern	CS	A
city of *candidate*	0.8303	92%	city guide to *candidates*	0.0749	52%
candidate is a large city	0.3866	89%	*candidate* is the capital city	0.0559	89%
cities near *candidates*	0.2644	52%	*candidate* is the largest city	0.0425	85%
city centre of *candidate*	0.1646	97%	cities in *candidates*	0.0271	6%
cities like *candidate*	0.1041	86%	cities from *candidates*	0.0239	29%

In order to evaluate our hypothesis that patterns with higher confidence score values correlates to good accuracy results, we first selected the 10 more effective patterns for each class, according to our CS. Then, we used the selected patterns individually as both extractors and discriminators for the extraction task, collecting 500 snippets for each pattern. Next, we took the 100 best candidate instances learned by each new pattern and we calculated accuracy on this sample. Analyzing the results in Table 1, we can observe that most of the learned patterns obtained high accuracy scores (column A) in the extraction task, such as "city centre of *candidate*" achieving accuracy up to 97%, and "city of *candidate*" scoring 92%. These patterns present high frequency of co-occurrence with actual instances of the *City* class, e.g., "*city centre of Brussels*" and "*city of Ottawa*". On the other hand, some misclassification occurred with the patterns "*cities in candidates*" and "*cities from candidates*". Despite these two patterns have been classified in top 10 in the previous step, they did not achieve acceptable accuracy results here. This happened because these patterns are not frequently followed by instances of the *City* class, e.g., "*cities in France*", "*cities from Brazil*", leading to an extraction of wrong candidate instances.

The above results of UMOPOW suggest that it produces satisfactory performance in terms of high accuracy values for the majority of the learned patterns. In order to keep the control of the accuracy of the instance learning process, we decided to promote only the best 5 linguistic patterns classified by Formula 3 for each class per iteration.

As a final remark, we considered to conduct comparative evaluations with other approaches presented in Related Work section, but that would only be possible if the compared approaches were under the same experimental setup (same corpus, same domain ontology, etc). Since we are using the Web as a big corpus, and considering the dynamic nature of it, we cannot provide a fair and direct comparison in this case.

5 Conclusions and Future Work

We have proposed an unsupervised method for ontology population, the UMOPOW, which is based on a confidence-weighted metric for assessing candidate instances extracted from the Web. In this method, we split up the entire learning process into several simpler steps in an iterative cycle, which is executed for each class of the input ontology. In addition, this method is able to learn specific extraction patterns that expand an initial set of domain-independent patterns. We presented an evaluation of the UMOPOW on two tasks: candidate instance classification and pattern learning.

Although we achieved encouraging results, there are many opportunities for improvement. Thus, a detailed quantitative analysis of the actual contribution of each weight factor would suggest the more reliable factors for instance ranking. Moreover, further work is needed for improving accuracy by using more efficient filters, allowing the elimination of false candidate instances. Finally, we intend to evaluate the impact on accuracy when the learning module considers the initial and the learned set of extraction patterns at the same time.

Acknowledgments. The authors would like to thank the National Council for Scientific and Technological Development (CNPq/Brazil) for financial support (Grant No. 140791/2010-8).

References

1. Berners-Lee, T., Hendler, J., Lassila, O.: The Semantic Web. Scientific American 284(5), 34–43 (2001)
2. Cimiano, P.: Ontology Learning and Population from Text Algorithms, Evaluation and Applications. Springer, New York (2006)
3. Wimalasuriya, D.C., Dou, D.: Ontology-Based Information Extraction An introduction and a Survey of Current Approaches. Journal of Information Science 36(3), 306–323 (2010)
4. Etzioni, O., Cafarella, M., Downey, D., Kok, S., Popescu, A., Shaked, T., Soderland, S., Weld, D., Yates, A.: Web-Scale Information Extraction in KnowIt All (Preliminary Results). In: 13th Intl. Conference on World Wide Web (WWW 2004), pp. 100–110. ACM (2004)
5. McDowell, L.K., Cafarella, M.: Ontology-Driven, Unsupervised Instance Population. Web Semantics: Science, Services and Agents on the World Wide Web 6(3), 218–236 (2008)
6. Geleijnse, G., Korst, J.: Learning Effective Surface Text Patterns for Information Extraction. In: Workshop on Adaptive Text Extraction and Mining (ATEM 2006) at the 11th Conference of the European Chapter of the Association for Computational Linguistics (EACL 2006), pp. 1–8. ACL (2006)
7. Downey, D., Etzioni, O., Weld, D.S., Soderland, S.: Learning Text Patterns for Web Information Extraction and Assessment. In: Workshop on Adaptive Text Extraction and Mining (ATEM 2004) at the 19th Nat. Conf. on Artificial Intelligence (AAAI 2004). AAAI (2004)
8. Hearst, M.: Automatic Acquisition of Hyponyms from Large Text Corpora. In: 14th Conference on Computational Linguistics (COLING 1992), vol. 2, pp. 539–545. ACL (1992)
9. Oliveira, H., Lima, R., Gomes, J., Ferreira, R., Freitas, F., Costa, E.: A Confidence–Weighted Metric for Unsupervised Ontology Population from Web Texts. In: Liddle, S.W., Schewe, K.-D., Tjoa, A.M., Zhou, X. (eds.) DEXA 2012. LNCS, vol. 7446, pp. 176–190. Springer, Heidelberg (2012)
10. Pedersen, T.: Information Content Measures of Semantic Similarity Perform Better Without Sense-Tagged Text. In: Human Language Technologies 2010 Annual Conference of the North American Chapter of the Association for Computational Linguistics (HLT 2010), pp. 329–332. ACL (2010)
11. Lin, D.: An Information-Theoretic Definition of Similarity. In: 15th Intl. Conference on Machine Learning (ICML 1998), pp. 296–304 (1998)
12. Wu, Z., Palmer, M.: Verb Semantics and Lexical Selection. In: 32nd Annual Meeting of the Association for Computational Linguistics (ACL 1994), pp. 133–138. ACL (1994)
13. Monlla, C.V.: Ontology-Based Information Extraction. Dissertation Thesis, Polytechnic University of Catalunya (2011)

Minimum Cluster Size Estimation and Cluster Refinement for the Randomized Gravitational Clustering Algorithm

Jonatan Gomez[1], Elizabeth León[1], and Olfa Nasraoui[2]

[1] Alife & Midas Research Groups
Computer Systems Engineering
Universidad Nacional de Colombia
{jgomezpe,eleonguz}@unal.edu.co
[2] Knowledge Discovery & Web Mining Lab
Dept. of Computer Engineering & Computer Science
University of Louisville
olfa.nasraoui@louisville.edu

Abstract. Although clustering is an unsupervised learning approach, most clustering algorithms require setting several parameters (such as the number of clusters, minimum density or distance threshold) in advance to work properly. In this paper, we eliminate the necessity of setting the minimum cluster size parameter of the Randomized Gravitational Clustering algorithm proposed by Gomez et al. Basically, the minimum cluster size is estimated using a heuristic that takes in consideration the functional relation between the number of clusters and the clusters with at least a given number of points. Then a data point's region of action (region of the space assigned to a point) is defined and a cluster refinement process is proposed in order to merge overlapping clusters. Our experimental results show that the proposed algorithm is able to deal with noise, while finding an appropriate number of clusters without requiring a manual setting of the minimum cluster size[1].

Keywords: data mining, data clustering, gravitational clustering, cluster refinement, cluster size estimation.

1 Introduction

Clustering is a learning technique that accepts unlabeled data points (data records) and classifies them into different groups or clusters according to some similarity measure (points assigned to the same cluster have high similarity between them, while points assigned to different clusters have low similarity between them) [1,6,7,11,13]. Although clustering is considered an unsupervised learning approach, most of the clustering algorithms require the setting of some

---

[1] This paper was partially funded by a Colciencias Grant (1101-521-28885). J. Gomez was partially funded by the 2010-2011 Fulbright Visiting Scholar Program Grant.

J. Pavón et al. (Eds.): IBERAMIA 2012, LNAI 7637, pp. 51–60, 2012.

parameters like the number of clusters k. Such is the case of partitional algorithms like k-means [11]. However, finding the right clusters is a difficult task since clusters can vary in shape, size and density and can suffer from the presence of noise. In fact, the presence of noise can deteriorate the results of many of the clustering techniques that are based on the Least Squares estimate [13]. DBSCAN [3] is a density-based clustering algorithm used to discover arbitraily shaped clusters in the presence of noise. Basically, a concept of data point neighborhood is defined as the set of points located within a distance smaller than a certain threshold (**Epsilon**). Then points are categorized into *core* point (if they have at least a number of predefined neighbors (**MinPoints**)), *border point* if they have fewer than such a predefined number of neighbors and belong to some neighborhood of a core point and *noise* point if they have fewer than such a predefined number of neighbors and do not belong to some neighborhood of a core point. Then, a cluster is defined as a set of density-conected points that is maximal with respect to density-reachability. One difficulty in using DBScan is its sensitivity to the setting of the parameters Epsilon and MinPoints [8].

Data clustering algorithms inspired by natural phenomena such as natural evolution [10,12], and gravitational force have also been proposed in order to tackle these problems. In particular, gravitational clustering algorithms are a type of agglomerative hierarchical algorithms that are based on concepts inspired from field theory in physics [14,9], but suffer from the relatively high complexity of the algorithm. One such case is the GC algorithm [14] that simulates the universal gravitational system by considering each data point as a particle in a space exposed to gravitational fields. A unit mass is associated with each data point, and they are moved toward the cluster centers due to gravitational fields. In [4,5], a gravitational clustering algorithm (RGC) that is robust to noise and does not require the number of clusters was proposed. Like GC, it is inspired from gravitational theory, however it redefined the clustering target and the dynamics of the system, thus reducing the time complexity of the original GC to less than quadratic in addition to being able to resist noise. The computational complexity was reduced mainly by considering only a sample instead of all the other data points when making a decision about moving a given data point. Both interacting data points are moved according to a simplified version of the Universal Gravitational Law and Newton's Second Motion Law. Points that are close enough end up merged into virtual clusters. Finally, the *big crunch* effect (convergence to one single big cluster at the end) was eliminated by introducing a cooling mechanism similar to the one used in simulated annealing.

In this paper, we extend the RGC algorithm by defining a heuristic for estimating the minimum cluster size parameter that is based on analyzing the behavior of the number of clusters (c_m) with at least m points. A notion of data point's *region of action* based on the merging process is defined and a heuristic for refining the extracted clusters (merging overlapping clusters), based on the newly developed notion of data point's *region of action*. The remainder of this paper is organized as follow. An overview of the Randomized Gravitational Clustering algorithm is done in Sect. 2. Then we introduce the heuristic for estimating the minimum cluster size, the data points' region of action concept and the cluster refinement heuristic in Sect. 3 and 4. Our Experimental results are presented in Sect. 5, and finally, some conclusions are drawn in Sect. 6.

2   Randomized Gravitational Clustering (RGC)

Gravitational clustering is an agglomerative hierarchical clustering algorithm based on the concepts of field theory in physics [9,14]. The algorithm simulates a gravitational system, following Newton's gravitational law, where each data point is considered as a single particle, with unit mass, exposed to some gravitational fields in the feature space (defined by the data set) and is moved toward the cluster centers due to these gravitational fields generated by other data points. Finally, the hierarchy of emergent clusters of particles is extracted [14]. When two particles are close enough to be merged, they are considered to belong to the same cluster, one of them is removed from the simulation, and the mass of the other is increased by the amount of the mass of the particle being removed. The process is stopped when only one particle remains in the system. The main problem with Wright's algorithm is its high time complexity, $O\left(N^3\right)$, with respect to the size of the data set (N) [9]. Also, the gravitational clustering algorithm does not automatically detect noise. In order to reduce the time complexity of the Gravitational clustering algorithm, Gomez et al proposed a randomized version in [4], that modifies four components of the original algorithm: First, every particle is moved according to the gravitational force field induced by a single randomly selected particle. In this way, Equation 1 is used for defining the force vector applied to a given particle and Equation 2 is used for moving, in an asynchronous fashion[2], both particles (the particle under consideration and the randomly selected one).

$$F_{x,y} = \frac{Gm_x m_y}{d_{x,y}^2} \tag{1}$$

$$y_{t+1} = y_t + \frac{Gm_x m_y}{\left\|\overrightarrow{d_{x,y}}\right\|^3}\overrightarrow{d_{x,y}} \tag{2}$$

Second, when the given particles are close enough to be merged, both of them are kept in the system and an optimal disjoin-union set structure (see [2]) is updated to track the formation of clusters. Since no data points are removed from the system, nor are modifications on the mass of the particles considered, Equation 2 is simplified as follows:

$$y_{t+1} = y_t + \overrightarrow{d_{x,y}}\frac{G}{\left\|\overrightarrow{d_{x,y}}\right\|^3} \tag{3}$$

---

[2] The original gravitational clustering works in a synchronous fashion, since every change movement is computed for every particle before they are moved.

Algorithm 1 Randomized Gravitational Clustering

RGC(x, **G**, $\triangle(G)$, **M**, ε)
1. **for** i=1 to N **do**
2.   MAKE(i)
3. **for** i=1 to M **do**
4.   **for** j=1 to N **do**
5. k = random point index such that $k \neq j$
6.   MOVE(x_j , x_k)   *//Move both points using Eq 3.*
7.   **if** $d_{x_j,x_k} \leq \varepsilon$ **then** UNION(j, k)
8.   G = (1-$\triangle(G)$)*G
9. **for** i=1 to N **do**
10.   FIND(i)
11. **return** disjoint-sets

Algorithm 2 Cluster Extraction.

GETCLUSTERS(clusters, α, N)
1. newClusters = $\emptyset$
2. **for** i=0 **to** number of clusters **do**
4.   **if** size(cluster$_i$) $\geq \alpha$ **then**
5.   newClusters = newClusters $\cup$ { cluster$_i$ }
6. **return** newClusters

Third, a cooling factor ($\triangle(G)$), that reduces the "Gravitation constant" value G, is introduced in order to reduce or eliminate the big crunch effect. In this way, a new parameter, the number of iterations (M), is introduced. Fourth, a parameter (α) is used to determine the minimum number of data points that a cluster should include in order to be considered a valid cluster.

Algorithm 1 shows the randomized gravitational clustering algorithm (**RGC**) producing the disjoint-union set structure while Algorithm 2 is used for extracting the set of clusters that are considered valid.

In [5], Gomez et al introduced two elements in the RGC algorithm: the first one to reduce the effect of the data set size in the system's dynamics and the second one to automatically set the initial gravitational constant value. In order to determine an appropriate value of G, an extended bisection search algorithm is used [2]. Basically, the value of G is considered appropriate if the number of clustered points is close to $\frac{N}{2}$, i.e. $\frac{N}{2} \pm \tau$, after $\lfloor \sqrt{N} \rfloor$ iterations (these values were obtained after analyzing the behavior of the cluster formation when running the RGC algorithm on different data sets). If more than half of the points ($\frac{N}{2}$) are clustered, then G is reduced, otherwise G is increased.

3 Estimation of the Minimum Cluster Size (α)

The minimum cluster size, i.e., the number of data points that a cluster should contain in order to be considered a valid cluster, can be estimated by analyzing

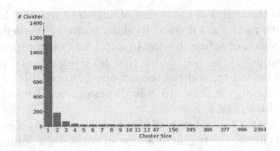

Fig. 1. Expected relation between the number of cluster with at least m points

the behavior of the number of clusters (c_m) with at least m points. First, noise points are expected to be far enough from any other point, thus reducing the possibility of being merged into clusters, so noisy points would be merged in clusters with a low number of points. Second, noise is expected to be present in different regions of the space, so it is expected that the number of clusters with a low number of points (noise points) will be high. Third, it is expected that real clusters will be defined by a large number of points. Fourth, it is expected, in general, that the number of clusters defining the data set is very small compared to the number of points represented by such clusters. Figure 1 shows the expected behavior of the number of clusters c_m with at least m points.

Therefore, we compute the behavior of c_m and obtain the size α where the slope is closest to $\frac{\pi}{4}$, i.e., we choose the value α where the number of clusters ((nc) with at least α points is higher than the value α ($nc > \alpha$), see Fig. 1.

4   Data Point Region of Action and Cluster Refinement

Due to the random nature of the merging process of the RGC algorithm, it is possible that some good points, points that already belong to some cluster, will not be assigned to some cluster. Moreover, it is possible that some 'overlapping' clusters will not be merged at all. In order to tackle these disadvantages, we introduce a notion of a data point's *region of action* based on the merging process and we propose a heuristic for refining the extracted clusters based on this notion. Due to the dynamic behavior of the RGC, it is possible not only to track the cluster formation, but also to track the real distance (distance in the original space before points were moved) between points that have been merged. This distance gives us an indication of the strength of attraction force exerted by the region of action of the data point. In this way, we associate with every data point k, two values: the aggregated merging distance of data point k (noted d_k) and the total number of data points that data point k has being merged with (noted n_k). Notice that d_k and n_k can be computed in constant time, by incrementing d_k and n_k every time that a data point j is merged with data point k (just by adding to d_k the distance between data points k and j and by adding one to n_k). Finally, we compute the average merging distance ($\overline{d_k} = \frac{d_k}{n_k}$) of data point

k, and we use it as the radius of the region of action (a hyper-sphere centered at the data point with radius $\overline{d_k}$) defined by data point k. We define the concept of a data point's region of action, having in mind two main objectives: The first one is to be able to determine the cluster that an unknown and potentially new data point should belong to, and the second one is to be able to refine clusters by merging 'overlapping clusters'. In this direction, we define the sub-cluster relation between clusters as follows:

One cluster c_1 is said to be a **sub-cluster** of a cluster c_2 if every data point x of cluster c_1 falls inside the region of action of some data point y in cluster c_2. As expected, two clusters will be merged if one of them is a sub-cluster of the other one. This process can be repeated until no further clusters are merged.

5   Experimental Results

Experiments were conducted on synthetic data sets with Gaussian clusters and with clusters of different shapes.

5.1   Gaussian Cluster Data Sets

Tests were conducted on four synthetic data sets with different cluster densities and sizes, and with different levels of noise (10% and 20%), see Fig. 2.

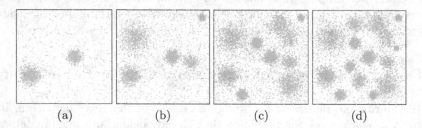

(a)   (b)   (c)   (d)

Fig. 2. Data sets with Gaussian clusters: (a) Two clusters, (b) Five clusters, (c) Ten clusters, and (d) Fifteen clusters

Due to the lack of space, we show the results for only the most challenging data set, i.e. the ten clusters' data set with 20% noise. Figure 4 shows the typical clustering result obtained after each 500 iterations, up to the end of the process (when the stopping criterion is applied). Notice that the majority of data points inside the clusters are moving towards the cluster centers (see first column) while almost all noisy points remain still or barely move. As expected, clusters emerge as in a dynamic system , first the most dense clusters (see point labels' column at iteration 250) and then the less dense clusters (see point labels' column at iteration 1000). Moreover, noisy data points either do not form clusters or they form very tiny clusters. It can be seen that the proposed heuristic for determining the minimum size of valid clusters works well since almost every noise point is removed and only 'real' clusters are extracted (see third column). Finally, it looks like both the simplification of the heuristic for estimating the initial gravitational constant G and the heuristic for stopping the RGC algorithm work well, since, in general, no 'real' clusters were merged and the structure of the extracted clusters does not change much between the last two shown iterations (see iteration 1000 and 1500) indicating that no further changes are expected. Figure 5 shows the behavior of the PFRGC algorithm on all the four Gaussian clusters data sets (when applying the refinement to the extracted clusters) and compares them against the results obtained by DBScan. As can be noticed, some small clusters were merged with bigger clusters producing a more compact cluster model [3]. However, for the 15 cluster data set, PFRGC divided one of the clusters into a few smaller ones. This can be due to the fact that this cluster is not dense and is located between two very dense cluster. In the end, all the clusters are extracted and noise is removed.

5.2 Data Sets with Clusters of different Shapes

Tests were conducted on three Chameleon benchmark data sets, see Fig. 3.

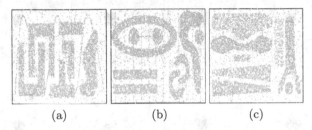

(a)   (b)   (c)

Fig. 3. Chameleon Data sets (a) Six clusters, (b) Nine Clusters, and (c) Eight clusters

Due to the lack of space, we show results for only the nine clusters' data set. Figure 6 shows the typical clustering result obtained after each 400 iterations up to the end of the process (when the stopping criteria is applied). As expected, the behavior is similar to the one observed on the data sets with Gaussian clusters. Interestingly, the majority of data points inside the clusters are seen to be moving towards some kinds of cluster cores (see first column) while almost all the noisy points remain still or barely move. In this way, any cluster shape is detected by the PFRGC algorithm. Notice that some 'overlapping' clusters are generated by the PFRGC, but such clusters are merged when using the refinement process, see Fig. 7. As expected, the behavior for all the data sets is similar to that observed on the nine cluster data set. However, for the eight clusters data set, PFRGC merges three clusters and splits one of them., which can be due to the fact that

---

[3] It is possible to apply the refinement process to the generated clusters before extracting them. However, we just perform it after extracting the clusters for simplifying the analysis of the refinement process.

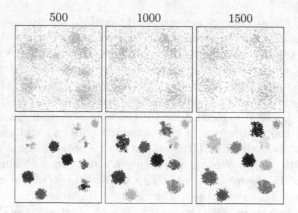

Fig. 4. Typical clustering result for the Gaussian 10 clusters data set with 20% noise each 500 iterations. Row one shows the position of the data points after the given number of iterations, and row two shows the extracted clusters after the given number of iterations.

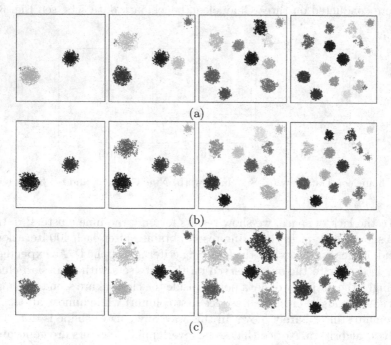

Fig. 5. Typical clustering results obtained by the RGC algorithm on the Gaussian data sets: (a) Extracted clusters, (b) Refined clusters, and (c) DBScan results with Max Distance 0.014 and MinPoints 5.

one of the clusters is not dense and is located very close to a dense cluster. As in the previous experiments, all the clusters are extracted and noise is removed. Notice that PFRGC generally performs better than DBScan .

400   800   1200

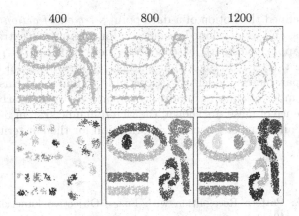

Fig. 6. Typical clustering result for the nine clusters chameleon data set (t7.10) after each 400 iterations. Row one shows the position of the points after the given number of iterations, and row two shows the extracted clusters after that many iterations.

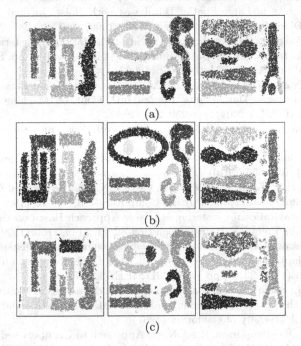

(a)

(b)

(c)

Fig. 7. Typical clustering results obtained by the RGC algorithm on the Chameleon data sets (last iteration): (a) Extracted clusters, (b) Refined clusters, and (c) DBScan results with Max Distance 0.014 and MinPoints 5

6   Conclusions

In this paper, we established a heuristic for estimating the minimum cluster size parameter by analyzing the behavior of the number of clusters (c_m) with at least

m points, we defined the notion of a data point's *region of action* based on the merging process, and we developed a heuristic for refining the extracted clusters (merging overlapping clusters), based on the notion of a data point's region of action. Since the PFRGC algorithm neither requires a special initialization, nor assumes a parametric model, PFRGC is able to find good clusters, without knowing the number of clusters in advance, regardless of their arbitrary shape, and in the presence of noise. As shown, the rich dynamic system behavior of the RGC algorithm allows us to get useful information for the clustering process.

References

1. Bezdek, J.C.: Pattern Recognition with Fuzzy Objective Function Algorithms. Plenun Press (1981)
2. Cormer, T., Leiserson, C., Rivest, R.: Introduction to Algorithms. McGraw-Hill (1990)
3. Ester, M., Kriegel, H., Sander, J., Xu, X.: A Density-Based Algorithm for Discovering Clusters in Large Spatial Databases with Noise. In: 2nd Intl. Conf. on Knowledge Discovery and Data Mining (KDD 1996), pp. 226–231. AAAI (1996)
4. Gomez, J., Dasgupta, D., Nasraoui, O.: A New Gravitational Clustering Algorithm. In: 3rd SIAM Intl. Conf. on Data Mining (SDM 2003), vol. 3, pp. 83–94. Society for Industrial and Applied Mathematics (2003)
5. Gomez, J., Nasraoui, O., Leon, E.: RAIN – Data Clustering Using Randomized Interactions between Data Points. In: 3rd Intl. Conf. on Machine Learning and Applications (ICMLA 2004), pp. 250–255 (2004)
6. Han, J., Kamber, M.: Data Mining – Concepts and Techniques. Morgan Kaufmann (2000)
7. Jain, A.K.: Data Clustering – 50 Years Beyond K-Means. Pattern Recognition Letters 31(8), 651–666 (2010)
8. Karypis, G., Han, E., Kumar, V.: CHAMELEON – A Hierarchical Clustering Algorithm Using Dynamic Model. IEEE Computer 32(8), 68–75 (1999)
9. Kundu, S.: Gravitational Clustering – A New Approach Based on the Spatial Distribution of the Points. Pattern Recognition 32(7), 1149–1160 (1999)
10. Leon, E., Nasraoui, O., Gomez, J.: A Scalable Evolutionary Clustering Algorithm with Self-Adaptive Genetic Operators. In: 2010 IEEE Congress on Evolutionary Computation (CEC 2010), pp. 4010–4017. IEEE (2010)
11. MacQueen, J.: Some Methods for Classification and Analysis of Multivariate Observations. In: 5th Berkeley Symposium on Mathematics, Statistics, and Probabilities, pp. 281–297. University of California (1967)
12. Nasraoui, O., Krishnapuram, R.: A Novel Approach to Unsupervised Robust Clustering Using Genetic Niching. In: 9th IEEE Intl. Conf. on Fuzzy Systems (FUZZ IEEE 2000), vol. 1, pp. 170–175 (2000)
13. Rousseeuw, P.J., Leroy, A.M.: Robust Regression and Outlier Detection. John Wiley & Sons (1987)
14. Wright, W.E.: Gravitational Clustering. Pattern Recognition 9(3), 151–166 (1977)

Online Cluster Prototype Generation for the Gravitational Clustering Algorithm

Elizabeth León, Jonatan Gómez, and Fabián Giraldo

Universidad Nacional de Colombia,
Computer Systems Engineering Department
{eleonguz,jgomezpe,fagiraldo}@unal.edu.co

Abstract. Data clustering is a popular data mining technique for discovering the structure of a data set. However, the power of the results depends on the nature of the clusters prototypes generated by the clustering technique. Some cluster algorithms just label the data points producing a prototype for the cluster as the full set of data points belonging to the clusters. Some techniques produce a single 'abstract' data point as the model for the full cluster losing the information of the shape, size and structure of the cluster. This paper proposes an on-line cluster prototype generation mechanism for the Gravitational Clustering algorithm. The idea is to use the gravitational system dynamic and the inherent hierarchical property of the gravitational algorithm for determining some summarized prototypes of clusters at the same time the gravitational clustering algorithm is finding such clusters. In this way, a cluster is represented by several different 'abstract' data points allowing the algorithm to find an appropriated representation of clusters that are found. The performance of the proposed mechanism is evaluated experimentally on two types of synthetic data sets: data sets with Gaussian clusters and with non parametric clusters. Our results show that the proposed mechanism is able to deal with noise, finds the appropriated number of clusters and finds an appropriated set of cluster prototypes.

Keywords: clustering, gravitational, hierarchical, prototype.

1 Introduction

The rapid development of information technologies have influenced major changes in may processes of science and industry [6,10,17,20]. Systems to capture, store, and manage data have evolved from primitive file processing systems to sophisticated and powerful database systems. The enormous amount of available data has exceeded the human abilities of exploring, analyzing and understanding such data, making necessary to use advanced computational data mining techniques such as data clustering.

Clustering is a learning technique that accepts unlabeled data points (data records) and classifies them into different groups or clusters according to some similarity measure. The grouping is done in such a way that points assigned to

J. Pavón et al. (Eds.): IBERAMIA 2012, LNAI 7637, pp. 61–70, 2012.
© Springer-Verlag Berlin Heidelberg 2012

the same cluster have high similarity between them, while points assigned to different clusters have low similarity between them . Different clustering techniques have been developed [2,6,7,15,18]. A partitional clustering algorithm starts with a selection of k samples from the data set to be clustered. These samples define the initial set of candidate cluster centers. Next, the algorithm assigns the data samples to these clusters based on some similarity measure. Finally, the candidate cluster centers are recomputed. This process is repeated until a stopping criteria is satisfied [6,15,20]. Hierarchical clustering algorithms build a hierarchical structure of the data (clusters) in an iterative process using one of two approaches : agglomerative or divisive. Agglomerative hierarchical clustering is a bottom-up approach. At the beginning, each data sample is a single cluster; then clusters are merged based on some similarity measure in an iterative process that stops when there is only one cluster remaining [6,20]. Divisive clustering is a top-down clustering approach that starts with all data samples belonging to one cluster , then splits this cluster recursively until each data sample forms its own cluster. Chameleon is an agglomerative hierarchical clustering algorithm based on a dynamic model [8]. It is a two-phase algorithm that operates on a sparse graph of the data to be clustered (requires a similarity matrix), in which nodes represent data items and links represent the similarity among the data items. Chameleon is able to find clusters of different shapes, densities, sizes, and can handle noise and artifacts.

Data clustering algorithms inspired by natural phenomena such as natural evolution [12,16], and gravitational force have also been proposed. In particular, gravitational data clustering algorithms are considered agglomerative hierarchical algorithms based on concepts of field theory in physics [9,19], but suffer from the problem of the complexity of the algorithm, such as the case of the GC algorithm [19], that simulates the universal gravitational system considering each data point as a particle in a space exposed to gravitational fields. A unit mass is associated with each data point, and they are moved toward the cluster centers due to gravitational fields. In [4,5], a gravitational clustering algorithm that is robust to noise and does not require the number of clusters was proposed. Like GC, it is inspired from the theory of gravitation, however it redefined the clustering target and the dynamics of the system, thus reducing the time complexity of the original GC to less than quadratic in addition to being able to resist noise. The computational complexity was reduced mainly by considering only a sample instead of all the other data points when making a decision about moving a given data point. Then, both interacting data points are moved according to a simplified version of the Universal Gravitational Law and Second Newton's Motion Law. Points that are close enough end up merged into virtual clusters. Finally, the *big crunch* effect (convergence to one single big cluster at the end) was eliminated by introducing a cooling mechanism similar to the one used in simulated annealing. Although, the Randomized Gravitational Clustering algorithm proposed by Gomez et al in [5] works well on a variety of data sets, it does not produced a model or prototype for the clusters as the k-means does.

In other work, Liu et al. proposed multi-prototype instead of single prototype in order to represent a cluster. For a given dataset, the dataset is partitioned into a relatively large number of small subclusters where each one is represented by a prototype.The squared-error clustering is employed in this stage to produce P prototypes [13].

Ben et al, proposed Guided fuzzy clustering with multi-prototypes. The algorithm starts with a sequence of splitting operations under the guidance of intra-cluster non-consistency. Using FCM (Fuzzy c-means), the dataset is first partitioned into p initial subclusters with each one represented by a prototype [1]. Finally, the prototypes are merged until there are only c cluster in the partition.

Luo et al, proposed a Multi-prototype Clustering Algorithm Based on Minimum Spanning Tree (MST). it is a split and merge scheme. In the split stage, the suitable patterns are determined to be prototypes in terms of their degrees in the corresponding MST, while in the merge stage, a two-step merge strategy is designed to group the prototypes [14].

The purpose of this paper is to introduce an on-line mechanism for the Rgc algorithm that is able to generate good prototypes for the found clusters at the same time it is finding such clusters. Basically, the gravitational system dynamics is used along with the inherent hierarchical property of the gravitational algorithm for determining some summarized prototypes of clusters at the same time the gravitational clustering algorithm is finding such clusters. Each certain number of iterations, the labeled data points are analyzed to determine if they define a cluster with a size higher than a threshold. Then, such sub-clusters are organized and summarized in a hierarchical structure that maintains the relation of such clusters with previously found sub-clusters. Finally, a cluster is represented by several different 'abstract' data points allowing the algorithm to find an appropriated representation of clusters that are found.

The remainder of this paper is organized as follow. An introduction to the Randomized Gravitational clustering algorithm is presented in Sect. 2. Then we introduce the on-line cluster prototype generation mechanism in Sect. 3. Our Experimental results are presented in Sect. 4, and finally, some conclusions are drawn in Sect. 5.

2   Randomized Gravitational Clustering (Rgc)

Gravitational clustering is an agglomerative hierarchical clustering algorithm based on the concepts of field theory in physics [9,19]. The algorithm simulates a gravitational system where each data point is considered as a single particle exposed to some gravitational fields in the feature space (defined by the data set) and is moved toward the cluster centers due to these gravitational fields generated by other data points. Therefore, the data clustering problem is solved by considering each data point as a particle[1], with unitary mass, in a space

---

[1] Notice that we talk about particle instead of data points, since, in general, particles are allowed to be defined as the fusion of several data points.

exposed to gravitational fields, then simulating the dynamics of this gravitational system following Newton's gravitational law, and finally extracting the hierarchy of emergent clusters of particles [19]. When two particles are close enough to be merged, they are considered to belong to the same cluster, one of them is removed from the simulation, and the mass of the other is increased by the amount of the mass of the particle being removed. The process is stopped when only one particle remains in the system. The main problem with Wright's algorithm is its high time complexity, $O\left(N^3\right)$, with respect to the size of the data set (N) [9]. Also, the gravitational clustering algorithm does not automatically detect noise.

In order to reduce the time complexity of the Gravitational clustering algorithm, Gomez et al proposed a randomized version in [4], that modifies four components of the original algorithm: First, every particle is moved according to the gravitational force field induced by a single randomly selected particle. In this way, Equation 1 is used for defining the force vector applied to a given particle and Equation 2 is used for moving, in an asynchronous fashion[2], both particles (the particle under consideration and the randomly selected one).

$$F_{x,y} = \frac{Gm_x m_y}{d_{x,y}^2} \tag{1}$$

$$y_{t+1} = y_t + \frac{Gm_x m_y}{\left\|\overrightarrow{d_{x,y}}\right\|^3}\overrightarrow{d_{x,y}} \tag{2}$$

Second, when the given particles are close enough to be merged, both of them are kept in the system and an optimal disjoin-union set structure (see [3]) is updated to track the conformation of clusters. Since no data points are removed from the system, neither modifications on the mass of the particles are considered, Equation 2 is simplified as follows:

$$y_{t+1} = y_t + \overrightarrow{d_{x,y}}\frac{G}{\left\|\overrightarrow{d_{x,y}}\right\|^3} \tag{3}$$

Third, a cooling factor $(\triangle(G))$, that reduces the "Gravitation constant" value G, is introduced in order to reduce or eliminate the big crunch effect. In this way, an extra parameter, the number of iterations (M), is introduced. Fourth, an extra parameter (α) is used to determine the minimum number of data points that a cluster should include in order to be considered a valid cluster. Algorithm 1 shows the randomized gravitational clustering algorithm (**Rgc**) producing the disjoint-union set structure.

In [5], Gomez et al introduced two elements in the RGC algorithm: the first one to reduce the effect of the data set size in the system dynamics and the second one to automatically set the initial gravitational constant value. In order to determine an appropriated value of G, an extended bisection search algorithm

---

[2] The original gravitational clustering works in a synchronous fashion, since every change movement is computed for every particle before they are moved.

Algorithm 1. Randomized Gravitational Clustering

Rgc(x, **G**, $\triangle(G)$, **M**, ε)
1. **for** i=1 **to** N **do**
2.   Make(i)
3. **for** i=1 **to** M **do**
4.   **for** j=1 **to** N **do**
5. k = random point index such that $k \neq j$
6.   Move(x_j , x_k)   //Move both points using Eq 3.
7.   **if** $d_{x_j, x_k} \leq \varepsilon$ **then** Union(j, k)
8.   G = (1-$\triangle(G)$)*G
9. **for** i=1 **to** N **do**
10. Find(i)
11. **return** disjoint-sets

---

is used [3]. Basically, the number of clustered points (points that were assigned to some cluster with two or more points), after some checking iterations of the RGC algorithm, is used as an indicator of the quality of G. In this way, the value of G is considered appropriated if the number of clustered points is close to $\frac{N}{2}$, i.e. $\frac{N}{2} \pm \tau$, after $\left\lfloor \sqrt{N} \right\rfloor$ iterations (these values were obtained after analyzing the behavior of the cluster formation when running the RGC algorithm on different data sets). If more than half of the points ($\frac{N}{2}$) are clustered, then G is reduced, otherwise G is increased.

3 Model for On-Line Cluster Prototypes Generation

Because the RGC algorithm can be seen as a hierarchical and agglomerative algorithm, it is possible to use the conceptual hierarchical structure created by RGC to on-line summarize the clusters (sub-clusters) being formed iteration through iteration, See Algorithm 2. Such analysis and summarization process are applied each certain number of iterations in order to allow the gravitational dynamic system to create new clusters and merge some old clusters (line **8a**, added to the RGC algorithm). When the prototypes generation module is applied, the union/disjoint set structure (labels structure) is analyzed in order to determine if new clusters prototypes or high level clusters prototypes are introduced. We considered a cluster as candidate prototype if such cluster contains a number of points higher than a certain predefined threshold α (line 4). Therefore, we check the labels structure to find clusters with size higher than the given threshold (line 4). Such new prototypes are added to the clusters prototype hierarchical structure as leaves (lines 5-7). Then, we check if old clusters are merged (clusters being re-labeled). If so, we introduce a high level cluster prototype (prototype defined by other cluster prototypes) as an inner node having as child nodes the cluster prototypes defining it, (lines 9-28). At the same time clusters prototypes are defined, they are also summarized, i.e., the average of the points defining the cluster is computed and store in the cluster prototypes hierarchy along with the cluster size (line 17). The same is done when two cluster prototypes are merged but taking in consideration the average and the size of the prototypes (additive property of the clusters prototype). Finally, some cluster prototypes can absorb some points. Such points information is also used in order to recompute the summarized information of the cluster (line 4).

Algorithm 2. Prototype Generation and RGCmodification

Rgc(x, G, $\triangle(G)$, M, ε, IS, α)
8.   G = (1-$\triangle(G)$)*G
8a.   **if** i=IS **then** PrototypeGeneration(α)
9.   **for** i=1 **to** N **do**
10.   ....

PrototypeGeneration(α)
1.   clustersIndex = GETCLUSTER()
2.   **for** k=0; **to** size (clustersIndex) **do**
3.   c = Get (clusterIndex, k)
4.   **if** size(c) > α && !absorbed(c.getLabel()) **then**
5.   **if**(!exist(c, groups)) **then**
6.   simple = create (SimpleGroup (c.getLabel, c));
7.   ADD (simple, groups)
8.   **else**
9.   composite={}, father = {} ,childrenGroup = {}
10.   **for** l=0 **to** size(groups) **do**
11.   **if**(groups(l).getLabel() == c.getLabel()) **then**
12.   father=groups(l);
13.   **else**
14.   **if**(getSets()[groups(l),getLabel()]==c.getLabel()) **then**
15.   ADD(groups(l),childrenGroup)
16.   ADD(groups(l).getLabel ,absorbedGroup)
17.   ADD(microCluster, summarization (groups(l)))
18.   **if**(size (childrenGroup>0)) **then**
19.   **if**(father instanceof SimpleGroup) **then**
20.   composite = Convert(father)
21.   **else**
22.   composite = father();
23.   ADD(childrenGroups ,composite)
24.   REMOVE (childrenGroups ,groups)
25.   REMOVE (father , groups)
26.   ADD(composite ,groups)
27.   **else**
28.   ADD(searchNewPoint(c.getIndex(), father)

Figure 1 shows an example of the application of the mechanism of clustering prototype generation (anaysis performed each two iterations and min cluster size α set to 3). At iteration 1 two clusters are formed: point 1 and 2 are merged, and points 8 and 9 are merged. At iteration 2, point 3 is absorbed by cluster {1,2}, and point 10 is absorbed by cluster {8,9}. Since iteration 2 is a summarization and analysis iteration (checkpoint) and the minimum cluster size is 3 for defining a cluster prototype then two clusters prototype are added in the clusters prototype hierarchy ({1,2,3} and {8,9,10}). When the checkpoint 2 is reached, a new cluster prototype ({5,6,7}) is formed and merged with cluster {1,2,3,4}. Notice that point 4 was absorbed by cluster {1,2,3}. So, a new hight level cluster prototype was added to the clusters prototype hierarchy.

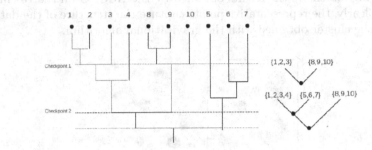

Fig. 1. Example of mechanism of clustering prototype generation. Left part shows the fusion of data points, right part shows the cluster prototype hierarchy obtained at each checkpoint.

4   Experimental Results

In order to determine the performance of the on-line cluster prototype generation mechanism, experiments were conducted on five synthetic data sets with different clusters density, size, shape and percentages of noise (10% and 20%) (see Fig. 2).

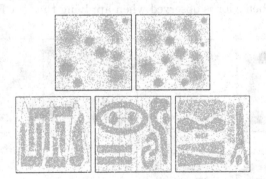

Fig. 2. Synthetic Data Sets. [Up] Data sets with Gaussian clusters (10 and 15 clusters with 10% noise). [Down] Chameleon data sets.

The last three data sets are taken from the chameleon data set collection [8]. The RGC with cluster prototypes (RGCPG) was run for 1000 iterations for each tested data set.

Figure 3.a shows the typical results obtained by the RGcPG algorithm when applied to the 10 cluster data set without noise and with 10% of noise. In this case 70 representative points (cluster prototypes) are obtained. These representative points capture the structure of the original data set, determines appropriately the clusters in the data set and are almost 1% of the original data set in size (from 6400 data points to 70 representative points). As can be noticed, noisy points are removed and no representative points are generated for noise data points. Figure 3.b shows the results obtained by the RGCPG on the 15 clusters data set. Clearly, the representative points capture the structure of the data set as well as the cluster obtained with the gravitational algorithm.

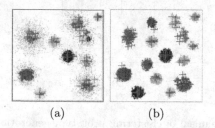

(a)   (b)

Fig. 3. Results on Gaussian cluster data sets. (a) 10 cluster data set, (b) 15 cluster data set.

Figure 4 shows the typical results obtained by the RGCPG algorithm when applied to the chameleon data sets. In the first chameleon data set (see Fig. 4.a), the RGcPG generates 149 representative points capturing the structure of the original data set, determining appropriately the clusters in the data set and are less than 2% of the original data set in size (from 8000 data points to 149 representative points). As can be noticed, noisy points are almost totally removed. Similar behavior is observed when applying the RGcPG algorithm to

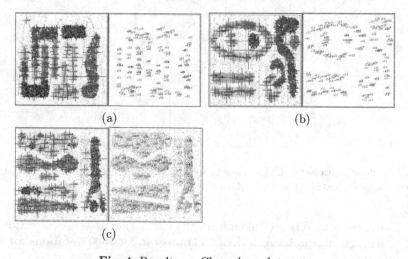

(a)   (b)

(c)

Fig. 4. Results on Chameleon data sets

the second and third chameleon data sets, see Fig. 4.b and 4.c. In these cases the set of representative points is shows the results obtained by the RGCPG on the 15 clusters data set. Clearly, the size of the set of representative points capture are 147 and 167 respectively, (close to the 2% of the data set).

Additionally, making a comparison with previous work, the gravitational algorithm performs the clustering process and select of prototypes in a single phase (Online), while in [1,13] requires two phases: in the first instance to partition the original data set and then join these prototypes in order to obtain the final result of the clustering process. Additionally, prototypes that represent groups with irregular shaped in some cases are few, being limited to 3 or 5 representative points, causing not represent the dynamic of data set.

5   Conclusions

The paper introduce a mechanisms for cluster summarization and clustering prototype generation using the randomized gravitational clustering algorithm proposed by Gomez et al in [5]. The summarization process, from the sub-cluster obtained by the gravitational clustering algorithm ensures that representative points are obtained while maintaining the original group structure. The effectiveness of the proposed summarization scheme, allows us to extend the original algorithm to be used in data streams [11]. Since a reduction up to 98% is obtained from the original data set without losing its structure and dynamic behaviors. This feature is crucial given the constraints of existing memory. Moreover, the summarization scheme can be extend using a heuristic for adapting the size of the sub-cluster. This would guarantee finding the most suitable set of representatives for a given set of points. In order to extend the algorithm to data stream, it is important to further study the effect of the mass in representative areas. If the mass is a function of number of points, it can cause new points in the flow to be quickly attracted to such previously found clusters. As shown, the rich dynamic system behavior of the RGC algorithm allows us to get useful information for the clustering process. In this direction, our future work will concentrate on exploring and understanding the dynamic system behavior, in such a way, that we can extend it to non Euclidean spaces, to deal with the curse of dimensionality when moving to high dimensional spaces, and making it work for data streams.

Acknowledgments. This paper was partially funded by a Colciencias Grant (1101-521-28885) and Vicerrectoría de Investigación de la Universidad Nacional de Colombia.

References

1. Ben, S., Jin, Z., Yang, J.: Guided Fuzzy Clustering with Multi-Prototypes. In: 2011 International Joint Conference on Neural Networks (IJCNN 2011), pp. 2430–2436. IEEE (2011)

2. Bezdek, J.C.: Pattern Recognition with Fuzzy Objective Function Algorithms. Plenun Press (1981)
3. Cormer, T., Leiserson, C., Rivest, R.: Introduction to Algorithms. McGraw Hill (1990)
4. Gomez, J., Dasgupta, D., Nasraoui, O.: A New Gravitational Clustering Algorithm. In: 3rd SIAM International Conference on Data Mining (SDM 2003), vol. 3, pp. 83–94 (2003)
5. Gomez, J., Nasraoui, O., Leon, E.: RAIN – Data Clustering using Randomized Interactions between Data Points. In: 3rd International Conference on Machine Learning and Applications (ICMLA 2004), pp. 250–255 (2004)
6. Han, J., Kamber, M.: Data Mining – Concepts and Techniques. Morgan Kaufmann (2000)
7. Jain, A.K.: Data Clustering – 50 Years Beyond K-Means. Pattern Recognition Letters 31(8), 651–666 (2010)
8. Karypis, G., Han, E., Kumar, V.: CHAMELEON – A Hierarchical Clustering Algorithm Using Dynamic Model. IEEE Computer 32(8), 68–75 (1999)
9. Kundu, S.: Gravitational Clustering – A New Approach Based on the Spatial Distribution of the Points. Pattern Recognition 32(7), 1149–1160 (1999)
10. Kuok, C.M., Fu, A.W., Wong, M.H.: Mining Fuzzy Association Rules in Databases. SIGMOD Record 27(1), 41–46 (1998)
11. Lee, W., Stolfo, S., Mok, K.: Mining in a Data-flow Environment –: Experience in Network Intrusion Detection. In: 5th ACM SIGKDD International Conference on Knowledge Discovery and Data Mining (KDD 1999), pp. 114–124. ACM (1999)
12. Leon, E., Nasraoui, O., Gomez, J.: Scalable Evolutionary Clustering Algorithm with Self-Adaptive Genetic Operators. In: 2010 IEEE Congress on Evolutionary Computation (CEC 2010), pp. 4010–4017. IEEE (2010)
13. Liu, M., Jiang, X., Kot, A.C.: A Multi-Prototype Clustering Algorithm. Pattern Recognition 42(5), 689–698 (2009)
14. Luo, T., Zhong, C., Li, H., Sun, X.: A Multi-Prototype Clustering Algorithm Based on Minimum Spanning Tree. In: 7th International Conference on Fuzzy Systems and Knowledge Discovery (FSKD 2010), pp. 1602–1607. IEEE (2010)
15. MacQueen, J.: Some Methods for Classification and Analysis of Multivariate Observations. In: 5th Berkeley Symposium on Mathematics, Statistics, and Probabilities, pp. 281–297. University of California Press (1967)
16. Nasraoui, O., Krishnapuram, R.: A Novel Approach to Unsupervised Robust Clustering Using Genetic Niching. In: 9th IEEE International Conference on Fuzzy Systems (FUZZ IEEE 2000), vol. 1, pp. 170–175 (2000)
17. Nurnberger, A., Pedrycz, W., Kruse, R.: Data mining tasks and methods – Classification – Neural Network Approaches. In: Klosgen, W., Zytkow, J. (eds.) Handbook of Data Mining and Knowledge Discovery. Oxford University Press (2002)
18. Rousseeuw, P.J., Leroy, A.M.: Robust Regression and Outlier Detection. John Wiley & Sons (1987)
19. Wright, W.E.: Gravitational Clustering. Pattern Recognition 9(3), 151–166 (1977)
20. Zhao, Y., Karypis, G.: Comparison of Agglomerative and Partitional Document Clustering Algorithms. In: SIAM Workshop on Clustering High-dimensional Data and Its Applications 2002, pp. 1–13 (2002)

Association Rule Visualization and Pruning through Response-Style Data Organization and Clustering

Leandro A.F. Fernandes and Ana Cristina Bicharra García

Fluminense Federal University (UFF), Computer Science Institute,
Rua Passo da Pátria 156, 24210-240, Niterói, RJ, Brazil
{laffernandes,bicharra}@ic.uff.br

Abstract. Association rules are a very popular non-supervised data mining technique for extracting co-relation in large set of data transactions. Although the vast use, the analysis of mined rules may be intricate for non-experts, and the technique effectiveness is constrained by the data dimensionality. This paper presents a pre-processing approach that uses (1) dual scaling in order to present the mined rules with some semantic contextualization that assists interpretation, and (2) mean shift clustering to reduce data dimensionality. We tested our model with real data collected from accident reports in petroleum industry.

Keywords: data mining, Apriori, association rules, pruning, dimension reduction, clustering, dual scaling, mean shift.

1 Introduction

Association rules (AR) are one of the most popular non-supervised data mining techniques that aim to discover relations between sets of variables. The popularity comes from the availability and efficiency of Apriori [1] family algorithms. AR are "if/then" statements, such as $X \Rightarrow Y$, that obey the following directives:

- $X \cup Y$ compose an itemset in which X and Y are sets of elements (or items) obtainable in the dataset; and
- All elements composing a rule are frequently find together in the dataset, *i.e.*, $(X \cup Y) \geq \sigma$, for which σ is the minimum support defined by the user; and
- The conditioning probability of finding the elements of right hand side of the rule (Y, the conclusion), given the left hand side elements of the rules (X, the conditions), is also high, *i.e.*, $(X \cup Y) \geq \gamma$, for which γ is the minimum confidence of the rule, defined by the user.

From the user's perspective, one of the main challenges of dealing with AR-based techniques is to perceive from the set of resulting rules whether there might be some relation among them, or whether the mining process may have been influenced by noisy data. Based on his/her perception, the user filters input data and set minimum support and confidence in an exploratory way in order to obtain

J. Pavón et al. (Eds.): IBERAMIA 2012, LNAI 7637, pp. 71–80, 2012.

better rules. Another challenge is that, typically, the number of AR generated
from a large dataset is at an unmanageable size. Increasing minimum support
threshold mitigate this problem. On the other hand, this strategy removes novel
and more interesting rules hidden behind low frequency appearance.

In this paper we propose mapping the input data into a response-style space
where AR may be graphically presented with some semantic contextualization
that emerges from the relationship among input data entries. The contextualization helps the user to best understand: (i) the influence of each element in
the composition of a rule; (ii) the possible influence of elements that were not
reported as part of any rule due to the values chosen as minimum support and
confidence; and (iii) to perceive the intrinsic relations among all mined rules.
Our approach is completely independent of the mining process itself. It is based
on *dual scaling* [15], a technique typically applied in marketing research on survey questionnaire data to generate a graphical representation of response-style
patterns among surveyed subjects and their preference over given stimuli.

As we demonstrate in this paper, the response-style space produced by dual
scaling guarantees that the spatial organization of mapped elements is consistent
with the expected relationship of those elements as part of the mined rules.
Such a relationship is approximated in the response-style space by the Euclidean
distance between mapped elements, *i.e.*, related elements are mapped close to
each other while unrelated elements are kept apart (see Fig. 1, right).

Since the use of dual scaling is independent of the mining process itself, in
this paper we show that it can be applied as a pre-processing stage and that
the organization of data in the response-style space can be explored in order
to prune elements that are unlikely to become part of any useful itemset (see
Fig. 1, left). The proposed pruning method is based on *anisotropic kernels mean
shift* [21], a non-parametric feature-space analysis technique that is typically
used for clustering in image and video segmentation.

2   Related Work

A great effort has been dedicated to address the combinatorial explosion issue typically related to AR-based approaches [2,3]. Reduction methods can be
classified considering the data discovery process phase, the amount of domain
dependence and the need for human interaction. Pre-processing methods aim to
filter the data to be mined, while post-processing methods aim to prune the output set, *i.e.*, to prune the generated AR. In either approach, reduction methods
can be domain dependent or independent. The use of statistic metrics, such as
support and confidence, and visualization techniques to highlight outliers and
filter are examples of domain-independent methods. Including existing domain
knowledge, such as domain taxonomy and ontology, to empower or weaken existing relationships are considered domain-dependent methods. Finally, the role of
human intervention defines the degree of subjectivity of the methods. The proposed approach is classified as an automatic pre-processing domain-independent
method for element pruning that also assists users in the analysis of minned AR.

Statistic measures, such as median, average, standard deviation and items' correlations, indicate outliers, inconsistent values or even irrelevant items that can be filtered by pre-processing techniques. In addition to filter, data can be transformed and combined to facilitate manipulation, for instance, transforming the "age" item (varying from 0 to 100 years) to "age range" (young, adult, middle age or old) or combining "height" and "weight" items into "mass corporal index".

While statistics compute data correlations, visualization techniques offer graphical representations to allow human perception on data correlations. The representation model should be comprehensible for the user, but also it should be able to group a high level of information. The idea behind visualization techniques is clusterization. Data dimensionality and data sparseness are addressed by presenting rules in clusters. Commonly, k-means is the clusterization algorithm considering a function of the number of transactions covered by different rules as the distance metric [4,13]. In this case, users must provide the number of clusters (k). Our research presents a new technique for clustering based on dual scale metric and without human definition on the expected number of clusters.

There are other visualization techniques for finding correlation in AR, such as: scatter plots for rules [2], grouped matrix visualizations, mosaic plots and their variant called Double-Decker [12], factorial planes and parallel coordinates plots [5,22]. The usefulness of visualization, as pruning techniques, has made it built-in components of most data mining software systems [6]. They differ with respect to the type of represented rules (one-to-one, many-to-one, *etc.*), to the number of associations that can be visualized, to the type of visualized information (items or measures characterizing the rules), to the number of dimensions (2D or 3D) and to the possibility to interact with the graph.

Domain knowledge can also be included in the pre-processing phase to enrich the mining process. Domain taxonomy [8] and domain ontology [11] are examples of using domain knowledge to guide and prune AR generation applied to market sales and petroleum domains, respectively. The combination of the pruning power offered by domain knowledge techniques with human perception offered by the proposed visualization technique is in our current future work list.

Although preventing rules of being generated should be preferred, most research effort to reduce AR output has been concentrated in post-processing techniques. Objective metrics based on statistics aim to decrease the number of extracted rules, maintaining the interestingness of the output AR. The most popular statistic measures include lift, conviction, X_2 test, leverage, Jaccard and cosine [20]. All these metrics are used monotonically. A rule with a higher value in a metric is more interesting than a rule with a lower one. Our pre-processing approach can be combined to any of these post-processing techniques.

Generalization is an alternative way of reducing the number of AR. Instead of specializing the relationships between antecedent and consequent parts and restricting rules to support values, taxonomy structures [8] organize concepts related with the "is-a" relation in function of their shared characteristics to reduce the amount of uninteresting itemsets. Item-Relatedness [18] measures the relatedness between the items of already discovered AR. The use of ontology to filter AR has been studied from the very beginning of AR development, but the domain dependency makes it harder to be systematically used [14,19].

3   The Proposed Approach

The approach proposed in this paper includes a visualization technique for mined AR (see Sect. 3.1) and an element pruning method (see Sects. 3.2 and 3.3). It is applied in the pre-processing stage in a straightforward way, and visualization results are used together with the mined rules.

3.1   Response-Style Space Construction

Dual scaling is a versatile method for the analysis of a wide range of dominance and categorical data types, including rank-order data, paired-comparisons, successive categories, contingency tables, multiple-choice data, and sorting data [15]. It is usually applied in the mapping of latent preferences/behaviors of surveyed subjects to a rating scale that is common among a certain group of individuals. With such a mapping, each surveyed subject and stimulus is represented as a point in the resulting response-style space. The latent preferences and behaviors of subjects emerge from the visual inspection of the distribution of subjects points along the axes of the space and from the distance between subjects points and stimuli points. For instance, one of the axes of the resulting response-style space may organize subjects in ascending order by "age" (*e.g.,* the left side of the axis includes children, while the right side includes teenagers and adults) and, within each age group, one may notice the presence of subgroups of subjects that approach a certain "film category" (*e.g.,* animations, cult, documentary, silent) and a "place" where subjects might prefer to see the movie (*e.g.,* at movie theater, at home). In this example, film categories and places are the stimuli.

Although dual scaling has been proposed for the analysis of preferences of human subjects, we claim that it is a more general approach which can be used to discover response styles on virtually any database that may be analyzed by AR learning techniques. In this work, we treat database entries as multiple-choice data and represent them in a $(1,0)$ response-pattern matrix with the form:

	Stem 1			Stem 2			Stem 3		
	a	b	c	a	b	c	a	b	c
Subject 1	1	0	0	0	1	0	1	0	0
Subject 2	0	1	0	1	0	0	0	0	1
Subject 3	1	0	0	0	0	1	1	0	0

where each transaction from the database is treated as a subject, and the elements are grouped as possible answers of some multiple-choice stem. In dual scaling, each column of the response-pattern matrix is a different stimulus. Thus, the use of several stems is for organizational purposes only (*e.g.,* transforming the "age" item into "age range" and keep the choices under the same steam).

Once we have the raw data converted into a $N \times m$ response-pattern matrix F, where N is the number of transactions and m the number of elements, we apply dual scaling to this incidence data as usual. Due to space restrictions, the formulation of dual scaling is not presented in this paper. See [16] for details.

The transactions points mapped to the response-style space are computed by dual scaling as the rows of the $N \times N_s$ matrix y_{normed}, while the mapped elements points are the rows of the $m \times N_s$ matrix $x_{projected}$. The maximum number of dimensions of the response-style is $N_s = (m - rank\,(F) + 1)$ (i.e., the total number of nontrivial solutions); and *projected* and *normed* denote whether a kind of point is projected onto the space spanned by the other kind of point. See [17] for a discussion on the importance of using projected and normed data for, respectively, mapped subjects and stimuli.

According to our experience, for viewing purposes it is sufficient to present to the user only the first two dimensions of the response-style space (i.e., the two most significant dimensions, capable of explain most data). However, for clustering purposes (see Sect. 3.2), the use of the first k_{max} dimensions is sufficient. Following the notation convention adopted in [17], the total information explained by each dimension of the response-style space is given by δ_k, where $k = \{1, 2, \cdots, N_s\}$. We have chosen the value of k_{max} subject to:

$$\arg\max_{k_{max}} \left(\sum_{k=1}^{k_{max}} \delta_k \right) \leq 16\%,$$

where 16% was defined empirically from our experiments.

In contrast to conventional application of dual scaling, here we are concerned neither on displaying the transactions points (y_{normed}) to the user nor using the transactions for clustering, pruning or thresholding. The rationale for our strategy lies on the fact that subsequent mining procedures will retrieve rules that are comprised only by the dataset elements. Therefore, the visualization is much cleaner when presenting only $x_{projected}$ points. Handling transactions and elements together while performing dual scaling was key for approximating and repealing elements in the response-style space. However, after computing the $x_{projected}$ points, the y_{normed} points can be disposed.

3.2   Clustering Dataset Elements

The Euclidean distance of points in the response-style space can be interpreted as how related those points are in some context. A context emerges from the existence of groups and subgroups of subjects (i.e, transactions) having similar preferences (i.e., containing approximately the same set of elements). Conventionally, the visual inspection of dual scaling charts is performed by looking for near points defining those groups and subgroups. Therefore, it is natural to expect that by clustering elements points in the response-style space one will get an indication of which elements are likely to be combined in the formation of itemsets that result in significant rules. In this work we perform clustering using the anisotropic kernel mean shift (AKMS) algorithm [21].

Mean shift [10] is an iterative procedure that treats the points in the feature space as probability density functions (PDFs), and makes local maxima of the underlying distribution correspond to dense regions in the feature space. Its original formulation estimates the local density using a radially symmetric kernel (*e.g.*, Gaussian kernels). Wang *et al.* [21] extended the mean shift procedure to use anisotropic kernels and make the shape, scale, and orientation of the PDF better adapt to the local density of the space. We follow Wang *et al.* and use multivariate Gaussian kernels while clustering dataset items. In our approach, the feature space correspond to the k_{max} most significant dimensions of the response-style space and the underlying density distribution is the concentration of mapped elements points in such a space. It is important to emphasize that the use of k_{max} dimensions does not characterize a reduction in the amount of data, since all mapped elements points $x_{projected}$ are used for clustering. Such a choice for a lower dimensional space helps to reduce the sparsity of points and, in a conservative way, it promotes the identification of more numerous clusters. This outcome is important for defining a safe element pruning scheme (see Sect. 3.3).

For each data point in the feature space, mean shift-based techniques perform a gradient ascent procedure on the local estimated density until convergence or until the maximum number of iterations is reached. The stationary points of this procedure represent the modes of the underlying distribution, while data points associated with the same stationary point are considered members of the same cluster. Due to space restrictions, the formulation of the AKMS procedure is not presented in this paper. See [21] for details.

Wang *et al.* applied the AKMS to color image and video segmentation. In such a case, the data points are comprised by spatial and color range coordinates. Our data is comprised only by spatial coordinates. Therefore, we simplified the original equations by removing the terms related to color range. In our experiments we set the initial spatial bandwidth h_0^s (see [21]) to the Euclidean distance of the two most distant $x_{projected}$ points in the dataset. Such a conservative choice for h_0^s guarantees that the initial PDF of data points will not be ill-defined, *i.e.*, it will not leave an actual neighbor point out of the limits of the neighborhood.

3.3   Element Pruning

The result of the clustering stage is a set of clusters comprised by the elements that are more likely to be combined in the composition of some itemset, and hence in the formation of some significant rule. Therefore, if a cluster includes only one element entry them it is unlikely that this element will be important to the formation of any interesting rule.

Our safe element pruning method consists on dispose all elements that are included in single-entry clusters. A cluster ends with only one data element when this element is repealed by the transactions and by the other elements during the application of dual scaling.

Complementary, we allow to the user to specify a threshold value $t_{pruning}$ for disposing all elements included in clusters having at most $t_{pruning}$ elements.

4   Proposal Evaluation

Brazilian petroleum reservoir is mostly located in offshore areas. Each exploration unit house hundreds of people to operate a production plant. The nature of the activity is highly risky and accidents happen, creating economic, environmental and human consequences. Government agencies regulate operation requiring that any accident, even small ones, must be reported. These reports are rich and enclose causal chains that should be fast identified to prevent recurrence. Reports must include a great deal of details such as the involved equipment, task, location and process specifications. Considering each accident report as a transaction, the itemset describing a transaction contains about 34 different attributes (or steams in the response-pattern matrix – Sect. 3.1). Each steam is composed of a different number of choices, totaling 722 elements (or stimuli, in dual scaling terms). This high dimensionality calls for pre-processing pruning to let mining feasible. This fact motivated us to use this domain as the application domain for our visualization technique.

For evaluating our proposal, we present a step-by-step example applied to the accident report domain. We consider a set of 5,000 transactions that reported real accidents from 2006-2009. In order to preserve the confidentiality of information, some elements were renamed (*e.g.*, "Company" and "Oil rig") or omitted (*e.g.*, "Executive management") in Figs. 1 and 2.

The mining process is divided into iterative *mining cycles*, in which each cycle consists of *four main steps*:

i) Prepare the data to be mined by selecting the sets of transactions and elements used;
ii) Calculate the response-style space (see Sect. 3.1) and perform clustering (see Sect. 3.2) and pruning (see Sect. 3.3);
iii) Run the association rule technique Apriori on the remaining elements; and
iv) Analyze the generated graphic.

In the first mining cycle we used a subset of transactions extracted from the original dataset. By applying filters we selected the 1,838 records related to accidents that led to losses in the production of oil and/or gas. In this mining cycle, all the 722 elements where considered while computing the response-style space. However, the set of 233 items identified as being unlikely to be part of any interesting rule were disposed by our pruning strategy, and only the 499 remaining elements were used in the Apriori procedure. Figure 1 (left) shows the organization of the elements in the response-style space. Close to the center of the image it is possible to identify a red star representing the conclusion itemset of all the 322 rules retrieved. Such an itemset is comprised by a single item: "Production loss". The green circles represent the items that compose some condition itemset. The label of most items was omitted for clarity. We show the location of items "Company 1, 2, 3 and 4" in order to demonstrate that the emergent overall organization of the space seems to be related to the occurrence of specific subsets of items in the records related to each company. In other words, the elements next to a company are more related to such a company

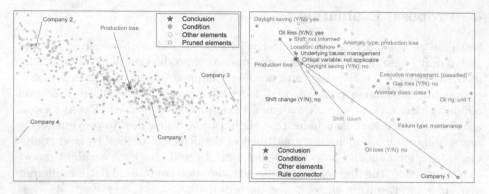

Fig. 1. Response-style space computed from 1,838 transactions reporting accidents related to production loss in four petroleum companies. The circles and squares at *left* represent, respectively, the 499 items (or elements) used in the mining procedure, and the 223 items pruned in a pre-processing stage. The green circles represent items that compose some condition itemsets, while the red star represents the conclusion itemset of all the 322 AR retrieved. A detailed view of one of the mined rules is presented at *right*. Note that it is possible to perceive the importance of each condition from its distance to the conclusion itemset. Please see electronic version for better visualization.

than to the others. Therefore, a possible interpretation of the graphic depicted in Fig. 1 (left) is that the mined rules are more likely to apply to "Company 1".

It is important to comment that, according to Sect. 3.1, clustering is performed in a k_{max}-dimensional space (in this mining cycle, $k_{max} = 27$) while visualization is presented in a 2D space. Hence, the existence of pruned elements mixed with significant ones in Fig. 1 (left) is just an illusion caused by the projection of data into a lower dimensional space.

Figure 1 (right) presents a detailed view of one of the mined rules. Notice that, by proximity, one can see that the antecedents of different rules, such as "Critical variable: not applicable" and "Shift: not informed", are strongly related to "Production loss". However, it turns out that these values are in fact irrelevant in the application domain. By post-pruning the rules that include these conditions we reduced the set of AR from 322 to 47 mined rules. Also, by inspecting the location of the "Shift" steam it was observed that the element "Steam: dawn" is the only shift that is close to mined rules. However, due to the parameterization of the Apriori algorithm, such an element was prevented to be pointed as a condition. In all experiments we used $\sigma = 30\%$ and $\gamma = 80\%$.

From the visual cues provided by the proposed visualization scheme we designed filters and performed a new mining cycle. In such a cycle we selected from the dataset a subset of 157 transactions related to accidents that happened during the dawn shift and led to losses in the production of oil and/or gas. Also, we removed from the set of items the steam choices that could assume the values "not informed" or "not applicable". The resulting response-style space is presented in Fig. 2 (left). The mining procedure retrieved only 55 rules, one of which is shown in Fig. 2 (right).

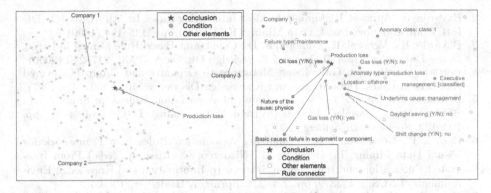

Fig. 2. Response-style space computed from 157 transactions reporting accidents related to production loss during the dawn shift. (left) 11 items are marked as a condition of one of the 55 mined rules. (right) Detailed view of the rule having "Failure in equipment or component", "Physical cause" and "Oil loss" as conditions that leads to "Production loss". Please see electronic version for better visualization.

In our experiments, we observed that the number and the composition of mined rules is the same both with and without the use of the proposed safe pruning approach. However, the pruning procedure helps reduce the amount of itemsets and hence helps to alleviate the computational load of the mining technique. For instance, without pruning, the mining process depicted in Fig. 1 would generate $\sim 2.21 \times 10^{217}$ itemsets in worst case. By applying our element-pruning scheme the amount of itemsets drops to $\sim 1.64 \times 10^{150}$ in worst case.

5 Summary and Future Work

This paper presented a data mining pre-processing visualization technique based on dual scale metric. The technique assists users to identify elements (items or attributes) that can be removed from the dataset leading to dimensionality reduction without impoverishing the quality of the extracted association rules. Although we did not obtain conclusive evidences, the placement of objects in a 2D space should also provide good hints of the adequate minimum support value to be used during association rules mining. There are some limitations to our approach. Mean shift is sensible to the initial bandwidth selection h_0^s. We adopt a conservative strategy to minimize this problem by increasing the value, however the iterative process will take longer and sometimes lead to unacceptable answer time. There are other approaches to minimize the bandwidth problem by using techniques dependent on the dataset entry [7,9]. Automatic bandwidth selection is still an open research issue that will be addressed in our future work.

References

1. Agrawal, R., Imielinski, T., Swami, A.: Mining Associations Between Sets of Items in Massive Databases. In: 1993 ACM SIGMOD Intl. Conf. on Management of Data (SIGMOD 1993), pp. 207–216. ACM (1993)

2. Bayardo, R., Agrawal, R.: Mining the Most Interesting Rules. In: 5th ACM SIGKDD Intl. Conf. on Know. Dis. & Data Mining (KDD 1999), pp. 145–154 (1999)
3. Bayardo, R., Agrawal, R., Gunopulos, D.: Constraint-Based Rule Mining in Large, Dense Databases. Data Mining and Knowledge Discovery 4(2-3), 217–240 (2000)
4. Berrado, A., Runger, G.C.: Using Metarules to Organize and Group Discovered Association Rules. Data Mining and Knowledge Discovery 14(3), 409–431 (2007)
5. Bruzzese, D., Davino, C.: Visual Mining of Association Rules. In: Simoff, S.J., Böhlen, M.H., Mazeika, A. (eds.) Visual Data Mining. LNCS, vol. 4404, pp. 103–122. Springer, Heidelberg (2008)
6. Buono, P., Costabile, M.F.: Visualizing Association Rules in a Framework for Visual Data Mining. In: Hemmje, M., Niederée, C., Risse, T. (eds.) From Integrated Publication and Information Systems to Information and Knowledge Environments. LNCS, vol. 3379, pp. 221–231. Springer, Heidelberg (2005)
7. Comaniciu, D., Ramesh, V., Meer, P.: The Variable Bandwidth Mean Shift and Data-Driven Scale Selection. In: 8th IEEE Intl. Conf. on Computer Vision (ICCV 2001), pp. 438–445. IEEE (2001)
8. Domingues, M.A., Rezende, S.O.: Post-Processing of Association Rules Using Taxonomies. In: 12th Portuguese Conf. on Artif. Intel. (EPIA 2005). pp. 192–197 (2005)
9. Einbeck, J.: Bandwidth Selection for Mean-Shift Based Unsupervised Learning Techniques – A Unified Approach Via Self-Coverage. Journal of Pattern Recognition Research 6(2), 175–192 (2011)
10. Fukunaga, K., Hostetler, L.: The Estimation of the Gradient of a Density Function, with Applications in Pattern Recognition. IEEE Trans. on Information Theory 21(1), 32–40 (1975)
11. Garcia, A.C.B., Ferraz, I., Vivacqua, A.S.: From Data to Knowledge Mining. Artif. Intel. for Eng. Design, Analysis and Manufacturing 23(4), 427–441 (2009)
12. Hofmann, H., Siebes, A., Wilhelm, A.: Visualizing Association Rules with Interactive Mosaic Plots. In: 6th ACM SIGKDD Intl. Conf. on Knowledge Discovery and Data Mining (KDD 2000), pp. 227–235. ACM (2000)
13. Lavrac, N., Flach, P., Zupan, B.: Rule Evaluation Measures – A Unifying View. In: Džeroski, S., Flach, P. (eds.) ILP 1999. LNCS (LNAI), vol. 1634, pp. 174–185. Springer, Heidelberg (1999)
14. Marinica, C., Guillet, F.: Filtering Discovered Association Rules Using Ontologies. IEEE Trans. on Knowledge and Data Eng. 22(6), 784–797 (2009)
15. Nishisato, S.: Elements of Dual Scaling – An Introduction to Practical Data Analysis. Psychology Press (1993)
16. Nishisato, S.: On Quantifying Different Types of Categorical Data. Psychometrika 58(4), 617–629 (1993)
17. Nishisato, S.: Gleaning in the Field of Dual Scaling. Psychometrika 61(4), 559–599 (1996)
18. Shekar, B., Natarajan, R.: A Framework for Evaluating Knowledge-Based Interestingness of Association Rules. Fuzzy Opt. and Dec. Making 3(2), 157–185 (2004)
19. Srikant, R., Agrawal, R.: Mining Generalized Association Rules. In: 21st Intl. Conf. on Very Large Databases (VLDB 1995), pp. 407–419. Morgan Kaufmann (1995)
20. Tan, P., Kumar, V., Srivastava, J.: Selecting the Right Objective Measure for Association Analysis. Information Systems 29(4), 293–313 (2004)
21. Wang, J., Thiesson, B., Xu, Y., Cohen, M.: Image and Video Segmentation by Anisotropic Kernel Mean Shift. In: Pajdla, T., Matas, J. (eds.) ECCV 2004. LNCS, vol. 3022, pp. 238–249. Springer, Heidelberg (2004)
22. Yang, L.: Visualizing Frequent Itemsets, Association Rules, and Sequential Patterns in Parallel Coordinates. In: Kumar, V., Gavrilova, M.L., Tan, C.J., L'Ecuyer, P. (eds.) ICCSA 2003, Part I. LNCS, vol. 2667, pp. 21–30. Springer, Heidelberg (2003)

Identifying Relationships in Transactional Data

Melissa Rodrigues[1], João Gama[1,2], and Carlos Abreu Ferreira[2,3]

[1] FEP - University of Porto, Porto Portugal
[2] LIAAD-INESC TEC, Porto, Portugal
[3] ISEP - Polytechnic Institute of Porto, Porto, Portugal

Abstract. *Association rules* is the traditional way used to study market basket or transactional data. One drawback of this analysis is the huge number of rules generated. As a complement to *association rules*, *Association Rules Network (ARN)*, based on *Social Network Analysis (SNA)* has been proposed by several researchers. In this work we study a real market basket analysis problem, available in a Belgian supermarket, using *ARNs*. We learn *ARNs* by considering the relationships between items that appear more often in the consequent of the *association rules*. Moreover, we propose a more compact variant of *ARNs*: the *Maximal Itemsets Social Network*. In order to assess the quality of these structures, we compute *SNA* based metrics, like *weighted degree* and *utility of community*.

Keywords: social network analysis, association rules network.

1 Introduction

Every day the consumers satisfy their needs with the acquisition of products and services that they choose according to factors such as the price, the brand and the quality. To study the behavior and preferences of the consumers *market basket analysis* can be a powerful tool to help food chains, recommendation systems and other businesses to promote their products or services.

The traditional way to find relationships among products available in transactional databases is to run an *association rule miner* [1] and obtain *association rules* that represent valuable knowledge. The *association rule miner* algorithm generates a set of rules and each rule is associated with one, or more, interest measures, like support and confidence. The problem with this approach is the huge number of rules found by the *association rule miner*, most of them are redundant and uninteresting. A more recent framework used in market basket analysis is to use *Social Networks Analysis (SNA)* [2]. Using this framework a *social network of products* is built [13]. Social networks of products are graph structures where vertices can be products and edges represent products bought together in the same transaction. These networks can represent valuable relationships among products.

In this work we study the problem of identifying meaningful relationships available in the transactions database of a Belgian supermarket. We use two

J. Pavón et al. (Eds.): IBERAMIA 2012, LNAI 7637, pp. 81–90, 2012.

different strategies to study this data. One strategy is to represent our data in a *global social network* (GSN), that includes all products, and use this representation to extract interesting information about the *best seller products*. We extract some interesting information about the products and network by computing statistical measures according to the vertex and according to the network. Moreover, we choose the *weighted degree* measure to find the *best seller products* [9]. The problem with this approach is that we have a large number of products and get highly complex networks that can not represent the motivation for two products appearing in the same transaction. To address this issue of our *GSN* we developed a new pipeline methodology that is grounded in the *Association Rule* analysis. First, we run an *association rule miner* to obtain the most interesting association rules. Then, and also to reduce the size of the ruleset, we put the focus on the most interesting products [13] and learn meaningful *Association Rules Networks (ARNs)* [12]. The most interesting products are the ones that appear more often in the consequent of the association rules found by the *association rule miner*. Moreover, we compute the same metrics that we use in the *SNA*, plus some communities measures used to detect and study *communities* [13] available in the obtained *ARNs*. We obtain some interesting results but we would like to study a more compact way to represent only the more meaningful relationships among products. Thus, we introduce in this work the *Maximal Itemsets Social Network (MISN)*. First we find the *maximal itemsets* [14] and then we generate the MISN.

The paper is organized as follows. In Sect. 2 we present some related work and concepts. In Sect. 3 we describe the methodology that we use to study our data and present the obtained results. Last, in Sect. 4, we conclude and present some work that we will develop in the near future.

2   Related Work

Identifying relationships in transactional data is the primary focus of *market basket analysis* [4,12,13].

According to [4], finding the hit-list of products in transactional data can be done by using an *association rule* framework but it is required to integrate the search for frequent itemsets within a microeconomic model. Otherwise we will obtain meaningless *association rules*. In this work the authors study a dataset of transactions acquired from a fully-automated convenience store and obtained interesting association rules. The authors also show that by exploring *frequent itemsets*, it is possible to identify the cross-sales potential of product items and use this information for better product selection.

Another work that discovers meaningful relationships among the products is [13]. In this work the authors model the data as a product network and present a new metric to study *communities*. To find interesting *communities* the authors introduce the *utility of community* metric. According to these authors, the set of *communities* and the *ARN* structure, along with the actual list of *association rules*, can provide important insights on the supermarket customer behavior. By exploring data collected from a convenience store they found several interesting communities. For instance, the community associated with the highest value of the *utility of community* metric shows that chips and salsa are complementary products and that people often buy these two products together.

3 Methodology and Analysis of the Results

In this section we present the methodologies that we use to identify meaningful relationships available in the *Retail* database [4] while presenting and analyzing the results that we obtained. First, we represent the entire transactional data using a *social network(GSN)* and study some statistical measures according to the vertex and according to the network. Second, grounded in the *association rule* framework we present a sequence of steps that uncover interesting relationships. We start by finding the most interesting *association rules* using the *Apriori* algorithm [1]. Then, to reduce the ruleset and network complexity, we select the *association rules* having each one of the five products that appear more often in the consequent of the ruleset and use these findings to generate five *ARNs*, one *ARN* for each one of the five most frequent products. We analyze the obtained *ARNs* using the same statistical measures that we use to study the *social network* plus measures suitable to study *communities*. Next, we introduce a more compact representation based on the *maximal itemsets* [14] that we found in the entire *Retail* dataset, we introduce the *MISN*. To study this later *social network* we use the same metrics that we use to study the ARNs.

Concerning to the *Retail* dataset [4], this dataset registers 250 transactions and 1209 products sold in a small Belgium supermarket during 5 years and a half. We do not have assess to the identification of any of the products. Each product identity is mapped into an integer number and here we work only with the coded data.

3.1 Social Network Analysis

In this section we use SNA to represent the entire set of *Retail* transactions into a *social network* of products [13]. In the next sections this network is called *GSN*. In this network representation, each product defines a vertex. And every two products appearing in the same transaction are represented by an edge. Using this mapping strategy we obtain the *social network* represented in Fig. 1. This network has 1209 vertices and 12257 edges. We use *Gephi software* [15] to draw the *social network* represented in this figure. To characterize, understand and explain the structure of this *social network* we compute and analyze a set of statistical metrics. We compute metrics for the vertices: *degree, weighted degree, betweenness and eigenvector centrality* and compute metrics for the network: *density, path length, number of the shortest paths, diameter and agglomeration coefficient* [2,10]. Moreover, due to the poor viewing, we use the *Fruchterman Reingold* algorithm [7] to improve the networks' perception.

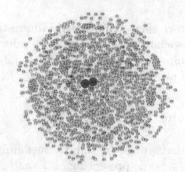

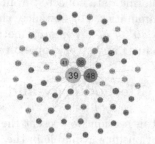

Fig. 1. Social network of *Retail* database   **Fig. 2.** *MISN* of *Retail* database

In Table 1 we present the average value of each metric that we use to analyze the vertices of the generated *social network,* the one presented in Fig. 1. We can see that each vertex is connected to approximately 20 vertices. Regarding the *weighted degree*, the total weight average of the edges in each vertex is 21.838. On the other hand, the average value of the metric *betweenness* shows that a given vertex appears 810 times in the shortest paths of the *Social Network*. Last, by inspecting the average *eigenvector centrality* we can see that the vertices are connected about 0.057 among them.

In Table 2 we present the metrics that we use to analyze our *social network*. We see that we have a low *density* (0.017) network. This means that the network is far to become complete (complete networks have density equal to 1). The analysis of the metric *average length path* indicates that the average distance between all vertices pairs in the network is 2.364. Moreover, we can say that there exist 1436418 different shortest paths. Furthermore, we can see that the longest distance between two vertices, *diameter*, is 5 edges. The network presents a high *agglomeration coefficient* value (0.886) which suggests a tendency of the network to form cliques.

In Table 3 we present the five products with the highest *weighted degree* in the *social network*. The *weighted degree* is defined as the sum of the weights of all edges connected to a particular vertex [9]. Using this metric, we identify the five *best seller products*: **39**, **48**, **38**, **41** and **32**. Then, we represent the network of each product using *self-social networks*. These individual structures represent only the direct edges among each one of the best seller products and all the others products. We analyze these structures and get an *agglomeration coefficient* equal to zero. This shows that the *best seller* products play a central role and they can be seen as a communication channel among products [8]. Moreover, we get for all five *self-social networks* a *diameter* equal to 2.

Table 1. Statistical measures by vertex   **Table 2.** Statistical measures by network

Av. degree	Av. weighted degree	Av. betweenness	Av. eigenvector centrality	Density	Av. length path	Nr of shortest paths	Diameter	Av. agglomeration coefficient
20.276	21.838	810.300	0.057	0.017	2.364	1436418	5	0.886

Table 3. Products with highest *weighted degree*

Products	Weighted degree
39	1155
48	1092
38	618
41	556
32	233

3.2   Association Rules-Based Approaches

In this section, grounded in the *association rule framework*, we use method-ologies to reduce the complexity of the social networks. We learn an *ARN* for each one of the most interesting products. Moreover, we introduce the *MISN*, a more compact representation of the entire *Retail* database that uses the *maximal itemsets*.

Association Rules. We use association rules to explore the relationships be-tween items frequently purchased together. These rules have two parts, the *an-tecedent* part and the *consequent* part. For instance, in a supermarket dataset we can obtain the following rule: $\{cake, bread\} => coffee$. This rule represents a partial implication that means that people buying cake and bread also buy coffee. To find *association rules* there exist a wide number of algorithms that we can use [1,6]. In this work we will use the *Apriori* algorithm [1] to find the most interesting rules. The *Apriori* algorithm can be parameterized to find both the *association rules* and the most *frequent itemsets* [1]. Moreover we can use a naive post processing strategy to find the subset of *maximal itemsets*. An itemset is *maximal* if it is *frequent* but none of their proper *supersets* is *frequent* [14].

Typically, when we run an *association rule miner* to find either the *frequent itemsets* or the *association rules* on a database of transactions, we get a huge number of uninteresting and redundant patterns. If we increase the minimum *support* or *confidence* thresholds we get a small number of patterns but we can fail to detect interesting itemsets or rules having a support or/and confidence value lower than the user-defined values. To address this issue we can use low support and confidence thresholds and compute additional metrics like *convic-tion, cosine or lift* [6] to select the most interesting *association rules*. In this work we compute the *lift* metric of each *association rule* to find rules having negative or positive association. In Table 4 we present a subset of association rules that we obtained by running *Apriori* algorithm to find *association rules*. We use the implementation available in *arules* package of the *R Project software* [16]. We set the *support* threshold value equal to 0.01, the *confidence* threshold equal to 0.50 and the minimum *lift* value of each rule equal to 2. With this setting we obtained 115 rules. Without the *lift* constrain and using the other two parameters we get 288 rules, i.e., by using *lift* we prune 173 rules.

Association Rules Networks. Here we learn an *ARN* for each one of the top 5 most frequent products available in the consequent of the 115 association rules presented in the previous section. Then we analyze each one of the *ARNs*.

Table 4. Three association rules that we found by setting $lift > 2$

Rule Nr.	Antecedent		Consequent	Support	Confidence	Lift
2	281	=>	38	0.012	1	3.676
274	36,39,48	=>	38	0.016	1	3.676
288	36,38,39,48	=>	41	0.012	0.75	3.074

According to [12], an *ARN* can show the direct and indirect associations among the products. Each *ARN* is a unique direct hypergraph that is associated with only one target-product. Each rule is represented by the directed edge where the itemsets in the rule antecedent are the source-vertices and the target item in the consequent of the rule is the destiny-vertex. These authors present the following sequence of steps to learn an *ARN:* **1)** Given a database D and the minimum support and confidence threshold, find all *association rules* using an algorithm such as *Apriori*; **2)** Choose a frequent item z that appears in the consequent of a ruleset and built the direct hypergraph that flows to this target-vertex z; **3)** Prune the constructed hypergraph of opposite hypercycles and hyperedges. The resulting hypergraph is an *ARN*.

We analyze the *ARNs* using the metrics described in Sect. 3.1, we compute metrics according to the vertex and according to the network. However, due to space limitations we can only say that we obtained lower *degree* and *weigthed degree* values when we compare with the values that we obtained in the *GSN* (see Sect. 3.1). They express few relationships but still get a value higher than the ones obtained when analyzing the *social self-networks*. We also find that the *density* is high in the *ARNs* as they represent just the most interesting rulesets. As *ARNs* have less relationships compared to the relationships of the *GSN*, their *agglomeration coefficient* is lower, which means a lower tendency to form cliques.

Here we also study the *communities* in each *ARN*. A *community* is a group of vertices densely connected that has high concentrations of edges connecting vertices within the group and has low concentrations of edges connecting to other groups. The metric used to detect this property is called *modularity* [11,5]. *Modularity*, Q, values range between -1 and 1:

$$Q = \sum (e_{II} - a_I^2) \tag{1}$$

where, e_{II} is the fraction of edges that join the vertices to other vertices in the community I and a_I is the fraction that remains in the community I.

To evaluate these groups, a new measure called *utility of community* $U(G_i)$ was proposed by [13]. This measure includes two parts: *information* and *information density* and its range is between 0 and 1. *Information*, $I(G_i)$, is the sum of the weights of the *intra-community* edges, $I(G_i) = a_0 + \sum P(p_1|p_2)$. *Information density* $D(G_i)$ give us the information of the vertex i in the graph G_i, in a given *community*, in other words, its *weighted degree*, $D(G_i) = \frac{I(G_i)}{|V_i|}$. This way we can define the *utility of the community*:

$$U(G_i) = \frac{2I(G_i)D(G_i)}{I(G_i) + D(G_i)} \tag{2}$$

Table 5. Statistical measures by vertex of the *MISN*

Av. degree	Av. weighted degree	Av. betweenness	Av. eigenvector centrality
3.806	6.484	34.371	0.199

Table 6. Statistical measures by network of the *MISN*

Density	Av. length path	Nr. of short paths	Diameter	Av. agg. coefficient	Modularity
0.062	2.127	3782	3	0.534	0.255

There are several algorithms to detect *communities*, so in this work we use an algorithm of *modularity optimization*, the *Blondel Algorithm* [5]. This algorithm has two phases. Consider a weighted network where each vertex is a community, the first phase is to calculate the *modularity gain* of all neighbors. If a vertice has a *modularity gain* (ΔQ) higher in a neighbor community, it will be allocated to this community. This process continues until there is no improvement. After creating the network, the second phase is to apply again the first phase of the algorithm to the weighted network [3,5].

In this work we follow this methodology to discover *communities* in the five *ARNs*. The *ARNs* correspond to the products **38**, **41**, **48**, **32** and **36** and we analyze each network by computing the same metrics that we used in Sect. 3.1. Moreover, we analyze communities available in each *ARN* by computing some special purpose measures: *modularity, representation percentage and utility of community*.

ARNs provided us to discover expressive relationships between some popular products. In these informative *ARNs* we could imagine a similar need, such as complementary, or products purchased in the nights, for instance. According to [13], *ARNs* and *association rules* failed to find relationships that fall outside the specified support and confidence thresholds.

Maximal Itemsets Social Network (MISN). Here we introduce the *MISN* to get a more compact network representation than the *GSN* that we found in Sect. 3.1. We believe that the *MISN* will help us to discover meaningful relationships in the entire transactions database. To obtain the *MISN* we run the *Apriori algorithm* to find all *frequent itemsets* and then use a naive strategy to find the *maximal itemsets*. Using this strategy we found 117 *maximal itemsets*. Then, we translate the *maximal itemsets* into an adjacency list. Next, we use the adjacency list to generate the *MISN*. Finally, we analyze the statistical measures of the *MISN* and detect the *communities*. We also compare the *MISN* communities, where the target products appear, with the corresponding *ARNs* communities.

In Table 5 we present *MISN* vertex statistical measures. The metric *degree* shows that the average number of edges connecting to a vertex is approximately 4 edges. This table also shows that the average *weighted degree* is 6.484. Concerning the measure *betweenness*, that reflects the number of times that a given vertex appears in the *shortest paths* of the network, we get an average value of 34. In the last column we present the metric *eigenvector centrality*. We can see that each vertex is connected to 0.199 of the vertices.

Relatively to the metric *density* presented in Table 6 we get a density of 0.062, which reflects that the *MISN* is far to be complete. The measure *average length*

Table 7. Communities, products, representation percentage and utility in *MISN*

Communities	Products	Rep. percentage	Utility
1 (violet)	48,859,798,96,260,359,147,357,179,365,548,186,258,242,101,45,493,649,730,11,65	33.87	0.385
2 (light green)	39,79,152,384,150,259,155,272,225,312,9,249,475,278,237,809,255	27.42	0.269
3 (dark green)	248,41,348,956,37,89,105,561,110	14.52	0.235
4 (red)	178,32,170	4.84	0.167
5 (blue)	38,55,604,589,281,161,390,36,740,441,286,47	19.35	0.326

path reveals that 2.127 is the average distance between all the pairs of vertices. In the total, 3782 is the sum of all *shortest paths* among each pair of vertices. The longest distance between any two vertices is obtained using the *diameter* metric, which in this case is of 3 edges. The average *agglomeration coefficient* is 0.534 and this value shows the tendency to cliques formation, which are complete subgraphs where any two vertices are connected at least by a edge. In this case, we can see in Figure 2 a central clique, composed by the products **41, 38, 39** and **48**, for instance, which correspond exactly to the products with higher *weighted degree* in the *MISN* and in the *GSN*.

Here, we also study the five products that have the higher *weighted degree* (**39, 48, 38, 41** and **32**). Suppose that these products can be *bread, apples, cheese, coffee* and *sugar*. We imagine these because they satisfy needs in all meals, like *bread* can be necessary for the breakfast, lunch and dinner and their function can be complementary with other products, like *cheese* with ham, a meal composed by rice, tomatoes, beef, *apples* and *sugar*.

Beyond the representation and statistical metrics, it is important to analyze the communities. In this sense, we apply again the *Blondel algorithm*. This way we can obtain the number of discovered *communities*, the *representation percentage* in the entire network and the *utility of community*. The *MISN* modularity has the value of 0.255, so it has a significant community structure [10] and we identified 5 communities, as we can see in Fig. 2.

The *utility of community* helped to quantify the importance of each community in the *MISN*, according to the weights of the edges and the vertices' *weighted degree*. This is the contribution that the groups provide to the *social network*, excluding the illusory effect of the representation percentage, that just take into account the number of the vertices comprised in each *community*. This way, we sort the *communities* of the *MISN* using the *utility* metric: the *community* **1** with 0.385, the *community* **5** with 0.326, the *community* **2** with 0.269, the *community* **3** with 0.235 and finally the *community* **4** with 0.167. In the Table 7 we can see that the second community (second row) in the *MISN* has the second

Table 8. Community of the target-product, products, representation percentage and utility of the community of each *ARN*

Chosen ARN	Com. of the target-product (ARN)	Products	Rep. percentage	Utility of the community
38	1	38,55,281,32,589,604,170,740	40	0.242
41	2	41,38,441,105,390,32,37,248	50	0.504
48	1	48,798,357,11,859,96,147	35	0.24
32	1	32,178,39	100	0.889
36	1	36,740	50	0.40

higher *percentage of representation*, but its *utility of community* (0.269) is lower than the *utility of community* of community five (0.326). Therefore, communities that include a higher number of products do not always correspond to the communities with highest *utility of community*.

Comparing the communities of the *MISN* network with the communities of the five *ARNs* (products **38, 41, 48, 32** and **36**), we found (see Table 8) that: 50% of the products contained in the community of the *38*-ARN that contains the product **38** are also contained in community **5** of the *MISN* (see Table 7), that also contains the product **38**; 37.5% of the products contained in the community of the **41**-ARN that contains the product **41** are also contained in community **3** of the *MISN*, that also contains the product **41**; 66.7% of the products contained in the community of the **32**-ARN that contains the product **32** are also contained in the community **4** of the *MISN*; 100% of the products that appear in the ARN community of the **48**-ARN that contains the product **48** and in the community of the **36**-ARN that contains product **36**, appear, respectively, in the communities **1** and **5** of the *MISN*. Thus, we concluded that the *MISN* is a good approach to discover meaningful relationships and that most of the *communities* of the chosen products in the *ARNs* are well represented in the *MISN*.

4   Conclusions

In this work we explore different representations of our supermarket transactional data and discovered very interesting and meaningful relationships. We start by building a *social network* of products, our *GSN*, and found that this representation generates a highly complex network. This can be the result of representing all products bought together, including the ones that were bought without a common motivation. Then we use the *association rules* to explore the relationships between the products. The problem with this approach is the huge number of *association rules* found by any association rule miner. Then we introduce the *lift* measure to get a small and more interesting set of rules. This way, we get some interesting rules but we need to search for a global overview on the products. Thus, we select the top five frequent products in the consequent of the lift-pruned rules and generate five *ARNs*. We analyze each one of the five *ARNs* using a set of metrics and search for the *best seller products*, the products having the highest *weighted degree*. Moreover, we found that the *agglomeration coefficient* has lower values for the *social self-networks* when compared with the values that we obtained in the *ARNs*. This is explained by the *social self-networks* representation structure. *Social self-networks* represent the edges between the vertices and the *best seller vertex*, not taking into account possible edges between the vertices. Last, we use the *maximal itemsets* that we find in the entire dataset to generate a more compact network, the *MISN*. Overall we can say that the *best seller products*, according to the measure *weighted degree*, computed from the *GSN*, do not correspond to the products that appear more often in the consequent of the *association rules*, but to the products with higher *weighted degree* in the *MISN*.

In the future, we will search for other interest measures for the *association rules* to obtain high interesting association rules and explore the *cliques* available in the *MISN* to group products that share a significant level of connections.

Acknowledgments. This work is funded by the ERDF - through the COMPETE Programme and by National Funds through the FCT Project KDUS.

References

1. Agrawal, R., Srikant, R.: Fast Algorithms for Mining Association Rules. In: 20th Intl. Conf. on Very Large Data Bases (VLDB 1994), pp. 487–499 (1994)
2. Albert, R., Barabasi, A.: Statistical Mechanisms of Complex Networks. Reviews of Modern Physics 74, 47–97 (2002)
3. Blondel, V.D., Guillaumem, J., Lambiotte, R., Lefebrvre, E.: Fast Unfolding of Communities in Large Networks. Journal of Statistical Mechanics: Theory and Experiment P10008, 1–12 (2008)
4. Brijs, T., Swinnen, G., Vanhoof, K., Wets, G.: Using Association Rules for Product Assortment Decisions – A Case Study. In: 5th ACM SIGKDD Int. Conf. on Knowledge Discovery and Data Mining (KDD 1999), pp. 254–260. ACM (1999)
5. Easley, D., Kleinberg, J.: Networks, Crowds, and Markets – Reasoning About a Highly Connected World. Cambridge University Press (2010)
6. Faceli, K., Lorena, A.C., Gama, J., Carvalho, A.: Inteligência Artificial – Uma Abordagem de Aprendizado de Máquina. Livros Técnicos e Científicos (2011)
7. Fruchterman, T., Reingold, E.M.: Graph Drawing by Force-Directed Placement. Software: Practice and Experience 21(11), 1129–1164 (1991)
8. Kretschmer, H., Kretschmer, T.: Application of a New Centrality Measure for Social Network Analysis to Bibliometric and Webometric Data. In: 1st IEEE Int. Conf. of Digital Information Management (ICDIM 2006), pp. 199–204. IEEE (2006)
9. Lopez-Fernandez, L., Robles, G., Gonzalez-Barahona, J.M.: Applying Social Network Analysis to the Information in CVS Repositories. In: 1st International Workshop on Mining Software Repositories (MSR 2004), pp. 101–105 (2004)
10. Newman, M.E.J.: The Structure and Function of Complex Networks. Society for Industrial and Applied Mathematics Review 45(2), 167–256 (2003)
11. Newman, M.E.J.: Fast Algorithm for Detecting Community Structure in Networks. Physical Review E 69(6), 066133, 1–5 (2004)
12. Pandey, G., Chawla, S., Poon, S., Arunasalam, B., Davis, J.: Association Rules Network – Definition and Applications. Statistical Analysis and Data Mining 1(4), 260–279 (2009)
13. Raeder, T., Chawla, N.: Market Basket Analysis with Networks. Social Network Analysis and Mining 1(2), 97–113 (2011)
14. Gouda, K., Zaki, M.: Efficiently Mining Maximal Frequent Itemsets. In: 2001 IEEE International Conference on Data Mining (ICDM 2001), pp. 163–170. IEEE (2001)
15. Bastian, M., Heymann, S., Jacomy, M.: Gephi – An Open Source Software for Exploring and Manipulating Networks. In: 3rd Intl. AAAI Conf. on Weblogs and Social Media (ICWSM 2009), pp. 361–362. AAAI (2009)
16. R Core Team: R – A Language and Environment for Statistical. R Foundation for Statistical Computing (2012)

Time Series Discretization Based on the Approximation of the Local Slope Information

Willian Zalewski[1,2], Fabiano Silva[1], Huei Diana Lee[2],
Andre Gustavo Maletzke[2], and Feng Chung Wu[2]

[1] Federal University of Parana – UFPR, Curitiba, Brazil
Formal Methods and Artificial Intelligence Laboratory – LIAMF
{wzalewski,fabiano}@inf.ufpr.br
http://www.inf.ufpr.br
[2] State University of West Parana – UNIOESTE, Foz do Iguassu, Brazil
Bioinformatics Laboratory – LABI
{andregustavom,hueidianalee,wufengchung}@gmail.com
http://www.foz.unioeste.br/labi

Abstract. In the last decade symbolic representations approaches have
shown effectiveness for knowledge discovery in time series, such as the
Symbolic Aggregate Approximation (SAX). However, SAX doesn't preserve the local slope information of the time series because it uses only the
mean values of the segments. The modification Extended SAX (ESAX)
proposed to treat this problem by the dimensionality increase. In this
paper, we present a symbolic representation method that preserves the
behavior of local slope characteristics in the symbolic representations of
the time series. The proposed method was evaluated with three different
discretization approaches and compared with the SAX and the ESAX algorithms. The experimental evaluation, using artificial and real datasets
with 1-nearest-neighbor classification, demonstrate the method effectiveness to reduce the error rates of time series classification and to keep the
local slope information in the symbolic representations.

Keywords: time series, knowledge discovery, symbolic representation,
classification, dimensionality reduction.

1 Introduction

The traditional data mining algorithms were developed to analyze data without
temporal relation. However, the storage increase of continuous data with temporal interdependencies, such as time series, has motivated the development of
new data mining approaches [1,2]. The time series are collections of observations made chronologically and this type of data is present in almost all domains
such as business, industry, medicine, science and entertainment. Time Series
Data Mining (TSDM) is a relatively new area that uses data mining methods
adjusted to take into consideration the temporal nature of data [3,4].

Over the last decade many interesting TSDM techniques were proposed and
have shown to be useful in many applications [5]. Specifically, symbolic representations have demonstrated to be a very effective tool to reduce the dimensionality

J. Pavón et al. (Eds.): IBERAMIA 2012, LNAI 7637, pp. 91–100, 2012.

of the time series [2,6,7,8] and to preserve the underlying information and produce interpretable symbols within the domain [1,9].

The most common symbolic representation is the Symbolic Aggregate Approximation (SAX) [2]. The variation Extended SAX (ESAX) was proposed to keep the slope information into symbolic representation. However, the ESAX algorithm causes the increase of the dimensionality and uses additional values of the raw data that can be affected by the noise presence [10].

In previous work [11] we proposed a initial symbolic representation method to preserve the approximated local slope information between the time series observations. In this work, we extend the previous work by presenting a sliding window function to transform the time series data. Furthermore, we propose and evaluate the application of different discretization approaches.

The rest of this paper is organized as follows. Section 2 presents background on time series data mining and related works. Section 3 introduces our symbolic method. Section 4 contains an experimental evaluation of the symbolic method on a variety of the time series datasets. In Sect. 5 the effectiveness of the symbolic method is also analyzed. Finally, Sect. 6 presents the conclusions and directions for future works.

2   Background and Related Works

In the context of TSDM, the time series representation is a fundamental problem because direct manipulation of high dimensional data in an efficient way is extremely difficult in traditional data mining techniques. A common approach is to use a time series representation based on some dimensionality reduction technique, while preserving the relevant characteristics of a particular dataset [1,8]. Many numerical time series representation approaches have been proposed in the literature to reduce the high dimensionality [2,5].

There are domains, such as medicine and finances, where symbolic representation rather than numerical analysis is needed to produce more comprehensive knowledge of the time series [12]. Many works have also considered symbolic representations of time series, such as Shape Description Alphabet (SDA); Interactive Matching of Patterns with Advanced Constraints in Time Series Databases (IMPACTS); *Clipping*; *Persist*; and Piecewise Vector Quantized Approximation (PVQA) [2,3,5].

Most of the symbolic representations cited are affected by two main aspects. Firstly, the intrinsic dimensionality of the symbolic representation is the same as the raw data, thus the data mining algorithms scale poorly with high dimensionality. Second, the unavoidable noise presence in time series can produce meaningless symbols. The SAX is the first symbolic approach that applies dimensionality reduction technique as a preprocessing step, in this case the PAA algorithm [2]. The smoothing property of the PAA contributes to minimize the noise effect.

Piecewise Aggregate Approximation: To transform m-dimensional vector space X to an w-dimensional vector space Y, the data is divided into w equal-size segments, and the mean value of each segment is used to represent original time series with lower w-dimension. The time series $T = \{t_1, \ldots, t_m\}$ of length m can be represented in w-dimensional space by a vector $\overline{T} = \{\overline{t}_1, \ldots, \overline{t}_w\}$ and the ith element of $\overline{T}$ is calculated by the Equation 1 [2]:

$$\overline{t}_i = \frac{w}{m} \sum_{j=\frac{m}{w}(i-1)+1}^{\frac{m}{w}i} t_j \tag{1}$$

Symbolic Aggregate Approximation: The SAX symbolic representation is performed in two steps. First the PAA algorithm is applied to the raw time series (see Fig. 1(a)). Second, the distribution space (y-axis) is divided into equiprobable regions under a Gaussian curve and the mean segment values from PAA are converted into symbols corresponding to each segment [2]. The SAX symbolic representation can be defined by the function $SAX(\overline{T}, w, a) = \hat{T} = \{\hat{t}_1, \ldots, \hat{t}_w\}$ where $\hat{t}_i$ represent the ith symbol, w is the number of segments and a is the alphabet size. In Fig. 1(b) is presented a SAX example of a symbolic sequence **baabccbc** with the alphabet $\{a, b, c\}$.

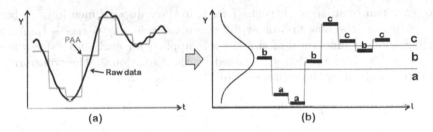

Fig. 1. (a) PAA application example and (b) SAX application example

In the last decade, SAX has been widely applied to many fields and obtained good results [2,5]. However, the smoothing effect by only using the PAA algorithm may lose useful information, especially the segment slope information. Furthermore, the equiprobable feature of SAX symbols produces low performance for non-uniform time series [7].

The ESAX approach proposed in [10] is based in addition to the mean value two new symbols for each segment representation, the maximum value and the minimum value of the interval. The ESAX symbolic representation can be defined by the function $ESAX(\overline{T}, w, a) = \hat{T} = \{\hat{t}_1, \ldots, \hat{t}_w\}$ where $\hat{t}_i = \{p_{min}, p_{mid}, p_{max}\}$ is the ith symbolic segment, w is the number of segments and a is the alphabet size. The position of the symbols p_{min} (minimum value), p_{mid} (mean value) and p_{max} (maximum value) in each symbolic segment is determined by the increasing order. However, the ESAX approach has some problems, such as the dimensionality increase by three times the dimensionality of the SAX approach. Furthermore, the selection of the maximum value and minimum value in each segment can be affected by the noise presence in these points.

In [11] was proposed a symbolic representation method to preserve the approximated local slope information between the time series observations based on the first order differences calculus to the PAA representation and the k-means algorithm to create the symbols. But, this approach also presents some problems such as computing cost to define the initial centers in k-means application and the need to use some training set to create the symbols.

3 Symbolic Representation Method

In this section we present a new symbolic representation method for time series. The method is performed in three sequential steps: Dimensionality Reduction; Data Transformation; and Symbol Creation. The first step is performed by the application of PAA algorithm (Equation 1).

In this work, we proposed an intermediate step between dimensionality reduction and symbolic representation. The data transformation step is used to keep approximated information about the local slope of the time series. In this step, we calculated the first order differences between the adjacent values $\overline{T}$ produced by PAA algorithm.

For each pair of adjacent elements $(i, i+1)$ in the reduced dimension $\overline{T}$, where $1 \leq i \leq w - 1$, the new first order difference value is $\delta(i) = \overline{t}_{i+1} - \overline{t}_i$. After, a sliding window function θ of size three is applied for each $\delta(i)$ value where $1 \leq i \leq w - 3$. The function θ is defined by the Equation 2. The transformed time series is given by the values $\Theta = \{\theta(1), \dots, \theta(w - 3)\}$.

$$\theta(i) = \frac{\delta(i) + 2 \times \delta(i + 1) + \delta(i + 2)}{2} \tag{2}$$

The sliding window function θ is used to emphasize continuous adjacent segments in the same direction and to minimize the transitions between adjacent segments with different directions.

Symbol creation is performed based on time series produced by the data transformation step. A discretization algorithm is used to divide in k groups the values $\{\theta(1), \dots, \theta(w - 3)\}$ and to calculate k centroids $C = \{c_1, .., c_k\}$. The values in C are used to associate the values in Θ to symbols. The k value represents the alphabet size for symbolic representation.

The symbol is defined by a function called $Symb$ (Equation 3) that receives a $\theta(i)$ value and the centroids $\{c_1, .., c_k\}$ as input to compute the correspondent symbol.

$$Symb(\theta(i), C) = which.min(\{|c_1 - \theta(i)|, \dots, |c_k - \theta(i)|\}) \tag{3}$$

where the function $which.min$ finds the c_j value that has the minimum difference to the $\theta(i)$ value, where $1 \leq j \leq w - 3$.

The function $Symb$ is applied for each value in Θ and the result set is the symbolic representation $\hat{T}$ of the time series T. The values of the symbols in $\hat{T}$ is the approximated difference value between the points in $\overline{T}$ representation. Thus, it is possible to associate to the symbols one meaningful information, such as the slope angle which is given by $\alpha = tan^{-1}(c_j)$. By example, suppose the symbolic sequence CBBDACD considering the alphabet size $a = 4$ and the respective centroids $C = \{+2.5, +1.3, -1.2, -2.8\}$ we can represent the sequence by the approximated angles values $(-50°, +52°, +52°, -70°, +68°, -50°, +68°)$.

In the symbol creation to compute the centroids we proposed three different approaches:

Equal Fixed-Values Discretization (EFVD): In this approach the values from the data transformation step are divided into equal-sized regions between the predefined values $min = tan(-90° \times \pi/180)$ and $max = tan(+90° \times \pi/180)$. In Fig. 2(a) is presented a figurative example considering the alphabet size $a = 4$ where the regions can be viewed as a distribution of angles and the set of symbols $\{A, B, C, D\}$ is associated to the mean value of each region. In this example the centroids are $\{A = +67.5°, B = +22.5°, C = -22.5°, D = -67.5°\}$.

Equal Width Discretization (EWD): This discretization method is performed by dividing the range value, provided by the data transformation step, into equal width regions. In this approach should be used a set of time series to build the intervals. For each region, the mean of the values are calculated and associated to one symbol. The figurative example presented in Fig. 2(b) uses a alphabet size $a = 4$ and the set of symbols $\{A, B, C, D\}$. In this approach the symbol values depend of the contained values in the time series used to the discretization.

Equal Frequency Discretization (EFD): This discretization method is similar to the EWD algorithm, but in this approach the range value is divided into equal frequency of values in each region (see Fig. 2(c)).

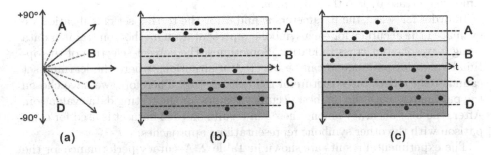

Fig. 2. Discretization algorithms: (a) EFVD; (b) EWD and (c) EFD

4   Experimental Evaluation and Results

In this section we present an extensive empirical comparison between the symbolic representations SAX, ESAX and our method with the proposed discretizations approaches EFVD, EWD and EFD. As suggested in [13], we performed an initial experimental classification to the symbolic representations using one nearest neighbor classifier and Euclidean Distance as similarity measure between two symbolic sequences. The method codification and the experimental tests was built using R Language.

In our experiments we used 20 time series datasets provided by the UCR Time Series Data Mining Archive [13] that contains artificial and real-world data. The dataset features are presented in Table 2, such as dataset name, the number of classes (NC), the size of training set (STr), the size of testing set (STe) and the time series length (LS).

Table 1. Summary of datasets

Dataset Name	NC	STr	STe	LS	Dataset Name	NC	STr	STe	LS
Synthetic Control	6	300	300	60	FaceFour	4	24	88	350
Gun-Point	2	50	150	150	Lightning2	2	60	61	637
CBF	3	30	900	128	Lightning7	7	70	73	319
FaceAll	14	560	1690	131	ECG	2	100	100	96
OSU Leaf	6	200	242	427	Adiac	37	390	391	176
Swedish Leaf	15	500	625	128	Yoga	2	300	3000	426
50words	50	450	455	270	Fish	7	175	175	463
Trace	4	100	100	275	Beef	5	30	30	470
Two Patterns	4	1000	4000	128	Coffee	2	28	28	286
Wafer	2	1000	6174	152	Olive Oil	4	30	30	570

We performed experiments on different combinations of dimensionality reduction and alphabet size for each dataset and for each symbolic representation method. The alphabet size a was evaluated in the interval from 2 until 20 and the dimensionality w in the interval from 2 until 50% of time series length. Each time we increase by two the value of w.

In order for select the parameters w and a for the testing set classification we evaluated the accuracy for each symbolic representation method on training data using leave-one-out cross validation. Sometimes, the correct selection of the optimal values of parameters can be affected in situations where the learning set cannot fully reflect the structure of the test set [14]. Therefore, we have chosen the parameters with the ten best accuracy results for the testing data evaluation. After, the best accuracy among these ten results on each dataset is used for comparison with the other symbolic representations approaches.

The experimental results are shown in Table 2. Accuracy performance for the methods SAX, ESAX, EFVD, EWD and EFD are presented in the 2nt, 3rd, 4th, 5th and 6th columns, respectively (the best accuracy results are bolded). Also the parameters w and a are presented for the methods ESAX, EFVD, EWD and EFD in the 7th, 8th, 9th and 10th columns, respectively (the w value for SAX is a third of ESAX).

As recommended in [15], in order to show that an algorithm is useful, it is necessary predict ahead of time when the method will have superior accuracy. They proposed the calculus of the function $gain = A/B$ to measure the *expected gain* (on training data) and the *actual gain* (on testing data). The values A and B represents the accuracy performance for a method A and for a method

Table 2. Experimental 1-NN classification results

Name Dataset	Accur. SAX	Accur. ESAX	Accur. EFVD	Accur. EWD	Accur. EFD	w/a ESAX	w/a EFVD	w/a EWD	w/a EFD
ECG200	0.9000	0.8700	**0.9500**	0.9400	0.9400	96/7	38/19	38/19	42/19
Synthetic	**0.9867**	0.9833	0.9633	0.9567	0.9500	36/13	14/17	12/10	12/10
Coffee	0.8929	**0.9643**	**0.9643**	0.9286	**0.9643**	396/19	20/3	46/13	52/20
CBF	0.9170	0.8989	0.9456	**0.9856**	0.9478	30/14	22/11	8/5	20/9
Beef	0.5667	0.5400	**0.8000**	0.6333	0.6000	84/16	190/2	50/20	202/10
Trace	0.7300	0.7100	0.8100	0.8200	**0.8700**	132/16	82/7	106/8	48/6
SwedishLeaf	0.7648	0.7984	0.8272	0.8144	**0.8432**	126/18	58/20	58/20	48/18
OliveOil	0.1667	0.1667	0.8333	0.8333	**0.9000**	12/2	220/20	200/18	212/19
OSULeaf	0.5290	0.5248	0.5579	0.5620	**0.5827**	156/11	58/17	82/8	170/4
Lightning2	0.7705	0.7869	**0.8197**	0.7869	0.7705	18/19	76/8	52/16	24/18
Lightning7	**0.6576**	0.5480	0.5617	0.6165	0.5891	18/11	24/19	8/6	4/3
Gun Point	0.8200	0.8267	0.9067	**0.9333**	0.9267	18/19	44/19	50/19	46/7
FaceFour	0.7387	0.8523	0.7728	0.8296	**0.8750**	36/18	16/4	28/2	26/7
FaceAll	0.7006	0.7172	**0.7385**	0.7379	0.7299	108/14	36/19	40/19	38/14
Adiac	0.1637	0.1586	0.5729	0.6599	**0.7238**	240/19	52/20	82/16	80/18
50words	0.6022	**0.6726**	0.6374	0.6506	0.6286	48/7	20/14	24/12	32/7
Fish	0.6915	0.6972	0.8343	0.8458	**0.8629**	312/15	120/19	68/17	202/8
Two Patterns	**0.9370**	0.7340	0.9085	0.8890	0.8980	54/5	24/5	18/15	18/9
Yoga	0.8220	0.8230	0.8180	**0.8320**	0.8220	576/16	78/10	106/16	104/6
Wafer	0.9924	0.9926	0.9889	**0.9940**	0.9932	78/4	12/3	48/2	42/2

B, respectively. In Fig. 3 is presented the comparison gain for $EFVD/ESAX$, EFD/EFD and $EFD/ESAX$. We remove the datasets $OliveOil$ ($gain > 5$) and $Adiac$ ($gain > 2.5$) to the best visualization of the charts. The region TP (True Positive) indicates: the method A is more accurate than B for training and testing; the region TN (True Negative): the method B is more accurate than A for training and testing; the region FN (False Negative): the method A is more accurate than B for testing but not for training; the region FP (False Positive): the method B than A is more accurate for testing but not for training.

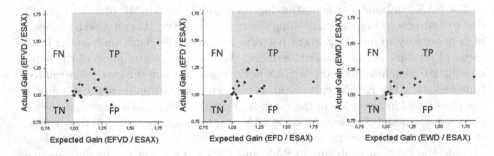

Fig. 3. Gain accuracy comparisons

In Fig. 4 we summarize some results by plotting the dimensionality reduction performance for each dataset into pairwise scatter plots. The points above the diagonal line indicate that the method in the horizontal-axis has a greater dimensionality reduction, and the points below the diagonal line indicate that the method in the vertical-axis has a greater dimensionality reduction.

In the statistical evaluation of the symbolic representations performance, we use the approach applied in [14]. The Iman and Davenport version of the F-test is used to test the null-hypothesis that all symbolic representations have the same performance and the observed differences are merely random. As post hoc test we used the Nemenyi test to compare all methods to each other.

In our accuracy analysis the corresponding critical value is equal to 3.92 for $\alpha = 0.05$ (mean ranks: SAX=3.88, ESAX=3.70, EFVD=2.73, EWD=2.28, EFD=2.33). The null-hypothesis that all methods has the same accuracy is rejected (p-value is 0.025). In the post hoc test the rejected comparisons are: EWDvsSAX, EFDvsESAX, EWDvsESAX and SAXvsEFD.

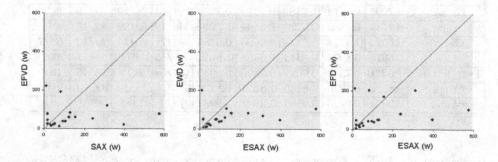

Fig. 4. Dimensionality reduction comparisons

5   Discussion

Time series data mining techniques have become an important tool to discover novel relevant patterns that can help in decision making process. The human decision making in time series analysis is commonly based on domain expert perceptions [9]. In this cases, a symbolic representation is preferred instead a numerical representation [12] and the symbols should preserve the underlying information [6].

The SAX symbolic representation has been widely used in the literature [2,5,7] due to fast processing and smoothing the noise. However, this approach causes a high possibility to miss important patterns in time series data, such as the local trend of the time series [10]. Furthermore, the Gaussian assumption of the symbols distribution has effects on the SAX performance for non-uniform or correlated time series [7]. The ESAX representation was proposed to minimize the missing of the local trend information of the symbols, but the ESAX has a poor dimensionality reduction and presents the same SAX problems for non-uniform time series.

In this context, we proposed a new symbolic representation method to exclude the existing problems in SAX and ESAX. Our method introduces one intermediate step between dimensionality reduction and symbol creation to preserve the approximated local slope information into the symbols. We also introduce three new discretization algorithms: EFVD, EWD and EFD. The last two are our modifications of existing methods.

The classification accuracy and the dimensionality reduction are the parameters of interest evaluated in this work. In particular, to the approaches based on the preservation of the slope information is desirable to maintain a similar performance or better than SAX to these parameters.

According the charts in Fig. 4 we can see that our method outperforms the dimensionality reduction of the ESAX for most datasets. Furthermore, the results presented in Fig. 3 demonstrate the ability of our method to predict ahead of time when it will have superior accuracy or not. Note in the charts that the most points are into region TP.

Comparing our method EFVD/EWD/EFD and the SAX/ESAX approaches for each dataset accuracy (results in Table 2) we can observe some very good improvement cases, such as for the datasets *Beef*, *Olive Oil*, *Adiac* and *Fish*. By the other hand, SAX/ESAX approaches do not present expressive improvement for any dataset. For the dimensionality reduction, only the *Olive Oil* dataset presented a poor result to our method.

The statistical evaluation indicates that our method using the EFD and EWD discretization approaches, are more accurate than SAX and ESAX for one nearest neighbor classification. For EFVD, no statistical significant difference in comparison to the other approaches, therefore we can consider that the EFVD have equivalent accuracy performance them. Furthermore, the EFVD discretization do not need to use a training set to calculate the centroids in a previous step, such as need EWD and EFD.

The experimental evaluation presented in this work has demonstrated the competitivity of our method in comparison to SAX and ESAX. In particular, our method is a good symbolic representation alternative to preserve the local slope information, instead ESAX, since has better performance on dimensionality reduction and classification accuracy.

6   Conclusions and Future Works

In this paper we have presented a symbolic representation method to preserve the slope information between the time series segments. We have performed a evaluation on 20 widely used datasets including artificial and real-world time series. The experimental results analysis demonstrate the effectiveness of our representation method in time series classification for low error rates and for dimensionality reduction in comparison with SAX and ESAX approaches.

Future works include the application of the other techniques on our method to improve the dimensionality reduction, such as Adaptive Piecewise Constant Approximation; evaluate other distance measures, such as Dynamic Time Warping and others Lp-norms; and also test different classification algorithms.

Acknowledgments. We would like to acknowledge Dr. Eamonn Keogh for his experimental datasets.

References

1. Antunes, C.M., Oliveira, A.L.: Temporal Data Mining – An Overview. In: Workshop on Temporal Data Mining at the 7th ACM SIGKDD International Conference on Knowledge Discovery and Data Mining (KDD 2001), pp. 1–15 (2001)
2. Lin, J., Keogh, E., Lonardi, S., Chiu, B.: A Symbolic Representation of Time Series, with Implications for Atreaming Algorithms. In: 8th ACM SIGMOD Workshop on Research Issues in Data Mining and Knowledge Discovery (DMKD 2003), pp. 2–11. ACM (2003)
3. Karamitopoulos, L., Evagelidis, G.: Current Trends in Time Series Representation. In: 11th Panhellenic Conference on Informatics (PCI 2007), pp. 217–226 (2007)
4. Laxman, S., Sastry, P.S.: A Survey of Temporal Data Mining. Sadhana 31(2), 173–198 (2006)
5. Fu, T.C.: A Review on Time Series Data Mining. Engineering Applications of Artificial Intelligence 24(1), 164–181 (2010)
6. Hugueney, B.: Adaptive Segmentation-Based Symbolic Representations of Time Series for Better Modeling and Lower Bounding Distance Measures. In: Fürnkranz, J., Scheffer, T., Spiliopoulou, M. (eds.) PKDD 2006. LNCS (LNAI), vol. 4213, pp. 545–552. Springer, Heidelberg (2006)
7. Pham, N.D., Le, Q.L., Dang, T.K.: Two Novel Adaptive Symbolic Representations for Similarity Search in Time Series Databases. In: 12th International Asia-Pacific Web Conference (APWEB 2010), pp. 181–187. IEEE (2010)
8. Ding, H., Trajcevski, G., Scheuermann, P., Wang, X., Keogh, E.: Querying and Mining of Time Series Data – Experimental Comparison of Representations and Distance Measures. VLDB Endowment 1(2), 1542–1552 (2008)
9. Batyrshin, I., Sheremetov, L.: Perception-Based Approach to Time Series Data Mining. Applied Soft Computing 8(3), 1211–1221 (2008)
10. Lkhagva, B., Suzuki, Y., Kawagoe, K.: New Time Series Representation ESAX for Financial Applications. In: 22nd International Conference on Data Engineering Workshops (ICDEW 2006), pp. 17–22. IEEE (2006)
11. Zalewski, W., Silva, F., Lee, H.D., Maletzke, A.G., Wu, F.C.: A Symbolic Representation Method to Preserve the Characteristic Slope of Time Series. In: 21st Brazilian Symposium on Artificial Intelligence, SBIA 2012 (to appear, 2012)
12. Alonso, F., Martinez, L., Perez-Perez, A., Santamaria, A., Valente, J.P.: Modelling Medical Time Series Using Grammar-Guided Genetic Programming. In: Perner, P. (ed.) ICDM 2008. LNCS (LNAI), vol. 5077, pp. 32–46. Springer, Heidelberg (2008)
13. Keogh, E., Zhu, Q., Hu, B., Hao, Y., Xi, X., Wei, L., Ratanamahatana, C.A.: The UCR Time Series Classification/Clustering Homepage (2011), www.cs.ucr.edu/~eamonn/time_series_data/
14. Gorecki, T., Luczak, M.: Using Derivatives in Time Series Classification. In: Data Mining and Knowledge Discovery, pp. 1–22 (in press, 2012)
15. Batista, G.E.A.P.A., Wang, X., Keogh, E.J.: A Complexity-Invariant Distance Measure for Time Series. In: 11th SIAM International Conference on Data Mining (SDM 2011), pp. 699–710 (2011)

Enhancing the Performance of SVM on Skewed Data Sets by Exciting Support Vectors

José Hernández Santiago[1], Jair Cervantes[1],
Asdrúbal López-Chau[2], and Farid García Lamont[1]

[1] Posgrado e Investigación, UAEM-Texcoco, Av. Jardín Zumpango s/n
Fraccionamiento El Tejocote, Edo. Mex., C.P. 56259
chazarra17@gmail.com
[2] UAEM, Centro Universitario UAEM Zumpango, Camino viejo a Jilotzingo
continuación calle Rayón, Valle Hermoso Zumpango, México, C.P. 55600
alchau@uaemex.mx

Abstract. In pattern recognition and data mining a data set is named skewed or imbalanced if it contains a large number of objects of certain type and a very small number of objects of the opposite type. The imbalance in data sets represents a challenging problem for most classification methods, this is because the generalization power achieved for classic classifiers is not good for skewed data sets. Many real data sets are imbalanced, so the development of new methods to face this problem is necessary. The SVM classifier has an exceptional performance for data sets that are not skewed, however for imbalanced sets the optimal separating hyper plane is not enough to achieve acceptable results. In this paper a novel method that improves the performance of SVM for skewed data sets is presented. The proposed method works by exciting the support vectors and displacing the separating hyper plane towards majority class. According to the results obtained in experiments with different skewed data sets, the method enhances not only the accuracy but also the sensitivity of SVM classifier on this kind of data sets.

Keywords: SVM, skewed data sets, imbalanced data sets, SMOTE.

1 Introduction

A data set is said skewed or imbalanced whether it contains a large number of objects of certain type (majority class) and a very small number of objects of the opposite type (minority class). There are many real world applications that present a remarkable imbalance in their training data sets, for example in fraud detection problems, the imbalance ratio can be from 100 to 1 up to 100,000 to 1 [12], another examples are the classification of protein sequences [3,5,17], medical diagnosis [10], intrusion detection and text classification [13,14]. Recent experiments [1,9,18] show that the performance of most classification methods is affected when they are applied on skewed data sets, this is more evident when the imbalance ratio is large. The imbalance of data sets considerably affects the

J. Pavón et al. (Eds.): IBERAMIA 2012, LNAI 7637, pp. 101–110, 2012.

performance of most classifiers, because in general they are designed to reduce
the global mean error regardless classes distribution and therefore the decision
boundaries are biased to the majority class in the training phase. Support Vector
Machine (SVM) classifier is currently one of the most important classification
techniques[5], it achieves better classification accuracy over other methods such
as artificial neural networks [2], decision trees and Bayesian classifiers[3,19] in
some applications. The generalization power of SVM is one of its most remarkable characteristics, the reason of the excellent generalization can be explained
by the statistic learning theory [16] related to maximum margin separating hyper planes. In spite of maximum margin, in the case of skewed data sets the
slanting to majority class of decision boundary (separating hyper plane) negatively impacts in achieved accuracy because minority class can be considered as
noise and therefore ignored by classifier. Sensitivity and specificity are measures
commonly used to detect this. The development of new techniques to enhance
the performance of classifiers such as SVM to be applied on skewed data sets
is an important challenge in the areas of pattern recognition, data mining and
learning machines. Some authors have proposed methods to reduce the negative
effect of imbalance of data sets. Under sampling and over sampling methods
intent to balance the data sets by randomly selecting a small number of objects
from majority class and taking all or doubling the objects from minority class [1].
A drawback with this is approach is that if objects that are support vectors (SV-
objects that define the separating hyper plane) are removed then the separating
hyper plane is different from optimal one and accuracy, sensibility and sensitivity are damaged. In addition doubling the number of objects in minority class
increases training time of SVM, whose complexity is about O(n2) [3]. Chawla
et al [4] proposed Synthetic Minority Over sampling Technique (SMOTE) that
generates artificial objects to be included as members of the minority class.
SMOTE takes an object from minority class and produces a new version of it by
multiplying each feature of original object times a random number between 0 an
1 and adding up this result to the original features. SMOTE does not include a
data selection step to recover more important objects from data set. According
to the results presented in [4] the technique is better than under sampling and
over sampling. Applying SMOTE along with over sampling was proposed in [1].
That method also introduces a scheme to penalize errors depending on the majority (decrease cost) or minority class (increase cost), such combination makes
denser the distribution of minority class and puts closer the separating hyper
plane from the majority class. In [17] different penalization criteria are used to
produce similar effect in separating hyper plane. In [18] a kernelized version of
SMOTE is proposed. Some other proposals inspired in SMOTE can be seen in
[7,8,11]. In [9] an algorithm to populate the minority class is proposed. The new
objects are generated by computing the similarity and dissimilarity among pairs
of objects. Genetic algorithms have been used to face the problem of classification on skewed data sets. In [20] a genetic algorithm is used to balance skewed
data sets, the method produces better results than simple random sampling.

In this paper a new sampling technique to enhance the performance of SVM on skewed data sets is presented. This novel method differs from previous mainly in that there is no necessity of changing original SVM formulation, add new penalization schemes or just randomly add up new artificial objects to data set, which can lead to unrepeatable experiments. In the proposed method a SVM is first trained using whole training set in order to find the SV. These SV are then "excited" to be forced to moved forward majority class, after that a few examples are added up to data set close to decision boundary to improve classification accuracy. This approach produces consistent results because examples are not put on arbitrary locations, but always close to decision boundaries.

The results presented in this paper show that accuracy obtained is improved, also the sensitivity and specificity of classifier is enhanced.

The rest of the paper is organized as follows. In Sect. 2 a brief overview on SVM and on metrics for testing classifiers on skewed data sets is presented. Section 3 presents the proposed method. The results of experiments are shown in Sect. 4. Discussion and Conclusions are in Sect. 5 and 6 respectively. The references are in the last part of this paper.

2   Preliminaries

2.1   Support Vector Machines

SVM are inspired on statistical learning theory developed by Vapnik on 70's [15]. This classifier is one of the most effective methods for complex binary classification problems, so it has been applied in many different fields. The training of SVM begins with a training set X_{tr} given as (1):

$$X_{tr} = \{(x_i, y_i)\}_{i=1}^{n} \tag{1}$$

with $x_i \in R^d$ and $y_i \in R\{+1, -1\}$. The classification function is determined as (2)

$$y_i = sign\left(\sum_{j=1}^{n} \alpha_i y_j K \langle x_i \cdot x_j \rangle + b\right) \tag{2}$$

where α_i are the Lagrange multipliers, $K\langle x_i \cdot x_j \rangle$ is the kernel matrix, and b is the bias. Deeper details can be found in [15].

2.2   Metrics for Testing Classifiers on Skewed Data Sets

Accuracy is most time the measurement used to evaluate and to compare a classifier method against other ones. For the special case of skewed data sets, using only accuracy as a metric for evaluating a classifier can lead to wrong conclusions, because minority class has a pretty small impact on accuracy compared with majority class. Consider for example a data set presenting an imbalance ratio of 99 to 1. A classifier that achieves 99% of accuracy is considered good for the general case, however for the skewed example such classifier is not useful.

In order to evaluate a classifier on large and skewed data sets, it is necessary to use a different metric. Medical and machine learning communities use more and more the sensitivity and specificity to evaluate the performance. Sensitivity is computed with (3)

$$S_n^{true} = \frac{T_P}{T_P + F_N} \tag{3}$$

and specificity is computed with (4).

$$S_n^{false} = \frac{T_N}{T_N + F_P} \tag{4}$$

With

T_P is the number of objects (true class +1) that have been predicted as class +1.

T_N is the number of objects (true class) that have been predicted as -1.

F_P is the number of objects (true class -1) that have been predicted as class +1.

F_N is the number of objects (true class +1) that have been predicted as class -1.

Sensitivity is the proportion of positive examples that are correctly identified, whereas the specificity is the proportion of negative examples that are correctly identified.

In addition to these numeric performance metrics mentioned above, the area under the ROC curve (AUC),is also used in this paper. Receiver Operating Characteristic (ROC) analysis is a widely used method for analyzing the performance of binary classifiers. The area under the ROC curve represents how separable two objects are.

A ROC curve can be generated using the labels of the input data set and the classifier output. A detail description on how to plot a ROC curve also can be found in [6].

The most important advantage of ROC analysis is that it is not necessary to specify the misclassification costs. The visual and numeric metrics associated with this method allow for great flexibility in performance analysis.

3   Proposed Method

In order to reduce the effect of imbalance in data sets, we propose to excite the SV that belong to minority class, and force the decision boundary to move forward majority class. The main advantage of the proposed method is that the performance of SVM is enhanced. New points are generated taking as a guide the optimal separating hyperplane and added close to it. This is different to other methods such as SMOTE, where some points are just randomly generated and added up to training set without considering the decision boundary.

The steps of the method can be stated as follows.

1. Separate majority and minority class examples. The examples in minority class form a partition called X_r^+, and the rest of the examples form the majority class partition X_r^-.
2. Under sample. Some objects from the majority class (X_r^-) are randomly selected, the subset is renamed as X_r^-.
3. Train SVM. A SVM is trained using only X_r^+ and X_r^-, the idea in this step is to identify the SV.
4. Excite SV. Once the support vectors have been identified, those that belong to minority class are excited by moving them forward majority class.

The direction of movement is chosen according to (5) and (6)

$$\nu_i = \frac{x_{svi}^+ - x_{ij}^-}{\left\| x_{ij}^- - x_{svi}^+ \right\|_2}, \ i = 1, ..., |X_r^-| \tag{5}$$

with

$$x_{ij}^- = \min_j \left\| x_{svi} - x_{svj} \right\|_2, \ j = 1, ..., |X_r^+| \tag{6}$$

where
$x_{svi}^- \in SV$ of X_r^-
$x_{svj}^+ \in SV$ of X_r^+
The SV of minority class are then moved forward majority class using (7). The step size of the movement is ϵ, the values of ϵ are between 1×10^{-3} and 1×10^{-6}.

$$x_{svi} - x_{svi} + \epsilon \cdot \nu_i \tag{7}$$

This displacement of SV belonging to minority class moves the decision boundary towards majority class improving the classification accuracy, sensitivity and sensibility.

The algorithm 1, represents the entire process followed by our proposal:

In the Algorithm $Data_{new}(X_{sr}^+, X_{sr}^-)$ represent the data points created from the first hyperplane using the ecs (6)(7) and (8). H_2 represents the tunned hyperplane obtained with the data points created and original data points.

4   Experiments

In this section the results the proposed method on skewed data sets are presented.

Training a SVM involves the choosing of some parameters. Such parameters have an important effect on the performance of classifier. In all the experiments we use the radial basis function (RBF) as kernel, this function is defined in (8).

$$K(x_i - x_j) = e^{(\gamma \| x_i - x_j \|)}, \gamma > 0 \tag{8}$$

Cross validation and grid search was used to find parameters in (8) and also for computing the regularization parameter of SVM. We use model selection to get the optimal parameters. The hyper-parameter space is explored on a two

---

Algorithm 1. Training Algorithm

Input
X : A skewed data set
Output
$H_f : \{x_i \in SV\}$
Begin
$X_r^+ \leftarrow 0$ // Training set with positive labels starts empty
$X_r^- \leftarrow 0$// Training set with negative labels starts empty
$X_r^+ \leftarrow \{x_i \in X : y_i = +1\}$, i=1,...,p
$X_r^+ \leftarrow \{x_i \in X : y_i = +1\}$, i=1,...,n
$SV \leftarrow getSV(X_r^+, X_r^-)$ //Obtain the SV
repeat
Get support vectors SV_+, SV_- from H_1
Move SV according to (7)
Create $Data_{new}(X_{sr}^+, X_{sr}^-)$ from $SV_+, SV_- \in H_1$
    $H_2 \leftarrow$ trainSVM with $X_r^+, X_r^- \cup X_{sr}^+, X_{sr}^-$ //Compute tunning hyper plane
    $SV \leftarrow getSV(X_r^+, X_r^- \cup X_{sr}^+, X_{sr}^-)$ //Obtain SV
Acc(t)$\leftarrow TestSVMH_2(X_{rt}^+, X_{tr}^-)$ //Test accuracy
while (Acc(t)-Acc(t-1) > 0)
return $H_f(X_{RD}^+, X_{RD}^-)$
End

Table 1. Data sets

Data set	Cm(+1)	CM(-1)	Dim	Imbalance ratio
australian	307	383	14	1:1.248
diabetes	268	500	8	1:1.866
german_numer	300	700	24	1:2.333
yeast1	429	1,055	8	1:2.459
vehicle0	199	647	18	1:3.251
ecoli1	77	259	7	1:3.364
new-thyroid1	35	180	5	1:5.143
ecoli2	52	284	7	1:5.462
segment0	329	1,979	19	1:6.015
glass6	29	185	9	1:6.379
yeast3	163	1,321	8	1:8.104
page-blocks0	559	4,913	10	1:8.789
cleveland-0_vs_4	13	164	13	1:12.615
shuttle-c0-vs-c4	123	1,706	9	1:13.870
p-blocks-1-3_vs_4	28	444	10	1:15.857
shuttle-c2-vs-c4	6	123	9	1:20.500
glass5	9	205	9	1:22.778
yeast4	51	1,433	8	1:28.098
yeast5	44	1440	8	1:32.727
yeast6	35	1,449	8	1:41.400

dimensional grid with $\gamma = [10^{-2}, 10^{-1}, 10^{0}, 10^{1}]$ and the regularization parameter $C = [10^{0}, 10^{1}, 10^{2}, 10^{3}, 10^{4}]$. In the experiments all data sets were normalized and the 10 fold cross validation method was applied for the measurements. A number of 30 runs were executed in each experiment. For creating the training set and testing sets, the 80% and 20% of elements of each data set were randomly selected respectively.

4.1   Datasets

The KEEL data sets are imbalanced ones (Public available at http:// sci2s.ugr.es/ keel/datasets.php). Table 1 shows the datasets used in the experiments. In order to measure the performance of the proposed method in different scenarios, the data sets chosen have an imbalance ratio from 1 to 1.248 up to 1 to 41.4.

Table 2. Performance of the proposed method

Data set	(average)				(std dev)			
	AUC	S_n	S_n^v	S_n^f	AUC	S_n	S_n^v	S_n^f
australian	0.897	0.941	0.941	0.783	0.024	0.021	0.021	0.049
diabetes	0.847	0.857	0.857	0.730	0.024	0.034	0.034	0.018
german_numer	0.686	0.880	0.880	0.602	0.028	0.040	0.040	0.048
yeast1	0.797	0.773	0.773	0.722	0.018	0.019	0.019	0.029
vehicle0	0.981	0.982	0.982	0.938	0.009	0.012	0.012	0.021
ecoli1	0.959	0.987	0.987	0.869	0.023	0.028	0.028	0.029
new-thyroid1	0.998	1.000	1.000	0.989	0.004	0.000	0.000	0.014
ecoli2	0.959	0.890	0.890	0.954	0.035	0.099	0.099	0.019
segment0	1.000	0.995	0.995	1.000	0.000	0.007	0.007	0.000
glass6	0.982	0.940	0.940	1.000	0.030	0.097	0.097	0.000
yeast3	0.978	0.969	0.969	0.939	0.009	0.021	0.021	0.013
page-blocks0	0.973	0.852	0.852	0.976	0.010	0.031	0.031	0.007
cleveland-0_vs_4	1.000	0.950	0.950	0.994	0.000	0.158	0.158	0.020
shuttle-c0-vs-c4	1.000	1.000	1.000	1.000	0.000	0.000	0.000	0.000
page-blocks-1-3_vs_4	1.000	1.000	1.000	1.000	0.000	0.000	0.000	0.000
shuttle-c2-vs-c4	1.000	1.000	1.000	1.000	0.000	0.000	0.000	0.000
yeast4	0.953	0.710	0.710	0.975	0.034	0.057	0.057	0.007
yeast5	0.994	0.900	0.900	0.990	0.007	0.115	0.115	0.006
yeast6	0.981	0.857	0.857	0.975	0.012	0.095	0.095	0.012

In Table 2 the reader can observe the full test results, the standard deviations for S_n^{false}, S_n^{true} and AUC were included to compare against other methods shown in Table 3.

In order to compare the results of the proposed method, Table 3 shows the results achieved by the following methods.

- SVM (first column of Table 3).
- Under sampling method (second column).

Table 3. Results of other state of the art methods

Data Set	SVM				Under sampling			
	AUC	S_n	S_n^T	S_n^F	AUC	S_n	S_n^T	S_n^F
australian	0.89	0.73	0.73	0.88	0.89	0.81	0.81	0.85
glass6	0.98	0.86	0.86	0.99	0.97	0.92	0.92	0.90
yeast3	0.98	0.69	0.69	0.98	0.97	0.90	0.90	0.93
page-blocks0	0.96	0.53	0.53	1.00	0.95	0.82	0.82	0.94
cleveland-0_vs_4	0.98	0.20	0.20	1.00	0.90	0.80	0.80	0.78
page-blocks-1-3_vs_4	1.00	0.50	0.50	1.00	0.98	0.96	0.96	0.89
shuttle-c2-vs-c4	1.00	0.90	0.90	1.00	1.00	1.00	1.00	0.95
glass5	0.99	0.00	0.00	1.00	0.91	1.00	1.00	0.79
yeast4	0.75	0.00	0.00	1.00	0.89	0.81	0.81	0.88
yeast5	0.99	0.10	0.10	1.00	0.99	1.00	1.00	0.91
yeast6	0.92	0.00	0.00	1.00	0.94	0.89	0.89	0.89
Data Set	Oversampling				SMOTE			
	AUC	S_n	S_n^T	S_n^F	AUC	S_n	S_n^T	S_n^F
australian	0.88	0.75	0.75	0.87	0.87	0.93	0.93	0.67
glass6	0.97	0.90	0.90	0.99	0.98	0.92	0.92	0.99
yeast3	0.98	0.92	0.92	0.94	0.98	0.85	0.85	0.96
page-blocks0	0.97	0.83	0.83	0.96	0.97	0.66	0.66	0.98
cleveland-0_vs_4	0.97	0.40	0.40	0.99	0.97	0.50	0.50	0.99
page-blocks-1-3_vs_4	1.00	0.90	0.90	0.98	1.00	0.94	0.94	1.00
shuttle-c2-vs-c4	1.00	0.90	0.90	1.00	1.00	1.00	1.00	1.00
glass5	1.00	1.00	1.00	0.93	1.00	1.00	1.00	0.98
yeast4	0.84	0.34	0.34	0.97	0.89	0.52	0.52	0.98
yeast5	0.99	0.64	0.64	0.99	0.99	0.85	0.85	0.98
yeast6	0.94	0.74	0.74	0.97	0.95	0.73	0.73	0.97

- over sampling method (third column)
- SMOTE algorithm (fourth column).

It is notable that when imbalance ratio is large, the performance achieved by the proposed method is much better that the obtained by using traditional SVM or the other methods.

5   Discussion

Many works on imbalanced classification use ROC-Curves in order to show the performance of the proposed algorithms. However, in some cases ROC curves are not sufficient to evaluate the performance of a classifier on skewed datasets, because it is possible to achieve a good AUR — S_n^t with a regular classifier.

In our experiments we use four evaluation metrics to show the performance of proposed method. Due to the nature of the SVM, the decision surface relies on the positive/negative support vectors, hence SVM is less sensitive to the statistical prosperities of the features. In this way, to create new data points can be unfavorable, because in some extreme cases, a single misclassified example of the minority class can create a significant drop in the classifier performance. in order face this disadvantage, the proposed method only use the data points created when the performance is improved.

It can be seen in the tables of results that the improvement on the classifier performance is better when the imbalance radio is large. In some datasets with small imbalance radio, there is not improvement in the performance. In datasets with large imbalance radio the threshold can be flexibly set, the goodness of the decision surface learned from the training data determines the classification accuracy. In our experiments, we showed that the SVM could learn a good decision surface generating data points along of the decision surface.

6   Conclusions

Current classification methods produce good results when they are applied on data sets that are balanced, however for the specific case of skewed data sets most classifiers cannot obtain acceptable results because decision boundaries are computed regardless minority and majority class.

In this paper a novel method that enhances the performance of SVM for skewed data sets was presented. The method reduces the effect of imbalance ratio by exciting SV and moving separating hyper plane toward majority class. The method is different from other state of the art methods in that it does not simply adds artificial objects to training sets, instead the new objects are added close to optimal separating hyperplane, which has the effect of dramatically increasing the performance of SVM on skewed data sets.

According to the experiments, the proposed method produces the most noticeable results when the imbalance ration if greater than 10.

References

1. Akbani, R., Kwek, S., Japkowicz, N.: Applying Support Vector Machines to Imbalanced Datasets. In: Boulicaut, J.F., Esposito, F., Giannotti, F., Pedreschi, D. (eds.) ECML 2004. LNCS (LNAI), vol. 3201, pp. 39–50. Springer, Heidelberg (2004)
2. Arbach, L., Reinhardt, J., Bennett, D., Fallouh, G.: Mammographic Masses Classification – Comparison Between Backpropagation Neural Network (BNN), K Nearest Neighbors (KNN), and Human Readers. In: IEEE Canadian Conference on Electrical and Computer Engineering (CCECE 2003), vol. 3, pp. 1441–1444. IEEE, Washington, DC (2003)
3. Cervantes, J., Li, X., Yu, W.: Splice Site Detection in DNA Sequences Using a Fast Classification Algorithm. In: IEEE International Conference on Systems, Man and Cybernetics (SMC 2009), pp. 2683–2688. IEEE, Washington, DC (2009)
4. Chawla, N.V., Bowyer, K.W., Hall, L.O., Kegelmeyer, W.P.: SMOTE – Synthetic Minority Over-Sampling Technique. Journal of Artificial Intelligence Research 16(1), 321–357 (2002)

5. Dror, G., Sorek, R., Shamir, R.: Accurate Identification of Alternatively Spliced Exons Using Support Vector Machine. Bioinformatics 21(7), 897–901 (2005)
6. Fawcett, T.: An Introduction to ROC Analysis. Pattern Recognition Letters 27(8), 861–874 (2006)
7. Guo, H.: Learning from Imbalanced Data Sets with Boosting and Data Generation – The DataBoost–IM Approach. ACM SIGKDD Explorations Newsletter 6(1), 30–39 (2004)
8. Hu, S., Liang, Y., Ma, L., He, Y.: MSMOTE – Improving Classification Performance When Training Data is Imbalanced. In: 2nd International Workshop on Computer Science and Engineering (WCSE 2009), vol. 2, pp. 13–17. IEEE, Washington, DC (2009)
9. Koknar-Tezel, S., Latecki, L.: Improving SVM Classification on Imbalanced Data Sets in Distance Spaces. In: 9th IEEE International Conference on Data Mining (ICDM 2009), pp. 259–267. IEEE, Washington, DC (2009)
10. Kononenko, I.: Machine Learning for Medical Diagnosis – History, State of the Art and Perspective. Artificial Intelligence in Medicine 23(1), 89–109 (2001)
11. Nguyen, H.M., Cooper, E.W., Kamei, K.: Borderline Over-Sampling for Imbalanced Data Classification. International Journal of Knowledge Engineering and Soft Data Paradigms 3(1), 4–21 (2011)
12. Provost, F., Fawcett, T.: Robust Classification for Imprecise Environments. Machine Learning 42(3), 203–231 (2001)
13. Sebastiani, F.: Machine Learning in Automated Text Categorization. ACM Computing Surveys 34(1), 1–47 (2002)
14. Tan, S.: Neighbor-Weighted K-Nearest Neighbor for Unbalanced Text Corpus. Expert Systems with Applications 28(4), 667–671 (2005)
15. Vapnik, V.N.: The Nature of Statistical Learning Theory. Springer-Verlag New York, Inc., New York (1995)
16. Vapnik, V.N.: Statistical Learning Theory. Wiley-Interscience (1998)
17. Veropoulos, K., Campbell, C., Cristianini, N.: Controlling the Sensitivity of Support Vector Machines. In: 16th International Joint Conference on Artificial Intelligence (IJCAI 1999), pp. 55–60 (1999)
18. Zeng, Z.Q., Gao, J.: Improving SVM Classification with Imbalance Data Set. In: Leung, C.S., Lee, M., Chan, J.H. (eds.) ICONIP 2009, Part I. LNCS, vol. 5863, pp. 389–398. Springer, Heidelberg (2009)
19. Zhang, Y., Chu, C.H., Chen, Y., Zha, H., Ji, X.: Splice Site Prediction Using Support Vector Machines with a Bayes Kernel. Expert Systems with Applications 30(1), 73–81 (2006)
20. Zou, S., Huang, Y., Wang, Y., Wang, J., Zhou, C.: SVM Learning from Imbalanced Data by GA Sampling for Protein Domain Prediction. In: 9th International Conference for Young Computer Scientists (ICYCS 2008), pp. 982–987. IEEE, Washington, DC (2008)

Study on the Impact of Affinity on the Results of Data Mining in Biological Populations

Paweł Skrobanek[1], Olgierd Unold[1], Ewa Walkowicz[2],
Henryk Maciejewski[1], and Maciej Dobrowolski[2]

[1] Institute of Computer Engineering, Control and Robotics,
Wroclaw University of Technology, Wybrzeże Wyspiańskiego 27, 50-370 Wrocław, Poland
[2] Department of Horse Breeding and Riding, Wroclaw University of Environmental and Life
Sciences, Kożuchowska 6, 51-631 Wrocław, Poland
{henryk.maciejewski,olgierd.unold,pawel.skrobanek}@pwr.wroc.pl,
{ewa.walkowicz,maciej.dobrowolski}@up.wroc.pl

Abstract. In biological populations genetic correlations between individuals are the result of genetic relatedness. In its standard form, the data is not stored in a way that lets users easily take into account the information in the processes of data mining. The aim of this study was to verify whether and to what extent inclusion of this additional information (in the form of grandparents and great grandparents of data) affects the results of data mining. This paper is one of the stages of interdisciplinary research project investigating a population of Silesian horses. The database contains breeding history of roughly the complete population of Silesian horses bred in Poland over the last 50 years. Tests were conducted with a subset of individuals known to their parents due to the assumption that we try to predict characteristics of offspring, knowing the characteristics of ancestors (parents, grandparents, great grandparents).

Keywords: genetic dependences in data mining, biological population data base, prediction.

1 Introduction

The most important task of the breeder is such selection of parental individuals, that their progeny would give the chance to obtains a breeding progress, i.e. was better (more efficient, faster, healthier etc.) that their parents. Currently, it is possible to perform the direct genetic analysis [1, 2], but for the population from many years ago it is only possible to perform the analysis indirectly - using the characteristics of their ancestors. Therefore, in planning process the breeder selects parents in such a way to get certain features of the child. Usually it is being done on the basis of the ranking of the fathers and mothers obtained using methods such as BLUP [3]. Every phenotypes of the trait are summary results of the genetics background and environmental effects. But of these two factors, which determined animal value, only genetic values of the parents (and also other ancestors) are passed to the offspring and can influence their phenotypic values. Of course offspring phenotypic values are also influenced by

J. Pavón et al. (Eds.): IBERAMIA 2012, LNAI 7637, pp. 111–119, 2012.

environmental factors, but they are independent and could be significantly different from those of their parents 'or grandparents' generation.

There are many methods that use phenotypic features to estimate genetic value of selected features, which indicate what can be expected in the next generation provided there will not be significant changes in the environmental conditions.

A heritability of traits provides also very important information. Breeders select animals characterized by the highest level of desirable features that they want to strengthen in the offspring. This method works well for the features with high heritability level where the phenotypic value at the same time provides a solid foundation of genetic traits that will be inherited in offspring. Therefore, the high rate of heritability of a feature indicates the possibility of its improvement based on the phenotypic value of parents.

Database of biological populations usually contain information about an individual (its characteristics) and information about its parents. The question that arose during the work of our team was as follows: will the enlargement of the data on the characteristics of earlier ancestors (grandparents and great grandparents) have an impact on improving the quality of the results? As the subject of research of our team is the population of Silesian horses [4], experiments were conducted on these data, and results of the most interesting of these are outlined later in this work.

2   Data and Methodology

2.1   Data

We analyzed almost complete population of the Silesian horses stallions bred in Poland after 1945 year [5]. The data set used in the study contains 16069 observations with known value of born year and information on at least one parent. These observations were used in predictions. Some details are given in subsection together with description of experiments (see next section).

The experimental data, as was described earlier, have been prepared from three generations: parents, grandparents, great grandparents – the identifiers of individual relatives are shown in Fig. 1.

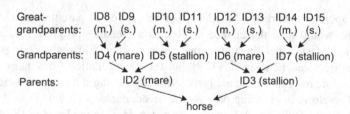

Fig. 1. Identifiers for parents, grandparents and great-grandparents

According to Fig.1, we use the following notation for height, girth and circumference of ancestors, respectively: IDn_H, IDn_G, IDn_C where $n \in \{2,...,15\}$. For example ID2_H means height of mother, ID4_H – height of grand-mother.

Table 1 shows some information about data: the minimal value (min), the maximal value (max), the arithmetic mean. The distance is equal to the difference between max and min (distance = max-min). Extract (dataset without protected data) from Silesian horse database can be found in [4].

Table 1. Information about height, girth and cannon circumference with data set

	Height	Girth	Cannon Circ.
arithmetic mean	159	195	22
max	176	240	27
min	140	157	2[*)]
distance	36	83	25

*) the value shows that some data in data base are incorrect (although the data were processed and cleaned)

2.2   Methodology

An important element of the breeding is the proper selection of individuals for reproduction. Breeders would like to obtain offspring with specific characteristics, therefore for the experiments a feature has to be chosen – we chose height (one of the important parameters describing a horse). Experiments were conducted in the field of prediction:

- whether the height of the offspring will be above a certain threshold,
- exact height of the offspring.

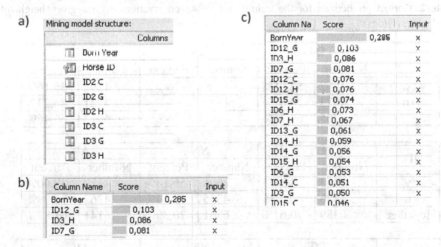

Fig. 2. Input features used in experiments a) mother and father (M&F), b) 4 most important features (4F), c) 16 most important features (16F)

Each of the experiments were performed for three sets of characteristics (see Fig. 2):

- prediction based on information about parents,
- prediction based on the four most important attributes (score was calculated with the algorithm supplied with the tool including in Visual Studio 2008),
- prediction on the basis of the 16 most important attributes.

In Tables 2 - 6 (see Sect. 3) the following notation will be used:

- M&F - for the analysis performed on the features shown in Fig. 1a,
- 4F – for the analysis performed on the features shown in Fig. 1b,
- 16F - for the analysis performed on the features shown in Fig. 1c.

Features describing each of the individuals: height, girth, cannon circumference. Microsoft Visual Studio 2008 and Microsoft SQL Server 2008 R2 was chosen as a test software. Three methods, the best for our set of data, were chosen: decision trees (DT), neural networks (NN), association rules (AR). In addition, the set of data was divided into two parts:

- data of 10945 individuals (including 9048 with measurements of their height) that were born before 1999 (as a training set),
- data of 5124 individuals (including 525 with measurements of their height) that were born since 2000 (as a set for evaluating the quality of the algorithms).

The main purpose of the evaluation of the quality was not the sole evaluation of quality of the predictions, rather verification whether additional information about extended ancestors in learning process also affect the quality of the results with respect to predictions without this additional information. Evaluation of quality was performed only for individuals with the measurement of their height.

Table 2. Correct predictions for the training set (9048 observations with a given height of 10945 observations)

M&F	DT		NN		AR	
	Number	Percent	Number	Percent	Number	Percent
y (yes)	1892	52,95%	-	-	1292	36,16%
n (no)	4373	79,87%	-	-	4721	86,23%
together	6265	69,24%	-	-	6013	66,46%

4F	DT		NN		AR	
	Number	Percent	Number	Percent	Number	Percent
y	1963	54,94%	2006	56,14%	1379	38,60%
n	4426	80,84%	4355	79,54%	4762	86,98%
together	6389	70,61%	6361	70,30%	6141	67,87%

16F	DT		NN		AR	
	Number	Percent	Number	Percent	Number	Percent
y	2098	58,72%	1960	54,86%	2131	59,64%
n	4200	76,71%	4363	79,69%	3918	71,56%
together	6298	69,61%	6323	69,88%	6049	66,85%

Table 3. False predictions for the training set (9048 with a given height of 10945 observations)

	M&F			4F			16F		
	DT	NN	AR	DT	NN	AR	DT	NN	AR
y as n	1681	-	2281	1610	1567	2194	1475	1613	1442
n as y	1102	-	754	1049	1120	713	1275	1112	1557
yas "missing"	0	-	0	0	0	0	0	0	0
n as "missing"	0	-	0	0	0	0	0	0	0

Table 4. The results of prediction using a set of test (525 with a given height)

	correct prediction					
	DT		NN		AR	
M&F	Number	Percent	Number	Percent	Number	Percent
y	343	72,98%	-	-	225	47,87%
n	26	47,27%	-	-	41	74,55%
together	369	70,29%	-	-	266	50,67%

	correct prediction					
	DT		NN		AR	
4F	Number	Percent	Number	Percent	Number	Percent
y	421	89,57%	447	95,11%	161	34,26%
n	13	23,64%	7	12,73%	46	83,64%
together	434	82,67%	454	86,48%	207	39,43%

	correct prediction					
	DT		NN		AR	
16F	Number	Percent	Number	Percent	Number	Percent
y	470	100,00%	435	92,55%	400	85,11%
n	0	0,00%	9	16,36%	16	29,09%
together	470	89,52%	444	84,57%	416	79,24%

3 Case Study

3.1 Experiment 1

The question „whether the horse reaches the height above some fixed value?" is important, because a horse which is too low or too height cannot be considered a race horse. For this reason, the first experiment consisted in predicting, whether the child would be the height above the average height of a designated population (above 159 cm). Result of prediction may have three values: y-yes, n-no, "nothing" - missing value. The experimental results are presented in Tables 2. – 4:

- Table 2. – correct predictions for the training set,
- Table 3. – false predictions for the training set,
- Table 4. – correct predictions for the test set.

Summary:

- all results presented in Tables 2 - 4 indicate that the prediction based on the parental data generate the worst results, thus the genetic correlations can influence on the results and it is appropriate to expand the input sets of information regarding ancestors. It is interesting that for the population of Silesian horses the greatest impact on the results have the characteristics of father and his ancestors (see Fig. 2) – it may be due to the large amount of missing data (e.g. 997 records with missing height, about 25% of records with one parent missing),
- significantly increasing the number of features influences the results, but can also cause their deterioration,
- results obtained on the basis of the training set generate similar results for the test set, which allows, for example, for the selection of different algorithms to predict the correlation type "above" and "below" the threshold.

3.2   Experiment 2

Table 5. Correct predictions for the training set (9048 with a given height)

Features			max	average	No. of prediction ±3 cm	No. of prediction ±6 cm
M&F	DT	to high	19,37	3,86	2430	4646
		to low	-15,02	-2,86		
	NN	-	-	-	-	-
		-	-	-		
	AR	to high	19,37	4,70	1967	4669
		to low	-14,63	-2,72		
4F	DT	to high	19,37	3,65	5909	8082
		to low	-18,02	-2,95		
	NN	to high	19,37	3,44	5813	8005
		to low	-16,91	-3,00		
	AR	to high	16,09	2,81	6311	8177
		to low	-17,91	-3,98		
16F	DT	to high	19,37	3,86	5176	7650
		to low	-15,02	-2,86		
	NN	to high	17,25	3,41	5941	8024
		to low	-15,02	-3,06		
	AR	to high	13,09	2,94	6317	8155
		to low	-17,91	-3,70		

Table 6. Correct predictions for the test set (525 observations)

No. of features			max	average	No. of prediction ±3 cm	No. of prediction ±6 cm
M&F	DT	to high	22,25	3,28	141	254
		to low	-12,63	-3,39		
	NN	-	-	-	-	-
		-	-	-		
	AR	to high	16,37	1,94	95	133
		to low	0,00	-		
4F	DT	to high	16,37	1,94	95	133
		to low	-12,63	-4,01		
	NN	to high	16,37	1,93	84	118
		to low	-15,91	-4,38		
	AR	to high	13,09	0,74	38	38
		to low	-15,91	-6,28		
16F	DT	to high	22,25	3,28	141	254
		to low	-12,63	-3,39		
	NN	to high	16,37	2,75	96	154
		to low	-17,02	-4,31		
	AR	to high	13,09	1,08	38	39
		to low	-15,91	-6,38		

The second experiment consisted in predicting the "real" height of the offspring (a foal). For the evaluation of the quality of predictions average deviation of all measurements from the values measured was assumed, and above all the number of horses for which the prediction does not deviate significantly (difference was at most 3 cm) from the measurement of the horse. It should be noted that the measurements of the horses are made with 0.5 cm accuracy.

As the training set and the test set, as previously, complete data sets were used, but the evaluation could be conducted only on individuals with a given height values (with exclusion of observations with missing data).

The experimental results are presented in Tables 5 – 6:

• Table 5. – correct predictions for the training set,
• Table 6. – correct predictions for the test set,

Summary

The results obtained with use of the training set for the number of correctly predicted height (divergence from the measured values not greater than 3 cm) are better when we use the data of extended ancestors than just information of the parents. On the contrary it is not the same for the calculations performed with use of the test set. In the second case the predictions calculated using AR method are even worse that predictions based on the parental data. The main cause of this problem seems to be the change of guidelines for the height of horses over the last few decades – currently the horses are higher than their ancestors. For other methods, however, the results obtained for the cases 4F and 16F are not worse than for M & F - for the neuronal network we fail to generate results, probably due to the large amount of missing data (e.g. 997 records with missing height, about 25% of records with one parent missing, therefore without half of ancestors). More information about data of Silesian horses are given in [5]. Methods of dealing with features selection are a separate object of study and preliminary results are shown in [6].

4   Conclusions

In nature inheritance of genes results in fact that the descendants are in some way "similar" to the parents.

In the present paper it is shown that also in data mining, information about the ancestors can have a significant impact on the results. Empirical studies conducted in this work show that the results obtained from these data are in most cases better than without them. However, there are situations, such as the situation described in subsection 3.2. when they can worsen the results of certain methods.

Therefore using the information regarding the ancestors (even distant) seems to be as important for the analysis of biological data of the population as performing studies based on both - the training set and the methods of selecting features to specific algorithms, and then selecting the best working methods to predict the results of breeding.

Since the guidelines for both breeding and the environment are evolving, the most beneficial is to use predictions for the near future as well as conducting periodic tests described in the previous paragraph

Acknowledgments. This work was supported by the grant N516 415138 from the Ministry of Science and Higher Education.

References

1. Albertsdóttir E., Eriksson S., Sigurdsson, Árnason T.: Genetic Analysis of 'Breeding Field Test Status' in Icelandic Horses. Journal of Animal Breeding and Genetics 128(2), 124–132 (2011)
2. Hamann, H., Distl. O.: Genetic Variability in Hanoverian Warmblood Horses Using Pedigree Analysis. Journal of Animal Science 86(7), 1503–1513 (2008)
3. Tavernier A.: Advantages of BLUP Animal Model for Breeding Value Estimation in Horses. Livestock Production Science 20(2), 149–160, (1988)

4. Dataset of the Silesian Horses Population – An Extract from the Database (The Protected Information are Omitted, such as Personal Data of Breeders), http://www.silesian.pwr.wroc.pl/database.html
5. Walkowicz E., Unold O., Maciejewski H., Skrobanek P.: Zoometric Indices in Silesian Horses in the Years 1945-2005. Annals of Animal Science 11(4), 555–565 (2011)
6. Unold O., Dobrowolski M., Maciejewski H., Skrobanek P., Walkowicz E.: A GA-Based Wrapper Feature Selection for Animal Breeding Data Mining. In: Corchado, E., et al. (eds.) Hybrid Artificial Intelligent Systems, HAIS 2012. LNCS 7209, pp. 200–209. Springer, Heidelberg (2012)

Hierarchical Classification of Gene Ontology with Learning Classifier Systems

Luiz Melo Romão[1] and Julio César Nievola[2]

[1] Universidade da Região de Joinville - UNIVILLE
CEP 89201-974 - Joinville - SC - Brasil
luizmromao@gmail.com
[2] Pontifícia Universidade Católica do Paraná - PPGIA
CEP 80215-901 - Curitiba - PR - Brasil
nievola@pucpr.ppgia.br

Abstract. The Gene Ontology (GO) project is a major bioinformatics initiative with the aim of standardizing the representation of gene and gene product attributes across species and databases. The classes in GO are hierarchically structured in the form of a directed acyclic graph (DAG), what makes its prediction more complex. This work proposes an adapted Learning Classifier Systems (LCS) in order to predict protein functions described in the GO format. Hence, the proposed approach, called HLCS (Hierarchical Learning Classifier System) builds a global classifier to predict all classes in the application domain and its is expressed as a set of IF-THEN classification rules, which have the advantage of representing more comprehensible knowledge. The HLCS is evaluated in four different ion-channel data sets structured in GO terms and compared with a Ant Colony Optimisation algorithm, named hAnt-Miner. In the tests realized the HLCS outperformed the hAnt-Miner in two out of four data sets.

Keywords: learning classifier systems, hierarchical classifications problems, gene ontology.

1 Introduction

Conceived in 1975 by John Holland [9], the Learning Classifier System (LCS) consists of a set of rules called classifiers. The LCS develops a model of intelligent decision-making, using two biological metaphors, evolution and learning, where learning guides the evolutionary component to move in the direction of the best rules.

The LCS has been used with great success in several areas like robotics [10], environment navigation [13,19], function approximation [8], data mining [14] and others. And their main approaches are XCS [5,12,19], ACS [4] and UCS [3]. However, the topic of this work, hierarchical classification problems, has not been directly addressed by these and neither other approach of LCS.

In classification problem, a set of instances is described by a set of predictive attributes associated with a class attribute. The classification task of data mining

J. Pavón et al. (Eds.): IBERAMIA 2012, LNAI 7637, pp. 120–129, 2012.
© Springer-Verlag Berlin Heidelberg 2012

consists of building, in a training phase, a classification model that maps each instance t_i to a class c ∈ C of the target application domain, with $i = 1, 2, ...,$ n, where n represents the number of instances in the training set [1].

However, several classification scenarios have real problems that are much more complex. Cases such as text categorization, web content searches, prediction of protein function (focus this work), among others, are problems in which the class label is structured hierarchically. This type of problems exists when one or more classes are divided into sub-classes or grouped into super-classes, which makes the creation of the classification model even more complex. In this case, the classes are arranged in a hierarchical structure, like a tree or a directed acyclic graph (DAG), and the difference between these structures create greater complexity for the DAG solutions.

In this work we present an Learning Classifier Systems (LCS) adapted to resolve hierarchical classification problems. The proposed approach, called HLCS (Hierarchical Learning Classifier System) will be used for predicting protein functions described in the Gene Ontology (GO). The GO project is a major bioinformatics initiative with the aim of standardizing the representation of gene and gene product attributes across species and databases [2]. The classes in GO are structured in the form of a DAG, in which the terms are represented as graph nodes and in which they are organized from the general to the more specific. The protein function prediction links biological functions to proteins. This knowledge can help researchers better understand diseases, drug development, and preventive medicine, among others.

The HLCS builds a global classifier to predict all classes in the application domain and the classifier is expressed as a set of IF-THEN classification rules, which have the advantage of representing more comprehensible knowledge to biologist users and according to [7] is more understandable than other models such as neural networks, support vector machines and others.

The remainder of this paper is organized as follows: Section 2 discusses the hierarchical classification concept and how to distinguish hierarchical problems. Section 3 describes HLCS architecture and explains the operation of each of its components. Section 4 presents the computational results of the proposed method. Finally, Sect. 5 draws the conclusion of this paper and discusses future research directions.

2   Hierarchical Classification Problems

The concept of hierarchical classification is proposed in [17] as a specific type of structured classification problem, where the output of the classification algorithm is defined by a class taxonomy.

The class taxonomy, was explored in [20], as a hierarchical concept defined over a partially established set $(C, \prec)$, where C is a finite set that enumerates all the concepts of class in the application and the $\prec$ relation represents the relationship "IS-A". Thus, "IS-A" is defined in [17] relationship as asymmetric, anti-reflexive and transitive.

The solutions to the hierarchical classification problems can be differentiated by the type of algorithmic approach. Basically, the hierarchical classification of algorithms can be classified into local and global. However is important to make clear that most of the solutions that work with hierarchical problems use the local model in the training phase to build the classification model. This model trains a binary classifier for each node of the class hierarchy. In this case, it is necessary to use N independent local classifiers, one for each class except the root node. Therefore, the number of classifiers to be trained can be very large in situations where there are many classes. Moreover, in using the local approach, the technique can provide inconsistent results, because there is no guarantee that the class hierarchy will be respected.

In the global approach, a single classification model is built from the training set, taking into account the hierarchy of classes as a whole during a single execution of the classifier algorithm. In the global approach, the fact that the algorithm maintains hierarchical relationships between classes during the phases of training and testing makes the outcome of the prediction better understood.

According to [17], the global approach is still underexploited in the literature and it deserves more investigation because it builds a singular coherent classification model. However, to the user, the output of a global classifier approach might be easier to understand/interpret than the one from a local classifier approach, due to the typically much smaller size of the classification model produced by the former approach, as mentioned earlier. This is the case for instance in [18], where the number of rules generated by the global approach is much smaller than the number of rules generated by the local approaches used in their experiments. This paper proposes a new model of global classification.

3   The Proposed HLCS

The Hierarchical Learning Classifier System (HLCS) algorithm proposed in this paper uses as a development model the Learning Classifier System (LCS) and presents a comprehensive solution to hierarchical classification problems building a global classifier to predict all classes in the application domain.

In order to work with the class hierarchy, the HLCS presents a specific component for this task which is the evaluation component of the classifiers. This component has the task of analysing the predictions of classifiers considering the class hierarchy. In addition to this, the HLCS architecture consists of the following modules: population of classifiers, GA component, performance component and credit assignment component, which interacts internally.

The details of each one the HLCS components follow below.

3.1   Classifier Population and Evaluation Component

The size of the population of classifiers ($SizePop$) is defined by the HLCS algorithmic settings. The set of all classifiers is the predictive model. Each classifier C_i ($0 < i \leq SizePop$) of the HLCS comprises: a n set of conditions (where

n=number of attributes of an training instance), the class value and the classifier quality measure.

$$C_i=[(Cond_0 \text{ and...and } Cond_n)(ClassValue)(Q_{classifier})]$$

Each condition has three parameters: OP, VL, A/I, where: OP: operator relation (= or !=), VL: condition value and A/I: the choice of an active or inactive attribute, which determines if the condition will be used in the classifier or not.

In order to form each classifier, the HLCS randomly chooses an instance of the training base as a model. For each attribute of an training instance, a condition in the classifier is created. At the beginning, the conditions start with the operator relation (OP) "=". The condition value (VL) receives the value attribute of the training instance and whether the condition will be active (A) or inactive (I) is randomly determined.

The last step in the creation of the initial population of classifiers is define the quality of the classifier. ($Q_{classifier}$). To calculate the quality of the classifier two factors are considered: the percentage of positive classes predicted (*recall*) and the hierarchical control evaluation of the classifier (*evaluation_h*). The evaluation represents the predictive ability of the classifier, considering not only the class in question, but all the class antecedents in the hierarchy. This process is performed by the evaluation component which is essential for the HLCS to solve problems with hierarchical structures in DAG.

The evaluation is a way of considering the predictions made by the classifiers in the hierarchy of the problem. Principally, in the case of the prediction of protein function, is very important in biological terms, the knowledge of all classes that are part of a function, from the root to the most specific class. Based on this principle, this evaluation is responsible for promoting the classifiers that are close to their main goal, taking into consideration the quality of the classifier that predict at least some kind of antecedent class from the real class.

Through the evaluation component, the HLCS is able to verify whether an answer is correct, partially correct or incorrect, as shown in Fig. 1. With this model, it is possible to make the reward given to the classifier more dynamic, according to its prediction.

The correct prediction occurs when the predicted class is equal to the real class, as shown in Fig. 1a. In this case, according to Equation 1, the value of the classifier evaluation is 1.

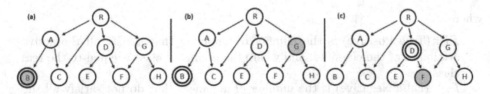

Fig. 1. (a) Example of correct prediction. (b) Example of incorrect prediction. (c) Example of partially correct prediction. In the examples, the double line circle represents the predicted class and the gray circle the real class.

The incorrect prediction occurs when the predicted class is not equal to the real class and as well as not being part of the real class antecedents, discarding the root node. In Figure 1b the class predicted (B) is outside hierarchy of class real (G). In this case, according to Equation 1, the value of the classifier evaluation is 0.

The prediction is considered partially correct when the algorithm misses the real class but hits at least one antecedent of this class, except the root node. In this case, according to Equation 1, it is then necessary to calculate the distance between the real class and the predicted class. In Fig. 1c the distance between the class predicted (D) and the class real (F) is only one edge, then the value of the classifier evaluation is 0.5.

Therefore, for each prediction, the HLCS achieves the $evaluation\_h(i)$ where, $(0 < i \leq$ number of instances) of the classifier as follows:

$$evaluation\_h(i) = \begin{cases} 1, & \text{if Correct} \\ 0, & \text{if Incorrect} \\ \frac{1}{1+(distance_{p,c})}, & \text{if Partially Correct} \end{cases} \qquad (1)$$

where:

- $distance_{p,c}$: this is the number of edges between the real class and predicted class. This value is calculated using Dijkstra's algorithm to find the shortest path. This distance is valid, only if there is at least one common node preceding the real class and predicted class, discarding the root node.

The final evaluation is then calculated as the sum of the evaluations and this value is incorporated into its quality, as shown in Equation 2.

$$evaluation\_h = \sum evaluation\_h(i) \qquad (2)$$

With this, the quality of the classifier is calculated as follows:

$$Q_{classifier} = recall * evaluation\_h \qquad (3)$$

$$recall = \frac{TP}{(TP + FN)} \qquad (4)$$

where:

- TP: (True Positive) is the number of instances that satisfy all the active attributes of the classifier, and where the predicted class is equal to the real class;
- FN: (False Negative) is the number of instances that do not satisfy all the active attributes of the classifier where the predicted class is equal to the real class.

This process is then repeated for all population of classifiers.

3.2   Performance Component

After creating the initial population, the process of learning and development of classifiers begins. In the first stage, the HLCS randomly chooses an training instance and compares with the classifiers of population. The comparison is made between the attributes of the training instance and the conditions of the classifier. These classifiers, whose active conditions are equal to the training instance attributes, form a action set, and are conducted to the performance component where they will participate in a competition.

The performance component is used to analyse the classifiers and evaluate the learning process. The classifier that obtains the highest bid ($eBid$) will have the chance of predicting the class of the training instance. The calculation of $eBid$ is shown in Equation 5.

$$eBid = 1 + ((\frac{total - actives}{total}) * Q_{classifier}) * (1 + Mod) \tag{5}$$

where:

- $Q_{classifier}$: the classifier quality measure;
- Mod: a random value that represents a modulation characterized by a noise with a normal distribution with mean 0 and variance 1;
- $total$: total classifier conditions;
- $actives$: total classifier active conditions.

In order to analyse the result of the prediction in the training instance and define the reward of the classifier, the credit assignment component is called.

3.3   Credit Assignment Component

The credit assignment component has the function of analysing the outcome of the classifier prediction of the training instance. The credit assignment is implemented by a modification of bucket brigade algorithm, and its analysis is re-passed to the classifier quality measure. If the winner classifier correctly predicts the training class instance, it gets a reward, as shown in Equation (6). Otherwise, the classifier receives a punishment for the prediction error, defined in Equation (7). In the case of an error, the evaluation component will interact to determine the degree of error according to the hierarchy of classes of instance.

$$Q_{classifier} = Q_{classifier} * (1 + PR + evaluation\_h) \tag{6}$$

$$Q_{classifier} = Q_{classifier} * (1 - PR + evaluation\_h) \tag{7}$$

where:

- PR: : the percentage of reward defined in the HLCS settings;
- $evaluation\_h$: Defined in Equation 2.

3.4 GA Component

The GA component is responsible for creating and modifying the classifiers so that they become more efficient. This component uses Genetic Algorithms (GA), which are based on probabilistic techniques that mimics the process of natural evolution. Through the crossover and mutation genetic operators, the classifiers evolve and their quality improve.

For this purpose, a genetic algorithm is applied to the classifiers in the action set. Two classifiers are selected by a tournament method, recombined, and mutated. The resulting offspring classifiers, if presenting a higher quality, are inserted in the population while other are deleted to keep the number of classifiers in the population constant.

The following algorithm show the entire procedure for creating the HLCS global model.

```
program HLCS Model
01 begin
02      for(i = 1 to SizePop)
03          generate initial population();
04          evaluate classifier quality measure();
05      end for
06      for(j = 1 to Number Generation)
07          for(k = 1 to Number Competitions)
08              id_instance = select random id instance();
09              for(i = 1 to SizePop)
10                  if((compare(instance(id_instance),classifier(i))))
11                      add classifier(i) to Action Set();
12                  end if
13              end for
14              for(i = 1 to Size Action Set)
15                  evaluate eBid classifier(i);
16                      if(classifier(i).eBid > best_eBid)
17                          best_eBid = classifier(i).eBid;
18                          id_best_eBid = i;
19                      end if
20              end for
21              if(compare(class(id_instance),class(id_best_eBid))
22                  evaluation_h = 1;
23                  Q_classifier = Q_classifier * (1 + PR + evaluation_h);
24              else
25                  if(is part of the real class antecedents)
26                  evaluation_h = 1/(1 + (distance_p,c);
27                  Q_classifier = Q_classifier * (1 - PR + evaluation_h);
28                  else
29                  evaluation_h = 0;
30                  Q_classifier = Q_classifier * (1 - PR + evaluation_h);
31                  end if
32              end if
33              crossover(Action Set);
34              mutation(Action Set);
35          end for
36      end for
37 end.
```

4 Computational Results

The HLCS was tested with data sets involving ion-channel proteins functions and compared with the hAnt-miner method [15]. Details about data sets and hAnt-miner method in [15].

In order to evaluate the algorithms we have used the metrics of hierarchical precision (hP), hierarchical recall (hR) and hierarchical F-measure proposed by [11]. These measures are, in fact, extended versions of the known measures like precision, recall and F-measure, tailored to the scenario of hierarchical classification.

The comparison results between the proposed HLCS method and the hAnt-Miner method are shown in Table 1. In all experiments, the parameters of HLCS were set to: 'SizePop=50', 'NumberGeneration=10', 'NumberCompetitions=10', 'Crossover=80%', 'Mutation=0.5%'. We have made no attempt to optimise these parameters for the data sets used in the experiments.

Table 1. Hierarchical measures of precision (hR), recall (hR) and F-measure (hF) values (mean ± standard deviation) obtained with the 10-fold cross-validation procedure in the four data sets. In the 'hF' column, the best result is shown in bold.

| | hAnt-Miner | | |
	hP	hR	hF
DS1 AA	0.56 ± 0.06	0.55 ± 0.06	0.56 ± 0.06
DS1 InterPro	0.82 ± 0.04	0.81 ± 0.04	**0.81 ± 0.04**
DS2 AA	0.63 ± 0.02	0.59 ± 0.02	0.61 ± 0.01
DS2 InterPro	0.83 ± 0.01	0.75 ± 0.01	**0.79 ± 0.01**

| | HLCS | | |
	hP	hR	hF
DS1 AA	0.84 ± 0.02	0.64 ± 0.03	**0.73 ± 0.02**
DS1 InterPro	0.54 ± 0.03	0.65 ± 0.02	0.59 ± 0.02
DS2 AA	0.86 ± 0.04	0.58 ± 0.03	**0.69 ± 0.01**
DS2 InterPro	0.64 ± 0.04	0.61 ± 0.03	0.63 ± 0.02

In order to measure if there is any statistically significant difference between the hierarchical classification methods being compared, we have employed the Wilcoxon signed-ranks test as strongly recommended for this case by [6]. This test proved that there is no statistically significant difference between the hF measure values of the two classifier at a confidence level of 95%.

However, the values show that the HLCS had best results on some measures when compared whit hAnt-Miner method. The HLCS outperformed the hAnt-Miner in two out of four data sets, namely 'DS1 AA' and 'DS2 AA'. This data set consists of real attributes, while the others data set are composed with boolean attributes. Since most data sets in real problems contains real attributes, shows that the HLCS is more robust than hAnt-Miner when dealing with this type of problem.

5   Conclusions

This paper presented a new Learning Classifier Systems, named HLCS, for the hierarchical classification problem of predicting protein functions using the Gene

Ontology. The HLCS is the first global approach based on Learning Classifier Systems for the prediction of hierarchical problems. The proposed HLCS discovers a single global classification model in the form of an ordered list of IF-THEN classification rules which can predict GO terms at all levels of the GO hierarchy, satisfying the parent-child relationships between GO terms. In order to work with the class hierarchy, the HLCS presents a specific component which has the task of analysing the predictions of classifiers considering the class hierarchy. With this component, the HLCS is able to verify whether an answer is correct, partially correct or incorrect making the reward given to the classifier more dynamic, according to its prediction.

The advantage of HLCS in contrast to other approaches is their adaptability. Based on the LCS model, the HLCS makes constant iterations of environmental samples to create their classification rules, making it a more flexible classification model.

The results comparing HLCS with the hAnt-Miner algorithm show that the HLCS had best results on some measures and this proves that the use of LCS models can be an alternative to the hierarchical classification problems. During the experiments we observed the need to better define the parameters used in the algorithm HLCS, in order to optimize the performance and robustness of the model system and achieve the most significant conclusions.

According to [16] the modern LCS research community is still small, but rapidly expanding. This expansion should result in a better exploitation of the suitability of LCS for application in complex real-world problems, due to their high power of expression combined with a very readable formalism for the human expert. As future research, we intend to evaluate this method on a larger number of datasets and compare it against other global hierarchical classification approaches. Although in this paper the HLCS was applied only to a biological data set, it is generic enough to be applied to other hierarchical classification data sets.

Acknowledgments. We want to thank Dr. Fernando E. B. Otero for kindly providing us with the datasets used in these experiments.

References

1. Alves, R., Delgado, M.: Multi-label Hierarchical Classification of Protein Functions with Artificial Immune Systems. In: Bazzan, A.L.C., Craven, M., Martins, N.F. (eds.) BSB 2008. LNCS (LNBI), vol. 5167, pp. 1–12. Springer, Heidelberg (2008)
2. The Gene Ontology Consortium: Gene Ontology – Tool for the Unification of Biology. Nature Genetics 25(1), 25–29 (2000)
3. Bernado-Mansilla, E., Garrell, J.M.: Accuracy-Based Learning Classifier Systems – Models, Analysis and Applications to Classification Tasks. Evolutionary Computing 11(3), 209–238 (2003)
4. Butz, M.V., Goldberg, D.E., Stolzmann, W.: Introducing a Genetic Generalization Pressure to the Anticipatory Classifier Systems – Part I - Theoretical Approach. In: Whitely, D., Goldberg, D.E., Cantu-Paz, E., Spector, L., Parmee, I.,

Beyer, H.G. (eds.) Genetic and Evolutionary Computation Conference (GECCO 2000), pp. 34–41. Morgan Kaufmann (2000)

5. Butz, M.V., Kovacs, T., Lanzi, P.L., Wilson, S.W.: Toward a Theory of Generalization and Learning in XCS. IEEE Transactions on Evolutionary Computation 8(1), 28–46 (2004)

6. Demšar, J.: Statistical Comparisons of Classifiers Over Multiple Data Sets. The Journal of Machine Learning Research 7, 1–30 (2006)

7. Freitas, A.A., Wieser, D.C., Apweiler, R.: On the Importance of Comprehensible Classification Models for Protein Function Prediction. IEEE/ACM Transactions on Computational Biology and Bioinformatics 7(1), 172–182 (2010)

8. Hamzeh, A., Rahmani, A.: A New Architecture of XCS to Approximate Real-Valued Functions Based on High Order Polynomials Using Variable-Length GA. In: 3rd International Conference on Natural Computation (ICNC 2007), vol. 3, pp. 515–519. IEEE (2007)

9. Holland, J.H.: Adaptation in Natural and Artificial Systems – An Introductory Analysis with Applications to Biology, Control and Artificial Intelligence. MIT Press, Cambridge (1992)

10. Hurst, J., Bull, L.: A Neural Learning Classifier System with Self-Adaptive Constructivism for Mobile Robot Control. Artificial Life 12(3), 942–951 (2006)

11. Kiritchenko, S., Matwin, S., Fazel, A.F.: Functional Annotation of Genes Using Hierarchical Text Categorization. In: BioLINK SIG Meeting – Linking Literature, Information and Knowledge for Biology (BioLINK 2005), pp. 1–4 (2005)

12. Kovacs, T.: Learning classifier systems resources. Soft Computing 6(3-4), 240–243 (2002)

13. Lanzi, P., Loiacono, D.: Classifier Systems that Compute Action Mappings. In: 2007 Annual Conference on Genetic and Evolutionary Computation (GECCO 2007), pp. 1822–1829. ACM (2007)

14. Orriols-Puig, A., Casillas, J., Bernadó-Mansilla, E.: Fuzzy- UCS – Preliminary Results. In: 2007 Annual Conference on Genetic and Evolutionary Computation (GECCO 2007), pp. 2871–2874. ACM (2007)

15. Otero, F., Freitas, A.A., Johnson, C.: A Hierarchical Classification Ant Colony Algorithm for Predicting Gene Ontology Terms. In: Pizzuti, C., Ritchie, M., Giacobini, M. (eds.) EvoBIO 2009. LNCS, vol. 5483, pp. 68–79. Springer, Heidelberg (2009)

16. Sigaud, O., Wilson, S.: Learning Classifier Systems – A Survey. Soft Computing 11(11), 1065–1078 (2007)

17. Silla, C.N., Freitas, A.A.: A Survey of Hierarchical Classification Across Different Application Domains. Data Mining and Knowledge Discovery 22(1-2), 31–72 (2011)

18. Vens, C., Struyf, J., Schietgat, L., Džeroski, S., Blockeel, H.: Decision Trees for Hierarchical Multi-Label Classification. Machine Learning 73(2), 185–214 (2008)

19. Wilson, S.W.: Classifier Fitness Based on Accuracy. Evolutionary Computation 3(2), 149–175 (1995)

20. Wu, F., Zhang, J., Honavar, V.: Learning Classifiers Using Hierarchically Structured Class Taxonomies. In: Zucker, J.D., Saitta, L. (eds.) SARA 2005. LNCS (LNAI), vol. 3607, pp. 313–320. Springer, Heidelberg (2005)

Detecting Survival Patterns in Women with Invasive Cervical Cancer with Decision Trees

Ricardo Timarán Pereira[1], Maria Clara Yepez Chamorro[2],
and Andrés Calderón Romero[1]

[1] Facultad de Ingeniería, Departamento de Sistemas
[2] Centro de Estudios en Salud,
Universidad de Nariño Ciudad Universitaria Torobajo, San Juan de Pasto, Colombia
{ritimar,mcych,aocalderon}@udenar.edu.co

Abstract. In this paper the first results of the process of extracting survival patterns in diagnosed women with invasive cervical cancer with classification techniques from data reported in population-based cancer registry of the municipality of Pasto (Colombia) for a time period of 10 years are presented. The generated knowledge will allow to understand the different socioeconomic and clinical factors affecting the survival of this population group. This knowledge will support effective decision making of government agencies and private health sector in relation to the approach of public policies and prevention programs designed to detect new cases of women with this disease early.

Keywords: survival patterns, invasive cervical cancer, data mining, classification task.

1   Introduction

Invasive cervical cancer is a preventable disease. However, it still is a serious health public problem which has a bigger impact in developing countries. Some facts and figures show 83.1% of cases and 85.5% of deaths in those regions [1].

From results of The National Cancer Institute of Colombia (NCI), cervical cancer shows the highest rates in regions such as Orinoquía and Amazon and also in the Department of Nariño.

For the Department of Nariño, during the period between 2002 and 2006, the NCI reported an estimated crude rate of cancer incidence of 130.9 per 100,000 women. Similarly, a mortality rate of 51.9 per 100,000 women was reported. During the same period, the estimated crude rate of cancer incidence and mortality rate of cervical cancer was 23.8 and 8.7 per 100,000 inhabitants respectively [2].

In the the municipality of Pasto, capital of the department of Nariño, the Population-based Cancer Registry (PCR) in the period 1998 to 2002, reported an Age-adjusted Incidence Rate (AAIR) of cancer for men and women of 142.5 per 100,000 inhabitants, with stomach cancer in men with a higher incidence (41.2) and cervical cancer in women with an AAIR of 50.4 per 100,000 women [3]. According to the

J. Pavón et al. (Eds.): IBERAMIA 2012, LNAI 7637, pp. 130–139, 2012.

health indicators of the municipality of Pasto, death rates for neoplasms of uterus in 2001 and 2002 were 7.6 and 7.0 per 100,000 women. For 2006, it was reported a mortality rate of 10.2 per 100,000 women. However, it ignores the situation of women in Pasto, once they have been diagnosed with invasive cervical cancer in which the probability of death increases.

Some studies [1, 4, 5], show that when cervical cancer is detected and treated early, usually it can be cured. The survival rate of five years for pre-invasive cervical cancer is 100 percent and for early-stage invasive cancer is 91%. The survival rate of five years decrease to 70% for cervical cancers detected in all stages combined [4].

Another research reported that the prognosis of cervical cancer is dependent on socio-economic and demographic characteristics of the patient. The clinical stage at diagnosis, treatment scheme and the time elapsed between diagnosis and treatment and its continuity are key variables affecting survival of patients [6].

The above studies are based on information processed by basic statistical analysis, which considers variables and their primary relationships firstly, regardless of the real relationships among data which are usually hidden and can only be discovered using a more complex data processing, which is only possible with data mining [7].

In the last decade, data mining and statistical analysis have been widely used in the industry of health care. When these methods are used together with information from large amounts of data can help to health professionals to make decisions and improve service [8].

While the statistics raises hypotheses to be validated from available data, Data Mining discovers patterns from the data which through its interpretation are able to propose, for example in the case of invasive cervical cancer, survival patterns which are difficult to found using just statistical tasks.

Data mining is emerging as a technology that aims to help understand the contents of a database. In general, the data is the raw material. At the moment that users attach special meaning to this data, it becomes information. When experts build a model, they build an interpretation of the available information. If it represents an added value, therefore, it is referred as knowledge [9, 10]. In this context, data mining emerges as the next step in the process of data analysis.

Nowadays, medical experts do not have objective tools that help them make a decision regarding the optimal treatment for a patient. Using the information that they believe important, data mining intends to find patterns and relationships between variables so as to predict in advance, in the specific case of cervical cancer, those factors that affect the survival of women with this disease. In this context, this study aims to characterize and classify the population of cervical cancer patients using data mining techniques, hoping to find underlying relationships in the data which cannot be identified by classical statistical treatment.

At the University of Nariño, municipality of Pasto and even in the Department of Nariño, research projects whose aims are building models from the recorded data and using data mining techniques to find early detection patterns of any cancer, had not been considered yet.

In this research project was intended to find patterns of survival of women diagnosed with invasive cervical cancer using techniques of knowledge discovery from data reported in population-based cancer registry of the municipality of Pasto for a time period of 10 years (1998 - 2007). Such patterns will generate knowledge about social, economic and clinical factors that affect the survival of this group of patients and will serve to support for effective decision making of government agencies and private health sector in relation to public policy and prevention programs designed to detect new cases of women with this disease early.

This paper is organized into sections. In the next section describes as carried out the extraction of patterns of survival in women with invasive cervical cancer. The final section presents conclusions and future work.

2   Survival Patterns Discovery Process

Knowledge Discovery in Databases (KDD) is the extraction of implicit, previously unknown, and potentially useful information from data [11]. KDD is basically an automatic process that combines discovery and analysis. The KDD process is interactive and iterative, involving numerous steps with many decisions made by user. This process usually involves preprocessing the data, make data mining and visualize the results [12-15]. In the process of discovering survival patterns of women with invasive cervical cancer, the following steps were performed:

2.1   Selection Step

The main goal of this step is selecting a data set from internal or external sources of data, or focusing on a subset of variables or data samples, on which discovery is to be performed. Internal sources are selected from the REGCANDB database, which is part of the REGCAMP software. The REGCANDB contains a Population-based Cancer Registry of the municipality of Pasto which stores around 17350 cases of different types of cancer since 1998 until 2007, covering the observation period of this study. Main external sources were selected from the Individual Health Services Delivery Registry - RIPS and the Potential Beneficiaries of Social Programs Information System - SISBEN of the municipality of Pasto (both acronyms come from their names in Spanish).

RIPS stores a basic data set with the minimal information about the Social Security System in Health. It is used for government agencies for process management, regulation and control. Data inside relate to the identification of health service provider, the user who receives the service, the service itself and the reason that led to: diagnosis or external cause.

SISBEN stores all socio-economic data provided in the survey of beneficiaries in order to determine a score of socioeconomic classification that places the recipient at a certain level (1-6).

Other external sources that were selected to complement missing information or to obtain other data were: private clinics, public and private hospitals, state social enterprises, health services providing companies, pathology laboratories and Health Specialized services Institutes.

From the REGCANDB database, just the records about women with invasive cervical cancer and the most representative attributes for each factor were selected. Different external data sources were used for replacing missing data. As a result of this stage, the CANCERDB database was created. It was built using the database management system PostgreSQL [16, 17]. Initially, CANCERDB consists of a single table, called CANCER, with 39 attributes and 507 records.

2.2 Preprocessing Step

The goal at this stage is to obtain clean data, i.e. data without null or outlier values, in order to retrieve high quality patterns. Through ad-hoc queries on the CANCER table, the quality of the data available for each of its attributes was thoroughly analyzed.

Keeping in mind the importance of the attributes in this research, different strategies were implemented to replace null values, for example: using statistical techniques such as mean, median and mode or deriving new values from other attributes or through external sources. For instance, missing values for attributes *fecha_n* (date of birth of the patient), *lugar_n* (birthplace of the patient) and fecha_*defun* (date of death of the patient) were updated using the National Registry Database. Missing values for attributes *regimen* (health system which the patient belongs to), *escolaridad* (educational level of the patient at diagnosis), *parentesco* (relationship to head of household), *ocupacion* (occupation of the patient) were updated from the SISBEN database. Finally, missing values for attributes *fecha_consulta_rips* (date of last patient visit to the health system) and diag_*principal_rips* (diagnosis of the last visit to the health system) were updated using the RIPS database.

The attributes with a high percentage of null values such as *quimio* (88.76%, determines whether the patient received chemotherapy), *braqui* (100%, determines whether the patient received brachytherapy) and *paliativo* (100%, determines whether the patient received palliative treatment) were eliminated.

2.3 Transformation Step

Data transformation includes any process that modifies the form of the data. The aim of this stage is to transform the data source in a dataset ready to apply any of the different techniques of data mining. Among the operations performed to transform the data are: elimination of the least relevant attributes, creation of new attributes by deriving them from others (keeping or replacing these attributes) and / or modification of the type of attributes (using discretization or continuity methods).

In order to facilitate patterns extraction, it was created new attributes derived from others in the CANCER table. Table 1 describes these new attributes.

The *comuna* attribute collects the different urban districts and rural areas in the municipality of Pasto. The new attribute replaces the name of each of the twelve urban districts for a number (1 to 12) and sets the value of 13 for the rural sector.

The new values for the *estrato* attribute and their description are shown in Table 2.

The *region* attribute groups the different municipalities of Nariño department in eight regions: North, South, Central, Western Andean, Pacific, Pasto, Putumayo, and Others. The values 'Others' refers to others municipalities of Colombia.

Table 1. New Attributes of CANCER Table

ATTRIBUTE	DESCRIPTION
barrio	Neighborhood of the patient in the city of Pasto at the moment of diagnosis.
comuna	Urban district or rural sector which the neighborhood belongs to.
estrato	Socio-economic level of the patient at the moment of diagnosis.
region	Geographic region of birth of the patient.
edaddx	Age of the patient at the moment of diagnosis.
cabezaflia	Determine if the patient is a single parent head of household.
tipovivienda	This is the patient's type of dwelling.
fuentedeagua	Water collection system of the patient at home.
puntajesisben	Score of the patient in the SISBEN System. It is used to calculate the SISBEN level.
nivelsisben	SISBEN level.
vivomuerto	Determine if the patient is alive or dead at the end of 2007.
nmeses	Number of months the patient live since the moment of diagnosis.

Table 2. *Estrato* Attribute Values

ESTRATO	DESCRIPTION
1	Very low
2	Low
3	Medium low
4	Medium
5	Medium high
6	High

Table 3. *Edaddx* Attribute Values

EDADDX	RANGE
1	15-28
2	29-41
3	42-54
4	55-67
5	68-80
6	81-93

In some cases, it is necessary to convert a numeric attribute to nominal values. This process is known as discretization [18]. For this reason, taking into account the different numerical values of the *edaddx*, attribute, these were discretized to nominal values, taking into account same size intervals and using the maximum and minimum as reference.

In the discretization process of attribute, it was used six same-sized intervals (*Ti*). They were calculated taking into account the difference between the maximal value (*Vmax* = 93 year old) and the minimal value (*Vmin* = 15 year old). The result was divided by the number of intervals (*Ni* = 6). The final results are shown in Table 3.

Nivelsisben attribute values depend on the score obtained by the patient in the respective citizen survey which is registered in the *puntajesisben* attribute. The final levels and how they are assigned are shown in Table 4.

Table 4. *Nivelsisben* attribute values

NIVEL SISBEN	URBAN AREA SCORE	RURAL AREA SCORE
1	0-36	0-18
2	37-47	19-30
3	48-58	31-45
4	59-69	46-61
5	70-86	62-81
6	87-100	82-100

Table 5. New Tables in CANCERDB

TABLE	DESCRIPTION
t507a22all	General table with 507 cases of cervical cancer (334 alive and 173 dead) and 22 attributes to be considered in the study.
t507a15econ	Table with 507 cases of cervical cancer and 15 attributes related to socio-economic factors.
T507a09clinico	Table with 507 cases of cervical cancer and 9 attributes related to clinical factors.

Table 6. Description of the most relevant attributes for this research

ATTRIBUTE	DESCRIPTION
region	Place of birth of the patient.
comuna	Urban district or rural sector which the neighborhood belongs to.
estrato	Socio-economic level of the patient at the moment of diagnosis.
edaddx	Patient age at the moment of diagnosis.
estadocivil	Marital status of the patient at the moment of diagnosis.
ocupacion	Occupation of the patient at the moment of diagnosis.
escolaridad	Educational level of the patient at the moment of diagnosis.
regimen	Health system of the patient at the moment of diagnosis.
nivelsisben	Level of the patient in SISBEN Database.
cabezaflia	Determines whether the patient is head of household or not.
tipovivienda	This is the patient's type of dwelling.
fuentedeagua	Water collection system of the patient at home.
discapacidad	Determines whether the patient has a disability or not.
fuente	Institutions where the cancer was diagnosed.
metododx	Method used for diagnosis.
morfologia	Morphology of the cancer.
locesp	Specific location for the cancer.
radio	Radiotherapy was part of the treatment.
cirugia	Surgery was part of the treatment.
biopsia	Determines whether a biopsy was performed.
nmeses	Number of months of life of patients since the moment of diagnosis.
vivomuerto	Determines whether the patient is alive or dead until the finish of the study.

Finally, in order to generate new knowledge about the social, economic and clinical factors that impact on the survival of diagnosed women with invasive cervical cancer, the most representative attributes for each factor were selected from the CANCER table. Depending on the factor, new tables with those attribute were created in the CANCERDB database. The remaining of attributes in CANCER table was removed. The descriptions of these tables are shown in Table 5.

A detail description of each of the 22 attributes more relevant for this research is shown in Table 6. These attributes form the table called *t507a22all*. The 15th attributes to consider as socioeconomic factors form the *t507a15econ* table. They are the first 13 attributes of the *t507a22all* table plus the last two (*nmeses* and *vivo_muerto* attributes). The 9th attributes which are considering as clinical factors form the *t507a09clinico* table. They are the last 9th attributes of the *t507a22all* table.

2.4   Data Mining Step

The goal of the data mining step is the search and discovery for unexpected and interesting patterns from data. In this process, intelligent task are applied such as *classification* [11, 19, 20], *clustering* [21, 22], *sequential patterns* [23], *associations* [12] among others.

The data mining task chosen for the process of discovering survival patterns in women with invasive cervical cancer was classification using a decision trees technique.

Data classification provides results from a supervised learning process. Data classification is a two-step process. In the first step, a model is built describing a predetermined set of data classes. The input data, also called the training set, consists of multiple examples (records), each having multiple attributes or features and tagged with a special class label. In the second step, the model is used to classify future test data for which the class labels are unknown [15, 24].

Decision tree classification is the most popular model, because it is simple and easy to understand [15, 25, 26]. A decision tree is a flow-chart-like tree structure, where each internal node denotes a test on an attribute, each branch represents an outcome of the test, and leaf nodes represent classes. The top-most node in a tree is the root node [15].

A decision tree classifier is built in two phases: a growth phase and a pruning phase. In the growth phase, the tree is built by recursively partitioning the data until all members belong to the same class. In the pruning phase, many branches are removed with the goal of improving classification accuracy on data [20].

The classification rules were obtained with the Weka data mining tool (Waikato Environment for Knowledge Analysis), using the J48 algorithm, which implements the algorithm C.45 [27], and utilizing data repositories described in Table 6.

Weka was developed at the University of Waikato (New Zealand) under a GPL license. This tool allows applying, analyzing and evaluating the most relevant techniques of data analysis, mainly those from machine learning, for any kind of dataset [28]. Weka is one of the popular suites used in the area of knowledge discovery in recent years.

The J48 algorithm is based on the use of the gain ratio criterion. Consequently, those variables with greater number of different values do not have benefit in the selection. Furthermore, the algorithm incorporates a classification tree pruning once it has been induced [8].

T507a22all repository was used to discover general patterns that affect the survival in women with invasive cervical cancer. The *vivomuerto* attribute (334 alive and 173 dead) was chosen as the class, using a confidence C = 0.7 and a number of records per node   M = 20. Figure 1 shows the obtained results with Weka tool.

Similarly, the t507a15econ and t507a09clinico repositories were used, respectively, to determine socioeconomic and clinical factors that affect the survival in women with invasive cervical cancer. The *vivomuerto* attribute was set as the class with a confidence C = 0.7 and a number of records per node M = 10.

```
weka.classifiers.trees.J48 -C 0.7 -M 20
=== Classifier model (full training set)
===
J48 pruned tree
------------------
nmeses <= 37
|   cabezaflia <= 0
|   |   nivelsisben = 1: VIVO (50.0/20.0)
|   |         nivelsisben  =  7:   MUERTO
(165.0/38.0)
|   |    nivelsisben = 2: VIVO (33.0/6.0)
|   |    nivelsisben = 3: VIVO (4.0/1.0)
|   |    nivelsisben = 4: VIVO (1.0)
|   cabezafamilia > 0: VIVO (42.0/4.0)
nmeses > 37: VIVO (212.0/15.0)

Number of Leaves  :    7
Size of the tree  :    10

Correctly Classified Instances
416              82.0513 %
Incorrectly Classified Instances
91               17.9487 %
```

Fig. 1. Classification Rules with Weka Tool

2.5   Evaluation Step

The objective of this final stage is the interpretation of the obtained results in order to consolidate the discovered knowledge with two goals in mind. First, to integrate it into other systems for further action, and second, to compare it with previously discovered knowledge.

According to the results, women survivors are those that pass the threshold of the 37 months after being diagnosed with invasive cervical cancer. If women do not exceed that threshold, who survives are those that are heads of household. In the case they are not heads of households, women survivors are those that are mainly classified in levels 1 or 2 of SISBEN.

Some socioeconomic factors affecting the survival in women with invasive cervical cancer are: to be head of household, not having any disability, membership of a subsidized health system and be aged between 29 and 41 years at diagnosis.

Among the discovered classification rules with   clinical factors are: if the morphology was a *Carcinoma NOS,* women have more chance of survive. Similarly, if the treatment involved a surgery, women have a chance of survive if the morphology was *Squamous cell carcinoma, NOS.* In the other hand, if during the treatment was not involved a surgery, the source of diagnosis was a hospital or clinic and the morphology was a *Squamous cell carcinoma, NOS*, women with chance of survive should exceed the threshold of 11 months after the diagnosis.

3   Conclusions and Future Work

According to the results obtained in the process of discovering survival patterns in women with invasive cervical cancer using classification decision trees, from the population-based cancer registry of the municipality of Pasto, for an observation period of 10 years, the main survival factor is the number of months that elapse after the moment of diagnosis. If it is greater than 37 months the patient survives. Otherwise, other factors, both socioeconomic and clinical, come into play.

Considering the total number of analyzed cases of cervical cancer in this study, 65.9% survived and of these 63.5% are over the threshold of 37 months after the cancer diagnosis.

Future work in this research includes the implementation of other techniques such as association and clustering to determine affinities, similarities and relationships between socioeconomic and clinical factors in women who survived and who died, taking into account the total number of cases of cervical cancer analyzed in this study.

References

1. Castro, M., Vera, L., Posso, H.: Epidemiología del Cáncer de Cuello Uterino-Estado del Arte. Revista Colombiana de Obstetricia y Ginecología 57(3), 182–189 (2006)
2. Pardo, C., Cendales, R.: Incidencia Estimada y Mortalidad por Cáncer en Colombia 2002-2006, p. 79. Informe Instituto Nacional de Cancerología, E.S.E, Bogotá, D.C., Colombia (2010)
3. Bolaños, H., Hidalgo, A., Yépez, M.C.: Incidencia de Cáncer en el Municipio de Pasto, Periodo 1998-2002. Editorial Universitaria, San Juan de Pasto, Colombia (2007)
4. Ferlay, J., Bray, F., Pisani, P., Parkin, D.M.: Cancer Incidence, Mortality and Prevalence Worldwide, Version 2.0. IARC Cancer Base 5. IARC Press, Lyon (2002)
5. Asport, S., Rivero, T.: Plan Nacional de Control de Cáncer de Cuello Uterino 2004-2008. Informe Ministerio de Salud y Deportes, La Paz, Bolivia (2004)
6. Merle, J.L.: Análisis de la Situación del Cáncer Cérvico Uterino en América Latina y el Caribe. OPS, Washington (2004)
7. Mora, R.: El Papel de la Minería de Datos en la Detección y Diagnóstico de Cáncer. Universidad de Salamanca, Salamanca, Spain,
   http://sistemaminergescon.blogspot.com/
8. Hernández, E., Lorente, R.: Minería de Datos Aplicada a la Detección de Cáncer de Mama. Universidad Carlos III, Madrid, Spain, http://www.it.uc3m.es/jvillena/irc/practicas/08-9/14.pdf

9. Cabena, P., Hadjinian, P., Stadler, R., Verhees, J., Zanasi, A.: Discovering Data Mining from Concept to Implementation. Prentice Hall (1997)
10. Timarán, R.: Una Mirada al Descubrimiento de Conocimiento en Bases de Datos. Ventana Informática 20, 39–58; Centro de Investigaciones, Desarrollo e Innovación, Facultad de Ingeniería, Universidad de Manizales, Manizales, Colombia(2009)
11. Witten, I., Frank, E.: Data Mining: Practical Machine Learning Tools and Techniques with Java Implementations, p. 365. Morgan Kaufmann Publishers, San Francisco (2000)
12. Agrawal, R., Srikant, R.: Fast Algorithms for Mining Association Rules. In: 20th International Conference on Very Large Data Bases (VLDB 1994), pp. 487–489 (1994)
13. Chen, M., Han, J., Yu, P.: Data Mining: An Overview from Database Perspective. IEEE Transactions on Knowledge Data Engineering 8(6), 866–883 (1996)
14. Piatetsky-Shapiro, G., Brachman, R., Khabaza, T.: An Overview of Issues in Developing Industrial Data Mining and Knowledge Discovery Applications. In: 2nd International Conference on Knowledge Discovery and Data Mining (KDD 1996), pp. 89–95. AAAI Press (1996)
15. Han, J., Kamber, M.: Data Mining Concepts and Techniques. Morgan Kaufmann Publishers, San Francisco (2001)
16. Stonebraker, M., Rowe, L.A.: The Design of Postgres. In: ACM SIGMOD International Conference on Management of Data (SIGMOD 1986), pp. 340–355 (1986)
17. Momjian, B.: PostgreSQL- Introduction and Concepts, p. 455. Addison-Wesley, New York (2001)
18. Hernández, J., Ramirez, M.J., Ferri, C.: Introducción a la Minería de Datos. Pearson Prentice Hall, Madrid (2005)
19. Quinlan, J.R.: Induction of Decision Trees. Machine Learning Journa 1(1), 81–106 (1986)
20. Wang, M., Iyer, B., Scott, V.J.: Scalable Mining for Classification Rules in Relational Databases. In: International Database Engineering and Application Symposium (IDEAS 1998), pp. 58–67 (1998)
21. Ng, R., Han, J.: Efficient and Effective Clustering Method for Spatial Data Mining. In: 20th International Conference on Very Large Data Bases (VLDB 1994), pp. 144–155 (1994)
22. Zhang, T., Ramakrishnan, R., Livny, M.: BIRCH: An Efficient Data Clustering Method for Very Large Databases. In: ACM SIGMOD International Conference on Management of Data (SIGMOD 1996), pp. 103–114 (1996)
23. Agrawal, R., Srikant, R.: Mining Sequential Patterns. In: 11th International Conference on Data Engineering (ICDE 1995), pp. 3–14 (1995)
24. Agrawal, R., Ghosh, S., Imielinski, T., Iyer, B., Swami, A.: An Interval Classifier for Database Mining Applications. In: 18th International Conference on Very Large Data Bases (VLDB 1992), pp. 560–573 (1992)
25. Sattler, K., Dunemann, O.: SQL Database Primitives for Decision Tree Classifiers. In: 10th International Conference on Information and Knowledge Management (CIKM 2001), pp. 379–386 (2001)
26. Timarán, R., Millán, M.: New Algebraic Operators and SQL Primitives for Mining Classification Rules. In: 5th IASTED International Conference on Computational Intelligence (CI 2006), pp. 1–5 (2006)
27. Quinlan, J.R.: C4.5: Programs for Machine Learning, p. 299. Morgan Kaufmann Publishers, San Francisco (1993)
28. Garcia, D.: Manual de Weka, http://www.metaemotion.com/diego.garcia.morate/download/weka.pdf

Using SOM Maps for Clustering and Visualization of Diamond Films Deposited by HFCVD Process

Leandro A. Pasa[1], José Alfredo F. Costa[2],
Marcelo C. Tosin[3], and Fábio A. Procópio de Paiva[4]

[1] UTFPR, Medianeira/PR, Brasil
pasa@utfpr.edu.br
[2] UFRN, Departamento de Engenharia Elétrica, Natal/RN, Brasil
jafcosta@gmail.com
[3] UEL, Departamento de Engenharia Elétrica, Londrina/PR, Brasil
tosin@uel.br
[4] IFRN, Campus Zona Norte, Natal/RN, Brasil
fabio.procopio@ifrn.edu.br

Abstract. Diamond is a material with unique properties to be exploited in various applications. The deposition of diamond thin films on surfaces enables its use in mechanics, electronics and optics, among others. To ensure the quality of crystals is important to control the parameters involved in the deposition process. In this study we used the SOM algorithm for clustering and visualization of the parameters of a reactor for deposition of diamond thin films, which together with scanning electron microscopy and Raman spectroscopy, collaborated in reactor calibration. The results show the importance of temperature in this process.

Keywords: SOM, hot filament chemical vapour deposition, diamond thin films.

1   Introduction

The interest in synthesizing diamonds is due to its physical and chemical stable properties, enabling unique technological applications in different fields like electronics, mechanics and optics. There are basically two methods for synthesizing diamonds. The first one consists in submitting graphite to high pressure and high temperature, reaching the region where the diamond is the stable phase. This method is known as HPHT - High Pressure and High Temperature. The second method is the synthesis of diamond at low pressures in the metastable region. Among these low pressure processes are the CVD - Chemical Vapor Deposition. It is a process that involves depositing a solid material on a substrate by activating the precursors in gaseous phase and making them react chemically. The hydrocarbon is dissociated into atomic hydrogen and active carbon. The carbon is deposited on a substrate in the tetrahedral form (diamond). This is a slow process because the atoms are deposited one by one to form a solid film adhered to the substrate.

J. Pavón et al. (Eds.): IBERAMIA 2012, LNAI 7637, pp. 140–148, 2012.

The major advantage of this kind of growth processes is that the diamond can be deposited as thin film on substrates of different geometries and thicknesses, allowing its use in components for use in several areas.

Carbon, in its pure form, appears in several allotropic, crystalline and amorphous forms. Two types of crystalline carbon are diamond and graphite, although there are other elements whose links form a crystal lattice. Among the amorphous forms, we may cite carbon fiber, amorphous carbon, coal and DLC - Diamond Like Carbon, which is an amorphous form and maintains some of the characteristics of diamond [1]. Besides these, there are several other elements formed from carbon atoms. For this reason, it is necessary to maintain tight control over the deposition parameters, to ensure that there is, mainly, the deposition of diamond crystals.

In this study, the Self Organizing Maps (SOM) algorithm was used for clustering and visualization of the parameters involved in a HFCVD process - Hot Filament Chemical Vapor Deposition, detailed in the next section. The parameters of each film deposition were purposely varied to calibrate the reactor to reach the best depositions.

The paper is organized as follows: Section 2 presents the key concepts about the HFCVD process; Sect. 3 describes a brief introduction to SOM maps; Sect. 4 shows the methodology used in the films deposition; Sect. 5 shows the details about the clustering using the SOM. And in the last section, the conclusions are presented.

2   The HFCVD Process

In the HFCVD process (Hot Filament Chemical Vapor Deposition), the reaction occurs in a chamber, as shown in Fig. 1. There is a metallic filament, generally made of tungsten, positioned between 3 and 10 mm above the substrate [2]. Usually, the substrate used is monocrystalline silicon, because it has high melting point, crystal structure and thermal expansion coefficient similar to diamond and has a relatively low cost [3], although other substrates may also be used, such as molybdenum, titanium, and copper, among others [4].

The carbon used in the process comes from the ethyl alcohol, methane or other hydrocarbon [5]. The hydrocarbon is dissolved in hydrogen and injected into the chamber at a constant rate, with a ratio of around 0.5%.

The filament is connected to a DC power source and it reaches an average temperature of 2000 °C while warming the substrate to a temperature of about 800 °C. At this temperature, tungsten catalyzes the formation of atomic hydrogen (H^0) which, together with the thermal process, decomposes the hydrocarbon dissolved in activated carboxyl, for example CH_3, CH_2, CH, CHOH, among others. The H^0 and these radicals reach the substrate, where it begins to emerge diamond deposits.

The process begins with the formation of seeds and carbon atoms will be deposited around them. The nucleation process can be accelerated with a pretreatment of the substrate, also called seeding. It consists, for example, directly sprinkling diamond powder on the substrate or a diamond slurry sonication treatment.

The deposited films can be identified by their crystal morphology analyzed by optical microscopy and the Raman spectrum typical for crystalline diamond [6]. The Raman spectroscopy identifies the different phases of carbon, like diamond, nanocrystalline diamond, graphite, amorphous carbon, DLC (Diamond Like Carbon) and hydrogenated carbon [7-8]. For the diamond, the typical wavelength peak occurs in 1333 cm^{-1}. For graphite, the peak occurs in the Raman spectrum from 1500 cm^{-1} and 1600 cm^{-1}.

It is important to determine and control the parameters involved in the process to define the conditions under which there is diamond films growth and to prevent defects occurring in the crystal formed.

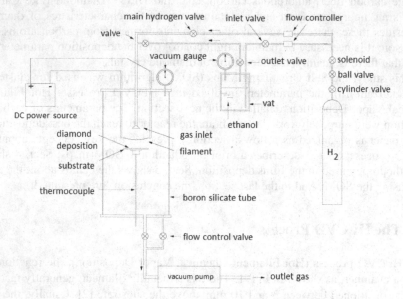

Fig. 1. Schematic view of the HFCVD chamber

3   Self-Organizing Maps (SOM)

The SOM is one of the main models of neural networks at present and is used in countless applications. Unlike other neural network approaches, the SOM is a type of neural net based on competitive and unsupervised learning [9]. The network essentially consists of two layers: an input layer I and an output layer U with neurons generally organized in a 2-dimensional topological array. The input to the net corresponds to a p-dimensional vector, x, generally in the space R^p. All of the p components of the input vector feed each of the neurons on the map. Each neuron i can be represented by a synaptic weight vector $w_i = [w_{i1}, w_{i2},..., w_{ip}]T$, also in the p-dimensional space. For each input pattern x a winner neuron, c, is chosen, using the criterion of greatest similarity:

$$\|x - w_c\| = \min_i\{\|x - w_i\|\} \tag{1}$$

where $\|.\|$ represents the Euclidian distance. The winner neuron weights, together with the weights of the neighboring neurons, are adjusted according to the following equation:

$$w_i(t + 1) = w_i(t) + h_{ci}(t)[x(t) - w_i(t)] \tag{2}$$

where t indicates the iteration of the training process, $x(t)$ is the input pattern and $h_{ci}(t)$ is the nucleus of neighborhood around the winner neuron c.

Once the SOM training algorithm has converged the computed feature map displays important statistical characteristics of the input space, which can be summarized as follows [10]:

(i) Vector quantization: the basic objective of SOM is to store a large set of input vectors by finding a smaller set of prototypes that provides a good approximation to the input space.

(ii) Topological ordering: the features map computed by SOM is ordered topologically. Similar input vectors are mapped close to each other, while dissimilar ones are mapped far apart.

(iii) Density Matching: the SOM reflects the probability distribution of data in the input space. Regions in the input space in which the input patterns are taken with a high probability of occurrence are mapped onto larger domains of the output space, and thus have better resolution than regions in the output space from which input patterns are taken with a low probability of occurrence.

There are some studies that apply SOM for visualization and analysis of processes in several areas. Pilsung [11] developed a virtual metrology system for an etching process in semiconductor manufacturing based on various data mining techniques that can not only predict the metrology measurement accurately, but also detect possible faulty wafers with a reasonable confidence. Abonyi [12] applied SOM on the analysis of an industrial polyethylene plant and demonstrates that the SOM is very effective in the detection of the typical operating regions related to different product grades, and the model can be used to predict the product quality based on measured process variables. Rasanen [13] presents an approach for dynamic process state monitoring and applied it in a circulating fluidized bed energy plant. That was based on a self-refreshing modification of the self-organizing map where previously learned data was used recursively to avoid catastrophic forgetting. The results of the simulations showed that method is a useful tool for monitoring process states. Sanchez [14] describes a virtual sensor design for coating thickness estimation in a hot dip galvanising line based on local models using SOM. Domínguez [15] proposes a method that defines a new visual exploration tool, called dissimilarity map for the visual comparison of industrial processes.

4   Diamond Depositions

Twenty one 21 diamond films depositions were made, each one consisted of 18 parameters: substrate area, pressure in the chamber, the main stream gas, ethanol flow, the bubbler (vat) valve opening, pressure in the bubbler, main valve opening, the thermocouple voltage, the substrate temperature, electrical current source, voltage source, the ethanol temperature, the ethanol vapor pressure, hydrogen line pressure, filament diameter, distance between filament and the substrate, deposition time, the percentage of carbon. The samples numbers 1 - 5 were deposited on silicon substrates and not passed through the seeding process. Samples 6 - 14 were deposited on silicon substrates and the sowing was carried with tungsten powder with a particle size of

Table 1. Samples separation into groups

Group	Deposition	Sample
1	None	1, 2, 3, 4 e 5
2	No diamond	8, 9, 11, 12, 13, 14 e 15
3	Diamond	6, 7, 10, 16, 17, 18, 19, 20, 21

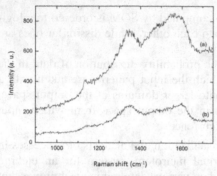

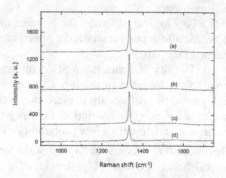

Fig. 2. Raman spectrum for sample 15   **Fig. 3.** Raman spectrum for sample 16

Fig. 4. Scanning microscopy image for sample 6   **Fig. 5.** Scanning microscopy image for sample 16

about 12 microns. The sample numbers 15 - 19 were deposited on silicon substrates, and the sowing was carried out with diamond powder with a particle size of about 1 micron. Samples 20 and 21 were deposited on substrates of pure titanium and the sowing was also performed with the diamond powder with a particle size of about 1 micron.

The analyzes carried out by scanning electron microscopy and Raman spectroscopy show the existence of three groups of samples, as shown in Table 1. Group 1 represents a sample where there was not the deposition of any material. Group 2 represents samples where there was no diamond deposition, but other allotropic carbon forms. Group 3 represents the diamond crystals deposition.

The Raman spectrum of the sample 15, shown in Fig. 2, reveals a prevalence of graphite deposition, since the Raman shift peak is near 1600 cm^{-1}, curve (a) at the periphery and the curve (b) in the center of sample. In sample 16, there were crystals deposition in diamond lattice, with a Raman shift peak around 1330 cm^{-1} as shown in Fig. 3, curves (a) and (b) at the periphery and the curves (c) and (d) in the center of the sample.

Figure 4 shows the scanning electron microscopy image for sample number 6 corresponding to diamond deposition. In Fig. 5, the image shows diamond crystals formation in the sample 16.

5   Clustering and Visualizations

The database used in this paper contains 21 records, divided into three classes, namely: 5 instances for the first class, 7 instances for second class and 9 instances for third class. The first class indicates that there was no material deposition, the second class indicates that there was material deposition, but not diamond crystals and the third class indicates diamond deposition.

Data were normalized, because SOM uses the Euclidean distance to measure distances between vectors. As the ranges of the variables are different, standardization is necessary so that a variable does not stand out compared to other.

The SOM Toolbox is contains function for creation, visualization and analysis of self-Organizing Maps [16]. It is a software package for Matlab computing environment available free of charge from http://www.cis.hut.fi/projects/somtoolbox.

Viewing the results produced by the SOM Toolbox it is necessary to set some parameters for initialization, training and viewing the map. In the initialization it was used the function *som_lininit* function, that initializes a SOM linearly, and for training it was used the *som_batchtrain* function, that trains the SOM with the given data using the batch training algorithm.

The SOM parameters configuration that were used for clustering and data visualization were: the variance is normalized to one, linear initialization of weights, batch training mode, gaussian neighborhood function, 3000 epochs and size of the map 12x12.

After training, the map is displayed in the U-Matrix, with the function *som_show*. In the U-Matrix different colors are used to represent the distances between neurons. A light shade means that they are close, as a darker can be interpreted as a separator clusters. Figure 6 shows the U-matrix color in three different classes, each one representing a cluster of samples. Figure 7 shows the map containing the sample clustering represented by their respective numbers, as follows:

- Red – class 1, no material deposition;
- Yellow – class 2, no diamond deposition, but other allotropic carbon forms;
- Blue – class 3, diamond deposition.

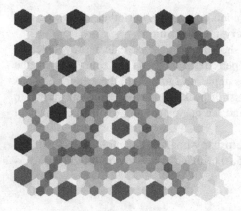

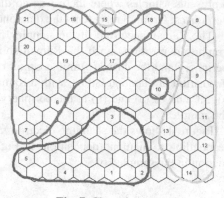

Fig. 6. The U-Matrix   **Fig. 7.** Clustering map

The sample 10 and sample 15 was intentionally marked to show they are arranged outside the cluster they belong to.

Observing Figs. 6 and 7, it is possible to see that the sample 15 (without diamond deposition) was placed between the samples of group 3, which had diamond deposition and away from the samples that did not result in the deposition of diamond, group 2. It can be explained by the deposition parameters in the sample: as well as the samples of group 3, this one was sowing with diamond powder and the other parameters values result in values similar to group samples, except the substrate temperature, which was 10% below the ideal temperature during deposition. The low temperature did not favor the formation of diamond crystals. The sample number 10 (with diamond deposition) was placed next to samples which showed no diamond deposition. This sample showed parameter values similar to other samples of the second group, but the substrate temperature was good throughout the deposition process, while the other group samples were deposited at a temperature below the minimum required to result in diamond crystals deposition.

Another way to understand the U-Matriz is show in Fig. 8. The valleys represent each cluster and de montains represent the distance between them.

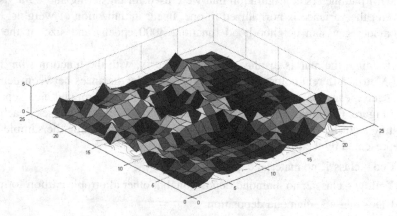

Fig. 8. The U-Matrix surface

Table 2. Quantization error for different map sizes

Map Size	Qe	Te
8x8	1.0066	0
10x8	0.8001	0
10x10	0.6353	0
12x10	0.4300	0
12x12	**0.2431**	0

The quality of the map generated was evaluated with the function *som_quality* through two measurements: Quantization error (Qe) and topographic error (Te). The quantization error represents the average distance of each input vector to the neuron. The topographic error represents the proportion of data vectors in which the first and second winning neurons are not adjacent units. The results obtained for the two metrics are Qe = 0.2431 and Te = 0. It shows, respectively, that the neuron is properly seated on the input vectors and the map represents the data input topology. Table 2 shows the results for the quantization error and topographic error for different map sizes.

6   Conclusions

SOM Toolbox was used to clustering and visualization of the deposition parameters of thin diamond films by HFCVD process. These parameters were used for calibration of a reactor. Analyzing the samples 10 and 15, it is clear how important is the substrate temperature during the process. In the map generated it can be seen that the separation of the samples are consistent with the results of analyzes by scanning electron microscopy and Raman spectroscopy, of the deposited films, showing the algorithm's effectiveness in clustering similar data, helping to identify the optimal parameters for deposition in this reactor.

References

1. Grill, A.: Diamond-Like Carbon State of the Art. Diamond and Related Materials 8(2-5), 428–434 (1999)
2. Matsumoto, S.: Development of Diamond Synthesis Techniques at Low Pressures. Thin Solid Films 368(2), 231–236 (2000)
3. Riley, D.J., Alexander, M.S., Latto, M.N., May, P.W., Pastor-Moreno, G.: A Simple Route to Ohmic Contacts on Low Boron-Doped CVD Diamond. Diamond and Related Materials 12(9), 1460–1462 (2003)
4. Ristic, G.S., Bogdanov, Z.D., Zec, S., Romcevic, N., Dohcevic-Mitrovic, Z., Miljanic, S.S.: Effect of the Substrate Material on Diamond CVD Coating Properties. Materials Chemistry and Physics 80(2), 529–536 (2003)
5. May, P.W., Everitt, N.M., Trevor, C.G., Ashfold, M.N.R., Rosser, K.N.: Diamond Deposition in a Hot-Filament Reactor Using Different Hydrocarbon Precursor Gases. Applied Surface Science 68(3), 299–305 (1993)

6. Spear, K.: Diamond (Ceramic Coating of the Future. Journal of the American Ceramic Society 72(2), 171–191 (1989)
7. Breza, J., Kadlečíková, M., Veselý, M., Frgala, Z., Kudrle, V., Janča, V., Janík, J., Buršík, J.: Raman Bands in Microwave Plasma Assisted Chemical Vapour Deposited Films. Microelectronics Journal 34(11), 1075–1077 (2003)
8. Willard, H.H., Merrit Jr., L.L., Dean, J.A., Settle Jr., F.A.: Instrumental Methods of Analysis. Wadsworth Publishing Company (1988)
9. Kohonen, T.: Self-Organizing Maps, 2nd edn. Springer, Berlin (1997)
10. Gonçalves, M., Andrade Netto, M.L., Costa, J.A.F.: Land-Cover Classification Using Self-Organizing Maps Clustered with Spectral and Spatial Information. In: Mwasiagi, J.I. (ed.) Self-Organizing Maps Applications and Novel Algorithm Design, vol. 1, pp. 299–322. InTech, Viena (2011)
11. Pilsung, K., Hyoung-joo, L., Sungzoon, C., Dongil, K., Jinwoo, P., Chan-Kyoo, P., Seungyong, D.: A Virtual Metrology System for Semiconductor Manufacturing. Expert Systems with Applications 36(10), 12554–12561 (2009)
12. Abonyi, J., Nemeth, S., Vincze, C., Arva, P.: Process Analysis and Product Quality Estimation by Self-Organizing Maps with an Application to Polyethylene Production. Computers in Industry 52(3), 221–234 (2003)
13. Rasanen, T., Kettunen, A., Niemitalo, E., Hiltunen, Y.: Self-Refreshing SOM for Dynamic Process State Monitoring in a Circulating Fluidized Bed Energy Plant. In: 3rd International IEEE Conference on Intelligent Systems (IS 2006), pp. 344–349. IEEE (2006)
14. Sanchez, A.P., Blanco, I.D., Cuadrado-Vega, A.A., Diez-Gonzalez, A.B., Carrera, F.O., Rubio, V.L.: Virtual Sensor Design for Coating Thickness Estimation in a Hot Dip Galvanising Line based on Interpolated SOM Local Models. In: 28th IEEE Annual Conference of the Industrial Electronics Society (IECON 2002), vol. 2, pp. 1584–1589 (2002)
15. Domínguez, M., Fuertes, J.J., Díaz, I., Prada, M.A., Alonso, S., Morán, A.: Monitoring Industrial Processes with SOM-Based Dissimilarity Maps. Expert Systems with Applications 39(8), 7110–7120 (2012)
16. Vesanto, J., Himberg, J., Alhoniemi, E., Parhankangas, J.: Self-Organizing Map in Matlab: the SOM Toolbox. In: 1999 Matlab DSP Conference, pp. 35–40 (1999)

Selection and Fusion of Neural Networks via Differential Evolution

Tiago P.F. de Lima, Adenilton J. da Silva, and Teresa B. Ludermir

Center of Informatics, Federal University of Pernambuco
Av. Jornalista Anibal Fernandes, s/n CEP 50.740-560
Cidade Universitria, Recife - PE, Brazil
{tpfl2,ajs3,tbl}@cin.ufpe.br

Abstract. This paper explores the automatic construction of multi-classifiers systems based on a combination of selection and fusion. The method proposed is composed by two phases: one for designing the individual classifiers and one for clustering patterns of training set and search a set of classifiers for each cluster found. In our experiments, we adopted the artificial neural networks in the classification phase and self-organizing maps in clustering phase. Differential evolution with global and local neighborhoods has been used in this work in order to optimize the parameters and performance of the techniques used in classification and clustering phases. The experimental results have shown that the proposed method has better performance than manual methods and significantly outperforms most of the methods commonly used to combine multiple classifiers for a set of 4 benchmark problems.

Keywords: classifier selection, classifier fusion, artificial neural network, self-organizing map, differential evolution.

1 Introduction

The aim of designing a pattern recognition system is to achieve the best possible classification performance for the given task. In general, a number of classifiers are tested in these systems, and the most appropriate one is chosen for the problem at hand. In an attempt to improve recognition performance of individual classifiers, a common approach is to combine multiple classifiers, forming Multi-Classifier Systems (MCS), also known as ensembles or committees [10,11,12]. The main motivation for using MCS derives from the idea that a pool of different classifiers can offer complementary information about patterns to be classified, improving the effectiveness of the overall recognition process [12]. Algorithms for the construction of MCS may take two main approaches: Classifier Fusion (CF) and Classifier Selection (CS). In the CF techniques, individual classifiers are applied in parallel and their outputs are aggregated using a function (e.g. arithmetic rule, majority vote, another different classifier) to achieve a group consensus [10]. In the CS, the idea is to define some regions of competence in the feature space and attempts to determine the most competent or a subset with the most competent classifiers in each region [11,12,18].

J. Pavón et al. (Eds.): IBERAMIA 2012, LNAI 7637, pp. 149–158, 2012.

While manual design of MCS may be appropriate when there are experienced humans experts with sufficient prior knowledge of the problem to be solved, it is certainly not the case for those real-world problems about which we do not have much prior knowledge. Thus, the focus of this paper is to propose an automatic method (called SFDEGL) that uses a combination of Selection and Fusion (SF) via Differential Evolution with Global and Local neighborhoods (DEGL). The preference for DEGL was motivated by studies that show a better performance in multiobjective optimization [7]. For the classification phase the preference for Artificial Neural Networks (ANN) was motivated by the success in many types of problems with degrees of complexity and different application fields [12]. In the clustering phase, the Self-Organizing Maps (SOM) was chosen because it is one of the classical techniques shows better performance [3].

This paper is organized as follows. Section 2 explains theoretical justification. Section 3 presents the DE and DEGL algorithms. The artificial neural networks optimizing is presented in Sect. 4 and in Sect. 5 selection and fusion optimizing. In Sect. 6 the experiments are described and the results are presented. Finally, in Sect. 7 the conclusion and future works are presented.

2   Theoretical Justification

Let $D = \{D_1, D_2, \cdots, D_L\}$ be a set of L classifiers and $E = \{E_1, E_2, \cdots, E_n\}$ be a set of N ensembles formed from D. The construction of our system is realized by grouping the training set regardless of the class labels in $K > 1$ regions denoted by $R_1, R_2, \cdots, R_K$. For each region $R_j, j = 1, 2, \cdots, K$ is designated an ensemble from E which have the highest accuracy in R_j. Let $E^* \in E$ be the ensemble with the highest average accuracy over the whole features space. Denote by $P(E_i|R_j)$ the probability of correct classification by ensemble E_i in region R_j. Consider $E_{i(j)}$ the ensemble designated for region R_j. The overall probability of correct classification of our system is described in Equation (1),

$$P_c = \sum_{j=1}^{K} P(R_j)P_c(R_j) = \sum_{j=1}^{K} P(R_j)P(E_{i(j)}|R_j) \tag{1}$$

where $P(R_j)$ is the probability that an input $\mathbf{x}$ drawn from the distribution of the problem falls in R_j. To maximize P_c, we assign $E_{i(j)}$ so that

$$P(E_{i(j)}|R_j) \geq P(E_t|R_j), t = 1, \cdots, N. \tag{2}$$

Thus, from Equations (1) and (2), we have that

$$P_c \geq \sum_{j=1}^{K} P(R_j)P(E^*|R_j) \tag{3}$$

Equation (3) shows that the combined scheme performs equal or better than the best ensemble E^*, regardless of the way the features space has been partitioned. However, the model might overtrain, giving a deceptively low training error. Hopefully, nominating an ensemble when it is better than the others will be a basis of a combination scheme less prone to overfitting and spurious errors.

3   Evolutionary Algorithms

Differential Evolution (DE) is a simply evolutionary algorithm for real parameter optimization. DE was firstly proposed by Storn and Price [16] and DE and its variations have been applied with success in different problems [4,17]. Recently DE has also been applied to search for near optimal artificial neural networks parameters [15]. In this section we explain DE and its variation DE with global and local neighborhoods (DEGL) [6].

3.1   Differential Evolution

DE is a population based algorithm that can be used to optimize a numerical function $f : R^D \to R$. DE creates a population P with NP vectors (or individuals) with dimension D. Each individual $X_{i,G} = (x_{j,i,G})$, where $x_{i,j,G}$ is the attribute j of individual i in generation G, is randomly set to a possible solution within the search space. Algorithm 1 shows how DE affects the population until achieve the stopping criterion.

Algorithm 1: Differential Evolution

---

1 **begin**
2   Create a random initial population of NP individuals
3   Evaluate each individual
4   **while** *termination criterion not met* **do**
5   **for** i 1 to NP **do**
6   Select basis vector $X_{basis,G}$
7   Randomly choose $X_{r1,G} \neq X_{basis,G}$
8   Randomly choose $X_{r2,G} \neq X_{r1,G} \neq X_{basis,G}$
9   Calculate the vector donor
                $V_{i,G} = X_{basis,G} + F(X_{r1,G} - X_{r2,G})$
10   Generate $j_{rand} = \text{randint}(1,D)$
11   **for** $j = 1$ to D **do**
12   **if** $j = j_{rand}$ *or* $rand(0,1) < CR$ **then**
13                     $U_{j,i,g} = V_{j,i,g}$
14   **else**
15                     $U_{j,i,g} = X_{j,i,g}$
16   **end**
17   **end**
18   **if** $f(X_{i,G}) \leq f(U_{i,G})$ **then**
19                 $X_{i,G+1} = X_{i,G}$
20   **else**
21                 $X_{i,G+1} = U_{i,G}$
22   **end**
23   **end**
24   **end**
25 **end**

3.2   DE with Local and Global Neighborhood

The DEGL algorithm was proposed in 2009 by Das and Abraham [6]. DEGL uses a neighborhood with ring topology and positive radius $k < (NP - 1)/2$. The neighborhood of a vector $X_{i,G}$ consists of vectors $X_{i-k,G}, \cdots, X_{(i,G)}, \cdots, X_{i+k,G}$. In DEGL for each member in population is created a local donor vector $\mathbf{L}$ described in Equation (4), where $nbest_i$ is the vector with smallest fitness in the neighborhood of $X_{i,G}$ and the integers p and q are randomly selected in the interval $[i - k, i + k]$ with $p \neq q \neq i$.

$$L_{i,G} = X_{i,G} + \alpha \cdot (X_{nbest_i} - X_{i,G}) + \beta \cdot (X_{p,G} - X_{p,G}) \qquad (4)$$

For each member in population a global donor vector $\mathbf{G}$ is created as described in Equation (5), where $gbest$ is the index of the best vector in the population at generation G and r_1 and r_2 are integers randomly selected in the interval $[1, NP]$ with $r_1 \neq r_2 \neq i$ and α and β are scaling factors.

$$g_{i,G} = X_{i,G} + \alpha \cdot (X_{gbest,G} - X_{i,G}) + \beta \cdot (X_{r_1,G} - X_{r_2,G}) \qquad (5)$$

Local and Global donor vectors are combined to compose the vector $V_{i,G}$ as described in Equation (6).

$$V_{i,G} = \omega \cdot g_{i,G} + (1 - \omega) \cdot L_{i,G} \qquad (6)$$

Mutation in DEGL follows Equations (4), (5) and (6), the rest of algorithm DEGL is exactly as the Algorithm 1. The parameter ω is crucial in DEGL [6] and it can be updated in 4 different ways: (i) linear increment where $\omega_G = G/G_{max}$; (ii) Exponential Increment, where $\omega_G = exp(\frac{G}{G_{max}} \cdot \ln(2)) - 1$; (iii) Random Weight Factor, where each individual has a different weight factor $\omega_{i,G}$ randomly selected in interval $(0,1)$; (iv) Self-Adaptive Weight Factor, where each individual has a weight factor $\omega_{i,G}$. The weight factor $\omega_{i,G}$ is initialized in $(0.0, 1.0)$ and is updated in each generation following Equation (7), where, $\omega_{G_{best},G}$ is the weight factor associated with the best individual $\mathbf{X}_{G_{best},G}$.

$$\omega_{i,G} = \omega_{i,G} + F \cdot (\omega_{G_{best},G} - w_{i,G}) + F \cdot (\omega_{r_1,G} - \omega_{r_2,G}) \qquad (7)$$

4   Artificial Neural Network Optimization

As the performance of ANN depends on the architecture and the weights, without using an optimization method, users would have to specify such parameters, falling in the problem of which parameters cannot be the best for a particular problem. Therefore, it is desirable to have an algorithm to find the best possible set of ANN parameters. Thus, for the construction of the set D, the DEGL algorithm was used for 30 generations with 15 individuals randomly generated through a direct encoding scheme, inspired in the works [1,14], as shown in Table 1. The number of individuals and generations were set empirically.

Table 1. Coding scheme of an individual in the ANN optimization

Training Algorithm	Training algorithm Parameters	Epochs	Layers	Neurons	Transfer Functions

The first part of the individual corresponds to the type of training algorithm used and its size is determined by the number of algorithms included in the search process. For this part were considered three algorithms: Resilient Backpropagation (RPROP), Levenberg-Marquardt (LM) and Scaled Conjugate Gradient Backpropagation (SCG). RPROP is used when the highest value is in the first attribute of this part; LM is used when the highest value is in the second attribute and otherwise SCG.

The second part involves the parameter values from the learning algorithm specified in the previous part. Each parameter has a predetermined position, therefore when the algorithm is chosen, it is possible recover: learning rate (lr), increment to weight change ($delt_{inc}$), decrement to weight change ($delt_{dec}$), initial weight change ($delta_0$) and maximum weight ($delta_{max}$), for the RPROP; initial Mu (μ), Mu decrease factor (μ_{dec}), Mu increase factor (μ_{inc}) and maximum Mu (μ_{max}), for the LM; and change in weight for second derivative approximation (σ) and regulating the indefiniteness of the Hessian (λ), for the SGC. All these parameters have real values with the intervals described in Table 2, but they are not directly encoded. They are initialized between $[-1.0, 1.0]$ and a linear map is used to obtain the real values of the parameters.

Table 2. Parameters

Parameter	lr	$delt_{inc}$	$delt_{dec}$	$delta_0$	μ	μ_{dec}	μ_{inc}	μ_{max}	σ	λ
Min. Value	0.006	1	0.3	0.042	0.0006	0.06	6	$6 \cdot 10^9$	$3 \cdot 10^{-5}$	$3 \cdot 10^{-7}$
Max. Value	0.014	2	0.7	0.098	0.0014	0.14	14	$1.4 \cdot 10^{10}$	$7 \cdot 10^{-5}$	$7 \cdot 10^{-7}$

The third part contains information about the numbers of training epochs. If the number of epochs is very large, the network will learn irrelevant aspects of training data. If the number of epoch is very small, the network will be unable to learn the training data. Therefore, the maximum number of training epochs is equal to 100, and it is determined by the position of the attribute with the highest value in this part.

The fourth part contains information on the hidden layers. According to [5], from extension of the Kolmogorov theorem, we need at most two hidden layers, with a sufficient number of units per layer to produce any mappings. It was also proved by [5] that only one hidden layer is sufficient to approximate any continuous function. Nevertheless, in complex problems the use of two hidden layers can facilitate and improve the generalization. Therefore in this paper the neural networks have a maximum of 2 hidden layers. To determinate the number of hidden layers is considered the attribute with the highest value in this part.

The fifth part encodes the number of hidden neurons in each layer. This part considers the maximum number of neurons per layer equal to n. Therefore, this part has 2 sections with dimension $2 \cdot n$. The first n attributes correspond to the first layer and and the next n attributes correspond to the second layer. The number of neurons in each layer is defined by the position of the attribute with the highest value in their respective section. The literature states that the best networks are those with a small number of neurons [13], so we use the maximum number of neurons $n = 10$.

The last part is represented with a 2-tuple vector, and the transfer function is defined by the position of the attribute value with the highest value. If this value is the first attribute then the function Tang-sigmoid is used, otherwise the function Log-sigmoid is used. The transfer function of the output layer is always Pure-linear.

After the initial structure is set, the ANN is trained and for the fitness is considered Equation (8). This equation is composed by: I_{val} - validation error; I_{tra} - training error; I_{hid} - number of hidden layers; and I_{nod} - total number of hidden neurons.

$$I_{fit} = \alpha \cdot I_{val} + \beta \cdot I_{tra} + \gamma \cdot I_{hid} + \delta \cdot I_{nod} \tag{8}$$

In Equation 8, the constants were found empirically as follows: $\alpha = 0.8$, $\beta = 0.145$, $\gamma = 0.05$ and $\delta = 0.005$. These definitions imply that when apparently similar individuals are found, those that have the least training error, structural complexity will prevail. The I_{val} and I_{tra} values are calculated using equation (9), where N and P are the total number of outputs and number of training patterns, respectively; d and o are the desired output (target) and network output (obtained), respectively.

$$I_{nmse} = \frac{100}{PN} \sum_{j=1}^{P} \sum_{i=1}^{N} (d_i - o_i)^2 \tag{9}$$

5   Selection and Fusion Optimization

Our idea of SF is divide-to-conquer, in which the supervised data set used for training are clustered using an unsupervised technique. Such division can be observed as a task to discover the best data clusters without considering the labels of the data set. It is worth mentioning that data clustering is an NP-hard problem when the number of clusters exceeds three [2]. Therefore, many researchers have employed EA to perform the search for the appropriated number of clusters [9]. In this way, to designate an ensemble for each region, the DEGL algorithm was employed for 10 generations with 35 individuals randomly generated following a coding scheme, as shown in Table 3. The number of individuals and generations were set empirically.

The first part of these individuals controls the number of nodes/clusters. The max number of clusters in this work was empirically set to 16. The number of clusters is determined by the position of the attribute with the highest value.

Table 3. Coding scheme of an individual in the SF optimization

Dimension	Train Epochs	Fusion Rules	Number of Designated	Designated

The second part contains information about the numbers of the SOM training epochs. The maximum number of training epochs was defined empirically equal to 10, and it is determined by the position of the attribute with the highest value in this part.

The third part considers the fusion rules for each region. We used six fusion methods: maximum, mean, median, minimum, product and vote. Thus, this part is represented with a 6-tuple vector, and the fusion rule is defined by the position of the attribute with the highest value.

The fourth part is responsible for define the number of designated in each region R_j, $j = 1, 2, \cdots, d$. It considers the maximum number of designated equal to s_{max}. Therefore, this part has d sections with dimension $d \cdot s_{max}$. The first s_{max} attributes correspond to the first region, the next s_{max} attributes correspond to the second region, and so on. The number of designated s for each region is defined by the position of the attribute with the highest value in their respective section. We use empirically the maximum number of classifiers per region $s_{max} = 6$.

The last part involves the designated from each region. This part has d sections with dimension $d \cdot L$, where L is the length of set D. The first L attributes correspond to the first region. The next L attributes correspond to the second region, and so on. In each section, the first attribute represents the classifier D_1, the second attribute represents the classifier D_2, and so on. Therefore when the number of designate s is defined in the previous part, it is possible recover the s highest values for each region in their respective section.

After the initial structure is set, the SFDEGL is trained and for the fitness is considered Equation (10). This equation is composed by: I_{mct} - misclassification in training; I_{nmel} - is the perceptual number of clusters that has no associated examples in training data set; and I_{act} represents the perceptual number of active clusters over the maximum number of active clusters allowed.

$$I_{fit} = \alpha \cdot I_{mct} + \beta \cdot I_{nmel} + \gamma \cdot I_{act} \tag{10}$$

In Equation (10), the constants were found empirically as follows: $\alpha = 0.55$, $\beta = 0.4$ and $\gamma = 0.05$, and are used to control the contribution of each one over the fitness value, and consequently, to guide the search process to find solutions with an equilibrium between such information.

6   Experiments and Results

The experiments were conducted using 4 well-known classification problems found in the UCI repository [8]. To perform the experiments, we used 10 two-fold iterations. At each iteration, the data were randomly divided by the stratification into 70% for training and 30% for testing. The first part was divided

(70% for training and 30% for validation set in the ANN optimization) and the other part was used only to test the final solution. The patterns were normalized to the range $[-1.0, 1.0]$.

Table 4 presents the performance with the misclassifications of the test set, executed in Matlab 2012, and some classical methods. The classical methods considered, executed in Java language with Weka 3.6.6, were bagging (BAG), MultiBoosting (MB), AdaBoost.M1 (ADBO) and Multilayer Perceptron (MLP). The results were expressed as follows: mean (standard deviation). A paired t-test with 90% confidence level was applied to determine whether the differences among the methods were statistically significant. In each line the boldface result means that the method is better than all classical methods. The DEGL emphasized results mean that the method is better than classical methods with non-emphasized results.

Table 4. Misclassification in test set

Problem	MCS							SC
	SFDEGL lin	SFDEGL exp	SFDEGL rand	SFDEGL sa	ADBO	BAG	MB	MLP
Cancer	*0.0335*	*0.0292*	*0.0292*	*0.0278*	0.0368	0.0368	0.0335	0.0421
	(0.0100)	*(0.0073)*	*(0.0083)*	*(0.0146)*	(0.0144)	(0.0115)	(0.0101)	(0.0147)
Diabetes	*0.2309*	**0.2248**	*0.2330*	*0.2322*	0.2652	0.2569	*0.2404*	0.2609
	(0.0197)	**(0.0190)**	*(0.0170)*	*(0.0170)*	(0.0374)	(0.0286)	*(0.0277)*	(0.0418)
Heart	**0.1652**	*0.1728*	*0.1746*	*0.1721*	0.2181	0.1804	0.1956	0.2199
	(0.0241)	*(0.0136)*	*(0.0156)*	*(0.0159)*	(0.0114)	(0.0145)	(0.0153)	(0.0127)
Heartc	**0.1670**	**0.1714**	**0.1736**	**0.1769**	0.2242	0.1967	0.2307	0.2209
	(0.0242)	**(0.0270)**	**(0.0376)**	**(0.0281)**	(0.0312)	(0.0317)	(0.0439)	(0.0409)
Mean	0.1491	0.1495	0.1526	0.1522	0.1861	0.1677	0.1750	0.1859

As it can be observed from Table 4, in most number of problems, at least one of the variants of SFDEGL method achieved better and significant performances when compared with the classical methods. This shows the potential of SF method when EA are correctly employed to optimize classification and clustering techniques. The disadvantage of the SFDEGL method, as demonstrate in Table 5, is that performing the search is very time consuming in comparison with the classical methods. The time is measured in minutes of processing on a computer with Microsoft Windows operational system, 8.0 GB of RAM and a processor Intel Core i7 of 3.40 GHz.

The length of time required for each execution when compared with the classical methods is the main disadvantage of SFDEGL method. While SFDEGL take an average time of 6 minutes, the classical methods take less than 0.5 minute to perform the same task. This huge time difference can be explained by the EA use and also by complexity of the classification and clustering techniques. For high-dimensional problems, the SFDEGL method may need a long time. Thus, for applications for which computational time is a problem, SFDEGL should not

Table 5. Mean time of processing for one interaction

Problem	MCS							SC
	SFDEGL lin	SFDEGL exp	SFDEGL rand	SFDEGL sa	ADBO	BAG	MB	MLP
Cancer	5.0589	5.2985	5.2857	5.2032	0.0428	0.0438	0.0437	0.0044
Diabetes	5.6694	5.0598	5.5599	5.3286	0.0384	0.0440	0.0438	0.0044
Heart	8.8787	7.7036	8.0440	7.8499	0.2945	0.3912	0.3751	0.0392
Heartc	3.9385	4.0562	3.8941	4.4071	0.0651	0.1312	0.0762	0.0132
Mean	5.8864	5.5295	5.6959	5.6972	0.1102	0.1525	0.1347	0.0153

be used; however, the MCS found with SFDEGL has better performance than the classical methods. SFDEGL could be applied in problems where training can be executed offline.

7 Conclusions and Future Works

The methodology is concerned with the development of a method that aims to automatic construct of MCS, based on a combination of SF. First, the set of classifiers is constructed. Second, the training data set is clustered to form regions and we decided one ensemble, from the set of classifiers, to make the decision in each region. For this purpose, hybridizations of recent advances in EA with classical algorithms for classification and data clustering have been proposed. The method SFDEGL showed to be a promising tool, with good results in comparison with classical methods. However, its main limitation is related to the large amount of time required for the solutions to be found. Even so, good results motivate the continuation of studies to advance the search for more effective methods for the construction of MCS.

As future work, the time complexity of SFDEGL must be analyzed, and ways of reducing time consumption must be proposed. A possible idea is to exploit multiprocessor architectures to reduce the computational cost of SFDEGL; differential evolution could be parallelized, for example, in a CUDA GPU. To reduce search time one can also try to develop a less cost activation function, using for example no using a local search algorithm. Another possible future work is to use meta-learning algorithm to select DEGL parameters and weight factor update rule.

References

1. Almeida, L.M., Ludermir, T.B.: A Multi-Objective Memetic and Hybrid Methodology for Optimizing the Parameters and Performance of Artificial Neural Networks. Neurocomputing 73(7-9), 1438–1450 (2010)
2. Brucker, P.: On the Complexity of Clustering Problems. Optimization and Operations Research 157, 45–54 (1978)

3. Chen, Y., Qin, B., Liu, T., Liy, Y., Li, S.: The Comparison of SOM and K-means for Text Clustering. Computer and Information Science 3(2), 268–274 (2010)
4. Cong, A., Cong, W., Lu, Y., Santago, P., Chatziioannou, A.: Differential Evolution Approach for Regularized Bioluminescence Tomography. IEEE Transactions on Biomedical Engineering 57(9), 2229–2238 (2010)
5. Cybenko, G.: Approximation by Superpositions of a Sigmoidal Function. Mathematics of Control, Signals, and Systems (MCSS) 2(4), 303–314 (1989)
6. Das, S., Abraham, A., Chakraborty, U., Konar, A.: Differential Evolution Using a Neighborhood-Based Mutation Operator. IEEE Transactions on Evolutionary Computation 13(3), 526–553 (2009)
7. Das, S., Suganthan, P.: Differential Evolution – A Survey of the State-of-the-Art. IEEE Transactions on Evolutionary Computation 15(1), 4–31 (2011)
8. Frank, A., Asuncion, A.: UCI Machine Learning Repository (2010), http://archive.ics.uci.edu/ml
9. Hruschka, E., Campello, R., Freitas, A., de Carvalho, A.: A Survey of Evolutionary Algorithms for Clustering. IEEE Transactions on Systems, Man, and Cybernetics, Part C: Applications and Reviews 39(2), 133–155 (2009)
10. Kittler, J., Hatef, M., Duin, R., Matas, J.: On Combining Classifiers. IEEE Transactions on Pattern Analysis and Machine Intelligence 20(3), 226–239 (1998)
11. Kuncheva, L.: Clustering-and-Selection Model for Classifier Combination. In: 4th International Conference on Knowledge-Based Intelligent Engineering Systems and Allied Technologies (KES 2000), vol. 1, pp. 185–188 (2000)
12. Kuncheva, L.: Combining Pattern Classifiers – Methods and Algorithms. Wiley-Interscience (2004)
13. Liao, K., Fildes, R.: The Accuracy of a Procedural Approach to Specifying Feedforward Neural Networks for Forecasting. Computers & Operations Research 32(8), 2151–2169 (2005)
14. da Silva, A., Mineu, N., Ludermir, T.: Evolving Artificial Neural Networks Using Adaptive Differential Evolution. In: Kuri-Morales, A., Simari, G.R. (eds.) IBERAMIA 2010. LNCS, vol. 6433, pp. 396–405. Springer, Heidelberg (2010)
15. Slowik, A.: Application of an Adaptive Differential Evolution Algorithm With Multiple Trial Vectors to Artificial Neural Network Training. IEEE Transactions on Industrial Electronics 58(8), 3160–3167 (2011)
16. Storn, R., Price, K.: Differential Evolution – A Simple and Efficient Heuristic for global Optimization over Continuous Spaces. Journal of Global Optimization 11, 341–359 (1997)
17. Vasile, M., Minisci, E., Locatelli, M.: An Inflationary Differential Evolution Algorithm for Space Trajectory Optimization. IEEE Transactions on Evolutionary Computation 15(2), 267–281 (2011)
18. Woods, K., Kegelmeyer Jr., W.P., Bowyer, K.: Combination of Multiple Classifiers Using Local Accuracy Estimates. IEEE Transactions on Pattern Analysis and Machine Intelligence 19(4), 405–410 (1997)

Prototype Selection with Compact Sets and Extended Rough Sets

Yenny Villuendas-Rey[1,3], Yailé Caballero-Mota[2], and María Matilde García-Lorenzo[3]

[1] Computer Science Department, University of Ciego de Ávila, Carr. a Morón km 9 ½, Cuba
yennyv@informatica.unica.cu
[2] Computer Science Department, University of Camagüey, Circunv. Norte km 3 ½, Cuba
yaile.caballero@reduc.edu.cu
[3] Computer Science Department, University of Las Villas, Carr. a Camajuaní, km 5 ½, Cuba
mmgarcia@uclv.edu.cu

Abstract. In this paper, we propose a generalization of classical Rough Sets, the Nearest Neighborhood Rough Sets, by modifying the indiscernible relation without using any similarity threshold. We also combine these Rough Sets with Compact Sets, to obtain a prototype selection algorithm for Nearest Prototype Classification of mixed and incomplete data as well as arbitrarily dissimilarity functions. We introduce a set of rules to a priori predict the performance of the proposed prototype selection algorithm. Numerical experiments over repository databases show the high quality performance of the method proposed in this paper according to classifier accuracy and object reduction.

Keywords: prototype selection, compact sets, rough sets.

1   Introduction

Case based reasoning is one of the key topics in Artificial Intelligence. Among case based classifiers, the nearest neighbor (NN) classifier is one of the most simple and widely-used. However, it needs to store completely the training instances, and to determine the class of a new pattern, it needs to compare it with every instance in the training set. In addition, noisy or mislabeled instances can degrade the NN accuracy. Several prototype selection [1-3] and prototype generation [4] methods have been proposed so far to overcome these drawbacks, but dealing with mixed data types and arbitrarily dissimilarities is still a challenge for Nearest Prototype Classification. Recently, Rough Sets have been used to both feature and instance selection [5, 6], but the complete possibilities of them have not been exploited. On the other hand, the capabilities of error-based editing methods and condensing methods have not been combined in order to obtain a reduced and accurate prototype set for mixed data types. To achieve this objective, we introduce a generalization of classical Rough Sets, the Nearest Neighborhood Rough Sets and combine them with Compact Set structuralization. The main contributions of this paper are: The redefinition of the positive regions of the decision classes in the context of Neighborhood Rough Sets, without using any similarity threshold, the combination of error-based editing and

J. Pavón et al. (Eds.): IBERAMIA 2012, LNAI 7637, pp. 159–168, 2012.

condensing approaches to prototype selection, to obtain a highly reduced and accurate prototype set, a graceful handling of mixed and incomplete data, as well as arbitrarily dissimilarity functions and a set of rules to a priori predict the performance of the proposed prototype selection method in a dataset.

The contribution is organized as following: in the next section, we cover some general concepts about Compact Sets and Rough Sets. Then, we introduce the proposed prototype selection schema. Section 4 covers the proposed rules and its use for a priori determining the performance of our algorithm. This section also contains several numerical experiments to determine the performance of the proposal with respect state of the art prototype selection methods, using different dissimilarity functions. Section 5 gives the conclusions.

2   General Concepts of Compact Sets and Rough Sets

2.1   Rough Sets

Rough Set Theory (RST) has proved usefulness for data analysis, and it has offered an attractive theoretic base for the solution of many problems within Machine Learning. Rough Sets Theory was proposed by Pawlak in 1982 [7]. RST philosophy is based on the assumption that each object x of an universe U has associated a certain amount of information (data and knowledge), expressed by means of some attributes that describe the object x. In RST, the basic structure of information is the Information System. An Information System is a pair S= (U, A), where U is a non-empty finite set of objects called the Universe and $A=\{a_1, a_2,...,a_n\}$ is a non-empty finite set of attributes. The classification data is represented as a Decision System, which is any Information System of the form $DS = A \cup \{d\}$, where $d \notin A$ is the decision attribute. Each attribute a_i is defined over a domain v_i. in RST, exists a function f: $UxA \rightarrow V$, $V=\{v_1,v_2,...,v_n\}$ such that $f(x,a_i) \in v_j$ for each $a_i \in A$, $x \in U$, called Information function [7]. The decision attribute d induces a partition of the universe U of objects. Let be the sets $Y_i=\{x \in U: x(d)=i\}$, $\{Y_1,...,Y_b\}$ is a collection of equivalence classes, called decision classes, where the objects belong to the same class if and only if they have the same value at the decision attribute d. Classical definitions of lower and upper approximations of concepts were originally introduced with reference to an indiscernible relation, which assumed to be an equivalence relation. The previous definitions of RST consider indiscernible the objects having the same values of a subset of attributes B, that is, the objects (x,y) are indiscernible if x(i)=y(i) for each attribute $i \in B$, where x(i) denotes the value of attribute i in object x. When dealing with continuous attributes, an indiscernible relation defined as previous is not appropriate, since some closed values may be similar, but discernible. An extension of the classical RST is to modify the concept of indiscernible objects, such that the similar objects according to a similarity relation R are grouped together in the same class. The similarity relations generate similarity classes, for ach object $x \in U$. The similarity class of x according to a similarity relation R is denoted by $R(x)$, and defined below.

$$R(x) = \left\{ y \in U : yRx \right\} \tag{2.2}$$

An example of extension of the RST based on similarity relations was presented by Slowinski and Vanderpooten [8]. Let be $X \subseteq U$ and R a binary, reflexive relation over U, and R^{-1} the inverse of R. They defined the lower and upper approximations of a set X as the following:

$$R_*(X) = \left\{ x \in U : R^{-1}(x) \subseteq X \right\} \tag{2.3}$$

$$R^*(X) = \left\{ x \in U : R^{-1}(x) \cap X \neq \phi \right\} \tag{2.4}$$

These generalizations allow handling mixed data, and using specific similarity functions. As shown, Rough Set Theory has several advantages to data analysis. It is based on the original data only and does not need any external information; no assumptions about data are necessary, and it is suitable for analyzing both quantitative and qualitative features [5].

2.2   Compact Sets

In Pattern Recognition, particularly in the Logical Combinatorial Approach, exist several data structuralization procedures [9-11]. One of them is the Compact Sets structuralization. Compact Sets are the connected components of a Maximum Similarity Graph (MSG). A Maximum Similarity Graph is a directed graph that connects each object with its most similar neighbors. Formally, let be $G = (X, \theta)$ a MSG for a set of objects X, with arcs θ. In this graph, two objects $x_i, x_j \in X$ form an arc $(x_i, x_j) \in \theta$ if $\max_{x \in X}\{sim(x_i, x)\} = sim(x_i, x_j)$, where $sim(x_i, x_j)$ is a similarity function. Usually $sim(x_i, x_j) = 1 - \Delta(x_i, x_j)$ and $\Delta(x_i, x_j)$ is a dissimilarity function. In case of ties, the Maximum Similarity Graph establishes a connection between the object and each of its nearest neighbors. As mentioned before, Compact Sets are the connected components of such graph. Formally, a subset $N \neq \emptyset$ of X is a Compact Set if and only if [11]:

$$a) \forall x_j \in X \left[x_i \in N \wedge \left(\begin{array}{c} \max\limits_{\substack{x_i \in X \\ x_i \neq 0_j}}\{sim(x_i, x_j)\} = sim(x_i, x_j) \\ \vee \max\limits_{\substack{x_i \in X \\ x_i \neq x_j}}\{sim(x_j, x_i)\} = sim(x_j, x_i) \end{array} \right) \right] \Rightarrow x_j \in N$$

$$b) \forall x_i, x_j \in N, \exists x_{i_1}, \cdots, x_{i_q} \in N \left[\begin{array}{c} x_i = x_{i_1} \wedge x_j = x_{i_q} \wedge \forall p\,\{1, \cdots, q-1\} \\ \left[\begin{array}{c} \max\limits_{\substack{x_t \in X \\ x_t \neq 0_{i_p}}} \left\{ sim\left(x_{i_p}, x_t\right)\right\} = sim\left(x_{i_p}, x_{i_{p+1}}\right) \\ \vee \max\limits_{\substack{x_t \in X \\ x_t \neq x_{i_p}}} \left\{ sim\left(x_{i_{p+1}}, x_t\right)\right\} = sim\left(x_{i_{p+1}}, x_{i_p}\right) \end{array} \right] \end{array} \right]$$

c) Every isolated object is a Compact Set, degenerated.

As well as Rough Sets, Compact Sets have several advantages to data analysis. They do not assume any properties of data, do not need any parameter for their construction, except of the similarity function to compare two objects, and directly handle mixed as well as incomplete data. In addition, the objects are connected only to their most similar objects in the training matrix, which is valuable information particularly in high Bayes risk zones. The arcs between objects also contribute to predict the certainty of the correct classification of an object [12].

3   Prototype Selection with Compact Sets and Extended Rough Sets

3.1   Nearest Neighborhood Rough Sets as Extended Rough Sets

One of the generalizations made to Rough Set Theory is the one introduced by Hu et al. [6], the Neighborhood Rough Sets. Given an arbitrary object $x \in X$, a set of attributes $B \subseteq A$, and a dissimilarity function Δ, the neighborhood $\partial_B(x)$ of x in B is defined as the set of objects which dissimilarity values with respect x, taking into consideration only the attributes in B, is lower than a threshold ∂.

$$\partial_B(x) = \{y | y \in X, \Delta^B(x, y) \le \partial\} \tag{3.1}$$

As mention by Hu et al., a neighborhood granule degrades to an equivalent class if the threshold $\partial = 0$. In this case, the objects in the same neighborhood granule are equivalent to each other. Also, a neighborhood relation N on the universe U can be written as a relation matrix $M(N) = (r_{ij})_{n \times n}$, (equation 2.6) and if Δ satisfies the properties of reflexivity and symmetry, N will also satisfy these properties [6].

$$r_{i,j} = \begin{cases} 1 & if \ \Delta^B(x_i, x_j) \le \partial \\ 0 & otherwise \end{cases} \tag{3.2}$$

However, to use Neighborhood Rough sets, it is needed to set the similarity threshold ∂, which is very difficult in practice. To overcome this drawback, it is introduced the Minimum Neighborhood Rough Sets. This approach, does not to use any similarity threshold, instead, it is based on a redefinition of the neighborhood $\partial_B(x_i)$ of x_i in feature space B using the Maximum Similarity Graph concepts. The neighborhood of an object x_i will be formed by its predecessors (the objects whose nearest neighbor is x_i) and its successors (the nearest neighbors of x_i) in a Maximum Similarity Graph. The new nearest neighborhood $N_B(x_i)$ of x_i in feature space B can be written as:

$$N_B(x_i) = \{x_j | (x_i, x_j) \in \theta \lor (x_j, x_i) \in \theta\} \tag{3.3}$$

where are the arcs in a Maximum Similarity Graph. Some objects will have a pure neighborhood, that is, a neighborhood composed only by objects of the same class, and others will have a heterogeneous neighborhood. The former will be included in the lower approximation of the decision classes and the later will be in the upper approximation. Let be $Y_i \in Y$ a decision class, its positive region is given by:

$$POS_B(Y_i) = x_i \,|x_i \in X, \forall_{x_j \in N_B(x_i)}, x_i(d) = x_j(d) = Y_i \qquad (3.4)$$

So, the positive region of the decision classes will be formed by objects with pure neighborhood, while boundary region is the set of samples having a heterogeneous neighborhood.

3.2   Prototype Selection Based on Nearest Neighborhood Rough Sets

The proposed approach works in two stages: editing stage and condensation stage. On the editing stage, it uses the previously introduced Neighborhood Rough Sets to smooth classification boundaries for Nearest Neighbor classifiers, removing the objects not included in the positive region of the decision classes. The objects not in the positive region have an uncertainty degree about of their correct classification. Those objects are either having a nearest neighbor of different class (a successor in the Maximum Similarity Graph), or being the nearest neighbor of an object of another class (a predecessor in a Maximum Similarity Graph). Although the Nearest Neighbor classifier can be beneficiated with this smoothing process, it includes an additional processing on condensation stage to reduce the training matrix. To accomplish this objective, the algorithm computes compact sets of the remaining objects (the ones in the positive region of each decision class). Taking into consideration that all noisy objects are not included in the Compact Sets computation (CS), and that the CS is made class by class, much condensation is obtained, because objects of the same class usually are very similar to each other. In addition, the algorithm condenses each compact set to a single object, a representative prototype p (see Fig. 1).

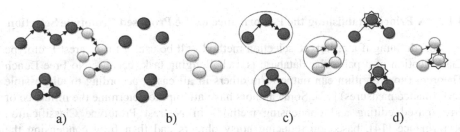

a)   b)   c)   d)

Fig. 1. Proposed algorithm. It first computes a Maximum Similarity Graph of the objects (a) and then computes the Positive Region of the decision (b). Then, it computes the Compact Sets of each class (c) and then selects a representative prototype for each Compact Set (d).

The algorithm (see Fig. 2) selects as representative prototype the object that maximizes the similarity with respect to other objects in the compact set CS, that is, the object for which the similarity value is the maximum. It uses Rough Sets to detect noisy or mislabeled objects in the editing stage, and detect the structure of classes using Compact Sets The algorithm is based on the original data only and does not need any additional information; no assumptions about data are needed, and it is suitable for dealing with both quantitative and qualitative features, and with missing values.

Two stage algorithm for Nearest Prototype Classification
Inputs: Training set T, Attribute set B, Dissimilarity Δ. Outputs: Prototype set P

Editing Stage
1. Obtain a Maximum Similarity Graph, $G = (T, \theta)$ of the objects in T
2. Compute the positive region of the Decision System as:
$POS_B(Y) = \bigcup_i POS_B(Y_i)$, where
$POS_B(Y_i) = x_i \mid x_i \in X, \forall_{x_j \in N_B(x_i)}, x_i(d) = x_j(d) = Y_i$
3. Remove the objects not included in the positive region of the Decision System
$T = T - POS_B(Y)$
Condensing Stage
4. $P = \emptyset$
5. For each decision class Y_i:
    5.1. Compute compact sets CS_i of $POS_B(Y_i)$
       For each $cs \in CS_i$
    5.1.1. Select a representative prototype p as:
$$p = \underset{o \in cs}{\operatorname{argmax}}\left\{\sum_{i \in cs} sim(o, i)\right\}$$
    5.1.2. $P = P \cup \{p\}$
6. Return P

Fig. 2. Algorithm for Nearest Prototype Classification

4 Experimental Results

4.1 A Priori Establishing the Performance of the Proposed Prototype Selection

A priori defining if a prototype selection method will be useful for Nearest Prototype Classification of a particular database is a challenging task, because No Free Lunch Theorem (no algorithm can outperform others in all cases, according to all possible performance measures) [13]. Some authors have attempt to determine the influence of error based editing and condensing methods in Nearest Prototype Classification performance [14], based on reducing noisy objects and then fully condensing the remaining training set. However, on unbalanced data sets, the minority class may be entirely deleted by the editing method. As the proposed algorithm exploits the boundary smoothing property of error based editing and the reduction of condensing algorithms, it is needed to a priori determine in which kind of data our proposal will have a good performance, and in which data it should not be applied. To accomplish this objective, a set of rules was designed. Although several data characteristic can be taken into consideration to determine the proposed algorithm performance, it is considered that class balance and class overlapping are the main influences in Nearest Prototype Classification. Class balance influences error-based editing methods, because the objects of minority class can be considered as noisy objects, and then deleted by the editing procedure. In this study, the class balance was measured using the Imbalance Ratio (IR), as the ratio between object count of majority class and object count of minority class. On the other hand, class overlapping also impacts classifier accuracy, increasing the Bayes's risk. Class overlapping (CO) was measure as the ratio of objects having a Nearest Neighbor of different class. Both data characteristic are used to decide to apply or not the algorithm, introducing a set of simple learning rules (see Fig. 3). To test the efficiency of the proposed rules, fifteen databases of the Machine Learning Repository of University of California at Irvine [15] were used. The description of used databases is given in Table 1.

Table 1. Description of the databases used in numerical experiments, and results of the proposed rules in predicting the performance of our algorithm. In bold the exception

Databases	Attributes (Categorical -Numerical)	Obj.	Missing values	IR	CO	Predicted result	Real result
anneal	29-9	798	x	86.51	0.05	Good	Good
autos	10-16	205	x	23.13	0.25	Bad	Bad
breast-c	9-0	286	x	2.36	0.50	**Bad**	**Good**
car	6-0	1728		18.69	0.75	Bad	Bad
colic	15-7	368	x	1.72	0.22	Good	Good
cylinder	20-20	512	x	1.36	0.23	Bad	Bad
dermat.	1-33	366	x	5.62	0.06	Good	Good
heart-h	7-6	294	x	1.77	0.22	Good	Good
ionosphere	0-34	351		1.78	0.13	Good	Good
labor	6-8	57		1.85	0.14	Good	Good
molecular	58-0	105		1.05	0.24	Good	Good
tae	2-3	151		1.09	0.40	Bad	Bad
trains	29-4	10	x	1.25	0.43	Bad	Bad
vehicle	0-18	946		1.10	0.30	Good	Good
vowel	3-9	990		1.12	0.01	Good	Good

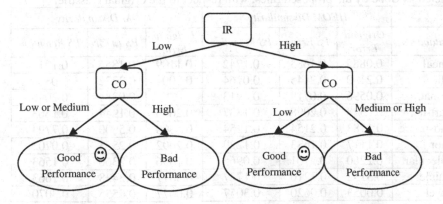

Fig. 3. Rules to determine the performance of the algorithm

The IR and CO for every database were calculated, and the rules below were applied. Then, the algorithm was run (see Table 1). To apply the rules, it is consider IR to be low if IR< 10, and high otherwise. In case of CO, it is considered CO≤0.20, medium 0.20<CO≤0.35 and high CO>0.35. These thresholds were obtaining by discretizing the values of CO and IR in three intervals (low, medium and high), and two intervals (low and high), respectively. It is consider the algorithm to have a good performance if the difference in classifier error on testing data is lower than 10%, and to have a bad performance otherwise. The results show that the proposed rules are able to predict the performance of the prototype selection algorithm accurately, with only one exception, the breast-c database. However, on most cases the rules are good enough to predict the algorithms performance. Another advantage of the proposed set of rules with respect to other validation procedures is that it does not need to apply the prototype selection schema into an independent dataset, to predict performance. It is only needed to compute the values of Class Overlapping and Imbalance Ratio, and then decide if the prototype selection schema will perform good or not.

4.2   Description of the Experiments

To compare the performance of the proposed prototype selection algorithm, four prototype selection methods were selected. Among them, there are two editing methods, MSEditA and MSEditB, proposed in [12] and two condensing methods, the Generalized Condensed Nearest Neighbor (GCNN) [16] and CSESupport [17]. To compare the results, 10-fold cross validation was used and both classifier error and object retention rates were measured. Classifier error (Error) was computed as the ratio of misclassified objects, and object retention was calculated as the ratio between selected prototypes and the amount of objects in the dataset. The experiment were carried out with two dissimilarity functions, HEOM and HVDM proposed in [18].

As shown in Table 2, the proposed PS obtains a highly reduced prototype set, without a significant drop on classifier accuracy. However, to establish if the differences in performance of the proposed PS with respect to the original classifier

Table 2. Results of the new Prototype Selection (PS) schema in databases predicted as Good by the proposed rules, with respect to the original classifier

Databases	HEOM Dissimilarity			HVDM Dissimilarity		
	Original Error	PS Error	PS Retention	Original Error	PS Error	PS Retention
anneal	0.0885	0.1685	0.1742	0.1109	0.1856	0.1717
colic	0.2190	0.2445	0.0764	0.2004	0.2222	0.0385
dermat.	0.0596	0.0719	0.1913	0.0294	0.0384	0.2040
heart-h	0.2548	0.2098	0.1837	0.2606	0.1944	0.1663
ionosphere	0.1783	0.2154	0.1254	0.5000	0.5000	0.7794
labor	0.1117	0.1683	0.1229	0.2092	0.2583	0.0702
molecular	0.2260	0.2701	0.0965	0.1096	0.2366	0.1563
vehicle	0.3132	0.3216	0.1727	0.3017	0.3438	0.1663
vowel	0.0053	0.0620	0.3057	0.0077	0.0555	0.3070

Table 3. p-values of the Wicoxon test comparing PS aginst others, according to classifier error and object redcution. In bold significant differences in performance.

HEOM dissimilarity			HVDM dissimilarity		
Our Method vs.	Error	Object retention	Our Method vs.	Error	Object retention
Original	0.139	**0.000**	Original	0.066	**0.000**
MSEditA	0.575	**0.005**	MSEditA	0.173	**0.005**
MSEditB	0.028 *	**0.005**	MSEditB	0.241	**0.005**
GCNN	0.074	**0.005**	GCNN	0.066	**0.005**
CSESupport	0.721	0.114	CSESupport	0.139	**0.044**

* our method had worse performance.

and other prototype selection algorithms were significant or not, it was used the Wilcoxon test, with a 95% confidence. It was applied the test four times (Error with HEOM dissimilarity, Retention with HEOM dissimilarity, Error with HVDM dissimilarity and Retention with HVDM dissimilarity). In each case, it was compared the performance of the proposed PS with respect to the original classifier and every other prototype selection algorithm. Table 3 shows the resulting p-values of the test.

As shown in Table 3, our proposal does not heavily depend of the dissimilarity function used. According to classifier error, the proposal obtains very good results. It ties with the original classifier and with all other methods except MSEditB using HEOM dissimilarity, having p-values of the Wilcoxon test greater than 0.05. In addition, it obtains the best results according to object reduction, being significantly better than every other method, except CSESupport with HEOM dissimilarity (p-values lower than 0.05). It is important to mention that the proposed method maintains the classifier accuracy using only a very reduced prototype set. The above results show that the Nearest Neighborhood Rough Set and Compact Set prototype selection algorithm leads to an edited set with high accuracy and also with much less objects than the original training set. The proposed approach also allows handling imbalanced datasets, but with lower class overlapping. It also handles balanced data with highly or medium class overlapping. However, to effectively deal with highly imbalanced and overlapped dataset, it is needed to explore other characteristics of Rough Sets, such as the limit region of the decision.

5   Conclusions

Nearest Prototype Classification offers several advantages to Nearest Neighbor classifiers. However, dealing with mixed data is still a challenge for prototype selection algorithms. In this article it is introduced a novel technique to Nearest Prototype Classification, and it is given a set of rules to a priori determine the performance of the proposed algorithm. It is based on the newly introduced Nearest Neighbor Rough Sets, and it combines error-based editing and condensation. Numerical experiments show the prototype selection algorithm maintains classifier accuracy, using only a reduced prototype set.

References

1. García-Osorio, C., Haro-García, A., Gaecía-Pedrajas, N.: Democratic Instance Selection A Linear Complexity Instance Selection Algorithm Based on Classifier Ensemble Concepts. Artificial Intelligence 174(5-6), 410–441 (2010)
2. Nikolaidis, K., Goulemas, J.Y., Wu, Q.H.: A Class Boundary Preserving Algorithm for Data Condensation. Pattern Recognition 44(3), 704–715 (2011)
3. Zafra, A., Gibaja, E.L., Ventura, S.: Multiple Instance Learning with Multiple Objective Genetic Programming for Web Mining. Applied Soft Computing 11(1), 93–102 (2011)
4. Triguero, I., Derrac, J., García, S., Herrera, F.: A Taxonomy and Experimental Study on Prototype Generation for Nearest Neighbor Classification. IEEE Transactions on Systems, Man, and Cybernetics, Part C: Applications and Reviews 42(1), 86–100 (2012)
5. Caballero, Y., Bello, R., Salgado, Y., García, M.M.: A Method to Edit Training Set Based on Rough Sets. Intl. Journal of Computational Intelligence Research 3(3), 219–229 (2007)
6. Hu, Q., Yu, D., Liu, J., Wu, C.: Neighborhood Rough Sets Based Heterogeneous Feature Selection. Information Sciences 178(18), 3577–3594 (2008)
7. Pawlak, Z.: Rough Sets. Intl. Journal of Parallel Programming 11(5), 341–356 (1982)
8. Slowinski, R., Vanderpooten, D.: A Generalized Definition of Rough Approximations Based on Similarity. IEEE Trans. on Knowledge and Data Eng. 12(2), 331–336 (2000)
9. Ruiz-Shulcloper, J., Guzmán-Arenas, A., Martinez Trinidad, J.F.: Logical Combinatorial Approach to Pattern Recognition Feature Selection and Supervised Classification. Editorial Politécnica, Mexico (2000)
10. Martínez Trinidad, J.F., Guzmán-Arenas, A.: The Logical Combinatorial Approach to Pattern Recognition An Overview through Selected Works. Pattern Recognition 34(4), 741–751 (2001)
11. Ruiz-Shulcloper, J., Abidi, M.A.: Logical Combinatorial Pattern Recognition A Review. In: Pandalai, S.G. (ed.) Recent Research Developments in Pattern Recognition, pp. 133–176. Transword Research Networks, USA (2002)
12. García-Borroto, M., Villuendas-Rey, Y., Carrasco-Ochoa, J.A., Martínez-Trinidad, J.F.: Using Maximum Similarity Graphs to Edit Nearest Neighbor Classifiers. In: Bayro-Corrochano, E., Eklundh, J.-O. (eds.) CIARP 2009. LNCS, vol. 5856, pp. 489–496. Springer, Heidelberg (2009)
13. Wolpert, D.H., MacReady, W.G.: No Free Lunch Theorems for Optimization. IEEE Transactions on Evolutionary Computation 1(1), 67–82 (1997)
14. Dasarathy, B.V., Sanchez, J.S., Townsend, S.: Nearest Neighbour Editing and Condensing Tools Synergy Exploitation. Pattern Analysis & Applications 3(1), 19–30 (2000)
15. Merz, C.J., Murphy, P.M.: UCI Repository of Machine Learning Databases. Dept. of Information and Computer Science. University of California at Irvine, Irvine (1998)
16. Chou, C.H., Kuo, B.A., Cheng, F.: The Generalized Condensed Nearest Neighbor Rule as a Data Reduction Technique. In: 18th International Conference on Pattern Recognition (ICPR 2006), vol. 2, pp. 556–559. IEEE (2006)
17. García-Borroto, M., Villuendas-Rey, Y., Carrasco-Ochoa, J.A., Martínez-Trinidad, J.F.: Finding Small Consistent Subset for the Nearest Neighbor Classifier Based on Support Graphs. In: Bayro-Corrochano, E., Eklundh, J.-O. (eds.) CIARP 2009. LNCS, vol. 5856, pp. 465–472. Springer, Heidelberg (2009)
18. Wilson, R.D., Martinez, T.R.: Improved Heterogeneous Distance Functions. Journal of Artificial Intelligence Research 6, 1–34 (1997)

Improving SMOTE with Fuzzy Rough Prototype Selection to Detect Noise in Imbalanced Classification Data

Nele Verbiest[1], Enislay Ramentol[2], Chris Cornelis[1,3], and Francisco Herrera[3]

[1] Dept. of Applied Mathematics and Computer Science, Ghent University, Belgium
Nele.Verbiest@UGent.be
[2] Dept. of Computer Science, University of Camagüey, Cuba
enislayr@yahoo.es
[3] Dept. of Computer Science and AI, University of Granada, Spain
chriscornelis@ugr.es,
herrera@decsai.ugr.es

Abstract. In this paper, we present a prototype selection technique for imbalanced data, Fuzzy Rough Imbalanced Prototype Selection (FRIPS), to improve the quality of the artificial instances generated by the Synthetic Minority Over-sampling TEchnique (SMOTE). Using fuzzy rough set theory, the noise level of each instance is measured, and instances for which the noise level exceeds a certain threshold level are deleted. The threshold is determined using a wrapper approach that evaluates the training Area Under the Curve of candidate subsets. This proposal aims to clean noisy data before applying SMOTE, such that SMOTE can generate high quality artificial data.

Experiments on artificial data show that FRIPS in combination with SMOTE outperforms state-of-the-art methods, and that it particularly performs well in the presence of noise.

Keywords: SMOTE, imbalanced classification, AUC, fuzzy rough set theory.

1 Introduction

Imbalanced classification has become an important field in data mining. In contrast to traditional classification, it deals with datasets where one or more classes are under-represented. In this paper we consider the two-class case where one class (the majority or negative class) is over-represented and the other class (the minority or positive class) is under-represented. The Imbalance Ratio (IR, the size of the majority class divided by the size of the minority class) characterizes the imbalance of the datasets: a dataset with IR 1 is perfectly balanced, while datasets with a higher IR are more imbalanced.

Standard data mining techniques might not always work well for the imbalanced problem, as their results are often biased towards the majority class. One cause for this is that data mining techniques are often based on global quantities

J. Pavón et al. (Eds.): IBERAMIA 2012, LNAI 7637, pp. 169–178, 2012.
© Springer-Verlag Berlin Heidelberg 2012

like classification accuracy. Instead of classification accuracy, one may use the Receiver Operating Characteristic (ROC) curve. It plots the ratio of correctly classified minority instances against the ratio of correctly classified majority instances. As a result, the Area Under the ROC Curve (AUC, [2]) can be used to evaluate data mining techniques for imbalanced data. It reflects the trade-off between correctly classified minority and majority instances.

Many techniques have been developed for imbalanced data, both on the classifier level and on the data level. In this work we focus on the data level, i.e., on preprocessing techniques that transform datasets such that they are better suited for the imbalanced classification task. More specifically, we focus on the Synthetic Minority Over-sampling TEchnique (SMOTE, [4]) that forms new minority instances by interpolation to balance the dataset.

As SMOTE is sometimes too forceful in adding new minority instances, some improvements on the technique have been studied. E.g., Borderline-SMOTE [11] only re-samples border instances, while SMOTE with Tomek links and SMOTE-ENN [1] apply data cleaning after re-sampling the minority instances.

In this paper, we present another improvement of SMOTE that cleans the data before applying SMOTE, that is, we try to remove noisy instances from the data, such that the quality of the instances introduced by SMOTE is better. As there is no reason to assume that only the majority instances can be noisy, we both remove minority and majority instances.

We proceed as follows: for each instance, we calculate its noise level using a measure based on fuzzy rough set theory [7]. Next, we remove all instances that have a noise level higher than a certain threshold, which is determined by a wrapper procedure that evaluates different thresholds based on the training AUC of the resulting subsets of instances. After this data preprocessing, we finally apply SMOTE. We call this technique Fuzzy Rough Imbalanced Prototype Selection (FRIPS) and call it FRIPS-SMOTE when it is applied in combination with SMOTE.

Note that we use the term *prototype* selection instead of *instance* selection. The reason for this is that our technique is specifically developed to improve the K Nearest Neighbor (KNN, [5]) classifier. In the KNN context, instance selection is often called prototype selection [8].

We use KNN because it is a simple classification method that does not impose assumptions on the data. Due to its local nature it has low bias, more specifically, the error rate of 1NN asymptotically never exceeds twice the optimal Bayes error rate We use the 1NN classifier as this classifier is most susceptible to noisy data.

The remainder of this paper is structured as follows: In Sect. 2.1 we introduce a noise measure based on fuzzy rough set theory, that is used in the FRIPS algorithm introduced in Sect. 2.2. In Sect. 3.1 we describe the set-up of the experimental evaluation. In Sect. 3.2 we present the results of the experimental evaluation, which show the good performance of FRIPS. We conclude and suggest future research directions in Sect. 4.

2   Fuzzy Rough Imbalanced Prototype Selection

2.1   A Noise Measure Based on Fuzzy Rough Set Theory

We consider a decision system $(X, \mathcal{A} \cup \{d\})$ that consists of a set of instances $X = \{x_1, \ldots, x_n\}$, a set of continuous attributes $\mathcal{A} = \{a_1, \ldots, a_m\}$ and a fixed decision attribute $d \notin \mathcal{A}$. The value of an attribute $a \in \mathcal{A}$ for an instance $x \in X$ is denoted by $a(x)$, and we assume that these values are normalized, that is, $a(x) \in [0,1]$ for all $x \in X$ and $a \in \mathcal{A}$. The class of each instance is denoted by $d(x)$ and can take two values: 0 or 1.

In [16], the following measure was introduced, based on fuzzy rough set theory, to express how noisy an instance $x \in X$ is [7]:

$$\forall x \in X : \alpha(x) = OWA_W \underbrace{\frac{1}{\sum_{i=1}^m \delta_{a_i}(x,y)}}_{y \in \{z \in X | d(x) \neq d(z)\}}. \tag{1}$$

In this formula, for each attribute $a \in \mathcal{A}$, δ_a is a distance measure defined as follows:

$$\forall x, y \in X : \delta_a(x,y) = (a(x) - a(y))^2. \tag{2}$$

As we assume that all attributes are normalized, this distance returns a value between 0 and 1.

The OWA_W [18] operator is an aggregation operator that, given a series of values $a_1, \ldots, a_p \in \mathbb{R}$ and a weight vector $W = \langle w_1, \ldots, w_p \rangle$ that fulfills $\forall i \in 1, \ldots, p : w_i \subset [0,1]$ and $\sum_{i=1}^p w_i = 1$, is given by:

$$OWA_W(a_1, \ldots, a_p) = \sum_{i=1}^p w_i b_i, \tag{3}$$

where $b_i = a_j$ if a_j is the ith largest value in $a_1, \ldots, a_p$. That is, the values are ordered and then a weighted average is applied to these values. In our case, the weights are defined by:

$$\forall i \in 1, \ldots, p : w_i = \frac{2(p - i + 1)}{p(p+1)}. \tag{4}$$

As these weights are decreasing, OWA_W is a softening of the maximum operator, which can be represented by the weight vector $(1, 0, \ldots, 0)$.

Note that the noise value $\alpha(x)$ is proportional to the distance to instances from other classes. When many instances from other classes are close to x, the noise value will be high.

2.2   Fuzzy Rough Imbalanced Prototype Selection

The noise measure described in the previous subsection can be used to apply prototype selection: instances with a low noise value should be retained, while instances with high noise values should be removed. The difficulty is now to find a good threshold for the noise values.

The FRIPS algorithm proceeds as follows: the noise values of all instances are considered and any of these values is used as threshold. Each threshold corresponds to a subset of instances, namely those instances that have a noise value not higher than the threshold. These subsets are evaluated by measuring their training AUC. The threshold corresponding with the subset of instances that has the best training AUC is finally selected. In case there is more than one optimal threshold, the median of all thresholds is chosen.

In Algorithm 1, the procedure that calculates the training AUC is given. As we use the 1NN algorithm [5] in the experiments as final classifier, we also use this classification rule in the FRIPS procedure. The confusion matrix C is initialized in Line 2. Then we classify all instances in X using the leave-one-out procedure: to classify a training instance x w.r.t. a subset S of all training instances, we look up the nearest neighbor of x in the entire set S if x is not contained in S, and in $S \setminus \{x\}$ otherwise. For each classified instance we update C and at the end we calculate the AUC based on C.

The final FRIPS procedure is described in Algorithm 2. In Line 2 and 3, the candidate noise thresholds are calculated. In Line 4 to 6, the training AUC of the complete training set is calculated. In order to do that, the nearest neighbors of all instances need to be calculated. In the loop going from Line 8 to 19, the candidate thresholds are evaluated. As we evaluate them in decreasing order, the nearest neighbors do not need to be re-calculated for all instances in each iteration: only the instances that have neighbors that are removed in Line 9 need to be re-calculated. As a result, we can keep the running-time of the FRIPS algorithm under control. In Line 20, the final noise threshold is selected and the instances that have a noise value lower than or equal to this threshold are returned in Line 22.

Algorithm 1 trainAUC, procedure to measure the AUC of a subset of instances using a leave-one-out approach.

1: **input:** Reduced decision system $(S, \mathcal{A} \cup \{d\})$ $(S \subseteq X)$.

2: Initialize confusion matrix $C = \begin{pmatrix} 0 & 0 \\ 0 & 0 \end{pmatrix}$

3: **for** $x \in X$ **do**

4:     **if** $x \in S$ **then**

5:         Find the nearest neighbor nn of x in $S \setminus \{x\}$

6:         $C(d(x), d(nn)) \leftarrow C(d(x), d(nn)) + 1$

7:     **else**

8:         Find the nearest neighbor nn of x in S

9:         $C(d(x), d(nn)) \leftarrow C(d(x), d(nn)) + 1$

10:     **end if**

11: **end for**

12: **Output** AUC based on C.

Algorithm 2 FRIPS

1: **input**: Decision system $(X, \mathcal{A} \cup \{d\})$
2: Calculate $\alpha(x_1), \ldots, \alpha(x_n)$
3: Remove duplicates and order the α values from step 2: $\alpha_1 > \alpha_2 > \ldots > \alpha_p$
4: opt.alphas $\leftarrow \{\infty\}$
5: Calculate nearest neighbors of all instances
6: auc.opt $\leftarrow trainAUC(X, \mathcal{A} \cup \{d\})$
7: auc.current $\leftarrow$ auc.opt
8: **for** $\alpha = \alpha_2, \ldots, \alpha_p$ **do**
9:     Remove instances x for which $\alpha(x) > \alpha$, the resulting set of instances is S
10:    **if** Number of remaining instances > 1 **then**
11:       Recalculate nearest neighbors of instances for which current nearest neighbor
          was removed in step 9
12:       auc.current $\leftarrow trainAUC(S, \mathcal{A} \cup \{d\})$
13:       **if** auc.current $>$ auc.opt **then**
14:          opt.alphas $\leftarrow \{\alpha\}$
15:       **else if** auc.current $=$ auc.opt **then**
16:          opt.alphas $\leftarrow$ opt.alphas $\cup \{\alpha\}$
17:       **end if**
18:    **end if**
19: **end for**
20: best.alpha $=$ median(opt.alphas)
21: Remove instances x for which $\alpha(x) > best.alpha$, the resulting set of instances is
    S
22: **Output** $(S, \mathcal{A} \cup \{d\})$

---

3 Experimental Study

In this section we evaluate the performance of our algorithm. In Sect. 3.1 we present the datasets used for the experimentation and list the algorithms to which we compare our algorithm. In Sect. 3.2 we present and discuss the obtained results.

3.1 Experimental Set-Up

We use the datasets that were constructed by Napierała et al. in [12]. All datasets are binary and are randomly and uniformly distributed in a two-dimensional feature space. The minority class takes three different shapes in the feature space: the *subclus* data has 3 rectangles of minority instances, in the *clover* data the minority instances form a flower with five elliptic petals, and the *paw* datasets have three elliptic subregions of minority instances, of which two subregions are close to each other. The datasets are constructed with 600 or 800 instances. In case of 600 instances, the IR is 5, in case of 800 instances, the IR is 7.

To test if FRIPS can handle noise, we use the same data, where the borders of the subregions in the minority class were disturbed. The Disturbance Ratio (DR) is 0, 30, 50, 60 and 70 % , where the DR is the ratio of the width of the overlapping minority subregion compared to the total width of the subregion. As a result, there are 30 datasets: there are three shapes, with 600 or 800 instances and 5 DR levels.

We compare our algorithms to several state-of-the-art approaches. We consider the SMOTE algorithm itself and the following improvements of it:

- SMOTE with data cleaning using Tomek Links (SMOTE-TL [1])
- SMOTE with data cleaning using the Edited Nearest Neighbour technique (SMOTE-ENN [1])
- Borderline SMOTE, where only border instances are re-sampled (SMOTE-BL1[11])
- A variation on SMOTE-BL1 where the synthetic instances are closer to the minority class (SMOTE-BL2[11])
- SMOTE weighting the minority instances according to their safe-level (SMOTE-SL [3])
- SMOTE with data cleaning using Rough Set Theory (SMOTE-RSB,[13])
- SMOTE with data cleaning using Fuzzy Rough Set Theory (SMOTE-FRS, [14])

Furthermore, we also consider the SPIDER [15] algorithm, which removes majority instances that result in misclassifying instances from the minority class and over-samples minority instances that are surrounded by majority instances [15]. The last algorithm we use is SPIDER2: a two-phase version of the SPIDER algorithm presented in [12]. In the first phase noisy majority instances are removed or relabeled, in the second phase noisy minority examples are amplified.

We use a 5 fold cross validation strategy: each dataset is divided in 5 folds, and the instances of each fold (test data) are classified using the remaining folds as training data. The training data is preprocessed using the state-of-the-art techniques, FRIPS and FRIPS-SMOTE, and afterwards the test data is classified using the 1NN rule applied on the training data. We report the average AUC over all test folds. All procedures are implemented in the Keel[1] software platform.

3.2 Results

In Fig. 1, the average AUC values over all 30 datasets are given for each method. It can be seen that all preprocessing techniques improve the KNN classification. The state-of-the-art techniques SMOTE-ENN and SMOTE-TL improve SMOTE quite well. On the other hand, SMOTE-RSB and SMOTE-FRS, both techniques that try to improve SMOTE by deleting instances from the dataset processed by SMOTE, do not improve SMOTE. FRIPS improves SMOTE but is not better than SMOTE-TL. On the other hand, if we use FRIPS to clean the data before applying SMOTE, we obtain very good results.

To see if FRIPS-SMOTE significantly outperforms the state-of-the-art results, we perform the statistical Wilcoxon test [17]. This is a non-parametric pairwise test that aims to detect signifcant differences between two sample means; that is, the behavior of the two implicated algorithms in the comparison. For each

---

[1] www.keel.es

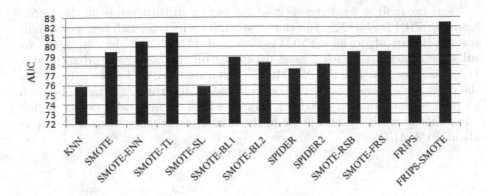

Fig. 1. Average AUC values over all datasets for each method

Table 1. Observed values of the Wilcoxon test, Friedman test and Holm's post-hoc test, comparing FRIPS-SMOTE to state-of-the-art algorithms

FRIPS-SMOTE vs.	Wilcoxon R+	R-	p-value	Friedman Friedman Ranking	Holm p-value
KNN	459.0	6.0	0.000003	10.9	0
SMOTE	400.0	35.0	0.000076	5.2167	0.012532
SMOTE-ENN	386.0	79.0	0.001537	4.6833	0.043861
SMOTE-TL	349.0	116.0	0.015566	3.4	0.361218
SMOTE-SL	459.0	6.0	0.000003	11.0333	0
SMOTE-BL1	432.0	33.0	0.000036	6.4833	0.000143
SMOTE-BL2	424.0	41.0	0.000078	6.8167	0.000032
SPIDER	452.0	13.0	0.000006	8.4833	0
SPIDER2	455.0	10.0	0.000004	7.5833	0.000001
SMOTE-RSB	417.0	48.0	0.000136	5.3167	0.011839
SMOTE-FRS	418.5	46.5	0.00012	5.5333	0.006762
FRIPS-SMOTE	-	-	-	2.55	-

comparison we compute $R+$, the sum of ranks of the Wilcoxons test in favor of FRIPS-SMOTE, $R-$, the sum of ranks in favor of the other methods, and also the p-value obtained for the comparison. The observed values of the statistics are listed in Table 1. As the p-value is always lower than 0.05, we can conclude that FRIPS-SMOTE outperforms all state-of-the-art algorithms at the 5% significance level.

Besides, we perform a statistical analysis conducted by non-parametric multiple comparison procedures [6,10,9]. We use Friedman's procedure to compute the set of ranks that represent the effectiveness associated with each algorithm. In addition, we compute the adjusted p-value with Holm's test. The Friedmann rankings are given in Table 1, together with Holm's adjusted p-values. FRIPS-SMOTE obtains the highest ranking and outperforms all algorithms except SMOTE-TL at the 5% significance level.

Next, we analyze what the effect of the border disturbance is on the performance of FRIPS-SMOTE. Therefore, we compare it to the two best-performing state-of-the-art algorithms: SMOTE-ENN and SMOTE-TL. In Fig. 2, the results are depicted for each dataset depending on the border disturbance ratio. From this, we see that FRIPS-SMOTE performs more or less equally well as the other algorithms if no border noise is added, but that it performs better if an intermediate amount of border noise is added. It must also be noted that all methods are highly susceptible to the border disturbance: there is a drop of about 10 % AUC.

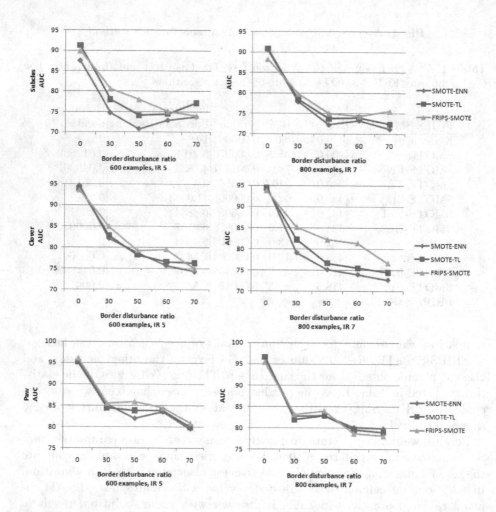

Fig. 2. Results for each dataset, comparing the results with different border disturbance ratios

4   Conclusions and Future Work

In this paper, we have presented a new improvement of the SMOTE over-sampling technique, FRIPS-SMOTE. It cleans the data before applying SMOTE by measuring the noise of every instance using fuzzy rough set theory, and selecting a noise threshold using a wrapper approach that evaluates candidate thresholds w.r.t. the corresponding training AUC.

Experiments on artificial data show that FRIPS-SMOTE outperforms state-of-the-art methods, and that it particularly performs well if the borders of the minority classes are disturbed.

In the future we want to take this work a step further by applying further data cleaning techniques on the dataset preprocessed by FRIPS-SMOTE. Moreover, we want to experiment with other prototype selection techniques, and we want to study the impact of FRIPS-SMOTE on real datasets.

Acknowledgment. This work was partially supported by the projects P10-TIC-0685 and P11-TIC-7765.

References

1. Batista, G.E.A.P.A., Prati, R.C., Monard, M.C.: A Study of the Behavior of Several Methods for Balancing Machine Learning Training Data. SIGKDD Explorations 6(1), 20–29 (2004)
2. Bradley, A.P.: The Use of the Area Under the ROC Curve in the Evaluation of Machine Learning Algorithms. Pattern Recognition 30(7), 1145–1159 (1997)
3. Bunkhumpornpat, C., Sinapiromsaran, K., Lursinsap, C.: Safe-Level-SMOTE – Safe-Level-Synthetic Minority Over-Sampling TEchnique for Handling the Class Imbalanced Problem. In: Theeramunkong, T., Kijsirikul, B., Cercone, N., Ho, T.-B. (eds.) PAKDD 2009. LNCS, vol. 5476, pp. 475–482. Springer, Heidelberg (2009)
4. Chawla, N.W., Bowyer, K.W., Hall, L.O., Kegelmeyer, W.P.: SMOTE – Synthetic Minority Over-Sampling Technique. Journal of Artificial Intelligence Research 16, 321–357 (2002)
5. Cover, T., Hart, P.: Nearest Neighbor Pattern Classification. IEEE Transactions on Information Theory 13(1), 21–27 (1967)
6. Derrac, J., García, S., Molina, D., Herrera, F.: A Practical Tutorial on the Use of Nonparametric Statistical Tests as a Methodology for Comparing Evolutionary and Swarm Intelligence Algorithms. Swarm and Evolutionary Computation 1(1), 3–18 (2011)
7. Dubois, D., Prade, H.: Rough Fuzzy Sets and Fuzzy Rough Sets. International Journal of General Systems 17(2-3), 191–209 (1990)
8. García, S., Derrac, J., Cano, J.R., Herrera, F.: Prototype Selection for Nearest Neighbor Classification – Taxonomy and Empirical Study. IEEE Transactions on Pattern Analysis and Machine Intelligence 34(3), 417–435 (2012)
9. García, S., Fernández, F., Luengo, J., Herrera, F.: A Study of Statistical Techniques and Performance Measures for Genetics-Based Machine Learning – Accuracy and Interpretability. Soft Computing 13(10), 959–977 (2009)

10. García, S., Alcalá Fernandez, J., Luengo, J., Herrera, F.: Advanced Nonparametric Tests for Multiple Comparisons in the Design of Experiments in Computational Intelligence and Data Mining – Experimental Analysis of Power. Information Sciences 180(10), 2044–2064 (2010)

11. Han, H., Wang, W., Mao, B.: Borderline-SMOTE – A New Over-Sampling Method in Imbalanced Data Sets Learning. In: Huang, D.-S., Zhang, X.-P., Huang, G.-B. (eds.) ICIC 2005. LNCS, vol. 3644, pp. 878–887. Springer, Heidelberg (2005)

12. Napierala, K., Stefanowski, J., Wilk, S.: Learning from Imbalanced Data in Presence of Noisy and Borderline Examples. In: Szczuka, M., et al. (eds.) RSCTC 2010. LNCS, vol. 6086, pp. 158–167. Springer, Heidelberg (2010)

13. Ramentol, E., Caballero, Y., Bello, R., Herrera, F.: SMOTE-RSB* – A Hybrid Preprocessing Approach Based on Oversampling and Undersampling for High Imbalanced Data-Sets Using Smote and Rough Sets Theory. Knowledge and Information Systems (2011) (in press)

14. Ramentol, E., Verbiest, N., Bello, R., Caballero, Y., Cornelis, C., Herrera, F.: Smote-frst – A New Resampling Method Using Fuzzy Rough Set Theory. In: 10th International FLINS Conference on Uncertainty Modeling in Knowledge Engineering and Decision Making, FLINS 2012 (in press, 2012)

15. Stefanowski, J., Wilk, S.: Selective Pre-processing of Imbalanced Data for Improving Classification Performance. In: Song, I.-Y., Eder, J., Nguyen, T.M. (eds.) DaWaK 2008. LNCS, vol. 5182, pp. 283–292. Springer, Heidelberg (2008)

16. Verbiest, N., Cornelis, C., Herrera, F.: Fuzzy Rough Prototype Selection (submitted)

17. Wilcoxon, F.: Individual Comparisons by Ranking Methods. Biometrics Bulletin 1(6), 80–83 (1945)

18. Yager, R.R.: On Ordered Weighted Averaging Aggregation Operators in Multicriteria Decisionmaking. IEEE Transactions on Systems, Man and Cybernetics 18(1), 183–190 (1988)

Fitness Function Obtained from a Genetic Programming Approach for Web Document Clustering Using Evolutionary Algorithms

Carlos Cobos[1], Leydy Muñoz[1], Martha Mendoza[1], Elizabeth León[2], and Enrique Herrera-Viedma[3]

[1] Computer Science Department, Universidad del Cauca, Colombia
{ccobos,cmunoz,mmendoza}@unicauca.edu.co
[2] Systems and Industrial Engineering Department, Engineering Faculty, Universidad Nacional de Colombia, Colombia
eleonguz@unal.edu.co
[3] Department of Computer Science and Artificial Intelligence, University of Granada, Spain
viedma@decsai.ugr.es

Abstract. Web document clustering (WDC) is an alternative means of searching the web and has become a rewarding research area. Algorithms for WDC still present some problems, in particular: inconsistencies in the content and description of clusters. The use of evolutionary algorithms is one approach for improving results. It uses standard index to evaluate the quality (as a fitness function) of different solutions of clustering. Indexes such as Bayesian Information Criteria (BIC), Davies-Bouldin, and others show good performance, but with much room for improvement. In this paper, a modified BIC fitness function for WDC based on evolutionary algorithms is presented. This function was discovered using a genetic program (from a reverse engineering view). Experiments on datasets based on DMOZ show promising results.

Keywords: genetic programming, web document clustering, clustering of web results, Bayesian information criteria.

1 Introduction

In recent years, web document clustering (WDC) -clustering of web results- has become a very interesting research area [1]. Web document clustering systems seek to increase the coverage (amount) of documents presented for the user to review, while reducing the time spent in reviewing documents [2]. Web document clustering systems are called web clustering engines. Among the most prominent are Carrot, SnakeT, Yippy, KeySRC and iBoogie [3]. Such systems usually consist of four main components: search results acquisition, preprocessing of input, construction and labeling of clusters, and visualization of resulting clusters [1].

The **search results acquisition** component begins with a query defined by the user. Based on this query, a document search is conducted in diverse data sources, in this case in traditional web search engines such as Google, Yahoo! and Bing. In

J. Pavón et al. (Eds.): IBERAMIA 2012, LNAI 7637, pp. 179–188, 2012.

general, web clustering engines work as meta search engines and collect between 50 to 200 results from traditional search engines. These results contain, as a minimum, a URL, a snippet and a title [1].

The **preprocessing** of search results comes next. This component converts each of the search results into a sequence of words, phrases, strings or general attributes or characteristics, which are then used by the clustering algorithm. There are a number of tasks performed on the search results, including: removal of special characters and accents, conversion of the string to lowercase, removal of stop words, stemming of the words and the control of terms or concepts allowed by a vocabulary [1].

Once preprocessing is finished, **cluster construction and labeling** is begun. This stage makes use of three types of algorithm [1]: data-centric, description-aware and description-centric. Each of these builds clusters of documents and assigns a label to the groups. Data-centric algorithms are the algorithms traditionally used for data clustering (partitional, hierarchical, density-based, etc.) [1, 4-10]. Description-aware algorithms put more emphasis on one specific feature of the clustering process. For example, they might put a priority on the quality of the labeling of groups and as such achieve results that are more easily interpreted by the user. An example of this type of algorithm is Suffix Tree Clustering (STC) [8]. Description-centric algorithms, meanwhile [1, 7, 11-15] are designed specifically for WDC, seeking a balance between the quality of clusters and the description (labeling) of clusters. An example of such algorithms is Lingo [11].

Finally, in the **visualization** step, the system displays the results to the user in folders organized hierarchically. Each folder seeks to have a label or title that represents well the documents it contains and that is easily identified by the user. As such, the user simply scans the folders that are actually related to their specific needs. The presentation folder tree has been adopted by various systems such as Carrot2, Yippy, SnakeT, and KeySRC, because the folder metaphor is already familiar to computer users, but there are others visualization schemes [1].

The two predominant problems with existing web clustering algorithms are inconsistencies in cluster content and in cluster description [1]. The first problem refers to the content of a cluster that does not always correspond to the label. Also, that navigation through the cluster hierarchies does not necessarily lead to more specific results. The second problem refers to the need for more expressive descriptions of the clusters (cluster labels are confusing).

Lately, evolutionary algorithms have been used to solve web clustering problems [16-18]. Bayesian Information Criteria (BIC) and Davies-Bouldin (DB) index have been used as a fitness function, but results can be improved upon. This is the main motivation of the present work, in which a new fitness function for web clustering evolutionary algorithms is put forward. This new function, obtained using a genetic program, is based on BIC, but it incorporates the average distance between centroids of the clustering solution and in preliminary experiments indeed shows better results.

The remainder of the paper is organized as follows. Section 2 presents related work. Section 3 presents the genetic program and the fitness function for the web clustering evolutionary algorithms obtained. Section 4 shows the experimental results on DMOZ and AMBIENT datasets using the obtained fitness function; in this section results are also compared with BIC. Finally, some concluding remarks and suggestions for future work are presented.

2   Related Work

In general, clustering algorithms can be classified into [19]: hierarchical, partitional, density-based, grid-based, and model-based algorithms, among others. The algorithms most commonly used for WDC have been the hierarchical and the partitional [4]. The hierarchical algorithms generate a dendogram or a tree of groups. This tree starts from a similarity measure, among which are: single link, complete link and average link. In relation to WDC, the hierarchical algorithm that brings the best results in accuracy is called UPGMA (Unweighted Pair-Group Method using Arithmetic averages) [5].

In partitional clustering, the most representative algorithms are: k-means, k-medoids, and Expectation Maximization. The k-means algorithm is the most popular because it is easy to implement and its time complexity is $O(n)$, where n is the number of patterns or records, but it has serious disadvantages: it is sensitive to outliers, it is sensitive to the selection of the initial centroids, it requires prior definition of the number of clusters, and the obtained clusters are only hyper spherical in shape [8]. Bisecting k-means [4, 7] algorithm (2000) combines the strengths of the hierarchical and partitional methods reporting better results concerning the accuracy and the efficiency of the UPGMA and the k-means algorithms.

The first algorithm to take the approach based on frequent phrases shared by documents in the collection was put forward in 1998 and called Suffix Tree Clustering (STC) [7, 8]. Later in 2001, the SHOC (Semantic, Hierarchical, Online Clustering) algorithm was introduced [12]. SHOC improves STC and is based on LSI and frequent phrases. Next in 2003, the Lingo algorithm [11, 20] was devised. This algorithm is used by the Carrot2 web searcher and it is based on complete phrases and LSI with Singular Value Decomposition (SVD). NMF (also in 2003) is another example of these algorithms. It is based on the non-negative matrix factorization of the term-document matrix of the given document corpus [21]. This algorithm surpasses the LSI and the spectral clustering methods in document clustering accuracy but does not care about cluster labels. Another approach was proposed by the Pairwise Constraints guided Non-negative Matrix Factorization (PCNMF) algorithm [22] in 2007. This algorithm transforms the document clustering problem from an un-supervised problem to a semi-supervised problem using must-link and cannot-link relations between documents. In 2007, the Dynamic SVD clustering (DSC) [14] algorithm was made available. This algorithm uses SVD and minimum spanning tree (MST). This algorithm has better performance than Lingo. In 2009, KeySRC was put forward [23]. KeySRC was built on top of STC with part-of-speech pruning and dynamic selection of the cut-off level of the clustering dendrogram. It outperforms STC, Lingo, Credo, and EP (Essential Pages). Finally, in 2010, a new algorithm for web clustering algorithm based on Word Sense Induction was proposed [24]. This algorithm outperforms STC, Lingo and KeySRC but it is computationally costly.

In relation to a frequent word sets model for WDC, in 2002, FTC (Frequent Term-Based Text Clustering) and HFTC (Hierarchical Frequent Term-Based Text Clustering) algorithms became available [15]. These algorithms use combinations of frequent words (association rules approach) shared in the documents to measure their proximity in the text clustering process. Then in 2003, FIHC (Frequent Item set-based

Hierarchical Clustering) was introduced [13], which measures the cohesion of a cluster using frequent word sets, so that the documents in the same cluster share more of the frequent word sets than those in other groups. These algorithms provide accuracy similar to that reported for Bisection k-means, with the advantage that they assign descriptive labels to associate clusters.

Looking at partitional clustering from an evolutionary approach: in 2007, three hybridization methods between the Harmony Search (HS) [25] and the k-means algorithms [26] were compared. These were: sequential hybridization method, interleaved hybridization method and the hybridization of k-means as a step of HS. As a general result, the last method was the best choice of the three. Later, in 2008 [9, 25, 27], based on the Markov Chains theory the researchers demonstrated that the last algorithm converges to the global optimum. Next, in 2009, a Self-Organized Genetic [28] algorithm was devised for text clustering based on the WordNet ontology. In this algorithm, a modified LSI model was also presented, which appropriately gathers the associated semantic similarities. This algorithm outperforms the standard genetic algorithm [29] and the k-means algorithm for WDC in similar environments. In 2010, two new algorithms were put forward. The first one, called IGBHSK [18] was based on global-best harmony search, k-means and frequent term sets. The second one, called WDC-NMA [17] was based on memetic algorithms with niching techniques. These two researches outperform obtained results with Lingo (Carrot2) over few datasets. Finally, in 2011 a memetic algorithm based on roulette wheel selection, 2 point crossover and replace the worst was proposed. It was designed from a hyper heuristic approach and its fitness function is based on BIC expressed by formula (1).

$$BIC = n * Ln\left(\frac{SSE}{n}\right) + k * Ln(n) \tag{1}$$

Where n is the total number of documents, k is the number of clusters,
SSE is the sum of squared error expressed by formula (4).

3   The Genetic Program and the New Fitness Function

The genetic program used to generate the new fitness function uses a gene representation based on tree of expressions, one and two-point crossover of two parents, three kinds of mutation approaches, rank selection to generate new generation, and random re-initialization when premature convergence is detected. The fitness function of the genetic program is based on maximizing the F-measure (commonly used in information retrieval and classification tasks) extracted from a table of multiple solutions of k-means for several web clustering problems, including the "ideal" solution.

In order to evaluate the F-measure (weighted formulas used by Weka [30]) given a collection of clusters $\{C_1, C_2, ... C_k\}$ with respect to a collection of ideal clusters $\{C_1^i, C_2^i, ... C_h^i\}$, these steps are followed: (a) find for each ideal cluster C_n^i a distinct cluster C_m that best approximates it in the collection being evaluated, and evaluate $P(C, C^i)$, $R(C, C^i)$, and $F(C, C^i)$ as defined by (2), (b) Calculate the weighted F-measure (F) based on (3).

$$P(C, C^i) = \frac{|C \cap C^i|}{|C|}, R(C, C^i) = \frac{|C \cap C^i|}{|C^i|}, and \; F(C, C^i) = \frac{2 * P(C, C^i) * R(C, C^i)}{P(C, C^i) + R(C, C^i)} \tag{2}$$

Where C is a cluster of documents and C^i is an ideal cluster of documents

$$F = \frac{2 * P * R}{P + R} \; where \; P = \frac{1}{T} \sum_{j=1}^{h} |C_j^i| * P(C_m, C_j^i), \; R = \frac{1}{T} \sum_{j=1}^{h} |C_j^i| *$$
$$R(C_m, C_j^i), \; and \; T = \sum_{j=1}^{h} |C_j^i| \tag{3}$$

Table 1 shows the table that the genetic program seeks to optimize (maximize the average F-measure in all problems). A total of 50 web clustering problems based on DMOZ datasets was used. For each problem, a total of 630 solutions was created using k-means (30 with 2 clusters, 30 with 3 clusters, and so on until 30 with 22 clusters). For each solution, several values were registered, namely: n (number of documents), k (number of clusters), SSE (standard sum of squared error based on formula (4)), weighted SSE (WSSE based on formula (5)), minimum distance between centroids (MNDBC expressed by formula (6)), average distance between centroids (ADBC expressed by formula (7)), maximum distance between centroids (MXDBC expressed by formula (8)), and F-measure (calculated based on current solution and ideal solution). An additional row for each problem was included; the "ideal" solution with all previously mentioned attributes.

$$SSE = \sum_{j=1}^{k} \sum_{i=1}^{n} \left(P_{i,j} * \left(1 - SimCos(x_i, c_j) \right)^2 \right) \tag{4}$$

Where $P_{i,j}$ is 1 if the document xi belongs to cluster j and 0 if otherwise, and c_j is the centroid of the cluster j.

$$WSSE = \sum_{j=1}^{k} |C_j| \sum_{i=1}^{n} \left(P_{i,j} * \left(1 - SimCos(x_i, c_j) \right)^2 \right) \tag{5}$$

Where $|C_j|$ is the number of documents in cluster j.

$$MNDBC = Minimize_{i=1,..k-1, j=i+1,..k} (d_{i,j}) \tag{6}$$

$$Where \; d_{i,j} = 1 - SimCos(c_i, c_j)$$

$$ADBC = \frac{2}{n \times (n-1)} \sum_{i=1}^{k-1} \sum_{j=i+1}^{k} \left(1 - SimCos(c_i, c_j) \right) \tag{7}$$

$$MXDBC = Maximize_{i=1,..k-1, j=i+1,..k} (d_{i,j}) \tag{8}$$
$$Where \; d_{i,j} = 1 - SimCos(c_i, c_j)$$

The genetic program seeks to maximize the formula (9) and it can be summarized by Fig. 1.

Table 1. Dataset to optimize (maximize F-measure) based on attributes. There are 50 problems (P) and 631 solutions (S) for each problem.

P	S	N	K	SSE	WSSE	MNDBC	ADBC	MXDBC	F-measure
	1	121	2	71.09	36.98	0.89	0.89	0.89	57.93
	2	121	2	71.84	36.04	0.83	0.83	0.83	56.66
1	...								
	630	121	22	31.26	2.17	0.54	0.94	0.54	48.75
	ideal	121	4	56.50	17.60	0.91	0.96	0.91	100.00
...									
	1	132	2	89.65	70.83	0.93	0.93	0.93	9.48
	2	132	2	90.92	73.90	0.85	0.85	0.85	10.86
50	...								
	630	132	22	37.24	2.27	0.63	0.97	0.63	54.03
	ideal	132	10	50.69	5.19	0.77	0.96	0.77	100.0

$$FF = \frac{\sum_{i=1}^{P} SelectFBest(p_i, exp)}{P}$$

$SelectFBest(p_i, exp) = Fmeasure \mid Minimize(exp\ in\ p_i\ over\ all\ S)$

Where P is the total number of problems, p_i is the problem i, exp is the expression in genetic chromosome, Fmeasure is the value of F-measure in Table 1, and S is the list of 631 solutions for each problem. SelectFBest is a function that applies the current expression on chromosome to each solution (S), selects the solution with the minimum value for the expression and returns the F-measure for that solution.

(9)

```
01   Initialize algorithm parameters.
02   Randomly initialize population, which encode expressions as a Tree.
03   Calculate fitness value for each solution in population using (9).
04   For Generation = 1 to MNG
05       For I = 1 to PS step by 2
06           Select chromosome I as parent1 from current population.
07           Select chromosome I+1 as parent2 from current population.
08           Generate two intermediate offspring based on parent1 and
             parent2 using one or two point crossover and include them
             in population.
09           Calculate fitness value for offspring using (9).
10       Next For
11       Apply mutation using usual gene mutation, transposition of in-
         sertion sequence (IS) elements or root transposition, calculate
         fitness value for each new solution, and include new solutions
         in current population.
12       Select PS solutions from current population to the new genera-
         tion using Rank selection.
13       If Premature Convergence then Re-initialize population keeping
         best solution and calculate fitness value for each chromosome
         in population using (9).
14   Next For
15   Select and return best chromosome.
```

Fig. 1. Pseudo-code for the genetic program

Initialize Algorithm Parameters: in this research, the optimization problem lies in maximizing the FF function expressed by (9). The algorithm needs the following parameters: Population Size (PS), Mutation Rate (MR), and Maximum Number of Generations (MNG) to stop the algorithm execution.

Representation and Initialization: each solution has an expression and the objective function value. The expression is a tree of different arguments ($0 for n, $1 for k, $2 for SSE, $3 for WSSE...) and functions (+, -, *, /, and ln for natural logarithmic).

Crossover: with 50% of probability a one point crossover is executed, otherwise a two point crossover is executed. In a one point crossover, if the length of the parent's chromosomes is the same, a random point in the first expression is defined, so that the offspring are the results of swapping parts of chromosomes at that point. In a two point crossover, two different points are randomly generated based on the parent's chromosomes, so that the offspring are the results of swapping the content of parents at those points.

Mutation: A low probability of mutation (MR) is applied to solutions in population. If a solution is selected to mutate, one of three different options can be used, namely: usual gene mutation, transposition of IS elements, or root transposition. In usual gene mutation a position in the tree (expression) is randomly selected and changed for another, also randomly generated (arguments are changed for other arguments and functions are changed for other functions). Transposition of IS elements is done by copying a randomly selected region of genes into the head of the chromosome (into a randomly selected position). The first gene of the chromosome's head is not affected – it cannot be selected as target point. Root transposition is achieved by inserting a new chromosome root and shifting the existing one. The method first of all randomly selects a function gene in the chromosome's head. The starting point of the sequence to be put into chromosome's head is found. It then randomly selects the length of the sequence making sure that the entire sequence is located within the head. Once the starting point and the length of the sequence are known, it is copied into the head of the chromosome, shifting elements already existing.

The genetic algorithm was executed and several expressions obtained an average F-measure of 90%. Several expressions included the relation between SSE and ADBC involved in a natural logarithmic function. With this information, an adaptation of BIC called Balanced BIC was proposed. The Balanced BIC is expressed by (10).

$$BBIC = n * Ln\left(\frac{SSE}{n \times ADBC}\right) + k * Ln(n)$$

Where n is the total number of documents, k is the number of clusters,   (10)
SSE is the sum of squared error expressed by formula (4), and ADBC is
the average distance between centroids expressed by formula (7)

4   Experimentation

Fifty (50) datasets based on The Open Directory Project (or DMOZ available online at http://www.unicauca.edu.co/~ccobos/wdc/wdc.htm) and forty four (44) datasets of AMBIENT (AMBIguous ENTries available online at http://credo.fub.it/ambient) were used to evaluate the obtained function. Precision and F-measure (the harmonic means of precision and recall) [9] were used to evaluate the quality of solution using weighted formulas from Weka [30]. Finally, the memetic algorithm obtained in [16] was used to compare BIC and Balanced BIC. Results are shown in Table 2.

Table 2. Precision (P) and F-measure (F) obtained at different number of generations (G) using BIC and Balanced BIC. In addition, the number of clusters (k) is shown when the ideal average value is 7,9 for AMBIENT and 6 for DMOZ. Detailed results can not be shown due to restrictions in the length of the paper.

| | Average on AMBIENT datasets | | | | | | | Average on DMOZ datasets | | | | | |
| | BIC | | | Balanced BIC | | | | BIC | | | Balanced BIC | | |
G	k	P	F	K	P	F	G	k	P	F	k	P	F
100	5,6	65,95	53,39	6,1	68,11	55,17	18	7,9	79,91	70,48	8,4	81,05	71,08
105	5,7	66,09	53,39	6,2	68,32	55,36	19	8,0	80,32	70,68	8,5	81,5	71,24
110	5,7	66,30	53,44	6,2	68,50	55,35	20	8,1	80,73	70,86	8,5	81,88	71,45
115	5,7	66,43	53,41	6,2	68,73	55,40	25	8,3	82,51	71,73	8,8	83,82	72,7
120	5,8	66,61	53,47	6,3	68,96	55,45	30	8,5	83,88	72,48	9	85,48	73,49

In general, balanced BIC obtained better values of precision and F-measure than BIC over all generations, but balanced BIC assigned a greater value of k (number of groups) than BIC fitness function. Better values of Precision and F-measure in the early generations of memetic algorithm helped the algorithm to find better solutions in less time (an important consideration in WDC). A multi-objective genetic program can be used to optimize F-measure and the number of clusters [31]. Balanced BIC improve BIC with 95% of confidence based on Wilcoxon non-parametric statistical hypothesis test [32] over individual results on AMBIENT and DMOZ dataset at same number of generation.

5   Conclusions and Future Work

Genetic programming was used to define a new fitness function for evolutionary WDC algorithms. This new function, called Balanced BIC, presents better results than BIC over 50 datasets based on DMOZ using a specific evolutionary algorithm. A reverse engineering approach was used to transform the web document clustering problem into an optimization problem seeking an expression that maximizes F-measure. The goal can be changed, for example, so that it maximizes precision, recall or accuracy; this would depend on the problem in hand.

As future work, the authors plan to test the Balanced BIC function on a variety of datasets including ODP-239 (available online at http://credo.fub.it/odp239) and MORESQUE (available online at http://lcl.uniroma1.it/moresque).

Some improvements to the genetic program are planned, e.g. use of other clustering attributes (SSE by individual clusters, average distance from centroids to general center) in the data set; inclusion of different index (such as BIC and DB) as initial solution in the genetic program; inclusion of more functions in the program such as Exponential and Log10; and design of a new multi-objective program based on NSGA-II to optimize F-measure and the number of clusters at the same time.

Acknowledgments. This work has been carried out with support from the Federal Financing of Projects FuzzyLIng-II TIN2010-17876, Andalucian Excellence Projects TIC5299 and TIC-5991, and the Universidad del Cauca under Project VRI-2560.

References

1. Carpineto, C., Osiński, S., Romano, G., Weiss, D.: A Survey of Web Clustering Engines. ACM Computing Surveys 41(3), 17:1–17:38 (2009)
2. Baeza-Yates, R., Ribeiro-Neto, B.: Modern Information Retrieval. Addison-Wesley (1999)
3. Carpineto, C., D'Amico, M., Romano, G.: Evaluating Subtopic Retrieval Methods - Clustering Versus Diversification of Search Results. Information Processing & Management 48(2), 358–373 (2012)
4. Hammouda, K.: Web Mining - Clustering Web Documents A Preliminary Review. Dept. of Systems Design Engineering. University of Waterloo (2001)
5. Jain, A.K., Dubes, R.C.: Algorithms for Clustering Data. Prentice-Hall, Inc. (1988)
6. Steinbach, M., Karypis, G., Kumar, V.: A Comparison of Document Clustering Techniques. In: KDD 2000 Workshop on Text Mining, pp. 1–20. ACM (2000)
7. Li, Y., Chung, S.M., Holt, J.D.: Text Document Clustering Based on Frequent Word Meaning Sequences. Data & Knowledge Engineering 64(1), 381–404 (2008)
8. Oren, Z., Oren, E.: Web Document Clustering - A Feasibility Demonstration. In: 21st Annual International ACM SIGIR Conference on Research and Development in Information Retrieval (SIGIR 1998), pp. 46–54. ACM (1998)
9. Mahdavi, M., Abolhassani, H.: Harmony K-Means Algorithm for Document Clustering. Data Mining and Knowledge Discovery 18(3), 370–391 (2009)
10. Berkhin, P., Kogan, J., Nicholas, C., Teboulle, M.: A Survey of Clustering Data Mining Techniques. In: Grouping Multidimensional Data, pp. 25–71. Springer (2006)
11. Osiński, S., Weiss, D.: A Concept-Driven Algorithm for Clustering Search Results. IEEE Intelligent Systems 20(3), 48–54 (2005)
12. Zhang, D., Dong, Y.: Semantic, Hierarchical, Online Clustering of Web Search Results. In: Yu, J.X., Lin, X., Lu, H., Zhang, Y. (eds.) APWeb 2004. LNCS, vol. 3007, pp. 69–78. Springer, Heidelberg (2004)
13. Fung, B., Wang, K., Ester, M.: Hierarchical Document Clustering Using Frequent Itemsets. In: 3rd SIAM Intl. Conference on Data Mining (SDM 2003), pp. 59–70. SIAM (2003)
14. Mecca, G., Raunich, S., Pappalardo, A.: A New Algorithm for Clustering Search Results. Data & Knowledge Engineering 62(3), 504–522 (2007)
15. Beil, F., Ester, M., Xu, X.: Frequent Term-Based Text Clustering. In: 8th ACM SIGKDD Intl. Conf. on Know. Discovery and Data Mining (KDD 2002), pp. 436–442. ACM (2002)
16. Cobos, C., Mendoza, M., Leon, E.: A Hyper-Heuristic Approach to Design and Tuning Heuristic Methods for Web Document Clustering. In: IEEE Congress on Evolutionary Computation (CEC 2011), pp. 1350–1358. IEEE (2011)
17. Cobos, C., Montealegre, C., Mejía, M., Mendoza, M., León, E.: Web Document Clustering based on a New Niching Memetic Algorithm, Term-Document Matrix and Bayesian Information Criterion. In: IEEE Congress on Evolutionary Computation (CEC 2010), pp. 4629–4636. IEEE (2010)
18. Cobos, C., Andrade, J., Constain, W., Mendoza, M., León, E.: Web Document Clustering Based on Global-Best Harmony Search, K-means, Frequent Term Sets and Bayesian Information Criterion. In: IEEE Congress on Evolutionary Computation (CEC 2010), pp. 4637–4644. IEEE (2010)

19. Jain, A.K., Murty, M.N., Flynn, P.J.: Data Clustering - A Review. ACM Computing Surveys 31(3), 264–323 (1999)
20. Osiński, S., Weiss, D.: Carrot 2 - Design of a Flexible and Efficient Web Information Retrieval Framework. In: Szczepaniak, P.S., Kacprzyk, J., Niewiadomski, A. (eds.) AWIC 2005. LNCS (LNAI), vol. 3528, pp. 439–444. Springer, Heidelberg (2005)
21. Wei, X., Xin, L., Yihong, G.: Document Clustering Based on Non-Negative Matrix Factorization. In: 26th Annual International ACM SIGIR Conference on Research and Development in Informaion Retrieval (SIGIR 2003), pp. 267–273. ACM (2003)
22. Zhong-Yuan, Z., Zhang, J.: Survey on the Variations and Applications of Nonnegative Matrix Factorization. In: 9th International Symposium on Operations Research and Its Applications (ISORA 2010), pp. 317–323. ORSC & APORC (2010)
23. Bernardini, A., Carpineto, C., D'Amico, M.: Full-Subtopic Retrieval with Keyphrase-Based Search Results Clustering. In: IEEE/WIC/ACM Intl. Joint Conferences on Web Intelligence and Intelligent Agent Technologies (WI-IAT 2009), pp. 206–213. IEEE (2009)
24. Navigli, R., Crisafulli, G.: Inducing Word Senses to Improve Web Search Result Clustering. In: Conference on Empirical Methods in Natural Language Processing (EMNLP 2010), pp. 116–126. Association for Computational Linguistics (2010)
25. Geem, Z., Kim, J., Loganathan, G.V.: A New Heuristic Optimization Algorithm - Harmony Search. Simulation 76(2), 60–68 (2001)
26. Forsati, R., Meybodi, M.R., Mahdavi, M., Neiat, A.G.: Hybridization of K-Means and Harmony Search Methods for Web Page Clustering. In: IEEE/WIC/ACM Intl. Conf. on Web Intell. and Intell. Agent Technology (WI-IAT 2008), pp. 329–335. IEEE (2008)
27. Mahdavi, M., Chehreghani, M.H., Abolhassani, H., Forsati, R.: Novel Meta-Heuristic Algorithms for Clustering Web Documents. Applied Mathematics and Computation 201(1), 441–451 (2008)
28. Song, W., Li, C.H., Park, S.C.: Genetic Algorithm for Text Clustering Using Ontology and Evaluating the Validity of Various Semantic Similarity Measures. Expert Systems with Applications 36(5), 9095–9104 (2009)
29. Song, W., Park, S.: Genetic Algorithm-Based Text Clustering Technique. In: Jiao, L., Wang, L., Gao, X., Liu, J., Wu, F. (eds.) ICNC 2006, Part I. LNCS, vol. 4421, pp. 779–782. Springer, Heidelberg (2006)
30. Hall, M., Frank, E., Holmes, G., Pfahringer, B., Reutemann, P., Witten, I.H.: The WEKA Data Mining Software - An Update. ACM SIGKDD Explorations Newsletter 11(1), 10–18 (2009)
31. Lopez-Herrera, A.G., Herrera-Viedma, E., Herrera, F.: A Study of the Use of Multi-Objective Evolutionary Algorithms to Learn Boolean Queries - A Comparative Study. Journal of the American Society for Information Science and Technology 60(6), 1192–1207 (2009)
32. Wilcoxon, F.: Individual Comparisons by Ranking Methods. Biometrics Bulletin 1(6), 80–83 (1945)

On the Estimation of Predictive Evaluation Measure Baselines for Multi-label Learning

Jean Metz, Luís F.D. de Abreu, Everton A. Cherman, and Maria C. Monard

Institute of Mathematics and Computer Science (ICMC)
University of São Paulo in São Carlos (USP/São Carlos)
P.O. Box 668, Zip Code 13561-970
São Carlos, SP, Brazil
jean@metzz.org, lfdorelli@grad.icmc.usp.br,
{echerman,mcmonard}@icmc.usp.br

Abstract. Machine learning research relies to a large extent on experimental observations. The evaluation of classifiers is often carried out by empirical comparison with classifiers generated by different learning algorithms, allowing the identification of the best algorithm for the problem at hand. Nevertheless, previously to this evaluation, it is important to state if the classifiers have truly learned the domain class concepts, which can be done by comparing the classifiers' predictive measures with the ones from the baseline classifiers. A baseline classifier is the one constructed by a naïve learning algorithm which only uses the class distribution of the dataset. However, finding naïve classifiers in multi-label learning is not as straightforward as in single-label learning. This work proposes a simple way to find baseline multi-label classifiers. Three specific and one general naïve multi-label classifiers are proposed to estimate the baseline values for multi-label predictive evaluation measures. Experimental results show the suitability of our proposal in revealing the learning power of multi-label learning algorithms.

Keywords: machine learning, multi-label classification, baseline classifiers.

1 Introduction

In *single-label learning*, each example in the dataset is associated with only one class, which can assume several values. The task is called binary classification if there are only two possible class values (Yes/No), and multi-class classification when the number of class values is greater than two [1]. In contrast to single-label learning, *multi-label learning* enables an example to belong to several classes simultaneously. The main difference between multi-label learning and single-label learning is that classes in multi-label learning are often correlated [3], while the class values in single-label learning are mutually exclusive. Multi-label learning has received much attention from the machine learning community due to the increasing number of new applications where examples are annotated with more than one class [2, 5–7].

J. Pavón et al. (Eds.): IBERAMIA 2012, LNAI 7637, pp. 189–198, 2012.

Machine learning research relies to a large extent on experimental observations. Whenever a new learning algorithm is proposed, its performance is compared to existing algorithms. To this end, it is usual to execute the algorithms on several selected datasets from different domains, and the quality of the resulting classifiers are evaluated using appropriate predictive measures. The final step consists of statistically verifying the hypothesis of improved performance of the new algorithm [4].

In any case, as a first step it is important to previously compare any new algorithm with the results obtained by a classifier constructed by a naïve learning algorithm, which can be used as a baseline from which the baseline of predictive measures can be calculated. Any new learning algorithm must be able to construct a classifier with better predictive performance measures than the naïve classifier. In single-label learning, this classifier is the one constructed by only looking at the class values, *i.e.*, the attributes that describe the examples in the dataset are not seen by the naïve learning algorithm. Having only this information, and due to the fact that the classification of a new instance has only two possible outcomes, correct or incorrect, the best it can do is to construct a classifier which always classifies a new instance with the majority class.

However, unlike single-label classification, multi-label classification should also take into account partially correct classification. As the predictive measures of multi-label classifiers highlight different aspects of partially correct classifications, the task is not as straightforward as for single-label classifiers, due to the fact that a naïve multi-label classifier which maximizes/minimizes one multi-label measure does not necessarily maximize/minimize the others.

This work proposes a simple way to find the naïve multi-label classifiers which focus on maximizing/minimizing one multi-label predictive measure at a time, and from it the baseline of the specific predictive measure can be calculated, as well as a way to find only one naïve multi-label classifier which can be used as a baseline for all the predictive measures. Similar to single-label, the multi-label naïve learning algorithms which construct these classifiers should only access the dataset multi-labels. To the best of our knowledge, this simple idea of constructing naïve multi-label classifiers to be used as a baseline for multi-label learning has not been previously considered by the community.

Our proposal is illustrated by three multi-label predictive measures frequently used to evaluate multi-label classifiers, which are used in a set of experiments on benchmark datasets. The rest of this work is organized as follows: Section 2 briefly presents multi-label learning and the predictive measures used in this work. Section 3 describes our proposal, which is evaluated in Sect. 4. The conclusions and future work are presented in Sect. 5.

2   Multi-label Classification and Evaluation Measures

Let D be a training set composed of N examples $E_i = (\mathbf{x}_i, Y_i)$, $i = 1..N$. Each example E_i is associated with a feature vector $\mathbf{x}_i = (x_{i1}, x_{i2}, \ldots, x_{iM})$ described by M features X_j, $j = 1..M$, and a subset of labels $Y_i \subseteq L$, where

$L = \{y_1, y_2, \dots y_q\}$ is the set of q labels. Table 1 shows this representation. In this scenario, the multi-label classification task consists of generating a classifier H, which given an unseen instance $E = (\mathbf{x}, ?)$, is capable of accurately predicting its subset of labels Y, i.e., $H(E) \to Y$.

Table 1. Multi-label data

	X_1	X_2	$\dots$	X_M	Y
E_1	x_{11}	x_{12}	$\dots$	x_{1M}	Y_1
E_2	x_{21}	x_{22}	$\dots$	x_{2M}	Y_2
$\vdots$	$\vdots$	$\vdots$	$\ddots$	$\vdots$	$\vdots$
E_N	x_{N1}	x_{N2}	$\dots$	x_{NM}	Y_N

Multi-label learning methods can be organized into two main categories: algorithm adaptation and problem transformation [8]. The first one consists of methods which extend specific learning algorithms in order to handle multi-label data directly. The second category is algorithm independent, allowing the use of any state of the art single-label learning algorithm to carry out multi-label learning. It consists of methods which transform the multi-label classification problem into either several binary classification problems, such as the Binary Relevance (BR) approach, or one multi-class classification problem, such as the Label Powerset (LP) approach. Both approaches are used in this work and are described next.

The BR approach decomposes the multi-label learning task into q independent binary classification problems, one for each label in L. To this end, the multi-label dataset D is first decomposed into q binary datasets D_{y_j}, $j = 1..q$ which are used to construct q independent binary classifiers. In each binary classification problem, examples associated with the corresponding label are regarded as positive and the other examples are regarded as negative. Finally, to classify a new multi-label instance BR outputs the aggregation of the labels positively predicted by the q independent binary classifiers. As BR scales linearly with size q of the label set L, it is appropriate for not a very large q. However, it experiences the deficiency in which correlation among the labels is not taken into account.

The LP approach transforms the multi-label learning task into a multi-class learning task. To this end, LP considers every unique combination of labels in a multi-label dataset as one class value of the correspondent multi-class dataset. In other words, each $E_i = (\mathbf{x}_i, Y_i)$, $i = 1..N$, is transformed into $E_i = (\mathbf{x}_i, l_i)$ where l_i is the atomic label representing a distinct label subset. Considering this, unlike BR, LP takes into account correlation among the labels. However, as the number of class values of the correspondent multi-class dataset is given by the number of distinct label subsets in D, the main drawback of this approach is that some class values in the multi-class dataset may be associated with a very small number of instances, making the multi-class dataset highly imbalanced.

The performance of multi-label classifiers can be evaluated using several different measures. Some of these measures are adaptations from the single-label classification problem, while others were specifically defined for multi-label tasks. Unlike single-label classification where the classification of a new instance has only two possible outcomes, correct or incorrect, multi-label classification should also take into account partially correct classification. A complete discussion on the performance measures for multi-label classification tasks is out of the scope of this paper, and can be found in [8]. In what follows, we briefly describe the predictive measures used in this work to illustrate our proposal in order to evaluate how well a multi-label classifier H constructed using a training set D predicts the actual set of labels for each instance. The measures are *Hamming-Loss*, *Subset-Accuracy* and *F-Measure*, defined by Equations 1, 2 and 3, respectively, where Δ represents the symmetric difference between two sets, Y_i is the set of true labels and Z_i is the set of predicted labels, $I(\text{true}) = 1$ and $I(\text{false}) = 0$.

$$Hamming\text{-}Loss(H, D) = \frac{1}{N} \sum_{i=1}^{N} \frac{|Y_i \Delta Z_i|}{|L|} \tag{1}$$

$$Subset\text{-}Accuracy(H, D) = \frac{1}{N} \sum_{i=1}^{N} I(Z_i = Y_i) \tag{2}$$

$$F\text{-}Measure(H, D) = \frac{1}{N} \sum_{i=1}^{N} \frac{2|Y_i \cap Z_i|}{|Z_i| + |Y_i|} \tag{3}$$

All these performance measures have values in the interval [0..1]. For *Hamming-Loss*, the smaller the value, the better the multi-label classifier performance is, while for the other measures, greater values indicate better performance.

3   Proposed Multi-label Baselines

Unlike single-label learning where the most naïve classifier used as the baseline is the one that always predicts the majority class by simply considering that the classification of a new instance has only two possible outcomes, in multi-label learning the predictive measures consider different aspects of partially correct classification. In other words, a naïve multi-label classifier which maximizes/minimizes one multi-label measure does not necessarily maximize/minimize the other measures. To this end, we propose a simple way to find the naïve multi-label classifiers which focus on maximizing/minimizing one predictive measure at a time, and from it the baseline of the specific predictive measure is calculated. We also propose a way to find a unique naïve multi-label classifier which can be used as a baseline for all the predictive measures. In both cases, similarly to single-label learning, the naïve classifiers are determined by only analyzing the dataset multi-labels, *i.e.*, the attributes that describe the examples are not considered.

The naïve multi-label classifiers which maximize/minimize one multi-label predictive measure at a time are explained next.

Hamming-Loss, defined by Equation 1, is the percentage of correct labels not predicted and incorrect labels which are predicted. Thus, we need to find the multi-label Z that minimizes Equation 1. As N and $|L|$ are constants, this can be done by minimizing $\sum_{i=1}^{N} |Y_i \Delta Z|$, where

$$|Y_i \Delta Z| = \sum_{j=1}^{|L|} I(y_{ij} \neq z_j) \qquad (4)$$

and y_{ij} denotes the value of label y_j in the multi-label Y_i of example E_i, *i.e.* positive if $y_j \in Y_i$, negative otherwise. To minimize *Hamming-Loss*, for each multi-label Y_i we need to maximize the possibility that $y_j \in Z$, such that $I(y_{ij} \neq z_j) = 0$. Thus, all labels with a frequency $> 50\%$ should be included in Z. The naïve classifier which minimizes *Hamming-Loss* will be called *Hamming-Loss$_B$*.

Subset-Accuracy, defined by Equation 2, is a very strict evaluation measure as it requires the exact match of the predicted and the true multi-label to maximize its value, *i.e.* $I(Z = Y_i) = 1$. It is easy to see that by choosing Z as the most frequent multi-label in the dataset, the *Subset-Accuracy* measure is maximized. The naïve classifier which maximizes *Subset-Accuracy* will be called *Subset-Accuracy$_B$*.

To illustrate, consider the dataset in Table 2(a). Table 2(b) shows the frequency of each distinct multi-label in the dataset and Table 2(c) the label frequencies.

Table 2. Multi-label and label distribution in dataset D with $L = \{y_1, y_2, y_3, y_4\}$

(a) Dataset D		(b) Multi-labels frequency		(c) Labels frequency	
	Y	Y	$frequency(Y_i)$	y_j	$frequency(y_j)$
E_1	$Y_1 = \{y_1, y_3\}$	$\{y_1, y_3\}$	$2/5$	y_1	$4/5$
E_2	$Y_2 = \{y_1, y_2\}$	$\{y_1, y_2\}$	$1/5$	y_2	$3/5$
E_3	$Y_3 = \{y_1, y_3\}$	$\{y_2\}$	$1/5$	y_3	$2/5$
E_4	$Y_4 = \{y_2\}$	$\{y_1, y_2, y_4\}$	$1/5$	y_4	$1/5$
E_5	$Y_5 = \{y_1, y_2, y_4\}$				

The multi-label Z which minimizes *Hamming-Loss* is $Z = \{y_1, y_2\}$ since the frequency of each of these labels is $> 50\%$, and the one which maximizes *Subset-Accuracy* is $Z = \{y_1, y_3\}$ which is the most frequent multi-label in D.

F-Measure, defined by Equation 3, is commonly used in information retrieval and frequently used to assess the overall performance of classifiers. It is often described as the harmonic mean of the *Precision* and *Recall* multi-label measures, which are defined by Equations 5 and 6 respectively.

$$Precision(H, D) = \frac{1}{N} \sum_{i=1}^{N} \frac{|Y_i \cap Z_i|}{|Z_i|} \quad (5) \qquad Recall(H, D) = \frac{1}{N} \sum_{i=1}^{N} \frac{|Y_i \cap Z_i|}{|Y_i|} \quad (6)$$

Precision computes the percentage of predicted labels that are relevant, while *Recall* computes the percentage of relevant labels that are predicted. As can be observed, maximizing *Recall* by itself is straightforward, since $Z = L$ maximizes $\sum_{i=1}^{N} |Y_i \cap Z|$. However, finding a Z which maximizes *Precision* is not straightforward, as $|Z|$ would be in the denominator. To this end, a procedure similar to the one explained next for *F-Measure* should be used.

To maximize *F-Measure*, we need to find the multi-label Z which maximizes Equation 3. This can be done by maximizing $\sum_{i=1}^{N} \frac{2|Y_i \cap Z|}{|Z|+|Y_i|}$, where Z should maximize $|Y_i \cap Z|$ but with few labels since $|Z|$ is in the denominator. Algorithm 1 finds this Z.

Algorithm 1: Finds multi-label Z which maximizes *F-Measure*

---

1 $V \leftarrow$ List of labels in L ordered by frequency
2 $D \leftarrow$ Dataset
3 $max \leftarrow 0$
4 $Z \leftarrow Z_m \leftarrow \emptyset$
5 **for** $i \leftarrow 1$ *to* q **do**
6 $\quad$ $Z_m \leftarrow Z_m \cup \{V_i\}$
7 $\quad$ $P \leftarrow$ *F-Measure*(Z_m, D)
8 $\quad$ **if** $max < P$ **then**
9 $\quad\quad$ $max \leftarrow P$
10 $\quad\quad$ $Z \leftarrow Z_m$
11 **Return** Z

For the toy dataset in Table 2(a), the multi-label which maximizes *F-Measure* is $Z = \{y_1, y_2\}$. The naïve classifier which maximizes *F-Measure* will be called *F-Measure$_B$*.

Taking this into account, either directly or by algorithms similar to Algorithm 1, it is possible to find the naïve multi-label classifier to maximize/minimize a specific measure, from which we can find the baseline for that measure. However, the other measures are not necessarily maximized/minimized.

Considering this disadvantage, it would be appropriate to look for a unique naïve multi-label classifier which, although does not necessarily maximizes/minimizes each predictive measure, it can be used as a global baseline for all predictive measures. Let us call this classifier *General$_B$*.

The rationale behind *General$_B$* consists of building a ranking of the single-labels in L according to their relative frequencies, and including the top most frequent single-labels in Z. Assuming the most frequent single-labels are in higher positions, as shown in Table 2(c), let σ be the number of the top single-labels to be included in Z. We are then left with the problem of *how to find σ* such that Z is representative, *i.e.*, with a reasonable number of single-labels and at the same time avoiding to be too strict (including too few single-labels) or too flexible (including too many single-labels). Since we are interested in finding Z that best represents the multi-label distribution in the dataset, we could use the label cardinality, which represents the average size of the multi-labels in the dataset, defined by Equation 8, to find the value of σ. In this work, we define σ as $[CR(D)]$, where $[x]$ is the closest integer value of x.

To illustrate, the value of σ for the dataset in Table 2(a) is given by Equation 7. Thus, the multi-label Z predicted by *General$_B$* is $Z = \{y_1, y_2\}$.

$$\sigma = [CR(D)] = [\frac{2+2+2+1+3}{5}] = [2] = 2 \tag{7}$$

Using the specific naïve classifiers *Hamming-Loss$_B$*, *Subset-Accuracy$_B$* and *F-Measure$_B$* or the global naïve classifier *General$_B$*, baselines for multi-label predictive measures can be calculated. These baselines should provide further information about other classifiers' learning power. In fact, the performance of the classifier generated by a multi-label learning algorithm should be better than the performance of naïve classifiers. Next, we show a set of experiments carried out using benchmark datasets.

4   Experiments and Results

The proposed naïve classifiers were implemented using Mulan[1], a package of Java classes for multi-label classification based on Weka[2]. The multi-label transformation approaches *BR* and *LP* were used to generate the other classifiers, whose predictive measures were compared with the correspondent baselines. All the reported results were obtained using 5×2 paired folds cross-validation.

4.1   Datasets and Setup

The experiments were carried out using eight multi-label datasets from four different domains obtained from the Mulan's repository. Table 3 shows, for each dataset, the domain (Domain); the number of examples (N); the number of features (M); the number of labels $(|L|)$; the Label Cardinality (CR), which is the average number of single-labels associated with each example (Equation 8); the Label Density (DE), which is the normalized cardinality (Equation 9); and the number of Distinct Combinations (Dis) of labels.

Table 3. Description of the datasets used in the experiments

Dataset	Domain	N	M	$|L|$	$CR(D)$	$DE(D)$	Dis
bibtex	text	7395	1836	159	2.402	0.015	2856
corel5k	images	5000	499	374	3.522	0.009	3175
emotions	music	593	72	6	1.869	0.311	27
enron	text	1702	1001	53	3.378	0.064	753
medical	text	978	1449	45	1.245	0.028	94
scene	images	2407	294	6	1.074	0.179	15
tmc2007-500	text	28596	500	22	2.158	0.098	1341
yeast	biology	2417	103	14	4.237	0.303	198

$$CR(D) = \frac{1}{N} \sum_{i=1}^{N} |Y_i| \qquad (8) \qquad\qquad DE(D) = \frac{1}{N} \sum_{i=1}^{N} \frac{|Y_i|}{|L|} \qquad (9)$$

The specific versions of the *BR* and *LP* approaches used in this work are the ones available in Mulan. For each of these approaches, we used two different base learning algorithms: Naïve Bayes (NB) and the Support Vector Machines algorithm SMO, both implemented in the Weka tool-kit and executed with default parameters.

---

[1] http://mulan.sourceforge.net
[2] http://www.cs.waikato.ac.nz/ml/weka/

4.2   Results and Discussion

Table 4 shows the results obtained for each classifier and their correspondent baselines, *i.e.*, specific and general. Light gray cells represent cases where the multi-label classifier underperforms the specific baseline, whilst dark gray cells show cases for which the classifier underperforms both the specific and the general baselines.

Table 4. Classifiers' predictive measures and baselines

Dataset	Classifiers				Baselines	
	Hamming-Loss					
	BR (SMO)	*LP* (SMO)	*BR* (NB)	*LP* (NB)	*Hamming-Loss_B*	*General_B*
bibtex	0.02	0.02	0.06	0.02	0.02	0.03
corel5k	0.01	0.02	0.01	0.02	0.01	0.01
emotions	0.20	0.21	0.26	0.23	0.31	0.33
enron	0.06	0.06	0.19	0.06	0.06	0.07
medical	0.01	0.01	0.03	0.03	0.03	0.04
scene	0.11	0.10	0.24	0.14	0.18	0.27
tmc2007-500	0.06	0.05	0.11	0.06	0.09	0.11
yeast	0.20	0.21	0.30	0.24	0.23	0.26
	Subset-Accuracy					
	BR (SMO)	*LP* (SMO)	*BR* (NB)	*LP* (NB)	*Subset-Accuracy_B*	*General_B*
bibtex	0.15	0.21	0.07	0.15	0.06	0.00
corel5k	0.01	0.04	0.00	0.02	0.01	0.00
emotions	0.27	0.34	0.20	0.28	0.14	0.07
enron	0.11	0.16	0.00	0.14	0.10	0.00
medical	0.64	0.67	0.17	0.32	0.16	0.16
scene	0.51	0.68	0.17	0.54	0.17	0.17
tmc2007-500	0.31	0.42	0.15	0.33	0.09	0.05
yeast	0.14	0.25	0.10	0.20	0.10	0.05
	F-Measure					
	BR (SMO)	*LP* (SMO)	*BR* (NB)	*LP* (NB)	*F-Measure_B*	*General_B*
bibtex	0.38	0.37	0.28	0.22	0.10	0.10
corel5k	0.13	0.16	0.18	0.11	0.20	0.18
emotions	0.58	0.65	0.62	0.60	0.46	0.30
enron	0.50	0.51	0.33	0.42	0.46	0.42
medical	0.75	0.77	0.26	0.41	0.24	0.23
scene	0.61	0.73	0.56	0.63	0.30	0.20
tmc2007-500	0.69	0.72	0.61	0.68	0.45	0.43
yeast	0.61	0.62	0.54	0.57	0.58	0.55

It is possible to observe that the base learning algorithm used in the *BR* and *LP* approaches have a strong influence on the learning process. Both approaches present weak performance when using NB as the base learning algorithm, while significantly better results are achieved when using SMO, especially for the *BR* approach.

Concerning *Hamming-Loss*, it is possible to observe that not only the *BR* (NB) classifier presents very poor performance comparing with the baselines, but also the other classifiers were incapable of outperforming the *Hamming-Loss_B* and *General_B* baselines for most datasets. More specifically, 56.25% of the classifiers show *Hamming-Loss* values below the specific *Hamming-Loss_B* baseline, while 25% are below the *General_B* baseline. Therefore, for only 43.75% of the experiments the multi-label algorithms were capable of outperforming the two naïve baseline (*Hamming-Loss_B* and *General_B*).

Regarding *Subset-Accuracy*, the *BR* (NB) algorithm underperforms both baselines for three out of eight datasets, and for the *yeast* dataset this combination is only better than the *General$_B$* baseline. When using SMO as the base learning algorithm, both the *BR* and *LP* approaches show higher *Subset-Accuracy* values, outperforming the baselines in 15 out of 16 cases. Nevertheless, although the baseline values for *Subset-Accuracy* are quite low, only for some datasets the multi-label classifiers achieve a significant improvement over the baselines, for example *medical* and *scene* datasets. Concerning all datasets and the *Subset-Accuracy* measure, the weakest performance is observed for *BR* (NB) with the datasets *corcl5k* and *enron*, resulting in zero *Subset-Accuracy* value. This weak performance might be related to the high values of $CR(D)$, $|L|$ and *Dis*. Summing up, 15.62% of the cases are below the specific baseline *Subset-Accuracy$_B$*, while 9.37% are also below the *General$_B$* baseline. It is worth noticing that the *Subset-Accuracy* measure requires a perfect match between the true and predicted multi-label. Therefore, partially correct classifications are not accounted for by *Subset Accuracy*.

Similar results are observed when considering *F-Measure*, since for some datasets the classifiers could not perform better than the baselines. Precisely, the *F-Measure* of 25% of the experiments are below the specific *F-Measure$_B$* baseline, while 21.87% are also below the *General$_B$* baseline for *F-Measure*. These weak performances happen with datasets *corel5k*, *enron* and *yeast*, mainly when NB is used as the base learning algorithm. The only exception is for dataset *corel5k*, for which the *F-Measure* is below the specific and general baselines in all experiments. Positive results are also observed in this scenario, since 75.00% of the results are above the baseline values for *F-Measure*, indicating that, although it is hard to predict the exact multi-label, it is possible to predict a subset of the true multi-label associated to each instance. These partially correct classifications represent the learning capability of the multi-label classifiers, which can be estimated as the difference between the baseline and the respective *F-Measure* value obtained from the classifier prediction.

Recall that *Hamming-Loss$_B$*, *Subset-Accuracy$_B$* and *F-Measure$_B$* were tailored to find the Z which minimizes/maximizes one specific measure. Accordingly, it is expected that they present better values for the specific measure they are based on, while sacrificing the others. On the other hand, *General$_B$* was tailored to allow a global analysis of the classifier, finding a Z to estimate the baseline for all predictive measures.

Table 5 gives an insight into the behaviour of the proposed baselines. It shows, for each predictive measure considered in this work, the average ranking among the baselines in all datasets. Observe that in all cases the specific baseline is

Table 5. Average ranking of the baseline methods over all datasets

	Subset-Accuracy$_B$	Hamming-Loss$_B$	F-Measure$_B$	General$_B$
Subset-Accuracy	1	3	4	2
Hamming-Loss	3	1	4	2
F-Measure	3	4	1	2

ranked first for the corresponding measure and is at a lower rank for the other measures, while $General_B$ is always ranked second.

5 Conclusions

This work proposes a simple way of constructing naïve multi-label algorithms to find baselines for multi-label predictive measures, which should be used as a first step to evaluate already proposed, as well as new multi-label learning algorithms. These baselines allow us to reveal the learning power of any multi-label algorithm, which must be able to construct a classifier whose predictive measures are better than at least the baselines provided by $General_B$. As future work, we plan to carry out a thorough literature review to search for experimental evaluations of multi-label learning algorithms in benchmark datasets in order to classify these published results taking into account the baselines proposed in this work.

Acknowledgements. The authors would like to thank the anonymous referees for their comments on this paper. This research was supported by the Brazilian Research Council FAPESP.

References

1. Alpaydin, E.: Introduction to Machine Learning. MITP (2004)
2. Cherman, E.A., Metz, J., Monard, M.C.: Incorporating Label Dependency into the Binary Relevance Framework for Multi-Label Classification. Expert Systems with Applications 39(2), 1647–1655 (2012)
3. Dembczynski, K., Waegeman, W., Cheng, W., Hüllermeier, E.: On Label Dependence in Multi-Label Classification. In: 2nd International Workshop on Learning from Multi-Label Data (MLD 2010) at the 27th International Conference of Machine Learning (ICML 2010), pp. 5–12 (2010)
4. Demžsar, J.: Statistical comparison of classifiers over multiple data sets. Journal of Machine Learning Research 7(1), 1–30 (2006)
5. Feng, S., Xu, D.: Transductive Multi-Instance Multi-Label learning algorithm with application to automatic image annotation. Expert Systems with Applications 37(1), 661–670 (2010)
6. Qi, G.J., Hua, X.S., Rui, Y., Tang, J., Mei, T., Zhang, H.J.: Correlative Multi-Label Video Annotation. In: 15th International Conference on Multimedia (MULTIMEDIA 2007), pp. 17–26. ACM (2007)
7. Trohidis, K., Tsoumakas, G., Kalliris, G., Vlahavas, I.: Multilabel Classification of Music into Emotions. In: 9th International Conference on Music Information Retrieval (ISMIR 2008), pp. 325–330 (2008)
8. Tsoumakas, G., Katakis, I., Vlahavas, I.: Mining Multi-label Data. In: Maimon, O., Rokach, L. (eds.) Data Mining and Knowledge Discovery Handbook, pp. 667–685. Springer (2010)

Towards Web Spam Filtering
with Neural-Based Approaches

Renato Moraes Silva[1], Tiago A. Almeida[2], and Akebo Yamakami[1]

[1] School of Electrical and Computer Engineering, University of Campinas – UNICAMP,
13083-852, Campinas, SP, Brazil
{renatoms,akebo}@dt.fee.unicamp.br
[2] Department of Computer Science, Federal University of São Carlos – UFSCar,
13565-905, Sorocaba, SP, Brazil
talmeida@ufscar.br

Abstract. The steady growth and popularization of the Web increases the competition between the websites and creates opportunities for profit in several segments. Thus, there is a great interest in keeping the website in a good position in search results. The problem is that many websites use techniques to circumvent the search engines which deteriorates the search results and exposes users to dangerous content. Given this scenario, this paper presents a performance evaluation of different models of artificial neural networks to automatically classify web spam. We have conducted an empirical experiment using a well-known, large and public web spam database. The results indicate that the evaluated approaches outperform the state-of-the-art web spam filters.

Keywords: web spam, spam classifier, artificial neural network, pattern recognition.

1 Introduction

Nowadays, the volume of information in the Web is explosively increasing. As a consequence, search engines have become important tools to help users find desired information. Then, the higher the relevance of a page, the greater the chance that page appears in search results and is clicked. This, combined with the current competitive business gives birth several malicious methods that try to circumvent the search engines by manipulating the relevance of web pages to increase the return of investment [1]. Such a technique is known as web spamming which can be composed by *content spam* and *link spam*. According to Araujo and Martins-Romo [2], content spam is a technique that alters the logical view that a search engine has over the page contents, for instance, by inserting invisible popular keywords that have no connection with the actual content of the page. On the other hand, link spam consists of the creation of a link structure to increases the relevance of pages in search engines that rank the importance of pages using the relation of the amount of links pointing to it.

Web spam is undesirable because in addition to deteriorate the search results, still can expose users to malicious content that installs malwares on their computers and can steal sensitive information, as passwords, financial information, or web-banking credentials.

J. Pavón et al. (Eds.): IBERAMIA 2012, LNAI 7637, pp. 199–209, 2012.

Recent estimates suggest that at least 1.3% of all search queries of the Google search engine contain results that link to malicious pages [3].

Given this scenario, there is a common sense that it is very necessary to put forward efficient techniques to automatically detect web spam. Previous studies focus only on the analysis of the relation of web links [4, 5], the web pages content [6, 7], or both [8–10]. In this paper, we evaluate the combination of different models of artificial neural networks with these three strategies to automatically detect samples of web spam. We have conducted an empirical experiment using a well-known, large, and public web spam database and the reported results indicate that the evaluated approaches outperform currently established web spam filters.

This paper is organized as follows: Sect. 2 presents related work regarding web spam detection. Sect. 3 introduces the basic background of the evaluated artificial neural networks. The experiment protocol and main results are presented in Sect. 4. Finally, Sect. 5 offers the main conclusions and guidelines for future work.

2   Related Work

Castilho *et al.* [10] a web spam detection system that combines link-based features and content-based features. In addition, they use the web graph topology by exploiting the link structure among hosts and proposed features that were used in several other relevant works and in important events, such as the *Web Spam Challenge Track* I and II.

Svore *et al.* [11] present a method for detecting web spam that use content-based features and the rank-time. The experiments were performed using SVM classifier with linear kernel using the rank-time features into query-independent and query-dependent. The results indicate that the first method performs better than the second one.

Noi *et al.* [12] present a method based on a combination of graph neural network model and probability mapping graph self organizing maps. The two models are organized into a layered architecture, consisting of a mixture of unsupervised and supervised learning methods. The found results indicate that the proposed approach was comparable with established methods at that time.

Shengen *et al.* [1] propose to derive new features for web spam detection, using genetic programming, from existing link-based features and use them as the inputs to support vector machine and genetic programming classifiers. According to the authors, the classifiers that use the new features achieve better results compared with the features provided in the original database.

Largillier and Peyronnet [13] consider that spammers use web pages with specific dedicated structure around a given target page, to increase its PageRank. The authors propose a technique for identification of web spam which deals with spam links, analyzing the frequency language associated with random walks amongst those dedicated structures. The results indicate that the proposed technique is efficient since it was able to identify spam using a few simple patterns.

3   Artificial Neural Network

Artificial neural network (ANN) is a parallel and distributed method made up of simple processing units called neurons, which has computational capacity of learning and generalization. In this system, the knowledge is acquired through a process called train-ing or learning that is stored in strength of connections between neurons, called synaptic weights [14].

A basic model of ANN has the following components: a set of synapses, an integra-tor, an activation function, and a bias. So, there are different models of ANN depending on the choice of each component [14].

In the following, we briefly present each model we have evaluated in this work.

3.1 Multilayer Perceptron Neural Network

A multilayer perceptron neural network (MLP) is a perceptron-type network that has a set of sensory units composed by an input layer, one or more intermediate (hidden) layers, and an output layer of neurons [14]. By default, MLP is a supervised learn-ing method that uses the backpropagation algorithm which can be summarized in two stages: *forward* and *backward* [15].

In the *forward* stage, the signal propagates through the network, layer by layer, as follows: $u_j^l(n) = \sum_{i=0}^{m^l - 1} w_{ji}^l(n) y_i^{l-1}(n)$, where $l = 0, 1, 2, ..., L$ are the indexes of net-work layers. So, $l = 0$ represents the input layer and $l = L$ represents the output layer. On the other hand, $y_i^{l-1}(n)$ is the output function relating to the neuron i in the previous layer, $l - 1$, $w_{ji}^l(n)$ is the synaptic weight of neuron j in layer l and m^l corresponds to the number of neurons in layer l. For $i = 0$, $y_0^{l-1}(n) = +1$ and $w_{j0}^l(n)$ represent the bias applied to neuron j in layer l [14].

The output of neuron j in layer l is given by $y_j^l(n) = \varphi_j(u_j^l(n))$, where φ_j is the activation function of j. Then, the error can be calculated by $e_j^l(n) = y_j^l(n) - d(n)$, where $d(n)$ is the desired output for an input pattern $x(n)$.

In *backward* stage, the derivation of the backpropagation algorithm is performed starting from the output layer, as follows: $\delta_j^L(n) = \varphi_j'(u_j^L(n)) e_j^L(n)$, where φ_j' is the derivative of the activation function. For $l = L, L - 1, ..., 2$, is calculated: $\delta_j^{l-1}(n) =$ $\varphi_j'(u_j^{l-1}(n)) \sum_{i=1}^{m^l} w_{ji}^l(n) * \delta_j^l(n)$, for $j = 0, 1, ..., m^l - 1$.

Consult Haykin [14] and Bishop [15] for more information.

Levenberg-Marquardt Algorithm. The Levenberg-Marquardt algorithm is usually employed to optimize and accelerate the convergence of the backpropagation algo-rithm [15]. It is considered a second order method because it uses information about the second derivative of the error function.

Considering that the error function is given by mean square error (MSE), the equation used by Gauss-Newton method to update the network weights and to minimize the value of MSE is $W_{i+1} = W_1 - H^{-1} \nabla f(W)$.

The gradient $\nabla f(W)$ can be represented by $\nabla f(W) = J^T e$ and the Hessian matrix can be calculated by $\nabla^2 f(W) = J^T J + S$, where J is a Jacobian matrix and $S = \sum_{i=1}^{n} e_i \nabla^2 e_i$. It can be conclude that S is a small value when compared to the product of the Jacobian matrix, so the Hessian matrix can be represented by $\nabla^2 f(W) \approx J^T J$.

Therefore, updating the weights in Gauss-Newton method can be done by $W_{i+1} = W_1 - (J^T J)^{-1} J^T e$.

One limitation of the Gauss-Newton method is that a simplified Hessian matrix can not be reversed. Thus, the Levenberg-Marquardt algorithm updates the weights by $W_{i+1} = W_i - (J^T J + \mu I)^{-1} J^T e$, where I is the identity matrix and μ a parameter that makes the Hessian a positive definite matrix.

More details can be found in Bishop [15] and Hagan and Menhaj [16].

3.2 Kohonen's Self-Organizing Map

The Kohonen's self-organizing map (SOM) is based on unsupervised competitive learning. Its main purpose is to transform an input pattern of arbitrary dimension in a one-dimensional or two-dimensional map in a topologically ordered fashion [14, 17].

The training algorithm for a SOM can be summarized in two stages: competition and cooperation [14, 17].

In the competition stage, a random input pattern (x_j) is chosen, the similarity between this pattern and all the neurons of the network is calculated by the Euclidean distance $id = \arg \min_{\forall i} \|x_j - w_i\|$ where $i = 1, ...k$, and the index of the neuron with lowest distance is selected.

In cooperation stage, the synaptic weights w_{id} that connect the winner neuron in the input pattern x_i is updated. The weights of neurons neighboring the winner neuron are also updated by $w_i(t + 1) = w_i(t) + \alpha(t)h(t)(x_i - w_i(t))$, where t is the number of training iterations, $w_i(t+1)$ is the new weight vector, $w_i(t)$ is the current weight vector, α is the learning rate, $h(t)$ is the neighborhood function and x_i is the input pattern.

The neighborhood function $h(t)$ is equal to 1 when the winner neuron is updated. This is because it determines the topological neighborhood around the winning neuron, defined by the neighborhood radius σ. The amplitude of this neighborhood function monotonically decreases as the lateral distance between the neighboring neuron and the winner neuron increases. There are several ways to calculate this neighborhood function, and one of the most common is the Gaussian function, defined by $h_{ji}(t) = \exp\left(\frac{-d_{ji}^2}{2\sigma^2(t)}\right)$, where d_{ji} is the lateral distance between winner neuron i and neuron j. The parameter $\sigma(t)$ defines the neighborhood radius and should be some monotonic function that decreases over the time. So, the exponential decay function $\sigma(t) = \sigma_0 \exp\left(-\frac{t}{\tau}\right)$ can be used, where σ_0 is the initial value of σ, t is the current iteration number and τ is a time constant of the SOM, defined by $\tau = \frac{1000}{\log \sigma_0}$.

The competition and cooperation stages are carried out for all the input patterns. Then, the neighborhood radius σ and learning rate α are updated. This parameter should decrease with time and can be calculated by $\alpha(t) = \alpha_0 \exp\left(-\frac{t}{\tau}\right)$, where α_0 is the initial value of α, t is the current iteration number and τ is a time constant of the SOM which can be calculated as presented in the cooperation stage.

3.3 Learning Vector Quantization

The learning vector quantization (LVQ) is a supervised learning technique that aims to improve the quality of the classifier decision regions, by adjusting the feature map through the use of information about the classes [14].

According to Kohonen [17], the SOM can be used to initialize the feature map by defining the set of weight vectors w_{ij}. The next step is to assign labels to neurons. This assignment can be made by majority vote, in other words, each neuron receives the class label in that it is more activated.

After this initial step, the LVQ algorithm can be employed. Although, the training process is similar to the SOM one, it does not use neighborly relations. Therefore, it is checked if the class of the winner neuron is equal to the class of the input vector x, and it is updated as follows:

$$w_{id}(t+1) = \begin{cases} w_{id}(t) + \alpha(t)(x_i - w_{id}(t)), \text{ equal class} \\ w_{id}(t) - \alpha(t)(x_i - w_{id}(t)), \text{ different class} \end{cases}$$

where α is the learning rate, id is the index of the winner neuron and t is the current iteration number.

3.4 Radial Basis Function Neural Network

A radial basis function neural network (RBF), in its most basic form, has three layers. The first one is the input layer which has sensory units connecting the network to its environment. The second layer is hidden and composed by a set of neurons that use radial basis functions to group the input patterns in clusters. The third layer is the output one, which is linear and provides a network response to the activation function applied to the input layer [14]. The activation function most common for the RBFs is the Gaussian, defined by $h(x) = \exp\left(-\frac{(x-c)^2}{r^2}\right)$, where x is the input vector, c is the center point and r is the width of the function.

The procedure for training a RBF is performed in two stages. In the first one, the parameters of the basic functions related to the hidden layer are determined through some method of unsupervised training, as K-means.

In the second training phase, the weights of the output layer are adjusted, which corresponds to solve a linear problem [15]. According to Bishop [15], considering an input vector $x = [x_1, x_2, ..., x_n]$, the network output is calculated by $y_k = \sum_{j=1}^{m} w_{kj} h_j$, where $x = [w_{k1}, w_{k2}, ..., x_{km}]$ are the weights, $h = [h_1, h_2, ..., h_m]$ are the radial basis functions, calculated by a function of radial basis activation.

After calculating the outputs, the weights should be updated. A formal solution to calculate the weights is given by $w = h^\dagger d$, where h is the matrix of basis functions, $h^\dagger$ represents the pseudo-inverse of h and d is a vector with the desired responses [15].

Consult Haykin [14], Bishop [15] and Orr [18] for more information.

4   Experiment and Results

To give credibility to the found results and in order to make the experiments reproducible, all the tests were performed with the public and well-known WEBSPAM-UK2006 collection[1]. It is composed by 77.9 million web pages hosted in 11,000 hosts

---

[1] *Yahoo! Research: "Web Spam Collections".* Available at http://barcelona.
research.yahoo.net/webspam/datasets/

in the UK domains. It is important to note that this corpus was used in *Web Spam Challenge*[2] *I* and *II*, that are the most known competitions of web spam detection techniques.

In our experiment, we have followed the same competition guidelines. In this way, we have used three sets of 8,487 feature vectors employed to discriminate the hosts as spam or ham. Each set is composed by 6,509 hosts labeled as ham and 1,978 labeled as spam. The organizers provided three sets of features: the first one composed by 96 content-based features [10], the second one composed by 41 link-based features [19] and the third one composed by 138 transformed link-based features [10], which are the simple combination or logarithm operation of the link-based features.

4.1 Protocol

We evaluated the following well-known artificial neural networks (ANNs) algorithms to automatically detect web spam: multilayer perceptron (MLP) trained with the gradient descent (MLP-GD) and Levenberg-Marquardt (MLP-LM) methods, Kohonen's self-organizing map (SOM) with learning vector quantization (LVQ) and radial basis function neural network (RBF).

We have implemented all the MLPs with a single hidden layer and with one neuron in the output layer. In addition, we have employed a linear activation function for the neuron of output layer and an hyperbolic tangent activation function for the neurons of the intermediate layer. We have initialized the weights and biases with random values between $[-1, 1]$ and normalized the data to this interval by $x = 2 * \frac{x - x_{min}}{x_{max} - x_{min}} - 1$, where x is the array with all the feature vectors and x_{min} and x_{max} are, respectively, the smallest and largest value in the array x. Also, we have performed such data normalization for SOMs with LVQ and RBFs.

Regarding the parameters, in all simulations, we have employed the following stopping criteria: maximum number of iterations be greater than a threshold θ, the mean square error (MSE) of the training set be smaller than a threshold γ or when the MSE of the validation set increases (checked every 10 iterations).

The parameters used for each ANN model were chosen empirically, by trial-and-error method, and are presented in Table 1

Table 1. Parameters of the neural networks

Parameter	MLP-GD	MLP-LM	RBF	SOM + LVQ
θ	10,000	500	-	2,000
γ	0.001	0.001	-	0.01
step learning α	0.005	0.001	-	-
Number of neurons in the hidden layer	100	50	10	120
Neighborhood function	-	-	-	One-dimensional
Initial neighborhood radius σ	-	-	-	4

Note that, as Table 1 presents, for the simulations using the RBFs, we have not employed any stopping criteria because the training method is not iterative, as pointed out in Sect. 3.

---

[2] *Web Spam Challenge:* http://webspam.lip6.fr/

To address the algorithms performance, we used a random sub-sampling validation, which is also known as Monte Carlo cross-validation [20]. Such method provides more freedom to define the size of training and testing subsets. Unlike the traditional k-fold cross-validation, the random sub-sampling validation allows to do as many repetitions were desired, using any percentage of data for training and testing. In this way, we divided each simulation in 10 tests and calculated the arithmetic mean and standard deviation of the following well-known measures: accuracy rate (Acc%), spam recall rate (Rcl%), specificity (Spc%), spam precision rate (Pcs%), and F-measure (FM) [21]. In each test, we have randomly selected 80% of the samples of each class to be presented to the algorithms in the training stage and the remaining ones were separated for testing.

4.2 Results

In this section, we report the main results of our evaluation. Table 2 presents the performance achieved by each ANN using each set of feature vectors. Bold values indicate the highest score acquired by each ANN and values preceded by the symbol "*" indicate the highest score in each performance measure.

Table 2. Results achieved by each evaluated neural network for WEBSPAM-UK2006 dataset

	Content	Links	Trans. Links	Content+Links
	MLP trained with the gradient descent method			
	Mean	Mean	Mean	Mean
Acc	86.2±1.2	86.4±1.3	88.3±0.9	*89.3±0.7
Rcl	57.0±4.6	61.6±3.1	**75.2±2.2**	74.2±3.2
Spc	**95.0±0.4**	93.9±0.9	92.1±1.4	94.0±0.9
Pcs	77.5±2.7	75.3±2.9	73.9±3.1	**79.5±2.5**
FM	0.656±0.039	0.677±0.026	0.745±0.014	**0.767±0.016**
	MLP trained with the Levemberg-Marquardt method			
Acc	88.6±1.4	88.1±1.6	80.0±0.8	**92.1±0.6**
Rcl	69.3±4.2	70.8±6.6	74.9±3.9	*81.7±2.0
Spc	94.2±1.2	93.0±0.7	93.1±0.4	**95.3±0.2**
Pcs	77.6±4.6	74.1±3.7	76.1±2.1	*84.4±1.9
FM	0.731±0.032	0.723±0.049	0.754±0.27	*0.830±0.008
	RBF			
Acc	79.7±0.6	76.7±0.4	**81.7±0.9**	76.8±0.3
Rcl	26.7±2.8	4.8±1.3	**38.9±3.9**	5.5±1.4
Spc	95.8±0.7	*98.6±0.3	94.8±0.06	98.4±0.4
Pcs	65.8±3.3	50.3±7.9	**69.3±2.5**	50.4±5.2
FM	0.379±0.030	0.087±0.024	**0.497±3.5**	0.098±0.024
	SOM + LVQ			
Acc	80.6±0.8	77.3±0.9	**85.1±1.5**	78.2±0.4
Rcl	29.2±2.6	15.4±3.6	**62.7±5.6**	17.5±1.3
Spc	96.3±0.6	96.0±1.2	91.9±0.5	**96.6±0.5**
Pcs	**70.4±4.0**	54.4±7.4	69.9±2.6	61.3±3.5
FM	0.412±0.030	0.238±0.046	**0.660±0.042**	0.272±0.018

According to the results, it is clear that the MLP trained with Levenberg-Marquardt method achieved the best performance. On the other hand, the SOM and RBF accomplished poor results. Note that, although the best set of results was acquired when all the features were used (content-based and link-based features), in average, the transformed link-based features offered a more balanced classification if we take into account all the classifiers performance.

If we compare the algorithms performance achieved by each set of features, we can note that, in general, the best results were achieved by MLPs using the combination of content-based and link-based features. However, for RBF and SOM, the results achieved by using these set of features were much inferior than those one achieved by using transformed link-based features. On the other hand, if we compare only the results achieved by the ANNs using the content-based with the link-based features, we can see that, in general, the networks acquired better performances when content-based features were employed.

It is important to note that the results shown in Table 2 also indicate that, in general, the ANNs have more successful to identify ham hosts than spam ones (specificity rate higher than spam recall rate). Thus, we suspected that the low capacity of spam recognition was due to the fact that the data is unbalanced. Consequently, the large difference between the number of ham samples and spam used for training the ANNs could cause the classifier biased in class with larger number of samples. So, we decided to use the same number of data in the two classes in the training stage. In this way, in each of the ten tests for each simulation, 1,978 samples of each class were randomly selected to be exposed to the classifiers and new simulations were performed keeping the proportion of 80% of the samples of each class for training and 20% for testing. Table 3 presents the classification results.

The results in Table 3 indicate that the ANNs trained with the same number of samples in each class improved the performance of all classifiers. If we compare these results with the ones presented in Table 2, we can see that the F-measure was higher in almost all the simulations, except in the simulation with SOM using the link-based features and combination of the link-based features with content-based features. Note that, with this new configuration, the MLP with gradient descent method achieved the best performance.

Again, we observed that the MLPs are more efficient when the combination of content-based and link-based features is used. However, for RBF and SOM, the best results were again achieved when transformed link-based features were employed.

To show that the evaluated ANNs are really competitive, in Table 4 we present a comparison between the best results achieved by the evaluated methods and the top performance techniques available in the literature. To offer a fair evaluation, we have implemented all the compared approaches and tested them by using the same dataset with unbalanced classes, features and protocol employed in our ANNs. We set exactly the same parameters as described in the papers or, otherwise, we kept the default values. In resume, we have implemented the bagging of decision trees [6, 10] and boosting of decision trees [6] using the WEKA library and the linear support vector machines (SVM) [11] using the LIBSVM library. For the genetic programming [1], we just report the same results available in the paper since the authors adopted the same dataset and protocol we have used.

Table 3. Results achieved by each evaluated neural network for WEBSPAM-UK2006 dataset using balanced classes in the training stage

	Content	Links	Trans. Links	Content+Links
	MLP trained with the gradient descent method			
	Mean	Mean	Mean	Mean
Acc	84.7±1.6	83.9±1.9	87.4±1.6	*89.1±1.4
Rcl	82.9±2.0	90.2±2.6	89.6±2.2	*92.6±2.4
Spc	86.4±2.4	77.9±3.0	85.2±1.1	85.6±2.0
Pcs	86.1±2.4	80.0±2.9	85.9±2.0	86.7±2.1
FM	0.845±0.015	0.848±0.019	0.877±0.019	*0.895±0.013
	MLP trained with the Levemberg-Marquardt method			
Acc	87.6±1.5	86.4±1.7	86.3±2.7	88.4±2.1
Rcl	86.5±2.0	92.1±3.8	87.5±4.0	91.9±3.5
Spc	88.8±1.9	81.1±2.6	85.2±3.6	85.0±3.3
Pcs	*89.1±2.4	82.3±2.6	85.8±3.3	85.6±2.7
FM	0.877±0.017	0.868±0.019	0.866±0.027	0.886±0.021
	RBF			
Acc	63.6±1.3	65.9±3.5	75.7±1.8	66.7±0.8
Rcl	45.6±1.9	79.5±2.6	75.2±4.3	72.3±2.3
Spc	81.6±1.5	52.2±8.7	76.1±5.6	61.1±3.3
Pcs	71.3±2.1	62.7±3.8	76.2±3.2	65.1±1.3
FM	0.556±0.016	0.700±0.019	0.755±0.018	0.684±0.007
	SOM+LVQ			
Acc	66.9±0.7	77.2±0.5	86.0±0.4	78.1±0.6
Rcl	59.7±5.9	11.6±1.9	64.7±2.9	16.6±1.6
Spc	74.2±5.5	*97.1±0.5	92.5±0.09	96.7±0.9
Pcs	70.1±2.9	54.9±4.8	72.3±1.8	61.4±6.3
FM	0.642±0.026	0.191±0.028	0.683±0.013	0.260±0.021

Table 4. Comparison between the results achieved by the evaluated neural networks and the top performance classifiers available in the literature

Classifiers	Pcs	Rcl	FM
Best results available in the literature			
Castilho et al. [10], Ntoulas et al. [6] - content	81.5	68.0	0.741
Svore et al. [11] - content	55.5	86.5	0.677
Ntoulas et al. [6] - content	78.2	68.2	0.728
Shengen et al. [1] - links	69.8	76.3	0.726
Shengen et al. [1] - transformed links	76.5	81.4	0.789
Best results achieved by the neural networks			
MLP + Levenberg - content+links	79.5	74.2	0.767
MLP + Gradient - content+links	84.4	81.7	0.830
MLP + Levenberg - content+links (balanced classes)	85.6	91.9	0.886
MLP + Gradient - content+links (balanced classes)	86.7	92.6	0.895

The comparison indicates that the MLPs are very suitable to deal with the problem. Note that, both the MLP trained with gradient descent as the MLP trained with the Levemberg-Marquardt method achieved the highest performances. Their results are comparable with the top-performance methods such as bagging [6, 10] and boosting algorithm [6]. However, taking into account the spam precision and recall rates it is clear that the MLP trained with the gradient descent method using the complete set of features outperformed all the compared approaches.

5   Conclusions and Future Work

In this paper, we have presented a performance evaluation of different models of artificial neural networks used to automatically classify real samples of web spam using content-based features, link-based features, the combination of both and transformed link-based features.

The results indicate that, in general, the multilayer perceptron neural network trained with the gradient descent and Levenberg-Marquardt methods are the best evaluated models, especially when the combination of the link-based and content-based features are employed. Both methods outperformed established techniques available in the literature such as decision trees [10], SVM [11] and genetic programming [1].

Furthermore, since the data we used in our experiment is unbalanced, the results also indicate that all the evaluated techniques are superior when trained with the same amount of samples of each class. It is because the models tend to be biased to the benefit of the class with the largest amount of samples.

Overall, we have also concluded that Kohonen's self-organizing map and radial basis function neural network were inferior than the multilayer perceptron neural networks in all the simulations independent on the chosen set of features.

Actually, we are working to propose new set of features and new possible combinations in order to enhance the classifiers prediction.

References

1. Shengen, L., Xiaofei, N., Peiqi, L., Lin, W.: Generating New Features Using Genetic Programming to Detect Link Spam. In: 2011 Intl. Conf. on Intelligent Computation Technology and Automation (ICICTA 2011), pp. 135–138. IEEE (2011)
2. Araujo, L., Martinez-Romo, J.: Web Spam Detection – New Classification Features Based on Qualified Link Analysis and Language Models. IEEE Transactions on Information Forensics and Security 5(3), 581–590 (2010)
3. Egele, M., Kolbitsch, C., Platzer, C.: Removing Web Spam Links from Search Engine Results. Journal in Computer Virology 7(1), 51–62 (2011)
4. Shen, G., Gao, B., Liu, T., Feng, G., Song, S., Li, H.: Detecting Link Spam Using Temporal Information. In: 6th Intl. Conf. on Data Mining (ICDM 2006), pp. 1049–1053. IEEE (2006)
5. Gan, Q., Suel, T.: Improving Web Spam Classifiers Using Link Structure. In: 3rd Intl. Work. on Adversarial Information Retrieval on the Web (AIRWeb 2007), pp. 17–20. ACM (2007)
6. Ntoulas, A., Najork, M., Manasse, M., Fetterly, D.: Detecting Spam Web Pages Through Content Analysis. In: 15th Intl. Conf. on World Wide Web (WWW 2006), pp. 83–92. ACM (2006)

7. Silva, R.M., Almeida, T.A., Yamakami, A.: Artificial Neural Networks for Content-based Web Spam Detection. In: 14th Intl. Conf. on Artificial Intelligence (ICAI 2012), pp. 1–7 (2012)

8. Bíró, I., Siklósi, D., Szabó, J., Benczúr, A.A.: Linked Latent Dirichlet Allocation in Web Spam Filtering. In: 5th Intl. Work. on Adversarial Information Retrieval on the Web (AIRWeb 2009), pp. 37–40. ACM (2009)

9. Abernethy, J., Chapelle, O., Castillo, C.: Graph Regularization Methods for Web Spam Detection. Machine Learning 81(2), 207–225 (2010)

10. Castillo, C., Donato, D., Gionis, A.: Know Your Neighbors – Web Spam Detection Using the Web Topology. In: 30th Annual Intl. ACM SIGIR Conf. on Research and Development in Information Retrieval (SIGIR 2007), pp. 423–430. ACM (2007)

11. Svore, K.M., Wu, Q., Burges, C.J.: Improving Web Spam Classification Using Rank-Time Features. In: 3rd Intl. Work. on Adversarial Information Retrieval on the Web (AIRWeb 2007), pp. 9–16. ACM (2007)

12. Noi, L.D., Hagenbuchner, M., Scarselli, F., Tsoi, A.: Web Spam Detection by Probability Mapping Graphsoms and Graph Neural Networks. In: Diamantaras, K., Duch, W., Iliudis, L.S. (eds.) ICANN 2010, Part II. LNCS, vol. 6353, pp. 372–381. Springer, Heidelberg (2010)

13. Largillier, T., Peyronnet, S.: Using Patterns in the Behavior of the Random Surfer to Detect Webspam Beneficiaries. In: Chiu, D.K.W., Bellatreche, L., Sasaki, H., Leung, H.-f., Cheung, S.-C., Hu, H., Shao, J. (eds.) WISE Workshops 2010. LNCS, vol. 6724, pp. 241–253. Springer, Heidelberg (2011)

14. Haykin, S.: Neural Networks – A Comprehensive Foundation, 2nd edn. Prentice Hall, New York (1998)

15. Bishop, C.M.: Neural Networks for Pattern Recognition. Oxford Press, Oxford (1995)

16. Hagan, M.T., Menhaj, M.B.: Training Feedforward Networks with the Marquardt Algorithm. IEEE Transactions on Neural Networks 5(6), 989–993 (1994)

17. Kohonen, T.: The Self-Organizing Map. Proceedings of the IEEE 78(9), 1464–1480 (1990)

18. Orr, M.J.L.: Introduction to Radial Basis Function Networks. Center for Cognitive Science, UK (1996)

19. Becchetti, L., Castillo, C., Donato, D., Leonardi, S., Baeza-Yates, R.: Using Rank Propagation and Probabilistic Counting for Link-Based Spam Detection. In: Workshop on Web Mining and Web Usage Analysis (WebKDD 2006), pp. 1–10. ACM (2006)

20. Shao, J.: Linear Model Selection by Cross-Validation. Journal of the American Statistical Association 88(422), 486–494 (1993)

21. Witten, I.H., Frank, E.: Data Mining – Practical Machine Learning Tools and Techniques, 2nd edn. Morgan Kaufmann, San Francisco (2005)

A Graph-Based Approach for Transcribing Ancient Documents

Graciela Lecireth Meza-Lovón

Universidad Nacional de San Agustín
UNSA - Arequipa, Perú
gmezalovon@unsa.edu.pe
Universidad Católica San Pablo
UCSP - Arequipa, Perú
gmezal@ucsp.edu.pe

Abstract. Over the last years, the interest in preserving digitally ancient documents has increased resulting in databases with a huge amount of image data. Most of these documents are not transcribed and thus querying operations are limited to basic searching. We propose a novel approach for transcribing historical documents and present results of our initial experiments. Our method divides a text-line image into frames and constructs a graph using the framed image. Then Dijkstra algorithm is applied to find the line transcription. Experiments show a character accuracy of 79.3%.

Keywords: handwriting recognition, graph theory, support vector machines, shortest path algorithms.

1 Introduction

In the last decade, word wide libraries have invested a great amount of effort in digitalizing handwritten historical documents and in storing them in different image formats. Although paleography experts, historians and other researchers can query these image databases, such queries are mostly restricted to author, title, year of publication or subject. These restrictions are due to the fact that the great majority of document images are not transcribed into a textual electronic format, and consequently, users cannot carry out queries based on the content of the document images.

Even though considerable progress has been made in generic handwriting recognition technology over the last decades[2, 5–7, 12], the transcription of handwritten historical documents remained mostly unexplored. But as the interest in document digitization projects oriented to publish such information increased, the necessity of more specialized queries became imperative.

Querying words contained in historical collections was initially carried out by Manmatha et al. [13–15], who proposed a word spotting method based on Dynamic Type Warping and clustering techniques. Using these techniques, Manmatha et al. were able to create a word index, on which queries were performed.

J. Pavón et al. (Eds.): IBERAMIA 2012, LNAI 7637, pp. 210–220, 2012.

Other non-training methods to retrieve word images were presented by Leydier et al. [9–11]. Even though content-based queries can be done using these methods their purpose was not to transcribe documents.

Pioneer work on transcribing ancient documents was made by Toselli et al. [20] and Romero-Gómez et al. [18, 19]. Roughly speaking, a transcription system is two-fold: on the one hand, it has a core based on a handwritten text recognition (HTR) model; and on the other hand, it has a post-editing module by means of which a transcription expert corrects the mistakes made by handwritten text recognition system. In this context, Toselli et al. [20] and Romero-Gómez et al. [18, 19] proposed an approach in which a HTR system (based on Hidden Markov Models) is improved by the expert feedback; that is, the interaction with the experts makes the HTR update its parameters and yield a more accurate output. The whole framework is supported by a statistical model.

In this paper, we focus on the handwritten text recognition but not on the post-editing module. We present HTR system for transcribing historical documents which is based on a graph representation. Line images can be represented by a sequence of non-overlapping fixed-width regions called frames. To transcribe a text-line image, we first divide the image into frames, then using the framed image, a character classifier previously trained and the minimum and maximum number of frames that any character spreads over, we create a graph in which the path with maximum cost is used to find the line transcription.

This paper is organized as follows. Sections 2 and 3 formulate our problem and provide an overview of the whole method. Section 4 describes the pre-processing methods applied to our corpora. Section 5 presents the classifier we use and the technique to extract features. Later, we introduce our recognition method, which is based on frame segmentation and graph theory, in Sect. 6, and we describe its evaluation in Sect. 7. Finally, our conclusions and future work is presented in Sect. 8.

2   Problem Setting

We assume that text-line images have been extracted from page images. Formally, we denote a feature vector by $\mathbf{x}$, and represent a text-line image as a sequence of feature vectors $\overline{\mathbf{x}} = (\mathbf{x_1}, \ldots, \mathbf{x_T})$, where $\mathbf{x_t} \subset \mathbb{R}^d$. Furthermore, a line transcription $\bar{l}$ is composed of a sequence of characters, $\bar{l} = (l_1, \ldots, l_N)$ where $l_n \in \Sigma$, for all n, $1 \leq n \leq N$. Σ is the set of characters in the Spanish alphabet, plus the space character; and Σ^* is the set of all finite-length sequences over Σ; thus $\bar{l} \in \Sigma^*$. Moreover, note that N is not fixed since the number of characters in $\bar{l}$ varies from one line image to another.

Next, the goal of our research is stated as follows: given a sequence of feature vectors $\overline{\mathbf{x}}$ representing a line image, to search for a sequence of characters $\bar{l}' \in \Sigma^*$, with the highest conditional probability,

$$\bar{l}' = \arg\max_{\bar{l} \in \Sigma^*} p(\bar{l}|\overline{\mathbf{x}}) \tag{1}$$

However, a direct search is not feasible since the number of possible sequences is exponential in the number of events. A tractable approximation to find $\bar{l}'$ is proposed in this paper. The next section describes an overview of the whole method.

3   Overview

Since for solving the aforementioned problem we use text-lines images, the first step of our method is to prepare the data and extract text-line images, so they can be used in posterior stages. To accomplish that, we perform several tasks which include: 1) correcting the skew of the text-lines with respect to the x-coordinate, 2) splitting the page images into text-lines images, 3) correcting the handwriting slant and 4) normalizing the text-lines images so they have the same height measures (see Sect. 4).

The second step is to split the text-lines into frames. Subsequently, we select part of the data to train a character classifier, namely SVM (see Sect. 5.1). More precisely, we divide the selected text-lines into character images, extract gradient features from them (see Sect. 5.2), and pass them to a SVM to be trained. Besides we compute max_f and min_f using the selected text-lines (see Sect. 6.1).

Lastly, for the recognition stage, we construct a graph for every text-line image of the remaining data 1) by adding edges and nodes, as well as 2) by associating a character class (e.g. 'a', 'm') and a cost to each edge (see Sect. 6.1). In regard to 2), we extract subimages from the text-line image in question, and calculate their gradient features. Afterwards we find the shortest path of the graph, traverse it, and meanwhile we take the character class associated to its edges. By doing this we obtain the optimal sequence of characters (see Sect. 6.2).

4   Data Preparation

The data used in our experiments consists of gray-scale images, on which we applied procedures to improve images quality and to extract the text-lines from them. First, similarly to the method described in [1], we fixed the pages skew (the slope of the text-lines introduced during the page scanning process) by applying a heuristic which consists in simulating text-line rotations with angles ranging from -18° to 18°; and then choosing the angle that produces the horizontal projection profile with both the greatest variance and the highest peak.

After skew correction operation, we segmented the page image into text-line images. For this purpose, we applied horizontal projection profile to a page image, and subsequently we identified the profile valleys. Generally speaking, such valleys correpond to the spaces between lines, and therefore they were used to segment page images.

Then, aiming to bring the slating handwriting to the upright position, we corrected the slant. To this end, we detected the angle α between the hand-writing and the y-coordinate, and then we smeared the image using the detected angle. The angle α can be derived from central moments μ as follows, $\alpha = \arctan(\mu_{11}/\mu_{02})$; $\mu = \sum_{x=1}^{N} \sum_{y=1}^{N} (x - x_c)^g (y - y_c)^h p(x,y)$, where x_c and

y_c are the centroid coordinates of the image and $p(x, y)$ is the pixel intensity at position (x, y). The point (x_c, y_c) was estimated from the geometric moment as explained in [3]. Then we smeared the image by applying a horizontal shear transform to every pixel (x, y), obtaining for each of them a new intensity value $p(x', y')$ in which, $x' = x - (y - y_c)\tan(\alpha)$ and $y' = y$.

Moreover, we need the central, ascender and descender areas (see Fig. 1) of all the text-line images to be the same height, in order to make the recognition process size invariant. To this end, the text-line images were normalized similarly as done in [17]. First, we found the mid-line using the horizontal projection profile; secondly, we delimited the central area by finding the x-line and base-line; and finally, we normalized the central, ascender (region above the x-line) and descender (region below the base-line) areas according to height ratios given by the user.

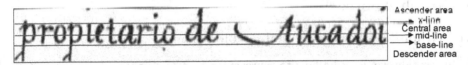

Ascender area
x-line
Central area
mid-line
base-line
Descender area

Fig. 1. Line Normalization

5   Training and Feature Extraction

5.1   Support Vector Machines

Support Vector Machines (SVM) [4] aims to find an optimal separating hyperplane, defined as one which provides the maximal distance (maximal margin), between the hyperplane and the closest input samples (support vectors) of two classes. Finding the hyperplane with the maximal margin can be formulated as an optimization problem subject to certain restrictions. In addition, SVM maps, through a kernel function, the input data into a higher dimensional space in which a linear separation is feasible.

In this work, part of the text-lines images obtained from previous stage was used to train and test a SVM. Firstly, we divided the text-lines into character images; secondly, we extracted gradient features from the images according to what is described in Sect. 5.2. Finally we used the 90% of the feature vectors for training, and the reminder to test SVM. Furthermore, we used the LIBSVM library[1] which not only predict the class for a test pattern, but also provides the probabilities associated to each class.

5.2   Gradient Features

Using gradient features we aim at finding the gradient strengths for each pixel intensity $p(x, y)$ of an image. To that end, we followed the method by Fujisawa

---

[1] http://www.csie.ntu.edu.tw/~cjlin/libsvm/

et al. [8], who proposed to apply the Robert's Cross Operator [16] which calculates the gradient vector of the pixel (x, y) using diagonal directions; more precisely, Fujisawa et al. estimated both the gradient magnitude s and the direction α of pixel (x, y) via $s(x, y) = \sqrt{\triangle u^2 + \triangle v^2}$ and $\theta(x, y) = \arctan\left(\triangle v/\triangle u\right)$, where $\triangle u = \partial p/x = p(x + 1, y + 1) - p(x, y)$ and $\triangle v = \partial p/y = p(x + 1, y) - p(x, y + 1)$. Generally, the direction of the gradient is quantized in 32 angle intervals of $\pi/16$ each. The common procedure to extract gradient features is first to divide vertically and horizontally an image into non overlapping blocks of the same size, and secondly, to accumulate for each block the strength of the gradient in each of the 32 directions. By doing this, we obtained a feature vector $\mathbf{x} = (\mathbf{x_1} \ldots, \mathbf{x_T})$, $\mathbf{T} = 32 * B$, where B represents the number of blocks in which the image was divided.

6   Graph Approach

6.1   Graph Representation of Text-Line Images

In this section we describe how to represent a text-line image as a graph. This description must be applied to every text-line image to be recognized. A text-line image is divided into frames, $f_1, f_2, \ldots, f_N$, where each frame f_i is an area of fixed size, with a starting point p_i corresponding to the x-coordinate where the frame starts (see Fig. 2(a)). Moreover, note that characters spreads over a certain number of frames; e.g., Fig. 2(b) illustrates character 'i' and 's' spreading over 3 and 5 frames respectively. So, from a set of characters we find the minimum min_f and maximum max_f number of frames that a character can take up.

We construct a graph using the line image, the frame width, min_f and max_f. In such a graph, a node s represents the x-coordinate where a frame starts, and the edge leaving node s represents the number of frames that must be taken from the x-coordinate.

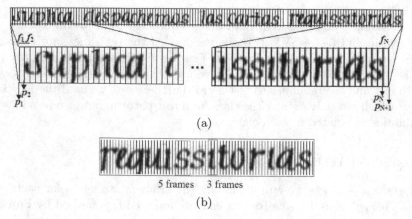

(a)

5 frames   3 frames

(b)

Fig. 2. a) Image segmented into frames. b) Character 'i' and 's'.

Not every path of the graph is valid in our method; more precisely, valid paths start at p_1 and end at $p_N + 1$. This is because we analyze the whole text-line image; that is, from p_1 to $p_N + 1$. The first node we create is $p_i, i = 1$ and it corresponds to zero x-coordinate. Then we add $(max_f - min_f + 1)$ edges leaving p_1. Each of these edges is associated to a subimage that starts at position p_1 and whose width is determined by a particular number of frames n in the range $[min_f, max_f]$. Gradient features are extracted from the subimage just as described in Sect. 5.2, and tested by a previously trained SVM, which yields both the most likely class and its class probability. Thus every edge is related to a subimage, a class and a probability estimate (cost of an edge) as shown in Fig. 3(a). Moreover, every time an edge is added, its ending node p_n is added as well, where $n = i + k + 1$. We repeat this procedure until we reach $p_N + 1$.

To illustrate this procedure consider Fig. 3(a) and assume that $max_f = 5$ and $min_f = 3$ were previously computed. First, we add both the initial node p_1 and 3 edges leaving p_1, namely, e_{14}, e_{15} and e_{16}. The edge e_{14} corresponds to taking the subimage that spreads over 3 frames from position p_1. From this subimage we extract gradient features and test them using a SVM which gives the most likely class and its class probability; subsequently, the ending node p_4 is added. This is interpreted as follows: if we start at position p_1 and test 3 frames (3 fs), we end up at position p_4. The same holds for e_{15} and e_{16} (see Fig. 3(a)). After creating p_4, p_5, p_6, we add 3 edges from p_4 as well as their corresponding ending nodes p_7, p_8, p_9 (see Fig. 3(b)). The same is applied to p_5, p_6, p_7 (Fig. 3(c)(d)(e)). Figure 3(f) shows the complete graph for the text-line image in Fig. 3(a).

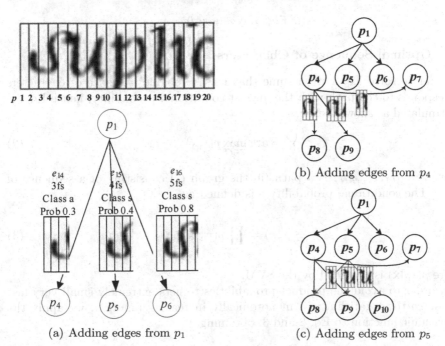

(a) Adding edges from p_1

(b) Adding edges from p_4

(c) Adding edges from p_5

Fig. 3. Contruction of the graph

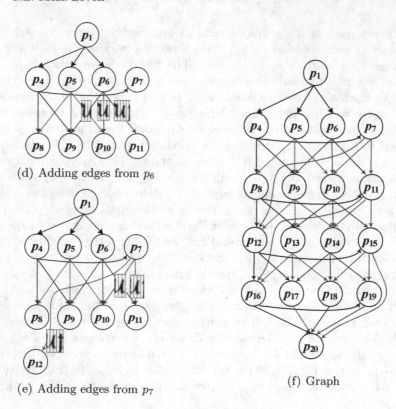

(d) Adding edges from p_6

(e) Adding edges from p_7

(f) Graph

Fig. 3. (*continued*)

6.2   Optimal Sequence of Characters

In order to solve Eq. 1 we assume that most probable sequence of characters corresponds to the path with the highest conditional probability; hence Eq.1 is reformulated as shown below,

$$\overline{r}' = \arg \max_{\overline{r} \in G} p(\overline{r}|\overline{\mathbf{x}}), \tag{2}$$

where $\overline{r} = (r_1, \ldots, r_N)$ is a path (in the graph G) consisting of a sequence of edges. The conditional probability p is defined as

$$p(\overline{r}|\overline{\mathbf{x}}) = \prod_{n=1}^{N} p(r_n|\mathbf{x}), \tag{3}$$

where $p(r_n|\mathbf{x})$ is provided by the SVM.

In order to avoid the product probabilities to gets extremely small very fast and since the logarithm is a monotonically increasing function, we apply the logarithmic function to Eq. 2 and 3, obtaining

$$\overline{r}' = \arg \max_{\overline{r} \in G} \ln(p(\overline{r}|\overline{\mathbf{x}})) \tag{4}$$

and

$$\ln(p(\overline{r}|\mathbf{x})) = \sum_{n=1}^{N} \ln(p(r_n|\mathbf{x})). \tag{5}$$

Note that instead of $\ln p$, we can assign the cost $c = 1/\ln p$ to an edge. By doing this we can convert the highest probability path problem into the lowest probability path one, which can be solved by applying any shortest path algorithm, such as Dijkstra. However, note that according to the description for constructing the graph, exposed in Sect. 6.1, Dijkistra algorithm favours paths with fewer number of edges; or from other perspective, the algorithm is biased to choose paths with edges associated to wider subimages (bigger number of frames). Consequently, we need to adapt the algorithm to keep all the paths well-balanced in length. To this end, we modified the cost estimation such that the new c' assigned to an edge is $f * c$, where f is the number of frames tied up to the edge.

7 Experiments and Results

For assessing the proposed method, we used a corpus of 550 page images of handwritten Spanish text written by a single author. The corpus, which we abbreviate as ECA, was created from a historical book called "Ejecutoría y certificación del escudo de armas de los apellidos Echapare, Loigorri, Virto y Casado" written in 1756 and stored in the "Biblioteca del Patrimonio Bibliográfico", Spain. Besides, in order to compare the results of our system with those of the literature, we employed the IAMDB[2], a laboratory database created by the Research Group on Computer Vision and Artificial Intelligence, Universitã Bern, which consists of 1539 pages (forms) of scanned text, 5685 sentences, written by 657 writers who contributed samples of their handwriting (see Fig. 4) .

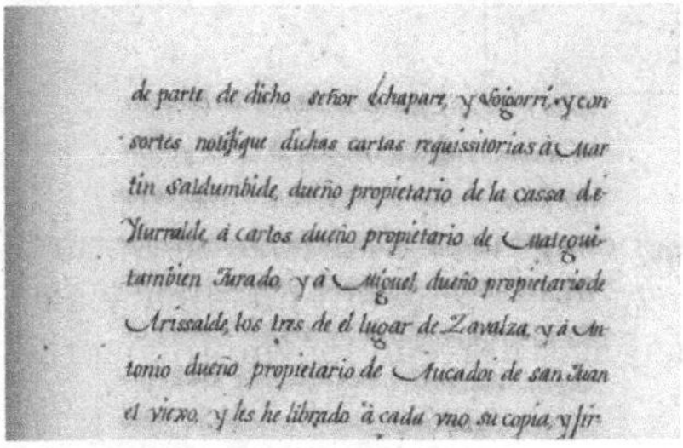
de parte de dicho señor Echapare, y Loigorri, y con
sortes notifique dichas cartas requissitorias à Mar
tin Saldumbide, dueño propietario de la cassa de
Iturralde, à Carlos dueño propietario de Mategui
tambien Jurado y à Miguel, dueño propietario de
Arissalde, los tres de el lugar de Zavalza, y à An
tonio dueño propietario de Aucadoi de san Juan
el viexo, y les he librado à cada vno su copia, y fir

(a)

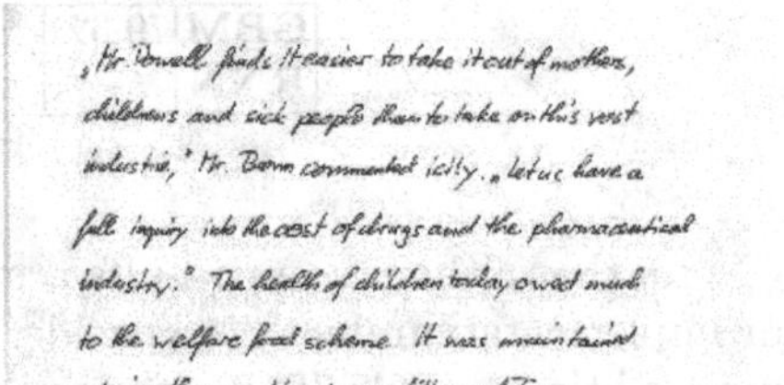
„Mr. Powell finds it easier to take it out of mothers,
childrens and sick people than to take on this vast
industry," Mr. Benn commented icily. „Let us have a
full inquiry into the cost of drugs and the pharmaceutical
industry." The health of children today owed much
to the welfare food scheme. It was maintained
during the war. Now in conditions of Tory
affluence it seemed it could not be carried on.

(b) Fragment from IAMDB.

Fig. 4. Fragments of a page from a) ECA and b) IAMDB

[2] `http://www.iam.unibe.ch/fki/databases/iam-handwriting-corpus`

Since our work includes neither a language model nor a word dictionary, we did not use the word accuracy to asset the performance, but instead we used the character accuracy, which is defined as:

$$A = 100 \times (1 - \frac{i + s + d}{L}),$$

where i, s, d, are the number of insertions, substitutions and deletions summed over the whole test set and L is the total length of the set transcriptions.

Table 1 summarizes the statistics of the corpora and shows the number of samples used in the experiments. The accuracies obtained from SVM using EAC and IAMDB are presented in Table 2. Furthermore, we obtained $max_f = 9$ and $min_f = 5$ for ECA and $max_f = 9$ and $min_f = 4$ for IAMDB. The character accuracy achieved by applying the Graph-Based Model(GBM) is shown in Table 3.

Table 1. Statistics of ECA and IAMDB

	Number of			Number of Characters SVM		Number of
	pages	lines	characters	training	testing	Characters GBM
ECA	50	9982	39498	7150	795	31553
IAMDB	50	531	15636	2814	313	12509

Table 2. Results for ECA and IAMDB using SVM

Character Accuracy (%)	
ECA	IAMDB
98.83±0.5%	91.43±1.35%

Table 3. Main Results for our method using ECA and IAMDB

	Character Accuracy(%)	
	ECA	IAMDB
GBM	79.3%	72.57%
RNN	-	81.8%

Note, that although our results are not as good as those shown in literature, our implementation does not consider a language model, a word dictionary and a post-editing module. Therefore we believe there is still room for improving the system performance.

8   Conclusions and Future Work

We present a method for transcribing handwritten text that is based on a graph representation for a text-line image. We assessed our method using real data, more precisely, a historical book written in Spanish, and obtained a character accuracy of 79.3%. We believe that our approach has potential in recognizing handwriting; therefore, we intend to develop a complete system that include: 1) a dictionary, which helps us to correct misspelling words; 2) a language model, which is useful to capture the properties of the language, and to predict the next word in a sequence; and finally 3) a graph model that captures transitions between characters.

References

1. Baird, H.S.: The Skew Angle of Printed Documents. In: O'Gorman, L., Kasturi, R. (eds.) Document Image Analysis, pp. 204–208. IEEE Computer Society Press (1995)
2. Burger, T., Kessentini, Y., Paquet, T.: Dempster-Shafer Based Rejection Strategy for Handwritten Word Recognition. In: 2011 Intl. Conf. on Document Analysis and Recognition (ICDAR 2011), pp. 528–532. IEEE (2011)
3. Cheriet, M., Kharma, N., Liu, C.L., Suen, C.: Character Recognition Systems: A Guide for Students and Practitioners. Wiley & Sons Inc. (2007)
4. Cortes, C., Vapnik, V.: Support-Vector Networks. Maching Learning 20(3), 273–297 (1995)
5. Frinken, V., Bunke, H.: Self-Training for Handwritten Text Line Recognition. In: Bloch, I., Cesar, R.M. (eds.) CIARP 2010. LNCS, vol. 6419, pp. 104–112. Springer, Heidelberg (2010)
6. Frinken, V., Fischer, A., Bunke, H.: Combining Neural Networks to Improve Performance of Handwritten Keyword Spotting. In: Gayar, N.E., Kittler, J., Roli, F. (eds.) MCS 2010. LNCS, vol. 5997, pp. 215–224. Springer, Heidelberg (2010)
7. Frinken, V., Fischer, A., Bunke, H., Fornés, A.: Co-training for handwritten word recognition. In: Intl. Conf. on Document Analysis and Recognition (ICDAR 2011), pp. 314–318. IEEE (2011)
8. Fujisawa, Y., Shi, M., Wakabayashi, T., Kimura, F.: Handwritten Numeral Recognition Using Gradient and Curvature of Gray Scale Image. In: 5th Intl. Conf. on Document Analysis and Recognition (ICDAR 1999), pp. 277–300. IEEE (1999)
9. Leydier, Y., Lebourgeois, F., Emptoz, H.: Omnilingual Segmentation-freeWord Spotting for Ancient Manuscripts Indexation. In: 8th Intl. Conf. on Document Analysis and Recognition (ICDAR 2005), pp. 533–537 (2005)
10. Leydier, Y., Lebourgeois, F., Emptoz, H.: Text Search for Medieval Manuscript Images. Pattern Recogntion 40(12), 3552–3567 (2007)
11. Leydier, Y., Ouji, A., LeBourgeois, F., Emptoz, H.: Towards an Omnilingual Word Retrieval System for Ancient Manuscripts. Pattern Recognition 42(9), 2089–2105 (2009)
12. Liwicki, M., Bunke, H.: Feature Selection for HMM and BLSTM Based Handwriting Recognition of Whiteboard Notes. International Journal of Pattern Recognition and Artificial Intelligence 23(5), 907–923 (2009)
13. Rath, T.M., Manmatha, R.: Word Spotting for Historical Documents. International Journal on Document Analysis and Recognition 9(2), 139–152 (2007)
14. Rath, T.M., Manmatha, R.: Features for Word Spotting in Historical Manuscripts. In: 7th Intl. Conf. on Document Analysis and Recognition (ICDAR 2003), pp. 218–222. IEEE (2003)

15. Rath, T.M., Manmatha, R.: Word Image Matching Using Dynamic Time Warping. In: 2003 IEEE Computer Society Conference on Computer Vision and Pattern Recognition, vol. 2, pp. 521–527 (2003)
16. Roberts, L.G.: Machine Perception of Three-Dimensional Solids. Ph.D. thesis, Dept. of Electrical Engineering, Massachusetts Institute of Technology (1963)
17. Romero, V.: Multimodal Interactive Transcription of Handwritten Text Images. Ph.D. thesis, Departamento de Sistemas Informáticos y Computación, Universidad Politécnica de Valencia (2010)
18. Romero, V., Pastor, M.: Computer assisted transcription of text images. In: Toselli, A., Vidal, E., Casacuberta, F. (eds.) Multimodal Interactive Pattern Recognition and Applications, pp. 61–98. Springer (2011)
19. Romero, V., Rodríguez-Ruiz, L.: Computer assisted transcription: General framework. In: Toselli, A., Vidal, E., Casacuberta, F. (eds.) Multimodal Interactive Pattern Recognition and Applications, pp. 47–60. Springer (2011)
20. Toselli, A.H., Romero, V., Pastor, M., Vidal, E.: Multimodal Interactive Transcription of Text Images. Pattern Recognition 43(5), 1814–1825 (2010)

Differential Diagnosis of Hemorrhagic Fevers Using ARTMAP

William Caicedo, Moisés Quintana, and Hernando Pinzón

Computer Science Department at Universidad Tecnológica de Bolívar,
Parque Industrial y Tecnológico Carlos Vélez Pombo, Km 1 Vía Turbaco,
Cartagena, Colombia
Napoleón Franco Pareja Children Hospital - Casa del Niño, Bruselas Transversal 36
No. 36-33, Cartagena, Colombia
caicedo77@gmail.com, mquintana@unitecnologica.edu.co,
hesapire_2@hotmail.com

Abstract. The differential diagnosis of endemic hemorrhagic fevers in tropical countries is by no means an easy task for medical practitioners. Several diseases often overlap with others in terms of signs and symptoms, thus making this diagnosis a difficult, error-prone process. Machine Learning algorithms possess some useful qualities to tackle this kind of pattern recognition problems. In this paper, a neural-network-based approach to the differential diagnosis of Dengue Fever, Leptospirosis and Malaria, using the Adaptive Resonance Theory Map (ARTMAP) family is discussed. The use of an Artificial Immune System (CLONALG) led to the identification of a subset of symptoms that enhanced the performance of the classifiers considered. Training, validation and testing phases were conducted using a dataset consisting of medical charts from patients treated in the last 10 years at Napoleón Franco Pareja Children Hospital in Cartagena, Colombia. Results obtained on the test set are promising, and support the feasibility of this approach.

Keywords: machine learning, neural networks, ARTMAP, hemorrhagic fever, dengue, leptospirosis, malaria, differential diagnosis.

1 Introduction

Dengue, Leptospirosis and Malaria are diseases belonging to a group known as Hemorrhagic Fevers [16,23]. The initial manifestations of such diseases may be consistent with indeterminate febrile illnesses, and because of that they can be easily confused with other conditions or even between them [22]. Despite similar symptoms, etiologies and treatment are very different for each one of these diseases, and that makes it especially important to achieve high performance, clearly defined diagnostic mechanisms, since early diagnosis improves patients prognosis. In order to perform diagnosis, medical practitioners rely on semiological attributes discussed in the relevant literature, but the highly variable characteristics of this diseases imply high variability in terms of signs and symptoms present in patients; making it very hard to come up with a plausible

J. Pavón et al. (Eds.): IBERAMIA 2012, LNAI 7637, pp. 221–230, 2012.

diagnostic hypothesis. Besides, laboratory tests available to confirm potential diagnoses have variable confidence and sometimes it takes too long for results to be available. All these issues play against an accurate and opportune diagnosis, and lead often to the wrong ones. Several studies [1,13,18,19] point out situations where an epidemic outbreak of one disease masks out a significant portion of cases from some other disease. On the other hand in tropical countries like Colombia, Dengue, Leptospirosis and Malaria are diseases with mandatory notification to disease control public entities, since they are considered public health risks, making it even more pressing to find ways to obtain accurate early diagnoses. Machine learning techniques have historically offered important resources in the form of Computer Aided Diagnosis software, by considering diagnosis as a pattern recognition problem. The idea behind this kind of applications is not to replace medical personnel but to provide additional tools for decision making, and contributing to enhanced patient care.

Among machine learning techniques, a particular family of neural networks based on the Adaptive Resonance Theory (ART) have been used with positive results, reported in the specialized literature [12,14,20]. In this paper, we state the use of an Adaptive Resonance Theory Neural Network (ARTMAP) to perform differential diagnosis of Dengue, Leptospirosis and Malaria, with a subset of inputs identified by means of an Artificial Immune System based on Clonal Selection Theory (Clonalg).

2 Dengue, Leptospirosis and Malaria

Dengue, Leptospirosis and Malaria are febrile diseases which are endemic in tropical countries, and in Colombia they are subject to mandatory notification to government health institutions, and considered public health risks, because of their contagion dynamics and the possible mortal consequences of their most severe forms. An important characteristic of these three diseases (and other hemorrhagic fevers) is that in their mild forms they can be practically indistinguishable (in terms of clinical signs) from common cold, or even between themselves. Hemorrhagic manifestations can be present in severe forms, contributing to death of the patient. Despite all similarities regarding symptoms and clinical signs, these diseases are very different in terms of etiology, transmission vectors and infection mechanisms; all of this implies different treatments. It is worth noting that an early and correct treatment improves patient prognosis.

2.1 Dengue Fever

Dengue fever is a syndrome caused by several viruses transmitted by arthopodes (aedes aegypti mosquito mainly), characterized by biphasic fever, myalgia and/or arthralgia, leucopenia and lymphadenopathy. Severe dengue with hemorrhagic manifestations is an often fatal complication that can lead to Dengue Shock Syndrome (DSS), characterized by abnormalities in hemostasis and capillary permeability [15]. There is a general consensus regarding existence of four antigenically distinct members into into the Dengue subgroup, inside Flavivirus genus. Dengue fever is an illness characterized by high fever, absence of chills, frontal headache, myalgia, arthralgia, retro-ocular pain, exanthema (petequial, specially), "white islands in a sea of red" sign, facial erythema (blush), leukopenia with lymphocytosis, thrombocytopenia, among others symptoms [23], with severity varying according to patient age.

2.2 Leptospirosis

Leptospirosis is a zoonosis present worldwide, caused by spirochaete of the genus Leptospira. Leptospira infect a variety of wild and domestic animals that excrete the microorganism in their urine. Humans, which get infected by contact with sick animals or through exposition to water contaminated with urine of infected animals, develop an acute febrile illness which can be followed by a more severe and sometimes fatal condition (Weils disease), that may include jaundice, renal failure, meningitis, myocarditis, hemorrhagic pneumonia and hemodynamic collapse. Until discovery of the agent causing Leptospirosis, it was diagnosed erroneously as Yellow Fever or Malaria [22]. Even today confusion persists between Leptospirosis and other febrile illnesses as Dengue, Hepatitis, Malaria and Influenza, to mention a few.

2.3 Malaria

Malaria is a disease caused by any of the following microorganisms: Plasmodium Falciparum, Plasmodium Vivax, Plasmodium Ovale and Plasmodium Malariae. From those, in Colombia only P. Falciparum and P. Vivax are found. Cyclic fever is the hallmark of malaria, and occurs shortly after or during rupture of red cells and the release of merozoites into the bloodstream. In the case of infection by P. Ovale or P. Vivax, this release cycle occurs every fourty-eight hours, producing the malignant tertians (fever each third day); and in the case of infection by P. Malarie each 72 hours, giving rise to the malignant quartans (fever each fourth day). P. Falciparum tends to produce continuous fever with intermittent peaks, instead of the well-defined cycles of P. Vivax and P. Ovale. Malaric crisis has some very well defined characteristics, to the extent that it is a definitive clinical manifestation of the disease. After a prodrome of variable duration, malaric crisis has three stages: Chills that can last from fifteen minutes to several hours, high fever for several hours and coinciding with the release of merozoites to the blood stream; and finally sweating, fatigue and defervescence.

2.4 Differential Diagnosis of Dengue, Leptospirosis and Malaria

Diseases considered in this work share a series of symptoms and signs that can make diagnosis difficult. However, according to a systematic revision of the relevant literature [10,19,21], and expert opinions from staff in Napoleón Franco Pareja Children Hospital - Casa del Niño, a preliminary symptoms and signs list for the differential diagnosis between the three diseases was constructed. The list was used to construct a dataset for the training, validation and testing of the proposed classifiers. Table 1 describes the structure of the list and shows the included symptoms and signs and the disease for which they are predictors.

Table 1. Signs and symptoms for the differential diagnosis and the importance relative to each disease

Sign/Symptom	Dengue	Leptospirosis	Malaria
Age	x	x	x
Fever type (continuous or cyclic)	x	x	x
Positive tourniquet sign	x		
Anorexia	x		
Chills		x	x
Headache type (frontal or global)	x	x	
Retro-ocular pain	x		
Arthralgia	x		
Myalgia	x	x	
Exanthema localization	x	x	
White islands in a sea of red	x		
Itch	x		
Facial erythema (blush)	x		
Hyponatremia		x	
Opportunistic infections			x
Elevated CPK		x	
Renal compromise		x	x
Jaundice		x	
Pharyngitis		x	
History of contact with dogs or rodents		x	
Contact with rainwater/stagnant water		x	
Calf pain		x	
Hemoglobin level			x
Leukocyte count	x	x	
Lymphocyte count	x	x	
Neutrophil count	x	x	
Month of medical consult	x	x	x
Days of fever	x	x	x
Hematocrit level	x		x

3   Adaptive Resonance Theory (ART) and ARTMAP Neural Networks

3.1   Adaptive Resonance Theory - ART

Adaptive Resonance Theory (ART) was initially proposed by Grossberg as an attempt to resolve the stability-plasticity dilemma [4]. With neural networks as the Multilayer Perceptron, there is the risk of forgetting already memorized patterns when learning new ones, and the solution proposed by Grossberg included a similarity measure designed to avoid this catastrophic forgetting of patterns. ART networks are a special type of competitive network, where neuron activation depends on the similarity between the pattern stored in its weights and the input being considered, similarly to a Kohonen Self-Organizing Map [17]. ART spans a family of neural networks that includes ART1 [4] (binary values), ART2 [5], ART3 [6] and Fuzzy ART [8] among others, which use unsupervised learning; and FuzzyARTMAP [7], ARTMAP-IC [9] and Default ARTMAP [3] among others, which use supervised learning. ART is inspired in the mechanisms of the mammal visual system, and specifically in the way the brain interprets signals coming from the retina.

3.2   ART1

An ART1 network is composed by two layers of neurons. The first layer represents the network Short Term Memory (STM), and the second represents the network Long Term Memory (LTM). When a pattern is presented to the network, it is stored in the STM, and then each neuron in LTM receives a copy of the pattern stored in STM and a competition takes place between the neurons, which results in only one neuron with non-zero activation. This kind of competition is called a Winner-Take-All (WTA) competition, and it is inspired in the activation of certain zones of the cerebral cortex in response to certain stimulus. The connection between STM and LTM layers is filtered by the Bottom-Up weight matrix and the Top-Down weight matrix, which communicate, respectively STM layer with LTM layer (Bottom-Up) and in the opposite way, closing a circuit (Top-Down).

Learning in ART1. ART1 (and in general all models in the ART family) can operate under two modes of learning: Slow learning and fast learning. In slow learning mode (Grossberg models original mode of learning), convergence of weights requires several presentations for each pattern, since in each iteration just a fraction of the pattern is actually learnt (the learning rate β is less than 1); whereas in fast learning mode it is assumed that the pattern is presented during a sufficient time to guarantee convergence in only one iteration (learning rate is equal to one). In practice fast learning is often preferred, since it allows learning in few iterations, with the possible disadvantage of getting different internal memories depending of the order of presentation of the inputs. In any case, ART1 learning mechanisms guarantee that the learning weights will converge after a finite number of iterations.

3.3   ARTMAP

ARTMAP is a neural model that consists of an ART network and an associative memory (map) for supervised training applications. The internal ART network attempts to predict the class where the input vector belongs, and if the prediction is not correct, the vigilance parameter is raised (its value increases to the minimum needed to cause the inhibition of the selected neuron plus a small value ϵ) according to an algorithm called Match-Tracking (MT) and the input pattern is presented again forcing the network to make a correct prediction. This process is repeated until the ART network selects a memory/neuron that predicts correctly the input vector class or (if every neuron in LTM is inhibited) until the creation of a new category in LTM, adding a new neuron that will code the new pattern; and at this point, vigilance returns to its original value. For a detailed description, the interested reader can consult [7].

4 Training, Validation and Testing of the ARTMAP Classifiers

4.1 Dataset Construction

In order to construct a dataset for training, validation and testing, medical charts from the last ten years were collected at Napoleón Franco Pareja Children Hospital in Cartagena, Colombia. The medical chart was selected for inclusion if there were laboratory confirmed diagnosis of dengue, Leptospirosis or Malaria or a very strong confirmatory opinion from senior medical staff.The resulting dataset is comprised by medical charts of 136 patients, and it was divided in three parts, one for training, one for model selection (validation) and one for testing. Stratified random sampling with proportional assignment was used to populate the sets. The final distribution is shown in table 2.

Table 2. Data distribution between training, validation and test sets

Set	Dengue	Leptospirosis	Malaria	Total
Training	51	11	8	70
Validation	24	5	4	33
Test	23	5	5	33

4.2 Training

After partition, the classifiers were trained using the training set. The training mode chosen for the networks was fast learning, which guarantees perfect learning (zero percent error) in few iterations. To reduce the possibility of overfitting the training set, only one training iteration was performed (early stopping).

4.3 Validation

The validation process was centered in finding a subset of symptoms and signs that maximized the performance of the classifiers (feature selection). The idea

Table 3. Parameter values used in each network

Neural network	alpha	initial epsilon	MT	Q	CAM Power
FuzzyARTMAP	0,1	0	-0,01	N/A	N/A
ARTMAP-IC	0,1	0	-0,001	9	N/A
DefaultARTMAP2	0,1	0	-0,001	N/A	4

was to reduce model complexity in order to minimize computational times and improve the generalization bounds. This problem was formulated as an combinatorial optimization problem, and an artificial immune system (CLONALG) was used. Clonalg [11] is an optimization algorithm based on the Clonal Selection Theory [2].

During validation (operating with the whole set of predictors) the parameter values maximizing model performance on the validation set were identified (table 3). Model performance on the validation set is shown in table 4.

Table 4. Results (Recall) on the validation set using all predictors

Neural network	Dengue	Leptospirosis	Malaria
FuzzyARTMAP	91,67% (22/24)	80% (4/5)	50% (2/4)
ARTMAP-IC	87,5% (21/24)	100% (5/5)	50% (2/4)
DefaultARTMAP2	87,5% (21/24)	100% (5/5)	50% (2/4)

Feature Selection. Optimization algorithms seek to minimize (or maximize) an objective function. Solutions can be restricted to certain feasible region (constrained optimization) or not, according to the problem. In this work, the objective function is the classifier performance, and the search space is given by all possible subsets of symptoms and signs that can be used as input; and no restrictions were considered. Every B-cell (immune agent) used a binary encoding, where one represented the presence of a particular sign/symptom, and zero its absence. Measures used to assess performance are a fundamental issue here, and in this case precision, recall and F1-score were chosen as performance measures, since the dataset classes are skewed in favor of Dengue. The formula used to calculate F1-Score is shown in equation 3. It is worth noting that the F1-Score is used in binary classification problems, and since the problem stated in this work is not binary (multi-class classification), the macro-averaging [24] technique to handle multiclass problems was used.

$$precision = \frac{truepositives}{truepositives + falsepositives} \tag{1}$$

$$recall = \frac{truepositives}{truepositives + falsenegatives} \tag{2}$$

$$F1 = 2 * \frac{precision * recall}{precision + recall} \tag{3}$$

After execution of the artificial immune system (10 iterations, 30 B-cells, 300 clones per B-cell) using each neural network, several subsets of symptoms and signs that maximized the performance of each classifiers were obtained (100% F1 score). A specific subset of nineteen symptoms and signs was particularly good, since it maximized the performance of the three classifiers used (Fuzzy, IC and DefaultARTMAP).

4.4   Final Tests

Once validation determined the parameter values and the subset of symptoms and signs that maximized the classifiers performance, final tests were conducted using the test set. Results are shown in table 5.

Table 5. Test set results (recall per class and Macro F1-Score) using symptoms and signs determined by validation

Neural Network	Dengue	Leptospirosis	Malaria	Macro F1-Score
FuzzyARTMAP	91,30% (21/23)	80% (4/5)	40% (2/5)	0,725
ARTMAP-IC	91,30% (21/23)	60% (3/5)	80% (4/5)	0,768
DefaultARTMAP2	91,30% (21/23)	60% (3/5)	60% (3/5)	0,736

4.5   Analysis of the Results Obtained

Test set results obtained by the networks show ARTMAP-IC with a slight advantage in terms of F1-score and accuracy. In general, performance of the three classifiers appears to be very good discriminating Dengue cases from the rest (91,30% of correct diagnoses), which can be explained by the higher amount of Dengue data available for training. On the other hand, models present greater performance variability for class Leptospirosis (60% - 80% of correct diagnoses), and this phenomena is even more pronounced for class Malaria (40% - 80% of correct diagnoses); this variability can be explained also by the limited amount of training cases available for these two clases.

It is interesting to note that distributed prediction models (ARTMAP-IC and Default ARTMAP) offer better results, outperforming FuzzyARTMAP. This is consistent with results available in the relevant literature. Each trained classifier generated 13 categories in layer LTM, which corresponds to a compression factor of 81%, which suggests that results obtained in the test set are not due to overfitting, and offer a reliable estimator for the generalization performance of the classifiers.

5   Conclusions

Dengue, Leptospirosis and Malaria are zoonosis that prevail in tropical countries, even having very different etiological nature, they share several symptoms and clinical signs at different stages, and that makes the differential diagnose a complicated one. This paper stated an ARTMAP based approach to the diferential diagnosis of these three diseases, and the use of an Artificial Immune System for the identification of a set of symptoms and signs that maximized the performance of the classifiers. Test set results obtained show that an ARTMAP-IC classifier is able to perform differential diagnosis with confidence enough to be used by medical staff as a computational aid.

References

1. Brown, M., Vickers, I., Salas, R., Smikle, M.: Leptospirosis in Suspected Cases of Dengue in Jamaica, 2002-2007. Tropical Doctor 40(2), 92–94 (2010)
2. Burnet, F.: The Clonal Selection Theory of Acquired Immunity. Vanderbilt University Press (1959)
3. Carpenter, G.: Default ARTMAP. In: International Joint Conference on Neural Networks (IJCNN 2003), vol. 2, pp. 1396–1401. IEEE (2003)
4. Carpenter, G., Grossberg, S.: A Massively Parallel Architecture for a Self Organizing Neural Pattern Recognition Machine. Computer Vision, Graphics, and Image Processing 37(1), 54–115 (1987)
5. Carpenter, G., Grossberg, S.: ART 2 – Self-organization of Stable Category Recognition Codes for Analog Input Patterns. Applied Optics 26(23), 4919–4930 (1987)
6. Carpenter, G., Grossberg, S.: ART3 – Hierarchical Search Using Chemical Transmitters in Self-Organizing Pattern Recognition Architectures. Neural Networks 3(2), 129–152 (1990)
7. Carpenter, G., Grossberg, S., Markuzon, N., Reynolds, J., Rosen, D.: Fuzzy ARTMAP – A Neural Network Architecture for Incremental Supervised Learning of Analog Multidimensional Maps. IEEE Transactions on Neural Networks 3(5), 698–713 (1992)
8. Carpenter, G., Grossberg, S., Rosen, D.: Fuzzy ART – Fast Stable Learning and Categorization of Analog Patterns by an Adaptive Resonance System. Neural Networks 4(6), 759–771 (1991)
9. Carpenter, G., Markuzon, N.: ARTMAP-IC and Medical Diagnosis – Instance Counting and Inconsistent Cases. Neural Networks 11(2), 323–336 (1998)
10. Chadwick, D., Arch, B., Wilder-Smith, A., Paton, N.: Distinguishing Dengue Fever from Other Infections on the Basis of Simple Clinical and Laboratory Features – Application of Logistic Regression Analysis. Journal of Clinical Virology 35(2), 147–153 (2006)
11. De Castro, L.N., Von Zuben, F.J.: Learning and Optimization Using the Clonal Selection Principle. IEEE Transactions on Evolutionary Computation 6(3), 239–251 (2002)
12. Downs, J., Harrison, R., Kennedy, R., Cross, S.: Application of the Fuzzy ARTMAP Neural Network Model to Medical Pattern Classification Tasks. Artificial Intelligence in Medicine 8(4), 403–428 (1996)
13. Ellis, T., Imrie, A., Katz, A., Effler, P.: Underrecognition of Leptospirosis During a Dengue Fever Outbreak in Hawaii, 2001-2002. Vector-Borne and Zoonotic Diseases 8(4), 541–547 (2008)

14. Goodman, P., Kaburlasos, V., Egbert, D., Carpenter, G., Grossberg, S., Reynolds, J., Rosen, D., Hartz, A.: Fuzzy ARTMAP Neural Network Compared to Linear Discriminant Analysis Prediction of the Length of Hospital Stay in Patients with Pneumonia. In: IEEE Intl. Conf. on Systems, Man and Cybernetics (ICSMC 1992), vol. 1, pp. 748–753 (1992)
15. Halstead, S.E. (ed.): Dengue, Tropical Medicine – Science and Practice. Imperial College Press (2008)
16. Kgrostad, D.: Plasmodium Species (Malaria). In: Mandell, G., Bennet, J.E., Dolin, R. (eds.) Principles and Practice of Infectious Diseases, pp. 2818–2831. Churchill Livingstone (2000)
17. Kohonen, T.: Self-Organized Formation of Topologically Correct Feature Maps. Biological Cybernetics 43(1), 59–69 (1982)
18. Levett, P., Branch, S., Edwards, C.: Detection of Dengue Infection in Patients Investigated for Leptospirosis in Barbados. The American Journal of Tropical Medicine and Hygiene 62(1), 112–114 (2000)
19. Libraty, D.H., Myint, K.S.A., Murray, C.K., Gibbons, R.V., Mammen, M.P., Endy, T.P., Li, W., Vaughn, D.W., Nisalak, A., Kalayanarooj, S., Hospenthal, D.R., Green, S., Rothman, A.L., Ennis, F.A.: A Comparative Study of Leptospirosis and Dengue in Thai Children. PLoS Neglected Tropical Diseases 1(3), e111 (2007)
20. Markuzon, N., Gaehde, S., Ash, A., Carpenter, G., Moskowitz, M.: Predicting Risk of an Adverse Event in Complex Medical Data Sets Using Fuzzy ARTMAP Network. Artificial Intelligence in Medicine – Interpreting Clinical Data. Technical Report Series, pp. 93–96 (1994)
21. Potts, J., Rothman, A.: Clinical and Laboratory Features that Distinguish Dengue from Other Febrile Illnesses in Endemic Populations. Tropical Medicine & International Health 13(11), 1328–1340 (2008)
22. Tappero, J., Ashford, D., Perkins, B.: Leptospira Species (Leptospirosis). In: Mandell, G., Bennet, J.E., Dolin, R. (eds.) Principles and Practice of Infectious Diseases, pp. 2495–2501. Churchill Livingstone (2000)
23. Tsai, T.: Flaviviruses. In: Mandell, G., Bennet, J.E., Dolin, R. (eds.) Principles and Practice of Infectious Diseases, pp. 1714–1735. Churchill Livingstone (2000)
24. Yang, Y.: An Evaluation of Statistical Approaches to Text Categorization. Information Retrieval 1(1), 69–90 (1999)

Conversing Learning: Active Learning and Active Social Interaction for Human Supervision in Never-Ending Learning Systems

Saulo D.S. Pedro and Estevam R. Hruschka Jr.

Federal University of Sao Carlos, UFSCar Sao Carlos, Brazil

Abstract. The Machine Learning community have been introduced to NELL (Never-Ending Language Learning), a system able to learn from web and to use its knowledge to keep learning infinitely. The idea of continuously learning from the web brings concerns about reliability and accuracy, mainly when the learning process uses its own knowledge to improve its learning capabilities. Considering that the knowledge base keeps growing forever, such a system requires self-supervision as well as self-reflection. The increased use of the Internet, that allowed NELL creation, also brought a new source of information on-line. The social media becomes more popular everyday and the AI community can now develop research to take advantage of these information, aiming to turn it into knowledge. This work is following this lead and proposes a new machine learning approach, called *Conversing Learning*, to use collective knowledge from web community users to provide self-supervision and self-reflection to intelligent machines, thus, they can improve their learning task. The Conversing Learning approach explores concepts from Active Learning and Question Answering to achieve the goal of showing what can be done towards autonomous Human Computer Interaction to *automatically* improve machine learning tasks.

Keywords: machine learning, social web, crowdsourcing, self-supervision, never-ending learning system.

1 Introduction

Machine Learning (ML) has been an effervescent research topic in the last years. New algorithms and new approaches have been proposed bringing relevant contribution to the AI community in general, and also, enhancing learning capabilities of computational systems. A new and relevant approach for machine learning systems is called *Active Learning* (AL). The basic principle behind active learning [3,10] is to improve machine learning algorithms performance by selecting specific training data. Following along these lines, active machine learning algorithms can achieve better accuracy with fewer training instances if they can choose the data from which they learn. In this sense, an active learning system should identify the most relevant training instances, and then, use them in its learning process.

When exploring principles behind AL, some researchers have proposed the idea of *Interactive Learning* (IL) [5,9] where AL is performed not only once, and the learning process is continuous during a number of iterations. In such an approach, after each

J. Pavón et al. (Eds.): IBERAMIA 2012, LNAI 7637, pp. 231–240, 2012.

iteration, the system interacts with the user and may pose queries (usually in the form of unlabeled data instances to be labeled) that will help improving the learning results in the next iteration.

Another recent and relevant research topic in Machine Learning is the *Never-Ending Learning* approach that focus on proposing algorithms and models to build learning systems that learn cumulatively forever, using what they have learned yesterday to improve their ability to learn better today, and keep learning indefinitely. The first Never-Ending Learning system described in the literature was proposed in [2] and is called NELL (Never-Ending Language Learner). NELL has been continuously running since January 2010, attempting to perform two main tasks each day[1]: first, it attempts to *read* or extract facts from text found in hundreds of millions of web pages (e.g., playsInstrument(George_Harrison, guitar)). Second, it attempts to improve its reading competence, so that tomorrow it can extract more facts from the web and more accurately than today. So far, NELL has accumulated over 15 million candidate beliefs by reading the web, and it is considering these at different levels of confidence.

In addition to the aforementioned ideas and approaches, the quick development of new technologies in communication and in data storage and processing allows companies to deliver better quality and widespread projects in sharing content and communication. The popularity and power of social media connects more people everyday and all kinds of subjects are discussed worldwide through social media applications. All these factors together resulted in a growing interest of Artificial Intelligence (AI) and ML researchers in exploring web communities to solve new and traditional problems. As already presented by [6], the information available in social web has potential to be turned into high valued content.

We believe that the conjunction of all previously discussed achievements put us in a privileged position to propose an new type of learning system, that takes advantage of Active Learning, Interactive Learning, Never-Ending Learning techniques and the Web Communities. In this sense, we believe that Never-Ending Learning systems can go beyond IL and can autonomously search (in a proactive way) for human supervision on the Web whenever it needs to confirm any information (or to label training instances). Therefore, even if an user cannot give any feedback to the system (as users do in an *Interactive Learning* approach), the system should be capable of autonomously finding answers from other sources (i.e. on the web communities), thus, helping to refine and improve its learning capabilities even when a specific user cannot give any feedback. In this work, we call such a system: Conversing Learning System (CLS). In such a system, the acquired knowledge can be exploited to help supervision and knowledge revision tasks. Thus, the proposed approach allows self-supervision and self-reflection for learning systems. The possibility of self-supervision, self-reflection and knowledge revision is even more relevant in systems that learn forever like NELL. It is interesting to mention, that looking for answers or feedback on specific themes on web communities is a natural behavior of many human Internet users. Many people ask questions on specific forums (on the Web), as well as, many other ones offer advice and guidance. In this work, we intend to show how a Never-Ending Learning system (like NELL) can

---

[1] http://rtw.ml.cmu.edu

autonomously use the content available on two Web communities (Yahoo!Answers[2] and Twitter[3]) to bring better quality and accuracy to its learning methods.

The main contributions of this paper are: (i) Presenting a *Conversing Learning* (CL) system that can be used to help NELL to be self-supervised and to autonomously review its knowledge base (KB) contents; and (ii) Exploring the use of two different Web communities and discuss the main differences regarding the conversing learning aspects.

2 Related Work

NELL is the first Never-Ending Learning system described in the literature. It was developed at Carnegie Mellon University [2] and uses its acquired knowledge to learn better each day. The research team fed the system with an initial ontology and seeds. The system, then, takes advantage of the combination of several algorithms to continuously induce new knowledge from millions of web pages. The combination of the algorithms is itself a kind of self-supervision, but the system also counts on some shallow human supervision to ensure it is free from errors, thus avoiding concept drifting.

Even not focusing on the definition of a CLS, the work proposed in [7] (where the SS-Crowd component was described) is, to our knowledge, one of the first steps towards Conversing LearningCL. In that paper, the authors bring many interesting contributions to the idea proposed in our work. Thus, we've based the experiments (presented in Sect. 4) on a SS-Crowd implementation. In a nutshell, SS-Crowd takes (from a targeted learning system) potentially wrong knowledge, then, converts the specific knowledge into a question and query Yahoo!Answers community about the persistence of the question through their eyes. The answers from the community represent the belief that the knowledge from the learning system is right or wrong. SS-Crowd uses a predefined filter to combine the obtained answers and *decide* if the community answered in a positive or negative way. This *decision* can then be used to feedback NELL with information that indicates the differences between the knowledge acquired by the learning system with the knowledge from the web community. The Macro-Question/Answer approach is one of the key ideas behind SS-Crowd [7].

The idea of taking advantage on the redundancy of information from large content available on the web is focused in [4] to resolve QA problems. In that work, the amount of data available on-line makes answer extraction easier and the task presents a good performance even working on large datasets and simple natural language processing. Another interesting use of human generated content is presented on [1] the work applies frequently asked questions (FAQ) instead of traditional text files as a source to retrieve answers for a QA problem. Also, it introduces the FAQFinder system and an approach to reduce the costs of natural language processing to understand complex questions. The system proposed matching the user's questions with existing questions on FAQ files.

In this paper we explore the usage of SS-Crowd in Twitter as well as in Yahoo!Answers communities. In addition we investigate the use of a supervised learning method to learn to interpret the answers from both Web Communities. Twitter has been the focus of recent interesting researches. The work in [11] presents a network

---

[2] http://answers.yahoo.com/
[3] https://twitter.com/

of stream-based measures called Tweetonomy that combines messages, users and content of messages to allow the measure to compare stream aggregations. Also, the work presented in [8] proposes a method to generate answers to status of Twitter users. Although the method is not intended to be a dialog machine, it succeeded in generating meaningful answers to the twitter statuses.

The collected intelligence as mentioned in [6], is the data retrieved from the social web and contains high valued information to web semantic development. Gruber suggests that the real collective intelligence comes from the creation of knowledge which is impossible to be obtained manually, and also from new ways of learning through the recombination of data from social web. Gruber describes the class of systems that can deliver at this opportunity as *collective knowledge systems* and he suggests four key properties that characterizes them. They are: user generated content, human-machine synergy, increasing results with scale and emergent knowledge.

3 Conversing Learning

A *Conversing Learning* (CL) system should be capable of autonomously looking for human collaboration to enhance a ML system. The collaboration can be used to perform self-supervision and self-reflection tasks. Here, we define the behavior of a CL System (CLS) based on Web communities, its differences from Active and Interactive Learning and our concerns to improve communication among machines and users.

Researchers in Human Computer Interaction (HCI), have worked on how users interact with machines, focusing mainly on making the user's experience more useful and friendly. In these cases, most of communication improvements targets the human users. In CL instead, we want humans to help improving machine tasks, which means, the application of Reversed Human Computer Interaction (RHCI) [7]. In our approach, the communication improvements target the machine and not the human user. To autonomously improve Machine Learning tasks based on human supervision, we had to focus in an environment where the computer can autonomously get help from humans. Thus, it is important that a CL system identifies the following questions: (i) which knowledge should be put to humans attention? (ii) Who are the humans that the machine should look for help? (iii) How to understand human answers? (iv) How to infer knowledge from human answers?

In this work, to demonstrate CL capabilities, we explore new possibilities with the SS-Crowd algorithm. The algorithm was first presented on [7] and uses NELL' knowledge base (KB) to get together a machine that aims to learn as humans do and a machine that resolves its questions as humans do. SS-Crowd algorithm can be summarized by the following automatic tasks: (i) Take facts from the KB. (ii) Build a human understandable question from the facts. (iii) Query the web community with the questions. (iv) Gather and resolve the answers (classify them as positive or negative). (v) Combine the answers and produce a combined opinion from the community about the persistence of the facts. Although we expect CL to bring some insights to enhance SS-Crowd capabilities, it is important to clarify that particular improvements on this system are not the focus of our research. Instead, we want to explore the possibilities and important issues of using Web communities in learning tasks aiming to present CL as a series of new capabilities and concerns.

Popular AI applications like spam trackers already presented good solutions using systems based on Interactive Learning approaches. With machine learning techniques, a spam tracker may have its own set of initial rules (or facts) to find spam messages. The spam trackers apply Active Learning to select candidate messages to be labeled as spam by the users. The tracker keeps interactively asking the user and updates it's policy rules to identify new spams. In the spam tracker case (following the Interactive Learning approach) the e-mail owner is the only human that can interact with the machine, and the machine has no need (and no capability) to look for help anywhere else. Therefore, the machine prompts the user with questions and *passively* waits for collaboration.

An IL spam tracker depends on the user to complete its IL task. Thus, with no interaction with other humans and no *proactive* search for extra collaboration. In CL, on the contrary, we want the system to *actively* look for help in other sources when needed. In addition, tagging e-mails may not be a long effort task for a regular user, but other Machine Learning tasks, such as Never Ending Learning might have a large set of data to be verified and the opinion of a single user may not be enough to feed the system accurately. A CLS can share the validation task among several human users and use their different opinions as an advantage to provide redundancy. The core difference between CL task to other learning tasks resides in (proactive and) automatically seeking for information from human users instead of passively waiting for their collaboration. Looking for help from many (and any) humans user may lead the IL task to lose precision and confidence due to noisy feedback. To rely on the human generated content, and answer the questions raised by CL, we defined the following capabilities that should be taken into consideration.

Active Learning Approach: When the KB of the learning system is large, it might be unpractical to put every bit of knowledge to human validation, therefore it is necessary to prioritize the knowledge that is going to be validated by the web community. Also, querying the users for more information than it is usually done, will constrain the user to keep collaborating because they will not be able to track all the messages from the ML system. In Machine Learning we are used to actively select (from the dataset) the information that is more adequate to the ML system intents, that is, Active Learning. And this is what we are doing here, it is important to select the bit of knowledge that brings better benefits when asked to a web community.

Scope of the Web Users: The effectiveness of asking for human feedback can be different from a community to another. The web communities available online have different users and different intents. Although we can communicate with users in almost any community, they might react in a different way. The culture, expertise, age and language are just a few factors that will change our feedback message. For an example, a travel suggestion application that reads from a KB would be better fed from users of travel web communities than an open question answering community like Yahoo! Answers, but you would have to deal with the drawback of querying a smaller set of users with the risk of collecting a smaller set of feedback.

Driven Feedback: When we are working with human generated content, the answers (gotten from human users) might be too noisy or too complex to be interpreted. If that is the case, the algorithm can miss part of the feedback. An alternative to cope with such cases is to encourage human users to provide *machine friendly* content. A good example of such an idea is implemented in [7] where the SS-Crowd algorithm prompts Yahoo! Answers users to answer just *yes* or *no* for their questions. Such approach restricts the answers from the users and the algorithm can be structured to focus on content easier to read. As in the case of scope, the drawback of such approach is to find a smaller amount of contributions. Although we consider this is imperative to enable accurate results in CL, the recent advances in Natural Language Processing (NLP) and IR indicates that machines will be able to better and better understand human generated content in the next years, and soon, we would not need to push the user to an specific kind of answer.

System Identity: It is known that the human communication behavior changes as the interlocutor changes. If you target web users that know about the machine nature of who is asking, they might feel either cornered and shy or stimulated when returning feedback. Researchers have already been doing it through Amazon's Mechanical Turk[4], where users are stimulated with specific instructions to feedback a system they know it is as a machine. If the community is used to help academic research, it is likely that the feedback will be more *machine friendly*. Showing ourselves as a machine, or not, depend on the intents of the application of CL but in either way, it is important to know the aspects of the community we are asking for feedback and to ensure that this usage of the social media does not bypass its security and privacy policies.

4 Experiments and Results

To explore CL principles, and also, to study the interaction of different web communities, we ran the SS-Crowd algorithm using Twitter as well as Yahoo!Answers as a source for human feedback. Although Twitter interface is not intended to perform as a QA system, users often use it to get answers for *question posts*, so we are miming these users and behaving the same way. Considering that the work in [7] already put the SS-Crowd algorithm to test Yahoo! Answers, we are using here the same algorithm and adding Twitter as a second source of information.

With the method proposed in this paper, we want to explore how can we apply CL by implementing its capabilities in a real case where NELL would benefit from the obtained results. We are also going to explore how the behavior of different communities could affect the benefits of using social media as a source of information for learning tasks. As a measure of achievement, we took the very same rules used in [7]. We had a set of 62 NELL's rules that were (automatically) converted (by SS-Crowd) into questions and then, were posted as questions in both communities. The questions generated 350 answers in Yahoo! Answers and 72 answers in Twitter. All those results were given as input to a classifier to learn how to interpret answers from both communities. In our experiments each question receives several kinds of sentences as answers and the SS-Crowd algorithm determines if those answers are approving or rejecting the the validity of the rule. If the algorithm cannot make such decision then the rule is marked as unresolved.

During the execution of the experiments, we noticed how user's collaboration differ from one community to another. In Yahoo! Answers, users are not aware that our

---

[4] https://www.mturk.com

Table 1. Total of approved, rejected and unresolved answers from Yahoo! Answers and Twitter

	Approved	Rejected	Unresolved
Twitter	51	17	4
Yahoo! Answers	124	168	58

questions are generated by a machine. In Twitter instead, we made that clear. As an instant effect, users came to us asking how restrictive should they be about the rule being evaluated. We answered them to be as restrictive as they think they should be, so we keep our intents to not interfere in the user's opinion. Knowing the original intents of the question, the users in Twitter are more *machine friendly*, they actually try to help the learning system (considering that they are NELL's *followers*).

In Yahoo! Answers, people are encouraged to earn *points* and *respect* by answering questions. Users collaborate giving answers even when they are not sure about the answer. This behavior reflects in our results as a higher amount of collaboration. In Twitter instead, the collaboration has some restrictions. The user has to be *following* NELL to receive its updates (questions in our case). This means that the user is previously interested in the subject and because of this interest, while the amount of collaboration decreases, its quality increases a lot. The example below extracted from our results explains it in a practical manner.

Question: *(Yes or No?) If athlete Z is member of team X and athlete Z plays in league Y, then team X plays in league Y.*

Answer sampled from a Twitter user: *No. (Z in X)* ∧ *(Z in Y)* → *(X in Y)*

Answer sampled from a Yahoo! Answers users: *NO, Not in EVERY case. Athlete Z could be a member of football team X and he could also play in his pub's Friday nights dart team. The Dart team could play in league Y (and Z therefore by definition plays in league Y). This does not mean that the football team plays in the darts league!*

As we can infer from the examples, users from both communities are giving us the same opinion through different answers. The first contains a simple *No* answer and a justification in a logic-like format while, the latter, is pure natural language and includes an example. Everything that we need from both answers is the *No* and since the first answer is shorter, the SS-Crowd is more accurate to extract the opinion from it. In Table 1, we notice more unresolved answers in Yahoo! Answers (16.5%) answers than in Twitter (5.5%) answers. It is also important to notice that the Yes/No nature of the question facilitates the resolution of tasks like this. This feature is the *driven feedback* discussed in Sect. 3 and is part of the SS-Crowd original algorithm. Overall, as illustrated in the example, we can state that if the users are different, the system is different and the answers are different.

The CLS should be able to find how useful is the community contribution. If the human collaboration is not good enough, the system may take an action to help users to provide better feedback. This interaction between the learning system and the users aiming to allow human feedback in machine learning tasks is the main focus of CL.

We know that the *machine friendly* collaboration of Twitter users is good to our intents since it allows more accurate validation of knowledge. We also know that a QA environment such as Yahoo! Answers is more participatory and we have users from all kind of expertise and experience. Thus, we have on one side a more accurate and smaller set of answers and in the other a larger set of answers, human *identity* and an unbiased crowd. Those different biases present in each community were important to help us deciding upon using these specific communities. Examining the simple sum of the totals of answers from both communities, we found that users from Yahoo! Answers and Twitter have a substantial difference in their opinion, which is good to our intents. The results also pointed that users from one community disagree with users from the other community in 45% of the answers. This increases our belief that we are not dealing with redundant information (but with independent sources).

A CLS with multiple independent sources of human collaboration could use collective knowledge to improve its own ability to keep looking for information. Therefore, performing a self-revision task. To implement such capability, we gathered information from SS-Crowd implementation with Twitter and Yahoo! Answers and represented the data as attributes to a classifier. Thus, the system is capable of assisting SS-Crowd to identify where to look for better information on web communities. The attributes retrieved from SS-Crowd are as follows: (i) Total number of rules resolved as approved and rejected by users in Twitter. (ii) Total number of rules resolved as approved and rejected by users in Yahoo! Answers. (iii) The best answer from Yahoo! Answer. (iv) The combined resolution of answers to a single question (taken from SS-Crowd task #5 in Sect. 3).

We believe that the classifier can be used to infer more valuable knowledge from the behavior of the communities. If we are applying CL to improve learning system KB, such a classifier could bring the possibility to choose what information from the web community makes difference to that specific learning system. In our experiments we used the attributes to feed traditional classifiers and observed how the combination of different social media sources and the improved interaction with users, through Conversational Learning, could give us a deeper understanding of the machine knowledge validated through the eyes of humans.

To apply the CL idea in our experiments, we used the attributes retrieved from SS-Crowd to create 62 tuples (one for each rule) to train traditional classifiers. The learning task of the binary classifier is to identify whether a rule is right or wrong. The dataset composed by those instances (tuples) were previously labeled with the judgment of NELL's developers and the tests were performed using a 10-fold cross-validation. With the outputs, we can measure the relevance of the attributes and decide which of them are suitable to our intents. Although the average difference indicates no redundant information, it does not guarantee that every attribute are not independent. We know that some attributes may represent our problem better than others, and to resolve this matter, we decided to run the classifiers in a ablation strategy removing attributes from the dataset. Therefore, we are going to analyze how the classifier accuracy behaves in the lack of attributes.

When comparing both systems' outputs, it is possible to notice that Yahoo! Answers attributes are more relevant to the CLS. The system could benefit from this inference to assign a different behavior for Yahoo! Answers collaboration, specially for the rejections, as evidenced in Table 2. On the other hand, when using a single community as source of human feedback, the use of Twitter brought better results than Yahoo!Answers (last two lines in Table 2).

Table 2. Classifier average correct classification rates over 10-fold cross validation using a dataset containing 62 instances

Removed Attribute	Classifier		
	NaiveBayes	C4.5	ID3
None Removed	74.19	77.41	75.80
YahooApproved	75.80	74.19	75.80
YahooRejected	**69.35**	**69.35**	**72.58**
YahooUnresolved	75.80	79.03	80.64
TwitterApproved	75.80	61.29	61.29
TwitterRejected	74.19	83.87	77.41
TwitterUnesolved	70.96	75.80	75.80
YahooBest	77.41	75.80	77.41
YahooCombined	74.19	75.80	75.80
YahooOnly	70.96	77.41	74.19
TwitterOnly	**77.41**	**79.03**	**79.03**

As we already mentioned, the *identity* of the CLS and the knowledge of the humans about a subject might interfere in their decisions. While Twitter users gives us more straightforward response (which matches the NELL's developers), the Yahoo! Answers users gives more complex and more in-depth feedback. In a few words, while Twitter users improves a ML in self-supervision, Yahoo! Answer users help the ML system to ensure its completeness, that is, the system comprehension of all possibilities of the knowledge acquired.

In a nutshell, the results of our classifier can tell which attributes are more relevant to the rule validation task. The classifier loses accuracy when the YahooRejected attribute is removed. Implementing such a classifier can help the CLS to tune itself in a self-supervised self-reflection task and to be able to be more effective. The classification task can also report to the ML system, which bit of the knowledge base could benefit from deeper investigation.

5   Conclusions and Future Work

In this work, CL was proposed and implemented using NELL as a case study. Such a learning process is intended to autonomously help to improve ML tasks actively looking for human assistance from different sources (in a *Active-Learning-oriented approach*. To achieve that, the presented case study took advantage from the web communities and their wide popularity and also their millions of users. We presented our concerns and some directions on how to solve problems of low confidence when relying on human generated content. We also showed how CLSs are related to Active Learning and Interactive Learning. To allow CLSs to effectively communicate with humans, we explored some "reversed" techniques such as Reversed Human Computer Interaction as well as Reversed Macro Question/Answeras defined in [7].

The case study was implemented based on SS-Crowd and three traditional classifiers (Naive-Bayes, C4.5 and ID3). Experiments were performed using Twitter and Yahoo!Answers as source for the human feedback. The results obtained in the performed experiments revealed that the CL approach was able to correctly label data that can be stored in NELL's knowledge base and help the system in its never-ending learning task. Also, it was possible to observe that Twitter and Yahoo!Answers classifier attributes contributed in different ways to the classification task. In this sense, Twitter's attributes alone were capable of giving the higher classification accuracy to the classifiers. However, the list of used attributes can still be extended to take advantage of other information from web communities such as reputation and earned points.

Since the SS-Crowd algorithm has a few issues with unresolved answers (e.g. decide if an answer is *yes* or *no*), an interesting future work can focus on extending the keyword base approach [7] with more detailed information from the web community (like opinion analysis and sentiment analysis). We also intend to increase the datasets used in the experiments to learn more subtleties from CL approach.

References

1. Burke, R.D., Hammond, K.J., Kulyukin, V.A., Lytinen, S.L., Tomuro, N., Schoenberg, S.: Question Answering from Frequently Asked Question Files – Experiences with the FAQ Finder System. Tech. rep., University of Chicago, Chicago, IL, USA (1997)
2. Carlson, A., Betteridge, J., Kisiel, B., Settles, B., Hruschka Jr., E.R., Mitchell, T.M.: Toward an Architecture for Never-Ending Language Learning. In: 24th Conference on Artificial Intelligence (AAAI 2010), pp. 1306–1313. AAAI (2010)
3. Cohn, D.A., Ghahramani, Z., Jordan, M.I.: Active Learning with Statistical Models. Journal of Artificial Intelligence Research 4, 129–145 (1996)
4. Dumais, S., Banko, M., Brill, E., Lin, J., Ng, A.: Web Question Answering – Is More Always Better? In: 25th Annual International ACM SIGIR Conference on Research and Development in Information Retrieval (SIGIR 2002), pp. 291–298. ACM, NY (2002)
5. Godbole, S., Harpale, A., Sarawagi, S., Chakrabarti, S.: Document Classification Through Interactive Supervision of Document and Term Labels. In: Boulicaut, J.F., Esposito, F., Giannotti, F., Pedreschi, D. (eds.) PKDD 2004. LNCS (LNAI), vol. 3202, pp. 185–196. Springer, Heidelberg (2004)
6. Gruber, T.: Collective Knowledge Systems – Where the Social Web Meets the Semantic Web. Web Semantics 6(1), 4–13 (2008)
7. Pedro, S.D.S., Hruschka Jr., E.R.: Collective Intelligence as a Source for Machine Learning Self-Supervision. In: 4th International Workshop on Web Intelligence and Communities (WIC 2012), pp. 5:1–5:9. ACM (2012)
8. Ritter, A., Cherry, C., Dolan, W.B.: Data-Driven Response Generation in Social Media. In: 2011 Conference on Empirical Methods in Natural Language Processing (EMNLP 2011), pp. 583–593. ACL (2011)
9. Settles, B.: Closing the Loop – Fast, Interactive Semi-Supervised Annotation with Queries on Features and Instances. In: 2011 Conference on Empirical Methods in Natural Language Processing (EMNLP 2011), pp. 1467–1478. ACL (2011)
10. Settles, B.: Active Learning, Synthesis Lectures on Artificial Intelligence and Machine Learning, vol. 6. Morgan and Claypool (2012)
11. Wagner, C., Strohmaier, M.: The Wisdom in Tweetonomies – Acquiring Latent Conceptual Structures from Social Awareness Streams. In: 3rd International Semantic Search Workshop (SEMSEARCH 2010), pp. 6:1–6:10. ACM (2010)

Spoken Digit Recognition in Portuguese Using Line Spectral Frequencies

Diego F. Silva, Vinícius M.A. de Souza, Gustavo E.A.P.A. Batista,
and Rafael Giusti

Instituto de Ciências Matemáticas e de Computação – Universidade de São Paulo
{diegofsilva,vsouza,gbatista,rgiusti}@icmc.usp.br

Abstract. Recognition of isolated spoken digits is the core procedure for a large and important number of applications mainly in telephone based services, such as dialing, airline reservation, bank transaction and price quotation, only using speech. Spoken digit recognition is generally a challenging task since the signals last for short period of time and often some digits are acoustically very similar to each other. The objective of this paper is to investigate the use of machine learning algorithms for digit recognition. We focus on the recognition of digits spoken in Portuguese. However, we note that our techniques are applicable to any language. We believe that the most important task for successfully recognizing spoken digits is the attribute extraction. Audio data is composed by a huge amount of very weak features, and most machine learning algorithms will not be able to build accurate classifiers. We show that Line Spectral Frequencies (LSF) provides a set of highly predictive coefficients for digit recognition. The results are superior than those obtained with state-of-the-art methods using Mel-Frequency Cepstrum Coefficients (MFCC) for digit recognition. In particular, we show that the choice of the right attribute extraction method is more important than the specific classification paradigm, and that the right combination of classifier and attributes can provide almost perfect accuracy.

Keywords: speech recognition, machine learning, spoken digit recognition, line spectral frequency.

1 Introduction

In the last decades, research on speech and speaker recognition has attracted a huge amount of interest, mainly due to the enormous number of applications involving such technology. A few examples are biometric authentication, in which a user voice is used to allow or deny access to a system; and accessibility, in which a user is able to control equipments or navigate on the Internet just using speech, facilitating these tasks to physically-impaired people.

An important speech recognition application, especially useful for telephone service providers, is the recognition of isolated spoken digits. Examples of such services are telephone dialing using speech, airline reservation, banking transactions, price quotation, etc. By using this type of interaction, companies can

J. Pavón et al. (Eds.): IBERAMIA 2012, LNAI 7637, pp. 241–250, 2012.

make their services more user-friendly when compared to, for instance, entering numbers on the telephone keypad. This is even more evident when the procedure is done through mobile devices, in which there is not a physically detached keyboard for dialing.

Digit recognition might seem an easy task when compared to recognition of spoken words in general. However, spoken digits recognition is challenging due to two main reasons [9]:

1. Spoken digits are of short acoustic duration, typically a few seconds of speech;
2. Some digits are acoustically very similar to each other (for example, "one" and "nine").

The objective of this paper is to investigate the use of machine learning algorithms for digit recognition. We focus on the recognition of digits spoken in Portuguese. However, we note that our techniques are applicable to any language. We believe that the most important task for successfully recognizing spoken digits is attribute extraction. Machine learning algorithms are fully dependent on predictive attributes to build precise classifiers. In speech recognition, and in sound recognition in general, the raw (audio) data is composed of a huge amount of very weak features, and most machine learning algorithms will not be able to build accurate classifiers, mainly due to the curse of dimensionality.

We show that Line Spectral Frequencies (LSF) provides a set of highly predictive coefficients for digit recognition. The results are superior to those obtained with state-of-the-art methods using Mel-Frequency Cepstrum Coefficients (MFCC) for digit recognition. In particular, we show that the choice of the right attribute extraction method is more important than the specific classification paradigm, and that the right combination of classifier and attributes can provide almost perfect accuracy.

This paper is organized as follows: Section 2 reviews the related work on spoken digit recognition using machine learning techniques. Section 3 briefly introduces the general ideas behind MFCC and LSF. This section also reviews the dynamic windowing pre-processing technique used to extract local coefficients, as well as to generate attribute vectors with fixed length. Section 4 describes the database of spoken digits used in our experiment and the techniques used to segment the data. Section 5 presents our experimental design and discusses the obtained results. Finally, Sect. 6 provides the conclusions and possible future work.

2   Related Work

As previously mentioned, spoken digit recognition is the core of several important applications. Due to its relevance, several papers have been published on this topic for diverse languages such as Japanese [8], English [1], Arabic [2,6], Hindi [13], Bengali [5] and Urdu [3]. In general, these papers have a common framework, in which MFCC are used as principal attributes in conjunction with a classifier induced by a machine learning system.

We scanned the literature searching for papers that proposed approaches and/or evaluated them on spoken digits in Portuguese, and we discovered that there is an enormous lack of research work on that language. To the best of our knowledge, the only pieces of work that considered the Portuguese language were the work of Rodrigues and Trancoso [15], in which MFCC and Hidden Markov Models were used to recognize digits in Portuguese with an accuracy of 99.40%, and, more recently, Bresolin et al. [4], which compared wavelet-based attributes to MFCC for recognizing digits, obtaining an accuracy of 92.97% for the best configuration of attributes based on wavelet and 92.87% for MFCC in speaker-independent digit recognition.

In our work, we show that LSF coefficients provide a more accurate set of attributes than MFCC for digit recognition in Portuguese. With the right combination of LSF coefficients and classifier our approach achieved almost perfect classification accuracy in the same database used in [4].

3   Attribute Extraction Methods

As previously discussed, machine learning algorithms are highly dependent on predictive features in order to build accurate classifiers. In this section we provide a brief description of two well-known methods for attribute extraction, namely Mel-Frequency Cepstrum Coefficients (MFCC) and Line Spectral Frequencies (LSF). The main purpose of these methods is to perform a representational change of the original audio data, from a high-dimensional weak-feature domain to a low-dimensional strong-feature domain.

We start describing the technique of dynamic windowing. The importance of this technique is two-fold: first, the window allows extracting local attributes from smaller parts of the signal and characterizing signal changes in time; second, the dynamic setting allows adjusting the size of the window so that every signal results in the same number of attributes.

3.1   Dynamic Windowing

Usually, speech recognition involves the classification of signals with different durations. This variability occurs not only inter-classes, because different words have different lengths, but also intra-classes, because different speakers usually have different paces. Data with varying length is a problem for several machine learning algorithms that expect a fixed-size attribute-value table as input. We use dynamic windowing as a strategy to overcome that issue.

Dynamic windowing is a simple strategy that breaks a signal of arbitrary length into a set of feature vectors. Each feature vector is the collection of features extracted from a segment of the original signal, which is obtained from a sliding window of width w_s. The value of w_s is dependent on the length of the signal s and the number of windows required. Furthermore, each window has an overlap with the previous, as can be seen in Fig. 1. This overlap must be large enough so that information in the signal transitions are not lost. An overlap higher than 50% is commonly used.

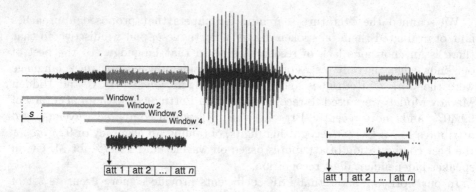

Fig. 1. In the dynamic windowing strategy, the feature extraction uses a sliding window of width w, proportional to a preset number of windows, with an overlap of size s between consecutive windows. So, a n−dimentional feature vector is extracted for each window.

In our experiments, we set the window width w_s according to Equation 1 below:

$$w_s = \lceil \frac{e}{1-o} \rceil \tag{1}$$

where o is the overlapping rate in the range between 0 and 1 and e is the window width disregarding overlapping between consecutive windows. The value of e can be obtained from Equation 2 below:

$$e = \lceil \frac{l_s}{n} \rceil \tag{2}$$

where l_s is the signal length and n is the number of windows.

Obviously, the dynamic window strategy should be used with a word of caution: the existence of signals with considerable difference in duration will make the window sizes, and consequently the step sizes, have a large variance. Large step sizes may cause a loss of detail on how the signal evolves in time when features are extracted.

3.2   Mel-Frequency Cepstrum Coefficients

The Mel-Frequency Cepstrum Coefficients are probably the most commonly used attributes in speech processing tasks, such as speaker and speech recognition [18]. Briefly, to calculate those coefficients, we first take the magnitudes of frequency components using an acoustically-defined scale called *mel*, originated from the study of Stevens et al. [16], which relates physical frequencies to the frequencies perceived by the human auditory system. Next, we apply a Discrete Cosine Transform, widely used in data compression [17]. The MFCC are the cepstrum coefficients obtained from this operation. Equation 3 shows the conversion from frequency (f) to mel-frequency (m).

$$m = 2595 \times log_{10}(1 + \frac{f}{700}) \tag{3}$$

3.3   Line Spectral Frequencies

Linear Prediction (LP) is a technique used in many speech applications, such as recognition, compression and modeling [14,10]. LP is based on the fact that a speech signal can be described by Equation 4.

$$\hat{x}_k = \sum_{i=1}^{p} a_i x_{k-i} \qquad (4)$$

where k is the time index and p is the order of LP – i.e., the number of employed LP coefficients. The a_i coefficients are calculated in order to minimize the prediction error by means of a covariance or auto-correlation method.

Equation 4 can be rewritten in the frequency domain with a $z-$transform [11]. In this way, a short segment of speech is assumed to be generated as the output of an all-pole filter $H(z) = 1/A(z)$, where $A(z)$ is the inverse filter such that:

$$H(z) = \frac{1}{A(z)} = \frac{1}{1 - \sum_{i=1}^{p} a_i z^{-i}} \qquad (5)$$

The Line Spectral Frequencies (LSF) representation, introduced by Itakura [7], is an alternative way to represent LP coefficients. In order to calculate LSF coefficients, the inverse filter polynomial is decomposed into two polynomials $P(z)$ and $Q(z)$:

$$P(z) = A(z) + z^{p+1}A(z^{-1}) \text{ and } Q(z) = A(z) - z^{p+1}A(z^{-1})$$

where $P(z)$ is a symmetric polynomial and $Q(z)$ is an antisymmetric polynomial. The roots of $P(z)$ and $Q(z)$ determine the LSF coefficients.

LSF is well suited for quantization and interpolation [12]. Therefore LSF can represent the speech signal, mapping a large signal to a small number of coefficients, better than other LP representations.

4   Spoken Digits Database

In this section, we describe the database used in our experiments. In order to promote the comparison to literature results and facilitate the reproducibility of our results, we used a publicly available database created by Bresolin et al. [4]. We believe that the use of public data restricts any bias that could possibly arise if we decided to create our own database.

We are also highly committed to reproducibility of our results. Therefore, we created a paper website[1] in which we published every source code and data used in this paper.

---

[1] http://www.icmc.usp.br/~diegofsilva/IBERAMIA2012

4.1   Database Description

The database consists of spoken digits in Portuguese collected during a period of three months, from eighty-two men aged between 18 and 42 years-old. The sampling rate of the recording is 22,050Hz. Altogether, the database has 216 sequences of 10 digits (0 − 9) each, totalling 10 classes and 2,160 examples. Thus, it is a balanced dataset considering the class distribution.

Table 1 presents the approximated pronunciation of the 10 digits in English and by the International Phonetic Alphabet symbols (IPA[2]).

Table 1. Portuguese digits, approximate English pronunciation and IPA symbols

Digit	Portuguese Writing	Pronounce	IPA	Digit	Portuguese Writing	Pronounce	IPA
0	zero	zeh-ro	['zɛru]	5	cinco	seen-coh	['siŋku]
1	um	oom	[ũ]	6	seis	say-z	['sejʃ]
2	dois	doy-z	['doiʃ]	7	sete	seh-chee	['sɛtʃi]
3	três	treh-z	['trejʃ]	8	oito	oy-too	['ojtu]
4	quatro	kwah-troh	['kwatru]	9	nove	noh-vee	['nɔvi]

4.2   Signal Pre-processing

Each audio recording is related to one speaker who pronounces all digits from 0 to 9. Therefore, the recordings are not separated for each digit, rather each file

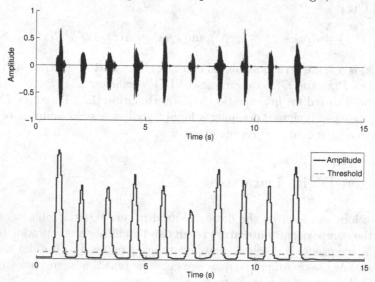

Fig. 2. Segmentation scheme. It's calculated the mean amplitude in the original signal (top) using a sliding window to form a vector that defines a confidence level for the existence of an interesting signal in the window (bottom). Finally, it is set a threshold for acceptance.

---

[2] http://www.langsci.ucl.ac.uk/ipa/

records one phrase encompassing the pronunciation of all digits. It was necessary to segment each file into 10 fragments, each one containing one digit.

As the signal-to-noise ratio of these signals is relatively high, it was possible to use a simple amplitude-based detector. First, the signal is normalized, dividing the values in each window by the highest value observed. Thus, the relative amplitudes will be within the interval between −1 and 1. After that, the mean amplitude within a sliding window is calculated and used as confidence estimate. The greater the calculated amplitude, the greater the confidence that the window contains part of a spoken signal. Finally, we set an acceptance threshold so that the portions above the threshold are indicative of a spoken digit. We save the segments above the threshold in separate files. This detection method is shown in Fig. 2.

The audio files were generated by speakers pronouncing the digits in numerical order. Thus, the task of labeling signals after segmentation is trivial.

5   Experiments and Results

Our main goal is to show that LSF coefficients can be used as features to provide highly accurate classifiers for spoken digits recognition. We compared MFCC with 13 coefficients against LSF with orders 24 and 48. These numbers of co-efficients were used because it is known that 13 MFCC and 12 LP coefficients are sufficient to characterize speech signals. Furthermore, it is common to use a multiple of the number of LP coefficients as the LSF order.

We compare the methods on 12 different scenarios. Each scenario is a different setting of some classification algorithm. The algorithms we use for classification and their related settings are shown in Table 2. We chose these algorithms because they are frequently used and the authors report good classification performance on signal recognition papers. Nearest neighbor classifiers were induced with inverse distance weighting approach.

Table 2. Experiment scenarios description

Scenario	Inducer/settings
1-NN	Nearest Neighbor
5-NN	5-Nearest Neighbor weighted by inverse distance
7-NN	7-Nearest Neighbor weighted by inverse distance
9-NN	9-Nearest Neighbor weighted by inverse distance
SVM-Poly1	Support Vector Machine with Polynomial Kernel with Degree 1
SVM-Poly2	Support Vector Machine with Polynomial Kernel with Degree 2
SVM-Poly3	Support Vector Machine with Polynomial Kernel with Degree 3
SVM-RBF0.01	Support Vector Machine with RBF Kernel wit Gamma=0.01
SVM-RBF0.05	Support Vector Machine with RBF Kernel wit Gamma=0.05
SVM-RBF0.1	Support Vector Machine with RBF Kernel wit Gamma=0.1
NB	Naïve Bayes
RF	Random Forest

For both approaches, MFCC and LSF, features were extracted via dynamic windowing strategy. The width and step size of the sliding window were such that for each signal a set of 25 feature arrays was generated and each adjacent pair of windows had an overlapping area of 75%. Therefore, each feature extraction method generated a dataset where each instance consisted of $25 \times n$ attributes, n being the number of extracted features. In other words, each signal was transformed into an instance with 325, 600 and 1,200 attributes for the 13-MFCC, 24-LSF and 48-LSF strategies, respectively.

Ten-fold cross-validation was used to partition the data sets into training and test sets. In order to reduce results variance by chance we have repeated this process ten times, randomizing the order of examples between two consecutive executions, i.e., we performed 10×10-fold cross-validation.

Our classification results are summarized on Table 3. Values are mean accuracy and standard deviation on accuracy for a set of 10×10-fold cross-validation. Each line stands for an inducer applied on the dataset produced from the features extracted by the method on the column. The most accurate classification algorithm on each method is highlighted.

Table 3. Mean accuracy and standard deviation for the three analyzed methods on the 12 scenarios

Scenario	MFCC	24 LSF	48 LSF
1-NN	86.33 (2.15)	92.92 (1.51)	**93.03 (1.64)**
5-NN	89.52 (1.88)	95.57 (1.19)	**95.66 (1.27)**
7-NN	89.61 (1.85)	95.82 (1.32)	**95.98 (1.37)**
9-NN	90.20 (1.82)	96.13 (1.26)	**95.67 (1.24)**
SVM-Poly1	97.96 (0.86)	98.85 (0.69)	**99.30 (0.57)**
SVM-Poly2	97.88 (0.93)	98.77 (0.70)	**99.31 (0.57)**
SVM-Poly3	97.91 (0.90)	98.75 (0.72)	**99.17 (0.63)**
SVM-RBF0.01	93.62 (1.71)	97.93 (0.95)	**98.64 (0.83)**
SVM-RBF0.05	96.88 (1.17)	98.54 (0.83)	**98.70 (0.77)**
SVM-RBF0.1	97.19 (1.04)	**98.32 (0.88)**	98.02 (0.90)
NB	90.63 (1.66)	**94.86 (1.46)**	94.72 (1.35)
RF	91.83 (1.90)	**96.36 (1.23)**	95.89 (1.37)

Each single execution of the 10-fold cross-validation produced a confusion matrix, from which we were able to assess accuracy values and what are the errors types committed by the classifier. One example of such confusion matrices may be seen on Table 4. This particular matrix shows the results of one of the 10 executions of the SVM-Poly2 inducer on the dataset generated with features extracted by the 48 LSF method. As the original matrix was very sparse, we omitted zeroes from the table for the sake of presentation.

Results show that our extraction methods (24/48 LSF) outperformed the original MFCC extraction method every time. In order to allow for better confidence on the results, we performed the Wilcoxon statistical test. The Wilcoxon test is recommended for comparing pairs of grouped populations. The Wilcoxon test

Table 4. Confusion matrix for one of the test of the SVM-Poly2 inducer on the dataset with features extracted by 48-LSF

		Actual									
		Zero	Um	Dois	Três	Quatro	Cinco	Seis	Sete	Oito	Nove
	Zero	214							3		
	Um		216							1	
	Dois			214						3	
Predicted	Três				216						
	Quatro					215					1
	Cinco						216	1	1		
	Seis							215			
	Sete	2							212		
	Oito			2						212	
	Nove					1					215
Acc. (%)		99.07	100	99.07	100	99.54	100	99.54	98.15	98.15	99.54

indicate that 24 and 48 LSF, despite not being comparable to each other with statistical significance, performed better than the original MFCC approach with 95% of significance for the analyzed dataset and classification algorithms.

6   Conclusions

In this study, we investigated the spoken digit recognition using a database of sounds corresponding to digits spoken in Portuguese. For this task, we investigated the use of LSF coefficients and compared to performance obtained using MFCC, commonly used descriptors in speech recognition. Both descriptors were extracted with dynamic windowing strategy. We used four classification algorithms, with parameter variations.

We demonstrated that the LSF coefficients are highly predictive attributes when classifying spoken digits. Our results showed that these attributes outperformed MFCC for all classifiers analyzed, providing an almost perfect classification performance.

Although the results presented in this study are restricted to the recognition of digits in Portuguese, all the techniques discussed may be used for other speech signals of short duration. Some examples are the recognition of vowels and isolated words.

As future work, we intend to evaluate the use of LSF coefficients in recognition of digits and other related areas in other languages, with the use of dynamic windowing and with Hidden Markov Models and nearest neighbors using the Dynamic Time Warping distance, which does not require that the vectors attributes having the same length.

Acknowledgments. This work is partially financially supported by FAPESP and CAPES.

References

1. Abushariah, A., Gunawan, T., Khalifa, O., Abushariah, M.: English Digits Speech Recognition System Based on Hidden Markov Models. In: Intl. Conf. on Computer and Communication Engineering (ICCCE 2010), pp. 1–5. IEEE (2010)
2. Alotaibi, Y.: Investigating Spoken Arabic Digits in Sspeech Recognition Setting. Information Sciences 173(1), 115–139 (2005)
3. Azam, S., Mansoor, Z., Mughal, M., Mohsin, S.: Urdu Spoken Digits Recognition Using Classified MFCC and Backpropgation Neural Network. In: Computer Graphics, Imaging and Visualisation (CGIV 2007), pp. 414–418. IEEE (2007)
4. Bresolin, A.A., Neto, A.D.D., Alsina, P.J.: Digit Recognition Using Wavelet and SVM in Brazilian Portuguese. In: International Conference on Acoustics, Speech and Signal Processing (ICASSP 2008), pp. 1545–1548. IEEE (2008)
5. Ghanty, S., Shaikh, S., Chaki, N.: On Recognition of Spoken Bengali Numerals. In: International Conference on Computer Information Systems and Industrial Management Applications (CISIM 2010), pp. 54–59. IEEE (2010)
6. Hu, X., Zhan, L., Xue, Y., Zhou, W., Zhang, L.: Spoken Arabic Digits Recognition Based on Wavelet Neural Networks. In: IEEE International Conference on Systems, Man, and Cybernetics (SMC 2011), pp. 1481–1485. IEEE (2011)
7. Itakura, F.: Line Spectrum Representation of Linear Predictor Coefficients of Speech Signals. The Journal of the Acoustical Society of America 57, S35 (1975)
8. Kondo, K., Kamata, H., Ishida, Y.: Speaker-Independent Spoken Digits Recognition Using LVQ. In: IEEE World Congress on Computational Intelligence (WCCI 1994), vol. 7, pp. 4448–4451 (1994)
9. Kopparapu, S., Rao, P.: Enhancing Spoken Connected-Digit Recognition Accuracy by Error Correction Codes – A Novel Scheme. Sadhana 29(5), 559–571 (2004)
10. Markel, J., Gray, A.: Linear Prediction of Speech. Springer (1976)
11. Oppenheim, A., Schafer, R., Buck, J.: Discrete-Time Signal Processing. Prentice-Hall (1989)
12. Paliwal, K., Kleijn, W.: Quantization of LPC Parameters. In: Speech Coding and Synthesis, pp. 433–466. Elsevier (1995)
13. Panwar, M., Sharma, R., Khan, I., Farooq, O.: Design of Wavelet Based Features for Recognition of Hindi Digits. In: Intl. Conference on Multimedia, Signal Processing and Communication Technologies (IMPACT 2011), pp. 232–235 (2011)
14. Rabiner, L., Schafer, R.: Digital Processing of Speech Signals. Prentice-Hall (1978)
15. Rodrigues, F., Trancoso, I.: Digit Recognition Using the SPEECHDAT Corpus. In: 2nd Conference on Telecommunications (CONFETELE 1999), pp. 1–4 (1999)
16. Stevens, S.S., Volkmann, J., Newman, E.B.: A Scale for the Measurement of the Psychological Magnitude Pitch. Journal of the Acoustical Society of America 8(3), 185–190 (1937)
17. Watson, A.: Image Compression Using the Discrete Cosine Transform. Mathematica Journal 4(1), 81–88 (1994)
18. Zhen, B., Wu, X., Liu, Z., Chi, H.: On the Importance of Components of the MFCC in Speech and Speaker Recognition. In: 6th International Conference on Spoken Language Processing (ICSLP 2000), pp. 487–490 (2000)

Technique to Neutralize Link Failures for an ACO-Based Routing Algorithm

Delfín Rupérez Cañas, Ana Lucila Sandoval Orozco,
and Luis Javier García Villalba

Grupo de Análisis, Seguridad y Sistemas (GASS)
Departamento de Ingeniería del Software e Inteligencia Artificial
Facultad de Informática, Despacho 431
Universidad Complutense de Madrid
C/ Profesor José García Santesmases s/n
Ciudad Universitaria, 28040 Madrid, Spain
{delfinrc,asandoval,javiergv}@fdi.ucm.es

Abstract. Ad hoc networks are formed by wireless devices distributed
without a predefined infrastructure using a technique called multi-hop
communication. A particular case is mobile ad hoc networks, which operate within dynamic environments. This determines the necessity of
paying special attention to the routing problem. Traditional techniques
are not particulary efficient at making the bioinspired algorithms more
relevant. These techniques are based on the analysis of the behavior of
some animals, especially in the process of obtaining food. A set of these
techniques or algorithms are known as the ACO (Ant Colony Optimization) which is based on the particular behavior of ants. A representative
protocol from this kind is AntOR, routing protocol for mobile ad hoc
hybrid, multipath and adaptive. In this article a variant of AntOR is
proposed which causes the protocol AntOR-UDLR. This approach consists of replacing the link failure notification messages sent in a broadcast manner by unicast messages, which are sent to the predecessor of
the node reporting the link failure, until the source of the data session
is reached. The simulation results show that AntOR-UDLR improves its
predecessor according to all analyzed metrics.

Keywords: bioinspired algorithm, routing protocol, mobile ad hoc
networks, ant colony optimization, link failure, unicast.

1 Introduction

Given dynamic topology of mobile ad hoc networks, that is, given the continuous joining and departing of nodes in a mobile ad hoc network, designing of
efficient routing protocols is not an easy task because it is not directly applicable
for standard routing solutions. There is a group of algorithms called Bioinspired
which have their adaptive capabilities as a main characteristic. This proves particularly relevant in this type of environment. Within these algorithms there has
been particular reference made in literature to the concept of *Swarm* Intelligence

J. Pavón et al. (Eds.): IBERAMIA 2012, LNAI 7637, pp. 251–260, 2012.
© Springer-Verlag Berlin Heidelberg 2012

[1], inspired by the social behavior of insects and other animals to solve complex problems. *Swarm* Intelligence is a set of methods to solve difficult optimization problems both static and dynamic problems using cooperative agents, usually called ants. These model a stigmergy behavior, which means the collaboration through a physical medium. Each insect smells the pheromone trail that other ants leave. This seemingly simple behavior solves complex problems. The ant behavior that they carry out of acquiring the food is the principle of the *Ant Colony Optimization* (ACO) algorithms [2]. This algorithm makes reference to the concept of ant as the agent that plays a particular role. It also uses the concept of *forward* ant (that goes from the source node to the destination) and *backward* ant (in the opposite direction).

This article presents the so-called protocol AntOR-UDLR (AntOR - Unicast Disjoint Link Route), variant of AntOR-DLR [3]. The main idea of this algorithm is to replace the link failure notification messages sent in broadcast manner by one-hop and unicast messages sent to the predecessor node of a valid path to a reachable destination. This paper is divided into 5 sections with the first section introducing the concept. In Sect. 2 we discuss the most relevant related work in the routing based on ACO. In Sect. 3 we present AntOR-UDLR explaining the major differences with regard to AntOR-DLR. In the following Sect. 4 we analyze the results of the simulation where AntOR-UDLR, AntOR-DLR and OLSR are compared. Finally we offer conclusions and lines of future work in Sect. 5.

2   Related Work

Many ACO algorithms have been proposed in the literature. These algorithms can be classified, as well as the traditional ones, in proactive, reactive, and hybrid. Proactive protocols frequently need to exchange packets between mobile nodes and to continuously update their routing tables. On the other hand, reactive protocols are that deal of reducing the overhead which produce proactive protocols but they have more latency. As a combination of proactive and reactive part we have hybrid protocols, among it, the following should be noted.

Ant-AODV [4], hybrid routing protocol based on ACO and on the routing protocol AODV, as its name suggests, it tries to take advantage of both. To overcome some of the disadvantages of AODV, as is the overhead generated by the increase of control message, this hybrid technical is utilized, that highlights the node connectivity and decreases the End-to-End delay, as well as the latency of route setup process. Ant-AODV similarly to other protocols such as ADRA [5] was designed without taking into account techniques to help to find the shortest routes and mechanisms to mitigate the congestion problem.

HOPNET [6] is based on a technique in which the ants jump from one zone to another one. The algorithm has characteristics extracted from the ZRP and DSR protocols, being highly scalable, compared with other hybrid protocols. This algorithm consists of proactive route setup in the area of node vicinity, and communication between zones reactively on demand is done when it sends packets from a zone to another. When the number of nodes is small the continuous movement of peripheral nodes constantly attempts to discover new routes, which causes more delay than in other hybrid routing protocols.

But undoubtedly the most representative is AntHocNet [7]. It constitutes a hybrid, adaptive and multipath protocol that takes into account the dynamic topology and other characteristics of the MANETs, presenting a hybrid mode of operation: it is reactive because it has agents operating in the route setup to destinations and proactive due to other agents collecting information to discover new routes in the prevention against link failure. It is multipath because it establishes different paths to send the information to the destination. Finally, it is adaptive because it suits the traffic and network conditions. In the operation of AntHocNet the following steps or phases can be distinguished:

- Routing information setup: The source node sends reactive agents to discover the first available route to the destination.
- Data routing: Data is sent through the nodes to the destination using the route information and can use a multihop technique, which involves sending data through intermediate nodes. These nodes act as routers.
- Path maintenance and exploration: Information about existing routes is proactively updated and the discovery of new ones is possible.
- Management of link failures: Management failures occur when a node is outside the scope of the network or does not receive control messages which are responsible for informing a node of its closest neighbours (who are one hop), and so on. This phase deals with such failures.

However, it is necessary to improve some aspects as the overhead produced in the route setup phase. This overhead is produced because it does not include techniques to monitor the number of ants that move over the network. Also, the use of disjoint route could improve the efficiency of the algorithm.

Finally, AntOR [3] is a protocol based on AntHocNet but it differs from this in the following characteristics: i) it is a protocol that works in two separate modes: Disjoint-link and Disjoint-node; ii) it takes into account the pheromone separation in the diffusion process; iii) Use of the *distance* metric in path exploration. In such protocol there are two kinds of routes: Disjoint-node and Disjoint-link. The first corresponds to routes in which nodes are not shared and the latter refers to routes in which links are not shared. In AntHocNet a same route can simultaneously have regular and virtual pheromone values. In the proposed protocol a route cannot have both a regular pheromone value and a virtual pheromone simultaneously; this technique improves the efficiency of the algorithm. Finally, it uses the *distance* metric, where AntOR takes into account the number of hops for the routes which have been found to be the best. In this manner, a proactive ant is controlled to ensure it does not go through more nodes than those established by the limit of the number of hops. This hop limit is established according to the best routes (less distance in number of hops) previously calculatedy.

3   AntOR-UDLR

In this article we present a new protocol which is a variant of AntOR-DLR [3]. We chose AntOR-DLR instead of AntOR-DNR because of the comparison done in [8] which showed that it is more beneficial. One of the aspects that the design of this new algorithm pursues is to reduce the overhead in the network. Before specifying it we must differentiate between *unicast* and *broadcast* messages. *Unicast* means that the information from a unique sender to a unique receiver is sent, unlike the broadcast system that sends data to the whole network in an indiscriminate way. *Unicast* mode checks through control messages that the channel is free to transmit. This fact implies more delay to have with respect to broadcast messages, but it has the advantage that it produces fewer collisions, losing fewer messages.

3.1   Specification

The main idea of this approach is to replace the notification messages sent in *broadcast* mode by simple messages sent the precursor of a valid path to a reachable destination. We mean with valid route that route with has pheromone value greater than zero and belongs to the active session of a particular destination. When a node detects the link failure in its neighbour, it communicates such a failure to its predecessor through a *unicast* message, repeating that message to its predecessor until the source node of the data session is reached. This causes the source to launch a *forward* ant in the route setup phase. It may be the case that the node, that detects the link failure, has two or more overlapped data sessions. This causes the failure communication to have to do different predecessors, due to the distinct source data session. Next we explain how to manage the link failures in AntOR-DLR and AntOR-UDLR.

Link Failure Management: In mobile ad hoc networks the link failures can occur by physical changes, such as when a node is switched off or moved, or due to changes that affect the connectivity of wireless communication, such as the increase in the transmission range or a decrease in the utilized transmission power. Since the MANETS are dynamic, these events occur frequently, and the routing algorithms of such a network must be prepared to deal with them efficiently. The first step in the management of link failures is the detection. Once the failure is detected, the next step is the neutralization of the failure. This stage is where AntOR-UDLR differs from AntOR-DLR, significantly improving the performance of the routing algorithm. Then we enter the core concepts of link failures management.

Link Failure Management in AntOR-DLR: Before analyzing the link failure management in this protocol, we should comment AntOR-DLR offers some basic protection components. These components are the route setup process and proactive route maintenance process. The first one allows the source nodes to rebuild the entire route if needed and the second one provides protection in a proactive manner through the creation of new paths, which can serve as backup for the routing. In AntOR-DLR the link failure is detected whether protocols from the lower layers inform of the transmission failure about control or data packet, or if a node does not receive the corresponding message HELLO from its neighbors. As mentioned, when a failure is detected, we process it to neutralize it. At this phase, AntOR-DLR behaves in the the following way. In AntOR-DLR, the first task that occurs when there is a failure node is that the node detecting the failure removes it from its neighbors table. Then the routing table with the new pheromone information is updated. Finally, it is responsible for neutralizing the failure taking into account the following factors:

a. If there is no route at the source a reactive *forward* ant is sent.
b. If there is no route at an intermediate node and it is dealt with by a data packet that had been forwarding when the failure occurred, a route repair *forward* ant is sent. If there is no reply from the corresponding repair *backward* ant in a certain time period a link failure notification message is sent in broadcast mode, reporting the unreachable destination.
c. When there is a link failure, due to the fact that the corresponding consecutive message HELLO has not been received in a while or because a unicast control message is lost, and if it is dealt with intermediate nodes in the following way is processed: a link failure notification message is created informing about unreachable destinations and this message in broadcast mode is sent.

Link Failure Management in AntOR-UDLR: The algorithm of link failure detection is the same as in AntOR-DLR. The only thing that changes is the way to deal with the corresponding failure. Here is where we comment on the new characteristics.

As AntOR-DLR, the first fact that occurs when there is a node failure in AntOR-UDLR is the node that perceives the failure removes it its neighbors table. Then the routing table with the new pheromone information is updated. Finally, it is processed similarly to AntOR-DLR:

a. If there is no route at source node, a reactive *forward* ant is sent.
b. If there is no route at an intermediate node, and it is dealt with by a data packet that had been forwarding when the failure occurred, a route repair *forward* ant is sent. If there is not reply from the corresponding repair *backward* ant repair in a given time period, a message in *unicast* mode to the precursor of the route is sent informing about the unreachable destination. The node that receives this message updates the routing table and forwards this message to the precursor of the route to the destination. This process is repeated as many times as needed until the source node of the data session is reached.
c. If there is no route at the intermediate node, and it is dealt with by a control packet (a HELLO message is not consecutively received at every certain interval or a unicast control message), no message is not sent. This last option may prevent those routes from repairing correctly, because in this case any operation is not performed. To fix this we create a new functionality: when an intermediate node, which is routing data and does not find a valid route,

i.e., a route with a regular pheromone value greater than zero, sends a *unicast* message to all one-hop neigbours, so that they update their routing tables. It is necessary to send this message to all neighbors, because otherwise we do not have information of the predecessor by not finding a valid route. When one of these neighboring nodes has a valid route to the destination, it forwards the *unicast* message the precursor of the route. This process is repeated as often as needed until the source node is reached.

3.2 Algorithm Design

AntOR-UDLR has a *unicast* message of link notification (ULN), which has a simple structure. It contains two IP addresses: *Session Destination Address* and *Session Source Address*. The first address makes reference to the destination of the data session with a valid route and the second to the source. These two addresses are essential for the functioning of the algorithm. We use the destination address because, when there is a link failure, the node, which detects it, has to indicate the destination in that message, so that the predecessor nodes can process it properly and decide if they must forward such a message depending on whether they detect or not valid route to that destination. The source address is important because it indicates to the node that receives the message ULN, if the source node has been reached or not, by checking if the source address encapsulated in the message is the same than the main address from the node.

---

1 {src, dst} = GetInformation(ULN)
2 **if** *CheckValidRoute(dst)* **then**
3 | **if** *CURRENT_NODE* = *src* **then**
4 | | *Send(RFA)*
5 | **else**
6 | | *TTL = TTL - 1*
7 | | *{ pre } = GetPrecursor(dst)*
8 | | *ReSend (pre, ULN)*
9 | **end**
10 **end**

Algorithm 1: Link failure neutralization process

According to Algorithm 1, in line 1 we get the source and destination associated with the data session. This information is extracted from the ULN message. In line 2 we check if there is a valid route (active session and value of regular pheromone greater than zero) to the destination *dst*. In positive case, in line 3 whether the current node (which receives the message ULN) is equivalent to src is checked. If we have reached the source of the data session we perform a new route setup (line 4), in case contrary we re-forward message ULN (lines 6-8). In 6 we subtract a unit to the value of the field Time to live (TTL). This field in the packet header is included. In line 7 we obtain the precursor *pre*, so that in 8 we forward message ULN to such a precursor.

3.3 Functioning

The following example explains how to treat a link failure at an intermediate node, when data message is transmited and we cannot fix the route (case b of "Link failure management in AntOR-UDLR"). Figure 1 shows a network formed by 5 nodes, where the source and destination node corresponds to the letters A and E respectively. We mark the failed or deactivated node in red which causing the link failure between C and D. Node C notifies its predecessor B, with a simple *unicast* message, that the destination E is unreachable. On receiving the node B this message forwards it to its predecessor A discounting a unit to the TTL value of such a message. Finally when A receives this message and executes a new route setup process because it is the source node.

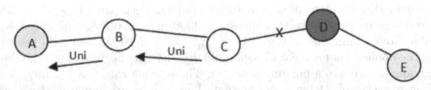

Fig. 1. Example of Link-failure Manage (I)

Figures 2(a) and 2(b) show another scenario in which the new functionality is seen (case c of "Link failure management in AntOR-UDLR" in Sect. 3.1) This scenario (see Fig. 2(a)) consists of 6 nodes where the source and destination of a session of data are represented by the letters A and E respectively. A node forwards the data packet to the reachable destination E through the next hop B.

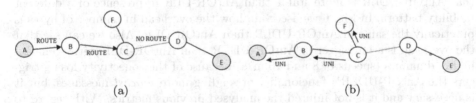

(a)   (b)

Fig. 2. Example of Link-failure Manage (II)

Upon receiving node B the data packet correctly, forwards it to C with destination E. Now node C has to relay it, but cannot find the route to the next hop

D, so that the information cannot be routed to the destination successfully. At this moment, we apply the new functionality (see Fig. 2(b)), by sending a *unicast* message to all neighbours. To be able to send the corresponding message to all neighbours it must find the IP addresses of each one of them in the neighbors table. A *unicast* message is sent by IP address of the found neighbor, rather than a broadcast message; because the sending in unicast mode is more efficient as explained at the beginning of this section. Nodes F and B receive the message sent by C, but do not receive D because it is removed from the neighbors table of C since it originated the failure. Node F processes the message but does not forward it, because it does not belong to the valid route to the destination E. Instead, node B forwards it to node A, since it belongs to this data session. Upon receiving Node A this message, it sends a *forward* ant to proceed with a new route setup.

4   AntOR-UDLR vs. AntOR-DLR

The characteristics of the simulations in Simulator NS-3 were: We used randomly distributed 100 nodes with transmission range of 300 m. The nodes are moved according to the *Random WayPoint* (RWP) pattern with pause time of 2 s. The scenario was rectangular with dimensions 3000 m × 1000 m. The speed was variable from a minimum of 0 m/s to 10 m/s. It used 10 random data sessions using the application protocol *Constant Bit Rate* (CBR) beginning to send data at random from 0 s to a maximum of 60 s. The sending rate was 512 bit/s, i.e., sending a packet of 64 bytes per second. The maximum simulation time was established to 300 s. It employed a total of 5 runs in the experiment. Fig. 3 and 4 show the Throughput and ratio respectively. Both have similiar behaviour, but using a different scale. In this scenario and with this new algorithm we achieve a ratio of 77% in adverse conditions of speed and dimensions because it is a rectangular scenario which does not help in the packets reception. The square scenarios have a better node distribution and have a more regular and uniform movement. In Fig. 5 we appreciate how the Average End-to-End Delay is lower in AntOR-UDLR than AntOR-DLR at all times. This behavior makes us think that AntOR-UDLR is more stable than AntOR-DLR in presence of a different mobility pattern. In Fig. 6 we ascertain how the overhead in number of bytes is practically the same in AntOR-UDLR than AntOR-DLR. Also we can see that the overhead is a bit bigger in AntOR-UDLR than AntOR-DLR with scenarios highly dinamics (speeds of 8 and 10 m/s) because of the conectivity losing triggers the AntOR-UDLR's funcionality of sending more *unicast* messages, but it is necessary and it is not injured the analysed previous metrics. With regard to OLSR we can appreciate how AntOR-UDLR and AntOR-DLR improve it in all metrics except Average End-to-End Delay. OLSR is a proactive protocol and it has a high overhead and low delay.

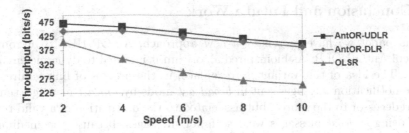

Fig. 3. Throughput

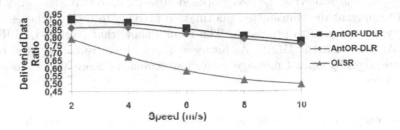

Fig. 4. Delivered Data Ratio

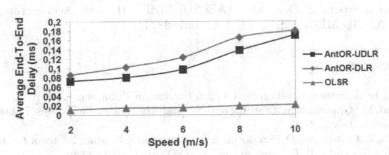

Fig. 5. Average End-To-End Delay

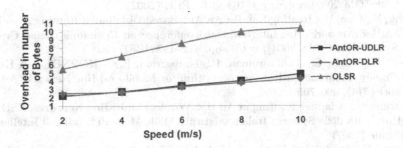

Fig. 6. Overhead in number of Bytes

5   Conclusion and Future Work

In this paper we have presented a new approach, AntOR-UDLR, of routing protocol AntOR-DLR. As bioinspired algorithm it is suited to dynamic environments. The idea of this variant is to replace, in the process of link failure, the failure notification messages sent in *broadcast* mode by *unicast* message, sent to the predecessor to the source, but associated to the destination of a valid route. Also, using *unicast* messages we lose fewer messages, because the medium is checked before transmitting, i.e., if the medium we want to send is free; this fact does not happen when it is sent through *broadcast* mode. With this new protocol we have aimed at achieving the two proposed objectives: to reduce network traffic and to prevent the transmitted information arriving to nodes unnecessarily, i.e., they do not need to process it. The results show that AntOR-UDLR improves AntOR-DLR and OLSR. As future work we aim at replacing local route repair messages by unicast message, as well as evaluating more metrics as could be the Jitter.

Acknowledgments. This work was supported by the Ministerio de Industria, Turismo y Comercio (MITyC, Spain) through the Project Avanza Competitividad I+D+I TSI-020100-2011-165 and the Agencia Española de Cooperación Internacional para el Desarrollo (AECID, Spain) through Acción Integrada MAEC-AECID MEDITERRÁNEO A1/037528/11.

References

1. Kennedy, J.: Swarm Intelligence. Morgan Kaufmann Publishers (2001)
2. Dorigo, M.: Optimization, Learning and Natural Algorithms. PhD thesis. Politecnico di Milano, Italy (1992)
3. García, L.J., Rupérez, D., Sandoval, A.L.: Bioinspired Routing Protocol for Mobile Ad Hoc Networks. IET Communications 4(18), 2187–2195 (2010)
4. Marwaha, S., Tham, C.K., Srinavasan, D.: Mobile Agents Based Routing Protocol for Mobile Ad Hoc Networks. In: IEEE Global Telecommunications Conference (GLOBECOM 2002), vol. 1, pp. 163–167. IEEE (2002)
5. Zheng, X., Guo, W., Renting Liu, R.: An Ant-Based Distributed Routing Algorithm for Ad-Hoc Networks. In: International Conference on Communications, Circuits and Systems (ICCCAS 2004), vol. 1, pp. 412–417. IEEE (2004)
6. Wang, J., Osagie, E., Thulasiraman, P., Thulasiram, R.K.: HOPNET – A Hybrid Ant Colony Optimization Routing Algorithm for Mobile Ad Hoc Network. Ad Hoc Networks 7(4), 690–705 (2009)
7. Ducatelle, F.: Adaptive Routing in Ad Hoc Wireless Multi-Hop Networks. PhD thesis, Università della Svizzera Italiana, Istituto Dalle Molle di Studi sull Intelligenza Artificiale (2007)
8. Rupérez, D., Sandoval, A.L., García, L.J., Kim, T.H.: A Comparison Study between AntOR-Disjoint Node Routing and AntOR-Disjoint Link Routing for Mobile Ad Hoc Networks. In: Tai-hoon, K., et al. (eds.) MulGraB 2011, Part II. CCIS, vol. 263, pp. 300–304. Springer, Heidelberg (2011)

A Combination of Specialized Differential Evolution Variants for Constrained Optimization

Luis-Alfredo Gordián-Rivera and Efrén Mezura-Montes

Laboratorio Nacional de Informática Avanzada (LANIA) A.C.
Rébsamen 80, Centro, Xalapa, Veracruz, 91000, México
iie.alfredogordian@gmail.com, emezura@lania.mx

Abstract. A novel approach based on three differential evolution variants to solve numerical constrained optimization problems is presented. Each variant competes to get more vectors for reproduction from the population. Such competition is based on two performance measures for convergence and solution improvement. Two of the variants adopted in this work were precisely proposed to deal with constrained search spaces. Two experiments are carried out: one to analyze the behavior of each variant with respect to the features of the problem solved and another to compare the performance of the proposed approach with respect to state-of-the-art multi-operator algorithms. The results obtained show that the specialized variants are more useful in the search, either combined or just using one of them. Finally, the final results of the proposed approach were highly competitive, and better in some cases, with respect to those of the algorithms used in the comparison.

Keywords: evolutionary algorithms, differential evolution, constrained optimization.

1 Introduction

Nowadays, the usage of metaheuristic algorithms to solve complex optimization problems has become very popular. Among such algorithms, evolutionary computing has been successfully applied, particularly, in numerical optimization problems [1]. However, evolutionary algorithms (EAs) in their original versions were designed to deal with unconstrained search spaces. On the other hand, several optimization problems have constraints in their definitions. This has motivated the design of techniques to incorporate feasibility information within an EA to sample constrained search spaces [2].

This work precisely focuses on the constrained numerical optimization problem (CNOP), which, without loss of generality can be formulated as follows:
Find x which optimizes $f(x)$
subject to: $g_j(x) \leq 0, j = 1, \ldots, m$ and $h_k(x) = 0, k = 1, \ldots, p$
where $x \in \mathbb{R}^n$ is the vector of solutions $x = [x_1, x_2, \ldots, x_n]^T$ and each x_i, $i = 1, \ldots, n$ is limited by lower and upper limits $L_i \leq x_i \leq U_i$. If the feasible region is $\mathcal{F}$ and the whole search space is $\mathcal{S}$, then $\mathcal{F} \subseteq \mathcal{S}$. For an inequality

J. Pavón et al. (Eds.): IBERAMIA 2012, LNAI 7637, pp. 261–270, 2012.

constraint that satisfies $g_j(\boldsymbol{x}) = 0$, the constraint is active at $\boldsymbol{x}$. All equality constraints are active at all solutions of $\mathcal{F}$. To handle equality constraints they are transformed into inequality constraints as follows $|h_k(\boldsymbol{x})| - \epsilon \leq 0$, where ϵ is the tolerance value allowed(a very small value).

It is well-known by the No Free Lunch Theorems [3] that there is not an algorithm which ensures to outperform other algorithms in all search problems, i.e. an algorithm will not present the same good performance in all problem classes.

This feature has motivated the development of new ways to improve the performance of an algorithm in a wider set of problems. Regarding CNOPs, there are proposals based on multiple operators within the same algorithm [4,5] and even multiple algorithms with multiple operators in a single approach [6]. However, based on a recent review of the state-of-the-art such efforts in constrained numerical optimization are still scarce [2]. Moreover, to the best of the authors' knowledge, the aforementioned proposals mostly report final results, while the behavior of the multiple operators has been overlooked. Furthermore, in those multiple-operator EAs for constrained optimization, no operators adapted for CNOPs have been considered.

On the other hand, among those EAs usually adopted to solve CNOPs, differential evolution (DE) has been the most preferred due to its better performance in such type of optimization problems [2].

All the aforementioned is the main motivation of this research, where three DE variants, two of them specifically adapted to solve CNOPs, are incorporated into a single algorithm. Two performance measures are used as criteria to adaptively give those more successful variants more chances to generate offspring. Therefore, a competition of operators is promoted and analyzed. The aim is, besides giving empirical evidence of the performance of the proposed approach, analyzing the behavior of the approach so as to detect which DE variants are preferred depending of the features of the CNOP being solved.

This paper is organized as follows. Section 2 details the DE variants adopted. Section 3 describes the adaptive mechanism to control those DE variants. The experimental design and results are presented in Sect. 4. Finally, some conclusions and the future work are shown in Sect. 5.

2   DE Variants Adopted

DE works with a population P with NP vectors, i.e, potential solutions of an optimization problem [7]. The population evolves by using two variation operators: recombination (usually discrete) and differential mutation based on differences between vectors chosen at random from P. At each iteration t, each vector $\boldsymbol{x}_{i,t}$ in $P(t)$, called parent vector at this time, uses the differential mutation to generate a mutation vector $\boldsymbol{v}_{i,t}$. After that, by using the recombination operator between the parent and mutation vectors, an offspring vector $\boldsymbol{u}_{i,t}$ is generated (see Eq. 1).

$$u_{j,i,t} = \begin{cases} v_{j,i,t} \text{ if } rand_j[0,1) \leq CR \text{ or } j = j_{rand} \\ x_{j,i,t} \text{ otherwise} \end{cases} \tag{1}$$

where $rand_j[0,1)$ is a uniform random number distributed between 0 and 1, j_{rand} is randomly chosen index from $\{1,2,\ldots,n\}$, and $0 \leq CR \leq 1$ determines the similarity of the offspring with respect to the mutation vector. Such offspring then competes with its parent $x_{i,t}$ in a greedy selection to choose the one that will be part of the next population $P(t+1)$.

Three differential mutation variants are mixed in a competition scheme within the same algorithm to solve CNOPs in this current work. They are the following:

1. **Original mutation operator**: This mutation operator is used in the most popular DE variant called DE/rand/1/bin [7], where the mutation vector $v_{i,t}$ is generated by three vectors chosen at random. The scaled difference (by a user-defined parameter F) between two of them ($x_{r1,t}$ and $x_{r2,t}$) defines the search direction and the third one, $x_{r3,t}$, is used as a base vector (see Eq. 2).

$$v_{i,t} = x_{r3,t} + F(x_{r1,t} - x_{r2,t}) \tag{2}$$

2. **Modified differential evolution (MDE)**: Proposed in [8] to deal with CNOPs, where two differences are computed: (1) between the best vector in the current population $x_{best,t}$ and a randomly chosen vector $x_{r2,t}$, and (2) between the parent vector $x_{i,t}$ and another randomly chosen vector $x_{r1,t}$. Both differences are scaled by two different factors F_α and F_β, respectively. Finally, a third randomly chosen vector $x_{r3,t}$ is used as a base vector (see Eq. 3).

$$v_{i,t} = x_{r3,t} + F_\alpha(x_{best,t} - x_{r2,t}) + F_\beta(x_{i,t} - x_{r1,t}) \tag{3}$$

It is important to note that MDE generates n_o offspring per parent vector and the best one is the one which competes against its parent.

3. **Adaptative Differential Evolution (ADE)**: Proposed in [9] to solve CNOPs and based on a multi-parent schema where, for each individual $x_{i,t}$ in $P(t)$, the mutation vector $v_{i,t}$ is generated as in Eq. 4:

$$v_{i,t} = x_{i,t} + \sum_{k=1}^{K} w_k * (x_{r_k,t} - x_{r_{k+1},t}) \tag{4}$$

where, $r_1, r_2, \ldots, r_K \in \{1,2,\ldots,NP\}$, are K integers different among each other and different from i (the index of the parent vector), and $x_{r_{K+1},t} = x_{r_1,t}$. The weighted values w_k are calculated as indicated in Eq. 5:

$$\xi = randn(1,K), w = \xi/sum(\xi) \tag{5}$$

where, $randn(1,K)$ is a vector with K normally distributed random numbers, $sum(\xi)$ is the sum of all components of the vector ξ, and $w = [w_1,\ldots,w_K]$. Eqs. 4 and 5 are used K times to generate K vectors by recombination. The best of them is chosen as the offspring to compete against its parent.

3   Proposed Approach

As it was mentioned in Sect. 1, the three DE mutation variants will compete to generate offspring in a single population at each generation. Such competition will be based on two performance measures, one for measuring convergence and another for measuring the improvement of the best solution at each generation:

- **Convergence difference (CD)**: it is based on the convergence measure P_m proposed in [10], where the Euclidean distance between the center of the population and the individual farthest from it is computed. The center of the population O_p is calculated as the average position of all individuals in P as detailed in Eq. 6:

$$O_p = \frac{\sum_{i=1}^{NP} x_i}{NP} \tag{6}$$

Then, P_m is defined in Eq. 7

$$P_m = max \parallel x_i - O_p \parallel_E, i = 1, ..., NP. \tag{7}$$

Thus, the convergence difference of two populations is presented in Eq. 8:

$$CD = P_m(P(t-1)) - P_m(P(t)) \tag{8}$$

where $P(t-1)$ is the population before the application of the DE variant and $P(t)$ is the population after the application of the DE variant.
- **Progress ratio (PR)**: originally proposed in [11] to measure improvement within the feasible region of the search space. In this work this measure is slightly modified in such a way that it is used to evaluate the ability on an algorithm to improve its best feasible solution at each generation as indicated in Eq. 9:

$$PR = \left| \ln \sqrt{\frac{f_{min}(t-1)}{f_{min}(t)}} \right| \tag{9}$$

where $f_{min}(t-1)$ is the best feasible objective function value in $P(t-1)$ and $f_{min}(t)$ is the best feasible objective function value in $P(t)$.

The proposed algorithm works in a similar way as DE does it. However, unlike traditional DE where only one DE variant is used to generate the offspring of each vector in the population, the three variants described in Sect. 2 compete to get more vectors to reproduce. The initial population $P(0)$ of NP vectors is divided in three sub-populations ($P_1(0)$, $P_2(0)$, and $P_3(0)$) of equal size ($s_1(0) = s_2(0) = s_3(0)$). Each sub-population is assigned to each one of the three DE variants. Moreover, each DE variant is assigned a value which determines its strength. The initial strength value for each DE variant (at generation 0) is 1 ($ST_{v1}(0) = ST_{v2}(0) = ST_{v3}(0) = 1$) and if for some reason it falls below 1 it is reset to 1.

Each DE variant then generates the offspring for each vector in its sub-population. After all offspring are generated by each DE variant in its corresponding sub-population, the two performance measures are computed for all three sub-populations, considering in each case the current sub-population $P_{sp}(t)$ and the set of offspring recently generated $P'_{sp}(t+1)$, $sp = 1, 2, 3$.

The process to update the strength values is through comparisons among the values of the performance measures obtained by each DE variant as follows: (1) if one DE variant outperforms other variant in both performance measures, a value of 1 is added to the strength of the best one and a value of 1 is subtracted to the strength of the outperformed DE variant, (2) if no DE variant is better than the other two, a value of 1 is added to the strength value of all of them, (3) if two DE variants have a tie in one measure value, the value of the remaining measure breaks the tie.

Based on the strength values updated at each generation of the approach, the size of each sub-population is also updated accordingly by using a so-called *portion* value for each sub-population, which is calculated in Eq. 10:

$$portion_i(t+1) = \frac{ST_{vi}(t)}{\sum_{j=1}^{3} ST_{vj}(t)}, i = 1, 2, 3 \tag{10}$$

Thereby, for each DE variant its sub-population size for the next generation can be calculated as indicated in Eq. 11:

$$s_i(t+1) = s_i(t) * portion_i(t+1); i = 1, 2, 3 \tag{11}$$

If $s_i(t+1) < 5$, vectors from other sub-populations are taken to maintain a minimum size of 5 vectors. At the end of the generation, the population is randomly merged to allow each DE variant to work with different vectors at each generation.

The constraint-handling technique adopted in this work is the set of feasibility rules proposed by Deb [12]. They are used as criteria to choose between the parent vector and its child as follows:

- Between 2 feasible vectors, the one with the highest fitness value is preferred.
- If one vector is feasible and the other one is infeasible, the feasible vector is preferred.
- If both vectors are infeasible, the one with the lowest sum of constraint violation ($\sum_{j=1}^{m} max(0, g_j(\boldsymbol{x})) + \sum_{k=1}^{p} max(0, |h_k(\boldsymbol{x})| - \epsilon|)$) is preferred.

The complete details of the proposed approach are in Algorithm 1.

4 Experiments and Results

To evaluate the performance of the proposed approach two experiments were designed: (1) an analysis of the behavior of each DE variant depending of two features of the CNOP solved, and (2) a comparison of final results with respect to state-of-the-art EAs, two with multiple operators to solve CNOPs; they are

---

Algorithm 1. Pseudocode of the proposed approach

Require: number of iterations CH, population size NP
1: Generate $P(0)$ of size NP at random and evaluate each vector in $P(0)$
2: Divide $P(0)$ in three sub-populations $P_1(0)$, $P_2(0)$, and $P_3(0)$ with equal size $s_1(0) = s_2(0) = s_3(0)$
3: $ST_{v1}(0) = ST_{v2}(0) = ST_{v3}(0) = 1$
4: $t = 0$
5: **while** $t \leq CH$ **do**
6:    Apply DE variants ($v1$, $v2$, and $v3$) to their corresponding sub-population $P_1(t)$, $P_2(t)$, and $P_3(t)$ to generate offspring $P_1'(t+1)$, $P_2'(t+1)$, and $P_3'(t+1)$ and evaluate each new vector generated
7:    Calculate CD (Eq. 8) and PR (Eq. 9) for each sub-population sp based on $P_{sp}(t)$ and $P_{sp}'(t+1)$, $sp = 1,2,3$
8:    Update the strength values for each DE variant $ST_{v1}(t)$, $ST_{v2}(t)$, and $ST_{v3}(t)$
9:    Calculate $portion_i(t+1)$, $i = 1,2,3$ (Eq.10)
10:   Update the sub-population sizes $s_i(t+1)$, $i = 1,2,3$ (Eq.11)
11:   Generate the population for the next generation $P(t+1)$ by selecting, based on Deb's rules, the best vector between parent and child for each sub-population $P_{sp}(t)$ and $P_{sp}'(t+1)$, $sp = 1,2,3$
12:   Shuffle the new population $P(t+1)$
13:   Distribute the vectors in $P(t+1)$ based on the updated sizes for the sub-populations $s_i(t+1)$, $i = 1,2,3$, to each sub-population $P_{sp}(t+1)$, $sp = 1,2,3$
14:   $t = t+1$
15: **end while**

---

the self-adaptive multi-operator genetic algorithm (SAMO-GA) and the self-adaptive multi-operator differential evolution (SAMO-DE) [6] and finally the elitist teaching-learning-based optimization (TLBO) algorithm [13]. Thirteen well-known test problems with different features were used in both experiments and their descriptions can be found in [6]. A summary of their main features is presented in Table 1.

The proposed approach used the following parameter values: NP=21, CH = 5000 (260,000 evaluations were carried out per independent run). For each DE variant the parameter values, as suggested in their references, were the following for DE: $CR = 0.7$ and $F = 0.9$, ADE: $CR = 0.5$, $K = 3$, MDE: $CR = 0.7$, $F_\alpha = 0.9$, $F_\beta = 0.4$, $N_o = 3$

For the first experiment, the average sub-population sizes per iteration on 30 independent runs for representative test problems were plotted. The aim is to analyze the adaptive behavior the proposed approach has depending on the features of the CNOP solved.

Figure 1 shows the sub-population sizes for problems with different estimated sizes of the feasible region. As it can be seen, for large feasible regions, even if the three variants start with different sizes (i.e., different strengths), they tend to converge to a similar value before the first half of the search. The opposite is observed for small feasible regions (problem g10) where one DE variant (ADE in

Table 1. Features of test problems. *"n"*: dimensions, *"LI"*, *"NI"*, *"LE"*, *"NE"*: linear inequality, nonlinear inequality, linear equality and nonlinear equality constraints, respectively, *"a"*: active constraints, and *"ρ"*: estimated feasible region size.

Function	n	Type of function	ρ	LI	NI	LE	NE	a
g01	13	quadratic	0.0003%	9	0	0	0	6
g02	20	nonlinear	99.9973%	0	2	0	0	1
g03	10	nonlinear	0.0026%	0	0	0	1	1
g04	5	quadratic	27.0079%	0	6	0	0	2
g05	4	nonlinear	0.0000%	2	0	0	3	3
g06	2	nonlinear	0.0057%	0	2	0	0	2
g07	10	quadratic	0.0000%	3	5	0	0	6
g08	2	nonlinear	0.8581%	0	2	0	0	0
g09	7	nonlinear	0.5199%	0	4	0	0	2
g10	8	linear	0.0020%	3	3	0	0	6
g11	2	quadratic	0.0973%	0	0	0	1	1
g12	3	quadratic	4.7697%	0	1	0	0	0
g13	5	nonlinear	0.0000%	0	0	0	3	3

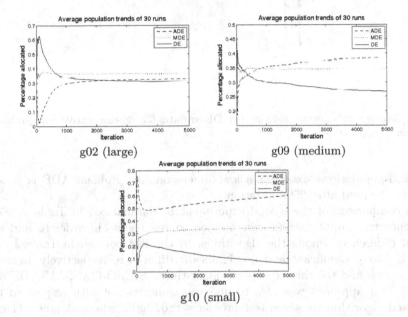

g02 (large)   g09 (medium)

g10 (small)

Fig. 1. Average sub-population size per DE variant for representative test problems based on estimated size of the feasible region

this case) dominates the other two since the beginning. A behavior "in the middle" can be observed for medium sized feasible regions, where ADE dominates, but its dominance is lower with respect to MDE. In all three cases, the original DE was the least used variant.

Figure 2 presents the sub-population sizes for problems with different dimensionalities. For a high dimensionality test problem the two specialized DE variants to solve CNOPs, have the same strength after iteration 3000 while the traditional DE variants is almost unused. For a test problem with a medium dimensionality an interesting difference in strengths is observed between 1000 and 2000 iterations. After that, the three DE variants are used with almost the

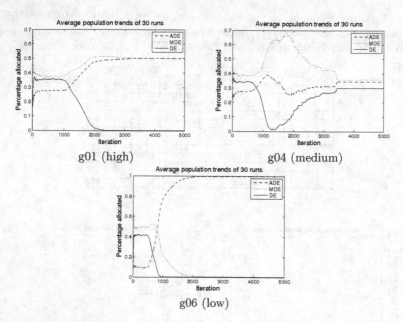

Fig. 2. Average sub-population size per DE variant for representative test problems based on dimensionality

same sub-populations sizes. For a low dimensionality problem ADE is almost the only one used after 2000 iterations.

The comparison of the second experiment is summarized in Table 2. 95%-confidence two-sample t-tests were applied to the results in order to find significant differences among the algorithms. In the last column in Table 2 "√" and "X" mean significant and no significant difference, respectively, between our approach and the three compared algorithms (SAMO-GA, SAMO-DE and TLBO). Our approach was able to find the same results with respect to the compared algorithms in seven test problems (g01, g04, g06, g08, g09, g11 and g12). Moreover, the t-test results confirmed that our approach outperformed the other three algorithms in test problem g10, while outperforming SAMO-GA and TLBO in problem g05 (no significant difference was obtained with SAMO-DE). In problem g07, based on the t-test results, our approach outperformed SAMO-GA and no significant difference was observed with respect to SAMO-DE and TLBO. In problem g13, our approach outperformed TLBO but was outperformed by SAMO-GA and SAMO-DE. Finally, our approach was outperformed in problems g02 and g03 (problems with a nonlinear objective function, a high-dimensionality and nonlinear constraints). The overall results of the comparison against state-of-the-art approaches suggest a competitive performance of our approach and even better with respect to other multi-operator EAs as in problems g07 and g10.

Table 2. Statistical comparison of the proposed approach against state-of-the-art EAs

Problem/Optimal	Stat	Our approach	SAMO-GA	SAMO-DE	TLBO	t-test
g01	Best	-15.0000	-15.0000	-15.0000	-15.0000	
-15.0000	Average	-15.0000	-15.0000	-15.0000	-15.0000	X X X
	Std. dev	0.00E+0	0.00E+0	0.00E+0	0.00E+00	
g02	Best	-0.803603	-0.803591	-0.803619	-0.803619	
-0.803619	Average	-0.782710	-0.796048	-0.798735	-0.803619	√ √ √
	Std. dev	20.1E-03	5.8025E-03	8.8005E-03	0.00E+00	
g03	Best	-1	-1	-1	-1	
-1.	Average	-0.988	-1	-1	-1	√ √ √
	Std. dev	23.5E-03	0.00E+00	0.00E+00	1.40E-04	
g04	Best	-30665.539	-30665.539	-30665.539	-30665.539	
-30665.539	Average	-30665.539	-30665.539	-30665.539	-30665.539	X X X
	Std. dev	1.4138E-11	0.00E+00	0.00E+00	0.00E+00	
g05	Best	5126.484	5126.497	5126.497	5126.484	
5126.484	Average	5126.591	5127.976	5126.497	5168.7194	√ X √
	Std. dev	585.7E-03	1.1166E+00	0.00E+00	5.41E+01	
g06	Best	-6961.814	-6961.814	-6961.814	-6961.814	
-6961.814	Average	-6961.814	-6961.814	-6961.813875	-6961.814	X X X
	Std. dev	4.6252E-12	0.00E+00	0.00E+00	0.00E+00	
g07	Best	24.307	24.306	24.306	24.306	
24.306	Average	24.309	24.411	24.310	24.310	√ X X
	Std. dev	2E-03	4.5905E-02	1.5888E-03	7.11E 03	
g08	Best	-0.095825	-0.095825	-0.095825	0.005825	
-0.095825	Average	-0.095825	-0.095825	-0.095825	-0.095825	X X X
	Std. dev	1.4115E-17	0.00E+00	0.00E+00	0.00E+00	
g09	Best	680.630	680.630	680.630	680.630	
680.630	Average	680.630	680.634	680.630	680.630	X X X
	Std. dev	1.9868E-07	1.4573E-03	1.1567E-05	0.00E+00	
g10	Best	7049.365	7049.248	7049.248	7052.488	
7049.28	Average	7050.373	7144.40311	7059.813	7143.45	√ √ √
	Std. dev	771.8E-03	6.7860E+01	7.856E+00	1.13E+02	
g11	Best	0.75	0.75	0.75	0.75	
0.75	Average	0.75	0.75	0.75	0.75	X X X
	Std. dev	1.1292E-16	0.00E+00	0.00E+00	7.06E-05	
g12	Best	-1	-1	-1	-1	
-1	Average	-1	-1	-1	-1	X X X
	Std. dev	0.00E+00	0.00E+00	0.00E+00	0.00E+00	
g13	Best	0.05390	0.05394	0.05394	0.13314	
0.05394	Average	0.33032	0.05403	0.05394	0.83851	X X √
	Std. dev	333.0E-03	5.9414E-05	1.7541E-08	2.26E-01	

5   Conclusions and Future Work

This paper has presented the combination of three differential evolution variants, two of them designed for constrained search spaces, to solve CNOPs. Two performance measures, one for convergence and another to measure the improvement of the best solution so far, where used as criteria to assign more (or less) vectors to each variant. Two experiments were carried out: (1) one to analyze the behavior of each DE variant depending of the features of the CNOP and (2) another to compare the final results of the proposed approach with respect to three state-of-the-art EAs (two of them multi-operator-based). The results of the first experiment showed that for large or medium size feasible regions or medium dimensionalities, the three DE variants are used with a similar frequency, being the traditional DE/rand/1/bin the least used. For a small feasible region or a low dimensionality test problem, one DE variant (ADE) clearly dominated the other two. For a high-dimensionality test problem the two specialized DE variants to solve CNOPs (ADE and MDE) were clearly preferred. The results of the second experiment suggest a competitive performance of the proposed approach with respect to state-of-the-art algorithms, mostly in problems with a combination of linear and nonlinear inequality constraints (g07 and g10). The next paths of research include adding new performance measures, using new DE variants, and solving more benchmark and mechanical design problems.

Acknowledgments. The authors acknowledge support from CONACyT through project 79809.

References

1. Eiben, A., Smith, J.E.: Introduction to Evolutionary Computing. Springer (2003)
2. Mezura-Montes, E., Coello Coello, C.A.: Constraint-Handling in Nature-Inspired Numerical Optimization – Past, Present and Future. Swarm and Evolutionary Computation 1(4), 173–194 (2011)
3. Wolpert, D.H., Macready, W.G.: No Free Lunch Theorems for Optimization. IEEE Transactions on Evolutionary Computation 1(1), 67–82 (1997)
4. Mallipeddi, R., Suganthan, P., Pan, Q., Tasgetiren, M.: Differential Evolution Algorithm with Ensemble of Parameters and Mutation Strategies. Applied Soft Computing 11(2), 1679–1696 (2011)
5. Wang, Y., Cai, Z., Zhang, Q.: Differential Evolution with Composite Trial Vector Generation Strategies and Control Parameters. IEEE Transactions Evolutionary Computation 15(1), 55–66 (2011)
6. Elsayed, S.M., Sarker, R.A., Essam, D.L.: Multi-Operator Based Evolutionary Algorithms for Solving Constrained Optimization Problems. Computers and Operations Research 38(12), 1877–1896 (2011)
7. Price, K., Storn, R., Lampinen, J.: Differential Evolution – A Practical Approach to Global Optimization. Springer (2005)
8. Mezura-Montes, E., Velázquez-Reyes, J., Coello Coello, C.A.: Modified Differential Evolution for Constrained Optimization. In: 2006 IEEE Congress on Evolutionary Computation (CEC 2006), pp. 332–339. IEEE Press (2006)
9. Youyun, A., Hongqin, C.: An Adaptive Differential Evolution Algorithm to Solve Constrained Optimization Problems in Engineering Design. Engineering 2(1), 65–77 (2010)
10. Feoktistov, V.: Differential Evolution – In Search of Solutions. Springer (2006)
11. Mezura-Montes, E., Coello, C.A.C.: Identifying On-line Behavior and Some Sources of Difficulty in Two Competitive Approaches for Constrained Optimization. In: IEEE Congress on Evolutionary Computation (CEC 2005), vol. 2, pp. 1477–1484. IEEE Press (2005)
12. Deb, K.: An Efficient Constraint Handling Method for Genetic Algorithms. Computer Methods in Applied Mechanics and Engineering 186(2), 311–338 (2000)
13. Rao, R.V., Patel, V.: An Elitist Teaching-Learning-Based Optimization Algorithm for Solving Complex Constrained Optimization Problems. International Journal of Industrial Engineering Computations 3, 535–560 (2012)

Sensitivity Analysis of an Autonomous Evolutionary Algorithm

Jesús-Antonio Hernández-Riveros and Daniel Villada Cano

Universidad Nacional de Colombia
Facultad de Minas, Cra. 80. 65 - 223, Medellín
{jahernan,dvilladc}@unal.edu.co

Abstract. When applying any heuristic, the user faces difficulties on deciding on the control parameters of the method. A generic sensitivity analysis to measure the interdependencies of the parameters from an autonomous evolutionary algorithm and their influence in the final result is shown. The Multi Dynamics Algorithm for Global Optimization is the base of the experiment. With only two parameters, it is a quasi-free parameter autonomous algorithm. The impact on the quality of the results on several multimodal standard problems applying different instances of those parameters has been studied. Excellent outcomes for sensitivity levels from 10^0 to 10^{-5} are found. The Logit model is used to determine the functioning parameters of the MAGO and for their mutual effects. Depending on the problem type, its dimensionality, and the expected precision, this work gives *a priori* configuring for the best performance of the MAGO.

Keywords: parameter control, multidynamics optimization, autonomous search.

1 Introduction

Evolutionary Algorithms (EA) are recognized by their capacity to find the global optimum. Their probability of obtaining a solution depends, not only on the problem in process, the individuals' representation and the fitness function, but especially on the control parameters setting. In the field of parameter setting for EA most of the literature is concerned on independently searching for the best values without considering the influence of these parameters on the EA performance and among them. The chosen parameters determine whether the EA will find a satisfactory solution, and whether it works efficiently. There are different approaches to deal with the problem of controlling the EA parameters [1-3]; they go from the offline static point of view, passing by the on line dynamic changing, until the continuous self-adaptation. The Multi Dynamics Algorithm for Global Optimization (MAGO) is an autonomous evolutionary algorithm which is inspired on estimation distribution algorithms, Lagrangian evolution, and statistical control [16]. It is autonomous in the sense that regulates its own behavior and not need human intervention [4]. In real situations, the population size and the number of generations are handled by the user upon the context of the problem. MAGO has only these two parameters, which could be removed. But before removing them, it is necessary to know how they behave. This paper

J. Pavón et al. (Eds.): IBERAMIA 2012, LNAI 7637, pp. 271–280, 2012.

addresses the application of a statistical method for modeling response variables –the Logit Model, to determine the suitable values of the two control parameters of the MAGO. Obtaining a good solution with the MAGO, as in other heuristics, is a function of the complexity of the problem being solved and particularly of the control parameters setting. The contribution of this work is to know the probability of success of the MAGO on problems before any attempt to solve them. The parameters interdependencies are also learned through the Logit model. Knowing a priori the value of MAGO's control parameters for a class of problem and how the chosen values mutually affect them, relieves the user from a time-consuming task and from a considerable effort. This approach, extensible to any EA, is developed over commonly used multimodal, multidimensional, scalable, non-separable, standard functions. This paper is organized as follows. Next section describes the Logit Model. Section 3 details the Multidynamics Algorithm for Global Optimization. The experiment and the obtained results are presented in Sect. 4. The paper finishes with some conclusions.

2   The Logit Model

Regression methods are fundamental in data analysis when describing the relationship between a response variable and the explanatory variables [5]. Logistic regression is a statistical modeling method used to explain discrete decision process. It determines the functional relationship among a dependent variable and the independent variables. This task is realized through the Logit transform: the natural logarithm of the odds that some discrete event will occur. The Logit model has been applied in medicine and social sciences and little in industry [6]; generally to find a linear relation among a categorical response and several continuous or categorical variables. Logit model also appropriately defines the unit of change for the independent variables. Logit model produces a structure representing the probability distribution of data. The Logit model or logistic regression [7] for k decision variables x_k and the probability that the event z occurs in a number of trials, given x_k, can be expressed as in equation (1).

$$F(z) = e^z / (e^z + 1) \tag{1}$$

where z is $z = \beta_0 + \beta_1 x_1 + \beta_2 x_2 + \beta_3 x_3 + ...+ \beta_k x_k$. The parameter β_0 is the propensity of z to be true independent of the parent's state. The effects of variables, $\beta_1, \beta_2,$ " β_k, measure the marginal change in the Logit for a unit change of x_k, and identify the z dependency upon each parent independently of each other. $F(z)$ is the probability that z occurs given x_k. The Logit model was created to be used on discrete variables, but in this paper it is being applied on a continuous problem. A neighborhood around the optimum of the test function is defined as the event z for the Logit model. Different levels of accuracy were established, from 10^0 to 10^{-5}. The goal is to know how MAGO, a non-deterministic algorithm for optimization, is dependable while working on continuous functions. The MAGO's convergence probability to the global optimum is determined through the Logit model. A value of 1 will be assigned to F(z), if the final performance of the MAGO with a certain configuration sets down in the predefined neighborhood. Otherwise, a value 0 is assigned. The Logit model reflects the success rates of the MAGO. For each level of problem accuracy and each MAGO's configuration, a Logit is developed. The decision variables are the control parameters of MAGO. The convergence probability to predefined vicinity using any configuration of the MAGO parameters could also be pre-known through the Logit.

3   Multidynamics Algorithm for Global Optimization

The MAGO is a heuristic for optimization problems based on dynamical schemes of evolution. The population is autonomously separated in subsets that are permanently reallocated throughout the searching space trying to find the global optimum. MAGO starts with a uniform randomly distributed population over the searching space. The exploration is performed through the new individuals from three subpopulations with independent dynamics. The cardinality of each group changes at each generation according to a rule inspired in statistical control. Each subpopulation is independently guided, balancing exploration and exploitation, by means of a novel combination of techniques, such as Lagrangian evolution, statistical population distribution, and self-organization. MAGO uses a greedy criterion in one subset looking for the goal while simultaneously exploring the rest of the searching space and increasing diversity in the population by mass movement with the other subsets. The Island Model GA also works with subpopulations [18]. But in this model, more parameters are added to the genetic algorithm: number of islands, migration size, migration interval, which island migrate, how migrants are selected and how to replace individuals. Instead, in MAGO only two parameters are needed: number of generations and population size.

3.1   Dynamical Cardinality of Subpopulations

Best practice in EA is between a priori and a posteriori knowledge. A posteriori knowledge is acquired through solving problems. This is expressed on the internal parameters of operation, those depending on the method; such as the crossover rate, the population's proportion that is subject of random changes, the size of subpopulations, and the rotation angles, etc. The most satisfactory internal parameters must be provided by the user after empirical evidence. In addition, the user must specify some external parameters depending on the problem, a priori knowledge. In real-world problems, the population size is determined by the available data, the expected response time affects the number of generations, and the stopping criteria is chosen upon the context. MAGO inspires in statistical quality control for a self-adapting management of the population. In control charts it assumed that if the mean process is out of some limits, the process is suspicious of being out of control. Actions should be taken to drive the process to the control limits [8]. MAGO takes advantage of the concept of control limits to divide the population in three groups with different behavior: the Emergent Dynamics (ED), Crowd Dynamics (CD) and Accidental Dynamics (AD) according to the first, second and third deviation of the actual population, respectively. To get the cardinality of each dynamics, consider the dispersion matrix of the population, $S(j)$, at generation j, and its diagonal, $diag(S(j))$. If $Pob(j)$ is the set of potential solutions being considered at generation j, the groups can be defined in (2).

$$G_1 =\{ \text{ x} \in Pob^{(j)}/x_M^{(j)} - \sqrt{(diag(S^{(j)}))} <= x <= x_M^{(j)} + \sqrt{(diag(S^{(j)}))} \}, \tag{2}$$

$$G_2 =\{(x \in Pob^{(j)}/x_M^{(j)} - 2\sqrt{(diag(S^{(j)}))} < x <= x_M^{(j)} + \sqrt{(diag(S^{(j)}))}), \text{ or}, (x_M^{(j)} + \sqrt{(diag(S^{(j)}))} <= x < x_M^{(j)} + 2\sqrt{(diag(S^{(j)}))}\}$$

$$G_3 =\{ (x \in Pob^{(j)}/ x <= x_M^{(j)} - 2\sqrt{(diag(S^{(j)}))}), \text{ or}, x >= x_M^{(j)} + 2\sqrt{diag(S^{(j)})}) \}$$

where: Pob(j) = G1 U G2 U G3. If N1, N2 and N3 are the cardinalities of the sets G1, G2 and G3, then the cardinalities of the ED, the CD and the AD are set, respectively. This way of defining the elements of each group is dynamical by nature. The cardinalities depend on the whole population dispersion in the generation j. As MAGO iterates, the ED tends to concentrate N1 individuals around the best one. The CD tends to concentrate N2 individuals around the mean of the actual population. These actions are reflected in lower values of the standard deviation in each of the problem variables. The AD, with N3 individuals, keeps the population dispersion at an adequate level. The locus of the best individual is different from the population's mean. As the evolution advances, the location of the best individual and of the population's mean could be closer. This is used to self-control the population diversity.

The ED is composed of N1 fittest individuals. The N1 fittest individuals are transformed using a kind of direction-based search in order to incorporate the information of the very best individual. Each transformed individual is compared with its parent and the one with better performance is kept for the new population. ED does not directly apply direction-based search. It displaces N1 fittest toward the best one, as in Lagrangian evolution. A simplex group or three trial individuals are not used. A movement in a straight line of a fit individual toward the best one occurs. If this movement generates a better individual, this one passes to the next generation; otherwise its predecessor passes on with no changes. For each individual $x_i^{(j)}$ at generation j a shifted one is created according to the rule in equation (3),

$$x_T^{(j)} = x_i^{(j)} + F^{(j)}(x_B^{(j)} - x_i^{(j)}), \tag{3}$$

$$F^{(j)} = S^{(j)} / \| S^{(j)} \|$$

where $x_B^{(j)}$ is the best individual. To incorporate information of the current relations among the variables, the factor $F(j)$ depending on the covariance matrix is chosen in each generation. $S(j)$ is the population covariance matrix at generation j. This procedure compiles the differences among the best individuals and the very best one. The covariance matrix of the updated population takes into account the effect of the evolution. This information is propagated on new individuals. ED has the role of making fast convergence and conserving best solutions until now.

The CD is created sampling N2 individuals from a uniform distribution. Its lower and upper bounds are determined by the mean and dispersion of the population in generation j, as is shown in equation 4. This group looks for potential solutions in a neighborhood of the population mean. It explores regions of the space that have not been covered by the ED. At the beginning the neighborhood is wide, but with successive generations, the dispersion vanishes and the neighborhood size is reduced. As the evolution advances the location of the best individual and of the population's mean will be closer, indicating stagnation or that the stopping criterion is near. Depending on the precision level for the goal, a decision should be taken.

$$LB^{(j)} = x_M^{(j)} - \sqrt{(\text{diag}(S^{(j)}))}, \tag{4}$$

$$UB^{(j)} = x_M^{(j)} + \sqrt{(\text{diag}(S^{(j)}))},$$

The CD explores potential regions, different from the most promising one. The algorithm EMNA [9] works similarly as the CD but with elite of fixed cardinality given by the user, with a greater probability of stagnation.

AD is the smallest group. N3 individuals are sampled from a uniform distribution over the whole space, just like the initial population. This dynamics could abruptly change the evolution path to a better solution, relocating the fittest individual, relocating the population's mean and reassigning the cardinalities N1 and N3. The AD cardinality tends to a steady state, with a lower magnitude in relation to the others. AD introduces diversity continuously even though the other dynamics have already converged, maintains the exploration of the whole space, and guarantees numerical stability for the covariance matrix.

The use of covariance matrix to set an exploring distribution can also be found in [9]. Where sampling from a Gaussian distribution with an intricate adapted covariance matrix new individuals are created in only one dynamics to explore the promising region. In MAGO a simpler distribution, is used. In each generation, ED shapes the promising region displacing the fittest individuals toward the best. With a uniform distribution and with varying limits explores the potential regions through the CD and keeps diversity via the AD with a uniform distribution over the whole space. MAGO's pseudocode is in Table 1.

Table 1. Pseudocode of the MAGO

1: j := 0, Random initial population generation uniformly distributed over the searching space.
3: **repeat**
4: Evaluate each individual with the objective function.
5: Calculate the sampling population dispersion matrix.
6: Calculate the cardinalities N1, N2 and N3 of the groups G1, G2 and G3.
7: Select N1 best individuals, modify them according to equation (2), make them to compete and translate the winners towards the best one. Pass the fittest to the next generation j + 1.
8: Sample from a uniform distribution in hyper rectangle [LB$^{(j)}$, UB$^{(j)}$] N2 individuals and pass them to generation j + 1.
9: Sample from a uniform distribution over the whole searching space N3 individuals and pass them to generation j + 1.
10: j = j + 1
11: **until** an ending criterion is satisfied.

3.2   The Control Parameters of MAGO

Because the behavior of EAs depends on initial conditions, they should be dealt with in the same way as in chaotic systems. It is necessary to previously find a setup of the EA for a given problem or continuously adjust the control parameters. Usually, an adequate setup of an EA for a problem is not viable for another. Setting the control parameters of EAs has been an open challenge from the early stages of the field [1]. Most of the literature on EA's control parameters is on making self-adaptive the parameters [2, 3, 10]. This approach has not been successful at all because it cannot be applied for the whole set of parameters at the same time. An alternative is reducing the number of parameters. This should be viewed carefully so that some parameters are not just hidden away [11].The parameters control of an EA can be of offline or online. Online setting can be classified as dynamic (a prescribed schedule), adaptive (a feedback mechanism rewarding parameters), and self-adaptive (parameters evolve according to their impact on the fitness) [12]. The behavioral parameters of MAGO are self-adaptive because of its design. Being MAGO a real-code EA, its structural parameters depend on the problem taken at hand. Nowadays, there is a growing interest in techniques for removing the need for a human in the process of designing an effective method to solve a problem [12, 13]. MAGO belongs to this paradigm of autonomous searching. This paper deals with a design of an experiment applying the Logit model as the first step to remove all the parameters from MAGO, making MAGO genuinely autonomous and knowing a priori its probability of success.

4   Experiment and Results

In the taxonomy of parameter setting given by Eiben et al [10] MAGO has a self-adaptive parameter control. However, MAGO self-adjusts its parameters on the fly while generating offspring according to the distribution of parents. An experiment was designed to know the MAGO's quality answer solving a problem. Only two parameters deliberately varied: population size and number of iterations. The experiment aims to know the robustness of those parameters and also their interactions, subjected them to a precision threshold on the problem solution, meaning this that they cannot be set one by one. This is an algorithm configuring approach instead of being a parameter tuning. Tuning deals with the values of parameters to solve a specific problem but after experimenting with it, producing a posteriori knowledge. Algorithm configuring is about classes of problems and the value of parameters should be known before trying a specific problem, producing a priori knowledge.

In the experiment design these parameters are the factors. Each factor has six levels: 50, 100, 200, 400, 600, and 1000. There are $2^6=64$ combinations. Some authors recommend 20 or 30 repetitions for each level [14] but here, for a more meaningful response, each combination is repeated 60 times for each benchmark problem (a standard function, its dimensionality and the solution threshold). Five standard functions: Camel, Schwefel, Rastrigin, Goldstein and Griewank [17] are used. These functions with different dimensions and solution thresholds represent several behaviors that the user resembles with the problem at hand. The dimensions considered were 3, 6, 12 and 24. The precision threshold varies from 10^0 to 10^{-7}. The same random initial population is used for every test. The aim is to know the standard performance indices [15] of the MAGO. Mean Best Fitness, Reliability (success rate), efficiency (average number of evaluations to a solution) and a normalized efficacy (0 as the worst, 1 as the best) are the Overall Performance indices. The Evolving Performance indices are Best-so-far (BSF) and the Average-of-Current-Population (ACP). BSF in the MAGO case coincides with the Best-of-Current-Population. Worst-of-Current-Population was not necessary because the accidental dynamics.

The variances of the different dynamics tend to a steady state. When cardinality is zero, there is a sign of possible stagnation and its dynamics is forced to appear again. Typical behaviors of cardinalities are shown in Fig. 1a. Average fitness of all dynamics tends to a neighborhood and the best individual is around it. See Figure 1b. If the average location of each dynamics is the same, there is a sign of diversity loss. In this case the CD is shifted far away from the average location of the ED. Overall

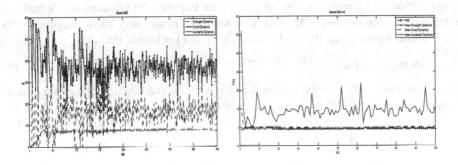

Fig. 1. MAGO Dynamics. Camel Function, 24D, N=600, NG= 400; a) Cardinality b) Fitness

Table 2. Performance indices for Camel Function, a) D12, 10^{-3}; b) D24, 10^{-3}

a) D12

		NG 50	100	200	400	600	1000
BSF	50	-1,031	-1,031	-1,031	-1,031	-1,028	-1,030
ACP	50	-0,661	-0,822	-0,862	-0,807	-0,837	-0,823
BSF	100	-1,031	-1,031	-1,031	-1,031	-1,031	-1,031
ACP	100	-0,886	-0,960	-1,004	-1,020	-1,020	-1,008
BSF	200	-1,031	-1,031	-1,031	-1,031	-1,031	-1,031
ACP z	200	-0,821	-0,997	-0,919	-1,002	-1,022	-1,028
BSF		-1,031	-1,031	-1,031	-1,031	-1,031	-1,031
ACP	400	-0,829	-0,832	-0,999	-1,018	-1,018	-1,027
BSF		-1,031	-1,031	-1,031	-1,031	-1,031	-1,031
ACP	600	-0,947	-0,979	-0,982	-1,018	-1,023	-1,026
BSF		-1,031	-1,031	-1,031	-1,031	-1,031	-1,031
ACP	1000	-0,952	-0,974	-1,021	-1,012	-1,019	-1,026
MBF		-0,812	-0,831	-0,845	-0,825	-0,812	-0,846
Efficiency		0,700	0,080	0,040	0,565	0,850	0,986
Efficacy		0,787	0,805	0,819	0,800	0,787	0,820
Reliability	50	0,017	0,033	0,050	0,067	0,000	0,000
MBF		-0,981	-1,009	-1,013	-1,027	-1,017	-1,026
Efficiency		0,500	0,430	0,410	0,870	0,783	0,796
Efficacy		0,951	0,978	0,982	0,996	0,986	0,995
Reliability	100	0,150	0,500	0,750	0,917	0,833	0,883
MBF		-1,000	-1,024	-1,030	-1,032	-1,032	-1,032
Efficiency		0,180	0,760	0,370	0,855	0,928	0,970
Efficacy		0,969	0,992	0,998	1,000	1,000	1,000
Reliability z	200	0,467	0,900	0,950	1,000	1,000	1,000
MBF		-0,993	-1,022	-1,031	-1,032	-1,032	-1,032
Efficiency		0,180	0,250	0,710	0,958	0,900	0,989
Efficacy		0,963	0,990	0,999	1,000	1,000	1,000
Reliability	400	0,617	0,917	0,983	1,000	1,000	1,000
MBF		-0,947	-1,018	-1,032	-1,032	-1,032	-1,032
Efficiency		0,760	0,780	0,810	0,945	0,982	0,980
Efficacy		0,918	0,986	1,000	1,000	1,000	1,000
Reliability	600	0,800	0,933	1,000	0,983	1,000	1,000
MBF		-1,019	-1,030	-1,031	-1,032	-1,032	-1,032
Efficiency		0,680	0,610	0,880	0,845	0,948	0,970
Efficacy		0,987	0,998	1,000	1,000	1,000	1,000
Reliability	1000	0,833	0,967	0,967	1,000	1,000	1,000

b) D24

		NG 50	100	200	400	600	1000
BSF		-1,0097	-1,004	-1,010	-1,015	-1,017	-1,008
ACP	50	-0,728	-0,570	-0,594	-0,578	-0,566	-0,538
BSF		-1,031	-1,028	-1,029	-1,031	-1,031	-1,031
ACP	100	-0,819	-0,841	-0,825	-0,803	-0,820	-0,804
BSF		-1,031	-1,031	-1,031	-1,031	-1,031	-1,031
ACP z	200	-0,770	-0,819	-0,929	-0,883	-0,940	-0,941
BSF		-1,031	-1,031	-1,031	-1,031	-1,031	-1,031
ACP	400	-0,879	-0,968	-0,931	-0,905	-1,009	-1,012
BSF		-1,031	-1,031	-1,031	-1,031	-1,031	-1,031
ACP	600	-0,802	-0,849	-0,948	-1,013	-0,985	-0,968
BSF		-1,031	-1,031	-1,031	-1,031	-1,031	-1,031
ACP	1000	-0,932	-0,895	-0,934	-0,991	-0,988	-1,027
MBF		-0,653	-0,636	-0,622	-0,537	-0,601	-0,538
Efficiency		0,000	0,000	0,000	0,000	0,000	0,000
Efficacy		0,633	0,617	0,602	0,521	0,582	0,522
Reliability	50	0,000	0,000	0,000	0,000	0,000	0,000
MBF		-0,797	-0,849	-0,842	-0,825	-0,848	-0,808
Efficiency		0,620	0,000	0,000	0,783	0,818	0,846
Efficacy		0,772	0,823	0,817	0,799	0,822	0,784
Reliability	100	0,017	0,000	0,000	0,017	0,033	0,033
MBF		-0,920	-0,901	-0,916	-0,969	-0,897	-0,922
Efficiency		0,740	0,240	0,870	0,960	0,927	0,968
Efficacy		0,892	0,873	0,888	0,939	0,870	0,894
Reliability z	200	0,083	0,083	0,033	0,183	0,133	0,167
MBF		-0,962	-0,983	-0,980	-0,993	-0,990	-0,988
Efficiency		0,540	0,790	0,820	0,978	0,950	0,931
Efficacy		0,932	0,953	0,950	0,962	0,960	0,958
Reliability	400	0,167	0,250	0,333	0,433	0,417	0,500
MBF		-0,981	-0,992	-1,002	-1,021	-1,023	-1,029
Efficiency		0,140	0,800	0,065	0,738	0,933	0,785
Efficacy		0,951	0,962	0,972	0,990	0,992	0,998
Reliability	600	0,283	0,417	0,567	0,750	0,783	0,850
MBF		-1,013	-1,011	-1,020	-1,025	-1,030	-1,032
Efficiency		0,640	0,350	0,795	0,893	0,878	0,914
Efficacy		0,982	0,980	0,988	0,994	0,998	1,000
Reliability	1000	0,383	0,600	0,750	0,867	0,967	1,000

and Evolving Performance indices for a benchmark problem are shown on Table 2 revealing the impact of parameter values on efficiency, efficacy and reliability of MAGO. Increasing population means better efficacy, and generations, better efficiency. If a user is confronting a problem with 24 variables and needs at least a success rate of 85%, searching in Table 2 may chose: 600 individuals and 1000 generations or 1000 individuals and 400 generations. These tables are also suitable for comparison matters. If a user resembles the problem at hand with a tested benchmark problem and must work with a population size, using the Logit can choose the number of generations for certain success rate. If a user imposes the population size and the number of generations to the MAGO, with the Logit model may know the probability of a solution for the given threshold. The Logit model is in equation (6).

$$SR\,(n, ng) = (\,a + e^{\beta 0 + \beta 1*n + \beta 2*ng + \beta 3*n*ng} \,/\, (1 + e^{\beta 0 + \beta 1*n + \beta 2*ng + \beta 3*n*ng})\,) \tag{5}$$

where, SR denotes the success rate of the MAGO for some function on certain dimensionality and a threshold. $\beta 1$ is the effect of the number of individuals and $\beta 2$ is the effect of the number of generations and $\beta 3$ the effect of the mutual interaction. The Logit Model for some benchmark problems are displayed on Fig. 2.

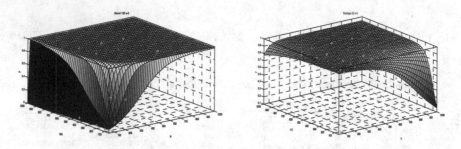

Fig. 2. Logit Model Estimation, a) Camel Function, 12D, 10^{-3}; b) Rastrigin Function, 6D, 10^{-3}

The parameter's values with their confidence interval for the Logit model on a threshold of 10^{-3} are shown in Table 3. An example of taking advantage of this Logit model follows: Let be a problem with 12 variables. A threshold of 10^{-3} for the solution is considered satisfactory. If a user may resemble that problem with the topology of the Camel function, and wants to run with 800 individuals and 900 iterations, the calculation of the Logit will inform a success probability of 0.9491. Before trying with the problem the user could know other success probabilities for other parameter combinations. Average success rates for benchmark problems are found in Table 4. The Emergent, the Crowd and the AD through the evolution have different locations and cardinalities. When contrasting the average location of each dynamics with its average fitness there is a signal of stagnation or having found a solution. Depending of the desired threshold if the three dynamics have the same average location while having each one the same average fitness, a decision is taken to continue the process or relocate the CD away from the Emergent. Figure 4 illustrates the movement from the dynamics of MAGO during the evolution process.

Table 3. Parameters of logit Model. Camel Function

	D3	D6	D12	D24
	Camel Function			
β_0	1.8 (0.2765, 3.324)	0.001956 (-16.69, 16.69)	-0.4396 (-1.294, 0.4149)	1.426 (-1.207, 4.059)
β_1	-0.001585 (-0.004168, 0.0009979)	-0.01664 (-0.3487, 0.3155)	-0.01665 (-0.02631, -0.006987)	0.0006898 (-0.005419, 0.006799)
β_2	0.01578 (-0.009826, 0.04139)	0.01273 (-0.3207, 0.3462)	-0.02528 (-0.03697, -0.01359)	-0.0003896 (-0.005051, 0.004272)
a	-0.01181 (-0.02719, 0.003567)	-0.01413 (-0.03309, 0.004818)	-0.05092 (-0.09048, -0.01136)	-0.5694 (-0.8886, -0.2502)
β_3	1.297e-005 (-3.093e-005, 5.688e-005)	0.0004126 (-0.006232, 0.007057)	0.0004504 (0.0002557, 0.0006451)	6.345e-006 (-3.313e-005, 4.582e-005)
	Rastrigin Function			
β^0	5.589 (1.439, 9.739)	-2.845 (-3.464, -2.227)	0.3842 (-0.2073, 0.9756)	1.225 (0.8657, 1.583)
β_1	-0.008043 (-0.01341, -0.002674)	0.04282 (0.03306, 0.05259)	0.007912 (0.001844, 0.01398)	0.005666 (0.002093, 0.009238)
β_2	-0.00498 (-0.00992, -3.924e-005)	-0.001944 (-0.004001, 0.0001138)	0.0001319 (-0.001026, 0.00129)	-9.252e-005 (-0.0008237, 0.0006386)
a	-0.05698 (-0.1274, 0.01346)	-0.01802 (-0.03365, -0.00239)	-0.4716 (-0.5168, -0.4264)	-0.8127 (-0.8355, -0.7899)
β_3	2.823e-005 (2.274e-006, 5.418e-005)	4.171e-005 (3.183e-006, 8.024e-005)	-6.206e-007 (-1.129e-005, 1.004e-005)	1.392e-006 (-5.402e-006, 8.186e-006)

Table 4. Average Reliability for some tested Benchmark Problems

	D3						D6					
	e-5	e-4	e-3	e-2	e-1	e0	e-5	e-4	e-3	e-2	e-1	e0
Camel	0,11286	0,88190	0,95238	0,98619	0,99954	1,00000	0,09905	0,88333	0,95762	0,98667	0,99815	1,00000
Goldstein	0,03981	0,23194	0,64213	0,89583	0,94954	0,97454	0,03889	0,23981	0,57639	0,76528	0,85278	0,93796
Schwefel	0,00000	0,00046	0,00093	0,00417	0,01250	0,04444	0,00000	0,00046	0,00417	0,00741	0,01435	0,03611
Rastrigin	0,79537	0,83426	0,87546	0,91343	0,93704	0,93796	0,82731	0,84259	0,85463	0,86713	0,87870	0,88889
Griewank	0,29954	0,34676	0,42130	0,55787	0,97762	1,00000	0,39286	0,40048	0,41333	0,42571	0,47083	0,99907

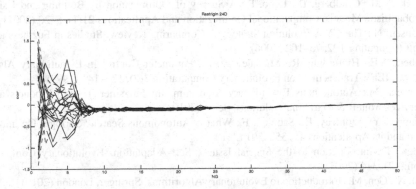

Fig. 3. MAGO evolution process. Movement of the dynamics (Rastrigin Function, 24D, 10^{-3})

5   Conclusions

A user working with an autonomous algorithm should only be concerned with the information of the problem. Performance indices of the MAGO, designed in this direction, have been introduced. In real-world, the value of some parameters is determined by the problem itself; the running time has an effect on the number of generations, the available data on the population size, and the precision threshold on the stopping criterion. The first two items may be self-governed inside the MAGO. Knowing only, both, the class to which the problem belongs and the expected solution threshold, values for these two parameters were found. For the tested benchmark problems, when lower dimensions and a threshold of 10^{-3}, with a population of 200 individuals and a number of generations of 400 is enough to get a solution with a probability of 0.85. Similar calculations are available for other combinations. For dimensions, large than 24, the minimum values are 1000 for individuals and generations. When calculating the Logit model with the parameter values chosen by the user is easy to know a priori the probability of success for different dimensionalities and precision thresholds. If MAGO runs autonomously is possible to get the confidence interval of the result. Further study is required to classify families of general problems as a tool to facilitate the development of fully autonomous algorithms. Future work aims to test more benchmark problems removing supervising all the behavioral and structural parameters but respecting the user's possibility of managing them.

References

1. Grefenstette, J.J.: Optimization of Control Parameters for Genetic Algorithms. IEEE Transactions on Systems, Man, and Cybernetics 16(1), 122–128 (1986)
2. Eiben, A.E., Smith, J.E.: Introduction to Evolutionary Computation. Springer (2003)
3. Lobo, F.G., Lima, C.F., Michalewicz, Z. (eds.): Parameter Setting in Evolutionary Algorithms. Springer (2007)
4. Hernández, J.A., Ospina, J.D.: A Multi Dynamics Algorithm for Global Optimization. Mathematical and Computer Modelling 52(7), 1271–1278 (2010)
5. Czepiel, S.A.: Maximum Likelihood Estimation of Logistic Regression Models - Theory and Implementation. czep.net, http://czep.net/stat/mlelr.pdf (accessed January 17, 2012)
6. Jihong, Y., Muammer, K., Jay, L.: A Prognostic Algorithm for Machine Performance Assessment and its Application. Production Planning & Control 15(8), 796–801 (2004)
7. Hosmer, D.W., Lemeshow, S.: Applied Logistic Regression. Wiley, New York (1989)
8. Pelikan, M., Goldberg, D., Lobo, F.: A Survey of Optimization by Building and Using Probabilistic Models. Computational Optimization and Applications 21(1), 5–20 (2002)
9. Hansen, N.: The CMA Evolution Strategy A Comparing Review. Studies in Fuziness and Soft Computing 192, 75–102 (2006)
10. Eiben, A.E., Hinterding, R., Michalewicz, Z.: Parameter Control in Evolutionary Algorithms. IEEE Transactions on Evolutionary Computation 3(2), 124–141 (1999)
11. Šprogar, M.: Autonomous Evolutionary Algorithm. In: Fuerstner, I. (ed.) Products and Services from R & D to Final Solutions. Sciyo (2010)
12. Hamadi, Y., Monfroy, E., Saubion, F.: What is Autonomous Search? Springer Optimization and its Applications 45, 357–391 (2010)
13. Bäck, T.: Introduction to the Special Issue (Self-Adaptation. Evolutionary Computation 9(2), 3–4 (2001)
14. Yu, X., Gen, M.: Introduction to Evolutionary Algorithms. Springer, London (2010)
15. Suganthan, P.N., Hansen, N., Liang, J.J., Deb, K., Chen, Y.P., Auger, A., Tiwari, S.: Problem Definitions and Evaluation Criteria for the CEC 2005 Special Session on Real-Parameter Optimization. Tech. Report 2005005. Kanpur Genetic Algorithms Lab. (2005)
16. Montgomery, D.C.: Introduction to Statistical Quality Control. Wiley (2008)
17. Hedar, A.R.: Global Optimization Test Problems (2011), http://www-optima.amp.i.kyoto-u.ac.jp/member/student/hedar/Hedar_files/TestGO.html (accessed December 22, 2011)
18. Skolicki, Z., De Jong, K.: The Influence of Migration Sizes and Intervals on Island Models. In: 2005 Conference on Genetic and Evolutionary Computation (GECCO 2005), pp. 1295–1302. ACM (2005)

Progressive Minimal Criteria Novelty Search

Jorge Gomes[1], Paulo Urbano[1], and Anders Lyhne Christensen[2,3]

[1] LabMAg, Faculdade de Ciências da Universidade de Lisboa, Portugal
[2] Instituto Universitário de Lisboa (ISCTE-IUL), Lisboa, Portugal
[3] Instituto de Telecomunicações, Lisboa, Portugal
{jgomes,pub}@di.fc.ul.pt, anders.christensen@iscte.pt

Abstract. We propose progressive minimal criteria novelty search (PM-CNS), which is an extension of minimal criteria novelty search. In PMCNS, we combine the respective benefits of novelty search and fitness-based evolution by letting novelty search freely explore new regions of behaviour space as long as the solutions meet a progressively stricter fitness criterion. We evaluate the performance of our approach in the evolution of neurocontrollers for a swarm of robots in a coordination task where robots must share a single charging station. The robots can only survive by periodically recharging their batteries. We compare the performance of PMCNS with (i) minimal criteria novelty search, (ii) pure novelty search, (iii) pure fitness-based evolution, and (iv) with evolutionary search based on a linear blend of novelty and fitness. Our results show that PMCNS outperforms all four approaches. Finally, we analyse how different parameter setting in PMCNS influence the exploration of the behaviour space.

Keywords: novelty search, evolutionary swarm robotics, deception.

1 Introduction

Deception is one of the biggest challenges in evolutionary robotics (ER). Because of deception, some fitness functions misguide the search towards local optima, ultimately resulting in poor solutions to the problem. The more complex the goal task is, the harder it may be to define a non-deceptive fitness function. The interactions between a robot and its environment are often complex, even in simple tasks. Fitness functions in ER are therefore prone to be deceptive. The problem is exacerbated in multirobot systems in which numerous, distributed local interactions can result in distinct self-organised global behaviours.

Recently, Lehman and Stanley [5] proposed a radically different evolutionary approach called *novelty search* (NS). NS searches for novel behaviours regardless of their fitness quality, and thus overcomes deception by ignoring the objective. In NS, behaviours are scored based on how different they are from previously evaluated behaviours. The approach has been successfully applied to many different domains, including evolutionary robotics [2,6,8,10]. Besides avoiding getting stuck in local optima, it was demonstrated that NS is able to find more diverse and less complex solutions, when compared to objective-based evolution [5].

J. Pavón et al. (Eds.): IBERAMIA 2012, LNAI 7637, pp. 281–290, 2012.

As NS is guided by behavioural innovation alone, its performance can be greatly affected when searching through vast behaviour spaces [1,4], since it may spend most of its time exploring behaviours that are irrelevant for the goal task. To address this problem, Lehman and Stanley [4] proposed *minimal criteria novelty search* (MCNS). MCNS is an extension of NS where individuals must meet some domain-dependent minimal criteria to be selected for reproduction. In [4], the authors applied MCNS in two maze navigation tasks and demonstrated that MCNS evolved solutions more consistently than both novelty and fitness-based search. However, MCNS suffers from two major drawbacks: domain knowledge is required to define suitable minimal criteria; and it may be necessary to bootstrap the search with a genome specifically evolved to satisfy the criteria.

To address the problem of vast behaviour spaces, Cuccu and Gomez [1] proposed to base selection on a linear blend of novelty and fitness (henceforth referred to as *linear blend*). They have applied the approach to the deceptive Tartarus problem, and found that linear blend outperformed both novelty and fitness-based search. Mouret [8] proposed novelty-based multiobjectivisation, which is a Pareto-based multi-objective evolutionary algorithm. A novelty objective is added to the task objective in a multi-objective optimisation. The technique was applied to a deceptive maze navigation problem. Compared with pure novelty search, the multiobjectivization obtained only slightly better results. Other evolutionary techniques that combine behavioural diversity with fitness-guided evolution are presented and compared in [9].

In recent work [2], we successfully applied NS to evolutionary swarm robotics. In this paper, we extend our study by applying variants of NS that combine novelty and fitness, and by studying a different task. We also introduce *progressive minimal criteria novelty search* (PMCNS), which extends MCNS in two ways: (1) PMCNS uses a fitness threshold as the minimal criteria, avoiding the necessity of specifying criteria by hand; (2) starting from the lowest possible fitness score, the criterion is increased dynamically, thereby limiting novelty search to regions of the behaviour space with an increasingly higher fitness. The criterion's monotonous increase depends on the fitness profile of the current population.

We compare the performance of PMCNS against four related methods: NS; fitness-based evolution; linear blend; and MCNS. We use a swarm robotics task in which multiple robots must share a single battery charging station in order to survive. The charging station only has room for one robot and the robots must therefore evolve effective coordination strategies. We use NEAT to evolve the neurocontrollers for the robots in the swarm. NEAT uses speciation to maintain genetic diversity and evolves both the neural network topology and synaptic weights, allowing solutions to become gradually more complex.

2   Background

2.1   Novelty Search

Implementing novelty search [5] requires little change to any evolutionary algorithm aside from replacing the fitness function with a domain dependent novelty metric. The novelty metric measures how different an individual is from other individuals with respect to behaviour. In NS, there is a constant evolutionary pressure towards behavioural innovation. The novelty of an individual is computed with respect to the behaviours of an archive of past novel individuals and to the current population. The archive is initially empty, and new behaviours are added to it if they are significantly different from the ones already there, i.e., if their novelty is above a dynamically computed threshold.

The novelty metric characterises how far the new individual is from the rest of the population and its predecessors in behaviour space, based on the sparseness at the respective point in the behaviour space. A simple measure of sparseness at a point is the average distance to the k-nearest neighbours at that point, where k is a constant empirically determined. Intuitively, if the average distance to a given point's nearest neighbours is large then it is in a sparse area; it is in a dense region if the average distance is small. The sparseness at each point is given by Eq. 1, where μ_i the ith-nearest neighbour of x with respect to the behaviour distance metric $dist$, which typically is the Euclidean distance between domain-dependent behaviour characterisation vectors.

$$\rho(x) = \frac{1}{k} \sum_{i=1}^{k} dist(x, \mu_i) \; . \tag{1}$$

Candidates from more sparse regions of this behavioural search space then receive higher novelty scores, thus guiding the search towards what is new, with no other explicit objective.

2.2 Minimal Criteria Novelty Search

Minimal criteria novelty search [4] is an extension of NS that relies on a task-dependent minimal criteria. In MCNS, if an individual satisfies minimal criteria, it is assigned its normal novelty score, as described above. If an individual does not satisfy the minimal criteria, it is assigned a score of zero and is only considered for reproduction if there are no other individuals in the population that meet the criteria. That implies that until an individual is found that satisfies the criteria, search will be random. Therefore, it may be necessary to seed MCNS with a genome specifically evolved to meet the criteria, in case it is unlikely to generate individuals satisfying them in the initial population.

2.3 Linear Blend of Novelty and Fitness

Cuccu and Gomez [1] proposed a linear blend of novelty and fitness score, as a form of sustaining diversity and improving the performance of standard objective search. Their approach constrains and directs the search in the behaviour space. Each individual i is evaluated to measure both fitness, $fit(i)$, and novelty, $nov(i)$, which after being normalised (Eq. 2) are combined according to Eq. 3.

$$\overline{fit}(i) = \frac{fit(i) - fit_{min}}{fit_{max} - fit_{min}}, \quad \overline{nov}(i) = \frac{nov(i) - nov_{min}}{nov_{max} - nov_{min}} \; , \tag{2}$$

$$score(i) = (1 - \rho) \cdot \overline{fit}(i) + \rho \cdot \overline{nov}(i) \ . \tag{3}$$

The parameter ρ controls the relative weight of fitness and novelty, and must be specified by the experimenter through trial and error. fit_{min} and nov_{min} are the lowest fitness and novelty scores in the current population, and fit_{max} and nov_{max} are the corresponding highest scores. The linear blend was applied to the deceptive Tartarus problem, with a large behaviour space, and performance was compared for different values of ρ. The best results were produced with values of ρ between 0.4 and 0.9.

3   Progressive Minimal Criteria Novelty Search

We propose an extension to Minimal Criteria Novelty Search. The objective is to take advantage of the behaviour space restriction provided by MCNS, without having to pre-define domain dependent minimal criteria. In our algorithm, the minimal criterion is a dynamic fitness threshold – individuals with a fitness score greater than the threshold meet the criterion.

Note that although in NS the fitness score does not influence the evolution, typically a fitness function must be specified anyway, in order to be able to identify the best controllers found by NS. In this way, our algorithm does not require the definition of task-specific minimal criteria or any other additional measures. As pre-defining a fixed fitness threshold would raise the same issues as in MCNS (choosing the criteria and bootstrapping the search), we progressively increase the minimal criterion (fitness threshold) during the evolutionary process. The idea behind the increasing fitness criterion is to progressively restrict the search space, to avoid spending much time on the least fit behaviours.

The minimal criterion starts at the theoretical minimum of the fitness score (typically zero), so all controllers initially meet the criterion. In each generation, the new criterion is found by determining the value of the P-th percentile of the fitness scores in the current population, i.e., the fitness score below which P percent of the individuals fall. The P-th percentile ($0 \leq P < 100$) of N ordered values is obtained by first calculating the ordinal rank n:

$$n = \frac{P}{100} \times N + \frac{1}{2} \ , \tag{4}$$

rounding the result to the nearest integer, and then taking the value v_n that corresponds to the rank n. Only increases in the minimal criterion are allowed, and in order to smooth out the changes, the minimal criterion from the previous generation is used to compute the criterion for the current generation:

$$mc_g = mc_{g-1} + \max(0, (v_n - mc_{g-1}) \cdot S) \ , \tag{5}$$

where mc is the minimal criterion, and S is the smoothing parameter. The score of each individual in the population is then calculated according to:

$$score(i) = \begin{cases} nov_i & \text{if } fit_i \geq mc_g \\ 0 & \text{otherwise} \end{cases} \ , \tag{6}$$

where nov_i and fit_i is the novelty score and the fitness score of the individual i, respectively. The parameter P controls the exigency of the minimal criterion (0 – all individuals meet the criterion, 1 – only the individual with the highest fitness meets the criterion). The smoothing parameter S controls the speed of the adaptation of the minimal criterion (0 – no changes at all, 1 – the value from the previous generation is not considered).

The operation of the novelty archive was not modified, and works as in NS [5]. Even individuals that do not meet the minimal criterion are still added to the repository if their behaviour is sufficiently novel.

4 Experiments

4.1 Setup

The experiments used a resource sharing task, where a swarm of 5 homogeneous robots must coordinate in order to allow each member periodical access to a single battery charging station. The charging station only has room for one robot. To survive, each robot will have to possess several competencies: navigate and avoid walls, find and position itself on the charging station to recharge, and effectively share the common resource with the other robots.

The simulated environment is modelled in a customised version of the Simbad 3d Robot Simulator [3]. The environment is a 4 m by 4 m square arena bounded by walls. The charging station is placed in the centre of the arena. The robots are based on the physical characteristics of the the e-puck educational robot [7], but do not strictly follow its specification. Each simulated robot has 8 IR sensors evenly distributed around its chassis for the detection of obstacles (walls or other robots) up to a range of 10 cm, and 8 sensors dedicated to the detection of other robots up to a 25 cm range.

Each robot starts with full energy (1500 units) and lose energy over time. In order to charge, the robots must remain still (maintain the same position) inside the charging station, which has the same diameter as a robot. Each robot is additionally equipped with (1) a ring of 8 sensors for the detection of the charging station up to a range of 1 m; (2) a boolean sensor that indicates whether the robot is inside the charging station or not; (3) an internal sensor that reads the current energy level of the robot. If a robot runs out of energy, it stops working, and remains immobile until the end of the simulation.

We test each controller 10 times in varying initial conditions. The set of possible initial positions only includes those from where a robot cannot sense the charging station. Each simulation lasts for 400 s of simulated time.

The controllers of the robots are time recurrent neural networks. The implementation of NEAT used in the evolution is the Java-based NEAT4J (version 1.0).[1] NS was implemented over NEAT following the description and parameters in [5], with a k value of 15 and a dynamic archive threshold [4]. This dynamic threshold ensures a reasonable flow of individuals to the archive (an average

---

[1] http://neat4j.sourceforge.net/

rate of 3 individuals per generation). The NEAT parameters are the same for all evolutionary methods: the crossover rate is 25%, the mutation rate 10%, the population size 200, the compatibility threshold is dynamic, targeting 10 species, and each evolution runs for 250 generations. The remaining parameters are set to their default values in the NEAT4J implementation.

We used two slightly different setups in our experiments. In setup A, the robots lose a fixed 10 units of energy per second. In setup B, the robots lose energy proportionally to the power used by their motors, at a rate between 5 and 10 units of energy per second. In both setups, the charging station charges a robot at a rate of 100 units of energy per second.

The fitness function F used to evaluate the controllers is a linear combination of the number of robots alive at the end of the simulation and the average energy of the robots throughout the entire simulation:

$$F = 0.9 \cdot \frac{|a_T|}{N} + 0.1 \cdot \sum_{t=1}^{T} \sum_{i=1}^{N} \frac{e_{i_t}}{T N e_{max}} \ , \tag{7}$$

where $|a_T|$ is the number of robots alive in the end of the simulation, T is the length of the simulation, N is the number of robots in the swarm, e_{i_t} is the energy of the robot i at instant t, and e_{max} is the maximum energy of a robot.

The behaviour characterisation, that is used to compute the behavioural difference in NS and its variants, is closely related to the fitness function. It is composed by just two measures: (1) the number of robots alive at the end of the simulation; and (2) the average energy of the alive robots throughout the simulation. The behaviour characterisation is defined by:

$$\mathbf{b} = \left(\frac{|a_T|}{N}, \sum_{t=1}^{A} \sum_{i \in a_t} \frac{e_{i_t}}{A \cdot |a_t| \cdot e_{max}} \right) \ , \tag{8}$$

where A is the number of time steps in which there was at least one robot alive and a_t is the set of alive robots at instant t.

4.2   Results

Fitness Performance. To study how PMCNS and the four related evolutionary methods are influenced by the deceptiveness of the problem, we evaluated and compared their performance in two different setups. Despite being intuitively similar, the setup B leads to deception, while the setup A does not. In setup B, where energy consumption depends on wheel speed, the fitness function is deceptive. It often leads the fitness-based evolution to a very poor local maxima where all the robots remain static, in order to conserve energy and survive more time. Naturally, no one charges and none of the robots reach the end of simulation alive, resulting in a low fitness score. The results can be seen in Fig. 1.

In both setups, PMCNS significantly outperforms both fitness-based evolution and NS. PMCNS is also significantly better than linear blend in setup A, and

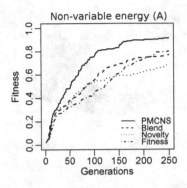
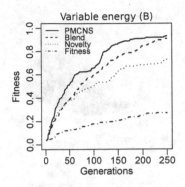

Fig. 1. Average fitness score of the best individual found so far in each generation, with each method. The values are averaged over 10 evolutionary runs for each experiment. Linear blend has $\rho = 0.75$ and PMCNS has $P = 0.5$. Other parameter values were tested but these ones gave the best results.

can on average achieve high fitness scores sooner than linear blend in setup B. Statistical significance was verified with Student's t-test with $p < 0.05$.

The original MCNS was also tested by defining a fixed fitness threshold as the minimal criterion. Values of 0.03, 0.07, 0.10 and 0.20 were tested for the fitness threshold. Evolution was only able to bootstrap with a fitness threshold of 0.03. In this case, the fitness trajectory was slightly worse than pure NS. With greater fitness thresholds, the evolution could not find individuals with a fitness score that surpassed the threshold, and thus MCNS effectively acted as a random evolution, achieving on average a best fitness of 0.065.

Behaviour Space Exploration. The behaviour space exploration (see Fig. 2) is similar in PMCNS and linear blend. However, PMCNS clearly has a greater focus in the behaviours with higher fitness scores. It finds behavioural diversity where it is most relevant – in the zones of successful behaviours. It is interesting to note that although PMCNS might be viewed as technique to restrict the search space, it was actually able to find a broader behavioural diversity than NS alone, with respect to the novelty measure used. The explanation for this is that the growing minimal criterion creates a pressure to explore behaviour zones associated with higher fitness – which, in a complex task, are typically the hardest ones to reach. The analysis of the space explored by fitness-based evolution confirms its poor performance. It gets stuck in local maxima with low fitness.

PMCNS could find a broad diversity of successful behaviours (where every robot survives), as it can be seen in Fig. 2. There are successful behaviours with average energy ranging from 800 to 1150 units. Observing some of these behaviours confirms this diversity: (1) The robots go towards the charging station and stay there, when another one arrives, the first moves away from the station and returns after a period of time; (2) similar to (1), but they never go farther than the station sensor range (1 m); (3) the robots go towards the station, circle

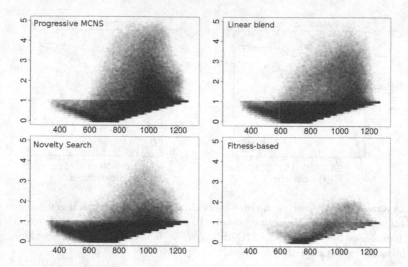

Fig. 2. Behaviour space exploration in setup B. The x-axis is the average energy level of the robots still alive, the y-axis is the number of robots alive at the end of the simulation. Each individual evolved is mapped according to its behaviour. Darker zones mean that there were more individuals evolved with the behaviour of that zone.

around it at a very close distance and when their energy level reaches 1000 units, they enter the station to charge and leave when they are full; (4) similar to (3), but they start charging with an energy level below 400 units and only charge until their energy level reaches 1000 units.

Algorithm Parameters. P is the most important parameter in the PMCNS algorithm. It determines the exigency of the minimal criterion, and consequently, the percentage of population individuals that receive a non-zero score. Three values of P were tested: 25%, 50% and 75%. Figure 3 shows how this parameter affects the fitness trajectory, the progression of the minimal criterion, and the number of individuals that are above the minimal criterion in each generation.

The results show that a high value of P (75%) is prejudicial to the evolutionary process, because the minimal criterion is too strict. Lower values of P are preferred, where only a smaller percentage of the population does not meet the minimal criterion. Analysing the behaviour space explored for each parameter setting, we found that with $P = 50\%$, the search had a greater focus on the high fitness behaviour zones, when compared to the variant with $P = 25\%$. With $P = 75\%$, the search covered a very narrow zone of the behaviour space, and actually explored the high-fitness zones less. A possible explanation for this is that the search got stuck in low-fitness behaviour zones, probably due to the high level of elitism associated with a strict minimal criterion.

The smoothing parameter S was set to 0.5 in all experiments. Variations of this parameter within reasonable limits ($0.25 - 0.75$) did not have a profound impact on the performance of PMCNS.

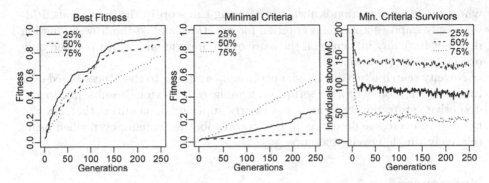

Fig. 3. Left: how the P parameter of PMCNS affects the fitness trajectory. Middle: the progression of the minimal criteria value over the generations. Right: the average number of individuals above the minimal criterion in each generation. Results are from the experiments with setup B.

5 Conclusions

We presented a new method, *progressive minimal criteria novelty search*, for combining fitness and novelty in evolutionary search. We extended *minimal criteria novelty search* by using a dynamic fitness threshold as the minimal criteria, pushing exploration of behaviour space towards zones of higher fitness. We experimented with a swarm robotics task where robots must share a resource in order to survive. We compared the new algorithm with MCNS with a fixed fitness threshold as minimal criteria, novelty search alone, fitness-based evolution, and a linear blend of novelty and fitness scores.

PMCNS could effectively overcome the drawbacks of MCNS while achieving a better performance. The fitness score was successfully used as minimal criterion. It was clearly advantageous to use a progressive minimal criterion, compared to a fixed minimal criterion in MCNS. The bootstrap problem was also overcome, as the minimal criterion starts from the minimum fitness score and only grows if the fitness profile of the current population also increases.

Both PMCNS and linear blend performed significantly better than pure NS and fitness-based evolution in the deceptive setup. In the non-deceptive setup, they were at least as good. Our experiments showed that the fitness performance of NS can be further improved by using the fitness function – even when this fitness function is deceptive. In both PMCNS and linear blend, the behaviour space exploration was greater and more uniform than in NS alone. This result suggests that the fitness function can actually help NS to explore the behaviour space, by creating an additional pressure to explore zones associated with higher fitness, which typically are more difficult to reach in complex tasks.

In terms of fitness trajectory, PMCNS was significantly better than linear blend. PMCNS also explored more the behaviour zones associated with higher fitness scores. This is relevant because it suggests that PMCNS creates a pressure to evolve a diversity of successful individuals. As opposed to the linear blend, where the fitness function is always influencing the score of the individuals, PM-CNS only imposes a minimal criterion for selection, and so the fitness function does not have any influence on the score of the individuals, which is based only on the novelty measure.

Novelty search alone displayed a performance similar to the fitness-based evolution in the non-deceptive setup, confirming our previous results [2]. In the deceptive setup, novelty search was clearly superior. It confirms that NS can be used to overcome deception in the swarm robotics domain, even when using relatively simple novelty measures.

References

1. Cuccu, G., Gomez, F.J.: When Novelty Is Not Enough. In: Chio, C.D., et al. (eds.) EvoApplications 2011, Part I. LNCS, vol. 6624, pp. 234–243. Springer, Heidelberg (2011)
2. Gomes, J., Urbano, P., Christensen, A.L.: Introducing Novelty Search to Evolutionary Swarm Robotics. In: Dorigo, M., Birattari, M., Blum, C., Christensen, A.L., Engelbrecht, A.P., Groß, R., Stützle, T. (eds.) ANTS 2012. LNCS, vol. 7461, pp. 85–96. Springer, Heidelberg (2012)
3. Hugues, L., Bredeche, N.: Simbad – An Autonomous Robot Simulation Package for Education and Research. In: Nolfi, S., et al. (eds.) SAB 2006. LNCS (LNAI), vol. 4095, pp. 831–842. Springer, Heidelberg (2006)
4. Lehman, J., Stanley, K.O.: Revising the Evolutionary Computation Abstraction – Minimal Criteria Novelty Search. In: 2010 Genetic and Evolutionary Computation Conference (GECCO 2010), pp. 103–110. ACM, New York (2010)
5. Lehman, J., Stanley, K.O.: Abandoning Objectives – Evolution through the Search for Novelty Alone. Evolutionary Computation 19(2), 189–223 (2011)
6. Lehman, J., Stanley, K.O.: Evolving a Diversity of Virtual Creatures through Novelty Search and Local Competition. In: 2011 Genetic and Evolutionary Computation Conference (GECCO 2011), pp. 211–218. ACM, New York (2011)
7. Mondada, F., Bonani, M., Raemy, X., Pugh, J., Cianci, C., Klaptocz, A., Magnenat, S., Zufferey, J.C., Floreano, D., Martinoli, A.: The e-puck, a Robot Designed for Education in Engineering. In: 9th Conference on Autonomous Robot Systems and Competitions (Robotica 2009), pp. 59–65. IPCB, Castelo Branco (2009)
8. Mouret, J.: Novelty-Based Multiobjectivization. In: Doncieux, S., Bredèche, N., Mouret, J.B. (eds.) New Horizons in Evolutionary Robotics. SCI, vol. 341, pp. 139–154. Springer, Heidelberg (2011)
9. Mouret, J.B., Doncieux, S.: Encouraging Behavioral Diversity in Evolutionary Robotics – An Empirical Study. Evolutionary Computation 20(1), 91–133 (2012)
10. Risi, S., Vanderbleek, S.D., Hughes, C.E., Stanley, K.O.: How Novelty Search Escapes the Deceptive Trap of Learning to Learn. In: 2009 Genetic and Evolutionary Computation Conference (GECCO 2009), pp. 153–160. ACM, New York (2009)

Fisherman Search Procedure

Oscar José Alejo Machado[1], Juan Manuel Fernández Luna[2],
Juan Francisco Huete Guadix[2], and Eduardo R. Concepción Morales[1]

[1] Departamento de Informática, Universidad de Cienfuegos,
Cienfuegos, Cuba
{alejo,econcep}@ucf.edu.cu
[2] Departamento de Ciencias de la Computación e I.A.,
E.T.S.I. Informática y de Telecomunicación. CITIC-UGR,
Universidad de Granada, Granada, Spain
{jmfluna,jhg}@decsai.ugr.es

Abstract. Optimization is used in diverse areas of science, technology and business. Metaheuristics are one of the common approaches for solving optimization problems. In this paper we propose a novel and functional metaheuristic, Fisherman Search Procedure (FSP), to solve combinatorial optimization problems, which explores new solutions using a combination of guided and local search. We evaluate the performance of FSP on a set of benchmark functions commonly used for testing global optimization methods. We compare FSP with other heuristic methods referenced in literature, namely Differential Evolution (DE), Particle Swarm Optimization (PSO) and Greedy Randomized Adaptive Search Procedures (GRASP). Results are analyzed in terms of successful runs, i.e., convergence on global minimum values, and time consumption, demonstrating that FSP can achieve very good performances in most of the cases. In 90% of the cases FSP is located among the two better results as for successful runs. On the other hand, with regard to time consumption, FSP shows similar results to PSO and DE, achieving the best and second best results for 82% of the test functions. Finally, FSP showed to be a simple and robust metaheuristic that achieves good solutions for all evaluated theoretical problems.

Keywords: metaheuristics, global optimization, search procedures.

1 Introduction

Metaheuristic techniques are used to solve hard problems (generally NP-hard problems) instead of or in conjunction with exact algorithms. When the problem dimension becomes very large, exact algorithms may not be useful since they are computationally too expensive. In these cases, approximate algorithms (which do not guarantee to find an optimal solution) are a very effective alternative. Metaheuristics are approximate algorithms which encompass and combine constructive methods, local search strategies, local optima escaping strategies and population-based search. They include, but they are not restricted

J. Pavón et al. (Eds.): IBERAMIA 2012, LNAI 7637, pp. 291–299, 2012.

to: Tabu Search [1], Simulated Annealing [2], Evolutionary Computation [3], Memetic Algorithms [4], Scatter Search [5], Iterative Improvement (Hill climbing et similia), Ant Colony Optimization [6], Particle Swarm Optimization (PSO) [7], Greedy Randomized Adaptive Search Procedure (GRASP) [8], Iterated Local Search [9,10] and Variable Neighborhood Search [11].

Metaheuristics are strategies to design heuristic procedures. Therefore, metaheuristics types are defined according to the type of procedures referred by them. Some of the fundamental types are metaheuristics for relaxation procedures, constructive processes, neighbourhood searches and evolutive procedures.

Some metaheuristics arise by combining different types of metaheuristics, as GRASP [8] that combines a constructive phase with a phase of search improvement. Other metaheuristics are centered in the use of some type of computational resource or special formulation such as neural networks, ant systems or the constraint programming and they are not included clearly in none of the four previous types.

In general, one way or another, all metaheuristics can be conceived as strategies applied to search processes.

In fact, in this work a new metaheuristic, named Fisherman Search Procedure (FSP), is introduced. This search algorithm explores new solutions using a combination of guided search and local search. This metaheuristic was designed with the purpose of developing useful and practical solutions for a wide variety of combinatorial optimization problems.

The main advantages are the following: easy implementation, it provides an explicit description of the model-based idea and the own conception of this metaheuristic allows it to be applied to a large number of classical combinatorial optimization problems, as well as to those that arise in real-world situations in different areas of applied sciences, engineering, and economy.

In order to introduce our metaheuristic, as well as the experimentation to evaluate its performance, the rest of the paper is organized as follows. In Sect. 2, the FSP Approach is formally introduced. Section 3 is devoted to describe the settings of the experimental study that allows evaluating the performance and the computational time of the new proposed algorithm, as well as the results obtained, comparing them with several metaheuristics referenced in literature. Finally, in Sect. 4 we conclude our work and point out some directions for future research.

2 FSP Approach

In this section, a new metaheuristic for combinatorial optimization problems is formally described. The "FSP" is a global optimization method, inspired by the cognitive behavior and the dexterities observed in a fisherman. This method explores new solutions using a combination of guided search and local search. The algorithm is shown in Table 1.

Initially, we set N capture points in the whole fishing area (search space). Basically each capture point is composed of a position vector, x_i (coordinated in

Table 1. The FSP algorithm

```
1:   Input: T, N, L and M
2:   for i=1 to N do
3:      Initialize x_i
4:      Evaluate x_i
5:      Instantiate p_i
6:      Update g_best
7:   end for
8:   for i=1 to T do
9:      for j=1 to N do
10:        while ((L ≠ 0) and (find improvements)) do
11:           for k=1 to M do
12:              Update y_jk with expression (1)
13:              Evaluate y_jk
14:              Update p_j
15:           end for
16:        end while
17:        Update x_j
18:        Update g_best
19:     end for
20:     Apply a strategy to update the width coefficient c
21:  end for
22:  Output: g_best
```

the search space) and a memory of the best solution found by the fisherman in the neighborhood of the capture point p_i. Let $x_i \in X$, where $X = \{x_1, x_2, ..., x_N\}$ denotes the set of position vectors of the capture points.

The fisherman's global memory is defined as g_{best} (for example, the best among the capture points).

Following a fishing trajectory, the fisherman throws the fishing network L times in each capture point. The fishing network represents a set of position vectors $y_{ij} \in Y$, $Y = \{y_{i1}, y_{i2}, ..., y_{iM}\}$, created and defined starting from a reference point, where y_{ij} denotes the jth vector in x_i, $i = 1, 2, ..., N$; $j = 1, 2, ..., M$. The value M represents the quantity of network's position vectors.

The equation to create the network's position vectors, is the following:

$$y_{ij} = x_i + A_j \tag{1}$$

Where A_j is a N-dimensional vector composed of random numbers in the range $[-c,c]$, where c is real number denominated width coefficient.

The network position vectors are evaluated and if some of them has an fitness value better than p_i of the capture point from where the launching was performed, the capture point is updated with this new position and the fisherman network is redefined again considering this better solution as the new reference vector. When updating the p_i value for the ith capture point, if p_i is better than g_{best}, the latter is also updated.

The whole fishing procedure is repeated T times. After each iteration, the improvement rate in each capture point is analyzed. If the function value in p_i for the ith capture point improves with respect to previous iteration, we recommend to decrease the value of the width coefficient, with the idea of reducing the risk of skipping the global minimum, in the case when the solution is close to it. This strategy pursues the intuitive idea of narrowing the holes of the fishing network to guarantee the capture. On the other hand, if the function value in p_i for the ith capture point does not improve, the value of the width coefficient is increased, with the idea of reaching other fishing areas (search spaces). In this last case, if a better function value is found, we update the p_i value for the ith capture point and reset the width coefficient to its initial value.

3   Experimentation and Evaluation

In this section we present the experimental results of the evaluation stage of our proposal in terms of successful runs and time consumption. We carry out comparisons considering other metaheuristics and interesting proposals referenced in literature. For evaluation, we have used a set of benchmark functions broadly used to test the behavior and convergence of heuristic methods. Finally, we show and analyze the results of the achieved performance by the different methods.

3.1   The Benchmark Functions

In order to evaluate the novel metaheuristic, a test suite of benchmark functions previously introduced by Molga and Smutnicki [12] was used (see Table 2). The ranges of search spaces, dimensionalities, and global minimum function values (ideal values) are also included in Table 1. In each case n is the dimension size of the function, f_{min} is its ideal value, and $S \subset R^n$ is the search space. The problem set contains a diverse set of problems, including unimodal as well as multimodal functions, and functions with correlated and uncorrelated variables.

Functions f_1 - f_3 are unimodal. Functions f_4 and f_5 are multimodal functions where the number of local minima increases exponentially with the problem dimension. Functions f_6 - f_{11} are low-dimensional functions which have only a few local minima.

3.2   Selected Metaheuristics for Comparison

With the intention of comparing FSP with other heuristic procedures, we selected GRASP, DE and PSO methods. This selection was carried out with the goal of evaluating the behavior of the method proposed with similar algorithms (GRASP) and with other completely different ones (DE and PSO), demonstrating the potentialities of FSP in the resolution of optimization problems.

Table 2. The employed benchmark functions

Functions	n	S	f_{min}
$f_1(\vec{x}) = \sum\limits_{i=1}^{n} x_i^2$	5	$[-5.12, 5.12]^n$	$f_1(\vec{0}) = 0$
$f_2(\vec{x}) = \sum\limits_{i=1}^{n} (i \cdot x_i^2)$	5	$[-5.12, 5.12]^n$	$f_2(\vec{0}) = 0$
$f_3(\vec{x}) = \sum\limits_{i=1}^{n} \sum\limits_{j=1}^{i} x_j^2$	2	$[-65.536, 65.536]^n$	$f_3(\vec{0}) = 0$
$f_4(\vec{x})$ $\sum\limits_{i=1}^{n} \left[-x_i \sin\left(\sqrt{|x_i|}\right) \right]$	$= 2$	$[-500, 500]^n$	$f_4(420.\vec{9}687) = -418.9829n$
$f_5(\vec{x}) = \sum\limits_{i=1}^{n} |x_i|^{i+1}$	2	$[-1.0, 1.0]^n$	$f_5(\vec{0}) = 0$
$f_6(x_1, x_2) = \left(x_2 - x_1^2\right)^2 + (1 - x_1)^2$	2	$[-1.9, 2.0]$	$f_6(1,1) = 0$
$f_7(x, y)$ $(x - 13 + ((5 - y)y - 2)y)^2 + (x - 29 + ((y+1)y - 14)y)^2$	$= 2$	$[-1, 12]$	$f_7(5,4) =$ 0, $f_7(11.41, -0.8986) =$ 18.0842
$f_8(x_1, x_2)$ $a\left(x_2 - bx_1^2 + cx_1 - d\right)^2 +$ $e(1 - f)\cos(x_1) + e$	$= 2$	$[-\pi, 13]$	$f_8(-\pi, 12.275) =$ 0.397887, $f_8(\pi, 2.275) =$ 0.397887, $f_8(9.42478, 2.475) =$ 0.397887
$f_9(x, y)$ $(1.5 - x(1 - y))^2 +$ $\left(2.25 - x\left(1 - y^2\right)\right)^2 +$ $\left(2.625 - x\left(1 - y^3\right)\right)^2$	$= 2$	$[0.0, 5.0]$	$f_9(3, 0.5) = 0$
$f_{10}(x_1, x_2)$ $\left(4 - 2.1x_1^2 + \frac{x_1^4}{3}\right)x_1^2 + x_1x_2 +$ $(-4 + 4x_2^2) x_2^2$	$= 2$	$x_1[-3,3]$, $x_2[-2,2]$	$f_{10}(-0.0898, 0.7126) =$ -1.0316, $f_{10}(0.0898, -0.7126) =$ -1.0316
$f_{11}(x_1, x_2)$ $[1 + (x_1 + x_2 + 1)^2 (19 - 14x_1 + 3x_1^2 - 14x_2 + 6x_1x_2 + 3x_2^2)] \cdot$ $[30 + (2x_1 - 3x_2)^2 (18 - 32x_1 + 12x_1^2 + 48x_2 - 36x_1x_2 + 27x_2^2)]$	$= 2$	$[-2, 2]$	$f_{11}(0, -1) = 3$

GRASP is a multi-start metaheuristic in which each iteration consists basically of two phases: construction and local search. One possible shortcoming of the standard GRASP framework is the independence of its iterations, i.e., the fact that it does not learn from the history of solutions found in previous iterations. This is so because the basic algorithm discards information about any solution encountered that does not improve the function value. Information gathered from good solutions can be used to implement memory-based procedures to influence the construction phase, by modifying the selection probabilities associated with each element of the restricted candidate list (RCL).

PSO is a population-based stochastic optimization technique developed by Russell C. Eberhart and James Kennedy in 1995 [7], inspired by social behavior of bird flocking or fish schooling. The main advantages are: insensitive to scaling of design variables, simple implementation, easily parallelized for concurrent processing, derivative free, very few algorithm parameters, very efficient global search algorithm. In spite of this, it presents the disadvantage of a slow convergence in refined search stage (weak local search ability).

DE algorithm has been introduced by Storn and Price [15]. DE is a method of optimization belonging to the category of evolutionary Computation. It maintains a population of solutions candidates, to which a mutation and recombination procedure to generate new individuals is applied. The new individuals are chosen according to the value of its performance function. The main characteristic of DE is the use of test vectors, which compete with the current population individuals in order to survive. One of their biggest advantages is that it overcomes the standard drawbacks of the genetic algorithms: premature convergence and lack of good local search ability. However, DE sometimes has a limited ability to move its population large distances across the search space and would have to face stagnation.

Although, FSP not always outperforms the other methods, it solves some of their inconveniences, e.g. the independence of iterations in GRASP, the weak capacity of local search of PSO and the limited ability to face stagnation in DE.

3.3   Evaluation

The algorithms used for comparison are GRASP [8], Particle Swarm Optimization with inertia weight and constriction factor (PSO-w-cf) [13,14], and Differential Evolution (DE) algorithm [15]. In all experiments, a total of 30 runs are made. The experiment results are listed in Table 3, where Func. = Functions, Algo. = Algorithms, Best stands for the best function value over 30 runs, Mean indicates the mean best function values, and Time stands for the average CPU time (in seconds) consumed within the fixed number of generations. Succ. Runs stands for the success number over 30 runs. All results are reported with a precision level of 1e-02.

The initial population is generated uniformly and randomly in the range as specified in Table 1. The parameters of (PSO-w-cf) are: learning rate $c_1=c_2=2$, inertia weight linearly decreased from 0.9 to 0.4 with run time increasing, constriction factor $\chi = 0.729844$ and the maximum velocity v_{max} is set at 20% of the dynamic range of the variable on each dimension. The parameters of DE are: mutation f=0.75, recombination cr=0.5, number of objective vectors NVO=6 and strategy s=4.

The parameters of FSP are: number of launchings from 3 to 5, width coefficient was adjusted by the own method always beginning in 0.20 and the number of points of the fishing network is fixed between 50 and 100, according to the characteristics of the functions.

All algorithms are run on a PC with Intel(R) Core(TM) i5 CPU 2.53GHz.

The results of 30 independent runs for benchmark functions f_1 - f_{11} are summarized in Table 3. From Table 2, FSP is successful over all the 30 runs for f_5, f_7 and f_9. For f_4, it is successful in only 20% of all runs, but it outperforms all other algorithms. For the functions 1,6 and 8, FSP always outperforms GRASP and DE methods in successful runs. For f_1, FSP is successful in 23% of the runs

Table 3. Performance of the algorithms

Func.	Algo.	Best	Mean	Time	Succ.Runs
	DE	1.7328e-02	9.5487e-02	2.58	05
f_1	PSO-w-cf	8.3241e-13	3.6998e-11	**0.98**	**30**
(De Jong's)	GRASP	1.4805e-01	1.17728420	76.1	00
	FSP	1.4058e-02	7.7205e-02	2.21	07
	DE	1.6242e-02	8.8914e-02	9.21	04
f_2	PSO-w-cf	6.1828e-10	9.1778e-09	**1.04**	**30**
(Axis parallel	GRASP	0.42167256	1.67167256	85.3	00
hyper-ellipsoid)	FSP	1.7272e-02	9.3354e-02	9.91	02
	DE	6.1984e-05	7.1452e-05	0.06	**30**
f_3	PSO-w-cf	1.2611e-04	2.2155e-04	**0.03**	**30**
(Rotated	GRASP	4.1835e-03	3.1987e-02	1.51	00
hyper-ellipsoid)	FSP	1.7315e-03	1.7956e-02	0.06	08
	DE	-837.96586	-837.36187	**0.06**	02
f_4	PSO-w-cf	-837.96586	-837.12575	0.08	05
(Schwefel's)	GRASP	-837.91124	-837.21545	7.74	00
	FSP	-837.90581	-837.61520	0.08	06
	DE	1.7257e-05	8.5222e-04	**0.01**	18
f_5	PSO-w-cf	1.9099e-05	6.6587e-04	**0.01**	21
(Sum of different	GRASP	2.9311e-04	3.1533e-03	0.06	00
power functions)	FSP	8.6995e-06	1.9112e-05	**0.01**	**30**
	DE	8.4157e-03	2.4723e-02	**0.01**	00
f_6	PSO-w-cf	1.6448e-05	5.3687e-04	**0.01**	**16**
(Rosenbrock	GRASP	5.7065e-04	1.2365e-03	0.05	00
or Banana)	FSP	1.5161e-05	2.8734e-04	**0.01**	14
	DE	5.1626e-04	1.1234e-03	0.07	**30**
f_7	PSO-w-cf	1.0961e-04	3.5698e-03	**0.06**	23
(Freudenstein	GRASP	1.9228e-03	1.4589e-02	1.09	11
and Roth)	FSP	3.0940e-03	1.1090e-03	**0.06**	**30**
	DE	0.39781959	0.40254578	**0.03**	01
f_8	PSO-w-cf	0.39788737	0.39998751	**0.03**	**25**
(Branins's)	GRASP	0.39782849	0.41587485	0.67	01
	FSP	0.39787495	0.39954781	**0.03**	12
	DE	1.3211e-03	3.6587e-02	**0.03**	18
f_9	PSO-w-cf	1.8051e-05	2.7624e-04	**0.03**	**30**
(Beale)	GRASP	3.3778e-04	9.5874e-03	1.07	20
	FSP	5.5255e-04	1.4423e-03	**0.03**	**30**
	DE	-1.0316284	-1.0375987	0.04	**08**
f_{10}	PSO-w-cf	-1.0316625	-1.0335411	0.04	01
(Six-hump	GRASP	-1.0310172	-1.0405474	0.99	00
camel back)	FSP	-1.0316738	-1.0381120	0.04	02
	DE	3.00000082	3.00054785	**0.03**	**30**
f_{11}	PSO-w-cf	3.00711378	3.01965874	**0.03**	21
(Goldstein-Price's)	GRASP	3.00664548	3.09925453	0.71	17
	FSP	3.00285013	3.01125478	**0.03**	23

and has less time consumption than GRASP and DE. For f_6 and f_8, FSP is successful in 46% and 40% of the runs respectively, for both cases, and has less time consumption than GRASP and the same as DE. For f_{10} and f_{11}, FSP is successful in 46% and 40% runs respectively and is better than GRASP and PSO-w-cf methods to achieve the desired accuracy. For this function, it also has less time consumption than GRASP and the same as PSO-w-cf. In f_2 and f_3, FSP overcomes GRASP in computational time and successful runs.

The results with benchmark functions allow us to conclude that FSP is suitable for solving optimization problems for unimodal and multimodal functions with satisfactory (second best) convergence ability. Compared to classic GRASP metaheuristic, FSP has better search ability and less time consumption, expressed in terms of successful runs and total runtime, respectively, for the benchmark functions. Moreover, FSP has a competitive performance for all benchmark functions, compared to PSO-w-cf and DE.

4   Conclusions

In this paper, we have proposed a new metaheuristic called Fisherman Search Procedure. This search algorithm explores new solutions using a combination of guided and local search. Our metaheuristic was designed with the purpose of developing good solutions for a wide variety of combinatorial optimization problems.

The main advantages are the following: it provides an explicit description of the model-based idea, easy implementation and the conception of this metaheuristic allows it to be applied to a large number of classical combinatorial optimization problems, as well as to those that arise in real-world situations in different areas of science, technology and business.

Finally, we conclude that FSP has better search ability and less time consumption, expressed in terms of successful runs and total runtime, respectively, for the benchmark functions, compared to classic GRASP metaheuristic. In 90% of the cases FSP is located among the two better results as for successful runs. On the other hand, with regard to time consumption, FSP shows similar results to PSO and DE, achieving the best and second best results for 82% of the test functions.

As future work, we plan to analyze the quality of the solution with other benchmark test functions. We will also apply FSP to combinatorial problems in different areas. On the other hand, we will implement parallelization strategies and hybridization with other metaheuristics.

Acknowledgments. This work has been supported by the Spanish Ministerio de Ciencia e Innovación by means of the Project TIN2008-06566-C04-01.

References

1. Glover, F., Laguna, M.: Tabu Search. Kluwer Academic Publishers, Dordrecht (1997)
2. Kirkpartick, S., Gelatt, C.D., Vecchi, M.P.: Optimization by Simulated Annealing. Science 220(4598), 671–680 (1983)
3. Calegari, P., Coray, G., Hertz, A., Kobler, D., Kuonen, P.: A Taxonomy of Evolutionary Algorithms in Combinatorial Optimization. Journal of Heuristics 5(2), 145–158 (1999)
4. Moscato, P.: Memetic Algorithms – A Short Introduction. In: Corne, D., Dorigo, M., Glover, F. (eds.) New Ideas in Optimization, pp. 219–234. McGraw-Hill, London (1999)
5. Glover, F.: Scatter Search and Path Relinking. In: Corne, D., Dorigo, M., Glover, F. (eds.) New Ideas in Optimization, pp. 297–316. McGraw-Hill, London (1999)
6. Dorigo, M., Gambardella, L.M.: Ant Colony System – A Cooperative Learning Approach to the Travelling Salesman Problem. IEEE Transactions on Evolutionary Computation 1(1), 53–66 (1997)
7. Eberhart, R.C., Kennedy, J.: A new Optimizer Using Particles Swarm Theory. In: 6th International Symposium on Micro Machine and Human Science (MHS 1995), pp. 39–43. IEEE (1995)
8. Resende, M.G.C., Ribeiro, C.C.: Greedy Randomized Adaptive Search Procedures. In: Glover, F., Kochenberger, G. (eds.) Handbook of Metaheuristics. International Series in Operations Research & Management Science, vol. 57, pp. 219–249. Springer, Heidelberg (2003)
9. Stützle, T.: Local Search Algorithms for Combinatorial Problems – Analysis, Algorithms and New Applications. DISKI – Dissertationen zur Künstliken Intelligenz, Infix (1999)
10. Stützle, T.: Iterated Local Search for the Quadratic Assignment Problem. Technical report, TU Darmstadt (1999)
11. Hansen, P., Mladenovic, N.: An Introduction to Variable Neighborhood Search. In: Voss, S., et al. (eds.) Metaheuristics – Advances and Trends in Local Search Paradigms for Optimization, pp. 433–458. Kluwer Academic Publishers (1999)
12. Molga, M., Smutnicki, C.: Test Functions for Optimization Needs. Technical report (2005), http://www.zsd.ict.pwr.wroc.pl/files/docs/functions.pdf
13. Shi, Y., Eberhart, R.: A Modified Particle Swarm Optimizer. In: IEEE World Congress on Computational Intelligence (WCCI 1998), pp. 69–73. IEEE (1998)
14. Clerc, M., Kennedy, J.: The Particle Swarm – Explosion, Stability, and Convergence in a Multidimensional Complex Space. IEEE Transactions on Evolutionary Computation 6(1), 58–73 (2002)
15. Storn, R., Price, K.: Differential Evolution – A Simple and Efficient Adaptive Scheme for Global Optimization over Continuous Spaces. Technical report TR-95-012, International Computer Science Institute, Berkeley, CA, USA (1995)

Adaptation of Robot Behaviour through Online Evolution and Neuromodulated Learning

Fernando Silva[1], Paulo Urbano[1], and Anders Lyhne Christensen[2]

[1] LabMAg, Faculdade de Ciências, Universidade de Lisboa (FC-UL)
{fsilva,pub}@di.fc.ul.pt
[2] Instituto de Telecomunicações & Instituto Universitário de Lisboa (ISCTE-IUL)
anders.christensen@iscte.pt

Abstract. We propose and evaluate a novel approach to the online synthesis of neural controllers for autonomous robots. We combine online evolution of weights and network topology with neuromodulated learning. We demonstrate our method through a series of simulation-based experiments in which an e-puck-like robot must perform a dynamic concurrent foraging task. In this task, scattered food items periodically change their nutritive value or become poisonous. Our results show that when neuromodulated learning is employed, neural controllers are synthesised faster than by evolution alone. We demonstrate that the online evolutionary process is capable of generating controllers well adapted to the periodic task changes. An analysis of the evolved networks shows that they are characterised by specialised modulatory neurons that exclusively regulate the output neurons.

Keywords: neural networks, online adaptation, neuroevolution, neuromodulated learning, odNEAT.

1 Introduction

Evolutionary computation techniques have been widely studied and applied in the field of robotics as a means to automate the design of robotic systems [1]. In evolutionary robotics (ER), robot controllers are typically based on artificial neural networks (ANN). The connection weights and sometimes the topology of the ANN are optimised by an evolutionary algorithm (EA), a process termed as *neuroevolution*. Evolutionary synthesis of controllers is usually performed offline in simulation, which presents a number of limitations. When a suitable neurocontroller is found, it is deployed on real robots. Since no evolution or adaptation takes place online, the controllers are fixed solutions that remain static throughout the robot's lifetime. If environmental conditions or task parameters become distinct from those encountered during offline evolution, the evolved controllers may be incapable of solving the task as they have no means to adapt.

Online evolution is a process of continuous adaptation that potentially gives robots the capacity to respond to changes in the task or in environmental conditions by modifying their behaviour. An EA is executed on the robots themselves

J. Pavón et al. (Eds.): IBERAMIA 2012, LNAI 7637, pp. 300–309, 2012.
© Springer-Verlag Berlin Heidelberg 2012

as they perform their tasks. This way, robots may be capable of long-term self-adaptation. In recent years, different approaches to online evolution have been proposed (see for instance [2,3,4]). Notwithstanding, in such contributions, online neuroevolution has been limited to evolving weights in fixed-topology ANNs. In a recent study [9], we proposed a novel approach called odNEAT. odNEAT is an online, distributed, and decentralised EA for online evolution in groups of robots, that evolves both weights and network topology. The network topology is therefore a product of a continuous evolutionary process.

Online evolution is a form of online adaptation that acts at genotype level. Controllers produced are static as they do not change their parameters *while* they are controlling the robot. While evolution produces phylogenetic adaptation, online learning operates on a much shorter time-scale. Learning acts at phenotypic level and gives each individual controller the capacity to self-adjust during task-execution. Several studies indicate that learning can accelerate the evolution of good solutions, a phenomenon known as the Baldwin effect [5].

Agents controlled by ANNs can learn from experience by dynamically changing their internal synaptic strengths. This mechanism is inspired by how organisms in nature adapt to cope with dynamic and unstructured environments as a result of synaptic plasticity [13]. In this paper, we synthesise behavioural control for autonomous robots based on online evolutionary computation and online learning. We combine evolution of weights and network topology (odNEAT) with *neuromodulation* [12]. Neuromodulation is a form of synaptic modification involving modulatory neurons that diffuse chemicals at target synapses. Modulation has been suggested as essential for stabilising classical Hebbian plasticity and memory [15].

We demonstrate our method in a simulated experiment where an e-puck-like robot [8] must perform a dynamic concurrent foraging task. The robot must locate and consume scattered food items. When a food item is consumed, a new item of the same type is randomly placed in the environment. At regular time intervals, food items change their nutritive value, or become poisonous. Besides learning to forage, the robot must therefore be able to adapt and change its foraging policy in order to survive. To the best of our knowledge, the contribution presented here is the first demonstration of online learning and online evolution of both the weights and the ANN topology in multirobot systems.

2   Background

In this section, we first discuss evolution of plastic ANNs, with a focus on the neuromodulation-based model, and we then review odNEAT, which we extended to incorporate neuromodulated plasticity.

2.1   Artificial Evolution of Neuromodulated Plasticity

Synaptic plasticity is considered a fundamental mechanism behind memory and learning in biological neural networks [14]. In ANNs, the modification of internal synaptic connection strengths can be performed according to a generalised

Hebbian plasticity rule [13]. Synaptic weights are updated based on pre- and post-synaptic neuron activities as follows:

$$\Delta w = \eta \cdot [Axy + Bx + Cy + D], \tag{1}$$

where η is the learning rate, x and y are the activation levels of the pre-synaptic and post-synaptic neurons. w is the connection weight and $A - D$ are the correlation term, pre-synaptic term, post-synaptic term, and constant weight decay or increase, respectively. By tuning these parameters, it is possible to evolve distinct forms of synaptic plasticity. ANN controllers can thus implement learning and memory by means of recurrent connections, plastic Hebbian connections, or a combination of the two.

The adaptation capabilities of fixed-topology plastic Hebbian ANNs were demonstrated in [7]. In a light-switching task, a mobile robot Khepera had to turn on a light switch and then navigate towards a gray area at the opposite end of the environment. The evolved plastic Hebbian controllers managed to solve the task much faster than fixed-weight networks. The plastic controllers also exhibited a larger variety of successful behaviours and robustness to environmental changes. With a similar setup, it was shown that dynamic environments promote the genetic expression of plastic connections over static ones [6].

Although the use of plastic ANNs can increase performance, recent studies indicate that in more complex tasks, both plastic and fixed-weight ANNs have limited learning capabilities [11,12,13]. In this context, controlling synaptic plasticity through *neuromodulation* was presented as a more powerful and biologically plausible approach [14]. In biological neural networks, neuromodulation has been suggested as essential for stabilising classical Hebbian plasticity and memory [15]. In a neuromodulated network, specialised modulatory neurons control the amount of activity-dependent plasticity between pairs of standard control neurons. This process is illustrated in Fig. 1.

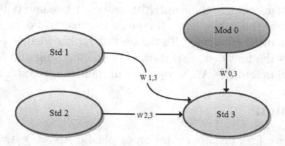

Fig. 1. Neuromodulated plasticity. A modulatory neuron, Mod 0, transmits a modulatory signal to Std 3. Modulation affects the learning rate for synaptic plasticity of weights $w_{1,3}$ and $w_{2,3}$. The weights are part of the incoming connections for the standard control neuron being modulated.

The advantage of adding neuromodulation is that ANNs become capable of changing the degree of synaptic plasticity on specific neurons at specific times, i.e., deciding when learning should start and stop. In addition to its standard activation value a_i, each neuron i also computes its modulatory activation m_i as follows:

$$a_i = \sum_{j \in Std} w_{ji} \cdot o_j, \tag{2}$$

$$m_i = \sum_{j \in Mod} w_{ji} \cdot o_j, \tag{3}$$

where w_{ji} is the connection weight between pre- and post-synaptic neurons j and i. o_j is the output of a pre-synaptic neuron j. The weight between neurons j and i, with $j \in Std$, undergoes synaptic modification as follows:

$$\Delta w_{ji} = tanh(m_i/2) \cdot \eta \cdot [Ao_j o_i + Bo_j + Co_i + D]. \tag{4}$$

2.2 odNEAT: An Online Evolutionary Algorithm

odNEAT [9] is an online, distributed and decentralised version of NEAT [10]. The NEAT method, one of the most prominent neuroevolution (NE) algorithms, is capable of optimising both the topology of the network and its connection weights. NEAT starts with a population of simple networks with no hidden neurons. Topologies are gradually *complexified* by adding new neurons and connections through structural mutation. This scheme allows NEAT to find the right level of complexity for the task while avoiding *a priori* specification of the network topology. NEAT has proven successful in diverse control and decision-making problems, such as double pole balancing, outperforming several methods that use fixed topologies [11]. The important features of NEAT for the purpose of this paper are that NEAT evolves *both* the weights and the topology of an ANN, while maintaining a healthy diversity of complexifying structures simultaneously. Complete descriptions of the method are available in [9,10,11].

odNEAT was originally designed to run across a distributed group of agents whose objective is to evolve and adapt while operating in the environment. In this contribution, experiments were performed with a single robot. Therefore, we only describe odNEAT's important characteristics when applied to a single agent. The agent is controlled by an ANN that represents a candidate solution to the current task. The agent maintains a virtual energy level representing its task performance. The fitness value is defined as the average of the energy level, sampled at regular time intervals.

The agent maintains a set of chromosomes (the genetic encoding of candidate ANNs) and their respective fitness scores in an internal repository. The repository stores the current and previous active chromosomes. When the energy level reaches zero, the current chromosome is considered unfit for the task. A new chromosome is then created based on NEAT's genetic operators. First, two parents are selected, each one via a tournament selection of size 2. Offspring is created through crossover of the parents' genomes and mutation of the new chromosome. Newly created chromosomes are guaranteed a minimum amount of time α during which they control the agent, a *maturation period*.

odNEAT's genetic encoding was augmented with a new modulatory neuron type in order to encode neuromodulated plasticity. Each time a new neuron is added through structural mutation, it is randomly assigned a standard or modulatory role. We augmented the genetic encoding with the learning parameters in Eq. 4. The five parameters are separately encoded and evolved in the range [-1,1] for A-D, and [-100,100] for η. It is important to note that there is no Lamarckian inheritance: weight modifications during lifetime are not passed on to offspring.

3   Experimental Setup

The concurrent foraging task used in this study is performed in an arena with different types of items that can be consumed. To assess how the robot adapts through time, we applied odNEAT with and without neuromodulation. The robot loses energy at a constant rate and must learn to find food items. There are two types of items, red items and pink items. At regular time intervals, the nutritious food items become poisonous or less nutritive and vice-versa. The robot is able to sense the type of nearby items but cannot determine the nutritive value of an item without consuming it. When an item is consumed, a new item of the same type is placed randomly in the arena. This way, the task remains dynamic while the sum of the energy value of the food items in the environment is kept constant.

The motivation for the concurrent foraging task is twofold: (i) since the robot loses energy at a constant rate, it is required to evolve efficient exploration behaviours, (ii) when a poisonous item is consumed, the robot must be able to change its food gathering policy in order to survive.

3.1   Robot Model and Behavioural Control

The simulated robot is modelled after the e-puck, a small (75 mm in diameter) differential drive robot capable of moving at speeds of up to 13 cm/s [8]. We have equipped the robot with an omni-directional camera similar to the one employed by the *s-bot* robots [16]. The image recorded is processed to calculate the distance, the red colour component, and the blue colour component of the closest object in each of the eight 45° sectors. The camera has a range of 50 cm and is subject to noise (simulated by adding a random Gaussian component within $\pm$ 5% of each of the three components' saturation value). Besides the camera, the robot has an internal energy level, comfort and discomfort sensors. The energy sensor allows the robot to perceive its virtual energy level. The remaining sensors indicate if the robot has consumed a poisonous or nutritious food item. Note that the comfort sensor does not indicate to the robot the nutritive value of a consumed food item. That information is reflected by the energy sensor, which the robot also has to learn to interpret.

The robot is controlled by an ANN synthesised by odNEAT. The ANN's connection weights $\in [-10, 10]$. The input layer consists of 27 neurons: (i) three for each 45° sector, measuring the red and blue colour components, and distance of the closest object, (ii) one neuron for each of the virtual sensors (energy, discomfort and comfort). The output layer contains three neurons, one for each wheel of the robot, and one for the gripper. The gripper enables the robot to consume the closest food item within a range of 2 cm (if any).

3.2 Experimental Parameters

The environment is a 3 x 3 meter square arena surrounded by blue walls. The virtual energy level is limited to the range [0,100] energy units. The robot is capable of surviving for approximately 17 minutes without consuming (nutritious) food as energy decreases at a rate of 0.1 units/sec. When the energy level reaches zero, a new controller is generated and assigned maximum energy (100 units). In the generation of the new controller, two parents are selected from the local repository. Crossover and mutation are performed with probabilities 0.25 and 0.4, respectively. During mutation, the probability of adding a new neuron is 0.1 while a new connection is added with probability 0.05. Each connection weight is perturbed with probability 0.02 and a maximum magnitude of 2.5. The local repository is capable of storing 30 chromosomes. Performance was found to be robust to moderate changes in these parameters.

In our experimental setup, the nutritive value of the different types of food change periodically. Periods are composed of four phases of equal duration. At the beginning of each phase, the energy value of the different types of food items is set as listed in Table 1. Each experiment lasts for 100 hours of simulated time.

Table 1. The energy value of red and pink food items during the four phases. Values listed are in energy units.

	Phase 1	Phase 2	Phase 3	Phase 4
Red item	5	8	-3	3
Pink item	3	-3	8	5

4 Results and Discussion

4.1 Effects of Neuromodulated Learning

To assess the impact of neuromodulated learning on the robot's task performance, we performed three sets of evolutionary experiments characterised by distinct phase durations p_d: (i) $p_d = 9$ min, (ii) $p_d = 90$ min, and (iii) $p_d = 900$ min. For each configuration, we placed five food items of each type and performed 30 independent runs. We consider those controllers stable that manage to survive at least 25 times the minimum survival time, i.e., approximately 7 hours of simulated time.

The results obtained are listed in Table 2. Considering the average number of evaluations (controllers tested) required for producing stable solutions, odNEAT combined with neuromodulation required approximately 23.3% to 28.2% fewer evaluations than odNEAT without neuromodulation. odNEAT alone failed to achieve stability in two evolutionary runs, one for $p_d = 9$ min and one for $p_d = 90$ min. In these runs, the long lasting controllers operated for 4.04 and 6.69 hours, respectively. For $p_d = 9$ min and $p_d = 90$ min, differences in the number of evaluations are not statistically significant ($\rho > 0.20$ and $\rho > 0.15$ respectively, Student's t-test). For $p_d = 900$ min, the differences are statistically significant ($\rho < 0.01$). These results suggest that, as the task-requirements become more stable, so does the performance of odNEAT with neuromodulation.

Table 2. Summary of the results obtained for each of the three phase durations tested. The table lists the failure rate (runs without stable controllers), average number of evaluations required before stable solutions are evolved, and the average maximum age and gathered energy per period in each experimental setup.

Experimental setup with odNEAT				
Phase duration	Failure Rate	Evaluations	Max Age (mins)	Gathered Energy
9 mins	3.33%	39.02	3404.98 ± 1668.31	343.43 ± 35.38
90 mins	3.33%	49.28	2886.88 ± 1399.20	3491.03 ± 334.49
900 mins	0%	40.40	3041.81 ± 1446.78	42526.94 ± 6897.61
Experimental setup with neuromodulated odNEAT				
Phase duration	Failure Rate	Evaluations	Max Age (mins)	Gathered Energy
9 min	0%	29.52	3351.12 ± 1358.34	354.39 ± 46.19
90 min	0%	37.79	2799.34 ± 1650.21	3530.82 ± 336.66
900 min	0%	28.99	3074.33 ± 1283.85	45199.64 ± 6680.48

Table 3. Summary of the number of nodes and connections added to the initial network topology by each evolutionary method. Results for each configuration are averaged over 30 evolutionary runs.

Evolutionary Method	Phase Duration	Augmented Connections	Augmented Neurons
odNEAT	9 mins	26.43 ± 12.30	9.47 ± 3.95
odNEAT	90 mins	30.26 ± 17.32	10.41 ± 4.65
odNEAT	900 mins	25.17 ± 12.82	9.60 ± 4.31
odNEAT + NeuroMod	9 mins	22.89 ± 14.98	8.48 ± 4.83
odNEAT + NeuroMod	90 mins	29.32 ± 11.31	10.82 ± 3.91
odNEAT + NeuroMod	900 mins	28.91 ± 11.57	10.50 ± 3.57

Depending on the experimental setup, the most stable controller of each run operated from approximately 47 hours to 57 hours of simulated time before the experiment was terminated. This result indicates that the evolutionary process is capable of evolving controllers well adapted to the periodic changes in the nutritive value of the food items. In terms of gathered energy per period, neuromodulated solutions perform slightly better. ANNs evolved with and without neuromodulation have a similar topological complexity. The initial topology

of stable solutions was augmented with a comparable number of connections
and neurons (see Table 3). Topologies are synthesised faster by odNEAT with
neuromodulation. This result suggests that when neuromodulation is present,
odNEAT performs a more efficient exploitation of a given network topology. In
fixed-weight networks, fine-grained adjustment of connection weights can only be
achieved through mutation. Modulated networks allow for a different expression
of a given topology's potential, and are advantageous even when task requirements do not change for a long time ($p_d = 900$ mins). When modulatory neurons
are present, solutions are synthesised after fewer controller evaluations, probably
due to the modification of internal dynamics by each network.

4.2   Structural Role of Neuromodulation

The results presented above show that neuromodulated learning allows for faster
synthesis of stable controllers. In this section, we analyse the structural role of
neuromodulation on the most stable controllers of each independent run in order
to determine how it affects internal neural dynamics.

Table 4. Summary of the most stable controllers in each independent run. The table
lists the augmented and modulatory neurons, and augmented and modulatory connections in each network.

Phase Duration	Aug. Neurons	Mod. Neurons	Aug. Connections	Mod. Connections
9 mins	9.73 ± 4.88	4.97 ± 2.92	23.93 ± 13.28	6.37 ± 4.39
90 mins	11.97 ± 4.02	6.07 ± 2.99	30.57 ± 10.58	7.93 ± 4.34
900 mins	10.10 ± 5.07	5.03 ± 3.36	25.67 ± 13.34	6.97 ± 4.90

Table 4 shows the average complexity of each stable solution. Approximately
half of the augmented neurons have a modulatory role. Modulatory actions are
localised as each of these neurons typically connects to one or two other neurons. A common topological characteristic between evolved solutions is that the
majority of modulatory connections have output neurons as targets. In fact, the
evolutionary process often leads to the appearance of specialised neurons that
exclusively regulate output neurons as listed in Table 5. Depending on the experimental setup, 59% to 69% of the modulatory neurons are specialised units.
6% to 9% of the specialised neurons modulate more than one output neuron.
For $p_d = 9$ and $p_d = 900$ mins, differences in the number of specialised neurons
are statistically significant ($\rho < 0.05$, Student's t-test). Analysis of experimental
data shows that there is a higher regulatory activity of outputs for the setups of
$p_d = 9$ mins and $p_d = 90$ mins. In these scenarios, controllers experience more
environmental changes during task-execution. Food gathering policies must be
flexible and change whenever a nutritious item becomes less nutritive or poisonous. With the increase of phase durations, the task becomes less dynamic
and the percentage of specialised neurons decreases. Existing specialised neurons increasingly focuses on movement (left and right wheels) and less on the
gripping and food consumption actions.

Table 5. Summary of the specialised neurons for the best solutions of each evolutionary run. The table lists the percentage of modulatory neurons that are specialised in regulating the output actions, and the percentage of specialised neurons that regulate each output. LW and RW represent the left and right wheel, respectively.

Phase Duration	Specialised Reg. Neurons (%)	LW (%)	RW (%)	Gripper (%)
9 mins	69 ± 20	34	34	38
90 mins	62 ± 24	40	32	35
900 mins	57 ± 26	50	30	29

5   Conclusions and Future Work

In this paper, we have introduced a novel approach to the online synthesis of behavioural control for autonomous robots. We combined odNEAT and neuromodulated learning. While odNEAT evolves online both the weights and the topology of neural controllers, neuromodulation allows each individual controller to actively modify its internal dynamics. We demonstrated our method through a series of simulation-based experiments in which an e-puck-like robot had to perform a dynamic concurrent foraging task. We showed that odNEAT with neuromodulation outperforms simple odNEAT by requiring fewer evaluations to produce stable solutions. Results indicate that neuromodulated learning is beneficial even when task requirements do not change for a long time.

We showed that the evolutionary process generates controllers well adapted to the periodic changes in the nutritive value of the food items. Depending on the experimental setup, the most stable controller in each run operated from approximately 47 hours to 57 hours of simulated time before the experiment was terminated. The controllers had thus become resilient to changes in task requirements and they could have operated for longer if they had been given more time. In order to determine the structural and functional role of neuromodulation, we analysed the evolved topologies of the most stable solutions. Evolved networks are characterised by specialised neurons dedicated to regulating the output neurons.

The immediate follow-up work to this study includes the analysis of the neural activation patterns and weight changes to better understand the neural dynamics and the decision-making mechanisms underlying the robot's behaviour.

References

1. Floreano, D., Keller, L.: Evolution of Adaptive Behaviour in Robots by Means of Darwinian Selection. PLoS Biology 8(1), e1000292 (2010)
2. Watson, R.A., Ficici, S.G., Pollack, J.B.: Embodied Evolution – Embodying an Evolutionary Algorithm in a Population of Robots. In: Congress on Evolutionary Computation (CEC 1999), pp. 335–342. IEEE Press, Piscataway (1999)

3. Huijsman, R.J., Haasdijk, E., Eiben, A.E.: An On-Line On-Board Distributed Algorithm for Evolutionary Robotics. In: Hao, J., Legrand, P., Collet, P., Monmarché, N., Lutton, E., Schoenauer, M. (eds.) 10th International Conference on Evolution Artificielle (EA 2011). Online Proceedings, pp. 119–129 (2011), http://www.info.univ-angers.fr/ea2011/doc/EA2011_ProceedingsWeb.pdf

4. Haasdijk, E., Eiben, A.E., Karafotias, G.: On-line Evolution of Robot Controllers by an Encapsulated Evolution Strategy. In: IEEE Congress on Evolutionary Computation (CEC 2010), pp. 1–7. IEEE Press, Piscataway (2010)

5. Hinton, G.E., Nowlan, S.J.: How Learning Can Guide Evolution. Complex Systems 1(3), 495–502 (1987)

6. Floreano, D., Urzelai, J.: Evolutionary Robots with On-line Self-organization and Behavioral Fitness. Neural Networks 13(4-5), 431–443 (2000)

7. Urzelai, J., Floreano, D.: Evolution of Adaptive Synapses – Robots with Fast Adaptive Behavior in New Environments. Evolutionary Computation 9(4), 495–524 (2001)

8. Mondada, F., Bonani, M., Raemy, X., Pugh, J., Cianci, C., Klaptocz, A., Magnenat, S., Zufferey, J., Floreano, D., Martinoli, A.: The e-puck, a Robot Designed for Education in Engineering. In: 9th Conference on Autonomous Robot Systems and Competitions (Robotica 2009), vol. 1, pp. 59 65. IPCB (Instituto Politécnico de Castelo Branco) (2009)

9. Silva, F., Urbano, P., Oliveira, S., Christensen, A.L.: odNEAT: An Algorithm for Distributed Online, Onboard Evolution of Robot Behaviours. In: 13th International Conference on the Simulation and Synthesis of Living Systems (ALIFE 2012), pp. 251–258. MIT Press, Cambridge (2012)

10. Stanley, K.O., Miikkulainen, R.: Evolving Neural Networks through Augmenting Topologies. Evolutionary Computation 10(2), 99–127 (2002)

11. Stanley, K.O.: Efficient Evolution of Neural Networks through Complexification. PhD thesis. The University of Texas at Austin, Austin, TX (2004)

12. Soltoggio, A., Bullinaria, J.A., Mattiussi, C., Dürr, P., Floreano, D.: Evolutionary Advantages of Neuromodulation Plasticity in Dynamic, Reward-based Scenarios. In: 11th International Conference on the Simulation and Synthesis of Living Systems (ALIFE 2008), pp. 569–579. MIT Press, Cambridge (2008)

13. Niv, Y., Joel, D., Meilijson, I., Ruppin, E.: Evolution of Reinforcement Learning in Uncertain Environments – A Simple Explanation for Complex Foraging Behaviors. Adaptive Behavior 10(1), 5–24 (2002)

14. Katz, P.: Beyond Neurotransmission – Neuromodulation and Its Importance for Information Processing. Oxford University Press, Oxford (1999)

15. Bailey, C.H., Giustetto, M., Huang, Y.-Y., Hawkins, R.D., Kandel, E.R.: Is Heterosynaptic Modulation Essential for Stabilizing Hebbian Plasticity and Memory? Nature Reviews Neuroscience 1(1), 11–20 (2000)

16. Ampatzis, C., Tuci, E., Trianni, V., Christensen, A.L., Dorigo, M.: Evolving Self-Assembly in Autonomous Homogeneous Robots: Experiments with Two Physical Robots. Artificial Life 15(4), 465–484 (2009)

A Hierarchical Clustering Strategy to Improve the Biological Plausibility of an Ecology-Based Evolutionary Algorithm

Rafael Stubs Parpinelli[1,2,*] and Heitor Silvério Lopes[2]

[1] Applied Cognitive Computing Group
Santa Catarina State University
Joinville, Brazil
[2] Bioinformatics Laboratory
Federal Technological University of Paraná
Curitiba, Brazil
parpinelli@joinville.udesc.br,
hslopes@utfpr.edu.br

Abstract. It is well known that, in nature, populations are dynamic in space and time. This means that the formation of habitats changes over time and its formation is not deterministic. This work uses the concepts of ecological relationships, ecological successions and probabilistic formation of habitats to build a cooperative search algorithm, named ECO. This work aims at exploring the use of a hierarchical clustering technique to probabilistically set the habitats of the computational ecosystem. The Artificial Bee Colony (ABC) was used in the experiments in which benchmark mathematical functions were optimized. Results were compared with ABC running alone, and the ECO with and without the use of hierarchical clustering. The ECO algorithm with hierarchical clustering performed better than the other approaches, possibly thanks to the ecological interactions (intra and inter-habitats) that enabled the co-evolution of populations and to a more bio-plausible probabilistic strategy for habitats definition. Also, a critical parameter was suppressed.

Keywords: optimization, cooperative search, co-evolution, habitats, ecology, hierarchical clustering, single-link algorithm, biological plausibility.

1 Introduction

The search for biologically plausible ideas, models and computational paradigms always drew the interest of computer scientists, particularly those from the Natural Computing area [2]. The main feature of bio-plausible systems is the use of natural inspirations at some degree where the designers of these systems generally aim to achieve biologically plausible functionalities in non-biological contexts, such as the optimization of engineering problems.

* Authors would like to thank the Brazilian National Research Council (CNPq) for the research grant to H.S. Lopes; as well as to UDESC (Santa Catarina State University) and FUMDES program for the doctoral scholarship to R.S. Parpinelli.

J. Pavón et al. (Eds.): IBERAMIA 2012, LNAI 7637, pp. 310–319, 2012.
© Springer-Verlag Berlin Heidelberg 2012

The concept of optimization can be abstracted from several natural processes such as in the evolution of the species, in the behavior of social groups, in the dynamics of the immune system, in the strategies of searching for food and in the ecological relationships of different populations. Most of these cases were the source of inspiration to the development of algorithms for optimization, such as the evolutionary computation (EC) and swarm intelligence (SI) that currently offer a wide range of strategies for optimization [4,10].

It is worth mentioning that most bio-inspired algorithms only focus on and take inspiration from specific aspects of the natural phenomena. However, in nature, biological systems are interlinked to each other, e.g. biological ecosystems [1,7].

In [9] the authors first introduce the potentiality of some ecological concepts (e.g., habitats, ecological relationships and ecological successions) presenting a simplified ecological-inspired algorithm. In this work we use a hierarchical clustering algorithm [8,6] as a biologically plausible strategy for creating habitats in an ecological-inspired system. The aim is to compare the results obtained by the implementation of the algorithm with the use of ecological concepts, without the use of ecological concepts (application of stand alone algorithms), and with the use of hierarchical clustering.

2   Hierarchical Clustering

Hierarchical clustering refers to methods that produce a nested series of partitions [11]. Single-link and complete-link algorithms are the most popular hierarchical clustering algorithms. These two algorithms differ in the way they characterize the similarity between a pair of clusters. In the single-link method, the distance between two clusters is the minimum of the distances between any two points (or patterns) in the different clusters. In the complete-link algorithm, the distance between two clusters is the maximum of all pairwise distances between any two points in the different clusters. In either case, two clusters are merged to form a larger cluster based on the minimum distance criteria. In this work we use the single-link algorithm.

A hierarchical algorithm yields a dendrogram representing the nested grouping of patterns and similarity levels at which groupings change [8]. Table 1 gives a distance matrix sample for five items (1 - 5). In our context, each item represents the centroid of a given population and the distance matrix is computed using the Euclidean distance metric. The single-link algorithm returns the linkage information needed to build a dendrogram (see Table 2) in a matrix with three columns and $NQ - 1$ rows where NQ is the number of items [6]. In Table 2, each row identifies a node and represents a link between clusters. The first column identifies the nodes, and the two subsequent columns identify the clusters that have been linked. Negative items represent newly formed binary clusters. The third column contains the distance between these objects. The dendrogram of Fig. 1 shows the series of merges that result from using the single-link technique. The height at which two clusters are merged in the dendrogram reflects the distance of the two clusters. The dendrogram can be broken into different levels to yield different clusterings of the data. For example, if we define a cutoff level at 3.0 in the y-axis, three clusters are formed: one with items 1 and 2; other with items 4 and 5; and other with item 3.

Table 1. Distance matrix for five items

Items	1	2	3	4	5
1	0.0	0.5	4.3	3.8	4.8
2	0.5	0.0	4.7	3.3	4.4
3	4.3	4.7	0.0	6.2	6.6
4	3.8	3.3	6.2	0.0	1.1
5	4.8	4.4	6.6	1.1	0.0

Table 2. Single-link result for the data in Table 1

Node	Item$_{left}$	Item$_{right}$	Distance
1	1	2	0.8
2	4	5	2.7
3	-1	-2	3.8
4	3	-3	5.7

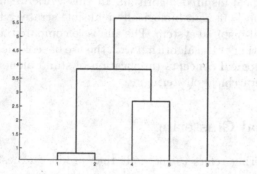

Fig. 1. Dendrogram generated using linkage information from Table 2

3   The Proposed Ecological-Inspired Approach

The ecological-inspired algorithm, named ECO, represents a new perspective to develop cooperative evolutionary algorithms. The ECO is composed by populations of individuals (candidate solutions for a problem being solved) and each population evolves according to an optimization strategy. Therefore, individuals of each population are modified according to the mechanisms of intensification and diversification, and the initial parameters, specific to each optimization strategy. The ECO system can be modeled in two ways: homogeneous or heterogeneous. A homogeneous model implies that all populations evolve in accordance to the same optimization strategy, configured with the same parameters. Any change in the strategies or parameters in at least one population characterises a heterogeneous model.

The ecological inspiration stems from the use of some ecological concepts, such as: habitats, ecological relationships and ecological successions [1,7]. Once dispersed in the search space, populations of individuals established in the same region constitute an ecological habitat. For instance, in a multimodal hyper-surface, each peak can become a promising habitat for some populations. A hyper-surface may have several habitats. As well as in nature, populations can move around through all the environment. However, each population may belong only to one habitat at a given moment of time t. Therefore, by definition, the intersection between all habitats at moment t is the empty set.

With the definition of habitats, two categories of ecological relationships can be defined. Intra-habitats relationships that occur between populations inside each habitat, and inter-habitats relationships that occur between habitats [1,7].

In ECO, the intra-habitat relationship is the mating between individuals. Populations belonging to the same habitat can establish a reproductive link between their individuals, favoring the co-evolution of the involved populations through competition for mating. Populations belonging to different habitats are called reproductively isolated.

The inter-habitats relationship are the great migrations. Individuals belonging to a given habitat can migrate to other habitats aiming at identifying promising areas for survival and mating.

In addition to the mechanisms of intensification and diversification specific to each optimization strategy, when considering the ecological context of the proposed algorithm, the intra-habitats relationships are responsible for intensifying the search and the inter-habitats relationships are responsible for diversifying the search.

Inside the ecological metaphor, the ecological successions represent the transformational process of the system. In this process, populational groups are formed (habitats), relations between populations are established and the system stabilizes by means of the self-organization of its components.

Algorithm 1 shows the pseudo-code of the proposed approach. In this algorithm, the ecological succession loop (lines 3 to 12) refers to iterations of the computational ecosystem. In line 4, evolutive period, each population evolves (generations/iterations) according to its own criteria. The metric chosen to define the region of reference is the centroid and represents the point in the space where there is a longest concentration of individuals of population i. For a detailed description refer to [9].

3.1   Habitats Formation Using Hierarchical Clustering

A key concept of the proposed ECO system is the definition of habitats (line 6 in Algorithm 1). In [9] the definition of habitats is performed deterministically by the use of a user defined proximity threshold ρ. In this work we use a hierarchical clustering algorithm to setup the habitats where each cluster represents a habitat. Hence, the habitats are defined probabilistically taking into account the distance information returned by the single-link algorithm. This gives more biological plausibility to the system once, in nature, the habitats are not defined deterministically as done in [9]. Also, this approach suppress the control parameter ρ.

To create probabilistically the habitats we use the linkage information returned by the single-link algorithm (see Table 2). The distance information are used as probabilities to drive the formation of habitats in a top-down strategy (see Algorithm 2). It is a top-down strategy because it starts from the top of the dendrogram (farthest clusters) and goes down to the bottom of the dendrogram (closest clusters).

After some initializations, the first step in Algorithm 2 is to scale linearly the single-link distances in order to be able to work with this information as probabilities (line 6). We choose to work within the closed interval of $[0.01, 0.99]$ in order to give one more biologically plausible feature to the system. Hence, concerning the lower bound, it means that as close as two populations are from each other, there is still 1% of chance of not grouping these two populations. There is a small chance to the closest populations not belong to the same habitat. Concerning the upper bound, it means that as far as two populations are from each other, there is still 1% of chance of grouping these two populations. There

---

Algorithm 1. Pseudo-code for ECO

1: Consider $i = 1, \ldots, NQ$, $j = 1, \ldots, NH$ and $t = 0$;
2: Initialize each population Q_i^t with n_i random candidate solutions;
3: **while** stop criteria not satisfied **do** {Ecological succession cycles}
4:     Perform evolutive period for each population Q_i^t;
5:     Apply metric C_i to identify the region of reference for each population Q_i^t;
6:     Using the C_i values, define the NH habitats;
7:     For each habitat H_j^t define the communication topology CT_j^t between populations Q_{ij}^t;
8:     For each topology CT_j^t, perform interactions between populations Q_{ij}^t;
9:     Define communication topology TH^t between H_j^t habitats;
10:    For TH^t topology, perform interactions between H_j^t habitats;
11:    Increase t;
12: **end while**

Algorithm 2. Pseudo-code for probabilistic habitats formation

1: $NH = 0$;
2: $nodeCount = 0$;
3: $curNode = NQ - 1$;
4: $curHabitat = 0$;
5: Create $H_{curHabitat}$ with no items;
6: Linearly scalonate the single-link distances;
7: **while** $nodeCount < NQ - 1$ **do**
8:     **if** $rand \geq Distance(curNode)$ **then** {Group items}
9:         $H_{curHabitat} = curNode.item_{left}$ and $curNode.item_{right}$;
10:        $nodeCount = nodeCount + 1$;
11:    **else** {Separate items}
12:        $H_{curHabitat} = curNode.item_{nearest}$;
13:        $NH = NH + 1$;
14:        Create H_{NH} with no items;
15:        $H_{NH} = curNode.item_{farthest}$;
16:        $nodeCount = nodeCount + 1$;
17:    **end if**
18:    Update $curHabitat$;
19:    Update $curNode$;
20: **end while**
21: Return NH;
22: Return H_j where $j = 1, \ldots, NH$;

is a small chance to the farthest populations belong to the same habitat. Table 3 gives the linearly scaled values for the example of Table 2.

After that, the algorithm enters a loop until all nodes are analyzed (lines 7 to 20). The $nodeCount$ variable counts the number of analyzed nodes. Inside this loop a probabilistic conditional statement decides if the items will be grouped together or separated in two groups (line 8). Notice that the distance between items influence directly the probabilistic decision. The closer two items are from each other, the larger the chance to group these two items together. The opposite holds for the farthest items. If two items are decided to be grouped together, the current habitat ($H_{curHabitat}$) receives the left and the right items from the node being analyzed ($curNode$) (lines 9 and 10). If two items are decided to be separated from each other, it is necessary to decide which item stays and which item will belong to a new habitat. As a general rule, the closest item from the current group stays and the farthest item creates a new habitat (lines 12 to 16).

Next steps are to update the next habitat and the next node to be analyzed. The $curHabitat$ variable is updated to the absolute value of the first habitat with a negative item inside (newly formed binary clusters) (line 18). The $curNode$ variable is updated to the absolute value of the first negative item inside $H_{curHabitat}$ (line 19). Finally, the algorithm returns the number of habitats (NH) and the habitats themselves (H_j) (lines 21 and 22, respectively).

3.2   Intra-habitats Communication

Once the habitats are probabilistically defined, the next step in Algorithm 1 (line 7) is the definition of the communication topology for each habitat. Differently from the work done in [9], in this work the definition of intra-habitats communication topology does not use any proximity threshold. Again, aiming at improving the biological plausibility of the system, here, we use a communication topology that is probabilistically defined.

For a habitat with more than one population, intra-habitat communication occurs in such a way that each population inside the habitat chooses another population to perform communication. Here, the distance between populations influence directly the probabilistic decision. The closer two populations are from each other the higher is the chance of these two populations communicate. The opposite happens with farthest populations.

All the non-mentioned procedures of Algorithm 1 remain the same as published in [9].

Table 3. Linearly scaled values for distance

Node	Item$_{left}$	Item$_{right}$	Distance
1	1	2	0.01
2	4	5	0.39
3	-1	-2	0.62
4	3	-3	0.99

4   Experiments and Results

Experiments were conducted using four benchmark functions extensively used in the literature for testing optimization methods [3]. Each function to be minimized was tested with 10 and 200 dimensions. The first function ($f_1(\boldsymbol{x})$ with $-100 \leq x_i \leq 100$) is known as generalized F6 Schaffer function. The second function ($f_2(\boldsymbol{x})$ with $-5.12 \leq x_i \leq 5.12$) is the Rastrigin function. The third function ($f_3(\boldsymbol{x})$ with $-600 \leq x_i \leq 600$) is the Griewank function. Finally, the fourth function ($f_4(\boldsymbol{x})$ with $-30 \leq x_i \leq 30$) is the Rosenbrock function.

The parameters of the ECO algorithm are: number of populations (N-POP) that will be co-evolved, the initial population size (POP-SIZE), number of cycles for ecological successions (ECO-STEP), the size of the evolutive period (EVO-STEP) that represents number of function evaluations in each ECO-STEP, the tournament size (T-SIZE) and the proximity threshold ρ. In this development (ECO-C), with definition of habitats using hierarchical clustering, the proximity threshold ρ is suppressed.

In all experiments the initial population size was set to POP-SIZE = 10. Studies about the adjustment of parameters have not been carried out yet. Hence, all the parameters of the algorithm were defined empirically [9].

In all experiments, the Artificial Bee Colony Optimization (ABC) algorithm [5] was used in a homogeneous model, i.e. all populations use this algorithm with the same control parameters.

For the number of dimensions (D) equal to 10, the parameters used were N-POP = 100, ECO-STEP = 100, EVO-STEP = 100, T-SIZE = 5 e $\rho = 0,5$. With this configuration, the total number of function evaluations was 10,000 for each population. For $D = 200$, some parameters were redefined: N-POP = 200, ECO-STEP = 500, EVO-STEP = 200. With this adjustment of parameters, for 200 dimensions, the total number of function evaluations was 100,000 evaluations for each population.

Table 4 shows the averaged results obtained for the benchmark functions. For both dimensions, $D = 10$ and $D = 200$, the results obtained by each configuration of the algorithms are presented (columns 2 to 4). The ecological-inspired framework was tested using three configurations. The first configuration implements Algorithm 1 as described in Sect. 3, with the definitions of habitats using the proximity threshold ρ, topologies and ecological relations (ECO$_{ABC}$, fourth column of Table 4). The second configuration implements Algorithm 1 and enables the ability to probabilistically create habitats using the single-link clustering information upon the proposed Algorithm 2 (ECO-C$_{ABC}$, third column of Table 4). The third configuration disables the ability to create habitats and, consequently, topologies and interactions are not defined. This third configuration simulates the evolution of completely isolated populations, and they evolve without exchanging information (ABC, second column of Table 4). For each configuration, the algorithm was run 30 times. For each dimension, the third line (*Global Best*) in Table 4 shows the average and standard deviation of the best result obtained by all populations in all runs.

Table 4. Obtained results for the benchmarck functions

$f_1(x)$	$D = 10$		
Model	ABC	ECO_{ABC}	$ECO\text{-}C_{ABC}$
Global Best	4.6569 ± 0.8	1.1344 ± 0.2	1.0687 ± 0.2
	$D = 200$		
Model	ABC	ECO_{ABC}	$ECO\text{-}C_{ABC}$
Global Best	27.5936 ± 0.73	20.2792 ± 0.4	19.8027 ± 0.5
$f_2(x)$	$D = 10$		
Model	ABC	ECO_{ABC}	$ECO\text{-}C_{ABC}$
Global Best	$10^{-11} \pm 0.0$	0.0000 ± 0.0	0.0000 ± 0.0
	$D = 200$		
Model	ABC	ECO_{ABC}	$ECO\text{-}C_{ABC}$
Global Best	62.1453 ± 0.0	$10^{-05} \pm 0.0$	$10^{-05} \pm 0.0$
$f_3(x)$	$D = 10$		
Model	ABC	ECO_{ABC}	$ECO\text{-}C_{ABC}$
Global Best	$10^{-06} \pm 0.0$	$10^{-13} \pm 0.0$	$10^{-18} \pm 0.0$
	$D = 200$		
Model	ABC	ECO_{ABC}	$ECO\text{-}C_{ABC}$
Global Best	$10^{-07} \pm 0.0$	$10^{-11} \pm 0.0$	$10^{-11} \pm 0.0$
$f_4(x)$	$D = 10$		
Model	ABC	ECO_{ABC}	$ECO\text{-}C_{ABC}$
Global Best	0.0098 ± 0.0	0.0086 ± 0.0	0.0082 ± 0.0
	$D = 200$		
Model	ABC	ECO_{ABC}	$ECO\text{-}C_{ABC}$
Global Best	13036.1 ± 1100.4	137.00 ± 42.0	1.8778 ± 1.7

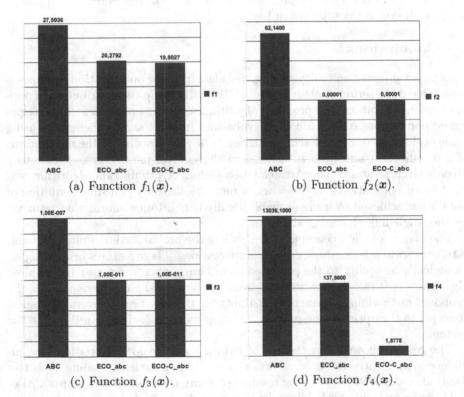

(a) Function $f_1(x)$.   (b) Function $f_2(x)$.

(c) Function $f_3(x)$.   (d) Function $f_4(x)$.

Fig. 2. Bar graph off each benchmark function with $D = 200$

Analyzing the ABC and ECO$_{ABC}$ we can observe that the ecological-inspired approach obtained much better results than the algorithm executed without the concepts of habitats for all functions. This gain is mainly due to the ecological interactions (intra and inter-habitats) that enabled the co-evolution of populations. Analyzing the results for the ecological-inspired approach with probabilistic habitat definition, ECO-C$_{ABC}$, we can observe that the results were equivalent or better for all functions when compared with the ecological-inspired approach without the use of clustering strategy (ECO$_{ABC}$). This analysis indicates that the behavior of the ecological algorithm does not change when using the proposed hierarchical clustering strategy to probabilistically setup the habitats and communication topology. It is worth mentioning that with this strategy a critical parameter (ρ) is suppressed. Also, one can notice that the results obtained by ECO-C$_{ABC}$ for function $f_4(x)$ with $D = 200$ was much better than the ECO$_{ABC}$ approach. This result indicates that the value for the ρ parameter present in ECO$_{ABC}$ was not the best choice and should be optimized. With the new application of hierarchical clustering this problem is cleary solved. Moreover, the ECO-C$_{ABC}$ was the best approach for all functions. In Fig. 2 we can visually verify the results for $D = 200$, where the x-*axis* shows the different approaches and the y-*axis* represents the *Global Best* values of each approach and are shown at the top of each bar.

5   Conclusions

This paper presents an ecological-inspired algorithm for optimization that uses a hierarchical clustering strategy to probabilistically setup the distribution of populations into habitats. The proposed algorithm uses cooperative search strategies where populations of individuals co-evolve and interact among themselves using some ecological concepts. Each population behaves according to the mechanisms of intensification and diversification, and the control parameters, specific to a given search strategy. The Artificial Bee Colony Optimization algorithm was used in all populations. In this work, a more biologically plausible definition of habitats is achieved by using probabilistically the distance information returned by the single-link clustering algorithm.

The main ecological concepts addressed are the probabilistic definition of habitats, ecological relationships, ecological successions. These features bring a higher biological plausibility to the proposed algorithm, opposed to most bio-inspired algorithms that take inspiration only from one biological phenomenon. Thus, the proposed methodology opens the possibility for the insertion of several ecological concepts in the optimization process, bringing more biological plausibility to the system.

The results showed that the use of habitats and ecological relationships influence significantly the co-evolution process of populations, leading to better solutions (when compared to the results not using the ecological concepts). Also, the use of a probabilistic habitats definition inside the ECO framework improved the results and, mainly, suppressed the proximity threshold ρ, a critical control parameter that should be set by the user.

This work is still under development and as future work we intend to analyze the influence of the remaining control parameters (number of ecological successions, evolutive period, and number of populations) on the quality of solutions, as well as to add other search strategies in the proposed model. Currently, in order to bring more biological plausibility to the system, other ecological concepts are being modeled, and efforts are doing to eliminate control parameters.

References

1. Begon, M., Townsend, C.R., Harper, J.L.: Ecology – From Individuals to Ecosystems, 4th edn. Blackwell Publishing, Oxford (2006)
2. de Castro, L.N.: Fundamentals of Natural Computing – An Overview. Physics of Life Reviews 4(1), 1–36 (2007)
3. Digalakis, J.G., Margaritis, K.G.: An Experimental Study of Benchmarking Functions for Evolutionary Algorithms. International Journal of Computer Mathematics 79(4), 403–416 (2002)
4. Engelbrecht, A.P.: Computational Intelligence: An Introduction, 2nd edn. Wiley, Chichester (2007)
5. Karaboga, D., Akay, B.: A Comparative Study of Artificial Bee Colony Algorithm. Applied Mathematics and Computation 214(1), 108–132 (2009)
6. Legendre, P., Legendre, L.: Numerical Ecology. Elsevier, Amsterdam (1998)
7. May, R.M.C., McLean, A.R.: Theoretical Ecology: Principles and Applications. Oxford University Press, Oxford (2007)
8. Murtagh, F., Contreras, P.: Algorithms for Hierarchical Clustering – An Overview. Data Mining and Knowledge Discovery 2(1), 86–97 (2012)
9. Parpinelli, R.S., Lopes, H.S.: An Eco-inspired Evolutionary Algorithm Applied to Numerical Optimization. In: 3rd World Congress on Nature and Biologically Inspired Computing (NaBIC 2011), Salamanca, Spain, pp. 466–471 (2011)
10. Parpinelli, R.S., Lopes, H.S.: New Inspirations in Swarm Intelligence – A Survey. International Journal of Bio-Inspired Computation 3(1), 1–16 (2011)
11. Xu, R., Wunsch, D.: Survey of Clustering Algorithms. IEEE Transactions on Neural Networks 16(3), 645–678 (2005)

An Intelligent System Based on Discrete Cosine Transform for Speech Recognition

Washington Silva and Ginalber Serra

Federal Institute of Education, Science and Technology
Department of Electroelectronics,
Laboratory of Computational Intelligence Applied to Technology
Av. Getúlio Vargas, 04, Monte Castelo, CEP: 65030-005, São Luis, Maranhão, Brazil
http://www.ifma.edu.br

Abstract. This paper proposes a genetic-fuzzy system for speech recognition. In addition to pre-processing, with mel-cepstral coefficients, the Discrete Cosine Transform (DCT) is used to generate a two-dimensional time matrix for each pattern to be recognized. A genetic algorithm is used to optimize a Mamdani fuzzy inference system in order to obtain the best model for final recognition. The speech recognition system used in this paper was named Hybrid Method Genetic-Fuzzy Inference System for Speech Recognition (**HMFE**).

Keywords: speech recognition, fuzzy system, optimization, genetic algorithm, discrete cosine transform.

1 Introduction

Parameterization of an analog speech signal is the first step in speech recognition process. Several popular signal analysis techniques have emerged as standards in the literature. These algorithms are intended to produce a 'perceptually meaningful' parametric representation of the speech signal: parameters that can emulate some behavior observed in human auditory and perceptual systems. Actually, these algorithms are also designed to maximize recognition performance [1,2]. The problem of pattern recognition might be formulated as follows: Let S_k classes, where $k = 1,2,3...K$, and $S_k \subset \Re^n$. If any pattern space is take with dimension $\Re^x$, where $x \leq n$, it should transform this space into a new pattern space with dimension $\Re^a$, where $a < x \leq n$. Then assuming a statistical measure or second order model for each S_k, through a covariance function represented by $\left[\Phi_x^{(k)}\right]$, the covariance matrix of the general pattern recognition problem becomes:

$$[\Phi_x] = \sum_{k=1}^{K} P(S_k) \left[\Phi_x^{(k)}\right] \tag{1}$$

where $P(S_k)$ is a distribution function of the class S_k, *a priori*, with $0 \leq P(S_k) \leq 1$. A linear transformation operator through the matrix $\mathbf{A}$ maps the pattern space in a transformed space where the columns are orthogonal basis vectors

J. Pavón et al. (Eds.): IBERAMIA 2012, LNAI 7637, pp. 320–329, 2012.

of this matrix $\mathbf{A}$. The patterns of the new space are linear combinations of the original axes as structure of the matrix $\mathbf{A}$. The statistics of second order in the transformed space are given by:

$$\Phi_{\mathbf{A}} = \mathbf{A}^T[\Phi_x]\mathbf{A} \tag{2}$$

where $\Phi_{\mathbf{A}}$ is the covariance matrix which corresponds to the space generated by the matrix $\mathbf{A}$ and the operator $[\cdot]^T$ corresponds to the transpose of a matrix. Thus, it can extract features that provide greater discriminatory power for classification from the dimension of the space generated [3]. One of the most widespread techniques for pattern speech recognition is the "Hidden Markov Model" (HMM) [4]. A well known deficiency of the classical HMMs is the inadequate modeling of the acoustic events related to each state. Since the probability of recursion to the same state is constant, the probability of the acoustic event related to the state is exponentially decreasing. A second weakness of the HMMs is that the observation vectors within each state are assumed uncorrelated, and these vectors are correlated [5],[6].

1.1   Proposed Methodology

In this paper, a speech signal is encoded and parameterized in a two-dimensional time matrix, with four parameters of the speech signal. After coding, the mean and variance of each pattern are used to generate the rule base of Mamdani fuzzy inference system. The mean and variance are optimized using genetic algorithm in order to have the best performance of the recognition system. Consider as patterns the brazilian locutions (digits): $'0','1','2','3','4','5','6','7','8','9'$. The Discrete Cosine Transform (DCT) [7],[8] is used for encoding the speech patterns. The use of DCT in data compression and pattern classification has been increased in recent years, mainly due to the fact its performance is much closer to the results obtained by the Karhunen-Loève transform which is considered optimal for a variety of criteria such as mean square error of truncation and entropy [9,10]. This paper demonstrates the potential of DCT and fuzzy inference system in speech recognition [11,12]. These two tools have shown good results in the temporal modeling of speech signal[13].

2   Speech Recognition System

The proposed recognition system HMFE block diagram is depicted in Fig.1.

2.1   Pre-processing Speech Signal

Initially, the speech signal is digitized, so it is divided in segments that are windowed and encoded in a set of parameters defined by the order of mel-cepstral coefficients (MFCC). The DCT coefficients are computed and the two-dimensional time DCT matrix is generated, based on each speech signal to be recognized.

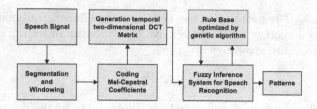

Fig. 1. Block diagram of the proposed recongnition system HMFE

Mel-Cepstrais Coefficients Coding. Experiments on human perception have shown that complex sound frequencies within a certain bandwidth of a nominal frequency should not be individually identified. When one of the components of this sound is out of bandwidth, this component can not be distinguished. Normally, it is considered a critical bandwidth for speech from 10 % to 20 % of the center frequency of the sound. One of the most popular way to map the frequency of a given sound signal for perceptual frequencies values, i.e., to be capable of exciting the human hearing range is the Mel-Scale [2].

2.2   Two-Dimensional Time Matrix DCT Coding

The two-dimensional time matrix as the result of DCT in a sequence of T mel-cepstral coefficients observation vectors on the time axis, is given by:

$$C_k(n,T) = \frac{1}{N} \sum_{t=1}^{T} mfcc_k(t) cos \frac{(2t-1)n\pi}{2T} \tag{3}$$

where $mfcc$ are the mel-cepstral coefficients, and $k, 1 \leq k \leq K$, is the k-th (line) component of t-th frame of the matrix and $n, 1 \leq n \leq N$ (column) is the order of DCT. Thus, the two-dimensional time matrix is obtained[12], where the interesting low-order coefficients k and n that encode the long-term variations of the spectral envelope of the speech signal[6]. Each frame of a given example of the word P generates a total of K mel-cepstral coefficients and the significant features are taken for each frame along time. The N-th order DCT is computed for each mel-cepstral coefficient of same order within the frames distributed along the time axis, i.e., c_1 of the frame t_1, c_1 of the frame t_2, ...,, c_1 of the frame t_T, c_2 of the frame t_1, c_2 of the frame t_2, ...,, c_2 of the frame t_T, and so on, generating elements $\{c_{11}, c_{12}, c_{13}, ..., c_{1N}\}$, $\{c_{21}, c_{22}, c_{23}, ..., c_{2N}\}$, $\{c_{K1}, c_{K2}, c_{K3}, ..., c_{KN}\}$, and the matrix given in equation (3). Therefore, a two-dimensional time matrix DCT is generated for each example of the word P. In this paper, a two-dimensional time matrix generated has order $(K = 2) \times (N = 2)$. Finally, the matrices of mean CM_{kn}^j (4) and variances CV_{kn}^j (5) are generated. The parameters of CM_{kn}^j and CV_{kn}^j are used to produce gaussians matrices C_{kn}^j which will be used as fundamental information for implementation of the fuzzy recognition system. The parameters of this matrix will be optimized by genetic algorithm.

$$CM_{kn}^j = \frac{1}{M} \sum_{m=0}^{M-1} C_{kn}^{jm} \tag{4}$$

$$CV_{kn}^j(var) = \frac{1}{M-1} \sum_{m=0}^{M-1} \left[C_{kn}^{jm} - \left(\frac{1}{M} \sum_{m=0}^{M-1} C_{kn}^{jm} \right) \right]^2 \qquad (5)$$

where M=10.

2.3 Rule Base Used for Speech Recognition

Given the fuzzy set A input, the fuzzy set B output, should be obtained by the relational max-t composition. This relationship is given by.

$$B = A \circ Ru \qquad (6)$$

where Ru is a fuzzy relation rules base. The fuzzy rule base of practical systems usually consists of more than one rule. There are two ways to infer a set of rules: Inference based on composition and inference based on individual rules [14], [15]. In this paper the compositional inference is used. Generally, a fuzzy rule base is given by:

$$Ru^l : IF \ x_1 \ is \ A_1^l \ and...and \ x_n \ is \ A_n^l \ THEN \ y \ is \ B^l \qquad (7)$$

where A_i^l and B^l are fuzzy set in $U_i \subset \Re$ and $V \subset \Re$, and $x = (x_1, x_2, ..., x_n)^T \in U$ and $y \in V$ are input and output variables of fuzzy system, respectively. Let M be the number of rules in the fuzzy rule base; that is, $l = 1, 2, ...M$.

From the coefficients of the matrices $\mathbf{C}_{kn}^j$ with $j = 0, 1, 2, ..., 9$, $k = 1, 2$ and $n = 1, 2$ generated during the training process, representing the mean and variance of each pattern j a rule base with $M = 40$ individual rules is obtained and given by:

$$Ru^j : IF \ C_{kn}^j \ THEN \ y^j \qquad (8)$$

In this paper, the training process is based on the fuzzy relation Ru^j using the Mamdani implication. The rule base Ru^j should be considered a relation $R(X \times Y) \to [0,1]$, computed by:

$$\mu_{Ru}(x, y) = I(\mu_A(x), \mu_B(y)) \qquad (9)$$

where the operator I should be any t-norm [16]. Given the fuzzy set A' input, the fuzzy set B' output might be obtained by **max-min** composition. For a minimum t-norm and max-min composition it yields:

$$\mu_{(Ru)}(x, y) = I(\mu_A(x), \mu_B(y)) = min(\mu_A(x), \mu_B(y)) \qquad (10)$$

$$\mu_{(B')} = max_x min_{x,y}(\mu_{A'}(x), \mu_{(Ru)}(x, y)) \qquad (11)$$

2.4 Generation of Fuzzy Patterns

The elements of the matrix C_{kn}^j were used to generate gaussians membership functions in the process of fuzzification. For each trained model j the gaussians memberships functions $\mu_{c_{kn}^j}$ are generated, corresponding to the elements c_{kn}^j of the two-dimensional time matrix $\mathbf{C}_{kn}^j$ with $j = 0.1, 2, 3, 4, 5, 6, 7, 8, 9$, where j is the model used in training. The training system for generation of fuzzy patterns is based on the encoding of the speech signal $s(t)$, generating the parameters of the matrix C_{kn}^j. Then, these parameters are fuzzified, and they are related to properly fuzzified output y^j by the relational implications, generating a relational surface $\mu_{(Ru)}$, given by:

$$\mu_{Ru} = \mu_{c_{kn}^j} \circ \mu_{y^j} \tag{12}$$

This relational surface is the fuzzy system rule base for recognition optimized by genetic algorithm to maximize the speech recognition. The decision phase is performed by a fuzzy inference system based on the set of rules obtained from the mean and variance matrices of two dimensions time of each spoken digit. In this paper, a matrix with minimum number of parameters (2×2) in order to allow a satisfactory performance compared to pattern recognizers available in the literature. The elements of the matrices $\mathbf{C}_{kn}^j$ are used by the fuzzy inference system to generate four gaussian membership functions corresponding to each element $c_{kn}^j \big|^{k=1,2;n=1,2}$ of the matrix. The set of rules of the fuzzy relation is given by:

$$IF \quad c_{kn}^j \big|^{k=1,2;n=1,2} \quad THEN \quad y^j \tag{13}$$

Modus Ponens

$$IF \quad c_{kn}^{'j} \big|^{k=1,2;n=1,2} \quad THEN \quad y^{'j} \tag{14}$$

From the set of rules of the fuzzy relation between antecedent and consequent, a data matrix for the given implication is obtained. After the training process, the relational surfaces is generated based on the rule base and Mamdani implication method. The final decision for the pattern is taken according to the $max - min$ composition between the input parameters and the data contained in the relational surfaces. The process of defuzzification for the pattern recognition is based on the **mean of maxima (mom)** method given by:

$$\mu_{y'^j} = \mu_{c_{kn}^{'j}} \circ \mu_{(Ru)} \tag{15}$$

$$y' = mom(\mu_{y'^j}) = mean\{y|\mu_{y'^j} = max_{y \in Y}(\mu_{y'^j})\} \tag{16}$$

2.5   Optimization of Relational Surface with Genetic Algorithm

The continuous genetic algorithm (GA) is configured with a population size of 100, generations of 300, with mutations probability of 15% and two individuals chromosomes with 40 gens each, to optimize a cost function with 80 variables, which are the mean and variances of the patterns to be recognized by the proposed fuzzy recognition system [17],[18]. The genetic algorithm was used to optimize the variations of mean and variances of each pattern in order to maximize the successful recognition process. For example, for the pattern of the spoken word "*zero*" is generated ten two-dimensional time matrix. For each element of the matrix C_{kn}^j coefficients are determined with variations minimum and maximum , and the coefficient $c_{11} \in [c_{11(minimum)}\ c_{11(maximum)}]$, $c_{12} \in [c_{12(minimum)}\ c_{12(maximum)}]$, $c_{21} \in [c_{21(minimum)}\ c_{21(maximum)}]$, $c_{22} \in [c_{22(minimum)}\ c_{22(maximum)}]$. Thus, it has eight time varying parameters for each pattern which correspond to eighty parameters to be optimized by genetic algorithm , [19],[20].

3   Experimental Results

3.1   System Training

The patterns to be used in the recognition process were obtained from ten speakers who are speaking the digits 0 until 9. After pre-processing of the speech signal and fuzzification of the matrix C_{kn}^j, its fuzzifieds components $\mu_{c_{kn}^j}$ had been optimized by the GA that maximize the total of successful recognition. The optimization process was performed with 16 realizations of the genetic algorithm, whose results are shown in Fig.2. The best result of the recognition processing by HMFE is shown in Fig.3. The total number of hits using GA was 92 digits correctly identified in the training process. The relational surface generated for this result was used for validation process.

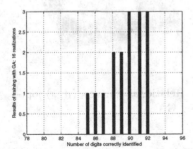
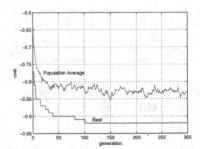

Fig. 2. Histogram for 16 realizations of the training process with the HMFE

Fig. 3. Plot of the best results obtained in the training process

The best individual in the first generation is shown in Fig. 4. In this case the total number of correct answers was 46 digits correctly identified. The ralational surface of the best individual in the first generation is shows in Fig. 5.

The optimum individual, HMFE, presents the features in Fig. 6 and Fig. 7.

3.2   System Test – Validation

In this step, 100 locutions uttered in a room with controlled noise level and 500 locutions uttered in an environment without any kind of noise control were used. For every ten examples of each spoken digit, was generated two-dimensional time matrix cepstral coefficients $\mathbf{C}_{kn}^j$ and they were used in the test procedure. Were performed six types of tests:

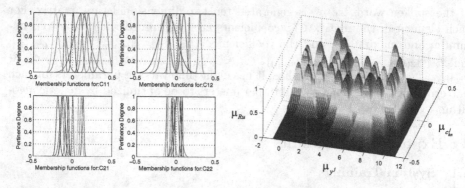

Fig. 4. Membership functions for c_{kn}^j in the 1st generation

Fig. 5. Relational surface (μ_{Ru}) in the 1st generation

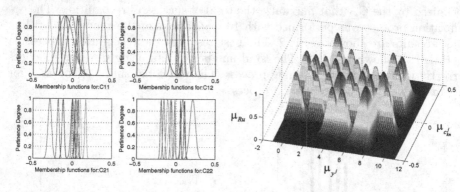

Fig. 6. Membership functions for c_{kn}^j optmized by GA

Fig. 7. Relational surface (μ_{Ru}) optmized by GA

Training: Recognition Optimized by HMFE (5 Female and 5 Male Speakers)
TEST 1: Validation - Strictly speaker dependent recognition, where the words used for training and testing were spoken by a same group of 10 speakers(5 Female and 5 Male Speakers).
TEST 2: Validation test- Recognition based on the partial dependence of the speaker with two examples for each ten examples of each digit(Female Speaker).
TEST 3: Validation test- Recognition based on the partial dependence of the speaker with two examples for each ten examples of each digit(Male Speaker).
TEST 4: Validation test- Recognition independent of the Speaker, where the speaker does not have influence in the training process(Female Speaker).
TEST 5: Validation test- Recognition independent of the Speaker, where the speaker does not have influence in the training process(Male Speaker).

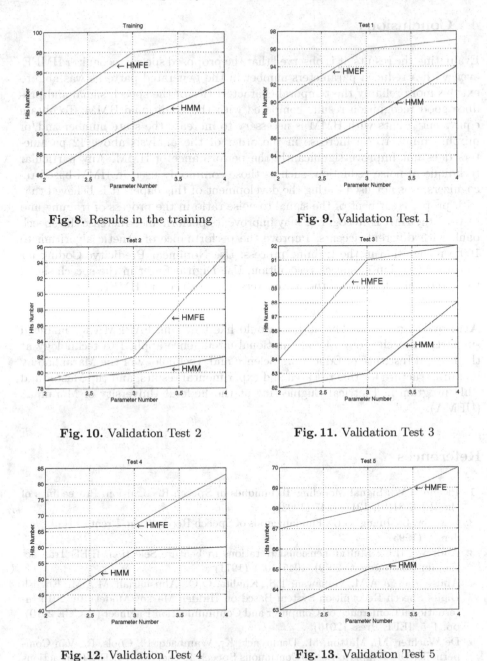

Fig. 8. Results in the training

Fig. 9. Validation Test 1

Fig. 10. Validation Test 2

Fig. 11. Validation Test 3

Fig. 12. Validation Test 4

Fig. 13. Validation Test 5

Figures 8 to 13 present the comparative analysis of the HMM with two, three and four states, two, three and four gaussians mixtures by state and order analysis, i.e., the number of mel-cepstral parameter equal 12 and HMFE with two, three and four parameters for speech recognition.

4   Conclusions

Evaluating the results, it is observed that the proposed speech recognizer HMFE, even with a reduced parameters number in the generated patterns was able to extract more reliably the temporal characteristics of the speech signal and produce good recognition results compared with the traditional HMM. To obtain equivalent results with HMM is necessary to increase the state number and/or mixture number. An increase in the order of the analysis above 12 parameters does not improve significantly the performance of HMM. Any particular technique of noise reduction, such as those commonly used in HMM-based recognizers, was not used during the development of this paper. It is believed that with proper treatment of the signal to noise ratio in the process of training and testing, the HMFE Recognizer may improve its performance:Increase the speech bank with different accents; Improve the performance of genetic algorithm to 100% recognition in the training process; Use Nonlinear Predicitve Coding for feature extraction in speech recognition; Use Digital Filter in the speech signal to be recognized; Increase the parameters number used in HMFE.

Acknowledgments. The authors would like to thank FAPEMA for financial support, research group of computational intelligence applied to technology at the Federal Institute of Education, Science and Technology of the Maranhão by its infrastructure for this research and experimental results, and the Master and PhD program in Eletrical Engineering at the Federal University of Maranhão (UFMA).

References

1. Picone, J.W.: Signal Modeling Techiniques in Speech Recognition. Proceedings of the IEEE 81(9), 1215–1247 (1993)
2. Rabiner, L., Juang, B.H.: Fundamentals of Speech Recognition. Prentice Hall, New Jersey (1993)
3. Andrews, H.C.: Multidimensional Rotations in Feature Selection. IEEE Transaction on Computers C-20(9), 1045–1051 (1971)
4. Abushariah, A.A.M., Gunawan, T.S., Khalifa, O.O., Abushariah, M.A.M.: English Digits Speech Recognition System Based on Hidden Markov Models. In: 2010 International Conference on Computer and Communication Engineer (ICCCE 2010), pp. 1–5. IEEE Press (2010)
5. De Wachter, M., Matton, M., Demuynck, K., Wambacq, P., Cools, R., Van Compernolle, D.: Template-Based Continuous Speech Recognition. IEEE Transactions on Audio, Speech, and Language Processing 15(4), 1377–1390 (2007)
6. Fissore, L., Laface, P., Ravera, F.: Using Word Temporal Structure in HMM Speech Recognition. In: 1997 IEEE International Conference on Acoustics, Speech, and Signal Processing (ICASSP 1997), vol. 2, pp. 975–978. IEEE Press (1997)
7. Ahmed, N., Natarajan, T., Rao, K.R.: Discrete Cosine Trasnform. IEEE Transaction on Computers C-23(1), 90–93 (1974)

8. Zhou, J., Chen, P.: Generalized Discrete Cosine Transform. In: 2009 Pacific-Asia Conference on Circuits, Communications and Systems (PACCS 2009), pp. 449–452. IEEE Press (2009)
9. Hua, Y., Liu, W.: Generalized Karhunen–Loeve Transform. IEEE Signal Processing Letters 5(6), 141–142 (1998)
10. Effros, M., Feng, H., Zeger, K.: Suboptimality of the Karhunen Loéve Transform for Transform Coding. IEEE Transactions on Information Theory 50(8), 1605–1619 (2004)
11. Zeng, J., Liu, Z.Q.: Type-2 Fuzzy Hidden Markov Models and Their Application to Speech Recognition. IEEE Transactions on Fuzzy Systems 14(3), 454–467 (2006)
12. Azar, M.Y., Razzazi, F.: A DCT Based Nonlinear Predictive Coding for Feature Extraction in Speech Recognition Systems. In: 2008 IEEE International Conference on Computational Intelligente for Measurement Systems and Applications (CIMSA 2008), pp. 19–22. IEEE Press (2008)
13. Silva, W.L.S., Serra, G.L.O.: Proposta de Metodologia TCD-Fuzzy para Reconhecimento de Voz. In: X Simpósio Brasileiro de Automação Inteligente (SBAI 2011), pp. 1054–1059. SBA Press (2011)
14. Wang, L.X.: A Course in Fuzzy Systems and Control. Prentice Hall (1994)
15. Gang, C.: Discussion of Approximation Properties of Minimum Inference Fuzzy System. In: 29th Chinese Control Conference (CCC 2010), pp. 2540–2546 (2010)
16. Babuška, R.: Fuzzy Modeling for Control. Kluwer Academic Publishers (1998)
17. Haupt, R.L., Haupt, S.E.: Practical Genetic Algorithms. John Wiley & Sons, Inc. (2004)
18. Zhou, E., Khotanzad, A.: Fuzzy Classifier Design Using Genetic Algorithms. Pattern Recognition 40(12), 3401–3414 (2007)
19. Weihong, Z., Shunqing, X., Ting, M.: A Fuzzy Classifier Based on Mamdani Fuzzy Logic System and Genetic Algorithm. In: 2010 IEEE Youth Conference on Information Computing and Telecommunications (YC-ICT 2010), pp. 198–201. IEEE Press (2010)
20. Zhang, X., Wang, X., Zhang, S., Yu, F.: Approximating the True Domain of Fuzzy Inference Sentence with Genetic Algorithm. In: 7th International Conference on Fuzzy Systems and Knowledge Discovery (FSKD 2010), pp. 114–118. IEEE Press (2010)

Multiobjective Genetic Fuzzy PID Control Design for Uncertain Dynamic Systems

Danúbia Soares Pires and Ginalber Luiz de Oliveira Serra

Federal Institute of Education, Science and Technology
Department of Electroelectronics,
Laboratory of Computational Intelligence Applied to Technology
Av. Getúlio Vargas, 04, Monte Castelo, CEP: 65030-005, São Luis, Maranhão, Brazil
danubiapires@ifma.edu.br, ginalber@ifma.edu.br

Abstract. In this paper, a robust fuzzy digital PID control strategy, via multiobjective genetic algorithm, based on the gain and phase margins specifications, with applications to uncertain dynamic systems with time delay, is proposed. A multiobjective genetic strategy is defined to tune the fuzzy controller parameters, so the gain and phase margins of the fuzzy control system are close to the specified ones. Computational results show the efficiency of the proposed methodology through the accuracy in the gain and phase margins of the fuzzy PID control system compared to the specified ones and tracking of the reference trajectory compared to Ziegler-Nichols method.

Keywords: robust control, fuzzy system, digital PID controller, uncertain dynamic system, multiobjective genetic algorithm.

1 Introduction

A control is robust when the adjustment mechanism of the controller takes account of certain classes of parametric uncertainties and dynamics of the plant to be controlled. The controller is designed to make the control system stable, in spite of the uncertainties or parametric changes in the plant to be controlled, so as to establish tracking of the reference trajectory within the frequency range of interest. The robust control area has a rich literature on different techniques for design, analysis and applications. However, since designers and engineers need to deal with industrial plants increasingly complex, taking into account structural and dynamic features such as nonlinearities, uncertainties, parametric variations, time delay, among others, several methods of robust control has been proposed, allowing in their formulation the use of constraints and performance requirements [1,2]. In [3], the stabilization of a discrete time robust control system based on reference model, is achieved. In [4], the design of robust control for perturbed systems, is presented. In [5], a fuzzy PID control to improve the stability of hydraulic position servo system, is proposed.

Furthermore, fuzzy controllers have been a good alternative for control of complex dynamic systems, once that the fuzzy structure based on rules are able

J. Pavón et al. (Eds.): IBERAMIA 2012, LNAI 7637, pp. 330–339, 2012.

to treat uncertainties, nonlinearities and time delay problems [6]. In this paper, a model based robust fuzzy digital PID control strategy, via multiobjective genetic algorithm, based on the gain and phase margins specifications, with applications to uncertain dynamic systems with time delay, is proposed.

2 Mathematical Analysis of Additive Unstructured Uncertainty

Consider the real dynamic system transfer function $H(z, \nu)$, given by:

$$H(z, \nu) = \frac{b_\alpha + b_{\alpha-1}z^{-1} + \ldots + b_1 z^{-\alpha+1} + b_0 z^{-\alpha}}{1 + a_{\beta-1}z^{-1} + \ldots + a_1 z^{-\beta+1} + a_0 z^{-\beta}} + \Delta_A(z, \nu) \tag{1}$$

where Δ_A is the additive uncertainty, a and b are the coefficients of the nominal dynamic system transfer function, v is a time varying scheduling variable of the uncertainty Δ_A z is the Z-Transform operator, α and β are the orders of the numerator and denominator of the nominal transfer function.

The structure of $\Delta_A(z, \nu)$ is usually unknown but $\Delta_A(z, \nu)$ is assumed satisfying an upper bound in the frequency domain, i.e,

$$|\Delta_A(\omega, \nu)| \leq \nu_A(\omega), \forall(\omega) \tag{2}$$

for some known function $\nu_A(\omega)$. From (1) and (3) is defined a family of plants described by:

$$\prod_A = \{H / |H(\omega, \nu) - H(\omega)| \leq \nu_A(\omega)\} \tag{3}$$

where:

$$\omega = \frac{1 - z^{-1}}{1 + z^{-1}} \tag{4}$$

3 Identification of TS Fuzzy Model Based on Clustering Algorithm

3.1 Antecedent Parameters Estimation

In this paper, the TS fuzzy model antecedent parameters are estimated by fuzzy C-Means (FCM) clustering algorithm, which is based on minimizing the functional given by:

$$J(Z; U, V) = \sum_{i=1}^{c} \sum_{k=1}^{N} (\mu_{ik})^m \|z_k - v_i\|_A^2 \tag{5}$$

where

$$U = [\mu_{ik}] \in M_{fc} \tag{6}$$

is a fuzzy partition matrix of Z,

$$V = [v_1, v_2, ..., v_c], v_i \in \Re^n \tag{7}$$

is a vector of cluster prototypes (centers), determined by:

$$D_{ikA}^2 = \|z_k - v_i\|_A^2 = (z_k - v_i)^T A (z_k - v_i) \tag{8}$$

which is a squared inner-product distance norm, where z_k represents the elements of each column of the data matrix Z and v_i is associated with the coordinates of the clusters centers.

The FCM algorithm is realized using the following steps: given the data set Z and the initial partition matrix $U^{(0)} \in M_{fc}$, choose the number of clusters $1 < c < N$, the tolerance $\epsilon > 0$ and the weighting exponent $m > 1$.

Repeat for $l=1,2,...$

1- Compute the cluster prototypes (means):

$$v_i^{(l)} = \frac{\sum\limits_{k=1}^{N} \mu_{ik}^{(l-1)} z_k}{\sum\limits_{k=1}^{N} \left(\mu_{ik}^{(l-1)}\right)^m}, 1 \leq i \leq c \tag{9}$$

2- Compute the distances:

$$D_{ikA}^2 = \left(z_k - v_i^{(l)}\right)^T A \left(z_k - v_i^{(l)}\right), 1 \leq i \leq c, 1 \leq k \leq N \tag{10}$$

3- Update the partition matrix:
If $D_{ikA} > 0$ for $1 \leq i \leq c, 1 \leq k \leq N$,

$$\mu_{ik}^{(l)} = \frac{1}{\sum\limits_{j=1}^{c} (D_{ikA}/D_{jkA})^{2/(m-1)}}, \tag{11}$$

otherwise
$\mu_{ik}^{(l)} = 0$ if $D_{ikA} > 0$, and $\mu_{ik}^{(l)} \in [0, 1]$ with $\Sigma_{i=1}^c \mu_{ik}^{(l)} = 1$.
Until $\|U^{(l)} - U^{(l-1)}\| < \epsilon$.

3.2   Consequent Parameters Estimation

Consider the transfer function $G_P^i(z)$ as i-th rule consequent sub-model of the TS fuzzy inference system, given by:

$$G_P^i(z) = \frac{b_0^i + b_1^i z^{-1} + \ldots + b_\beta^i z^{-\beta}}{1 + a_1^i z^{-1} + a_2^i z^{-2} + \ldots + a_\alpha^i z^{-\alpha}}, \tag{12}$$

where:

- z is a complex variable, based on Z-transform;
- $a_{1,2,...,\alpha}^i$ and $b_{1,2,...,\beta}^i$ are the parameters of i-th sub-model;

− α and β are the orders of the numerator and denominator of $G_P^i(z)$, respectively.

The TS fuzzy dynamic model presents the following structure:

$$\tilde{y}(k) = \sum_{i=1}^{l} \gamma^i(k)[b_0^i u(k)+\ldots+b_\beta^i u(k-\beta)-a_1^i y(k-1)-a_2^i y(k-2)-\ldots-a_\alpha^i y(k-\alpha)]$$
(13)

In matricial form, results:

$$\tilde{\mathbf{Y}}(\mathbf{k}) = \Gamma^1 \mathbf{X}(\mathbf{k})\Theta^1 + \ldots + \Gamma^i \mathbf{X}(\mathbf{k})\Theta^i \tag{14}$$

where:

$$X(k) = \left[\, u(k)\big|u(k-1)\big|\ldots\big|u(k-\beta)\big|y(k-1)\big|-y(k-2)\big|\ldots\big|-y(k-\alpha)\,\right] \tag{15}$$

is called the regressors matrix,

$$\Theta^i = \begin{bmatrix} b_0^i \\ b_1^i \\ \vdots \\ b_\beta^i \\ a_1^i \\ a_2^i \\ \vdots \\ a_\alpha^i \end{bmatrix} \tag{16}$$

is the vector of the sub-model parameters in i-th rule,

$$\Gamma^i = \begin{bmatrix} \gamma^i(0) & 0 & \ldots & 0 \\ 0 & \gamma^i(1) & \ldots & 0 \\ \vdots & \vdots & \ddots & \vdots \\ 0 & 0 & \ldots & \gamma^i(N) \end{bmatrix} \tag{17}$$

is the diagonal weighting matrix of i-th rule,

$$\tilde{\mathbf{Y}}(\mathbf{k}) = \begin{bmatrix} \tilde{y}(0) \\ \tilde{y}(1) \\ \vdots \\ \tilde{y}(N) \end{bmatrix} \tag{18}$$

is the output vector of fuzzy model.

Considering the output vector of the uncertain dynamic system as

$$\mathbf{Y(k)} = \begin{bmatrix} y(0) \\ y(1) \\ \vdots \\ y(N) \end{bmatrix} \tag{19}$$

applying the least squares algorithm in order to reduce the approximation error between the outputs of the fuzzy model and the uncertain dynamic system, the parameters vector of the sub-models in the consequent space can be estimated as follow:

$$\Theta^1 = (\mathbf{X}^{'} \Gamma^1 \mathbf{X})^{-1} \mathbf{X}^{'} \Gamma^1 \mathbf{Y(k)}$$
$$\Theta^2 = (\mathbf{X}^{'} \Gamma^2 \mathbf{X})^{-1} \mathbf{X}^{'} \Gamma^2 \mathbf{Y(k)}$$
$$\vdots$$
$$\Theta^l = (\mathbf{X}^{'} \Gamma^l \mathbf{X})^{-1} \mathbf{X}^{'} \Gamma^l \mathbf{Y(k)} \tag{20}$$

4   Strategy for Robust Fuzzy Digital PID Controller Design

4.1   Tuning Formulas for Model Based Control via Gain and Phase Margins Specifications

The TS fuzzy inference system to be used as model of the uncertain dynamic system $H(z, \nu)$, presents the $i|^{[i=1,2,\ldots,l]}$-th rule given by:

$R^{(i)}$: IF $\widetilde{y}(k-1)$ IS $F^i_{k|\widetilde{y}(k-1)}$ THEN

$$G^i_P(z) = \frac{K^i}{a^i z^2 + b^i z + c^i}$$

where a^i, b^i, c^i, and K^i are the parameters to be estimated by least square algorithm. The variable $\widetilde{y}(k-1)|^{[t=1,2,\ldots,n]}$ belongs to fuzzy set $F^i_{k|\widetilde{y}(k-1)}$ with a value $\mu^i_{F_{k|\widetilde{y}(k-1)}}$ defined by a membership function $\mu^i_{\widetilde{y}(k-1)} : R \to [0,1]$, with $\mu^i_{F_{k|\widetilde{y}(k-1)}} \in \mu^i_{F_{1|\widetilde{y}(k-1)}}, \mu^i_{F_{2|\widetilde{y}(k-1)}}, \mu^i_{F_{3|\widetilde{y}(k-1)}}, \cdots, \mu^i_{F_{p_{\widetilde{y}(k-1)}|\widetilde{y}(k-1)}}$, where $p_{\widetilde{y}(k-1)}$ is the partitions number of the universe of discourse related to linguistic variable $\widetilde{y}(k-1)$. The TS fuzzy digital PID controller, according to Parallel Distributed Compensation (PDC), presents the $j|^{[j=1,2,\ldots,l]}$-th rule given by:

$R^{(j)}$: IF $\widetilde{y}(k-1)$ IS $F^j_{k|\widetilde{y}(k-1)}$ THEN

$$G^j_c(z) = K^j_P + K^j_I \left(\frac{T(z+1)}{2(z-1)} \right) + K^j_D \left(\frac{2(z-1)}{T(z+1)} \right)$$

where K_P, K_I, and K_D are proportional, integral, and derivative controller gains, respectively. Therefore, the TS fuzzy controller $G_c(\widetilde{y}(k-1), z)$ is a weighted sum of local linear PID sub-controllers:

$$G_c(\tilde{y}(k-1), z) = \sum_{j=1}^{l} \gamma_j(\tilde{y}(k-1)) \times \left(K_P^j + K_I^j \left(\frac{T(z+1)}{2(z-1)} \right) + K_D^j \left(\frac{2(z-1)}{T(z+1)} \right) \right)$$

(21)

and the TS fuzzy model, $G_p(\tilde{y}(k-1), z)$, by weighted sum of local linear sub-models:

$$G_p(\tilde{y}(k-1), z) = \sum_{i=1}^{l} \gamma_i(\tilde{y}(k-1)) \frac{K^i}{a^i z^2 + b^i z + c^i}$$

(22)

In the direct path of closed-loop control system, considering the TS fuzzy model, the time delay $R_2(z)$, and the fuzzy digital PID controller, it has:

$$G_c(\tilde{y}(k-1), z) G_p(\tilde{y}(k-1), z) = \sum_{j=1}^{l} \sum_{i=1}^{l} \gamma_i(\tilde{y}(k-1)) \gamma_j(\tilde{y}(k-1)) \times$$

(23)

$$\times \left(K_P^j + K_I^j \left(\frac{T(z+1)}{2(z-1)} \right) + K_D^j \left(\frac{2(z-1)}{T(z+1)} \right) \right) \times \frac{K^i}{a^i z^2 + b^i z + c^i} R_2(z)$$

The gain and phase margins of the fuzzy control system are given by:

$$arg[G_c(\tilde{y}(k-1), e^{j\omega_p}) G_P(\tilde{y}(k-1), e^{j\omega_p})] = -\pi$$

(24)

$$A_m = \frac{1}{|G_c(\tilde{y}(k-1), e^{j\omega_p}) G_P(\tilde{y}(k-1), e^{j\omega_p})|}$$

(25)

$$|G_c(\tilde{y}(k-1), e^{j\omega_g}) G_P(\tilde{y}(k-1), e^{j\omega_g})| = 1$$

(26)

$$\phi_m = arg[G_c(\tilde{y}(k-1), e^{j\omega_g}) G_P(\tilde{y}(k-1), e^{j\omega_g})] + \pi$$

(27)

where the gain margin is given by (24) and (25), and the phase margin is given by (26) and (27), respectively. The ω_p is called phase crossover frequency and ω_g is called gain crossover frequency.

4.2 Multiobjetive Genetic Strategy for Controller Tuning

The GA proposed in this paper to optimize the parameters K_P^j, K_I^j, and K_D^j of fuzzy digital PID controller in the j-th rule from the gain and phase margins specifications, presents the cost function given by [7]:

$$Custo = |A_{mcal} - A_{mesp}| + |P_{mcal} - P_{mesp}|$$

(28)

where A_{mcal} and A_{mesp} correspond to the gain margin computed and specified, respectively; P_{mcal} and P_{mesp} correspond to the phase margin computed and specified, respectively. The crossover between two chromosomes, used by the multiobjective genetic algorithm generates two new offspring by a simple crossover operator, which performs a weighted sum between the genes of the parents in order to generate the offspring, as follow:

$$
\begin{aligned}
cromossomo_1 &= [p_{m1}, p_{m2}, p_{m3}..., p_{mn}] \\
cromossomo_2 &= [p_{p1}, p_{p2}, p_{p3}..., p_{pn}] \\
d_{new1} &= \beta * p_{mn} + (1 - \beta) * p_{pn} \\
d_{new2} &= \beta * p_{pn} + (1 - \beta) * p_{mn}
\end{aligned}
\tag{29}
$$

where the terms p_{mn} and p_{pn} represent the n genes mother chromosome (cromossomo$_1$) and genes father chromosome (cromossomo$_2$) respectively, d_{new} is new offspring generated from two chromosomes and β is a random value between 0 and 1. The mutation operator used in this paper selects randomly a gene from the chromosome of the population and change its value to any other, within the range of possible values that the gains of the fuzzy controller can take. The best chromosome of the previous generation is kept for the next generation, which is complemented by selected parents and the result of the mutation on the offspring. The stages of evaluation, classification, partner selection, crossover, mutation, and formation of the new population are repeated at each iteration of the algorithm.

5   Computational Results

To illustrate the efficacy of the proposed method, according to sampling time $T = 10ms$, the nominal transfer function is given by:

$$
H(z) = \frac{2.469 * 10^{-5}z^2 + 4.938 * 10^{-5}z + 2.469 * 10^{-5}}{z^2 - 1.975z + 0.9753}
\tag{30}
$$

and the additive uncertainty $\Delta_A(z, \nu)$, used has the following transfer function:

$$
\Delta_A(z, \nu) = \frac{T(z + 1)}{(2 + \nu T)z - 2 + \nu T}
\tag{31}
$$

where ν is a random parameter. The real transfer function of the uncertain dynamic system to be controlled, considering the additive uncertainty, results in the following expression:

$$
H(z, \nu) = \frac{2.469*10^{-5}z^2 + 4.938*10^{-5}z + 2.469*10^{-5}}{z^2 - 1.975z + 0.9753} + \frac{T(z+1)}{(2+\nu T)z - 2 + \nu T}
\tag{32}
$$

In the identification procedure, it was used the input and output signals of the uncertain dynamic system, as shown in Fig. 1, respectively. In order to estimate the fuzzy sets corresponding to input linguistic variable $\tilde{y}(k)$, the FCM algorithm was implemented for 2 clusters, weighting exponent $m=1.2$ and tolerance $\epsilon=0.01$. The efficiency of the identified model and the fuzzy sets obtained are shown in Fig. 2, respectively. From the data input and output of the uncertain dynamic system, taking into account the weights of fuzzy sets, the least squares algorithm was applied for parameter estimation of the consequent sub-models, resulting in

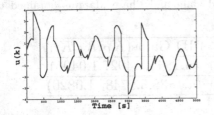 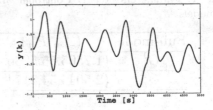

Fig. 1: System Identification: Input Signal and Output Signal, respectively

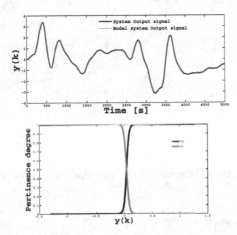

Fig. 2. Model validation and Membership Functions, respectively

the fuzzy model structure of the uncertain dynamic system to be controlled, given by:

$$\text{IF } \widetilde{y}(k-1) \text{ IS F1 , THEN } G_p^1 = \frac{0.0026}{z^2 - 1.2671z + 0.2707} \tag{33}$$

$$\text{IF } \widetilde{y}(k-1) \text{ IS F2 , THEN } G_p^2 = \frac{0.0023}{z^2 - 1.3075z + 0.3113} \tag{34}$$

From the multiobjetive genetic strategy proposed in this paper, specifying the appropriate gain and phase margins for the fuzzy control system, and considering the fuzzy model of the uncertain dynamic system with time delay of $L = 0.5s$, the parameters of the fuzzy digital PID controller were obtained, according to table. 1.The parameters of fuzzy digital PID controller obtained by the multiobjetive genetic strategy proposed was compared to Ziegler-Nichols Method [8].

The multiobjective genetic algorithm used the following parameters: 300 generations, random initial population of 100 chromosomes, each chromosome comprising three genes, the selection rate of 50% and the mutation rate of 30%. It can be seen the efficiency of the proposed methodology in the model based PID controller design, since the gain and phase margins obtained of the fuzzy control system are very close to the specified ones (2,55°). The Bode Diagram of submodels is shown in Fig.3. The temporal response performance of the proposed

Table 1. Parameters of PID Controller and Gain and Phase Margins obtained to sub-models

Sub-model	(A_m, P_m)	PID Gains(K_P, K_I, K_D)
G_p^1	$(1.7505, 55.5960°)$	$(6.1846, 1.4927, 1.0405)$
G_p^2	$(2.5044, 54.7174°)$	$(4.1838, 3.9748, 1.0820)$

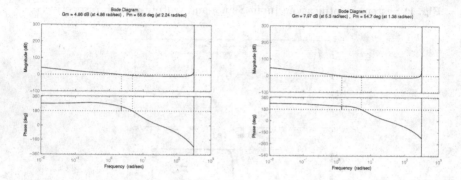

Fig. 3. Bode Diagram of G_p^1 and Bode Diagram of G_p^2

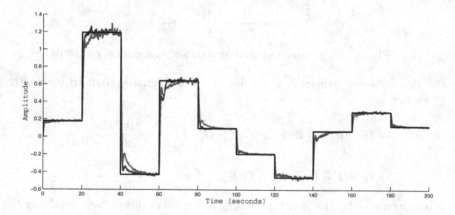

Fig. 4. Temporal response performance of the proposed methodology: black (reference signal), blue (robust fuzzy PID controller), red (ziegler-nichols fuzzy PID controller)

methodology is shown in Fig.4: black (reference signal), blue (robust fuzzy PID controller), red (ziegler-nichols fuzzy PID controller).

6   Conclusions

In this paper, a methodology for robust fuzzy digital PID control design of the uncertain dynamic systems with time delay, was proposed. The control scheme was efficient to ensure, through the multiobjetive genetic approach, that the design criteria are met, the accuracy of the gain and phase margins obtained by the fuzzy control system, as well as the tracking of the reference trajectory.

Acknowledgments. The authors thank to FAPEMA for financial support of this research and to PPGEE-UFMA for encouraging the development of this work.

References

1. Ozdemir, I.Y.A.: Design of Model-Reference Discrete-Time Sliding Mode Power System Stabilizer. In: 2008 International Workshop on Variable Structure Systems (VSS 2008), pp. 325–330. IEEE (2008)
2. Lin, F., Brandt, R.D., Saikalis, G.: Self-tuning of PID Controllers by Adaptive Interaction. In: 2000 American Control Conference (ACC 2000), vol. 5, pp. 3676–3681. IEEE (2000)
3. Okuyama, Y.: Model-Reference Type Discretized PID Control for Continuous Plants. In: 2010 SICE (Society of Instrument and Control Engineers) Annual Conference (SICE 2010), pp. 1402–1405. IEEE (2010)
4. Pahuja, P., Rai, H.M.: Design of Robust Control for Perturbed Systems Using QFT. In: 2nd International Conference on Advanced Computing and Communication Technologies (ACCT 2012), pp. 219–224. IEEE (2012)
5. Lin-ke, Y., Jian-ming, Z., Qi-long, Y., Ji-ming, X., Yan, L.: Fuzzy PID Control for Direct Drive Electro-hydraulic Position Servo System. In: 2011 International Conference on Consumer Electronics, Communications and Networks (CECNet 2011), pp. 370–373. IEEE (2011)
6. Petrov, M., Ganchev, I., Taneva, A.: Fuzzy PID Control of Nonlinear Plants. In: 1st International IEEE Symposium Intelligent Systems (SISy 2011), vol. 1, pp. 30–35. IEEE (2002)
7. Haupt, R.L., Haupt, S.E.: Practical Genetic Algorithms. John Wiley & Sons, Inc. (2004)
8. Jacquot, R.G.: Modern Digital Control Systems. Marcel Dekker Inc. (1995)

Functional State Estimation Methodology Based on Fuzzy Clustering for Complex Process Monitoring

Henry Sarmiento[1,2], Claudia Isaza[3], and Tatiana Kempowsky-Hamon[4,5]

[1] ICARO Research Group, Politécnico Colombiano Jaime Isaza Cadavid, Medellín, Colombia
[2] GEPAR Research Group, Universidad de Antioquia, Medellín, Colombia
phosm984@jaibana.udea.edu.co
[3] MICROE Research Group, Universidad de Antioquia, Medellín, Colombia
cisaza@udea.edu.co
[4] CNRS, LAAS, 7 Avenue du Colonel Roche, F-31400 Toulouse, France
[5] Univ de Toulouse, LAAS, F-31400 Toulouse, France
tkempows@laas.fr

Abstract. In order to prevent faults, many methodologies have been proposed for process monitoring. When it is difficult to obtain a classical model, the use of fuzzy clustering techniques allow the identification of classes that can be associated to the process functional states (normal, alarms, faults). This paper presents a methodology for predicting functional states in order to prevent critical situations. Using the process historical data and combining fuzzy clustering techniques with Markov's chains theory a fuzzy transition matrix is constructed. This matrix called *WFT* is used later online in order to predict the next functional state of the monitored process. The methodology was tested in a boiler subsystem, and a water treatment plant.

Keywords: fuzzy clustering and classification, Markov chains, complex process, functional state prediction.

1 Introduction

In the industrial environment, the human operator or expert can perform multivariable analysis to identify functional states and track the system evolution, in order to correct or prevent possible problems, avoid failures, or restore the system if it fails; this is relatively simple in noncomplex processes, especially if the number of variables is reduced [1]. In complex processes, the monitoring system, based on the identification of the current functional state, allow the operator to quickly understand the current behavior of the system. One of the techniques used to identify the functional states in a process is data clustering [2]. With this technique, complex patterns in the historical data of a process can be identified and associated to functional states, which may be useful for situation assessment, fault diagnosis and as support in the decision making process, in order to find solutions to problems with high complexity variables [3]. To prevent a critical fault, it is interesting to estimate the next functional state of the process at each sample time. In this way, the ability to implement forecasting techniques constitutes a valuable tool for the optimal operation of a process. Recently,

J. Pavón et al. (Eds.): IBERAMIA 2012, LNAI 7637, pp. 340–349, 2012.
© Springer-Verlag Berlin Heidelberg 2012

advances in pattern recognition have resulted in the development of methods for state identification based on features extracted from specific signals. Statistical Process Control (SPC) [4], Hidden Markov Models (HMM) [5, 6], and Fuzzy Transition Probabilities (*FTP*) [7] are among the methods used for the estimation of states. In the last few years Artificial Intelligence (*AI*) methods such as Neural Networks (*NN*), Fuzzy Logic (*FL*), Genetic and Evolutionary Computation (*GC*, *EC*), and Support Vector Machines (*SVM*) have increasingly been used for monitoring complex processes [8]. In general, the most used methods are based on, or include, probabilities or fuzzy sets for estimating functional states.

FTP [7] combines the effectiveness of methods based on probabilities and that of methods based on fuzzy sets, but it only works to detect progressive failures. These failures are associated with degrading processes.

This article introduces a new methodology which allows estimating, for the next sample time, the fuzzy membership degrees of the process to the different functional states. The proposed methodology is based on the *FTP* . In online mode and using the estimated membership degrees the next functional state is predicted. This estimation becomes vital for the process operator in determining the actions to take in order to maintain the required control, security and reliability of the process.

Section 2 describes the methodological proposal of *FTP* (the basis for the new proposal). A detailed description of the new prediction method is presented in Sect. 3. The results obtained by applying the methodology to two real processes, a boiler subsystem and a water treatment plant, are analyzed in Sect. 4. Finally, Sect. 5 includes conclusions and future work.

2   *FTP* Based on Markov Chains for the Monitoring of Industrial Processes

According to Du and Yeung [7], it is possible to obtain the Fuzzy Transition Probabilities (*FTP*) starting from a representative historical dataset of a process.

The methodology includes two parts: First, an offline training allows to obtain fuzzy probabilities [9] associated with every sample and the *FTP*. Secondly, the *FTP* is used to estimate the next state. The second part is an online step.

Offline, a specific analogy is proposed in which *FTP*s take the same structure as the probability of transition of Markov chains theory [10]. That is:

$$FP_j(S_{t+1}) = \sum_{k=1}^{m} FP_{kj} * FP_k(S_t), \ j = 1,2,...,m. \tag{1}$$

where, $FP_j(S_{t+1})$ is the fuzzy probability estimated for sample $t+1$ to state j. This value can be associated with the probability of the process to change to state j at the next time sample $t+1$. $FP_k(S_t)$ is the Fuzzy Probability of the current measurement vector to belong to functional state (class) k. FP_{kj} is the fuzzy transition probability from state k to state j, and m is the number of states in the process.

The specified condition in (2) must be satisfied.

$$1 = \sum_{j=1}^{m} FP_{kj}, \ k = 1,2,...,m. \tag{2}$$

In particular, the methodology was developed for processes where there is no backward transition. This characteristic was included in the mathematical formulation changing the upper limit of the sum as $k=j$. The proposal of Du and Yeung is limited to processes where there is no return to previous states, and defined according to equation (3)

$$FP_j(S_{t+1}) = \sum_{k=1}^{j} FP_{kj} * FP_k(S_t), \ j = 1,2, ..., m.   \quad (3)$$

Based on (3), a group of linear equations is obtained, where FP_{kj} is solved by means of the Least Squares (LS) method. Then, by normalizing the solution, the transition probability function can be found.

Online, the proposed methodology in Du and Yeung [7], allows the calculation of the fuzzy probabilities for the current sample, $FP_k(S_t)$ and, using the FP_{kj} found offline, the fuzzy probabilities for the next sample $FP_j(S_{t+1})$ (estimation) is obtained by evaluating (1). And, according to the maximum fuzzy probability in $FP_j(S_{t+1})$, the estimated state is defined. FTP methodology was specially oriented toward mechanical systems with degrading states [11].

Since, most of industrial processes present the possibility to return to previous states, the FTP Methodology is not applicable in a general form, and in addition, this methodology depends on the classification method proposed in Du and Yeung [7].

3   Fuzzy Memberships Prediction Method

In order to predict (in online mode) the next functional state for the monitored system, a general methodology based on fuzzy clustering methods is proposed. This approach is based on the FTP theory presented in Sect. 2. This new algorithm allows to predict the fuzzy membership degrees associated with sample at time $t+1$, i.e. $\mu_k(S_{t+1})$ $(k=1,2,...,m)$, based only on the current fuzzy membership degrees at time t, i.e. $\mu_k(S_t)$ $(k=1,2,...,m)$. These fuzzy membership degrees are obtained using any fuzzy clustering or classification algorithm. The estimated functional state at $t+1$ is associated with the maximum value of the membership degrees.

The methodology has two principal steps: an offline training stage to obtain what we have called Weights of Fuzzy Transition (WFT), and an online stage to predict the next functional state of the process.

In Fig. 1, the steps of the proposed method are presented. Black lines indicate the sequence of the steps to follow both offline training and online monitoring. Dotted lines indicate the information obtained in a specific offline step which is required in an online step.

In the training stage, to estimate the WFT matrix, the membership degrees of historical data to the functional states of the process are used. These membership degrees are obtained using any fuzzy clustering algorithm. For this proposal, in a similar way to the FTP theory, we propose to work the Markov chains with the historical fuzzy membership degrees; then, (1) is modified as follows:

$$\mu_j(S_{t+1}) = \sum_{k=1}^{m} WFT_{kj} * \mu_k(S_t), \ j = 1,2, ..., m   \quad (4)$$

The above proposal is supported by the theory presented by Dubois and Prade [12]. They demonstrated a bijective relation (bijective mapping) between a probability measure p_i and a possibility measure π_i (or membership degree). Then, it is possible to calculate the probabilities in terms of possibility measures (5), and the possibilities in terms of probability measures (5).

$$\forall_i = 1, ..., n \quad p_i = \sum_{j=i}^{n} \frac{1}{j}(\pi_j - \pi_{j+1}); \quad \forall_i \quad \pi_i = \sum_{j=1}^{n} min(p_i, p_j) \quad (5)$$

Thus, the behavior of discrete event systems expressed in probabilities and/or possibilities –where the probabilities are obtained from the possibilities or vice versa– preserves the same pattern and relationship between values.

It should be noted that in equation (4), unlike the proposed equation in Du and Yeung [7], the sum is extended to $k=m$ in the upper limit. In this way, the calculation of bidirectional transitions between functional states is included. Based on (4) a group of linear equations –(8),(9) and (10)– is constructed, and a solution for *WFT* is obtained using Least Squares Method (LSM), since the solution of the linear system with more equations than unknown values may have multiple solutions, then we restraint the solution to values equal or greater than zero. In equation (6), *x* corresponds to *WFT* vector, and matrix *A* and vector *b* correspond to fuzzy membership degrees organized according to equations (7) and (8).

$$E = \|A * x' - b\|, \quad \forall x' \geq 0 \quad (6)$$

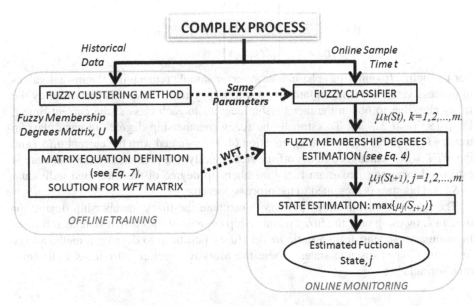

Fig. 1. General diagram of the prediction methodology

In the offline stage, in order to obtain the fuzzy membership degrees matrix, U, any fuzzy clustering method can be applied to the historical data (e.g. Fuzzy C-Means –*FCM*–, Gustafson-Kessel –*GK*–, Learning Algorithm for Multivariable Data Analysis –*LAMDA*–, among others)[13, 14]. Where, μ_{rk} is an element of matrix *U*, *r* corresponds to the measurement vector for each sample ($r=1,2,...,N$ where *N* is the number of samples) and *k* corresponds to the class ($k=1,2,...,m$). These membership degrees μ_{rk} allow to construct the system of equations obtained from (4).

The matrix representation for equation (4) is given by equation (7). It is solved to obtain the Weights of Fuzzy Transition (*WFT* vector).

$$[\mu(S_{2...N})] = [\mu(S_{1...(N-1)})] * [WFT_{kj}] \tag{7}$$

$$\text{where, } [\mu(S_{2...N})] = \begin{bmatrix} \mu_1(S_2) \\ \vdots \\ \mu_1(S_N) \\ \vdots \\ \mu_m(S_2) \\ \vdots \\ \mu_m(S_N) \end{bmatrix}, [WFT_{kj}] = \begin{bmatrix} WFT_{11} \\ \vdots \\ WFT_{1m} \\ \vdots \\ WFT_{m1} \\ \vdots \\ WFT_{mm} \end{bmatrix} \tag{8}$$

and,

$$[\mu(S_{1...(N-1)})] = \begin{bmatrix} \begin{vmatrix} \vec{A_1} & \vec{0} & \cdots & \vec{0} \\ \vec{0} & \vec{A_1} & \cdots & \vec{0} \\ \vdots & \vdots & \ddots & \vdots \\ \vec{0} & \vec{0} & \cdots & \vec{A_1} \end{vmatrix} \begin{vmatrix} \vec{A_2} & \vec{0} & \cdots & \vec{0} \\ \vec{0} & \vec{A_2} & \cdots & \vec{0} \\ \vdots & \vdots & \ddots & \vdots \\ \vec{0} & \vec{0} & \cdots & \vec{A_2} \end{vmatrix} \cdots \begin{vmatrix} \vec{A_m} & \vec{0} & \cdots & \vec{0} \\ \vec{0} & \vec{A_m} & \cdots & \vec{0} \\ \vdots & \vdots & \ddots & \vdots \\ \vec{0} & \vec{0} & \cdots & \vec{A_m} \end{vmatrix} \end{bmatrix} \tag{9}$$

$$\vec{0} = \begin{bmatrix} 0 \\ 0 \\ \vdots \\ 0 \end{bmatrix}, \vec{A_i} = \begin{bmatrix} \mu_i(S_1) \\ \mu_i(S_2) \\ \vdots \\ \mu_i(S_{N-1}) \end{bmatrix} \quad i = 1,2,...m.$$

For the online (monitoring) phase, a new vector sample (containing the instant values of process variables) is taken into the monitoring system, where it is processed by the fuzzy classifier to obtain the membership degrees to each class at the current time t, i.e. $\mu_k(S_t)$ $(k=1,2,...,m)$. To estimate the fuzzy membership degrees to each class in time $t+1$, i.e. $\mu_j(S_{t+1})$ $(j=1,2,...,m)$, equation (4) is evaluated with the current $\mu_k(S_t)$ and the *WFT* vector calculated in the offline step. Finally, the predicted functional state is estimated using the maximum fuzzy membership degree of the estimated individual $\mu_j(S_{t+1})$. This state is presented to the process operator.

The proposed methodology permits to estimate the fuzzy membership degree for time $t+1$, by using only the fuzzy membership degrees of the current sample at time t. In summary, we start from a static model (fuzzy partition) to develop a methodology for estimation of discrete states, where the Markov structure introduces a discrete-time formulation.

4   Application in Industrial Processes

The proposed method was tested in two complex processes: a boiler subsystem –where the methodology application is explained in detail–, and a water treatment plant [15]. *LAMDA* [13] was used as the fuzzy clustering algorithm, because this algorithm has been successfully applied to the monitoring of industrial processes [15-18], nevertheless any other fuzzy clustering method can be used.

4.1   Boiler Subsystem

The steam generator was designed as a scaled version to pilot a real steam generator of a nuclear plant. Operation of the process is the following: the feed water flow is generated by a pump that propels water to a boiler. To maintain constant water level in the boiler, an On–Off controller operates via the pump. Therefore, the heat power value of the boiler will depend on the steam accumulator pressure. When the accumulator pressure drops below a minimum value, the heat resistance that gives the maximum heat power is activated, and when achieving a maximum pressure the heat resistance is cut off to maintain the pressure in the set-point. The historical data contains 601 training samples, 1800 test samples, and, 5 descriptor variables, corresponding to physical measures: the feed water flow, heat power, boiler pressure, boiler level and output steam flow. With the objective of homogenizing the influence of the own dimensions of the variables, the data is normalized with respect to the maximum and minimum value of each variable [18].

The fuzzy membership degrees (matrix U) for each historical sample were obtained by applying LAMDA algorithm. Five classes were identified by the fuzzy clustering method. Each sample was classified according to their maximum membership degree. In Table 1, the 5 resulting classes were associated to functional states after previous validation (100% clustering performance) by the process expert.

Table 1. Subsystem of boiler: states

Class	State
C1	Normal Operation
C2, C3	Pressure Regulation
C4	Level Regulation
C5	Level and Pressure Regulation

Table 2. Estimation for sample 200 in training database

$\mu_k(S_t)$	$\mu_j(S_{t+1})$	Estimated $\mu_j(S_{t+1})$
$\mu_1(S_{199})$=0,2030	$\mu_1(S_{200})$=0,2030	$\mu_1(S_{200})$=0,2116
$\mu_2(S_{199})$=0,7901	$\mu_2(S_{200})$=0,7883	$\mu_2(S_{200})$=0,7769
$\mu_3(S_{199})$=0,5357	$\mu_3(S_{200})$=0,5338	$\mu_3(S_{200})$=0,5382
$\mu_4(S_{199})$=0,2332	$\mu_4(S_{200})$=0,2305	$\mu_4(S_{200})$=0,2305
$\mu_5(S_{199})$=0,2611	$\mu_5(S_{200})$=0,2604	$\mu_5(S_{200})$=0,2611
Assigned, Expected State: C2.	Assigned Expected State: C2.	Estimated Expected State: C2.

The expected classes (given by the expert) are shown in Fig. 2a), where the horizontal axis in each point corresponds to each of the samples for the database and the vertical axis corresponds to the classes which are defined according to the maximum membership degree given by the classifier. For comparison, the x-axis in the figures of Estimated classes is defined from $t=2$ up to N, this is necessary since the prediction function needs an initial value sample. Based on matrix U, values are assigned to (7). The WFT vector is then calculated solving (7). With the resulting WFT, the next functional state is estimated.

To verify the performance of the proposed method, every single sample of the training database is taken as if it was the sample at time t, $\mu_k(S_t)$, and the next fuzzy membership degrees $\mu_j(S_{t+1})$ are estimated for time $t+1$ by evaluating (4). Taking the maximum $\mu_j(S_{t+1})$ the estimated state is defined. The predicted states for each sample of the training database are shown in Fig. 2b).

As an example for the training database, in Table 2, vector $\mu_k(S_t)$ –for sample 199–, vector $\mu_j(S_{t+1})$ –for sample 200–, and the estimated vector $\mu_j(S_{t+1})$ –for sample 200– are shown in the first, second and third column respectively.

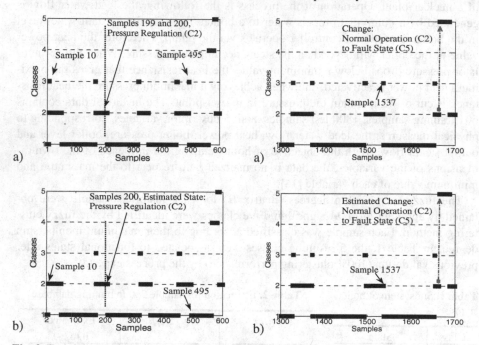

Fig. 2. Training database. a) Expected, b) Estimated classes.

Fig. 3. Test database (1300 - 1700 samples). a) Expected, b) Estimated classes.

In the last row of Table 2, the assigned states according to the resulting maximum fuzzy membership degrees, and the expected state by the expert are presented. Pressure Regulation (C2) is the estimated state for sample 200 based on sample 199. The estimation corresponds to the expected assignation (see Fig. 2). For the training database (600 samples), a comparison between the expected states (see Fig. 2a) and the estimated states (see Fig. 2b) was made. There were only 2 errors in the estimated states; samples 10 and 495 were expected in C2, but estimated in C3. Nevertheless C2 and C3 are both pressure regulation. Then, *WFT* was used to estimate the state at *t+1*, by taking each of the samples of the test database as the state at instant *t*. The test database, with 1799 samples, includes the transition from "Pressure Regulation" C2 to "Fault" C5 not present in the training database, and on the contrary state C4 "Regulation Level" is not present. For the test database, expected states (see Fig. 3a) and estimated states (see Fig. 3b) were compared. There was only one error. Sample 1537 was estimated in "pressure regulation" C2 but it was expected in C3 which corresponds to the same "Pressure regulation". Moreover, the transitions "Normal Operation" C2 to "Fault" C5 were correctly estimated, and as expected no prediction to state C4 was registered. The estimation was correct in 98.8% of the cases within the training database, and 99.83% of the cases within the test database.

4.2   Water Treatment Plant

The "SMAPA" water treatment plant (Tuxtla-Mexico), has a nominal capacity to process 800 l/s per day. Raw water is collected from the river "Grijalva" and pumped to the plant. The water treatment plant includes two main processes, clarification and filtration. The behavior of the plant depends on the turbidity parameters and the consumption of chemical agents [17].

The training database is built up using 105 samples. Four variables were chosen to monitor the process: turbidity at the decanters input, filter backwashing frequency, the coagulant added dose, and the difference between input and output turbidity. The data for testing contained 105 samples. In the training stage –using *LAMDA* algorithm– 6 classes were identified. The classes were associated with states according to Table 3.

Only 5 classes were validated by the expert in the process, i.e. 98% of clustering performance was obtained because two samples were misclassified in C6(see Fig. 4a).

Table 3. Water plant: functional states

Class	C1	C2	C3	C4	C5	C6
State	Normal Op. (end of rain)	Normal Op	Alarm	High sludge	Critical state	Spurious class

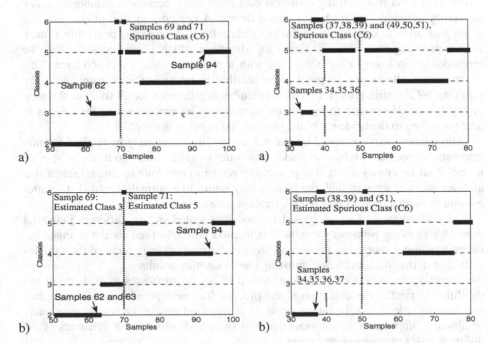

Fig. 4. Training database (50-100 samples). a) Classifier, b) Estimated.

Fig. 5. Test database (30-80 samples). a) Classifier, b) Estimated.

Applying the proposed methodology for the training database (104 samples), the estimated states are shown in Fig. 4b). There were three errors. Sample 62 and 63 were estimated in "Normal operation" C2 (samples expected in "Alarm state" C3), sample 94 was estimated in "High sludge" C4 (sample expected in "Critical state" C5). Sample 70 was estimated in "Spurious Class" C6 (sample expected in "Critical state" C5). Whereas sample 69 was estimated in C3 "Alarm" but expected in Spurious class" C6, and sample 71 which was also expected in "Spurious Class" C6 was estimated in C5 "Critical state", thus avoiding the undesired "spurious class".

This same situation was evidenced in the results obtained for the test database. Here, data samples 37, 38, 39, 49, 50 and 51 were classified in the "Spurious class" C6 (see Fig. 5a), but by using the proposed method, only samples 38, 39 and 51 were estimated in the "Spurious class" C6. (see Fig. 5b).

Classes according to fuzzy classification and estimated classes for the test database are presented in Fig. 5a) and Fig. 5b) respectively. The global estimation was correct in 98% of the cases within the training database, and in 92% of the cases within the validation set.

5   Conclusions

A methodology for functional state prediction of complex industrial processes is proposed in this paper. This methodology is based on the calculation of a Weighted Fuzzy Transition matrix using historical data from the process and combining fuzzy clustering techniques with Markov chains theory. A key contribution of our proposal is the possibility to use any fuzzy clustering/classification technique providing a fuzzy membership degrees matrix U. This is an advantage which allows implementing the methodology in a very simple way and with a relatively short execution time. This characteristic allows our proposal to be feasible in an online implementation. The resulting WFT matrix provides predicted membership degrees for all functional states, giving useful information to the process operator so he can determine the actions to take according to the tendency of the process that is being observed.

The methodology proposed by Du and Yeung in [7] can only be applied for non renewable processes, we have extended it in order to generalize it so it can be applied to industrial processes where it is possible to return to previous functional states (i.e. after an alarm or a minor fault the process may return to a normal/degraded state after passing through a transition or reconfiguration state).

The performance of the proposed method was tested in two different industrial processes showing promising results. The method correctly predicts the changes between functional states. For the second process the methodology reduced the samples classified in the spurious class, improving the monitoring results.

Currently, the methodology is being tested in "slow" processes to evaluate its capabilities to predict the evolution of the process (i.e. next possible state) more than one time sample ahead. In future works, it is intended to use the results previously obtained, to implement an automata that will show and estimate the dynamics of the different states of complex processes.

Acknowledgements. This work was supported by the agreement COLCIENCIAS (COL) – ECOSNord (FRA), and CODI Universidad de Antioquia (COL).

References

1. Isermann, R.: Fault-Diagnosis Systems: An Introduction from Fault Detection to Fault Tolerance. Springer, New York (2006)
2. Zio, E., Di Maio, F.: Processing Dynamic Scenarios from a Reliability Analysis of a Nuclear Power Plant Digital Instrumentation and Control System. Annals of Nuclear Energy 36(9), 1386–1399 (2009)
3. Aguilar-Martín, J.: Inteligencia Artificial para la Supervisión de Procesos Industriales. ULA, Mérida (2007)
4. De Noord, O.E.: Improvements to Multivariate Data Analysis and Monitoring of Batch Processes by Multilevel Methods. Journal of Chemometrics 26(6), 340–344 (2012)
5. Tobon-Mejia, D.A., Medjaher, K., Zerhouni, N., Tripot, G.: HMM for Failure Diagnostic and Prognostic. In: IEEE Prognostics and System Health Management Conference (PHM 2011), pp. 1–8 (2011)
6. Daidone, A., Di Giandomenico, F., Chiaradonna, S., Bondavalli, A.: Hidden Markov Models as a Support for Diagnosis: Formalization of the Problem and Synthesis of the Solution. In: 25th IEEE Symp. on Reliable Distributed Systems (SRDS 2006), pp. 245–256 (2006)
7. Du, R., Yeung, K.: Fuzzy Transition Probability(ANew Method for Monitoring Progressive Faults. Part 1 – The Theory. Eng. App. of Art. Intell. 17(5), 457–467 (2004)
8. Roth, J., Djurdjanovic, D., Yang, X.: Quality and Inspection of Machining Operations: Tool Condition Monitoring. J. Manufacturing Science and Engineering 132, 1–16 (2010)
9. Baldwin, J., Martin, T., Pilsworth, B.: Firl, Fuzzy and Evidential Reasoning in Artificial Intelligence. John Wiley & Sons, Inc., New York (1995)
10. Ross, S.M.: Stochastic Processes. John Wiley & Sons, Inc., New York (1996)
11. Du, R., Yeung, K.: Fuzzy Transition Probability – A New Method for Monitoring Progressive Faults. Part 2 – Applications. Eng. App. of Art. Intell. 19(2), 145–155 (2006)
12. Dubois, D., Prade, H.: Unfair Coins and Necessity Measures – Towards a Possibilistic Interpretation of Histograms. Fuzzy Sets and Systems 10(1), 15–20 (1983)
13. Aguilar-Martín, J., Lopez De Mantaras, R.: The Process of Classification and Learning the Meaning of Linguistic Descriptors of Concepts. In: Gupta, M.M., Sanchez, E. (eds.) Approximate Reasoning in Decision Analysis, pp. 165–175. North-Holland (1982)
14. Ali, A., Karmakar, G., Dooley, L.: Review on Fuzzy Clustering Algorithms. J. of Advanced Computations 2(3), 169–181 (2008)
15. Sarmiento, H., Isaza, C.: Identification and Estimation of Functional States in Drinking Water Plant Based on Fuzzy Clustering. In: Bogle, D., Fairweather, M. (eds.) 22nd European Symposium on Computer Aided Process Engineering (ESCAPE 2012), pp. 1317–1321. Elsevier (2012)
16. Hedjazi, L., Kempowsky-Hamon, T., Despènes, L., Le Lann, M., Elgue, S., Aguilar-Martin, J.: Sensor Placement and Fault Detection Using and Efficient Fuzzy Feature Selection Approach. In: 49th IEEE Conf. on Decision and Control (CDC 2010), pp. 6827–6832 (2010)
17. Isaza, C., Diez-Lledo, E., Hernandez de Leon, H., Aguilar-Martin, J., LeLann, M.V.: Decision Method for Functional States Validation in a Drinking Water Plant. In: 10th IFAC Computer Appl. in Biotechnology (CAB 2007), pp. 359–364 (2007)
18. Kemposky, T., Subias, A., Aguilar-Martin, J.: Process Situation Assessment – From a Fuzzy Partition to a Finite State Machine. Eng. App. of Art. Intell. 19(5), 461–477 (2006)

Unsupervised Feature Selection Based on Fuzzy Clustering for Fault Detection of the Tennessee Eastman Process

C. Bedoya, C. Uribe, and C. Isaza

Dept. of Electronic Enginnering, Universidad de Antioquia, Colombia
{cabedoya,cesar.uribe,cisaza}@udea.edu.co

Abstract. The large number of components involved in the operation of industrial processes increases its complexity, together with the likelihood of failure or unusual behaviors. In some cases, industrial processes solely depend on plant operator experience to prevent and identify failures. It has been shown that automatic identification of failures within functional states of the process brings support to the operator performance, reducing the incidence of accidents and defective products. However, increasing use of automatic measurement systems generates large amounts of information that hinders fault detection. Obtaining adequate fault identification systems requires the use of the most informative variables to cope with large amounts of data by intelligently removing redundant and irrelevant variables. In this paper, an unsupervised methodology based on fuzzy clustering is applied on fault identification of the Tennessee Eastman process. Results show that an optimal variable subset improves the classification percentages and avoid the use of unnecessary variables.

Keywords: feature selection, fault detection, fuzzy clustering, Tennessee Eastman process.

1 Introduction

In the absence of a mechanistic model it is possible to detect abnormal situations in complex industrial processes using classification techniques. Fuzzy logic presents the advantage to express the membership degree of an observation (historical data) to several classes or functional states [1]. But in large amounts of data, variables are usually highly correlated with non-linear behavior which hinders data-based identification and isolation of faults. Appropriate fault identification requires the most relevant and informative variables to be used.

Feature selection is often used as a way to reduce the high dimensionality of the data, improving storage requirements, computational cost and fault identification results [2]. Several authors have proposed methods for feature selection in complex industrial processes: Patterson et al. [3], proposed a methodology for Feedback Variable Selection for Control of Semiconductor Manufacturing Processes. Fei and Huan [4], proposed a feature selection method based on the spatial distribution of subgraph features in graph data and apply their method on several chemical processes. Jun et al.

J. Pavón et al. (Eds.): IBERAMIA 2012, LNAI 7637, pp. 350–360, 2012.

[5], make use of partial least squares regression for variable selection in an Automobile Assembly process. These cases show the utility of feature selection methods in a wide area of real life applications.

The Tennessee Eastman process, developed by Downs and Vogel [6] and proposed in 1993 has been widely used as study case in the development of methodologies for process monitoring. Shi and Huang [7] proposed a wavelet BP neural network structure for monitoring and fault detection of this process. Hsu and Chen [8] performed the fault detection for this process by using a support vector machine. Mao et al. [9], make use of principal component analysis (PCA) and sliding windows to detect failures in this process.

Some authors have also proposed feature selection procedures for the Tennessee Eastman Process: Senoussi et al. [10] similarly to Wu and Wang [11] selected 3 fault states and found the number of features needed to detect properly those 3 faults. Da Silva et al. [12] developed individual classifiers for each fault and determined the number of variables required to detect each fault individually.

This paper, focus on feature selection for fault identification of the Tennessee Eastman Process using a fuzzy clustering methodology [13], and a wrapper feature selection method [14, 15] to reduce the number of descriptors provided by the process. The method founds a minimum number of features required to detect a greater or equal number of faults than those found in previous works. It takes into account all process variables and it does not require isolating faults individually and developing particular classifiers to each one in order to obtain a better classification.

In the Tennessee Eastman Process all faults cannot be detected with the same effort, there are some fault states more difficult to identify than others. Five of the most commonly used and less difficult to identify failures were selected to expose the performance of the wrapper feature selection method, then five of the most rare and difficult to identify failures were selected to demonstrate its efficiency.

This paper is presented as follows. Section 2 explains the wrapper feature selection method; Sect. 3 presents the application to the Tennessee Eastman process, as well as the analysis of experimental results and discussion. Finally in Sect. 4 conclusions and future work are presented.

2 Feature Selection Method

There are different approaches in feature selection; the most used are the wrapper and the filter [16]. A wrapper approach is based on the idea that a subset of features obtained with an induction algorithm guided by some performance measure leads to a better feature subset [16]. The feature subset with the highest performance is chosen as the final set on which to run the induction algorithm. The filter approach selects features using a preprocessing step, even though they are usually faster. The main disadvantage of this approach is that it ignores the effects of the selected feature subset on the performance of the induction algorithm [16] (in this case a fuzzy clustering algorithm).

Recently a wrapper approach guided by a clustering algorithm was proposed in [14, 15] capable of finding a reduced number features to identify functional states of a process, but it was limited in its applications. Figure 1 shows a scheme of the presented wrapper feature selection method which performs a partially directed search based on quality measures. First, the process data set (*V*) is preprocessed, obtaining a normalized and transformed matrix (*V'*). The obtained matrix (*V'*) is divided in *n* subsets each described by *n-1* of the *n* available descriptors or features. These subsets are processed one by one by the clustering algorithm obtaining the membership degree matrix *U* for each case (which contains the membership degrees of each vector or individual to each class). The obtained partitions are evaluated through a cluster validation index, obtaining a value *Q* that measures the partition quality. An optimization algorithm is used to improve the results of the clustering method by trying to find a better partition for each feature subset using only the membership degree matrix *U* (given by any fuzzy clustering method) and the performance index *Q*. *Q* is then used as criterion to eliminate the least informative and more irrelevant feature. The remaining features are used as a base set for the next iteration.

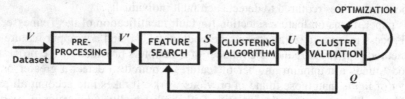

Fig. 1. Wrapper feature selection method

2.1   Preprocessing

In most cases, the clustering algorithm does not yield good classifications when the pure signals taken from the process are used directly in it. The Tennessee Eastman process faults are usually characterized by changes in the power of the signals, thus a power calculation in a sliding window (eq. 1) was chosen. Where $x(i, n)$ is the datum i belonging to the feature n, n is the number of feature of the original feature set $FS(\mathfrak{R}^n)$ and W is the window size. Sliding windows were used previously for the calculation of this kind of statistics in the Tennessee Eastman process [7, 9]. This prepossessing was selected because emphasizes the signal amplitude changes.

$$P(i,n) = \frac{\sum_{i=1}^{W}|x(i,n)|^2}{W} \tag{1}$$

2.2   Feature Search

To eliminate the less informative features it is necessary to implement a search strategy which organizes the subset distribution such as Sequential Backward Elimination (SBE) [17]. In SBE the feature subset (*S*) starts with all the *n* features available. The partition given by the clustering algorithm is evaluated with all the *n* variables through the performance index *Q*. Then, subsets of *n-1* variables are created where each data subset has a single variable eliminated. Each data subset is evaluated by the performance index; the variable that is not present in the data subset with the highest

Q is eliminated. The process is repeated iteratively with all the remaining variables until all the n variables are eliminated. SBE is a directed search algorithm and it does not perform an exhaustive search with all possible combinations among variables, thus giving suboptimal solutions. SBE is part of a greater category called sequential search algorithms; they add or subtract features by using a local search strategy. However there are some other strategies like exponential (e.g. branch and bound) and randomized (e.g. genetic algorithms) that are less inaccurate but require additional exigencies [18]. SBE gives suboptimal solutions due to its hill climbing search strategy. This local search strategy does not guarantee to find the best possible solution since the wrapper algorithm may be stack on a local optimum. Despite all its weaknesses, SBE becomes in a good search algorithm because of its simplicity and significant results (even if they are suboptimal).

2.3   Clustering Algorithm

A clustering algorithm is used to obtain the data clusters associated to the functional states of the process. Wrapper feature selection methods allow the use of any existing fuzzy clustering algorithm because the feature relevance analysis depends only on the membership degree matrix. In this work the LAMDA methodology is used as fuzzy clustering algorithm, but it is possible to use any other fuzzy clustering method.

LAMDA (Learning Algorithm for Multivariate Data Analysis) is an unsupervised fuzzy classification methodology [13] that has been used for detection of states, faults and monitoring tasks in complex industrial processes [14, 15, 19]. It does not require the number of classes as an input parameter as most of the fuzzy clustering algorithms and it works with data that can be quantitative (numeric) and/or qualitative (symbolic) [19]. This clustering algorithm is based on the use of marginal information available by means logical connectors to their respective representation in classes, groups or concepts such qualitative as quantitative. The LAMDA methodology generates and recognizes classes using as criterion the global adequacy degree (GAD) of each individual to each class given by the logical connectors.

The marginal adequacy degree (MAD) which is the membership degree of each descriptor of each individual to each class is calculated using a Gaussian possibility function (see eq. 2).

$$MAD(x_j/u_{kj}, \sigma_{kj}) = e^{\frac{1}{2}\left(\frac{x_j - \mu_{kj}}{\sigma_{kj}}\right)^2} \tag{2}$$

Where x_j is the individual (one vector V in one t-sample with the values of the j variables in that t-sample), u_{kj} and σ_{kj} are the mean and standard deviation values for each descriptor j in each k class respectively.

After calculating the membership degree of each individual to each generated class, the global adequacy degree (GAD) is calculated using aggregation rules previously established by logical connectors (see eq. 3), and taking into account the contribution of all descriptors.

$$GAD(x/c_k) = \alpha T(MAD(x_1/c_k), ... MAD(x_n/c_k))$$
$$+ (1 - \alpha)S(MAD(x_1/c_k), ... MAD(x_n/c_k)) \tag{3}$$

Where á is an exigency index, 0<á<1, $T(f_1, ... f_n)$ is the t-norm $(min(f_1, ... f_n)$ for this case), $S(f_1, ... f_n)$ is the s-norm $(max(f_1, ... f_n)$ for this case) and n is the number of features.

When the algorithm starts, only one class has been predefined and it is known as the Non-Information class (NIC). This class gives the same adequacy degree to all data. The first individual is classified in the NIC class because it is considered unrecognized, then, a new class is created and initialized with the NIC parameters, modified by the data values as additional information. Similarly, if an individual has a membership degree lower than the NIC threshold it cannot be classified within a class, it is put in the NIC and a new class is created. If an individual can be classified within a class, the mean and standard deviation values of the class are updated to contain the new entry value.

The membership degree matrix is the matrix which contains all the classified vectors GADs.

2.4   Performance Index

For each group of selected variables (at each iteration), the cluster validity index CV, (see eq. 4), measures the quality of the cluster in terms of the separation among classes and its data dispersion.

$$CV = \frac{D_{is}}{N} \cdot D^*{}_{min} \cdot \sqrt{K} \tag{4}$$

Where N is the number of data samples available, K is the total number of classes, D_{is} is the partition dispersion (eq. 5) and D^* is the ultrametric distance between the fuzzy set A and the fuzzy set B (see eq. 6).

$$\cdot D_{is} = \sum_{k=1}^{K} 1 - \frac{\sum_{n=1}^{N} \delta_{k,n} \cdot e^{\delta_{k,n}}}{N \cdot \mu_{M,k} \cdot e^{\mu_{M,k}}} \tag{5}$$

Where $\delta_{k,n} = \mu_{M,k} - \mu_{k,n}$, $\mu_{M,k} = max(\mu_{k,n}) \forall n, n \in [1, N]$ y $\mu_{k,n}$ is the membership degree of the individual n to class k.

$$D^*(A, B) = 1 - \frac{\sum_{n=1}^{N} min\,(\mu_{A,k}, \mu_{B,k})}{\sum_{n=1}^{N} max\,(\mu_{A,k}, \mu_{B,k})} \tag{6}$$

The partition with most compacted and separated classes is the partition with the highest CV value.

The CV only depends on the membership degree matrix (this contains the membership degrees of each data to each class). CV depends neither on the data values nor on the geometric structure of the classes, which makes it independent of the clustering method [20].

2.5   Optimization Algorithm

This algorithm only depends on the properties of the membership degree matrix provided by the clustering algorithm and the separation among classes [20]. It measures the partition quality with a performance index (CV) and merges the two most similar classes, then the CV is calculated again, and the process continues until a partition with only two classes is obtained. To estimate the most similar classes, the fuzzy similarity measure $G(A, B)$ is used (see eq. 7). The two most similar classes are merged using maximum S-norm. Finally, the highest CV value is used to select the best partition.

$$G(A, B) = 1 - D^*(A, B) \tag{7}$$

The optimization algorithm is an optional stage and it may not be included in the wrapper feature selection method. When it is not included, the CV is calculated with the partition given by the variable subset. When the optimization algorithm is used, the CV is calculated with the optimal partition.

3   Application to the Tennessee Eastman Process

The Tennessee Eastman Process (TEP) is a benchmark process control problem developed by the Eastman Kodak Company in collaboration with the University of Tennessee, to be a tool in the study, research, evaluation, and improvement of process control technologies [6]. This process describes a complete chemical plant with 5 main subsections that produces two exothermic chemical reactions starting from four gaseous reactants.

The TEP has 53 variables, 12 manipulated and 41 measured variables (22 variables responsible of continuous measurements for the process and 19 compositions). All variables and their names are shown in Table 1.

Table 1. Tennessee Eastman process features

#	Name	#	Name	#	Name
1	A feed	19	Stripper steam flow	37	D Product analysis
2	D feed	20	Compressor work	38	E Product analysis
3	E feed	21	Reactor cooling temp.	39	F Product analysis
4	A and C feed	22	Separator cooling temp.	40	G Product analysis
5	Recycle flow	23	A Reactor feed analysis	41	H Product analysis
6	Reactor feed rate	24	B Reactor feed analysis	42	D feed flow
7	Reactor pressure	25	C Reactor feed analysis	43	E feed flow
8	Reactor level	26	D Reactor feed analysis	44	A feed flow
9	Reactor Temperature	27	E Reactor feed analysis	45	A and c feed flow
10	Purge rate	28	F Reactor feed analysis	46	Comp. recycle valve
11	Product separator temp.	29	A Purge gas analysis	47	Purge value
12	Product separator level	30	B Purge gas analysis	48	Separator pot liquid flow
13	Product separator pressure	31	C Purge gas analysis	49	Stripper product flow
14	Prod. separator underflow	32	D Purge gas analysis	50	Stripper steam valve
15	Stripper level	33	E Purge gas analysis	51	Reactor cooling water
16	Stripper pressure	34	F Purge gas analysis	52	Condenser cooling water
17	Stripper underflow	35	G Purge gas analysis	53	Agitator speed
18	Stripper temperature	36	H Purge gas analysis		

In the Tennessee Eastman process it is possible to simulate 20 pre-established fault states. Table 2 shows the faults selected as study case. Faults IDV(1,2,4,7,8) are the most commonly used in literature as study case [7, 12, 21-23]. IDV(14) is occasionally used [7, 8, 22]. IDV(16,17,18,19) faults are unknown and are rarely used in previous literature. In other papers when these last four faults are used, the classification algorithm has unsatisfactory results [9, 24], presenting a challenge for the fault identification algorithms.

Table 2. Process faults

Name	Process Disturbances
IDV(1)	A/C feed ratio, B composition constant
IDV(2)	B composition, A/C ratio constant
IDV(4)	Reactor cooling wáter inlet temperature
IDV(7)	C header pressure loss—reduced availability
IDV(8)	A,B,C feed composition
IDV(14)	Reaction kinetics
IDV(16)	Unknown
IDV(17)	Unknown
IDV(18)	Unknown
IDV(19)	Unknown

Ten thousand data for each of the 53 available features were collected for this experiment. To test the fault identification the data were divided in proportions 70% for training (variable selection and training clustering algorithm) and 30% for test (recognition) sets respectively. Faults in the simulation are produced after a normal state. The Pre-processing stage presented in Sect. 2 was applied to each variable. The number of samples used in the normal state is the same number used for the fault condition in training and test datasets.

4   Experimental Results and Discussion

Ten faults were detected by the clustering algorithm. Using the training data (70% of the total data) the most informative variables were selected. In Table 3 the classification results for the training set and the test data set (30% of the total data) with the 53 variables and with the selected variables (31) are presented.

The method chose 31 of 53 variables, thus obtaining the optimal feature subset Fs=[1,2,3,5,8,9,12,14,15,16,17,18,19,21,22,24,26,31,34,36,37,39,40,41,42,43,45,47,49,51,52]. Figure 2 shows the CV values through the SBE search. The optimal feature subset Fs is obtained when the maximum CV value (0.00346) is attained.

Table 3 shows a comparison among the results obtained in the fault identification for training and test sets. The comparison was made using the correct classification percentage of the obtained LAMDA classification. á=1 is used as exigency level.

In most cases the correct classification percentage is approximately equal or greater when the wrapper feature selection method is used in comparison with the classification made with all TEP features, but using 22 variables less (see Table 3).

The variables selected by the wrapper method are used to the fault identification in the recognition data set. The recognition results show that the used methodology allows identifying the most important variables to improve the fault detection. Faults IDV(1) and IDV(8) can be detected only using the classification made by the clustering algorithm with all variables in the training data set. The wrapper feature selection method is not totally useful when the training set is used for the fault identification of IDV(1) and IDV(8), but it is necessary for the recognition data set. The use of this wrapper feature selection method ensures and enhances the identification of all failures in test and training data sets due to the clustering algorithm is not able by itself of make the fault identification of IDV(1) and IDV(8) in the recognition set as it does in the training set.

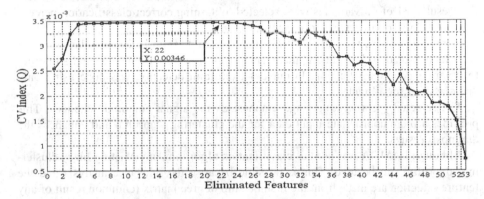

Fig. 2. CV values during the wrapper search

Table 3. Training and Test classification percentages for each fault

	Training		Test-Recognition	
Features	**53**	**31**	**53**	**31**
Fault	*All features*	*Feat. selection*	*All features*	*Feat. selection*
IDV (1)	96,183	87,277	77,727	91,769
IDV (2)	91,152	98,391	71,501	96,667
IDV (4)	50,000	89,341	63,082	95,384
IDV (7)	50,000	83,544	50,000	87,692
IDV (8)	90,512	89,231	50,000	84,077
IDV (14)	80,916	81,170	50,000	89,333
IDV (16)	90,102	93,401	50,000	81,470
IDV (17)	50,000	94,162	60,770	92,307
IDV (18)	50,000	77,862	80,769	84,613
IDV (19)	50,000	92,621	96,154	97,142

The results are comparable with previous works that uses supervised learning approaches. The classification percentage is over 90% in average for the IDV(1,2,4,7,8,14) faults, similar results were found in [7, 8, 12, 24]. These faults are generally the least difficult to detect. When the last four faults are compared with [24], their fault identification (fault IDV (16) (96%), fault IDV (17) (91%), fault IDV (18) (81%) and fault IDV (19) (83%)) is not as good as the recognition results presented here. Results also show better performance than [9], where the fault identification results are 11.13%, 10%, 91.63% and 64.38% for the faults IDV (16), IDV (17), IDV (18) and IDV (19) respectively.

5   Conclusions and Future Work

This wrapper approach reduces significantly the number of redundant and non-informative variables in high dimensional data sets and improves the fault identification results. 31 of 53 variables were selected, obtaining correct classification percentages over 90% (in average) for recognition.

In previous works the fault identification was made from individual classifiers for each fault, isolating the fault and the normal operation state from other faults in order to obtain a good classification. In our case, the fault detection was done using only one classifier for all faults.

The selected preprocessing stage emphasizes the signal amplitude changes. This provides a more appropriate input data for the clustering algorithm and enhances the diagnosis results.

Although LAMDA was used as classification algorithm, any existing fuzzy clustering algorithm can be used. This is possible because the relevance analysis and the feature selection are made from the membership degree matrix (common result of any fuzzy clustering method).

Future work consists in the use of several validation indexes and feature search algorithms in the wrapper feature selection method that can improve the fault identification results on the Tennessee Eastman process.

Acknowledgments. This project was supported by the committee for research development (CODI) -Universidad de Antioquia- Colombia and the ECOSNORD program – COLCIENCIAS, Colombia. We thank GEPAR group for providing an appropriate and useful environment to develop this research.

References

1. Gentil, S.: Supervision Des Procedes Complexes. Hermes Science Publications (2007)
2. Morita, M.E., Sabourin, R., Bortolozzi, F., Suen, C.Y.: Unsupervised Feature Selection Using Multi-Objective Genetic Algorithm for Handwritten Word recognition. In: 7th Intl. Conference on Document Analysis and Recognition (ICDAR 2003), pp. 666–670 (2003)

3. Patterson, O.D., Dong, X., Khargonekar, P., Nai, V.N.: Methodology for Feedback Variable Selection for Control of Semiconductor Manufacturing Processes, Part 1 – Analytical and Simulation Results. IEEE Transactions on Semiconductor Manufacturing 16(4), 588–597 (2003)
4. Fei, H., Huan, J.: Structure Feature Selection for Chemical Compound Classification. In: 8th Intl. Conference on BioInformatics and Bioengineering (BIBE 2008), pp. 1–6 (2008)
5. Jun, C.-H., Lee, S.-H., Park, H.-S., Lee, J.-H.: Use of Partial Least Squares Regression for Variable Selection and Quality Prediction. In: 39th Intl. Conference on Computers & Industrial Engineering (CIE 2009), pp. 1302–1307 (2009)
6. Downs, J., Vogel, E.: A Plant-Wide Industrial Process Control Problem. Computers and Chemical Engineering 17(3), 245–255 (1993)
7. Shi, H., Huang, C.: A BP Wavelet Neural Network Structure for Process Monitoring and Fault Detection. In: 6th World Congress on Intelligent Control and Automation (WCICA 2006), pp. 5675–5681 (2006)
8. Hsu, C., Chen, L.: Integrate Independent Component Analysis and Support Vector Machine for Monitoring Non-Gaussian Multivariate Process. In: 4th Intl. Conference on Wireless Communications, Networking and Mobile Computing (WiCOM 2008), pp. 1–4 (2008)
9. Mao, Z., Zhao, Y., Zhou, L.: A Flexible Principle Component Analysis Method for Process Monitoring. In: 4th Intl. Conference on Natural Computation (ICNC 2008), pp. 18–21 (2008)
10. Senoussi, H., Chebel-Morello, B., Denaï, M., Zerhoun, N.: Feature Selection for Fault Detection Systems (Application to the Tennessee Eastman Process. In: 7th IEEE Conference on Automation Science and Engineering (CASE 2011), pp. 189–194 (2011)
11. Wu, H., Huang, D.: Kernel Fisher Discriminant Analysis Using Feature Vector Selection for Fault Diagnosis. In: 2nd Intl. Symposium on Intelligent Information Technology Application (IITA 2008), pp. 109–113 (2008)
12. Da Silva, A., Galvao, R.: Fault Detection Using Linear Discriminant Analysis with Selection of Process Variables and Time Lags. In: 11th IEEE Intl. Conference on Industrial Technology (ICIT 2010), pp. 217–222 (2010)
13. Piera-Carrete, N., Desroches, P., Aguilar-Martin, J.: Variation Points in Pattern Recognition. Pattern Recognition Letters 11, 519–524 (1990)
14. Uribe, C., Isaza, C., Gualdron, O., Duran, C., Carvajal, A.: A Wrapper Approach Based on Clustering for Sensors Selection of Industrial Monitoring Systems. In: 5th Intl. Conference on Broadband, Wireless Computing, Communication and Applications (BWCCA 2010), pp. 482–487 (2010)
15. Uribe, C., Isaza, C.: Unsupervised Feature Selection Based on Fuzzy Partition Optimization for Industrial Processes Monitoring. In: 4th Intl. Conference on Computational Intelligence for Measurement Systems and Applications (CIMSA 2011), pp. 1–5 (2011)
16. Kohavi, R., John, G.: Wrappers for Feature Subset Selection. Artificial. Intelligence 97(1-2), 273–324 (1997)
17. Devakumari, D., Thangavel, K.: Unsupervised Adaptive Floating Search Feature Selection Based on Contribution Entropy. In: 2010 Intl. Conference on Communication and Computational Intelligence (INCOCCI 2010), pp. 623–627 (2010)
18. Aha, D., Bankert: A Comparative Evaluation of Sequential Feature Selection Algorithms. In: Fisher, D., Lenz, Hans, J. (eds.) Artificial Intelligence and Statistics V. Lecture Notes in Statistics, vol. 112, pp. 199–206. Springer, Heidelberg (1995)

19. Lamrini, B., Le Lann, M.V., Benhammou, A., Lakhal, E.: Detection of Functional States by the 'LAMDA' Classification Technique – Application to a Coagulation Process in Drinking Water Treatment. Comptes Rendus - Physique 6(10), 1161–1168 (2005)
20. Isaza, C., Orantes, A., Kempowsky, T., Le Lann, M.V.: Contribution of Fuzzy Classification for the Diagnosis of Complex Systems. In: 7th IFAC Symposium on Fault Detection, Supervision and Safety of Technical Processes (SafeProcess 2009), pp. 1132–1137 (2009)
21. Xu, J., Hu, S.: Fault Detection for Process Monitoring Using Improved Kernel Principal Component Analysis. In: 2010 Intl. Conference on Artificial Intelligence and Computational Intelligence (ICAI 2009), pp. 334–338 (2009)
22. Li, G., Alcala, C., Qin, S., Zhou, D.: Generalized Reconstruction-Based Contributions for Output-Relevant Fault Diagnosis with Application to the Tennessee Eastman Process. Transactions on Control Systems Technology 19(5), 1114–1127 (2011)
23. Yu, C., Pan, Q., Cheng, Y., Zhang, H.: A Kernel-Based Bayesian Classifier for Fault Detection and Classification. In: 7th World Congress on Intelligent Control and Automation (WCICA 2008), pp. 124–128 (2008)
24. Lee, J., Kang, B., Shin, K., Kang, S.: Online Process Monitoring Scheme for Fault Detection Based on Independent Component Analysis (ICA) and Local Outlier Factor (LOF). In: 40th Intl. Conference on Computers and Industrial Engineering (CIE 2010), pp. 1–6 (2010)

On Modelling Virtual Machine Consolidation to Pseudo-Boolean Constraints

Bruno Cesar Ribas[1,3], Rubens Massayuki Suguimoto[2], Razer A.N.R. Montaño[1],
Fabiano Silva[1], Luis de Bona[2], and Marcos Castilho[1]

[1] LIAMF - Laboratório de Inteligência Artificial e Métodos Formais
[2] LARSIS - Laboratório de Redes e Sistemas Distribuídos
Federal University of Paraná
[3] Universidade Tecnológica Federal do Paraná - Campus Pato Branco
{ribas,rubensm,razer,fabiano,bona,marcos}@inf.ufpr.br

Abstract. Cloud Computing is a new paradigm of distributed computing that offers virtualized resources and services over the Internet. To offer Infrastructure-as-a-Service (IaaS) many Cloud providers uses a large data center which usage ranges 5% to 10% of capacity in average. In order to improve Cloud data center management and resources usage a Virtual Machine (VM) consolidation technique can be applied to increase workloads and save energy. Using VM consolidation, we introduce an artificial intelligence consolidation based in Pseudo-Boolean (PB) Constraints to find a optimal consolidation. To evaluate our PB consolidation approach we used the DInf-UFPR and Google Cluster scenario and the formulas are solved with two state-of-the-art solvers.

Keywords: pseudo-Boolean, satisfiability, optimization, cloud, consolidation.

1 Introduction

Cloud Computing is a new paradigm of distributed computing that offers virtualized resources and services over the Internet [1,7]. Using Cloud Computing it is possible to offer a pool of easily usable and accessible virtualized resources. These resources can be dynamically reconfigured to adjust to a variable load (scale), allowing also for an optimum resource utilization. This pool of resources is typically exploited by a pay-per-use model in which guarantees are offered by the Infrastructure Provider by means of customized SLAs [16].

One of the service model offered by Clouds is Infrastructure-as-a-Service (IaaS) in which virtualized resource are provided as virtual machine (VM). With VMs, users obtain a personalized and isolated execution environment to execute applications. A VM also uses virtualized resources such virtual CPU, virtual RAM, virtual network and virtual storage devices.

Many Cloud providers use a large data center in order to offer IaaS. Data centers contains a huge amount of physical resources (server, disks, wired networks). Unfortunately, most of large data center usage ranges from 5% to 10% of capacity on average. In order to maximize the resources utilization by virtualized resources, a IaaS Cloud

J. Pavón et al. (Eds.): IBERAMIA 2012, LNAI 7637, pp. 361–370, 2012.

provider can apply server consolidation technique [4,11,17] for VM reallocation on physical servers. This consolidation is also denoted as VM Consolidation.

A server consolidation can increase workloads on servers from 50% to 85% where they can operate more energy efficiently [5] and, in some cases, a consolidation can save 75% of energy [3]. Reallocating virtualized resources allow to shutdown physical servers, reducing cooling costs, headcount, hardware management and energy consumption costs.

To maximize Cloud data center usage, an optimal VM consolidation has been topic of research in Cloud Computing. There are works [2,4,11,17] that uses *Linear Programming* formulation or distributed algorithms to guarantee the optimal resource utilization. Different from these approaches we introduce an artificial intelligence approach based on Pseudo-Boolean (PB) [13] formulation to solve the optimization problem. We perform experiments using DInf-UFPR datacenter and Google Cluster to evaluate our approach based on real scenarios.

In Sect. 2 we present related works to consolidation in Clouds. Section 3 describes the Pseudo-Boolean formulation. In Sect. 4 we evaluate the proposed approach using data from real scenario. Finally, in Sect. 5 we present a conclusion and future works.

2   Related Works

Advances in virtualization technology allowed migration of VMs or entire virtual execution environment across physical resources. It also allowed a VM consolidation which has been investigated with different aspects [3,12,15] such performance of VM, energy consumption, costs of resource and costs of migration. Optimal VM consolidation has been explored and solved using *Linear Programming* formulation [2,4] and Distributed Algorithms [11] approaches.

Marzolla *et al.* [11] presents a gossip-based algorithm called *V-Man*. Each physical server (host) run *V-Man* with an *Active* and *Passive* threads. *Active* threads request a new allocation to each neighbor sending to them the number of VMs running. The *Passive* thread receives the number of VMs, calculate and decide if current node will pull or push the VMs to requested node. The algorithm iterate and quickly converge to an optimal consolidation, maximizing the number of idle hosts.

Ferreto *et. al.* [4] presents a *Linear Programming* formulation and add constraints to control VM migration on VM consolidation process. The migration control constraints uses CPU and memory to avoid worst performance when migration occurs.

Bossche *et. al.* [2] propose and analyze a *Binary Integer Programming* (BIP) formulation of cost-optimal computation to schedule VMs in Hydrid Clouds. The formulation uses CPU and memory constraints and the optimization is solved by *Linear Programming*.

Different from above approaches, we introduce an artificial intelligence solution based on *Pseudo-Boolean* formulation to solve the problem of optimal VM consolidation.

3   Pseudo-Boolean Optimization

A Pseudo-Boolean function in a straightforward definition is a function that maps Boolean values to a real number. The term pseudo-Boolean is given to these functions that are not

Boolean but remains very close to Boolean functions [8,10,13]. In a *Pseudo-Boolean* (PB) formula, variables have Boolean domains and constraints, know as PB constraints [13], are linear inequalities with integral coefficients. In *PB Optimization*, a cost function is added to a PB formula.

PB functions are a very rich subject of study since numerous problems can be expressed as the problem of optimizing the value of a PB function. PB constraints offer a more expressive and natural way to express constraints than clauses and yet, this formalism remains close enough to the *Satisfiability* (SAT) [8,10] problem to benefit from the recent advances in SAT solving.

Simultaneously, PB solvers benefit from the huge experience in *Integer Linear Programming* (ILP) and, more specifically, *0-1 programming*. This is particularly true when optimization problems are considered. Inference rules allow to solve problems polynomially when encoded with PB constraints while resolution of the problem encoded with clauses requires an exponential number of steps. PB constraints appear as a compromise between the expressive power of the formalism used to represent a problem and the difficulty to solve the problem in that formalism [13].

In this work we use PB constraints instead of raw Boolean because each Boolean variable has an integer coefficient that maps the structure of the servers and VMs in terms of processing power (CPU) and memory (RAM). With this construction there is no need to transform the formula into a CNF since PB can represent all that is necessary.

We take advantage of *PB optimization* [13] that are implemented on PB solvers, where we create one more PB constraint. This constraint does not have the inequality to express the upper bound of the constraint but is set as an objective constraint to the solver to find the minimal value that this constraint can assume while respecting all other constraints.

A detailed description of modern SAT solver, maximum satisfiability and Pseudo-Boolean optimization can be found, respectively in [8,10,13].

3.1 PB Formulation to Optimal VM Consolidation

The goal of our problem is to deploy K VMs $\{vm_1 \ldots vm_K\}$ inside N hardwares $\{hw_1 \ldots hw_N\}$ while minimizing the total number of active hardwares. Each VM vm_i has an associated needs such as number of VCPU and amount of VRAM needed while each physical hardware hw_j has an amount of available resources, number of CPU and available RAM.

In order to create the PB Constraints each hardware consists of two variables, one that relates hw_i to the amount of RAM hw_i^{ram} and one that relates to the amount of CPU hw_i^{proc}. Per hardware, a VM has 2 variables, one to relate the VM vm_j required amount of VRAM vm_j^{ram} to the hardware hw_i amount of RAM hw_i^{ram}, denoted as $vm_j^{ram \cdot hw_i}$. The another variable relate the required VCPU vm_j^{proc} to the amount of CPU available hw_i^{proc}, denoted as $vm_j^{proc \cdot hw_i}$. The total amount of VM variables is $2 \times N$ variables.

Our main objective is to minimize the amount of active hardware. This constraint is defined in 1. Each hw_i is a Boolean variable that represents one hardware that, when *True*, represents that hw_i is powered on and powered off otherwise.

$$minimize: \sum_{i=1}^{N} hw_i \tag{1}$$

To guarantee that the necessary amount of hardware is active we include two more constraints that implies that the amount of usable RAM and CPU must be equal or greater than the sum of resources needed by VM. These constraints are defined at 2 and 3, respectively.

$$\sum_{i=1}^{N} RAM_{hw_i} \cdot hw_i^{ram} \geq \sum_{j=1}^{K} RAM_{vm_j} \cdot vm_j^{ram} \tag{2}$$

$$\sum_{i=1}^{N} PROC_{hw_i} \cdot hw_i^{proc} \geq \sum_{j=1}^{K} PROC_{vm_j} \cdot vm_j^{proc} \tag{3}$$

To limit the upper bound of hardwares, we add two constraints per host that limit:

Available RAM per Hardware: This constraint dictates that the sum of needed ram of virtual machines must not exceed the total amount of ram available on the hardware, and it is illustrated in constraint 4;

Available CPU per Hardware: This constraint dictates that the sum of VCPU must not exceed available CPU, and it is illustrated in constraint 5.

$$\forall hw_i^{ram} \in hw_N^{ram} \left(\sum_{j=1}^{K} RAM_{vm_j} \cdot vm_j^{ram \cdot hw_i} \leq RAM_{hw_i} \right) \tag{4}$$

$$\forall hw_i^{proc} \in hw_N^{proc} \left(\sum_{j=1}^{K} PROC_{vm_j} \cdot vm_j^{proc \cdot hw_i} \leq PROC_{hw_i} \right) \tag{5}$$

Finally we add one constraint per VM to guarantees that the VM is running in exactly one hardware. These constraints can be seen on constraint 6.

$$\forall vm_i \in vm_K \left(\sum_{j=1}^{N} vm_i^{proc \cdot hw_j} \cdot vm_i^{ram \cdot hw_j} \cdot hw_j^{proc} \cdot hw_j^{ram} = 1 \right) \tag{6}$$

With this model we have $(2 \times N + 2 \times N \times K)$ variables and $(2 + 2 \times N + K)$ constraints with one more constraint to minimize in our PB formula. It is possible to get these amounts because it is a non-linear formula since constraint 6 has a sum of four multiplication.

Note that additional constraints, such as requiring minimal latency between VM, minimal guarantee of bandwidth, migration costs and others will add additional complexity to the problem and are left for future works.

4 Experiments

For the implementation and evaluation of the PB Constraints, we wrote a simple program that reads the amount of physical hardware followed by its amount of RAM and CPU, the amount of VM and its requirements of virtual memory (VRAM) and virtual processing power (VCPU), and solved the formula using open source PB solver/optimizer *Sat4j-PB* [6] and *BSOLO* [9].

We use two workloads to perform our PB consolidation approach. The first is the datacenter of Informatic Departament of Federal University of Paraná (DInf-UFPR), which are used to deploy VMs to offer services and execution environments for experiments of researches and students. The second is the Google Cluster Data project which has traces about machines and tasks running in Google servers. Tasks have resource requirements as well as VMs.

To evaluate both workloads we used the First-Fit and Round-Robin approaches to allocate the VMs on resources to compare with our PB optimal solution. With Round-Robin we expect to find the worst case and with First-Fit a medium case of consolidation.

We also used a *subset of workloads* to see the progress on the use of different amount of VM or tasks. A *subset of workload* is the larger subset of VMs or tasks which sum of VCPU requirements does not exceed σ percent of sum of physical servers CPU capacities. In this experiment we assume σ equals to 25%, 50% and 75%.

4.1 Better Use of DInf-UFPR Datacenter

In DInf-UFPR Datacenter we separated a set of physical server and VMs totalizing 9 servers and 22 VMs. The configuration are as follows on Table 1. The number of CPU and VCPU is given by the amount of processing cores and RAM and VRAM is given by amount of memory in Gigabytes.

To evaluate our approach in this scenario, we took the subset of VMs present in Table 2. The table shows information about subsets with respective sum of VCPU, sum of VRAM and amount of VMs.

As a result, Table 3 show the execution time, in seconds, of PB solvers for current scenario with above subsets workload. The table also shows respective amount of variables and amount of PB constraints generated from formula. Figure 1 presents the number of active servers for each subset. Each subset was executed using Round-Robin, First-Fit and PB consolidation with Sat4j-PB and BSOLO solver.

The results obtained in DInf-UFPR scenario show that PB optimal consolidation has a better result of First-fit, but it is very close to optimal due to little amount of servers. As expected, Round-Robin presents the worst-case of consolidation.

4.2 Google Cluster Data Project

Google Cluster Data [1] is a Google project to intend for the distribution of data about workloads running on Google Cluster. The workloads contains data traces about *12k* machines describing events and resource capacity of each server. The traces also describes around *132k* tasks workloads with respective resource requirements.

---

[1] http://code.google.com/p/googleclusterdata/

Table 1. Hardwares and VM description for DInf-UFPR scenario

(a) Hardware description.

Host	RAM	CPU
hw1	30	4
hw2	18	4
hw3	10	8
hw6	10	8
hw5	30	4
prd3b	125	32
prd3d	125	32
prd3c	125	32
tesla1	62	16
SUM	535	140

(b) VMs desciptions.

VM	VRAM	VCPU	VM	VRAM	CPU
planetmon	12	4	db	2	1
vc3-blanche	8	4	devel	4	2
alt	10	8	salinas	5	2
dalmore	10	8	vc3-colombard	8	2
mumm	10	8	vc3-educacional	2	2
priorat	5	8	vc3-newcastle	4	2
talisker	32	8	vc3-qef1	2	2
bowmore	20	12	vc3-qef2	2	2
alt-marcadle	80	16	vc3-qef3	2	2
alt-murphy	93	24	vc3-qef4	2	2
caporal	18	4	alt-guinness	120	32
			SUM	451	155

Table 2. Workload subsets with σ equals to 25%, 50% and 75% and respective sums of VRAM, VCPU and amount of VMs for DInf-UFPR scenario

Workload Percent	$\sum$ VRAM	$\sum$ VCPU	Amount of VMs
25%	51	23	11
50%	81	39	14
75%	138	71	18

Table 3. Variables and constraints generated and execution time for DInf-UFPR scenario using BSOLO and Sat4j-PB solvers

Formula	Variables	Constraints	BSOLO	Sat4j-PB
hw9-vm25p	108	25	**0.004**	**0.101**
hw9-vm50p	198	30	**0.004**	**0.109**
hw9-vm75p	288	35	**0.004**	**0.118**

Due to the long period to perform PB consolidation using all *12k* machines and *132k* workloads we selected five subset of machines. The size of each subset are **32, 64, 128, 256, 512** machines. For each size of subset machines, we used the above *subset of workload* to perform experiments. Table 4 shows the amount of resources used to evaluate PB consolidation and others allocation approaches. Values of CPU and RAM are normalized in a scale relative to the largest capacity of the resource on any machine in the period of trace. The value of the largest capacity is *1.0*.

As a result, Table 5 shows time results for the set of formulas explained above. For each instance was given a time limit of 7200 seconds. When the solver run out of time limit and did not found any solution it is show a Time Limit Exceeded (TLE). If the solver caught a Segmentation Fault signal a Runtime Error (RTE) is thrown as a result.

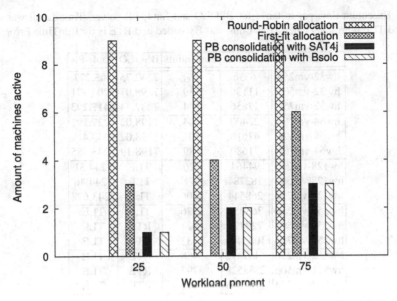

Fig. 1. Number of active hardware for each approach for DInf-UFPR scenario

Table 4. Workload subsets for each subset of machines. The workload has a σ equals to 25%, 50% and 75% and respective sum of VRAM, VCPU and amount of tasks for Google Cluster scenario.

#Machines	RAM	CPU	Workload %	$\sum$ VRAM	$\sum$ VCPU	#Tasks
32	14.9813	17.0000	25%	3.7375	4.3475	98
32	14.9813	17.0000	50%	5.7048	8.5640	173
32	14.9813	17.0000	75%	9.5204	12.7674	278
64	32.2117	34.5000	25%	5.7281	8.6389	174
64	32.2117	34.5000	50%	13.8382	17.2724	371
64	32.2117	34.5000	75%	19.3733	25.8826	559
128	61.8284	68.0000	25%	13.5025	17.0473	368
128	61.8284	68.0000	50%	26.3261	34.3367	713
128	61.8284	68.0000	75%	39.0425	51.0215	1048
256	121.5035	134.5000	25%	26.2943	33.9555	712
256	121.5035	134.5000	50%	49.0585	67.2507	1407
256	121.5035	134.5000	75%	75.6842	10.08777	2119
512	246.7420	275.2500	25%	50.9854	68.8945	1432
512	246.7420	275.2500	50%	100.1324	137.8664	2771
512	246.7420	275.2500	75%	206.4426	148.0852	4035

Figures 2a, 2b, and 2c respectively shows the result of amount actives machines for 32, 64, 128 and 256 subset of machines. For each subset, we perform the Round-Robin, First-Fit and PB consolidation approaches using Sat4j-PB and BSOLO solvers.

Unfortunately none of the tested solvers were able to find a satisfiable assignment for the larger formulas such subsets of 512 machines and 256 machines and only two

Table 5. Execution time per instance for BSOLO and Sat4j-PB solver. Time Limit was set to 7200s and TLE represents when Time Limit was Exceeded and RTE is for RunTime Error.

Formula	Variables	Constraints	BSOLO	Sat4j-PB
hw32-vm25p	6336	164	7242.75	**305.277**
hw32-vm50p	11136	239	7198.01	7204.971
hw32-vm75p	17856	344	7237.44	**6417.293**
hw64-vm25p	22400	304	7198.02	7227.192
hw64-vm50p	47616	501	7198.02	7243.419
hw64-vm75p	71680	689	7198.19	7243.385
hw128-vm25p	94464	626	TLE	7244.51
hw128-vm50p	182784	971	TLE	7244.46
hw128-vm75p	268544	1306	TLE	7243.678
hw256-vm25p	365056	1226	TLE	TLE
hw256-vm50p	720896	1921	RTE	TLE
hw256-vm75p	1085440	2633	RTE	TLE
hw512-vm25p	1467392	2458	RTE	TLE
hw512-vm50p	2838528	3797	RTE	TLE
hw512-vm75p	4132864	5061	RTE	TLE

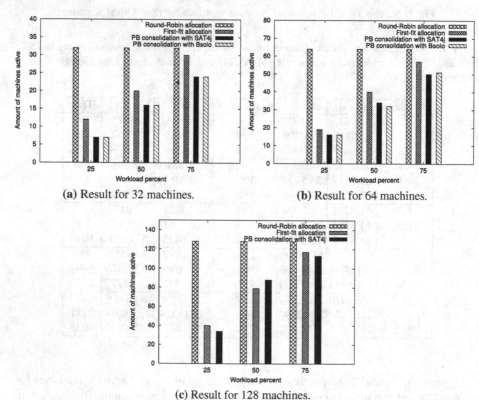

(a) Result for 32 machines.

(b) Result for 64 machines.

(c) Result for 128 machines.

Fig. 2. Number of active machines using Round-Robin, First-Fit and PB consolidation with Sat4J-PB and BSOLO solvers for Google Cluster scenario

instances reached optimum objective assignment. A non optimum solution can be easily identified in test case of 128 machines with 50% load where in Fig. 2c the First-Fit algorithm were able to optimize better than the PB Solver. Table 5 shows that the biggest formulas tested solver were not even able to find one satisfiable assignment to the formula, as can be identified as RTE and TLE. The RTE has many possibilities of errors caused in the solver execution, and it discussion is out of the scope of this work. The TLE means that it took too much time to find any satisfiable assignment with 7200 seconds time limit.

With the present result, we can confirm the VM consolidation by PB formulation approach is a valid formulation. When the Cloud has only a few resources, both physical and virtual, state-of-the-art solvers can prove optimal consolidation very fast. Within larger instances, PB solvers could not find the optimal, and in most of the cases they do not found any consolidation.

5   Conclusions

This paper presented a VM consolidation model using a artificial intelligence based on Pseudo-Boolean (PB) Constraints. A PB Constraints can be used to optimize costs, i.e minimizing the amount of active hardware. With a PB approach it is easily add extra restrictions to VM consolidation that would not be easily done with a First-fit or Round-Robin algorithms.

Unfortunately, follow experimental results, PB solvers were not able to solve the formulas of a huge test scenario such as Google Cluster. Also the benefit of running time was not as good as others approaches such First-fit algorithm.

Despite the fact tested solvers were not powerful enough to complete all formulas in a practical time we can use these formulas as a good benchmark to improve PB solvers.

We are interested in going on investigating some important research direction. First, we want to extend our solution and implement it inside a Cloud Management System (i.e. OpenNebula [14]) as an optimizer module. After we are interested to add some important restrictions such as network dependency of VMs and create classes of VMs to make better use of network interfaces of hosts.

References

1. Armbrust, M., Fox, A., Griffith, R., Joseph, A.D., Katz, R.H., Konwinski, A., Lee, G., Patterson, D.A., Rabkin, A., Stoica, I., Zaharia, M.: Above the Clouds: A Berkeley View of Cloud Computing. Tech. rep., EECS Department, University of California, Berkeley (2009)
2. Bossche, R., Vanmechelen, K., Broeckhove, J.: Cost-Optimal Scheduling in Hybrid IaaS Clouds for Deadline Constrained Workloads. In: 3rd IEEE International Conference on Cloud Computing (CLOUD 2010), pp. 228–235. IEEE Computer Society (2010)
3. Corradi, A., Fanelli, M., Foschini, L.: Increasing Cloud Power Efficiency through Consolidation Techniques. In: 2011 IEEE Symposium on Computers and Communications (ISCC 2011), pp. 129–134. IEEE Computer Society (2011)
4. Ferreto, T.C., Netto, M.A.S., Calheiros, R.N., De Rose, C.A.F.: Server Consolidation with Migration Control for Virtualized Data Centers. Journal of Future Generation Computer Systems 27(8), 1027–1034 (2011)

5. Harmon, R., Auseklis, N.: Sustainable IT Services – Assessing the Impact of Green Comput-ing Practices. In: 2009 Portland International Conference on Management of Engineering & Technology (PICMET 2009), pp. 1707–1717. IEEE Computer Society (2009)
6. Le Berre, D.: SAT4j – A Reasoning Engine in Java Based on the SATisfiability Problem, http://www.sat4j.org
7. Leavitt, N.: Is Cloud Computing Really Ready for Prime Time? Journal of Computer 42(1), 15–20 (2009)
8. Li, C.M., Manyà, F.: MaxSAT, Hard and Soft Constraints. In: Biere, A., Heule, M.J.H., van Maaren, H., Walsh, T. (eds.) Handbook of Satisfiability, vol. 185, ch. 19, pp. 613–631. IOS Press (2009)
9. Manquinho, V.: BSOLO – A Solver for Pseudo-Boolean Constraints, http://sat.inesc-id.pt/~vmm/research/
10. Marques-Silva, J.P., Lynce, I., Malik, S.: Conflict-Driven Clause Learning SAT Solvers. In: Biere, A., Heule, M.J.H., van Maaren, H., Walsh, T. (eds.) Handbook of Satisfiability, vol. 185, ch. 4, pp. 131–153. IOS Press (2009)
11. Marzolla, M., Babaoglu, O., Panzieri, F.: Server Consolidation in Clouds through Gossiping. In: IEEE International Symposium on a World of Wireless, Mobile and Multimedia Networks (WoWMoM 2011), pp. 1–6. IEEE Computer Society (June 2011)
12. Mehta, S., Neogi, A.: ReCon: A Tool to Recommend Dynamic Server Consolidation in Multi-cluster Data Centers. In: 2008 IEEE Network Operations and Management Sympo-sium (NOMS 2008), pp. 363–370. IEEE Computer Society (2008)
13. Roussel, O., Manquinho, V.: Pseudo-Boolean and Cardinality Constraints. In: Biere, A., Heule, M.J.H., van Maaren, H., Walsh, T. (eds.) Handbook of Satisfiability, vol. 185, ch. 22, pp. 695–733. IOS Press (2009)
14. Sotomayor, B., Montero, R.S., Llorente, I.M., Foster, I.: Virtual Infrastructure Management in Private and Hybrid Clouds. IEEE Internet Computing 13(5), 14–22 (2009)
15. Umeno, H., Parayno, C., Teramoto, K., Kawano, M., Inamasu, H., Enoki, S., Kiyama, M., Aoyama, T., Fukunaga, T.: Performance Evaluation on Server Consolidation using Virtual Machines. In: 2006 SICE-ICASE International Joint Conference (SICE-ICCAS 2006), pp. 2730–2734. IEEE Computer Society (2006)
16. Vaquero, L.M., Rodero-Merino, L., Caceres, J., Lindner, M.: A Break in the Clouds – Towards a Cloud Definition. Journal of ACM SIGCOMM Computer Communication Re-view 39(1), 50–55 (2008)
17. Vogels, W.: Beyond Server Consolidation. Journal of ACM Queue 6(1), 20 (2008)

Analysis of Poisson's Ratio Effect on Pavement Layer Moduli Estimation - A Neural Network Based Approach from Non-destructive Testing

Gloria Beltrán[1,2,*] and Miguel Romo[1]

[1] Instituto de Ingeniería, Universidad Nacional Autónoma de México, México D.F, México
gbeltranc@iingen.unam.mx, mromo@iingen.unam.mx
[2] Facultad de Ingeniería, Universidad Nacional de Colombia, Bogotá, Colombia

Abstract. The structural condition of pavements can be evaluated properly by non-destructive surface deflection testing. Based on measured deflection responses of pavements to impact load, it is possible to estimate layer moduli through back analyses. For that purpose, typical constant values of Poisson's ratio are commonly assumed for each layer material. In this work a thorough investigation to assess Poisson's ratio influence on pavements response modeling is carried out. To this end, Artificial Neural Networks are proposed to Poisson's ratio estimation from deflection testing data. A comparative analysis of pavement responses obtained under constant and variable conditions of Poisson's ratio is performed.

Keywords: neural networks, pavements, Poisson's ratio, non-destructive testing.

1 Introduction

The remaining life and maintenance decisions of existing pavements are highly dependent on structural conditions exhibited throughout their service. Particularly, flexible pavements are considered as multilayer systems under repeated loading, whose structural response and performance significantly depend on the features of pavement layers: thickness, type of materials, mechanical properties such as strength and stiffness. Layer moduli are commonly used to represent the layer stiffness, which can be back-calculated from non-destructive surface deflection testing, conducted on existing pavements. To this end, constant values of Poisson's ratio, related to strain behavior, are usually assumed for each layer.

An analysis is carried out in this investigation to verify the influence of a dynamic range of Poisson ratio on pavements response modeling, since previous studies have mentioned the negligible effect that constant assumption of Poisson ratio has on layer moduli estimation.

An approximate non-conventional solution via Artificial Neural Networks - ANNs, is considered in this work to Poisson's ratio estimation. Previous investigations have shown the exceptional ability of ANNs for parameter identification problems related to pavements, but most of the reported cases were developed using synthetic

J. Pavón et al. (Eds.): IBERAMIA 2012, LNAI 7637, pp. 371–380, 2012.

deflection testing data or hypothetical pavement systems. Although good estimates have been achieved, the ability of ANNs modeling was constrained by the selected range and distribution of training synthetic data.

This paper presents further attempts using a database with wide ranges of responses obtained from deflection tests, performed on three and four layer pavement systems, including traditional layer structuring and pavements having a subbase stiffer than the granular base.

Assessment of the resulting ANN modeling shows its forecasting capabilities and efficiency. Further model validation is performed by verifying the coherence between predicted behavior and measured responses.

2   Mechanical Behavior of Flexible Pavements

Each vehicular load pulse on pavement surface is gradually transferred to depth, inducing a particular state of stresses and strains, depending on pavement features. The emphasis on studying the structural behavior of pavements has been focused on the strength and stiffness of the constituent layers, and the stresses – strains responses shown in Fig. 1, induced by repeated load.

The estimation of parameters related to stiffness, such as layer moduli and Poisson's ratio, are based on the most basic concept of elasticity: the relationship between applied stress and strain response. For existing pavements, layer moduli can be determined from in situ Non-destructive Testing – NDT, to know the structural capacity under actual environmental conditions.

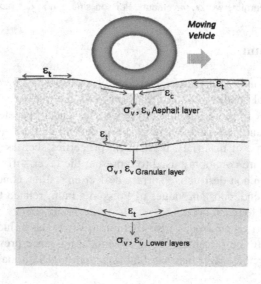

Fig. 1. Stress and strain state under traffic loading

Under axial loading, the Poisson's ratio is defined as lateral strain divided by axial deformation, as illustrated in Fig. 2. It constitutes one of the input parameters to the response models used in the mechanical empirical methods of design.

Poisson's ratio can be determined through laboratory testing, but for practical purposes constant typical values are generally assumed for each layer, due to the narrow margin of variation suggested for paving materials [5], as shown in Table 1.

Although some previous studies have mentioned the negligible effect that constant assumption of Poisson ratio has on layer moduli estimation [1 a 4], it was also recommended that Poisson's ratio of the lower layers should be carefully assumed, because small variations may cause important differences in the moduli estimation of overlaying pavement layers [5].

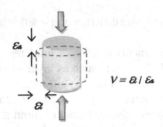

Fig. 2. Poisson's Ratio definition (v)

Table 1. Typical values of Poisson's ratio

Layer	Poisson's ratio
Asphalt Concrete	0.30 – 0.40
Granular Base	0.20 – 0.40
Cement-stabilized soil	0.10 – 0.30
Cohesive soil	0.25 – 0.45

3   Impact Load Deflection Test - Deflection Basin

The structural condition of pavements can be evaluated properly by non-destructive surface deflection testing. Impulse load devices such as Falling Weight Deflectometer (FWD) and Heavy Weight Deflectometer (HWD) are probably the most commonly used for this purpose, because they simulate properly traffic loading features such as type, magnitude and time-passing vehicle loading.

FWD and HWD devices apply an impulse load (Q) through a mass in free-fall on a circular plate placed on the pavement surface; vertical displacement response (D1, D2,..., Di), is recorded by various sensors located at different distances from the impact point, as shown in Fig. 3.Accordingly, a deflection basin can be defined; the maximum displacement, known as peak deflection, occurs beneath the loading point.

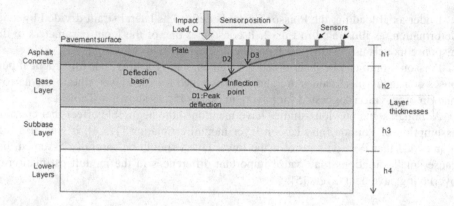

Fig. 3. Impact load deflection test - deflection basin

Deflection response of pavements to impact load tests depends on applied load, layer thicknesses, mechanical parameters such as layer moduli and Poison's ratios.

Scopes and limitations of testing should be considered for proper interpretation of deflection data: all parameters derived, represent the loading and environmental conditions at time of testing. It should also be borne in mind that most analytical methods are not suitable to analyze the response when either extensive deterioration or thin layers exist in the pavement [5].

4   Traditional Solution to Parameter Identification Problem

Based on measured responses of pavements to deflection tests, parameter related to mechanical behavior can be estimated through back analyses.

In common practice, the problem is reduced to a basic principle of action (applied load) and response (deflections), both related by any law of soil material behavior known (e.g., elastic, critical state, viscoelastic, etc). In those approaches, Poisson's ratio is supposed constant for each layer and seed moduli are assumed to compute theoretical deflections. Moduli are then back-calculated through an iterative process trying to match computed and measured deflections by minimizing an error function until certain criteria for acceptance is met.

Although the non-linearity in material behavior can be considered into traditional analyses, the cost and the computational complexity considerably increase; therefore, simplified hypothesis such as linear behavior of materials have to be assumed in these approaches to solve the problem efficiently. Despite the limitations, estimations obtained are widely accepted given the complexity of pavement's behavior.

5   Artificial Neural Networks

Since stiffness parameters identification problem is non-linear, multivariate and complex, a non-conventional solution via ANNs is considered to map properly the pavement responses measured in field.

ANNs are computational tools where learning and adaptation converge to develop "intelligent" software that allows modeling complex and variable systems. ANNs use prior knowledge to solve a problem and by incorporating new information throughout a time-learning process increases their forecasting capabilities. Accordingly, problems can be treated more rationally either when multivariate models for regression computations are developed or pattern recognition from a data set is the issue.

ANNs are formed by interconnected-processing neurons that receive, process and transmit signals or information to others which are connected [6]; each link has associated a value called weight, which can be fitted to simulate any feature or behavior in particular.

An ANN is a parallel multilayer structure formed by an input layer, hidden layers and an output layer; each one is constituted by neurons. Its results depend largely on how the neurons are interconnected (architecture) and the strength of these connections (weights values). Complex architectures have been associated commonly to nonlinear, multi-dimensional problems. Typical elements of an ANN system are: Learning rule, error function, input function, transfer function, all of which have to be defined by a trial and error process.

There are two stages in ANN model development: 1) Training stage, where learning is achieved from input-output data sets; the learning process could be: supervised if desired outputs are given for the specified inputs or reinforced if desired outputs are not known for sure but there is hint on them [7]. 2) Testing stage where the ability of ANN to yield reasonable outputs for new data sets, is evaluated; all performance statistics must be reported on the testing data. When suitable results are obtained in both stages, the resulting ANN is said to be a model capable of carrying out reliable predictions out from unknown data sets.

For parameter identification problems via ANN, input variables and desired outputs are presented to the network, which assigns initial values to weights which are adjusted by successive iterations. After each iteration, the network provides outputs that are compared with desired outputs until a given error criterion is satisfied; then it is said that the network has learned the input-output relationships naturally.

It is worth mentioning that once a well-trained ANN is developed, it can be used for fast and reliable predictions. Furthermore, by introducing plasticity (the ability to always learn) into the ANN, new information in long-term memory can be assimilated. Henceforth, ANN capabilities are enhanced.

6 Application

A 28 km road length with two lanes was selected as the case of study. Available parameters listed in Table 2 were selected to create the database for Poisson's ratio estimation.

Table 2. General database

Data Type	Parameters
Pavement system	Measured layer depth
Deflection testing: On right lane: 278 tests On left lane: 280 tests	Applied load, Q (ton) Measured deflections Sensors position

Figure. 3 shows the main parameters related to deflection testing. Applied loads vary between 4 and 7 tons; seven sensors located at 0.0 m, 0.3 m, 0.45 m, 0.6 m, 0.9 m, 1.2 m and 1.8 m away from loading point, allowed deflection basin measurement.

As illustrated in Fig. 4 and Table 3, there are two types of pavement systems within the 28 km road stretch considered in this study: a three-layer system from kilometer 119 to 127, where the stiffness decreases with depth and a four-layer pavement system having a subbase stiffer than the granular base; the asphalt layer of the former system is thicker than in the latter.

Available information on the road right lane was selected to train the ANN and the left lane dataset was used for the testing stage. To predict Poisson's ratio, twelve variables were selected for the input set: one load level, layer depths (4) and seven surface pavement deflections in each test. In the output of the training set, typical values of Poisson's ratio were assumed for each layer material: 0.3, 0.4, 0.35 and 0.45 for asphalt layer, granular base, stabilized subbase and lower layer respectively.

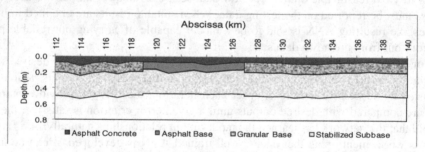

Fig. 4. Structural pavement systems along the road stretch considered

Table 3. Ranges of layer thicknesses (m)

Layer	Three-layer system	Four-layer system
Asphalt layer	0.15 – 0.20	0.06 – 0.10
Granular base	0.00	0.11 – 0.13
Stabilized subbase	0. 29 - 0.31	
Lower layers	3.00	

The ANN configuration used was the supervised three-layer feed-forward model illustrated in Fig. 5, with Multilayer Normal Feed Forward – MLN architecture and Quick Propagation – QP learning algorithm. This configuration has proved to be efficient for a parameter identification problem in a previous study [8].

In this study the approximation between target Poisson's ratios (υ_{Targ}) and estimated via ANN (υ_{ANN}) was evaluated by the Mean Absolute Error function, MAE convergence criterion, defined by:

$$MAE = \sum |(Dijmeas - Dijcomp)|)/M \qquad (1)$$

Where:

Dijmeas = measured deflection at sensor i for basin j
Dijcomp = computed deflection at sensor i for basin j
M = The number of basins times the number of sensors

The resulting dynamic ranges of Poisson's ratios on the testing set are given in Table 4. It is observed that most of the predicted υ_{ANN} are within reasonable values for each layer of pavements studied here.

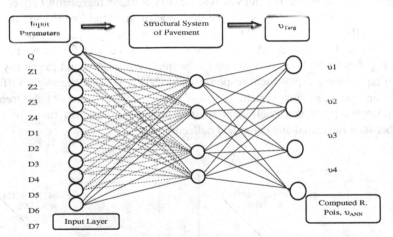

Fig. 5. ANN-based backcalculation model

Table 4. Poisson's ratios estimated via ANN

Layer	υ_{ANN}
Asphalt Concrete	0.24 – 0.35
Granular Base	0.31 – 0.42
Stabilized Subbase	0.29 – 0.40
Lower Layers	0.41 – 0.48

The highest values of Poisson's ratio along the asphalt layer were obtained for the intermediate three-layer pavement system, where an asphalt base is a constituent of the surface layer. Also, lower values were obtained in the stabilized subbase than in the base, as expected.

The layer moduli estimation process, under constant assumption of Poisson's ratio was conducted in the prior study [8], by means of a supervised-learning ANN modeling. At that time, constant values of Poisson's ratios were introduced in the input set along with measured deflection basins, applied load and layer thicknesses. Likewise, layer moduli back-calculated by Orozco [9] via layer-elasticity theory, from the same deflection testing database, was used as initial approximation of target outputs in the ANN training process.

With Poisson's ratios computed in this work - υ_{ANN}, the whole process was repeated to estimate another set of layer moduli. The obtained layer moduli for each scenario were used for a deflection-basin verification process, conducted by means of ANN modeling as well. Now, measured deflection basins were the target outputs and the computed moduli via ANN were considered as inputs for each option. The forecasting reliability was judged on the basis of the accuracy their computations matched the field-measured deflection basins.

Matching accuracy was defined according to the similarity with the characteristics of a perfect match, which is achieved when exists a linear regression between computed and measured deflections such that the slope of the trend line (b) and the determination coefficient (r2) are equal to one and the intercept value (a) is zero.

Estimated and measured deflections are in good agreement for both options, as seen in Fig. 6, which allows concluding on the quality of results and the ability of the ANN to reproduce the pavement response under NDT. Despite the slight difference between the two scenarios, variable Poisson's ratio yield to values of the trend line slope, intercept point and coefficient of determination, closer to those of perfect match between measured and computed deflections.

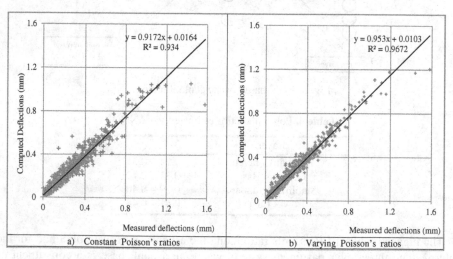

Fig. 6. Deflections measured and computed - left lane

7   Conclusions

In this paper, an ANN model with three-layer feed-forward MLN architecture and QP learning algorithm was used to estimate Poisson's ratio and layer moduli of pavements.

The predicted Poisson's ratios remain within reasonable values for each layer. It was found that pavement features are well mapped by the ANN model.

Deflection-basin verification process via ANNs was helpful to compare predictions with field measurements. Layer moduli estimated using variable Poisson's ratio, are able to reproduce more closely, the pavement field-measured deflection basins: values of the trend line slope and coefficient of determination were close to one, the intercept was nearly zero and 2% of error (MAE) was obtained.

The analysis of results, allow thinking about the convenience of assuming pre-established hypotheses regarding the influence of Poisson's ratio in the estimates of layer moduli. In fact, if proper simulation of the actual physical phenomenon of pavements is intended, it is very convenient to eliminate the uncertainty associated with such assumptions.

Finally, based on the high quality of results obtained, it seems reasonable to conclude that ANNs arc confidently enough that can be used for Poisson's ratio and layer moduli predictions for flexible pavements.

Acknowledgements. The authors acknowledge the comments of Dr. Raúl V. Orozco and the support provided by Instituto de Ingeniería-UNAM, Universidad Nacional de Colombia and CLAF- ICyTDF.

References

1. Uzan, J.: Advanced Backcalculation Techniques. In: Von Quintus, H.L., Bush, A.J., Baladi, G.Y. (eds.) Non Destructive Testing of Pavements and Backcalculation of Moduli. STP-1198, vol. 2, pp. 3–37 (1994)
2. Ullidtz, P.: Will Nonlinear BackcalculationHelp. In: Tayabji, S.D., Lukanen, E.O. (eds.) Non Destructive Testing of Pavements and Backcalculation of Moduli. STP 1375, vol. 2, pp. 14–22 (2000)
3. Huang, Y.: Pavement Analysis and Design. Prentice-Hall Inc., Upper Saddle River (2003)
4. ARA Inc. & ERES Consultants Division: Guide for Mechanistic-Empirical Design of New and Rehabilitated Pavement Structures. Final Report, Part 2, National Cooperative Highway Research Program-NCHRP, TRB, NRC (2004)
5. ASTM D5858-96: Standard Guide for Calculating In Situ Equivalent Elastic Moduli of Pavement Materials Using Layered Elastic Theory. ASTM West Conshohocken, Pa (2003)
6. Haykin, S.: Neural Networks, a Comprehensive Foundation, 2nd edn. Prentice Education Inc. (1999)

7. Logical Designs Consulting Inc.: ThinksPro Neural Networks for Windows, User's Guide. LogicalDesignsConsulting Inc. (1996)
8. Beltran, G., Romo, M.: Estimación de módulos elásticos en pavimentos usando redes neuronales artificiales. In: 14th Pan-American Conference on Soil Mechanics and Geotechnical Engineering (PanAm CGS-GC 2011), pp. 1–9 (2011)
9. Orozco, R.V.: Evaluación de pavimentos flexibles con métodos no destructivos. Engineering PhD Thesis, UNAM. México, D.F (2005)

On Modeling Connectedness in Reductions from Graph Problems to Extended Satisfiability

Ricardo Tavares de Oliveira, Fabiano Silva,
Bruno Cesar Ribas, and Marcos A. Castilho

Departamento de Informática, Universidade Federal do Paraná
POBox 19081, 81531-980, Curitiba, Brazil
{rtoliveira,fabiano,ribas,marcos}@inf.ufpr.br
http://www.inf.ufpr.br

Abstract. In this paper we present an efficient way to encode connectedness in reductions from graph problems to SAT and MaxSAT. We show and prove linear reductions from Minimum Path and Clique and a quadratic reduction from Steiner Tree, although others NP-complete and NP-hard problems can be reduced with this complexity as well. These reductions use a new class of operators that extends the traditional set of connectors of propositional logic.

Keywords: polynomial reductions, satisfiability, maximum satisfiability, Steiner tree, clique.

1 Introduction

Due to the big effort put on SAT and MaxSAT solvers in the last years, the interest on reductions from many NP problems to (Max)SAT has grown, mainly hard problems from the Graph Theory.

However, it's not trivial to reduce problems in graphs that requires the solutions to be *connected* in an efficient way. There are formulas easily built that states the requirement of *complete* connected subgraphs (cliques), as shown in [3]. These reductions are linear in the size of the complement of the given graph, which can be large for sparse graphs. Also, creating a boolean formula that states that a solution must be a connected graph, but not necessarily a complete one, is not trivial.

One can build a formula that states that a certain graph must be a (connected) tree by modeling a depth-first transversal [1]. It's not trivial to build such a formula efficiently. Also, approximated reductions encode connectedness by enumerating some (not all) paths between pair of vertices [2]. These reductions require a large number of encoded paths to guarantee a solution.

We suggest a simpler way to build such reductions by allowing the resulting formula to have operators other than the classic ones $(\neg, \wedge, \vee)$. It's possible to convert these new operators to formulae with the classic ones in linear time. Also, these operators can be implemented on non clausal SAT solvers. With them, we reduce Steiner Tree and Hamiltonian Cycle, for instance, in quadratic time in the size of the given graph. Also, we reduce the decision version of Clique in linear time in the size of the given graph.

J. Pavón et al. (Eds.): IBERAMIA 2012, LNAI 7637, pp. 381–391, 2012.
© Springer-Verlag Berlin Heidelberg 2012

Section 2 presents the new defined operators. Section 3 shows reductions from graph problems to SAT or MaxSAT. Section 4 shows experimental results, and Sect. 5 concludes and describes some future works.

2   Definition of the New Used Operators

Let $\mathbb{B} = \{0,1\}$ be the set of truth values, where 0 is equivalent to $false$ and 1 is equivalent to $true$. An operator of arity k is a function $o : \mathbb{B}^k \to \mathbb{B}$ that associates a truth value for k truth values.

Let $H \subseteq \{0, ..., k\}$ be a finite set of non-negative integer numbers. Let's define the **Choose-H** (C_H) operator in the following way:

$$C_H(f_1, f_2, ..., f_k) = \begin{cases} 1, \text{if} \sum_{i=1}^{k} f_i \in H \\ 0, \text{otherwise} \end{cases}$$

This operator assumes the true value if and only if the number of true arguments is in H. The operator $C_{\{0,2\}}(f_1, ..., f_k)$, for instance, assumes 1 if there is exactly 0 or 2 true values among $f_1, ..., f_k$, and 0 otherwise. When H is an unit set $H = \{x\}$, we write C_x instead of $C_{\{x\}}$ for simplicity.

The operator can be clearly implemented as a disjunction of $|H|$ counters and comparators. These circuits can be converted to a CNF formula in linear time [4]. Also, if H has constant size, then the entire operator can be converted also in linear time by renaming the resulting formulae.

It's worth mentioning that the operators $\wedge$, $\vee$ and $\neg$ can be directly translated to some *Choose* operator with the following properties: $(f_1 \wedge ... \wedge f_k) = C_k(f_1, ..., f_k)$; $(f_1 \vee ... \vee f_k) = C_{\{1,...,k\}}(f_1, ..., f_k)$; $\neg f_1 = C_0(f_1)$. Also, the property $\neg C_H(f_1, ..., f_k) = C_{\{0,...,k\}\setminus H}(f_1, ..., f_k)$ holds.

These operators allow us to count the number of true values among a certain set of variables. In our reductions, we use them to force the degree of certain vertices, as shown in Sect. 3.

3   Reductions from Problems in Graphs

We present in this section some reductions from problems in graphs to SAT and MaxSAT using the operators presented in Sect. 2. We start by showing reductions from Path Checking and Minimum Path. Although these problems are in P, these reductions are used as subroutines while reducing NP problems.

3.1   Path Checking

Let $G = (V, E)$ be a graph and let $v_a, v_b \in V$ be a pair of distinct vertices in G. Let's recall that a (single) path P between v_a and v_b with length k in G is a sequence P of edges in E, $P = (e_1, e_2, ..., e_k)$, with the following properties:

- $v_a \in e_1$ and there is no edge in $P \setminus \{e_1\}$ containing v_a;
- $v_b \in e_k$ and there is no edge in $P \setminus \{e_k\}$ containing v_b;

- $|e_i \cap e_{i+1}| = 1$ and there is no edge in $P \setminus \{e_i, e_{i+1}\}$ that contains the vertex in $e_i \cap e_{i+1}$, for all $1 \leq i < k$.

The Path Checking problem consists of, given G, v_a and v_b, checking whether there is a path between v_a and v_b in G.

Let $f_p(G, v_a, v_b)$ be a boolean formula that is satisfiable if and only if there is at least one path between v_a and v_b in the graph G. Also, any model A for this formula describes a subgraph $G_p(A)$ of G that contains at least one path between the given vertices. This formula can be built in the following way:

- Let's associate, for each $e_i \in E$, a boolean variable ϱ_i, and let $\mathscr{E} = \{\varrho_i : e_i \in E\}$. In a given assignment $A : \mathscr{E} \to \mathbb{B}$ for $f_p(G, v_a, v_b)$, $A(\varrho_i) = 1$ if and only if e_i is in the subgraph described by A. The described graph $G_p(A)$ is defined then as the subgraph of G induced by the edge set $\{e_i \in E : A(\varrho_i) = 1\}$;
- Let $\mathscr{N}(v_i) = \{\varrho_j \in \mathscr{E} : e_j \in N(v_i)\}$ be the set of variables associated with the *edges* in $N(v_i)$, the neighbourhood of v_i. Let's force the degree $d()$ of both vertices v_a and v_b to be 1, i.e., $d(v_a) = d(v_b) = 1$ in the described subgraph. This can be done with the constraints $C_1(\mathscr{N}(v_a))$ and $C_1(\mathscr{N}(v_b))$;
- For each other vertex $v_i \in V \setminus \{v_a, v_b\}$, let's force its degree to be 0 or 2 in the required subgraph. This can be done with the constraint $C_{\{0,2\}}(\mathscr{N}(v_i))$.

The formula $f_p(G, v_a, v_b)$ is built then as a conjunction of these constraints:

$$f_p(G, v_a, v_b) = C_1(\mathscr{N}(v_a)) \wedge C_1(\mathscr{N}(v_b)) \wedge \qquad (1)$$
$$C_{\{0,2\}}(\mathscr{N}(v_1)) \wedge C_{\{0,2\}}(\mathscr{N}(v_2)) \wedge ... \wedge C_{\{0,2\}}(\mathscr{N}(v_m))$$

where $\{v_1, v_2, ..., v_m\} = V \setminus \{v_a, v_b\}$.

To prove that there is one path between v_a and v_b in G if and only if $f_p(G, v_a, v_b)$ is satisfiable, it's enough to show the following two theorems:

Theorem 1: If there is a path $P = (e_1, ..., e_k)$ between v_a and v_b in G, then there is a model $A : \mathscr{E} \to \mathbb{B}$ for $f_p(G, v_a, v_b)$ for which $G_p(A)$ contains P.

Proof: Let A be the assignment that assigns 1 to and only to variables associated to edges in P, i.e., $A(\varrho_i) = 1$ if $e_i \in P$, and $A(\varrho_i) = 0$ otherwise. Clearly $G_p(A)$ contains only the edges in P. Let's show that A satisfies $f_p(G, v_a, v_b)$.

The edge e_1 is the only edge in P that contains v_a, since P is a simple path as defined above. Thus, $d(v_a) = 1$ in $G_p(A)$, satisfying $C_1(\mathscr{N}(v_a))$. For the same reason, e_k, the last edge in P, is the only edge in it that contains v_b, and thus $C_1(\mathscr{N}(v_b))$ is satisfied as well.

Since P is a simple path with length k, e_i and e_{i+1} share exactly one vertex, say v_i, for each $1 \leq i < k$. The edges e_i and e_{i+1} are the only edges in P that contains v_i. Thus, $d(v_i) = 2$ in $G_p(A)$, which satisfies the constraint $C_{\{0,2\}}(\mathscr{N}(v_i))$. For all the vertices v_j that are not in any edge of P, there is no edge in $N(v_j)$ present in $G_p(A)$. This satisfies the constraint $C_{\{0,2\}}(\mathscr{N}(v_j))$ as well, since $d(v_j) = 0$ in the described graph.

Hence, A satisfies all the given constraints, satisfying $f_p(G, v_a, v_b)$.   □

Theorem 2: Let A be a complete assignment of $\mathcal{E}$. If A satisfies $f_p(G, v_a, v_b)$, then there is a path between v_a and v_b in the graph $G_p(A)$.

Proof: Let A be a complete assignment of $\mathcal{E}$ that satisfies $f_p(G, v_a, v_b)$. Assume that $G_p(A)$ doesn't contain a path between v_a and v_b. v_a and v_b belong to different connected components of $G_p(A)$. Let $G'_p(A, v_a)$ be the subgraph of $G_p(A)$ consisting of the connected component v_a belongs to.

Since A satisfies $f_p(G, v_a, v_b)$, $d(v_a) = 1$ in $G_p(A)$ and, since $G'_p(A, v_a)$ is a connected subgraph of G containing v_a, $d(v_a) = 1$ in $G'_p(A, v_a)$ as well.

Since A satisfies $f_p(G, v_a, v_b)$, all vertices in $V \setminus \{v_a, v_b\}$ have even degree (0 or 2) in $G_p(A)$. Also, except for v_a, the only vertex that has odd degree (1) in $G_p(A)$ is v_b, which is not in $G'_p(A, v_a)$, as stated. Due to this, v_a is the only vertex in $G'_p(A, v_a)$ that has odd degree. So there's an odd number of vertices (only one, v_a) with odd degree in $G'_p(A, v_a)$.

It's well know that there must be an even number of vertices with odd degree in any graph. Since $G'_p(A, v_a)$ is a graph, the conclusion above is an absurd. Hence, a connected component of $G_p(A)$ with v_a and without v_b cannot exist, and thus there is a path between v_a and v_b in the graph $G_p(A)$.   □

There are $|E|$ variables in the formula. Also, there are $|V|$ constraints in it, one for each vertex in G. The arity of each one is equal to the degree of the corresponding vertex in G. Hence, the number of elements in the entire formula is bounded to $|V|$ plus the sum of the degrees of the vertices in G, $2|E|$. Hence, the size of the resulting formula is linear in the size of the given graph.

3.2   Minimum Path

Once reduced, Path Checking can be used to reduce Minimum Path to MaxSAT.

Let's describe the (Partial Weighted) MaxSAT problem as, given a hard formula f_h, a set of soft formulae $f_s = \{f_{s_1}, f_{s_2}, ..., f_{s_{|f_s|}}\}$ and a function $w_s : f_s \to \mathbb{N}$ that associates a weight to each soft formula, finding a model for f_h that maximizes the sum of the weights of the satisfied soft formulae.

Let $w : E \to \mathbb{N}$ be a function that associates, for each edge in a given graph G, a natural weight. The weight of a path P is the sum of the weights of the edges in P. The minimum path problem consists of, given G, w and a pair $v_a, v_b \in V$, finding a path between v_a and v_b whose weight is minimum.

Minimum Path can be reduced to MaxSAT by defining a hard formula that states that there must be a path between the given pair of vertices, and a set of soft formulae that states that the path must be minimum.

The hard formula can be $f_p(G, v_a, v_b)$ as described above. Each soft formula can be defined simply as the unit clause $(\neg \varrho_i)$ with weight $w(e_i)$, for each $e_i \in E$. These formulae indicate the willing of maximizing the sum of the weights of the edges not present in the desired path, minimizing then the weight of such a path.

There is a minimum path P between v_a and v_b in the given graph if and only if there is an optimal solution A for the given instance for which $G_p(A)$ contains only P. This is shown by the following two theorems:

Theorem 3: If $A : \mathscr{E} \to \mathbb{B}$ is a solution for the given MaxSAT instance, then $G_p(A)$ contains exactly a minimum path between v_a and v_b.

Proof: Let $A : \mathscr{E} \to \mathbb{B}$ be a model for $f_p(G, v_a, v_b)$ and let m be the sum of the satisfied soft formulae by A.

Since each soft formula consists only of the clause $(\neg\varrho_i)$ with weight $w(e_i)$ for each $e_i \in E$, m is equal to the sum of the weights of the edges not present in $G_p(A)$. Let $M = \sum\limits_{e_i \in E} w(e_i)$ be the sum of the weights of all edges in G.

Since MaxSAT consists of maximizing m, the sum of the weights of the edges in $G_p(A)$, $M - m$, is minimized. Thus, if A is optimal, then the sum of the weights of all edges in $G_p(A)$ is minimum. Also, according to the theorem 2, there is a path between v_a and v_b in $G_p(A)$. Then, $G_p(A)$ is a subgraph of G that contains a path between the given vertices and whose sum of its edges is minimum. Clearly $G_p(A)$ is a subgraph consisting of a required minimum path.

Hence, if A is an optimal solution, then $G_p(A)$ contains only a minimum path between the given pair of vertices.   □

Theorem 4: Let P be a minimum path between v_a and v_b in a given graph G. There is an optimal assignment A that is a solution for the built MaxSAT instance for which $G_p(A)$ contains exactly the edges in P.

Proof: Let P be a minimum path between v_a and v_b in the given graph.

Consider the assignment A shown in theorem 1. A satisfies $f_p(G, v_a, v_b)$, and $G_p(A)$ contains only the edges in P. Let $w(P)$ be the weight of the path P. Since $A(\varrho_i) = 1$ for each $e_i \in P$, all and only the soft formulae corresponding to an edge in P is unsatisfied by A. Thus, the sum of the weights of all satisfied soft formulae (the objective function of MaxSAT) is equal to $M - w(P)$. Since $w(P)$ is minimum, $M - w(P)$ is maximum.

Hence, A is an optimal solution for the given MaxSAT instance.   □

Since $|f_p(G, v_a, v_b)|$ is linear in the size of the given graph G as stated in Sect. 3.1, and since there is only an unit clause in f_s for each edge in G, this reduction is still linear in the size of G.

3.3   Connectedness Checking

The reduction from Minimum Path can be used as subroutine to reduce others NP problems, such as Steiner Tree. To reduce it, however, it's necessary to reduce Connectedness Checking firstly.

Let $G = (V, E)$ be a graph and $S \subseteq V$ be a subset of the vertices in G. The Connectedness Checking problem consists of checking whether all vertices in S are connected, i.e., there is a path in G between s_i and s_j, for all $s_i, s_j \in S$.

Let's built a formula $f_c(G, S)$ that is satisfiable if and only if all vertices in S belongs to the same connected component in G. Analogously to $f_h(G, v_a, v_b)$, any model A for $f_c(G, S)$ describes a subgraph $G_c(A)$ of G in which all vertices in S are connected. This formula can be built in the following manner:

- Let $G_1, G_2, ..., G_{|S|-1}$ be $|S|-1$ graphs, all of them identical to G. Also, let $e_{i,j}$ be the edge i in the graph G_j. Let's associate, for each $e_{i,j} \in \cup_{j=1}^{|S|-1} E(G_j)$, a boolean variable $\varrho_{i,j}$. Let $\mathscr{E}_j = \{\varrho_{i,j} : e_i \in E(G_j)\}$ and $\mathscr{E} = \cup_{j=1}^{|S|-1} \mathscr{E}_j$. Given a model $A : \mathscr{E} \to \mathbb{B}$ for $f_c(G, S)$, $G_c(A)$ is then defined as the union of all graphs $G_{j_p}(A_j)$, where A_j is the assignment A restricted to the variables in $\mathscr{E}_j$, i.e., $A_j = \{(\varrho_{i,j}, A(\varrho_{i,j})) : \varrho_{i,j} \in \mathscr{E}_j\}$;
- Let $S' = (s_1, ..., s_{|S|})$ be a permutation of the set S. Let's state that there must be a path between each pair of adjacent vertices in S', in each graph. This can be done with the constraints $f_p(G_j, s_j, s_{j+1})$ for all $1 \le j < |S|$.

$f_c(G, S)$ is defined then as a conjunction of these constraints, i.e.,

$$f_c(G, S) = f_p(G_1, s_1, s_2) \wedge f_p(G_2, s_2, s_3) \wedge ... \wedge f_p(G_{|S|-1}, s_{|S|-1}, s_{|S|}) \quad (2)$$

Let's show that $f_c(G, S)$ is satisfiable if and only if all vertices in S are connected in G. To do so, let's prove the following theorems:

Theorem 5: If all vertices in S are connected in G, then there is a model $A : \mathscr{E} \to \mathbb{B}$ for $f_c(G, S)$ for which all vertices in S are connected in $G_c(A)$.

Proof: Since all vertices in S belongs to the same connected component of G, there is a path in G between each pair of adjacent vertices in S'. Let P_j be the path between the vertices s_j and s_{j+1}. As shown in theorem 1, there is a model $A_j : \mathscr{E}_j \to \mathbb{B}$ for the formula $f_p(G_j, s_j, s_{j+1})$, for all $1 \le j < |S|$. Also, $G_{j_p}(A_j)$ contains P_j.

Let $A : \mathscr{E} \to \mathbb{B}$ be the union of all $A_j : \mathscr{E}_j \to \mathbb{B}$ described above. Since A_j satisfies $f_p(G_j, s_j, s_{j+1})$, A satisfies all the constraints in $f_c(G, S)$, and thus is a model for it. Also, since $G_c(A)$ is defined as the union of all $G_{j_p}(A_j)$ that contains P_j, $G_c(A)$ contains a path between each adjacent pair of vertices in S'. Due to transitivity, $G_c(A)$ contains a path between all pairs of elements in S and, thus, contains a connected subgraph of G that contains all vertices in S. $\square$

Theorem 6: Let A be a complete assignment of $\mathscr{E}$. If A is a model for $f_c(G, S)$, then all vertices in S are connected in $G_c(A)$.

Proof: Let $A : \mathscr{E} \to \mathbb{B}$ be a model for $f_c(G, S)$. Since A satisfies the formula $f_p(G_j, s_j, s_{j+1})$ for all $1 \le j < |S|$, there is a path P_j between the vertices s_j and s_{j+1} in the graph $G_{j_p}(A_j)$ as shown in theorem 2, where A_j is the assignment A restricted to the variables in $\mathscr{E}_j$.

Since $G_{j_p}(A_j)$ is a subgraph of $G_c(A)$, there is a path in $G_c(A)$ for all $1 \le j < |S|$ as well. Due to transitivity, there is a path between each pair of vertices in S in $G_c(A)$, thus all vertices in S are connected in this subgraph of G. $\square$

There are $|S| - 1$ constraints in $f_c(G, S)$. Each of them has $|V| + 2|E|$ elements, as shown in Sect. 3.1. Hence, the size of this formula, which has $|E|(|S| - 1)$ variables, is equal to $(|V| + 2|E|)(|S| - 1)$. It's quadratic in the size of the graph in the worst case. However, it's worth mentioning that $|S| \leq |V|$, and, if $|V| \leq |E|$, the size of the formula is smaller than $(|V| + |E|)^2$.

3.4   Steiner Tree

The Steiner Tree problem consists of, given a graph $G = (V, E)$, a set of its vertices $S \subseteq V$ and a function $w : E \to \mathbb{N}$ that associates a weight to each edge in G, finding a subgraph of G that is connected, contains all the vertices in S and whose weight is minimum. The weight of a subgraph is equal to the sum of the weights of its edges. Clearly an optimal subgraph is always a tree. The problem is known to be NP-hard [5].

Steiner Tree can be reduced to MaxSAT if the hard formula states that all vertices in S are connected, and the soft formulae state that the required graph must have the minimum sum of weights of its edges.

The hard formula is defined as $f_c(G, S)$ as described above. Each soft formula is defined as $f_{s_i} = (\neg \varrho_{i,1} \land ... \land \neg \varrho_{i,|S|-1})$ with weight $w(e_i)$, for each $e_i \in E$.

The correctness of this reduction is shown by the following two theorems. Their proof were omitted due to space limitations. However, they can be proved using theorems shown in Sect. 3.1, 3.2 and 3.3.

Theorem 7: If $A : \mathscr{E} \to \mathbb{B}$ is a solution for the reduced instance to MaxSAT, then $G_c(A)$ is an optimal tree containing the vertices in S.

Theorem 8: Let T be an optimal tree of G that contains all vertices in S. There is a model A for $f_c(G, S)$ that is a solution for the given MaxSAT instance for which $G_c(A)$ contains only T.

The number of elements in $f_c(G, S)$ is equal to $(|V| + 2|E|)(|S| - 1)$, as shown in Sect. 3.3. Also, There are $|E|$ formulae in f_s with size $|S| - 1$ each. Hence, the sum of the size of all the formulae is equal to $(|V| + 3|E|)(|S| - 1)$. This reduction is also quadratic in the size of the given graph in the worst case, but smaller than $2(|V| + |E|)^2$ if $|V| < |E|$.

This reduction is partially based on ideas from a previously published approximated reduction from Steiner Tree to MaxSAT [2]. After a pre-processing step, the reduction presented in [2] generates a CNF instance with $|E| + k(|S| - 1)$ variables and $O(|E| + k|E|(|S| - 1))$ clauses, where k is an approximation factor. k is not polynomial for exact reductions. Our reduction is exact, quadratic and doesn't require a pre-processing step.

Using similar ideas, it's possible to reduce other NP problems than Steiner Tree to SAT and MaxSAT. One can reduce Hamiltonian Cycle, for instance, stating that all vertices in V must be connected and that the degree of each one in the resulting subgraph must be exactly 2. This reduction is also quadratic in the worst case. It's not covered in this paper due to space limitations.

3.5   Clique

As shown in previous sections, it is possible to build a formula stating that some (possible all) vertices of a graph must be connected in a solution in quadratic time, in the worst case. However, reductions can be simplified when the required solution consists of a complete connected subgraph, i.e., a clique.

A clique of size k in a graph G is a complete subgraph of G with exactly k vertices. The decision problem Clique consists of, given G and $k \in \mathbb{N}$, checking whatever there is a clique of size k in G. In this paper we assume $k > 1$, since the problem is trivial for other cases. Clique is a NP-complete problem [5].

Clique can be reduced to SAT by building a formula $f_K(G, k)$ that is satisfiable if and only if there is a clique of size k in G. Also, any model A for $f_K(G, k)$ describes a subgraph $G_K(A)$ of G consisting of a required clique. This formula can be built in the following way:

- Analogously to the reduction from Minimum Path, let's associate a binary variable ϱ_i for each $e_i \in E$, and let $\mathscr{E}$ be the set of all these variables. Given a model $A : \mathscr{E} \to \mathbb{B}$ for $f_K(G, k)$, $G_K(A)$ is defined then as the subgraph of G induced by the edge set $\{e_i \in E : A(\varrho_i) = 1\}$.
- Let's state that there must be exactly k vertices in $G_K(A)$ with degree $k-1$. This can be done with the constraint, where $\{v_1, v_2, ..., v_{|V|}\} = V$:
$$C_k(C_{k-1}(\mathcal{N}(v_1)), C_{k-1}(\mathcal{N}(v_2)), ..., C_{k-1}(\mathcal{N}(v_{|V|})))$$
- Also, let's state that all others $|V| - k$ vertices must have degree 0 in $G_K(A)$. This can be done with the constraint
$$C_{|V|-k}(C_0(\mathcal{N}(v_1)), C_0(\mathcal{N}(v_2)), ..., C_0(\mathcal{N}(v_{|V|}))).$$

$f_K(G, k)$ can then be built as the conjunction of the given two constraints:

$$f_K(G, k) = C_k(C_{k-1}(\mathcal{N}(v_1)), C_{k-1}(\mathcal{N}(v_2)), ..., C_{k-1}(\mathcal{N}(v_{|V|}))) \wedge \quad (3)$$
$$C_{|V|-k}(C_0(\mathcal{N}(v_1)), C_0(\mathcal{N}(v_2)), ..., C_0(\mathcal{N}(v_{|V|})))$$

This reduction to SAT is correct, as shown by the two following theorems:

Theorem 9: If there is a clique of size k in G, then $f_K(G, k)$ is satisfiable.

Proof: Let G' be a clique of size k in G, and let A be the assignment that associates 1 to the variables corresponding to the edges in G', i.e., $A(\varrho_i) = 1$ if and only if $e_i \in E(G')$.

Since G' is a complete subgraph, all vertices in $V(G')$ have the same and maximum possible degree in it, equal to $|V(G')| - 1$. Since G' has k vertices, $|V(G')| = k$ and thus the degree of all k vertices in it is equal to $k - 1$. Hence, there are exactly $k - 1$ edges in the neighbourhood of v_i in the clique, for all $v_i \in V(G')$. Since this sentence is valid for exactly k vertices, A satisfies the first constraint of $f_K(G, k)$.

Also, all the others $|V| - k$ vertices in G do not belong to G', and thus none (0) of the edges in their neighbourhood are in the clique. Hence, A satisfies the second constraint of $f_K(G, k)$ as well, and thus satisfies the entire formula. $\quad \square$

Theorem 10: If $f_K(G, k)$ is satisfiable, then G contains a clique of size k.

Proof: Let A be a model for $f_K(G, k)$. Since A satisfies the second constraint of $f_K(G, k)$, there are at least $|V| - k$ vertices for which no edges in $G_K(A)$ connects them, since their degree is zero. Hence, there are at most k vertices in $G_K(A)$.

Also, since A satisfies the first constraint of the formula, there are at least k vertices for which there is at least one edge in $G_c(A)$ connecting it, since we assume $k - 1 \geq 1$. $G_K(A)$ has at most and at least k vertices with positive degree. Hence, there are exactly k vertices in $G_K(A)$.

Since A satisfies the first constraint of $f_K(G, k)$, the degree of any vertex in $G_K(A)$ is equal to $k - 1$. This degree is maximum, since there are k vertices in $G_K(A)$. Hence, any vertex in the subgraph is directly connected to all others vertices in it, and thus $G_K(A)$ is a clique of size k.

Since $G_K(A)$ is a subgraph of G, G contains a clique of size k. □

The number of elements in both the first and second constraints of $f_K(G, k)$ is proportional to the number of vertices in G plus the sum of the degrees of all vertices in G, $2|E|$. To be exact, there are $4|E| + 2|V| + 3$ elements in the entire formula, which has $|E|$ variables. Hence, the size of this formula is linear in the size of the given graph.

The decision problem Clique can be used to solve the optimization problem Maximum Clique. The problem can be solved by binary searching k or by incrementing k until the formula is unsatisfiable.

4   Experimental Results

We implemented all described reductions. The resulting formulae were converted to CNF by using recursive counters [4] with variable injections. Our implementation can be downloaded at *http://www.inf.ufpr.br/rtoliveira* .

We compare the size of the resulting formulae and the time taken by a (Max)SAT solver to solve them against earlier published reductions. We use Lingeling [7] to solve SAT instances, and MiniMaxSAT [3] to solve MaxSAT ones. Both solvers were run on an *Intel(R) Core(TM)2 Duo CPU E8400, 3 GHz, 4 Gb RAM, Ubuntu 10.10 OS*.

The reduction from Steiner Tree was compared against a straightforward, not optimized implementation of a depth-first transversal (DFT) representation [1]. The tested instances were obtained from the SteinLib benchmark [6].

Table 1 shows the results. The column $|V|/|E|/|S|$ describes the size of the elements of the graph. *No. Vars.* and *No. Claus.* indicate the number of boolean variables and the number of clauses in the resulting formulae, respectively. *Time* describes the time took by the solver to solve the instance. The value *TLE* indicates that the instance was not solved within one hour.

One can observe that our reduction generates formulae which are smaller and can be solved faster than the DFT reduction. It's worth mentioning, however, that DFT's authors themselves point the ineffectiveness of this reduction [1].

Table 1. Experimental results of reductions from Steiner Tree

		Presented Reduction			DFT		
Instance	$|V|/|E|/|S|$	No.Vars	No.Claus.	Time	No.Vars.	No.Claus.	Time
b01	50/63/9	2367	7309	2.87s	15939	1032075	TLE
b02	50/63/13	3363	10330	3.56s	15939	1032079	TLE
b03	50/63/25	6711	20705	10.18s	15939	1032091	TLE
b04	50/100/9	4748	14816	TLE	40100	4080209	TLE

It's also possible to notice that the size of a formula is not proportional to the time a SAT solver takes to solve it. The formula generated from the instance b04 is smaller, but is not solved as fast as the formula generated from b03.

The presented reduction from Clique was compared against the simpler reduction from Maximum Clique to MaxSAT, linear in the complement of the given graph (LCOMP), as shown in [3]. The conversion from our reduced instances to CNF generated formulae larger than the ones generated by LCOMP, mainly due to the large number of encoded half and full adders. Using LCOMP is more efficient than converting our formulae to CNF, even for random sparse graphs (with density 1%).

It's worth mentioning, however, that formulae generated by our reduction from Clique have $4|E| + 2|V| + 3$ elements before the conversion to CNF, while the hard formula generated by LCOMP have $\binom{|V|}{2} - |E|$ clauses with size 2.

Also, before the conversion to CNF, instances generated by our reduction from Steiner Tree have $|E|(|S| - 1)$ variables (aprox. 5 times less than the number of variables after the conversion, for the tested instances), and $(|V| + 3|E|)(|S| - 1)$ elements (aprox. 4 times less than the number of clauses for the same instances).

As discussed in Sect. 5, this motivate the direct implementation of the Choose operators in a non clausal SAT solver. This would discard the need to convert the formulae to CNF.

5   Conclusions and Future Work

We presented *Choose-H*, a class of operators that simplifies reductions from problems in graphs to SAT and MaxSAT. As shown in Sect. 2, any classical formula can be directly converted to use only these operators. Also, these operators can be converted to classical formulae in linear time, if $|H|$ is constant.

Our experiments showed that, when converted to CNF, the formulae generated by our reduction from Steiner Tree are smaller and can be solved faster than ones generated by the previously presented exact reduction. However, they are not small enough, as our experiments with the reduction from Clique also showed.

A possible way to take advantage of smaller formulae is to adapt some non clausal SAT solver to make it solve MaxSAT instances with *Choose* operators, using Branch and Bound, like MiniMaxSAT [3]. We intend to implement the operators in some free, open source non clausal SAT solver.

It will not be needed to create new variables in the formulae, since, given a (partial) assignment, the solver can count and compare the number of true values among the arguments of an operator in a trivial way. This will keep the number of variables of an instance in its minimum, $|\mathscr{E}|$.

Also, since any classical formula can be converted to use the *Choose* connectors, we are motivated to create a new non clausal SAT solver that handles these operators only. Efficient internal data structures are being studied and implemented to optimize the Boolean Constraint Propagation Procedure on these connectors.

References

1. Kautz, H., Selman, B., Jiang, Y.: A General Stochastic Approach to Solving Problems with Hard and Soft Constraints. In: The Satisfiability Problem – Theory and Applications, pp. 573–586. American Mathematical Society (1996)
2. Menai, M.E.B.: A Logic-Based Approach to Solve the Steiner Tree Problem. In: Iliadis, Maglogiann, Tsoumakasis, Vlahavas, Bramer (eds.) Artificial Intelligence Applications and Innovations III. IFIP AICT, vol. 296, pp. 73–79. Springer, Heidelberg (2009)
3. Heras, F., Larrosa, J., Oliveras, A.: Minimaxsat – An Efficient Weighted Max-Sat Solver. Journal of Artificial Intelligence Research 31(1), 1–32 (2008)
4. Muller, D.E., Preparata, F.P.: Bounds to Complexities of Networks for Sorting and for Switching. Journal of the ACM 22(2), 195–201 (1975)
5. Karp, R.M.: Reducibility Among Combinatorial Problems. In: Complexity of Computer Computations, pp. 85–103. Plenum Press (1972)
6. Koch, T., Martin, A., Vos, S.: Steinlib: An Updated Library on Steiner Tree Problems in Graphs. Technical Report ZIB 00-37. Zuse Institute Berlin (2000)
7. Biere, A.: Lingeling, Plingeling, Picosat and Precosat at SAT race 2010. Technical Report 10/1, FMV Reports Series. Institute for Formal Models and Verification, Johannes Kepler University (2010)

Towards Socio-Chronobiological Computational Human Models

Francisco Campuzano, Emilio Serrano, and Juan A. Botía

University of Murcia, Murcia, Spain
{fjcampuzano,emilioserra,juanbot}@um.es

Abstract. Testing and validating Ambient Intelligence (AmI) services by living labs is not always feasible. The costs involved, specially when considering a large number of users, may be prohibitive. In these cases, an artificial society is required to test the AmI software in a simulated environment. Numerous methodologies deal with the modeling of agents, but this paper contributes with a methodology capable of modeling human beings by using agents, *CHROMUBE*. This methodology is extended in this paper to include social interactions in its models. This extension of the methodology employs an architecture which maximizes code reuse and allows developers to model numerous kind of interactions (p.e.: voice, e-mail conversations, light panels ads, phone calls, etcetera). An implementation of the architecture is also given with *UbikSim* and a case study illustrates its use and potential.

Keywords: ambient intelligence, testing, validation, social simulation, chronobiology, interactions.

1 Introduction

Ambient Intelligence (AmI) [15] brings us the possibility of a new world where computing devices are spread everywhere. These devices allow human beings to interact in physical world environments in an intelligent and unobtrusive way. These environments should be aware of the needs of people. For that reason, AmI environments offer different services whose main goal is to augment live quality of people. As any software, these services need to be tested and validated. The use of living labs [16] is a typical approach to test and to validate AmI environments. A living lab is a real environment that emulates the final environment where the system under test is going to be deployed. However, this approach is not feasible in scenarios with a large number of users involved due to the high costs associated with its deployment.

As an alternative, new approaches based on simulation are emerging. Simulation implies the creation of a virtual physical space which combines real and simulated features. Some components as the system under test could be real while another components (users, sensors and appliances) are simulated. Various attempts following this approach can be found in the literature; Ubiwise,

J. Pavón et al. (Eds.): IBERAMIA 2012, LNAI 7637, pp. 392–401, 2012.

TATUS, UbiREAL [12] and UbikSim [17] are examples of this. Among this examples, only UbikSim addresses the simulation of users realistically by combining this tool with *CHROMUBE*.

In addition to the development of UbikSim, previous works [6] have introduced *CHROMUBE* (CHROnobiology for Modeling hUman BEhavior). Unlike related works which propose methodologies for the agent based modeling, CHROMUBE allows developers to model realistic AmI users with the purpose of testing and validating AmI systems. The main ideas behind this methodology are the following. (1) It is possible to create realistic human behaviors and simulate them for the validation of AmI environment's services or applications. (2) Chronobiology, an area of science which studies how time affects living organisms, can help in the characterization of human behaviors. (3) Sensor data gathered from the AmI environment allow *CMHBs* (Computational Models of Human Behavior) to be created. CHROMUBE has been successfully employed to validate AmI environments with isolated users, e.g. elders living independently in their own house. On the other hand, this methodology still lacks mechanisms to model and validate social interactions in the CMHBs. There is a great number of AmI scenarios, e.g. evacuation services, where the communication among humans must be considered to model a realistic society. Besides, different social roles for different human models must also be included since they have an important influence over the behavior presented.

The contribution of this paper is an extension of CHROMUBE in general and its modeling phase in particular to simulate human behaviors including social interactions, i.e. building socio-chronobiological computational human models. To build such models, this methodology guide developers step by step in the construction of an architecture based on two components: hierarchical automaton of behaviors (*HAB*) and hierarchical automaton of interactions (*HAI*). The paper shows how this component-based architecture allows developers to model a large number of interactions such as voice, e-mail conversations, light panels ads, phone calls, etc. UbikSim [2], available online, has been extended to include not only the code to follow the methodology so as to build instances of this architecture for specific cases, but also numerous examples to maximize the software reuse. Moreover, independently of CHROMUBE and UbikSim, this paper offers a breakdown of the major design decisions that any developer has to deal with to include interactions in social simulations.

The paper is structured as follows. Section 2 outlines the basic ideas of CHROMUBE and presents the extension for the modeling phase. Section 3 defines how to obtain behavior models in CHROMUBE and Sect. 4 explains the process of including social interactions in these behavior models. Section 5 illustrates the application of previous sections in a concrete case study. Section 6 gives related works. Finally, Sect. 7 outlines conclusions and future work.

2   A Methodology to Develop Realistic Human Models

CHROMUBE [6] addresses the problem of obtaining realistic human models to validate AmI services by social simulations. This methodology is capable of

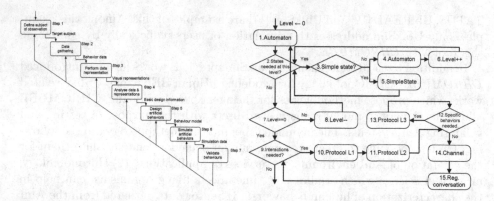

Fig. 1. Methodological process to obtain and validate computational models of human behavior (on the left). Detail of the modeling step (on the right). Figures available online [1].

generating and validating a realistic CMHB, i.e. one that reproduces a behavior which is highly similar to that used as a source, by using techniques of chronobiology. Chronobiology is the field of biology that studies the mechanisms and alterations of each organism's temporal structure [10]. Some Chronobiology methods employed in CHROMUBE to ensure that the human models are realistic are the use of *actograms* and *plexograms* to characterize the activity rate of people and how their activity varies depending on time. CHROMUBE appears graphically represented in Fig. 1 on the left. A more detailed explanation of CHROMUBE is available online http://ants.dif.um.es/staff/emilioserra/ubiksim/IBERAMIA/ [1].

As explained in the introduction, this paper extends the step 5 of CHROMUBE, design of artificial behaviors, providing CHROMUBE with the possibility of modeling interactions among the human models. Fig. 1 on the right shows the guideline for this design in a flow diagram. Before explaining this detail of the methodology, the following sections introduce the general architecture that developers have to adapt to their specific purposes. The resulting CHMBs are the inputs for the step 6 of CHROMUBE (Simulate artificial behaviors). The case study follows this extension of the methodology and simulates the resulting models in UbikSim [2].

3   Hierarchical Automaton of Behaviors

This section discusses the *Hierarchical Automaton of Behaviors* (HAB) that allows humans to be modeled realistically. Previous works [6] have introduced this automaton, but this paper gives a methodology for its design (see Fig. 1 on the right) and an implementation available online [2] to be tested by the reader interested. Furthermore, this paper combines a HAB with a hierarchical automaton of interactions (HAI) which is explained in Sect. 4 to build an architecture for the interactions among human models whose main components are depicted in

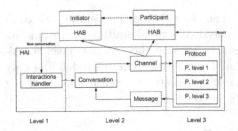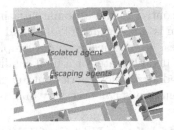

Fig. 2. Architecture for the interactions among human models, main components (on the left). Simulation with UbikSim (on the right).

Fig. 2 on the left. An implementation of this architecture is included in UbikSim, Fig. 2 on the right shows a simulation in UbikSim which is deployed in Sect. 5.

In essence, a HAB is composed of: a list of pending transitions ordered by priority, a method for creating new transitions (adding them to the list), a current state (state with the control) and a default state (state that takes control of the automaton when the list of pending transitions is empty). An *interpreter* [6] makes the automaton advance every step of the simulation. The main actions of the interpreter are described below. (1) Firstly, *new pending transitions* are generated from the *current state* to another. (2) Then, the interpreter checks whether the current state is completed (or still empty) to undertake the next transition in the list, the one with higher priority. (3) If the list is empty, the *default state* is taken as current state. (4) If the current state is not finished but there is a transition with highest priority in the list, the interpreter gives the control to the latter. Finally, (5) the current state takes control to undertake an action. In our proposal, the HAB control is performed transparently to the developer. The complete code of the interpreter is omitted for the sake of brevity (see code online [1]). The following section outlines the main components to model behaviors using a HAB and the main decisions to be made when implementing it.

3.1   Main Components of a HAB

Hierarchical automaton means that each state is itself another automaton, a *subordinate automaton*, and therefore, it has the same components. By default, the architecture presented assumes that an automaton ends and returns the control when the time assigned as a parameter in its creation is over, or if there is no default state given and no transitions pending. Note that the main automaton (level 0), the highest in the hierarchy, never ends if a cyclic behavior wants to be modeled (and therefore a default state must be given). UbikSim offers the class *Automaton* to define a HAB extending it. The tasks to be implemented by the developer are: (1) creating new transitions, (2) getting the default state, and (3) including an ending condition for the automaton if needed.

The states at the bottom of the hierarchy (with no subordinate automata) implements simple behaviors. The developer must create one of these simple states when defining an action which will be performed in one step to immediately return control to the automaton father. The class that defines simple states in UbikSim is *SimpleState*. (1), (2), and (3), needed in the definition of Automaton instances, are not necessary for simple states because they do not have: transitions, a default state, or a final condition. These states requires redefining only a method *step* which carries out an "atomic" action (in the sense that modeling an automaton is not necessary due to its simplicity).

3.2 Modeling a HAB in CHROMUBE

Figure 1 on the right explains the methodology for the creation of a HAB in steps 1 to 8. Firstly, an abstraction level 0 is supposed to create an automaton (step 1). Then, the developer considers whether to add new states to the automaton at that level (step 2). If so, the next decision is whether the state is simple or not (step 3). If it is not simple, an *Automaton* is created (step 4). If it is simple, a *SimpleState* is introduced (step 5). For both cases, steps 4 or 5, some details are required such as the maximum execution time and the priority of the state (see [6]). The previous section details the key decisions to be addressed in implementing Automaton and SimpleState extensions. If an automaton has been created, the subordinate states must be defined. In this case, the abstraction level is increased (step 6) and the developer returns to step 2 to define these subordinate states. Once there are no more states to be added at the current level (step 2), step 7 checks if the abstraction level is zero to start modeling the interactions. In the level is not zero, the level is reduced and the developer returns to step 1 to include transitions to the subordinate states in the currently considered automaton.

This methodology describe a top-down approach which involves the breaking down of a human behavior to gain insight into its compositional sub-behaviors. Code reuse is a major concern of the architecture presented. Some example automata implemented in UbikSim [2] that can be used or combined to create a specific HAB are: *SimpleMove* (to allow an agent to move in a straight line); *DoNothing* (do nothing, typically used as default state); *Move* (move to a room or a particular position establishing automatically an optimal path in the map), this automaton has several subordinate SimpleMove automata; *MoveAndStay* (which allows an agent to move to a room and stay in a certain time), this automaton has as subordinate automata DoNothing and Move.

4 Hierarchical Automaton of Interactions

There are plenty of related works which propose a model of social agents. In contrast, this paper offers an architecture which is able to model human beings considering their social interactions. This section details the *Hierarchical Automaton of Interactions* (HAI) to be combined with the HAB discussed above in order to model these social interactions in CMHBs. The HAI is a hierarchical automaton in three levels: InteractionsHandler, Conversations and Protocols. Besides, Protocols have three different levels of abstraction, see Fig. 2 on the left.

The control of the HAI is illustrated in Fig. 2 on the left. An initiator, an agent which wants to start an interaction, calls the *InteractionsHandler* to register a conversation with a protocol and a channel. The handler passes control to the conversation in every step of the simulation. The conversation passes control to a protocol (if it is allowed by the channel). The protocol produces messages in the conversation, marks the end of the conversation, and makes the participants react (usually causing new transitions in the HAB). The following section discusses these elements in more detail and explains the decisions required when implementing a HAI.

4.1   Main Components of the HAI

The main components of the HAI are: messages, protocols (three levels), channels, conversations and InteractionHandler. They are explained below.

The communication implemented is based on a *Message* passing, but this mechanism is used to model various types of conversations (voice, email, phone, etc). Messages have the typical elements of a FIPA ACL message [8].

The *Protocol* is the message producer and has three different levels of abstraction. A *first level* is responsible for performing tasks that are implemented for a protocol regardless of the semantics exchanged. Its objectives are: (1) providing the set of performatives, i.e. communicative acts [8], that can follow a given performative in the protocol; (2) determining if the protocol is finished for a given message and if this end has been successful or not; and (3) verifying, given a conversation that has followed this protocol, if the protocol has been followed correctly. When a protocol is used for specific purposes, is used in a *second level of abstraction*. At this level, the problem is no longer deciding the next performative, but deciding the semantics or content for the following message. That is, (4) the semantics of a received message must be studied in addition to its performative to select the next message to be sent. This level is also responsible for (5) selecting a set of participants for the conversation and (6) reacting once the protocol has been completed, i.e., changing the behavior of the participants based on the results of a conversation. Finally, at *a third level of abstraction*, each agent can have (7) different preferences to fulfill a protocol, so there are as many instances of the second level as preferences needed.

The protocol produces messages assuming that the agents are in an appropriate state of the HAB and that the messages are correctly received. However, the messages must not always reach their destination. The requisites to decide whether a message is received or not are implemented in the *Channel*. In particular, the channel is responsible for five different tasks listed below. (1) *Initialize participants* reserves the use of the channel when necessary (e.g for a phone call). (2) *Channel free to send* decides if the person modeled is available to send a message through the channel in a conversation (e.g. having a cell phone and not being already calling). (3) *Channel free to receive* is also necessary because in some channels the proper sending does not imply that the recipient receives the message (e.g modeling a interaction by e-mail). (4) *Discard message* when a message does not reach its destination at once (e.g. voice is ruled out, but a e-mail is not). (5) *Finish participants* undertakes tasks after the end of a conversation on the channel (e.g. releasing a channel reservation if it was made in (1)).

A *Conversation* uses a channel, a protocol of level 1 and 2, and, if necessary, specific protocols of the participants (level 3) to generate messages. The conversation is a protocol and "channels" interpreter. The conversations are registered by the HAB in the *InteractionsHandler*, another interpreter which manages the different conversations. These interpreters acts in a transparent manner without requiring additional code as the interpreter of the HAB explained in Sect. 3 (see source code online [1]).

4.2   Modeling a HAI in CHROMUBE

Fig. 1 on the right explains the methodology for the creation of a HAI in steps 9 to 15. Step 9 checks whether it is necessary to add interactions among the humans modeled. If so, the developer implements a protocol of the first level of abstraction that can be used for different purposes (step 10). Afterwards, this protocol is extended for a particular purpose, e.g. FIPA-request-for-meeting (step 11). Step 12 checks if some people have different behaviors at the second level of the protocol to create a third level of abstraction (step 13). Once all the necessary protocol implementations are developed, the channel is implemented (step 14). Finally, the HAB is modified to register a conversation in the *InteractionsHandler*, including the protocols and the channel newly created.

Again, as in the case of the HAB, a HAI can be constructed using components available in the implementation of the approach presented [2]. In this case, however, is usually necessary to implement protocols for level 2 and 3 ad-hoc because the semantics of interactions often depends on the specific purposes of the simulation. Some examples of classes already defined in UbikSim are: channels (channelVoice, channelPhone, channelEmail, etc.) and protocols of level 1 (FipaRequest, FipaContractNet, SimpleMessage, etc).

5   Case Study

This case study models an emergency evacuation in a real department at a university (see map of the department and figure of the environment simulated online [1]). The purpose is to illustrate the construction of a HAB and a HAI in a particular case. In a first approximation, the department faculty remain working in her office by default. Then, one of the professors start fleeing to the stairs and loudly warning of an emergence on her way. The expected outcome is a viral effect that produces the spread of the emergency behavior.

Following the methodology of Fig. 1 on the right, a class *AutomatonProfessor* is implemented with the behavior of professors in the department (step 1). This automaton represents the abstraction level 0. After step 2 and 3, a "working" automaton must be modeled. The *Move* automaton provided by UbikSim for movements along complex environments is used to make agents go to their offices (step 4). Back in *AutomatonProfessor* this new working automaton is used as default state (step 1; after steps 6, 2, 7, 8 and 1). After step 2, 3 and 4; a new automaton *Escape* is created. The level of abstraction is increased (step 6) to design the new states of this automaton of level 1. Step 4 is simplified again by using predefined UbikSim automata: *Move* (to "goToStairs") and *Disappear* (to remove the agent after the escape). Returning to the design of *Automaton-Professor* (steps 2, 7, 8 and 1), a transition is included to *Escape*.

After modeling the HAB, the social interactions are included in the HAI. *SingleMessage*, included in UbikSim, is employed as protocol of level 1 (step 10) to send a single message of performative *inform*. Step 11 creates *SingleMessage-WarningOfFire* to include: the semantics ("Fire" as content of the message), participants of the conversation (all staff), and the reaction of the receptors (generating a transition in the HAB to *Escape*). Step 12 and 13 considers the possibility of heterogeneous reactions to the alarm, i.e. some agents could tend to panic, which are not modeled in this case. Step 14 models *ChannelVoice*, already given by UbikSim, which does not require initialization or ending by the participants, either has restrictions when sending. In contrast, the messages that are not received after a step are ruled out and the successful reception depends on the distance among participants. Finally, step 15 goes to *Escape* to register the conversation in the *InteractionHandler*.

Figure 2 on the right shows a snapshot of the simulation. Multiple agents escaping can be observed in red. An agent at the upper left corner has not received the warning because of its isolation from the rest. A second strategy can generate more movement transitions in the HAB to pass through several key points in the building so as to spread the warning. A third strategy, which is the one that the department actually has, can designate organizers and a series of offices to be evacuated by each of these organizers. For the sake of brevity, the model of these last two alternative strategies are not included in this paper. However, all these variations can be easily reproduced by the interested reader including more "move" transitions in the basic HAB modeled here. The graphical representation of the HAB modeled and the classes implemented to reproduce this case study in UbikSim are available online [1]. The authors also strongly recommend to watch the video showing a run of the simulation for the three evacuation strategies modeled [1].

6   Related Works

Regarding engineering realistic human behaviors, various approaches have been proposed to create autonomous characters. Garcia-Valverde et al. [9], defined human behaviors as states in a hierarchical automata and probabilistic transitions between them. In approaches [18] and [5], the behavioral models described also use a hierarchical structure of finite state automata.In the work of Chittaro et al. [7], the behavior sequences are modeled through probabilistic automata (Probabilistic Finite-State Machine, PFSMs). Arthur [4] develops agents using a parameterised learning automaton with a vector of associated actions that can be weighted to choose actions over time the way humans would. Anastassakis et al. [3] present an approach where every character is provided with a small KBS (Knowledge-Based System) for intelligent reasoning. A reasoning system is also used by Noser et al. [13]. Both methods are very flexible, but defining the knowledge base is a complex and time-consuming task. Liu et al. [11] use a distributed intelligent multi-agent system for modeling complex and dynamic user behavior. Most alternative approaches just rely on reading variables to simulate interactions without offering the developer any guideline. The extension of CHROMUBE presented in this paper offers a concrete methodology and a complete architecture to model social interactions.

7   Conclusions and Future Works

This paper extends *CHROMUBE* (CHROnobiology for Modeling hUman BEhavior), in particular its step of modeling, with an architecture to build sociochronobiological computational human models. For this purpose, the architecture includes a hierarchical automaton of interactions which defines protocols with several levels of abstraction, channels which decide if messages can be sent and received, and interpreters which make the messages flow in a transparent manner. The methodology offers concrete steps to adapt the architecture to specific cases and the major issues in the modeling of these interactions have been discussed. Besides, an implementation of the architecture has also been given [2] and a case study illustrates the potential of the methodology to model societies to test and validate Ambient Intelligence (AmI) services. Additional unpublished material is available online [1].

Since the case study presented is based on fire safety and security policies of a department, our main future work is to apply the methodology and architecture presented in scenarios where sensors can gather information of the real human beings (e.g. hospitals or geriatrics). The use of *sociometers* [14] will allow us to register physical movements, capture vocal inflections and face to face interactions. Patterns that represent the degree of engagement between conversing people can be identified analyzing these data to be modeled with the architecture presented in this paper and subsequently validated.

Acknowledgment. This research work is supported in the scope of the Research Projects TSI-020302-2010-129, TIN2011-28335-C02-02 and through the Fundación Séneca within the Program 04552/GERM/06.

References

1. Additional material for this paper,
   http://ants.dif.um.es/staff/emilioserra/ubiksim/IBERAMIA
2. Ubiksim website, http://ubiksim.sourceforge.net/
3. Anastassakis, G., Panayiotopoulos, T., Ritchings, T.: Virtual Agent Societies with the mVITAL Intelligent Agent System. In: de Antonio, A., Aylett, R.S., Ballin, D. (eds.) IVA 2001. LNCS (LNAI), vol. 2190, pp. 112–125. Springer, Heidelberg (2001)

4. Arthur, W.: On Designing Economic Agents that Behave like Human Agents. Journal of Evolutionary Economics 3(1), 1–22 (1993)
5. Becheiraz, P., Thalmann, D.: A Behavioral Animation System for Autonomous Actors Personified by Emotions. In: 1998 Workshop on Embodied Conversational Characters, WECC 1998 (1998)
6. Campuzano, F., Botia, J., Villa, A.: Chronobiology Applied to the Development of Human Behavior Computational Models. Journal of Ambient Intelligence and Smart Environments (to appear)
7. Chittaro, L., Serra, M.: Behavioral Programming of Autonomous Characters Based on Probabilistic Automata and Personality. Computer Animation and Virtual Worlds 15(34), 319–326 (2004)
8. FIPA: FIPA ACL Message Structure Specification (2002)
9. García-Valverde, T., García-Sola, A., Lopez-Marmol, F., Botia, J.A.: Engineering Ambient Intelligence Services by Means of MABS. In: Demazeau, Y., et al. (eds.) Trends in PAAMS. AISC, vol. 71, pp. 37–44. Springer, Heidelberg (2010)
10. Halberg, F., Carandente, F., Cornelissen, G., Katinas, G.S.: Glossary of Chronobiology, Chronobiologia, vol. 4. Intl. Society for Chronobiology (1977)
11. Liu, Y., O'Grady, M.J., O'Hare, G.M.P.: Scalable Context Simulation for Mobile Applications. In: Meersman, R., Tari, Z., Herrero, P. (eds.) OTM 2006 Workshops. LNCS, vol. 4278, pp. 1391–1400. Springer, Heidelberg (2006)
12. Nishikawa, H., Yamamoto, S., Tamai, M., Nishigaki, K., Kitani, T., Shibata, N., Yasumoto, K., Ito, M.: UbiREAL – Realistic Smartspace Simulator for Systematic Testing. In: Dourish, P., Friday, A. (eds.) UbiComp 2006. LNCS, vol. 4206, pp. 459–476. Springer, Heidelberg (2006)
13. Noser, H., Thalmann, D.: Towards Autonomous Synthetic Actors. In: Kunii, T., Luciani, A. (eds.) Synthetic Worlds. John Wiley and Sons (1995)
14. Pentland, A.S.: Honest Signals – How They Shape Our World. The MIT Press (2008)
15. Ramos, C.: Ambient Intelligence – A State of the Art from Artificial Intelligence Perspective. In: Neves, J., Santos, M.F., Machado, J.M. (eds.) EPIA 2007. LNCS (LNAI), vol. 4874, pp. 285–295. Springer, Heidelberg (2007)
16. de Ruyter, B., van Loenen, E., Teeven, V.: User Centered Research in Experience-Lab. In: Schiele, B., et al. (eds.) AmI 2007. LNCS, vol. 4794, pp. 305–313. Springer, Heidelberg (2007)
17. Serrano, E., Botia, J.: Validating Ambient Intelligence Based Ubiquitous Computing Systems by Mans of Artificial Societies. Information Sciences (2010) (in press)
18. Thalmann, D., Musse, S., Kallmann, M.: Virtual Humans' Behaviour – Individuals, Groups, and Crowds. In: International Conference on Digital Media Futures, pp. 1–14 (1999)

Development of a Code Generator
for the ICARO Agent Framework

José M. Gascueña[1], Elena Navarro[1],
Antonio Fernández-Caballero[1], and Juan Pavón[2]

[1] Universidad de Castilla-La Mancha, Departamento de Sistemas Informáticos &
Instituto de Investigación en Informática de Albacete (I3A), 02071-Albacete, Spain
{JManuel.Gascuena,Elena.Navarro,Antonio.Fdez}@uclm.es
[2] Universidad Complutense de Madrid, Facultad de Informática
Departamento de Ingeniería del Software e Inteligencia Artificial
c/ Profesor José García Santesmases, s/n, 28040-Madrid, Spain
jpavon@fdi.ucm.es

Abstract. ICARO is a software framework to implement multi-agent
systems (MAS) that promotes the use of different organizational and behavioural patterns. This has been extensively used in several projects and
the conclusion is that productivity could be improved with the support of
an agent-oriented modelling language. This would allow the specification
of MAS at a higher level during design phases. Then, there is a need for
code generation from the specifications to the ICARO framework. The
INGENIAS Development Kit (IDK) supports both the specification of
MAS models with all the characteristics that are required to implement
MAS with ICARO and a set of facilities for code generation. This paper
shows how ICARO is integrated with the IDK with the development of
two IDK modules (code generator and code update) for the implementation of ICARO reactive agent applications.

Keywords: multi-agent system, agent-based software engineering, code
generation.

1 Introduction

Code generators are useful tools for software development due to the evident benefits that their exploitation provides [4]. One is an improved productivity as the
time necessary to perform coding tasks is reduced. Another important benefit is
that the quality of the developed systems is also improved, as the generated code
(usually) does not have bugs. Multi-agent systems (MAS) are not an exception.
Several tools for developing MAS applications [18] already provide functionalities to generate code for a given agent programming language or framework. For
example, PDT [14], the supporting tool of the Prometheus methodology [15],
offers a code generation facility to automatically produce JACK agent language
code [21]. Taom4E [13], a tool for the development of software following the
TROPOS methodology [12], includes functionalities to generate code for Jadex

J. Pavón et al. (Eds.): IBERAMIA 2012, LNAI 7637, pp. 402–411, 2012.

language [3]. DDE [19] is an environment for the development of MAS that is based on a Domain Specific Modeling Language for MAS and supports code generation for JACK and JADE languages [1].

ICARO [7] is a software framework to implement MAS that promotes the use of different organizational and behavioural patterns. The differentiating factor from other agent oriented programming frameworks and languages [2] is the use of component patterns for modeling MAS. Moreover, while other agent based platforms that are FIPA-compliant (e.g. JADE) are focused mainly on communication standards, ICARO focuses on providing high level software components for easy development of complex agent behavior, agent coordination, and MAS organization. Regrettably, there are no tools for modeling MAS applications and generating code for this framework. ICARO has been extensively used in several projects [7] and the conclusion is that productivity could be improved with the support of an agent-oriented modelling language. This would allow the specification of MAS at a higher level during design phases. Then, there is a need for code generation from the specifications to the ICARO framework.

The contribution of this paper is to present our experience of developing two software modules that solve this gap: (1) a code generator module, and (2) a module for code update. These two modules have not been developed from scratch but the INGENIAS Development Kit (IDK) [10], the tool supporting the agent-oriented software engineering methodology named INGENIAS [16], has been used. IDK provides a template based proprietary mechanism for developing new modules able to automatically generate code for any target language. As far as we know, this kind of functionality is not provided for any other tool for designing MAS applications (e.g., PDT, Taom4E, DDE). A developer who wants to use other tools to implement the functionality implemented in this work with IDK (code generator and code update) has to be familiar with the IDK models and the structure of the xml files that store the specification of the design models.

2   Principals of ICARO and IDK

ICARO framework [7] provides high level software components that facilitate the development of agent applications. It provides engineers with concepts and models, together with a customizable MAS design and Java code fully compatible with software engineering standards, which can be integrated in the most popular IDEs. Moreover, it is independent of the agent architecture allowing developers to create new architectures and integrate them into the framework. This is a clear difference with regard to other agent frameworks, such as JACK [21] or JADE [1], which provide a middleware, instead of an extensible architecture, to establish the communications among agents. An additional advantage is that the framework already implements functionalities for automatic component management, application initialization and shutdown, reducing the developers' workload and ensuring that the components are under control. These last functionalities are not usually provided by other frameworks. Moreover, ICARO provides support to build reactive [7] and cognitive [8] agents.

On the other hand, the IDK [10] offers a graphical editor for modelling MAS applications and functionality for developing new modules able to automatically generate code for any target language. Graphical editor is generated from the INGENIAS meta-model [17], which can be extended introducing new concepts and relations needed to build new MAS applications. After that the IDK is regenerated again from the new meta-model specification. An advantage of this approach is that changes in the definition of meta-model can be easily applied to generate personalized editor. Regarding the modules, they can be developed following a general process based on both the definition of specific templates for each target platform, and procedures to retrieve information from INGENIAS models [9]. Currently, IDK incorporates modules to generate code for JADE language from design artifacts as well as documentation in HTML format for these artifacts. Moreover, there is also available a module, named *code uploader*, which can be used to keep the code components design artifacts updated with changes made in the implementation.

3   Case Study: IDK Modules for ICARO

The development of IDK modules to support ICARO as the target platform chosen for the final implementation of a multi-agent system application has followed a "bottom-up" approach. In first place, the INGENIAS structures necessary to specify all concepts and their relations for an application implemented in ICARO are identified. Then, a module is gradually developed, which automates the task of ICARO code generation from INGENIAS specifications in line with the identified conceptual relations. Finally, a new module is developed to provide the ability to upgrade the specification of a model from changes made in the implementation. A detailed description of the general process for developing IDK modules can be found in [17].

The next subsections provide a description about relations between INGENIAS and ICARO concepts, as well as the development of the modules to generate code for ICARO and to support the update of code, respectively.

3.1   Conceptual Relation between INGENIAS and ICARO

First, it is worth noting some details of the figures used in this section to describe the relationship between INGENIAS and ICARO. The right side of the figures correspond to the notation chosen to express a fragment of a model using ICARO concepts and the left side is the notation used to express the same fragment but in terms of INGENIAS language.

Any communications between the components implemented to develop a new executable ICARO application can be summarized as follows. First, an *event* is an entity for exchanging information between the producer of the event and potential receivers. An event is used for communication and information delivery from a resource to its agent or among agents. Thus, agents send events through their use interfaces and, in the same way, a resource also uses the use interface

Fig. 1. Modeling an agent using resource's services

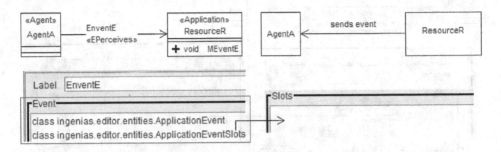

Fig. 2. Modeling an agent's perception

of an agent to send it an event. Second, an agent uses the resource use interface to request the services (methods) it offers.

From our point of view, the concepts of reactive application agent and application resource used in ICARO can be modeled in INGENIAS by using the concepts of agent and application, respectively. For example, when establishing a relationship *ApplicationBelongsTo* between an agent and an application, it is understood that the agent uses the services offered by the resource (see Fig. 1). In particular, the actions that agents execute on the environment are represented by this structure. Services are modeled as application methods.

The sending of information from a resource to an agent is modeled in IN-GENIAS by establishing a relationship *EPerceives* between the agent and the application that represents the resource (see Fig. 2). In INGENIAS, this information falls within the relationship *EPerceives* that is modeled with an event of type *ApplicationEvent* whether a resource simply sends a signal to the agent. But, it is modeled with an event of type *ApplicationEventSlots* whether more information has to be sent. In the latter case, the information and its type is modeled with entities *slots*.

Now, the sending of information among reactive agents is modeled in IN-GENIAS by specifying an entity of type *InteractionUnit* and relating it to the producer and consumer agents by means of the relationships *UInitiates* and *UICollaborates*, respectively (see Fig. 3). If the producer sends information, then this information is included in the unit of interaction through an entity of type *FrameFact* containing the necessary *slots* to transport it. Conversely, if it only sends a signal, then it does not include a *FrameFact*. Visually, it is possible to know that a unit of interaction includes a *FrameFact* because it shows the "Info" attribute (the value shown is the identifier of the *FrameFact*).

Whenever an ICARO user wants to implement the behavior of a reactive agent, he has to create an automaton which is modeled with a state diagram. In

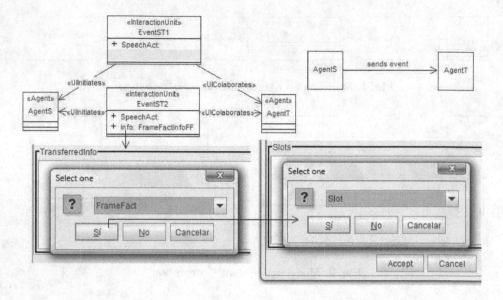

Fig. 3. Modeling a communication among agents

particular, the following five structures, availabe in INGENIAS "state diagram", have been identified to specify any automaton (see Fig. 4):

- To represent the initial state, a relationship is established between an "InitialNode" entity and the state.
- To represent a final state, a relationship is established between an "EndNode" entity and the state.
- To represent a transition between two different states, a "WFollowGuarded" relationship is established between these states, and a transition is specified using the syntax event / semantic action in its "Condition" attribute. The event represented in the state diagram is related to an *ApplicationEvent* or *ApplicationEventSlots* entity when the event is sent by a resource (see Fig. 2), or to an *InteractionUnit* entity if the event is sent by an agent (see Fig. 3). The semantic action takes the same name of the task created in the components diagram.
- The IDK tool does not permit to explicitly represent relationships that cycle over the same entity. To fix this issue, a fourth structure is considered as described next. To represent a transition that comes back to the same state, first a copy of the state is made, afterwards a "WFollowGuarded" relation is established from the copied state to the original state, and finally the transition is specified following the syntax described in the previous structure.
- Universal transitions of an automaton of an ICARO reactive agent are valid for any state of an automaton. That is to say, when the event arrives, actions are executed and the next state is reached, regardless of the automaton current state. The solution for graphically representing them in INGENIAS is to have a "UniversalState" to represent any state, which makes the role of

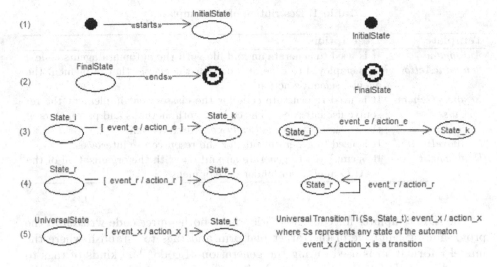

Fig. 4. Modeling an agent's automaton

the "source" state of the universal transition. Obviously, "UniversalState" has not to be used with a different meaning.
- Finally, notice that the agent's name is assigned to the state diagram as a criterion to identify the agent's behavior.

The XML file that describes the organization of an ICARO application represents the deployment of the application. The IDK tool offers the possibility of creating deployment diagrams. The number of instances of each type of agent is specified using entities such as *DeploymentPackage* and/or *DeploymentUnitByType*. However, the existence of an application instance is conditioned by the existence of the instance of an agent. For this reason, it is necessary to find an alternative way of independently expressing the number of instances of agents and applications, such as in ICARO. The solution is to create an environment model and to follow the following steps: (1) copy all the agents and applications, (2) relate them with entities of type *UMLComment*, and (3) set in attribute *Text* of *UMLComment* the number of instances to be deployed. Obviously, this process can be repeated to create different deployment configurations.

3.2   Code Generation Module

In order to generate code for the ICARO-T Framework, the *IIF* IDK module has been developed. For this aim, the *IIFGenerator* class is extended so that its constructors have, in a similar way to any IDK code generator, the templates that the *IIF* module uses. Moreover, the extended *IIFGenerator* class also implements the abstract methods defined in *BasicCodeGeneratorImp*. It is worth noting that the development of the *IIF* module has been simplified by defining a template for each artifact that an ICARO user has to implement (see Table 1).

Table 1. Description of the templates

Template	Description
Automaton	It is used to generate an xml file with the automata agents code.
SemanticAction	It is employed to generate code for the classes that implement the agents' semantic action.
ResourceGenera-torClass	It is used to generate code for the classes that implement the re-source use interfaces. The code of both methods and parameters of these classes is automatically generated as well.
ResourceUseItf	It is used to generate code for the resource use interfaces.
Deployment	It is employed to generate an xml file with the organization of the ICARO application under development.

The IDK templates for code generation have both source code written in the programming language of the target platform and tags to establish where the model information is used during the generation of code. The kinds of tags to be used in an IDK template are very limited [9]: *program* is the main tag of the document, *repeat* means that the text enclosed by this tag has to be copied and pasted to have a duplicate, *v* represents a variable, and *saveto* is used to save the enclosed text into a file. Therefore, it can be stated that the IDK code generation technology is more straightforward and easy to learn than other technologies for code generation, such as XSLT [20] o XPAND [11]. However, IDK exhibits a disadvantage: it does not allow developers to reuse templates so that they have to copy and paste those fragments to be reused hindering the code generator maintainability.

Next, the elements used by the IIF module to generate code for the intermediate states of an ICARO reactive agent automaton are shown. With this aim, the *automaton* template specifies the following pattern: for each (first repeat) intermediate state defined by the *intermediateState* variable, generate code for each (second repeat) transition that starts from such intermediate state.

```
@@@repeat id="intermediateStates"@@@
<state intermediateId="@@@v@@@intermediateState@@@/v@@@">
  @@@repeat id="isTransitions"@@@
    <transition input="@@@v@@@event@@@/v@@@"
                action="@@@v@@@action@@@/v@@@"
                nextState="@@@v@@@nextState@@@/v@@@"/>
  @@@/repeat@@@
</state>
@@@/repeat@@@
```

When the IIF module is executed using a model created with IDK, a sequence of data is generated. For instance, in the following a sketch of the sequence of an agent automaton is shown.

```
<repeat id="intermediateStates">
  <v id="intermediateState" entityID="" attID="" >IS1</v>
```

```
<repeat id="isTransitions">
    <v id="event" entityID="" attID="" >EV1</v>
    <v id="action" entityID="" attID="" >A1</v>
    <v id="nextState" entityID="" attID="" >NSA</v>
</repeat>
<repeat id="isTransitions">
    <v id="event" entityID="" attID="" >EV2</v>
    <v id="action" entityID="" attID="" >A2</v>
    <v id="nextState" entityID="" attID="" >NSB</v>
</repeat>
</repeat>
```

Finally, it is worth noting that the IIF module performs a matching between the templates and the data retrieved from the model. Next, following our example, it is shown the code generated by IIF for an intermediate state and two transitions that starts from it.

```
<state intermediateId="IS1">
    <transition input="EV1" action="A1" nextState="NSA"/>
    <transition input="EV2" action="A2" nextState="NSB"/>
</state>
```

3.3 Module to Support Code Update

Another important aspect to consider when developing of a code generator is to provide developers with facilities that prevent manually written code from being overridden by subsequent generator runs. The applied solution has been to integrate in the *IIF* module a facility for marking protected regions where the developers can manually write code. The start and end of a protected region is marked by means of comments. A file can have as many protected regions as necessary, labeled each one with a unique identifier. For instance, the classes that implement the agents' semantic actions have a protected region for each semantic action established in the state diagram that specifies the agent automaton. The following fragment of code shows an example of this type of region, where *ACTIONID* has to be replaced with the identifier of the related semantic action.

```
//#start_nodeIDACCION:ACTIONID <--ACTIONID-- DO NOT REMOVE THIS
//#end_nodeIDACCION:ACTIONID <--ACTIONID-- DO NOT REMOVE THIS
```

The *IIF* module uses the specification of the model to generate code. Therefore, it is necessary to store a copy of the code manually written in the protected regions. In this way, each time the *IIF* module is run, each protected region is overridden with the code manually written by the developer.

Another module, named *ICAROTCodeUploader*, has been developed that is in charge of synchronizing code and design. When it is executed, the design specification is updated with the regions of the code generated. This module, unlike the *IIF* module, does not require templates for its definition.

4   Conclusions

In this paper, the development of two modules (code generator and code update) that provide support for the implementation of ICARO reactive agent applications has been described. These modules are integrated in the IDK tool. It is worth pointing out that the time spent learning how to develop and implement the *IIF* and the *ICAROTCodeUploader* modules described in section 3 was two months and fifteen days. This effort is worth as new applications are modelled and implemented because the productivity is improved. The main reason is that the time necessary for coding is reduced because the developer does not need to learn the structure, location and naming rules of ICARO applications files.

We would like to point out that the presented modules have been validated through its use in the development of two different applications. The first application [5] was developed to face the problem of a collection of robots patrolling around a surveillance environment. The second application [6] was developed for monitoring and controlling the normal and anomalous situations that happen when humans access to a specific area.

During the development of both applications, the developer only had to write manually the body of both the resources methods and semantic actions along with some auxiliary classes. The remaining code was automatically generated by using as input the models created with the IDK. However, in order to provide the code generator with more powerful capabilities we are currently developing an extension for generating the event notification code.

Acknowledgements. This work is partially supported by the Spanish Ministerio de Ciencia e Innovación / FEDER under projects TIN2010-20845-C03-01 and TIN2008-06596-C02-01, and by the Spanish Junta de Comunidades de Castilla-La Mancha / FEDER under projects PII2I09-0069-0994 and PEII09-0054-9581.

References

1. Bellifemine, F., Caire, G., Greenwood, D.: Developing Multi-Agent Systems with JADE. John Wiley and Sons (2007)
2. Bordini, R.H., Dastani, M., Dix, J., El Fallah Seghrouchni, A.: Multi-Agent Programming – Languages, Tools and Applications. Springer (2009)
3. Braubach, L., Pokahr, A., Lamersdorf, W.: Jadex – A BDI-Agent System Combining Middleware and Reasoning. In: Unland, R., Calisti, M., Klusch, M. (eds.) Software Agent-Based Appl., Platforms and Development Kits, pp. 143–168. Springer (2005)
4. Gascueña, J.M., Navarro, E., Fernández-Caballero, A.: Model-Driven Engineering Techniques for the Development of Multi-Agent Systems. Engineering Applications of Artificial Intelligence 25(1), 159–173 (2012)
5. Gascueña, J.M., Navarro, E., Fernández-Caballero, A.: VigilAgent for the Development of Agent-Based Multi-robot Surveillance Systems. In: O'Shea, J., Nguyen, N.T., Crockett, K., Howlett, R.J., Jain, L.C. (eds.) KES-AMSTA 2011. LNCS, vol. 6682, pp. 200–210. Springer, Heidelberg (2011)

6. Gascueña, J.M., Navarro, E., Fernández-Caballero, A.: VigilAgent Methodology: Modeling Normal and Anomalous Situations. In: Pérez, J.B., Corchado, J.M., Moreno, M.N., Julián, V., Mathieu, P., Canada-Bago, J., Ortega, A., Caballero, A.F. (eds.) Highlights in Practical Applications of Agents and Multiagent Systems. AISC, vol. 89, pp. 27–35. Springer, Heidelberg (2011)
7. Gascueña, J.M., Fernández-Caballero, A., Garijo, F.J.: Using ICARO-T Framework for Reactive Agent-Based Mobile Robots. In: Demazeau, Y., Dignum, F., Corchado, J.M., Pérez, J.B. (eds.) Advances in PAAMS. AISC, vol. 70, pp. 91–101. Springer, Heidelberg (2010)
8. Lacouture, J., Gascueña, J.M., Gleizes, M.-P., Glize, P., Garijo, F.J., Fernández-Caballero, A.: ROSACE: Agent-Based Systems for Dynamic Task Allocation in Crisis Management. In: Demazeau, Y., Müller, J.P., Rodríguez, J.M.C., Pérez, J.B. (eds.) Advances on PAAMS. AISC, vol. 155, pp. 255–260. Springer, Heidelberg (2012)
9. Gómez-Sanz, J.J.: INGENIAS Agent Framework – Development Guide, version 1.0. Technical Report, Universidad Complutense de Madrid (2008), http://grasia.fdi.ucm.es/main/myfiles/guida.pdf
10. Gómez-Sanz, J.J., Fuentes, R., Pavón, J., García-Magariño, I.: INGENIAS Development Kit – A Visual Multi-Agent System Development Environment. In: 7th Conference on Autonomous Agents and Multi-agent Systems (AAMAS 2008), pp. 1675–1676. IFAAMAS (2008)
11. Gronback, R.C.: Eclipse Modeling Project – A Domain-Specific Language Toolkit. Addison-Wesley (2009)
12. Morandini, M., Penserini, L., Perini, A.: Modelling Self-Adaptivity – A Goal-Oriented Approach. In: 2nd IEEE International Conference on Self-Adaptive and Self-Organizing Systems (SASO 2008), pp. 469–470 (2008)
13. Morandini, M., Nguyen, C.D., Penserini, L., Perini, A., Susi, A.: Tropos Modeling, Code Generation and Testing with the Taom4E Tool. In: 5th International i* Workshop (iStar 2011), pp. 172–174 (2011)
14. Padgham, L., Thangarajah, J., Winikoff, M.: Prometheus Design Tool. In: 23th AAAI Conference on Artificial Intelligence (AAAI 2008), pp. 1882–1883 (2008)
15. Padgham, L., Winikoff, M.: Developing Intelligent Agents Systems – A Practical Guide. John Wiley and Sons (2004)
16. Pavón, J., Gómez-Sanz, J.J., Fuentes, R.: The INGENIAS Methodology and Tools. In: Henderson-Sellers, B., Giorgini, P. (eds.) Agent-Oriented Methodologies, pp. 236–276. Idea Group Publishing (2005)
17. Pavón, J., Gómez-Sanz, J.J., Fuentes, R.: Model Driven Development of Multi-Agent Systems. In: Rensink, A., Warmer, J. (eds.) ECMDA-FA 2006. LNCS, vol. 4066, pp. 284–298. Springer, Heidelberg (2006)
18. Pokahr, A., Braubach, L.: A Survey of Agent-Oriented Development Tools. In: El-Fallah-Seghrouchni, A., Dix, J., Dastani, M., Bordini, R.H. (eds.) Multi-Agent Programming – Languages, Tools and Applications, pp. 289–329. Springer (2009)
19. Warwas, S., Hahn, C.: The DSML4MAS Development Environment. In: 8th Conference on Autonomous Agents and Multi-agent Systems (AAMAS 2009), pp. 1379–1380 (2009)
20. Willians, I.: Beginning XSLT and XPath – Transforming XML Documents and Data. Wiley Publishing Inc. (2009)
21. Winikoff, M.: Jack Intelligent Agents – An Industrial Strength Platform. In: Bordini, R.H., Dastani, M., Dix, J., El-Fallah-Seghrouchni, A. (eds.) Multi-Agent Programming Languages, Platforms Applications, pp. 175–193. Springer (2005)

Implementation and Assessment of Robot Team Cooperation Models Using Deliberative Control Components

José M. Gascueña[1], Francisco J. Garijo[2], Antonio Fernández-Caballero[1], Marie-Pierre Gleizes[2], and Pierre Glize[2]

[1] Universidad de Castilla-La Mancha, Departamento de Sistemas Informáticos & Instituto de Investigación en Informática de Albacete (I3A), 02071-Albacete, Spain
{JManuel.Gascuena,Antonio.Fdez}@uclm.es
[2] IRIT - Institut de Recherche en Informatique de Toulouse
118 route de Narbonne, 31062 Toulouse Cedex 4, France
fgarijo@pdi.ucm.es, {gleizes,glize}@irit.fr

Abstract. This paper proposes an organizational framework and an approach for development of cooperation models for teams of Autonomous Adaptive Vehicles (AAV), using goal-driven control components. The framework and the approach are illustrated through the development and assessment of task allocation in multi-robot teams. Two cooperation models have been implemented: i) a team model based on the Adaptive Multi-Agent Systems (AMAS) theory, where task responsibility is agreed between team peers, by exchanging individual estimations of the degree of difficulty and priority to achieve the task; ii) a hierarchical model where an AAV manager asks team members estimations and then assigns the task. Experimentation for team-cooperation assessment has been done taking into consideration environmental changes, communications and internal failure. The most significant results reported in this work concerns team coordination in stressing situations. The experimental setting and team performance figures are detailed in the paper.

Keywords: adaptive multi-agent systems, agent framework, robotics, distributed task allocation, cooperation models.

1 Introduction

Component based approaches are increasingly used to deal with heterogeneity and complexity of robotic systems [2]. A key advantage of componentization is to allow development of simulated models which could be seamlessly deployed fully or in part into the robot hardware. Ongoing work on robot simulation tools are also in this direction [3]. This paper proposes a component based layered architecture for Autonomous Adaptive Vehicles (AAV) which control is based on a deliberative goal driven agent pattern [10]. High-level deliberative control facilitates development and experimentation with different behaviour models by bridging the gap between analysis, design and implementation. It also allows

J. Pavón et al. (Eds.): IBERAMIA 2012, LNAI 7637, pp. 412–421, 2012.

reusability, and ease traceability of the control process which is based on high level constructs close to human behaviour. However common pitfalls are: hard integration with software engineering standards, poor performance, and difficulty to control the deliberative process. Therefore, integration of symbolic deliberative components with imperative components is still a challenge.

This paper describes an architectural framework for implementing teams of AAVs capable to achieve individual and collective mission goals by taking into account unexpected changes in the environment, internal failure and availability of mission resources. The work is part of the research effort undergone in the ROSACE (Robots and Embedded Self-Adaptive Communicating Systems) project (http://www.irit.fr/Rosace,737), where the experimental setting is based on a simulated fire forest crisis management scenario where AAV teams should cooperate among themselves and with a Control Center broadcasting requests for helping potential victims jeopardized by fire. Ongoing work in ROSACE joints research efforts on MultiAgent System (MAS) coordination in other domains such as poisonous material accidental release in a city [4]. In the Combined System (http://combined.decis.nl) project, agents are used to implement a collaborative decision system for handling crisis situations. They are responsible for the coordinate tasks, plan actions and reroute information of different actors from different rescue organizations. Users can also benefit from agents' information using a dedicated geo-spatial language named OpenMap, and a dedicated interaction language named Icon. Multi-agent-based Distributed Perception Networks (DPN) are also another relevant application of multi-agent systems to crisis management by intelligently aggregating information coming from a network of sensors [11]. Our works focus on sensor and data, and the intelligence is embedded outside the devices, which implies a notable delegation for a tier of computing services. While most of the experimental results focus on simulated coordination for *best cases*, the most significant results reported in this work concerns team coordination in stressing situations. Performance testing has been done considering different team size, tasks to be achieved, and AAV deployment in different processing nodes in order to assess the impact of communication.

The rest of the paper is organized as follows. Section 2 outlines the architectural principles for AAV design, and the rationale for adopting a goal oriented approach for implementing AAV control and team-cooperation. This approach is illustrated with the development of two cooperation models in the ROSACE project experimental setting: i) AMAS (Adaptative Multiagent System) model where each team member evaluates the cost to achieve the goal, sends its evaluation to their peers and then assumes the goal if it has the most suitable evaluation; ii) hierarchical model where a manager, asks each peer to estimate the evaluation of a given goal, then it proceeds to assign the goal to the most suitable peer. Section 3 details assessment metrics, and testing results using different configuration made up of various team size and number of victims to rescue. Stress testing has been done to compare both functional issues and performance issues on the AMAS model and the hierarchical model. Finally, conclusions and open issues are summarized in Sect. 4.

2   A Goal Oriented Approach for AAV Control and Cooperation

The proposed approach relies on a multi-layered component based architecture, which is populated by manageable components offering their services to other components through standard interfaces (see Fig. 1). The AAV behaviour is governed by the Robot Global Control Component (RGC) which gathers elaborated information from the rest of the components, makes choices, orders execution of actions, monitors results, and sends control information to relevant components when is necessary.

RGC is implemented with a declarative goal processor [5] that manages a goal space, and a working memory. Strategic and tactics criteria for generating goals and executing tasks and actions, in order to try to achieve goals, are defined by means of situation-action rules, where the situation part specifies a partial state of the working memory including the objective and its internal state, and

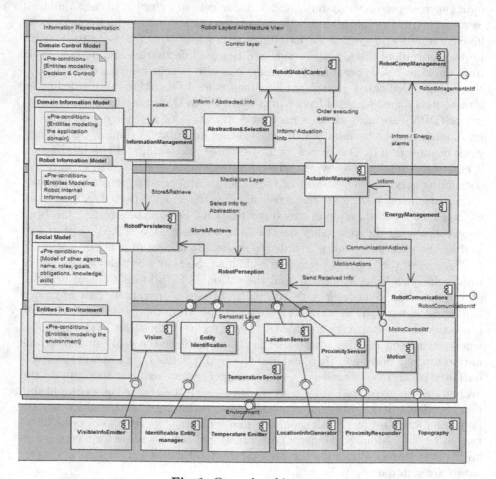

Fig. 1. General architecture

the action part contains statements for executing tasks. The processing cycle is droved by incoming information which is stored in the working memory. Then control rules are used to decide either to generate new goals, to focus on a new goal, to verify the resolution of pending goals, or to proceed to the resolution of pending goals by executing new tasks and actions. Componentization allows seamless integration of real or simulated components, then facilitating modelling, encapsulation and reuse of control strategies and cooperation models.

2.1   Using the Approach for Developing Team-Cooperation Models

Work on team-cooperation focus on evaluating different control architectures and cooperation models allowing an AAV-team achieve efficiently mission goals. The experimental setting for AAV operation is based on fire forest crisis management scenarios. The AAV team is situated in the intervention area to help people jeopardized by fire. The Control Center (CC) broadcast requests to help potential victims indicating the priority, location, and additional detail when needed.

The team should be capable of interpreting and evaluating the CC requests taking into account their current work-load, then decide which member of the team would assume the goal for helping the victim, and finally the team-mate who have accepted the responsibility for the goal should proceed to help the victim. When new requests for helping victims are sent by the CC, the team should reallocate their current goals in order to satisfy the new demands.

Initial experiments have started implementing the AMAS cooperation model [9], [1], [8]. AAVs are supposed to have a cooperative attitude which allows them to take decisions in order to sharing resources and/or assuming goals (tasks), avoiding possible conflicts. The generic process for team-cooperation to achieve this common goal is the following.

Each AGV: (i) estimates the cost to achieve the new goal; (ii) sends its estimated cost to the team members; (iii) receives estimated costs from team members, and (iv) takes a decision to assume the goal based on the estimations received from its peers. Three cases might happen. (C1) The agent has the best estimation: it sends to their peers its proposal to achieve the goal, and waits to receive their confirmation. (C2) There are other team-mates better suited than him to achieve the goal: it sends them the agreement for them to achieve the goal. (C3) The agent has the optimal cost, but it is tied with other team-mates: the tied peers add an randomly generated number to their estimations, and send the new estimation to tied peers, in order to allow one of them to take the responsibility of the goal.

Goal Allocation and Cost Estimation. A formal definition for the multi-robot goal allocation problem can be defined as *"given a number of goals, G_1, G_2, ..., G_t, a team of robots, R_1, R_2, ..., R_r, and a function $F_{eval}(G_i, R_k)$, that specifies the evaluation function (cost) of allocating goal G_k for the robot R_r, find the assignment that allocates the goal for the robot with lowest cost according the established criterion by the evaluation function"*. The cost evaluation function is calculated as follows. Goals consist on helping victims which should be rescued according to its priority. When there two victims with the same priority the victim that was notified first will be helped first. $PriV_v$ is the priority of victim

V_v. $Q_R = V_1, V_2, ..., V_{new}, ..., V_{n-1}, V_n$ is an ordered list by priority of victims that are assigned for robot R, where the new notified victim (V_{new}) is the victim that is being considered by the team in order to decide which robot will be responsible for its rescue. $D(V_i,V_k)$ is the distance between the victims V_i and V_k. $D(R_r,V_1)$ is the distance between the robot R_r and the first victim (V_1) located in Q_R. The distance is calculated using the Euclidean distance formula, in three-dimensions. Length(Q) is the number of victims of Q. Using these concepts, for goal (victim) allocation the evaluation function is defined as follows:

$$\text{If VPD} > \text{RE then } F_{eval} = -1.0$$

$$\text{else } F_{eval} = W_1 * VPD + W_2 * AT \tag{1}$$

where RE is the robot available energy; VPD is the path distance to visit each victim belonging to Q (see equation 2); AT is the required time for attending victims belonging to Q (see equation 3); W_1, W_2 and W_3 are weights for VPD, AT and $PriV_v$ values. For the experiments the weight values are $W_1 = 10.0$; $W_2 = 3.0$; $W_3 = 3.0$.

$$VPD = D(R_r, V_1) + \sum_{i=1}^{n=Length(Q)-1} D(V_i, V_{i+1}) \tag{2}$$

$$AT = \sum_{i=1}^{n=Length(Q)} W_3 * PriV_i \tag{3}$$

Performance evaluation of the goal allocation algorithm is based on the following three parameters. (1) The time required for a goal to be assigned to a team-mate. This time is calculated using the processor real time clock, as the time difference between the instant when the control center sends the request, and the instant when the goal to help the victim was accepted by a team-mate. (2) Goal distribution among team members. (3) The cost of the robot team, which corresponds to the highest cost of the goals assumed by each team member.

Dealing with Uncooperative Peers. Cooperation comes out from the need by each agent to get information from their team mates to achieve their own goals. The cooperation process is highly dependent on team-communication which quality cannot be guarantee in a hazardous and changing environment as the fire-forest. Cooperation might fail when communication is missing, and also due to internal processing factors such as lack of synchronization in the cooperation process, and malfunctioning of internal components like sensors, motion, vision, position, computing, and others. Consequently each agent should be capable to deal with situations where: i) they cannot communicate with their peers; ii) communication is possible but team-mates do not send the expected information, and/or they do not respond to requests; and iii) they send unexpected or out-dated information. In these cases individual decisions should be taken to achieve the goals/tasks requested by the CC. To cope with "worst cases" which correspond to real situations the AAV team model has been extended to take into account: deadlines for decision making, missing information from the team mates, the current workload of the AAV, and stressing requests from the CC.

A *hierarchical team model* has been implemented to have a reference for assessing the strengths and weakness of the AMAS model, and for the utilization of a "heavy deliberative control architecture" for implementing these models.

2.2   Implementation Approach Using ICARO's Deliberative Control

The ICARO framework has been used in ROSACE and in other areas to model AAVs using reactive patterns [6,7] which control is based on a Finite State Automata. The deliberative control pattern is based on a goal processor. AAV behaviour is characterized by: i) the set of goals which can be achieved; ii) the activities, process and actions needed to achieve the goals; iii) the information model representing the domain and environmental entities, the computing entities needed for representing goal achievement states, and intermediate results produced by activities and actions, and iv) the process defining the life cycle of goals. This is done through situation-action rules expressing conditions for: a) goal generation; b) goal focalization; c) goal achievement, and d) executing activities and actions to make it possible that pending goals satisfy their achievement conditions.

Goals are represented as classes from which multiple object instances can be generated. Activities and actions needed to achieve goals are represented as tasks. The work-flow of activities and actions needed to achieve goals are first defined with UML activity diagrams, and then implemented with situation-action rules. In AMAS team model, the goal resolution process is defined with 41 structured rules. From each behaviour model multiple distributed deployment instances might be generated. The ICARO framework provides deployment, monitoring and communication transparency among component instances.

The **AMAS team-model** is implemented with a common behaviour model for all AAVs. Teams are made up of cloning instances; they have the same goals, tasks, information model and goal-resolution rules. Requests sent by the CC are received by all team-members which generates similar goal instances: *helpVictim()* and *decideWhoShouldGo()*. Cooperation is modeled in the protocol for making collective decisions, that is, to achieve the goal *decideWhoShouldGo()*. This is done by exchanging cost estimations, and then deciding which member of the team is the best situated to help the victim.

Although all the team members participate voluntary on the decisions process, the way in which each AAV achieves their own goals is dependent on its situation in the environment and on its internal state which is characterized by information objects in its working memory including previous goals and the current focus representing the goal under resolution. Experimentation has been done for fine-tuning the model in order to: 1) allow the AAV takes individual decisions when collective decisions fails; 2) determine deadlines for expected information and for taking collective decisions. As most of these parameters are dependent of hardware and communication performance, they are defined as configurable.

The **hierarchical team-model** has two roles implemented with two behavioural models: a) the *AAV-boss* which is in charge of interpreting the requests from the CC and deciding which team-member should be assigned to achieve the goal; b) the *AAV-subordinate* which receives messages from his boss, first requesting to estimate their cost for achieving the goal, and then to accept/refuse proposals for assuming the goal. Subordinates might refuse proposals when they do not have the necessary means to achieve it, however the final decision to assign the goal correspond the boss. Deadlines for expected answers and deadlines for taking decisions are similar to the AMAS model. The information model is the same as for AMAS, goal and tasks might also be shared, however the boss role is implemented with 15 rules, and the subordinate role with 6 rules.

The system is implemented in java. It may run in a central node or in a network of processing nodes with OS windows/linux and virtual machine Java 6.xx. The rule processor used for implementing the deliberative agent pattern is based on Drools 5.x. and communication among AAVs is done through RMI. A public version will be available for demonstration during the conference.

3   Experimental Results

Metrics to assess both the model and the implementation approach using the deliberative architecture considers two main aspects: functional conformity and performance. Functional conformity focus on the quality of goal allocation, and goal distribution among team members. Performance considers the time needed for the team to assume goals for helping victims requested by the CC. Metric values have been gathered from testing experiments considering the following parameters: i) the team size and the number of victims to rescue; ii) the frequency of messages sent by the CC in order to assess the response of the team face up to stressing requests; iii) deployment in different processing nodes to assess the impact of real parallel processing and communication.

Experimentation in one central node has been done in a processor AMD Phenom II X4 at 3,20 GH with 4MB Ram and SO Windows 7. The two additional nodes for distributed experiments are based on Intel core I7 at 2,20 Ghz with 8Gb of Ram, SO windows 7 , and AMD Turion X2 at 2 Ghz , 2Gb of Ram and SO Windows XP. The most significant results are summarized below.

The **AMAS model** works as expected in situations where the CC sends requests at frequency greater than the time needed for deciding the responsibility to assume the goal. As the time required to take decisions increases with the size of the team, deadlines for waiting responses and for taking decision should also be increased to synchronize goal resolution. When deadlines are not met the same goal might be assumed by two or more team members, however this rarely happens. Tie-brakes for cost evaluation are satisfactorily solved.

Fig. 2 shows performance results for AAVs deployed in one central node and deployed in 3 nodes. Time for allocating goals is quite similar. Stressing requests degrade team performance due to the perturbation caused by the interpretation of incoming requests during collective decision making.

The first consequence of increasing the frequency of CC requests is desynchronising the process for achieving goals. CC messages are received at different time and processed at different speed by team-peers. When a team-member receives a request from the CC, it retrieves the victim's priority and generates new goals for helping the victim and for deciding who should assume that goal. If the priority

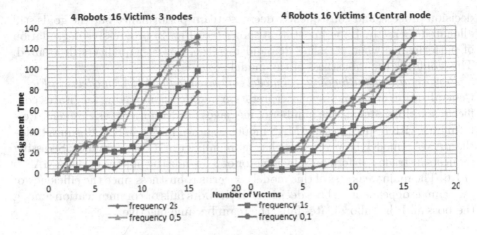

Fig. 2. AMAS model goal assignment

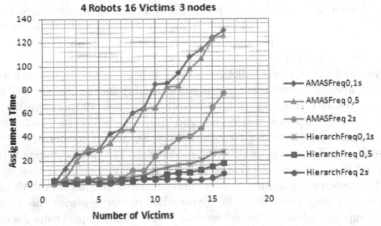

Fig. 3. AMAS model versus Hierarchical model

of the new victim is higher than the victim which decision is trying to achieve, it delays the resolution of the current goal and starts a new decision process to help this new victim. It is assumed that their team-mates will do the same, consequently it estimates its cost to achieve the goal and send it to its companions. However it happens that team-peers receive cost estimations and requests for sending its estimations before the message from the CC was processed. This lack of synchronization might lead to various peers taking the responsibility to assume the same goal. To deal with this situation, the peer receiving cost estimations, or requests for sending estimations about unknown victims, acts as if it were informed by its peer about the CC request. It trusts peer's information, and then it generates the goals and starts participating in the decision process. When the CC request arrives interpretation is already done. If the CC request cannot be received the AAV has been indirectly informed through its team-mates. Goal desynchronisation delays decisions due to multiple interruptions during the decision process, and consequently decrease team-performance but the goals still allocated correctly. Experimentation shows (see Fig. 2) progressive degradation of performance when stressing demand increase, however quality still assured. This confirms the robustness of the model.

Performance of the hierarchical model compared to the AMAS model is in Fig. 3. Centralization of CC message interpretation and decision making facilitates conflict resolution reducing the number of messages needed for goal assignment. Performance with respect to the AMAS model is shown in Fig. 3. It is 10 times faster than AMAS model, however stress has more impact in its performance. Stressing requests degrades performance by a factor of 3,3 while the impact in the AMAS is of 1,6. The main weakness of this model concerns robustness since the efficiency of the team is dependent on boss decisions. If the boss fails or communication among the boss and the subordinates fails, the team became inactive.

4   Conclusions and Future Challenges

Experimentation with decision models using deliberative architecture requires availability of engineering tools facilitating quick development, deployment and evaluation. Face to the wide range of papers devoted to team modeling, availability of systems allowing verification and extension of these models are scarce. Work have faced two related challenges: model validation taking into account realistic constraints, and engineering evaluation mainly focused on the utilization of heavy deliberative architecture for controlling the behaviour of complex entities such as AAVs. Experimentation has gone beyond "best cases" to be focused on stressing test cases in order to validate key aspects of cooperative decision making such as performance, quality and robustness. The most significant results are obtained in *worse case scenarios* were team-members should face up with internal failure, communication failure, and stressing requests. AMAS performance is significantly lower than the hierarchical model; however this weakness might be compensated by higher robustness. Stress decrease performance in both models, most significantly in the hierarchical model, but quality is guaranteed. Utilization of encapsulated deliberative architecture facilitates high level modeling, and the traceability of the collaborative decision making process, then allowing incremental development and bridging the gap between analysis design and implementation. Seemly creation of multiple parallel instances can be done without penalizing deployment and performance.

The current system is made up of open source, reusable, components provided by ICARO . Extensibility, manageability, integration and deployment might be done with most popular IDEs. This paves the way to the development and experimentation with new team models were teammates might change dynamically their role. For example, the implementation of a team which starts hierarchical but becomes AMAS when the boss looses connection with their peers, can be done without significant effort. Other models such as selecting a new boss or creating partial hierarchy for big teams might be quickly developed.

Future work aims to go beyond simulation to validate the models incorporated into actual AAVs evolving in a physical environment.

Acknowledgements. This work is supported by the French RTRA-STAE foundation (Reseau Thematique de Recherche Avancee Sciences et Technologies pour l'Aeronautique et l'Espace) in the scope of the ROSACE project. This work is also supported by the Spanish Ministerio de Ciencia e Innovación / FEDER under project TIN2010-20845-C03-01 and by the Spanish Junta de Comunidades de Castilla-La Mancha / FEDER under projects PII2I09-0069-0994 and PEII09-0054-9581.

References

1. Clair, G., Kaddoum, E., Gleizes, M.-P., Picard, G.: Self-Regulation in Self-Organising Multi-Agent Systems for Adaptive and Intelligent Manufacturing Control. In: 2nd IEEE Intl. Conf. on Self-Adaptive and Self-Organizing Systems (SASO 2008), pp. 107–116 (2008)
2. Domínguez-Brito, A.C., Santana-Jorge, F.J., Cabrera-Gámez, J., Hernández Sosa, J.D., Isern-González, J., Fernández-Perdomo, E.: Exploring Interfaces in a Distributed Component-based Programming Framework for Robotics. In: 4th Intl. Conf. on Agents and Artificial Intelligence (ICAART 2012), pp. 667–672 (2012)
3. Echeverria, G., Lassabe, N., Degroote, A., Lemaignan, S.: Modular Open Robots Simulation Engine – MORSE. In: 2011 IEEE Intl. Conf. on Robotics and Automation (ICRA 2011), pp. 46–51. IEEE (2011)
4. García-Magariño, I., Gutierrez, C., Fuentes-Fernández, R.: Organizing Multi-Agent Systems for Crisis Management. In: 7th Ibero-American Workshop in Multi-Agent System (IBERAGENTS 2008), pp. 69–80 (2008)
5. Garijo, F., Bravo, S., Gonzalez, J., Bobadilla, E.: BOGAR LN – An Agent Based Component Framework for Developing Multi-Modal Services Using Natural Language. In: Conejo, R., Urretavizcaya, M., Pérez-de-la-Cruz, J.-L. (eds.) CAEPIA/TTIA 2003. LNCS (LNAI), vol. 3040, pp. 207–220. Springer, Heidelberg (2004)
6. Gascueña, J.M., Fernández-Caballero, A., Garijo, F.J.: Using ICARO-T Framework for Reactive Agent-Based Mobile Robots. In: Demazeau, Y., Dignum, F., Corchado, J.M., Pérez, J.B. (eds.) Advances in PAAMS. AISC, vol. 70, pp. 91–101. Springer, Heidelberg (2010)
7. Gascueña, J.M., Fernández-Caballero, A., Navarro, E., Serrano-Cuerda, J., Cano, F.A.: Agent-Based Development of Multisensory Monitoring Systems. In: Ferrández, J.M., et al. (eds.) IWINAC 2011, Part I. LNCS, vol. 6686, pp. 451–460. Springer, Heidelberg (2011)
8. Georgé, J.-P., Peyruqueou, S., Régis, C., Glize, P.: Experiencing Self-adaptive MAS for Real-Time Decision Support Systems. In: Demazeau, Y., et al. (eds.) PAAMS 2009. AISC, vol. 55, pp. 302–309. Springer, Heidelberg (2009)
9. Gleizes, M.-P., Camps, V., Georgé, J.-P., Capera, D.: Engineering Systems Which Generate Emergent Functionalities. In: Weyns, D., Brueckner, S.A., Demazeau, Y. (eds.) EEMMAS 2007. LNCS (LNAI), vol. 5049, pp. 58–75. Springer, Heidelberg (2008)
10. Lacouture, J., Gascueña, J.M., Gleizes, M.-P., Glize, P., Garijo, F.J., Fernández-Caballero, A.: ROSACE: Agent-Based Systems for Dynamic Task Allocation in Crisis Management. In: Demazeau, Y., Müller, J.P., Rodríguez, J.M.C., Pérez, J.B., et al. (eds.) Advances on PAAMS. AISC, vol. 155, pp. 255–260. Springer, Heidelberg (2012)
11. Maris, M., Pavlin, G.: Distributed Perception Networks for Crisis Management. In: 3rd Intl. Conf. on Information Systems for Crisis Response and Management (ISCRAM 2006), pp. 376–381 (2006)

Improving the Tracing System in PANGEA
Using the TRAMMAS Model

Luis Búrdalo[1], Andrés Terrasa[1], Vicente Julián[1], Carolina Zato[2], Sara Rodríguez[2],
Javier Bajo[2], and Juan M. Corchado[2]

[1] Department of Computer Systems and Computation
Polytechnic University of Valencia
Valencia, Spain
{lburdalo,aterrasa,vinglada}@dsic.upv.es
[2] Department of Computer Science and Automation
University of Salamanca
Salamanca, Spain
{carol_zato,srg,jbajope,corchado}@usal.es

Abstract. This paper presents the integration of the tracing model TRAMMAS
in an agent platform called PANGEA. This platform allows to developed multiagent systems modeled as Virtual Organizations. The concepts of roles, organizations and norms are fully supported by the platform assuring flexibility and
scalability. Before TRAMMAS, this platform uses a Sniffer Agent to trace the
information reducing its scalability as a centralized mechanism. TRAMMAS
proposes the use of event tracing in multiagent systems, as an indirect interaction and coordination mechanism to improve the amount and quality of the information that agents can perceive in order to fulfill their goals more efficiently.
Moreover, the event tracing system can help reducing the amount of unnecessary information.

Keywords: agent platform, multiagent systems, virtual organizations, IRC
protocol, tracing systems.

1   Introduction

Distributed multi-agent systems (MAS) have become increasingly sophisticated
in recent years, with the growing potential to handle large volumes of data and
coordinate the operations of many organizations [21]. In these systems, each agent
independently handles a small set of specialized tasks and cooperates to achieve the
system-level goals and a high degree of flexibility [10]. Multiagent systems have
become the most effective and widely used form of developing this type of application in which communication among various devices must be both reliable and efficient. One of the problems related to distributed computing is message passing, which
is in turn related to the interaction and coordination among intelligent agents. Consequently, a multiagent architecture must necessarily provide a robust communication
platform and control mechanisms.

J. Pavón et al. (Eds.): IBERAMIA 2012, LNAI 7637, pp. 422–431, 2012.

This article presents a multiagent platform based on a Virtual Organization (VO) paradigm. In this paradigm, the social behavior (based on abstractions such as norms, teams, organizations, roles, commitments, etc.) plays and important role and it has to be incorporated as a decentralized mechanism. This platform called PANGEA (Platform for Automatic coNstruction of orGanizations of intElligent Agents) includes a robust communication model that allows intelligent agents to connect from a variety of devices. On the other hand, TRAMMAS is a tracing model that is incorporated to the platform to improve the amount and quality of the information that agents can perceive from both their physical and social environment, in order to fulfill their goals more efficiently.

The remainder of the paper is structured as follows: the next section introduces some previous works made in tracing systems. Section 3 presents an overview of the TRAMMAS model. Section 4 explains the inclusion of TRAMMAS inside PANGEA. Next, Section 5 presents a case study and some results. Finally, Section 6 shows some conclusions.

2 Related Work

The tracing systems within the multiagent architectures have been traditionally used for tasks of "debugging" and the control of certain agents' behavior.

The most outstanding example of this case is the Sniffer Agent and the Introspecter Agent of JADE [23]. The Sniffer Agent allows registering all the messages sent and received by the MAS and later, by means of a log file, to examine its content. The Introspecter Agent allows knowing all the events related to the life cycle of an agent, the messages sent and received as well as its behavior. Nevertheless, in this model all the communication flow is centralized and must pass through this agent to be analyzed and later, registered. Once the information is in the log files, humans must study it since is not prepared for the treatment by agents. The own agents cannot extract log information and the procedure cannot be automated. JADEX [8] provides a Conversation Center, which allows a user to send messages directly to any agent while it is executing and to receive answers to those messages from a user-friendly interface. The JACK [7, 12] multiagent platform supports monitoring communication between agents by means of Agent Interaction Diagrams. It also provides a Design Tracing Tool, to view internal details of JACK applications during execution, and a Plan Tracing Tool, to trace the execution of plans and the events that handle them. Other examples of tracing facilities provided by platforms are ZEUS's [13] Society Viewer and Agent Viewer, which display organizational inter-relationships among agents and their messages and agent's internal state. Also, JASON [11] provides a Mind Inspector tool to examine agents' internal state.

Apart from those tools provided by multiagent platforms themselves, there are many tracing facilities provided by third party developers. This is the case of Java Sniffer [14], developed by Rockwell Automation based on JADE's Sniffer Agent. Another third party tool based on JADE's Sniffer Agent is ACLAnalyser [16], which intercepts messages interchanged by agents during the execution of the application and stores them in a relational database, which can be lately inspected to detect social pathologies in the MAS. These results can be combined with data mining techniques to help in the multiagent system debugging process [17]. MAMSY, the management tool presented in [18] lets the system administrator monitorize and manage a MAS running over the Magentix multiagent platform [19]. MAMSY provides graphical tools to interact with the MAS and visualize its internal state at run time. In [20], the authors describe an advanced visualization tools suite for MAS developed with ZEUS, although the authors also claim these tools could be used with Common-KADS.

As previously mentioned, the multiagent system that is proposed is based on Virtual Agent Organizations [6]. Consequently, the PANGEA platform makes it possible to create open systems that resolve the inflexibility of a multiagent system. The new open and collaborative architectures require a control focused on the interaction and global knowledge rather than autonomous behaviors. For this reason, traceability has become a key point for the distributed knowledge. As it can be appreciated, tracing facilities in MAS are usually conceived as debugging tools to help in the validation and verification processes. It is also usual to use these tracing tools as help for those users which have to understand how the MAS works. Thus, generated events are designed to be understood by a human observer who would probably use them to debug or to validate the MAS and tracing facilities are mostly human-oriented in order to let MAS users work in a more efficient and also comfortable way. Some multiagent platforms provide their own tracing facilities, although there is also important work carried out by third party developers. However, even those tracing facilities which were not designed by platform developer teams are usually designed for a specific multiagent platform. This reason leads us to integrate TRAMMAS with our platform to probe its independency and to achieve a distributed way to share knowledge between our PANGEA agents in a distributed way.

3   TRAMMAS Overview

Multiagent systems can be considered to be formed by a set of tracing entities or components which are susceptible of generating and/or receiving certain information related to their activity as trace events. A trace event is a piece of data representing an action which has taken place during the execution of an agent or any other component of the multiagent system. Each trace event has these attributes [14]:

- Event type: Trace events can be classified according to the nature of the information which they represent. This event type is necessary for tracing entities in order to be able to interpret the rest of the data attached to the trace event.
- Time stamp: Global time at which the event took place, necessary to be able to chronologically sort events produced anywhere in the multiagent system.
- Origin entity: The tracing entity which originated the event.
- Attached data: Additional data which could be necessary to correctly interpret the trace event. The amount and type of these data will depend on the event type. Some trace events may not need any additional information.

Tracing entities can be considered to be playing two different tracing roles. When they are generating trace events, tracing entities are considered Event Source entities (ES). When they are receiving trace events, tracing entities are considered Event Receiver entities (ER). Any tracing entity can start and stop playing any of these two roles, or both, at any time.

This architecture considers three different kinds of tracing entities: Agents, artifacts and aggregations.

On the one hand, agents are all those autonomous and proactive entities which define the multiagent system behavior. On the other hand, artifacts are all those passive elements in the multiagent system (databases, physical sensors and actuators, etc.) susceptible of generating events at run time or receiving them as an input [25]. Artifacts can combine in order to perform more complex tasks, generating or receiving trace events as a tracing individual. From the point of view of the tracing system, these combinations of artifacts are also modeled as single artifacts.

If the multiagent system supports aggregations of agents (or agents and artifacts), such as teams or organizations, then such aggregations are considered by the tracing system as single tracing entities, in the sense that trace events can be generated from or delivered to these entities as tracing individuals. Agents and artifacts within an aggregation are still tracing entities and thus, they can also generate and receive trace events individually, not only as members of the aggregation.

From the point of view of the architecture, the multiagent platform can be seen as a set of agents and artifacts. Therefore, the components of the platform are also susceptible of generating and receiving trace events.

When a tracing entity is playing the ER tracing role, the tracing system provides it with a stream, which can be seen as a special mailbox where the Trace Manager delivers the trace events for this ER entity. These streams can either be pieces of memory or log files. In both cases, the ER entity which owns the stream has to limit its size in order not to overload its resources.

Event types are modeled in this architecture as tracing services. A tracing service is a special service which is offered by an ES entity to share its trace events, in a similar way to a traditional service. Each ES entity can offer different tracing services, and the same tracing service can be offered by many different ES entities.

As with traditional services, when an ER entity is interested in receiving trace events of a specific event type, which are generated by a given ES, it has to request the corresponding service. From that moment on, the Trace Manager starts recording the corresponding trace events and delivering them directly to the ER stream until the ER cancels the request. The Trace Manager only records those trace events, which have been requested by an ER entity, so that no resources are spent in recording and delivering trace events, which have not been requested by any ER entity.

The Trace Manager provides a list of all the available tracing services and the ES entities, which offer them. When an ES entity wants to offer any tracing information, it must inform the Trace Manager in order to publish the corresponding tracing service so that other tracing entities can request it if they are interested in its trace events. When a tracing entity does not want to receive certain trace events anymore it has to cancel the request to the corresponding tracing service.

In order to let ES entities decide which ER entities can receive their trace events, when an ES entity publishes a tracing service, it has also to specify which agent roles are authorized to request that service to that ES entity (direct authorization). In this way, when an ER entity wants to request a tracing service to an ES, it has to be able to assume one of the authorized agent roles. ER entities which are authorized to request a tracing service to certain ES entity can also authorize other roles to request the same tracing service to that ES entity. This is defined as authorization by delegation. In this way, the tracing system maintains an authorization graph for each tracing service which is being offered by each ES. This authorization graph is dynamic, since tracing entities can add and remove authorizations at run time. When an authorization, direct or by delegation, is removed, all those delegated authorizations which depended on the removed one are also removed.

The tracing system does not control which entities can assume each role in order to request or to add authorizations for a tracing service. It is the multiagent platform which has to provide the necessary security mechanisms no prevent agents from assuming inappropriate roles.

4   Description of PANGEA Including TRAMMAS

Developing PANGEA, we are looking for a platform that can integrally create, manage and control VOs. When launching the main container of execution, the communication system is initiated; the agent platform then automatically provides the following agents to facilitate the control of the organization:

- OrganizationManager: the agent responsible for the actual management of organizations and suborganizations. It is responsible for verifying the entry and exit of agents, and for assigning roles. To carry out these tasks, it works with the OrganizationAgent, which is a specialized version of this agent.
- InformationAgent: the agent responsible for accessing the database containing all pertinent system information.
- ServiceAgent: the agent responsible for recording and controlling the operation of services offered by the agents.
- NormAgent: the agent that ensures compliance with all the refined norms in the organization. For example, preventing an agent to take an unauthorized role.
- Sniffer: manages the message history and filters information by controlling communication initiated by queries.

One of the most important features that characterize the platform is the use of the IRC protocol for communication among agents. Internet Relay Chat (IRC) is a Real Time Internet Protocol for simultaneous text messaging or conferencing. This protocol is regulated by 5 standards: RFC1459 [1], RFC2810 [5], RFC2811 [4], RFC2812 [2] y RFC2813 [3]. This allows for the use of a protocol that is easy to implement, flexible and robust. The open standard protocol enables its continuous evolution. There are also IRC clients for all operating systems, including mobile devices.

All messages include the following format: *prefix command command-parameters\r\n*. The prefix may be optional in some messages, and required only for entering messages; the command is one of the originals from the IRC standard. For the diffusion of the defined trace event taking into account the format of the IRC messages, the event attributes have been included as parameters of the messages. The communication platform is able to treat the messages according to its format and to distribute them suitably.

In line with this design, the inclusion of TRAMMAS in PANGEA is relatively easy. As previously commented, a tracing service is a special service which is offered by an ES entity to share its trace events. Therefore, the unique existing condition is that, as far as possible, an ES entity should implement its tracing service as a Web Service. This allows the ServiceAgent of PANGEA to offer the services to all the agents in the rest of suborganizations.

An *EventTracing Suborganization* has been included to create the tracing system. Figure 1 shows the agents and its relationships. This suborganization carry out the tasks that the model TRAMMAS assign to the Trace Manager. Four agents form the suborganization:

- TraceEntityAgent in charge of registering and managing all the tracing entities.
- TracingServicesAgent in charge of registering and managing tracing services offered by ES entities.
- SubscriptionAgent, which stores and manages subscriptions to each tracing service and ES entity.
- AuthorizationAgent which stores and manages the authorization needed for each tracing service and ES entity.

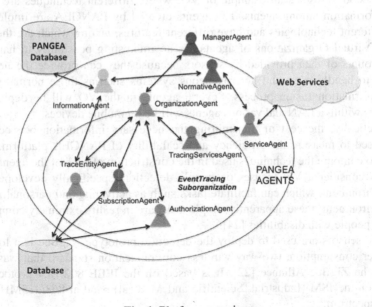

Fig. 1. Platform overview

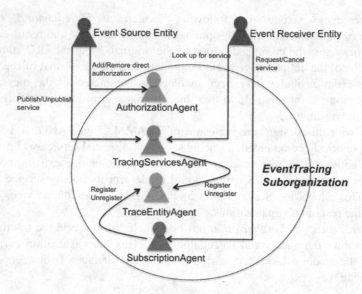

Fig. 2. Interactions between agents in the EventTracing Suborganization

Figure 2 shows how tracing entities interact with the *EventTracing Suborganization*.

5   Case Study and Results

The case study presents an example of VO, where different techniques are used to share information among agents. The agents created by PANGEA are implemented using different technologies and have different features, among which are the use of sensors. Virtual Organizations of agents are an interesting possibility to handle the large amounts of data provided by sensors because they can provide the necessary capacity to handle open and heterogeneous systems such as those normally found in the information fusion process. Several agents in the VO will be deployed on computers within a LAN and various agents will be on mobile devices.

Theoretically, the cost of transmitting the necessary information between them can be used to measure the efficiency and scalability of PANGEA platform. It also enables to compare the techniques used in the construction of each of the agents.

Let us consider a VO focuses on people detection, specifically developed for a work environment, which can facilitate tasks such as activating and personalizing the work environment; these apparently simple tasks are in reality extremely complicated for some people with disabilities [24].

ZigBee sensors are used to deploy the detection prototype. ZigBee is a low cost, low power consumption, two-way wireless communication standard that was developed by the ZigBee Alliance [22]. It is based on the IEEE 802.15.4 protocol, and operates on the ISM (Industrial, Scientific and Medical) band at 868/915MHz and a 2.4GHz spectrum.

The proposed proximity detection system is based on the detection of presence by a localized sensor called the control point which has a permanent and known location. Once the Zigbee tag carried by the person has been detected and identified, its location is delimited within the proximity of the sensor that identified it. Consequently, the location is based on criteria of presence and proximity, according to the precision of the system and the number of control points displayed. The parameter used to carry out the detection of proximity is the RSSI (Received Signal Strength Indication), a parameter that indicates the strength of the received signal. This force is normally indicated in mW or using logarithmic units (dBm). 0 dBm is equivalent to 1mW. Positive values indicate a signal strength greater than 1mW, while negative values indicate a signal strength less than 1mW [24].

In our Case Study we have a distribution of computers and laptops in a real office environment, separated by a distance of 2 meters. The activation zone is approximately 90cm, a distance considered close enough to be able to initiate the activation process. It should be noted that there is a "Sensitive Area" in which it is unknown exactly which computer should be switched on; this is because two computers in close proximity may impede the system's efficiency from switching on the desired computer. Tests demonstrate that the optimal distance separating two computers should be at least 40cm.

The agents share certain information about the state of the sensors so that other agents can carry out the detection in an optimal way. For instance, important increases in the RSSI of sensors may be indicative of a proximity to a computer and so on.

The example considers the transmission of relevant information of sensors between agents which may be interested. The internal reasoning process by which agents receive information from sensors is out of scope of this work. The case study will be considered to be in a general situation where there are n_{sens} agents in charge of controlling n sensors in the system and there is a total amount of n_{rem} remarkable situations to be reported to agents. Table I shows the number of transmissions as a function of the number of remarkable situations occurred in the system. The number of transmissions in the worst case is in the same order for both techniques (broadcast and the *EventTracing Suborganization*). However, the best case is constant for event tracing while it is higher using broadcasting.

Table 1. Summary of best and worst case costs as a function oft he number of N_{sens} agents for a constant number of remarkable situation ($K_{remarkable}$)

Number of transmissions for n_{rem} situations		
	Best Case	*Worst Case*
Broadcast	$k_{remarkable}*(2+n_{sens})$	$k_{remarkable}*(2+n_{sens})$
EventTracing Suborganization	0	$k_{remarkable}*(2+n_{sens})$

Results show that the event tracing technique provides a way to coordinate different agents in charge of sensors without having to contact directly with none of them. The amount of information interchanged among agents in the system is reduced to the minimum necessary, which makes the system more efficient and scalable.

6   Conclusions

This paper has presented a platform called PANGEA, which has been improved thanks to TRAMMAS. PANGEA has great potential to create open systems, and more specifically, virtual agent organizations. This architecture includes various tools that make it easy for the end user to create, manage and control these systems. One of the greatest advantages of this system is the communication platform that, by using the IRC standard, offers a robust and widely tested system that can handle a large number of connections, and that additionally facilitates the implementation for other potential extensions. Before TRAMMAS, the Sniffer agent offers services that can be invoked to study and extract message information but this was centralized and limited if we want to create a platform for building Large-Scale Agent-Based Systems.

TRAMMAS offers an additional indirect communication mechanism which lets agents and other entities in the system generate trace events, as well as receiving events generated by other entities. The incorporation of this model to PANGEA has improved the way in which entities and agents perceive each other and their environment, which in turn improves the way in which high-level social abstractions can be developed and incorporated to the multiagent system.

Finally, the event tracing suborganization can help reducing the amount of unnecessary information which has to be transmitted and processed, while keeping agents' internal logic as simple as possible and thus, contributing to the scalability and feasibility of VOs.

Acknowledgment. This work has been partially supported by the MICINN project TIN 2009-13839-C03-03.

References

1. Oikarinen, J., Reed, D.: Internet Relay Chat Protocol. RFC 1459, IETF (1993)
2. Kalt, C.: Internet Relay Chat(Client Protocol. RFC 2812, IETF (2000)
3. Kalt, C.: Internet Relay Chat(Server Protocol. RFC 2813, IETF (2000)
4. Kalt, C.: Internet Relay Chat(Channel Management. RFC 2811, IETF (2000)
5. Kalt, C.: Internet Relay Chat(Architecture. RFC 2811, IETF (2000)
6. Foster, I., Kesselman, C., Tuecke, S.: The Anatomy of the Grid Enabling Scalable Virtual Organizations. International Journal of High Performance Computing Application 15(3), 200–222 (2001)
7. Agent Oriented Software Pty Ltd.: JACK^{TM} Intelligent Agents Teams Manual. s.l.. Agent Oriented Software Pty. Ltd. (2005)
8. Pokahr, A., Braubach, L.: JadexTool Guide. p. 66. University of Hamburg, Germany (2008)
9. Helsinger, A., Wright, T.:Cougaar A Robust Configurable Multi Agent Platform. In: 2005 Aerospace Conference AC 2005. pp.1–10. IEEE (2005)
10. Gruver, W.: Technologies and Applications of Distributed Intelligent Systems. IEEE MTT– Chapter Presentation, Waterloo, Canada (2004)

11. Bordini, R.H., Hübner, J.F., Vieira, R.: Jason and the Golden Fleece of Agent-Oriented Programming. In: Bordini, R., Dastani, M., Dix, J., El FallahSeghrouchni, A. (eds.) Multi-Agent Programming – Languages. Platforms and Applications, vol. 15, pp. 3–37. Springer, Heidelberg (2005)
12. Agent Oriented Software Pty. Ltd.: Jack Intelligent AgentTracing and Logging Manual, p. 85 (2008)
13. Collis, J., Ndumu, D., Nwana, H., Lee, L.: The Zeus Agent Building Tool-kit. BT Technology Journal 16(3), 60–68 (1998)
14. Búrdalo, L., Terrasa, A., García-Fornes, A., Espinosa, A.: Towards Providing Social Knowledge by Event Tracing in Multiagent Systems. In: Corchado, E., Wu, X., Oja, E., Herrero, Á., Baruque, B. (eds.) HAIS 2009. LNCS, vol. 5572, pp. 484–491. Springer, Heidelberg (2009)
15. Tichy, P., Slechta, P.: Java Sniffer 2.7 User Manual (2006)
16. Botia, J., Hernansaez, J., Skarmeta, F.: Towards an Approach for Debugging MAS Through the Analysis of ACL Messages. In: Lindemann, G., Denzinger, J., Timm, I.J., Unland, R. (eds.) MATES 2004. LNCS (LNAI), vol. 3187, pp. 301–312. Springer, Heidelberg (2004)
17. Botia, J., Hernansaez, J., Gomez-Skarmeta, A.: On the Application of Clustering Techniques to Support Debugging Large-Scale Multi-Agent Systems. In: Bordini, R., Dastani, M., Dix, J., El FallahSeghrouchni, A. (eds.) PROMAS 2006. LNCS (LNAI), vol. 4411, pp. 217–227. Springer, Heidelberg (2007)
18. Sanchez-Anguix, V., Espinosa, A., Hernandez, L., Garcia-Fornes, A.: MAMSY: A Management Tool for Multi-Agent Systems. In: Demazeau, Y., Pavón, J., Corchado, J.M., Bajo, J. (eds.) PAAMS 2009. AISC, vol. 55, pp. 130–139. Springer, Heidelberg (2009)
19. Alberola, J., Mulet, L., Such, J., Gacía-Fornes, A., Espinosa, A., Botti, V.: Operating System Aware MultiagentPlatform Design. In: 5th European Workshop on Multi-Agent Systems (EUMAS 2007), pp. 658–667 (2007)
20. Ndumu, D.T., Nwana, H.S., Lee, L.C., Haynes, H.R.: Visualization and Debugging of Distributed MultiagentSystems. Applied Artificial Intelligence 13(1-2), 187–208 (1999)
21. Helsinger, A., Thome, M., Wright, T.: Cougaar – AScalable, Distributed Multi-Agent Architecture. In: IEEE International Conference on Systems, Man and Cybernetics (SMC 2004), vol. 2, pp. 1910–1917. IEEE (2004)
22. ZigBee Standards Organization: ZigBee Specification Document 053474r13. ZigBee Alliance (2006)
23. Bellifemine, F., Caire, G., Trucco, T., Rimassa, G., Mungenast, R.: JADE Administrator's Guide. TILAB (2007)
24. Villarrubia, G., Sánchez, A., Zato, C., Bajo, J., Rodríguez, S., Corchado, J.M.: Proximity Detection Prototype Adapted to a Work Environment. In: Novais, P., Hallenborg, K., Tapia, D.I., Rodríguez, J.M.C. (eds.) Ambient Intelligence - Software and Applications. AISC, vol. 153, pp. 51–58. Springer, Heidelberg (2012)
25. Omicini, A., Ricci, A., Viroli, M.: Artifacts in the A&AMeta-Model for Multi-Agent Systems. Autonomous Agents and Multi-Agent Systems 17(3), 432–456 (2008)

A Private Reputation Mechanism for n-Player Games

Pedro Mariano and Luís Correia

LabMAg – Dep. de Informática
Faculdade de Ciências
Universidade de Lisboa
Portugal
plmariano@di.fc.ul.pt,
Luis.Correia@di.fc.ul.pt

Abstract. In n-player games a focal player may choose $n-1$ players to play a round of the game. It makes sense that this choice might be informed, meaning that the focal player tries to choose the best $n-1$ players from the population. Reputation is a mechanism that allows such informed choice. In this paper we present a private reputation mechanism that can be applied to any n-player game. Our solution targets the case when a player cannot identify the partner responsible for his payoff. Players collect information from previous interactions and build an imprecise reputation of their candidate partners. This information is used in future interactions to select the best partners. Results show that when there are not enough good partners, our mechanism is able to select the top $n-1$ best partners.

Keywords: partner selection, cooperation, reputation.

1 Introduction

Cooperation dilemmas appear in a variety of social situations [2]. The dilemma can be solved if a player can choose partners that are cooperative. This has been shown in 2 player game models (e.g. [1]) and in n-player games (e.g. [9]). However in the beginning of interaction, players do not know each other. Therefore they need a means to obtain information about the cooperating character of potential partners.

In order to evaluate some entity, one can assign it a reputation. This involves repeated interactions with that entity [2]. A reputation value can be formed by the interactions one has with that entity, by observing the interactions of the entity with some third-party, or by obtaining information from some third-party. This may be called the *reputation obtention process*.

Using reputation information a player may select the most reputed partners when forming a team to play a game or, in general, to engage in some cooperating activity. In such models, dynamics will tend to a state where a focal player only interacts with cooperators. A problem may arise if there are not enough cooperators, for instance if some potential partners behave stochastically. In such cases, a player has to find the best partners.

In this paper we improve a generic partner selection model [9] augmenting it with a reputation mechanism including the reputation obtention process. The previous model

J. Pavón et al. (Eds.): IBERAMIA 2012, LNAI 7637, pp. 432–441, 2012.

is generic in the sense that is applicable to any n-player game. However, it behaves poorly when there are fewer than $n - 1$ cooperators. The reputation mechanism we develop addresses the problem of selecting the top $n - 1$ best partners.

We assume that the player only uses his payoff in order to build a partner reputation. Such reputation can be considered imprecise because the player does not know each partner's actions. This model maintains the generality property in the sense that it can be used with any n-player game.

2   Related Work

In our approach a player obtains a reputation representation of other players from results of games he played with them. Reputation is then used by a focal player to choose partners whenever needed. If a player chooses partners with higher reputation he should benefit his outcome in the game. Similar approaches have been followed to study evolution of cooperation [11,13], sometimes combined with other features such as punishment [3] that favour emergence of cooperation.

Previous work [14] has investigated partner choice based on binary reputation of players, in the Prisoner's Dilemma (PD) game. However, a binary reputation is too coarse and does not allow a gradation of reputation. This gradation seems to better correspond to real situations where a binary classification is seldom realistic.

When players assess their peers, this information may be shared with others. This is used in artificial markets where sellers and buyers rate each other [5,6]. Sabater and Sierra [15] review some models of computational reputation management. They present models where reputation is built from direct interactions or from information given by others. These, as well as other works on player reputation [7,12] require perfect identification of players.

Kreps and Wilson [8] study the effect of imperfect information about players payoffs in building a reputation about opponents strategies. This is applied to firms competing for a market, in a scenario with a dominant firm and others that, one at a time, may challenge the dominance. Brandts and colleagues [4] made a similar study in loan decision making.

However all these cases use two player games. In [16] a Public Good Provision (PGP) game of three players is used with reputation. A focal player gets perfect knowledge of his neighbors actions in a network of contacts and, for each round, he can choose two partners based on their reputation. The measure of reputation is the number of cooperative actions a player has performed. A similar measure is also used in [10] in a 5-player PGP, also with perfect reputation information.

In the case we are addressing a player does not obtain direct information about individual actions of his partners. We consider that a player only obtains information from his own payoff. This means that he cannot directly identify partners that have not cooperated, nor obtain some kind of signal from them. This is a situation that often occurs in human interaction. In a group of people sometimes is not possible to pinpoint who shirked from contributing. We find that for instance in a n-player snow-drift type game. Suppose a bus that has to be pushed by several individuals. No one knows exactly if a specific individual is cooperating. One can only assess the global outcome in the form of the progress of the bus.

To the best of our knowledge no previous research has dealt with imperfect reputation information in n-player games. This happens for instance in a PGP game when only the player's own payoff is known without access to the individual actions of the players. In such case, the only situation with perfect information is when all players cooperate. Otherwise each player has an uncertainty about the other $n - 1$ players' actions. One or more of them may have defected. Our work tackles this situation in two ways from the point of view of the focal player. One is to have the player using imperfect reputation knowledge to choose his successive partnerships, and the other is to have him gathering individual reputation information from the result of a PGP type game.

We chose a private reputation model that extends the random partner selection model described in [9]. In the present work, a player associates to each potential partner a single value that measures his utility. This value is updated from direct interactions with partners, considering all partners in a game as equally responsible for the outcome. Our classification system is independent of the game being played, which contrasts with others [3] that are game specific.

3 Model Description

We describe the proposed reputation mechanism that was built on top of a partner selection model. We begin by describing the main features of this model (for details see [9]) and finish with the description of the new model using the reputation mechanism.

3.1 Random Partner Selection

Whenever a focal player needs to play a game, he selects one of the combinations of partners stored in vector **c**. Each combination has a probability of being selected. This probability is stored in vector **p**. The length of these vectors is represented by parameter l, pool size. In this model, when a focal player selects his game partners, they cannot refuse playing.

After a player has played the game with partner combination c_k, he compares the utility obtained u with utility threshold u_T. If the utility is higher or equal than the threshold, no changes occur. If the utility is lower than the threshold, the corresponding probability is decreased by factor δ, and the combination is replaced. The following equation represents the probability update policy for the used combination k:

$$p_k^{t+1} = \begin{cases} \delta p_k^t & \text{if } u < u_T \\ p_k^t & \text{if } u \geq u_T \end{cases}. \tag{1}$$

The probabilities of other combinations are updated as follows (to maintain unit sum):

$$p_i^{t+1} = \begin{cases} p_i^t + \dfrac{(1-\delta)p_k^t}{l-1} & \text{if } u < u_T \\ p_i^t & \text{if } u \geq u_T \end{cases}. \tag{2}$$

The used combination is replaced by a new one if the utility is lower than u_T:

$$c_k^{t+1} = \begin{cases} \text{rnd}(\mathscr{C}) & \text{if } u < u_T \\ c_k^t & \text{if } u \geq u_T \end{cases}. \tag{3}$$

If a new combination is to be added, it is previously checked against the ones in the combination vector. If it is identical to any of those, a new one is drawn until it is unique. The overall behaviour of this model is that good combinations remain in the probability vector because they are not replaced and absorb the probabilities of bad combinations.

3.2 Partner Selection with Reputation

In the new model, reputation is used only when a new combination must be drawn in order to replace a combination deemed unacceptable. To represent reputation, a focal player assigns a weight to each possible partner. These weights are stored in vector **w**. When a new combination is drawn, the probability of partner i being selected is proportional to his weight:

$$P(X = i) = \frac{w_i}{\sum_j w_j} \quad . \tag{4}$$

Therefore a weight represents the desire to choose the corresponding player as a partner. It can be considered as his reputation. Higher values mean a partner has a higher reputation and thus should be chosen more often.

We consider that the n-player game does not allow the focal player to identify the partner that has done a particular action. In light of equation (4), the model assumes that a player can correctly identify the partners in a combination.

Weights are updated after knowing the result of playing a game with selected combination c_k according to:

$$w_j^{t+1} = w_j^t(1 - p_k^t) + (u - \underline{u})p_k^t \quad , \tag{5}$$

where $j \in c_k$ and $\underline{u}$ is the lowest utility obtainable by the player.

The initial value of the weight vector may depend on the game. An optimistic approach is to define every initial weight to be the utility obtained by a player using a strategy belonging to a Pareto Optimum profile. This is tantamount to consider that all players are cooperative until shown otherwise.

Weight domain is the domain of the utility, but translated by $\underline{u}$ in order to always have positive weights even when the game has negative values. We can interpret the dynamics of equation (5) as assigning to any partner the utility the focal player obtained while playing with him, discounted by probability p_k associated to the combination c_k where the partner is.

Algorithm 1 details the partner selection based on reputation. The parameters of the algorithm are the strategy s used by the player, his set of candidate partners $\mathcal{N}$, the game he is going to play, $\mathcal{G}$, and the parameters of the partner selection model: pool size l, probability update factor δ, utility threshold u_T, and d that is a boolean indicating whether combinations in the vector are all distinct or repetitions are allowed.

Figure 1 lists the parameters of the model 1a and sketches the player architecture 1b.

Require: $s, \mathcal{N}, \mathcal{G}, l, \delta, u_T, d$
  $w^0 \leftarrow f(\mathcal{G})$
  $\mathbf{p}^1 \leftarrow \{p_i^1 : p_i^1 = 1/l \wedge 1 \leq i \leq l\}$
  $\mathbf{c}^1 \leftarrow \{c_i^1 : c_i^1 = \text{rnd}(\mathcal{C}) \wedge 1 \leq i \leq l\}$
  $\mathbf{w}^1 \leftarrow \{w_\alpha^1 : w_\alpha^1 = w^0 \wedge \alpha \in \mathcal{N}\}$
  for $t = 1$ **to** N_I **do**
    select combination of partners from $\mathbf{c}^t$ using $\mathbf{p}^t$
    play game $\mathcal{G}$ and obtain u
    compute $\mathbf{p}^{t+1}$ using equations (1) and (2) with δ, u_T and u
    compute $\mathbf{c}^{t+1}$ using equation (3) with $\mathbf{w}^t$, u_T, u and d
    compute $\mathbf{w}^{t+1}$ using equation (5)
  end for

Algorithm 1. Partner selection with reputation model algorithm

Environment	
$\mathcal{G}$	n-player game
$\mathcal{N}$	set of candidate partners

Player	
s	strategy for game $\mathcal{G}$
l	pool size
δ	probability update factor
u_T	utility threshold
d	distinct combinations flag
$\mathbf{p}$	probability vector
$\mathbf{c}$	combination vector
$\mathbf{w}$	weight vector

(a) Parameters.

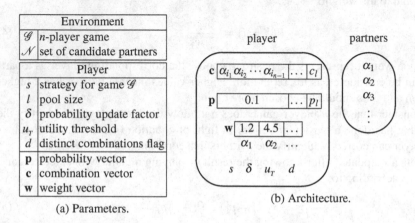

(b) Architecture.

Fig. 1. Player description. The table shows the parameters that effect the player.

4   Experimental Analysis

4.1   Analysis Description

In order to evaluate the partner classification model, we have performed an experimental analysis of algorithm 1. We have varied some of the required parameters of the algorithm, namely the set of candidate partners $\mathcal{N}$, the number of players in game $\mathcal{G}$, pool size l, probability update factor δ, and whether the combination vector has repeated combinations or not, d. Parameters l, δ and d are intrinsic to the partner selection model and are independent of the game $\mathcal{G}$. The tested values of these parameters are shown in Table 1a.

As the focus of this paper is the partner classification model and not any particular game $\mathcal{G}$, we have used an abstract game. Players are characterised by a probability to act acceptably. In this game there are only two payoffs: one if all players act acceptably, zero otherwise. With this choice of game payoff, parameter u_T was set to an arbitrary value between zero and one (exclusive). The number of players, n, varied between three and five (see Table 1b).

The set of candidate partners $\mathcal{N}$ had always eight distinct partners, with varying degrees to act acceptably. Several sets $\mathcal{N}$ were tested. Their compositions are shown in Table 1d. In sets $\mathcal{N}_1$ to $\mathcal{N}_3$ the probability to act acceptably varies linearly, each set including one partner with probability one. In set $\mathcal{N}_4$ there are two linear groups of partners: one with probabilities from 0.5 down to $1/8$, and the other group with probabilities from 1 down to $29/32$.

Table 1. Parameters values used in the two sets of experiments

(a) Partner selection algorithm.

l	4	6	8	10
δ	0	0.2	0.4	0.6	0.8
d	true false

(b) Game.

n	3	4	5

(c) Other parameters.

N_I number of iterations	10000
N_R number of runs	30

(d) Candidate partners. Numbers represent probability to behave acceptably.

$\mathcal{N}_1$	{1/8	2/8	3/8	4/8	5/8	6/8	7/8	1}
$\mathcal{N}_2$	{9/16	10/16	11/16	12/16	13/16	14/16	15/16	1}
$\mathcal{N}_3$	{25/32	26/32	27/32	28/32	29/32	30/32	31/32	1}
$\mathcal{N}_4$	{1/8	2/8	3/8	4/8	29/32	30/32	31/32	1}

Each run of the algorithm consisted in N_I iterations. For each parameter combination we ran the algorithm a certain number of runs, N_R, in order to obtain statistical significant data. The values of these parameters are shown in Table 1c.

We ran two sets of experiments. In the *control* set we only used random selection of partners, i.e., the weight vector was absent from the player architecture, see Fig. 1. In the *reputation* set we used partner selection with reputation. The purpose of these two sets was to assess the influence of the reputation model.

An aspect related to the implementation of the weight update policy pertains the possibility of zero weights. It may happen that all weights drop to zero as a consequence of a series of games where the player always obtained the lowest payoff, see equation (5). After such series, there is an indeterminacy in equation (4). However, in this state all partners should have the same probability of being selected. To circumvent this problem, weights are never allowed to drop to zero, but are instead set to ε.

4.2 Experimental Results

During a run of algorithm 1, we recorded in each iteration the partners selected by the focal player, and the payoff obtained by the focal player. Figures 2 and 3 show a summary of this data, respectively.

Regarding the partners selected by the focal player, the major result is that in the *reputation* experiments the focal player selects more often the partners with higher probability. In the *control* experiments all partners are usually selected the same number of times. Due to space limitations we only depict a few cases. Figure 2 shows results from simulations with candidate partners $\mathcal{N}_1$ and $\mathcal{N}_4$, with probability and combination vectors size set to $l = 10$, with probability update factor set to $\delta = 0.8$, and with distinct ($d = true$) or repetitions ($d = false$) in the combination vector. The vertical axis shows the percentage of the number of games played between the focal player and some partner, shown on the horizontal axis.

Results of $\mathcal{N}_4$ with $d = true$ (not depicted) are similar to those of $\mathcal{N}_1$ in the same conditions. For $d = false$ we clearly notice a difference in the selection preference between the two probability groups in $\mathcal{N}_4$, which does not happen in $\mathcal{N}_1$ (not depicted). Results from $\mathcal{N}_2$ and $\mathcal{N}_3$ and for other values of parameters follow the same pattern of dependency on the partner probabilities of acceptable behaviour.

Figure 3 shows the payoff obtained by the focal player along the iterations. Each point was obtained by averaging payoffs of N_R runs. Afterwards, we averaged points within a sliding window with a size of 30 iterations, to better observe tendencies. When we compare the results from *reputation* experiments and *control* experiments, the payoff

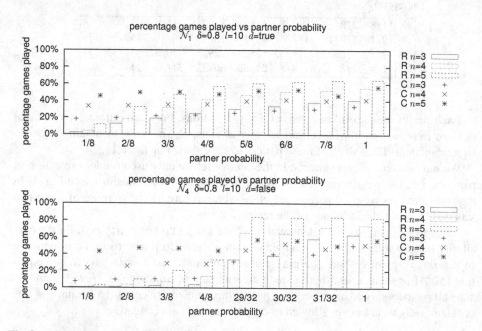

Fig. 2. Percentage of games played by focal player versus partner probability. Parameters values in both plots are $\delta = 0.8$, $l = 10$ and $n = \{3,4,5\}$. Top: $\mathcal{N}_1$ and $d = true$. Bottom: $\mathcal{N}_4$ and $d = false$ The numbers in the horizontal axis represent partner's probability for each of the candidate partners (see Table 1d). Bars represent results from *reputation* experiments (letter R in the key), while points represent results from *control* experiments (letter C in the key). Each value is the average result of N_R runs.

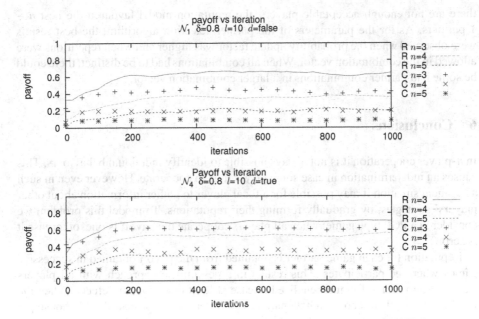

Fig. 3. Focal player payoff versus iteration, truncated at 1000 iterations for better visibility (from then on values are stable). Parameters values in both plots are $\delta = 0.8$, $l = 10$ and $n = \{3, 4, 5\}$. Top: $\mathcal{N}_1$ and $d = false$. Bottom: $\mathcal{N}_4$ and $d = true$. Lines represent results from set *reputation* (letter R in the key), while points represent results from set *control* (letter C in the key). Data is the average result of 30 runs.

obtained in the first set is always higher. This means that reputation improved the focal player's payoff. The plots also show a rapid increase of this payoff which stabilises before 200 iterations.

5   Discussion

We have performed experiments with a reputation model that was built on top of a partner selection algorithm. The partner selection algorithm maintains a vector of partner combinations along their probability to be selected. Good combinations never leave the vector and absorb the probabilities of bad combinations.

When there are no good combinations, because there are not enough good partners, the partner selection algorithm will keep drawing combinations with bad and average partners. To address this problem we have developed a reputation model. This model is characterised by a weight update policy that does not add a new parameter, but only depends on the payoff obtained by the player, the partner weight, and the probability of selecting the combination where the partner is. This greatly reduces the complexity of the model.

The results showed that the reputation model improved the payoff obtained by the focal player. This improvement was observed in games with five players. Even when there are not enough acceptable players, the reputation model favoured the best $n -$ 1 partners. As for the parameters of the partner selection algorithm, the best results were observed when the probability update factor was higher and when repetitions were allowed in the combination vector. When all combinations had to be distinct, there could be some bad partner combinations in a larger combination vector.

6   Conclusions

In n-player cooperation it is not always possible to identify individual behaviours. This causes an indetermination in case some player fails to cooperate. However even in such a stringent situation it may possible for a focal player to gather information about other players' strategies, by gradually forming their reputations. To model this problem we considered a PGP type game: when all players cooperate the payoff is one, otherwise it is zero.

Reputation for each game partner is obtained from the payoff obtained in successive games where he participates. This results in a pessimistic approach with all players from a group of $n - 1$ being penalized in case at least one of them defects. When the focal player needs to choose a new partner combination, the probability of choosing a player as partner is proportional to his reputation.

Results show that this reputation information, for slight it might be, enables higher payoffs for the focal player. Payoff differences between experiments using the reputation model and control experiments decrease with increasing number of partners n.

Future work will focus on experimenting different reputation assignments and on other partner selection procedures. The number n of players in a game may influence the modifications to the current reputation. With higher n the modification of an individual reputation should be lower than with smaller n because the uncertainty about individual responsibility in a negative result is higher. Partner selection taking into account reputation values can me made more or less greedy and this may have significant influence in the results.

In this paper we analysed the behaviour of a focal player with constant partners. We intend to analyse the behaviour of a dynamic population of players all of them being able to initiate a game and selecting their partners. This means that the set of candidate partners also changes, which is akin to an open environment.

References

1. Aktipis, C.A.: Know When to Walk Away – Contingent Movement and the Evolution of Cooperation. Journal of Theoretical Biology 231(2), 249–260 (2004)
2. Axelrod, R.: The Evolution of Cooperation. Basic Books (1984)
3. Brandt, H., Hauert, C., Sigmund, K.: Punishment and Reputation in Spatial Public Goods Games. Proceedings of the Royal Society of London, Series B: Biological Sciences 270(1519), 1099–1104 (2003)
4. Brandts, J., Figueras, N.: An Exploration of Reputation Formation in Experimental Games. Journal of Economic Behavior & Organization 50(1), 89–115 (2003)

5. Dellarocas, C.: Goodwill Hunting – An Economically Efficient Online Feedback Mechanism in Environments with Variable Product Quality. In: Padget, J., Shehory, O., Parkes, D., Sadeh, N., Walsh, W.E. (eds.) AMEC 2002. LNCS (LNAI), vol. 2531, pp. 238–252. Springer, Heidelberg (2002)
6. Dellarocas, C.: The Digitization of Word-of-Mouth – Promise and Challenges of Online Reputation Systems. Management Science 49(10), 1407–1424 (2003)
7. Janssen, M.A.: Evolution of Cooperation in a One-Shot Prisoner's Dilemma Based on Recognition of Trustworthy and Untrustworthy Agents. Journal of Economic Behavior & Organization 65(3), 458–471 (2008)
8. Kreps, D.M., Wilson, R.: Reputation and Imperfect Information. Journal of Economic Theory 27(2), 253–279 (1982)
9. Mariano, P., Correia, L.: Evolution of Partner Selection. In: Lenaerts, T., Giacobini, M., Bersini, H., Bourgine, P., Dorigo, M., Doursat, R. (eds.) 11th European Conference on the Synthesis and Simulation of Living Systems (ECAL 2011), pp. 487–494. MIT Press (2011)
10. McIntosh, C., Sadoulet, E., Buck, S., Rosada, T.: Reputation in a Public Goods Game – Taking the Design of Credit Bureaus to the Lab. Working Paper
11. Milinski, M., Semmann, D., Krambeck, H.J.: Reputation Helps Solve the "Tragedy of the Commons". Nature 415(6870), 424–426 (2002)
12. Nowak, M.A., Sigmund, K.: Evolution of Indirect Reciprocity by Image Scoring. Nature 393, 573–577 (1998)
13. Nowak, M.A., Sigmund, K.: Evolution of Indirect Reciprocity. Nature 437(7063), 1291–1298 (2005)
14. Ohtsuki, H., Iwasa, Y.: Global Analyses of Evolutionary Dynamics and Exhaustive Search for Social Norms that Maintain Cooperation by Reputation. Journal of Theoretical Biology 244(3), 518–531 (2007)
15. Sabater, J., Sierra, C.: Review on Computational Trust and Reputation Models. Artificial Intelligence Review 24(1), 33–60 (2005)
16. Wu, T., Fu, F., Wang, L.: Partner Selections in Public Goods Games with Constant Group Size. Physical Review E 80(2), 026121:1–8 (2009)

Moral Coppélia -
Combining Ratio with Affect in Ethical Reasoning

Matthijs A. Pontier[1], Guy Widdershoven[2], and Johan F. Hoorn[1]

[1,2] VU University Amsterdam,
[1] Center for Advanced Media Research Amsterdam (CAMeRA@VU),
De Boelelaan 1081, 1081HV Amsterdam, The Netherlands
{m.a.pontier,j.f.hoorn}@vu.nl
[2] VU University Medical Center, Amsterdam, The Netherlands
g.widdershoven@vumc.nl

Abstract. We present an integration of rational moral reasoning with emotional intelligence. The moral reasoning system alone could not simulate the different human reactions to the Trolley dilemma and the Footbridge dilemma. However, the combined system can simulate these human moral decision making processes. The introduction of affect in rational ethics is important when robots communicate with humans in a practical context that includes moral relations and decisions. Moreover, the combination of ratio and affect may be useful for applications in which human moral decision making behavior is simulated, for example, when agent systems or robots provide healthcare support.

Keywords: moral reasoning, machine ethics, cognitive modeling, cognitive robotics, emotion modeling, emotional computing.

1   Introduction

Due to a foreseen lack of resources and healthcare personnel to provide a high standard of care in the near future [24], robots are increasingly being used in healthcare. By providing assistance during care tasks, or fulfilling them, robots can relieve time for the many duties of care workers. Previous research shows that robots can genuinely contribute to treatment. For example, Robins et al. [20] used mobile robots to treat autistic children. Wada and Shibata [23] developed Paro, a robot shaped like a baby-seal that interacts with users to encourage positive mental effects. Interaction with Paro has been shown to improve users' moods, making them more active and communicative with each other and caregivers. Banks, Willoughby and Banks [2] showed that animal-assisted therapy with an AIBO dog helped just as good for reducing loneliness as therapy with a living dog.

As their intelligence increases, robots increasingly operate autonomously. With this development, we increasingly rely on the intelligence of these robots. Because of market pressures to perform faster, better, cheaper and more reliably, this reliance on machine intelligence will continue to increase [1]. These developments request that we should be able to rely on a certain level of ethical behavior from machines. As Rosalind Picard [17] nicely puts it: "the greater the freedom of a machine, the more it

J. Pavón et al. (Eds.): IBERAMIA 2012, LNAI 7637, pp. 442–451, 2012.

will need moral standards''. Particularly when machines interact with humans, which they increasingly do, we need to ensure that these machines do not harm us or threaten our autonomy. Therefore, care robots require moral reasoning. We need to ensure that their design and introduction do not impede the promotion of values and the dignity of patients at such a vulnerable and sensitive time in their lives [22].

As a first step to enable care robots in doing so, Pontier and Hoorn [19] developed a rational moral reasoning system that is capable of balancing between conflicting moral goals. The three moral goals considered in the system were respecting autonomy, beneficence, and non-maleficence.

In the well-known theory in biomedical ethics of Beauchamp & Childress [3], justice is added as the fourth moral principle. This is the primary value underlying ethical decisions in using utilitarian or Kantian theory [16]. Care providers may want decision-support systems to assist in allocating resources (i.e., linking the patient to the doctor that serves its needs best). During this process, dilemmas or 'wicked problems' might emerge which involve questions about how resources can be distributed fairly among patients. In entertainment settings, questions about fairness may arise as well; for example, a companion robot may have to decide on which person it should direct its attention. In accordance with the above described considerations, we added justice as a fourth moral principle to the system.

Thereby we match to the principlism of Beauchamp & Childress [3]. However, this theory has been criticized for being one-sided. It focuses on balancing principles through rational argumentation. Thereby it may lead to underexposing the role of social processes of interpretation and communication [15]. This criticism is in line with current research in moral psychology, which emphasizes the role of social processes in moral decision making.

For decades, research on moral judgment has been dominated by rationalist models, in which moral judgment is thought to be motivated by moral reasoning. However, more recent research indicates moral reasoning is just one of the factors motivating moral judgment. According to some researchers, moral reasoning is even usually a post hoc construction, generated after judgment has been reached (e.g., [9]).

Both reason and emotion are likely to play important roles in moral judgment. Greene et al. [8] find that moral dilemmas vary systematically in the extent to which they engage emotional processing and that these variations in emotional engagement influence moral judgment. Their study was inspired by the difference between two variants of an ethical dilemma: the Trolley dilemma and the footbridge dilemma.

In the Trolley dilemma, a runaway trolley is headed for five people who will be killed if it proceeds on its present course. The only way to save them is to hit a switch that will turn the trolley onto an alternate set of tracks where it will kill one person instead of five. Ought you to turn the trolley in order to save five people at the expense of one? Most people say yes.

In the Footbridge dilemma, as before, a trolley threatens to kill five people. You are standing next to a large stranger on a footbridge that spans the tracks, in between the oncoming trolley and the five people. In this scenario, the only way to save the five people is to push this stranger off the bridge, onto the tracks below. He will die if you do this, but his body will stop the trolley from reaching the others. Ought you to save the five others by pushing this stranger to his death? Most people say no.

According to Greene et al. [8], there is no set of consistent, readily accessible moral principles that captures people's intuitions concerning what behavior is or is not appropriate in these and similar cases. In other words, the different human moral decision-making processes in the Trolley dilemma and the Footbridge dilemma (and similar dilemmas) cannot be explained by rational principles alone. Therefore, human moral-decision making processes cannot be simulated in a moral reasoning system based on pure principlism.

Greene et al. [8] hypothesized that the crucial difference between the Trolley dilemma and the Footbridge dilemma lies in the latter's tendency to engage people's emotions in a way that the former does not. They proposed that the thought of pushing someone to his death is emotionally more salient than the thought of hitting a switch that will cause a trolley to produce similar consequences. Our conjecture is that this is related to the issue that the person in the footbridge is a concrete human being (although a stranger) standing close by, whereas the people on the railway track are positioned equally far away (by chance). And it is this emotional response that accounts for people's tendency to treat these cases differently.

The fMRI and behavioral results of Greene's et al. [8] studies supported this hypothesis Moral-personal dilemmas (those relevantly similar to the Footbridge dilemma) engage emotional processing to a greater extent than moral-impersonal dilemmas (those relevantly similar to the Trolley dilemma), and these differences in emotional engagement affect people's judgments.

To be able to capture these human moral decision making processes, we integrated the moral reasoning system of Pontier and Hoorn [19], which did not include emotional considerations, but merely rational principles, with Silicon Coppélia [10], a computational model of emotional intelligence that is capable of affective decision making. We hypothesized that, by combining moral reasoning and affective decision making into Moral Coppélia, human moral decision making processes could be simulated that could not be simulated using the moral reasoning system alone.

2   Method

2.1   About the Rational Moral Reasoning System

In the rational moral reasoning system [19], the agent tries to estimate the morality of actions by holding each action against the moral principles inserted in the system and picking actions that serve these moral goals best. The agent calculates the estimated level of Morality of an action by taking the sum of the ambition levels of the moral goals multiplied with the beliefs that the particular actions facilitate the corresponding moral goals. When moral goals are believed to be better facilitated by a moral action, the estimated level of Morality will be higher. The following formula is used to calculate the estimated Morality of an action:

$$\text{Morality(Action)} = \Sigma_{\text{Goal}}(\text{ Belief(facilitates(Action, Goal)) * Ambition(Goal))}$$

As can be seen Fig. 1, this can be represented as a weighted association network, where moral goals are associated with the possible actions via the belief strengths that these actions facilitate the three moral goals.

In six simulation experiments, the system reached the same conclusions as expert ethicists [19]. For example, consider the hypothetical situation that a patient with

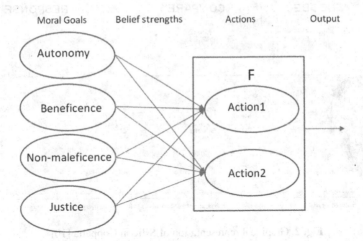

Fig. 1. Moral reasoner shown in graphical format

incurable cancer refuses chemotherapy that will let him live a few months longer, relatively pain free, but refuses the treatment due to the false belief that he is cancer-free. In this case, both the system and expert medical ethicists advise to try to convince the patient of the need of undergoing the chemotherapy, because the patient is not capable of fully autonomous decision making and his decision will lead to harm (dying sooner) and denies him the chance of a longer life (a violation of the duty of beneficence), which he might later regret.

2.2   About Silicon Coppélia – A Model of Emotional Intelligence

Previous work described how certain dimensions of the design of virtual characters were perceived by users and how they responded to them [21]. A series of user studies resulted in an empirically validated framework for the study of user-character interaction with a special focus on the explanation of user engagement and use intentions. This framework was summarized in a schema called Interactively Perceiving and Experiencing Fictional Characters (I-PEFiC). We formalized the I-PEFiC framework and made it the basic mechanism of how virtual characters and robots build up affect for their human users [5]. In addition, we designed a special module for affective decision-making (ADM) that made it possible to make decisions based on rational as well as affective influences, hence I-PEFiC^{ADM} [11].

To further advance I-PEFiC^{ADM} into the area of emotion regulation, we also included EMA [13]: an appraisal-based model of emotion generation and coping, and CoMERG [4]: a Cognitive Model for Emotion Regulation based on Gross' theory. Together, the three approaches cover a large part of appraisal-based emotion theory and all three boil down to appraisal models of emotion [6]. We therefore decided to integrate the three models of affect into one computational model that we called Silicon Coppélia [10]. Figure 2 drafts Silicon Coppélia in a graphical format.

Silicon Coppélia is software consisting of a loop with a particular situation as input, and actions as output, leading to a new situation. In this loop there are three phases: the encoding, the comparison, and the response phase. The virtual human

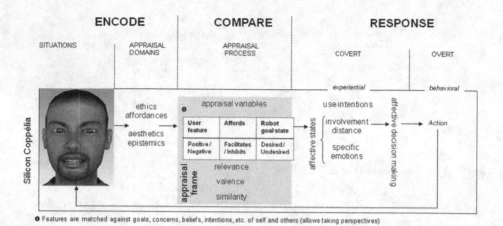

Fig. 2. Graphical representation of Silicon Coppélia [10]

is programmed in such a way, that it follows the perception and appraisal paths as given in Fig. 2 and explained below. In doing so, the virtual human 'perceives' its interaction partner (either human or artificial).

In the *encoding* phase, the virtual human 'perceives' another character (i.e., the respondent in this study) in terms of Ethics (good vs. bad), Affordances (aid vs. obstacle), Aesthetics (beautiful vs. ugly), and Epistemics (realistic vs. unrealistic).

In the *comparison* phase, the virtual human retrieves beliefs about actions that facilitate or inhibit the desired or undesired goal-states. This is to calculate a general expected utility of each action. The virtual human also determines certain appraisal variables, such as the belief that someone is accountable for accomplishing goal-states or not. These variables and the perceived features of others are related to the virtual human's goals and concerns, to appraise them for their level of Relevance (relevant or irrelevant) and Valence (positive or negative outcome expectancies).

In the *response* phase of the model, the results of the comparison phase lead to processes of Involvement with, and Distance toward the other, and to the emergence of certain Use Intentions: the virtual human's willingness to employ the other as a tool to achieve its own goals. Note that both overt (behavioral) and covert (experiential) responses can be executed in this phase. Emotions such as hope, joy, and anger are generated using appraisal variables (e.g., the perceived accountability of others, and likelihood of goal-states).

Finally, the virtual human applies an *affective decision-making module* to calculate the expected satisfaction of possible actions. In this module, affective influences and rational influences are combined in the decision-making process. Involvement and Distance felt toward the interaction partner give input for the affective influences in the decision-making process, whereas Use Intentions and general expected utility represent the more rational influences. However, no moral principles were included in the decision-making process yet. When the virtual human selects and performs an action, a new situation emerges, and the model loops back to the first phase.

In a speed-dating experiment [18], participants did not experience differences in the perceptions, emotions and decision-making behavior between an avatar controlled by Silicon Coppélia versus the same avatar controlled by a human confederate.

2.3   Integration of the Two Systems into Moral Coppélia

To integrate the moral reasoning system and Silicon Coppélia into Moral Coppélia, the moral principles were included in the appraisal process, and the affective-decision making module was added to the moral reasoning. This leads to the following formula to calculate the expected satisfaction of an action. In this formula, w_{eu}, w_{mor}, w_{pos} and w_{neg} represent weights in calculating the expected satisfaction.

$$ExpectedSatisfaction(Agent1, Action, Agent2) =$$
$$w_{eu} * ExpectedUtility +$$
$$w_{mor} * \qquad Morality(action) +$$
$$w_{pos} * \qquad (1 - abs(positivity - bias_{Involvement} * Involvement)) +$$
$$w_{neg} * (1 - abs(negativity - bias_{Distance} * Distance))$$

The agent prefers actions with a high level of expected utility for itself. Further, it prefers actions with a high level of (rational) morality, which could be seen as expected utility for everyone. The more emotional influences consisted of preferring actions with a positivity level close to the level of (biased) involvement, and a negativity level close to the (biased) level of distance. The biases account for individual defaults (being a positively or negatively oriented person).

3   Simulation Results

To examine the behavior of the moral reasoning system alone, we first tested the behavior of the rational moral reasoning alone in the trolley dilemma and the Footbridge dilemma in Experiment 1. To investigate the added value of Silicon Coppélia's affective decision-making, we then tested the behavior of the integrated system Moral Coppélia in the Trolley dilemma in Experiment 2, and in the Footbridge dilemma in Experiment 3.

3.1   Experiment 1: Rational Moral Reasoning Only

Table 1. Parameter settings and results for footbridge and Trolley dilemma

	Autonomy	Non-Malef	Benef	Justice	**Morality**
Kill 1 to save 5	-0.5	0.5	0.8	-0.2	**0.05**
Do Nothing	0	-0.8	-0.5	0	**-0.20**

An initial experiment was performed to test the behavior of the moral reasoning system alone, by setting all weights in the affective decision making module to 0, except w_{mor} for the influence of moral reasoning in the decision-making process.

In accordance with various expert ethicists (see acknowledgements), we set the contribution of actions to the four moral principles to the same levels for the trolley and Footbridge dilemma. The parameter settings and experimental results can be found in Table 1.

Because both dilemmas were represented by the exact same parameter settings, the system came to the exact same outcome for both the Trolley dilemma and the Footbridge dilemma. In both variants of the dilemma, killing one to save five was considered ethically better (morality = 0.05) than doing nothing (morality = -0.20). Thus, in both variants of the dilemma the agent killed one person to save five others.

3.2   Experiment 2: Trolley Dilemma with Ratio and Affect Combined

Table 2. Parameter settings for the Trolley dilemma

W_{pos}	W_{neg}	W_{eu}	W_{mor}
0.1	0.1	0.1	0.7

In experiment 2, we simulated the Trolley dilemma in the integrated model. The possible end-states in the system, '1 dead' and '5 dead' were both undesired goals. The ambition level for '1 dead' was set to -0.5, and the ambition level for '5 dead' to -1. The agent believed the action 'Kill 1 save 5' would certainly lead to '1 dead' and 'Do nothing' would certainly lead to '5 dead'. Killing the stranger was regarded an extremely negative action towards him (positivity = -1; negativity = 1), whereas letting him live at the cost of the five others was regarded an extremely positive action towards him (positivity = 1; negativity = -1). The remaining parameters in Silicon Coppélia were set at standard values that represent perceiving a stranger. This led to a small amount of involvement (0.15) and distance (0.07) towards the stranger that would be killed by hitting the switch.

The resulting expected satisfaction for 'Kill 1 to save 5' was 0.04, whereas the resulting expected satisfaction for 'Do nothing' was 0.03. Thus, the agent hit the switch and killed the stranger to save the five others.

3.3   Experiment 3: Footbridge Dilemma with Ratio and Affect Combined

According to Greene et al. [8], moral-personal dilemmas (such as the Footbridge dilemma) engage emotional processing to a greater extent than moral-impersonal dilemmas (such as the Trolley dilemma) and these differences in emotional engagement affect people's judgments. Therefore, the weights for the affective influences W_{pos} and W_{neg} were set to 0.2, a higher level than for the Footbridge dilemma. The remaining parameters were set to the same levels as Experiment 2.

Table 3. Parameter settings and results for the Footbridge dilemma

W_{pos}	W_{neg}	W_{eu}	W_{mor}
0.2	0.2	0.1	0.5

Because of the increased emotional processing compared to Experiment 2, the agent felt more restrained to kill one person so to save five. Therefore, the expected satisfaction of this action decreased to 0.02. This caused the agent to do nothing, and the five people on the track were killed.

4   Discussion

In this paper, we presented Moral Coppélia, which is an integration of a moral reasoning system [19] and Silicon Coppélia [10], a system for the generation and regulation of affect for (virtual) others. The resulting system can simulate human decision making processes in the ethical domain that cannot be simulated by a rational reasoning system. More specifically, the different choices that are typical for human decision behavior in response to the Trolley dilemma and the Footbridge dilemma could be simulated by the integrated system, whereas in the moral reasoning system without Silicon Coppélia, this was not possible.

The rational but cold ethical behavior that could be simulated by the moral reasoning system was made more humane by adding affective decision-making. This is important for effective communication about moral decisions. Solutions that seem ethically best to the objective observer are often perceived as harsh by the people involved [14]. It is often counter-productive to propose a solution and communicate about this 'like a robot', without any empathy for the people involved. Moral Coppélia can be used to act more human-like in situations like this. The feedback loop in Silicon Coppélia enables the robot to adapt its behavior to individuals. Additionally, the robot could project Moral Coppélia in its human interaction partners to estimate their ethical viewpoints and predict their emotional reactions to certain proposals and actions.

There are many applications, in which robots and computer agents should not behave ethically 'perfect' in a rationalist sense. They should be able to distinguish between right and wrong. In a training simulation or serious game, police officers may not always be effective when they 'play it nicely.' Sometimes they have to break the moral rules (e.g., lie or cheat) to achieve a higher goal (e.g., prevent a murder). Further, in entertainment settings, we often like characters that are a bit naughty [12]. Morally perfect characters may even be perceived as boring (ibid.). The need to be context-sensitive and not rigidly follow rational principles is not limited to such more or less atypical situations. It is actually crucial in all human interaction. A rationalist moral agent is insensitive to social processes of understanding, which are crucial for human interaction, especially in the context of care for dependent people. Certain authors even claim that it is impossible not to lie during the day [7].

Our experiments show that a system which integrates moral reasoning and emotion comes to decisions which do more justice to everyday moral concerns than a system that is based on principlist reasoning alone. The Silicon Coppélia software introduces an affective component to ethical decision making that can deal with inconsequent human choices in solving moral dilemmas. In application, a robot system could show empathy and understanding for the moral choice (e.g., "I won't enter his house") that a user makes. Nonetheless, the robot may insist that the affective choice is traded for a rational one ("But you have to do it anyway. The patient may die"). To push the envelope, the robot system could even propose to do the job for the user ("Shall I do it for you?"). The robot does the dirty job and the user comes out 'clean'. In itself, this makes interesting scenarios to have participants evaluate the ethical position of robot as well as user, which could be used to improve the moral reasoner in relation to affective decision making.

In future research, we wish to transform the Trolley and the Footbridge dilemma to a healthcare setting. The idea is to let care professionals work with a robot helper, a Caredroid, on a fictitious medical case.

A medical equivalent of the Footbridge dilemma would be: Five people are waiting to have an organ transplant. If they are not operated immediately, they will die. At the Intensive Care unit, someone who crashed in a car accident is in a coma. That person has the right organs for all five transplant patients. Should the person in coma die to save the other five?

It would be especially interesting to apply the new system to real life dilemmas, such as the decision whether or not to inform relatives about the outcome of a genetic test on a patient which may be relevant to their health. Another case could be whether or not to enter the house of a patient who is in need of care, but refuses to cooperate.

In the different scenario's we will run, the Caredroid offers various solutions, also the one in which it proposes that the user does not have to take responsibility and that the Caredroid will do the dirty job for him or her. We plan to sample think-aloud protocols of other care professionals in which we record the arguments in support or against the ethical behavior and decisions of the Caredroid and its user. A set of judges (e.g., Medical Ethical Committee) will then classify the data as arguments of Autonomy, Beneficence, Non-maleficence, Justice and affective influences. This will provide insight into the priorities of the various arguments and argument clusters, informing the design of a Caredroid that will be acceptable to care professionals because it knows what it can propose and what not.

As is, the moral reasoner with affective components only allows choosing from given decision options in scenarios. We additionally want to explore what happens if the Caredroid proposes alternatives that include more information than what is offered by the isolated dilemma. What do care professionals say and what is the conclusion of a Medical Ethical Committee if the Caredroid escapes from wicked problems through creativity? For example, what is our moral position if the Caredroid buys us time by suggesting that the transplant patients should be connected to the coma patient so that the six of them live symbiotically together until a definite solution is found and no one has to die?

Acknowledgements. This study is part of the SELEMCA project within CRISP (grant number: NWO 646.000.003). We would like to thank Joel Anderson and Margo van Kemenade for some interesting discussions.

References

1. Anderson, M., Anderson, S., Armen, C.: Toward Machine Ethics: Implementing Two Action-Based Ethical Theories. In: Machine Ethics: Papers from the AAAI Fall Symposium. Association for the Advancement of Artificial Intelligence, Menlo Park, CA (2005)
2. Banks, M.R., Willoughby, L.M., Banks, W.A.: Animal-Assisted Therapy and Loneliness in Nursing Homes - Use of Robotic versus Living Dogs. Journal of the American Medical Directors Association 9, 173–177 (2008)
3. Beauchamp, T.L., Childress, J.F.: Principles of Biomedical Ethics. Oxford University Press, New York (2001)
4. Bosse, T., Pontier, M.A., Siddiqui, G.F., Treur, J.: Incorporating Emotion Regulation into Virtual Stories. In: Pelachaud, C., Martin, J.C., Andre, E., Chollet, G., Karpouzis, K., Pele, D. (eds.) IVA 2007. LNCS (LNAI), vol. 4722, pp. 339–347. Springer, Heidelberg (2007)
5. Bosse, T., Hoorn, J.F., Pontier, M.A., Siddiqui, G.F.: Robot's Experience of Another Robot: Simulation. In: Sloutsky, V., Love, B.C., McRae, K. (eds.) CogSci 2008, pp. 2498–2503 (2008)

6. Bosse, T., Gratch, J., Hoorn, J.F., Pontier, M.A., Siddiqui, G.F.: Comparing Three Computational Models of Affect. In: Demazeau, Y., Dignum, F., Corchado, J.M., Pérez, J.B., et al. (eds.) Advances in PAAMS. AISC, vol. 70, pp. 175–184. Springer, Heidelberg (2010)
7. DePaulo, B.M., Kashy, D.A., Kirkendol, S.E., Wyer, M.M., Ep-stein, J.A.: Lying in Everyday Life. Journal of Personality and Social Psychology 70(5), 979–995 (1996)
8. Greene, J.D., Sommerville, R.B., Nystrom, L.E., Darley, J.M., Cohen, J.D.: An fMRI Investigation of Emotional Engagement in Moral Judgment. Science 293(5537), 2105–2108 (2001), doi:10.1126/science.1062872
9. Haidt, J.: The Emotional Dog and Its Rational Tail - A Social Intuitionist Approach to Moral Judgment. Psychological Review 108(4), 814–834 (2001)
10. Hoorn, J.F., Pontier, M.A., Siddiqui, G.F.: Coppélius' Concoction: Similarity and Complementarity Among Three Affect-related Agent Models. Cognitive Systems Research Journal, 33–49 (2012)
11. Hoorn, J.F., Pontier, M.A., Siddiqui, G.F.: When the User is Instrument to Robot Goals. In: 7th IEEE/WIC/ACM International Conference on Intelligent Agent Technology (IAT 2008), pp. 296–301 (2008)
12. Konijn, E.A., Hoorn, J.F.: Some Like It Bad. Testing a Model for Perceiving and Experiencing Fictional Characters. Media Psychology 7(2), 107–144 (2005)
13. Marsella, S., Gratch, J.: EMA: A Model of Emotional Dynamics. Cognitive Systems Research 10(1), 70–90 (2009)
14. Noddings, N.: Caring – A Feminine Approach to Ethics and Moral Education. University of Calfiornia Press, Berkeley and Los Angeles (1984)
15. Ohnsorge, K., Widdershoven, G.A.M.: Monological versus Dialogical Consciousness – Two Epistemological Views on the Use of Theory in Clinical Ethical Practice. Bioethics 25(7), 361–369 (2011)
16. Pantazidou, M., Nair, I.: Ethic of Care: Guiding Principles for Engineering Teaching & Practice. Journal of Engineering Education 88(2), 205–212 (1999)
17. Picard, R.: Affective Computing. MIT Press, Cambridge (1997)
18. Pontier, M.A.: Virtual Agents for Human Communication - Emotion Regulation and Involvement-Distance Trade-Offs in Embodied Conversational Agents and Robots. Doctoral dissertation, VU University, Amsterdam (2011)
19. Pontier, M.A., Hoorn, J.F.: Toward Machines that Behave Ethically Better than Humans Do. In: Proceedings of the 34th International Annual Conference of the Cognitive Science Society, CogSci 2012 (in press, 2012)
20. Robins, B., Dautenhahn, K., Boekhorst, R.T., Billard, A.: Robotic Assistants in Therapy and Education of Children with Autism: Can a Small Humanoid Robot Help Encourage Social Interaction Skills? Journal of Universal Access in the Information Society 4, 105–120 (2005)
21. Van Vugt, H.C., Hoorn, J.F., Konijn, E.A.: Interactive Engagement with Embodied Agents: An Empirically Validated Framework. Computer Animation and Virtual Worlds 20(2-3), 195–204 (2009)
22. Van Wynsberghe, A.: Designing Robots for Care; Care Centered Value-Sensitive Design. Journal of Science and Engineering Ethics (in press, 2012)
23. Wada, K., Shibata, T.: Social Effects of Robot Therapy in a Care House. JACIII 13, 386–392 (2009)
24. WHO.: Health topics: Ageing (2010), http://www.who.int/topics/ageing/en/

Combining Rules and CRF Learning for Opinion Source Identification in Spanish Texts

Aiala Rosá[1,2], Dina Wonsever[1], and Jean-Luc Minel[2]

[1] Facultad de Ingeniería, Universidad de la República, Montevideo, Uruguay
{aialar,wonsever}@fing.edu.uy
[2] Université Paris Ouest Nanterre la Défense, Nanterre, France
jminel@u-paris10.fr

Abstract. In this work we present a system for the automatic annotation of opinions in Spanish texts. We focus mainly in the definition of a TFS-style model for the predicates of opinion and their arguments, in the creation of a lexicon of opinion predicates and in two additional variants for identifying the source of opinions. The original system extracts opinions and all its elements (predicate, source, topic and message) based on hand-coded rules, the first variant uses a CRF model for learning the source, assuming that the predicate is already tagged, and the second variant is a combined version, with the result of source recognition via the rule-based system being added as an additional attribute for training the CRF model. We found that this hybrid system performs better than each of the systems evaluated separately. This work involved the construction of several resources for Spanish: a lexicon of opinion predicates, a 13,000 word corpus with whole opinion annotations and a 40,000 word corpus with annotations of opinion predicates and sources.

Keywords: opinion extraction, hybrid approach, rule-based system, conditional random fields.

1 Introduction

An interesting task for various Natural Language Processing applications is the identification of the points of view or positions of different sources, generally people of public importance, about different topics. To answer questions such as *What is X´s opinion on the topic Y?*, *Who said something on the subject Y?*, *Who approves or disapproves of some issue Y?*, it is essential to be able to extract occurrences of opinions of different persons, in journalistic texts such as editorials or news articles.

There are systems (Appinions[1], EMM News Explorer[2]) that offer such services for English. These systems rely on different types of resources such as specialized lexicons and annotated corpora, besides general-purpose resources in natural language processing (i.e., taggers, lexical databases like WordNet, parsers, etc.).

---

[1] appinions.com
[2] emm.newsexplorer.eu

J. Pavón et al. (Eds.): IBERAMIA 2012, LNAI 7637, pp. 452–461, 2012.

In the case of Appinions, an important resource is the MPQA corpus [20], which contains annotations for different elements of an opinion (source, topic, polarity, etc.). This system also uses dictionaries of subjective words [7].

Other work on the identification of opinions is also based on the use of a specialized vocabulary: positive and negative verbs and adjectives [8], or verbs that introduce reported speech [9, 11].

For recognition of the sources, [18] defines a repertoire of source introducing predicates (SIP), where each entry has an associated semantic class and some syntactic information.

There are no specific resources for opinion extraction in Spanish so we had to rely on general purpose lexical resources. These resources proved useful as an initial basis, but they had to be adapted, and to be contrasted with examples from a corpus. This is the case of ADESSE[3], a lexical database for Spanish that provides lists of verbs belonging to different semantic classes and numerous corpus examples showing different syntactic configurations of the arguments inside each semantic class. Its adaptation to the type of text that we are interested in (journal articles) is not trivial, since many of the examples come from literary texts, where we find highly ambiguous cases, such as for instance occurrences of the verbs *greet*, *pray* or *sign* within the class communication (*"Ojalá que venga", reza. / "I hope he comes", he prays; Nunca dejé de rezar por ti. / I kept praying for you.*).

In a previous paper [15] we presented a rule-based system for the recognition of opinions and their elements (the predicate, the source, the topic and the message) in Spanish journalistic texts. In the present paper we focus primarily on opinion source identification. We report on the use of a CRF classifier for source recognition; on a combined system that includes the rule-based system output as an input attribute for training, significantly improving the results of the rule-based system and the CRF system; and on a specialized co-reference resolution module for the recovery of omitted sources. The combined system for source recognition achieves 83% of exact F-measure, this result being similar to those reported for English and Chinese [6, 11, 21].

The following resources were created and will be publicly available: a) a lexicon of 155 opinion predicates in which for every element we provide syntactic and semantic information, necessary for the recognition of different patterns for the predicates and their arguments, b) two annotated corpora: a 13,000 token corpus annotated with opinions and their elements and a 40,000 token corpus annotated with predicates and sources.

The organization of this paper is as follows. In Sect. 2 we present some works related to the source recognition task. In Section 3 we present our definition for opinion. In Sect. 4 we describe an opinion predicate lexicon. In Sect. 5 we present the automatic systems for source recognition: we first describe briefly the rule-based system and then we present the CRF classifier, the combined system and the co-reference module for opinion sources. Finally, we conclude in Sect. 6.

2   Related Work

Regarding the identification of opinions, one of the most important references is the annotation schema for opinions and emotions presented in [20]. This model specifies

---

[3] adesse.uvigo.es

the different kinds of expressions to be considered for the study of opinions: explicit mentions of private states (*The U.S. fears a spill-over*), speech events expressing private states (*"The U.S. fears a spill-over," said Xirao-Nima*), expressive subjective elements (*The report is full of absurdities*), and objective speech event (*Sargeant O'Leary said the incident took place at 2:00pm*). In our work we have considered most of these expressions, except the expressive subjective elements, so we included in our study all cases of reported speech (objective and subjective).

To our knowledge, there are not systems for opinion source identification in Spanish texts. Different works focus on source identification for English [2, 3, 5, 6, 8, 21] and Chinese [11]. Almost all these authors apply machine learning methods, only [11] has developed a rule-based system obtaining better results than most of the listed systems. Some authors [8, 21] use a semantic role tagger, this tool is considered very important for source identification by some authors who have studied this problem [17, 18]. We did not have access to this type of resource for Spanish.

In addition, there are some works on reported speech identification, the typical mechanism for citation. Both studies analyzed [9, 14] propose rule systems. In the first case, the speech verb, the source and the reported clause are identified for each reported speech instance. In the second case, only direct speech is recognized.

3   Opinion Definition

In our work, the concept of opinion covers all the expressions attributed to different sources by the author of the text, including those in which the source transmits an objective content. We identify four relevant elements for the opinion:

- the predicate: expression that indicates the presence of an opinion (verbs like *opinar/say, rechazar/reject*; nouns like *opinión/opinion, rechazo/rejection* and source indicators like *según, de acuerdo con / according to*),
- the source: opinion holder,
- the topic: explicit subject on which the opinion is expressed,
- the message: content of the opinion.

In our analysis the predicate is the central element of the opinion and the remaining elements are its arguments.

In example (1) we show the different elements of the opinion using the following notation: underlined source, predicate in bold, topic in italics and message shaded in gray.

(1)
Consultado *sobre la lentitud de los procesos judiciales uruguayos*, <u>Carranza</u> **respondió**: "Hay una situación de un muy alto número de presos sin condena, hay que agilizar los procesos".

[*Consulted about the slowness of the Uruguayan judicial processes, Carranza said, "There is a situation of a very high number of unsentenced prisoners, we must speed up processes."*]

Most instances of opinions in texts do not contain all the defined elements. The topic, for instance, is not very common. The source is sometimes absent, mainly when it can be recovered from context. In Sect. 5.4 we present a module for recovering missing sources.

4   Opinion Predicate Lexicon

Automatic opinion recognition is built around the identification of an opinion-introducing predicate. A predicate lexicon is essential to identify these elements.

The lexicon we built contains 100 verbs and 55 nouns, mostly extracted from our development corpus. The rules system evaluation (presented in section 4.1) showed that the lexicon had good coverage (91 %) on the evaluation corpus.

For each lexicon entry a type is assigned, according to a model we defined for predicates, where the syntactic and semantic properties of the predicates and their arguments are described. These properties make it possible to identify the source, the topic and the message within the syntactic structures in which the predicates occur.

The model focuses on predicates, mostly verbal predicates, and the other opinion elements (source, topic and message) are arguments for these predicates. It is specified in the language of Typed Feature Structures (TFS) [13].

The type system defined for verbal predicates is based on the hierarchically organized semantic classes of ADESSE and each subtype inherits properties or restrictions specified by TSF structures. In Figure 1 we show the hierarchical organization for opinion verbs. Semantic classes in bold belong to ADESSE classification.

We have defined one semantic property (semantic orientation, with possible values positive, negative or neutral) and several syntactic-semantic properties:

- The semantic role of the grammatical subject of the opinion verb, which can take the values *source* (OV_SS) or *topic* (OV_ST), resulting in the first binary branching of the tree.
- The possibility of accepting the topic of the opinion as an object complement of the verb (OV_SS_NO_NEU: evaluation, acceptation and some sensation verbs) or of not accepting it (OV_SS_BEL_COM: belief and communication verbs). In addition, OV_SS_BEL_COM are neutral and OV_SS_NO_NEU have a semantic orientation positive (OV_SS_POS) or negative (OV_SS_NEG).
- The possibility of accepting a subordinate construction containing the opinion message (OV_SS_BEL_REP: belief and reported speech verbs) or of not accepting it (OV_SS_TALK: verbs like "talk").
- The possibility of topicalisation for the opinion topic, usually with the preposition *sobre /about* (OV_SS_BEL_REP: belief and reported speech verbs).

Our model also includes nominal predicates for which the main feature we specified is the opinion element introduced by the Spanish preposition *de*: in some cases this preposition introduces the source (*la delcaración del presidente* / *the president statement*), in other cases it can introduce the source or the topic (*el anuncio del presidente* / *the president's announcement* or *el anuncio de su llegada* / *the announcement of his arrival*).

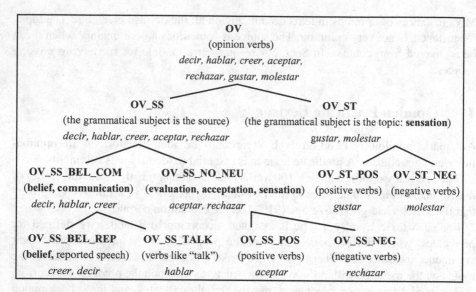

Fig. 1. Opinion Verbs: Types Hierarchy, some examples are shown for each class[4]

5   An Automatic Opinion Identification Tool

5.1   A Rule-Based System

We developed a rule-based system, based on contextual rules [22], that uses the predicate lexicon for the identification of the opinions and their elements. Example (2) shows the system output:

```
(2)
<opinion so="pos">
        <source so="neu">Mujica</source>
        <predicate so="pos">respaldó</predicate>
        <topic so="neu">importante inversión minera</topic>
</opinion>
[Mujica supports a major mining investment.]
```

We defined five rule modules: one for each opinion element (predicate, source, topic and message) and a final module for the whole opinion. For each element, except for the message, a semantic orientation (so) value (neutral, positive or negative) is assigned. Finally, the semantic orientation of the whole opinion is calculated, based on the values of the elements. A more detailed description of the rule-based system was provided in [15], [16].

---

[4] decir/say, hablar/talk,speak, creer/believe, aceptar/accept, rechazar/reject, molestar/annoy, gustar/please,like.

The rule system was evaluated on a 13,000 token corpus, including 300 opinion instances. Table 1 shows exact and partial results.

Table 1. Results obtained with the rule-based system

	Predicate	Source	Topic	Message	Opinion
Precision (exact)	92%	81%	67%	65%	52%
Precision (partial)	92%	93%	96%	95%	94%
Recall (exact)	91%	63%	45%	58%	42%
Recall (partial)	91%	72%	62%	84%	77%
F-measure (exact)	91.5%	71%	54%	61%	47%
F-measure (partial)	91.5%	81%	75%	89%	85%

There are several elements which are sometimes partially recognized, especially for the topic and the message which are usually longer than the predicate and source.

Results for the predicate show that the lexicon has good coverage, although there remains some place for improvement by adding new predicates (recall for predicate recognition is 91%).

5.2   Machine Learning Experimentation

In order to improve the results for source recognition, we applied a machine learning process, based on the Conditional Random Fields (CRF) model. CRF [10], a sequential discriminative probabilistic model, has proved to be successful in various applications of Natural Language Processing, such as nominal group segmentation, named entity identification and morphological tagging [19]. It has also been used in Opinion Mining for source recognition in English texts [5, 6] and to classify subjective sentences in English and Chinese texts [12].

We treat the problem of source recognition as a sequential classification problem, where we estimate the conditional probability of a sequence of output values (the class of each lexical unit) given an input sequence (observations).

We generated a manually annotated corpus of 40,000 tokens: 30,000 for training and 10,000 for testing. The training corpus contains 486 sources and the testing corpus contains 158 sources.

For training, we used morpho-syntactic attributes (word, lemma, POS-tag, number, gender and some special attributes that indicate which verbs, nouns and prepositions belong to the opinion predicate lexicon. The corpus includes an output attribute, based on the B-I-O notation, indicating whether a word is the beginning (B) of a source or interior (I) to a source. The value O is assigned to non source words. We performed several experiments [16], varying the way of combining the attributes, the number of elements to consider before and after the current element, and the use of bigrams for output values. The best results obtained were 66% in recall and 92% in precision.

To compare the two systems, we carried out a new evaluation of the rules system, just for source recognition, assuming all predicates were recognized, and using the same test corpus that we used for the CRF system evaluation. The rules system reaches the best results for recall, 73% rules / 66% CRF, while CRF is better for precision, 85% rules / 92% CRF (exact measures).

5.3   Combining the Rule-Based System with the CRF Classifier

An additional input attribute, based on the B-I-O notation, indicates whether a word was marked as a source or as part of a source by the rule-based system. Thus we obtained our third system: a combined system that inherits the benefits of each of the systems described above, reaching good results in precision, like CRF, and in recall, like the rule-based system. It is even one or two points higher on each measure compared to the best values of the original systems. This leads to an improvement of the F-measure (83%): 4 points on the rule-based system and 7 points on the CRF system.

We found that one of the advantages of the CRF system is the flexibility to include different elements in the sources, so that it achieves complete sources in some cases in which the rules system finds only partial sources (example 3).

(3)

Original text:	según[5] una denuncia efectuada por funcionarios del INAU ...
English translation:	*according to a complaint made by officials of INAU ...*
Expected annotation:	según [una denuncia efectuada por funcionarios del INAU]
Rules annotation:	según [una denuncia] efectuada por funcionarios del INAU
CRF annotation:	según [una denuncia efectuada por funcionarios del INAU]
CRF+rules annotation:	según [una denuncia efectuada por funcionarios del INAU]

On the other hand, the rule system performs better for sources of nominal predicates, which have a low frequency in the training corpus (example 4).

(4)

Original text:	en palabras[6] del economista Fernando Ribeiro ...
English translation:	*in the words of economist Fernando Riberio ...*
Expected annotation:	en palabras [del economista Fernando Ribeiro] ...
Rules annotation:	en palabras [del economista Fernando Ribeiro] ...
CRF annotation:	en palabras del economista Fernando Ribeiro ...
CRF+rules annotation:	en palabras [del economista Fernando Ribeiro] ...

5.4   Recovery of Omitted Sources and Co-reference Chains for Sources

As an additional improvement in the recognition of the opinion source, we count now with a module specialized in co-reference resolution [1], including the recovery of omitted sources, very frequent in Spanish due to the possibility of omitting the subject.

It is worth noticing that it is very common in news texts expressing opinions of politicians or governors, to write out the opinion spread in more than one sentence.

---

[5] In this case the predicate is *según / according to*.

[6] In this case the predicate is *palabras / words*.

For stylistic reasons, the source is not repeated in each subsequent sentence: it is rather omitted or spelled in a different form.

The algorithm deals with:

1- Recovery of omitted sources. This process is triggered by opinions with no recognized source, and is very similar to pronominal anaphora resolution.

2- Co-reference chains. For each opinion source, the system chooses between two possibilities: a. the source belongs to a previously started co-reference chain, b. the source initiates a new co-reference chain.

The method relies on the maximization of a function that ranks a source according to a scale of first mention features:

- Existence of proper nouns and appositions within the nominal group
- Indefinite determinant
- Definite determinant
- Demonstrative

If the function value is below the threshold for initiating a new chain, criteria for selecting an existing chain, based on morphological agreement and WordNet relations, are applied.

The co-reference module recovers 61% of omitted sources and achieves 84% of F-measure for the co-reference chain task. It is not easy to compare this number with similar work because of the difference in scenarios and languages, and even the proliferation of metrics for the co-reference task [4].

6   Conclusions

We report on a system for the automatic identification of source opinions in Spanish journalistic texts. To our knowledge, this is the first system for this task for the Spanish language. A set of linguistic resources has been generated and will be made publicly available: an opinion predicate lexicon, two annotated corpora and a software tool for the automatic recognition of the opinion elements. All these resources have been extensively tested. The combined system for source recognition achieves 83% of exact F-measure, this result being similar to those reported for other languages: 78.1% of partial F-measure for English [6], 78% of partial F-measure for Chinese [11] and 62.6% of exact F-measure for English [21]. A detailed comparison was not possible due to the difference in languages and scope of related work. Future directions of this work will focus on the identification of the theme within the message component, and in the inference of an affective orientation for opinions.

References

1. Acerenza, F., Rabosto, M., Zubizarreta, M., Rosá, A., Wonsever, D.: Resolución de correferencias entre fuentes de opiniones en español. In: XXXVIII Conferencia Latinoamericana en Informática (to appear, CLEI 2012)

2. Bethard, S., Yu, H., Thornton, A., Hatzivassiloglou, V., Jurafsky, D.: Automatic Extraction of Opinion Propositions and their Holders. In: AAAI Spring Symposium on Exploring Attitude and Affect in Text, pp. 20–27. The AAAI Press, Menlo Park (2004)

3. Bethard, S., Yu, H., Thornton, A., Hatzivassiloglou, V., Jurafsky, D.: Extracting Opinion Propositions and Opinion Holders Using Syntactic and Lexical Cues. In: Shanahan, J., Qu, Y., Wiebe, J. (eds.) Computing Attitude and Affect in Text – Theory and Applications. The Information Retrieval Series, vol. 20, pp. 125–141. Springer, Heidelberg (2006)

4. Cai, J., Strube, M.: Evaluation Metrics for End-to-End Coreference Resolution Systems. In: 11th Annual Meeting of the Special Interest Group on Discourse and Dialogue (SIGDIAL 2010), pp. 28–36. Association for Computational Linguistics, Stroudsburg (2010)

5. Choi, Y., Cardie, C., Riloff, E., Patwardhan, S.: Identifying Sources of Opinions with Conditional Random Fields and Extraction Patterns. In: Conference on Human Language Technology and Empirical Methods in Natural Language Processing (HLT-EMNLP 2005), pp. 355–362. Association for Computational Linguistics, Vancouver (2005)

6. Choi, Y., Breck, E., Cardie, C.: Joint Extraction of Entities and Relations for Opinion Recognition. In: 2006 Conference on Empirical Methods in Natural Language Processing (EMNLP 2006), pp. 431–439. Association for Computational Linguistics, Stroudsburg (2006)

7. Choi, Y., Cardie, C.: Learning with Compositional Semantics as Structural Inference for Subsentential Sentiment Analysis. In: 2006 Conference on Empirical Methods in Natural Language Processing (EMNLP 2008), pp. 793–801. Association for Computational Linguistics, Stroudsburg (2008)

8. Kim, S.-M., Hovy, E.: Extracting Opinions, Opinion Holders, and Topics Expressed in Online News Media Texts. In: 2006 Workshop on Sentiment and Subjectivity in Text (SST 2006), pp. 1–8. Association for Computational Linguistics, Stroudsburg (2006)

9. Krestel, R., Bergler, S., Witte, R.: Minding the Source – Automatic Tagging of Reported Speech in Newspaper Articles. In: 6th International Language Resources and Evaluation Conference (LREC 2008), pp. 2823–2828. ELRA (2008)

10. Lafferty, J., McCallum, A., Pereira, F.: Conditional Random Fields – Probabilistic Models for Segmenting and Labeling Sequence Data. In: 18th International Conference on Machine Learning (ICML 2001), pp. 282–289. ACM (2001)

11. Lu, B.: Identifying Opinion Holders and Targets with Dependency Parser in Chinese News Texts. In: Student Research Workshop at Human Language Technologies – 11th Annual Conference of the North American Chapter of the Association for Computational Linguistics (NAACL HLT-SRWS 2010), pp. 46–51. Association for Computational Linguistics, Stroudsburg (2010)

12. Nakagawa, T., Inui, K., Kurohashi, S.: Dependency Tree-based Sentiment Classification using CRFs with Hidden Variables. In: 11th Annual Conference of the North American Chapter of the Association for Computational Linguistics (NAACL HLT 2010), pp. 786–794. Association for Computational Linguistics, Stroudsburg (2010)

13. Pollard, C., Sag, I.A.: Information-Based Syntax and Semantics, Volume 1 – Fundamentals. CSLI Lecture Notes no. 13. Center for the Study of Language and Information (CSLI). University of Chicago Press, Stanford (1987)

14. Pouliquen, B., Steinberger, R., Best, C.: Automatic Detection of Quotations in Multilingual News. In: Recent Advances in Natural Language Processing (RANLP 2007), pp. 487–492 (2007)

15. Rosá, A., Wonsever, D., Minel, J.L.: Opinion Identification in Spanish Texts. In: Young Investigators Workshop on Computational Approaches to Languages of the Americas at Human Language Technologies – 11th Annual Conference of the North American Chapter of the Association for Computational Linguistics (NAACL HLT 2010), pp. 54–61. Association for Computational Linguistics, Stroudsburg (2010)
16. Rosá, A.: Identificación de opiniones de diferentes fuentes en textos en español. PhD Thesis. Universidad de la República (Uruguay) / Université Paris Ouest Nanterre La Défense (France) (2011)
17. Ruppenhofer, J., Somasundaran, S., Wiebe, J.: Finding the Sources and Targets of Subjective Expressions. In: 6th International Language Resources and Evaluation Conference (LREC 2008), pp. 2781–2788. ELRA (2008)
18. Saurí, R.: A Factuality Profiler for Eventualities in Text. PhD dissertation. Brandeis University (2008)
19. Sutton, C., McCallum, A.: An Introduction to Conditional Random Fields. arXiv, p. arXiv:1011.4088v1 (2010)
20. Wiebe, J., Wilson, T., Cardie, C.: Annotating Expressions of Opinions and Emotions in Language. Language Resources and Evaluation 39(2-3), 165–210 (2005)
21. Wiegand, M., Klakow, D.: Convolution Kernels for Opinion Holder Extraction. In: Human Language Technologies – 11th Annual Conference of the North American Chapter of the Association for Computational Linguistics (NAACL HLT 2010), pp. 795–803. Association for Computational Linguistics, Stroudsburg (2010)
22. Wonsever, D., Minel, J.-L.: Contextual Rules for Text Analysis. In: Gelbukh, A. (ed.) CICLing 2001. LNCS, vol. 2004, pp. 509–523. Springer, Heidelberg (2001)

Voice-QA: Evaluating the Impact
of Misrecognized Words on Passage Retrieval

Marcos Calvo[1], Davide Buscaldi[2], and Paolo Rosso[1]

[1] Grup d'Enginyeria del Llenguatge Natural i Reconeixement de Formes (ELiRF)
Departament de Sistemes Informàtics i Computació
Universitat Politècnica de València
Camí de Vera s/n, 46022, València, Spain
{mcalvo,prosso}@dsic.upv.es
[2] Institut de Recherche en Informatique de Toulouse
Université Paul Sabatier
118 Route de Narbonne, F-31062, Toulouse Cedex 9, France
davide.buscaldi@irit.fr

Abstract. Question Answering is an Information Retrieval task where
the query is posed using natural language and the expected result is a
concise answer. Voice-activated Question Answering systems represent
an interesting application, where the question is formulated by speech.
In these systems, an Automatic Speech Recognition module can be used
to transcribe the question. Thus, recognition errors may be introduced,
producing a significant effect on the answer retrieval process. In this work
we study the relationship between some features of misrecognized words
and the retrieval results. The features considered are the redundancy of
a word in the result set and its inverse document frequency calculated
over the collection. The results show that the redundancy of a word may
be an important clue on whether an error on it would deteriorate the
retrieval results, at least if a closed model is used for speech recognition.

Keywords: voice-activated question answering, passage retrieval, term
informativeness.

1   Introduction

Question Answering (QA) is an Information Retrieval (IR) task in which the
query is posed in natural language and the expected result is a concise answer.
Currently, most QA systems accept written sentences as their input, but in the
last years there has been a growing interest in systems where the queries are
formulated by voice; as can be seen in, for example, [2,5]. In fact, due to this
interest some Evaluation Conferences, such as the CLEF (Cross-Language Evaluation Forum) competition have included a voice-activated Question Answering
task in different languages [7].

In general, as it is shown in Fig. 1, a QA system is composed by an analysis
module, which determines the type of the question; a Passage Retrieval (PR)
module, which uses IR techniques to retrieve passages where the answer might

J. Pavón et al. (Eds.): IBERAMIA 2012, LNAI 7637, pp. 462–471, 2012.
© Springer-Verlag Berlin Heidelberg 2012

be contained; and an answer extraction module, which uses NLP techniques or patterns to extract the answer from the passages. In addition, if the input to the system are utterances, an Automatic Speech Recognition (ASR) module can be used to transcribe the vocal input. One option is to "plug" the ASR before the QA modules, in such a way that the input to the QA system is the sentence (or the n-best sentences) given by the ASR. Figure 1 shows the architecture of such a system, where the output is given back to the user by means of a Text-To-Speech synthesizer (TTS).

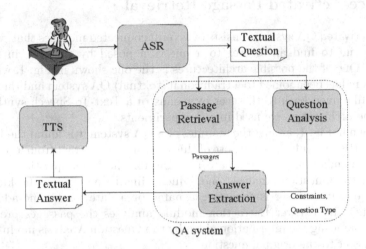

Fig. 1. Modules of a voice-activated Question Answering system

In these systems, recognition errors can strongly modify the meaning of the query. In fact, these errors are crucial in the case of Named Entities (NEs), since they are usually very meaningful words. Unfortunately, NEs are often very difficult to be recognized properly, sometimes because they are in a language different to the user's one, which makes this fact one of the biggest open challenges in voice-activated QA. From an IR perspective, NEs can be characterized by their high IDF (Inverse Document Frequency) and redundancy in the retrieved passages. Thus, our hypothesis is that recognition errors on words with a high IDF and that are redundant in the retrieved passages are key, since the object of the question is lost.

Our aim is to study the correlation between the recognition errors on question words with the above characteristics and the resulting errors in the PR module. We limited our study to this phase and did not take the full QA system because the errors in the other modules are so important that can mask the retrieval errors [4]. We computed the IDF of the words of the original sentence that were misrecognized by the ASR both over the document collection and the passages retrieved by the PR engine using the correct sentence. This experiment was performed for several language models with a different number of NEs.

The rest of the paper is structured as follows. In Sect. 2 we explain how a voice-activated Passage Retrieval system works. Then, in Sect. 3, we describe the Passage Retrieval system that we have used in the experimentation we report in this paper. In Sect. 4 a discussion about some interpretations of the IDF is provided and in Sect. 5 we present how we have measured the performance of the PR module. Next, we detail the experimentation performed and discuss the obtained results. Finally, we draw some conclusions.

2   Voice-Activated Passage Retrieval

A voice-activated QA system consists of several connected modules that, working together, aim to find an answer to a question posed by the user in natural language. One of the possible architectures is the one shown in Fig. 1, where an ASR system has been joined to a traditional (textual) QA system and the output is optionally given back to the user by means of a Text-To-Speech synthesizer. This is the architecture we used in our experiments.

As shown in Fig. 1, among the modules of a QA system it is found the Passage Retrieval (PR) module. The purpose of this module is to extract from a collection of texts a number of them that are relevant for the input question. Another module is the Question Analysis one, which aims to determine the kind of a question (e.g. if the user is expecting a name or a date) and some additional constraints. The Answer Extraction module analyses the passages previously retrieved and using the information given by the Question Analysis module looks up the answer to the original question.

The most critical part in a QA system is the Question Analysis module. In fact, in [4] it is shown that 41.6% of the errors in a Question Answering system derive from an error in the Question Analysis phase, with more than 33% due to the identification of the question type. Answer extraction is also an important source of errors, with 18.7% of the total number of errors in QA. However, Passage Retrieval is shown to be a limited source of errors, as mistakes derived from this module account only for 1.6% on the performance in QA.

For this reason, we have focused our work on the study of the effects of the ASR errors on Passage Retrieval, where the effects of a badly recognized question are directly reflected on the ranking of passages and can be detected. These effects can not be discovered using the complete QA system, since the errors in Question Analysis and Answer Extraction would mask most of the effects of the question recognition over the retrieval phase.

3   The JIRS Passage Retrieval System

In our study, we have used the JIRS Passage Retrieval system. This PR system uses a weighting scheme based on n-grams density. It was proved in [1] that this approach is more effective in the PR and QA tasks than other commonly used IR systems based on keywords and the well-known TF.IDF weighting scheme. So,

JIRS works under the premise that, in a sufficiently large document collection, question n-grams should appear near the answer at least once. The architecture of JIRS is shown in Fig. 2.

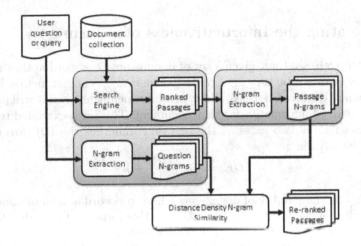

Fig. 2. Structure of the JIRS Passage Retrieval engine

The first step consists in extracting passages which contain question terms from the document collection, which is done using the standard TF.IDF scheme. Subsequently, the system extracts all question k-grams (with $1 \leq k \leq n$, where n is the number of terms of the question) from both the question and each of the retrieved passages. The output of the system is a list of at most M passages (in our experiments we set $M = 30$) re-ranked according to a similarity value calculated between the passages and the question. The similarity between the question q and a passage p is defined in Equation 1.

$$Sim(p, q) = \frac{\sum_{\forall x \in (P \cap Q)} \frac{h(x)}{1 + \alpha \cdot ln(1 + d(x, x_{max}))}}{\sum_{i=1}^{n} w(t_{q_i})} \tag{1}$$

In this equation P is the set of k-grams ($1 \leq k \leq n$) contained in passage p and Q is the set of k-grams in question $q = (t_{q_1}, \ldots, t_{q_n})$; n is the total number of terms in the question. $w(t)$ is the term-weight, determined by:

$$w(t) = 1 - \frac{log(n_t)}{1 + log(N)} \tag{2}$$

Here n_t represents the number of sentences in which the term t occurs and N is the number of sentences in the collection.

The weight of each k-gram $x = (t_{x_1}, \ldots, t_{x_k})$ is calculated by means of the function $h(x) = \sum_{j=1}^{k} w(t_{x_j})$.

Finally, the distance $d(x, x_{max})$ is calculated as the number of words between any k-gram x and the one having the maximum weight (x_{max}). α is a factor, empirically set to 0.1, that determines the importance of the distance in the similarity calculation.

4   Estimating the Informativeness of a Term

We can intuitively see that, given a set of documents D, a word w that appears in all of them will not be very informative, since it makes no distinction between the documents. However, if w is found in just one document, then it will probably be one of the most informative for that document. This idea, extended to all the range between these two cases, is the one that underlies the IDF formula [3], which can be written as

$$IDF = -log(\frac{|D(w)|}{|D|}) \tag{3}$$

where $|D(w)|$ is the number of documents where the word w is found and $|D|$ is the cardinality of the collection. According to this formula, the higher the IDF for a word w, the more relevant it is in the collection.

From a PR point of view, two interpretations can be given to the IDF depending on the set of documents considered. On one hand, if we calculate the IDF of a word over the whole document collection, this value represents how important is the word in it, which is called *term informativeness*. On the other, if the set is constituted by the passages retrieved by the PR engine given a query in which the word appears, the IDF can be used to calculate the *redundancy* of that word on this result set. In this case, a low IDF indicates a high redundancy. Due to the filter constituted by the PR phase, a redundant word in this set may not be a stop-word, but a term highly related to the query submitted to the system.

It might happen that, given a query containing a word w, it does not appear in any of the documents returned by the PR engine using this query. Thus, in order to avoid zeroes as a result of the division, in the case of the redundancy we have slightly modified the IDF formula by adding one to both elements of the fraction. This is shown in Equation 4.

$$redundancy = -log(\frac{|D(w)| + 1}{|D| + 1}) \tag{4}$$

5   Measuring the Performance of the Passage Retrieval Module

The output of the PR module is a ranked list of passages. So, it is interesting to know if this ranking would match what a user would expect from the PR system. Among the IR measures that are commonly used to take into account the position of the passages, we chose the Normalized Discounted Cumulative Gain (nDCG), since it is the one that best models the user's preferences, according to [6].

In order to calculate IR measures such as the nDCG, it is necessary to have a set of *relevance judgments*, which is a set of documents considered to be relevant for the query. In our case, this set was built using hand-made answer patterns and regular expressions to test if a passage contains the answer.

Normalized DCG at position π is defined as:

$$nDCG_\pi = \frac{DCG_\pi}{IDCG_\pi} \tag{5}$$

where $IDCG_\pi$ is the "ideal" DCG obtained by ranking all the relevant documents at the top of the ranking list, in order of relevance, and $DCG_\pi = rel_1 + \sum_{i=2}^{\pi} \frac{rel_i}{\log_2 i}$, where rel_i is the degree of relevance of the result at position i.

6   Experiments and Results

For our experiments we have used the questions in Spanish from the CLEF[1] QA 2003-2006 contests. The target collection (the set of documents where the answer should be found) is composed by documents of the EFE (Spanish news agency) of the years 1994 and 1995. The 1800 questions available were split into a set of 1600 for training and the remaining 200 for test. The latter were uttered by a specific user (because this corpus does not include utterances of the written questions) and constitute the input to the ASR.

We have trained a generic Language Model (LM) for the ASR with just the training questions, separating the NEs in a category. Then, we have added more elements to this set according to its frequency in the document collection. So, we can distinguish two types of LMs: the Open Named Entity models, which include only the N most frequent NEs taken from the target collection, and the Closed NE models, which include all the test NEs plus a number of the most frequent NEs taken from the same collection, in order to amount up to N Named Entities. In both cases the minimum number of NEs considered in the category was $4,000$ and the maximum $48,000$. As the original corpus does not have the NEs tagged in any way, previously to this process we automatically tagged the corpus using a POS-tagger.

For this experimentation we used both Open and Closed Named Entity models because they simulate different kinds of real applications of QA systems. On one hand, an Open NE model simulates a situation where the number of NE that the system has in its vocabulary is limited but the users are allowed to ask about whatever they want. On the other, the Closed NE model simulates a more restricted domain where the NEs the user can ask about are limited and known when building the system.

Once all the test questions were recognized using each one of these models, we considered two outputs from the ASR: the recognized sentences themselves and the Word Error Rate (WER). Then, we performed the Passage Retrieval process, taking the recognized sentences as its input.

---

[1] http://www.clef-campaign.org

As explained before, the ASR that works before the PR may modify the original sentence by introducing recognition errors. Thus, it would be interesting to relate the nDCG values obtained for each of the LMs to the ones achieved if the input to the PR process was composed by the correct test questions. For this reason, we have used as the measure of the Passage Retrieval performance for each LM the value *nDCG_diff* defined as in Equation 6, where nDCG(test_sents) stands for the nDCG obtained using the correct original sentence as the input for the Passage Retrieval module, while nDCG(recognized_sents) means the same but taking the output of the ASR module. The average nDCG obtained for the original test set is 0.584.

$$nDCG\_diff = nDCG(test\_sents) - nDCG(recognized\_sents) \qquad (6)$$

Finally, we have calculated the term informativeness and the redundancy of the words of the test queries that were misrecognized by the ASR. These calculations were done over the complete target collection and the passages retrieved by the PR engine using the full correct sentence. In the case of the redundancy, we have calculated a composition within each sentence, both using the mean and max operators. The use of these operators is motivated because in the recognized sentences there may be more than one error, so it is reasonable to consider both the word that would give the largest redundancy (max), and the average redundancy considering all the misrecognized words. Also, for both the redundancy and the term informativeness, and for each LM, we have averaged the results obtained for each sentence. The obtained figures are presented in Table 1.

Table 1. Results for the Closed and Open Named Entities Models

| # NE | | Closed NE Models | | | | | Open NE Models | | | |
| | | avg redund. | | | | | avg redund. | | | |
# NE	WER	mean	max	Term inf	nDCG_diff	WER	mean	max	Term inf	nDCG_diff
4000	0.265	**0.348**	**0.529**	2.329	**0.151**	0.333	0.522	0.755	2.379	0.265
8000	0.298	**0.419**	**0.606**	2.020	**0.183**	0.347	0.530	0.762	2.526	0.262
12000	0.305	**0.432**	**0.614**	2.011	**0.197**	0.351	0.531	0.750	2.455	0.273
16000	0.310	**0.448**	**0.636**	2.102	**0.192**	0.350	0.533	0.759	2.364	0.252
20000	0.310	**0.454**	**0.644**	2.143	**0.192**	0.348	0.534	0.760	2.389	0.248
24000	0.306	**0.456**	**0.648**	2.091	**0.195**	0.342	0.531	0.760	2.292	0.246
28000	0.312	**0.461**	**0.660**	2.159	**0.201**	0.344	0.526	0.755	2.297	0.242
32000	0.319	**0.487**	**0.689**	2.241	**0.208**	0.342	0.533	0.764	2.336	0.232
36000	0.319	**0.489**	**0.691**	2.293	**0.205**	0.344	0.534	0.766	2.388	0.229
40000	0.319	**0.496**	**0.698**	2.330	**0.199**	0.342	0.539	0.768	2.409	0.222
44000	0.321	**0.493**	**0.698**	2.298	**0.203**	0.345	0.536	0.768	2.390	0.226
48000	0.321	**0.493**	**0.698**	2.298	**0.204**	0.345	0.535	0.768	2.375	0.226

The different behaviour with respect to the number of NEs is due to the own nature of the models: in the closed NE models, the smaller the NE set, the lesser the probability of error is. This is opposed to what happens in the open models, where introducing new NEs increases the chances of finding the right NE among the elements of the set and so recognizing it properly.

With regard to the relationship between redundancy and nDCG in the retrieved passages, Table 1 shows that in the closed NE models the lower the redundancy of the misrecognized words, the lower the nDCG difference is (see also Fig. 3). Indeed, their Pearson correlation coefficient amounts to 0.9408. In the open NE models (see Fig. 4) this correlation is not observed. None of the models show a correlation between the nDCG and the term informativeness

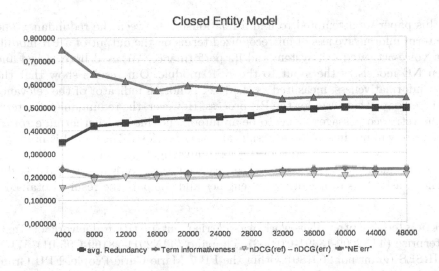

Fig. 3. Closed Entity Model Results. Term informativeness values have been divided by 10. "NE err": error on NEs.

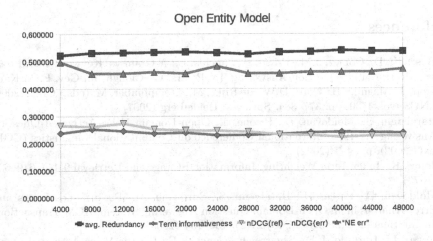

Fig. 4. Open Entity Model results. Term informativeness values have been divided by 10. "NE err": error on NEs.

of the misrecognized words, somehow surprising as we expected that errors on words with high IDF should be more important.

Our interpretation of these results is that in the closed NE models the errors on non-NE words, which may have a high redundancy in the result set, are very important. As shown on Table 1, the error on NEs is inversely proportional to redundancy, indicating that NEs are less redundant than some other words.

7 Conclusions and Future Work

In this paper we attempted to find a relationship between the redundancy and the term informativeness of misrecognized terms on the output of a PR module of a voice-activated QA system and its performance. We used both closed and open NE models as the input to the ASR module. Our results show that the term informativeness, measured as the IDF, is not an indicator of the relevance of the error on that term for the PR process. However, the redundancy of a term in the retrieved passages seems to be an important clue on whether an error on that term will produce a worse result, at least if a closed NE model is used.

As future work, it would be interesting to investigate the relationship between other informativeness measures on the misrecognized words and the nDCG differences, as well as to use other PR engines and compare the results obtained.

Acknowledgments. This work was carried out in the framework of Text-Enterprise (TIN2009-13391-C04-03), Timpano (TIN2011-28169-C05-01), WIQ-EI IRSES (grant no. 269180) within the FP 7 Marie Curie People, FPU Grant AP2010-4193 from the Spanish Ministerio de Educación (first author), and the Microcluster VLC/Campus on Multimodal Intelligent Systems (third author).

References

1. Buscaldi, D., Gómez, J.M., Rosso, P., Sanchis, E.: N-Gram vs. Keyword-Based Passage Retrieval for Question Answering. In: Peters, C., Clough, P., Gey, F.C., Karlgren, J., Magnini, B., Oard, D.W., de Rijke, M., Stempfhuber, M. (eds.) CLEF 2006. LNCS, vol. 4730, pp. 377–384. Springer, Heidelberg (2007)
2. Harabagiu, S., Moldovan, D., Picone, J.: Open-Domain Voice-Activated Question Answering. In: 19th International Conference on Computational Linguistics (COLING 2002), pp. 1–7 (2002)
3. Jones, K.: Index Term Weighting. Information Storage and Retrieval 9(11), 619–633 (1973)
4. Moldovan, D., Paşca, M., Harabagiu, S., Surdeanu, M.: Performance Issues and Error Analysis in an Open-Domain Question Answering System. ACM Transactions on Information Systems (TOIS) 21(2), 133–154 (2003)
5. Rosso, P., Hurtado, L.F., Segarra, E., Sanchis, E.: On the Voice-Activated Question Answering. IEEE Transactions on Systems, Man, and Cybernetics, Part C: Applications and Reviews 42(1), 75–85 (2012)

6. Sanderson, M., Paramita, M.L., Clough, P., Kanoulas, E.: Do User Preferences and Evaluation Measures Line Up? In: 33rd International ACM SIGIR Conference on Research and Development in Information Retrieval (SIGIR 2010), pp. 555–562. ACM, New York (2010)

7. Turmo, J., Comas, P., Rosset, S., Galibert, O., Moreau, N., Mostefa, D., Rosso, P., Buscaldi, D.: Overview of QAST 2009. In: Peters, C., Di Nunzio, G.M., Kurimo, M., Mandl, T., Mostefa, D., Peñas, A., Roda, G. (eds.) CLEF 2009. LNCS, vol. 6241, pp. 197–211. Springer, Heidelberg (2010)

A Classification Model with Corpus Enrichment for Toponym Disambiguation

Belém Priego Sánchez[1], María J. Somodevilla[1], Rafael Guzmán Cabrera[2], Ivo H. Pineda[1], and Maya Carrillo[1]

[1] FCC, Benemérita Universidad Autónoma de Puebla,
Av. San Claudio y 14 Sur, Col. San Manuel, Puebla, México
{belemps,mariajsomodevilla,ivopinedatorres,mcarrillr}@gmail.com
[2] DICIS, Universidad de Guanajuato,
Carretera Salamanca-Valle de Santiago Km 3.5+1.8 Km, Salamanca, México
guzmanc@ugto.mx

Abstract. This paper presents a method based on information retrieval to enrich corpus using bootstrapping techniques. A supervised corpus manually validated is provided, and then snippets are obtained from Web in order to increase the size of the initial corpus. Although this technique has already been reported in the literature, the main objective of this work is to apply it under the specific task of GEO/NO-GEO toponym disambiguation.The disambiguation procedure is evaluated by a classification model observing favorable results.

Keywords: toponym disambiguation, geographic information retrieval, corpus, classification model.

1 Introduction

In recent years, there has been a resurgence of an empiricist model of language processing. The raw material for this model is large volumes of unrestricted textual information better known as corpus. With this resurgence it appears also the need to develop techniques to facilitate treatment of these large data volumes.

The toponyms disambiguation is one of the Information Retrieval (IR) tasks, more specifically of Geographic Information Retrieval (GIR) and Question Answering (QA), including the generation of maps. It aims to relate place names with their geographic representation.

The Geo-information is abundant on the Web and digital libraries, for instance, collections of geo-referenced pictures (Flickr), news, databases of demographic information, among others. It is reported that approximately 80% of Web pages contain references to places [20]. Much of the information required is related to a given geographical context, i.e., finding the nearest restaurant, finding news about a certain country, as well as finding photographs taken in any specific community, among the most frequent. It has also documented that approximately 20% of queries on the Web have a geographic component, which

J. Pavón et al. (Eds.): IBERAMIA 2012, LNAI 7637, pp. 472–480, 2012.
© Springer-Verlag Berlin Heidelberg 2012

shows the importance of working with techniques for the treatment of certain terminology as in the case of toponyms. GIR belongs to a branch of information retrieval, and includes all research tasks that traditionally form the core of the IR, but also with an emphasis on Geographic and Spatial information.

In the task of GIR, the majority of users' requests are of type X in P, where P is a place name and X, the subject matter of the query. GIR addresses IR difficulties [5], such as geographic ambiguity (place names), for example: "there is a cathedral in St. Paul in London and one in Sao Paulo"; illdefined geographic regions, "near of the east"; complex geographic regions "near Russian cities" or "along the Mediterranean coast"; multilingual aspects: "Greater Lisbon" in English is the same as "Grande Lisboa" in Portuguese or "GroBraum Lissabon" in German and granularity in references to the countries "north of Italy".

The toponyms (place names) may be ambiguous and can have one of the two types of ambiguity GEO/GEO or GEO/NO-GEO. For GEO/GEO ambiguity a place name represents several places, for example: "Tripoli" is the name of 16 places. The GEO/NO-GEO case has the peculiarity that a place name refers to geographic entities (places) and non geographical entities (people, organizations, etc.), for example: "Benito Juarez" represents to a person and also places; "Java" is an island in Indonesia and a programming language. In both cases, the application domains are the extraction and information retrieval.

In this paper, the disambiguation of toponyms is addressed, specifically by GEO/GEO-NO type because it considers special characteristics closely associated with the spatial nature of the information. For this purpose, a corpus based method arises for the task of toponyms disambiguation since there is evidence indicating that these methods tend to be more accurate than those based on knowledge [8,11].

The remainder of this paper is structured as follows: Section 2 explains in detail the disambiguation of toponyms task, as well as the related work reported in the literature. The proposal presented is discussed in Sect. 3. Section 4 shows and discusses the experimental results. Finally, in Sect. 5 the conclusions and possible future work are reported.

2   Toponym Disambiguation

The disambiguation of toponyms is an important task within the geographic information retrieval. Recently, there has been great interest in this problem from different perspectives such as resource development for the evaluation of the toponyms disambiguation methods [12] and the use of these methods to improve resolution of the geographic scope in electronic documents [1], just to name a few. It would not be possible to study ambiguity of toponyms without studying also used resources such as databases, dictionaries and other supplies in the process to find the different meanings of a word. Throughout the investigation of methods for toponyms disambiguation, the choice of appropriate algorithm for this task has been extremely important. The chosen lexical resource greatly influences the discrimination of references to places.

Although the methods for the disambiguation of toponyms are very different, these have phases in common, such as those listed below:

1. **Remove the candidate's referents**. All possible regarding the location of a resource are extracted from a geographic knowledge resource (repositories of meaning: gazzetteer, ontology, etc.).
2. **Choosing the correct referent**. Apply a set of heuristics to determine all potential candidates who most probably has the correct meaning according to context (textual corpora) and the resources as a source of evidence.

Based on the above mentioned phases, this section includes a brief description of the most relevant works that have been developed in an interdisciplinary way for geographic information retrieval. The work of Smith and Crane [19] describes a system for toponyms disambiguation based on the digital library Perseo[1]. This disambiguation method calculates the geographical centroid of candidates and then removes all candidates located at a distance greater than twice the standard deviation from the centroid. Jones [9] reported some methods to extract geographic information from Web pages as part of SPIRIT[2] project, which includes the task of retrieval of spatial information through geographic ontologies, such as WordNet, where even (based on meanings of words in English) have been widely exploited to join to this project. Sang Ok [10] suggested the construction of a simple method that is capable of building a semi-automatic domain ontology through the analysis of many texts in a collection of unstructured documents, using word groupings (hub words). Varelas [21] proposes and implements a model to retrieve information of images and documents on the Web, using semantic similarity between concepts that are not geographically lexicon-like. Clough [6] proposes a heuristic based on the calculation of the punctuation of overlap between the context and the path to the hierarchical relation, i.e., the number of toponyms in common. Andrade and Silva [2] present a geographical similarity operator that calculates the ratio between two geographic locations and describes how to combine text classification, besides, different strategies are considered for the formulation of queries and to combine textual and geographic classification. Ledo and Sidorov [15] proposed a method of disambiguation of meanings of words using large lexical resources (explanatory dictionaries, dictionaries of synonyms, WordNet), this work is focused on the resolution of lexical ambiguity, which appears when the words. Leidner [12] concentrates on geographical names of popular sites, which defines the task of Toponym Resolution as the calculation of mapping occurrences of place names found in a text to its extensional semantic representation of the location to be referred. Leite y Ricarte [13], explore a framework to encode a geographic knowledge base composed of multiple related ontologies whose relationships are expressed as fuzzy. Buscaldi [4], on the other hand, aims to study the ambiguity of toponyms and the effects of resolution on GIR and QA applications as information retrieval using the Web. Dwivedi y Rastogi [7] investigated the critical aspects of the various approaches

---

[1] Disponible en: http://www.perseus.tufts.edu/hopper/

[2] Disponible en: http://www.geo-spirit.org/

to WSD [17], provide a breakdown of the rate of success of different approaches to WSD, as well its use in various application areas. Seco [16] formalized ontology of geographic space which provides a vocabulary of classes and relations to describe a given geographic area. Bensalem y Kholladi [3] present a heuristic for the disambiguation of toponyms in text based on the quantification of proximity in a tree hierarchical between toponyms. Lopez [14] suggest the development of techniques for toponyms disambiguation based on ontologies to deal with ambiguity in GIR queries. The method proposed is based on geographical proximity between toponyms in the same context using hierarchical relationships provided by the ontology, and the ontological hierarchical weighting, supplemented with the Haversine distance. This method resolves GEO/GEO ambiguity very well but does not completely resolve the ambiguity GEO/NO-GEO.

Considering the current state of the art presented above, it is possible to see the importance of the toponyms disambiguation task. The studies show different approaches and in some cases for very specific domains. However, no studies were found related to the Spanish language, and that was precisely what motivated the development of this work. The following section describes the proposed model for the treatment of ambiguous toponyms.

3   Proposal of the Classification Model

Since the ultimate goal of the research work is the toponyms disambiguation by supervised categorization techniques (probabilistic classifiers or support vector machines) requires essentially a supervised corpus to obtain an adequate classification model. To our knowledge, this corpus is not available for the task of toponyms disambiguation type GEO/NO-GEO. Therefore, we will use the technique proposed in [8] to create a training corpus using enrichment techniques for text collections. This supervised training corpus may then be used by any of the classifiers.

The steps for creation of the supervised corpus are shown in Fig. 1. Basically this is a bootstrapping technique, where a set of manually classified texts (initial corpus) is created, that is, it is enriched by a process of searching for sentences on the Web (snippets) followed by an evaluation in order to ensure the quality of the snippet to be added into the training corpus.

In our case, that is, the disambiguation of toponyms, creating an initial corpus manually tagged texts, means that (i.e., news) have a reference GEO (positive samples) or have a reference NO-GEO (negative samples). Since the toponyms GEO/NO-GEO are manually labeled in the initial corpus, then, it can trust the quality of this collection, however, it is important to ensure that samples (both positive and negative) are sufficiently representative, as to generalize the initial corpus, enriching it with samples extracted from the Web.

The initial corpus was extracted of written texts in Spanish from a collection of multilingual QA task news of CLEF[3] initiative. The procedure considered to sample the Web using any information retrieval system. In our case, we use the

---

[3] Revisar: http://www.clef-initiative.eu//

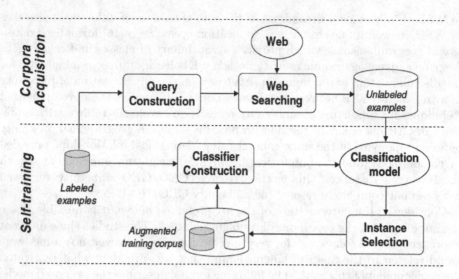

Fig. 1. Process for the enrichment of corpus from the Web [8]

Google API and queries were created from n-grams (bigrams and trigrams) of words extracted from the labeled news. Those n-grams that include the place name were only considered. For example, for the following piece of text (from a positive sample):

`En la ciudad de Guadalajara hubo un enfrentamiento ...`

The next five n-grams were obtained: {de Guadalajara}, {Guadalajara hubo}, {ciudad de Guadalajara}, {de Guadalajara hubo} and {Guadalajara hubo un}. These n-grams are used as query in Google and these search requests are launched to the Web in order to download information that contains some of the n-grams used as reference. The goal is to find more examples that potentially have a bearing on the toponyms in question. In our case, we asked 500 Google snippets for each query, resulting in a total of 2,500 snippets associated with a place name. Clearly, not all of them have the quality to be included in the training corpus (enrichment), and therefore its quality is evaluated using a classification model built on the positive and negative samples of the initial corpus. That is, if the snippet is classified as a positive sample with a threshold greater than 85%, then it is included in the initial corpus. The classification model is reconstructed, now considering the new sample and the process is repeated for a new snippet extracted from the Web. The process is performed for both positive samples and negative samples. The final training corpus is made up of 3.222 positive samples (type GEO) and 3.682 negative samples (type NO-GEO). After building the training corpus, then the process of disambiguation of toponyms is carried out.

Figure 2 shows the classification model proposed for disambiguation. Given a corpus of unstructured documents without identifying of toponyms andidates,

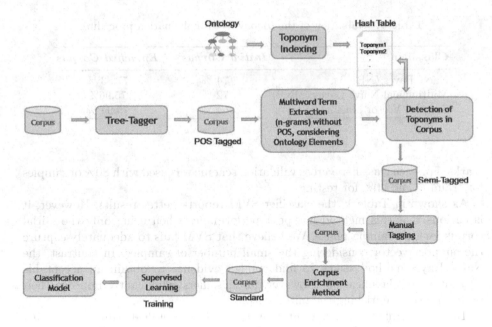

Fig. 2. Classification model for toponym disambiguation

each new is morphologically labeled in order to include the morphological categories as characteristics within a supervised classifier. Undoubtedly the most important feature is the class whose values are the labels NON-GEO and GEO, since they allow to determine whether an untagged notice containing or not a geographical reference (GEO/NO-GEO). In order to determine candidates toponyms in news, a spatial ontology is used, which describes the geographical area considering the natural and artificial geographic objects [18], and identify those terms in the news that are classified as toponyms in the ontology. This process simplifies the task of manually labeling the initial corpus.

The proposed disambiguation presented in this paper, considered three different classifiers: Naïve Bayes, Naïve Bayes Multinomial and Support Vector Machines. Since there is no standard corpus for evaluating the task of disambiguation of toponyms in Spanish, so a *baseline* classification results were used regardless of the enrichment process of the initial corpus. In the next section the results of applying the proposed methodology are presented.

4   Experimental Results

Table 1 shows the results of reference for the different types of classifiers used. These values correspond to the percentage of correctly classified instances for the initial corpus and also for the corpus enriched with information downloaded from the Web. In all cases, the context was determined based on a words bag, which contains the frequency of occurrence of words regardless of punctuation

Table 1. Evaluation of the toponyms disambiguation procedure

Classifier	*Initial Corpus*	*Enriched Corpus*
Naïve Bayes (NB)	74 %	77.83 %
Multinomial Naïve Bayes (MNB)	72 %	75.96%
Support Vector Machine (SVM)	64 %	79.94 %

marks. For each classifier a cross validation scheme was used with 80% of samples for training and 20% for testing.

As shown in Table 1, the classifier SVM reports better results. However, it is curious that this method has poor performance when using only the initial corpus for the training phase. We believe that SVM fails to adequately capture the support vector considering the small number of samples. In contrast, the Naïve Bayes method seems to find enough evidence to obtain an acceptable percentage of classification. However, all classifiers significantly improve their performance by enriching the initial corpus.

Table 2 shows the results of evaluation measures obtained when performing the disambiguation of toponyms, the lowest value of recall obtained indicates must be incorporated negative instances at training and testing sets.

Table 2. Evaluation measures of the toponyms disambiguation procedure

Classifier	Initial Corpus			Enriched Corpus		
	Precision	Recall	F-Measure	Precision	Recall	F-Measure
NB	0.778	0.221	0.344	0.842	0.424	0.563
MNB	0.839	0.161	0.270	0.893	0.447	0.595
SVM	0.786	0.213	0.335	0.833	0.425	0.562

The results show that when the corpus is enriched with information downloaded from the Web an increase the accuracy is achieved. This result allows us to appreciate the incorporation of information from the Web to the training set is useful in order to improve accuracy, which potentially it can be used even with not enough labeled training instances for a particular domain are available. However, it can be seen that there is a need to increase the size of the training and testing set by the incorporation of new unlabeled examples.

5   Conclusions and Future Work

The disambiguation of toponyms is an important task within the geographic information retrieval, noting that there is little research in this subject for Spanish language in comparison with other languages, specifically with the English language. Therefore, in this work a supervised corpus was created in order to generate an appropriate classification model for the toponyms disambiguation task type GEO/GEO NO for Spanish language.

In addition to creating a supervised corpus, a methodology for toponyms disambiguation has been evaluated and it was observed that the results were favorable. This performance is mainly due to the high quality of training instances and the incorporation of information downloaded from the Web, which guarantees a semantic relationship with the toponyms to disambiguate, considering the search patterns constructed on the basis of n-grams.

The approach presented in this paper focuses on the use of the method proposed for toponyms disambiguation; however, in the future it could use the same method for the disambiguation of the meaning of words in general.

References

1. Andogah, G.: Geographically Constrained Information Retrieval. Ph.D. thesis, University of Groningen, Groningen, Netherlands (May 2010)
2. Andrade, L., Silva, M.J.: Relevance Ranking for Geographic IR. In: Workshop on Geographic Information Retrieval (GIR 2006) at SIGIR 2006, pp. 1–4. ACM, New York (2006)
3. Bensalem, I., Kholladi, M.K.: Toponym Disambiguation by Arborescent Relationships. Journal of Computer Science 6(6), 653–659 (2010)
4. Buscaldi, D.: Toponym Ambiguity in Geographical Information Retrieval. In: 32nd international ACM SIGIR conference on Research and Development in Information Retrieval (SIGIR 2009), pp. 847–847. ACM, New York (2009)
5. Buscaldi, D.: Toponym Disambiguation in Information Retrieval. Ph.D. thesis, Universidad Politécnica de Valencia, Valencia, España (2010)
6. Clough, P.: Extracting Metadata for Spatially-Aware Information Retrieval on the Internet. In: 2005 Workshop on Geographic Information Retrieval (GIR 2005), pp. 25–30. ACM, New York (2005)
7. Dwivedi, S.K., Rastogi, P.: Critical Analysis of WSD Algorithms. In: 2009 International Conference on Advances in Computing, Communication and Control (ICAC3 2009), pp. 62–67. ACM, New York (2009)
8. Guzmán-Cabrera, R., Rosso, P., Montes-Y-Gómez, M., Villaseñor Pineda, L., Pinto-Avendaño, D.: Semi-supervised Word Sense Disambiguation Using the Web as Corpus. In: Gelbukh, A. (ed.) CICLing 2009. LNCS, vol. 5449, pp. 256–265. Springer, Heidelberg (2009)
9. Jones, C.B., Purves, R., Ruas, A., Sanderson, M., Sester, M., van Kreveld, M., Weibel, R.: Spatial Information Retrieval and Geographical Ontologies an Overview of the SPIRIT Project. In: 25th Annual International ACM SIGIR Conference on Research and Development in Information Retrieval (SIGIR 2002), pp. 387–388. ACM, New York (2002)
10. Koo, S.O., Lim, S.Y., Lee, S.J.: Building an Ontology Based on Hub Words for Information Retrieval. In: 2003 IEEE / WIC / ACM International Conference on Web Intelligence (WI 2003), pp. 466–469. IEEE, Los Alamitos (2003)
11. Lee, Y.K., Ng, H.T.: An Empirical Evaluation of Knowledge Sources and Learning Algorithms for Word Sense Disambiguation. In: ACL Conference on Empirical Methods in Natural Language Processing (EMNLP 2002), vol. 10, pp. 41–48. Association for Computational Linguistics, Stroudsburg (2002)

12. Leidner, J.L.: Toponym Resolution in Text – Annotation, Evaluation and Applications of Spatial Grounding of Place Names. Universal Press, Boca Raton (2008)
13. Leite, M.A.A., Ricarte, I.L.: Document Retrieval Using Fuzzy Related Geographic Ontologies. In: 2nd International Workshop on Geographic Information Retrieval (GIR 2008), pp. 47–54. ACM, New York (2008)
14. Lopez, A., Somodevilla, M.J., Vilarino, D., Pineda, I.H., De Celis, C.: Toponym Disambiguation by Ontology in Spanish – Geographical Proximity Between Place Names in the Same Context. In: AISS: Advances in Information Sciences and Service Sciences, pp. 282–289 (in press, 2012)
15. Ledo Mezquita, Y., Sidorov, G., Gelbukh, A.: Information Retrieval with Word Sense Disambiguation for Spanish. Computación y Sistemas 11, 288–300 (2008)
16. Naveiras, D.S.: Técnicas de indexación y recuperación de documentos utilizando referencias geográficas y textuales. Ph.D. thesis, Universidad de Coruña, Coruña, España (2009)
17. Navigli, R.: Word Sense Disambiguation – A Survey. ACM Computing Surveys 41(2), 10:1–10:69 (2009)
18. Priego-Sánchez, B., Somodevilla, M.J., Pineda, I.H., Hernandez, J.: Geontomex – una ontología espacial de méxico para la desambiguación de topónimos. In: Congreso Mexicano de Inteligencia Artificial, COMIA 2012 (2012)
19. Smith, D.A., Crane, G.: Disambiguating Geographic Names in a Historical Digital Library. In: Constantopoulos, P., Sølvberg, I.T. (eds.) ECDL 2001. LNCS, vol. 2163, pp. 127–136. Springer, Heidelberg (2001)
20. Spink, A., Wolfram, D., Jansen, M.B.J., Saracevic, T.: Searching the Web – The Public and Their Queries. Journal of the American Society for Information Science and Technology 52(3), 226–234 (2001)
21. Varelas, G., Voutsakis, E., Raftopoulou, P., Petrakis, E.G., Milios, E.E.: Semantic Similarity Methods in wordNet and Their Application to Information Retrieval on the Web. In: 7th Annual ACM International Workshop on Web Information and Data Management (WIDM 2005), pp. 10–16. ACM, New York (2005)

Semantic Role Labeling for Brazilian Portuguese: A Benchmark

Fernando Emilio Alva-Manchego and João Luís G. Rosa

Núcleo Interinstitucional de Linguística Computacional (NILC)
Instituto de Ciências Matemáticas e de Computação, Universidade de São Paulo
Av. Trabalhador São-carlense, 400 – Centro
13560-979 – São Carlos – SP – Brasil
{falva,joaoluis}@icmc.usp.br

Abstract. One of the main research challenges in Semantic Role Labeling (SRL) is the development of systems for languages other than English. For Brazilian Portuguese, a corpus with appropriate manually-annotated data, PropBank.Br, has recently become available. Proposals for implementing SRL systems using this corpus have already been made, but no standard way of comparing their results is available. We present a benchmark for comparing SRL systems for Brazilian Portuguese, based on the CoNLL Shared Tasks on SRL for English. Training and test data sets, evaluation metrics and a baseline system are provided as part of this benchmark. These resources have been used to implement a supervised SRL system which outperforms the baseline (17 points better in F_1 measure). Most importantly, the benchmark proved to be useful for evaluating the performance of SRL systems for Brazilian Portuguese.

Keywords: semantic role labeling, benchmark, supervised learning, natural language processing.

1 Introduction

Semantic Role Labeling (SRL) is a Natural Language Processing (NLP) task which identifies the semantic relations between the predicate (generally the verb) and the other sentence's constituents (the predicate's arguments). Basically, SRL determines *who* did *what* to *whom*, *when* and *where* [9]. Through this analysis of the meaning of sentences, it is possible to identify the events they describe and the participants involved [11].

It is worth noting that, even if the constituents of the sentence alternate syntactically, their semantic roles remain the same. In the example sentences[1] below, for predicate *quebrar* (to break), *a janela* (the window) alternates between object (S1 and S2) and subject (S3) while keeping the semantic role of `patient` (affected by the action). The same thing happens with *a pedra* (the stone) which is the `instrument` (used to performed the action) both when being part of a prepositional phrase (S1) and a subject (S2).

---

[1] The semantic roles in the examples are labeled under the PropBank annotation framework, which we will assume throughout this paper.

J. Pavón et al. (Eds.): IBERAMIA 2012, LNAI 7637, pp. 481–490, 2012.

$$[\textit{João}]_{A0} \; \textbf{quebrou} \; [\textit{a janela}]_{A1} \; [\textit{com a pedra}]_{A2}. \quad (S1)$$

$$[\textit{A pedra}]_{A2} \; \textbf{quebrou} \; [\textit{a janela}]_{A1}. \quad\quad\quad (S2)$$

$$[\textit{A janela}]_{A1} \; \textbf{quebrou} \; [\textit{ontem}]_{AM\text{-}TMP}. \quad\quad (S3)$$

Identifying the semantic roles of a predicate's arguments, considering their multiple syntactic alternations, is what makes SRL a challenging task. It has also proven useful in a variety of NLP applications, such as: information extraction, Q&A systems, automatic summarization and machine translation [9].

Most SRL systems rely on manually-annotated data in order to learn how to classify the constituents of a sentence into their corresponding semantic roles (given a target verb). For English, big lexical resources, such as PropBank [10], provide the necessary training examples for systems to learn properly. Since that's not the case for all other languages, one of the main research challenges in SRL is developing applications for languages other than English [9].

For Brazilian Portuguese, appropriate training data has been recently released in the PropBank.Br corpus [6]. This is a Brazilian Portuguese Treebank manually-annotated with semantic roles, following the guidelines of the PropBank project. Proposals have already been presented in [1,7] to use that corpus for developing SRL systems for Portuguese. However, there is no standard way of evaluating the systems so that their results can be properly compared. Having a standard way of evaluation could benefit the comparisson of different algorithms and methods when implementing SRL systems for Portuguese.

In this paper, a benchmark for evaluating SRL systems for Brazilian Portuguese is presented. It is based on the CoNLL Shared Tasks (STs) on constituent-based SRL [4,5], which have been widely used when evaluating SRL systems for English. The resources provided are training and test datasets, appropriate evaluation metrics and a baseline system for basic comparison. Results of a supervised system implemented using these resources are also presented. It obtained better performance than the baseline (17 point higher in F_1 score). Most importantly, results proved the usefulness of the benchmark when comparing SRL systems.

This paper is structured as follows: related work is described in Sect. 2, the procedure of building the benchmark is explained in Sect. 3, Sect. 4 describes the implementation of a supervised system using the benchmark and, finally, we conclude and outline some future work in Sect. 5.

2   Related Work

The STs regarding SRL have been widely used as benchmarks for English. The challenge consists on semantically analyse the propositions expressed by some target verbs in a given sentence. In particular, for each target verb, all constituents that could fill a semantic role must be identified and properly labeled. Manually-annotated data from the PropBank corpus is provided for training and testing the participant systems.

Even though the task remains the same, in each edition new information is given to the participants so as to explore new areas of improvement in the performance of the SRL systems: English constituent-based [4,5], English dependency-based [15] and multilingual dependency-based SRL [8].

As indicated in [9], most SRL systems rely on supervised learning methods for training classifiers capable of identifying and labeling semantic roles. This approach was used in [14] for European Portuguese. The CETEMPúblico section of the Bosque corpus was automatically annotated with P (predicate), ARGO (proto-agent) and ARG1 (proto-patient) labels according to the constituents' syntatic categories (verb, subject and object, respectively) and used as training data for two classifiers (SVM and CRF). Their best classifier (SVM) achieved a F_1 score of 31.1 for ARGO and 19.0 for ARG1. No indication of manual validation of the training data is given in their paper which could be the cause of the poor results.

For Brazilian Portuguese, two proposals have been given for developing SRL systems using the PropBank.Br corpus. In [1], the authors propose a semi-supervised approach using self-training and maximum entropy models. In [7], an architecture for neural networks is described, so that it can performed different NLP tasks, such as SRL. As far as we know, no results have yet been published regarding these proposed methods.

3   Building a Benchmark

Following the STs scheme, the bechmark provides: training and test data sets, evaluation metrics and a baseline system. These are described next.

3.1   Data

Sentences with information on predicate-argument structures were extracted from the PropBank.Br corpus. This was created based on the annotation of the Brazilian Portuguese section (CETENFolha) of the Bosque corpus from the Floresta Sintá(c)tica[2], which is a corpus annotated by the parser Palavras [2] and manually corrected by linguists [13]. The PropBank.Br corpus is composed of 4,213 sentences, which results in 7,107 propositions for 1,068 target verbs.

Following the PropBank annotation framework, each predicate is associated with two sets of roles: core and adjuncts. The former (A0-A5) have interpretations that are specific to that predicate, while the latter (AM-) are general arguments (such as location or time) whose interpretation is common accross predicates.

Data Format. Annotations of a sentence are given using a flat representation in columns, separated by spaces. Each column encodes an annotation by associating a tag with every word. The information provided for each sentence is explained in Table 1 and an example of a fully-annotated sentence is presented in Fig. 1.

---

[2] http://www.linguateca.pt/Floresta/principal.html

Table 1. Column format. Fields 10 and beyond are not available in the test set.

Number	Name	Description
1	ID	Token counter, starting at 1 for each new sentence
2	FORM	Word form or punctuation symbol
3	LEMMA	Gold-standard lemma of FORM
4	GPOS	Gold-standard part-of-speech tag
5	FEAT	Gold-standard morphological features
6	CLAUSE	Clauses in start-end format
7	FCLAUSE	Full clause information in start-end format
8	SYNT	Full syntactic tree
9	PRED	The semantic predicates in this sentence.
10...	ARG	Columns with argument labels for each semantic predicate following textual order.

```
1  Agora        agora       ADV     -         (S*  (FCL*  (FCL(ADVP*)    -          (AM-TMP*)   *
2  ,            ,           PU      -         *    *      *              -          *           *
3  os           o           ART     M|P       *    *      (CU(NP*        -          (A0*        *
4  soldados     soldado     N       M|P       *    *      *)             -          *           *
5  e            e           CONJ-C  -         *    *      *              -          *           *
6  a            o           ART     F|S       *    *      (NP*           -          *           *
7  polícia      polícia     N       F|S       *    *      *))            -          *)          *
8  estão        estar       V-FIN   PR|3P|IND *    *      (VP*           -          *           *
9  trabalhando  trabalhar   V-GER   -         *    *      *)             trabalhar  (V*)        *
10 juntos       junto       ADV     M|P       *    *      (ADVP*)        -          (AM-MNR*)   *
11 para         para        PRP     -         *    *      (PP*           -          (AM-PNC*    *
12 prender      prender     V-INF   -         (S*  (ICL*  (ICL(VP*)      prender    *           (V*)
13 os           o           ART     M|P       *    *      (NP*           -          *           (A1*
14 traficantes  traficante  N       M|P       *)   *)     *)))           -          *           *)
15 .            .           PU      -         *)   *)     *)             -          *           *
```

Fig. 1. An example of an annotated sentence in the training set.

Conversion Process. Sentences in the PropBank.Br corpus are in Tiger-XML format. When converting them to the flat column representation described previously, propositions of 905 sentences had to be discarded for the following reasons:

- **Wrongsubcorpus label:** During the annotation process, an instance was given this label if it presented an error in (i) parsing (e.g, a non annotated internal NP); (ii) corpus (ortographic or punctuation error, fragmented sentence); or (iii) invocation (verb in past participle used as adjective).
- **Disconected syntactic trees:** Sentences which had constituents that were not conected to another in the parse tree (i.e, child nodes without a parent).
- **Instances of verb *ser*:** Following the guidelines of the PropBank project, propositions whose target verb is *ser* (to be) weren't annotated.

Training and Test Sets. The STs provide training, development and test sets. Considering the amount of annotated propositions available in the PropBank.Br corpus, it was split in just training and test. For the CoNLL–X ST on multilingual dependency parsing [3], the Bosque corpus was properly divided in training and test data sets. We used the same sentences for each of our own data sets. If new sentences appeared in our corpus, they were added to the test set. The final statistics of the corpus are presented in Table 2.

Table 2. Counts on the data sets

	Training	Test	Total
Sentences	3,164	144	3,308
Tokens	57,744	2,352	60,096
Propositions	5,537	239	5,776
Verbs	1,001	164	1,023
Arguments	12,968	536	13,504
A0	2,934	124	3,058
A1	4,937	211	5,148
A2	1,063	38	1,101
A3	111	2	113
A4	74	1	75
A5	1	0	1
AM-ADV	349	20	369
AM-CAU	155	1	156
AM-DIR	13	2	15
AM-DIS	283	11	294
AM-EXT	80	1	81
AM-LOC	751	27	778
AM-MNR	392	18	410
AM-NEG	316	19	335
AM-PNC	166	5	171
AM-PRD	186	6	192
AM-REC	60	5	65
AM-TMP	1,097	45	1,142

3.2 Evaluation

The STs use three evaluation metrics: *precision* (percentage of the labels output by the system which are correct), *recall* (percentage of the true labels correctly identified by the system) and F_1 (harmonic mean of precision and recall). Since the input and output of the SRL systems are in the STs format, their official evaluation script, *srl-eval.pl*[3], is also used in our benchmark.

3.3 Baseline System

The baseline system in the STs uses a small set of simple rules for labeling semantic roles. These rules were adapted for Portuguese in order to build our own baseline, and are as follows:

---

[3] Publicly available in http://www.lsi.upc.edu/~srlconll/soft.html

1. Tag target verb as V.
2. Tag *não* in target verb clause as AM-NEG.
3. Tag first NP before target verb as A0.
4. Tag first NP after target verb as A1.
5. Tag *que* before target verb as A0.
6. Switch A0 and A1 if the target verb is in a passive VP. A VP is considered in passive voice if it contains verbs *ser* or *estar* and the part-of-speech tag of the target verb is V-PCP (participle).

One of the original rules (regarding modal verbs) couldn't be adapted since no appropiate syntactic annotation was available. The performance of the baseline system is presented in Table 3.

Table 3. Performance of the baseline system considering all propositions (training and test set) and just the ones in the test set. The overall results take into account all the semantic role labels in the corpus.

	Precision		Recall		F_1	
	All	Test	All	Test	All	Test
Overall	64.3%	64.6%	39.1%	40.9%	48.6	50.1
A0	51.6%	49.7%	72.2%	70.9%	60.2	58.5
A1	77.9%	79.4%	53.8%	53.1%	63.6	63.6
AM-NEG	79.6%	90.5%	89.6%	100.0%	84.3	95.0
V	96.1%	96.2%	96.1%	96.2%	96.1	96.2

4 Using the Benchmark

To evaluate the usefulness of the benchmark, a supervised SRL system was implemented and tested using the resources provided.

4.1 System Architecture

For a given verb, all constituents of the sentence are argument candidates, but just a small subset of them actually display a semantic role. Based on this consideration, a three-stage architecture is adopted so as to reduce the number of negative samples (constituents marked NULL) for the training stages.

Pruning. We use the pruning method of [16] to filter out constituents that are clearly not semantic arguments of the target verb. It is a recursive algorithm starting from the target verb. It first returns the siblings of the verb as candidates; then it moves to the parent of the verb, and collects the siblings again. The process goes on until it reaches the root. In addition, if a constituent is a PP, its children are also collected. For the example in Fig 2, for predicate *receber*, the output of the method will be: [*Ele*]NP, [*o valor a a vista*]NP, [*após 30 dias*]PP and [*30 dias*]NP.

[Ele]_{A0} *receberá* [o valor à vista]_{A1} [após 30 dias]_{AM-TMP}.

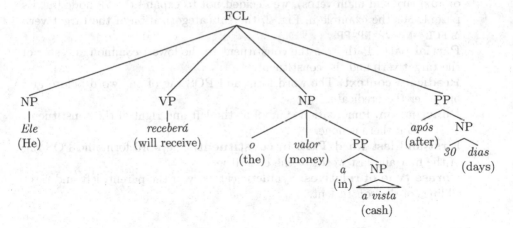

Fig. 2. Parse tree of a sentence in the training set

Argument Identification. For this step, we trained a binary classifier to identify whether a candidate is an argument or not. This subsystem receives as input the output of the prunning algorithm.

Argument Classification. In this stage, the system assigns labels to the argument candidates identified in the previous step. A multi-class classifier is trained to predict the semantic roles of the argument candidates. The classifier can also label an argument as NULL (not an argument) to discard it.

4.2   Features

We decided to use part of the feature set of ASSERT [12], which is one of the state-of-the-art SRL systems for English. Some adaptations were necessary considering the syntactic anotation of the sentences in our corpus. The final set of features consists of the following:

- **Predicate.** The word form and lemma of the target verb.
- **Path.** The syntactic path through the parse tree from the target verb to the constituent being classified. For example, in Fig 2, the path from *receberá* to *Ele* is VP↑FCL↓NP, where ↑ and ↓ represent going upwards or downwards in the tree, respectively.
- **Phrase type.** Syntactic category (NP, VP, etc.) of the constituent.
- **Position.** Whether the constituent is before or after the target verb.
- **Voice.** Whether the verb clause is in active or passive voice. The same strategy of Rule 6 of the baseline system was used.
- **Subcategorization.** The phrase structure rule expanding the target verb's parent node (normally a VP) in the parse tree. Given that Bosque doesn't

use traditional VP constituents but rather verbal chunks (consisting mainly of auxiliary and main verbs), we decided not to expand the VP node but its parent. For the example in Fig. 2, the subcategorization of the target verb is FCL→NP-VP-NP-PP.
- **Partial path.** Path from the constituent to the lowest common ancestor of the target verb and the constituent.
- **Predicate context.** The word form and POS tag of one word before and one after the predicate.
- **Punctuation.** Punctuation symbol at the left and right of the constituent, or NULL if there is none.
- **First and last word/POS in constituent.** The word form and POS tag of the first and last words of the constituent.
- **Phrase type of relatives.** Syntactic category of the parent, left and right siblings of the constituent.

4.3   Results and Discussion

We carried out experiments using Naive Bayes (NB) and Decision Tree (DT) algorithms for the identification and classification stages. The implementation of these algorithms provided in the NLTK Toolkit[4] were used. Both classifiers use the whole set of features described previously.

Following common practice, the SRL systems are evaluated in three tasks: **argument identification** (label each node as being an argument or not), **argument classification** (given gold argument candidates, label each one with the corresponding semantic role tag) and **combination of identification and classification** (the real case scenario). The results of these experiments are presented in Table 4.

Table 4. Results for argument identification, argument classification and combination of both for Naive Bayes (NB) and Decision Trees (DT) classifiers in the test set. For the classification task, since the system receives gold argument candidates, it won't miss or over-predict any argument. Therefore, only accuracy is presented.

Task	Precision		Recall		F_1		Accuracy	
	NB	DT	NB	DT	NB	DT	NB	DT
Identification	89.1%	**93.5%**	**94.9%**	91.6%	91.9	**92.6**	–	–
Classification	–	–	–	–	–	–	**64.1%**	57.5%
Ident. + Class.	**66.2%**	56.2%	**66.4%**	55.0%	**66.3**	55.6	–	–

Both classifiers performed better than the baseline when compared on F_1 scores. While the DT classifier performs better for the task of argument identification (only two labels), NB obtains better results when the task at hand

---

[4] http://nltk.org/

includes multiple classes[5]. Therefore, a final experiment was performed using DT for the first stage and NB for the second. The results (shown in Table 5) show that this approach is even better than the last two.

Table 5. Results of DT + NB compared to the baseline on the test set

	Precision		Recall		F_1	
	Baseline	DT+NB	Baseline	DT+NB	Baseline	DT+NB
Overall	64.6%	**68.0%**	40.9%	**66.6%**	50.1	**67.3**

5 Conclusions and Future Work

In this paper we present a benchmark for evaluating the performance of SRL systems for Brazilian Portuguese, based on the CoNLL STs. We provide training and test data sets, evaluation metrics and a rule-based baseline system. Furthermore, a supervised SRL system is implemented using these resources. This system outperforms the baseline in about 17 points of F_1 score. After the experiments, the benchmark has proven useful as a standard evaluation of the quality of SRL systems.

As future work, we will increase the information of the sentences in the data sets, specially regarding dependency information. Features that take into account the head of the constituent (really useful in SRL for English) couldn't be used since the gold parse trees available don't provide that type of information.

Simple training algorithms were used when implementing the SRL system, so as to just exemplify the usefulness of the benchmark's resources. The results obtained are poor when compared to the state-of-the-art systems for other languages. To improve them, experiments with more sophisticated learning algorithms (such as Maximum Entropy Models or Support Vector Machines) will be carried out.

Acknowledgments. The authors are grateful to FAPESP (Fundação de Amparo à Pesquisa do Estado de São Paulo, Brazil) for the research support under project numbers 2010/04647-0 and 2008/08245-4, which this paper is associated with. Also, the authors would like to thank the anonymous reviewers for their constructive criticism and useful suggestions.

References

1. Alva-Manchego, F., Rosa, J.L.: Towards Semi-supervised Brazilian Portuguese Semantic Role Labeling: Building a Benchmark. In: Caseli, H., Villavicencio, A., Teixeira, A., Perdigão, F. (eds.) PROPOR 2012. LNCS (LNAI), vol. 7243, pp. 210–217. Springer, Heidelberg (2012)

---

[5] The differences are statistically significant with $p < 0.0001$.

2. Bick, E.: The Parsing System PALAVRAS – Automatic Grammatical Analysis of Portuguese in a Constraint Grammar Framework. Aarhus University Press (2000)
3. Buchholz, S., Marsi, E.: CoNLL-X Shared Task on Multilingual Dependency Parsing. In: 10th Conference on Computational Natural Language Learning (CoNLL 2006), pp. 149–164. ACL, New York City (2006)
4. Carreras, X., Màrquez, L.: Introduction to the CoNLL-2004 Shared Task – Semantic Role Labeling. In: 8th Conference on Computational Natural Language Learning (CoNLL 2004) – Shared Task, pp. 89–97. ACL, Boston (2004)
5. Carreras, X., Màrquez, L.: Introduction to the CoNLL-2005 Shared Task – Semantic Role Labeling. In: 9th Conference on Computational Natural Language Learning (CoNLL 2005) – Shared Task, pp. 152–164. ACL, Ann Arbor (2005)
6. Duran, M.S., Aluísio, S.M.: Propbank-Br – A Brazilian Treebank Annotated with Semantic Role Labels. In: 8th International Conference on Language Resources and Evaluation (LREC 2012), Istanbul, Turkey, pp. 1862–1867 (2012)
7. Fonseca, E.R., Rosa, J.L.: An Architecture for Semantic Role Labeling on Portuguese. In: Caseli, H., Villavicencio, A., Teixeira, A., Perdigão, F. (eds.) PROPOR 2012. LNCS (LNAI), vol. 7243, pp. 204–209. Springer, Heidelberg (2012)
8. Hajic, J., Ciaramita, M., Johansson, R., Kawahara, D., Martí, M.A., Màrquez, L., Mayers, A., Nivre, J., Padó, S., Stepánek, J., Stranák, P., Surdeanu, M., Xue, N., Zhang, Y.: The CoNLL-2009 Shared Task: Syntactic and Semantic Dependencies in Multiple Languages. In: 13th Conference on Computational Natural Language Learning (CoNLL 2009) – Shared Task, pp. 1–18. ACL, Boulder (2009)
9. Màrquez, L., Carreras, X., Litkowski, K.C., Stevenson, S.: Semantic Role Labeling – An Introduction to the Special Issue. Computational Linguistics 34(2), 145–159 (2008)
10. Palmer, M., Gildea, D., Kingsbury, P.: The Proposition Bank – An Annotated Corpus of Semantic Roles. Computational Linguistics 31(1), 71–106 (2005)
11. Palmer, M., Gildea, D., Xue, N.: Semantic Role Labeling, 1st edn. Morgan & Claypool Publishers (2010)
12. Pradhan, S.S., Ward, W., Martin, J.H.: Towards Robust Semantic Role Labeling. Computational Linguistics 34(2), 289–310 (2008)
13. Santos, D., Bick, E., Afonso, S.: Floresta sintá(c)tica: apresentação e história do projecto. Encontro Um passeio pela Floresta Sintá(c)tica (Setembro 2007)
14. Sequeira, J., Gonçalves, T., Quaresma, P.: Semantic Role Labeling for Portuguese – A Preliminary Approach –. In: Caseli, H., Villavicencio, A., Teixeira, A., Perdigão, F. (eds.) PROPOR 2012. LNCS (LNAI), vol. 7243, pp. 193–203. Springer, Heidelberg (2012)
15. Surdeanu, M., Johansson, R., Meyers, A., Màrquez, L., Nivre, J.: The CoNLL 2008 Shared Task on Joint Parsing of Syntactic and Semantic Dependencies. In: 12th Conference on Computational Natural Language Learning (CoNLL 2008), pp. 159–177. ACL, Manchester (2008)
16. Xue, N., Palmer, M.: Calibrating Features for Semantic Role Labeling. In: 2004 Conference on Empirical Methods in Natural Language Processing (EMNLP 2004), pp. 88–94. ACL, Barcelona (2004)

Optimization Approach for the Development of Humanoid Robots' Behaviors

Luis Cruz[1,5], Luis Paulo Reis[1,4], Nuno Lau[2,6], and Armando Sousa[3,5]

[1] LIACC - Artificial Intelligence and Computer Science Lab., Univ. of Porto, Portugal
[2] IEETA - Institute of Electronics and Telematics Engineering of Aveiro, Portugal
[3] INESC-TEC - Institute for Systems and Computer Engineering of Porto, Portugal
[4] DSI/EEUM - Inf. Systems Dep., School of Engineering, Univ. Minho, Portugal
[5] FEUP - Faculty of Engineering of the University of Porto, Porto, Portugal
[6] DETI/UA - Electronics, Telecomm. and Informatics Dep., Univ. Aveiro, Portugal
ei06034@fe.up.pt, lpreis@dsi.uminho.pt, nuno.lau@ua.pt, asousa@fe.up.pt

Abstract. Humanoid robots usually have a large number of degrees of freedom which turns humanoid control into a very complex problem. Humanoids are used in several RoboCup soccer leagues. In this work, the SimSpark simulator of the Simulation 3D will be used. This paper presents an automatic approach for developing humanoid behaviors based on the development of a generic optimization system. The paper describes the adopted architecture, main design choices and the results achieved with the optimization of a side kick and a forward kick. For both skills, the optimization approach allowed the creation of faster and more powerful and stable behaviors.

Keywords: humanoids, soccer, simulation 3D, optimization, NAO, SimSpark.

1 Introduction

The advent of humanoid robots has brought new challenges in robotics and related fields. The development of behaviors with many degrees of freedom (DOF) is one of these challenges. Within RoboCup [7], an international robotic competition, researchers are challenged to many of these problems in order to have robots, including humanoids, playing soccer and performing other complex tasks.

The RoboCup Simulation 3D League uses a model of the humanoid robot NAO [4] and was created in order to promote research in techniques to make humanoid robots play soccer. The FCPortugal Team project was conceived as an effort to create intelligent players, capable of thinking like real soccer players and behave like a real soccer team competing in the RoboCup Simulation Leagues. The result of this kind of research may be extended to other domains, such as the use of real humanoid robots to perform social tasks such as helping the blind to cross streets or elderly people to perform tasks that became impossible for them to do alone.

J. Pavón et al. (Eds.): IBERAMIA 2012, LNAI 7637, pp. 491–500, 2012.

The use of simulated environments is very useful because it allows the developers to make arbitrary or complex tests in the simulator without using the real robot thus avoiding expensive material getting damaged [8].

In order to have a humanoid robot playing soccer, it has to walk in many directions, kick the ball, get up when necessary, etc. However, developing a behavior is not trivial as you have to control lot of DOF (NAO humanoid has 22) in a complex body shape where most configurations are not stable [9][13]. This makes the development of fast and stable behaviors a complex task. This paper presents an automatic approach to improve the development of such behaviors using generic optimization methods.

This paper starts by describing the problem in Sect. 2, then the designed optimization system and its main features in Sect. 3. The results achieved are presented in Sect. 4 and Sect. 5 presents the conclusion.

2   Problem Formulation

The official Robocup 3D simulation server is SimSpark [2], a generic physical multi-agent simulator system for agents in 3D environments. It simulates the physics dynamics of the real world in the context of a soccer game as well as the robots (physical dimensions, sensors and joints).

2.1   Humanoid Robot Behaviors

A behavior or skill consists in a intentional, repeatable action executed by the agent, such as getting up from a fall or kicking the ball. These can be specified once and executed as many times as necessary. The FCPortugal's agent has these behaviors specified and stored in XML files, providing the parameters of a behavior specification model. All behaviors are loaded when the agent starts.

A behavior defines the trajectories for all the humanoid joints. A joint trajectory can be defined by a set of points over an interval of time. A behavior specification model can be used to specify skills by computing different joint trajectories. There are various models for specifying skills, some of those used by the FCPortugal Team, including the StepBehavior model which uses step functions to model the trajectories, SlotBehavior model which uses a Sine Interpolation (SI) method [11,12,13], and the Central Pattern Generator model (CPG), based on the work of Behnke [1].

3   The Optimizer

The optimizer was designed in a distributed architecture allowing a behavior to be optimized using either a single computer or multiple computers connected via a network. Figure 1 depicts the configuration of the optimizer.

Once started, the optimizer server starts the simulator, the monitor and the agents using predefined shell scripts. It may start multiple simulators and their

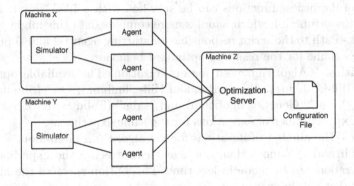

Fig. 1. Possible setup for the optimizer, running in multiple machines

respective monitors in different computers if specified. The agents connect to the simulation server and to the optimization server. Then the optimization server sends to the agents the behaviors to be executed and receives from them information about their execution used to compute the behavior performance.

The optimization server is the core of the system and it is multi-threaded. There is one thread per agent that provides the agent with the behavior to optimize, waits for the agent to finish executing the behavior, receives the experimental data sent by the agent and evaluates it, giving that generated behavior a score according to a specified objective function.

A shell script is responsible of starting the FCPortugal agents. This allows the agents to be started on the local or in a remote machine. Another shell script terminates the agents. In the current implementation, for convenience, the simulator script, that starts the simulator, is started from the agent script.

The scripts exist for both flexibility and to isolate the optimization server from the details of running the other components. Recompiling the optimization server each time we wanted to change the parameters of the agents, such as when the host of the simulation server changes, would be a poor design choice [12].

3.1   The Configuration File

In order to make this optimizer easier to use in different situations, a configuration file is used to specify the characteristics of the optimization and how the agent will execute the experiment. The main parameters are the following:

- **behavior** - Path to the XML specification file of the behavior to optimize.
- **type** - Type of behavior. It can be "StepBehavior", "SlotBehavior", "ExpediteSlotBehavior" or "CPGBehavior".
- **objectiveScript** - Path to the LUA script that evaluates the executed experiment and returns its fitness.
- **objective** - The evaluation method can be implemented directly in the optimizer code, instead of in a LUA script. This is not recommended since

most of the fitness functions can be specified with a LUA script. However, for a fitness function which handles more complex data this might be useful.

- **script** - Path to the script responsible for starting agent(s) and simulator(s).
- **name** - Name for the resulting optimized behavior.
- **algorithm** - Algorithm used for optimization. The available options are "hc" (Hill-Climbing), "hcr" (Random Hill-Climbing), "sa" (Simulated Annealing), "ga" (Genetic Algorithm) and "tabu" (Tabu Search).
- **numExp** - Number of executions for the same experiment.
- **nMax** - The number of iterations for the algorithms main loop.
- **numThread** - If more than one agent can execute the experiments, the optimization can be made in less time. This option specifies the number of agents that will be executing.
- **waitBefore** - Time in seconds that the agent will wait before executing the experiment. Ater a beam the agent loses some balance and this waiting time may be used to stabilize or to perform other preparation taks.
- **useGyroStabilization** - Instead of using the waitBefore option, another approach is possible. Using the data received from the agent's gyroscope, it is possible to know if the agent has enough stability to start the execution. The value in this parameter is a boolean (true/false).
- **waitAfter** - Time in seconds, the agent waits before collecting data about the experiment to be evaluated by the fitness function. This is useful, for instance when optimizing a kick as we need to know the final ball position.
- **beamBall** - The position of the ball in the start of each execution. Again, if when optimizing a kick we need to reset the ball position after each kick.
- **algorithm parameters** - the parameters of the algorithm such as the population size for genetic algorithms or the size of the tabu list for *Tabu Search*.
- **behavior optimization parameters** - specific parts of the behavior to be optimized such as which slots or steps for SlotBehaviors or StepBehaviors, respectively, which joints restrictions to enforce such as symmetries, etc.
- **minChange** - minimum value to change an optimization variable to obtain a neighboring solution - does not apply to time intervals
- **maxChange** - maximum value to change an optimization variable to obtain a neighboring solution - does not apply to time intervals
- **minChangeDelta** - minimum value to change an optimization variable that represents a time interval to obtain a neighboring solution;
- **maxChangeDelta** - maximum value to change an optimization variable that represents a time interval it to obtain a neighbouring solution.
- **serverRestartTime** - maximum amount of time the simulator can run without being restarted (in seconds). Further details in Sect. 3.5.

To process the configuration files *libconfig*[1] library is used. For this kind of configuration it is more compact and readable than XML. Besides, it is type-aware, which means that it is not necessary to do string parsing to the specified values [10].

---

[1] Further information in http://www.hyperrealm.com/libconfig/

3.2   Gyroscope Initial Stabilization

The time the agent has to wait before starting the experiment can be statically fixed in the configuration file or, alternatively, this time can be dinamically determined using information from the gyroscope. When this option is set the agent will wait until it receives from the gyroscope data values in the range of $]-5.0, 5.0[$. Then, the agent is ready to execute the behaviour.

3.3   Objective Function

In order to evaluate the experiment, the agent collects data and sends it to the server. The collected data includes: The time taken to execute the behaviour; A boolean indicating whether the agent fell; The agent's initial and final position; The distance travelled by the agent in each axis; The final agent's orientation; The ball's initial and final position; The distance travelled by the ball in each axis; The simulation time.

After receiving this data, the server evaluates the experiment. This is made calling the objective function (or fitness function). There are two ways to specify an objective function (or fitness function). The first is by implementing a C function and include it in the source code of the optimizer. The drawback of this approach is that whenever it is needed to create an objective function, some changes have to be made in the code. This requires some knowledge about the implementation code. Furthermore, it is necessary to recompile the optimizer. To handle this drawback, we used a scripting language known as Lua [5,6]. Lua is an embeddable scripting language with a simple C API and it has been widely used as a tool to customize applications. It has the usual control structures (whiles, ifs, etc.), function definitions with parameters and local variables, it also provides functions as first order values, closures, and dynamically created associative arrays (called tables) as a single, unifying data-structuring mechanism [3]. Using the Lua API, the objective function for the optimization can be implemented as a script in a separated file and it is only necessary to specify the path to it.

3.4   Optimization Algorithms

Several problems consist in finding the best configuration of a set of variable values to minimize (or maximize) some quantity known as the objective function, f. The independent variables that can change while searching for an optimum are known as decision variables. For some problems, the values that decision variables can take are specified by their domains and also through a number of conditions known as constraints.

The search space of a problem is defined as the set of all candidate solutions. A candidate solution is an instantiation of the decision variables, if it satisfies all the constraints of the problem it is called a feasible solution or just a solution. The solution space is the set of all (feasible) solutions. An optimal solution is a solution where the objective function evaluates to a minimum (or maximum). Computer algorithms that traverse the search space with the purpose of finding optimal solutions are called automatic optimization algorithms.

3.5   Adaptations Made in the Simulator

Whenever an experiment is made, the agent and ball positions change. In order to have the same conditions for every execution, it is necessary to undo these changes. It is necessary to have an automated way of controlling the agent and ball positions. So, a few changes were made in the simulation server.

The simulator has a feature that allows the creation of plugins. These plugins can be actions that make some changes in the simulation environment and they are triggered when the server receives some specific messages. The simulator had already a plugin that allowed the repositioning of the agent – the *Beam* plugin. However, this could only be done in the beginning of the games. As the optimizer needs to do this in every game states, a few changes were made in the *Beam* plugin. To reposition the ball, a similar plugin was created.

Another modification was to allow the game to automatically start. Originally the server only allowed manual starts. The duration of the game was also modified. In the original simulator, the server had to be reinitialized after less than 600 seconds of simulation, and each reinitialization took approximately 20 seconds. This is acceptable, but in order to speed up the optimization, this value was changed to a larger number.

4   Experimental Results

4.1   Side Kick Optimization

A good approach for developing new behaviors for the FCPortugal agent, is to start by creating a version of the behavior by hand. After that, the optimizer can be used to enhance it. In this experience, a side kick was developed using the Slot Behaviour model. The execution of the non optimized behaviour can be seen in Fig. 2. In a side kick the main objective is to get higher ball distances in less time and also not to have the ball going front or back. So, the fitness function awards solutions with these characteristics.

$$f(x) = \frac{bdist_y^3 * bell(bdist_x)}{\Delta t} \tag{1}$$

Fig. 2. Sequence of images showing the execution of the side kick skill

Table 1. Side kick optimization parameters

Parameter	Value
Number of experiments	5
Number of threads	1
Minimum Change for Angles	-5.0
Maximum Change for Angles	5.0
Minimum Change for Deltas	-0.3
Maximum Change for Deltas	0.3
Number of Iterations	500
Tabu List Size (Tabu Search)	1000
Wait for Gyroscope Stabilization	True
Time to Wait After the Experiment (sec)	3.0
Beam Ball Position	(0.0, 0.0)

Table 2. Side kick optimization results

	Ball Distance (m)	Duration (sec)	Best Solution (iteration)	Best Solution Time (simulation sec)	Total Time (simulation sec)
Original	1.42	1.14	-	-	-
Hill Climbing	2.75	0.89	266	9756	18042
Tabu Search	3.07	0.88	404	14553	17920

The function $bell(x)$ is the probability density function of a normal (or Gaussian) distribution. It is used in the fitness function with $\mu = 0.0$ (a.k.a. *mean*) and $\sigma^2 = 1.0$ (a.k.a. *variance*) with the aim of giving better fitness values to solutions in which the ball goes strictly to the side.

The optimization parameters used are shown in Table 1. The results achieved can be seen in Table 2. The best result reaches 3.07 meters of ball distance, executes in 0.88 seconds and was obtained with the Tabu Search algorithm.

The graphs of Fig. 3 present the evolution of the fitness score of the best and current solutions, for both Hill Climbing and Tabu Search methods. The blue lines represent the current experiment fitness and the red lines are the best fitness until that iteration. We can notice that the fitness of the solution that is being evaluated varies greatly, despite the very slight differences. Even though the Tabu Search only reached the best fitness at iteration 404, a solution with the same fitness as the best solution in Hill Climbing, was achieved in less time at iteration 63.

4.2   Forward Kick Optimization

Another behavior optimized was the forward kick. The behavior was already in use prior to being optimized but we wanted to maximize the distance achieved by the ball. The fitness function is represented in equation 2. Again, the function $bell(x)$ is used to ensure that the ball is kicked strictly forward.

$$f(x) = \frac{bdist_x^3 * bell(bdist_y)}{\Delta t} \tag{2}$$

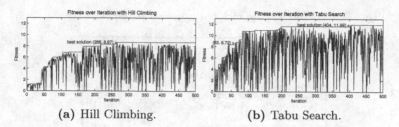

(a) Hill Climbing.   (b) Tabu Search.

Fig. 3. Graphs of the fitness over the iteration reported in the optimization of the side kick skill for both Hill Climbing and Tabu Search algorithms

Table 3. Forward kick optimization parameters

Parameter	Value
Number of experiments	6
Number of threads	1
Minimum Change for Angles	-5.0
Maximum Change for Angles	5.0
Minimum Change for Deltas	-0.3
Maximum Change for Deltas	0.3
Number of Iterations	500
Tabu List Size (Tabu Search)	1000
Wait for Gyroscope Stabilization	True
Time to Wait After the Experiment (sec)	4.0
Beam Ball Position	(0.0, 0.0)

Table 4. Forward kick optimization results

	Ball Distance (m)	Duration (sec)	Best Solution (iteration)	Best Solution Time (simulation sec)	Total Time (simulation sec)
Original	5.15	2.04	-	-	-
Hill Climbing	6.30	1.78	495	27419	27637
Tabu Search	5.65	2.04	356	20159	28258

Fig. 4. Sequence of images showing the execution of the front kick skill (not optimized)

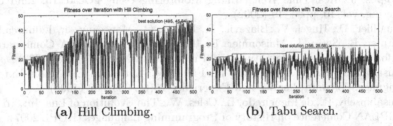

(a) Hill Climbing.   (b) Tabu Search.

Fig. 5. Graphs of the fitness over the iteration for the longest distance kick optimization with the Hill Climbing and Tabu Search methods

The Table 3 shows the parameters used in the experience. The results of this experiment are reported in the Table 4. The best results were achieved with Hill Climbing resulting in a kick that moves the ball 6.30 m. The skill duration was reduced from 2.04 s to 1.78 s. The graphs of Fig. 5 show the convergence of the optimization methods. The blue lines represent the fitness of the current experiment and the red lines are the best fitness until that iteration.

5   Conclusions

Humanoid robots are currently not able to perform as well as humans do some simple tasks, such as kicking a ball. This work offers an automated process of reducing this difference by improving existing behaviors with automatic optimization methods. The initial work was made to create an optimization framework for the behaviors of the FCPortugal Team 3D humanoid agent which inhabits the simulated world of the RoboCup 3D simulation server. This required both modifications to the agent, the simulation server and the creation of the optimizer itself. The configuration of the optimizer was designed to be easily used with different kinds of behaviors. Also, the use of scripts to implement the objective function, makes the optimization much more generic and easy to configure. Two behaviors were optimized in this work: a side kick and a front kick. Both were created using the SlotBehavior model and the results were very good.

The side kick reached the best results with the TS algorithm, having an improvement of 91% with the ball distance being raised from 1.38m to 2.64m. The forward kick optimization also achieved good results: from 5.15 meters of ball distance now the kick can get 6.30 meters, which is an improvement of 22%.

References

1. Behnke, S.: Online Trajectory Generation for Omnidirectional Biped Walking. In: IEEE International Conference on Robotics and Automation (ICRA 2006), pp. 1597–1603. IEEE (2006)
2. Boedecker, J., Asada, M.: SimSpark – Concepts and Application in the RoboCup 3D Soccer Simulation League. In: Workshop on The Universe of RoboCup Simulators, SIMPAR 2008, pp. 174–181 (2008)

3. Campos, J.: Real-Time Well Drilling Monitoring Using gOcad. In: 22nd Gocad Meeting, vol. 10, pp. 1–10 (2002)
4. Gouaillier, D., Hugel, V., Blazevic, P., Kilner, C., Monceaux, J., Lafourcade, P., Marnier, B., Serre, J., Maisonnier, B.: The NAO Humanoid – A Combination of Performance and Affordability. Arxiv Preprint p. arXiv:0807.3223 (2008)
5. Ierusalimschy, R., De Figueiredo, L., Filho, W.: Lua – An Extensible Extension Language. Software Practice and Experience 26(6), 635–652 (1996)
6. Ierusalimschy, R., de Figueiredo, L., Celes, W.: The Evolution of Lua. In: 3rd ACM SIGPLAN Conference on History of Programming Languages (HOPL 2007), vol. 2, pp. 1–26. ACM (2007)
7. Kitano, H., Asada, M., Kuniyoshi, Y., Noda, I., Osawa, E., Matsubara, H.: RoboCup – A Challenge Problem for AI. AI Magazine 18(1), 73–85 (1997)
8. Lund, H., Miglino, O.: From Simulated to Real Robots. In: 1996 IEEE International Conference on Evolutionary Computation (ICEC 1996), pp. 362–365. IEEE (1996)
9. MacAlpine, P., Urieli, D., Barrett, S., Kalyanakrishnan, S., Barrera, F., Lopez-Mobilia, A., Ştiurcă, N., Vu, V., Stone, P.: UT Austin Villa 2011 – A Champion Agent in the RoboCup 3D Soccer Simulation Competition. In: 11th Intl. Conf. on Autonomous Agents and Multiagent Systems (AAMAS 2012), pp. 1–8 (2012)
10. Mouton, C.: A Study of the Existing Libraries to Read from Configuration Files (from C++). Arxiv preprint p. arXiv:1103.3021 (2011)
11. Picado, H., Gestal, M., Lau, N., Reis, L.P., Tomé, A.M.: Automatic Generation of Biped Walk Behavior Using Genetic Algorithms. In: Cabestany, J., Sandoval, F., Prieto, A., Corchado, J.M. (eds.) IWANN 2009, Part I. LNCS, vol. 5517, pp. 805–812. Springer, Heidelberg (2009)
12. Rei, L., Reis, L.P., Lau, N.: Optimizing a Humanoid Robot Skill. In: 11th International Conference on Mobile Robots and Competitions (Robotica 2011), pp. 84–89 (2011)
13. Shafii, N., Reis, L.P., Lau, N.: Biped Walking Using Coronal and Sagittal Movements Based on Truncated Fourier Series. In: del Solar, J.R., Chown, E., Plöger, P.G. (eds.) RoboCup 2010. LNCS, vol. 6556, pp. 324–335. Springer, Heidelberg (2010)

Image Segmentation Based on Multi-Kernel Learning and Feature Relevance Analysis

S. Molina-Giraldo, A.M. Álvarez-Meza, D.H. Peluffo-Ordoñez,
and G. Castellanos-Domínguez

Signal Processing and Recognition Group - Universidad Nacional de Colombia,
Manizales, Colombia
{smolinag,amalvarezme,dhpeluffoo,cgcastellanosd}@unal.edu.co

Abstract. In this paper an automatic image segmentation methodology based on Multiple Kernel Learning (MKL) is proposed. In this regard, we compute some image features for each input pixel, and then combine such features by means of a MKL framework. We automatically fix the weights of the MKL approach based on a relevance analysis over the original input feature space. Moreover, an unsupervised image segmentation measure is used as a tool to establish the employed kernel free parameter. A Kernel Kmeans algorithm is used as spectral clustering method to segment a given image. Experiments are carried out aiming to test the efficiency of the incorporation of weighted feature information into clustering procedure, and to compare the performance against state of the art algorithms, using a supervised image segmentation measure. Attained results show that our approach is able to compute a meaningful segmentations, demonstrating its capability to support further vision computer applications.

Keywords: kernel learning, spectral clustering, relevance analysis.

1 Introduction

Image segmentation is an important stage in computer vision and image processing applications, it consists in splitting an image into disjoint regions such that the pixels have a high similarity according to a preset property or measure for each region and contrast difference among regions. The main goal is to obtain a proper segmentation that can be used in processes such as video object extraction [16], in which for partitioning the image into homogeneous regions that correspond to relevant objects, and then, to extract the moving object, the regions are merged according to temporal information of the sequence. Image segmentation is also used in object recognition systems [2]. Most of these systems partition the object to be recognized into sub-regions and attempt to characterize each region separately to simplify the matching process. Moreover, tracking systems that are region-based techniques [1] use the information of the entire objects regions. They track the homogeneous regions from the object by their

J. Pavón et al. (Eds.): IBERAMIA 2012, LNAI 7637, pp. 501–510, 2012.

color, luminance or texture. At the end, a merging technique based on motion estimation is carried out to obtain the complete object in the next frame.

Several image segmentation methods have been proposed, which can mainly be divided into the following categories: Histogram-based algorithms, which consider the histogram of an image as a probability density function of a Gaussian, hence the segmentation problem is reformulated as a parameter estimation followed by pixel classification. However, the parameter estimation and the selection of a global threshold in 3D histograms for color images represent a difficult task and could slant the algorithm to work with only some images. The second category are Boundary-based algorithms, the basic idea of this approach is that changes in pixels values among neighboring pixels inside a region is not as significant as changes in pixels values on the boundary of a region, therefore regions can be identified when the boundaries are detected. The main drawback of this approach is that boundaries may not be not totally closed. Many post-processing algorithms have been created in order to connect open boundaries [3], however these algorithms always tend to attain over-segmented results. Finally, Grouping-based algorithms aim to group pixels in the same cluster if they have similar patterns or characteristics, while pixels grouped into different clusters have different characteristics. Nonetheless, traditional grouping algorithms, e.g., Kmeans and Expected Maximization, tend to fall into local optimal, whereas spectral clustering algorithms can converge in a global optimal and can be used on arbitrary datasets [8]. Conventional spectral clustering algorithms used for image segmentation, use as input, similarity matrices based only on pixel intensity. Mostly, this information source is not enough to obtain a good performance by the spectral clustering algorithm.

In this sense, we propose a methodology for image segmentation based on a grouping approach that incorporates multiple sources of information for each input pixel by using a Multiple Kernel Learning (MKL) framework and a relevance analysis for the automatic weight selection of the MKL approach. Taking into account the survey of unsupervised measures presented in [17], we propose to use the unsupervised measure FRC [13] as a feedback control to determine a proper free parameter for the employed kernel. Also, we propose to use the Kernel Kmeans technique as spectral clustering algorithm and a post-processing stage to relabel clusters that are spatially split. Finally, a supervised measure Probabilistic Rand Index, described in [15], is used to objectively evaluate the proposed algorithm performance.

This paper is structured as follow. In Sect. 2.1 we describe the incorporation of multiple sources of information into the image segmentation problem by means of MKL. Section 2.2 explains the automatic weight selection of the MKL approach. In Sect. 3 we present the proposed image segmentation methodology. Section 4, describes the experimental scheme used for the proposed methodology and we expose the performed experiments. Finally in Sect. 5 and 6 discussions and conclusions over attained results are exposed.

2   Theoretical Background

2.1   Image Analysis by Multi-Kernel Learning

Recently, machine learning approaches have shown that the use of multiple kernels instead of only one can be useful to improve the interpretation of data [12]. Given a set of p feature representations for each image pixel $h_i = \{h_i^z : z = 1, \ldots, p\}$, based on the Multi-Kernel Learning (MKL) methods [7], the similarity among pixels can be computed via the function:

$$\kappa_\omega \left(h_i^z, h_j^z \right) = \sum_{z=1}^{p} \omega_z \kappa \left(h_i^z, h_j^z \right), \tag{1}$$

subject to $\omega_z \geq 0$, and $\sum_{i=1}^{p} \omega_z = 1$ $(\forall \omega_z \in \mathbb{R})$. Thereby, the input data can be analyzed from different information sources by means of a convex combination of basis kernels. Regarding to image segmentation procedures, each pixel of an image can be represented by including p different image features, which are properly combined by MKL as shown in (1), in order to enhance the performance of further spectral clustering stages. Nonetheless, as can be seen from (1), it is necessary to fix the ω_z free parameters, to take advantage, as well as possible, of each feature representation.

2.2   MKL Weight Selection Based on Feature Relevance Analysis

We propose to select the weights values ω_z in MKL by means of a relevance analysis over the original image features. This type of analysis is applied to find out a low-dimensional representations, searching for directions with greater variance to project the data, such as Principal Component Analysis (PCA). Although PCA is commonly used as a feature extraction method, it is useful to quantify the relevance of the original features, which also provides weighting factors taking into consideration that the best representation from an explained variance point of view will be reached [5]. Given a set of features $(\boldsymbol{\eta}_z : z = 1, \ldots, p)$ corresponding to each column of the input data matrix $\mathbf{X} \in \mathbb{R}^{r \times p}$ (a set of p features describing a pixel image h_i), the relevance of $\boldsymbol{\eta}_z$ can be identified as ω_z, which is calculated as $\boldsymbol{w} = \sum_{j=1}^{d} |\lambda_j \mathbf{v}_j|$, with $\boldsymbol{w} \in \mathbb{R}^{p \times 1}$, and where λ_j and $\mathbf{v}_j$ are the eigenvalues and eigenvectors of the covariance matrix $\mathbf{V} = \mathbf{X}^\top \mathbf{X}$, respectively.

Therefore, the main assumption is that the largest values of w_z lead to the best input attributes, since they exhibit higher overall correlations with principal components. The d value is fixed as the number of dimensions needed to conserve a percentage of the input data variability.

3   Weighted Gaussian Kernel Image Segmentation

Taking into account the above mentioned techniques, we propose a new image segmentation methodology called Weighted Gaussian Kernel Image Segmentation (WGKS). The main goal of the proposed methodology is to properly identify the objects contained in an image.

The first step of WGKS is to conform a feature space from the original image $H_{n\times m}$. In this sense, p different features are extracted for each pixel. Thus, a feature space $X_{r\times p}$ is obtained, with $r = n \times m$. A MKL framework is employed to identify the similarities among pixels, by combining the obtained features using a Gaussian kernel $G^z \in \mathbb{R}^{r\times r}$ as shown in (2)

$$G^z\left(x_i^z, x_j^z\right) = \exp\left(-\frac{1}{2}\left(\frac{\left|x_i^z - x_j^z\right|}{\left|x_j^z\right|\sigma}\right)^2\right),\tag{2}$$

where σ is the kernel band-width and the term $\left|x_j^z\right|$ in the denominator stands for comparing the samples x_i^z and x_j^z by means of a relative error. Therefore, as described in (1), a weighted gaussian kernel $G \in \mathbb{R}^{r\times r}$ can be inferred as $G = \sum_{z=1}^{p} w_z G^z$, where each ω_z is estimated by a feature relevance analysis over the original input space.

In order to exploit the data representation obtained by $\mathbf{G}$, a Kernel Kmeans algorithm [6] is used to segment the original image $\mathbf{H}$. Moreover, the number of groups k is calculated from an eigenvalue analysis over a weighted linear kernel, which is computed as $K_L = XWX^T$, where $W_{p\times p} = diag(w_{p\times 1})$, in a similar way as described in [11].

4   Experiments

To verify the effectiveness of the proposed methodology, natural images drawn from the Berkeley Image Segmentation Database are tested [9]. The Database contains hand-labeled segmentations made by 30 human subjects for 300 color images of 481×321 pixels. Natural images are in *jpg* format and human segmentation results in *seg* format. The images exhibit large variety of objects and real world scenes. For concrete testing, images are resized to 97×65, and the following features are extracted: RGB components, row position x, column position y, normalized rgb components, HSV components and YCbCr components. Thus, for each image an input feature space $X \in \mathbb{R}^{6305\times 14}$ is obtained.

It is important to note that for all the provided experiments the Kernel-Kmeans (KN-Kmeans) technique is used as a spectral clustering approach. Moreover, the Probabilistic Rand Index (PR) is employed as a supervised segmentation measure. The PR allows to compare a test segmentation with multiple hand labeled ground-truth images, through soft nonuniform weighting of pixel pairs as function of the variability in the ground-truth set [15]. Consider a set of manual segmentations $\{Y_1, \ldots, Y_T\}$ of an image H $\{h_1, \ldots, h_r\}$ consisting of r pixels. Let S be the segmentation that is to be compared with the manually labeled set. The label of point h_i is denoted by l_i^S in segmentation S, and by $l_i^{Y_t}$ in the manually segmented image Y_t, with $\{t = 1, \ldots, T\}$. It is assumed that each label $l_i^{Y_t}$ can take values in a discrete set of size l^{Y_t}, and correspondingly l_i^S takes one of the l^S values. The PR index chooses to model label relationships for each pixel pair by an unknown underlying distribution. It can be seen as if each human segmenter provides information about the segmentation Y_t of the

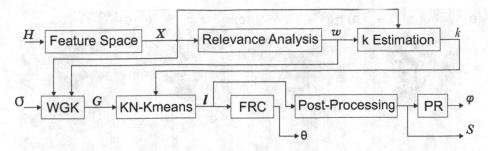

Fig. 1. WGKS scheme

image in the form of binary numbers $\delta(l_i^{Y_t} = l_j^{Y_t})$, for each pair of pixels (h_i, h_j). Therefore, this measure allows us to compare the segmented image by an image segmentation algorithm against a set of ground truth images as

$$\phi(S, Y) = \frac{1}{T} \sum_{t=1}^{T} \frac{1}{\binom{r}{2}} \sum_{ij} \left[\delta \left(l_i^S = l_j^S \right) \delta \left(l_i^{Y_t} = l_j^{Y_t} \right) + \delta \left(l_i^S \neq l_j^S \right) \delta \left(l_i^{Y_t} \neq l_j^{Y_t} \right) \right].$$

(3)

being ϕ the attained PR value. This measure is widely used because it can retains the uncertainty of the hand labeled segmentations, weighting it in a balanced way. Also, it has the capability to perform comparisons even if the number of groups of each segmented image is different [14].

Note that, the σ free parameter of the Gaussian kernel is selected from the set $\sigma = [0.15\,0.3\,0.45\,0.6\,0.75\,0.9]$, using as a cost function the unsupervised measure FRC [13]. Given the optimum σ value according to FRC, a post-processing stage is employed, which consists in relabeling clusters that are split into different groups. The proposed WGKS scheme is shown in Fig.1.

Two different experiments are performed. The first one aims to prove the effectiveness of the proposed WGKS approach when incorporating more information into the segmentation process with automatic parameter selection. To this end, image 388016 (blond-girl) of the Berkeley dataset is used. The WGKS segmentation result over blond-girl image is compared against GKS (WGKS with all equal weigths), and against traditional KN-Kmeans computing a gaussian kernel just over the RGB components. The attained segmentation results for blond-girl image are shown in Fig. 2, and the obtained relevance weights for WGKS are shown in Fig. 3.

The second kind of experiments are performed to compare the WGKS algorithm against a traditional image segmentation algorithm named Edge Detection and Image Segmentation System (EDISON), which is a low-level feature extraction tool that integrates confidence based edge detection and mean shift-based image segmentation [4]. The EDISON system has been widely used as a reference to compare image segmentation approaches [17,10]. For testing, the parameters of the EDISON system: scale bandwidth (b_s) and color bandwidth (b_c), are set as suggested in [10]. 50 randomly selected images from the Berkeley database are

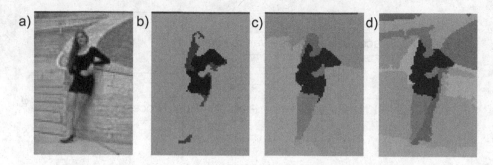

Fig. 2. a) Original Image, b) Single Gaussian Kernel RGB, c) GKS (WGKS Equally Weighted), d) WGKS

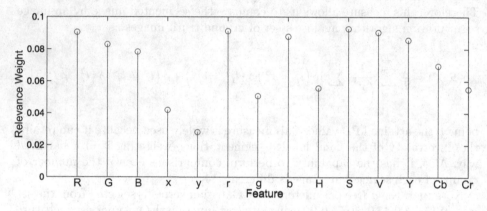

Fig. 3. Weight Selection by Relevance Feature Analysis for blond-girl Image 388016

used. The PR results for the second kind of experiments are presented in Fig. 4. Moreover, the mean estimated number of groups and the mean PR accuracy for all the 50 tested images are described in Table 1. Finally, some relevant results of the studied images are shown in Table 2 and Fig. 5.

Table 1. Segmentation Performance for 50 images drawn from the database

Method	k	ϕ
EDISON1	79.68 ± 47.65	0.660 ± 0.191
EDISON2	21.68 ± 25.53	0.473 ± 0.208
EDISON3	54.68 ± 43.46	0.589 ± 0.205
WGKS	9.862 ± 4.412	$\mathbf{0.742 \pm 0.142}$

k : Number of Groups, ϕ : PR measure.

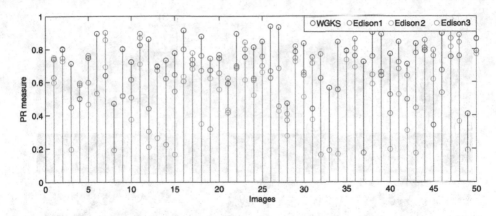

Fig. 4. Image segmentation results for 50 images. WGKS(b). EDISON1(r), EDISON2(g), EDISON3(m), are EDISON segmentation results using ($b_s = 7, 7, 20$) and ($b_c = 7, 15, 7$) respectively.

Table 2. Segmentation Performance for Images of Fig. 5

Method		a	b	c	d	e	f
EDISON	k	100	61	76	43	32	46
	ϕ	0.659	0.671	0.532	0.666	0.456	0.554
WGK	k	8	6	4	4	9	10
	ϕ	0.890	0.894	0.897	0.936	0.932	0.842

k : Number of Groups, ϕ : PR measure.

5   Discussion

From the image segmentation results attained for the blond-girl image, it can be seen how the single Gaussian kernel based segmentation using only RGB components poorly performs, lacking of extra information that could improves the estimation of the number of groups and the Kn-Kmeans clustering (see Fig. 2 b). The latter can be corroborated by a PR measure of 0.055. When the spatial and color spaces information are incorporated into the spectral clustering algorithm based on MKL, the performance improves dramatically, obtaining a PR or 0.721 (see Fig. 2 c). Finally, using the proposed WGKS methodology, the best result is achieved obtaining a PR of 0.774. It can be explained by the estimated weights using the relevance analysis, which allows to identify the most relevant features, avoiding redundant information which could affects the pixel representation (see Fig. 2 d).

The results for the 50 images are exposed in Fig.4. For the EDISON system 3 different combinations of parameters are used. The first combination (EDISON1) is set as $b_s = 7$ and $b_c = 7$, the second one as (EDISON2) $b_s = 7$ and $b_c = 15$ and the last one a as (EDISON3) $b_s = 20$ and $b_c = 7$. From the figure it can be observed that our methodology obtains the best results in most of the cases,

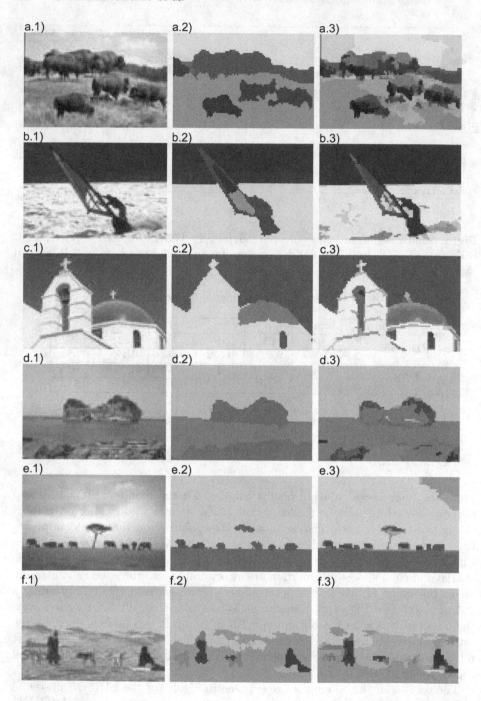

Fig. 5. Image segmentation results. (1) Original Images. (2) WGK. (3) EDISON.

obtaining the first place for 29 images, while EDISON 1 for 16. In Table 1 are exposed the mean results for the 50 images, it can be seen that the WGKS algorithm obtains the best results with the highest mean PR measure 0.742, furthermore, obtains the best stability for all images having the lowest standard deviation 0.142. It also can be seen that the EDISON system always obtains over-segmented results, generating a large amount of groups for each image, whereas the proposed algorithm can correctly identify the number of objects in the scene in most of the cases, it can be explained by the estimation of groups made by the eigenvalue analysis of the weighted linear kernel.

Image segmentation results attained by WGKS mehtodology, and EDISON system using $b_s = 7$ and $b_c = 7$ shown in Fig. 5 demonstrate that the proposed methodology produces more accurate and better segmentation results than the EDISON system, which clearly generate over-segmented images. The results in Table 2 expose that according to the PR measure, WGKS methodology generate very similar segmentations as those realized by each human person, identifying the objects present in the scene. By the other hand, EDISON system generates a large amount of groups for each image, hence, the PR measure penalizes the results, whereas the group estimation of our method was accurate for all images. It is important to note that all the approaches based on spectral techniques require a high computational cost due to the similarity matrix estimation.

6   Conclusions

We have proposed a grouping-based methodology for image segmentation called WGKS, which aims to incorporate different information sources by means of a MKL approach, each information source is weighted using a relevance analysis and a Kernel Kmeans algorithm is used to segment the resulting kernel. Experiments showed that the weighted incorporation of spatial and different color spaces information can enhance the data separability for further spectral clustering procedures. The attained results also showed that the estimation of the number of groups made by means of the eigenvalue analysis of the weighted linear kernel was accurate, supporting the performance of the spectral clustering algorithm. Moreover, the use of the FRC measure gave an effective feedback for the correct selection of the kernel bandwidth. As a future work, other different free parameter estimations are to be studied, as well as the extension for temporal analysis is to be designed such that the WGKS methodology can be performed and tested into a complete computer vision process. Furthermore, due to the complexity of the proposed WGKS, a GPU computation scheme could be proposed in order to achieve a real-time application over full size images.

Acknowledgments. This research was carried out under grants provided by a Msc. and two PhD. scholarships, and the project "ANÁLISIS DE MOVIMIENTO EN SISTEMAS DE VISIÓN POR COMPUTADOR UTILIZANDO APRENDIZAJE DE MÁQUINA", funded by Universidad Nacional de Colombia.

References

1. Ozyildiz, E., Krahnstöver, N., Sharma, R.: Adaptive Texture and Color Segmentation for Tracking Moving Objects. Pattern Recognition 35(10), 2013–2029 (2002)
2. Besl, P., Jain, R.: Three-Dimensional Object Recognition. ACM Computing Surveys 17(1), 75–145 (1985)
3. Canny, J.: A Computational Approach to Edge Detection. IEEE Transactions on Pattern Analysis and Machine Intelligence 8(6), 679–698 (1986)
4. Comaniciu, D., Meer, P.: Mean shift: A robust approach toward feature space analysis. IEEE Transactions on Pattern Analysis and Machine Intelligence 24(5), 603–619 (2002)
5. Daza-Santacoloma, G., Arias-Londoño, J.D., Godino-Llorente, J.I., Sáenz-Lechón, N., Osma-Ruíz, V., Castellanos-Dom'inguez, G.: Dynamic Feature Extraction – An Application to Voice Pathology Detection. Intelligent Automation and Soft Computing 15(4), 667–682 (2009)
6. Dhillon, I., Guan, Y., Kulis, B.: Kernel K-Means – Spectral Clustering and Normalized Cuts. In: 10th ACM SIGKDD International Conference on Knowledge Discovery and Data Mining (KDD 2004), pp. 551–556. ACM (2004)
7. Gonen, M., Alpaydin, E.: Localized Multiple Kernel Regression. In: 20th International Conference on Pattern Recognition (ICPR 2010), pp. 1425–1428. IEEE (2010)
8. Jung, C., Jiao, L., Liu, J., Shen, Y.: Image Segmentation Via Manifold Spectral Clustering. In: 2011 IEEE International Workshop on Machine Learning for Signal Processing (MLSP 2011), pp. 1–6. IEEE (2011)
9. Martin, D., Fowlkes, C., Tal, D., Malik, J.: A Database of Human Segmented Natural Images and its Application to Evaluating Segmentation Algorithms and Measuring Ecological Statistics. In: 8th IEEE International Conference on Computer Vision (ICCV 2001), vol. 2, pp. 416–423. IEEE (2001)
10. Pantofaru, C., Hebert, M.: A Comparison of Image Segmentation Algorithms. Tech. Rep. 336, Robotics Institute (2005)
11. Perona, P., Zelnik-Manor, L.: Self-Tuning Spectral Clustering. Advances in Neural Information Processing Systems 17, 1601–1608 (2004)
12. Rakotomamonjy, A., Bach, F.R., Canu, S., Grandvalet, Y.: SimpleMKL. Journal of Machine Learning Research 9, 2491–2521 (2008)
13. Rosenberger, C., Chehdi, K.: Genetic Fusion – Application to Multi-Components Image Segmentation. In: IEEE International Conference on Acoustics, Speech, and Signal Processing (ICASSP 2000), vol. 6, pp. 2223–2226. IEEE (2000)
14. Unnikrishnan, R., Pantofaru, C., Hebert, M.: A Measure for Objective Evaluation of Image Segmentation Algorithms. In: IEEE Conference on Computer Vision and Pattern Recognition – Workshops (CVPR 2005 Workshops), pp. 34:1–34:8 (2005)
15. Unnikrishnan, R., Pantofaru, C., Hebert, M.: Toward Objective Evaluation of Image Segmentation Algorithms. IEEE Transactions on Pattern Analysis and Machine Intelligence 29(6), 929–944 (2007)
16. Wang, D.: Unsupervised Video Segmentation Based on Watersheds and Temporal Tracking. IEEE Transactions on Circuits and Systems for Video Technology 8(5), 539–546 (1998)
17. Zhang, H., Fritts, J., Goldman, S.: Image Segmentation Evaluation – A Survey of Unsupervised Methods. Computer Vision and Image Understanding 110(2), 260–280 (2008)

Unsupervised Learning of Visual Object Recognition Models

Dulce J. Navarrete, Eduardo F. Morales, and Luis Enrique Sucar

Computer Science Department,
Instituto Nacional de Astrofísica, Óptica y Electrónica.
Luis Enrique Erro 1, 72840 Tonantzintla, México
{dj.navarrete,emorales,esucar}@inaoep.mx

Abstract. Object recognition from images is traditionally based on a large training set of previously annotated images which is impractical for some applications. Also, most methods use only local or global features. Due to the nature of objects some features are better suited for some objects, so researchers have recently combined both types of features to improve the recognition performance. This approach, however, is not sufficient for the recognition of generic objects which can take a wide variety of appearances. In this paper, we propose a novel object recognition system that: (i) uses a small set of images obtained from the Web, (ii) induces a set of models for each object to deal with polymorphism, and (iii) optimizes the contribution of local and global features to deal with different types of objects. We performed tests with both generic and specific objects, and compared the proposed approach against base classifiers and state-of-the-art systems with very promising results.

Keywords: object recognition, global features, local features, few images, multiple-classifiers.

1 Introduction

Consider a service robot that helps elderly people. Mary just acquired such a robot, and will like the robot to fetch a medicine she left in the kitchen and bring it to the bedroom. The robot, however, does not have a visual model of this particular medicine, so it searches for images in the Web, builds a model from a few images and then use this model to recognize it in an image.

Visual object recognition has been an area of research for several decades, in which important advances have been achieved in the last years. However, most object recognition systems: (i) require a large sample of annotated images of the object to be recognized [4], (ii) are usually focused on recognizing a particular class of object (i.e., faces) [6,9,15], (iii) many are based on local features which are good for recognizing specific objects (e.g., my cup) but are not so reliable for object categories (e.g., any cup), and (iv) fail with objects classes that have a high variability (e.g., recognizing apples - different colors, a single apple or a bunch of apples).

J. Pavón et al. (Eds.): IBERAMIA 2012, LNAI 7637, pp. 511–520, 2012.

In this work we have developed a general visual object recognition system that overcomes some of the previous limitations. It incorporates several novel features: (i) It starts with a small set of training images, obtained from the Web, and autonomously expand this initial set with artificial transformations for robustness against changes in scale, rotation and noise. (ii) It builds several classifiers to deal with polymorphism of objects. (iii) It automatically obtains an optimal combination of local and global features to recognize different types of objects.

A classifier ensemble is built for each object based on 12 images obtained with *Google Images*. We compared two selection strategies: (a) unsupervised –the first images returned by the search engine, (b) semi-supervised –a user selects a subset of images from the images returned by the search engine. Then each classifier is evaluated using a different set of positive and negative sample. We evaluated our object recognition system with 10 different objects from past editions of the Semantic Robot Challenge competition (SRVC) [1], that include specific objects and object categories, and with a set of images extracted from Google images used by other authors. The results are promising, with an average recognition rate of approximately 89.5% for specific objects and 78% for object categories. We also compared our method against other state-of-the-art systems trained with Web images. We obtained a clear superior performance, in terms of F-measure, using their same set of training images.

The rest of the paper is organized as follows. The next section summarizes related work. Section 3 describes the proposed method for object recognition and Sect. 4 presents the experiments and results. Finally, we conclude with directions for future work.

2   Related Work

The field of object recognition is very wide, so we focus on the most closely related work in 3 areas: (i) techniques that combine global and local features, (ii) methods based on multiple classifiers, and (iii) systems that make use of training images obtained from the Web.

Most object recognition methods are based either on global or local features (we do not consider in this review *structured* techniques). Global methods usually include color, texture and shape features, and are traditionally used for recognizing object categories. Local or key-point based methods model an object based on local descriptors and are more appropriate for recognizing specific objects [12], although recently there have been some extensions to recognize object categories [3]. There are few works that combine both types of features. In [10] they use global shape features, Fourier Descriptors combined with SIFT descriptors to help in improving the performance of object class recognition. In [18], the authors combine the advantages of appearance-based methods and key-point descriptors. First key-points are used for eliminating false matches, and then Local Binary Patterns confirm the match.

Recently, classifier ensembles have shown superior performance in several domains. In [14] a meta-level classifier produced the best results from nearest-neighbor classifiers that combined local and global features. In [8] the authors describe two alternative techniques for recognizing marine objects, one based on stacking and other on a hierarchical classifier, combining global and local features. In [7] the authors show a method based on hierarchical Dirichlet processes to generate intermediate mixture components for recognition and categorization.

Unsupervised object categorization relies on samples collected from the Web, some representative examples are [4,11,17]. Fergus et al. [4] apply probabilistic clustering methods to discover a mixture of visual topics in a collection of semi-organized image data.

Curious George [11] is a robot develop for the SRVC competition. Its object recognition component uses images retrieved from Computer Vision databases in the Web to build several classifiers based on SIFT features, shape and deformable parts models; which are combined for object recognition.

In [17] the authors propose an unsupervised learning algorithm for visual categories using potential images obtained from the web building on the work by Bunescu and Mooney [2]. The idea is to obtain several images by translating the category name into different languages and searching the web for images using those translated terms. The negative examples are collected from random images with obtained from different categories. They consider the fact that at least one of the positive images is truly a positive instance of the target concept while all the negative examples can be safely considered as negative instances of the target concept.

A multi-modal approach using text, metadata and visual features is used in [16]. Candidate images are obtained by a text-based web search querying on the object identier. The task is then to remove irrelevant images and re-rank the remainder. First, the images are re-ranked using a Bayes posterior estimator trained on the text surrounding the image and meta data features, and then the top-ranked images are improved by eliminating drawings and symbolic images using an SVM classifier previously trained with a hand labeled dataset.

Our unsupervised object recognition approach differs in three main aspects from previous work. It uses a smaller sample set of images which is expanded via transformations; this reduces the risk of introducing irrelevant images. It includes a learning mechanism that creates various visual models of the same category to deal with intraclass variability. It automatically weights the contribution of local and global features according to the object characteristics, as well as the rest of the model parameters via cross-validation.

3   Methodology

The general outline of the procedure for building a classification model for an object (specific or category) is the following (see Fig. 1):

1. A set of C training images for the *concept* to be learned are retrieved from the Web using Google Images.

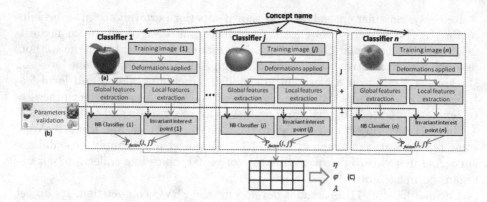

Fig. 1. Schematic representation of the object recognition system. A set of n classifiers is built, one for each sample image, generating d new images from each sample by applying different transformations. Global and local features are extracted from each image, and based on these two classifiers are trained, and combined. The parameters of the model are obtained via cross validation.

2. A series of transformations are applied to each training image, obtaining $|C|$ sets of d images each.
3. Global (color and texture) and local (SIFT key-points) features are extracted from each image in the extended training set ($C \times d$ images).
4. Two classifiers are trained for each of the $|C|$ sets of d images, one with the global features and other based on SIFT descriptors, so in total $2 \times C$ classifiers are obtained.
5. The local and global classifiers for each of the $|C|$ subsets are integrated via a linear weighted combination.
6. The set of $|C|$ classifiers are combined using a voting scheme.
7. The model parameters –weights for the linear combination of local and global features, thresholds for each classifier, and threshold for the combination of classifiers– are determined via cross-validation for each object.

Image Transformations

Inspired by [13], we generate several images from each sample (model) image via different transformations. This provides a training set for building a classifier for each model image. It also allows to select robust local features that are invariant to these transformations. The transformations include: (i) additive Gaussian noise, (ii) salt and pepper noise, (iii) rotations, (iv) changes in scale, and (v) changes in intensity. Five different levels are used for each transformation, so in total $5 \times 5 = 25$ images are generated.

Object Representation – Global and Local Features

An object is represented by a combination of global and local features extracted from the training images.

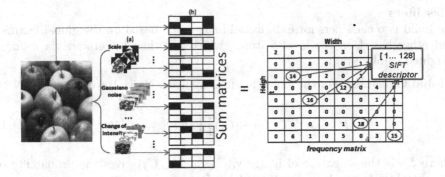

Fig. 2. SIFT key-points are obtained for the original image and the images obtained under the different transformations (scale, noise, intensity, etc.). The frequency of each point is collected in a *frequency matrix* and those points with higher frequency are selected as local features.

Global Features: Include color and texture information. To avoid the requirement of object segmentation we do not consider shape in this work. As color features we combine three different color models – RGB, HSV and CieLab , each is represented via a normalized histogram with 20 bins per channel.

As texture descriptors we used a Grey Level Co-occurrence Matrix (GLCM) and Gabor Filters. A GLCM is obtained for 4 different angles (0 , $\pi/4$, $\pi/2$ and $3\pi/4$), and for each one several statistical descriptors are obtained –contrast, correlation, energy and homogeneity. This gives $4 \times 4 = 16$ features. Gabor filters [5] are applied at the same 4 angles and with two different wavelengths, so in total there are 8 filters; for each one we obtain the mean and variance. This gives another $8 \times 2 = 16$ features.

The global feature vector has $3 \times 3 \times 20 = 180$ color descriptors and $16 + 16 = 32$ texture descriptors, which gives a total of 212 features. Considering that in the sample images usually the object of interest is approximately centered, we restrict the calculation of the global features to a central window of the image.

Local Features: As local features we use the SIFT descriptor [9]. The SIFT features are obtained for a sample image and all the transformations (25 images). For each SIFT point we count the number of repetitions in the set of images, and we select those that are preserved in at least v transformed images (in the experiments we set $v = 5$). To detect the matching SIFT points across the modified images, we obtain the coordinates of each key-point in the original model image, and these coordinates are geometrically mapped to the other images according to the corresponding transformation. With this process we obtain a set of *robust* SIFT descriptors for each model image, stable against affine transformations, noise and illumination variations. This process is illustrated in Fig. 2.

Classifiers

We build two classifiers for each model image, one based on the global features and other based on the local features, which are then integrated via a linear weighted combination.

Global Classifier: For the global features we use a Naïve Bayes classifier (NB):

$$P_{Global}(V_i, C_j) = P(C_j) \prod_{k=1}^{z} P(F_{ik} = f_{ik} | C_j) \tag{1}$$

where f_{ik} is the k feature of image V_i. $P_{Global}(V_i, C_j)$ gives the probability of concept C_j in image V_i given the z global features.

Local Classifier: For the local features we estimate the probability of concept C_j in image V_i based on the number of matching key-points between the model and test images (#matches). This probability, $P_{Local}(V_i, C_j)$, is estimated as:

$$P_{Local}(V_i, C_j) = \begin{cases} 1 - \frac{1}{\#matches+1}, & \#matches > 0 \\ 0.001, & \#matches = 0 \end{cases} \tag{2}$$

Classifier Combination: Local and global probabilities are combined via a weighted sum:

$$P_{fusion}(V_i, C_j) = \lambda P_{Global}(V_i, C_j) + (1 - \lambda) P_{Local}(V_i, C_j) \tag{3}$$

where λ is a parameter that gives different weight to the global or local features. A positive decision is obtained for classifier j if $P_{fusion}(V_i, C_j) > \eta$:

$$C_{decision}(V_i, C_j) = \begin{cases} 1, & P_{fusion}(V_i, C_j) \geqslant \eta \\ 0, & otherwise \end{cases} \tag{4}$$

This combined probability is obtained for each of the $| C |$ original training images. Thus, for a test image V_i, we obtain $P_{fusion}(V_i, C_j)$ for $j = 1.. | C |$. This process is depicted in Fig. 3. Finally, an object is recognized if at least φ classifiers give a positive classification:

$$R_{object}(V_i) = \begin{cases} 1, & \sum_{j=1}^{|C|} C_{decision}(V_i, C_j) \geqslant \varphi \\ 0, & otherwise \end{cases} \tag{5}$$

Parameter Adjustment: The model has 3 main parameters: (i) **Local-global Weight** ($\lambda : 0..1$) it determines the weight for the local vs. global features for each of the $| C |$ classifiers. (ii) **Classification Threshold** ($\eta : 0..1$) it sets the probability threshold so that each classifier gives a positive result if $P_{Global} > \eta$. (iii) **Recognition Threshold** ($\varphi : 1..|C|$) global threshold for combining the C classifiers, an object is recognized if at least φ classifiers give a positive classification.

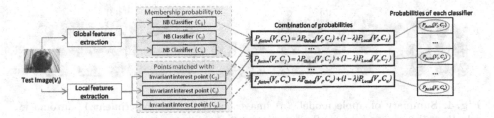

Fig. 3. For each test image the global and local features are extracted and from these the local and global probabilities are estimated based on the corresponding classifier, and then combined. This is repeated for each of the model images, obtaining $\mid C \mid$ probabilities.

The values of these parameters are automatically obtained by cross-validation in a set of validation images (also retrieved from the Web) to maximize the accuracy in the validation set.

4   Experiments and Results

We evaluated the proposed method in the recognition of some of the objects used in SRVC [1]. A robot is given several concepts that correspond to specific objects or object categories, and it has to search in the Web and build a model to recognize the objects in its environment. Thus, this competition provides a good testbed for our method. However, we can not make a direct comparison with competitors of SRVC, as they perform their tests in real environments[1] and we on images extracted from the Web.

We consider 10 objects from the SRVC, 5 specific (Colgate Total, Pepsi bottle, Coca-Cola can, Shrek DVD and Ritz crackers) and 5 categories (apple, banana, frying pan, white soccer ball, and eyeglasses). For each concept we used 12 positive examples for training obtained with Google Images, and 26 negative examples (images of indoor environments considering that a robot will search for the objects in this type of scenarios). Another 6 positive and negative examples (obtained from Web) are used as the validation set for tuning the parameters of the method. We used *precision, recall* and *accuracy* to quantitatively evaluate the performance of our method.

We performed two experiments. In Experiment 1 we used as training images the first 12 images returned by Google Images. For Experiment 2 we have a semisupervised scenario, where a person selects the training images among those 50 returned by the search engine. This could be a reasonable approach in some applications where a human can give some feedback to the robot (similar to intermediate relevance feedback). For testing we consider 40 new examples, 20 positive and 20 negative retrieved with Google Images (selected by a user).

---

[1] Their best reported results are in the order of 40% for object recognition in the competition.

Fig. 4. Summary of apple model. (a) images used for the experiment 1: automatic selection. (b) images used for the experiment 2: semi-supervised. (c) examples used as validation. (d) images of test for model.

We compared our method against three different base classifiers. First, building a classifier using only the global information from the training set. Second, storing all the local information (SIFT features) from all the training set and checking if a testing image matches any of the stored features. Third, combining local and global information with equal weight to both features. The results are summarized in Table 1.

From this table, it can be seen that the proposed approach very clearly outperforms the other base classifiers in terms of precision and accuracy. So it is evident that combining local and global features with an adjusted weight, depending on the characteristics of the images, and generating artificial images proves to be beneficial.In terms of the results for recall, although our proposed approach presents lower results, it should be noted that this can be explained as some results from the other classifiers are close to 100% but with a precision close to 50%, which means that they are building trivial classifiers that accept every image as positive.

As expected, the results for specific objects are higher (89.5% in Accuracy) than for general objects (78% in Accuracy). Also, better results are obtained

Table 1. Experimental results for the testing set in both scenarios. Using only global information (G), using only local information (L), combining both with equal weight (GL), and the proposed approach (GLM).

Experiment 1: Automatic selection

	Apple G	L	GL	GLM	Banana G	L	GL	GLM	Eyeglasses G	L	GL	GLM	Frying pan G	L	GL	GLM	White soccer ball G	L	GL	GLM	Average G	L	GL	GLM
Precision	57	60	52	64	70	57	57	69	59	51	58	89	53	46	52	71	60	51	52	80	60	53	54	**75**
Recall	100	90	55	55	70	20	75	80	95	90	100	80	100	80	100	75	85	76	100	80	**90**	71	86	74
Accuracy	63	65	52	63	70	53	60	72	65	52	65	85	55	43	55	73	58	85	72	95	64	53	57	**75**

	Coca Cola can G	L	GL	GLM	Colgate Total G	L	GL	GLM	DVD Shrek G	L	GL	GLM	Pepsi bottle G	L	GL	GLM	Ritz crackers G	L	GL	GLM	Average G	L	GL	GLM
Precision	54	88	62	89	51	78	74	100	63	76	60	93	54	64	60	80	54	85	64	100	55	78	64	**92**
Recall	100	75	100	85	100	90	100	90	100	95	100	70	100	55	100	60	100	85	100	90	**100**	80	**100**	79
Accuracy	58	82	70	88	53	82	82	95	70	83	67	83	58	62	67	73	58	85	72	95	59	79	72	**87**

Experiment 2: semi-supervised

	Apple G	L	GL	GLM	Banana G	L	GL	GLM	Eyeglasses G	L	GL	GLM	Frying pan G	L	GL	GLM	White soccer ball G	L	GL	GLM	Average G	L	GL	GLM
Precision	50	57	52	77	54	48	54	71	51	75	55	100	53	57	54	74	50	55	51	81	52	58	53	**81**
Recall	100	100	100	85	100	85	100	100	100	75	100	80	100	100	100	70	95	90	100	86	96	90	**100**	84
Accuracy	50	63	55	80	58	47	57	80	53	75	60	90	55	63	57	72	50	58	52	83	53	61	56	**81**

	Coca Cola can G	L	GL	GLM	Colgate Total G	L	GL	GLM	DVD Shrek G	L	GL	GLM	Pepsi bottle G	L	GL	GLM	Ritz crackers G	L	GL	GLM	Average G	L	GL	GLM
Precision	51	76	66	100	54	75	83	100	56	83	76	89	57	61	62	89	54	86	68	95	54	76	71	**95**
Recall	100	80	100	80	100	90	100	95	100	95	95	85	100	40	100	80	100	95	100	100	**100**	80	99	88
Accuracy	53	77	75	90	58	80	90	98	60	88	82	88	63	57	70	85	57	90	78	98	58	78	79	**92**

Table 2. Experiments with the same objects reported in [16,17] in terms of F-measure. *sMIL* is the method reported in [17], and *Schoroff* is the method reported in [16].

	Airplane			Guitar			Leopard			Motorbike		
	GLM	sMIL	Schoroff	GLM	sMIL	Schoroff	GLM	sMIL	Schoroff	GLM	sMIL	Schoroff
F-measure	41	26	23	51	23	25	50	24	25	72	25	25

	Watch			Car			Fase		
	GLM	sMIL	Schoroff	GLM	sMIL	Schoroff	GLM	sMIL	Schoroff
F-measure	60	26	25	52	25	n.a.	52	23	n.a.

with the semi-supervised experiments (86.5%) than with the automatic selection (81%). We believe that these results (average global accuracy of 83.75%) are very promising as the system only receives the name of the object (with a possible selection of relevant images by the user) and has to recognize an unknown instance of that object in new images.

We should emphasize, that contrary to traditional datasets used in the many computer vision tasks, we are using images obtained directly from the Web.

We also performed experiments with the same dataset that was used in [17] and in [16] with images extracted as well from Google Images. Our approach was trained with the first 12 images (for each category) from Google Downloads [4] and tested with Caltech-7. We compared the performance of those two approaches with our own in terms of F-measure and using, as they did, 5-fold cross validation. For this experiment the 12 validation samples are obtained from Google Downloads. The results are shown in Table 2.

We can appreciate, from the results shown in the Table 2, that our approach is clearly superior to the other related work using their training images.

5 Conclusions and Future Work

Object recognition without the need of supervised training and considering different appearances is still a challenging problem. In this work we have presented an approach based on multiple-classifiers that can recognize an unknown instance of an object given only the name of the object. The proposed approach obtains a small set of images from the Web, creates variants of those images for robustness against changes in scale, rotation and noise, induces several classifiers to deal with polymorphism of objects, extracts global and local features and obtains an optimal combination to recognize different types of objects. We performed several experiments with specific and generic objects and compared the proposed approach against base classifiers and state-of-the-art systems with very promising results. As future work, we plan to implement the system on a mobile robot to test our approach in a real environment. We also plan to test the sensitivity of our method according to the number of model images.

References

1. The Semantic Robot Vision Challenge (2011),
   http://www.semantic-robot-vision-challenge.org/

2. Bunescu, R.C., Mooney, R.J.: Multiple Instance Learning for Sparse Positive Bags. In: 24th International Conference on Machine Learning (ICML 2007), pp. 105–112. ACM (2007)
3. Chang, L., Duarte, M., Sucar, L., Morales, E.: A Bayesian Approach for Object Classification Based on Clusters of SIFT Local Features. Expert Systems With Applications 39(2), 1679–1686 (2012)
4. Fergus, R., Fei-Fei, L., Perona, P., Zisserman, A.: Learning Object Categories from Google"s Image Search. In: 10th IEEE International Conference on Computer Vision (ICCV 2005), vol. 2, pp. 1816–1823. IEEE (2005)
5. Gabor, D.: Theory of Communication. Journal of the Institution of Electrical Engineers-Part III: Radio and Communication Engineering 93(26), 429–441 (1946)
6. Grimson, W., Huttenlocher, D.: On the Sensitivity of the Hough Transform for Object Recognition. IEEE Transactions on Pattern Analysis and Machine Intelligence 12(3), 255–274 (1990)
7. Ji, Y., Idrissi, K., Baskurt, A.: Object Categorization Using Boosting Within Hierarchical Bayesian Model. In: 16th IEEE International Conference on Image Processing (ICIP 2009), pp. 317–320. IEEE (2009)
8. Lisin, D., Mattar, M., Blaschko, M., Learned-Miller, E., Benfield, M.: Combining Local and Global Image Features for Object Class Recognition. In: IEEE Computer Society Conference on Computer Vision and Pattern Recognition (CVPR 2005) - Workshops, vol. 03, pp. 47–54. IEEE (2005)
9. Lowe, D.: Distinctive Image Features from Scale-Invariant Keypoints. International Journal of Computer Vision 60(2), 91–110 (2004)
10. Manshor, N., Rajeswari, M., Ramachandram, D.: Multi-Feature Based Object Class Recognition. In: International Conference on Digital Image Processing (ICDIP 2009), pp. 324–329. IEEE (2009)
11. Meger, D., Muja, M., Helmer, S., Gupta, A., Gamroth, C., Hoffman, T., Baumann, M., Southey, T., Fazli, P., Wohlkinger, W., Viswanathan, P., Little, J., Lowe, D., Orwell, J.: Curious George – An Integrated Visual Search Platform. In: Canadian Conf. on Computer and Robot Vision (CRV 2010), pp. 107–114. IEEE (2010)
12. Mikolajczyk, K., Schmid, C.: A Performance Evaluation of Local Descriptors. IEEE Transactions on Pattern Analysis & Machine Intelligence 27(10), 1615–1630 (2005)
13. Ozuysal, M., Calonder, M., Lepetit, V., Fua, P.: Fast Keypoint Recognition Using Random Ferns. IEEE Transactions on Pattern Analysis and Machine Intelligence 32(3), 448–461 (2010)
14. Pereira, R., Lopes, L.S.: Learning Visual Object Categories with Global Descriptors and Local Features. In: Lopes, L.S., Lau, N., Mariano, P., Rocha, L.M. (eds.) EPIA 2009. LNCS, vol. 5816, pp. 225–236. Springer, Heidelberg (2009)
15. Rothganger, F., Lazebnik, S., Schmid, C., Ponce, J.: 3D Object Modeling and Recognition Using Affine-Invariant Patches and Multi-View Spatial Constraints. In: IEEE Computer Society Conference on Computer Vision and Pattern Recognition (CVPR 2003), vol. 2, pp. 272–277. IEEE (2003)
16. Schroff, F., Criminisi, A., Zisserman, A.: Harvesting Image Databases from the Web. In: 11th International Conference on Computer Vision (ICCV 2007), pp. 1–8. IEEE (2007)
17. Vijayanarasimhan, S., Grauman, K.: Keywords to Visual Categories – Multiple-Instance Learning for Weakly Supervised Object Categorization. In: IEEE Conf. on Computer Vision and Pattern Recognition (CVPR 2008), pp. 1–8. IEEE (2008)
18. Wang, Y., Hou, Z., Leman, K., Pham, N.T., Chua, T.W., Chang, R.: Combination of Local and Global Features for Near-Duplicate Detection. In: Lee, K.T., et al. (eds.) MMM 2011 Part I. LNCS, vol. 6523, pp. 328–338. Springer, Heidelberg (2011)

Hierarchical Markov Random Fields with Irregular Pyramids for Improving Image Annotation

Annette Morales-González[1], Edel García-Reyes[1], and Luis Enrique Sucar[2]

[1] Advanced Technologies Application Center. 7a # 21812 b/ 218 and 222,
Rpto. Siboney, Playa, P.C. 12200, La Habana, Cuba
{amorales,egarcia}@cenatav.co.cu
[2] Instituto Nacional de Astrofísica, Óptica y Electrónica, Puebla, Mexico
esucar@ccc.inaoep.mx

Abstract. Image segmentation and Automatic Image Annotation (AIA) are two important areas that still impose challenging problems. Addressing both problems simultaneously may improve their results since they are interdependent. In this paper we give a step ahead in that direction considering different segmentation levels simultaneously and possible contextual relations among segments in order to improve the automatic image annotation. We propose to include hierarchical relations among regions of an image in a Markov Random Field (MRF) model for annotation. This relations are obtained from irregular pyramids, which keep parent-child relations among regions through all the levels. Our main contribution is therefore the combination of the irregular pyramid approach with context modeling by means of hierarchical MRFs. Experiments run in a subset of the Corel image collection showed a relevant improvement in the annotation accuracy.

Keywords: Automatic image annotation, Markov random fields, irregular pyramids.

1 Introduction

Image segmentation and Automatic Image Annotation (AIA) are very important research areas in computer vision due to their relevance for many applications, such as image retrieval and scene understanding. However, the problems that arise in both fields are frequently addressed independently, disregarding the relation between them. Both fields suffer from the well-known semantic gap between low level image features and high level concepts, which is still a struggling point for researchers world-wide. Addressing both problems simultaneously may help closing the semantic gap and solving both more effectively.

Several approaches have been proposed in order to reduce the semantic gap. Probabilistic graphical models are a promising alternative used with the purpose of modeling in a more realistic fashion the context-dependent relations among

J. Pavón et al. (Eds.): IBERAMIA 2012, LNAI 7637, pp. 521–530, 2012.
© Springer-Verlag Berlin Heidelberg 2012

data. In particular, Markov Random Fields (MRF) [13] are employed in computer vision due to the possibility of modeling spatial neighborhood relations in images.

MRFs have been used for AIA in several works. In [15], a multiple MRF is proposed, where, instead of building a single MRF, they construct one MRF for each keyword in the vocabulary to capture different semantics among keywords. The proposal of [10] explores dependencies among features and several words. In [5] and [7], the co-occurrence information among words and the probabilities of occurrence of spatial relations between pairs of words respectively are used as interaction potential in an MRF model. While these approaches have focused on exploring dependencies among features and words, and between neighboring pairs of words, we propose to explore hierarchical relations among different segmentation levels of an image. Using hierarchies with MRF models is not a new idea. In [8] they propose a segmentation method using two levels of a hierarchy, where the region classification is performed independently at each level, and later combined within the MRF model. It has been used also for texture segmentation and denoising [9,3], where the hierarchy consists on two or three layers representing different characteristics of the image. The main difference with our proposal is that we will use a hierarchy of image partitions (represented as graphs) at different levels of resolution, and we will construct a MRF at each level that will be fed with the MRF information computed in adjacent levels, for the purpose of improving image annotation.

To obtain a hierarchical representation of images, we use irregular pyramids [1], which are hierarchical structures formed by combinatorial maps. The combinatorial map at each level of the pyramid is equivalent to a Region Adjacency Graph (RAG) [2] relative to a partition of the image. Irregular pyramids provide hierarchical relations among regions found at different levels, and topological relations among regions of the same level.

Our main contribution is therefore the combination of the irregular pyramid segmentation approach with context modeling for improving automatic image annotation. This involves using an additional potential in a MRF model, taking into account the hierarchical information among regions at different levels of the pyramid. A MRF will be modeled for each level of the pyramid, taking into account the initial labels (annotated with a base classifier) and contextual (hierarchical and spatial) relations among image regions. The best configuration of labels for each level will be computed in a bottom-top (taking information from lower levels) and top-bottom (taking information from lower and higher levels at the same time) processes, thus refining the initial annotation. Experiments performed in a subset of the Corel image collection showed that the proposal (called HMRF-Pyr) can clearly improve the annotation results and revealed the advantages of using hierarchical relations.

The remainder of this paper is as follows. Section 2 provides an overview of irregular pyramids. In Sect. 3 we present basic concepts regarding MRFs. The proposed approach is presented in Sect. 4, followed by the experimental evaluation in Sect. 5. Finally we present the conclusions and future work.

2   Irregular Pyramids Overview

An irregular graph pyramid is a stack of successively reduced graphs (being the base level the high resolution input image). In these graphs $G = (V, E)$ the vertices (V) represent cells or regions, and the edges (E) represent neighborhood relations of the regions. When we build an irregular pyramid from an image, each level represents a partition of the pixel set into cells, i.e. connected subsets of pixels. On the base level (level 0) of the pyramid, the cells represent single pixels and the neighborhood of the cells is defined by the 4-connectivity of pixels. A cell on level k (parent) is a union of neighboring cells on level $k - 1$ (children) [6]. Each graph is built from the graph below by selecting a set of surviving vertices and mapping each non surviving vertex to a surviving one. In this way, each surviving vertex represents all the non surviving vertices mapped to it and becomes their father [6]. This parent-child relations may be iterated down to the base level and the set of descendants of one vertex in the base level is named its receptive field (RF). Some of these concepts are illustrated in Fig. 1.

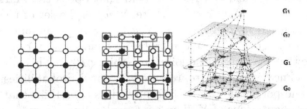

Fig. 1. Construction of the irregular pyramid. (a) Set of surviving vertices, depicted in black, (b) contraction kernels for this set and (c) irregular pyramid built using the contraction kernels from b.

Within the irregular pyramid framework the reduction process is performed by a set of edge contractions. The edge contraction collapses two adjacent vertices into one vertex and removes the edge. This set is called a Contraction Kernel (CK) [2]. The contraction of the graph reduces the number of vertices while maintaining the connections to other vertices.

This pyramid is able to represent several topological relations between regions. Besides the classical adjacency relationship encoded by the Region Adjacency Graph (RAG), each graph may also contain parallel edges and self-loops, representing several common boundaries and inclusion relations respectively [2].

Combinatorial pyramids [2] are introduced in order to properly characterize the inclusion relationship, which cannot be fully represented using graphs. In this case, the edges orientation around a vertex is needed. A Combinatorial Map (CM) may be understood as a planar graph encoding explicitly the orientation of edges called darts, each dart having its origin at the vertex it is attached to. A CM can be defined as $G = (D, \sigma, \alpha)$, where D is a set of darts (an edge connecting two vertices is composed of two darts $d1$ and $d2$, each dart belonging to only one vertex), α is the reverse permutation which maps $d1$ to $d2$ and $d2$ to $d1$ and σ is the successor permutation which encodes the sequence of darts encountered when moving around a vertex [2]. A combinatorial pyramid is then a stack of successively reduced combinatorial maps, having the advantages that each CM explicitly encodes the orientation of darts around each vertex

3 Markov Random Fields

Intuitively, Markov Random Fields [13] are undirected graphical models that combine information from a set of observations, and interaction information obtained by the relation with neighbors. Formally, we can say that $Y = \{Y_1, Y_2, ..., Y_n\}$ is called a random field, being Y_i random variables on a set of sites S, that can take values y_i in a set of labels L. This can be depicted as an undirected graph, where each vertex i represents the random variable Y_i and the edges represent direct dependence relations between variables. Henceforth, the terms "vertex" and "variable" shall be used interchangeably.

A Markov Random Field is a random field that obeys the Markov property $P(y_i|y_{i-1}, y_{i-2}, ..., y_1) = P(y_i|N(y_i))$, where $N(y_i)$ is the set of neighbors of y_i. This means that given its neighbor set $N(y_i)$, a vertex i is independent of all other vertices in the graph. The most probable configuration of labels Y^* for a MRF is the one that maximizes the joint probability $P(y)$. This joint probability is modeled by some restrictions represented by local probabilities, also known as potentials. The potentials can be interpreted as constrains that penalizes or favors certain configurations of Y. The joint probability is expressed as Eq. 1

$$P(y) = \frac{1}{Z} * \exp^{-U_p(y)} \tag{1}$$

where Z is the partition function or normalizing constant and $U_p(y)$ is the energy function. $U_p(y)$ is computed using the aforementioned potentials (Eq. 2).

$$U_p(y) = V_O(y) + \lambda \sum_I V_I(y, y') \tag{2}$$

$V_O(y)$ stands for the association (or unary) potential, which represents information coming from the observations. $V_I(y, y')$ is the interaction (or pairwise) potential and models the information obtained from neighboring vertices (y, y'). λ is a constant introduced to weight the relevance of the restrictions imposed by the potential functions. The Maximum A Posteriori (MAP) optimal configuration Y^* is obtained by minimizing the value of $U_p(y)$. Common methods for achieving this optimal configuration are the Iterated Conditional Modes (ICM), Simulated Annealing and Loopy Belief Propagation (LBP), among others [14].

Although higher order potentials could be used in the model (making y_i dependent on a number O of variables), we prefer to use only unary and pairwise potentials, since higher order potentials largely increase the computational cost for finding the optimal configuration.

4   Proposed Approach

The definition of MRFs (see Sect. 3) and most of its applications in images, deal with two basic relations: the relation of a region feature (observation) with a label, and the relation of neighboring labels. We are proposing to include in this framework a parent-child relationship, driven by the notion that in a hierarchical representation, the children regions may have a trustworthy vote regarding its parent's classification and viceversa.

We propose to build a MRF for each level of the pyramid, starting from bottom to top, and at each level l, the information regarding the best configuration of labels Y^*_{l-1} obtained in level $l-1$ is used as additional information to compute the current level's label configuration Y^*_l. When the top level is reached, the same process is repeated from top to bottom, now using Y^*_{l-1} and Y^*_{l+1} to compute Y^*_l. The MRF for each level will have the same structure of the underlying RAG in the irregular pyramid.

The Markovian neighborhood $N(y^l_i)$ of label y^l_i can be split into two neighborhoods: the spatial neighborhood and the hierarchical neighborhood. The spatial neighborhood of label y^l_i corresponding to vertex i, is composed by the labels assigned to all the vertices adjacent to i in the RAG of level l. The hierarchical neighborhood is formed by all the labels assigned to the Contraction Kernel of vertex i in level $l-1$ and by its parent's label in level $l+1$.

We propose to compute the energy function as depicted in Eq. 3.

$$U_p(y_l) = \lambda_O V_O(y^l_i) + \lambda_I \sum_i V_I(y^l_i, y^l_j) + \lambda_H \left(\sum_{ch} V_{Ch}(y^l_i, y^{l-1}_k) + V_P(y^l_i, y^{l+1}_m) \right)$$
(3)

This is an extension of Eq. 2, introducing $V_{Ch}(y^l_i, y^{l-1}_k)$ as a hierarchical potential that models the relation of label y^l_i (assigned to vertex i of level l of the pyramid) with its child label y^{l-1}_k, and $V_P(y^l_i, y^{l+1}_m)$ that models the relation of y^l_i with its parent label y^{l+1}_m. The label y^{l-1}_k was assigned to vertex k in level $l-1$ of the image pyramid by the MRF computed for this level. Vertex k belongs to the CK (see Sect. 2) of vertex i ($k \in CK(i)$). The observation, interaction and hierarchical potentials are weighted by λ_O, λ_I and λ_H respectively, and $\lambda_O + \lambda_I + \lambda_H = 1$.

Having stated the energy function, we defined each potential as follows. The association potential $V_O(y^l_i)$ is defined as in [5]. We use as base annotation system the k-nearest neighbors (KNN) classifier. In order to rank candidate labels for a given region we use the distance of the test instance to the top k-nearest neighbors as relevance weight. As presented in [5], relevance weighting is obtained using Eq. 4.

$$P^R(y^l_{ij}) = \frac{d_j(x^l_i)}{\sum^k_{n=1} d_n(x^l_i)}, \quad y^l_i \in Y, x^l_i \in X$$
(4)

where $d_j(x_i^l)$ is the Euclidean distance in the attribute space of observation x_j (corresponding to the j-nearest neighbor) to x_i^l (the test instance), being Y the set of labels and X the set of observations.

The association potential is then expressed as in Eq. 5,

$$V_O(y_i^l) = \frac{1}{P^R(y_i^l)} \qquad (5)$$

the interaction potential is defined in Eq. 6,

$$V_I(y_i^l, y_j^l) = \begin{cases} 0 & \text{if } y_i^l = y_j^l \\ 1 & \text{if } y_i^l \neq y_j^l \end{cases} \qquad (6)$$

the potential related with the children information is defined by Eq. 7 and the potential related with the parents information is presented in Eq. 8

$$V_{Ch}(y_i^l, y_k^{l-1}) = \begin{cases} 0 \text{ if } y_i^l = y_k^{l-1} \\ 1 \text{ if } y_i^l \neq y_k^{l-1} \end{cases} \qquad (7) \qquad V_P(y_i^l, y_m^{l+1}) = \begin{cases} 0 \text{ if } y_i^l = y_m^{l+1} \\ 1 \text{ if } y_i^l \neq y_m^{l+1} \end{cases} \qquad (8)$$

where $k \in CK(i)$ and $i \in CK(m)$.

The interaction potential penalizes neighbors with different labels with respect to the current vertex, while hierarchical potentials punish children or parents having different labels than the current vertex. In order to obtain the optimal configuration Y^*, we used the ICM algorithm, which is efficient and, although usually criticized for converging to local minimums, for this case the results were very similar to other more complex methods. This might indicate that for the current problem, ICM is actually converging to the global minimum.

5   Experiments

In order to validate our proposal, we ran experiments on a subset of the Corel image collection. Specifically, we used the CorelA subset developed by [4]. This dataset contains 205 natural scene images split into two subsets with 137 images for training and 68 images for testing. All images have been segmented using normalized cuts [12] and they have been manually annotated with 22 classes.

The irregular pyramids computed for these images have an average of 20 levels. For these experiments we tested all the levels ranging from level 6 to 16, in order to avoid extreme oversegmentations or undersegmentations. Following the idea of [11], we used as visual features for each vertex (region) of each graph, the quantization of the RGB values in 16 bins per channel, yielding a 48-dimensional color histogram, and a local binary pattern (LBP) histogram to characterize texture in the region.

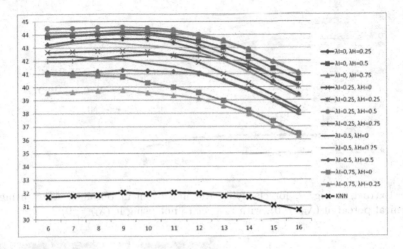

Fig. 2. Accuracy results in the CorelA dataset using different parameter combinations

The experiments were performed using as base annotation system u KNN classifier as implemented in [5]. We used this base classifier in order to be fair in the comparison, sticking to the conditions imposed by [7]. Nevertheless, we believe that, by using a more sophisticated classifier, our results can be improved. Since we used a different segmentation approach than the one used by [7] to label image regions, we measured the accuracy of the annotation at pixel level. Results can be seen in Table 1. The first three rows show the average accuracy over 10 runs obtained using the algorithms for each level of the pyramid. We are comparing the base classifier KNN with our hierarchical MRF approach (HMRF-Pyr) and the traditional MRF approach (without hierarchical relations). In row 4 we can see the relative improvement of HMRF-Pyr with respect to the KNN base classifier and row 5 shows the relative improvement of HMRF-Pyr over MRF. We tested several combinations of λ_O, λ_I and λ_H, having better results with 0.25, 0.25 and 0.5 respectively. This results can be analyzed in Fig. 2. Horizontal axis show the pyramid levels and vertical axis depict annotation accuracy (in %). For clarity, in Fig. 3 we can see an extract of Fig. 2, only showing the best results using the hierarchical information, the best results when this information is not used ($\lambda_H = 0$), and the base classifier KNN results.

In Fig. 4, some segmentation and annotation results can be seen for images of the CorelA set. From these results we can see that the HMRF-Pyr approach involving hierarchical and neighborhood relations improved the annotation accuracy with respect to the base classifier and with respect to the traditional MRF approach. This is consistent with the initial assumption that the annotation of children regions have influence in its father classification and viceversa.

Comparing our approach with other methods that were tested on this dataset, we can see that the highest annotation accuracy obtained by [7] is of 45.64%, while our best result is 44.6% (see Table 2). These results are similar (1 point difference), however some test conditions (segmentation method and low level

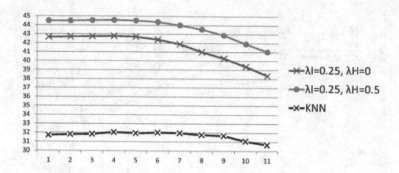

Fig. 3. Extract of Fig. 2, for clarifying the improvement obtained when using the hierarchical potential ($\lambda_H \neq 0$), with respect to not using it ($\lambda_H = 0$)

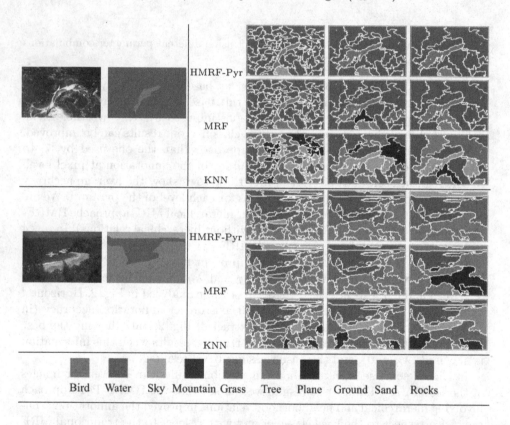

Fig. 4. Examples of Corel image annotation results. First column shows original images with its ground truth annotation mask in second column. Columns 4 to 6 show different pyramid levels. For each image, the first row of levels shows the annotation result with HMRF-Pyr, the second row shows the MRF annotation result and the third one shows the annotation result achieved with KNN. At the bottom we can find a color legend to understand the annotation results (best seen in color).

Table 1. Results obtained in the CorelA subset for each level of the pyramid

Algorithm	Pyramid levels										
	6	7	8	9	10	11	12	13	14	15	16
KNN	31.7%	31.8%	31.8%	32.0%	31.9%	32.0%	31.9%	31.7%	31.6%	31.1%	30.7%
MRF	42.2%	42.3%	42.2%	42.1%	41.8%	41.6%	41.2%	40.3%	39.7%	38.9%	37.9%
HMRF-Pyr	**44.5%**	**44.5%**	**44.5%**	**44.6%**	**44.5%**	44.4%	44.0%	43.5%	42.8%	41.9%	41.0%
Imp. HMRF-Pyr/KNN	12.8%	12.7%	12.7%	12.5%	12.6%	12.3%	12.0%	11.8%	11.2%	10.8%	10.3%
Imp. HMRF-Pyr/MRF	2.2%	2.1%	2.3%	2.5%	2.7%	2.8%	2.9%	3.1%	3.1%	3.0%	3.2%

Table 2. Comparison with other methods in the CorelA subset. Second column shows the accuracy of each algorithm. For those who use a base classifier (KNN), the accuracy of this classifier is shown in third column. Fourth column shows the relative improvement achieved by the algorithms over the base classifier.

Algorithm	Accuracy	KNN accuracy	Imp. from KNN
gML1 [4]	35.7%	-	-
gML1o [4]	36.2%	-	-
gMAP1 [4]	35.7%	-	-
gMAP1MRF [4]	35.7%	-	-
MRFs AREK [7]	45.6%	36.8%	8.8%
HMRF-Pyr	44.6%	32.0%	**12.8%**

features) are different and it is more relevant the gain with respect to the base classifier (last column of Table 2). For them, KNN scored 36.8%, while we obtained 32%. The best improvement for [7] over the base classifier was 8.82%, while our relative improvement is 12.8%. In our opinion, this relative improvement shows the importance of the hierarchical information in problems with context-dependent information, and the relevance of combining segmentation and annotation simultaneously. It can be seen in Fig. 4 that segmentation can be enhanced with annotation, simply by joining regions with the same label.

6 Conclusions

In this paper we proposed an approach that combines irregular pyramid segmentation with image annotation based on Markov Random Fields. MRFs allow to take into account contextual relations when performing the annotation, and we proposed an enhance to this model by using the hierarchical relations among regions of different levels of the irregular pyramid. As experimental results showed, hierarchical information actually provides relevant information to the annotation process, which combined with neighborhood information, can represent an important improvement with respect to the base classifier.

In future work, we have the intention of elaborating a multilevel segmentation/annotation algorithm where the structure of higher levels is modified by the lower levels information.

References

1. Brun, L., Kropatsch, W.: Introduction to Combinatorial Pyramids. In: Bertrand, G., Imiya, A., Klette, R. (eds.) Digital and Image Geometry. LNCS, vol. 2243, pp. 108–128. Springer, Heidelberg (2002)
2. Brun, L., Kropatsch, W.: Contains and Inside Relationships within Combinatorial Pyramids. Pattern Recognition 39(4), 515–526 (2006)
3. Cao, Y., Luo, Y., Yang, S.: Image Denoising Based on Hierarchical Markov Random Field. Pattern Recognition Letters 32(2), 368–374 (2011)
4. Carbonetto, P.: Unsupervised Statistical Models for General Object Recognition. Master's thesis, The Faculty of Graduate Studies, Dept. of Computer Science, Univ. of British Columbia, West Mall Vancouver, BC, Canada (2003)
5. Escalante, H.J., Montes, M., Sucar, E.: Word Co-occurrence and Markov Random Fields for Improving Automatic Image Annotation. In: 18th British Machine Vision Conf. (BMVC 2007), pp. 60.1–60.10 (2007)
6. Haxhimusa, Y., Kropatsch, W.: Segmentation Graph Hierarchies. In: Fred, A., Caelli, T.M., Duin, R.P., Campilho, A.C., de Ridder, D. (eds.) SSPR&SPR 2004. LNCS, vol. 3138, pp. 343–351. Springer, Heidelberg (2004)
7. Hernández-Gracidas, C., Sucar, L.E.: Markov Random Fields and Spatial Information to Improve Automatic Image Annotation. In: Mery, D., Rueda, L. (eds.) PSIVT 2007. LNCS, vol. 4872, pp. 879–892. Springer, Heidelberg (2007)
8. Keuper, M., Schmidt, T., Rodriguez-Franco, M., Schamel, W., Brox, T., Burkhardt, H., Ronneberger, O.: Hierarchical Markov Random Fields for Mast Cell Segmentation in Electron Microscopic Recordings. In: 8th IEEE Intl. Symp. on Biomedical Imaging (ISBI 2011), pp. 973–978. IEEE (2011)
9. Kim, D.H., Yun, I.D., Lee, S.U.: New MRF Parameter Estimation Technique for Texture Image Segmentation Using Hierarchical GMRF Model Based on Random Spatial Interaction and Mean Field Theory. In: 18th Intl. Conf. on Pattern Recognition (ICPR 2006), vol. 2, pp. 365–368. IEEE (2006)
10. Llorente, A., Manmatha, R., Rüger, S.: Image Retrieval Using Markov Random Fields and Global Image Features. In: ACM Intl. Conf. on Image and Video Retrieval (CIVR 2010), pp. 243–250. ACM (2010)
11. Morales-González, A., García-Reyes, E.: Simple Object Recognition Based on Spatial Relations and Visual Features Represented Using Irregular Pyramids. Multimedia Tools and Applications, 1–23 (2011) (in press), http://dx.doi.org/10.1007/s11042-011-0938-3
12. Shi, J., Malik, J.: Normalized Cuts and Image Segmentation. IEEE Transactions on Pattern Analysis and Machine Intelligence 22(8), 888–905 (2000)
13. Spitzer, F.: Random Fields and Interacting Particle Systems. Mathematical Association of America (1971), Notes on Lectures Given at the 1971 MAA Summer Seminar, Williamstown, MA
14. Szeliski, R., Zabih, R., Scharstein, D., Veksler, O., Kolmogorov, V., Agarwala, A., Tappen, M., Rother, C.: A Comparative Study of Energy Minimization Methods for Markov Random Fields with Smoothness-Based Priors. IEEE Transactions on Pattern Analysis and Machine Intelligence 30(6), 1068–1080 (2008)
15. Xiang, Y., Zhou, X., Chua, T., Ngo, C.: A Revisit of Generative Model for Automatic Image Annotation Using Markov Random Fields. In: IEEE Conf. on Computer Vision and Pattern Recognition (CVPR 2009), pp. 1153–1160 (2009)

Towards Automatic 3D Pose Tracking through Polygon Mesh Approximation

Manlio Barajas, Jorge Esparza, and J.L. Gordillo

Center for Intelligent Systems, Tecnológico de Monterrey, Monterrey, México
{mf.barajas.phd.mty,jo.esparza.phd.mty,jlgordillo}@itesm.mx
http://www.itesm.edu

Abstract. A method for visual 3D pose tracking of objects whose shape can be approximated to a polygon mesh it's presented. The proposed method takes advantage of the fact that polygon meshes may be composed of quadrilaterals, which can be tracked in 2D using standard plane tracking for which homography decomposition can be used to recover 3D pose information. Results show that it's feasible to do 3D pose tracking of polygon meshes using only one monocular camera and 2D tracking. This is a first step for a full automatic 3D pose tracking system, since planes can be detected without any priori knowledge using automatic plane detection methods.

Keywords: 3D tracking, 3D pose estimation, approximated 3D models, homography decomposition, cuboid tracking, polyhedral tracking, polygon mesh tracking, visual tracking, automatic object tracking.

1 Introduction

Visual 3D pose estimation of objects in real environments has been an important topic in literature because there are numerous fields which rely on precise localization systems and where the availability of other sensors systems is limited. Common visual approaches depend on depth information by means of stereo setups [9,14] or laser range data [12].

More closely to the visual tracking problem, approaches like [13] use standard tracking techniques with laser data with the objective of tracking more robustly multiple targets.

The application of 3D tracking in vehicle driving context has gained important attention. On one side, the need for dynamic obstacle is key component on autonomous driving [1] and vehicle assistance methods [11], but also out-of-board vehicle tracking is a key component in autonomous driving [6].

3D tracking may be accomplished by using full featured models [3,10] or by using approximated models [6]. While full featured models allow having a very exact representation of the real world entity, in not all situations is well suited having any sort of known 3D model. Approximated models can be used to overcome this constraint.

J. Pavón et al. (Eds.): IBERAMIA 2012, LNAI 7637, pp. 531–540, 2012.

In this work particular interest is set on tracking closed polygon meshes by using only 2D plane tracking. What is presented is a method for 3D tracking of an object that moves in an unknown 3D space. As it will be shown, this results in a very efficient way of tracking while being robust, since well developed plane tracking methods are used.

The use of plane tracking has an additional benefit: complex objects may be represented by planar surfaces which can be tracking using 2D plane tracking.

This work is presented as part of a more general method that deals with 3D pose tracking of unknown objects in unknown environments. We propose the use of polygon meshes for representing objects to be tracked after they have been discovered using an automatic plane detection method. For instance, [2,5,8] could be used to obtain the faces that are part of the unknown target object.

This article is divided as follows: section II will introduce work related to the problem of 3D tracking unknown objects in unknown environments and that is closely related to this work. On section III, theoretical background is provided as preparation for section IV, where a method for 3D tracking is presented. Section V shows a validation exercise of method proposed, that consists in tracking a cuboid. In section VI conclusions are presented.

2   Related Work

Literature on 3D tracking is very wide. Its applicability to almost all disciplines involves a large variety of methods. Here our purpose is exploring some methods that achieve 3D pose tracking by means of image alignment and that are related to our proposal.

Our work relies on homography decomposition for 3D reconstruction and standard 2D plane tracking. A close application of this is presented by Benhimane and Malis [7]. Efficient Second order Minimization algorithm is used for aligning 2D images over 8 parameters, for homography transforms. We also use this plane tracking method in our method. But while Benhimane's work it's focused on visual servoing, ours is aimed at full 3D object tracking.

There are other alternatives for 3D tracking in context of image alignment. Method presented by Cobzas and Sturm [4] take standard 2D tracking to a 3D pose parameter space (6 parameters, one for each DoF). A drawback is that, when changing the parametrization to handle 3D pose changes, it results that even some movements that could be tracked without a problem by tracking planes individually, can produce failure when tracking them using this parametrization. Another idea introduced by them are constraints between planes to make tracking more robust. For our work, in the future we will use a similar constrained tracking for increasing robustness on a per plane basis.

On the same line of parametrizing directly in euclidean space, Panin and Knoll [10] proposed a method for tracking objects that uses Mutual Information as similarity measure, instead of the common SSD, and perform a Levenberg-Marquardt optimization. Authors report performance of 2 *fps* because of the Mutual Information step. Our approach, on the other hand works at real time (more than 24 *fps*). Moreover, Panin's method requires at each iteration project-ing a full CAD model to image plane (and a z-test for determining visibility). Our tracker just requires this projection once per registration, and can be sim-plified to a partial 3D reconstruction. A drawback from our method is that it will be limited to polygon meshes, but that indeed a desired feature towards automatic plane detection.

Another approach to 3D pose tracking is that of Manz et al. [6]. In their work, they use custom simplified model for 3D pose tracking based on feature points. Their work shows robust performance on real time vehicle tracking. But this method has the disadvantage of requiring a fine tuning of descriptors and the model for each different tracked target. While this provides robustness, it's not suitable for dynamic models.

One of the ideas behind this work is avoiding 3D representations of objects. Because monocular cameras are used, tracking in 3D involve at some point tak-ing 2D image projections to 3D euclidean space. Handling 3D usually involves additional complexity (for example, building a 3D CAD model and rendering it). We have aimed at doing as much as possible on 2D space, and later interpreting the corresponding 3D representation.

3   Theoretical Background

Let's define the projection of a plane in euclidean space on image plane according to pinhole camera model. Let $\mathbf{m} = [x, y, z, 1]^T$ be a point that lies on plane π in real world coordinates using homogeneous coordinates. The projection of $\mathbf{m}$ on image plane $\mathbf{m}^* = [x^*, y^*, 1]^T$ is given by:

$$\mathbf{m}^* = \alpha \mathbf{KPm} \tag{1}$$

Where $\mathbf{P} = [\mathbf{R} \mid \mathbf{t}] \in \Re^{4 \times 4}$. $\mathbf{R}$ and $\mathbf{t}$ are the rotation and translation matrices respectively that relate real world and camera coordinate reference frames. α is a scaling factor.

3.1   Polygon Mesh Plane Based Model

A polygon mesh with n faces (quadrilaterals) can be defined in terms of the planes that conform it. That is:

$$C = \{\mathbf{P}_i \mid 1 \le i \le n\} \tag{2}$$

For any polygon mesh C there exist one transformation matrix $\mathbf{P}_i$ that maps real world coordinates to camera coordinate system for each plane π_i.

For all faces in polygon mesh C there exist at least one transformation matrix ${}^i\mathbf{T}_k$ that maps coordinate system from face k to face i coordinate referential (equation 3).

$$\forall \pi_i \in C \; \exists \; {}^i\mathbf{T}_k \mid \mathbf{P}_i = \mathbf{T}_k \mathbf{P}_k \tag{3}$$

Where $\mathbf{P}_i$ refers to the transformation matrix for plane π_i that maps real world coordinates to image coordinates. ${}^i\mathbf{T}_k$ is a transformation matrix that maps coordinate system of plane with transform $\mathbf{P}_k$ to $\mathbf{P}_i$.

Note that if dimensions of faces are unknown, finding transforms ${}^i\mathbf{T}_k$ requires finding vertex using plane intersection points to later recover width and height (or a proportion of them). As for this article, it's assumed that dimensions are provided.

3.2   Plane Tracking

Consider the homography $\mathbf{G} \in \Re^{3 \times 3}$:

$$\mathbf{m}^* = \alpha \mathbf{G} \mathbf{m} \tag{4}$$

In this case, $\mathbf{m} = [x, y, 1]^T$ and $\mathbf{m}^* = [x^*, y^*, 1]^T$ are points on image plane and transformed image plane respectively. Differently from pinhole camera model $\mathbf{KP}$, $\mathbf{G}$ is no longer a projective transform matrix. This homography matrix can be parametrized as shown in [16]:

$$\mathbf{W}(\mathbf{x}; \mathbf{p}) = \begin{pmatrix} 1 + p_1 & p_3 & p_5 \\ p_2 & 1 + p_4 & p_6 \\ p_7 & p_8 & 1 \end{pmatrix} \begin{pmatrix} x \\ y \\ 1 \end{pmatrix} \tag{5}$$

Provided a image T on which plane π is projected, and image I where the same plane π is projected but after some arbitrary change in pose in $\Re^3$, image alignment consist in finding the parameters set $\mathbf{p}$ (and consequently $\mathbf{G}$) that allows transforming image T into I.

The Efficient Second Order Minimization proposed by Malis in [15] is a image alignment which has higher convergence rate than other popular approaches [16]. This method works by iteratively updating parameters $\mathbf{p} := \mathbf{p} \circ \Delta\mathbf{p}$ where $\Delta\mathbf{p}$ can be evaluated as:

$$\Delta\mathbf{p} \approx -2(\mathbf{J}(\mathbf{e}) + \mathbf{J}(\mathbf{p}_c))^+(\mathbf{s}(\mathbf{p}_c) - s(\mathbf{e})) \tag{6}$$

Where $\mathbf{p}$ are the current parameters, $\mathbf{J}$ is the Jacobian, as presented in [16], and $\mathbf{s}$ is the current image, which can be evaluated using the current parameter set or the $\mathbf{0}$ set.

3.3   Homography Decomposition

Homography decomposition deals with reconstructing the 3D pose of a planar surface given its single or multi view projection on image plane. When working with plane tracking, usually only 8 parameters are used to accomplish tracking, which are mapped to the 3×3 homography transform (equation 5).

As shown in the pinhole camera model, transformation matrix of extrinsic parameters $\mathbf{P} = [\mathbf{R} \mid \mathbf{t}]$ is a matrix composed of rotation $\mathbf{R}$ and translation $\mathbf{t}$. In order for $\mathbf{P}$ to be a valid transformation, $\mathbf{R}$ must an orthonormal basis.

Using individual elements $h_{ij} : 1 \leq i, j \leq 3$ of $\mathbf{G}$, the following relations can be obtained:

$$\mathbf{r}_1 = \alpha \begin{bmatrix} \frac{h_{11} - c_x r_{31}}{f_x} \\ \frac{h_{21} - c_y r_{31}}{f_y} \\ h_{31} \end{bmatrix} \quad , \quad \mathbf{r}_2 = \alpha \begin{bmatrix} \frac{h_{12} - c_x r_{32}}{f_x} \\ \frac{h_{22} - c_y r_{32}}{f_y} \\ h_{32} \end{bmatrix} \tag{7}$$

Where the α factor is a normalizing factor and h_{ij} are the elements of homography matrix $\mathbf{G}$. c_x, c_y are center offset from camera intrinsic parameters. f_x and f_y are focal distances of the camera. From this, $\mathbf{r}_3$ can be obtained using cross product, as shown in equation 8.

$$\mathbf{r}_3 = \mathbf{r}_1 \times \mathbf{r}_2 \tag{8}$$

The normalizing factor is computed as:

$$\alpha = \frac{1}{\sqrt{\left(\frac{h_{11} - c_x r_{31}}{f_x}\right)^2 + \left(\frac{h_{21} - c_y r_{31}}{f_y}\right)^2 + 1}} \tag{9}$$

Finally, the translation vector it's obtained from the relation between the planar homography and the model:

$$\mathbf{t} = \alpha \begin{bmatrix} \frac{h_{13} - c_x}{f_x} \\ \frac{h_{23} - c_y}{f_y} \\ 1 \end{bmatrix} \tag{10}$$

The advantage of this decomposition method is that it only requires one view, and camera intrinsic parameters.

4   Polygon Mesh 3D Pose Tracking

Here it's presented a method for tracking the 3D Pose (3D orientation and 3D location) of a polygon mesh using only a monocular camera. This method is based on the homography decomposition of a face of the tracked polygon mesh for 3D reconstructing it. The tracking process is based on the fact that at any time at least one face of the object is seen by a camera. Then, it's only necessary to track this face in order to reconstruct the object. This process is summarized in figure 1.

4.1   3D Object Reconstruction

Our proposal is to track a polygon mesh using a single face. This method must also determine which face should be tracked. Here it's used a decomposition process to reconstruct the full 3D polygon mesh by starting from the current tracked plane.

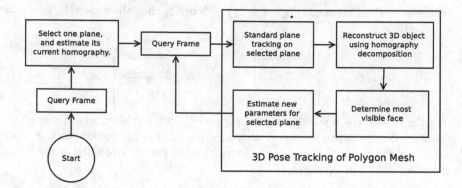

Fig. 1. Proposed process for tracking objects whose shape can be approximated to a polygon mesh. It's included the full registration process to illustrate required initialization step.

Let's start with the current tracked face, which is represented by plane $proj(\pi_c)$, where c denotes current and $proj$ is the projection of plane i on image. From this, and applying the decomposition process presented earlier (equations 7, 8, 9 and 10), it's possible to obtain the corresponding 3D pose of plane π_c.

Provided that dimensions for the object are known, reconstructing the full 3D object becomes simple. For each face, a transform from plane π_c can be obtained using equation 3. This is also applicable to determine current object center.

4.2 Plane Selection

From figure 1 it must be noted that there is no tight between modules. In the case of plane selection, we have chosen to use a method based on normal vector of each face, and the translation vector from camera to object. This method will output the face that has the larger area visible by the camera (provided equal face dimensions). Since visual tracking is going to be done over this area, it improves convergence to have a larger visible area.

Consider geometric setup depicted in figure 2. In this diagram it can be noted that to find the face which has the larger projection it's necessary to find the size of that projection first on virtual plane. Then, from virtual plane to image it's only needed and affine transform that preserves proportion.

Consider segments $\overline{AB}$ and $\overline{BC}$ and the following relations by trigonometric properties:

$$\overline{AB} = L \cos \theta_1 \tag{11}$$

$$\overline{BC} = L \cos \theta_2 \tag{12}$$

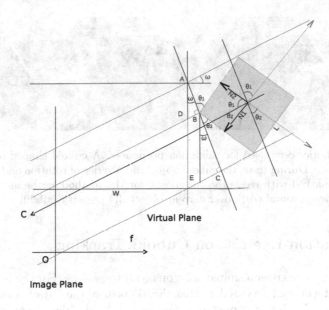

Fig. 2. Geometry for must aligned method for face selection. The method will report the face which has the wider visible area by the camera, regardless of its position or pose.

These are related to l_1 and l_2 as follows:

$$l_1 = \overline{AD} = \frac{\overline{AB}}{\cos\omega} = \frac{L\cos\theta_1}{\cos\omega} \tag{13}$$

$$l_2 = \overline{BE} = \frac{\overline{BC}}{\cos\omega} = \frac{L\cos\theta_2}{\cos\omega} \tag{14}$$

Taking the definition of angle between vectors, a general form for obtaining the projection on virtual plane of faces is given by:

$$\cos\theta_i = \frac{\mathbf{C}\cdot\mathbf{N}_i}{\|\mathbf{C}\|\|\mathbf{N}_1\|} \tag{15}$$

Because it's desired to find the normal that is must aligned, this problem can be defined as:

$$\operatorname*{argmax}_i l(i) = \left\{ \frac{L\cos\theta_i}{\cos\omega} \mid \forall i \, : \, 1 \le i \le 2 \right\} \tag{16}$$

This can be generalized for the case of a polygon mesh on $\Re^3$ with n faces as:

$$\operatorname*{argmax}_i l(i) = \{ \mathbf{C}\cdot\mathbf{N}_i \mid \forall i \, : \, 1 \le i \le n \} \tag{17}$$

Fig. 3. Synthetic scene used for validation porpouses. A cuboid shaped object moves over a 3D space. During tests, the cuboid object did a series of rotation and translations in $\Re^3$. Face marked with red is the one chosen for the method as the most visible. At any registration, ground truth over current object 3D pose is available.

5   Validation Exercise on Cuboid Tracking

Validation exercises over a simple polygon mesh were done. For these, a synthetic animation of a cuboid was used, so that the 3D pose of the object could be known on each frame. Each test consisted in having a cuboid object to execute a series of rotations and translations in $\Re^3$ in a way that would emulate a flying object. As a consequence, there were no large interframe displacements. A background image was entered to add difficulty to the tracking process.

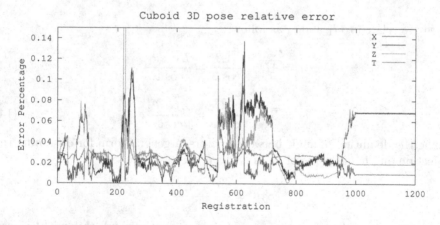

Fig. 4. Typical results from using our method for 3D pose tracking over 720×480 image sequences running at more than 24*fps*. Each series plots the error for pose estimation as a percentage. Relative error was calculated as $||\mathbf{v}_g - \mathbf{v}_c|| \, / \, ||\mathbf{v}_g||$, where $\mathbf{v}$ is vector $\mathbf{R}_x$ (X), $\mathbf{R}_y$ (Y), $\mathbf{R}_z$ (Z) or $\mathbf{t}$ (T). Subindex g denotes *ground truth* while c refers to *current estimate*.

On picture 4 results over this sequence of object motion and rotation are presented. In this plot, 3D pose estimation error for the tracked object is shown. Error is measured relative to the ground truth measure for each axis of rotation and the translation. In most of the cases is less than 10%. Error is produced because of plane tracking error, and sampling. In future work, a constrained plane tracking method will be used to reduce error on decomposition product of not fully valid plane tracking solutions. Also, tests on real objects will be presented.

From a theoretical perspective, our method may introduce error at face selection stage, since a fixed face size is considered. This is error has lees impact than the tracking process error, which is done at image level, and is prone to produce incorrect solutions.

Because our method relies on standard plane tracking [15], which solves an sum of squared differences expression with only 8 parameters, it works at more than $24fps$ on 720×480 image sequences.

6 Conclusions and Future Work

We have shown a method that allows tracking full featured objects by means of approximated models. This approach represents an important contribution in the sense that avoids dealing with a full featured model in situations where building such a model is not possible. More important, a method like this will also fit in situations where the model is not known, but can be discovered using automatic plane detection methods.

Another important feature of this work is the possibility of doing full 3D tracking in the 2D space. We show how using only homography decomposition and a simple transforms models (in $\Re^3$) it is possible to construct a 3D model of the target object.

3D pose estimation obtained is accurate, but there is important dependence on plane tracking and decomposition, which adds error to the pose estimation. Future work will deal with a constrained plane tracking process to increase robustness, while still preserving favorable properties of plane tracking using induced homography.

Approximated models are base of coarse to fine model refinement strategies (such as that employed in CAD model tessellation). In particular, to our research, we aim at discovering models for unknown objects in unknown environments. For these, we are studying model refinement parting from a cuboid shape until reaching a more complex mesh recursively.

Acknowledgements. Authors want to acknowledge Consejo Nacional de Ciencia y Tecnología (CONACyT) and e-Robots Research Chair from Tecnológico de Monterrey, Monterrey for supporting this research.

References

1. Bouchafa, S., Zavidovique, B.: Obstacle Detection "for Free" in the C-Velocity Space. In: 14th International IEEE Conference on Transportation Systems (ITSC 2011), pp. 308–313. IEEE (2011)

2. Bouchafa, S., Zavidovique, B.: c-Velocity: A Flow-Cumulating Uncalibrated Approach for 3D Plane Detection. International Journal of Computer Vision 97, 148–166 (2011)
3. Brown, J.A., Capson, D.W.: A Framework for 3D Model-Based Visual Tracking Using a GPU-Accelerated Particle Filter. IEEE Transactions on Visualization and Computer Graphics 18(1), 68–80 (2011)
4. Cobzas, D., Sturm, P.: 3D SSD Tracking with Estimated 3D Planes. In: 2nd Canadian Conference on Computer and Robot Vision (CRV 2005), pp. 129–134 (2005)
5. Košecká, J., Zhang, W.: Extraction, Matching, and Pose Recovery Based on Dominant Rectangular Structures. Computer Vision and Image Understanding 100(3), 274–293 (2005)
6. Manz, M., Luettel, T.: Monocular Model-Based 3D Vehicle Tracking for Autonomous Vehicles in Unstructured Eenvironment. In: IEEE International Conference on Robotics and Automation (ICRA 2011), pp. 2465–2471. IEEE (2011)
7. Benhimane, S., Malis, E.: Homography-Based 2D Visual Tracking and Servoing. The International Journal of Robotics Research 26(1), 661–676 (2007)
8. Micusik, B., Wildenauer, H.: Towards Detection of Orthogonal Planes in Monocular Images of Indoor Environments. In: IEEE International Conference on Robotics and Automation (ICRA 2008), pp. 999–1004. IEEE (2008)
9. Munozsalinas, R., Aguirre, E., Garciasilvente, M.: People Detection and Tracking Using Stereo Vision and Color. Image and Vision Computing 25(6), 995–1007 (2007)
10. Panin, G., Knoll, A.: Mutual Information-Based 3D Object Tracking. International Journal of Computer Vision 78(1), 107–118 (2007)
11. Prisacariu, V.A., Timofte, R., Zimmermann, K., Reid, I., Gool, L.V.: Integrating Object Detection with 3D Tracking Towards a Better Driver Assistance System. In: 20th International Conference on Pattern Recognition (ICPR 2010), pp. 3344–3347 (2010)
12. Shao, X., Zhao, H., Nakamura, K., Katabira, K., Shibasaki, R., Nakagawa, Y.: Detection and Tracking of Multiple Pedestrians by Using Laser Range Scanners. In: IEEE/RSJ International Conference on Intelligent Robots and Systems (IROS 2007), pp. 2174–2179. IEEE (2007)
13. Song, X., Zhao, H., Cui, J., Shao, X., Shibasaki, R., Zha, H.: Fusion of Laser and Vision for Multiple Targets Tracking Via On-Line Learning. In: IEEE International Conference on Robotics and Automation (ICRA 2010), pp. 406–411. IEEE (2010)
14. Tonko, M., Nagel, H.H.: Model-Based Stereo-Tracking of Non-Polyhedral Objects for Automatic Disassembly Experiments. International Journal of Computer Vision 37(1), 99–118 (2000)
15. Malis, E.: Improving Vision-Based Control Using Efficient Second-Order Minimization Techniques. In: IEEE International Conference on Robotics and Automation (ICRA 2004), vol. 2, pp. 1843–1848. IEEE (2004)
16. Baker, S., Matthews, I.: Lucas-Kanade 20 Years On – A Unifying Framework – Part 1. International Journal of Computer Vision 56, 221–255 (2004)

Embedding a Pose Estimation Module on a NCS-Based UGV

L.C. Carrillo-Arce, Christian Hassard, J.L. Gordillo, and Rogelio Soto

Center for Intelligent Systems, Tecnológico de Monterrey, Monterrey, México
{lc.carrillo.phd.mty,cr.hassard.phd.mty,jlgordillo,rsoto}@itesm.mx
http://www.itesm.edu

Abstract. Pose estimation is one of the most fundamental tasks in unmanned vehicles because many high level tasks depend directly on the vehicle localization. In this paper, an embedded pose estimation module based on the extended Kalman filter (EKF) is implemented in an autonomous vehicle with Network Controlled System (NCS) architecture. The implemented EKF fuses inexpensive sensor's data in order to provide a more precise estimation than using any of those sensors separately. Experimental results of tests with the vehicle in a parking lot show a comparison between pose estimation executed embedded on an low cost, low-speed micro-controller on the vehicle and in a remote high speed computer through a wireless link.

Keywords: pose estimation, extended Kalman filter, network controlled system, unmanned ground vehicle, CAN Bus.

1 Introduction

Pose estimation in autonomous vehicles is an important task that has received a lot of attention in the last decades. Usually this is done by fusing information from several sensors like INS, GPS, odometry among others. A very popular and effective technique to fuse information from different sensor sources is the Kalman filter.

In autonomous vehicles another trend is to use Distributed Controlled Systems (DCS) [1,2] thanks to advances and proved reliability of field bus technologies in commercial vehicles [3,4]. This helps to reduce the wiring in the vehicle and make the system modular, scalable and flexible.

Network Controlled Systems (NCS) is a particular case of a DCS in which the control loops are closed by an information network [5,6]. The defining feature of an NCS is that information is shared among components using the network. Figure 1 shows a general representation of a NCS, where sensors and actuators attached directly to the controlled system are connected to the network, as well as the controller, which may be in a remote location, thus closing the control loop [7].

In this paper, we present a comparison of an extended Kalman filter (EKF) when executed on a high-speed remote computer and when it was embedded on

J. Pavón et al. (Eds.): IBERAMIA 2012, LNAI 7637, pp. 541–550, 2012.

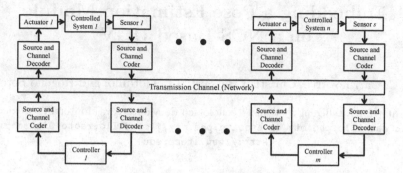

Fig. 1. Network Controlled System (NCS)

a low cost, low-speed micro-controller on the vehicle. The EKF fuses data from IMU, GPS, and odometry from a unmanned ground vehicle (UGV) instrumented with a NCS based on the Controller Area Network (CAN) bus. The main advantages of embedding the EKF on the vehicle NCS are: reduce the bandwidth usage of the wireless link; prevent dropped data; reduce the communication delay through the sensors and pose estimation module. Figure 2 presents both pose estimation schemes.

The following section will present an overview of the related work. Section 3 will explain how we applied the EKF to our ground vehicle. Section 4 will give a description of the vehicle, and the pose estimation module used in this research. In Sect. 5 we present the experimental setup and the results. Finally, in Sect. 6 we give the conclusions resulting from this research, and possible future work.

2   Related Work

The pose estimation of autonomous vehicles is a problem that has received considerable attention in the last decades due to its importance for higher-level functions like autonomous navigation. Kalman filtering, in its many variants, has been amply applied to solve this problem in many types of autonomous vehicles to fuse the information of whatever sensors the vehicle has, usually an Inertial Measurement Unit (IMU), vehicle odometry and GPS. Traditionally, this algorithm has been implemented on high-speed computers or devices with parallel processing capabilities.

In [8], there is a very good explanation of the Kalman filter, a detailed analysis, the characterization of the sensors they used and how they affect the filter, as well as some results. Even though this is a very good reference point and with excellent results, they do not specify the vehicle architecture or where the algorithm was executed. In [9], the authors applied Kalman filtering to an instrumented all-terrain vehicle, but the sensors used were too expensive (around USD 60,000) and the algorithm was executed on a computer on top of the vehicle.

While the common paradigm when using Kalman filters in autonomous vehicles is to fuse the information from the vehicle odometry, with an IMU and GPS,

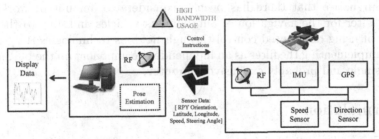

(a) Pose estimation executed on a computer, where data is received by a wireless network.

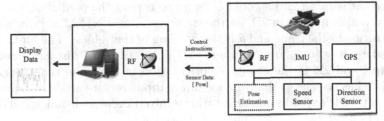

(b) Pose estimation running on the vehicle, where data is gathered through a more reliable wired network.

Fig. 2. Pose estimation approaches implemented on this research

in [10] the authors used Kalman filter between the odometry of an industrial instrumented vehicle and the triangulation from a laser mounted on the vehicle. In [11] they neglected the GPS, using instead a visual landmark recognition system. Still, both had very good results, proving that there are other ways to estimate the pose of an autonomous vehicle.

More recently, [12] present the analysis of fieldbus technologies for autonomous vehicles and how they would behave in some of their more critical tasks like navigation using Kalman filters, although their prototype was a wheelchair and the focus of the paper was on the real-time control of the vehicle with the distributed system. It is concluded that navigation algorithms can safely execute on the vehicle with a bus while other necessary control loops execute on real-time. In [13] there is an application of an unscented Kalman filter to get the navigation results of a commercial vehicle with IMU, GPS and a Compass where the algorithm was executed on a desktop computer on the back seat.

In other efforts, [14] implemented a Kalman filter to recognize the contour of roads for the navigation of autonomous vehicles, which can be combined with other pose estimation techniques to make a more reliable navigation algorithm. Finally, [15] implemented a floating-point Extended Kalman Filter embedded on a FPGA to work in the SLAM problem. This paper proved that a fast computer is not absolutely necessary to execute the Kalman filter, and they actually had better results by embedding the algorithm in their FPGA.

We can notice that there has been a considerable amount of work using Kalman filter for the navigation of autonomous vehicles and, due to the trend in these of using distributed control through fieldbus technologies [1,2], to find ways of implementing the filter as an independent component on the bus, instead of on a single and probably expensive computer.

3   Formulation

An EKF usually is divided into two main phases; first is prediction where a model function is used in order to calculate the state according to a theoretical model and an associated error; second is the correction phase where an external measurement is taken into account in order to correct the prediction.

In any vehicle moving in 2D, let the state vector $\mathbf{x} = [\mathbf{x}_x, \mathbf{x}_y, \mathbf{x}_\theta]^T$, where x, y is the position in the plane and θ is the heading of the vehicle. The input vector is defined by $\mathbf{u} = [\mathbf{u}_{\Delta D}, \mathbf{u}_{\Delta\theta}]^T$, where ΔD is the travelled distance between 2 time steps, and $\Delta\theta$ is the change of orientation in the same time period. As our vehicle has no sensors that provide direct input vector variables, Equation 1 translates vehicle's speed s and orientation θ into translated distance and change of orientation, which are our input vector variables.

$$\mathbf{u}_k = j(s, \theta) = \begin{bmatrix} \mathbf{u}_{\Delta D_k} \\ \mathbf{u}_{\Delta\theta_k} \end{bmatrix} = \begin{bmatrix} 2 \times \pi \times r \times s \times \Delta t \\ \theta - \mathbf{x}^+_{\theta_{k-1}} \end{bmatrix} \tag{1}$$

In order to apply EKF for vehicles pose estimation, we need a model to describe the vehicle pose in function of its last pose and input variables. This model is called kinematic model, and its result is also known as odometry. Equation 2 relates the vehicle odometry with the state prediction of the EKF.

$$\mathbf{x}^-_k = \begin{bmatrix} \mathbf{x}^-_{x_k} \\ \mathbf{x}^-_{y_k} \\ \mathbf{x}^-_{\theta_k} \end{bmatrix} = f(\mathbf{x}^+_{k-1}, \mathbf{u}_k) = \begin{bmatrix} \mathbf{x}^+_{x_{k-1}} + \mathbf{u}_{\Delta D_k} \cos{(\mathbf{x}^+_{\theta_{k-1}} + \mathbf{u}_{\Delta\theta_k})} \\ \mathbf{x}^+_{y_{k-1}} + \mathbf{u}_{\Delta D_k} \sin{(\mathbf{x}^+_{\theta_{k-1}} + \mathbf{u}_{\Delta\theta_k})} \\ \mathbf{x}^+_{\theta_{k-1}} + \mathbf{u}_{\Delta\theta_k} \end{bmatrix} \tag{2}$$

After the state is predicted, we need to predict the covariance matrix $\mathbf{P}$, which is represented as an ellipse in where the real pose could be in case it was not the one calculated. Equation 3 shows how to calculate the covariance prediction using the last covariance correction, and the noise associated to input variables $\mathbf{U}$.

$$\mathbf{P}^-_k = \mathbf{J}_{f\mathbf{x}_k} \mathbf{P}^+_{k-1} \mathbf{J}^T_{f\mathbf{x}_k} + \mathbf{J}_{f\mathbf{u}_k} \mathbf{U} \mathbf{J}^T_{f\mathbf{u}_k} \tag{3}$$

where $\mathbf{J}_{f\mathbf{x}}$ and $\mathbf{J}_{f\mathbf{u}}$ are the Jacobian matrix of the state function f, respect to the state and input variables respectively.

Once a measurement is performed, the correction phase of the EKF is executed. This phase begins calculating the Kalman gain, which will tell us how the prediction has to be corrected. Equation 4 shows how to calculate the Kalman gain.

$$\mathbf{K}_k = \mathbf{P}_k^- \mathbf{H}^T (\mathbf{H} \mathbf{P}_k^- \mathbf{H}^T + \mathbf{R}) \tag{4}$$

where $\mathbf{H}$ is how the measurement is related to the state, and $\mathbf{R}$ is the associated error of the measurement.

After computing the Kalman gain, we have to use it to fix our state prediction using measurement $\mathbf{z}$. Equation 5 shows how to calculate state correction from state prediction, Kalman gain, and the external measurement.

$$\mathbf{x}_k^+ = \mathbf{x}_k^- + \mathbf{K}_k (\mathbf{z}_k - \mathbf{x}_k^-) \tag{5}$$

Finally, we need to correct the covariance matrix using the Kalman gain and the predicted covariance. Equation 6 presents how to correct the covariance matrix.

$$\mathbf{P}_k^+ = (\mathbf{I} - \mathbf{K}_k \mathbf{H}) \mathbf{P}_k^- \tag{6}$$

After the correction phase, the EKF cycle concludes, and it is executed again at the next time step. For our experiments, this is the EKF filter that we implemented.

4   Research Platform

The vehicle used for this research is an electric ground vehicle from Johnson Industries (shown in Fig. 3a) originally designed to be driven by a human, that has been instrumented with the necessary components to provide some level of autonomy. In this vehicle, we implemented a NCS based on CAN bus as we show in Fig. 3b.

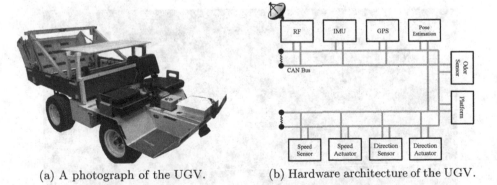

(a) A photograph of the UGV.   (b) Hardware architecture of the UGV.

Fig. 3. Research platform vehicle used and its architecture

We can see that the vehicle has many nodes connected to the network with three main control loops: vehicle's speed, involving a sensor in one of the front wheels and an electric motor to steer the vehicle; and retractable platform, that is a subsystem of the vehicle used to load and unload child vehicles.

CAN bus was chosen as the bus protocol thanks to its proven reliability in commercial vehicle applications [3,4], industrial applications, and research [12]. Other advantages of the CAN bus are its resistance to electromagnetic interference, which in electric vehicles has to be considered, and its ID priority-based communication protocol, that allows a higher-priority messages to access the bus first [16].

When the pose estimation module algorithm was executed on a remote computer (Dual-Core laptop computer running at 2.53 GHz with Hyper Threading), necessary data was gathered through a wireless link provided by an RF transceiver on the vehicle. Even when this link is reliable, we still have data loss and time delays added to process. In Section 5 will be presented how these delays affect directly to pose estimation performance.

When the pose estimation module was embedded on the vehicle (Low cost Arduino Uno R3 running at 16 Mhz), even when GPS and IMU had lower priority ID compared with the mentioned control loops, as the bus traffic is not too high, the pose estimation module was always able to receive the necessary data from these sensors.

5   Experiments and Results

In order to test the pose estimation system, we did experiments in an outdoor environment as shown in Fig.4. This area was selected because of the space and its GPS reception. In addition, Fig. 4 shows two trajectories described by the vehicle, which were used to calculate the vehicle pose error.

Fig. 4. Experimental area and real performed trajectory

The first path consisted on a simple 'C' shaped trajectory, which had two sharp turns. Figure 5 shows a comparison between the embedded and remote pose estimation algorithm results.

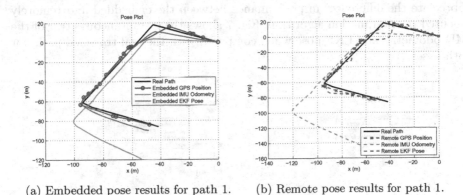

(a) Embedded pose results for path 1.   (b) Remote pose results for path 1.

Fig. 5. Comparison between embedded and remote pose results for path 1.

As shown in Fig. 5 the embedded pose estimation algorithm had a better performance than when executed remotely. We can see also a better performance in IMU odometry calculation when this calculation was embedded on the vehicle. For the second path, the vehicle travelled a 'S' shaped trajectory, which had more turns and more distance to travel. Figure 6 shows a comparison between the embedded and remote pose estimation algorithm results.

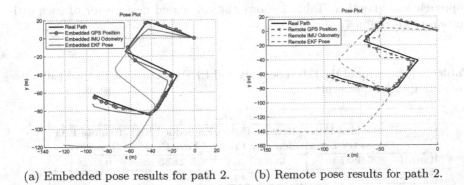

(a) Embedded pose results for path 2.   (b) Remote pose results for path 2.

Fig. 6. Comparison between embedded and remote pose results for path 2.

We can notice that, the embedded approach had a better performance than the remote one, again. Furthermore, the embedded calculation of the IMU odometry outperformed the remote IMU odometry calculation. In both experiments, the embedded EKF pose result behaved smoother than the remotely calculated EKF pose. It can be appreciated that the remote EKF pose sometimes got lost for a brief moment because data was lost during wireless communication, and then it would correct itself once GPS data reached the remote computer. To better appreciate the differences in performance between the embedded and remotely executed pose estimation algorithm, Fig. 7 shows the instantaneous error of the IMU odometry, and EKF pose when compared with the real travelled path, for both cases.

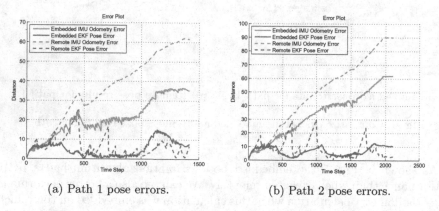

(a) Path 1 pose errors.   (b) Path 2 pose errors.

Fig. 7. Error for embedded and remote IMU odometry and EKF pose in both paths.

It can be observed that in both experiments, the remote EKF pose error gives spikes that were due to the wireless communication, while the embedded approach was smoother. Table 1 shows the calculated mean error of each estimation presented in 7.

Table 1. Mean error of the IMU odometry and EKF pose against the real path after completing both experiments

	Mean Error			
	Embedded IMU Odometry Error	Remote IMU Odometry Error	Embedded EKF Pose Error	Remote EKF Pose Error
Path 1	20.9557 m	35.6667 m	**5.2835 m**	6.3928 m
Path 2	33.6639 m	49.0897 m	**6.8828 m**	8.3677 m

These experiments showed, as summarized in Table 1, that the embedded approach had a better performance both in the calculation of the IMU odometry, as well as in the EKF pose estimation.

6 Conclusions and Future Work

This paper presented an implementation of an embedded EKF on a UGV as a module of its NCS. We showed a comparison between the performance of this filter, against the same filter executing on a remote computer, concluding that the embedded filter behaved slightly better, so that it can be safely applied embedded on the vehicle for high-level autonomy tasks.

The advantage of implementing the filter as a module of the UGV NCS is that now, it is fully independent of the rest of the vehicle systems, so any modification, like an upgrade, could be applied without the need of interfering in the rest of the systems. In addition, thanks to the philosophy used in the instrumentation of the vehicle, this module can be used on other vehicles instrumented with the same philosophy with minimal changes.

One of the contributions of this paper is that the EKF was implemented in an economic processor, which contributes to the development of a low cost, modular, robust, scalable and flexible UGV.

As future work, high-level functions such as exploration, mapping, and path planning will be implemented based on the obtained results to achieve a better degree of autonomy.

Acknowledgements. Authors want to acknowledge Consejo Nacional de Ciencia y Tecnología (CONACyT) and e-Robots Research Chair from Tecnológico de Monterrey, Monterrey for supporting this research.

References

1. Ataide, F., Santos, M.M., Vasques, F.: A Comparison of the Communication Impact in CAN and TTP/C Networks when Supporting Steer-by-Wire Systems. In: IEEE International Conference on Industrial Technology (ICIT 2004), pp. 1078–1083. IEEE (2004)
2. Bosque, J.D., Hassard, C., Gordillo, J.L.: Velocity Control of an Electric Vehicle Over a CAN Network. In: 10th Mexican International Conference on Artificial Intelligence (MICAI 2001), pp. 121–126. IEEE (2011)
3. Strobel, O., Rejeb, R., Lubkoll, J.: Communication in Automotive Systems – Principles, Limits and New Trends for Vehicles, Airplanes and Vessels. In: 12th International Conference on Transparent Optical Networks (ICTON 2010), pp. 1–6. IEEE (2010)
4. Navet, N., Song, Y., Simonot-Lion, F., Wilwert, C.: Trends in Automotive Communication Systems. Proceedings of the IEEE 93(6), 1204–1223 (2005)
5. Huo, Z., Fang, H., Ma, C.: Networked Control System – State of the Art. In: 5th World Congress on Intelligent Control and Automation (WCICA 2004), vol. 2, pp. 1319–1322. IEEE (2004)
6. Chow, M.-Y., Tipsuwan, Y.: Network-Based Control Systems – A Tutorial. In: 27th Annual Conference of the IEEE Industrial Electronics Society (IECON 2001), pp. 1593–1602. IEEE (2001)
7. Lihua, Z., Yuqiang, W., Lei, G., Haojie, C.: A Novel Research Approach on Network Control Systems. In: International Conference on Internet Computing in Science and Engineering (ICICSE 2008), pp. 262–265. IEEE (2008)

8. Kelly, A.: A 3D State Space Formulation of a Navigation Kalman Filter for Autonomous Vehicles. CMU-RI-TR-94-19. Carnegie Mellon University (1994)
9. Schonberg, T.: Positioning an Autonomous Off-Road Vehicle by Using Fused DGPS and Inertial Navigation. International Journal of Systems Science 27(8), 745–752 (1996)
10. Shoval, S., Zeitoun, I., Lenz, E.: Implementation of a Kalman Filter in Positioning for Autonomous Vehicles, and Its Sensitivity to the Process Parameters. The International Journal of Advanced Manufacturing Technology 13(10), 738–746 (1997)
11. Hague, T., Marchant, J.A., Tillett, N.D.: Ground Based Sensing Systems for Autonomous Agricultural Vehicles. Computers and Electronics in Agriculture 25(1-2), 11–28 (2000)
12. Nunes, U., Fonseca, J.A., Almeida, L., Arajo, R., Maia, R.: Using Distributed Systems in Real-Time Control of Autonomous Vehicles. Robotica 21(3), 271–281 (2003)
13. Zhang, P., Gu, J., Milios, E.E., Huynh, P.: Navigation with IMU/GPS/Digital Compass with Unscented Kalman Filter. In: IEEE International Conference Mechatronics and Automation (ICMA 2005), vol. 3, pp. 1497–1502 (2005)
14. Asif, M., Arshad, M.R., Yousuf, M., Zia, I., Yahya, A.: An Implementation of Active Contour and Kalman Filter for Road Tracking. International Journal of Applied Mathematics 37(2), 1–7 (2007)
15. Bonato, V., Marques, E., Constantinides, G.A.: A Floating-Point Extended Kalman Filter Implementation for Autonomous Mobile Robots. Journal of Signal Processing Systems 56(1), 41–50 (2008)
16. Bosch GmbH: CAN Specification – Version 2.0 (1991),
http://www.semiconductors.bosch.de/media/pdf/canliteratur/can2spec.pdf

Finding the Direction of an Odor Source by Using Biologically Inspired Smell System

B. Lorena Villarreal, Christian Hassard, and J.L. Gordillo

Center for Intelligent Systems, Tecnológico de Monterrey, Monterrey, México
{lvillarreal.bg,christian.hassard}@gmail.com,
jlgordillo@itesm.mx

Abstract. There is a wide area of applications for sniffing robots where different intelligent algorithms can be applied to follow the smell of precise odors. The localization of odor sources is one way to increase the efficiency and the speed of a multi-robot team in a disaster area during search and rescue applications. Then, the most important task is not the search but the localization of these odor sources, which inspired in nature, requires a stereo sensor to find the direction from where an odor is coming. The intention of this document is to prove that the robot heading can be aligned to the real odor flow direction improving the odor and localization task based on a designed and implemented biologically inspired nose system. Experiments compare the results when the nose system is implemented and when it is not.

Keywords: smell, odor source localization, bio-inspired nose system, nose system, nostrils, smell sense, CAN-Network, unmanned vehicles.

1   Introduction

The importance of smell in animals cannot be denied as olfaction is used for too many purposes in nature as scavenging and inspection, mating, recognition, hunting, avoiding predators. Even more, animals smell capability can be trained to find hazardous substances in the environment or during rescue tasks in disaster areas [1].

This is where a match between smell sensing and mobile robots for rescue applications can be made. Both areas have received considerable attention recently, but there is still a lot of work to be developed to increase its performance and effectiveness [2].

To understand a sniffing robot it is necessary to know that odors are volatile compounds and a mixture of different molecules and that the function of a smell sensor is to chemically react with these odorants and convert the chemical signal into an electrical or physical signal [3]. One of the difficulties of developing chemical sensors versus other sensors is that chemical reactions change the sensor, often in a way that is nonreversible. Therefore the system must be easy to maintain, meaning that the sensors should be exchangeable as fast as possible with minimum effort.

The main characteristics of commonly used smell sensors are the discrimination between odors and the sensitivity. The most important task of a sniffing robot is the

J. Pavón et al. (Eds.): IBERAMIA 2012, LNAI 7637, pp. 551–560, 2012.

odor source localization, which is not an easy task because the particles of smell are dispersed in the air by diffusion and flow with the wind by advection causing an important dependency on the environment. This is why, inspired on nature, odor source localization requires that the smell system has the capability of directionality which can be achieved by measurement strategies, in other words, applying intelligence.

Directionality as a single system has not been extensively implemented. The intention of this research is to analyze and justify that a single robot can find an odor source by using a biologically inspired stereo nose system.

In this implementation a ground vehicle instrumented with CAN Network is used to increase the robot adaptability and robustness of the designed smell sensor modules. Thanks to the reliability and flexibility of CAN networks applied on unmanned vehicles [4], this allows us to easily replace any sensor if needed.

There is some work involving odor source localization techniques in mobile robots. One perspective to solve the problem is when we consider that following the air flow and the odor trails the source could be found, because the odor flows with the wind and is carried by it. Lochmatter and Martinoli [2, 5] are developing three bio-inspired odor source localization algorithms. Another perspective is when no wind is present and the use of the concentration difference between two nostrils can be a solution. Two alternative strategies were implemented in [6] utilizing a direct sensor-motor coupling in a differential robot for finding an odor source indoors.

In the following section these algorithms are going to be explained, then on the third section the analysis of odor behavior is presented followed by the analysis of the bio-inspired nose system and the implementation design in Sect. 4. The experimental set-up and results are described in Sect. 5 and 6 respectively. Finally in Sect. 7 and 8 we present the future work and conclusions.

The intention of this paper is to prove that by using a complete bio-inspired nose system, the performance and the time to achieve the odor source localization task can be improved, since the robot has the ability to know the direction from where the source is emitting, and align its heading by using just gradient descend methods.

2   Related Background

In a typical environment some flow of air is present, and the odor flows with the wind. This behavior is the first obstacle of a sniffing robot and in this case to follow the air flow and the odor trails can be a solution to find the odor source. Some recent work is focusing on this kind of solution. Lochmatter and Martinoli [2, 5] developed three bio-inspired odor source localization algorithms, using a chemical sensor. The algorithms implemented in this research have the tendency of using the wind measurements to decide the best movement of the robot. They are also working on a simulation platform for the experimentation process [7]. Using local wind measurements is, however, currently not feasible in unventilated indoor environments because the wind speeds observed are usually too low [8].

When no air flow is present the use of the concentration difference between two nostrils can be a solution. Two alternative strategies were implemented in [6] utilizing a direct sensor-motor coupling in a differential robot. The speed of the motor on each tire of the robot is influenced directly by the averaged concentration measured by a chemical sensor array. The strategies are only differenced by the crossed or the uncrossed coupling connections of the sensor array and the motor. In this case, the odor source is a leaking alcohol device. In this research, with this particular kind of source, using a reactive robot, the major concentration values were not usually reached on the odor source [8]. This is probably caused by the excessive time of the leaking process, the dropping, the volatility of the chemical and because the time of exposure is too long, so the random walk of the diffusion process avoids having a real estimate of the odor source position and direction.

In [9] an odor grip map was presented, where the readings of the robot are convolved as soon as it moves using the radial symmetric two dimensional Gaussian function to create the next portion of the grid map. They used three different robot movement techniques: spiral, sweeping and instant gradient. From these, the sweeping movement was the most efficient, but the time is too long because it depends on the time it takes the robot to wander at a very low speed the whole area. Reactive gradient movement was a little faster, but usually gets stuck at a local maximum. From this research, a hound robot was presented by Loutfi et al. [10]. This robot discriminates odors and creates grid maps of these using the sweeping movement technique. A major drawback of this approach is that the volatility of the odor particles causes them to be quickly distributed in the room so, by the time the robot has finished its sweeping routine, the distribution of the odor could be completely different.

3   Diffusion-Advection Property

Odor can be propagated without air flows present by diffusion in a radial manner or by advection depending on the laminar air velocity.

Diffusion is the process by which matter is transported from one part of a system to another as a result of molecular motions [11]. This process is non-reversible and increases the entropy as the chemical reactions take place.

The Fick's law for diffusion says that the mass of a solute crossing a unit area per unit time in one direction is proportional to the solute concentration gradient in that direction.

$$\bar{q} = -D\,\partial C/\partial x = -D\nabla C = \partial c/\partial t \tag{1}$$

where q is a fluid flow, D is the diffusion coefficient which theoretically is a tensor, C is fluid concentration at certain measurement (x, or t).

The diffusion equation describes the transport of some kind of conserved quantity, in this case, odor concentration. In a two-dimensional x-y space:

$$\partial C/\partial t = D(\partial^2 C/\partial x^2 + \partial^2 C/\partial y^2) \tag{2}$$

Advection describes the diffusion process in a fluid moving at a uniform velocity, u, which is constant in time. Now the total flux is composed by two independent flows. The total mass flux q_T crossing a unit area perpendicular to the flow direction will consist of convective uc and diffusive q_D fluxes, resulting on the following advection-diffusion equation:

$$\frac{\partial c}{\partial t} = D\left(\frac{\partial^2 c}{\partial x^2} + \frac{\partial^2 c}{\partial y^2} + \frac{\partial^2 c}{\partial z^2}\right) - \left(u_x \frac{\partial c}{\partial x} + u_y \frac{\partial c}{\partial y} + u_z \frac{\partial c}{\partial z}\right). \tag{3}$$

It is composed by the concentration and wind gradients. When the air flow is high the diffusion process is overwhelmed but it should not be neglected unless the distance was too short. When no air flow is present, the odor propagation will be radial as in a simple diffusion.

4   Nose System

4.1   Nose Design

The animal kingdom and nature in general is a wide universe of solutions of simple but practical designs, and the olfactory system has not been left out. The obstacle behavior of odor molecules is represented by the reflection and image method. It means that the angle at which the wave is incident on the surface equals the angle at which it is reflected. It also means that the use of symmetric and equal obstacles would generate the same stop force in any nostril. This way the simple use of a septum would increase the differences of time of arrival and concentration between two nostrils depending on the direction of odor incidence [12]. If no air flow is present, the septum represents the same obstacle for all nostrils. The final nose system is composed by a septum and two nostrils, each one with an array of 3 alcohol sensors.

4.2   Sensor Model

The gas sensor MQ-3 consists of 6 terminals with two of them as repeaters. It reacts when some alcohol is present in the environment. It was selected because it is high sensitive and has a fast response. When the odor is detected, the resistance between two terminals varies and because the supply voltage is maintained the current over the load changes which generates different voltages on it. This voltage *Vin* is the one that is measured and analyzed.

The initial *Reference* for *Vin* is obtained in a calibration pre-experimental process, normally it consist in the lower voltage measured when no alcohol is present. The system maintains the *Reference* intact unless the actual measure was lower. Then it is updated. The *differential range* is considered the difference between *Vin* and the *Reference*. Finally the concentration change (% *C*) was also calculated as a normalization process as in [7]. Where *Vmax* is the maximum voltage ever measured.

$$\%C = (differential\ range)/(Vmax - Reference) * 100 \tag{4}$$

4.3   Nostril Design

The smell sense in nature is divided in stages, which are described as follows:

1. Aspiration process. At this stage the odor is carried by an air flow being inhaled
2. Conduction. At this stage a good sample of the odor is conducted to the sensor.
3. Sensing. In this stage all the sensor react and send the signal.
4. Processing. This is the algorithmic stage of the smell sense.
5. Transforming. The air is transformed to clean the sensory system.
6. Exhalation. The expulsion of the air through the nose and ventilation of the system.

All these stages are included in the smell system developed in this research to provide an efficient and optimized measurement. This system provides a desaturation level, the homogenization and sampling of environment.

The Nostril device has the ability to inhale and exhale, so after the measurement, the chamber is cleaned. Using this device, a desaturation of the sensors is present, optimizing the measurement and making it more realistic.

5   Experimental Set-Up

To simulate the advection behavior an odor source was considered. It consists in a container with alcohol gel and an air entrance that generates an almost laminar flow with a fixed magnitude.

As said before, inspired in nature, each nostril has the ability of inhalation and exhalation. Each of the individual sensors changes it resistance according to the concentration of alcohol, so we can read a change of voltage in a load resistor in series with the sensor. Figure 1 shows the experimental controlled area set-up and the source.

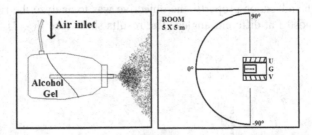

Fig. 1. Left: Odor Source. Right: Controlled environment set-up.

A tracked ground vehicle is used for the implementation. We added a CAN network subsystem to the vehicle, where we have the needed nodes for the smell system, without disrupting the original configuration of the vehicle. CAN network was used thanks to its proven reliability on commercial vehicles and on unmanned vehicles [13]. A microcontroller reads the nostrils voltages and puts the information in the bus while another module, a RF link, takes this information and broadcasts it to a near

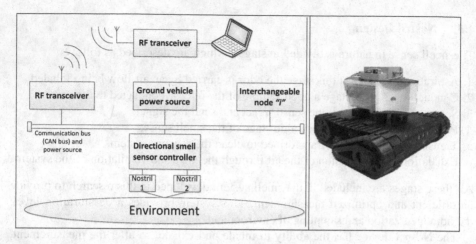

Fig. 2. Left: The subsystem architecture. Right: The vehicle and the odor system implemented.

computer for processing. Figure 2 shows the architecture used to add the odor sensor as a subsystem and a picture of the vehicle with the smell system.

6   Experimental Results

To test the odor sensor implemented in the vehicle, several experiments were made, with the vehicle in a fixed position while a directed odor source was aimed at the vehicle at several angles from the center of the sensor and a distance of 2m.

6.1   Advection Tests

When testing the advection property, the objective was to analyze the rise time delay between each nostril at different angles. The results show (see Fig. 3) that when the

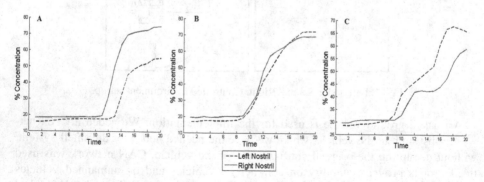

Fig. 3. Advection behavior results: A) Robot is facing 60° B) Robot is facing at 0°, C) Robot is facing at -60° and right nostril is the first in react

robot was facing at 60° the right nostril reacts 3 seconds earlier than the right nostril. The same happens at -60° but in this case the left nostril responds first. When the robot was facing 0° the reaction of both nostrils was almost at the same time.

These graphs show that the advection property is present because the time of arrival varied depending on the distance to the source.

The rising time delay between nostrils can be useful as a good estimate of the odor source direction and distance, it means that the air currents and the time of arrival to different sensors at different positions can be measured and the direction can be found. This can be helpful when the odor concentration saturate the sensors or exceeds the limits of the sensor and when the gas leak is intermittent.

6.2   Direction Tests

The biologically inspired nose system has the ability to detect the direction from where the odor is coming. To prove the increment of performance achieved in this research three different experiments were made. The first one is using two sensor arrays exposed to the environment. Figure 4 shows the results.

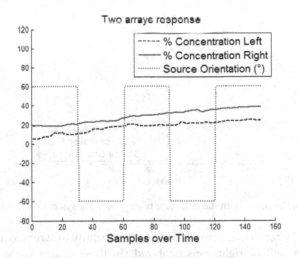

Fig. 4. Response when the biological system is not implemented

In these results we can see that the sensors do not respond with respect to the direction of the source as expected. A second experiment was made which included a septum in the design. Figure 5 shows the results of these experiments. When a septum is implemented the difference between nostrils seems to be positive when the robot is facing to the right and negative when the robot is facing to the left. Figure 6 shows the final experiments, whit the complete bio-inspired system.

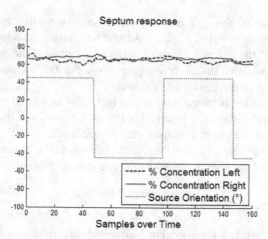

Fig. 5. Performance of direction finding task is increased when a septum is implemented

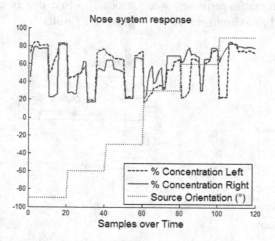

Fig. 6. Response with the complete biological nose system implemented

To compare the results, an error defined as the quantity of wrong perceptions of the source direction (left or right) was analyzed. In these results the error percentage without considering the measurements when the robot is facing at 0° was around 8.5%, which means that the performance to discriminate direction was increased from not possible to 91.5% by including a biologically inspired system.

The system can estimate a direction based on the difference between nostrils. Then we can choose the step size and the direction that the robot must align by ing $\theta_T * k$, where k can be defined by experimentation. Finally we can use these results to implement descend gradient method to find the odor source.

The following figure shows the direction estimate by the robot by using the stereo nose system at different orientations of the source in a controlled environment.

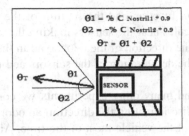

Fig. 7. Estimation of the robot heading depending on the nostrils measurements

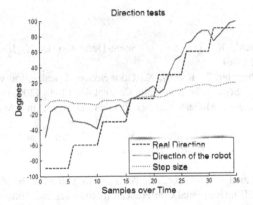

Fig. 8. Direction or heading estimate obtained by the robot perception

7   Future Work

In future work we will apply artificial intelligence and control techniques to improve the heading estimation of the robot, as well as performing the necessary experiments to prove that the instant gradient is good enough to find the odor source, using a bio-inspired physical design. The fundamental approach is to increase the efficiency in odor source localization techniques.

We will use a gradient function for each nostril with respect to time using a buffer of historic positions and the methodology of mean squares to determine a vector for the next movement of the robot. We can also consider wind measures and subtract both results as in the advection-diffusion equation. These approaches can be reached using AI techniques giving a real treatment to the uncertainties of the environment.

8   Conclusions

There are many applications where a sniffing robot can be used. This paper demonstrates that diffusion is present and that it can be measured even when a constant gas leak is present, just as long as the leak is always incrementing the actual concentration at that point.

Thanks to the inhalation function and the septum of the sensor, we were able to concentrate the odor molecules near the sensors making the readings between nostrils to be different relative to the direction of the odor. And in the other hand, the exhalation function helps us in the desaturation of the sensors and makes them ready to the next measure.

After the mentioned, and many other experiments we conclude that the designed odor sensor is capable of discriminating the direction an odor is flowing (right or left) in respect to the direction of the vehicle most of the time. Also we noticed that a nostril would react before the other if the odor flow reached it first by advection.

References

1. Browne, C., Stafford, K.: The Use of Scent-Detection Dogs. Irish Veterinary Journal 59(2), 97–102 (2006)
2. Martinoli, A., Lochmatter, T., Raemy, X.: Odor Source Localization with Mobile Robots. Bulletin of the Swiss Society for Automatic Control 46, 11–14 (2007)
3. Fraden, J.: Handbook of Modern Sensors Physics, Designs, and Applications. Springer (2003)
4. del Bosque, J., Hassard, C., Gordillo, J.L.: Velocity Control of an Electric Vehicle Over a CAN Network. In: 10th Mexican International Conference on Artificial Intelligence (MICAI 2011), pp. 121–126. IEEE (2011)
5. Martinoli, A., Lochmatter, T.: Theoretical Analysis of Three Bio-Inspired Plume Tracking Algorithms. In: IEEE International Conference on Robotics and Automation (ICRA 2009), pp. 2661–2668. IEEE (2009)
6. Lilienthal, A., Duckett, T.: Experimental Analysis of Smelling Braitenberg Vehicles. Advanced Robotics 18(8), 817–834 (2003)
7. Martinoli, A., Lochmatter, T.: Simulation Experiments with Bio-Inspired Algorithms for Odor Source Localization in Laminar Wind Flow. In: 7th International Conference on Machine Learning and Applications (ICMLA 2008), pp. 437–443. IEEE (2008)
8. Wadel, M., Lilienthal, A., Duckett, T., Weimar, U., Zell, A.: Gas Distribution in Unventilated Indoor Environments Inspected by a Mobile Robot. In: 11th International Conference on Advanced Robotics (ICAAR 2003), pp. 507–512 (2003)
9. Lilienthal, A., Duckett, T.: Building Gas Concentration Gridmaps with a Mobile Robot. Robotics and Autonomous System 48(1), 3–16 (2004)
10. Loutfi, A., Coradeschi, S., Lilienthal, A., Gonzalez, J.: Gas Distribution Mapping of Multiple Odour Sources Using a Mobile Robot. Robotica 27(2), 311–319 (2009)
11. Crank, J.: The mathematics of diffusion. Oxford University Press, New York (1976)
12. Villarreal, B.L., Gordillo, J.L.: Directional Aptitude Analysis in Odor Source Localization Techniques for Rescue Robots Applications. In: 10th Mexican International Conference on Artificial Intelligence (MICAI 2011), pp. 109–114. IEEE (2011)
13. Gurram, S.K., Conrad, J.M.: Implementation of CAN Bus in an Autonomous All-Terrain Vehicle. In: 2011 IEEE Southeast Con., pp. 250–254. IEEE (2011)

Fingerspelling Recognition with Support Vector Machines and Hidden Conditional Random Fields

A Comparison with Neural Networks and Hidden Markov Models

César Roberto de Souza, Ednaldo Brigante Pizzolato, and Mauro dos Santos Anjo

Universidade Federal de São Carlos, São Carlos, Brasil
{cesar.souza,ednaldo,mauro_anjo}@dc.ufscar.br

Abstract. In this paper, we describe our experiments with Hidden Conditional Random Fields and Support Vector Machines in the problem of fingerspelling recognition of the Brazilian Sign Language (LIBRAS). We also provide a comparison against more common approaches based on Artificial Neural Networks and Hidden Markov Models, reporting statistically significant results in k-fold cross-validation. We also explore specific behaviors of the Gaussian kernel affecting performance and sparseness. To perform multi-class classification with SVMs, we use large-margin Directed Acyclic Graphs, achieving faster evaluation rates. Both ANNs and HCRFs have been trained using the Resilient Back-propagation algorithm. In this work, we validate our results using Cohen's Kappa tests for contingency tables.

Keywords: gesture recognition, fingerspelling, sign languages, LIBRAS, support vector machines, hidden conditional random fields, neural networks, hidden Markov models, discriminative models.

1 Introduction

Human communication goes much further than the commonplace speaking, hearing, writing and reading activities. Whenever there is visual contact between a speaker and listeners, a whole continuum of information becomes available through the visual-gestural system. Moreover, when the phonological system is unavailable or damaged, the need for sign languages arises.

This work investigates the automatic recognition of sign languages. More specifically, we provide a comparison between recent advances and past approaches in pattern recognition to deal with the Brazilian Sign Language's manual alphabet. In the Brazilian Sign Language, henceforth LIBRAS, the use of the manual alphabet is only needed in specific occasions. Those occasions include, for example, explicitly spelling the name of a person or a location.

An example of a fingerspelling recognition system was given by [1], in which the authors considered an Artificial Neural Network (ANN) classification scheme based on a two stage architecture to deal with static gesture signs, followed by a bank of Hidden Markov Models (HMMs) to provide dynamic gesture classification. In this

J. Pavón et al. (Eds.): IBERAMIA 2012, LNAI 7637, pp. 561–570, 2012.

paper, we investigate the use of Support Vector Machines (SVMs) disposed in large-margin Decision Directed Acyclic Graphs (DDAGs) [2] to achieve static gesture classification, while at the same time providing comparisons against the ANN approach. Furthermore, we investigate the discriminative counterpart of the HMM-based classifiers given by Hidden Conditional Random Fields (HCRFs). We further explore the implications of those new models, their characteristics, advantages and drawbacks.

This paper is organized as follows. After this introduction, Sect. 2 gives a list of related works, raising some points of interest and discussions. Section 3 gives an overview of the gesture recognition field, its motivation and a brief literature review. Section 4 presents the methods, models and tools used in this work. In Sect. 5 we detail our experiments with fingerspelling recognition, presenting their results in Sect. 6. We then conclude our work, giving final considerations in Sect. 7.

2   Related Works

One of the earlier works on sign language recognition using HMMs were conducted by Starner [3] and colleagues [4]. His work with the American Sign Language (ASL) using a single camera had shown up to 99.2% accuracy. The success of his approach could be partially explained by a restricted vocabulary and the use of a grammar to make the problem tractable. Other correlated works were given by [5] in the recognition of the German Sign Language (*Deutsche Gebärdensprache*, DGS), and by [6] for the British Sign Language (BSL).

Besides [1], one of the most directly related works was developed by Dias et al. [7], who focused specifically on the movement aspect of the LIBRAS. By stating the problem in a convenient mathematical formulation, the authors provided a more tractable formalization of the movement recognition problem amendable to be solved by SOM networks, Learning Vector Quantization (LVQ) and fuzzy variants, attaining overall good results.

Moreover, other papers have already explored HCRFs [8] and other variants for gesture recognition. Morency et al. used LD-CRFs [9] to perform gesture recognition in continuous image streams, with excellent results. Elmezain et al. [10] also studied CRFs, HCRFs and LD-CRFs in the recognition of alphabet characters and numbers drawn in mid-air using hand trajectories, obtaining 91.52%, 95.28% and 98.05% for each model, respectively.

3   Gesture Recognition

Following a comprehensive survey conducted by Mitra and Acharya [11], one can say that gesture recognition methods have been traditionally divided into two main categories: Device-based and vision-based [5,7,10,12]. Device-based approaches often constrain the users to wear a tracking device, such as a tracking glove, resulting in less natural interaction. In this work we will focus only on vision-based approaches.

Gestures can be either static or dynamic. Static gestures, often known as *poses*, are individual still configurations performed by the user. They can often be registered in a single still image. On the other hand, dynamic gestures vary on time, and have to be captured as a sequence of still images (such as in the form of an image stream). Often, gestures have both elements, such as in the case of sign languages [11]. In this paper, we will be covering both gesture types.

Sign languages are natural languages, and therefore have their own structure and grammatical system. Unfortunately, sign languages (and gestures in general) are often ambiguous, in the sense that a specific sign can be used to denote different things depending on context. It is inevitable to make a parallel with the field of speech recognition: Juan and Rabiner reported how the paradigm shift — from generative to discriminative models — played a fundamental role in the field. The change was highly motivated by the fact that probability distributions governing acoustic speech signals could not be modeled accurately, turning Bayes decision theory "inapplicable under these circumstances" [13].

Discriminative models seem to show better performance than generative ones (although this claim is somewhat disputed, e.g. [14]). Nevertheless, there is an increasing literature interest in the application of CRFs, including applications in computer vision [10,15] and sign language recognition [9,12]. A comprehensive description of CRFs and HCRFs is given in [16].

4   Models and Tools

4.1   Artificial Neural Networks

As the name implies, at their creation ANNs had a strong biologic inspiration. However, despite their biological origins, they can be seen as simple functions $f: \mathbb{R}^n \to \mathbb{Y}$ mapping a given input $x \in \mathbb{R}^n$ to a corresponding output $y \in \mathbb{Y}$. The output vectors $y = \langle y_1, \ldots, y_m \rangle$ are also restricted to a specific subset of $\mathbb{R}^n$. Each $y_i \in y$ is restricted to a particular range according to the choice of activation function for the output neurons. In the case of a sigmoid activation function, this range is $[0; 1]$; in case of a bipolar sigmoid function, it is $[-1; 1]$.

The learning problem can be cast as a standard optimization problem, in which we would like to minimize divergence (such as measured by the error gradient) between produced outputs $\hat{y}$ and desired answers y. A promising method to minimize the error gradient is the Resilient Back-propagation algorithm (Rprop) [17], which is one of the fastest methods for gradient learning restricted solely to first-order information. Unlike other gradient based methods, such as Gradient Descent, in which the step size is always proportional to the gradient vector, Rprop takes into account only the direction of the gradient.

4.2   Support Vector Machines

Unlike ANNs, SVMs seem not to suffer from the curse of dimensionality (although the validity of this claim is again sometimes disputed, e.g. [18]). Nevertheless, SVMs have shown great performance in many real-world problems [12,19,20], including high dimensionality and large-scale ones. Its hyperplane decision function is given by

$$h(x) = sgn(\boldsymbol{\theta} \cdot \boldsymbol{x} + b) \underset{\omega_2}{\overset{\omega_1}{\lessgtr}} 0 \tag{1}$$

with $sgn(0) = 1$. Cortes and Vapnik [21] proposed finding a separating hyperplane using an approximate version of the Structural Risk Minimization principle: minimizing the structural risk through maximization of the classification margin, while at same time enforcing capacity control by controlling the margin's width. This problem could then be stated as a constrained optimization problem in the form

$$\underset{w,b,\xi}{min} \frac{1}{2} \|\boldsymbol{\theta}\|^2 + C \left(\sum_{i=1}^{n} \xi_i \right) \tag{2}$$

subject to $y_i(\boldsymbol{\theta} \cdot \boldsymbol{x}_l + b) \geq 1 - \xi_i$ in which $\xi_i \geq 0$ are slack variables and C is a regularization term imposing a weight to the training set error minimization in contraposition to minimizing model complexity. A large value for C would increase the variance of the model, risking overtting. A small C would, in turn, lead to possible underfitting. Considering the dual form of the optimization problem, by adding a nonlinear transformation $\varphi(\cdot): \mathbb{R}^n \rightarrow \mathcal{F}$ such that, when applied to the input tors $\boldsymbol{x}_l \in \mathbb{R}^n$, creates a projection in a high-dimensionality feature space $\mathcal{F}$, one can create a non-linear version of the SVM classifier as

$$h(\boldsymbol{x}) = sgn \left(\sum_{x_j \in SV} \alpha_j \, y_j \, \langle \varphi(\boldsymbol{x}_j), \varphi(\boldsymbol{x}) \rangle + b \right). \tag{3}$$

In this formulation, one can observe that the decision function can be expressed solely in terms of inner products in feature space. Those inner products can then be computed through a Mercer's kernel $k(\boldsymbol{x}, \boldsymbol{z}) = \langle \varphi(\boldsymbol{x}), \varphi(\boldsymbol{z}) \rangle$. Since φ does not have to be computed, the feature space $\mathcal{F}$ can have an arbitrarily high dimensionality.

4.3   Multiclass Classification Approaches

Considering its separating hyperplane formulation, the SVM is only a binary classifier, implying it can only decide between two classes at a time. Many approaches have been proposed to generalize SVMs to multiclass problems; one of the most promising being the Large-Margin Decision Directed Acyclic Graph (DDAG).

The most common approaches to multi-class classification in SVMs are the *one-vs-one* and *one-vs-all* strategies. For a decision problem over c classes, *one-vs-all* demands the creation of c classifiers, each trained to distinguish one class from the others. In the *one-vs-one* strategy, the problem is divided into $c(c - 1)/2$ sub-problems considering only two classes at a time. This leaves the problem of evaluating an increased number of machines for every new instance undergoing classification – which could easily become troublesome or prohibitive in time sensitive applications. The use of DDAGs allows one to conciliate the faster training times of the *one-vs-one* strategy with evaluation speed linear to the number of classes. For c classes, only $(c - 1)$ machines need to be evaluated [2].

4.4   Hidden Markov Models

Hidden Markov Models (HMMs) attempt to model the joint probability distribution of a sequence observations x and their relationship with time through a sequence of hidden states y. A HMM is described by a tuple $\lambda = (A, B, \pi)$ in which A denotes a matrix of possible state transition probabilities, B is a vector of probability distributions governing the observations and π is a vector of initial states probabilities. In the literature, HMMs are often described alongside with three associated canonical problems: evaluation, learning and decoding. Although we will not be discussing those in detail, a very comprehensive explanation is due to Rabiner [22].

Exploring the fact that an HMM is able to provide the likelihood for a given sequence x, it is possible to create a classifier by creating a model λ_i for each sequence label $\omega_i \in \Omega$. Treating each model λ_i as a density model conditioned to an associated class label ω_i, one can apply the Bayes' rule to obtain the a posteriori probability and then decide for the class with *maximum a posteriori*.

4.5   Hidden Conditional Random Fields

Conditional Random Fields (CRFs), first proposed in [23], attempt to model the conditional probability $p(x|y)$ directly. In a general definition [16], one can consider a factor graph G partitioned in a set of clique templates $\mathcal{C} = \{C_1, C_2, ..., C_P\}$. Each clique templates C_p specifies a set of sufficient statistics $\{f_{pk}(x_p, y_p)\}$ and parameters $\theta_p \in \mathfrak{R}^{K(p)}$, such that the general model for a CRF can then be written as

$$p(y|x) = \frac{1}{Z(x)} \prod_{C_p \in \mathcal{C}} \prod_{\Psi_c \in C_p} \Psi_c(x_c, y_c; \theta_p) \qquad (4)$$

with $\Psi_c(x_c, y_c; \theta_p) = exp\{\sum_{k=1}^{K(p)} \theta_{pk} f_{pk}(x_c, y_c)\}$ and in which $Z(x)$ is a normalization function to keep results as probabilities. It can be seen that a CRF denotes a family of Markov Random Fields defined over y for each new observation x. By choosing a specific set of features and initial values for the parameter vector, it is also possible to replicate the exact model of any given HMM, discrete or continuous. To replicate a discrete model, one could choose members from the two families of functions

$$f_{ij}^{edge}(y_t, y_{t-1}, x) = 1_{\{y_t = i\}} 1_{\{y_{t-1} = j\}} \qquad f_{io}^{node}(y_t, y_{t-1}, x) = 1_{\{y_t = i\}} 1_{\{x_t = o\}}$$

to form the feature vector and then initialize the parameter vector $\theta = \{\lambda, \mu\}$ with $\lambda_{ij} = \ln a_{ij}$ and $\mu_{io} = \ln b_{io}$, in which a_{ij} and b_{io} are elements from the A and B matrices of discrete HMMs, respectively.

However, unlike HMMs, CRFs assume the label sequence y is known during training. One possible solution to this problem is to handle y as latent variables. By adding a variable ω to designate class labels, and setting $\boldsymbol{y}$ to be hidden, one arrives at the Hidden Conditional Random Field (HCRF) formulation, given by

$$p(\omega|\boldsymbol{x}) = \frac{1}{Z(\boldsymbol{x})} \sum_{y} \prod_{C_p \in \mathcal{C}} \prod_{\Psi_c \in C_p} \Psi_c(\boldsymbol{x}_c, \boldsymbol{y}_c, \omega_c; \theta_p) \tag{5}$$

which can be computed by the same exact algorithms used to compute $Z(\boldsymbol{x})$ in the CRF case. The penalty paid for this extra flexibility is that the optimization problem is not convex anymore, so one has to deal with the problems of local minima. Nevertheless, one can also use the same Rprop algorithm as mentioned in Sect. 4.1 to mitigate those problems.

5   Experiments

5.1   Dataset

The data used in this study had been gathered as part of a previous work detailed in [1]. The whole dataset contains static gestures gathered from 45 subjects who articulated 27 static signs from the LIBRAS manual alphabet. It also contained dynamic gestures covering fingerspelling of 15 words. Static and dynamic gestures were stored as sequences of still images registered by a single camera in a controlled environment.

For the specific purpose of this experiment, a subset of 16,200 static gesture samples had been randomly selected from the original static sign set, with spurious or corrupted samples removed. Half of those samples were separated for testing purposes and the other half for training and validation. For the dynamic gesture set, we had 540 words containing 63,703 static signs. Hands were located from the still images using Otsu threshold with subsequent cropping and centering. The images were then dimensioned to 32x32 grayscale windows, forming vectors in $\mathbb{R}^{1024}$. Albeit not an optimal representation, this high-dimensionality approach has been done on purpose as part of the study, as it should be explained in the next section.

5.2   Static Gesture Recognition

The goal of this experiment is to perform a direct comparison between ANNs and SVMs without incorporating prior information into the problem (such as in the form of more elaborated features). Thus, we considered the same input dimensionality and output codes for both classifiers. For ANNs, we have created and tested multi-layer feed-forward networks with a single hidden layer and a varying number of hidden nodes using Rprop. All networks were created using bipolar sigmoid activation functions, with initial values given by Nguyen-Widrow's method. For SVMs, we used the Sequential Minimal Optimization (SMO) algorithm [24], together with the DDAG decision scheme [2] to achieve faster multi-class classification times. Parameter tuning for SVMs was performed using a coarse-to-fine grid-search (GS). We also investigated the effectiveness of using heuristic values for the Gaussian kernel based on the inter-quartile range of the input data norm statistics, as proposed by [25].

5.3   Dynamic Gesture Recognition

For the dynamic gesture recognition problem, we considered the same set of discrete features for both classifiers. After completing the previous experiment on static gesture recognition, we gathered the best static gesture classifiers to label all frames from all sequences in the dynamic gesture set. This procedure transformed our image stream data set in a more manageable set of discrete symbol sequences. We designed models containing one hidden state after each symbol in a given word. All models have been created considering the same forward-only topology for state transitions. All HMMs have been trained using Baum-Welch, and HCRFs have been trained using Rprop. Figure. 1 shows a schematic diagram of the system's architecture.

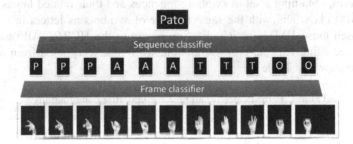

Fig. 1. Schematic representation for the recognition of the finger-spelled word "Pato" (Portuguese for "duck") using a two-stage classification architecture

6   Results and Discussion

We start describing our results for the static gesture recognition experiment with SVMs. For the Gaussian kernel, we found a behavior similar to the one described in [26]. We found out that C did not influence the performance of the classifier as much as would a proper choice for σ^2. Both the Kappa (κ) statistic and the average number of support vectors (SVs) for each classifier were mostly dependent on σ^2 rather than C, as shown in Fig. 2. It should be worth to point out that the heuristic choice for σ^2 not only resulted in overall good performance, but also resulted in less SVs.

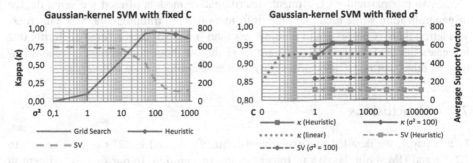

Fig. 2. Cuts of the grid-search procedure for Gaussian SVMs

For the ANN experiments, we found out that ANNs could approach the same SVM's performance rates, but at huge training costs, especially considering the costs on running multiple random initializations to ensure a good local minimum. The best values for κ were amid 300~500 neurons. However, the maximum performance obtained by ANNs ($\hat{\kappa}_{ANN} = 0.9249$) was very similar to the baseline linear SVM ($\kappa = 0.9268$) which can be seen in Fig. 2. Furthermore, the best SVM found ($\hat{\kappa}_{SVM} = 0.9586, \widehat{var}(\hat{\kappa}_{SVM}) = 5.10 \times 10^{-6}$) had also shown better results than the best ANN ($\hat{\kappa}_{ANN} = 0.9241, \widehat{var}(\hat{\kappa}_{ANN}) = 8.93 \times 10^{-6}$). Considering a κ test, the differences are statistically significant under a 0.05 significance level.

The next step was to create the dynamic gesture recognizers. After obtaining the best ANN and SVMs (in terms of higher κ), we tagged the entire dataset of continuous gestures, obtaining a set of symbol sequences and their related labels. First we created HMM classifiers with the same number of symbols as letters in each word. Then we used those HMMs as initialization points to the HCRFs. All results for κ were averaged using ten-fold cross-validation, with variance pooled from all validation runs, as shown in Table 1.

Table 1. Performance for all possible classifier combinations

Static Gesture	Dynamic Gesture	Training	Validation
		Kappa ± (0.95 C.I.)	Kappa ± (0.95 C.I.)
SVM	HMM	0.9469 ± 0.0207	0.8192 ± 0.1063
SVM	HCRF	0.9837 ± 0.0117	0.8332 ± 0.1032
ANN	HMM	0.9482 ± 0.0204	0.8035 ± 0.1092
ANN	HCRF	0.9903 ± 0.0090	0.8236 ± 0.1039

Results shown in Table 2 allow an interesting analysis. It can be seen that, albeit being the best combination, SVM+HCRF results in the validation set are not statistically different from others, meaning we cannot reject the hypothesis that validation results are equivalent. There is not enough evidence to conclude that validation results do not lie within a common range, as can be seen by noticing the overlap of confidence intervals.

However, the same is not true for the training results. It can be seen that training statistics are indeed significant. This opens up for an interesting interpretation of the results: in this particular experiment, discriminative models offered the same degree of generalization while retaining more information about training data. Since in cross-validation there is more data in training sets than in the validation set at each run, this indicates the models were able to learn more data without compromising generalization. In other words, HCRFs have shown greater learning ability with *less overfitting*.

7   Conclusions

In this paper, we detailed our experiments with SVMs and HCRFs in comparison to ANNs and HMMs in the task of fingerspelling recognition. In our first experiment in the task of static gesture recognition we achieved statistically significant results favoring SVMs over ANNs. However, despite the statistical significance and the better accuracy of the SVM models, our second experiment revealed how the choice of the gesture classifier had much greater impact than any particular choice of frame classifier. For either possible choice, using HCRFs instead of HMMs as the sequence classifiers resulted in an increased capacity for retaining training information while at same time providing comparable generalization ability. As a result, classifiers combining HCRFs and ANNs presented overall good results, with equivalent or even better accuracy than models combining HCRFs and SVMs.

However, due the high-dimensionality of the input vectors, the chance for the static gesture recognition problem being approximately linearly separable was high. As linear SVMs can be written in compact form, they were found to be able to offer similar or faster speeds than ANNs while providing comparable recognition rates. From a training perspective, SVMs were also much easier to learn. Training and selecting SVMs was simpler than dealing with the possible local-minima and long training times of ANNs. The cost of performing GS over multiple parameters could have been further reduced if we had focused only on heuristic values for σ^2, which would reduce the hyperparameter tuning problem to a single univariate search over C.

Acknowledgements. We would like to express our thanks to CNPq, for partially sponsoring this project; and also thank our anonymous referees for sharing their valuable comments and views with us.

References

1. Pizzolato, E.B., Anjo, M., Pedroso, G.: Automatic Recognition of Finger Spelling for LIBRAS Based on a Two-Layer Architecture. In: ACM Symposium on Applied Computing (SAC 2010), pp. 969–973. ACM (2010)
2. Platt, J., Cristianini, N., Shawe-Taylor, J.: Large Margin DAGs for Multiclass Classification. Advances in Neural Information Processing Systems 12(3), 547–553 (2000)
3. Starner, T.: Visual Recognition of American Sign Language Using Hidden Markov Models. Thesis (M.S.), Massachusetts Institute of Technology (1995)
4. Starner, T., Weaver, J., Pentland, A.: Real-Time American Sign Language Recognition Using Desk and Wearable Computer Based Video. IEEE Transactions on Pattern Analysis and Machine Intelligence 20(12), 1371–1375 (1998)
5. Bauer, B., Kraiss, K.-F.: Video-Based Sign Recognition Using Self-Organizing Subunits. In: 16th Intl. Conf. on Pattern Recognition (ICPR 2002), vol. 2, pp. 434–437. IEEE (2002)
6. Bowden, R., Windridge, D., Kadir, T., Zisserman, A., Brady, M.: A Linguistic Feature Vector for the Visual Interpretation of Sign Language. In: Pajdla, T., Matas, J. (eds.) ECCV 2004. LNCS, vol. 3021, pp. 390–401. Springer, Heidelberg (2004)
7. Dias, D., Madeo, R., Rocha, T., Bíscaro, H., Peres, S.: Hand Movement Recognition for Brazilian Sign Language – A Study Using Distance-Based Neural Networks. In: Int. Joint Conf. on Neural Networks (IJCNN 2009), pp. 2355–2362. IEEE (2009)
8. Wang, S., Quattoni, A., Morency, L.-P., Demirdjian, D.: Hidden Conditional Random Fields for Gesture Recognition. In: 2006 IEEE Conf. on Computer Vision and Pattern Recognition (CVPR 2006), pp. 1521–1527. IEEE (2006)

9. Morency, L.-P., Quattoni, A., Darrell, T.: Latent-Dynamic Discriminative Models for Continuous Gesture Recognition. In: IEEE Conf. on Computer Vision and Pattern Recognition (CVPR 2007), pp. 1–8. IEEE (2007)
10. Elmezain, M., Al-Hamadi, A., Michaelis, B.: Discriminative Models-Based Hand Gesture Recognition. In: 2nd Intl. Conf. on Machine Vision (ICMV 2009), pp. 123–127. IEEE (2009)
11. Mitra, S., Acharya, T.: Gesture recognition: A survey. IEEE Trans. on Systems, Man and Cybernetics - Part C: Applications and Reviews 37(3), 311–324 (2007)
12. Yang, H.-D., Sclaroff, S., Lee, S.-W.: Sign Language Spotting with a Threshold Model Based on Conditional Random Fields. IEEE Transactions on Pattern Analysis and Machine Intelligence 31(7), 1264–1277 (2009)
13. Juang, B., Rabiner, L.: Automatic Speech Recognition – A Brief History of the Technology. In: Encyclopedia of Language and Linguistics, 2nd edn., Elsevier (2005)
14. Ng, A., Jordan, M.: On Discriminative vs. Generative classifiers: A Comparison of Logistic Regression and Naive Bayes. In: Dietterich, T., Becker, S., Ghahramani, Z. (eds.) Neural Information Processing Systems, vol. 2, pp. 841–848. MIT Press (2001)
15. Quattoni, A., Collins, M., Darrell, T.: Conditional Random Fields for Object Recognition. In: Saul, L., Weiss, Y., Bottou, L. (eds.) Advances in Neural Information Processing Systems, vol. 17, pp. 1097–1104 (2005)
16. Sutton, C., McCallum, A.: Introduction to Statistical Relational Learning. In: Taskar, L. (ed.) An Introduction to Conditional Random Fields for Relational Learning. MIT Press (2007)
17. Igel, C., Hüsken, M.: Improving the Rprop Learning Algorithm. In: 2nd Intl. ICSC Symposium on Neural Computation (NC 2000), pp. 115–121 (2000)
18. Hastie, T., Tibshirani, R., Friedman, J.: The Elements of Statistical Learning: Data Mining, Inference, and Prediction, 2nd edn. Springer (2009)
19. Huang, L.: Variable Selection in Multi-Class Support Vector Machine and Applications in Genomic Data Analysis. ProQuest (2008)
20. Michel, P., El Kaliouby, R.: Real Time Facial Expression Recognition in Video Using Support Vector Machines. In: 5th International Conf. on Multimodal Interfaces (ICMI 2003), pp. 258–264. ACM (2003)
21. Cortes, C., Vapnik, V.: Support-Vector Networks. Machine Learning 20(3), 273–297 (1995)
22. Rabiner, L.R.: A Tutorial on Hidden Markov Models and Selected Applications in Speech Recognition. In: Waibel, A., Lee, K.-F. (eds.) Readings in Speech Recognition, pp. 267–296. Morgan Kaufmann Publishers Inc. (1990)
23. Lafferty, J., McCallum, A., Pereira, F.: Conditional Random Fields – Probabilistic Models for Segmenting and Labeling Sequence Data. In: 18th Intl. Conf. on Machine Learning (ICLM 2001), pp. 282–289. ACM (2001)
24. Platt, J.: Sequential Minimal Optimization – A Fast Algorithm for Training Support Vector Machines. Advances in Kernel Methods and Support Vector Learning 208, 1–21 (1998)
25. Caputo, B., Sim, K., Furesjo, F., Smola, A.: Appearance-Based Object Recognition Using SVMs – Which Kernel Should I Use? In: NIPS Workshop on Statistical Methods for Computational Experiments in Visual Processing and Computer Vision (2002)
26. Valentini, G., Dietterich, T.: Bias-Variance Analysis of Support Vector Machines for the Development of SVM-Based Ensemble Methods. The Journal of Machine Learning Research 5, 725–775 (2004)

Development of an Omnidirectional Kick
for a NAO Humanoid Robot

Rui Ferreira[1,2], Luís Paulo Reis[1,4], António Paulo Moreira[3,5], and Nuno Lau[2,6]

[1] LIACC – Artificial Intelligence and Computer Science Lab., University of Porto, Portugal
[2] IEETA – Institute of Electronics and Telematics Engineering of Aveiro, Portugal
[3] INESC-TEC – Institute for Systems and Computer Engineering of Porto, Portugal
[4] DSI/School of Engineering, University of Minho, Portugal
[5] DEEC/FEUP – Department of Electrical and Computer Engineering,
Faculty of Engineering of the University of Porto, Portugal
[6] DETI/UA – Electronics, Telecommunications and Informatics Department,
University of Aveiro, Portugal
{rui.ferreira,amoreira}@fe.up.pt, lpreis@dsi.uminho.pt,
nunolau@ua.pt

Abstract. This paper proposes a method to develop an omnidirectional kick behavior for a humanoid robot. The objective is to provide a humanoid with the ability to kick in different directions and to make kicks look more like those of a human player. This method uses a Path Planning module to create the trajectory that the foot must follow to propel the ball in the intended direction. Two additional modules are required when performing the movement: the Inverse Kinematics module computes the value of the joints to place the foot at a given position and the Stability module is responsible for the robot's stability. Simulation tests were performed using different ball positions, relative to the robot's orientation, and for various ball directions. The obtained results show the usefulness of the approach since the behavior performs accurately the intended motion and is able to kick the ball in all the desired directions.

Keywords: robotics, robotic behavior, autonomous agent, human behavior, robotic soccer.

1 Introduction

Robotic soccer has been an area of constant evolution and of major driving for the development of Artificial Intelligence and Intelligent Robotics [1]. Being soccer a complex game where the environment is dynamic and in real time, it raises exciting challenges and covers a wide area of research, from which stands out research in robotics, physics, biology, electronics, computer science and mechanics. Figure 1 shows two teams of robots playing a simulated soccer.

This work is related to the development of a new human like behavior for a humanoid robot for Portuguese soccer team FC Portugal, to equip a robot with the ability to kick a ball in various directions. The need to create this behavior arises from the necessity to perform a kick or a pass without having a preparation phase (phase used to put the robot at a precise position to perform the old front/side kick), during which the ball can be intercepted by an opponent.

J. Pavón et al. (Eds.): IBERAMIA 2012, LNAI 7637, pp. 571–580, 2012.

Fig. 1. Robots playing simulated 3D soccer

This behavior will be added to the list of all others previously developed in [2, 3] and enable a team of robots (NAO robots from Aldebaran), real or virtual ones, capable of playing a soccer match at RoboCup 3D Simulation League and Standard Platform League, using similar rules to real soccer, following the strategic framework previously developed in several related works [4-8].

Section 2 describes the implementation of the kick behavior as well as its constituent modules, Sect. 3 contains the practical results and experiments on the behavior, and finally, Sect. 4 gives the conclusions and presents some future work.

2   Omnidirectional Kick Development

2.1   Omnidirectional Kick

In general, kick behavior development is based on the use of keyframes for defining the trajectory of the foot. This method defines motion as a series of static values for the joints and then interpolates them sequentially to perform the movement. The main disadvantages of this approach are the inflexibility and the need of a preparation phase, in which the robot positions itself in order to kick the ball forward in the desired direction.

The idea of developing an omnidirectional kick is to make the kick more flexible and to kick the ball in any direction. To perform this, the robot has to compute the trajectory in real time and then make the foot follow this trajectory and propel the ball in the intended direction. If, during the movement, the ball position changes, the trajectory is updated and the foot movement adapts to this change, but only if the ball is still reachable by the foot.

The omnidirectional kick behavior consists mainly of three modules: Inverse Kinematics module, Path Planning module and Stability module. The Inverse Kinematics module is responsible for calculating the value of the joints of the leg that will perform the kick, the Path Planning module is responsible to compute a trajectory for the foot to propel a ball in some direction and the Stability module is responsible to stabilize the robot while performing the movement.

Fig. 2 shows some of the parameters required to develop the movement. A description of all used parameters can be seen in Table 1.

Fig. 2. Parameters used to create the movement.

Table 1. Parameters description

Parameter	Description
a	Distance from ball to curve start
b	Distance from ball to curve end
hP0	Bézier cubic curve parameters (height coordinate only). Useful to shape the curve and try different kicks)
hP1	
hP2	
hP3	
Duration	Duration of the kicking phase (see Fig. 3)
footOrientation	Angle between foot orientation and vector Ball2Target. This parameter is important to kick with different sections of the foot, e.g. front, side (inner/outer) or heel.

The behavior is divided into a computational part, in which all the computations needed to perform the movement are made, and an execution part, in which the actual movement is performed. Execution part consists of five phases:

- **Lean_Phase** – This is when the robot shifts is center of mass onto support leg.
- **Raise_Phase** – Phase where the robot raises the kick foot off the ground.
- **Kick_Phase** – When the robot kicks the ball. This is the main phase.
- **Return_Phase** – Phase when the robots returns it's kick leg to the base position, without putting the foot on the ground.
- **UnRaise_Phase** – This is when the robot shifts is center of mass to both legs while putting the kick foot on the ground.

Fig. 3 shows the building blocks of the behavior as well as the connections between them, inputs, outputs and generated data.

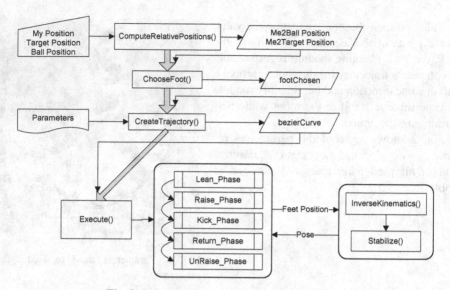

Fig. 3. Building blocks of the developed behavior

2.2   Inverse Kinematics Module

The Inverse Kinematics problem is to determine the value of each joint in order to put a part of our object at a given location in space. Some mechanical characteristics associated with our object, such as the number of joints, joints rotation/translation limits, can make the calculation complex and often raise difficulties to obtain a unique solution [9]. In this study we used a method adapted from [10] in which the geometric approach method was used to determine each joint from the leg of the robot NAO. Two mechanical problems make the solving of Inverse Kinematics complicated:

- The axes of the hip yaw are rotated by 45 degrees;
- The hip yaw axes of each leg are mechanically connected.

The input data is a homogeneous transformation matrix that contains the position and orientation of the desired foot target relative to a frame located at the robot pelvis. This matrix is represented by H_{Foot}^{Pelvis} . Next we have to determine the foot relative to the hip rotated frame [6].

$$H_{Foot}^{HipRot} = Rot_x(\pi/4) \cdot Trans_y(l_{dist}/2) \cdot H_{Foot}^{Pelvis\,1} \tag{1}$$

Assuming a triangle formed by the robot's thigh (lthigh) and lower leg (llowerleg), and the translational vector of H_{Foot}^{HipRot} (ltrans), and using law of cosines and atan2(), we can determine the value of the knee and ankle joints [6].

---

[1] $Rot_K(v)$ and $Trans_K(v)$ represents rotation and translation of value v along axis K, respectively, and l_{legs} = distance between legs.

The pitch, roll and yaw of the hip are determined by simple manipulation of the elements of H_{HipRot}^{Thigh} as seen in (2).

$$H_{HipRot}^{Thigh} = Rot_z\left(\theta_{hipYaw}\right) \cdot Rot_x\left(\theta_{hipRoll}\right) \cdot Rot_y\left(\theta_{hipPitch}\right)$$

$$= \begin{bmatrix} c_y c_z - s_x s_y s_z & -c_x s_z & c_z s_y + c_y s_x s_z \\ c_z s_x s_y + c_y s_z & c_x c_z & -c_y c_z s_x + s_y s_z \\ -c_x c_y & s_x & c_x c_y \end{bmatrix} \quad \text{2} \tag{2}$$

and H_{HipRot}^{Thigh} can be determined using

$$H_{HipRot}^{Thigh} = \left(H_{Thigh}^{Foot}\right)^{-1} \cdot \left(H_{Foot}^{HipRot}\right)^{-1} \tag{3}$$

$$H_{Thigh}^{Foot} = Rot_x\left(\theta_{ankleRoll}\right) \cdot Rot_y\left(\theta_{anklePitch}\right) \cdot$$
$$Trans_z\left(l_{lowerleg}\right) \cdot Rot_y\left(\theta_{knee}\right) \cdot Trans_z\left(l_{thigh}\right) \tag{4}$$

2.3   Path Planning Module

This module is responsible for creating a trajectory for the foot to follow in order to impose a motion to the ball in the desired direction. It makes use of Bézier curves [11] to determine a path between two points. These type of curves are defined as parametric curves and is easy to determine any point of the curve without using complex math (a simple equation gives the point). For our study we used a Bézier cubic curve (n=3) and the point can be determined using (5).

$$b(t) = \sum_{i=0}^{n} \binom{n}{i} \cdot t^i \cdot (1-t)^{n-1} \cdot p_i, \quad t \in [0,1] \tag{5}$$

2.4   Stability Module

The Stability module uses the center of mass equation [12] to determine if the ground projection of the center of mass (GCoM) is actually inside the polygon of the support foot. If not, it enters in a cycle where it will open one arm (on the same side of the supporting foot) until GCoM is in the desired location. In the extreme case where the arm movement is not enough a change in the hip and ankle roll angles of the supporting foot is also made to tilt the robot to a stable position.

3   Experiments and Results

In this section we show the results of several experiments performed to verify analytically the success of this work. We start by testing each module individually and then

---

2 c_x, c_y, c_z represents $\cos(\theta_{hipRoll})$, $\cos(\theta_{hipPitch})$, $\cos(\theta_{hipYaw})$, respectively.

test the whole behavior. The tests to each individual module are of great importance since the final behavior depends strongly of their success.

All points representing positions in the individual module tests are relative to a frame located at the robot pelvis (see Fig. 4).

3.1   Inverse Kinematics Module Tests

The main objective when testing this module is to verify its functionalities and limitations. It is necessary for it to operate with the minimum error possible because it is the base of the motion. A small error when computing the joints values makes

Fig. 4. Reference frame

the foot perform a wrong trajectory and propel the ball in the wrong direction. Table 2 shows the results of this test.

Table 2. Results of the Inverse Kinematics module tests

Target (x, y, z) (mm)	Average (x, y, z) (mm)	Standard Deviation (x, y, z) (mm)	Average-Target (x, y, z) (mm)
(0, -55, -150)	(3, -56, -148)	(1, 1, 3)	(3, -1, 2)
(-100, -55, -100)	(-89, -60, -99)	(1, 1, 0)	(11, -5, 1)
(100, -55, -100)	(100, -55, -105)	(7, 1, 3)	(0, 0, -5)
(0, -100, -100)	(7, -104, -108)	(2, 3, 3)	(7, -4, -8)
(500, -55, -10)	(214, -54, -16)	(1, 1, 2)	(-286, 1, -6)

3.2   Path Planning Module Tests

The main purpose when testing this module is to verify its trajectories creation. It is also necessary for it to operate with the minimum error possible because if the trajectory is miscalculated we will get a wrong movement, resulting in a wrong ball motion.

Fig. 5 shows 3 curves (linear, quadratic and cubic) created and the ability of the foot to follow these curves.

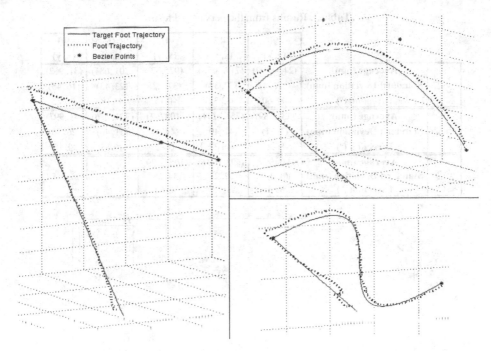

Fig. 5. Various curves created by Path Planning module and the trajectory executed by the foot

3.3   Omnidirectional Kick Tests

For the tests of the complete behavior we will test for:

— 3 positions (#1, #2 and #3) of the ball relative to the robot orientation (see Fig. 6);
— 5 kick directions (-90, -45, 0, 45 and 90 degrees), when possible.

Fig. 6. Ball Positions for the tests. Left is 'Position #1', center 'Position #2' and right is 'Position #3'

For each direction we performed the movement 10 times and 10 samples of the final ball position. We proceeded to get the average and standard deviation of the 10 samples and in the end we determined the resulting direction. This data is shown in Table 3 and Fig. 7.

Table 3. Results from the performed tests

		-90 (x, y)	-45 (x, y)	0 (x, y)	45 (x, y)	90 (x, y)
Pos. #1	Average (mm)	(24, -1009)	(719, -678)	(975, -2)	(701, 681)	(31, 962)
	Standard Deviation (mm)	(17, 38)	(37, 34)	(37, 22)	(23, 43)	(16, 45)
	Direction (°)	-88.60	-43.32	-0.15	44.18	88.12
Pos. #2	Average (mm)	(13, -989)	(758, -741)	(1082, 2)	(721, 676)	(31, 997)
	Standard Deviation (mm)	(7, 21)	(41, 40)	(44, 4)	(31, 40)	(26, 36)
	Direction (°)	-89.20	-44.37	0.12	43.15	88.19
Pos. #3	Average (mm)	(11, -991)	(693, -697)	(1053, -29)		
	Standard Deviation (mm)	(3, 23)	(22, 22)	(34, 18)		
	Direction (°)	-89.35	-45.15	-1.59		

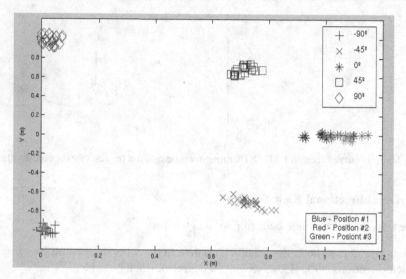

Fig. 7. Samples location for Positions #1, #2 and #3

By examining the results obtained from this test we can see that the behavior can perform the movement and propel the ball in various directions. From the table we can see the average final position of the ball of the 10 samples as well as the standard deviation, and from the average we determined the direction. The determined direction value, of each direction, only differs a few degrees from the intended target direction, which confirms the accuracy propelling the ball. The accompanying graphic serves only to have a visualization of the ball's final position of the 10 samples for each target direction. The samples are grouped by target direction. The parameters used on these tests were hand tuned. We can control the kick power by adjusting both the kick duration and the initial and final position.

To test the sensibility of the kick against different positions of the ball, relative to the robot, another test was made. This test consists of kicking the ball with a desired direction, using always the same values for the parameters, and only changing the ball initial position.

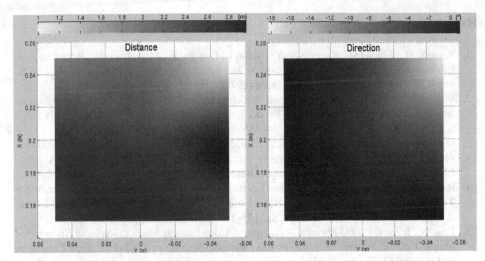

Fig. 8. Differences on the distance and direction due to different ball positions, for the same kick (forward kick, direction=0°)

The results obtained are shown in Fig. 8, where it is represented the distance and direction of the ball with a gradient value and the (x, y) coordinates refers to the ball's initial position relative to the kick foot.

The conclusion we take from these tests is that: if we configure the parameters of the behavior with some accuracy, we can get very good results. The problem is that, sometimes, it is not so easy to get the best parameters, becoming necessary the use of optimizers.

From Fig. 8 we can see that, if the ball is within a certain area relative to the kick foot, in almost 80% of that area it can kick the ball without losing accuracy.

4   Conclusions and Future Work

In this study we developed a behavior in order to provide a humanoid robot with the ability to perform an omnidirectional kick. The modularity of this behavior makes it perfect for future improvements or modifications.

The results obtained proved that the behavior performs accurately the desired motion. The Inverse Kinematics module, being the base of the behavior and with errors in the order of millimeters, is responsible for these satisfactory results. If it was not for the joints limitations it could reach any point within the working volume.

The Path Planning module proved to be very valuable when creating trajectories. With it, one can calculate any kind of trajectory easily, quickly and accurately.

Future work will be focused on improving the behavior, by optimizing it in order to perform faster and to drive the ball farther. This will be based on previous work developed on the area of machine learning and optimization applied to robotic soccer [13-16]. It will also be interesting to expand the behavior to perform heel kicks and to incorporate the kick in a walk/run motion.

References

1. Kitano, H., Asada, M., Kuniyoshi, Y., Noda, I., Osawa, E., Matsubara, H.: RoboCup – A Challenge Problem for AI and Robotics. In: Kitano, H. (ed.) RoboCup 1997. LNCS, vol. 1395, pp. 1–19. Springer, Heidelberg (1998)
2. Shafii, N., Reis, L.P., Lau, N.: Biped Walking Using Coronal and Sagittal Movements Based on Truncated Fourier Series. In: del Solar, J.R., Chown, E., Plöger, P.G. (eds.) RoboCup 2010. LNCS, vol. 6556, pp. 324–335. Springer, Heidelberg (2010)
3. Domingues, E., Lau, N., Pimentel, B., Shafii, N., Reis, L.P., Neves, A.J.: Humanoid Behaviors: From Simulation to a Real Robot. In: Antunes, L., Pinto, H.S. (eds.) EPIA 2011. LNCS, vol. 7026, pp. 352–364. Springer, Heidelberg (2011)
4. Reis, L.P., Lau, N., Oliveira, E.: Situation Based Strategic Positioning for Coordinating a Team of Homogeneous Agents. In: Hannebauer, M., Wendler, J., Pagello, E. (eds.) ECAI-WS 2000. LNCS (LNAI), vol. 2103, pp. 175–197. Springer, Heidelberg (2001)
5. Lau, N., Reis, L.P.: FC Portugal – High-level Coordination Methodologies in Soccer Robotics, Robotic Soccer. In: Lima, P. (ed.) Robotic Soccer, pp. 167–192. Itech Education and Publishing, Vienna (2007)
6. Lau, N., Reis, L.P., Certo, J.: Understanding Dynamic Agent's Reasoning. In: Neves, J., Santos, M.F., Machado, J. (eds.) EPIA 2007. LNCS (LNAI), vol. 4874, pp. 542–551. Springer, Heidelberg (2007)
7. Almeida, F., Lau, N., Reis, L.P.: A Survey on Coordination Techniques for Simulated Robotic Soccer Teams. In: 2010 Workshop on Multi-Agent Systems and Simulation (MAS&S 2010) at 2010 Multi-Agent Logics, Languages, and Organisations Federated Workshops (MALLOW 2010), pp. 47–54 (2010)
8. Mota, L., Reis, L.P., Lau, N.: Multi-Robot Coordination Using Setplays in the Middle-Size and Simulation Leagues. Mechatronics 21(2), 434–444 (2011)
9. Goldenber, A.A., Benhabib, B., Fenton, R.G.: A Complete Generalized Solution to the Inverse Kinematics of Robots. IEEE Journal of Robotics and Automation 1(1), 14–20 (1985)
10. B-Human Team: B-Human – Team Report and Code Release, ch. 5 (2011), http://www.b-human.de/downloads/bhuman11_coderelease.pdf (accessed February 2012)
11. Sederberg, T.: Bézier Curves. ch. 2, http://www.tsplines.com/resources/class_notes/Bezier_curves.pdf (accessed February 2012)
12. Tipler, P.A., Mosca, G.: Physics for Scientists and Engineers Extended Version, 5th edn. W.H. Freeman (2003)
13. Abreu, P.H., Moura, J., Silva, D.C., Reis, L.P., Garganta, J.: Performance Analysis in Soccer: a Cartesian Coordinates Based Approach Using RoboCup Data. Soft Computing 16(1), 47–61 (2012)
14. Faria, B.M., Reis, L.P., Lau, N., Castillo, G.: Machine Learning Algorithms Applied to the Classification of Robotic Soccer Formations and Opponent Teams. In: IEEE Conference Cybernetics and Intelligent Systems (CIS 2010), pp. 344–349. IEEE (2010)
15. Almeida, R., Reis, L.P., Jorge, A.M.: Analysis and Forecast of Team Formation in the Simulated Robotic Soccer Domain. In: Lopes, L.S., Lau, N., Mariano, P., Rocha, L.M. (eds.) EPIA 2009. LNCS (LNAI), vol. 5816, pp. 239–250. Springer, Heidelberg (2009)
16. Picado, H., Gestal, M., Lau, N., Reis, L.P., Tomé, A.M.: Automatic Generation of Biped Walk Behavior Using Genetic Algorithms. In: Cabestany, J., Sandoval, F., Prieto, A., Corchado, J.M. (eds.) IWANN 2009, Part I. LNCS, vol. 5517, pp. 805–812. Springer, Heidelberg (2009)

The Planning Net: Exploring the Petri Net Flow to Improve Planning Solvers

Marcos A. Schreiner, Marcos A. Castilho, Fabiano Silva, and Luis A. Kunzle

Artificial Intelligence Laboratory and Formal Methods LIAMF/UFPR,
Department of Informatics, Mail Box: 19081, Zip Code: 81531-980, Curitiba,
PR, Brazil
{maschreiner,marcos,fabiano,kunzle}@inf.ufpr.br

Abstract. In this paper the classical planning problem is formalized as
a Petri Net. We review the Graphplan notions of mutex relation and
maintenance actions based on the Petri Net flow. We classify pairs of
conflicting actions in terms of four different control structures, which are
used to build the Planning Net. The planning problem represented by
the net is translated into a SAT instance and then solved using a modern
SAT solver. We show the advantages of our method comparing our new
planner with Satplan in classical planning domains.

Keywords: planning problems, Petri net, planning net, satisfiability.

1 Introduction

One of the breakthroughs in the methods for solving planning problems was the
Graphplan [1]. It is based on a data structure which represents the search space
of a planning problem in a smart and economic way. It allows parallelism between
actions through the identification of mutually exclusive actions. The so called
Planning Graph is the basis for many algorithms which were proposed in the
past few years, among them we cite Satplan [3]. In Satplan, the Planning Graph
is converted to a satifiability problem. The solution of the planning problem is
obtained using fast and modern SAT solvers.

In this paper we will present a data structure based on Petri Nets. Petri Nets
are in fact a model that represents a system's structure and behavior because
it enables to represent states, events and information flow of a system based on
preconditions and effects. Our idea is to use the dynamics of the Petri Net in
order to improve from the Planning Graph, which is a static structure, and get
a faster planner.

In Silva [7], it has been proposed a planning method version with Petri Nets
that were called Petriplan. Its data structure had a similar representation with
relation to the Planning Graph. This representation allowed then the planning
problem to be solved by the reachability problem solution in Petri Nets.

This solver is not efficient as it could be, since it was surpassed by planners as
Satplan. The solver initially used was based in integer programming techniques.

J. Pavón et al. (Eds.): IBERAMIA 2012, LNAI 7637, pp. 581–590, 2012.

In this article we explore Petri Nets in a more effective way. We propose (i) a smarter way to use Petri Net flow; and (ii) a more precise way to classify the relation between actions. We will present a new data structure called the Planning Net.

Actually, in Graphplan, pairs of conflicting actions are classified as mutually exclusive based on two criteria: interference and competing needs. The conflicts between action pairs of the Planning Net are an improvement of the interference conflict. We specify a partial ordering of actions which is, theoretically, richer on information. We classify pairs of action in four different ways: given a pair of actions a and b, we define that they may occur in parallel, non-parallel, a precede b or they are mutually exclusives.

The Petri Net flow analysis showed the uselessness of the competing needs mutexes in the Planning Net. The reason is that the net flow ensures that pairs of actions in this mutex type do not occur in parallel. The net flow also allows reducing the number of maintenance actions on the net with relation to the Planning Graph. These actions are included only for the propositions that are deleted by some action belonging to the Planning Net.

As a result, we get a data structure which has more information than that of the Planning Graph. From this data structure it is possible to define a new SAT encoding to planning problems. We will show this new structure in this paper and compare our experimental results with Satplan.

2   Planning Net

A Petri Net is defined by a 4-tuple $R = <L, T, Pre, Post>$, where L is a finite and non-empty set of places of cardinality n; T is a finite and non-empty set of transitions of cardinality m; $Pre : L \times T \to \mathbb{N}$ is an input incidence function; and $Post : L \times T \to \mathbb{N}$ is an output incidence function.

A marked Petri Net is formally defined by the tuple $N = <R, M>$, where M is a vector of length n containing the initial marking, where $M(p)$ contains the number of place tokens p.

A Petri Net also has a dynamic behavior proportioned by the firing of enabled transitions in which occurrence results in the Net state change. A t transition is enabled by a M marking if, $\forall l \in L, M(l) \geq Pre(., t)$. The firing of a t transition in a M_i marking generates a new M' marking given by: $M' = M_i + Post(., t) + Pre(., t)$.

The problem of achieving a M_g marking from an initial M_i marking in an acyclic Petri Net may be mapped to the problem of finding a non-negative integer vector $\bar{s}$ in equation: $M_g = M_i + (Post - Pre) \cdot \bar{s}$

The Planning Net is an acyclic Petri Nets structure, where actions are represented by transitions. The propositions, preconditions and effects action, are represented by places. The negative effects are not represented, but are useful for calculating the ordering relations.

The Planning Net is built from a place L_{ini}, connected to a transition T_{ini}, which is connected to a place for every initial state proposition l_i^k, where i is

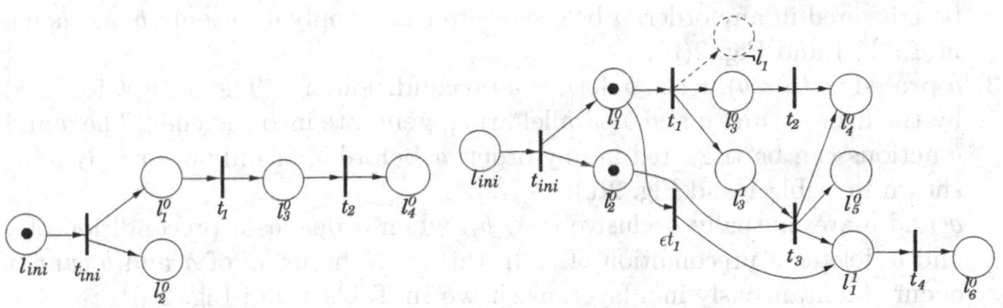

(a) Basic Planning Net   (b) Inclusion of actions in Planning Net

Fig. 1. Examples of Planning Net

the proposition index and k the place number that represents proposition i, as shown in Fig. 1.

One set of places is used to represent one proposition to avoid conflicts and to ensure that the result in Planning Net is acyclic. This set of places is created during the inclusion process for each transition.

A transition is added in the Planning Net if all preconditions are contained in the net. If the preconditions or effects are also another transition precondition, one new place should be created. The previous transition effects must be maintained, as shown in Fig. 1(b), with arcs (t_1, l_3^1).

If there is a transition in the Planning Net whose action removes the proposition represented by the created place, the maintenance of the previous transition effects is held by the transition, as shown by the transition ϵt_1 and arcs $(\epsilon t_1, l_1^1)$ and $(l_1^0, \epsilon t_1)$ (see Fig. 1(b)). If t_1 does not trigger, ϵt_1 allows the token flow in l_1^1 to other layers.

The Planning Net layer is different from that of the Planning Graph. A layer is composed of actions included in the net, copies and new places inserted as effect. The layer's temporal notion is relaxed.

The partial orderings between pairs of conflicting actions is an alternative to the Planning Graph's interference mutually exclusive actions. The Petri Net dynamics dispense the competing needs mutexes. The tokens flow prevents the transitions simultaneously trigger of the competing needs conflict.

We improve the inconsistence mutex notion by defining partial orderings between two actions a and b in the following way:

1. a and b are parallel ($a \parallel b$), when there is no inconsistency between a and b. The actions a and b can be triggered in any order: a before or after b, or both at the same time, or only a, or only b, as shown in Table 1 and Fig. 2(a);
2. a and b are non-parallel ($a \nparallel b$), where a deletes a b effect. In this case only parallel firing of the a and b generates inconsistency. The a and b actions can

be triggered in any order: a before or after b, or only a, or only b, as shown in Table 1 and Fig. 2(b);

3. a precede b ($a \lhd b$), when b deletes a precondition of a. The firing b followed by the firing a, and a and b parallel firing, generate inconsistency. The a and b actions can be triggered in any order: a before b, or only a, or only b, as shown in Table 1 and Fig. 2(c);

4. a and b are mutually exclusive ($a \Diamond b$), when a deletes a precondition of b and b deletes a precondition of a. In this case the firing of a and b cannot occur simultaneously in a layer, as shown in Table 1 and Fig. 2(d).

Based on the ordering relations it is possible to define valid and invalid subplans of two actions a and b occurring in two different layer steps. Table 1 illustrate these subplans, where | represents the parallel subplan, ; indicates the precedence between actions and λ is the empty subplan.

Table 1. Valid and invalid subplans of each ordering relation

Ordering relation.	Valid subplans	Invalid subplans
$a \parallel b$	$(a|b), (a), (b), (a;b), (b;a), \lambda$	
$a \mathbin{\shortmid\hspace{-0.3em}\shortmid} b$	$(a), (b), (a;b), (b;a), \lambda$	$(a|b)$
$a \lhd b$	$(a), (b), (a;b), \lambda$	$(a|b), (b;a)$
$a \Diamond b$	$(a), (b), \lambda$	$(a|b), (a;b), (b;a)$

In Fig. 2 we show the control structures of the Planning Net, that were built based on valid subplans between two actions a and b.

In the control structures of Fig. 2, the place I indicates the initial control in the layer and F the end control. The transitions θ and Φ, respectively, represents the beginning and end control of one or two actions, as to the ordering relation.

For example, the structure shown in Fig. 2(c): the token contained in place I enables the trigger θ_a or θ_b, because the valid subplans ($a \mathbin{\shortmid\hspace{-0.3em}\shortmid} b$) start with actions a or b. If θ_a is fired, the binary conflict between a and λ_a allows, respectively, a to run or not. The trigger a or λ_a create a token in the place which enables the end control transition a (Φ_a). The Φ_a trigger creates a token P_b, which represents the linkage between the layer steps and the ordering between actions.

The control structures can be grouped from places I and F. For example, the ordering relations ($b \parallel c$), ($a \mathbin{\shortmid\hspace{-0.3em}\shortmid} b$) and ($a \mathbin{\shortmid\hspace{-0.3em}\shortmid} c$) result in the composition of the control structures shown in Fig. 3.

In the composition of the control structures, only one control substructure can be fired at each layer step, as exemplified in Fig. 3. In the first step of each layer, the token contained in place I enables to be fired: the control substructure ($b \parallel c$), or the control substructure of action a. In the second step of each layer only one control substructure is enabled, which is ensured by the inclusion of

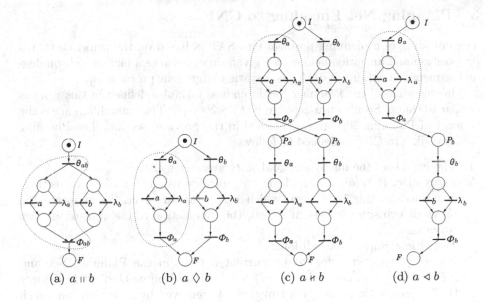

(a) $a \parallel b$ (b) $a \Diamond b$ (c) $a \nparallel b$ (d) $a \lhd b$

Fig. 2. Control structure used in the Planning Net

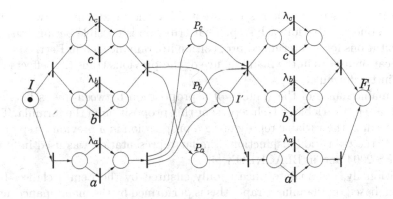

Fig. 3. Example of control structures composition

place I'. The parallel control structure allows the representation of more than one ordering relation. For example, the control substructure $(b \parallel c)$ is contained in the representation of structures $(a \nparallel b)$ and $(a \nparallel c)$.

Each transition that represents the execution of one action in the control structures composition is also linked with the preconditions and effects places of the action. The transition that represents the execution of one action is triggered if it belongs to a valid flow in the control structures composition and if the precondition places of the action contains a token.

3 Planning Net Encoding to CNF

The encoding of a planning problem into SAT is based on the principle that a proposition and an action belong to a given time, because a plan is a chronological sequence of actions and SAT is a static assignment problem [3].

The encoding of the Planning Net in clausal formulas defined in this work is similar to that of Satplan presented in ICAPS'2006 [4]. The main difference is the concept of Planning Net layer, explained in the previous section. The Planning Net encoding in CNF is defined as follows:

1. The literals of the initial and goal state are unary clauses;
2. Every place l_i^k belonging to a layer step implies disjunction of the transitions contained on this layer step, which has l_i^k as an effect. To maintain the previous transition effects, if $k > 0$, the disjunction of the transitions also contains l_i^{k-1};
3. Transitions imply preconditions;
4. For all propositions deleted by current actions in the Planning Net and for all these actions, a clause $(\neg l_i^k \vee \neg t)$ should be created. l_i^k is a place that represents a proposition i in the net, removed by an action, on which transition t belongs to the same step and layer as of l_i^k;
5. Mutually exclusive actions are represented by a set of disjunctions.

Due to item 2, a proposition is represented by the maximum of two variables per layer, one variable for each step. That criterion is possible because the other representations for a determined proposition are only needed in Petri Nets. This simplification assists in the maintenance of the previous transition effects represented in the formula.

The maintenance of the validity of a proposition between layers is encoded through a set of variables which represent this proposition in the formula. Therefore, in item 2, the variable representing a proposition in a previous step or layer is part of the transition disjunction. Similar representation was used in Satplan in ICAPS'2004 and in BLACKBOX [4].

Additionally, this maintenance is only ensured by the item 4 clause. In the encoding based on Planning Graph, this is performed by the maintenance actions and by the mutexes [3]. We show in Table 2 the differences between the encoding based on Planning Net and Satplan's.

Conflicts in the Planning Net are represented by binary clauses that restrict the validity of the actions, according to Planning Net ordering relations, described in Sect. 2. The control structures represent valid partial orderings. The conflict clauses represent invalid partial orderings.

For two mutually exclusive actions, a and b of some layer i, which is composed of two steps, the clauses: $(\neg a_i^1 \vee \neg b_i^1)$, $(\neg a_i^1 \vee \neg a_i^2)$, $(\neg a_i^1 \vee \neg b_i^2)$, $(\neg b_i^1 \vee \neg a_i^2)$, $(\neg b_i^1 \vee \neg b_i^2)$ and $(\neg a_i^2 \vee \neg b_i^2)$ are created. If the action a precedes action b, the same mutex clauses are created, except by $(\neg a_i^1 \vee \neg b_i^2)$, because it is a valid ordering. If a is a non-parallel to b, the same clauses are created mutex except $(\neg a_i^1 \vee \neg b_i^2)$ and $(\neg b_i^1 \vee \neg a_i^2)$. For parallel order relation additional clauses are not created.

Table 2. Comparison between Satplan and coding based in Planning Net

Coding based in Planning Net	Satplan
Base structure: Planning Net	Base structure: Planning Graph
Computes and encodes ordering relations	Computes mutex of interference, competing needs and propositions, but encodes interference and propositions
Relaxed layer	Layer not relaxed
Encodes maintenance clauses	Encodes maintenance actions and propositions mutex

The differences between the coding presented in this paper and that of Satplan result in formulas with different number of variables. Equation 1 describes the comparison between the number of variables R_i generated from the Planning Net up to layer i with Satplan's S_i number of variables, which contains generated variables from maintenance actions A_m.

$$R_i \leq 2(S_i - A_m) \tag{1}$$

In equation 1, A_m is eliminated from S_i, because in the Planning Net encoding, the new effects maintenance method does not result in variables in the formula. The result of this elimination is multiplied by two, because the Planning Net layers are relaxed. The number of variables R_i is less or equal than the result of the right side of the equation, because there may be a set of actions that are not contained in the second step of a layer.

4 Experimental Results

Experiments in the Planning Net were performed using 10 domains from the *ICAPS Competitions* website [2]. The results of these experiments were compared with the Satplan planner, which is among the best planners at this time.

All experiments of this work and other empirical tests have been validated by the *Plan Validator* [5], which certified the validity of the found plans.

The SAT solver used in the experiments with Planning Net and Satplan was the *lingeling*. This solver was one of three winners of the 2011 International SAT Competitions [6]. The experiments were performed on a AMD 2.8 GHz, with 8 cores, 10 GB of RAM and Debian GNU/Linux computer.

We show in Table 3 a comparative experiments between Planning Net and the Satplan. In the first six problems the execution time of the planner defined in this paper was better than Satplan.

The solving complexity of a formula in CNF does not depend only on the density and on the number of variables and clauses. In all experiments of this work the Planning Net encoding generated formulas with higher density than the

Table 3. Comparative results between Planning Net and Satplan

Problems	Satplan				Planning Net			
	Vars	Clause	Act plan	Time (s)	Vars	Clause	Act plan	Time (s)
Logistics 1	24539	221131	151	110.45	13303	172509	153	29.552
Logistics 2	–	–	–	timeout	24834	461445	224	950.67
TPP	43884	2665474	145	1608,142	68306	10445701	159	101,388
Storage 1	7369	362345	18	271,116	5453	786927	22	156,72
Storage 2	–	–	–	timeout	9508	2663990	29	321,22
Pipeworld	35025	7581085	44	465,32	26300	15137493	44	325,67
Elevador	6689	128525	27	119,9	5864	265995	27	801,5
Depots	5698	216423	73	55,73	20564	7075691	81	393,6
Driverlog 1	14049	248447	40	26,9	12186	479272	48	1319,5
Driverlog 2	76564	3677227	100	1681,32	–	–	–	timeout
Freecell	17582	6114100	30	253,05	15919	11159318	36	667,0
Satelite	18881	479761	43	38,97	14399	824851	48	263,4
Gripper	4476	57593	35	291,55	3224	53051	35	1321,326

formulas generated by Satplan. The clauses number in the formulas generated by Satplan is greater than the clauses number generated by the Planning Net, with exception of the Gripper and Logistic domains. The Planning Net generated fewer variables than the Satplan, except in the TPP e Depots domains.

The complexity of solving a formula depends on the domain structure combined with the formula encoding structures.

Another essential feature is the binary conflict clauses. We propose a partial ordering for the interference mutex and discard the competing needs. The partial ordering resulted in a better run-time than Satplan in some domains.

The encoding structure and the information type added to the formula are the main causes of the experimental results in this work. In the Logistics, TPP, Storage and Pipeworld domains, the Planning Net produces a more efficient encoding than the Planning Graph. In the Elevador, Depots, Driverlog, Freecell, Satelite and Gripper domains, the Planning Graph produces a more efficient encoding than the Planning Net.

Another relevant data in Table 3 is the length of the plans generated by the planners. The plans generated by Satplan are always smaller or equal than plans generated by the Planning Net. Through empirical tests performed with *BLACKBOX*, Kautz and Selman found that finding optimal plans is more difficult than finding sub-optimal ones [3].

The Satplan has postprocessing to remove (some of the) unnecessary actions of the plan. The postprocessing is useful because the SAT translation of the Planning Graph does not guarantee that every action that is true in the solution is actually needed in order to achieve the goals of the original plan [4].

We do not include this postprocessing step in our planner, but we obtained plans with the same length as Satplan's in Gripper, Elevador and Pipeworld. In the other seven domains the plans generated by our planner were longer.

We also performed an analysis of the information set included in the formula through the control structures. We made the combination of the mutex control structure with the other control structures, as shown in Table 4. The mutex only representation was more efficient in the Pipeworld, Elevator, Drivelog and Satellite domains.

Table 4. Information variation based in structure control

Problems	Complete	Mutex and non-parallel	Mutex and precede	Mutex
Logistica 2	950,6	894,1	**675,9**	805,3
TPP	**101,4**	141,2	110,2	108,5
Storage 2	321,2	**295,2**	302,1	352,9
Pipeworld 2	325,7	311,7	307,4	**186,9**
Elevador	801,5	887,7	664,8	**661,5**
Depots	393,6	343,6	**284,9**	470,2
Driverlog 1	1319,5	timeout	1663,6	**1112,8**
Freecell	667,0	**180,7**	824,7	198,1
Satelite	263,4	281,4	222,2	**190,1**
Gripper	1321,326	timeout	**609,264**	1075,042

In the Gripper and Depots domains, mutex and complete control structures have similar run-time. The combination of the precedes and mutex structures was more efficient. In the Gripper domain the combination of the non-parallel and mutex presented the worst results.

In the Freecell domain the combination of the non-parallel and mutex was more efficient. The run-time is less than Satplan's.

In the TPP domain the complete control structure was more efficient. The TPP domain used a large amount of memory.

The information set from the control structures that helps the search for the plan depends on the planning problem domain. In some domains, additional information may simplify the search for a solution while in other domains it may not.

5   Conclusions

In this work we presented the Planning Net, an efficient planner based on Petri Net. The Planning Net is more efficient that Satplan in four out of ten domains from the *ICAPS Competitions*. In the Logistics, TPP, Storage and Pipeworld domains, the Planning Net produces a more efficient encoding than Satplan. In the Elevator, Depots, Driverlog, Freecell, Satelite and Gripper domains, Satplan produces a more efficient encoding than Planning Net.

The classification of the conflicting action pairs in clauses using four different control structures assisted the SAT solver in the search for a satisfiable assignment. However, the information set from the control structures that helps the search for the plan depends on the planning problem domain. New studies in the Planning Net construction process for each domain are necessary to identify what information is important.

Another research that can be performed is the creation of propositions order relations in the Planning Net. The propositions conflict has more information than the actions conflict and this may produce better results when compared with actions order relations.

References

1. Blum, A., Furst, M.: Fast Planning through Planning Graph Analysis. In: 14th International Joint Conference on Artificial Intelligence (IJCAI 1995), pp. 1636–1642 (1995)
2. International Planning Competition - ICAPS, http://ipc.icaps-conference.org/
3. Kautz, H.A., Selman, B.: Pushing the Envelope – Planning, Propositional Logic, and Stochastic Search. In: Shrobe, H., Senator, T. (eds.) 13th National Conference on Artificial Intelligence (AAAI 1996) and 8th Innovative Applications of Artificial Intelligence Conference (IAAI 1996), pp. 1194–1201. AAAI (1996)
4. Kautz, H.A.: Deconstructing Planning as Satisfiability. In: 21st National Conference on Artificial Intelligence (AAAI 2006) and 18th Innovative Applications of Artificial Intelligence Conference (IAAI 2006), pp. 1524–1526. AAAI (2006)
5. VAL, The Automatic Validation Tool For PDDL, including PDDL3 and PDDL+ Strathclyde Planning Group, http://planning.cis.strath.ac.uk/VAL/
6. The international SAT Competitions web page, http://www.satcompetition.org
7. Silva, F., Castilho, M.A., Künzle, L.A.: Petriplan: A New Algorithm for Plan Generation (Preliminary Report). In: Monard, M.C., Sichman, J.M. (eds.) SBIA 2000 and IBERAMIA 2000. LNCS (LNAI), vol. 1952, pp. 86–95. Springer, Heidelberg (2000)

An Automated User-Centered Planning Framework for Decision Support in Environmental Early Warnings

Armando Ordonez[1], Vidal Alcázar[2], Daniel Borrajo[2], Paolo Falcarin[3],
and Juan Carlos Corrales[1]

[1] Universidad de Cauca
[2] Universidad Carlos III de Madrid
[3] University of East London
{jaordonez,jcorral}@unicauca.edu.co, valcazar@inf.uc3m.es,
dborrajo@ia.uc3m.es, falcarin@uel.ac.uk

Abstract. This paper presents the integration of automated planning in AUTO, a framework able to design plans of composed services for environmental early warning management. AUTO is based on three components: a request processing module that transforms natural language and context information into a planning instance; the automated planning and execution module based on an architecture for planning and execution, PELEA; and the Service Execution Environment for Web and Telco Services. The integration of a planning component provides two basic functionalities: the possibility of customizing the composition of services based on the preferences of the user and a middleware level that interfaces the execution of services in the environment.

Keywords: automated planning, service composition.

1 Introduction

Service Composition can be defined as the process of creating a composite process by combining available component services. It is used in situations where the request of a client cannot be satisfied by any single available service [1]. However, services may change, become available or unavailable and their number may also grow to unmanageable sizes, which makes impossible to manually generate a composition plan [11]. Previous works from both academia [14,6] and industry [1] have revolved around this topic. However, few academic approaches include implementations in production scenarios, and few works from the industry are open or easy to extrapolate to similar cases. This paper gathers experience from previous works and presents the integration of automated planning as a

---

[1] Some examples from the industry are Zypr http://www.zypr.net/, SIRI http://www.apple.com/iphone/features/siri.html and Vlingo http://www.vlingo.com/

J. Pavón et al. (Eds.): IBERAMIA 2012, LNAI 7637, pp. 591–600, 2012.
© Springer-Verlag Berlin Heidelberg 2012

key component of AUTO (an AUTOmated user-centric Telco and Web services composition framework) in the environmental early warning domain.

The goal of the environmental early warning field is to create contingency plans that help resolve potentially harmful or dangerous situations based on the information gathered from sensors and the input of relevant users. An example of such a situation would be evacuating all the villages close to a river after detecting that its level has risen beyond regular measurements or upon the request of an observer. In this case a contingency plan would include actions to monitor the river, determine affected areas, warn the villagers and coordinate the logistics of the evacuation.

Since the participation of a human is required in critical scenarios, we assume that all the requests are triggered by users. Besides, in rural environments the access to a device able to send a request in the format specified by the system may be limited. This means that the system should be able to process natural language so it can be initiated through simple communication means like a phone call or an SMS. Thanks to the rather restrictive process of composition in this domain, the main procedures and their associated services can be described using semantic annotations by experts, which allows a natural language recognition technique to be implemented without imposing many restrictions to the user. Moreover, this makes the integration of a planning process a much easier task. Although this depends on the domain, most of the principles discussed here are applicable to similar scenarios.

The overall functioning of the architecture is as follows: the user request is received in natural language from a given device and processed to determine the goals and preferences of the user. At the same time, information obtained from the sensors may be added to the request depending on the context. Next, the request is translated dynamically into a planning instance modeled using the Planning Domain Definition Language (PDDL) [3]. Then, the PDDL formatted request is sent to the High Level Replanner module of the Planning, Learning and Execution Architecture (PELEA) [4] in order to obtain and execute a plan that represents the composition of services. Finally, the composed plan is executed in a Jain SLEE [2] environment for convergent services.

In a previous work, we presented AUTO as a framework that dealt with the environmental early warning domain receiving input from natural language request [12]. However, the deliberative process was based on hierarchical planning, which has several limitations over domain-independent planners that use PDDL. First, it is a domain-dependent approach, so if there is a change in the domain an expert must encode the modifications. This encoding is usually much more difficult to define than modifications at the domain level, because it mixes domain knowledge with control knowledge. Second, most HTN planners like SHOP2 [10] find it difficult to use different metrics and cannot easily deal with user preferences. Third, HTN planners prune parts of the search space for performance reasons, which means that often low-quality solutions may be obtained in unexpected problems. Lastly, HTN planning cannot benefit from newer planners that

---

[2] JAIN SLEE v1.1 http://jcp.org/en/jsr/detail?id=240

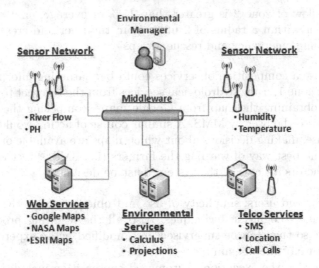

Fig. 1. Telecommunication and Web services interaction in Environmental Management Systems

may surpass the current state of the art as research in the area advances. In this context, the main contributions of this paper are: the automatic transformation of natural language queries into a general language like PDDL; the encoding of user preferences in the environmental early warning domain; and the inclusion of automated planning techniques in AUTO, aiming to fully integrate it with PELEA.

2 The Environmental Management Domain

A sketch of an environmental management system is presented in Fig. 1. The role of the environmental manager is to make decisions about the environmental alarms and crop management of a region. For this purpose he/she can request information from sensor networks deployed at several spots. The environmental manager can also use telecommunication (Telco for short) and Web services to process basic data and send information to both farmers and sensors. Available services often change dynamically and the resources may be limited.

As the environmental manager comes from fields like biology or agriculture, his/her technological background may be low. Furthermore, electronic devices in the area may be scarce. Thus, the preferred way to enter information to the system is by voice and in natural language. This way, users do not have to know how the system internally works and can make requests from regular mobile devices or landline phones. Commonly the user expresses his/her request informally; here are two examples:

- "I need to compute the hydrological balance of zone 1 and receive the resulting map to my cell phone"

— "the river flow of zone 2 is greater than 15% in average, emit an alarm to every farmer within a radius of 2 miles from the river and create an action map including emergency and rescue groups"

In the first case a composition of services could be: gathering information from the sensors in zone 1, using hydrological services from the Internet to process the sensed data, obtaining the map from Google maps, composing the final image and sending it to the user by MMS. A similar course of action would be done in the second case, making decisions about which maps are available or best suited to the case, the best way of warning the farmers (i.e. SMS, direct call, e-mail), etc. Several factors affect how the system must be designed:

— Usability for end users: simplicity of use and ubiquity forces the use of natural language recognition techniques. Also all the resulting processes must be readable so they can be supervised and modified by an expert due to the critical nature of the domain.
— Integration with the execution: Automated composition includes integration of Telco and Web functionalities, which requires specialized platforms.
— Reaction to change: planning systems deployed in dynamic environments must be able to react to potential changes during both the computation of the plans and the execution of the services.
— User preferences: multiple composition of services are often be possible, so the user may express his/her preferences in the request. Typical cases include minimizing the time of the execution of the composed services if it is an urgent request or minimizing the cost if there are no time constraints.

3   Automated Planning and Specification of the Domain

Automated planning is the task of finding a sequence of actions (plan) that leads to a state where some goals are achieved from a given initial state. Planning takes two inputs: a domain description and a problem description. Both are usually described using the standard language PDDL [3]. The domain file includes the types of the objects that may appear in the problems, a set of predicates/functions to be used to represent states and actions, and the actions set. Each problem file includes the initial state, the goals and, possibly, a metric.

If the domain and problem are specified in PDDL, almost all current domain-independent planners can be used to solve problems in our domain. Other paradigms related to domain-independent planning, like hierarchical planning, use representations on top of PDDL that tune the domain description towards some subset of solutions [10]. Usually, they are harder to generalize and reuse in other domains.

Here an overall description of the domain in PDDL will be given. First, the domain includes the definition of types of the objects that appear in the domain. As an example, these types might represent among others zones, users, communications means, etc.

```
(:types   zone user source map_step1 communication - object
          map_generation maptype - object)
```

Next, we have to define domain predicates and functions. As an example, we might define a predicate to express that we have already obtained some coordinates, or that we have already performed some sensing in a given zone. Predicates and functions have arguments that are typed.

```
(:predicates (coordinates_taken ?z - zone)
             (sensed  ?z - zone)
             (isolines ?z -zone) ...)


(:functions  (time) (cost)
             (messages ?m - communication)
             (access ?m - maptype)
             (source-cost ?m - source) ...)
```

Then, the domain actions model the different kinds of services. We describe now some of the actions on our domain. The *get_coordinates* action has as parameters: the user that performs the composition, the zone to be analyzed, the source of data (sensors, gps, database,...), and the type of communication to be used to gather coordinates (SMS, MMS, monitoring network,...). For this particular action there are no preconditions. Each source has associated different cost and time values, represented by the *source-cost* and *source-time* functions. We only show cost and time for simplicity.

```
(:action get_coordinates
    :parameters (?u - user ?z -zone ?m - source ?c - communication )
    :effect (and (coordinates_taken ?z) (sensed  ?z)
                 (increase (time) (source-time ?m))
                 (increase (cost) (source-cost ?m)) ...))
```

The *generate_map_from_vector_map* action has similar parameters: the user that perform the composition, the zone to be analyzed and the type of map to retrieve from internet (maps from NASA, free maps, maps by subscription). Some of the map services allow services a limited number of accesses. Therefore, each access decreases the number of available accesses. Consequently, when the number of services reaches zero it is necessary to update the subscription using the *update_subscription* action.

```
(:action generate_vector_map
    :parameters (?usr - user ?z - zone  ?mt - maptype)
    :precondition (and (sensed  ?z) (> (access ?mt) 0))
    :effect (and  (generated_map ?z)
                  (increase (time) (/ (time-map ?mt) 2))
                  (increase (cost) (/ (cost-map ?mt) 2))
                  (decrease (access ?mt) (access_quote))))
```

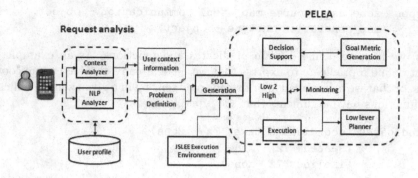

Fig. 2. Overall architecture of AUTO

```
(:action update_subscription
    :parameters (?usr - user ?z - zone ?m1 - map_step1  ?mt - maptype)
    :precondition (and (mapa1 ?m1) (sensed  ?z) (= (access ?mt) 0))
    :effect (and  (increase (access ?mt) (acccess_update))
                  (increase (time) (update_time))
                  (increase (cost) (update_cost))))
```

The same logic is applied to model the *inform* action. This action is on charge of sending alarms and important information to specific zones according to the device, network coverage, warning level or user preferences. The number of messages or calling credit is limited and eventually it is required to top it up. Due to lack of space we will omit the description of the actions *inform* and *top_up*, although they are similar to *generate_map_from_vector_map* and *update_subscription*. Similarly, other actions are also needed in the domain but here they will be omitted for brevity.

4   Architecture of the Framework

The architecture of AUTO is depicted in Fig. 2. The modules may be deployed in different machines so the processes load can be distributed. The access method can be both voice or text so AUTO can be accessed from a broad range of devices. In the literature, other alternatives have been proposed for user request treatment, such as Mashups [15] or service creation environments [8]. However, natural language offers a better mechanism for end users without expertise to express their requests [9].

The Natural Language Analysis decomposes the request in constitutive parts and infers semantically which words are verbs (possible actions), nouns (possible parameters), control flow or context information, whose function will be described later. The Context Analyzer uses three dimensions: user preferences, device capabilities and situational context that define parts of the initial state of the planning problem. Additional information may be added to the request from a database containing the profile of the user. The PDDL Generation module makes a translation from the processed request into a problem in PDDL. The data of the problem is obtained not only from the request but also from the information about the available services, which is why the PDDL Generation module requests information to the JSLEE Execution Environment at problem generation.

The automatically generated problem in PDDL is the input sent to PELEA, which performs the service composition using a domain-independent planner. The PDDL domain does not change, so PELEA uses the same domain definition for different service composition requests. In this work no monitoring is done, so currently the only task of PELEA is computing the plan and sending it to the JSLEE Execution Environment. In situations in which the status and characteristics of the services may change, though, PELEA would monitor the execution and replan or repair the current plan as needed.

AUTO uses a robust execution environment for telecommunications applications called Java Service Logic Execution Environment (JSLEE). The integration between PELEA and JSLEE is done in the execution module and allows the execution and the sensing of the state of the service composition. The execution module makes a dynamic association between the plan tasks and the JSLEE Service Building Blocks (SBB). SBBs are the basic components of the JSLEE architecture and call external Web services or Telco functionalities. The association between automated generated plans and SBB is done at run time, so changes in the environment can be easily dealt with.

5   Natural Language to PDDL

In AUTO, the transformation from natural language to PDDL is performed by a module composed by a set of underlying components. The functioning and implementation of this module has already been described elsewhere [12], so we will only provide here a rough description. The processing of the request in natural language is a set of sequential steps. First, the input is split into tokens, generating simple lexical units from complex sentences. Next, individual units are filtered and tagged according to their grammatical category. Additionally, each token is labeled as either "Control", "Functional" or "Situational" and classified according to three dimensions: device, user and situation. Next, information gathered from User Profile using the user's ID is added to the request. Finally, the request is translated into a planning instance from which a service composition is computed.

Every time a user makes a request a PDDL problem is generated. In this problem, the objects are defined, the predicates and functions initialized, the goals set and the metrics specified. The following is an example of how objects are defined and the functions are given values:

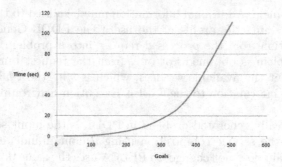

Fig. 3. Time needed to find composed services for an increasing number of goals

```
(:objects
    corpoamazonia - user
    farm1 farm2 farm3 - zone
    sms gps db - source
    sms mms voice - communication
    google nasa esri - maptype ...)

(:init
    (= (time) 0) (= (cost) 0) (= (topup_cost) 1)
    (= (source-time sms) 10) (= (source-time gps) 5)
    (= (source-cost sms) 5) (= (source-cost sms) 8) ...)
```

The goals are included as predicates that have to be achieved. The user preferences are encoded as a linear combination of the relevant criteria, namely *time* and *cost* because the standard way of encoding preferences in PDDL3, soft goals [3], offers no additional expressive power over regular metrics [7].

```
(:goal (and (informed farm1) (informed farm2) (informed farm3) ))
(:metric minimize (+ (* 1 (time)) (* 1 (cost)))))
```

6   Experimentation

To check the viability of the use of automated planning in AUTO some experimentation was done. First, we checked whether the system was able to scale up to requests that involve a high number of goals and services. An automatically generated instance was modified to increase the number of goals (farms that must be warned). The number of goals was increased from 20 to 400 in intervals of 50. Services, communication means, maptypes,... were left unmodified. The metric used for these problems was to minimize *time* plus *cost*. The planner used was CBP [2], a planner based on Metric-FF [5] with new heuristics designed to deal with numeric metrics.

Figure 3 shows how the time increases with the number of goals. In the experimentation, CBP behaves as expected, as the time increases exponentially.

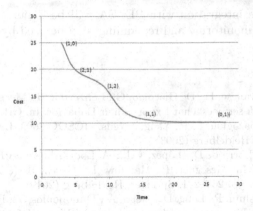

Fig. 4. Pareto front of solutions obtained by modifying α and β in the metric (in parenthesis)

However, CBP is still capable of finding a plan with 500 goals in less than 2 minutes while minimizing the metric. This is a performance competitive with "ad-hoc" algorithms for services composition [13].

Another of the advantages of automatic planning is the possibility of dealing with metrics by just changing the definition of the metric in the problem file. The aim was to obtain a broad range of plans that give priority to minimizing *time* over *cost* and vice versa so they suit the preferences of the user. This was done by modifying the weights of the aforementioned linear combination of *time* and *cost*. More precisely, the metric is $\alpha t + \beta c$, in which t is *time* and c is *cost*. This means that the plans should be diverse and adapt themselves well to changes in the parameters α and β, similar to multi-objective optimization algorithms. Figure 4 shows a set of non-dominated plans obtained by modifying α and β in the metric. As in multi-objective optimization, it forms a pareto front. This means that CBP is sensible to the changes and the plans are diverse enough to offer a valuable alternative to the user when needed.

7   Conclusions

In this paper we extend AUTO by integrating automated planning into an existing architecture as the deliberative process. This is a more general approach than the previously used technique that allows a greater flexibility both in terms of design and the implementation of the underlying algorithms. The main contribution is the automatic generation of planning instances in PDDL from natural language requests. Furthermore, we allowed the use of preferences modeling them as metrics of the planning instance. In the near future, we want to continue our research developing mechanisms for the automation of planning domain generation. Further experimentation with different planners will be done too so an increase in performance can be achieved. Additionally, we are extending the preferences criteria in order to get a better personalized experience for the user.

Finally, a complete integration with PELEA will be done, so features that it already offers, like monitoring and replanning, can be used by AUTO.

References

1. Berardi, D., Calvanese, D., De Giacomo, G., Lenzerini, M., Mecella, M.: Automatic Composition of E-services That Export Their Behavior. In: Orlowska, M.E., Weerawarana, S., Papazoglou, M.P., Yang, J. (eds.) ICSOC 2003. LNCS, vol. 2910, pp. 43–58. Springer, Heidelberg (2003)
2. Fuentetaja, R., Borrajo, D., López, C.L.: A Look-Ahead B&B Search for Cost-Based Planning. In: Meseguer, P., Mandow, L., Gasca, R. (eds.) CAEPIA 2009. LNCS, vol. 5988, pp. 201–211. Springer, Heidelberg (2010)
3. Gerevini, A., Haslum, P., Long, D., Saetti, A., Dimopoulos, Y.: Deterministic Planning in the Fifth International Planning Competition – PDDL3 and experimental evaluation of the planners. Artificial Intelligence 173(5-6), 619–668 (2009)
4. Guzmán, C., Alcázar, V., Prior, D., Onaindía, E., Borrajo, D., Fernández-Olivares, J., Quintero, E.: PELEA – A Domain-Independent Architecture for Planning, Execution and Learning. In: 6th Scheduling and Planning Applications Workshop (SPARK 2012), pp. 38–45 (2012)
5. Hoffmann, J.: The Metric-FF Planning System: Translating "Ignoring Delete Lists" to Numeric State Variables. Journal of Artif. Intel. Research 20, 291–341 (2003)
6. Hoffmann, J., Bertoli, P., Pistore, M.: Web Service Composition as Planning, Revisited – In Between Background Theories and Initial State Uncertainty. In: 22nd AAAI Conf. on Artificial Intelligence (AAAI 2007), pp. 1013–1018. AAAI (2007)
7. Keyder, E., Geffner, H.: Soft Goals Can Be Compiled Away. Journal of Artif. Intel. Research 36, 547–556 (2009)
8. Laga, N., Bertin, E., Glitho, R.H., Crespi, N.: Widgets and Composition Mechanism for Service Creation by Ordinary Users. IEEE Communications Magazine 50(3), 52–60 (2012)
9. Lim, J., Lee, K.H.: Constructing Composite Web Services from Natural Language Requests. Web Semantics – Science, Services and Agents on the World Wide Web 8(1), 1–13 (2010)
10. Nau, D., Au, T., Ilghami, O., Kuter, U., Murdock, J., Wu, D., Yaman, F.: SHOP2 – An HTN Planning System. Journal of Artif. Intel. Research 20, 379–404 (2003)
11. Oh, S.C., Lee, D., Kumara, S.R.T.: A Comparative Illustration of AI Planning-Based Web Services Composition. SIGecom Exchanges 5(5), 1–10 (2006)
12. Ordonez, A., Corrales, J.C., Falcarin, P.: Natural Language Processing Based Services Composition for Environmental Management. In: 7th International Conference on System of Systems Engineering, SoSE 2012 (2012)
13. Pistore, M., Traverso, P., Bertoli, P., Marconi, A.: Automated Synthesis of Executable Web Service Compositions from BPEL4WS Processes. In: Special Interest Tracks and Posters of the 14th Intl. Conf. on World Wide Web, WWW 2005 (2005)
14. Yelmo, J.C., del Álamo, J.M., Trapero, R., Martín, Y.S.: A User-Centric Approach to Service Creation and Delivery Over Next Generation Networks. Computer Communications 34(2), 209–222 (2011)
15. Zhao, Z., Bhattarai, S., Liu, J., Crespi, N.: Mashup Services to Daily Activities – End-User Perspective in Designing a Consumer Mashups. In: 13th International Conference on Information Integration and Web-based Applications and Services (iiWAS 2011), pp. 222–229. ACM (2011)

A Genetic Algorithm for Berth Allocation and Quay Crane Assignment

Mario Rodriguez-Molins[1], Federico Barber[1], María R. Sierra[2], Jorge Puente[2], and Miguel A. Salido[1]

[1] Instituto de Automática e Informática Industrial,
Universitat Politècnica de València Spain
{mrodriguez,msalido,fbarber}@dsic.upv.es
[2] Department of Computer Science, University of Oviedo Spain
{puente,sierramaria}@uniovi.es

Abstract. Container terminals are facilities where cargo containers are transshipped between different transport vehicles, for onward transportation. They are open systems that carry out a large number of different combinatorial problems that can be solved by means of Artificial Intelligence techniques. In this work, we focus our attention on scheduling a number of incoming vessels by assigning to each a berthing position, a mooring time and a number of Quay Cranes. This problem is known as the Berthing Allocation and Quay Crane Assignment problem. To formulate the problem, we first propose a mixed integer linear programming model to minimize the total weighted service time of the incoming vessels. Then, a meta-heuristic algorithm (Genetic Algorithm (GA)) is presented for solving the proposed problem. Computational experiments are performed to evaluate the effectiveness and efficiency of the proposed method.

Keywords: scheduling, planning, genetic algorithms, metaheuristics, berthing allocation, quay crane assignment.

1 Introduction

A container terminal is an open system with three distinguishable areas (berth, container yard and lanside areas) where there exist different complex optimization problems. For instance, berthing allocation or stowage planning problems are related to the berth area [13]; remarshalling problem or transport optimization in the yard area; and, planning and scheduling hinterland operations related to trains and trucks in the landside area [14].

Two planning and scheduling problems are studied in this paper, the Berth Allocation Problem (BAP) and the Quay Crane Assignment Problem (QCAP). The former is a well-known combinatorial optimization problem [10], which consists in assigning incoming vessels to berthing positions. The QCAP deals with assigning a certain number of QCs to each vessel that is waiting at the roadstead such that all required movements of containers can be fulfilled [1]. Once a vessel

J. Pavón et al. (Eds.): IBERAMIA 2012, LNAI 7637, pp. 601–610, 2012.

arrives at the port, it waits at the roadstead until it has permission to moor at the quay. The locations where mooring can take place are called berths. These are equipped with giant cranes, known as Quay Cranes (QC), that are used to load and unload containers which are transferred to and from the yard by a fleet of vehicles. These QCs are mounted on the same track (or rail) and, therefore they cannot pass each other. In a transshipment terminal, the yard allows temporary storage before containers are transferred to another ship or to another transportation mode (e.g., rail or road).

A comprehensive survey of BAP and QCAP is given by [1]. These problems have been mostly considered separately and with an interest mainly focused on BAP. However, there are some studies on the combined BAP+QCAP considering different characteristics of the berths and cranes [2,7,9,12,15]. In this paper, we present a formal mixed integer lineal programming for the combined BAP+QCAP that extends the model presented in [8], by managing a continuous quay line. In order to obtain optimized solutions in an efficient way, we develop a metaheuristic GA, so that compared with mathematical solvers obtains near-optimal solutions in competitive computational times.

The rest of the paper is organized as follows. In the next two sections we give a thorough description and a mathematical formulation of the problem. In Sect. 4 we give the details of the GA designed for the BAP+QCAP. Section 5 reports the results of the experimental study. Finally, in Sect. 6 we give the main conclusions of this work.

2   Problem Description

The objective in BAP+QCAP is to obtain an schedule of the incoming vessels with an optimum order of vessels mooring and a distribution of the docks and QCs for these vessels. Figure 1(b) shows an example of the graphical space-time representation of a berth plan with 6 vessels. Each rectangle represents a vessel with its handling time and length.

Our BAP+QCAP case is classified according to the classification given by [1] as:

- *Spatial attribute: Continuous layout.* We assume that the quay is a continuous line, so there is no partitioning of the quay and the vessel can berth at arbitrary positions within the boundaries of the quay. It must be taken into account that for a continuous layout, berth planning is more complicated than for a discrete layout, but it better utilizes the quay space [1].
- *Temporal attribute: Dynamic arrival.* Fixed arrival times are given for the vessels, so that vessels cannot berth before their expected arrival times.
- *Handling time attribute: Unknown in advance.* The handling time of a vessel depends on the number of assigned QCs (*QCAP*) and the moves required.
- *Performance measure: wait and handling times* The objective is to minimize the sum of the waiting (w_i) and handling times (h_i) of all vessels.

Let V be the set of incoming vessels. Following, we introduce the notation used for each vessel $i \in V$ (see Fig. 1(a)). The data variables are:

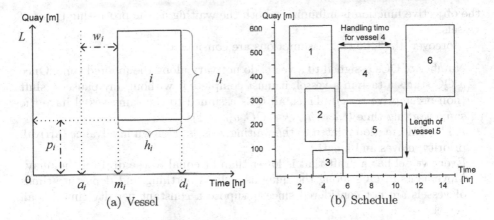

Fig. 1. Representation of the BAP+QCAP problem

- QC : Available QCs in the container terminal. All QCs carry out the same number of movements per time unit ($movsQC$), given by the container terminal.
- L : Total length of the berth in the container terminal.
- a_i : Arrival time of the vessel i at port.
- c_i : Number of required movements to load and unload containers of i.
- l_i : Vessel length.
- pr_i : Vessel priority.

The decision variables are:

- m_i : Mooring time of i. Thus, waiting time (w_i) of i is calculated as ($w_i = m_i - a_i$).
- p_i : Berthing position where i moors.
- q_i : Number of assigned QCs to i.
- u_{ik} : Indicates whether the QC k works (1) or not (0) on the vessel i.

The variables derived from the previous ones are:

- h_i : Loading and unloading time at quay (handling time) of vessel i. This time depends on q_i and c_i, that is : $\left(\frac{c_i}{q_i \times movsQC}\right)$.
- t_{ik} : Working time of the QC k that is assigned to vessel i.
- d_i : Departure time of vessel i ($d_i = m_i + h_i$).
- s_i, e_i : indexes for the first and last QC used in vessel i, respectively.

Our objective is to allocate all vessels according to several constraints minimizing the total weighted waiting and service time for all vessels:

$$T_s := \sum_{i \in V} (w_i + h_i) \times pr_i \qquad (1)$$

Note that this problem is a very special case of a multi-mode resource-constrained scheduling problem, where there exist shared resources (berth length), the duration of activities (mooring time) depends on the assigned resources (QCs), and the objective function is minimizing both the waiting as the processing times of vessels.

Moreover, the following assumptions are considered:

- Number of QCs assigned to a vessel do not vary along the moored time. Once a QC starts a task in a vessel, it must complete it without any pause or shift (non-preemptive tasks). Thus, all QCs assigned to the same vessel have the same working time ($t_{ik} = h_i, \forall k \in QC, u_{ik} = 1$)
- All the information related to the waiting vessels is known in advance (arrival, priority, moves and length).
- Every vessel has a draft that is lower than or equal to the draft of the quay.
- Movements of QCs along the quay as well as berthing and departure times of vessels are not considered since it supose a constant penalty time for all vessels.
- The components of the optimization function (Equation 1) can be independently weighted without requiring changes to our proposal.
- Simultaneous berthing is allowed, subject to the length of the berth.

And the following constraints must be accomplished:

- Moored time must be at least the same that its arrival time ($m_i \geq a_i$).
- It must be enough contiguous space at berth to moor a vessel of length (l_i).
- There is a safety distance (safeDist) between two moored ships. We assume 5% of the maximum length of two contiguous vessels.
- There must be at least one QC to assign to each vessel. The maximum number of assigned QCs by vessel depends on its length, since a safety distance is required between two contiguous QCs (safeQC), and the maximum number of QCs that the container terminal allows per vessel (maxQC). Both parameters are given by the container terminal.

3   Mathematical Formulation

In this section, the mathematical formulation for BAP+QCAP is presented. The given MILP model solves the BAP+QCAP by minimizing the function given by the Equation 1, where M denotes a sufficiently large number, subject to the given constraints:

$$m_i \geq a_i \quad \forall i \in V \tag{2}$$

$$w_i = m_i - a_i \quad \forall i \in V \tag{3}$$

$$p_i + l_i \leq L \quad \forall i \in V \tag{4}$$

$$q_i = \sum_{k \in QC} u_{ik} \quad \forall i \in V \tag{5}$$

$$1 \leq q_i \leq QC_i^+ \quad \forall i \in V \tag{6}$$

$$1 \leq s_i, e_i \leq |QC| \quad \forall i \in V \tag{7}$$

$$s_i \geq e_i \quad \forall i \in V \tag{8}$$

$$q_i = e_i - s_i + 1 \quad \forall i \in V \tag{9}$$

$$\sum_{k \in QC} t_{ik} \times \texttt{movsQC} \geq c_i \quad \forall i \in V \tag{10}$$

$$h_i = \max_{k \in QC} t_{ik} \quad \forall i \in V \tag{11}$$

$$t_{ik} - u_{ik} \times M \leq 0 \quad \forall i \in V, \forall k \in QC \tag{12}$$

$$h_i - M \times (1 - u_{ik}) - t_{ik} \leq 0 \quad \forall i \in V, \forall k \in QC \tag{13}$$

$$u_{ik} + u_{jk} + z_{ij}^x \leq 2 \quad \forall i, j \in V, \forall k \in QC \tag{14}$$

$$M \times (1 - u_{ik}) + (e_i - k) \geq 0 \quad \forall i \in V, \forall k \in QC \tag{15}$$

$$M \times (1 - u_{ik}) + (k - s_i) \geq 0 \quad \forall i \in V, \forall k \in QC \tag{16}$$

$$p_i + l_i \leq p_j - sd_{ij} + M \times (1 - z_{ij}^x) \quad \forall i, j \in V, \ i \neq j \tag{17}$$

$$e_i + 1 \leq s_j + M \times (1 - z_{ij}^x) \quad \forall i, j \in V, \ i \neq j \tag{18}$$

$$m_i + h_i \leq m_j + M \times (1 - z_{ij}^y) \quad \forall i, j \in V, \ i \neq j \tag{19}$$

$$z_{ij}^x + z_{ji}^x + z_{ij}^y + z_{ji}^y \geq 1 \quad \forall i, j \in V, \ i \neq j \tag{20}$$

$$z_{ij}^x, z_{ij}^y, u_{ik} \quad 0/1 \ \text{integer} \quad \forall i, j \in V, \ i \neq j, \forall k \in QC \tag{21}$$

The given formulation expands the model presented in [8] by adding the needed constraints to take into consideration QCs. Thereby, the handling time of vessels depends on the number of QCs and these QCs cannot pass each other when are relocated.

In the proposed model, there are two auxiliary variables: z_{ij}^x is a decision variable that indicates if vessel i is located to the left of vessel j on the berth ($z_{ij}^x = 1$); and, $z_{ij}^y = 1$ indicates that vessel i is moored before vessel j in time (see constraint 21). Moreover, Constraint 2 ensures that vessels must moor once they arrive at the terminal. Constraint 4 guarantees that a moored vessel does not exceed the length quay. Constraints 5, 6, 7, 8 and 9 assign the number of QCs to the vessel i. Constraint 10 establishes the needed handling time to load and unload their containers. Constraint 12 ensures that QCs that are not assigned QCs to i have t_{ik} zero. Constraint 13 forces all assigned QCs to i working the same number of hours. Constraint 11 assigns the handling time for vessel i. Constraint 14 avoids that one QC is assigned to two different vessels at the same time. Constraints 15 and 16 force the QCs to be assigned contiguously (from s_i up to e_i). Constraint 17 takes into account the safety distance between each two vessels. Constraint 18 avoids that one vessel uses a QC which should cross through the others QCs. Constraint 19 avoids that vessel j moors while the previous vessel i is still at the quay. Finally, constraint 20 establishes the relationship between each pair of vessels.

This mathematical model has been coded in IBM ILOG CPLEX Optimization Studio 12.3 as detailed in the Evaluation Sect. 5.

4   Genetic Algorithm

Algorithm 1 shows the structure of the GA we have considered herein. The core of this algorithm is taken from [4,5] and is quite similar to others generational genetic algorithms described in the literature ([3], [6] or [11]). In the first step, the initial population is generated and evaluated. Then, the genetic algorithm iterates over a number of steps or generations. In each iteration, a new generation is built from the previous one by applying the genetic operators of selection, reproduction and replacement. These operators can be implemented in a variety of ways and, in principle, are independent from each other. However, in practice all of them should be chosen considering their effect on the remaining ones in order to get a successful overall algorithm. The approach taken in this work is the following. In the selection phase all chromosomes are grouped into pairs, and then each one of these pairs is mated or not in accordance with a crossover probability (P_c) to obtain two offspring. Each offspring, or parent if the parents were not mated, undergoes mutation in accordance with the mutation probability (P_m). Finally, the replacement is carried out as a tournament selection (4:2) among each pair of parents and their offspring.

Algorithm 1. The genetic algorithm

Require: A BAP-QCAP instance P
Ensure: A mooring schedule for instance P
  1. Generate the initial population;
  2. Evaluate the population;
  while No termination criterion is satisfied **do**
    3. Select chromosomes from the current population;
    4. Apply the reproduction operators to the chromosomes selected at step 3. to generate new ones;
    5. Evaluate the chromosomes generated at step 4;
    6. Apply the replacement criterion to the set of chromosomes selected at step 3. together with the chromosomes generated at step 4.;
  end while
  return The schedule from the best chromosome evaluated so far;

The coding schema is based on permutations of vessels, each one with a given number of QCs. So a gene is a pair (i, q_i), $1 \leq q_i \leq \min(maxQC_i, maxQC)$, and a chromosome includes a gene like this for each one of the vessels. For example, for an instance with 5 vessels where the maximum number of QCs are 2, 3, 4, 3 and 2 respectively, two feasible chromosomes are the following ones:

$$c_1: (\ (1\ 1)\ (2\ 1)\ (3\ 1)\ (4\ 2)\ (5\ 1)\ )$$

$$c_2: (\ (3\ 2)\ (1\ 2)\ (2\ 2)\ (5\ 2)\ (4\ 3)\ )$$

Note that, the same vessel may have different number of QCs in each chromosome. In accordance with this encoding, a chromosome expresses the number of

QCs that each vessel is assigned in the solution and an order for building the schedule.

The order of vessels in chromosomes is used as a dispatching rule. Hence, we use the following decoding algorithm: the genes are visited from left to right in the chromosome sequence. For each gene (i, q_i) the vessel i is scheduled at the earliest mooring time with q_i consecutive QCs available, so that none of the constraints is violated. If there are several positions available at the earliest time, that closest to one of the berth extremes is selected. Also, the QCs are chosen starting from the same extreme of the berth.

For chromosome mating we have considered a classical crossover operator such as Generalized Position Crossover (GPX) which is commonly used in permutation based encodings. This is a two points crossover operator which work as follows. Let us consider two parents like:

$$p_1: (\,(1\ 1)\ |\ (2\ 1)\ (3\ 1)\ |\ (4\ 2)\ (5\ 1)\,)$$

$$p_2: (\,(3\ 2)\ |\ (1\ 2)\ (2\ 2)\ |\ (5\ 2)\ (4\ 3)\,)$$

Symbols "|" represent crossover positions, 1 and 3 respectively in this example, which are selected at random for each mating. Then two offsprings are built taking the substrings between positions 1 and 3 in each parent and then filling the remaining positions with the genes representing the remaining vessels taken from the other parent keeping their relative order. So in this case the two offsprings are:

$$o_1: (\,(1\ 2)\ |\ (2\ 1)\ (3\ 1)\ |\ (5\ 2)\ (4\ 3)\,)$$

$$o_2: (\,(3\ 1)\ |\ (1\ 2)\ (2\ 2)\ |\ (4\ 2)\ (5\ 1)\,)$$

For mutation we have implemented an operator that shuffles a random substring of the chromosome and at the same time changes the number of QCs assigned to each one of the shuffled genes at random, provided that the number of QCs is kept in between the proper limits for the vessel.

The initial population in generated at random, i.e. a random order for the vessels is chosen and each vessel i is assigned a number of QCs chosen uniformly in $[1, \min(maxQC_i, maxQC)]$. The termination condition is given in one of these three forms: (1) a number of generations, (2) a time limit or (3) a number of evaluations.

5   Evaluation

The experiments were performed in a corpus of 100 instances generated randomly, each one is composed of a queue from 5 to 20 vessels. These instances follow an exponential distribution for the inter-arrival times of the vessels ($\lambda = \frac{1}{20}$). The number of required movements and length of vessels are generated uniformly in $[100, 1000]$ and $[100, 500]$ respectively. In all cases, the berth length (L) is fixed to 700 meters; the number of QCs is 7 (corresponding to a determined MSC berth line) and the maximum number of QCs per vessel is 5 (maxQC); the safety distance between QCs (`safeQC`) is 35 meters and the number of movements that QCs carry out is 2.5 (`movsQC`) per time unit.

The two approaches developed in this paper, the GA and the MILP model, were coded using C++ and the IBM ILOG CPLEX Optimization Studio 12.3, respectively. They were solved on a Linux PC 2.26Ghz.

In the GA, the population size is 200. Mutation and crossover probabilities are $P_m = 0.1$ and $P_c = 0.8$, respectively. Due to the stochastic nature of the GA process, each one of the instances were solved 30 times and the results show the average obtained values.

Table 1 shows the results form CPLEX and GA averaged for each group of 100 instances with the same number of vessels (5 to 20). The timeout was 10 seconds. For CPLEX, the reported values are the average value of T_s for the solutions reached, the number of instances solved to optimality (#Opt), the number of instances solved without certify optimality (#NOpt) and the number of instances for which no solution is reached by the timeout (#NSol) The last two columns show the best and the average values of the solutions obtained by the GA in 30 runs. Obviously, in all cases, the objective function (T_s) increases as the number of incoming vessels increases from 5 up to 20.

Table 1. Comparision CPLEX with GA (timeout 10 secs)

|V|	CPLEX				GA	
	Avg T_s	#Opt	#NOpt	#NSol	Best T_s	Avg T_s
5	1723.75	98	2	0	1723.75	1723.75
6	2193.06	88	12	0	2189.63	2189.63
7	2702.46	66	34	0	2681.14	2681.67
8	3287.66	41	59	0	3219.80	3222.13
9	3891.09	24	76	0	3729.78	3734.72
10	4642.23	14	86	0	4337.10	4350.23
11	5453.31	6	94	0	4946.66	4971.86
12	6557.60	3	97	0	5552.09	5589.16
13	7944.50	2	98	0	6181.67	6236.60
14	9332.26	1	98	1	6854.33	6931.59
15	11578.40	0	98	2	7526.27	7631.98
16	13518.00	0	97	3	8290.95	8438.06
17	15105.80	0	94	6	8972.13	9163.65
18	17253.80	0	85	15	9694.16	9927.06
19	18390.40	0	65	35	10506.20	10787.79
20	20410.50	0	46	54	11395.52	11725.64

From these results, we can observe that CPLEX is not able to reach any optimal solution by the given timeout in at least 30% of the instances with 7 vessels or more. In addition, it can not get any optimal solution from 15 up to 20 vessels with this timeout. Moreover, for a number of instances with more than 14 vessels CPLEX is not able to reach a feasible solution. Regarding GA, all instances are solved and we can observe that the average values are better than those from CPLEX, the differences being in direct ratio with the number of vessels. Here, it is important to remark that GA reaches 1063 generations in 10 seconds.

However, the GA is able to converge in lower times. Figure 2 shows the GA convergence for one representative instance of 20 vessels, so that near-optimal values are obtained after 100 generations, taking 0.94 seconds. Furthermore, Fig. 3 shows how the average T_s for 10 vessels decreases as more computation time is allowed. In this experiment, the timeout was set to 5, 10, 20, and 60 seconds. As it can be observed, the GA approach does not require a large timeout (the improvement is lower than 1% beyond 5 seconds).

We remark that we have not been able to use previous test cases proposed in the literature because we assume a continuous berthing and non-preemtitive tasks [9,15]. However, even considering this more complex case, we can see that the results achieved are highly competitive against these previous approaches.

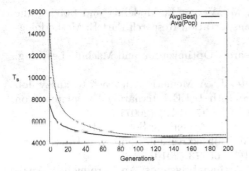

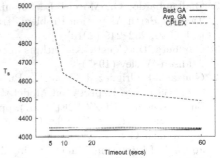

Fig. 2. Convergence of the Genetic Algorithm

Fig. 3. Average T_s for 10 vessels setting different timeouts

6   Conclusions

The competitiveness among container terminals causes the need to improve the efficiency of each one of the subprocesses that are performed within them. This paper focuses on two of the main related problems, the Berth Allocation and Quay Crane Assignment Problems, in an integrated way. To this end, a mixed integer lineal programming model and a Genetic Algorithm were developed. The MILP model was unable to get optimal solutions when a reasonable timeout is set or when the problem becomes harder (more than 10 vessels). Moreover, many of the instances were solved but without any guarantees of being the optimal ones since the timeout was reached. However, the GA approach is able to obtain near-optimal solutions in lower computational times and it also maintains a rapid convergence of the results even with large vessel queues. From these results, it is concluded the adequacy of a metaheuristic approach based on GA for solving the BAP+QCAP problem. This approach also extends the previous approaches given in the literature by adding features (as continuous quay line and non-preemptitive QC assignments) and it gives near-optimal solutions in a very competitive computational time. For future research, we propose devising some local search strategy that can be then combined with the GA or other metaheuristics such as GRASP, Tabu or Scatter Search.

Acknowledgments. This research has been supported by the Spanish Government under research project MICINN TIN2010-20976-C02-01 and TIN2010-20976-C02-02, and the predoctoral FPU fellowship (AP2010-4405).

References

1. Bierwirth, C., Meisel, F.: A Survey of Berth Allocation and Quay Crane Scheduling Problems in Container Terminals. European Journal of Operational Research 202, 615–627 (2010)
2. Giallombardo, G., Moccia, L., Salani, M., Vacca, I.: Modeling and Solving the Tactical Berth Allocation Problem. Transportation Research Part B: Methodological 44(2), 232–245 (2010)
3. Goldberg, D.: Genetic Algorithms in Search, Optimization and Machine Learning. Addison-Wesley (1985)
4. Gonzalez-Rodriguez, I., Vela, C., Puente, J.: A Memetic Approach to Fuzzy Job Shop Based on Expectation Model. In: 16th IEEE International Conference on Fuzzy Systems (FUZZ-IEEE 2007), pp. 692–697. IEEE (2007)
5. González-Rodríguez, I., Vela, C., Puente, J.: A Genetic Solution Based on Lexicographical Goal Programming for a Multiobjective Job Shop with Uncertainty. Journal of Intelligent Manufacturing 21(1), 65–73 (2010)
6. Holand, J.: Adaptation in Natural and Artificial Systems: An Introductory Analysis with Applications to Biology, Control and Artificial Intelligence. University of Michigan Press (1975)
7. Imai, A., Chen, H., Nishimura, E., Papadimitriou, S.: The Simultaneous Berth and Quay Crane Allocation Problem. Transportation Research Part E: Logistics and Transportation Review 44(5), 900–920 (2008)
8. Kim, K., Moon, K.: Berth Scheduling by Simulated Annealing. Transportation Research Part B: Methodological 37(6), 541–560 (2003)
9. Liang, C., Guo, J., Yang, Y.: Multi-Objective Hybrid Genetic Algorithm for Quay Crane Dynamic Assignment in Berth Allocation Planning. Journal of Intelligent Manufacturing 22, 471–479 (2011)
10. Lim, A.: The Berth Planning Problem. Operations Research Letters 22(2-3), 105–110 (1998)
11. Michalewicz, Z.: Genetic Algorithms + Data Structures = Evolution Programs. 3rd Revised and Extended Edition. Springer (1996)
12. Park, Y., Kim, K.: A Scheduling Method for Berth and Quay Cranes. OR Spectrum 25(1), 1–23 (2003)
13. Salido, M.A., Rodriguez-Molins, M., Barber, F.: Integrated Intelligent Techniques for Remarshaling and Berthing in Maritime Terminals. Advanced Engineering Informatics 25(3), 435–451 (2011)
14. Stahlbock, R., Voß, S.: Operations Research at Container Terminals – A Literature Update. OR Spectrum 30(1), 1–52 (2008)
15. Zhang, C., Zheng, L., Zhang, Z., Shi, L., Armstrong, A.: The Allocation of Berths and Quay Cranes by Using a Sub-Gradient Optimization Technique. Computers & Industrial Engineering 58(1), 40–50 (2010)

Constructing Real Test-Suites Using an Enhanced Simulated Annealing

Himer Avila-George[1], Jose Torres-Jimenez[2], and Vicente Hernández[1]

[1] Instituto Tecnológico Superior de Salvatierra, Madero 303, 38900 Salvatierra, Guanajuato, Mexico
hiavila@itess.edu.mx, vhernandez@dsic.upv.es
[2] CINVESTAV-Tamaulipas, Information Technology Laboratory, Km. 5.5 Carretera Victoria-Soto La Marina, 87130 Victoria Tamps., Mexico
jtj@cinvestav.mx

Abstract. In software systems, a common source of bugs are unexpected interactions among systems components. This risk is increased when the number of software components increases. To reduce this risk and ensure software quality, it may be necessary to test all interactions among the components. Combinatorial testing is a method that can reduce cost and increase the effectiveness of software testing for many applications. Covering arrays are combinatorial structures which can be used to represent test-suites. This paper presents a metaheuristic approach based on a simulated annealing algorithm for constructing covering arrays. The experimental design solved a benchmark reported in the literature and it is proposed a new bechkmark based on real test-cases. Experimental evidence showed that the simulated annealing algorithm equals or improves the obtained results by other approaches reported in the literature, finding the optimal solution in some of the solved cases.

Keywords: combinatorial testing, covering arrays, simulated annealing.

1 Introduction

Today's software applications are more complex: often operate in multi-layer environments, they operate under multiple platforms; they are designed in conditions fast and agile, and the requirements are more ambitious than ever. In this scenario, software testing has become a critical element to ensure quality and minimize the risk of malfuncion, at the same time that meet the requirements of the enterprises that use the software components.

Combinatorial testing is a method that can reduce cost and increase the effectiveness of software testing for many applications. It is based on constructing functional test-suites of economical size, which provide coverage of the most prevalent configurations. *Covering arrays* are combinatorial objects, that have been applied to do functional tests of software components. The use of covering arrays allows to test all the interactions, of a given size, among the input parameters using the minimum number of test cases.

J. Pavón et al. (Eds.): IBERAMIA 2012, LNAI 7637, pp. 611–620, 2012.

This paper aims at developing an enhanced simulated annealing (ESA) algorithm for finding near-optimal covering arrays. In contrast to other existing simulated annealing implementations developed for constructing covering arrays [7,12], our algorithm has the merit of improving three key features that have a great impact on its performance: (1) a method designed to generate initial solutions with maximum Hamming distance; (2) instead of using a single neighborhood function, the algorithm chooses between a set of predefined neighborhood functions according to an assigned probability to each function; and (3) an effective cooling schedule. The performance of the proposed simulated annealing algorithm is assessed with a benchmark, composed by 21 covering arrays of strengths two and three taken from the literature. The computational results are reported and compared with previously published ones, showing that our algorithm was able to improve 15 instances and to equal 6 previous best-known solutions on the selected benchmark instances. We propose a new benchmark composed of 58 instances corresponding to real test cases. We compare the results against those obtained from the best known tools in the literature.

The remaining of this paper is organized as follows: some techniques that have been used for constructing covering arrays are presented in Sect. 2, an overview of the proposed approach of simulated annealing with the details of its main components and values are described in Sect. 3, the experiments carried out with this approach are detailed in Sect. 4 and finally, Sect. 5 summarizes the main contributions of this work.

2   Background

Before discussing the different techniques for building test-suites based on covering arrays, we begin with some definitions. To generate interaction test-suites, a mathematical object called a covering array is often used.

2.1   Preliminary Definitions

Definition 1. *A covering array denoted by $CA(N; t, k, v)$ is an $N \times k$ array, each elements takes values from an alphabet of size $v = \{0, 1, \ldots, v-1\}$ such that every $N \times t$ subarray contains all t-tuples from $\{0, 1, \ldots, \}^t$ at least once. Here an $N \times t$ subarray is an $N \times t$ array obtained by selecting t of the columns, and deleting the remaining $k - t$ columns. In this subarray every row is a tuple.*

The strength of a covering array is t, which defines, for example, 2-way or 3-way coverage. The k columns of this array are called factors, where each factor has v values. A test-suite is an $N \times k$ array where each row is a test case. Each column represents a component and the value in the column is the level chosen. A covering array is optimal if it contains the minimum number of rows, the value N is known as the *Covering Array Number (CAN)*. The CAN is formally defined as: $CAN(t, k, v) = \min\{N : \exists\ CA(N; t, k, v)\}$. Given the values of t, k, and v, the optimal *covering array construction problem* (CAC) consists in constructing a $CA(N; t, k, v)$ such that the value of N is minimized. A lower bound for any covering array of strength t, is the product of the t greater alphabets of the variables.

For software testing, the fundamental problem is to determine $CAN(t, k, v)$. Because, it reduces the number of tests, the cost and the time expended on the software testing process.

A covering array has the same cardinality in all its parameters. However, most software systems do not have the same number of values for each factor, i.e., they do not have a single v. A more general structure can be defined that allows for variability in factor-value domain size. A mixed covering array (MCA) is a matrix in which the columns are variables and the rows are experiments, each variable can have different number of possible values (here comes the term MIXED), an each row indicates the value that each variable takes for that experiment. If all the combinations in pairs of variable appear at least once the MCA is denoted as of strength two, if all the combinations of triads of variables appear at least once the MCA is denoted as of strength three, and so on. An optimal MCA contains the minimum of experiments that exercise all the combinations defined by its strength.

Definition 2. *A mixed covering array $MCA(N; t, k, (v_1, \ldots, v_k))$ is an $N \times k$ array, M, having the following property. Each column i has symbols from the alphabet $[0, v_i - 1]$, and for $\{i_1, \ldots, i_t\} \subseteq \{1, \ldots, k\}$, if we consider the $N \times t$ subarray of M obtained by selecting columns $i_1, \ldots, i_t$, then there are $\prod_{i=1}^{t} v_i$ distinct t-tuples that could appear as a row. An MCA requires that each t-tuple appears at least once. A short notation for the mixed covering array can be given using the exponential notation $MCA(N; t, k, v_1^{q_1} v_2^{q_2} \ldots v_g^{q_w})$; the notation describes, that there are q_r parameters from the set $\{v_1, v_2, \ldots, v_k\}$ that takes v_s values.*

In this paper, when we use the term covering array refers to both uniform and mixed level covering arrays.

2.2   Example

Consider a hypothetical holiday-reservation system that has four components of interest shown in Table 1. There are three log-in types, three customer types, three reservation types, and three credit cards types. Different end users may use different combinations of components. To exhaustively test all combinations of the four parameters that have 3 options each from Table 1 would require $3^4 = 81$ tests. The four components are *factors*, and the three values for each factor are their *levels*.

It is possible to reduce the 81 tests required for exhaustive testing by employing a $CA(9; 2, 4, 3)$. Instead of testing every combination, all individual pairs of interactions are tested, the resulting test suite contains only 9 tests. The entire test suite covers every possible pairwise combination between components. The $CA(9; 2, 4, 3)$ is optimal given that a lower bound for any covering array of strength t, is the product of the t greater alphabets of the variables.

Table 1. A hypothetical holiday-reservation system

Log-in type	Customer type	Reservation type	Credit card type
New customer - not logged in	New customer	Cars	Visa
New customer - logged in	Frequent customer	Hotels	Mastercard
Frequent customer - logged in	Employee	Flights	American Express

Based on the example above, we note that it is easy to apply the combinatorial interaction testing. Combinatorial testing is a specification-based technique which requires no knowledge about the implementation details of the system under test. Note that the specification required by some forms of combinatorial testing is lightweight, as it only needs to identify a set of parameters and their possible values. This is in contrast with other testing techniques that require a complex operational model of the system under test.

2.3   Covering Arrays Construction Methods

Many algorithms and tools exist that construct covering arrays. Among them are: (a) algebraic methods, (b) recursive methods, (c) greedy methods, and (d) metaheuristics methods.

Mathematicians use some *algebraic and combinatorial methods* to construct covering arrays. Chateauneuf and Kreher [4] introduced a new method to construct covering arrays of strength three. Meagher and Stevens [13] extended the idea presented in [4], presenting a strategy for obtaining the starter vector by local search and the selection of a group action. Finally, Lobb et al. [11] presented a generalization of this method to permit any number of fixed points, permit an arbitrary group acting on the symbols, and permit an arbitrary group acting on the columns. Sherwood [15] described some algebraic constructions for strength-2 covering arrays developed from index-1 orthogonal arrays, ordered designs and covering arrays. Torres-Jimenez et al. [17] presented a method for constructing covering arrays using Galois fields and logarithm tables.

Williams [19] presented a tool called TConfig to construct covering arrays. TConfig constructs covering arrays using recursive functions that concatenate small covering arrays to create covering arrays with a larger number of columns. Moura et al. [14] introduced a set of recursive algorithms for constructing covering arrays based on covering arrays of small sizes.

The majority of commercial and open source test data generating tools use greedy algorithms for covering arrays construction (AETG [5], TVG [1], ACTS [10], DDA [3] and Jenny [9]); the greedy algorithms provide the fastest solving method.

Some metaheuristic algorithms, such as TS (Tabu Search) [8], SA (Simulated Annealing) [7,12,18], GA (Generic Algorithm) and ACO (Ant Colony Optimization Algorithm) [16] provide an effective way to find approximate solutions.

A simulated annealing metaheuristic (Henceforth called SAC) has been applied by Cohen et al. in [7] for constructing covering arrays. SAC starts with a randomly generated initial solution M which cost $c(M)$ is measured as the number of uncovered t-tuples. In their implementation, Cohen et al. use a simple geometric function $T_n = 0.9998T_{n-1}$ with an initial temperature fixed at $T_i = 0.20$. At each temperature, 2000 neighboring solutions are generated. The algorithm stops either if a valid covering array is found, or if no change in the cost of the current solution is observed after 500 trials.

Torres-Jimenez and Rodriguez-Tello [18] introduced a new SA implementation called ISA for constructing binary covering arrays. ESA is an extension of ISA to construct mixed-level covering arrays.

3   Metaheuristic Approach to Solve CAC Problem

This section presents the proposed method to build functional tests. The method is based on the construction of optimal o near-optimal covering arrays. We have developed an enhanced simulated annealing (ESA) in order to construct covering arrays. Next all the details of the simulated annealing implementation proposed are presented.

The following paragraphs will describe each of the components of the implementation of ESA. The description is done given the matrix representation of a covering array. A covering array can be represented as a matrix M of size $N \times k$, where the columns are the parameters and the rows are the cases of the test set that is constructed. Each cell $m_{i,j}$ in the array accepts values from the set $\{1, 2, \ldots, v_j\}$ where v_j is the cardinality of the alphabet of j-th column.

The *initial solution* M is constructed by generating M as a matrix with maximum Hamming distance. The Hamming distance $d(x, y)$ between two rows $x, y \in M$ is the number of elements in which they differ. Let r_i be a row of the matrix M. To generate a random matrix M of maximum Hamming distance the following steps are performed: (1) Generate the first row r_1 at random; (2) Generate s rows $c_1, c_2, \ldots, c_s$ at random, which will be candidate rows; (3) Select the candidate row c_i that maximizes the Hamming distance according to (1) and added to the i-th row of the matrix M; and (4) Repeat from step 2 until M is completed.

$$g(r_i) = \sum_{s=1}^{i-1} \sum_{v=1}^{k} d(m_{s,v}, m_{i,v}), \textbf{where } d(m_{s,v}, m_{i,v}) = \begin{cases} 1 \textbf{ if } m_{s,v} \neq m_{i,v} \\ 0 \textbf{ Otherwise} \end{cases} \quad (1)$$

The *evaluation function* $\mathcal{C}(M)$ is used to estimate the goodness of a candidate solution. Previously reported metaheuristic algorithms for constructing covering arrays have commonly evaluated the quality of a potential solution (covering array) as the number of combination of missing symbols in the matrix M [7,16]. Then, the expected solution will be zero missing. In ESA this evaluation function definition was used. Initially the computational complexity is equivalent to $O\left(N\binom{k}{t}\right)$, posterior calls to the evaluation function use local recalculation with a complexity, in the worst case, equivalent to $N \times \binom{k-a}{t-a}$ for $1 \leq a \leq t/2$.

Two *neighborhood functions* were implemented to guide the local search of ESA. The neighborhood function $\mathcal{N}_1(s)$ makes a random search of a missing

t-tuple, then tries by setting the j-th combination of symbols in every row of M. The neighborhood function $\mathcal{N}_2(s)$ randomly chooses a position (i, j) of the matrix M and makes all possible changes of symbol. During the search process a combination of both $\mathcal{N}_1(s)$ and $\mathcal{N}_2(s)$ neighborhood functions is employed by our simulated annealing algorithm. The former is applied with probability p, while the latter is employed at a $(1 - p)$ rate. This combined neighborhood function $\mathcal{N}_3(s, x)$ is defined in (2), where x is a random number in the interval $[0, 1]$.

$$\mathcal{N}_3(s, x) = \begin{cases} \mathcal{N}_1(s) & \text{if } x \leq p \\ \mathcal{N}_2(s) & \text{if } x > p \end{cases} \tag{2}$$

ESA uses a *geometrical cooling scheme*. It starts at an initial temperature T_i which is decremented at each round by a factor α using the relation $T_k = \alpha T_{k-1}$. For each temperature, the maximum number of visited neighboring solutions is L. It depends directly on the parameters (N, k and $\mathcal{V}$, where $\mathcal{V}$ is the maximum cardinality of M) of the studied covering arrays. This is because more moves are required for covering arrays with alphabets of greater cardinality.

The *stop criterion* for our simulated annealing is either when the current temperature reaches T_f, when it ceases to make progress, or when a valid covering array is found. In ESA a lack of progress exists if after ϕ (frozen factor) consecutive temperature decrements the best-so-far solution is not improved.

4   Experimentation and Results

The procedure described in the previous section was coded in C and compiled with gcc using the optimization flag -O3. It was run sequentially into a CPU Intel(R) Xeon(TM) a 2.8 GHz, 2 GB of RAM with Linux operating system. In all the experiments the following parameters were used for our simulated annealing implementation: Initial temperature $T_i = 4.0$; Final temperature $T_f = 1.0E-10$; Cooling factor $\alpha = 0.99$; Maximum neighboring solutions per temperature $L = N \times k \times \mathcal{V}^2$; Frozen factor $\phi = 11$; The neighborhood function $\mathcal{N}_1$ was applied using a probability $p = 0.3$, and the neighborhood function $\mathcal{N}_2$ was applied using a probability $p = 0.7$.

4.1   Comparing ESA with an Existing SA Implementation

The purpose of this experiment is to carry out a performance comparison of the bounds achieved by our ESA algorithm with respect to other SA solutions reported in the literature. For this experiment, we selected 21 instances presented earlier by Cohen et al. [6,7].

The results from this experiment are summarized in Table 2. A set of 12 instances of uniform level is shown in Table 2(a). Table 2(b) shows a set of 9 instances of mixed level. Column 1 describes the instance, column 2 shows the best size N found by SAC (reported in [6,7]), column 3 indicates the best size N found by ESA (* indicates that the instance is optimal, i.e., the product of the t greater alphabets of the variables), and the last column depicts the difference between the best result produced by ESA and SAC ($\Delta = ESA - SAC$).

Table 2. Comparison between ESA and SAC over a set of selected instances from [6,7]. Column 1 describes the instance, column 2 and 3 show the best size N found by SAC and ESA respectively, the last column depicts the difference between the best result produced by ESA and SAC ($\Delta = ESA - SAC$).

(a)				(b)			
	SAC	ESA	Δ		SAC	ESA	Δ
CA(2,100,4)	45	39	-6	$MCA(2,11,5^1 3^8 2^2)$	15	15*	0
CA(2,20,10)	183	155	-28	$MCA(2,75,4^1 3^3 92^3 5)$	21	20	-1
CA(2,16,6)	62	60	-2	$MCA(2,21,5^1 4^4 3^1 12^5)$	21	21	0
CA(2,16,7)	87	81	-6	$MCA(2,61,4^1 53^1 72^2 9)$	30	28	-2
CA(2,16,8)	112	102	-10	$MCA(2,19,6^1 5^1 4^6 3^8 2^3)$	30	30*	0
CA(2,17,8)	114	104	-10	$MCA(2,19,7^1 6^1 5^1 4^5 3^8 2^3)$	42	42*	0
CA(3,6,6)	300	258	-42	$MCA(3,6,5^2 4^2 3^2)$	100	100*	0
CA(3,8,8)	918	512*	-406	$MCA(3,10,6^6 4^2 2^2)$	313	305	-8
CA(3,9,9)	1490	1440	-50	$MCA(3,7,10^1 6^2 4^3 3^1)$	360	360*	0
CA(3,10,10)	2163	1300	-863				
CA(3,12,12)	4422	4091	-331				
CA(3,14,14)	8092	6956	-1136				

From Table 2(a) we can observe that ESA improves all the results obtained by SAC. The improvements are amazing, in three instances were reduced hundreds of rows, and in the case $CA(3, 14, 14)$ were reduced 1136 lines. Table 2(b) shows that ESA improves three instances and even the remaining six instances, five of these instances are optimal.

4.2 Constructing Test-Suites for Different Real-Case Software Components

The purpose of this experiment is to evaluate the performance of the proposed simulated annealing through the construction of different test suites for real cases of software components. The results of our simulated annealing are compared with those obtained by the following state-of-the-art procedures: TConfig [19], ACTS (IPOG) [10], Jenny [9] and TVG [1].

A real international company, which we named *xCompany* to avoid conflicts of interest, dedicated to custom software development is currently constructing the next software applications:

▷ App. A: An application designed to support Math students from First grade of Elementary School to High School. This system will help students to learn and practice math in a friendly way, using questions that will explain step by step how to get the expected result.

▷ App. B: An invoicing application for fullfiling the need in the local market generated by the electronic invoicing requirement published and made effective by SAT (Mexico's tax administration service).

▷ App. C: A software application to manage the tourist and industrial transport.

We have selected 12 representative test cases and created their corresponding covering arrays with strength $2 \leq t \leq 6$. Table 3 shows the 12 objects to be tested. Column 2 shows that corresponding software system. Column 3 shows a

Table 3. List of 12 representative cases for combinatorial testing

Test ID	App. ID	Description	Covering arrays
1	A	Hotel booking	$MCA(t, 6, 4^1 3^1 2^4)$
2	A	Control Panel, price variables	$MCA(t, 9, 6^6 2^3)$
3	A	Add section to blog	$MCA(t, 16, 5^1 4^4 3^9 2^2)$
4	A	Add Routes	$MCA(t, 6, 4^2 3^2 2^2)$
5	B	Additional informationon the invoice	$MCA(t, 9, 6^2 2^7)$
6	B	Configuration of thepre-invoice	$MCA(t, 6, 3^1 2^5)$
7	B	Add concept to the bill	$MCA(t, 6, 8^3 4^1 3^1 2^1)$
8	C	Teacher record	$MCA(t, 12, 3^8 2^4)$
9	C	School record	$MCA(t, 14, 4^1 3^{11} 2^2)$
10	C	List students	$MCA(t, 6, 2^6)$
11	C	Find student	$MCA(t, 4, 4^2 3^2)$
12	C	Add customer	$MCA(t, 13, 3^{10} 2^3)$

Table 4. Results of our simulated annealing compared against ACTS, Jenny, TVG, and TConfig. Column 1 shows the covering array ID corresponding to the Table 3. The next 4 columns show the best solution, in terms of N, found by ACTS, Jenny, TVG, and TConfig respectively. Column β represents the best solution, in terms of N, produced by the previous tools. Column 7 shows the best solution produced by ESA, the $\star$ means that the solution is optimal. Last column shows the difference between the best result produced by ESA and the best result obtained by the other tools examined in this work ($\Delta = ESA - \beta$).

(a) $t = 2$

ID	IPOF2	Jenny	TVG	TConfig	β	ESA	Δ
1	12	13	12	13	12	12*	0
2	50	53	58	54	50	42	-8
3	32	29	31	32	29	21	-8
4	17	20	18	16	16	16*	0
5	36	36	36	36	36	36*	0
6	9	9	8	8	8	7	-1
7	68	73	77	64	64	64*	0
8	17	17	18	17	17	13	-4
9	21	20	22	19	19	15	-4
10	8	8	8	7	7	6	-1
11	16	17	17	16	16	16*	0
12	18	19	19	17	17	14	-3
							-29

(b) $t = 3$

ID	IPOF2	Jenny	TVG	TConfig	β	ESA	Δ
1	34	34	33	33	33	24*	-9
2	368	372	423	366	366	357	-9
3	148	142	154	133	133	115	-18
4	49	58	58	53	49	48*	-1
5	122	89	84	74	74	72*	-2
6	20	18	19	18	18	18	0
7	512	533	543	514	512	512	0
8	57	58	61	58	57	48	-9
9	88	80	85	82	80	65	-15
10	13	14	12	12	12	12	0
11	50	55	51	53	50	48*	-2
12	68	65	69	68	65	52	-13
							-78

(c) $t = 4$

ID	IPOF2	Jenny	TVG	TConfig	β	ESA	Δ
1	72	70	70	72	70	60	-10
2	2219	2250	2462	2318	2219	1979	-240
3	665	611	640	607	607	570	-37
4	151	158	169	149	149	144*	-5
5	283	267	271	256	256	216	-40
6	38	37	37	36	36	30	-6
7	2056	2103	2134	2050	2050	2048*	-2
8	196	196	200	191	191	160	-31
9	312	296	305	313	296	259	-37
10	26	26	28	28	26	21	-5
11	144	144	144	144	144	144*	0
12	233	230	236	236	230	193	-37
							-450

(d) $t = 5$

ID	IPOF2	Jenny	TVG	TConfig	β	ESA	Δ
1	110	129	114	114	110	96*	-14
2	11103	11854	11947	11157	11103	7776*	-3327
3	2665	2517	2505	2473	2473	2188	-285
4	304	328	331	300	300	288*	-12
5	597	552	587	575	552	432	-120
6	54	70	64	48	48	48*	0
7	6150	6254	6239	6144	6144	6144*	0
8	591	593	604	624	591	471	-120
9	1100	1038	1037	1121	1037	958	-79
10	33	43	45	32	32	32*	0
11	-	-	-	-	0	-	-
12	755	744	763	792	744	657	-87
							-4044

(e) $t = 6$

ID	IPOF2	Jenny	TVG	TConfig	β	ESA	Δ
1	192	192	-	192	192	192*	0
2	52579	48071	48586	49644	48071	46656*	-1415
3	9759	9640	8740	9363	8740	8591	-149
4	576	576	-	576	576	576*	0
5	1165	1101	1170	1267	1101	898	-203
6	96	96	-	96	96	96*	0
7	12288	12288	12288	12288	12288*	12288	0
8	1636	1688	1673	1794	1636	1530	-106
9	3556	3473	3248	3662	3248	3141	-107
10	64	64	-	64	64	64*	0
11	-	-	-	-	-	-	-
12	2269	2269	2292	2412	2269	2150	-119
							-2099

description of the component to validate. Column 4 shows the specification of the cover covering array to build.

The detailed computational results produced by this experiment are listed in Table 4, here are displayed 5 subtables corresponding to strengths $t = 2$ through $t = 6$. Column 1 shows the results obtained from ACTS tool, we used the IPOF2 algorithm. Column 2 shows the results obtained from Jenny tool. Column 3 shows the results obtained from TVG tool, we used T-Reduce algorithm. Column 4 shows the results obtained from TConfig tool. Column 5 displays the best results for each case obtained in the first 4 columns ($\beta = \min{(ACTS, Jenny, TVG, TConfig)}$). Column 6 list the results obtained from ESA algorithm. The difference between the best result produced by ESA and the best solution obtained from the other four tools ($\Delta = ESA - \beta$) is depicted in the last column.

Again the results are striking, ESA gets the best levels in 41 cases and equals to the remaining bounds. It was constructed 24 optimum instances. Finally, we highlight the following two results: (1) $MCA(t, 9, 6^6 2^3) = 46,656$, this was reduced in 1415 the best bound obtained by the other four tools; (2) $MCA(t, 9, 6^6 2^3) = 46656$ this was reduced in 3327 the best bound obtained by the other four tools.

5   Conclusions

This paper presented a simple method to generate functional test cases from covering arrays. It was presented an enhanced simulated annealing algorithm, referred as ESA, that deals with the CAC problem. The key features of ESA are: (1) An efficient method to generate initial solutions using maximum Hamming distance; (2) A carefully designed composed neighborhood function which allows the search to quickly reduce the total cost of candidate solutions, while avoiding to get stuck on some local minimal; and (3) An effective cooling schedule allowing our simulated annealing algorithm to converge faster, producing at the same time good quality solutions.

The empirical evidence presented in this paper showed that our simulated annealing improved the size of the covering arrays in comparison with the tools that are among the best found in the state-of-the-art of the construction of covering arrays. In the first experiment, ESA gets 15 better bounds than SAC and even the others. In the second experiment, the performance of the proposed simulated annealing algorithm was assessed with a new benchmark, composed by 58 covering arrays of strengths two through six. The computational results, showing that our algorithm was able to find 41 better bounds and to equal the remaining.

Finally, the new covering arrays are available in CINVESTAV Covering Array Repository (CAR), which is available under request at http://www.tamps. cinvestav.mx/~jtj/CA.php. We have verified all covering arrays described in this paper using the tool described in [2].

Acknowledgments. This research work was partially funded by the following projects: CONACyT 58554, Calculo de Covering Arrays; 51623 Fondo Mixto CONACyT y Gobierno del Estado de Tamaulipas.

References

1. Arshem, J., Schroeder, P.J.: Test Vector Generator, TVG (2009), `http://sourceforge.net/projects/tvg`
2. Avila-George, H., Torres-Jimenez, J., Rangel-Valdez, N., Carrión, A., Hernández, V.: Supercomputing and Grid Computing on the Verification of Covering Arrays. The Journal of Supercomputing, 1–30 (2012) (published online: April 18, 2012)
3. Bryce, R.C., Colbourn, C.J.: The Density Algorithm for Pairwise Interaction Testing. Software Testing, Verification and Reliability 17(3), 159–182 (2007)
4. Chateauneuf, M., Kreher, D.L.: On the State of Strength-Three Covering Arrays. Journal of Combinatorial Designs 10(4), 217–238 (2002)
5. Cohen, D.M., Dalal, S.R., Parelius, J., Patton, G.C.: The Combinatorial Design Approach to Automatic Test Generation. IEEE Software 13(5), 83–88 (1996)
6. Cohen, M.B., Colbourn, C.J., Ling, A.C.: Constructing Strength Three Covering Arrays with Augmented Annealing. Discrete Math. 308(13), 2709–2722 (2008)
7. Cohen, M.B., Gibbons, P.B., Mugridge, W.B., Colbourn, C.J.: Constructing Test Suites for Interaction Testing. In: 25th Intl. Conf. on Software Engineering (ICSE 2003), pp. 38–48. IEEE (2003)
8. Gonzalez-Hernandez, L., Torres-Jimenez, J., Rangel-Valdez, N.: Construction of Mixed Covering Arrays of Strengths 2 through 6 Using a Tabu Search Approach. In: Discrete Mathematics, Algorithms and Applications 2 (in press, 2012)
9. Jenkins, B.: Jenny – A Pairwise Testing Tool (2011), `http://burtleburtle.net/bob/math/jenny.html`
10. Lei, Y., Kacker, R.N., Kuhn, D.R., Okun, V., Lawrence, J.: IPOG – A General Strategy for T-Way Software Testing. In: 14th Annual IEEE Intl. Conf. and Works. on the Eng. of Computer-Based Systems (ECBS 2007), pp. 549–556. IEEE (2007)
11. Lobb, J.R., Colbourn, C.J., Danziger, P., Stevens, B., Torres-Jimenez, J.: Cover Starters for Covering Arrays of Strength Two. Discrete Math. 312(5), 943–956 (2012)
12. Martinez-Pena, J., Torres-Jimenez, J., Rangel-Valdez, N., Avila-George, H.: A Heuristic Approach for Constructing Ternary Covering Arrays Using Trinomial Coefficients. In: Kuri-Morales, A., Simari, G.R. (eds.) IBERAMIA 2010. LNCS, vol. 6433, pp. 572–581. Springer, Heidelberg (2010)
13. Meagher, K., Stevens, B.: Group Construction of Covering Arrays. Journal of Combinatorial Designs 13(1), 70–77 (2005)
14. Moura, L., Stardom, J., Stevens, B., Williams, A.W.: Covering Arrays with Mixed Alphabet Sizes. Journal of Combinatorial Designs 11(6), 413–432 (2003)
15. Sherwood, G.B.: Optimal and Near-Optimal Mixed Covering Arrays by Column Expansion. Discrete Mathematics 308(24), 6022–6035 (2008)
16. Shiba, T., Tsuchiya, T., Kikuno, T.: Using Artificial Life Techniques to Generate Test Cases for Combinatorial Testing. In: 28th Annual Intl. Computer Software and Applications Conf (COMPSAC 2004), pp. 72–77. IEEE (2004)
17. Torres-Jimenez, J., Avila-George, H., Rangel-Valdez, N., Gonzalez-Hernandez, L.: Construction of Orthogonal Arrays of Index Unity Using Logarithm Tables for Galois Fields. In: Sen, J. (ed.) Cryptography and Security in Computing, pp. 71–90. InTech (2012)
18. Torres-Jimenez, J., Rodriguez-Tello, E.: New Bounds for Binary Covering Arrays Using Simulated Annealing. Information Sciences 185(1), 137–152 (2012)
19. Williams, A.W.: Determination of Test Configurations for Pair-Wise Interaction Coverage. In: 13th Intl. Conf. on Testing Communicating Systems – Tools and Techniques (TestCom 2000), pp. 57–72. Kluwer (2000)

Influence Diagram for Selection of Pedagogical Strategies in a Multi-Agent System Learning

Marta R. Bez[1], Cecília D. Flores[2], João M.L. Fonseca[2], Vinicius Maroni[2],
Paulo R. Barros[2], and Rosa M. Vicari[3]

[1] Universidade Feevale, Novo Hamburgo – RS – Brasil
[2] Universidade Federal de Ciências da Saúde de Porto Alegre – RS - Brasil
[3] Universidade Federal do Rio Grande do Sul, Porto Alegre – RS – Brasil

Abstract. An Influence Diagram is a simple visual representation of a decision problem that provides an intuitive way to identify and display the essential elements, including decisions, uncertainties, and objectives, and on how they influence each other. This paper discusses its use in the selection of pedagogical strategies in a multi-agent learning system for the health care practitioners: SimDeCS (Simulation for Decision Making in the Health Care Service). A clinical case is also presented and discussed.

Keywords: influence diagram, pedagogic strategy, probabilistic reasoning, medical education, simulation.

1 Introduction

The Influence Diagram (ID) appeared for the first time in the United States during the 1980's as a manner to represent a decision-making problem [1]. It is even more compact than a decision tree and can explicit the probabilistic dependencies among variables. According to [2], an ID is a graphical structure that allows the modeling of uncertain variables and decisions that explicitly reveal probabilistic dependency in a flux of information.

In accordance with the author, there are several benefits in the evaluation of a problem through ID operations such as: the algorithm executes the entire inference and analysis automatically; the analysis is available in a representation which is natural for decision making; the use of ID results in gains in processing as it considerably reduces the size of intermediary calculations and the need for greater memory spaces.

Recent work has shown the viability in the use of ID in processes where variables are uncertain and decisions need to be taken starting from the probabilistic dependency in a flux of information as, for instance, in the Medical field [3-5], the Communication area in multi-agent systems (MAS) [6, 7], and Risk Evaluation [8].

The ID is presented here in this paper in the selection of the best pedagogical strategy to be offered to a student during the execution of a clinical case simulation.

A simulation can be understood as a reproduction or the representation of a real scenario or process. It attempts to join together the main components of a scenario in

J. Pavón et al. (Eds.): IBERAMIA 2012, LNAI 7637, pp. 621–630, 2012.
© Springer-Verlag Berlin Heidelberg 2012

a coherent and integrated manner, enabling this environment to be modulated and also to evaluate the time course with or without the intervention of decision making.

Simulators for medical education may thus be understood broadly as tools that allow educators to maintain total control of pre-selected clinical settings, bypassing this stage of learning, and the discomfort and potential risks towards a real patient [9].

According to [10], the simulation brings clear advantages to the learning environment in general with specific applicability for medical education such as: it assists the student in understanding complex relations that otherwise would require expensive equipment or be dangerous; it allows the application of scientific and technical knowledge in an integrated and simultaneous manner; it permits the student to seek new methods and strategies for solving problems proposed by the simulator under study; providing a close to reality environment for training and the enhancement of acquired knowledge; eventually reduces risks whereas learning in real situations.

Simulators in the medical field in general, facilitate the estimation of decision making regarding the economic impact of employed strategies. It can be evaluated in parallel by means of decision trees with final results overlapping and in considering the economic impact of each one separately. Therefore education covers not only health care decisions, but it also completes instruction with a more realistic scenario that could be limited, or in not referring to resources and the feasibility of simulation.

The main goal in medical education is to acquire standards of excellence with the measurement of results in the learning process [9]. A specific subtype simulation aims to make the assessment of competence [11]. After the consolidation of a domain in medical knowledge by means of a student, the next step is to extract relevant conduct from that same area to a given situation, in the correct order of planning, and consider technical feasibility. The environment for the SimDeCS provides ways to quantify the process of acquiring competence.

The medical student can make use of the SimDeCS as a complementary tool in order to facilitate the development of his technical abilities and competence [12] concerning formulated diagnosis by following his own learning rhythm. The medical diagnosis formulation process can be seen composed by certain steps such as: medical interview, physical exam, formulation of diagnostic hypothesis, and a requisition (or not) of complementary exams. Once with the diagnosis at hand, the physician elaborates the conduct that may be the prescription of a certain medication, the solicitation of new exams, or forwarding to a specialist [13].

According to [14], the feedback is an essential component in a simulation. The student receives information during the entire simulation in the SimDeCS that permits and encourages him to search for the excellence in learning on what has been studied. Such information is selected by means of the ID that infers in which pedagogical strategy is most adequate for the student.

The next section is dedicated in presenting the SimDeCS simulation tool with special emphasis in the use of the Influence Diagram to select the strategy that will display the best utility in different moments of interaction. The parameters in use become the level of the student's declared confidence and credibility (expectation) that the system might have on the student. A clinical case concerning a Bayesian

Network (BN) for an adult migraine is presented and discussed in Sect. 3. The paper ends with closing remarks and future work perspectives.

2   Simulation for Decision Making in the Health Care Service

The stages in the simulation construction of the SimDeCS are as shown below in Fig. 1 where, in the sequence, each stage is accounted.

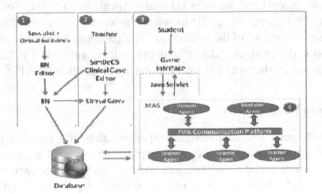

Fig. 1. Stages of the SimDeCS simulation construction

Stage 1: the specialist structures the knowledge of the medical domain in a BN by using Clinical Guidelines as a basic source. These guidelines attempt to compile the best available evidence in pertinent clinical problems towards primary attention and are made available through the Brazilian Society of Family Medicine and Community (SBMFC) in the form of texts, tables and flux sheets. Some of the SBMFC guidelines have been adopted to be modeled by Bayesian networks within the SimDeCS project.

Stage 2: Clinical cases are developed by a professor and represented in a BN that was previously built by the domain expert. Once symptoms and signs are freely made available on the BN, the professor propagates probabilities by emerging one or more diagnosis with its respective conducts, thus modeling the case that will be simulated by the students. The clinical cases are stored in a Data Bank (DB) being composed by the selected nodes by a professor for diagnosis, conduct and investigation stages. Additional information is also stored in the DB regarding the clinical case, as well as the patient's medical records. The network nodes that compose the clinical case are stored in a format of questions available during simulation. Once a question is made, the simulator consults the BN propagated by the professor and attains a reply that expresses the probability of the node at that instant in a colloquial way.

Stage 3: The Learner Agent interacts with students by means of a game. This game is the main form of interaction between SimDeCS and its students, presenting clinical cases and allowing students to model and submit their diagnostic hypothesis.

Stage 4: The SimDeCS MAS architecture is shown in area 4. The Learner Agent represents the student, gathering all concrete evidences about the status of his learning process. Based on these evidences, Learner Agent elaborates and updates the student's model, inferring the credibility that the system might have on the student, and also registering the self-confidence level declared by the student. Domain and Mediator Agents share the teacher's role in SimDeCS. The Domain Agent stores knowledge of the medical domain and evaluates the decisions taken by the student. The result is sent to the Mediator Agent in order to coordinate the interaction process. The interactions between the student and SimDeCS are seen as a process of Pedagogical Negotiation (PN), in which the Mediator Agent solves differences using teaching pedagogical strategies. The role of the Mediator Agent is to mediate the interactions between the student (Learner Agent) and the tutor (Domain Agent) at each stage of consultation with a patient. This agent uses an ID to select the strategy that will display the best utility in different moments of the interaction. The parameters in use become the level of the student's declared confidence and credibility, inferred by Learner Agent through the actions carried out by the student during simulation (see Fig. 2).

2.1   Influence Diagram (ID)

An Influence Diagram is a simple visual representation of a decision problem that provides an intuitive way to identify and display the essential elements; including decisions, uncertainties, and objectives, and on how they influence each other [15].

According to [15], Influence Diagrams are directed by acyclic graphs with three types of nodes (decision, chance, and a value node). Decision nodes, shown as squares, represent choices available to the decision-maker. Chance nodes, shown as circles, represent random variables (or uncertain quantities). Finally, the value node, shown in a diamond shape, represents the objective (or utility) to be maximized.

As formally presented, an ID is an oriented acyclic graph (DAG) $G = (N, E)$, where $N = P \cup D \cup \Psi$ becomes the set of nodes an E the set of arches, being that P, nodes of probability, are random variables (oval). Each node has a table of conditional probabilities in its association. In D we have the decision nodes with points of choice in action (rectangles). Its parent nodes may be other decision nodes or probability nodes. The utility nodes Ψ, has as its purpose the utility functions (lozenge). Each node has a table containing a utility description of the function of the variables associated to its parents, which can be probability or decision nodes. The conditional arches are those of utility or probabilistic nodes and represent probabilistic dependency [16].

An objective combines multiple sub-objectives or attributes, which may be in conflict as in energy costs, benefits, and environmental and health risks. Usually the objective is uncertain as decision analysts suggest maximizing the expected value, or more generally the expected utility, based on risk preference.

An arrow denotes an influence. An X influences Y means that knowing X would directly affect our belief or expectation about the value of Y. An influence expresses knowledge about relevance, and does not necessarily imply a causal relation.

As shown at the end of the previous section, important aspects are analyzed in the student's behavior during simulation: credibility and confidence.

Credibility is defined by the accompaniment carried out by the apprentice agent concerning the simulation process of the student. The apprentice agent delineates the credibility of the system regarding the student in one of the three following categories: High, Medium, or Low.

The credibility of the system on the student is calculated based on collected variables during simulation such as creating a record of the patient, the number of questioned bogus nodes, and the investigation process, which takes into consideration the questions carried out during anamnesis, physical examination and complementary exams as presented in the ID (see Fig. 2) and explained in the sequence.

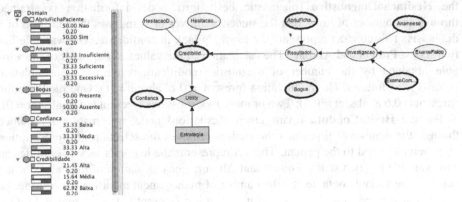

Fig. 2. Mediator Agent Influence Diagram for Pedagogical Strategy Selection

The values of the state of the nodes in the ID are determined in runtime from the LOG generated during the student's simulation by means of the LearnerAgent. The information is applied to the set of data by the MediatorAgent in order to obtain the final values of the state of nodes as clarified next.

The value for a **bogus** node (questions that do not have influence in the results) is obtained through the percentage of these types of questions done by the student in relation to the total of questions in the question bank. This variable in the ID is divided into two states: present and absent. The states of this node are established in the following manner: [0-10%] – (present = 0, absent=1), (10%-30%] – (present = 0,4 e absent = 0,6), (30%-100%] – (present = 1, absent =0).

The **AbriuFichaP** (open patient's record card) node is attained when simulation initializes through the student's act of access to the patient's record. The value is determined as a one for the "yes" state and a zero for the "no" state in case the student has created a record. On the other hand, a non-creation of a record results in a zero value for the "yes" state and a one value for the "no" state.

The information on the **Anamnese** (anamnesis) node is achieved through the percentage of questions in relation to the total of questions in the question bank. This variable has three states: Excessive, Sufficient, and Insufficient. The established states are as follows: [0-25%] - (insufficient = 1, sufficient = 0 & excessive = 0), (25%-75%] - (insufficient = 0, sufficient = 1 & excessive = 0), (75%-100%] - (insufficient = 0, sufficient = 0 & excessive = 1).

The **ExamesFisicos** (physical examination) node has its information by means of the percentage of accomplished exams in relation to what is available in the DB. This variable has states in knowledge: Excessive, Sufficient, and Insufficient. The states of this node will be established according to the percentage and will be distributed as follows: [0-25%] - (insufficient = 1, sufficient = 0 & excessive = 0), (25%-75%] - (insufficient = 0, sufficient = 1 & excessive = 0), (75%-100%] - (insufficient = 0, sufficient = 0 & excessive = 1).

The **ExamesComplementares** (complementary exams) node follows the same information used by physical exams as well as the identical states as shown above. For the **HesitacaoDiagnostico** (diagnostic hesitation) node, information is attained through the number of times that the student removes or withdraws the selection of a diagnosis. This conduct represents the learner's lack in confidence. This variable has two states: Present and Absent. The calculation of the values of the states of the variable obtained by the number of diagnostic modifications during the simulation process is as follows: No modification (present = 0 & absent = 1), One modification (present = 0,6 & absent = 0,4); Two or more modifications (present = 1 & absent = 0).

For the **HesitaConduta** (management hesitation) node, information is attained through the number of times that the student removes the selection of a prescription after being granted to the patient. This act represents the learner's lack in confidence. This variable has two states: Present and Absent. The calculation of the values of the states of the variable obtained by the number of management modifications during the simulation process is as follows: No modification (present = 0 & absent = 1), One modification (present = 0,6 & absent = 0,4); Two or more modifications (present = 1 & absent = 0).

The **confiança** (confidence) concerns on how safe a student feels when he executes the simulation. This is questioned in the beginning of the simulation and when leaving the investigation, diagnostic, and management modules, which may have the High, Medium or Low values [17, 18].

According to [17], the utility node in the ID makes a weighted average between the criterion that defines the utility of the problem to be decided and that should result in the choice of the best decision, which is good in all simultaneous criteria, but not necessarily the best when it comes to each individual node. A pedagogical strategy is generated once it is carried out by the student from the result of the combination of the possible states in the credibility and confidence nodes (see Table 1).

Table 1. Possible strategies to emerge in the Influence Diagram

		CREDIBILITY		
		HIGH	**MEDIUM**	**LOW**
CONFIDENCE	**HIGH**	Expansion	Contestation	Contestation
	MEDIUM	Evidence	Contestation	Orientation
	LOW	Support	Support	Orientation

2.2   Pedagogical Strategies

As shown in Table 1, five pedagogical strategies are available in the SimDeCS. The message to be carried out by the Mediator Agent to the student becomes dependent to the generated strategy from the ID and from the errors as described below:

Investigation errors (the patient's records did not open; adequate; excessive (over 90%); missing (less then 10%); bogus (over 25%); expensive and delayed); **Diagnostic errors** (correct; incomplete yet plausible; incomplete yet implausible); **Management errors** (correct; incorrect, consistent with diagnosis; correct, inconsistent with diagnosis; absence; expensive; delayed).

Orientation message: when the credibility of the system of the student is low and confidence is declared medium or low. In this case the simulator does not believe that the student will achieve his objectives and the learner demonstrates a lack of confidence in his work. This therefore aims to make the student review his procedures and the Mediator Agent should forward correction messages or alteration suggestions.

Expansion message: when the credibility of the system of the student is high and confidence is also declared high. In this case the simulator believes in the student's simulation potential, and the student has high confidence in his work. It aims to stimulate the student into searching extra knowledge and encourage his reasoning where, in this case, the Mediator Agent should send discussion messages.

Support message: when the credibility of the system of the student is high or medium and confidence is declared low. In this case the simulator believes in the student's simulation potential, yet the student shows himself lacking in confidence in the simulation. The approach in this type of strategy tends to encourage the student to proceed with his reasoning. The Mediator Agent should send messages with similar examples in the attempt to reinforce confidence in the student.

Contestation message: when the credibility of the system of the student is medium or low and confidence is declared high or medium. It takes place when the simulator does not believe that the student will be able to conclude his simulation in a satisfactory way. However, the student has high confidence in his knowledge. It aims to point out errors, arouse an auto-critical sense in the student, and mainly be the motivation to make the student review his reasoning and rebuild a procedure. The Mediator Agent should send experimentation, search and reflection messages.

Evidence message: when the credibility of the system of the student is high and confidence is declared medium. It happens when the simulator believes that the student has a potential, yet the student still proves to be insecure regarding the simulation. The approach in this kind of strategy seeks to incentive the student to go on with his reasoning by giving him reliability on his reckoning. The Mediator Agent should send messages with demonstrations of similar cases.

3   Case Study

This section presents a case study in order to demonstrate the strategies that emerge from the ID while using the simulator. The example case here represents a man with eventual headaches with sporadic arrival at a basic health station.

As a routine he says that he leaves home early in the morning and never has time to go to the station. The patient presents nasal obstruction and holocranial pain in less frequent episodes. It is expected that after the investigation carried out by the student, the choice by the apprentice will be the tension headache diagnosis and has as a conduct the prescription of an analgesic. However, during the investigation stage he asks the patient over 75% of the anamnesis inquiry options available in the simulator. This demonstrates to the Mediator Agent that he is insecure in the conduction of the case and thus will make a pedagogical strategy to appear in the form of a message.

The pedagogical strategy in use will make the displayed message to the student alter itself. Besides that, the strategy will be originated from the result out of the ID processing that considers the auto-confidence declared by the student. In this case, for example, excessive anamnesis with auto-declaration of high confidence and credibility inferred by the simulator as of being low will generate a pedagogical strategy of contestation (see Fig. 3 snippet) displaying the message: "You have made an excessive number of questions that may lead to a confusing diagnosis. Read again the questions and answers received in the investigation phase and reflect over the diagnosis in order to avoid it with another that is similar."

The student's option after the investigation stage is the diagnosis of sinusitis when it should be tension headache. In this manner, the simulator will consider the diagnosis as being incorrect yet plausible due to the fact that sinusitis is the second most probable node to appear in the BN from these symptoms.

The student, right after the diagnosis, chooses as a conduct the utilization of antimicrobial drugs and hence the simulator will present a message that the conduct is incorrect, yet coherent with the selected diagnosis. This information is obtained through the BN processing.

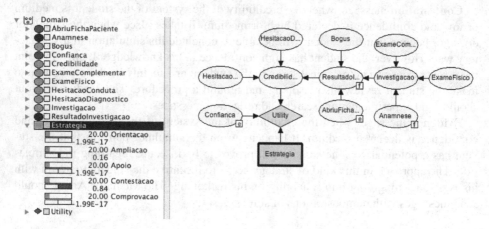

Fig. 3. Case study simulation results

4   Final Considerations

Our motivation relies on limitations detected on AMPLIA (Intelligent Probabilistic Multi-agent Learning Environment) [16, 17]. The main differential between Sim-DeCS and AMPLIA is its available interface for the student. With AMPLIA, the student would receive a BN editor and would build his own network, which would be compared to that of an expert. With the SimDeCS, the student receives a simulator with health cases prepared by professors in the form of a game with its basis on Bayesian networks created by specialists.

Another significant difference between both systems, which is the focus of this paper, is the structure of the ID where the AMPLIA would take into consideration a small number of variables. Variables were inserted in the SimDeCS that permits to accompany the student's course along the entire simulation. This way the main problems of medical students in the solution of clinical cases are taken into consideration so that a pedagogical strategy can emerge from the ID in which the learner can be kept up with throughout the entire simulation process.

Despite the analysis of other approaches to be followed for the pedagogical strategy decision making by the Mediator Agent, such as decision trees, the option was for the continuity in the use of the ID for several reasons. The ID shows the dependencies among variables more clearly than the decision tree does. Decision trees display more details on possible paths or scenarios through a sequence of branches from left to right. However, this detail presents a high cost: first all variables should be dealt with as being discreet even if they are continuous. In second place, the number of nodes in a decision tree exponentially increases with the number of variables and decisions.

The use of a structured simulator on BN permits the emulation of the medical diagnostic process with greater fidelity. In differentially valuing the correction of the student's decisions (credibility) compared to his own confidence in the same choices, it is possible to distinguish the suggested strategies through the simulator, thus attending the pedagogical requisite to particularize the needs of every single student. The fact that the same system can be used in different domains of knowledge, just by modifying the BN in use, becomes another differential. The choice for a MAS architecture also allows greater application autonomy once that the agents can perceive the environment and make decisions based on beliefs and self-objectives in an independent way, which also makes the cooperation for the resolution of conflicts possible, thus proposing intelligent solutions based on the knowledge of the domain expert.

The system is at its final stage of development with three networks (headache, dyspepsia and parasitosis) making it possible to mold around 80 clinical cases by professors who care to delineate his personal cases. Ten clinical cases have been prepared for the headache network for the students exercise.

With future improvements in the simulator, we intend to implement a time factor in order to permit that one or several correct or acceptable decisions at one point may be evaluated as incorrect if the opportune moment passes by, which is frequent in clinical decision making due to a patient's change of symptoms, with the appearance of new information in a return visit or a flaw in the initial proposed therapy. For this much, studies are being carried out with the intention to make use of Fuzzy ID (FID) [20] for the selection of pedagogical strategies to be executed by the Mediator Agent.

Acknowledgments. The authors gratefully acknowledge the Brazilian agencies, CAPES and UnA-SUS, for the partial support to this research project.

References

1. Clemen, R.T.: Making Hard Decisions – An Introduction to Decision Analysis. Duxbury Press (1991)
2. Shachter, R.D.: Evaluating Influence Diagrams. Operations Research 34(6), 871–882 (1986)
3. Kendrick, D.C., Bu, D., Pan, E., Middleton, B.: Crossing the Evidence Chasm – Building Evidence Bridges from Process Changes to Clinical Outcomes. Journal of the American Medical Informatics Association 14(3), 329–339 (2007)
4. Gómes, M., Bielza, C., Pozo, J.A.F., Ríos-Insua, S.: A Graphical Decision–Theoretic Model for Neonatal Jaundice. Medical Decision Making 27(3), 250–265 (2007)
5. Lee, R.C., Ekaette, E., Kelly, K.L., Craighead, P., Newcomb, C., Dunscombe, P.: Implications of Cancer Staging Uncertainties in Radiation Therapy Decisions. Medical Decision Making 26(3), 226–238 (2006)
6. Sun, L., Zeng, Y., Xiang, Y.: An Influence Diagram Approach for Multiagent Time-Critical Dynamic Decision Modeling. In: Zhang, B.-T., Orgun, M.A. (eds.) PRICAI 2010. LNCS, vol. 6230, pp. 674–680. Springer, Heidelberg (2010)
7. Zeng, Y., Xiang, Y.: Time-Critical Decision Making in Interactive Dynamic Influence Diagram. In: IEEE/WIC/ACM International Conference on Web Intelligence and Intelligent Agent Technology (WI-IAT 2010), pp. 149–156. IEEE (2010)
8. Liu, H., Zhang, C., Wan, Y.: Research on Information Engineering Surveillance Risk Evaluation Based on Probabilistic Influence Diagram. In: 2nd IEEE Intl. Conference on Information Management and Engineering (ICIME 2010), pp. 362–366. IEEE (2010)
9. Ziv, A., Ben-David, S., Ziv, M.: Simulation Based Medical Education – An Opportunity to Learn from Errors. Medical Teacher 27(3), 193–199 (2005)
10. Kincaid, J.P., Hamilton, R., Tarr, R.W., Sangani, H.: Simulation in Education and Training. In: Obaidat, M.S., Papadimitriou, G.I. (eds.) Applied System Simulation – Theory and Applications, pp. 437–456. Kluwer Academic Publlishers (2004)
11. Scalese, R.J., Obeso, V.T.S., Issenberg, B.: Simulation Technology for Skills Training and Competency Assessment in Medical Education. Journal of General Internal Medicine 23(Suppl. 1), 46–49 (2008)
12. Swanwick, T.: Understanding Medical Education – Evidence, Theory and Practice. Wiley-Blackwell (2010)
13. Epstein, R.: Assessment in Medical Education. New England Journal of Medicine 356(4), 387–396 (2007)
14. Ker, J., Bradley, P.: Simulation in Medical Education. In: Swanwick, T. (ed.) Understanding Medical Education – Evidence, Theory and Practice. Wiley-Blackwell (2007)
15. Pearl, J.: Probabilistic Reasoning in Intelligent Systems: Networks of Plausible Inference, 2nd edn., vol. 1, p. 552. Morgan Kaufmann, San Mateo (1988)
16. Gluz, J., Vicari, R., Flores, C., Seixas, L.: Formal Analysis of a Probabilistic Knowledge Communication Framework. In: Sichman, J.S., Coelho, H., Rezende, S.O. (eds.) IBERAMIA 2006 and SBIA 2006. LNCS (LNAI), vol. 4140, pp. 138–148. Springer, Heidelberg (2006)
17. Flores, C., Seixas, L., Gluz, J., Vicari, R.: A Model of Pedagogical Negotiation. In: Bento, C., Cardoso, A., Dias, G. (eds.) EPIA 2005. LNCS (LNAI), vol. 3808, pp. 488–499. Springer, Heidelberg (2005)
18. An, N., Liu, J., Bai, Y.: Fuzzy Influence Diagrams - An Approach to Customer Satisfaction Measurement. In: Lei, J. (ed.) 4th International Conference on Fuzzy Systems and Knowledge Discovery (FSKD 2007), pp. 493–497. IEEE (2007)

Multi-agent Model for Searching, Recovering, Recommendation and Evaluation of Learning Objects from Repository Federations

Paula Rodríguez[1], Valentina Tabares[1], Néstor Duque[2],
Demetrio Ovalle[1], and Rosa M. Vicari[3]

[1] Universidad Nacional de Colombia Sede Medellín
{parodriguezma,vtabaresm,dovalle}@unal.edu.co
[2] Universidad Nacional de Colombia Sede Manizales
ndduqueme@unal.edu.co
[3] Universidade Federal do Rio Grande do Sul
rosa@inf.ufrgs.br

Abstract. Nowadays there are many repositories that allow searching and retrieval of learning objects. However, these selected learning objects in many cases are not adequate to student's profiles. Hence, the construction of adaptive e learning recommender systems considering student cognitive characteristics requires customized searches to support teaching-learning processes. The use of intelligent agents is useful in order to get better results when learning objects are stored in large volume of repository federations. Thus, this paper proposes a model for learning object searching retrieving, recommendation, and evaluation modeled through the paradigm of multi-agent systems, called BROA. Finally, some results obtained from the BROA system are presented and discussed.

Keywords: AI in education, multi-agent system, MAS–CommonKADS, GAIA, learning objects repository federation, student-centered recommender system.

1 Introduction

The growth of digital information, high-speed computing, and ubiquitous networks has allowed for accessing to more information and thousands of educational resources. This fact has led to the design of new teaching-learning proposals, to share educational materials, and also to navigate through them [1]. Learning Objects (LOs) are distinguished from traditional educational resources for their easy and quickly availability through Web-based repository, from which they are accessed through their metadata. In order to maximize the number of LOs to which a student could have access, to support his/her teaching-learning process, digital repositories have been linked through centralized repository federations sharing in this way educational resources and accessing resources from others [2]. LOs must be tagged with metadata so that they can be located and used for educational purposes in Web-based environments [3]. Recommender systems are widely used online in order to assist users to

J. Pavón et al. (Eds.): IBERAMIA 2012, LNAI 7637, pp. 631–640, 2012.
© Springer-Verlag Berlin Heidelberg 2012

find relevant information [4]. Having a user profile allows a recommender system to help the student to find the most relevant LOs based on the student's needs and preferences. Intelligent agents are entities that have sufficient autonomy and intelligence to be able to handle specific tasks with little or no human supervision [5]. These agents are currently being used almost as much as traditional systems, making it a good choice to solve problems where autonomous systems are required and thus they work not only individually but also cooperate with other systems to achieve a common goal. The aim of this paper is to propose a model for LO searching, retrieving, recommendation, and evaluator modeled through the paradigm of multi-agent systems from repository federations. For doing so, the searching process needs a query string that is entered by the user and a similar relevance user profile according to the student's learning style (LS). The LO searching process is performed using local and remote repositories, or repository federations, that are accessible via web along with LO descriptive metadata. Since LO Repositories (LORs) are distributed, are different in design and structure, and not handle the same metadata standards. There is also a coordinator to be responsible for directing the search to different repositories according to their characteristics. The recommendation is made through collaborative filtering, searching for a similar profile to the user who is doing the quest to deliver a user pair LOs evaluated positively.

The rest of the paper is organized as follows: Section 2 outlines main concepts involved in this research. Section 3 describes some related works to the model proposed. Section 4 introduces the multi-agent model proposal based on both role and service models of GAIA methodology, and the analysis models of the MAS-CommonKADS methodology. A validation of the system's operation can be visualized is shown in Sect. 5. Finally, conclusions and future work are presented in Sect. 6.

2   Basic Concepts

2.1   Learning Objects, Repositories and Federations

According to the IEEE, a LO can be defined as a digital entity involving educational design characteristics. Each LO can be used, reused or referenced during computer-supported learning processes, aiming at generating knowledge and competences based on student's needs. LOs have functional requirements such as accessibility, reuse, and interoperability [6][7]. The concept of LO requires understanding of how people learn, since this issue directly affects the LO design in each of its three dimensions: pedagogical, didactic, and technological [7]. In addition, LOs have metadata that describe and identify the educational resources involved and facilitate their searching and retrieval. LORs, composed of thousands of LOs, can be defined as specialized digital libraries storing several types of resources heterogeneous, are currently being used in various e-learning environments and belong mainly to educational institutions [8]. Federation of LORs serve to provide educational applications of uniform administration in order to search, retrieve, and access specific LO contents available in whatever of LOR groups [9].

2.2   Recommender Systems

Recommender systems are aimed to provide users with search results close to their needs, making predictions of their preferences and delivering those items that could be closer than expected [10, 11]. In the context of LOs these systems seeks to make recommendations according to the student's characteristics and its learning needs. In order to improve recommendations, recommender systems must perform feedback processes and implement mechanisms that enable them to obtain a large amount of information about users and how they use the LOs [2, 12].

2.3   Multi-Agent Systems

Agents are entities that have autonomy in order to perform tasks by achieving their objectives without human supervision. The desirable characteristics of the agents are as follows [13]: **Reactivity**: they respond promptly to perceived changes in their environment; **Proactivity**: agents can take initiative; **Cooperation and Coordination:** they perform tasks communicating with other agents through a common language; **Autonomy**: agents do not require direct intervention of humans to operate; **Deliberation**: they perform reasoning processes to make decisions, **Distribution of Tasks**: each agent has definite limits and identified the problems to be solved; **Mobility**: they can move from one machine to another over a network; **Adaptation:** depending on changes in their environment they can improve their performance, and **Parallelism**: agents can improve performance depending on changes in their environment.

Multi-agent Systems (MAS) are composed of a set of agents that operate and interact in an environment to solve a specific and complex problem. This paradigm provides a new way of analysis, design, and implementation of complex software systems and has been used for the development of recommender systems [14].

2.4   Student Profile

The student profile stores information about the learner, its characteristics and preferences, which can be used to obtain search results according to its specificity. To handle a user profile can be used to support a student or a teacher in the LO selection according to its personal characteristics and preferences [14]. Gonzalez et al. [15] include in the student profile contextual characteristics that can be seen as transient values that are associated with environmental changes during one student's learning system session along with different physical and technological variables. Duque (2009) presents a combination of VARK y FSLSM models with good results to characterize the students profile and thus, provide students with learning materials tailored to their specific learning styles [16].

3   Related Works

Morales et al. (2007) present an architecture based on the multi-agent paradigm to identify and retrieve relevant LOs using the information request supplied by the user. In addition, this proposal includes aspects related to quality of LOs which are specified within their semantic description to improve the LO selection [17]. Authors propose a multi-agent architecture to retrieve LOs, however they do not use student cognitive characteristics such as learning styles in order to make recommendations. Gerling (2009) proposes an intelligent system to assist a user in finding appropriate LO, according to the search's subject by using the user profile which takes into account its characteristics, preferences, and LO *relative importance*.The recommender system incorporates an intelligent agent in order to retrieve educational resources on the Web, considering student's learning style [18]. However, the system's design only considers the utilization of one intelligent agent.

Duque (2009), in his doctoral thesis, proposes a multi-agent system for adaptive course generation. The system is composed of several intelligent agents: an agent for the student profile information; a domain agent, having the structure of the virtual course and the teaching material (TM); a HTN planner agent, and finally, a TM recovery agent which makes the process of TM search and retrieval [16]. This work focuses on creating customized virtual courses taking into account student's learning styles; however, it does not focus on LOs. Prieta (2010) proposes a multi-agent architecture for the process of search and retrieval of LO in distributed repositories. An additional functionality is provided to the system is making the LORs statistics on the number of results found and response time, then make future consultations in the LORs rated [19]. This system offers neither recommendations to the user nor customized searches based on the LO metadata. Casali (2011) presents an architecture and implementation of a recommender system prototype based on intelligent agents, whose goal is to return an ordered list of the most appropriate LOs according to the parameters that characterizes the user profile, language preferences and the interaction degree that the user wants to have with the LO. The search is performed in repositories having descriptive LO metadata which involves educational characteristics [14]. The main limitation of this research is that although some student characteristics are considered into the user profile the user learning styles were not taken into account.

4   Model Proposed

BROA (Spanish acronym for Learning Object Search, Retrieval & Recommender System) is a multi-agent system for searching, retrieving, recommendation and evaluator of LO, according to a search string entered by the user. The LOs resulting from the search are recommended based on the student's style of learning and other users' assessments. The Web-based LO search is performed over local and remote repositories, or by using LO repository federations through metadata descriptive LOs. Considering that LORs are distributed, they are different in design and structure, and hence they do not handle the same metadata standards. BROA was built under the MAS approach in order to exploit their advantages as follows: the *Parallelism of Tasks* for simultaneously searching in both local and remote LOR; the *Deliberation* ability for making decisions on which of LORs must perform the search and for performing user recommendations; *Cooperation*, *Coordination* and *Distribution* of tasks among agents by clearly identifying the problems to be solved by each agent and to define its limits. In our model each agent knows how LOs are stored and how each LO can be searched, accessed, and retrieved.

4.1   Development Methodology

There are different kind of methodologies for modeling MAS, such as GAIA characterized for analyzing and designing agent-oriented systems. The main key concepts of GAIA are the following: roles, which are associated with responsibilities, permissions, activities, and protocols [5]. Another well-known MAS design methodology is MAS-CommonKADS proposed by Iglesias in his doctoral thesis [20] which integrates knowledge and software engineering along with object-oriented protocols. An integration of both methodologies was used in order to model the BROA system. The

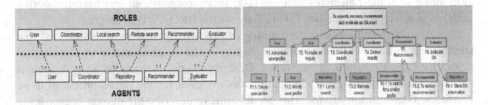

Fig. 1. Transformation of roles in agent's diagram   **Fig. 2.** Task Diagram

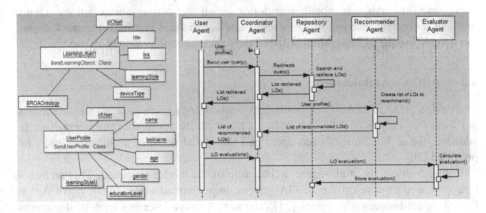

Fig. 3. Ontological Model   **Fig. 4.** Sequence diagram

Fig. 5. BROA's Architecture   **Fig. 6.** BROA's Web-based Interface

following is a brief description of each of these models: *Role Model* (GAIA): Allows the system designer to identify the expected functions of each of the entities that composes the system (goals, responsibilities, capabilities, and permissions). *Service Model* (GAIA): This model identifies all the services associated with each of the roles, its inputs, outputs, pre-conditions, and post-conditions. *Agent Model*: Describes the characteristics of each agent, specifying name, kind of agent, role, description, skills, services, activities, and goals. According to the GAIA methodology an agent can play several roles as shown in Figure 1, thus, a changing role diagram must be used in this case. *Task Model:* This model describes all the tasks that agents can perform along with the objectives of each task, its decomposition, and troubleshooting methods to solve each objective. Figure 2 shows the BROA's task diagram.

Expertise Model: Describes the ontologies (knowledge and its relationships) that agents need to achieve their objectives. Figure 3 shows an example of Ontological Model for LOs. *Communication Model:* Describes main interactions among humans and software agents along with human factors involved for the development of these interfaces. *Organization Model*: This model aims to describe the human organization in which the multi-agent system is involved along with the software agent organization structure. *Coordination Model*: Dynamic relationships among software agents are expressesed through this model. For doing so, all the conversations among agents must be described: interactions, protocols, and capabilities required. Figure 4 shows the BROA's sequence diagram that specifies main interactions among agents.

4.2   BROA's Architecture

The design phase of MAS-CommonKADS methodology takes as input all the models got from the analysis phase and transforms their specifications for implementation. In addition, the architecture of each agent and the global network architecture must be provided [20].

Figure 5 shows the multi-agent architecture of the model proposed. This architecture was used to develop the BROA system, implemented using JADE (Java Agent Development Framework) agents [21]. The next Section describes each of the agents of the BROA system along with the main interactions that exist among them.

4.2.1   Agent Description

User Agent: This agent communicates directly with the human user and whose role is representing him within the system along with communications with other agents (Coordinator and Evaluator). Also, the user agent manages the user's profile, enabling the creation and modification of profile's characteristics and preferences. Finally, this agent sends the query string to the coordinator agent in order to perform the LO search and the evaluation of the recommended LOs. *Coordinator Agent:* This agent is of deliberative nature since it takes care of redirectioning queries that the user makes to both the local and the remote repositories. This agent knows the repositories associated with the system and the information that each of them manages. In addition, it can access the user agent's profile to know what characteristics are useful for making a recommendation (learning style, educational level, language preference, among others). *Local and Remote Repository Agent:* Repository agents are responsible for making accurate LO searches in both local and remote repositories. This agent recognizes how LOs are stored inside the repositories, under what standard and type of metadata that manages. Also knows the type of search that can be performed within the repository and how to recover a particular LO stored. The local repository agent is also responsible for storing the LO evaluation given from an evaluator agent. Similarly, in the proposed architecture there is a repository for each LOR agent federation is local or remote. *Recommender Agent:* This agent makes two recommendations; the first stage is to find users registered in the system with similar profile to the user so having the same learning style and education level. The LOs selected by those users having a score greater or equal than 4 are shown. The second stage of recommendation is based on LOs recovered in all different repositories, based on user's LO query. This recommendation is based on the student's learning style. It is important to highlight that in the model proposed, the recommendation is based on the metadata that describes the LO and the information of learning style, educational level, and language preference of the registered student. In order to represent the agent's knowledge production rules were used, such as the following rule: *LearningStyle(Visual-Global) ∧ LearningResourceType(figure) ∨ LearningResourceType(graph) ∨ Learning ResourceType(slide) ∨ LearningResourceType(table) ∧ InteractivityLevel(medium) ∨ InteractivityLevel(high)*. When there is a failure of similar users, the system shows only the results of the second recommendation and then stored the user profile information and evaluated LOs, within the knowledge base. *Evaluator agent:* This agent manages the evaluation performed by a user to some of the LOs that have been explored. The evaluation is made through explicit qualification that is given by the selected student who rates the LO from 1 to 5 according to his/her own satisfaction.

4.2.2   Platform Design

The BROA's agent architecture was developed in JAVA, using JDOM for handling XML user's profiles. The local repository manager is stored in the PostgreSQL database that is characterized to be stable, with high performance, and great flexibility. The agent creation and management is made by using JADE platform using FIPA-ACL performatives [21]. The ontology creation was performed by using Protégé and finally, the Web integration was made based on the ZK framework. Figure 6 shows BROA's Web interface with the recommended and retrieved LOs. For the LO search process there was a student who had a Visual-sequential learning style and the search string used was: "computer science". Thus, a total of 196 LOs were recovered and only recommended, after a "learning style" filtering just 45 of them.

5   Experiments and Results

BROA system provides to the human user LO lists by using its interface. The first list is the result of the search made by the user according to his criteria. The second list presents list of recommended items to the user, which correspond to those LOs that are the most adapted to his own learning style.

To validate the BROA system a test was performed based on the keyword "computer science". In addition, a comparison was made with the results given by the system concerning the LOs recommended for users with different learning styles proposed by Duque [16]: Visual-Global, Visual-sequential, Auditory-Global, Auditory-sequential, Kinesthetic-Global, Kinesthetic-sequential, Reader-Global, Reader-sequential. Thus, virtual users with different profiles were generated and LOs from real repositories were recovered. Figure 7 shows the results got for the tests being performed. A total of 196 LOs were retrieved after the search process for students with different learning styles. Figure 7 (a) shows the quantity of LOs for each of the different learning styles. The BROA system makes a good recommendation process since the LOs provided are well adapted to the student's learning profile.

In order to evaluate the results of recommendations given by the system the Precision measure [22] was used which purpose is to analyze the quality of the retrieval.

$$(1) \ Precision = \frac{Relevant \ LOs}{Relevant \ LOs + \ Retrieved \ LOs}$$

Figure 7 (b) shows the results obtained by applying the Precison measure formula (1) to each learning style and additionaly comparing values obtained with and without recommendation when accesing LO Merlot repository.

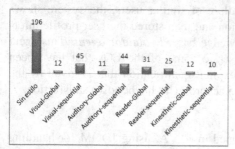
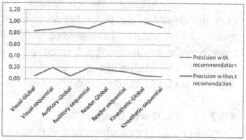

Fig. 7. a. LOs retrieved after search   **Fig. 7.** b. Precision

6   Conclusion and Future Work

This paper proposes a model for learning object searching, retrieving, recommendation, and evaluation modeled through the paradigm of MAS from repository federations. The BROA (Spanish acronym for Learning Object Search, Retrieval & Recommender System) system was built using this model. There is an agent in the BROA system dedicated to each repository accessed by the system. In order to facilitate LO searches, the agent knows how the LOs are stored, how is the way of accessing and recovering them, under what standard and type of metadata the LOs are stored and handled by the specific repository.. Those searches are performed in a local LOR, where the already evaluated LOs are stored, and also performed in remote LORs associated to the system. The BROA system offers two types of recommendation; the first one is based on finding similar profiles. This first recommendation approach has not already been implemented in this prototype. The second type of recommendation is by searching the metadata of the LO, taking into account the query performed by the user, the results are presented at the right side on Figure 6. The model proposed in this paper addressed issues such as working on LOs and learning styles and making recommendations by the system to the user based on customized searches using the LO metadata.In addition, the problem modeling using a MAS technique was an excellent option, that allowed the disintegration into functional blocks, without losing the systemic point of view, which leads to distributing the solution in diverse entities that require specific knowledge, processing and communication between each other. The MAS allowed a neutral vision in the model proposed.

It is envisaged as future work to add an interface agent to make context-aware adaptations, along with the list of LOs delivered by the system considering other issues such as type of device from where the query is made, bandwidth, among others. For the evaluation process, it is intended to make templates for the user to rate its opinion about recommended LOs (explicit evaluation). The agent should analyze the results of the explicit evaluation and use logs, to assign a rating to each LO. Also it is envisaged to improve the theoretical and practical basis of the first stage of recommendations made by the system through collaborative filtering techniques. The learning style for this prototype should be selected by the user, an additional future work aims to propose a learning style test that will define which kind of learning style the user who is logged in the system has.

Acknowledgements. The research reported in this paper was funded in part by the COLCIENCIAS project entitled "ROAC Creación de un modelo para la Federación de OA en Colombia que permita su integración a confederaciones internacionales" Universidad Nacional de Colombia, with code 1119-521-29361.

References

1. Peña, C.I., Marzo, J.-L., De la Rosa, J.L., Fabregat, R.: Un Sistema de Tutoría Inteligente Adaptativo Considerando Estilos de Aprendizaje. In: VI CongresoIberoamericano de InformáticaEducativa (IE 2002), pp. 1–12 (2002)
2. Li, J.Z.: Quality, Evaluation and Recommendation for Learning Object. In: International Conference on Educational and Information Technology (ICEIT 2010), vol. 2, pp. 533–537 (2010)
3. Gil, A.B., García, F.: Un Sistema Multiagente de Recuperación de Objetos de Aprendizaje con Atributos de Contexto. In: Workshop on Agents and Multi-agent Systems for Enterprise Integration (ZOCO 2007) at CAEPIA 2007, pp. 1–11 (2007)
4. Niemann, K., Scheffel, M., Friedrich, M., Kirschenmann, U., Schmitz, H.-C., Wolpers, M.: Usage-Based Object Similarity. Journal of Universal Computer Science 16(16), 2272–2290 (2010)
5. Wooldridge, M., Jennings, N.R., Kinny, D.: The Gaia Methodology for Agent-Oriented Analysis and Design. Autonomous Agents and Multi-Agent Systems 3(3), 285–312 (2000)
6. Ouyang, Y., Zhu, M.: eLORM – Learning Object Relationship Mining-based Repository. Online Information Review 32(2), 254–265 (2008)

7. Betancur, D., Moreno, J., Ovalle, D.: Modelo para la Recomendación y Recuperación de Objetos de Aprendizaje en Entornos Virtuales de Enseñanza/Aprendizaje. Avances en Sistemas e Informática 6(1), 45–56 (2009)
8. Prieta, F.D., Gil, A.B.: A Multi-agent System that Searches for Learning Objects in Heterogeneous Repositories. In: Demazeau, Y., Dignum, F., Corchado, J.M., Bajo, J., Corchuelo, R., Corchado, E., Fernández-Riverola, F., Julián, V.J., Pawlewski, P., Campbell, A., et al. (eds.) Trends in PAAMS. AISC, vol. 71, pp. 355–362. Springer, Heidelberg (2010)
9. Van de Sompel, H., Chute, R., Hochstenbach, P.: The aDORe Federation Architecture – Digital Repositories at Scale. International Journal on Digital Libraries 9(2), 83–100 (2008)
10. Chesani, F.: Recommendation Systems. In: Corso di Laurea in Ingegneria Informatica, pp. 1–32 (2007)
11. Mizhquero, K., Barrera, J.: Análisis, Diseño e Implementación de un Sistema Adaptivo de Recomendación de Información Basado en Mashups. Revista Tecnológica ESPOL (2009)
12. Sanjuán, O., Torres, E., Castán, H., Gonzalez, R., Pelayo, C., Rodriguez, L.: Viabilidad de la Aplicación de Sistemas de Recomendación a entornos de e-learning. Universidad Pontificia de Salamanca, Salamanca, Spain (2009)
13. Jennings, N.R.: On Agent-Based Software Engineering. Artificial Intelligence 117(2), 277–296 (2000)
14. Casali, A., Gerling, V., Deco, C., Bender, C.: Sistema Inteligente para la Recomendación de Objetos de Aprendizaje. Revista Generación Digital 16, 88–95 (2011)
15. González, H., Duque Méndez, N., Ovalle, C.D.: Técnicas Inteligentes para la Actualización Dinámica del Perfil del Usuario en un Sistema de Educación Virtual. Tendencias en Ingeniería de Software e Inteligencia Artificial (2009)
16. Duque, N.: Modelo Adaptativo Multi-Agente para la Planificación y Ejecución de Cursos Virtuales Personalizados. PhD Thesis. Universidad Nacional de Colombia (2009)
17. Morales, E., Gil, A.: Arquitectura para la Recuperación de Objetos de Aprendizaje de Calidad en Repositorios Distribuidos. In: SCHA – Sistemas Hipermedia Colaborativos y Adaptativos, II Congreso Español de Informática (CEDI 2007), vol. 1, pp. 31–38 (2007)
18. Gerling, V.B.: Un Sistema Inteligente para Asistir la Búsqueda Personalizada de Objetos de Aprendizaje. Universidad Nacional de Rosario (2009)
19. de la Prieta, F., González, A.G., Corchado, J.M., Sanz, E.: Sistema Multiagente Orientado a la Búsqueda, Recuperación y Filtrado de Objetos Digitales Educativos. In: VIII Jornadas de Aplicaciones y Transferencia Tecnológica de la Inteligencia Artificial (TTIA 2010), pp. 65–74 (2010)
20. Iglesias Fernández, C.Á.: Definición de una Metodología para el Desarrollo de Sistemas Multiagentes. PhD Thesis. Universidad Politécnica de Madrid (1998)
21. Bellifemine, F., Poggi, A., Rimassa, G.: JADE – A FIPA-Compliant Agent Framework. In: 4th International Conference and Exhibition on the Practical Application of Intelligent Agents and Multi-Agents (PAAM 1999), pp. 1–12 (1999)
22. Shani, G., Gunawardana, A.: Evaluating Recommendation Systems. In: Ricci, F., Rokach, L., Shapira, B., Kantor, P.B. (eds.) Recommender Systems Handbook, pp. 257–297 (2011)

An Agent Based Model for Integrating Intelligent Tutoring System and Virtual Learning Environments

Cecilia E.P. Giuffra and Ricardo Azambuja Silveira

Departamento de Informática e Estatística - Universidade Federal de Santa Catarina (UFSC)
Caixa Postal 476 – CEP: 88.040-900 - Florianópolis - SC – Brasil
{giuffra,silveira}@inf.ufsc.br

Abstract. Virtual learning environments (VLEs) are used in distance learning and classroom teaching as teachers and students support tools in the teaching–learning process, where teachers can provide material, activities and assessments for students. However, this process is done in the same way for all the students, regardless of their differences in performance and behavior in the environment. The purpose of this work is to develop an agent-based intelligent learning environment model inspired by intelligent tutoring to provide adaptability to distributed VLEs, using Moodle as a case study and taking into account students' performance on tasks and activities proposed by the teacher, as well as monitoring his/her study material access.

Keywords: virtual learning environments, intelligent tutoring, multi-agent.

1   Introduction

The number of students with computer access has increased substantially in recent years. A qualitative change in the teaching–learning process happens when we can integrate within an innovative view all technologies, including telematics, audiovisual, textual, oral and physical [11]. The fact of students seeking information on the computer converts them into more active students. "There are activities that can be performed with the computer, forcing the student to seek information, process it and use it to solve problems, allowing the understanding of what makes and the construction of their own knowledge" [18].

Virtual learning usually offers the same learning experience, during the course, for all students, without considering their specific needs. The problem is that the students are treated as if they always had the same profile, the same goals and the same knowledge [12].

In order to provide adaptability to learning environments, according to student characteristics, and to allow a greater interactivity degree between the learning environment and the users, the research points to the use of resources provided by artificial intelligence (AI) and in particular the use of multi-agent system-based architectures [15].

In agreement with this emerges the motivation of this research: to enhance the teaching–learning process in virtual learning environments using artificial intelligence techniques to make the environments more adaptive and more interactive. This paper

J. Pavón et al. (Eds.): IBERAMIA 2012, LNAI 7637, pp. 641–650, 2012.

proposes the use of agent-based intelligent tutoring systems architectures to get personalized teaching strategies, taking into account the student profile and his/her performance, exploring their skills as best as possible, in order to have better and more effective learning in an intelligent learning environment.

This paper is structured as follows: the second section presents the theoretical reference and related works, the third section presents the definition of the model, the fourth section presents an explanation about the model implementation and the last section presents the conclusions.

2   Background

Virtual learning environments are technological tools and resources using cyberspace to lead content and enable pedagogical mediation through the interaction between the educational process actors [14]. The use of these environments has increased significantly by the strong possibility of interaction between student and teacher that they offer, and by easy access anywhere and anytime. The virtual learning environments provide tools for interaction, such as forums and chats, and enable the provision of materials by teachers about the content of the course.

For Dillenbourg [6], virtual learning environments are not only restricted to distance learning. Web-based education is often associated with distance learning; however, in practice it is also widely used to support classroom learning. The author also comments that the difference between these two types of education is disappearing. Many students in distance courses do not live far from school, but have time constraints. Often they work. In addition, there are courses that combine distance and presence, which makes for more robust learning environments.

Virtual learning environments, at first, were used primarily in distance learning; now they also serve as support in classroom courses, as a teacher's tool to provide materials, to review tasks, to keep track of the students on course (activity logs) and also to evaluate them. For students, the environment facilitates the delivery of tasks, the obtaining of materials for the course and the monitoring of their evaluation.

Virtual learning environments can be enhanced with artificial intelligence techniques, using intelligent agents, having intelligent learning environments as result. An agent is an abstraction of something that can perceive its environment through sensors and can act upon that environment through actuators [16]. For Wooldridge [21], intelligent agents are those that have at least the following characteristics: autonomy, reactivity, proactivity and social ability.

In practice, systems with only one agent are not common. The most common are the cases of agents that inhabit an environment containing other agents. According to Bordini et al. [4], there are two major types of multi-agent systems: reactive and cognitive. The reactive acts under a stimulus-response scheme; the cognitive has, in general, few agents because each agent is a complex and computationally heavy system.

A rational agent is one who chooses his/her actions according to their own interests, given the belief that he/she has about the world. The Belief, Desire, Intention (BDI) model recognizes the importance of beliefs, desires and intentions in rational actions [20].

The BDI model represents a cognitive architecture based on mental states, and has its origin in the human practical reasoning model. An architecture based on the BDI model represents its internal processes through the mental states: belief, desire and intention, and defines a control mechanism that selects in a rational way the course of actions [7].

In the context of this work, an agent is considered as an autonomous entity, able to make decisions, respond in a timely manner, pursue goals, interact with other agents, and has reasoning and character. This agent is a of type BDI, with beliefs, desires and intentions, and operates in a virtual learning environment as an intelligent tutor.

Intelligent tutoring systems (ITS) are complex systems involving several different types of expertise: subject knowledge, knowledge of the student's knowledge, and pedagogical knowledge, among others. According to Santos et al. [17], an ITS is characterized for incorporating AI techniques into a development project and acts as a helper in the teaching–learning process.

According to Conati [5], intelligent tutoring systems are an interdisciplinary field that investigates how elaborate educational systems provide adapted instructions to the needs of students, as many teachers do.

ITS research has been investigating how to make computer-based tutors more flexible, autonomous and adaptive to the needs of each student by giving them explicit knowledge of the relevant components of the teaching process and reasoning skills to convert this knowledge into intelligent behavior.

To Giraffa and Viccari [9], ITS developments consider a cooperative approach between student and system. According to Oliveira [13], the goal of ITS is to complement or replace a human tutor, with the advantage of monitoring the student in each learning step.

Research in intelligent tutoring systems is concerned about the construction of environments that enable more efficient learning [8].

Intelligent tutoring systems offer flexibility in the presentation of material and have the major ability to respond to students' needs. They seek, in addition to teaching, learning relevant information about the student, providing an individualized learning. Intelligent tutoring systems have been shown to be highly effective in improving performance and motivation of students [10].

Intelligent tutoring systems in virtual learning environments potentiate the teaching–learning process, making the virtual environment into an intelligent learning environment. Intelligent learning environments use AI techniques to respond to students' needs, making that learning personalized [10].

According to [15], the intelligent learning environment must build and update the student model in terms of what he/she already knows, which can vary significantly from one student to another.

2.1   Related Works

In order to know the current status of recent research about virtual learning environments and the use of intelligent agents as tutors in these environments, we performed a systematic literature review. Among them, there were three items which were most closely related to the purpose of this study.

"Approach to an Adaptive and Intelligent Learning Environment" [1], which proposes an agent-oriented approach for the design and implementation of an adaptive and smart component for a virtual learning environment. The adaptivity in the model is defined as a system's ability to create and, during the learning process, uniformly upgrade the curriculum that satisfies the student's needs. The proposed model has three parts that describe the main features of intelligent and adaptive component. First, the student chooses the courses based on his/her needs, the level of excellence that he/she wants to achieve, and his/her preference concerning the type of study material. Second, the system will decide how to act – for example, show the material to the student, based on the belief (student model) that the system has about it. In the last part it is decided when to propose an evaluation test for the student or any other activity that can evaluate any specific knowledge in relation to the curriculum. After completing the evaluation, the belief about the student is updated.

"Cluster Analysis in Personalized E-Learning" [22]: this is a proposed system architecture in which teaching techniques and appropriate layouts are set to groups of students with similar preferences, created by applying clustering techniques. Teaching materials and content can be adapted to the needs of each group and different learning paths can be created. New students fill out a questionnaire to determine their learning style and their choices of usability and, according to this, the appropriate group is chosen for them. The idea of the proposed solution is to divide the process into two steps: first, to look for groups of students with a great similarity and detect those isolates. In the second step the groups are mixed in larger groups if necessary and the isolates are indicated. The objective of the experiment was to examine the performance of the proposed clustering technique for different student's data sets, depending on the choice of parameters.

"Supporting Cognitive Competence Development in Virtual Classrooms" [19]. The approach described in this article implements a mechanism to adaptively create self-assessment questionnaires in a Moodle environment. The Learning Management System (LMS) is capable of saving all online activities of the students in log files. This information can be used also to automatically generate intelligent feedback to the student. The questions are derived from an ontology of skills that is also used for indexing learning materials. The student traces through the learning materials used to determine the current state of "expected knowledge" or skills. The system includes two main agents: the goals manager agent, which guides the student in planning activities; and the content manager agent, which guides the student during the resources review. In this paper, an extension of the Moodle LMS – in which ontologies are used to structure the learning process by providing resources and generating questionnaires automatically for self-assessment of students – is presented.

In the conducted research to analyze the state of the art, papers were found dealing with adaptability in virtual learning environments, taking into account the students' needs, learning styles, usability preferences and their activities report (log).

In the first related paper, adaptability is based on the preferences of students regarding the study material, where the agent provides this material according to the information that he/she has about the student's preferences. In the second paper, the proposal is to provide different layouts to the students, taking into consideration similar preferences with regard to learning styles and usability choices. In the last related paper, self-assessment questionnaires, adaptively created in the virtual learning environment Moodle, and ontologies to index the learning materials are used.

This paper proposes to join data that can be obtained from the database (information of student performance and logs) that most virtual learning environments widely used usually have, in order to set the discipline in a personalized way for each student, with regards to the available material for the student as the activities proposed to him/her, exploring his/her skills and bypassing disabilities, always having a baseline with material and compulsory activities, and activities outside of this line divided into different levels of difficulty.

3   Definition of the Model

The aim of this work is to create an agent architecture and a knowledge base of these agents that compose an intelligent tutoring system with information obtained from the database of a teaching–learning virtual environment. For this, a case study is done based on the Moodle platform architecture, chosen because it is a platform widely used today, in addition to being consolidated from the standpoint of operation, and also to be formally used in the institution where the research is performed.

The model of agents "bedel" (agent of the discipline) and "tutor" (agent of the student) is defined; they are connected with the learning virtual environment through the database. The interface in which the teacher sets the priority and levels of the resources and tasks in the environment is developed. The database is adapted with the creation of the table of grade profiles of the students and the table of dependencies of resources and activities, configured by the teacher by means of a Moodle block into his discipline, and is made the integration of the actions of agents with the virtual learning environment Moodle.

The agents model (see Fig. 1) shows the agents "tutor" and "bedel" their actions, messages and perceptions, as well as their connection to the database. The actor "teacher" is the figure of the discipline teacher who inserts the resources and activities into the learning environment, sets the type of profile and sequence, and this information is stored in the database, so the agent "bedel" knows how to show them to students.

The database has information concerning the student, such as personal data, performance data and data from student interaction in the system. Every student interaction in the environment is saved in the base in the form of a log. Similarly, the student's performance in each of the activities and tasks is stored in the database and updated constantly every access and interaction of the student, providing rich material for the agent's performance.

The agents share the information from the database. The "tutor" updates the student profile and, if necessary, shows a message to him/her about his/her performance. The "bedel" obtains from the database the configuration of resources and activities in the discipline made by the teacher; it sets their preview and verifies if tasks were evaluated to send a message to the "tutor" who, upon receiving the message, updates the data of the student profile.

The model works as follows:

1. The teacher inserts the resources and creates tasks in the Moodle environment as usual. After that, he/she adds the tutor block in his/her discipline and configures the tutor setting for the dependencies of activities and resources, and their level (basic, intermediate and advanced), also by means of the Moodle environment. In addition, the teacher has the option to choose resources that must be shown to all students in a general way. The first reading (resource) and the first activity are shown for all students; therefore the teacher needs to indicate which they are. This information is stored in the database, where some tables which are necessary for the model are added. With this information, the "bedel" knows about resources and activities of the discipline and knows how the course should be developed for each type of student.

2. In the environment's database the grade_profile table (see Fig. 2) is also added, which contains a numeric value, calculated with the grades of the activities performed by students and the access made by them in different files provided by the teacher. This table is updated each time a teacher updates the worksheet with the grades of some of the tasks that he/she provides to students.

3. The grade_profile average of all students is computed and students are separated by profile into groups – basic, intermediate or advanced – according to their grade_profile. Whoever has average grades is in the average profile, whoever has grades below average is in the basic profile, and those who have grades above average are in the advanced profile.

4. Tasks are provided independently for each student, according to their performance in the previous tasks, and their access to previous reading material. The availability of tasks and resources is made by the "bedel" using the conditional access resource of Moodle.

5. Each time the tutor calculates the grade_profile it updates the belief base of the current profile of the student, which can go from basic to intermediate or advanced and vice-versa during the time that the course is offered.

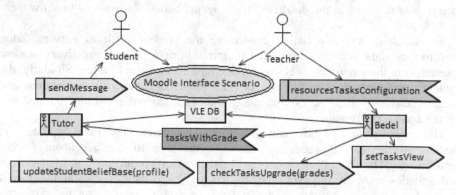

Fig. 1. Agent system model

The calculation of grade_profile is done as follows: The student grade of the last activity assessed by the teacher and the grade of the student access on reading that is a pre-requisite for activity are summed. If the student accesses the reading, two points in the activity grade are added. If he/she does not access, four points are added. This difference is given for increasing the possibility to the student who does not access the reading, to have a higher grade_profile and then go to a higher level task than the profile that he/she would belong to if he/she had a lower grade, stimulating him/her to read before accomplishing future activities.

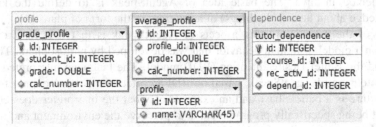

Fig. 2. Profile and dependence tables

After this, the average value of the grade_profile field is computed for all students. The lowest value considered for the profile average is 6; if the profile average is lower, it automatically becomes 6. For the student to be at an average profile, his/her grade_profile must be between 5.5 and 6.5; if the student has a grade_profile less than 5.5 he/she is on a basic profile and if he/she has grade_profile greater than 6.5 he/she is on an advanced profile.

The maximum value considered for the profile average is 8. If the average profile is greater than that, it automatically becomes 8. For the student to be at average profile, his/her grade_profile must be between 7.5 and 8.5, if the student has a grade_profile less than 7.5 he/she is on the basic profile and if he/she has a grade_profile greater than 8.5 he/she is on the advanced profile.

The student belongs to the average profile if his/her grade_profile is 0.5 less or more than the average grade_profile in his/her class; for example, if the grade_profile average is 7.5, he/she will be in the intermediate profile if he/she has a grade_profile between 7 and 8. The student who has a higher grade with more than 0.5 of difference with the average will be in the advanced profile and the student who has a lower grade with more than 0.5 of difference will be in the basic profile.

The student will have access to the material of their profile (basic, intermediate, advanced), according to the configuration of resources and tasks made by the teacher.

4 Implementation of the Model

The model integrates concepts of intelligent tutoring systems architectures with VLE's that have their use consolidated as Moodle, which are not adaptive for itself only, and can be potentiated with artificial intelligence techniques, resulting in intelligent learning environments which are shown to be adaptive and more suitable to the implementation of teaching defiant methodologies for the student.

The use of agents in the implementation of this model is important because of the agent's ability to adapt to environment changes, showing resources and activities to students in a personalized way, according to their performance in the discipline, and taking into account the teacher's initial settings.

For the agent implementation the Jason tool was used, which is an interpreter for an extended version of AgentSpeak, oriented agent programming language, implemented in Java. The basic idea of AgentSpeak is to define the know-how (knowledge about how to do things) of a program in the form of plans [3].

One of the most interesting aspects of AgentSpeak is that it is inspired by and based on a model of human behavior that was developed by philosophers. This model is called the Belief Desire Intention (BDI) model. The language interpreted by Jason is an extension of AgentSpeak, based on BDI architecture. A component of the agent architecture is a beliefs base and an example of what the interpreter does constantly, without being specifically programmed, is to perceive the environment and update the beliefs base accordingly with this [3].

The teaching–learning virtual environments are designed to enable the knowledge-building process. Different to conventional software, which seeks to facilitate the tasks achievement by user, learning environments incorporate the complexity to more flexible different forms of users (students), relations, to learn and to practice content, and to collaborate. These environments are used by students of various cognitive profiles [2].

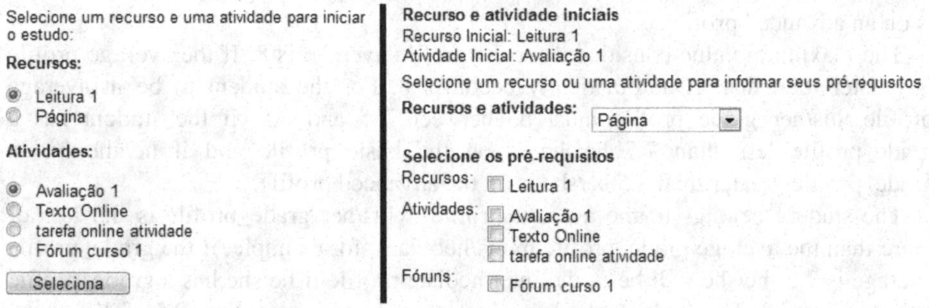

Fig. 3. Tutor configuration page (In Portuguese)

The version of virtual learning environment Moodle used for this work is 2.2, where the task condition resource is available, which allows the provision of content and activities with a restriction. This feature must be activated by the administrator of Moodle in the environment advanced settings, enabling the option "Enable tracking of completion" and "Enable conditional access." Moreover, in course settings, in "student progress" topic, the teacher must enable the completion tracking option.

With this feature enabled, tasks can be made available only to students who perform the pre-requisites set, which can be: a grade on a specific activity; the viewing of a resource; or his/her grade.

In this work, the availability of resources and activities is done taking into account the student's performance and his/her access in the system and is made available to the student depending on his/her grade_profile, computed according to his/her performance and participation in the discipline. The information between the agent system and the virtual learning environment are exchanged through the database of the learning environment which contains information about the pre-requisites and profiles of tasks and resources, defined by the teacher at a time to configure the tutor (see Fig. 3).

5   Conclusions

In this study is proposed a solution for virtual learning environments to assist teachers to provide activities and resources in a personalized way depending on the student's performance and his/her behavior in the discipline.

Students are assessed by their interaction in the discipline and the grades obtained in tasks, creating different profiles for groups of students with the same behavior. More advanced tasks are available for students who have improved performance, enabling more efficient learning, exploring students' skills, and maintaining a basic level for learning the discipline content.

Works related to virtual learning environments and adaptivity in general differentiate students by learning style – for example, a student who learns better with pictures than with reading lots of text.

In this work students are distinguished by their performance, taking into account the grades obtained, and their participation (access) in the various resources available in the discipline, creating an adaptive environment that constantly updates the profile of students, and therefore, a student with a basic profile, at the end of the course may have an average profile. These profile changes can be studied and displayed to the teacher, in an extension of this model.

References

1. Baziukaité, D.: Approach to an Adaptive and Intelligent Learning Environment. In: Elleithy, K., Sobh, T., Mahmood, A., Iskander, M., Karim, M. (eds.) Advances in Computer, Information, and Systems Sciences, and Engineering, pp. 399–406. Springer (2006)
2. Boff, E.: Collaboration in Learning Intelligent Environments mediated by a Social Agent Probabilistic. Ph.D. Thesis, Computer Science Course. Federal University of Rio Grande do Sul, Porto Alegre (2008) (in Portuguese)
3. Bordini, R.H., Hubner, J.F., Wooldridge, M.: Programming Multi-Agent Systems in AgentSpeak using Jason. Wiley, England (2007)
4. Bordini, R., Vieira, R., Moreira, A.F.: Fundamentos de Sistemas Multiagentes. In: Ferreira, C.E. (ed.) Jornada de Atualização em Informática (JAI 2001), vol. 2, pp. 3–44. SBC, Fortaleza (2001)
5. Conati, C.: Intelligent Tutoring Systems - New Challenges and Directions. In: 21st International Joint Conference on Artificial intelligence (IJCAI 2009), pp. 2–7 (2009)

6. Dillenbourg, P., Schneider, D.K., Synteta, P.: Virtual Learning Environments. In: Dimitracopoulou, A. (ed.) 3rd Hellenic Conference Information & Communication Technologies in Education, pp. 3–18 (2002)
7. Fagundes, M.: An Environment for Development of BDI Agents. Course Completion Work. Federal University of Pelotas (2004) (in Portuguese)
8. Frigo, L.B., Pozzebon, E., Bittencourt, G.: The Role of Intelligent Agents in Intelligent Tutoring Systems. In: World Congress on Engineering and Technology Education (WCETE 2004), pp. 667–671 (2004) (in Portuguese)
9. Giraffa, L.M.M., Viccari, R.M.: The Use of Agents Techniques on Intelligent Tutoring Systems. In: XVIII International Conference of the Chilean Society of Computer Science (SCCC 1998), pp. 76–83. IEEE (1998)
10. Lima, R.D., Rosatelli, M.C.: An Intelligent Tutoring System to a Virtual Environment for Teaching and Learning. In: IX Workshop de Informática na Escola, Campinas. Anais do XXIII Congresso da Sociedade Brasileira de Computação (2003) (in Portuguese)
11. Moran, J.M.: Computers in Education - Theory & Practice. Porto Alegre 3(1) (set. 2000); UFRGS. Postgraduate Program in Computer in Education, pp. 137–144 (in Portuguese)
12. Mozzaquatro, P.M., Franciscato, F., Ribeiro, P.S., Medina, R.D.: Modeling a Framework for Adaptation of Virtual Learning Environments Mobiles to Different Cognitive Styles. RENOTE - New Technologies in Education Journal 7(3) (2009) (in Portuguese)
13. Oliveira, C.L.V.: AutoExplC - Intelligent Tutoring System to Aid the Teaching of "C" Language Based on Learning by Self-Explanation of Examples. PUC, Campinas (2005) (in Portuguese)
14. Pereira, A.T.C., Schmitt, V., Álvares, M.R.C.: Virtual Learning Environments. Culture Bookstore (2007) (in Portuguese)
15. Silveira, R.A.: Ambientes Inteligentes Distribuídos de Aprendizagem. CPGCC da UFRGS, Porto Alegre (1998)
16. Russell, S., Norvig, P.: Artificial Intelligence - A Modern Approach. Prentice-Hall, Inc., New Jersey (2002)
17. Santos, C.T., Frozza, R., Dahmer, A., Gaspary, L.P.: DÓRIS - Pedagogical Agent in Intelligent Tutoring Systems. In: Cerri, S.A., Gouardéres, G., Paraguaçu, F. (eds.) ITS 2002. LNCS, vol. 2363, pp. 91–104. Springer, Heidelberg (2002)
18. Valente, J.A.: Computers in Education - Conform or Transform the School. p. 42 (2009)
19. Weinbrenner, S., Hoppe, H.U., Leal, L., Montenegro, M., Vargas, W., Maldonado, L.: Supporting Cognitive Competence Development in Virtual Classroom. In: 10th IEEE International Conference on Advanced Learning Technologies (ICALT 2010), pp. 573–577. IEEE (2010)
20. Wooldridge, M.: Reasoning about Rational Agents. The MIT Press, Cambridge (2000)
21. Wooldridge, M.: An Introduction to Multiagent Systems, 2nd edn. John Wiley & Sons Ltd., Hoboken (2009)
22. Zakrzewska, D.: Cluster Analysis in Personalized E-Learning Systems. Springer, Heidelberg (2009)

An Intelligent and Affective Tutoring System within a Social Network for Learning Mathematics

M.L. Barrón-Estrada[1], Ramón Zatarain-Cabada[1], J.A. Beltrán V.[1],
F.L. Cibrian R.[1], and Yasmín Hernández Pérez[2]

[1] Instituto Tecnológico de Culiacán, Juan de Dios Bátiz s/n, Col. Guadalupe,
Culiacán Sinaloa, 80220, México
[2] Instituto de Investigaciones Eléctricas, Cuernavaca, Morelos, México
{lbarron,rzatarain,abeltran,fcibrian}@itculiacan.edu.mx,
myhp@iie.org.mx

Abstract. In this paper we present an intelligent and affective tutoring system designed and implemented within a social network. The tutoring system evaluates cognitive and affective aspects and applies fuzzy logic to calculate the exercises that are presented to the student. We are using Kohonen neural networks to recognize emotions through faces and voices and multi-attribute utility theory to encourage positive affective states. The social network and the intelligent tutoring system are integrated into a Web application. We present preliminary results with different groups of students using this software tool.

Keywords: affective computing, intelligent tutoring systems, neural networks, fuzzy systems.

1   Introduction

The work of a human tutor is to teach and train a student through individualized instruction. This individualization that the human tutor performs with the student is done through different ways of adapting its educational materials to student needs. The aim of an Intelligent Tutoring System is not different: to deliver tutorial services that support personalized learning. Since its origins in 1970, the first generation of intelligent tutoring systems was more focused to work with cognitive aspects of the student [1-5]. However, if we want computers systems (including ITS) to be really smart and interact with us, we must grant them the ability to recognize emotions [6] and to react to them.

Affective computing is one of the most promising areas in the different fields of learning, and is nowadays a regular topic in most important conferences like intelligent tutoring systems (ITS), artificial intelligence in education (AIED), and advanced learning technologies (ICALT) among others. This topic attracts researchers from diverse fields including computer science, artificial intelligence, psychology, and education; and in most recent years we have seen an increasing

J. Pavón et al. (Eds.): IBERAMIA 2012, LNAI 7637, pp. 651–661, 2012.

number of affective intelligent tutoring systems developed for different learning fields [7-9].

Research on affective computing includes detecting and responding to affect. Affect detection systems observe and study the face, speech, conversation and other human features to detect frustration, interest, boredom, etc. using hardware sensors like web or blue eyes cameras [10, 11], microphones [12], and conversational dialogues [13]. On the other hand, affect response systems find the best way to handle and improve a student's negative emotion. There are excellent research works related to this problem [7, 9, 14].

In this paper we present an affective intelligent tutoring system embedded in a learning social network which is going to be used to improve poor results in ENLACE test (National Assessment of Academic Achievement in Schools in Mexico). ENLACE is the standardized evaluation of the National Educational System, applied to students in Grades 1-9 in public and private schools. This test is in Spanish and measures learning in math, Spanish, and a third subject that changes every year. The results of ENLACE applied in early 2011 to 14 million children from third to ninth elementary level, reveals that more than nine million students have an "insufficient" and "elemental" level in learning mathematics (http://www.enlace. sep.gob.mx/).

The paper's organization is as follows: in Sect. 2, we describe the system architecture of our Learning Social Network. In Sect. 3 we present the main structure of the affective tutoring system. Results are shown in Sect. 4 and conclusions and future work are discussed in Sect. 5.

2   Fermat Architecture

The Learning Social Network **Fermat** has the basic functionalities in all social networks, but its main feature is that it includes an ITS that offers the course content in a personalized style to users, as shown in Fig. 1.

Users of the network are associated with personal, academic and affective information in a profile, which is gathered from Fermat user navigation. The static profile contains the initial information of the user (e.g. personal and academic information). The dynamic profile will be updated according to the user interaction within the network and the ITS, considering during this interaction, cognitive and emotional aspects. According to [6], emotions are closely related to student learning, which in our point of view, represent a key factor to the student results.

Students' Cognitive states are measured according to the history that we obtain from the results of examinations of the user and the learning style computed by the neural network. Students' affective states are inferred by using sensors and neural networks that are supervising users' emotions.

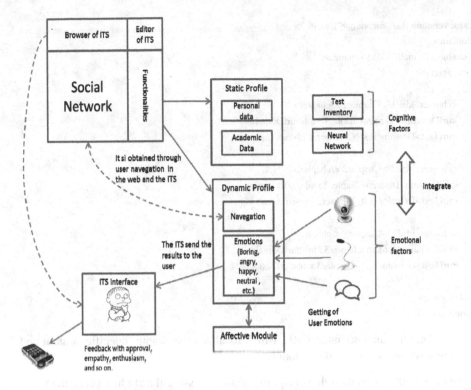

Fig. 1. Social Network for Affective Tutoring Systems

3 Fermat Affective ITS

The intelligent tutoring system (ITS) for Fermat adopts the traditional trinity model known as the four-component architecture where a user interface has access to three main modules: domain, student, and tutoring modules. Figure 2 shows the complete architecture of the Fermat ITS.

Domain Module: The knowledge acquisition and representation for the domain or expert module is a major problem which we handle through different concepts related to Knowledge Space Theory [15]. This theory provides a sound foundation for structuring and representing the knowledge domain for personalized or intelligent tutoring. It applies concepts from combinatory theory and we use it to model particular or personalized tutors according to different cognitive styles.

A course in Fermat can be seen as a discipline-specific knowledge space (a particular tree diagram) containing chapters which in turn are made by subjects. The total of nodes in the tree represents the expert knowledge. The domain module is stored as a XML document whose structure is shown below:

```xml
<?xml version="1.0" encoding="UTF-8"?>
<domain>
  <name> Domain Name  </name>
  <chapters>

    <chapter  id="1">Chapter1 </chapter>
    <urlDomain>Domain/Chapter1.xml</urlDomain>
    <urlTest>Domain/Test_Chapter1.xml</urlTest>

    <chapter  id="2">Chapter2 </chapter>
    <urlDomain>Domain/Chapter2.xml</urlDomain>
    <urlTest>Domain/Test_Chapter2.xml</urlTest>

    <chapter  id="1">Chapter3 </chapter>
    <urlDomain>Domain/Chapter3.xml</urlDomain>
    <urlTest>Domain/Test_Chapter3.xml</urlTest>

  </chapters>
</domain>
```

Each chapter has an associated URL, which localizes the chapter specific content and the diagnostic test of the student module.

Student Module: This module is responsible for assessing the student performance to establish their cognitive abilities and reasoning skills. It provides the information about student competencies and learning capabilities. Fermat identifies what the student's knowledge is through a diagnostic test. The test results show what the student knows and what he needs to learn. The Fermat student module can be seen as a subset (sub-tree implemented) of all knowledge possessed by the expert in the domain (module) and a student profile stores this, as shown in the right part of Fig. 2. The representation is based on a model called "Overlay", where the student's knowledge is a subset of the expert knowledge. As the student uses the intelligent tutoring system he expands this subset [16]. For every student there is a static profile, which stores particular and academic information, and a dynamic profile, which stores information obtained from the Fermat navigation and from emotion recognition.

When a student first accesses the ITS, he has to answer the diagnostic test, which allows the construction of the student knowledge space. In the diagnostic test each question has a difficulty ranking, and depending on this, we give different weights to the answers. Most difficult questions worth 3 points, intermediate questions worth 2 points and easy ones worth 1 point.

For the student's grade we use the following formula:

Student's Grade = Total Points scored / Sum of points in the questions

After the test results, a small algorithm establishes the level of student learning and the teaching method. Next, we present the algorithm for assigning the learning level and the teaching method for a student learning the topic of multiplications. The method is chosen according with the official Math program in Mexico's Public School.

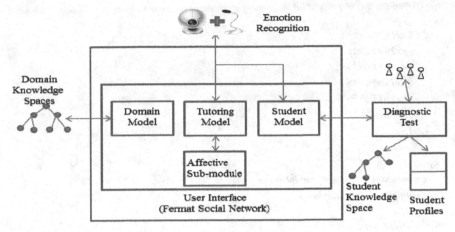

Fig. 2. Fermat Affective ITS

If (Grade < 4) Then
         Learning level = easy;   Method = Lattice
Else If (Grade < 5) Then
         Learning level = easy;   Method= traditional
Else If (Grade < 9) Then
         Learning level = Normal;   Method = traditional
Else
         Learning level = Difficult;   Method = Traditional

For the student's knowledge representation we use two categories: **Topics** where each time the student takes a topic, we store the history of subjects; and **student experience** that stores the history of grades by subject. Both are based on the Overlay model which allows us to know the subset of knowledge that the student knows.

Tutoring Module: The Fermat tutoring module is essentially based on ACT-R Theory of Cognition [3]. These types of tutoring systems are also named Model-Tracing Tutors or cognitive tutors. We implemented production rules (procedural memory) and facts (declarative memory) via a set of XML rules. Furthermore, we developed a new knowledge tracing algorithm (as part of the student module) based on fuzzy logic, which is used to track student's cognitive states, applying the set of rules (XML and Fuzzy rules) to the set of facts. The benefit of using fuzzy or vague rules is that they allow inferences even when the conditions are only partially satisfied. Next, we show a part of the set of production rules for multiplication operations, being the rules written in XML format:

```
<multiplication>
    <type problem="difficult" nProblems="...">
    <p1>
        < multiplying >17345</multiplying>
```

```
<multiplier>9</ multiplier >
<results>
  <r1>45</r1>
  <r2>40</r2>
  <r3>31</r3>
  <r4>66</r4>
  <r5>15</r5>
</results>
</p1>
...
<p...>
< multiplying >748392</ multiplying >
< multiplier >7</ multiplier >
<results>
  <r1>14</r1>
  <r2>64</r2>
  <r3>27</r3>
  <r4>58</r4>
  <r5>33</r5>
  <r6>52</r6>
</results>
</p...>
</problems>
```

Each topic divides the problem into different categories from 1 to n. The tutoring system reads the rules, and presents the exercises according to a level of difficulty in the problem. The student cannot move to the next state (input) unless he solves correctly all the exercises. During this transition he can ask for help and in case of mistake, an error message is displayed to help discover what the correct answer is. Once the student completes the exercise, the student profile is updated with information on the type and difficulty level of the exercise, as well as the amount of mistakes, assistances, and the time it took to solve the exercise. These variables (Difficulty, assistances, errors and time) will be required to decide the next exercise the student will take. For this we implemented a Fuzzy Expert System that eliminates arbitrary specifications of precise numbers and create smarter decisions, taking into account a more human reasoning. Fuzzy sets are described in Table 1 and Fig. 3 for output variable Difficulty.

Table 1. Fuzzy Values for Variable Difficulty

	Difficulty (%)	**Normalized Values**
Very Easy	0% - 10%	0 – 0.1
Easy	0% - 30%	0 – 0.3
Intermediate	20% - 80%	0.2 – 0.8
Difficult	70% - 100%	0.7 – 1.0
Very Difficult	90% - 100%	0.9 – 1.0

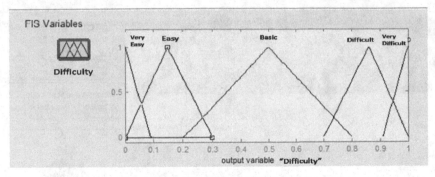

Fig. 3. Fuzzy Sets for Variable Difficulty

On the other hand, some of the fuzzy rules which establish the degree of difficulty of the next student's problem are:

If (Error is small) and (Assistance is small) and (Time is very fast) then (Difficulty is very difficult)

If (Error is small) and (Assistance is normal) and (Time is slow) then (Difficulty is difficult)

If (Error is big) and (Assistance is big) and (Time is very slow) then (Difficulty is very easy)

Affect Recognition and Handling: Emotions are detected by expression of the face and by voice. The method used for the detection of visual emotions is based on Ekman's theory |17|, which recognizes ten emotions. We only recognize 7 emotions: anger, disgust, fear, happiness, sadness, surprise, and neutral. To determine the emotion, we first take the image which is transformed to a more basic form. Based on this picture we get the feature points that minimize the set of input data to the neural network. We use a Kohonen Neural network with 20X20 input neurons and 2 output ones representing the emotion. For the detection of emotions in the voice, this is captured primarily through the computer microphone which is then normalized. Next we apply a technique to characterize components analysis (PCA) to the signal representing the voice. After using the SFFS method [18] we obtain an optimal set of features that will feed the neural network. Each neural network used to recognize emotions produces an output. All outputs of each neural network are integrated using fuzzy logic which gives us a final result that is the emotion of the user that the system recognizes.

Once the affective student state has been inferred, the affective sub-module has to respond accordingly. To do that, the tutor needs a model which establishes parameters that enable a mapping from the affective and knowledge student state to tutorial actions. The affective component of a tutorial action tries to promote a positive affective student state while the cognitive component tries to transmit knowledge. Figure 4 shows an interface of the Fermat Tutor with an affective agent represented by the Genie character of Microsoft agent.

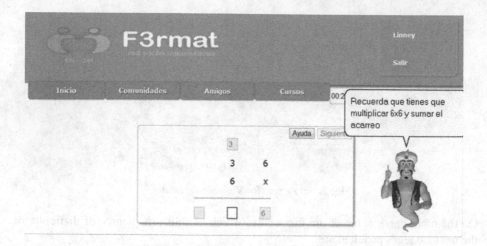

Fig. 4. Cognitive and affective feedback of Fermat ITS

The actions of the Genie are shown in Table 2. These actions were the results of studies conducted to evaluate the expressivity of the animated agents [19]. In these surveys, 20 teachers were asked to select appropriate affective actions to be presented according to several tutorial scenarios.

Table 2. Animations preferred by the teachers

Affective Action
Acknowledge
Announce
Congratulate
Confused
Get Attention
Explain
Suggest
Think

We want the agent's tutorial actions help students to learn and to foster a good affective state; hence we use decision theory to achieve the best balance between these objectives. The decision process is represented as a dynamic decision network.

Our model uses multi-attribute utility theory to define the necessary utilities [20]. That is, a Dynamic Decision network establishes the tutorial action considering two utility measures, one on learning and one on affect, which are combined to obtain the global utility by a weighted linear combination. These utility functions are the means that allow educators adopting the system to express their preferences towards learning and affect.

4   Results and Discussions

Fermat social network along with its intelligent tutor was evaluated by a group of children from third grade (see Fig. 5). There were 72 children from public and private schools who tested the tool and the tutoring system. Before the evaluation we offered a small introduction of 15 minutes with the environment of the tool. We evaluated the subject of multiplication. We applied a test with different exercises before and after the students used Fermat. Table 3 shows the results of a random sample of 10 students. We can see from the results a good improvement in most students (more in students with lower initial grades) using one of the two teaching methods for multiplication: traditional and lattice.

Fig. 5. Children testing Fermat in public and private schools

Table 3. Results, Course Level, and Learning Method for 10 students

Student	Initial Grade	Final Grade	Improvement %	Course Level	Method
1	4.74	7.89	31.5	difficult	Traditional
2	3.68	4.21	5.3	normal	lattice
3	3.68	7.89	42.1	difficult	lattice
4	7.89	8.42	5.3	difficult	Traditional
5	7.37	8.42	10.5	difficult	Traditional
6	10.00	10.00	0	difficult	Traditional
7	6.84	8.42	15.8	difficult	Traditional
8	8.42	8.42	0	difficult	lattice
9	8.42	9.47	10.5	difficult	Traditional
10	3.68	4.21	5.3	normal	lattice
Total %	6.78	8.12	13.4		

5   Conclusions and Future Work

One of the main advantages of using a social network for the learning process is to allow interaction and collaboration between individuals (instructors, students and parents), who share their connections under a scheme of learning communities around common learning interest. The social network keeps different roles for students, teachers, and parents.

Learnhub, Wiziq, and LectureShare are examples of social learning networks [21]. These networks provide an online education site for instructors and learners of all kinds. These users can create communities, share courses and lessons, have discussions, make quizzes, etc. However, learning material (courses, lessons, quizzes or tests) authored and used by the users, does not provide direct customized or intelligent instructions to the learners.

We need to do more testing with more students. We still are working with the emotion recognizer and we are adding more math operations to the ITS. We have implemented multiplications and divisions (elementary school). However, the initial results are encouraging. We are implementing our own recognizers because we need to use them in a Web platform where the social network and ITS may be access from any place and from any computer platform. We also need to add more sections to the ITS, in order to use the tool with real ENLACE tests and evaluate the impact of the tool with this national test.

Acknowledgments. The work described in this paper is fully supported by a grant from the DGEST in México.

References

[1] Carbonell, J.R.: AI in CAI – An Artificial Intelligence Approach to Computer-Aided-Instruction. IEEE Transactions on Man-Machine Systems 11(4), 190–202 (1970)

[2] Clancey, W.J.: Transfer of Rule-Based Expertise through a Tutorial Dialogue. PhD Thesis. Computer Science, Stanford University, Stanford, CA, USA (1979)

[3] Anderson, R., Boyle, C.F., Corbett, A.T., Lewis, M.W.: Cognitive Modeling and Intelligent Tutoring. Artificial Intelligence 42(1), 17–49 (1990)

[4] Aleven, V., Koedinger, K.: An Effective Metacognitive Strategy – Learning by Doing and Explaining with a Computer-Based Cognitive Tutor. Cognitive Science 26(2), 147–179 (2002)

[5] Woolf, B.P.: Building Intelligent Interactive Tutors. Morgan Kaufmann (2009)

[6] Picard, W.R.: Affective Computing. The MIT Press, Cambridge (1997)

[7] Arroyo, I., Woolf, B., Cooper, D., Burleson, W., Muldner, K., Christopherson, R.: Emotions Sensors Go to School. In: Diminitrova, V., Mizoguchi, R., Du Boulay, B., Graesser, A. (eds.) 14th International Conference on Artificial Intelligence in Education (AIED 2009), pp. 17–24. IOS Press (2009)

[8] Conati, C., Maclare, H.: Evaluating a Probabilistic Model of Student Affect. In: Lester, J.C., Vicari, R.M., Paraguaçu, F. (eds.) ITS 2004. LNCS, vol. 3220, pp. 55–66. Springer, Heidelberg (2004)

[9] D'Mello, S.K., Picard, R.W., Graesser, A.C.: Towards an Affective-Sensitive AutoTutor Special Issue on Inteligent Educational Systems. IEEE Intelligent Systems 22(4), 53–61 (2007)

[10] Essa, I.A., Pentland, A.: Facial Expression Recognition Using a Dynamic Model and Motion Energy. In: 5th IEEE International Conference on Computer Vision (ICCV 1995), pp. 360–367. IEEE, Cambridge (1995)

[11] Yacoob, Y., Davis, L.S.: Recognizing Human Facial Expressions from Log Image Sequences Using Optical Flow. IEEE Transactions on Pattern Analysis and Machine Intelligence 18(6), 636–642 (1996)

[12] Tosa, N., Nakatsu, R.: Life-Like Comunication Agent – Emotion Sensing Character 'MIC' and Feeling Session Character 'MUSE'. In: 3rd International Conference on Multimedia Computing and Systems (ICMCS 1996), pp. 12–19. IEEE (1996)

[13] Graesser, A., Lu, S.L., Jackson, G., Mitchell, H., Ventura, M., Olney, A., Louwerse, M.: AutoTutor – A Tutor with Dialogue in Natural Language. Behavior Research Methods 36(2), 180–192 (2004)

[14] Du Boulay, B.: Towards a Motivationally Intelligence Pedagogy – How Should an Intelligent Tutor Respond to the Unmotivated or the Demotivated? In: Calvo, R.A., D'Mello, S.K. (eds.) New Perspectives on Affect and Learning Technologies. Explorations in the Learning Sciences, Instructional Systems and Performance Technologies, vol. 3, pp. 41–52. Springer (2011)

[15] Doignon, J.-P., Falmagne, J.C.: Knowledge Spaces. Springer (1999)

[16] Günel, K.: Intelligent Tutoring Systems – Conceptual Map Modeling. Lambert Academic Publishing (2010)

[17] Ekman, P., Oster, H.: Facial Expressions of Emotion. Annual Review of Psychology 30(1), 527–554 (1979)

[18] Pudil, P., Novovičová, J., Kittler, J.: Floating Search Methods in Feature Selection. Pattern Recognition Letters 15(11), 1119–1125 (1994)

[19] Hernández, Y., Sucar, L.E., Arroyo-Figueroa, G.: Building an Affective Model for Intelligent Tutoring Systems with Base on Teachers' Expertise. In: Gelbukh, A., Morales, E.F. (eds.) MICAI 2008. LNCS (LNAI), vol. 5317, pp. 754–764. Springer, Heidelberg (2008)

[20] Clemen, R.T.: Making Hard Decisions. Duxbury Press, Belmont (2000)

[21] Ivanova, M.: Knowledge Building and Competence Development in eLearning 2.0 Systems. In: 12th International Conference on Knowledge Management and Knowledge Technologies (I-KNOW 2008), pp. 84–91 (2008)

Nearest Prototype Classification of Special School Families Based on Hierarchical Compact Sets Clustering

Yenny Villuendas-Rey[1,4], Carmen Rey-Benguría[2], Yailé Caballero-Mota[3],
and María Matilde García-Lorenzo[4]

[1] Computer Science Department, University of Ciego de Ávila, Carr. a Morón km 9 ½, Cuba
yennyv@informatica.unica.cu
[2] Educational Research Center, University "Manuel Ascunce", Carr. a Ceballos km 2 ½, Cuba
carmenrb@ucp.ca.rimed.cu
[3] Computer Science Department, University of Camagüey, Circunv. Norte km 3 ½, Cuba
yaile.caballero@reduc.edu.cu
[4] Computer Science Department, University of Las Villas, Carr. a Camajuaní, km 5 ½, Cuba
mmgarcia@uclv.edu.cu

Abstract. The family orientation process in Cuban Schools for children with Affective – Behavioral Maladies (SABM) involves clustering and classification of mixed type data with non-symmetric similarity functions. To improve this process, this paper includes some novel characteristics in clustering and prototype selection. The proposed approach uses a hierarchical clustering based on compact sets, making it suitable for dealing with non-symmetric similarity functions, as well as with mixed and incomplete data. The proposal obtains very good results on the SABM data, and over repository databases. In addition, the proposed clustering method is able to detect the true partitions of data and it was significantly better with respect to others according to external validity indexes. In prototype selection, the proposal obtains a highly reduced prototype set, while maintains the original classifier accuracy.

Keywords: special schools, nearest prototype classifiers, mixed data.

1 Introduction

In Cuba, the Ministry of Education has special educational schools for dealing with children with singular educational needs. Among them, there are Schools for children with Affective-Behavioural Maladies (SABM). In this kind of schools, the adequate orientation to the family of the children plays a key role to correct the deficiencies, and to insert effectively these children into society. That is why the personnel in charge of the family orientation process in the SABM of Ciego de Ávila characterize the familiar dynamics of each family, and then proceed to design a personalized strategy for each group of families with similar dynamics. To give an adequate orientation, the headings of the SABM proceed on two stages: Clustering and Classification. On stage 1, they cluster the families according to their characteristics, and on stage 2, they assign a new arrived family to the group of its closest family, using Nearest Prototype Classification (see Fig. 1).

J. Pavón et al. (Eds.): IBERAMIA 2012, LNAI 7637, pp. 662–671, 2012.

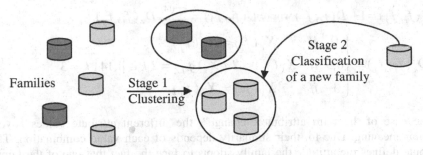

Fig. 1. Stages of the Family orientation process at SABM

Despite the challenges attached to clustering data, there is a need of structuralizing data in SABM School. In this domain, the description of each family has mixed and incomplete attributes. The data of the families of the SABM School of Ciego de Avila has fourteen attributes (see Table 1). These attributes measure the attitude of the family to the inclusion of a child in the SABM School, as well as the peculiarities of the family dynamic.

Table 1. Attributes that characterize the families

Att.	Name	Description
1.	impact	It exists impact or shock in the family
2.	attitude	The attitude adopted about the inclusion of a child in the SABM
3.	change	How the family reacts to the change, if they oppose (O), they resist (R), they have resignation (G) or they agree (A)
4.	guilty	If there are or there are not guilty feelings in the family
5.	clime	The kind of emotional clime, if it is positive or negative
6.	communication	The kind of communication that prevails in the family
7.	handling	The way the family handles the fact of including a child into the SABM
8.	relations	The way the interpersonal relations are developed into the family
9.	crisis	The kind of emotional crisis, by demoralization, disarranging, frustration, impotence or no crisis
10.	estimation	The way the self estimation of the family is
11.	consciousness	If there is or not consciousness of the reality
12.	linkage	If there is or not a favorable link with the SABM
13.	hopes	The hopes the family has to the future
14.	time	The time (in months) the child is at the SABM

The similarity function to compare the families was given by the family orientation experts. It is a non-symmetric similarity. Let be two families, fi and fj:

$$S(f_i, f_j) = 1 - D(f_i, f_j) \text{ where } D(f_i, f_j) = \sum_{k=1}^{14} D_k(f_i, f_j)$$

$$D_k(f_i, f_j) = \begin{cases} 0 & if & X_k(f_i) = X_k(f_j) \\ 0{,}5 & if & X_k(f_i) = ? \vee X_k(f_j) = ? \ k \in [1,14], k \neq 3 \\ 1 & if & X_k(f_i) \neq X_k(f_j) \end{cases} \tag{1}$$

In the case of the third attribute, "change", the different attribute values have a peculiar meaning. Due to, their similarity depends of each value combination. This attribute defines the attitude the family adopts to face the fact that one of the family members, a child, will be allocate into the SABM. Table 2 shows the comparison matrix of values for the attribute "change". As shown, the dissimilarity between values "Resistance" and "Resignation" differ from "Resignation" to "Resistance".

Table 2. Comparison matrix of the values for the attribute "change". Each cell shows the dissimilarity values of the pair (row vs. column). In bold the non-symmetric values.

Value	Opposition	Resistance	Resignation	Agreement
Opposition	0	0.2	0.8	1
Resistance	0.2	0	**0.4**	0.8
Resignation	0.8	**0.8**	0	0.4
Agreement	1	0.8	0.4	0

The main contributions of this paper are to cluster mixed type data, with non-symmetric dissimilarity functions, by using a hierarchical approach based on Compact sets structuralizations and to obtain a reduced prototype set. This approach obtains compact and separated clusters, and it is able to detect the true partitions of data, and outperforms other clustering techniques on real and repository data. It is also used representative instances of the clusters to form the final set of prototypes for the classification stage of the process. Despite the use of a non-symmetric similarity, this approach for the Nearest Prototype Classification stage obtains zero testing error on the SABM database, and is comparable to other Nearest Prototype algorithms over repository databases.

2   Hierarchical Clustering Based on Compact Sets

Taking into consideration the nature of the problem, which cases described by mixed features, and a non-symmetric similarity function used to describe the families; it is necessary to develop the hierarchical clustering algorithm based on compact sets (CSC). Compact sets structuralization is described in [1]. Let be G(X, θ) a Maximum Similarity Graph (MSG), which is a directed graph such that each instance x∈ X is connected to its most similar instance. A connected component of a MSG is a Compact Set (CS). All the instances connected between them belong to the same CS, such that the nearest neighbor of each instance is also in the same CS (see Fig. 2). The proposed method follows a hierarchical agglomerative approach to clustering, but merging CSs instead of objects.

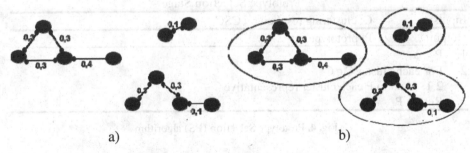

Fig. 2. a) Maximum Similarity Graph of instances and b) Compact Sets of instances

As many other hierarchical agglomerative clustering algorithms [2], it is used a multilayer clustering to produce the hierarchy. The algorithm starts by computing the Maximum Similarity Graph from dataset. Second, it is defined as initial groups each CS in the MSG. Then it merges the groups, until having the desired number of clusters. The merging is making with all possible groups that are more similar in a single step and it is avoided order dependence.

Compact Sets Clustering (CSC)		
Inputs:	k: number of groups	
	S: inter objects similarity function	
Output:	C: resulted clustering	

1. $C = \phi$
2. Create a Maximum Similarity graph using the similarity function S
3. Add to C each connected component of the graph created at step 1
   3.1. Select the cluster representative instance as in equation 2
4. While $|C| < k$
   4.1. Merge all more similar groups, using equation 1
   4.2. Recalculate cluster representative instance
5. Return C

Fig. 3. Compact Sets Clustering algorithm (CSC)

CSC algorithm uses the similarity between cluster representatives as inter group similarity function. Let be x and y the representatives of clusters Ci and Cj, respectively, and $S(x, y)$ is the similarity between those representatives. The similarity function between those clusters is:

$$sim(C_i, C_j) = S(x, y) , \text{ where} \tag{2}$$

The instances that maximize the overall inter-group similarity correspond to the representatives of the clusters. Formally, the representative instance r of a group Cj is:

$$r = arg \max_{x, y \in C_j} \{S(x, y)\} \tag{3}$$

Prototype Selection Stage	
Inputs:	C: clustering resulted by CSC
Output:	P: prototype set
1.	$P = \phi$
2.	For each cluster $C_i \in C$
	2.1. Add to P each cluster representative
3.	Return P

Fig. 4. Prototype Selection (PS) algorithm

In the classification phase, the representing object of each cluster was in the selected prototype set. The prototype set contains as many instances as groups in the clustering stage. Then, the Nearest Prototype Classification determines the class of the new families.

The algorithm proposed in this article includes several novel characteristics, differentiating it from previous clustering and prototype selection algorithms. It uses the connected components of a Maximum Similarity Graph as initial groups, instead as single objects. It also uses a data-dependent similarity function, which makes it applicable to several domains with non-metric similarities, such as social sciences and medicine. It selects representing objects of clusters as prototypes instead of constructing artificial objects for the Nearest Prototype Classification stage.

3   Clustering and Classification of the SABM School Data

The data of the families of the SABM School of Ciego de Avila, as mentioned before has described by mixed attributes that measure the attitude of the family to the inclusion of a child in the SABM School, as well as the peculiarities of the family dynamic. It is also used a non-symmetric similarity (equation 1) to compare family descriptions. In this section are addressed the results of the proposed method to clustering and classification of the SABM data. The first stage of the Family Orientation process is to cluster the families of the SABM. As no predefined number of clusters exists, it is needed to obtain several candidates clustering, and then select the one that best fits data. Among unsupervised cluster validity indexes, the Dunn's index measure how compact and well separated the clusters are. In order to determine the best cluster number, the data was clustering with cluster number varying from two to ten clusters, and then it was used the Dunn's index to select the partition that best fits data. Let be d(Ci,Cj) the dissimilarity between clusters, and Δ(Ci) the cluster size, the Dunn's validation index is the ratio between the minimum dissimilarity between two clusters and the size of the largest cluster.

$$D = \frac{\min\limits_{i=1..nc, j=1..nc, i \neq j} \{d(C_i, C_j)\}}{\max\limits_{i=1..nc} \{\Delta(C_i)\}} \tag{4}$$

where $d(C_i, C_j)$ is the dissimilarity between clusters, and $\Delta(C_i)$ is the cluster size.

To select the partition that best fits the family data, it is uses Dunn's index with complete – linkage and single – linkage as dissimilarity measure and cluster size measure, respectively. In Fig. 5, it is shown the results of cluster number varying (two to ten clusters). The best partition had seven clusters.

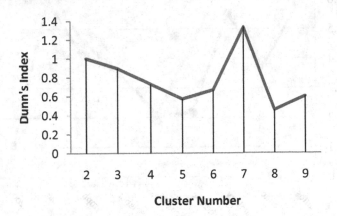

Fig. 5. Values of the Dunn`s index for the partitions obtained by CSC

For the classification stage, each instance had as class label the number of the cluster it was. By this, the original families constitute the training matrix for the classifier. However, a prototype reduction was needed to condense the training set, as prototype selection methods play a key role [3] in the context of Nearest Prototype Classification. The proposed approach selected the representatives of each cluster as prototypes. Thus, it obtained a much-reduced training matrix with only seven prototypes (one for each class). The 10 fold cross validation procedure facilitates testing the performance of the Prototype Selection Stage. The classifier trained with the whole data obtained zero testing error, despite the use of a non-symmetric similarity. In addition, the proposed Prototype Selection method was able to classify correctly every instance in the testing sets, having zero error too. This result shows the ability of this Prototype Selection approach to estimate correctly the class labels of instances.

4   Experimental Results

Nine mixed and incomplete databases of the Machine Learning repository of the University of California at Irvine (UCI) [4] are used in different experimentations. First, it is compared the performance of the CSC method with recently proposed clustering algorithms for mixed data [5, 6]. To compare the clustering results produced by the different algorithms, it is used the Cluster Error, as described in [6]. Lower values of Cluster Error indicate a high performance of the algorithms. The results are shown in Table 3 and Fig. 6.

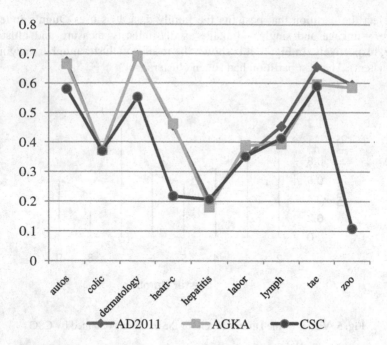

Fig. 6. Results of the Cluster Error of the methods over the UCI databases

Table 3. Cluster Error of the methods. Best results in bold

Databases	AD2011	AGKA	CSC
autos	0.6731	0.6650	**0.5804**
colic	**0.3695**	0.3724	**0.3695**
dermatology	0.6939	0.6910	**0.5519**
heart-c	0.4554	0.4615	**0.2178**
hepatitis	0.2064	**0.1803**	0.2064
labor	**0.3508**	0.3880	**0.3508**
lymph	0.4527	**0.3933**	0.4121
tae	0.6556	0.6158	**0.5894**
zoo	0.5940	0.5841	**0.1089**
Times Best	**2**	**2**	**7**

The Wilcoxon test (see Table 4) helps determining if the CSC significantly outperforms the other algorithms according to Cluster Error. It is define the null hypothesis as no differences in performance, and the alternative hypothesis as the proposed method outperforms the other method. It is used an alpha value of 0.05, with a 95% confidence level. The proposed method has a significant better performance than the AD2011 [6] and AGKA [5] methods, reflecting that the proposal is able to detect the underlying structure of data. It is compared the performance of the proposed Prototype Selection (PS) approach with some other prototype selection algorithms for mixed data [7-10] and with the original classifier (ONN), using all objects (Tables 5 and 6). Cluster count is set to 50, so 50 prototypes are selected, one for each cluster. As dissimilarity function is used the HOEM proposed by Wilson and Martinez [11].

Table 4. Results of the Wilcoxon test for pair wise clustering algorithms comparison

Our method	Asymptotical Significance
vs. AD2011	**0.028**
vs. AGKA	**0.036**

Table 5. Classifier error of the prototype selection methods. In bold the best results, and with * the errors lower than original classifier.

Databases	CSESupport	GCNN	NENN	PRS	PS	ONN
autos	0.3026	0.3023	0.6054	0.3311	0.3450	**0.2926**
colic	0.2310	0.1956*	**0.1819***	0.2176	0.3012	0.2064
dermatology	0.1172	0.0681	**0.0572***	0.0873	**0.0572***	0.0599
heart-c	0.2576	0.2282	**0.1621***	0.2312	0.2213*	0.2282
hepatitis	0.2325	0.1875	0.2079	0.2325	0.1937	**0.1741**
labor	**0.1000***	0.1566	0.1700	0.2066	0.1233*	0.1400
lymph	0.2361	0.2033	0.2433	0.2461	0.2033	**0.1823**
tae	0.3801	0.3841	0.7554	0.5691	0.5366	**0.3641**
zoo	**0.0300***	**0.0300***	0.1081	0.0490	0.0600	0.0400
Times better than ONN	2	2	3	0	3	

The proposal was able to outperform classifier accuracy in three databases, as well as NENN, and does not have a significant increase of classifier error in the remaining databases. Another quality measure of prototype selection methods is retention rate. Retention rate (RR) is calculated as the ratio between the amount of selected prototypes and the amount of instances in the original training set.

$$RR = \frac{|\text{Prototype set}|}{|\text{Training set}|} \qquad (5)$$

Table 6. Object retention rates of the prototype selection methods. In bold the best results.

Databases	CSESupport	GCNN	NENN	PRS	PS
autos	0.4277	0.9393	**0.1328**	0.4856	0.3155
colic	0.2936	1.0000	0.4616	0.3702	**0.0590**
dermatology	**0.1345**	0.7905	0.7562	0.5395	0.1982
heart-c	0.3447	0.9817	0.4518	0.3487	**0.2472**
hepatitis	0.3011	0.9971	0.5426	0.3606	**0.2000**
labor	**0.1638**	0.8887	0.4174	0.3392	0.2046
lymph	0.3304	0.9504	0.3686	0.4369	**0.1381**
tae	0.5798	1.0000	**0.0184**	0.3642	0.3252
zoo	**0.1166**	0.3851	0.8196	0.4873	0.1430
Times Best	3	0	2	0	**4**

The proposal gets the lower object retention rates in four databases, and keeps it lower than 35% in the remaining. These results are due to the selected amount of prototypes, established to be 50. Although the above results are very promising, again the Wilcoxon test (see Table 7) was used to establish the differences between the proposed approach and other algorithms, according to classifier error and object retention rates. Again, it is define the null hypothesis as no differences in performance, and the alternative hypothesis as the proposed method outperforms the other method. It is used an alpha value of 0.05, with a 95% confidence level.

Table 7. Results of the Wilcoxon test for pair wise prototype selection algorithms comparison

Asymptotical Significance for	Our method				
	vs. CSESupport	vs. GCNN	vs. NENN	vs. PRS	vs. Original
Classifier Error	0.678	0.263	0.327	0.314	0.051
Object retention	0.051	**0.008**	0.051	**0.008**	**0.008**

According to classifier error, the proposed Prototype Selection (PS) ties with other prototype selection algorithms, and with the original classifier. In addition, this approach has a significant better performance than two other methods according to object retention rates, according to a 95% of confidence. These results reflect that the proposed method is able to maintain classifier accuracy, using only a reduced number of prototypes. In addition, the nature of the PS algorithm makes it suitable for dealing with quantitative and qualitative features, absences of information and non-symmetric dissimilarity functions.

5   Conclusions

In Cuban special schools, the family orientation process has two stages: family clustering and family classification. This paper proposed a novel method for clustering and Nearest Prototype Classification. The proposed approach has its bases on hierarchical compact sets and handles mixed type data as well as non-symmetric similarity functions. It is compared the performance of the proposal with respect to existing clustering and prototype selection algorithms over repository and real Cuban special schools data. The proposal successfully clusters and classifies the families of children in Cuban special schools. This leads to a better orientation process, spending less time to correct the children deficiencies.

References

1. Ruiz-Shulcloper, J., Abidi, M.A.: Logical Combinatorial Pattern Recognition – A Review. In: Pandalai, S.G. (ed.) Recent Research Developments in Pattern Recognition. Transword Research Networks, pp. 133–176 (2002)
2. Jain, A.K., Dubes, R.C.: Algorithms for Clustering Data. Prentice Hall, Upper Saddle River (1988)
3. Triguero, I., Derrac, J., García, S., Herrera, F.: A Taxonomy and Experimental Study on Prototype Generation for Nearest Neighbor Classification. IEEE Transactions on Systems, Man, and Cybernetics, Part C: Applications and Reviews 42(1), 86–100 (2012)
4. Merz, C.J., Murphy, P.M.: UCI Repository of Machine Learning Databases. Department of Information and Computer Science. University of California at Irvine, Irvine (1998)
5. Roy, D.K., Sharma, L.K.: Genetic K-Means Clustering Algorithm for Mixed Numeric and Categorical Datasets. International Journal of Artificial Intelligence & Applications 1(2), 23–28 (2010)
6. Ahmad, A., Dey, L.: A K-Means Type Clustering Algorithm for Subspace Clustering of Mixed Numeric and Categorical Data. Pattern Recognition Letters 32(7), 1062–1069 (2011)
7. Hattori, K., Takanashi, M.: A New Edited K-Nearest Neighbor Rule in the Pattern Classification Problem. Pattern Recognition 33(3), 521–528 (2000)
8. Chou, C.H., Kuo, B.A., Cheng, F.: The Generalized Condensed Nearest Neighbor Rule as a Data Reduction Technique. In: 18th International Conference on Pattern Recognition (ICPR 2006), vol. 2, pp. 556–559. IEEE (2006)
9. Olvera-López, J.A., Carrasco-Ochoa, J.A., Martínez-Trinidad, J.F.: Prototype Selection Via Prototype Relevance. In: Ruiz-Shulcloper, J., Kropatsch, W.G. (eds.) CIARP 2008. LNCS, vol. 5197, pp. 153–160. Springer, Heidelberg (2008)
10. García-Borroto, M., Villuendas-Rey, Y., Carrasco-Ochoa, J.A., Martínez-Trinidad, J.F.: Finding Small Consistent Subset for the Nearest Neighbor Classifier Based on Support Graphs. In: Bayro-Corrochano, E., Eklundh, J.-O. (eds.) CIARP 2009. LNCS, vol. 5856, pp. 465–472. Springer, Heidelberg (2009)
11. Wilson, R.D., Martinez, T.R.: Improved Heterogeneous Distance Functions. Journal of Artificial Intelligence Research 6, 1–34 (1997)

Mining Social-Affective Data to Recommend Student Tutors

Elisa Boff[1] and Eliseo Reategui[2]

[1] Computer Science and Information Technology Center (CCTI),
University of Caxias do Sul - UCS, Caxias do Sul, Brazil
eboff@ucs.com
[2] PPGIE, Federal University of Rio Grande do Sul - UFRGS, Porto Alegre, Brazil
eliseoreategui@gmail.com

Abstract. This paper presents a learning environment where a mining algorithm is used to learn patterns of interaction with the user and to represent these patterns in a scheme called item descriptors. The learning environment keeps theoretical information about subjects, as well as tools and exercises where the student can put into practice the knowledge obtained. One of the main purposes of the project is to stimulate colaborative learning through the interaction of students with different levels of knowledge. The students' actions, as well as their interactions, are monitored by the system and used to find patterns that can guide the search for students that may play the role of a tutor. Such patterns are found with a particular learning algorithm and represented in item descriptors. The paper presents the educational application, the representation mechanism and learning algorithm used to mine social-affective data in order to create a recommendation model of tutors.

Keywords: recommender system, learning environment, colaboration, social-affective data.

1 Introduction

Mining data in educational environments is often used with two main purposes:

(1) to give educators a better understanding of how users learn with the system;
(2) to define different paths of study according to students' profiles learned from data.

The first goal may be achieved by using mining algorithms to identify patterns and represent them in a scheme that is easy to understand. The second goal can be pursued by employing a mechanism capable of using the patterns found to suggest topics related to the subjects being studied.

We used mining algorithms here in order to accomplish (1) and (2), and also to identify suitable student tutors that may help other students needing assistance.

Current research has shown the potentiality of cooperative learning, demonstrating that group work is fundamental for the cognitive development of the student [7] [8]. It is known that knowledge composition occurs on an individual basis, but cooperation (subjects acting together over the same topic, with common goals, interacting and

J. Pavón et al. (Eds.): IBERAMIA 2012, LNAI 7637, pp. 672–681, 2012.

exchanging ideas) is capable of involving all participants in learning [18]. In this perspective, motivating the students to interact can lead to an effective learning practice.

The recommendation service of tutors works in the sense of motivating group formation among the students. A group can be formed due to similarity and empathy of its members or to the necessity of support for the accomplishment of some task [1]. The latter can be motivated by prestige or status, economic benefits or the necessity and desire of contribution. Andrade et al. [1] also emphasize that the affective states of the individuals have significant importance in the interaction process. The authors complement affirming that some dimensions of the personality seem to have certain connections with the social performance in the interaction, but establishing an accurate relationship between them seems to be a complex task.

Our tutor recommendation service explores the social-affective dimension through the analysis of emotional states and social behavior of the users. A recommender system analyses students' interactions and finds suitable tutors among them as well as contents to be recommended. A specific algorithm was built to identify behavioral patterns in the students interaction, and to store this knowledge in structures called item descriptors [19]. The method proposed shows a good performance with respect to processing time and accuracy, and has an advantage over other techniques when it comes to understanding the knowledge elicited and letting users modify it. The first section of the paper gives an overview of the types of data collected from the interaction with the users. Then, the mechanism employed to represent knowledge is explained, in addition to its learning algorithm and recommendation process. Finally, preliminary results are discussed, as well as conceptual advantages and drawbacks of the approach. The last section of the paper offers conclusions and directions for future work.

2   Collecting Interaction Data

When students navigate in our learning environment, different types of data are collected from their interaction. By keeping the navigation history of every student, for example, we are able to identify navigation patterns and to use them in real-time recommendation of contents. For the recommendation of tutor colleagues, six other types of data are collected: Social Profile; Acceptance Degree; Sociability Degree; Mood State; Tutorial Degree and Performance.

The Social Profile (SP) is built during the communication process among students. The following information is collected during the interaction of the students through an instant message service:

- *Initiatives of communication*: number of times that the student had the initiative to talk with other pupils.
- *Answers to initial communications*: in an initial communication, number of times that the student answered.
- *Interaction history*: individuals with whom the student interacts or has interacted, and number of interactions.
- *Friends Group*: individuals with which the student interacts regularly, and number interactions.

Based on Maturana [15] we defined the Acceptance Degree (AD), which measures the acceptance a student has for another one. Such data is collected through a graphical interface that enables each student to indicate his/her acceptance degree for other students. This measure may also be considered from a point of view of Social Networks, which constitutes one of the most popular approaches for the analysis of human interactions. The most important concept in this approach is centrality. If an individual is central in a group, he/she is popular and gets a great amount of attention from the group members. As the AD is indicated by the students themselves based on their affective structures, the measurement can indicate diverse emotions, such as love, envy, hatred, etc. The average of all AD received by a student influences his/her Sociability Degree (SD).

The Mood State (MS) represents our belief in the capability of a student to play the role of a tutor if he/she is not in a positive mood state (although the student may have all the technical and social requirements to be a tutor). We consider three values for the MS: "bad mood", "regular mood" and "good mood". These states are indicated by the students in a graphical interface through corresponding clip-arts.

After a helping session, a small questionnaire is submitted to the student who got assistance. The goal of this questionnaire is to collect information about the performance of the tutor. The questions made are based on concepts from Social Networks and Sociometry, and may be answered by four qualitative values: "excellent", "good", "regular", and "bad". They are:

- How do you classify the sociability of your class fellow?
- How do you classify the help given by your class fellow?

The answer to the first question together with the average of the ADs of a student, form his/her Sociability Degree (SD). This measure indicates how other individuals see the social capability of this student.

The Tutorial Degree (TD) measures a student's pedagogical capacity to help, to explain and teach. This value is obtained from the answers given for the second question of the questionnaire above and from the marks the tutor got when he/she studied the contents for which he/she was asked for help. These marks were called Performance (P) and were used in the computation of the TD because when a tutor is not able to help another student it does not necessarily mean that the student is a bad tutor. He/she may simply not know very well the content for which his/her help was requested. Therefore, the answers of the students have to be "weighted".

A mining process determines relationships among these factors, and represents such relationships in item descriptors, which are later used for recommendation purposes.

3   The Item Descriptors

An item descriptor represents knowledge about when to recommend a particular item (a topic of study, an exercise, or a tutor) by listing other items found to be related to it. Users have features that may be classified as:

- *demographic:* data describing an individual, such as age, gender, occupation, address;
- *behavioral:* data describing tutoring and social capacity, navigation and study patterns.

It has been shown that both types of data are important when building a user profile [13] and inferring user's needs [5] [6]. Demographic material is represented here in attribute-value pairs. Behavioral information is represented by actions carried out by the user, such as the selection of a topic for reading. Emotional states and social behavior can either be inferred or collected explicitly in questionnaires.

While attributes used to define demographic features are typically single-valued, behavioral data is usually multi-valued. For instance, a person can only belong to one age group (demographic), but he/she may be friendly and patient at the same time (behavioral). Nevertheless, both types of information are represented in our model in a similar way. Let us examine an example of an item descriptor and its related items (Table 1).

Table 1. Item descriptor and related items

Descriptor d_n	
Correlated terms	**Confidence**
t_a	0.92
t_e	0.87
t_c	0.85
t_d	0.84
t_b	0.77

The descriptor has a *target (d_n)*, i.e. an item that may be recommended in the presence of some of its correlated terms. Each term's class and *confidence* (the strength with which the term is correlated with the target item) is displayed next to its identification.

We use *confidence* as a correlation factor in order to determine how relevant a piece of information is to the recommendation of a given item. This is the same as computing the conditional probability $P(d_j|e)$, i.e. the probability that the item represented by descriptor d_j is rated positively by a user given evidence e. Therefore, the descriptors can be learned through the analysis of actual users' records. For each item for which we want to define a recommendation strategy, a descriptor is created with the item defined as its target. Then, the confidence between the target and other existing demographic features and behavioral data is computed. This process continues until all descriptors have been created. For the recommendation of tutors, descriptors are built indicating the features of good and bad instructors.

4   The Recommendation of Tutors

Given a list of possible tutors $U=\{u_1, u_2,..., u_m\}$, the recommendation process starts with the gathering of demographic and behavioral information about each of them. Next, the data collected for each user is matched against a descriptor d_j which lists the most important features of good instructors, according to the terms $T=\{t_1,t_2,...,t_k\}$ stored in the descriptor. The system computes a score for each student that ranges from not similar (0) to very similar (1), according to the formula:

$$Score\ (d_j) = 1 - \Pi\ (Noise\ (t_p))$$

where $Score(d_j)$ is the final score of the descriptor d_j; $Noise(t_p)$ is the value of the *noise parameter* of term t_p, a concept used in noisy-OR probability models [19] and computed as $1 - P(d_j \mid t_p)$. The individual with the highest score is selected to assist the student needing assistance.

That expression contains an assumption of independence of the various t_p - which the designer of a practical system should be trying to achieve in the choice of terms. Ultimately the test of the assumption is in the users' perception of the quality of a system's recommendations: if the perception is that the outputs are fully satisfactory, this is circumstantial evidence for the soundness of the underlying design choices. The situation here is the same as in numerical taxonomy [22], where distances between topics i_d in a multidimensional space of attributes are given by metric functions where the choice of distinct dimensions should obviously aim to avoid terms that have mutual dependences. If the aim fails, the metric cannot - except occasionally by accident - produce taxonomic clusters C (analogous to sets of topics offered by a recommender system once a user has selected one member of C) that satisfy the users. This method is based on the assumption that any term matching the user's terms should increase the confidence that the descriptor holds the most appropriate recommendation. In a real-life example, let us suppose that we have a certain degree of confidence that a student who has shown a good ability in answering factorial exercises is our best bet to help another student who is having problem with the subject. Knowing that that same student is friendly and is in a good mood should increase the total confidence on his recommendation as a tutor, subject to not exceeding the maximum value of 1.

5   Validation and Discussion

An Environment for the Learning of Algorithms (A3) has been developed at the Department of Computer Science of the University of Caxias do Sul with the main goal of making the courses more dynamic, increasing the interest and participation of the students and providing an environment where students may interact in order to improve their knowledge. The environment presents students with the regular contents of algorithms, it proposes exercises, provides a forum for discussion and a tool for the testing and running of algorithms. Having been developed as a dynamic website, the system enables teachers and administrators to modify contents easily.

And most importantly, the system promotes the communication among students by suggesting individuals that may help others showing difficulty in learning a given topic. The A3 environment started to be tested in 2 courses at the Department. Descriptors were built manually in order to get the system to recommend contents and tutors. The data collected so far has not been sufficient for us to carry out conclusive experiments as to whether the system is making tutoring recommendations appropriately. However, initial experiments carried out and reported in Reategui [20] show that the item descriptors have a good performance in terms of processing time and accuracy, when compared with collaborative filtering, one of the most popular approaches in recommender systems. For the MovieLens database[1], for example, storing anonymous ratings of 3900 movies assigned by 6040 users, the item descriptors show an accuracy rate that is 6 points higher than that of the k-nearest neighbor algorithm. The Table 2 summarizes the results obtained.

Table 2. Scoring results for the MovieLens data set

Method	Scoring
Item Descriptors	65,7
k-nearest-neighbor (k=1)	39,3
k-nearest-neighbor (k=20)	54,9
k-nearest-neighbor (k=40)	59,7

The experiments were carried out considering neighborhoods with sizes 1, 20 and 40 (we did not observe any significant improvement in accuracy for the nearest-neighbor algorithm with neighborhoods larger than 40). The topic descriptors performed better than the k-nearest-neighbor algorithm, no matter what size of the neighborhoods was chosen.

Sarwar [21] have carried out a series of experiments with the same data set, employing the Mean Absolute Error (MAE) method to measure the accuracy of item-based recommendation algorithms. The results reported could not be compared directly with our own as the authors computed their system's accuracy using the MAE and considering integer ratings ranging from 1 to 5 (reaching values around 75%). In our experiment, we only took into account whether a user rated (1) or did not rate (0) an topic.

In order to evaluate the system's performance, we monitored how much time was spent by the system in order to recommend the 2114 topics in the test data set2. For k=1, the nearest-neighbor approach needed less time than the topic descriptors to perform the tests, though showing a lower rate of accuracy. However, for larger values of k (or simply larger numbers of users) the performance of the nearest-neighbor algorithm degrades, while that of the topic descriptors remains stable. Table 3 summarizes the results of the experiment.

---

1 MovieLens is a project developed in the Department of Computer Science and Engineering at the University of Minnesota (http://movielens.umn.edu).

Table 3. Performance results for the MovieLens data set

Method	Time spent in secs.
Topic Descriptors	32
k-nearest-neighbor (k=1)	14
k-nearest-neighbor (k=20)	43
k-nearest-neighbor (k=40)	86

In more realistic situations where the nearest-neighbor algorithm may have to access a database containing actual users' transactions, the nearest-neighbor approach may become impractical. For the same experiment described above, we tested the nearest-neighbor through access to an actual database, using k=10. A few hours was needed for the system to make the whole set of recommendations. Further validation results may be found in Reategui [19].

Another popular approach applied to recommender systems is *association rules* [14] (Mombasher, 2001). This technique use well-known inductive learning algorithms, such as *a priori* [2], to extract knowledge and represent them in "if ... then ..." rules format. The main advantage of such learning method relies on the robustness and stability of the algorithms available. Although being successfully applied in innumerable application areas, association rules are hard to modify while keeping the rule base consistent (e.g. adding new rules without contradicting existing ones). Keeping track of and trying to understand the large number of generated rules for each topic is another difficulty of this approach.

The item descriptor approach is different in that it represents knowledge in the form of descriptors and correlation factors. When compared with the other approaches in this respect, descriptors are interesting because they make it easy for users to understand as well as modify the knowledge represented. This is particularly important when the user wants to make the system respond in a certain way in given circumstances, e.g. if the teacher wants the system to recommend a certain reading when the student is viewing a particular topic.

The learning mechanism used on the item descriptors also exploits well-known methods to compute correlation factors and define the strength of the relationships among features and topics. The option to use term confidence instead of conditional probability to describe the model comes from the fact that other correlation factors that are not supported by probability theory are computed by the system, such as *interest* and *conviction* [4]. However, at present these are provided only to let the user analyze and validate the knowledge extracted from the database. We are currently testing different variations on the combination of these factors in the reasoning process.

Although the system learns and updates its descriptors in an offline process (therefore not critical for the application to recommend topics in real time), our learning algorithm is fairly simple and fast. Above all, it is faster than algorithms that group evidence and try to compute the relevance of each topic and then of each group of evidence.

Our model may also be compared with Hidden Markov Models (HMM), employed in tasks such as the inference of grammars of simple language [10], or the discovery of patterns in DNA sequences [3]. The two models are similar in that both use probability theory to determine the likelihood that a given event takes place. However, the actual methods used to compute probabilities of events are different: while HMM considers the product of the probabilities of individual events, we consider the product of noise parameters. Both models are based on the assumption that an output is statistically independent of previous outputs. This assumption may be limiting in given circumstances, but for the type of application we have chosen, we do not believe this to be a serious problem (e.g. as we have remarked above in our comments on indepencence). To take one practical example, the probability that a user studies topic C is very rarely dependent on the order in which users have read other topics (e.g. B before A, or A before B).

The recommendation method we use has the peculiarity of computing the correlation of individual terms initially, and then combining them in real time. This is analogous to finding first a set of rules with only one left-side term, followed at run time by finding associations between the rules. This is a good technique to avoid computing the relevance of all possible associations among terms in the learning phase.

Gomes [11] proposes a different recommendation strategy to identify tutors based on the computation of a utility function. Their strategy combines features in a mathematical expression to determine how effective a student can be for a given tutoring task. Compared to this approach, our mining and recommendation mechanism is more interesting in that it uses learning algorithms to learn a model from the available data automatically, identifying the importance of each utility function variable.

6   Conclusions

One important contribution of this work has been the definition of the types of data to be used in the mining and in the recommendation process of pupil tutors. Using the descriptors to calculate the relevance of terms individually, and then combining them at recommendation time through the use of the noisy-OR is also a novel approach. A similar use of the function can be found in research on expert systems [9], but not in applications for recommender systems. Initial results have shown that the approach can be very effective in large-scale practice for personalization purposes.

The use of social-affective information to promote the communication and collaborative learning among students is starting to be tested in the environment A3. The results obtained so far show that the use of Social Profile, Mood State, Performance Acceptance, Sociability and Tutorial Degree in tutor recommendation, is a promising alternative.

Although the data collected from students' interactions so far are not sufficient for us to draw assertive conclusions about the use of item descriptors to recommend tutors, other experiments have shown the adequacy of the approach in item recommendation.

The possibility to represent different types of information (demographic or behavioral) in a similar way seems to be advantageous when it comes to practical implementation issues. Previous work in the field has shown the importance of dealing with and combining such types of knowledge in recommender systems [17].

Current research on the identification of implicit user information also shows that recommender systems will have to manipulate different sorts of data in order to infer users' preferences [6].

One of our biggest challenges now concerns the automatic inference of students' affective states. At present we are using questionnaires and graphic interface controls to let the users indicate such states. Thus, little is done to automatically infer the social-affective information necessary for tutor recommendation. This will be one of our main research efforts in the near future.

References

1. Andrade, A., Jaques, P., Viccari, R., Bordini, R., Jung, J.: A Computational Model of Distance Learning Based on Vygotsky's Socio-Cultural Approach. In: International Conference on Artificial Intelligence on Education Multi-Agent Based Learning Environments Workshop (2001)
2. Agrawal, R., Srikant, R.: Fast Algorithms for Mining Association Rules. In: Proceedings of the 20th International Conference on Very Large Databases (1994)
3. Allison, L., Stern, L., Edgoose, T., Dix, T.I.: Sequence Complexity for Biological Sequence Analysis. Computers and Chemistry 24(1), 43–55 (2000)
4. Brin, S., Motwani, R., Ullman, J.D., Tsur, S.: Dynamic Topicset Counting and Implication Rules for Market Basket Data. SIGMOD Record (ACM Special Interest Group on Management of Data) 26(2), 255 (1997)
5. Buchner, A., Mulvenna, M.: Discovering Behavioural Patterns in Internet Files. In: Intelligent Tutoring Systems 1998. LNCS, vol. 1452 (1998)
6. Claypool, M., Brown, D., Le, P., Waseda, M.: Inferring User Interest. IEEE Internet Computing 5(6), 32–39 (2001)
7. Echeita, G., Martin, E.: Interação Social e Aprendizagem. Artes Médicas, Porto Alegre (1995)
8. Nitzke, J., Carneiro, M.L., Franco, S.: Ambientes de Aprendizagem Cooperativa Apoiada pelo Computador e sua Epistemologia. Informatica na educação: Teoria & Prática 5(1), 13–23 (2002)
9. Gallant, S.: Connectionist Expert Systems. Communications of the ACM 31(2), 152–169 (1988)
10. Georgeff, M.P., Wallace, C.S.: A General Selection Criterion for Inductive Inference. In: European Conference on Artificial Intelligence, ECAI 1984, Pisa, pp. 473–482 (1984)
11. Gomes, E.R., Boff, E., Viccari, R.: Social, Affective and Pedagogical Agents for the Recommendation of Student Tutors. In: 7th Intelligent Tutoring Systems, Workshop on Social and Emotional Intelligence on Learning Environments (2004)
12. Gomes, E.R., Silveira, R.A., Viccari, R.M.: Utilização de agentes FIPA em ambientes para Ensino a Distância. In: XI Congresso Iberoamericano de Educação Superior em Computação, CIESC 2003 (2003)
13. Krulwich, B.: LIFESTYLE FINDER (Intelligent User Profiling Using Large-Scale Demographic Data. Artificial Intelligence Magazine 18(2), 37–45 (1997)
14. Lin, W., Alvarez, S.A., Ruiz, C.: Collaborative Recommendation via Adaptive Association Rule Mining. In: Workshop on Web Mining for E-Commerce, KDD 2000 (2000)
15. Maturana, H.: Emoções e Linguagem na Educação e na Política. Ed. UFMG, Belo Horizonte (1998)

16. Mobasher, B., Dai, H., Luo, T., Nakagawa, M.: Effective Personalization Based on Association Rule Discovery from Web Usage Data. In: ACM Workshop on Web Information and Data Management (2001)
17. Pazzani, M.: A Framework for Collaborative, Content-Based and Demographic Filtering. Artificial Intelligence Review 13(5-6), 393–408 (1999)
18. Piaget, J.: Estudos Sociológicos. Companhia Editora Forense, Rio de Janeiro (1973)
19. Pradhan, M., Provan, G.M., Middleton, B., Henrion, M.: Knowledge Engineering for Large Belief Networks. In: Uncertainty in Artificial Intelligence. Morgan Kaufmann (1994)
20. Reategui, E., Campbell, J.A., Torres, R.: AAAI - The Nineteenth National Conference on Artificial Intelligence, Workshop on Semantic Web Personalization (2004)
21. Sarwar, B.M., Karypis, G., Konstan, J.A., Riedl, J.: Topic-Based Collaborative Filtering Recommendation Algorithms. In: 10th International World Wide Web Conference, WWW 2010 (2001)
22. Sneath, P.A., Sokal, R.R.: Numerical Taxonomy – The Theory and Practice of Numerical Classification. Freeman, San Francisco (1973)

A Case-Based Reasoning Approach to Support Teaching of Spanish as a Second Language in Indigenous Communities from Latin America

Jorge Bacca[1], Silvia Baldiris[1], Ramon Fabregat[1], Juan Guevara[2], and Dora Calderón

[1] Institut D'informàtica i Aplicacions, Universitat de Girona, Girona, Spain
{jorge.bacca;baldiris,ramon}@eia.udg.edu
[2] Universidad Distrital Francisco José de Caldas, Bogotá, Colombia
{jcguevarab,icalderon}@udistrital.edu.co

Abstract. Across Latin America 420 indigenous languages are spoken. Spanish is considered a second language in indigenous communities and is progressively introduced in education. However, most of the tools to support teaching processes of a second language have been developed for the most common languages such as English, French, German, Italian, etc. As a result, only a small amount of learning objects and authoring tools have been developed for indigenous people considering the specific needs of this population. This paper introduces Multilingual–Tiny as a web authoring tool to support the virtual experience of indigenous students and teachers when they are creating learning objects in indigenous languages or in Spanish language, in particular, when they have to deal with grammatical structures of Spanish language. Multilingual–Tiny has a module based on the Case-based Reasoning technique to provide recommendations in real time when teachers and students write texts in Spanish.

Keywords: authoring tool, second language acquisition, indigenous people, case-based reasoning.

1   Introduction

In bilingual virtual training programs for teachers that have and indigenous language as mother tongue [1, 2], there are some difficulties when teachers design and create learning objects to teach Spanish as a second language for indigenous population. Some of those difficulties were reported in [3] and are mainly related to the process of writing texts, in particular the use of grammatical gender and number in the Spanish language. The main cause of this situation is that in some indigenous languages there is no difference in grammatical gender, which means that do not have masculine or feminine distinction, or there are particular ways to express grammatical number that differs from Spanish language.

In consequence, teachers have to be aware of some rules in order to properly apply the grammatical rules of Spanish language and take care of teaching them correctly to their students. Nevertheless, in some cases, indigenous teachers of Spanish language

J. Pavón et al. (Eds.): IBERAMIA 2012, LNAI 7637, pp. 682–691, 2012.

use some didactic strategies designed to teach indigenous languages but they apply them to teach Spanish language. This situation can create some problems in students, because they do not reach a good Spanish level, so it will affect the learning process of other subjects in the future. As a result of these issues, some learning objects that are written by indigenous teachers in Spanish may contain some grammatical errors in the texts.

According to the context mentioned above the research question is: How to support the difficult task of indigenous teachers when they are designing learning objects to teach Spanish to indigenous students, in particular, when they have to deal with the grammatical gender and grammatical number?

As a solution, in this paper we introduce Multilingual-Tiny, a web authoring tool based on the TinyMCE [4] web content editor which consist of a complete set of plug-ins and online services for teachers to support them in the learning objects design and development. Multilingual-Tiny also has a module that applies Case-based reasoning (CBR), in order to provide recommendations (based on the grammatical structure of sentences) and taking into account the previous experience of skilled teachers from writing Spanish texts and well-formed texts obtained from internet. All of this process support teachers of Spanish language when they are creating their learning objects, mainly when they are writing texts in Spanish language.

The work presented in this paper has been designed in collaboration with a group of teachers of Spanish language with a wide expertise in intercultural and bilingual education from Colombia, Mexico, Peru, Bolivia, El Salvador and Nicaragua in the context of the ALTER-NATIVA project funded by the European Commission.

This document is organized as follows: In Sect. 2, some concerns about teaching Spanish as a second language are presented. In Sect. 3 the architecture design of Multilingual-Tiny is described, including the CBR cycle applied. Section 4 describes an illustrative scenario which present the complete process performed by Multilingual-Tiny and also how the CBR technique was applied. Finally in Sect. 5 the conclusions are presented.

2 Teaching Spanish as a Second Language

Teaching Spanish as a second language to indigenous communities is not a trivial task and suppose a challenge to governments and universities in which is important to promote effective Bilingual Intercultural Programmes (BIE) and at the same time, training teachers effectively in order to introduce Spanish in a coordinated bilingualism method [5], in which both, mother tongue or L1 and second language or L2 are developed at the same time. In this context, the mother tongue (which is an indigenous language), is acquired by a natural process [6]. The second language – L2, in this case, the Spanish language, is taught for facilitating indigenous people communication with Spanish-speakers and also to receive instruction in some knowledge areas which are taught in Spanish.

Despite of the efforts and advances obtained by applying the Bilingual Intercultural Programs in some countries such as Mexico and Peru, teachers of Spanish language may face some difficulties when they have to teach indigenous people how to read and write in Spanish and in the indigenous language [7] at the same time. Some of those difficulties are due to the fact that teachers of Spanish have an indigenous language as mother tongue and they learnt Spanish in a non systematic way. The consequence is that those teachers use the same strategies for teaching both languages, so it could be counterproductive in student's learning process [8].

When teaching Spanish, teachers usually can follow two complementary strategies: reading from textbooks and the language class [5]. The former, is a strategy in which teachers introduce and explains the topic in the indigenous language, after that, students read the book in Spanish language so that students identify vocabulary and pronunciation and finally, the teacher explains vocabulary or concepts that maybe students lost from the reading. The latter strategy is the language class, in which teachers of Spanish compare the indigenous language with the Spanish language in terms of grammar, vocabulary and structure in order to promote reflection and develop the meta-linguistic awareness [5].

In this context, in teacher's training, when universities are preparing indigenous students that will be future teachers of Spanish language for teaching in their indigenous communities, students have to develop competencies and skills in order to effectively apply the teaching strategies mentioned above and other didactic and pedagogic methods. Multilingual-Tiny, the web authoring tool developed, takes a relevant role in this task; giving recommendations to teachers to avoid grammatical errors. As a result, teachers can create quality educational content to teach Spanish language and create learning objects in their mother tongue.

3   Multilingual-Tiny Approach

Multilingual-Tiny is a web authoring tool developed in order to support indigenous students which will be future teachers of Spanish language in indigenous communities and teachers of this population, when they are creating learning objects, in particular, when they have to deal with some grammatical structures of sentences in Spanish language. Multilingual-Tiny consist of plug-ins and online services to provide a virtual environment to design and develop learning objects in Spanish and indigenous languages and has a module based on the case-based reasoning technique, to provide recommendations in order to avoid grammatical errors and develop quality educational content.

3.1   Architecture

The architecture of Multilingual-Tiny is depicted in Fig. 1. The architecture has 4 layers, from top to the bottom: The users layer, represent indigenous teachers and students that interact with Multilingual-tiny. The interface layer includes the authoring tool and shows the recommendations that come from the CBR module. The services layer, provides a group of services for text processing and includes the CBR based module to provide the recommendations. And finally the data access layer includes services for data storing, such as the case library. The following sections provide a detailed description of these layers.

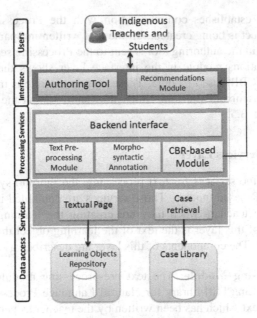

Fig. 1. Multilingual-Tiny Architecture

3.2   Users Layer

The users layer represent the users that interact with Multilingual-Tiny, for instance, indigenous students that will be future teachers of Spanish language in indigenous communities and indigenous teachers. These users interact with the interface layer to use the service for creating the learning objects.

3.3   Interface Layer and Authoring Tool

Interface layer includes the authoring tool and the recommendations. The authoring tool is based on the TinyMCE [4] web content editor, which is an open source Java-Script based web editor that provides a group of services in order to create web pages without worrying about HTML code, because HTML is generated by it. The authoring tool, can be integrated in the ATutor [9] e-learning platform or in other platforms. As a result teachers can easily create web pages which will be part of a course in ATutor e-learning platform as learning objects. Services provided by TinyMCE are:

- An editing area in which teachers can see the web page as it will be finally published. The editing area shows the page as it will be showed to students including colors, images, videos and the organization of that page.
- A plug-in developed to provide access to bilingual indigenous dictionaries so that teachers and students can search any word in Spanish or in their mother tongue.
- A plug-in which provides templates so that teachers can provide examples of text types to students, such as narrative, descriptive, argumentative or expositive texts.
- A group of services to give format to text and include videos and images.

The authoring tool establishes communication with the Processing services layer when a learning object is being created. All the text written in Spanish by indigenous teachers or students in the authoring tool is sent to the Processing services layer.

The recommendations module in the interface layer shows the recommendation that come from the CBR based module. These recommendations include suggestions on how to correct grammatical errors. More information about the recommendations are described in Sect. 3.5.

3.4   Processing Services Layer

This layer includes the services for text processing, the morpho-syntactic annotation module and the CBR based module. Those services are combined in order to provide recommendations to teachers when they are creating the learning objects to teach Spanish. The input of this layer is the text of the learning object that is being created in the authoring tool. The components of this layer are described as follows:

- **Text Pre-processing Module:** The text pre-processing module is based on the open source FreeLing [10] library for Natural Language Processing. The input of this module is a text which has been written by the teacher as part of a learning object. This text is automatically split into sentences and the resultant sentences are split into words. The result of this process will be the input of the morpho-syntactic annotation module.
- **Morpho-syntactic Annotation Module:** This module provides the morpho-syntactic annotation, which is a process of assigning tags for every word in the text, depending on the grammatical category. This process is based on the PoS (Part of Speech) tagging of FreeLing library. The input of this module is the output of the pre-processing module (which is a group of words). The part-of-speech tagging is based on the EAGLES [11] recommendations. EAGLES recommendations define a group of standard tags for every grammatical category. As a result, for each word of the text is assigned a tag depending on the context and grammatical structure of each sentence. The outputs of this module are groups of part-of-speech tags which represent a sentence. These tags will be an important component of the case representation in the case based reasoning module.
- **Cased-based Reasoning Module:** This module is based on the Case-based reasoning technique. It takes the output of the morphosyntactic annotation module, and executes the CBR cycle. As a result it provides the recommendations to indigenous teachers and students in order to correct grammatical errors when they write texts in Spanish language during learning objects creation. The module was built with jCOLIBRI framework [12], each case from the case library consists of a group of tags (part of speech tags) which represent a well-formed sentence. The CBR cycle, which includes 4 steps (Retrieve, Reuse, Review and Retain), is applied to grammatical sentence analysis in Spanish language and the process is depicted in Fig. 2.

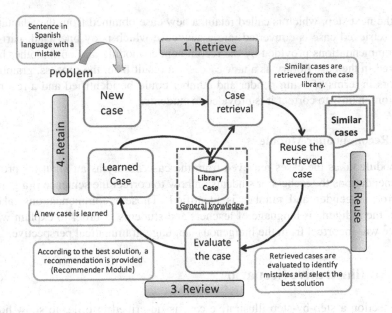

Fig. 2. CBR cycle applied to grammatical sentence analysis in Spanish language

The main steps of this process are:

1. The retrieve step: In this step a new case that comes from the morpho-syntactic annotation module, which is a new sentence, is compared with the cases stored in the case library by means of the similarity algorithm. As a result the most similar cases are retrieved. Both components are used:
   - Case library: Composed by a group of cases which are well-formed sentences in Spanish language obtained from a wide variety of texts from Internet. The case library is updated and new cases are stored when teachers add a new sentence structure. The case library is part of the Data Access layer which establishes communication with the services layer in order to store and retrieve cases.
   - Similarity Algorithm and Retrieve Component: Based on the JCollibri framework, the nearest neighborhood algorithm [13] is applied in order to retrieve the most similar cases when a new sentence is being analyzed. The local similarity function to apply in each attribute of the cases is the Overlap Coefficient [14], and the Global similarity function applied to compute the similarity is the Average Function from the jCOLIBRI framework.
2. The Reuse Step: In this step the K most similar cases obtained, by computing similarity, as described in the retrieve step, are selected and the CBR Module organizes the cases according with the weights defined by the Morpho-syntactic Annotation Module.
3. In the next step, review, the cases are evaluated in order to identify if the sentence is correct or if the sentence has a grammatical error. Besides, the case could be adapted or transformed to provide a recommendation about how to properly write the sentence. Further details about the overall process are depicted in Sect. 4.

4. In the next step, which is called retain, a new case obtained from the adaptation of the retrieved case is converted into a new case which is by one hand, part of the recommendations provided by the recommender module and on the other hand is stored in the case library as a new case. As a result from the process, grammatical errors in terms of using gender and number could be identified and a recommendation on how to correct it is provided to students.

3.5   Recommender Module

This module takes the cases retrieved from the case library as an input for providing recommendations to teachers or students on how to correct the sentence if a grammatical error in gender and number is identified. Those recommendations take into account the indigenous language of teachers and students in order to explain why the sentence was incorrect from the indigenous language grammatical perspective.

4   An Illustrative Scenario

In this section a step-by-step illustrative case is described in order to show how the CBR cycle is applied and how the grammatical sentence analysis in Spanish language is performed in order to provide recommendations to students and teachers.

- Step 1 - Writing the text: Indigenous students which are preparing to be future teachers of Spanish language write a text in the web content editor when they are creating learning objects. In this step it is probably that students make mistakes in terms of grammatical issues when they write a text in Spanish but they are frequently thinking in their mother tongue which is an indigenous language. For instance:
  - Me gustan el gatos blancos (sentence with a mistake in Spanish).
  - I like white cats (English translation only for illustrative purposes).

  The above sentence in Spanish has a mistake in the definite article ("el") because it is in singular form but it must be in plural form ("los").
- Step 2 – Text Pre-Processing (Morpho-syntactic annotation of the initial text): In this step the system takes the initial text and applies the morpho-syntactic part-of-speech annotation of the text according to EAGLES recommendations [11]. Taking the example mentioned above the morpho-syntactic annotation is depicted in Table 1. It is important to remark that in Table 1 for English language the sentence seems to be grammatically correct, but in Spanish language there is a mistake when using the definite article ("el") (which in English is "the") in singular form with a noun "gatos" (in English "cats") in plural form.
- Step 3 – Case retrieval: Based on the morpho-syntactic annotation from step 2, in which each word has a specific tag (as depicted in Table 1), a new case is created; this case is composed by the group of EAGLES tags. The new case could be: Case[PP1CS000, VMIP1P0, DA0MS0, NCMP000, AQAMP0]. This case is equivalent to the sentence: "Me gustan el gatos blancos" (in English: I like white cats). The new case is compared by means of the nearest-neighbor algorithm [13] with

cases previously stored in the case library. The most similar cases are retrieved. For instance, if the following case is retrieved: Case=[PP1CS000,VMIP1P0, DA0MP0,NCMP000,AQAMP0], with a computed similarity of 96% from the global similarity function. It is important to remark that cases stored in the case library have been obtained from texts without grammatical errors.

Table 1. Morpho-Syntactic annotation of the example

Word – Token		Part-of-speech tagging (EAGLES)	Meaning of the tag assigned to each word
Words in Spanish	Translation to English		
Me	I	PP1CS000	Personal pronoun, first person, common gender in singular form.
Gustan	Like	VMIP1P0	Main verb, indicative, present form, first person and plural.
El	the	DA0MS0	Define article, masculine, in singular form.
Gatos	cats	NCMP000	Common noun, masculine, in plural form.
Blancos	white	AQAMP0	Qualified adjective, masculine in plural.

- Step 1   Comparison of cases and recommendations: In this step a comparison between the new case and the most similar case retrieved is performed in order to find differences in terms of the sentence grammatical structure. By means of this comparison and the analysis performed is possible to identify for example if there are mistakes of grammatical gender or grammatical number which are common when indigenous people is learning Spanish. For instance the comparison of the example proposed ("Me gustan el gatos blancos" in English "I like white cats") with the case retrieved from the cases library is depicted in Fig. 3.

NewCase = [PP1CS000, VMIP1P0, **_DA0MS0_**, NCMP000, AQAMP0]

↓ Difference Identified

RetrievedCase = [PP1CS000, VMIP1P0, **_DA0MP0_**, NCMP000, AQAMP0]

Fig. 3. Comparing the example proposed with a retrieved case from case library

As a result of the comparison in this example, the system identifies a difference in the third element of the new case (DA0MS0) and the corresponding element of the retrieved case (DA0MP0). Those tags are described as follows:

- DA0MS0 = Definite article (DA), Neutral (0), Masculine (M), in singular form (S), is not a possessive article (0).
- DA0MP0 = Definite article (DA), Neutral (0), Masculine (M), in plural form (P), is not a possessive article (0).

The difference was identified around the use of the grammatical number: In the new case the article is in singular form, but in the retrieved case (which has been extracted from a text correctly spelled) the article is in plural form. When the mistake has been identified, a recommendation is provided in order to correct the sentence; this recommendation takes information from the case retrieved in the CBR cycle in order to suggest the correct form that the sentence should have. As a result indigenous students and teachers can also learn by interacting with the authoring tool. Figure 4 shows the graphical user interface of the CBR module.

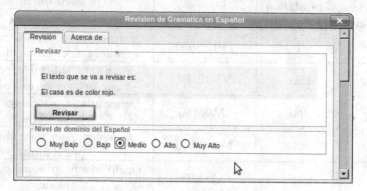

Fig. 4. CBR Module graphical interface

5   Conclusions and Future Work

The case-based reasoning technique applied to the process of sentence analysis in order to identify grammatical errors mainly in terms of grammatical number and gender, is an efficient technique due to the use of the past experience. Besides, the similarity algorithm, including the local similarity functions, the global similarity function and the retrieval process based on the K-NN algorithm in jCOLIBRI applied in the retrieval step works as it was expected in order to retrieve the most similar cases compared with a new case provided.

In short, this paper shows how to apply the case based reasoning technique for sentence analysis at grammatical level and to provide recommendations on how to correct mistakes in grammatical number and gender.

On the other hand, Multilingual-Tiny as an authoring tool to support indigenous students that will be future teachers of Spanish language when writing texts in Spanish, takes a relevant role in order to help students to improve their writing skills at grammatical level so that they will be proficient teachers of Spanish. Multilingual-Tiny also provides a group of services that allow creating learning objects and design activities in the context of learning Spanish as a second language. This tool can be considered an advance in information and communication technologies to support the training process of indigenous students in the context of bilingual intercultural programs.

Acknowledgements. The authors would like to thank to the European Commission for its support through the funding of the ALTERNATIVA Project (DCI-ALA/19.09.01/10/21526/245- 575/ALFA III (2010)88). They would also like to thank the Spanish Government for its support through the funding of the Augmented Reality in Adaptive Learning Management Systems for All (ARrELS - TIN2011-23930) and the Catalan Government for its support through the European Social Funds (SGR-1202).

References

1. UNICEF & PROEIB Andes.: Atlas Sociolingüístico de Pueblos Indígenas en América Latina–Tomo I. FUNPROEIB Andes, Bolivia (2009)
2. UNICEF – Oficina Regional para América Latina y el Caribe, http://www.unicef.org/lac/
3. Trillos, M.: Bilingüismo desigual en las escuelas de la Sierra Nevada de Santa Marta. Thesaurus LI(3), 401–486 (1996)
4. Moxiecode Systems AB–TinyMCE (2012), http://www.tinymce.com/
5. Hamel, R.E., Francis, N.: The Teaching of Spanish as a Second Language in an Indigenous Bilingual Intercultural Curriculum. Language, Culture and Curriculum 19(2), 171–188 (2006)
6. Lier, L.: The Ecology and Semiotics of Language Learning – A Sociocultural Perspective. Springer, Netherlands – Kluwer Academic Publishers, Boston (2004)
7. Valdiviezo, L.A.: Indigenous Worldviews in Intercultural Education – Teachers' Construction of Interculturalism in a Bilingual Quechua–Spanish Program. Intercultural Education 21(1), 27–39 (2010)
8. Arévalo, I., Pardo, K., Vigil, N.: Enseñanza de Castellano como Segunda Lengua en las Escuelas EBI del Peru. Dirección Nacional de Educación Bilingüe Intercultural (2004)
9. University of Toronto:ATutor Learning Management System (2012), http://atutor.ca/
10. Padró, L.: Analizadores Multilingües en FreeLing. Linguamatica 3(2), 13–20 (2011)
11. Expert Advisory Group on Language Engineering Standards (EAGLES): EAGLES Guidelines (1999), http://www.ilc.cnr.it/EAGLES96/browse.html
12. Recio, J.A., Díaz-Agudo, B., Gómez-Martín, M.A., Wiratunga, N.: Extending jCOLIBRI for Textual CBR. In: Muñoz-Ávila, H., Ricci, F. (eds.) ICCBR 2005. LNCS (LNAI), vol. 3620, pp. 421–435. Springer, Heidelberg (2005)
13. Yu, K., Ji, L., Zhang, X.: Kernel Nearest-Neighbor Algorithm. Neural Processing Letters 15(2), 147–156 (2002)
14. Achananuparp, P., Hu, X., Shen, X.: The Evaluation of Sentence Similarity Measures. In: Song, I.-Y., Eder, J., Nguyen, T.M. (eds.) DaWaK 2008. LNCS, vol. 5182, pp. 305–316. Springer, Heidelberg (2008)

Decision-Making Tool for Knowledge-Based Projects in Offshore Production Systems

Adriane B.S. Serapião[1], José R.P. Mendes[2], and Celso K. Morooka[2]

[1] UNESP, Univ Estadual Paulista – Rio Claro (SP), Brazil
adriane@rc.unesp.br
[2] UNICAMP, State University of Campinas – Campinas (SP), Brazil
{morooka,jricardo}@dep.fem.unicamp.br

Abstract. The development of an offshore field demands knowledge of many experts to choose the different components of an offshore production system. All the specialized parts of this knowledge are intrinsically related. The aim of this paper is to use Fuzzy Sets and knowledge-based systems to describe and formalize the phases of development of an offshore production system project, in order to share and to manage the required knowledge for carrying out a project, while at the same time proposing alternatives for the oil field configuration.

Keywords: offshore production system, petroleum engineering, decision-making tool, knowledge-based system, fuzzy system.

1 Introduction

The discovery of heavy oil fields in deep waters produces the necessity to study and develop methodologies for the oil well project and alternatives for offshore production systems. The development project of an offshore production system (OPS) involves a series of phases and procedures developed by many experts. However, many of the requirements used to define each phase are pieces of information shared during some decision-making procedures of the project. In fact, the result of developing a phase carried out by an expert team could be crucial for the development of the next phase under the responsibility of another team. The identification of requirements that should be shared and the integration of the decision-making processes on each aspect to be considered in the complete development of the oil field are extremely important to obtain the best possible performance of the OPS.

Nowadays the success of a company directly relates its intellectual capital to its collaborative work, in other words, with the efficiency of shared knowledge generated by its experts in their common action domain of problem resolution. A question that emerges from this is the difficulty of managing the acquired, used, modified, and available knowledge among experts. Therefore, it is necessary to find effective mechanisms for the extraction of best practices in the different activities of the company and make them available to all the members of the team, so that this knowledge could be effectively incorporated into the company's work routine as an auxiliary tool.

The way this knowledge is encoded is fundamental to its management. Furthermore, the recovery, practice and updating of knowledge many times reveal the necessity of

J. Pavón et al. (Eds.): IBERAMIA 2012, LNAI 7637, pp. 692–701, 2012.

sharing or integrating a great deal of other compartmentalized knowledge, or at least part of it. So, good modeling and good representation of knowledge are extremely necessary for their organization and classification. Thence, another important question about the representation of knowledge emerges, which is the characterization and unification of the vocabulary used by professionals in their area, in order to store, understand and share the structure of information their common action domain, since different words could be used in their description [1].

Although the existence of available knowledge in literature and professional practice can be observed, in Petroleum Engineering this information and knowledge are not easily used. Therefore, it is fundamental to consolidate and make these data available in an efficient and fast way for their use in the most diverse kinds of projects, among which, offshore oil fields projects. Nevertheless, there is a reduced number of projects of knowledge management system development in literature to be applied in the projection, analysis, supervision and operation of offshore oil systems [1–4].

In work by Franco et al. [5], specialized knowledge about processes and technical and environmental procedures that deal with oil and gas production were taken from technical literature information sources and joined together to propose a methodology to aid in the determination of the production unit, the equipment positioned not only in this unit but also at the bottom of the sea, and submarine layout for the development of an offshore oil field. In this methodology, specialized knowledge is encoded in the form of production rules that explain the reasoning of the engineers when taking decisions on the choice of the most adequate components for a new offshore production system.

Serapião et al. [6], using the theoretical methodology developed in [5], implemented a knowledge based system to make a single choice from alternatives of OPS. Since the specialized knowledge many times is full of subjectivities and linguistic expressions that facilitate the description of procedures that will be adopted in the carrying out of the development project of an oil field, both the treatment of the required information to the elaboration of the OPS project and the modeling and the codification of specialized knowledge were implemented using *Fuzzy Sets Theory* [7]. The vocabulary used by the experts to define the OPS, as well as the rules used in the decision-making processes were characterized and unified, in order to have homogeneity in the applied terms.

In the present work, by using fuzzy sets and frameworks, a knowledge based system, capable of helping an expert in consulting requirements of an offshore project in deep water fields, was developed, so that the data storage, manipulation, filtering and recovery could give guidance about the possible different scenarios for the development of an offshore oil field. A decision tool based on the methodology developed by Franco et al. [5] and implemented in the work carried out by Serapião et al. [6] was expanded to create the framework of an OPS used as support for the intelligent system. The purpose of this intelligent tool is to describe and share expert knowledge, in order to verify multiple possible development solutions of an oil field under different project conditions, allowing the expert to choose and conclude the best configurations for the OPS.

2   Conception of an Offshore Production System

The project of an OPS demands knowledge of different experts in the determination of each of their components. The decision processes in the development of an oil field unite different types of professionals from the petroleum area, such as geologists, reservoir engineers, drilling engineers, production engineers and economists; each one with a particular vision and particular criteria, related to different parts of the project. This means that each expert presents a different framework for the development of the oil field, based on some attributes (or criteria) that are considered more important in his/her domain. However, some of these attributes (*i.e.*, the number of wells) simultaneously influence the choice of some of the many components of the OPS that should be dimensioned by different experts, according to their function in the project. Furthermore, after its determination, a component could act as a necessary attribute to determine another component of the system. This is the case, for example, of well arrangement that after the layout is chosen becomes essential for the choice of the production unit; the type of mooring system of the production unit; and the use or not of a manifold. Generally, this means the necessity of an interaction of inherent concepts furnished by different experts to achieve success in the development of the oil field.

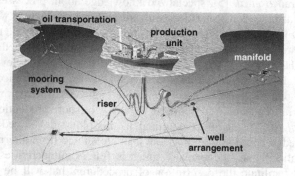

Fig. 1. Offshore Production System (modified from *www.offshore-technology.com*)

In his work, Franco *et al.* [5] gathered the expressed knowledge from different experts and catalogued the development of a petroleum field in literature, in order to propose a methodology for knowledge representation through the selection of some concepts and attributes used in the choice of components that determine the configuration of the petroleum field. According to this work, the concepts that indicate the most important components for the development of the petroleum field are: *well arrangement*; *use of manifold*; *type of production unit*; *mooring system of the production unit*; *riser type for the production unit;* and *type of transportation for production oil draining* (Fig. 1). Based on environmental and technical factors, the relevant attributes used to determine those components are: *reservoir area*; *reservoir depth; well type*; *number of wells*; *diary oil well flow rate*; *water depth*; *environmental condition*; *shore distance*; *existence of infra-structure near to the field;* and *oil storage capacity of the production unit*. Table 1 shows which attributes should be considered in the choice of each component (or concept) of the offshore production system, obtained from domain experts.

Due to the inter-dependence between the attributes and the concepts, as shown in Table 1, where some attributes are used in different concepts, and where concepts start being considered attributes used in other concepts, a sequential fixed process in decision-making was adopted so as to choose each component for OPS [5, 6]. Thus, the established order for the decision processes in a project is shown in Fig. 2.

Table 1. Relationship of concepts and attributes of the OPS

Concepts	Attributes
Offshore Production System	Well arrangement, Manifold, Production unit, Mooring system, Riser, Oil transportation
Well arrangement	Reservoir area, reservoir depth, well type and number of wells
Manifold	Number of wells, diary well flowrate and well arrangement
Production unit	Water depth, well arrangement, environmental condition, number of wells and diary well flowrate
Mooring system	Well arrangement, number of wells and production unit
Riser	Water depth, environmental condition and production unit
Oil transportation	Diary well flowrate, shore distance, existence of infra-structure near to the field and oil storage capacity of production unit

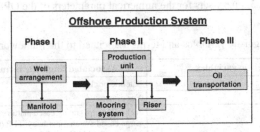

Fig. 2. Sequence of decision processes in the OPS

3   Fuzzy Sets and the Parameters of Offshore Production System

The attributes of the reservoir size, reservoir depth, number of wells, flow rate of the well, water depth, onshore distance, and oil storage capacity are intrinsically described as number values (for example, water depth of 1,500 meters) that should be considered for the OPS. However, the petroleum engineer uses linguistic associations many times to describe the instance of the attributes in the formulation of concepts and to evaluate the best possibilities for decision-making. Expressions like "deep water depth", "great number of wells" and "shallow depth" are frequently used in the daily reality of the engineer. Even so, the linguistic treatment would be associated to a certain subjectivity and would be less precise than numeric. This reduces the particularities of a practical situation and permits a better comprehension and judging of the real situation, bringing one near to the reasoning used by the engineer in situations that cannot be numerically described because of their complexity. So, linguistic terms have been used to replace the numeric description of the attributes of the OPS [6], according to *Fuzzy Sets Theory* [7]. Mamdani-type model was used to the fuzzy inference method.

The values of the attributes: type of well, environmental condition and existence of infra-structure near to the field are even expressed using a deterministic term and there is no need for it to be codified to another linguistic term. Therefore, they are already usually given and accepted among the experts.

For each numerical parameter of the OPS, linguistic terms (A) of a linguistic variable are associated with different membership degrees $\mu_A(x)$ in their discourse universe

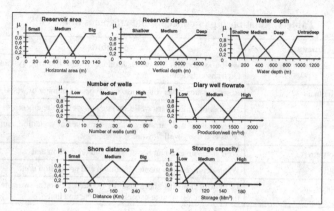

Fig. 3. Fuzzy sets for the numerical parameters of the OPS

Table 2. Linguistic variables and terms associated to the framework of OPS

	Linguistic variables	Associated linguistic terms (Instances)
Concepts	Well arrangement	Satellite or cluster
	Manifold	Yes or not
	Production unit	Jacket, jackup, gravity based platform, compliant tower, barge based system, spar buoy, TLP (tension leg), semi-submersible, FPSO or DPS.
	Mooring system	Conventional, guide line, turret system or tension leg
	Riser	Rigid, semi-rigid or flexible
	Oil transportation	Pipe, offloading or tanker
Attributes	Reservoir area	Small, medium or big
	Reservoir depth	Shallow, medium or deep
	Well type	Horizontal or vertical
	Number of wells	Low, medium or high
	Diary well flowrate	Low, medium or high
	Water depth	Shallow, medium, deep or ultra-deep
	Environmental condition	Mild, moderate or severe
	Shore distance	Small, medium or big
	Existence of infra-structure near to the field	Yes or not
	Oil storage capacity of production unit	Low, medium or high

(X) [7]. The linguistic label ($L(x)$) that better represents the transformation of the numerical value of a parameter in a linguistic term is given by the description with the highest membership degree of the linguistic variable in the universe discourse, according to Equation (1):

$$L(x) = \max\{\mu_A(x)\}, \text{ with } \mu_A(x): X \to [0, 1] \text{ and } x \in X \tag{1}$$

Figure 3 represents the fuzzy sets with triangular membership functions used to represent each numerical attribute of the OPS in a linguistic variable [6].

Table 2 presents a summary of the linguistic terms associated to each concept and to each instance (attribute) used in the conception of the OPS. In this way, Table 2 explains the adopted lexicon in the representation of the knowledge used in the development of an offshore production system.

Table 3. Rules of the *well arrangement* concept

Well arrange-ment	Number of wells	Well type	Reservoir depth	Reservoir area
	low	vertical	X	medium or big
	medium	vertical	X	X
Satellite	medium	horizontal	shallow	small or medium
	medium	horizontal	medium	small
	high	X	X	X
	low	vertical	X	small
	low	horizontal	X	X
Cluster	medium	horizontal	shallow	big
	medium	horizontal	medium	medium or big
	medium	horizontal	Deep	X

Table 3 contains the expert linguistic knowledge expressed on how to determine what type of *well arrangement* in a petroleum field, considering the attributes: *number of wells, well type, reservoir depth,* and *reservoir area*. The "×" symbol means that this attribute is not necessary to conclude which is the best alternative to the well arrangement. Table 3 should be read as a set of production rules. So, one of the possible scenarios represented in the concept '*Well arrangement* is a cluster' consists of this description of its attributes: '*Number of wells* is low'; '*Type of well* is vertical'; and '*Reservoir area* is small' [5, 6].

The knowledge on other concepts of OPS was described in an analogous way to the well arrangement. The knowledge of each concept of the OPS was implemented in distinct knowledge bases of the intelligent system. Manifold database contains 9 rules; the mooring system contains 20 rules; the production unit has 131 rules; the riser has 92 rules; and the oil transportation has 34 rules.

The system developed by Serapião *et al.* [6] uses this approach to deal with a set of numerical technical descriptions of an oil field to find its single best configuration in terms of choosing its components. The activated rules during the process of reasoning for determining the configuration are explained as feedback for the user.

4   Implementation of the Decision-Making Tool for the Offshore Production System

A computational tool was built for the knowledge acquisition according to our purposes, which supplies a representation of static knowledge formalized in a hierarchy of concepts and relations. This tool was developed in Delphi®Borland. The acquisition tool permits the user to configure, to specify and to store all the elements that explain the knowledge, such as concepts, attributes and relations. The tool permits the knowledge bases that describe the architecture of the OPS to be consulted. Figure 4 shows the simplified diagram that describes the offshore production system implemented as interrelated modules (each one for a specific concept) for decision-making about choosing the best configuration for an offshore production system.

The project of an offshore field involves a choice of six components of the OPS, as in Table 1. As mentioned before, each one of these components was described as a concept in a framework, in order to compose independent knowledge bases. A way to determine if the framework correctly represents the required knowledge to model a knowledge domain is to ask possible questions, such as:

- Which parameters are used to make the choice of the oil transporting system?
- Which is the well arrangement for high reservoir depth and horizontal wells?
- If manifold is not be used in an offshore field and the production unit is a semi-submersible, what are the possibilities of configuration for the rest of the processes (well arrangement, mooring system, riser, and oil transportation)?

The answers to these questions depend on the attributes (water depth, reservoir depth, etc.) of each concept (well arrangement, manifold, etc.), that are in fact, many times common among some concepts. Thus, an internal crossing of the instances and information (of the attributes or concepts) should be made to find the compatible answers. An ability of this type of system is to find multiple answers to any query, permitting visualization of all the possible alternatives (scenarios) to the solution of a question.

Complimenting the implemented system in [6], two different ways of using the knowledge bases were implemented: consulting using concepts, where an individual specific investigation of one of the concepts is required; and consulting using scenarios, where the integration between concepts and knowledge bases, in order to obtain a configuration of the whole project of the offshore production system is required.

4.1   Consulting Using Concepts

The option of consulting using concepts for a specific knowledge base is useful when one is willing to find the concepts that represent the associated knowledge to one of the components of the OPS, notwithstanding the other components of the system. Whenever a concept is selected by the instantiation of one or more of its attributes, it is possible to find all possible configuration alternatives for this concept, according to the automatic instantiation of the attributes that were not previously chosen.

Figure 5 shows a request to the placing of the question *"Which should be the well arrangement for high depth reservoirs and horizontal wells?"* and the generation of the possible concepts as an answer.

4.2   Consulting Using Scenarios

Consulting using a scenario module is shown in Fig. 6. In this module, given the initial instances of some attributes for any concepts of OPS, the instance of the other non-selected concepts is obtained, as well as all attributes related to the six concepts. This consulting allows the user to specify any initial parameters of OPS, crossing the information and relationships and receiving all complete possible scenarios as answers, according to the pre-established rules stored in the knowledge bases. When one of the resulted scenarios is selected, the values (instances) of all parameters (attributes) for this scenario emerge in other form.

Figure 6a represents the possible solutions to the question: *"If manifold is not used in an offshore field and if the standstill production unit would be sub-submersible type, what are the possibilities of configuration for the rest of the processes (well arrangement, mooring system, riser, and oil transportation)?"*.

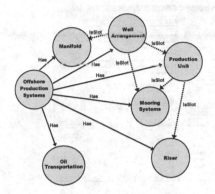

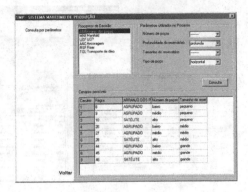

Fig. 4. Simplified framework's diagram of the decision-making tool for the OPS

Fig. 5. Consulting screen using concepts

The multiple scenarios for this kind of consulting mean that there are many configuration alternatives for the oil production field, when a partial initial condition is given. For example, a pipe could be the best oil transportation system in different conditions when the shore distance is small or medium, notwithstanding the storage capacity of the production unit. This infers to the same instance of the concept 'oil transportation', according to the activation of rules in the knowledge bases. So, all these possible combinations are presented as answers and appear many times. The divergence between the conditions that have produced the same answers can be understood checking the instances of the attributes of a concept in each case.

Because of this, the number of possible combinations is extremely high many times and the visualization and memorization of possibilities of different scenarios become difficult. In order to help the aggregation of results, the button 'Summary' (*Resumo*) in the tools' main screen (Fig. 6a) presents a brief table (Fig. 6b) containing the resumed possible scenarios, without a repetition of terms, or in other words, without a redundancy of scenarios.

5   Results

The complete system was evaluated with 34 examples of installed oil fields around the world. The real configurations of the oil fields were compared with the suggested configurations by the decision-making tool, obtaining 89.7% success with the same components (matching equal concepts). The main observed discrepancies are due to the fact that the adopted methodology to implement the decision-making tool does not consider (governmental or corporative) policies and economical factors as decision criterions to built the rules and the knowledge bases to choose the components of an OPS. Only environmental and technical factors are considered for that. In this way, although a technical solution can be the most adequate for an oil field, the oil company can adopt another more economically viable one.

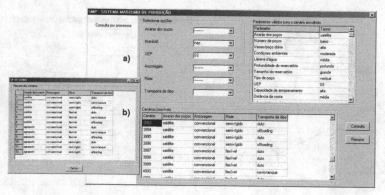

Fig. 6. Consulting screen using scenarios: a) Full screen, b) Screen of summarized scenarios

Table 4. Parameters used to choose the components of the OPS

Parameters	Instances
Reservoir area	Big
Reservoir depth	Medium
Well type	Horizontal
Number of wells	High
Diary well flowrate	High
Water depth	Medium
Environmental condition	Mild
Shore distance	Medium
Existence of infra-structure near to the field	Yes
Oil storage capacity of production unit	High

Table 5. Comparing results of suggested and real configurations of an oil field

Concepts	System Configuration	Real Configuration
Well arrangement	Satellite	Satellite
Manifold	Yes	Yes
Production unit	FPSO	Two Semi-submersibles and one FPSO
Mooring system	Conventional	Conventional and Turret
Riser	Semi-rigid	Semi-rigid
Oil transportation	Pipe	Pipe

A tested case example is presented here. This case is one of the 34 studied real oil fields. The parameters and instances considered in order to choose components of the known offshore production system are shown in Table 4. Using functionalities of chained structured queries in the decision-making tool and by sharing its results, the configuration of the offshore production system was defined. Considering the given parameters in Table 4, Fig. 4 shows the answer (satellite) for the query about well arrangement that was used to try to reproduce the real scenario. Table 5 presents the complete configuration obtained for all other components both by queries implemented in the decision-making tool and the real configuration of an existing oil field.

Some real oil fields have more than one production unit, because others units were introduced throughout time, according to the necessity and maturity of the field. The decision-making tool suggests always just a single solution for an initial production system. Thus, the final results can many times be partially compatible. This factor explains in part the statistical results (hit = 89.7%) comparing suggested and real configurations of OPSs for the six evaluated concepts.

6   Conclusions

The intelligent system has shown that frameworks help in the conceptual learning of the OPS model, exploring the context of the problem by making questions or consulting. This sheds light on the problem, allowing a wide visualization of its possible solutions. Thus, this knowledge-based system could be an additional tool to the teaching-learning process in the qualification of petroleum engineers in training to act in that area.

The description of the OPS as a framework facilitated the combinations of the multiple knowledge bases that describe each inherent process to the decision-making about the choice of components of the production system. It permitted the unified access to the knowledge bases on the mapping of the used terms by the experts through a language and a common mean of communication that correlates the technical jargon among them.

The modeling of reasoning based systems using framework applied to the construction of knowledge bases has shown a significant and rather useful process for the formalization and in the representation of this problem. That encourages us to expand the complexity of the problem and to incorporate new requirements of the project in the system, such as, for example, adding economical factors to aid in the choice of the components of the production system, in order to make it more realistic.

Acknowledgements. The authors would like to thank FAPESP and FUNDUNESP for the financial support.

References

1. Wang, X., Chan, C.W., Hamilton, H.J.: Design of Knowledge-Based Systems with the Ontology-Domain-System Approach. In: 14th International Conference on Software Engineering and Knowledge Engineering, Ischia, Italy, July 15-19, pp. 233–236 (2002)
2. Bargach, S., Martin, C.A., Smith, R.G.: Managing Drilling Knowledge for Improved Efficiency and Reduced Operational Risk. In: SPE/IADC Drilling Conference 67821 (2001)
3. Chao, K.M., Smith, P., Hills, W., Florida-James, B., Norman, P.: Knowledge Sharing and Reuse for Engineering Design Integration. Expert Systems with App. 14(3), 399–408 (1998)
4. Soh, C.K., Soh, A.K.: An Approach to Automate the Design of Fixed Offshore Platforms. Computers & Structures 46(4), 221–254 (1993)
5. Franco, K.P.M., Morooka, C.K., Mendes, J.R.P., Guilherme, I.R.: Desenvolvimento de um Sistema Inteligente para Auxiliar a Escolha de Sistema para Produção no Mar. In: 2o Congresso Brasileiro de P&D em Petróleo & Gás, Rio de Janeiro (2002) (in portuguese)
6. Serapião, A.B.S., Guilherme, I.R., Morooka, C.K., Mendes, J.R.P., Franco, K.P.M.: Um Sistema Inteligente para Escolha dentre Alternativas de Sistemas Marítimos de Produção. In: VI Simpósio Brasileiro de Inteligência Artificial, Bauru – SP, Brazil (2003) (in portuguese)
7. Klir, G.J., Yuan, B.: Fuzzy Sets and Fuzzy Logic – Theory and Applications, 1st edn. Prentice-Hall (1995)

An Intelligent Design Model for Offshore Petroleum Production Elements Layout

Ana Cristina Bicharra García[1], Bruno Vieira Guerra[2], Cristiana Bentes[3], and Luidi Simonetti[4]

[1] Computer Science Institute, Fluminense Federal University
`bicharra@ic.uff.br`
[2] Addlabs, Fluminense Federal University
`bvieira@addlabs.uff.br`
[3] Systems Engineering, State University of Rio de Janeiro
`cris@eng.uerj.br`
[4] Computer Science Institute, Fluminense Federal University
`lsimonetti@ic.uff.br`

Abstract. An offshore elements layout project consists of positioning oil wells, manifolds and platforms in offshore areas, as well as routing the pipelines that connect these elements. The design process involves a set of restrictions, a great number of decisions and an infinite number of design alternatives. This paper presents a new model to solve this problem based on combining two strategies: divide-and-conquer with Active Design Document. The idea is to generate a great number of alternative solutions and include the user as part of the problem solving. We developed a Computer Aided Design system based on this model, called ADDSUB. The focus of ADDSUB is not to propose the optimum solution for exploring the field, but to assist designers to easily create and analyze alternative solutions.

Keywords: pipeline design, offshore elements layout, intelligent systems, petroleum industry.

1   Introduction

The exploitation of oil reserves is a complex and multidisciplinary task that is vital to the petroleum industry. In an offshore field, the oil production flowlines and associated risers represent the most expensive part of operating the field. The flowline network is responsible for bringing the oil from a set of subsea wells to onshore refineries. The offshore subsea elements include oil wells, manifolds, platforms and pipelines. Arranging these elements to allow petroleum flow from subsea areas to the land, maximizing oil production and minimizing construction costs, comprises the project designer task.

Since elements, such as platforms, wells and pipelines, can be positioned in any place of a 3D space, spatial reasoning is required to address the problem domain. Additionally, the positioning of each design element restrains the positioning of the others and vice-versa, leading to a causal bidirectional graph

J. Pavón et al. (Eds.): IBERAMIA 2012, LNAI 7637, pp. 702–711, 2012.
© Springer-Verlag Berlin Heidelberg 2012

$G = (V, E)$, in which $v \in V$ represents each decision and $e \in E$ represents the causal relation among decisions. Besides the dependencies among decisions, the domain imposes a great deal of additional constraints such as avoiding pipeline crossing, or avoiding subsea hazard areas. The problem-solving process involves finding a set of parameter values (e.g., subsea elements positions) that satisfies a set of constraints. This problem description calls for constraint satisfaction methods. However, the infinite number of possible solutions combined with the great interdependence among decisions make CSP non-feasible due to the NP-completeness characteristic of the problem.

In this scenario, we tackle such a complex problem by proposing a model that combines a divide-and-conquer strategy with Active Design Documents (ADD) [6]. The main idea of our model is to decompose the problem graph into sub-graphs, generate a number of alternative solutions for each sub-graph and include the user as part of the problem-solving. The main advantage of our model is that it allows the use of different algorithms for the alternative solution generation, and the on-the-fly evaluation of the partial solutions. Another important feature of this model is that the algorithm for the sub-graph decisions can discretize the continuum world on-demand and use parallel processing for the time-consuming tasks.

We also developed an Intelligent Computer Aided Design system based on this model, called ADDSUB, that has been deployed at a Brazilian petroleum company to assist offshore designer to create a subsea design project. The focus of ADDSUB is not to propose the optimum solution for exploring the field, but to assist designers to easily create and analyze alternative solutions to reach a very good one.

The remainder of this paper is organized as following. In the next section we give a brief description of the offshore pipeline design domain. In Sect. 3, we describe our model, detailing how it solves such a complex problem. In Sect. 4, we show a case study of our model in ADDSUB. In Sect. 5, we discuss some related work. Finally, in Sect. 6, we present our conclusions and proposals for future work.

2   Domain

The main components of a subsea arrangement project are:

- offshore area: the seabed topography and hazards.
- reservoirs: subareas that previous studies (like seismic interpretation) estimate to contain oil.
- wells: produces oil from the reservoir to the platform.
- platforms: receives oil from the wells, processes it and exports to the land.
- manifold: equipment that interconnects a set of wells to the platform, reducing the number of pipelines entering the platform.
- pipelines: transport the oil from the wells to the platform. Can be rigid or flexible. Flexible pipelines are more stretchable for turns.

In an arrangement project, the offshore area to be explored, the reservoirs, and the platforms are predefined components. The development of the project consists of defining the number of manifolds to collect the oil, the placement of

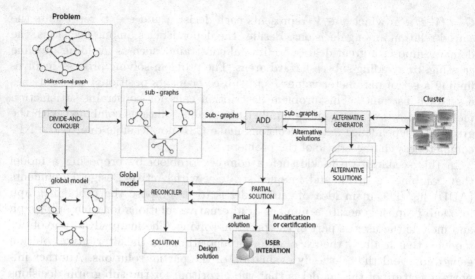

Fig. 1. Subsea arrangement model

each manifold, the placement of each well in the reservoir, the placement of each platform in the area, and the route of the pipelines.

There are a number of constraints that arrangement project must consider such as the pipelines cannot cross to each other, or a platform cannot be placed at too deep or too shallow water, among other restrictions.

The focus of a subsea arrangement project is to maximize oil recovery while minimizing the overall cost of the project. The overall cost of an arrangement project is summarized by the cost of the equipments installed, platform, manifolds, pipelines. What drives the difference in the arrangement solutions is the overall cost of the pipelines. Finding a minimum cost solution is a challenging task since a project has a combinatorial number of design possibilities to be assessed. In fact, the dimension of the search space of potential solutions for the arrangement is intractable, if we consider all the possibilities for the positioning of platforms, wells, manifolds and pipeline routing.

3   Intelligent Subsea Elements Arrangement Model

The model we propose to deal with the highly complex and connected problem of the subsea arrangement is described in Fig. 1. The problem is modeled as a bidirectional graph $G = (V, E)$, where $v \in V$ represents one decision of the problem, for example, positioning the platform, and $e \in E$ represents the causal relation between decisions. For example, if there is and edge from v_1 to v_2, then decision v_2 must follow decision v_1. The graph G is divided by the Divide-and-Conquer module into sub-graphs of higher level decisions, and a causal relation network is also defined to determine a sequence at which the sub-graphs are reconciled.

Currently, our model divides the subsea arrangement problem into the following sub-graphs higher level problems:

1. Wells clustering
2. Hierarchical wells clustering
3. Elements positioning (Platform, Manifold and Well Positioning)
4. Pipeline routing

Each of these sub-graphs comprises a series of decisions, and, in the following sections, we describe these decisions in detail. Each sub-graph is solved separately by the ADD module. The ADD module is responsible for managing the alternative solutions generated by the Alternative Generator module for the partial problem presented, and for managing the user interaction that validates or modifies the partial solution generated. The Alternative Generator module can apply a number of different algorithms for the same problem. The alternative solutions will be evaluated on-the-fly and the user interaction will provide feedback on the solutions presented. In addition, Alternative Generator module applies parallel processing in order to further improve the speed of the solution finding.

Despite the great number of alternative solutions evaluated by the ADD module, to avoid staying stuck in local optimums, our model has a Reconciler module. This module uses the causal relation network to recompute the order at which the partial solutions are generated. The Reconciler uses the causal relationship among the sub-graphs to integrate and adjust the set of partial solutions to generate the complete subsea element arrangement design.

3.1 Wells Clustering

When the offshore area is to be explored by more than one platform, this subgraph determines the groups of wells that will be explored by each platform. It involves solving a clustering problem.

As the number of platforms to exploit the area is previously defined, we use the well-known K-means clustering algorithm [10] to perform this grouping. Since the wells are not yet positioned, they are considered to be located at the center of the reservoir. The K-means algorithm split the wells into exactly k groups. The algorithm keeps track of the centroids of the groups, and works in iterations. Initially, the algorithm determines k random centroids for each group, and then iteratively refines the groups as follows:

1. For each well w_i, find the centroid that is closest to w_i, and assign w_i to the group of this centroid.
2. Update the centroid of each group based on the new constituent elements.

The algorithm terminates when there is no further change in the assignment of wells to groups.

After the clustering, the algorithm to assign a platform to a well group tests for each group G and each platform P_i, if the capacity of P_i complies with the sum of all the wells $w_i \in G$ productive capacity.

3.2   Hierarchical Wells Clustering

If manifolds are used to collect the oil from a set of wells, and send the oil to the platform, the wells clustering has to be done in a hierarchical fashion. After the first clustering, the wells are clustered again into subgroups that represent which wells will drain the oil prior to a manifold and then to the platform.

Since the number of manifolds is unlimited, we use an hierarchical clustering algorithm that recursively finds clusters in agglomerative mode [12]. The algorithm starts with each well being its own cluster, and does not require the number of clusters to be known in advance. At each step, the algorithm decides which clusters should be joined. The criterion for merging the cluster is to merge the closest pair of clusters, where "close" is defined by the measure of cluster distance. The merging steps stops when no more clusters are merged. We included a threshold for merging two clusters in order to comply with the constraint of the maximum distance of a manifold and a well. When no more merges are performed, the algorithm stops. After the subgroups are defined, they have to be further adjusted in order to conform with the constraints that a manifold cannot be located at more than 1500 meters distant to the wells and that a manifold collects oil from a limited number of wells.

3.3   Elements Positioning

This sub-graph deals with finding the best position for a platform, a manifold and a well, that is fundamental to the oil flow and to the pipelines length. The algorithm to position one of these elements is based on the discretization of the search area. The search area is discretized into a grid of q points, where the distance d between q_i and q_j is a system parameter.

The basic algorithm for an element positioning works in two stages. First, for each point q_i in the set, the algorithm computes if placing the element in q_i is *viable*. The viability test depends on the constraints imposed by the element in the search area. Then, for each *viable* q_j position, the algorithm computes the *cost* of routing the pipelines, considering the obstacles (hazards, anchors, etc), to q_j. The viable point with the smallest cost is chosen to be the element position.

For the platform positioning, the search area is defined as the bounding-box area that covers all the area where the reservoirs are located plus an extended area. The viability test performs two checkings at q_i: the water depth and the anchorage position. There is a minimum and a maximum water depth that each type platform can be placed, and the water depth of the platform cannot be smaller than the water depth of all the wells of the group. The anchorage of the platform cannot intersect with any other element or seabed hazards.

For the manifold positioning, the search area is also a bounding-box area that covers the reservoirs in the manifold subgroup. The viability test has to consider the constraints that the manifold cannot be placed over seabed hazards, the wells that connect to a manifold cannot be more than 1500 meters distant to the manifold, and the manifold cannot be placed over the platform anchorage area or the platform restriction area.

For the well positioning, the search area is defined as the reservoir area, and the viability test has to consider that a well cannot intersect any seabed hazard or any other element.

3.4   Pipeline Routing

Pipeline routing is a critical part of the subsea arrangement. The algorithm to determine the route of each pipeline projects the wells and the seabed onto a 2D space. The route of a pipeline has to consider the following constraints: the pipeline cannot intersect with the hazards, the pipelines cannot make arbitrary curves, the pipeline cannot cross other pipelines or other elements (wells, manifolds, platform anchorage). The hazards and the other elements are considered obstacles to the routes and are projected onto the 2D space as polygons. The algorithm to determine the route is based on robot path planning [11]. The robot path planning algorithm consider the case of a robot moving among a set of disjoint polygons S in the plane. Given a start position, p_{start} and a final position p_{goal}, the algorithm computes a shortest collision-free path from p_{start} to p_{goal}. To compute this shortest path the algorithm first builds a visibility graph, $G_V(S)$. The vertices of $G_V(S)$ are the vertices of S, plus p_{start} and p_{goal}. There is an edge between the vertices u and v if they are *visible* from each other, that means, if the segment $\overline{uv}$ does not intersect any obstacle in S.

After $G_V(S)$ is build, we do not use the well-known shortest path algorithm Dijkstra algorithm. Since Dijkstra is a greedy algorithm, we cannot implement the further restrictions such as the pipelines have a minimum allowed curvature radius. To solve this problem, we use a dynamic programming approach. We employ an algorithm similar to the Bellman-Ford algorithm [1,5]. This algorithm can be easily adapted to conform with the project constraints. The shortest path algorithm starts by finding, for each node v, the shortest path to t that uses at most 1 edge, or write down ∞, if there is no path. If for all v, the length of the shortest path to t that uses $i - 1$ edges is solved. The shortest path that uses i edges will first go to some neighbor x of v, and then take the shortest path from x to t that uses $i - 1$ or fewer edges, which is already solved. So, at each step, the minimum is taken over all neighbors x of v, accounting that a solution for the smaller problem is computed and the restrictions are satisfied.

Another decision concerning the pipeline routing is the order at which the pipelines are routed. Since two pipelines cannot cross each other, when a route is traced from the well w_i, this route can obstruct the route from the well w_j. So, the order at which the wells are chosen to trace the routes is fundamental for the overall length of the pipeline network. However, for a set of W wells, there are $|W|!$ number of orderings for the wells, which is intractable. In this way, we propose some heuristics for generating different orderings for the wells. The order that leads to the routes with the smallest cost is chosen.

The heuristics we used to generate different orderings performs a rotational line sweep. We define a half-line ρ, rotate ρ, and as ρ intersects a well w_i, it is inserted in the sequence S. Different heuristics are created with this method. The difference between them are: (i) the definition of ρ: it starts in the center of the platform and passes through the center of the bounding-box that encloses all the wells, or it is a vertical line crossing the platform, (ii) the division of the sequences: ρ can divide the wells into two sequences, S_1 and S_2, or the wells can be considered all in the same sequence, S, and (iii) the sweeping direction: clockwise, or counterclockwise.

3.5   Parallel Processing

Some of the algorithms included in the sub-graphs involve a huge amount of computation. Consequently, they require parallel processing to provide interactive results. The parallelization strategy employed exploits data parallelism by dividing the data into disjoint sets and assigning the computation of each set to a different processor. In this parallelization strategy, all the processors execute the same algorithm, but on different part of the data. For the positioning algorithms, this mapping is straightforward, for an area discretized with q points, and n processors, each processor will compute the subset of q/n points. For the routing algorithm, each processor will compute the route for a subset of the orders generated by the heuristics.

3.6   Solution Reconciling

Since each sub-graph separately solves only part of the problem, we define a causal relation network to determine a sequence at which the sub-graphs are solved to produce the complete solution. The dependency network follows the sequence shown in Sect. 3. However, the dependency network cannot be unidirectional, because the order at which each sub-graph is computed affect the overall result. For example, we define the routes of the pipeline after the wells are positioned, but the route of one pipeline obstructs the route of the others. So, sometimes after the route is traced, it would be better to place the well at another position.

In this way, the dependency network is bidirectional to allow backflow in the network. This backflow will guarantee the recomputation of the sub-graph in a different order to search for a better solution. The Reconciler module can be explicitly required by the user, and can be an iterative procedure, where the user defines the number of reconciler steps to be performed. In a reconciler step, we take into account all the previously computed sub-graph results and try to compute a better solution using the reverse order of the sequence of sub-graph computed in the previous iteration.

4   Case Study

We have implemented our model in an Intelligent Computer Aided Design system, called ADDSUB, that was developed in C++. ADDSUB has been deployed at a Brazilian petroleum company to assist offshore designer to create real-world subsea design projects. ADDSUB also provides a sophisticated graphic interface to allow the user to interact with the partial solutions provided. In this way, ADDSUB merges the designer experience with the capacity of the computer in searching for different alternatives.

ADDSUB is producing real advantages in terms of providing the designer a large number of project alternatives, all of them with a detailed explanation of the costs and the restrictions involved. The designer can save the alternative, or move around the elements positioned as needed. All the modifications can be stored and the user has on-the-fly evaluation of the modifications made.

For confidentiality reasons, we cannot provide data from real projects being developed under ADDSUB, but we can illustrate the behavior of ADDSUB using a fictional production field. The idea of this case study is to illustrate the benefits of ADDSUB in dividing the problem into sub-graphs, generating a number of alternative solutions and reconciling them with a global model.

Consider the offshore area and the reservoirs described in Fig. 2. If these reservoirs are to be explored by two platforms, the first sub-graph of ADDSUB proposes the grouping scheme presented in this figure. Each color represents a different group. In Fig. 3, we show the solution proposed by ADDSUB to platform positioning. For the manifold sub-graph, the algorithm found only one spatial cluster that comply with the systems constraints. The manifold is positioned according to Fig. 4. The route of the pipelines are traced as shown in Fig. 5. When a obstacle is inserted in the area, ADDSUB has to recompute the pipeline routes as shown in Fig. 6. However, this solution can be further improved, and Fig. 7 shows the result of the reconciling module.

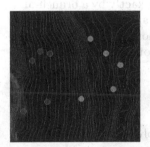 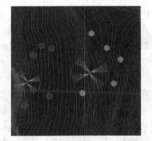 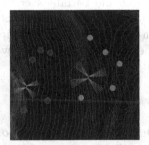

Fig. 2. Grouping   **Fig. 3.** Platforms placing   **Fig. 4.** Manifold placing

5 Related Work

Most of the available literature in the design and planning of infrastructure in oil production field deals with mathematical models for calculating the number of production platforms, their capacities, and the scheduling of well perforation. The problem has been initially presented by Devine and Lesso [4] that proposed a mathematical programming formulation for the development of offshore oil-fields at minimum cost. Garcia-Diaz *et al.* [7] presented a network representation

Fig. 5. Pipeline routing   **Fig. 6.** New routes   **Fig. 7.** Reconciled

for the same problem and proposed a Lagrangean relaxation solution method. Iyer and Grossmann [9] proposed a decomposition algorithm originally designed for process network optimization that solves part of the design problem in the reduced space of binary variables to determine the assignment of wells to platforms. Ierapetritou *et al.* [8] solved the problem of optimal vertical well locations using mixed integer and linear programming. Carvalho and Pinto [3] proposed an optimization model based on mixed-integer program to determine the existence of a given set of platforms and their potential connection with wells. None of these approaches, however, focus on the pipeline design.

In terms of the pipeline design, the work by Brimberg *et al.* [2] concentrated only on the configuration of the network and sizes of pipes used, the problem is expressed as a mixed-integer program, and solved both heuristically by Tabu Search and Variable Neighborhood Search methods and exactly by a branch-and-bound method. The works by Paton *et al.* [13] and Strandgaard [14] presented interactive 3D tools for pipeline routing. These tools, however, do not compute the route, they only allow the designer to draw the route on the seabed and adjust it as needed.

6   Conclusions

Our contribution consists of proposing a new problem-solving model to deal with the infinite number of possibilities in the offshore subsea arrangement elements design domain. Our model combines the divide-and-conquer with the Active Design Document strategies and includes the user into the problem-solving scheme.

The problem domain search space can be represented as a dense causal bidirectional graph in which each design decision influences the other decisions. Experts, in general, do the work mentally and come up with an entire solution at once. Our model breaks this graph into sub-graphs and solves them individually. As the sub-graph solutions are built, the system presents to the users for validation and acceptance. This interaction puts the users as part of problem-solving strategy. After building the partial solution, our model allows the solution reconciling. This reconciling step change the dependency direction of the causal network trying to adjust previous decisions. Since users can also change the solution or part of it, they act preventing the model to get stuck into local optimum.

Our model is being tested on top of a Computer Aided Design system we developed, called ADDSUB, currently in use at a Brazilian petroleum company. We are measuring ADDSUB solution quality in terms of costs, the amount of changes users have to do to reach a good solution (user effort) and the task duration with and without ADDSUB assistance (project duration). We expect ADDSUB will lead less expensive projects, easily modifiable and fast developed.

Further work consists of generalizing our model to other domains represented as bidirectional dependency dense graphs. We are also interested in comparing solution quality and processing complexity with other search strategies, such as genetic algorithm, to deal with local optimums.

References

1. Bellman, R.: On a Routing Problem. Quarterly of Applied Mathematics 16, 87–90 (1958)
2. Brimberg, J., Hansen, P., Lin, K.W., Mladenovic, N., Breton, M.: An Oil Pipeline Design Problem. Operations Research 51(2), 228–239 (2003)
3. Carvalho, M.C.A., Pinto, J.M.: An MILP Model and Solution Technique for the Planning of Infrastructure in Offshore Oilfields. Journal of Petroleum Science and Engineering 51(1-2), 97–110 (2006)
4. Devine, M.D., Lesso, W.G.: Models for the Minimum Cost Development of Offshore Oil Fields. Management Science 18(8), 378–387 (1972)
5. Ford, L.R., Fulkerson, D.R.: Flows in Networks. Princeton University Press (1962)
6. Garcia, A.C.: Active Design Documents A New Approach for Supporting Documentation in Preliminary Routine Design. Ph.D. thesis, Stanford University, Stanford, CA, USA (1992)
7. Garcia-Diaz, J., Startzman, R., Hogg, G.: A New Methodology for Minimizing Investment in the Development of Offshore Fields. SPE Production & Facilities 11(1), 22–29 (1996)
8. Ierapetritou, M.G., Floudas, C.A., Vasantharajan, S., Cullick, A.S.: Optimal Location of Vertical Wells – A Decomposition Approach. AIChE Journal 45(4), 844–859 (1999)
9. Iyer, R.R., Grossmann, I.E.: Optimal Planning and Scheduling of Offshore Oil Field Infrastructure Investment and Operations. Industrial & Engineering Chemistry Research 37(4), 1380–1397 (1998)
10. Lloyd, S.: Least Squares Quantization in PCM. IEEE Transactions on Information Theory 28(2), 129–137 (1982)
11. Lozano-Pérez, T., Wesley, M.A.: An Algorithm for Planning Collision-Free Paths Among Polyhedral Obstacles. Communication of the ACM 22(10), 560–570 (1979)
12. Murtagh, F.: A Survey of Recent Advances in Hierarchical Clustering Algorithms. The Computer Journal 26(4), 354–359 (1983)
13. Paton, M., Mayer, L., Ware, C.: Interactive 3D Tools for Pipeline Route Planning. In: MTS/IEEE Conference OCEANS 1997, pp. 1216–1221. IEEE (1997)
14. Strandgaard, T.: GeoLine3D – Analysis of Subsea Pipelines in a Virtual, Subsea World. Scandinavian Oil-Gas Magazine 7, 39–41 (2007)

MAS for Alarm Management System in Emergencies

Ana Cristina Bicharra García[1], Luiz Andre P. Paes Leme[1], Fernando Pinto[1],
and Nayat Sanchez-Pi[2]

[1] Computer Science Institute,
Fluminense Federal University
Rua Passo da Pátria, 156. Niterói. RJ. 24210-240. Brazil
{cristina,luis.andre,fernando}@addlabs.uff.br
[2] Computer Science Department,
Carlos III University of Madrid
Avda de la Universidad Carlos III, 22. Madrid. 28270. Spain
nayat.sanchez@uc3m.es

Abstract. Due to the imminent danger involved in the petroleum operation domain, only well trained workers are allowed to operate in offshore
oil process plants. Although their vast experience, human errors may happen during emergency situations as a result of the overwhelmed amount
of information generated by a great deal of triggered alarms. Alarm devices have become very cheap leading petroleum equipment manufacturers to overuse them transferring safety responsibility to operators. Not
rarely, accident reports cite poor operators' understanding of the actual
plant status due to too many active alarms. In this paper, we present
an alarm management system focused on guiding offshore platform operators' attention to the essential information that calls for immediate
action during emergency situations. We use a multi-agent based approach
as the basis of our alarm management system for assisting operators to
make sense of alarm avalanche scenarios.

Keywords: multi-agent systems, emergencies, alarm management, oil
industry, fault detection, sense making.

1 Introduction

Alarm management in emergency scenarios has become a topic of great concern in different economic sectors, such as nuclear, aeronautics and offshore oil
industry, due to the frequent accidents occurred in the last decades caused by inappropriate alarm management systems. Although great effort has been devoted
to plant's automation and cheap alarm device development, operators play an
important role mastering all information and adjusting equipments' behavior as
needed. The observations of our research are domain independent, but, in this
paper, we focus on the offshore oil process plant domain.

An alarm informs operators of the process plant unit' status and might require
immediate action. As the safety norms become more stringent and sensor devices

J. Pavón et al. (Eds.): IBERAMIA 2012, LNAI 7637, pp. 712–721, 2012.

become inexpensive and easier to embed, manufacturers have overused installing alarms into their equipments. Trained operators handle pretty well few, but not many, alarm information at a time. During a non-planned process plant shutdowns, operators face an avalanche of alarm information, frequently over 1000 alarms/minute, that must be understood, prioritized and reasoned to decide upon which action, if any, to take. This information overflow has been related as one of the major cause of several serious accidents in the last decade, such as the Mildford Haven refinery accident in the UK, on 24 July 1994, which resulted in a loss of 48 million pounds and two months of non-operation. The report of the Health and Safety Executive department [4] has identified as the accident cause the refinery operators' inability to identify what was really happening behind the large number of triggered alarms generated. The accident could be avoided if the alarm system had identified the cause of the problem, sorted alarm information and displayed only the most important ones so that the operator is able to act properly.

A process plant of a petroleum offshore unit is a complex artifact composed of independent equipments which interact with each other to receive petroleum from subsea reservoirs; treat it and export gas and oil to land refineries. Each equipment behaves and reacts to accomplish its own goal, such as compress gas or treat oil, but maintaining its behavior within the safety functioning range. Sensors and actuators are essential devices embedded in the equipments to monitor or control their behavior, respectively. These complementary devices are orchestrated by the process plant automation system that receives sensors information and triggers actuators actions, such as closing a valve.

Inspired by the distributed and encapsulated aspect of the process plant artifact physical model, we proposed a multi-agent-based alarm management system to synthesize the process plant situation during emergency situations. Each agent represents an equipment that understands about its expected and unexpected behavior within the process plant. During emergency scenarios, alarms related to expected behavior can be suppressed to lead operators' attention to unexpected behavior. Distinguishing expected from non-expected behavior during emergency scenarios and using this information to filter what to display to operators is the basis for our intelligent alarm management system proposal. In addition to proposing a model, we have implemented a prototype version and tested it in a controlled environment. We are currently deploying a version of the system to work within a Brazilian offshore petroleum process plant unit. The rest of the paper is structured as followed. The first section presents related work in the area of alarm management systems, focused on offshore oil process plant domain. Next, our multi-agent alarm management system is laid down, followed by a case study. Results are presented and a conclusions are outlined.

2   Related Work

We see three strategies to face the problem of information overflow: 1) mitigate wrong decisions, 2) predict problems to avoid avalanches and 3) real-time analysis of the avalanche to filter unimportant alarms and automatically diagnose problems. We propose the third strategy. Firstly, because mitigate bad decisions is not always possible or economically feasible for obvious reasons. Secondly, predictive methods are usually based on labeled examples or mathematical models which were not available. Moreover, predicting of problems could not avoid all shutdowns and, therefore, it would still be necessary to manage emergencies. Most existing alarm management approaches focus either on post-crisis information analysis (first strategy) or on more automation procedures (second strategy) [3,9,11]. None addresses the challenge of assisting operators to make sense of the situation DURING crisis scenarios.

Since our goal is to provide assistance during crisis, our system must be designed as a real-time application. We have investigated many different approaches in different industries (oil and electric power), such as conventional centralized structures [1,5,12,13], decentralized applications [2] and multi-agent system [3,6,8,9,11], but the last approach the best results concerning response time and flexibility to grow the application.

3   MAS for Alarm Management System

An emergency shutdown (SD) in a process plant unit is a safety measure, in general, triggered by automation systems (AS) to protect the equipment, the system, people operating the system and the environment. Each SD triggers a set of events designed by the automation designers to protect the unit. For example, during a shutdown of a specific equipment, it is expected that this equipment be contained and isolated from the rest. In order to accomplish these effects, the automation procedure imposes the closing of upstream and downstream valves. When shutting down a system or even the entire unit, many more events should be triggered. Of course, these events interact with each other and further automation procedures must specify the desired interactions. At the same time sensors monitor parameters' values for undesirable situations, sometimes these undesirable situations are the expected ones. For instance, a fast pressure drop downstream a pump might represent a pump cavity danger. However, the same information when associated with a pump turn-off means a correct and desirable behavior. As noted, in an emergency situation, a great deal of information is generated. It is extremely useful to establish priorities to set which alarms are actually important to be displayed to operators.

This scenario is very suited to agent architecture: each equipment, system or even a component can be modeled as autonomous agents. A sensor would be an agent, as well as valves, pumps, compressors, etc. An agent must know the effect of its good or ill behavior. If something unexpected occurs the agent can report the problem together with alarms which support its conclusion. But, there could be other agents which would be responsible for more complex diagnoses that could be based on the reasoning of other agents. For example, a vessel would be considered contained if all inlet and outlet valves are completely closed. In this case, each valve corresponds to a different agent responsible for diagnosing the actual state of the valves and the vessel to an agent responsible to diagnose the actual state of the vessel. The vessel agent reasoning rests on the diagnoses of the valve agents.

The differences between configurations of process plants is another key aspect which points towards the agents technology. Although the set of equipments of a process plant can not be dynamically changed, it can be changed over time or operated with different sets of active equipments. Moreover, two petroleum offshore units can be very different in terms of its process plant. Once Oil companies have to manage many different petroleum offshore unit, systems for asset management and control should be easily configurable and scalable. Agents technology perfectly fits in this kind of engineering problems due to the main characteristics of agents: autonomous reasoning, proactivity, configurability and scalability. During the years researchers have come to the conclusion that reactivity is also a very important characteristic that an intelligent agent should possess [7]. Reactivity is suitable for changing environments performing an appropriate response to some changes which have been recognized and perceived [10].

The objective of our approach is to work as an alarm information filter, receiving and sorting information sent by the automation supervisor system (AS), during a serious non-planned process plant shutdown, called here simply as STOP. This STOP situation causes an avalanche of alarm information. It is humanly impossible for process plant operators to understand not only what is happening with the process plant, but also, and more importantly, if it is being moving to a safe state, i.e. if the plant is properly being turned off. Thus, our proposed system can be seen as a assisted-stop system. The operator should only receive information related to unexpected alarms or danger degree escalation that may compromise the safety of the unit.

3.1 MAS Architecture

The Agents paradigm provides an excellent modeling abstraction for our intelligent alarm management system due to agent's human-like characteristics, including reasoning, proactivity, communication and adaptive behavior. Moreover, Alarm Management Systems in Emergency Situations beg for technologies that are transparent, so that the functional behavior in an emergency situation can be easily understood by operators.

Our model, illustrated in Fig. 1, represents an intelligent support system for alarms management in an offshore oil production domain. The MAS architecture is composed of four types of agents: Environment Agent, Automation Agent, Log Handler Agent, Log Analyser Agent and Blackboard Agent. The agents main functionalities are the following:

- **Environment Agent:** This agent monitors information from nature. It also manages information regarding the Oil Production Platform status such us the identification of a SD.
- **Automation Agent:** Automation System (AS). Events and alarms continuously monitored and identified by sensors embedded in the equipments

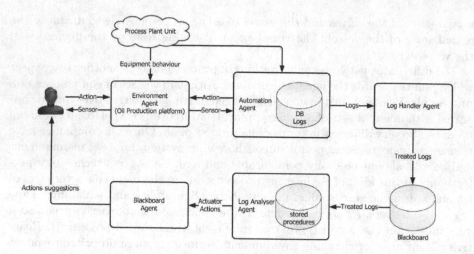

Fig. 1. Multi-Agent Architecture

are sent to the automation system (AS). Later, the AS triggers Actuators (pumps, valves, compressors, etc.) for actions (open/close, turn-on/turn-off). This agent creates a log of events which are sent to the Log Handler Agent.

- **Log Handler Agent:** This agent reads and parses the log of events in the blackboard to create structured information that can be further analyzed.
- **Log Analyser Agent:** This agent is actually a set of agents. Each agent understands about a equipment. Each agent selects, from the structured information stored in the blackboard, only the information that concerns its expertise. Its knowledge is written in terms of production rules describing expected and unexpected behaviors. Expected behaviors triggers an alarm information suppression action, that means an information removal from the blackboard.
- **Blackboard Agent:** This agent handles information that will be displayed to operators. It must handle information synchronization since many agents are reading and writing into its structure. It invokes the GUI where alarms information are shown to the final operator.

3.2   Ontology

We model the process plant domain using an ontology that emphasizes the component and monitoring characteristics of the artifact. Modeling this environment involves representing entities and relationships among these entities. The main concepts of the ontology and its description are as follows.

- **Equipment:** It is a component of a process plant.
- **Actuator:** It is a device, such as valves, pumps and compressors, which controls the equipment behavior.

- **Equipment behavior:** It represents the way the equipment behaves in order to achieve a desired functionality. Equipment behavior is measured through sensors.
- **Event:** It is an action over the actuators that might causes a change in the state of the alarm. For instance, the event "close" over the actuator "valve" should cause a decrease on oil flow in the pipeline.
- **Alarm:** It represents an abnormal state of the equipment behavior. The possible values are High (H), Very High (HH), Low (L) or Very Low (LL). HH and LL leads to equipment and even the entire unit shut down
- **Sensor:** It is a device that measures control variables.
- **Control Variable Status:** It indicates the variation of a measurement. A control variable status indicates for instance if the temperature is increasing.

An equipment is part of a process plant. Equipment achieves its goals though a set of behaviors such as oil level, pressure, temperature and flow that are monitored by sensors. Alarm is a special type of sensor that indicates an equipment behavior overtake danger threshold values. There are four types of alarms: Very high, high, low and very low alarm. There is also analogic sensors that measure the exact value of a given behavior. Automation controls equipment behaviors though events changing actuators status such as pump turn-off. Valves, pumps and compressors are examples of actuators.

3.3   Stored Procedure

The automation agent continuously harvest data from environment agents to identify emergencies and trigger shutdowns. It also sends harvested data to the Log Handler agent in the form of text messages.

The Log Handler agent interprets data from the automation system, filters useful data and publishes treated data in a blackboard which is stored in a relational table (see Fig. 2.a). Log Handler agents are platform specific because the syntactic rules of messages may vary between offshore units. It discards repeated messages, extracts structured data from unstructured messages, validate chronology of messages and identify the element (valve, pump, etc.) that messages refers to.

There are one analyser agent for each environment agent that should be monitored, i.e. a valve has a corresponding analyser which diagnoses its failures. If the valve does not close or open when it should do, its analyser publishes diagnoses and suggestions of actions to operators in the blackboard. The blackboard agent, then, filters what is important.

The rules are propositional implications in the conjunctive normal form where each clause states variable transitions or states of alarms, actuators and variables. It is stored in a relational table (see Fig. 2.b) as well. The inferences currently done are checking of actual state of valves, pumps, compressors, etc. and danger degree escalation. Danger degree escalation is when fire or gas leak happens in the same area of the initiator of the SD. The inferences of each agent can be accomplished through a set of relational operations over the two mentioned relations as shown in Fig. 2.c.

	BLACKBOARD		
DATE		OBJECT	OBSERVED
22-JAN-2010 23:37:00		ESD-2	INITIATED
22-JAN-2010 23:38:00		SDV1	CLOSED
22-JAN-2010 23:39:00		LVL-SG1	DECREASED
22-JAN-2010 23:41:00		PRS-SDV1	MAINTAINED

a)

	RULES		
ACTUATOR	TP	OBJECT	EXPECTED
SDV1	UB	LVL-SG1	DECREASE
SDV1	UB	SDV1	OPEN
SDV1	EB	LVL-SG1	NOT DECREASE
SDV1	EB	PRS-B1	DECREASE
SDV1	...		
B1	...		

b)

R1 $\leftarrow \sigma_{object=SDV122303}$ (RULES)

R2 $\leftarrow$ R1 $\bowtie$ BLACKBOARD

R3 $\leftarrow \Pi_{tp,if(obsserved=expected,true,false)}$ (R2)

R4 $\leftarrow \rho_{R3(tp,value)}$ (R3)

R5 $\leftarrow \sigma_{tp=UB}$ (R4)

R6 $\leftarrow \mathcal{G} OR_{value}$ (R5)

R7 $\leftarrow \sigma_{tp=EB}$ (R4)

R8 $\leftarrow \mathcal{G} AND_{value}$ (R7)

R10 $\leftarrow \Pi_{tp,not(value)}$ (R8)

R11 $\leftarrow \rho_{R3(tp,value)}$ (R10)

R12 $\leftarrow \mathcal{G} AND_{value}$ (R6 $\cup$ R11)

FALHA $\leftarrow \Pi_{value}$ (R12)

c)

Fig. 2. Agents processing

The rules for all agents are fed by automation experts though a special knowledge acquisition interface (not included in the main model) and stored in the knowledge-base. There are two types of rules: those depending only on the status of each equipment behavior and those that depend on a combination of equipments' behaviors. Therefore, there is a rule chain.

The log handler, analysers and blackboard agents are all implemented using stored procedures. This strategy allows for the designer of the system to easily distribute processing as needed taking advantage of database replication. To do so the designer has to setup the replication of the blackboard and rules relations and distribute the analyser agent procedures across the database replicas as needed. The log handler and blackboard agents can also be duplicated to increase robustness and decrease the probability of data loss of event log.

4   Case Study

Now we are going deeper into more details about the agents behavior. The environment and automation agents will not be covered because they do not differ from existing automation systems. As example of how to automatically manage alarms consider an atmospheric separator SG1 (see Fig. 3), which is part of a process plant. It is an equipment is which petroleum is separated into oil and gas. It is equipped with three sensors and four alarms that keep track of the level inside the vessel and a valve SDV1 (see Fig. 3) in the oil outlet of SG1. The sensors and alarms of the separator detect and indicate if the level is very high, high, normal, low and very low. When level is very high or very low the automation system triggers a shutdown, i.e. the AS takes a set of actions that

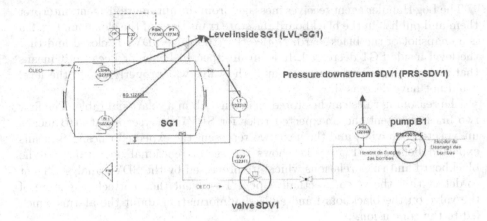

Fig. 3. Agents processing

stops the production process of the platform. One of the actions is to close the SDV1. It may happen that, because of the wear of the valve or malfunctioning of closing mechanism, the valve closes but do not completely seal the oil outlet or even do not close properly as commanded by automation system.

Then, the alarm management system has to extract from operational data (event logs) clues that could indicate that the valve is closed after a shutdown is initiated, otherwise the platform would be in an unsafe state until the valve is closed. Of course there will be other actions such as close the inlet valve of oil and the outlet valve of gas, but this actions will be monitored by other agents similarly.

Analysing the schema of the separator it can be seen that if the valve is closed it is unexpected that the valve will not declare itself closed. In the platform control system which we were dealing with all actuators declared its state. It is unexpected, as well, that the level inside SG1 will decrease. On the other hand, it is expected that the level will not decrease, i.e. will increase or maintain, depending on the state of the inlet valve. It is expected that pressure downstream SDV1 (see Fig. 3) decreases as well. The agent can then reason on observations of what is unexpected and expected and diagnose what is the actual state of the valve. If nothing unexpected has happened and everything expected have happened then the valve would be considered closed otherwise it might be open.

We propose to specify both unexpected and expected behavior rules. To better understand why, note that in the previous example the valve could be partially open, but an inlet flow could be compensating an outlet flow so that the level remains the same, i.e. the level will not decrease as unexpected behavior rules require. In this case, valve opening would only be detected by checking pressure downstream the valve in the expected behavior rule. Moreover, in terms of knowledge acquisition to configure reasoning rules of agents this approach facilitates one to remember what should be checked. If we want to assure that something was done it is natural to think in terms of what was unexpected and expected to happen.

The Log Handler agent receives messages from the automation agent, interpret them and publish in the blackboard the state transitions of the elements. Fig. 2.a is a snapshot of the blackboard. Notice that the valve SDV1 is closed and that the level inside SG1 decreased. It is an unexpected behavior because it means that level inside SG1 decreased, but if the valve was properly closed the level could not have decreased.

The reasoning rules can be stored as in Fig. 2.b in a relational table. The first two lines represent the unexpected rules for SDV1 analyser agent (UB means unexpected behavior) and the next two represent the expected rules (EB means expected behavior). Figure 2.c shows the set of relational operations on the blackboard and rules relations which are processed by the SDV1 analyser agent to detect that the valve is actually open. The agent then corrects the state of the valve on the blackboard and adds the information about the alarms which led to the conclusion.

We have tested the system in an environment where the automation agent generated up to 30 messages/second during a shutdown and that there was 200 analyser agents. The measured load capacity of the log handler agent was 40 messages/second and the average processing time for each analyser agent was 7 milliseconds.

	SHUT DOWN EXECUTION				ALARMS			
ESD	Date	ESD type	Begin	End	Total	Suppressed	Presented	% Suppresed
1	22/1/10	ESD-2	23:42:25:40	23:44:01:26	71	65	6	91,55%
2	22/1/10	ESD-2	23:45:36:06	23:47:59:22	58	52	6	89,66%
3	22/1/10	ESD-2	23:50:22:40	23:52:46:05	33	33	0	100,00%
4	30/3/10	ESD-2	13:34:15.84	13:35:59.34	27	27	0	100,00%
5	30/3/10	ESD-2	13:39:28.64	13:41:09.18	12	12	0	100,00%
6	19/4/10	ESD-3T	19:21:52.85	19:23:21.77	86	81	5	94,19%
7	20/4/10	ESD-3T	0:07:30.38	00:09:13.24	41	37	4	90,24%
8	19/5/10	ESD-3T	10:57:40.56	10:59:51.36	46	38	8	82,61%
9	18/6/10	ESD-3T	20:16:00.19	20:21:20.20	113	108	5	95,58%

Fig. 4. Results. Alarms suppressed

Figure 4 shows the results of the analyses of data from 9 SDs. The last column represents the percentage of alarm suppression. As shown, there are scenarios of 93,76

5   Conclusions

In this paper, we have presented an alarm management system that provides a solution for improving operators' situation awareness during emergency situations in offshore oil platforms. Oil process plant is a complex artifact composed of independent subparts that interacts with each other. The results of initial experiments run in our research lab using actual data information coming from SD scenarios have shown that only 6 percent of the total of the alarms were visualized to the operator which is an outstanding result. Additionally, operators confirmed that the suppressed information was unnecessary.

References

1. Aizpurua, O., Galan, R., Jimenez, A.: A new cognitive-based massive alarm management system in electrical power administration. In: 2008 7th International Caribbean Conference on Devices, Circuits and Systems, pp. 1–6. IEEE (April 2008)
2. Cochran, T., Bullemer, P., Nimmo, I.: Managing abnormal situations in the process industries parts 1, 2, 3. In: NIST Proceedings of the Motor Vehicle Manufacturing Technology (MVMT) Workshop (1997)
3. Dheedan, A., Papadopoulos, Y.: Model-Based Distributed On-line Safety Monitoring. In: The Third International Conference on Emerging Network Intelligence (EMERGING 2011), Lisbon, Portugal, pp. 1–7 (2011)
4. Health and Safety Executive: The Explosion and Fires at the Texaco Refinery, Milford Haven, 24 July 1994 (Incident Report). HSE Books (1997)
5. Heydt, G.T., Vittal, V., Phadke, A.G.: The strategic power infrastructure defense (SPID) system. A conceptual design. IEEE Control Systems 20(4), 40–52 (2000)
6. Hossack, J.A., Menal, J., McArthur, S.D.J., McDonald, J.R.: A multiagent architecture for protection engineering diagnostic assistance. In: 2003 IEEE Power Engineering Society General Meeting (IEEE Cat. No.03CH37491), vol. 2, p. 640. IEEE (2003)
7. Kornelije, R.: A Combination of Reactive and Deliberative Agents in Hospital Logistics. In: Proceedings of 17th International Conference on Information and Intelligent Systems, Croatia, pp. 63–70 (2006)
8. McArthur, S.D.J., Strachan, S.M., Jahn, G.: The Design of a Multi-Agent Transformer Condition Monitoring System. IEEE Transactions on Power Systems 19(4), 1845–1852 (2004)
9. Mendoza, B., Xu, P., Song, L.: A multi-agent model for fault diagnosis in petrochemical plants. In: 2011 IEEE Sensors A Applications Symposium, pp. 203–208. IEEE (February 2011)
10. Rabuzin, K., Malekovic, M., Cubrilo, M.: Resolving Physical Conflicts in Multiagent Systems. In: 2008 The Third International Multi-Conference on Computing in the Global Information Technology (iccgi 2008), pp. 193–199. IEEE (July 2008)
11. Sayda, A.F., Taylor, J.H.: Toward a Practical Multi-Agent System for Integrated Control and Asset Management of Petroleum Production Facilities. In: 2007 IEEE 22nd International Symposium on Intelligent Control, pp. 511–517. IEEE (2007)
12. Skogdalen, J.E., Vinnem, J.E.: Combining precursor incidents investigations and QRA in oil and gas industry. Reliability Engineering & System Safety 101, 48–58 (2012)
13. Zarri, G.P.: Knowledge representation and inference techniques to improve the management of gas and oil facilities. Knowledge-Based Systems 24(7), 989–1003 (2011)

Simulating Data Journalism to Communicate Hydrological Information from Sensor Networks

Martin Molina

Department of Artificial Intelligence
Technical University of Madrid, Spain
martin.molina@upm.es

Abstract. Presenting relevant information via web-based user friendly interfaces makes the information more accessible to the general public. This is especially useful for sensor networks that monitor natural environments. Adequately communicating this type of information helps increase awareness about the limited availability of natural resources and promotes their better use with sustainable practices. In this paper, I suggest an approach to communicating this information to wide audiences based on simulating data journalism using artificial intelligence techniques. I analyze this approach by describing a pioneer knowledge-based system called VSAIH, which looks for news in hydrological data from a national sensor network in Spain and creates news stories that general users can understand. VSAIH integrates artificial intelligence techniques, including a model-based data analyzer and a presentation planner. In the paper, I also describe characteristics of the hydrological national sensor network and the technical solutions applied by VSAIH to simulate data journalism.

Keywords: sensor networks, automated data journalism, intelligent knowledge-based system, multimedia-presentation system, computational sustainability.

1   Introduction

Sensor networks for monitoring natural environments usually generate important data that many potential users can use. Monitoring water in natural environments can help different types of users (e.g., municipalities, civil protection, consultants, scientist researchers or educators) make decisions related to agriculture, hydroelectric energy production, flood risk or climate change.

In general, it is important to communicate this type of information appropriately to increase the awareness of the limited availability of natural resources (i.e., water) and promote their better use with sustainable practices. It is thus useful to have web applications that make the information more accessible to the general public. However, these applications are often difficult to use because they present low-level information without adequate data interpretations and explanations.

In this paper, I describe an approach to improve communicating this type of information to wide audiences. This approach is based on data journalism, a professional practice in which journalists look for news in databases (usually online databases) and create a story understandable and useful to the general public.

J. Pavón et al. (Eds.): IBERAMIA 2012, LNAI 7637, pp. 722–731, 2012.

I suggest the idea of using artificial intelligence techniques to simulate data journalism and improve sensor data communication. I analyze this approach by describing a pioneer system called VSAIH, which looks for news using hydrological data from a national sensor network in Spain and creates news stories that are potentially useful to different types of users. VSAIH integrates artificial intelligence techniques, including a model-based data analyzer and presentation planner, to generate descriptions.

The remainder of this paper describes a national hydrological sensor network. I then describe how VSAIH simulates data journalism to communicate hydrological information from the sensor network.

2   A National Sensor Network

In Spain, there is a national hydrological sensor network called SAIH (SAIH is the Spanish acronym for Hydrological Automatic Information System) [6]. The SAIH network measures real-time hydrological data using thousands of sensors geographically distributed in rivers and basins in Spain. SAIH is a mature infrastructure that has collected hydrological data for over 20 years.

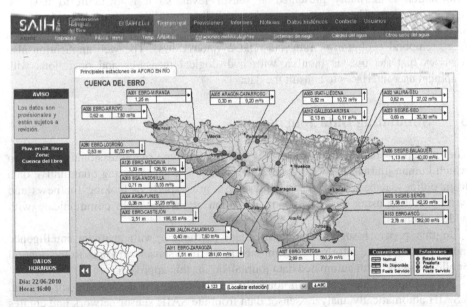

Fig. 1. Web application of the Ebro basin (provided by the *Confederación Hidrográfica del Ebro* in Spain)

The entire SAIH network is divided into nine sub-networks according to the main basins in Spain (e.g., Ebro, Tajo, Júcar). There are nine control centers in Spain, one for each sub-network. The information is recorded periodically and sent to the control centers (e.g., every 30 or 15 minutes). Control centers process and store the data in local databases. The Ministry of Environment of Spain coordinates the control centers and integrates the recorded data into a global database.

The SAIH system includes the following main types of sensors: pluviometers to measure rainfall at a certain geographic place, flow stations to measure water flow in river channels, level stations located at reservoirs or at river channels to measure the water level and volume stations located at reservoirs to measure the volume of stored water. The SAIH network also includes other sensors (e.g., sensors for gates in reservoirs, snow level) and telecommunication devices (e.g., radio emitter-receiver systems, optical fiber networks).

Because many users can use the data recorded by the SAIH network, the Ministry of Environment of Spain and the local governments related to the control centers created open web applications to help users freely consult the data. Figure 1 shows an example of a web application for one of the nine SAIH sub-networks (the Ebro basin). This screen shows a map of the Ebro basin where a user can consult real-time data about water flows and levels in rivers. It uses natural and intuitive presentations with graphics (usually maps and 2D charts for time series).

However, this type of web application presents some limitations when communicating information to general users. One main limitation is that the information is normally presented at sensor level, so it is difficult to have an aggregated view. The user must search sensor-by-sensor, consulting individual time series. It is difficult for the user to see the aggregated behavior of related information (e.g., temporal evolution of rain and related water flows). The web application also assumes that the user is familiar with hydrological measures and operations with graphical user interfaces to consult the data.

3   Simulating Data Journalism

The concept of data journalism [3, 11] identifies a type of professional practice in which human journalists look for news in databases (e.g., analyzing quantitative data from online databases). In general, journalists are experts at looking for news and writing stories using particular communication styles that help communicate with wide audiences.

In this paper, I suggest simulating data journalism with artificial intelligence methods to improve information communication from sensor networks to the general public. I use the term automated data journalism for this approach.

An example of automated data journalism in hydrology is the VSAIH application. VSAIH automatically analyzes sensor data from the SAIH sensor network and creates news stories that summarize relevant information. VSAIH generates news according to three different goals: flood risk management, water management, and sensor validation. These types of news are distributed in geographic areas according to the main river basins in Spain. There are ten areas that correspond to nine areas for sub-networks plus another geographic area for the whole nation. VSAIH thus includes 3 goals x 10 areas = 30 news generators.

Each generated piece of news follows the typical journalistic style used in newspapers. There is a headline that summarizes the main idea in a short sentence, and the body text develops the story to answer the usual journalistic questions (e.g., who, what, where) with evidential facts to support the affirmations. In this domain, it is important to provide adequate evidence presenting the actual sensor measures to help users trust the system's descriptions.

Flow above normal in the Jerte river at El Torno
  The Jerte River at El Torno has a recorded flow of 38 m3/s, which represents an increase of 8 m3/s compared to the previous hour. The normal flow at this point of the river is 5 m3/s. With respect to this flow, the following hydrological behavior can be highlighted. It has rained in the Tajo Basin over the past 24 hours. Cabezuela del Valle is the location with maximum rainfall over the past 24 hours with a value of 24 mm. The rainfall at Las Becillas was 22 mm, and the rainfall at Los Angeles Casar was 21 mm. The Jerte Reservoir at Plasencia has a recorded volume increase of 1.44 Hm3 over the past 24 hours.

Fig. 2. Generated summary related to flood risk management

Figure 2 shows an example of a generated news story related to flood risk management (it is a translation from the original Spanish text in Fig. 3). The headline describes that there is high flow in a river. The body text follows a discourse that gives answers to questions such as what (high flow), which hydrologic component (the Jerte river), and where (at El Torno). The body text gives information to help explain the causes (places with significant rain in the previous 24 hours).

In general, the text presents a qualitative interpretation of hydrological quantities (e.g., high flows, moderate rain). The description shows quantitative measures recorded by sensors, which are contrasted with other values (previous hour and normal value) to help quantify the relevance of the situation. The text also shows spatial and temporal aggregations, including maximum flow values in rivers and cumulative rain amounts in the previous 24 hours.

The news is presented to the user on a user interface designed as a digital newspaper. Many users are familiar with this type of presentation, so this design helps facilitate communication with a wide audience. The digital newspaper includes a first page that summarizes the most relevant news. The user can select a news story to display on a new page with more details. Figure 3 shows an example page. Tabs at the top of the page allow the user to select different types of news.

Most news includes graphics complementing the text descriptions. The presented graphics depend on the content of the news. There are maps with highlighted geographic points to show, for example, the spatial location of river sections with certain flow or places with significant rain. The points on the map are related to the text descriptions using hyperlinks. This helps the user better understand the text description (especially when the user is not familiar with certain geographic areas). There are also charts to show time series that describe temporal measure behaviors. There are also graphical animations that show information from meteorological radar or image satellites.

Fig. 3. Sample presentation page generated by the VSAIH application (Fig. 2 shows English translation)

4   The VSAIH Architecture

To generate news, VSAIH simulates two main tasks: (1) analyzing hydrological data, and (2) generating presentations to effectively communicate the news to general users. To support these tasks, the VSAIH architecture follows a knowledge-based approach with three knowledge models for the system, abstraction and presentation [12]. The system model represents the set of river basins in Spain. This model follows a component-based approach using single components (e.g., river sections, reservoirs, geographic places where the rain is measured) and aggregated components (e.g., rivers, basins) with quantitative attributes and qualitative states.

The system model is used to analyze sensor data with an abstraction model, which uses logic- and rule-based representations to abstract data. Abstraction is important for generating headlines and concise descriptions in the body text. Abstraction includes the following more specific tasks: interpret quantitative data (i.e., the value of flow 362 m3/s means an above-normal flow in the Segre river), select the most relevant states (i.e., a flow above normal is more relevant than light rain), aggregate information (i.e., the Guadalhorce river and Limonero reservoir are part of the Andalusian basin), and generalize properties (i.e., the qualitative states light rain and heavy rain can be generalized by the qualitative state rain).

VSAIH uses a particular notion of relevance to filter data. The degree of relevance of a state is directly proportional to the distance between the current and normal (or desirable) states. Relevance is thus context-dependent. A low water level in rivers or reservoirs is a desirable state for flood risk, but it is not desirable for water management (e.g., for agriculture or hydroelectric energy production).

PATTERN: *describe_with_causes_and_effects*
GOAL: *inform(x)*
CONDITIONS: *causes(x, c)* ∧ *effects(y, e)*
DISCOURSE: {*summarize_state(x)*, *elaborate_state(x)*,
                       elaborate_causes(c), *elaborate_effects(e)*}

PATTERN: *describe_state_of_single_component*
GOAL: *elaborate_state(x)*
CONDITIONS: *(state(y, s)* ∈ *x)* ∧ *single_component(y)* ∧ *quantity(y, q)*
DISCOURSE: {*elaborate_with_quantity(y, q)*,
                       contrast_to_previous (y, q),
                       contrast_to_average(y, q)}

Fig. 4. Example discourse patterns

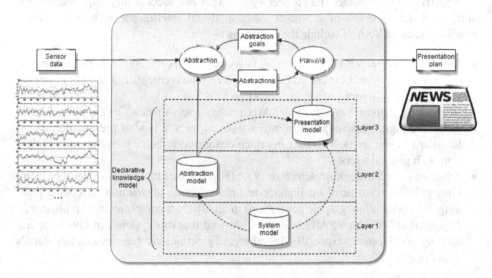

Fig. 5. Main VSAIH architecture components

VSAIH also uses a presentation model to generate the final descriptions. This model is represented as the knowledge base of a hierarchical planner following an HTN approach [8]. The model represents discourse strategies (called discourse patterns) to present the information. Figure 4 shows example discourse patterns. The planner generates the text description using partial text templates that are combined according to the hierarchical planning process. The planner also decides the most appropriate graphic to combine with texts (e.g., map or animation).

Figure 5 summarizes the main components of the VSAIH architecture. It includes the three models (the system, abstraction and presentation models) organized in three layers. The figure shows the main processes at the top (data analysis and presentation planning) and input/output relationships.

VSAIH generates news every hour using approximately 45,000 numerical measures (each page is generated in under 30 seconds). The first operational version of VSAIH was installed online in June 2008 using models corresponding to 3 river basins (Ebro, Segura and South of Spain). A second version was installed in May 2010 with improvements to the user interface and models corresponding to 9 river basins.

5   Discussion

Simulating data journalism can be an adequate solution for better communicating relevant information from sensor networks. VSAIH follows this approach to communicate information about water to a wide audience, using data measured by a national sensor network and presenting general descriptions that are useful for water management (e.g., for agriculture and energy production) and flood risk.

VSAIH can be considered a pioneer system that has successfully implemented the automated data journalism approach using artificial intelligence techniques. Some characteristics of VSAIH include the following:

- *News generators.* VSAIH includes 30 news generators to capture different types of news according to different goals (e.g., water management, risk floods or sensor validation in different geographic areas).
- *Interactive graphic newspaper.* VSAIH presents sets of news in an automatically generated digital newspaper with interactive graphics, a type of presentation that is familiar to most users. This user interface design contributes to better communication with general users.
- *Efficient computational architecture.* VSAIH processes thousands of sensors, combining different artificial intelligence techniques (e.g., abstraction, discourse planning, text generation, graphic generation) in an efficient computational architecture.
- *Practical utility.* The VSAIH evaluation showed that this system can save to operators up to 5 hours, especially in emergency situations (see evaluation details in [12]).

We are currently working on more advanced approaches to simulate data journalism. In general, our future work aims to design more general and flexible solutions. One challenge in designing this type of application is finding a balance between its efficiency (combining different AI techniques) and its generality and flexibility.

VSAIH efficiently generates text descriptions using a hierarchical planner with partial text templates. Instead of using templates, natural language generation techniques could provide more flexibility when generating descriptions [16, 17]. We are applying natural language generation techniques to automatically generate more complex and reusable narratives and geographic references [13]. We are also interested in identifying and formalizing discourses applicable to different domains.

VSAIH represents the hydrologic network using a system model following a component-approach. This is useful for certain sensor networks similar to the SAIH network. However, other networks (e.g., domains with moving sensors) can require different representations (e.g., event-based approaches) [14].

We are also interested in using general components for data analysis. VSAIH uses a particular data analyzer that was designed for this purpose. However, it is possible to use software libraries (for spatial and temporal reasoning) and tools (e.g., Weka or R) to implement data analyzers. Online data sources can help facilitate the development of data analyzers, thus reusing domain knowledge (e.g., geographic knowledge such as Open Street Maps [19]).

Finally, VSAIH presents the information using text in combination with graphics. Hyperlinks relate part of the text to the graphics. The relation between text and graphics could be improved with more flexible coordination, using solutions proposed in multimedia presentation systems [1].

6   Related Work

In general, researchers have explored the idea of combining computer systems and journalism from different perspectives. Computational journalism is a general field that involves applying information technologies to journalism activities [4, 7].

A more specific approach is summarizing news from documents by applying text summarization techniques and web mining [15]. This approach contrasts to the goal of VSAIH, as VSAIH automatically creates news stories by analyzing non-linguistic data instead of summarizing news from different documents.

The goal of a recent project called Stats Monkey is to develop a news generator for baseball games. This generator is similar to the news generators in VSAIH. Stats Monkey was initiated in 2009 and seems to apply a statistics-based approach with text templates[1] [10]. In contrast, VSAIH is an operational system, first installed online in 2008, that follows a complex knowledge-based approach with a collection of 30 news generators. Each news generator uses a model-based data analyzer and a hierarchical planner. VSAIH also includes a dynamically generated multimedia user interface as a multi-page digital newspaper to present the collection of generated news.

The VSAIH architecture includes components that are present in intelligent multimedia presentation systems [1] (e.g., presentation planning, text generation). Bateman et al. [2] explore how to automatically construct the page layout (using rhetorical relationships and design heuristics) with the $Dart_{bio}$ prototype. VSAIH uses a presentation planner to select the best page layout (from a prefixed set of layouts), which can efficiently and flexibly combine different types of text descriptions and graphics.

---

[1] We have not found scientific publications related to this project or an operational web application. It is thus difficult to know the degree of success of this project.

The text generation in VSAIH is similar to the goal of data-to-text systems, which generate natural language text from non-linguistic data [9, 18]. Compared to other data-to-text systems, VSAIH can generate complex narratives (with rhetorical relationships such as contrast, exemplify, cause and elaboration) because it uses a model-based data analyzer and a discourse planner with discourse patterns. As mentioned above, VSAIH uses text templates, i.e., it does not apply advanced natural language generation techniques that could provide more flexibility to the generated sentences.

VSAIH uses a system model to capture qualitative descriptions, as in physical reasoning [5]. As a main difference from other qualitative reasoning approaches, the VSAIH representation is designed to simulate abstraction instead of other tasks that require more precision (e.g., diagnosis or prediction). Compared to qualitative reasoning representations, the VSAIH representation is simpler and thus more efficient for both inference and knowledge acquisition.

7   Conclusions

Sensor networks for monitoring natural resources usually generate large amounts of data that are useful for many users. Monitoring water in natural environments can help different types of users, e.g., municipalities, civil protection, consultants, scientific researchers and educators, make decisions related to agriculture, energy production and flood risk. An adequate communication of this type of information can help increase awareness about the limited availability of natural resources and promote their better use with sustainable practices.

In this paper, I argue that simulating data journalism with artificial intelligence techniques can help communicate information from sensor networks to the general public. I illustrate this concept with the VSAIH system, a successful pioneer web-based application that follows this approach in hydrology.

VSAIH generates news from thousands of hydrological sensors using 30 specialized news generators and presents the news on a dynamically generated user interface designed as a digital newspaper. VSAIH combines an intelligent data analyzer using a model-based approach and a presentation planner to generate text-graphic presentations.

This type of solution has great applicability, especially for sensor networks that monitor natural environments. Our future research in this area aims to build general and flexible solutions that can help developers implement this type of application in different domains.

Acknowledgements. The research leading to these results has received funding from the European Union Seventh Framework Programme (FP7/2007-2013) under grant agreement PIOF-GA-2009-253331 (Project INTERACTIVEX). This work was also partially supported by the Ministry of Science and Innovation of Spain within the VIOMATICA project (TIN2008-05837). This work was also possible thanks to the support of the Ministry of Environment of Spain (*Dirección General del Agua, Ministerio de Medio Ambiente, Medio Rural y Marino*).

References

1. André, E.: The Generation of Multimedia Presentations. In: Dale, R., Moisl, H., Somers, H. (eds.) A Handbook of Natural Language Processing Techniques and Applications for the Processing of Language as Text, pp. 305–327. Marcel Dekker Inc., New York (2000)
2. Bateman, J., Kleinz, J., Kamps, T., Reichenberger, K.: Towards Constructive Text, Diagram, and Layout Generation for Information Presentation. Computational Linguistics 27(3), 409–449 (2001)
3. Bradshaw, P.: How to Be a Data Journalist. The Guardian (October 1, 2010)
4. Cohen, S., Li, C., Yang, J., Yu, C.: Computational Journalism A Call to Arms to Database Researchers. In: 5th Biennial Conference on Innovative Data Systems Research (CIDR 2011), pp. 148–151 (2011)
5. Davis, E.: Physical Reasoning. In: van Harmelen, F., Lifschitz, V., Porter, B. (eds.) Handbook of Knowledge Representation, pp. 597–620. Elsevier, Oxford (2007)
6. Dirección General del Agua: El Programa S.A.I.H. – Descripción y Funcionalidad, el Presente y el Futuro del Sistema. Ministerio de Medio Ambiente y Medio Rural y Marino (Spain) (2009), http://www.mma.es
7. Flew, T., Daniel, A., Spurgeon, C., Swift, A.: The Promise of Computational Journalism. Journalistic Practice 6(2), 157–161 (2012)
8. Ghallab, M., Nau, D., Traverso, P.: Automated Planning: Theory and Practice. Morgan Kaufmann (2004)
9. Hunter, J., Gatt, A., Portet, F., Reiter, E., Sripada, S.: Using Natural Language Generation Technology to Improve Information Flows in Intensive Care Units. In: 18th European Conference on Artificial Intelligence (ECAI 2008), pp. 678–682 (2008)
10. Infolab. Intelligent Information Laboratory at Northwestern University. Stats Monkey project (2012), http://infolab.northwestern.edu/projects/stats-monkey/
11. Lorenz, M.: Data Driven Journalism: What is There to Learn? In: Innovation Journalism Conference (IJ-7), Stanford, CA, June 7-9 (2010), http://datadrivenjournalism.net
12. Molina, M., Flores, V.: Generating Multimedia Presentations that Summarize the Behavior of Dynamic Systems Using a Model-Based Approach. Expert Systems with Applications 39, 2759–2770 (2012)
13. Molina, M., Stent, A.: A Knowledge-Based Method for Generating Summaries of Spatial Movement in Geographic Areas. International Journal on Artificial Intelligence Tools 19(4), 393–415 (2010)
14. Molina, M., Stent, A., Parodi, E.: Generating Automated News to Explain the Meaning of Sensor Data. In: Gama, J., Bradley, E., Hollmén, J. (eds.) IDA 2011. LNCS, vol. 7014, pp. 282–293. Springer, Heidelberg (2011)
15. Radev, D.R., Otterbacher, J., Winkel, A., Blair-Goldensohn, S.: NewsInEssence Summarizing Online News Topics. Communications of the ACM 48(10), 95–98 (2005)
16. Reiter, E.: NLG vs. Templates. In: 5th European Workshop on Natural Language Generation (1995)
17. Reiter, E., Dale, R.: Building Natural Language Generation Systems. Cambridge University Press, Cambridge (2000)
18. Reiter, E., Sripada, S., Hunter, J., Yu, J., Davy, I.: Choosing Words in Computer-Generated Weather Forecasts. Artificial Intelligence 67(1-2), 137–169 (2005)
19. Roth, M., Frank, A.: A NLG-based application for walking direction. In: ACL-IJCNLP 2009 Software Demonstrations (ACLDemos 2009), pp. 37–40 (2009)

Method Based on Context-Information to Improve User Experience on Mobile Web-Based Applications

Jordán Pascual Espada[1], Vicente García-Díaz[1], Rubén González Crespo[2],
Carlos Enrique Montenegro Marin[3], Oscar Sanjuán Martínez[4],
B. Cristina Pelayo García-Bustelo[1], and Juan Manuel Cueva Lovelle[1]

[1] Department of Computer Science, University of Oviedo, Asturias, Spain
{pascualjordan,garciavicente,cris.pelayo,cueva}@uniovi.es
[2] Department of Computer Science, Pontifical University of Salamanca, Madrid, Spain
ruben.gonzalez@upsam.es
[3] Universidad Distrital Francisco José de Caldas, Bogota, Colombia
cemontenegrom@udistrital.edu.com
[4] Department of Computer Science, Carlos III University, Madrid, Spain
oscar.sanjuan@uc3m.es

Abstract. Some of the technical characteristics of today's mobile devices and Smartphones, such as small displays and keyboards on touch displays contribute to restrict some aspects of user interfaces of software applications. These limitations are especially evident in mobile web applications. The user data entry process in mobile web applications is one of the most critical parts. Today many native mobile applications use the hardware elements from the device (sensors, cameras, GPS, etc) to obtain data directly from the context, preventing the user from having to enter them manually, this approach can improve the user experience, reducing the time spent on data entry and also reducing the odds of mistakes. This paper uses a technology that allows the development of mobile Web applications capable of managing the hardware elements of the device (similar to a native application) in order to extract information directly from the physical world. This technology is used to develop mobile web applications due to be submitted for evaluation processes in order to determine the degree of improvement in user experience that the context information could bring to the mobile web.

Keywords: mobile web, user interfaces, input data, user interaction, context information, mobile devices.

1 Introduction

The intelligent phone, commonly called "Smartphone", has become an emerging phenomenon for both personal and business use. Energy savings in their processors, operating systems, new generation mobiles and Internet connection to broadband have improved productivity and boosted the popularity of these devices [1]. Today, millions of people around the world use their Smartphones daily to browse web pages at anytime

J. Pavón et al. (Eds.): IBERAMIA 2012, LNAI 7637, pp. 732–741, 2012.
© Springer-Verlag Berlin Heidelberg 2012

from anyplace [2]. However, many of the Smartphones have hardware restrictions that can affect the interfaces of web applications, making the access to these from the mobile phone significantly more uncomfortable than from a PC [3]. The physical elements of the Smartphone that influence the user experience the most are [4]:

- Small/limited physical keyboards small/limited or the virtual keyboards displayed on the phone's display. Limited keyboards usually cause errors and contribute to slow down the data entry process.
- Small displays that can rotate. This type of display may cause difficulties for the user to view or select the Web elements and controls [5].
- Processors, Ram memory, storage, and limited computing resources in general.
- "Finger Pointing Device". The finger is less accurate than a mouse cursor.
- Connectivity elements that affect the quality of the the mobile device's connection.

Each of the cited elements has an impact on the user's experience using their mobile device's web applications, issues included: not being able to display a web page specifically without using the zoom and scroll functions, slowdowns in the execution of the pages, non-displayed components, connection losses or very slow data transmission, etc. This work will focus on the data entry of web applications.

Commonly, users enter their data in web applications by using text fields or handling other types of controls, such as checkboxes, radio buttons, lists, etc., the accuracy with which the user can type words or select items in a mobile device is constrained by the interfaces of physical inputs, such as displays and keyboards. Without a doubt, the reduced dimensions of these interfaces contributes to make the process of using Web applications from mobile devices an expensive one for many users, increasing the tendency to make mistakes and increasing the time required to enter information into the web application.

Many native mobile applications that are available for different platforms (iPhone OS, Android, Windows Phone, Symbian, etc) use some of the elements of the Smartphone's hardware (geolocation, light sensor, accelerometer, compass, microphone, camera, Near Field Communication, etc.) to capture contextual information [6] and prevent the user from having to enter it manually, i.e. by using the keyboard. This approach may not be valid for all kinds of systems because their implementation depends largely on the business logic of the application, but it certainly can be useful to simplify automatic data entry processes in many applications. Context information can improve the user's experience and makes compensation for the limited data input mechanisms of mobile devices [7].

There are many different definitions for "context information" [6] as it doesn't seem to be an entirely satisfactory definition. Some researchers have attempted to define this concept by examples [8-9]; other authors have sought more formal definitions [6-10]. Although it has not been possible to reach a completely accepted definition, most of the authors share similar concepts about what we are referring to include the context information. Normally, in the field of information systems context it refers to any information that comes from the real world.

Smartphones are very convenient for the capture and use of context information. These devices normally include many mechanisms such as sensors, microphones, cameras, etc. The number of mobile applications that use the information in context has grown considerably in recent years.

Many applications, such as the commercial ones or those belonging to the field of research, use information directly captured from the real world. This information is often used as an input for certain tasks: [11-12] how to use the GPS to automatically get your position, the camera to decode a barcode, the microphone to capture voice commands, the acceleration sensors to interact with the interfaces, etc.

Some technologies allow web applications to manage some types of context information such as location and motion sensors [13], the use of these proposals can simplify the process of data input by the user in many scenarios, but by focusing exclusively on a small set of context information types, the benefits at improving the user experience are limited. In addition, other proposals have attempted to integrate context-sensitivity (context aware) mobile Webs [14], most of these proposals do not address the impact of context information to improve the user experience, they are mainly focused on providing the mobile web applications with new technical capabilities or features, instead.

The aim of this study is to evaluate the potential benefits of the use of context information on the mobile web, in order to simplify and optimize the quality of procedures for data entry and improve the overall user experience. In this research we are using a context-aware web browser and a set of XML tags that allows developers to include context information requirements in the web applications, giving them the ability to manage the device's hardware elements that native mobile applications posses [15]. We will use this technology to develop several context-aware web applications, which will be evaluated and compared with other conventional web applications in order to determine the impact that the use of context information can bring at improving the user experience, this study will be focused on new possibilities of data-entry applications to the mobile web applications.

2   Background and Related Work

Many studies aim to improve the user's experience by using mobile devices to access Web applications. The improvement of the user's experience can come in many ways, because (as noted above) there are several problems associated to the mobile web (screen size, small keyboards or virtual computing capacity, etc.) [16]. One of the approaches in the underlying of the proposals is to adapt the contents of this website to the technical characteristics of the mobile device. In many cases, content adaptation is achieved by using a schema that defines the structure of the web from an analysis of the layout or from an algorithm that performs a partition of the content of the site in several blocks [17]. Other proposals use similar methods to modify the presentation of the content on the web to make it more efficient and satisfactory to the user that usually visits it from mobile devices with limited features [18-19]. Today's most popular Web applications already have specifically designed versions for mobile devices (Facebook, Youtube, Amazon, PayPal, Google, Ebay, etc). So instead of using methods to adapt the content so that it can be displayed on mobile devices, they choose to create a version optimized for its display on mobile devices.

Even if the display and presentation of the content of the web page are the main objectives on which are based most of the proposals of the authors is not the only aspect that affects the user's experience with mobile web applications [16]. Eliminating the need to zoom and scroll to fully display a website from a mobile phone is a great improvement for users. Sometimes, a better visual representation can help to improve mechanisms for data entry but it can't attack the problems of small/limited physical keyboards or virtual keyboards, which favor the errors and slows down the data entry process.

In addition to manual entry of users's data there are other methods to obtain data, the speech-recognition function is widely used, [20-21] it allows the user to use his voice as a control command. This functionality can be applied to the web, usually for data entry. To implement this technology there are different proposals that should normally be referred to in the web browser and sometimes also in the web application [22-23]. This input method can help the users to free themselves from having to type their data into applications. Sometimes, the speech-recognition function becomes a special requirement for some sites, as it promotes the use of applications for people with vision problems or reduced mobility. At present, there are elements of hardware device used in a generalized manner to facilitate the entry of data on the web. Aside from those microphones used for speech recognition there are APIs that detect the location [13] and sensors on the mobile device. Other proposals increase the number of types of background information that the web can handle, including: camera, light sensor, Bluetooth, etc. [15].

This research aims to use the background information on the mobile web to automate certain data entry processes that used to be performed manually, thus optimizing the quality of procedures and improving the overall user experience.

3   The Context Aware Web Browser

The context-aware web browser is proposed in two parts [15]:

1)   **Server side - Web Applications with Context Information XML Tags**. It defines an open set of XML tags (Context Information XML tags), these tags are included in the presentation layer of web applications, such as HTML code. Each tag expresses a request for specific context information. The traditional web browsers simply ignore the context Information XML tags that are unknown to them.

Each XML tag will be associated to a set of attributes; these attributes can be included as an optional way to configure the capture, processing or response. These tags will be processed on the client's part (context-aware web browser). According to the processed tag, the component determines the actions to be run on the client's device. Several of the context information XML tags are presented in the following table:

Table 1. Subset of context information XML Tags

Context Information XML Tag	Description
<magneticfield/>	Value of the magnetic field sensor. [X,Y,Z]
<orientation/>	Current value of sensor orientation. [X,Y,Z]
<accelerometer/>	Present value of motion sensor. [X,Y,Z]
<lightSensor/>	Present value of light sensor. [0.0-1.0]
<audiocapture/>	Get an audio recording using the microphone on the device. [Audio File]
<camera/>	Gets an image using the device camera. [Image File]
<location/>	Gets the current location of device. [Longitude, Latitude]
<camerabarcode/>	Use the device's camera as a visual scanner to decode a bar code. [String]
<cameraqrcode/>	Use the device's camera as a visual scanner to decode a QR code. [String]
<nfc/>	Uses the communications module of Near Field Communication to write or read labels. [String]
<bluetooth/>	Use the Bluetooth communications module to perform different actions, scanning, connections, sending and receiving data, etc.

2) Client-Side The context aware web browser. This application is responsible for processing the XML tags that express context information requirements. When the context aware web browser processes a context information XML tag, it notifies the user's requirement.

If the user accepts the request, that means that he allows the context aware web browser to manage the device hardware elements capable of satisfying that specific requirement. Once the user has accepted a request, the context aware web browser will run the scheduled task associated with the specific context information XML tag. Usually, scheduled tasks manage one of the elements of the device hardware, with the aim of capturing context information.

The context aware web browser has been specifically designed to display context aware Web applications. It also processes the traditional web languages (HTML, CSS, Javascript) in the same way as a classic web browser (Internet Explorer, Chrome, etc.)

4   Evaluated Mobile Web Applications

To assess the impact on user experience of the data entry by using context information in mobile web applications a particular scenario has been selected:

"implementation of price comparison products in nearby supermarkets", similar to the ShopSavvy application [25]. We have developed two web applications with the same functionality, the first uses traditional web technologies, HTML, CSS and PHP, and the second combines the use of traditional web technologies with context information XML tags, these tags allow the application to receive data directly from the context without the user having to enter them manually.

Both web applications require two elements to search for a product: 1) the user's current location, 2) a unique identifier of the product that can be a name or a bar code.

The context aware web application uses two context information XML tags. It uses a benchmark to perform a search of nearby supermarkets using the device's current location. This location is obtained by using the device's GPS chip, which will use the context XML tag <location/>. The second tag <camerabarcode/> involved will be used to allow the user to identify a product by scanning the bar code itself, instead of entering the product name on a form. The following figure (Fig.1) shows the implementation and appearance of part of the context aware web application:

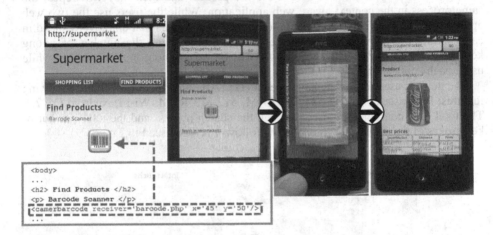

Fig. 1. <camerabarcode/> tag is displayed on the web to inform the user that there is a context-information requirement. When the user clicks on the <camerabarcode/> icon the web browser launches a scheduled task. The data collected by the task is sent to a web server to load the product information.

5   User's Evaluation

This section analyzes the behavior of the user and his level of satisfaction while using web applications that make use of the proposed specification. The following assessment has been done with the participation of 20 regular users of Smartphones. Those users have Smartphones and are used to manage both native applications and web applications from their device.

To perform these evaluations we have used two applications that previously had been developed and presented in Sect. 4. The mobile web applications enable users to search for the best price of a particular product in nearby supermarkets. For this to work, the application requires an identifier or a product name, and also the user's current location. All this data is sent to an external web service that returns the list of nearby supermarkets that sell that product.

The applications that are part of the evaluation process are:

1) **Web application with context information XML tags**: The web application used for evaluation is presented in the previous section. This web application was developed using PHP, HTML and introduces two types of context information XML tags.

2) **Web application**: This is a web application with the same functions of the previous one, the difference here is that the context information XML tags have been replaced by HTML forms. This application is less usable than the first one because it forces the user to enter all the information manually.

In this assessment, the users will use the two applications to perform a search for a product ("Coca-cola Can 33CL") in nearby supermarkets. First, the 20 users will use the classic Web application to search for the product and then they will repeat the same process in the context aware web application. While the users use the two web applications, their actions will be monitored to take the times that employees spend in each action, the number of display keystrokes required and the number of wrong keystrokes performed. Finally, each user will be asked about his satisfaction while using each application.

The devices used for testing have been a HTC Aria Smartphones with the following features: Processor 600 MHz 384 MB RAM, 512 MB ROM, Wi-Fi, Android OS 2.3. The total time consumed by users through the search process and the total number of keystrokes of the display are shown in the following charts (see Fig.2).

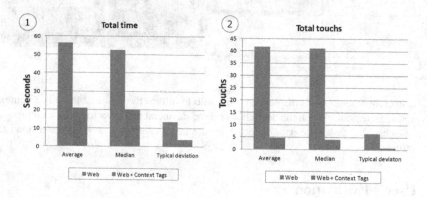

Fig. 2. (1) Graphical representation of the time consumed by users in carrying out actions under the use case. (2) Graphical Representation of the number of keystrokes display performed by users in the implementation of the for the use case.

The following graphic shows the number of errors committed by users, in full and on the number of display keystrokes. Of course, the total number of erroneous keystrokes increase depends on the keystrokes required to complete the search process, so we also analyzed the percentage of keystrokes errors obtained by completing the search process in the two applications (see Fig.3).

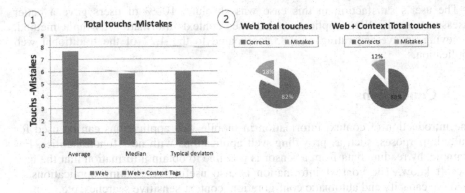

Fig. 3. (1)Graphic representation of the number of errors made in the display keystrokes made by users in the implementation of actions for the use case (2) Statistical comparison between the percentage of keystrokes of correct and wrong display performed by users in the implementation of actions for the use case

Once the search process was completed, the users rated their degree of satisfaction in each applications with a number from 0 to 10. 0 means "not satisfied at all" and 10 stands for "completely satisfied". The meaning of the results and evaluations obtained are shown in the chart below.

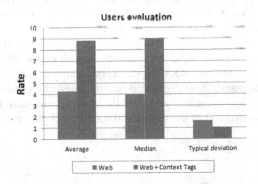

Fig. 4. The page shows the product and the information of nearby supermarkets that shell it

Although the results of this evaluation focus on a specific application, it can draw some valuable general conclusions. In several scenarios, the use of mobile web applications that use specific mechanisms to capture context information as input data can provide very significant benefits to the user experience.

In the case of this application, the contest aware web application has reduced the time spent on the data input by more than 60% and the data entry process requires 10 times less keystrokes than the prior display. Since the number of key display significantly reduced with the incursion of the context information, it has reduced the total number of errors. According to the results of the evaluations, the number of errors not only decreased in absolute sense, but also in relative terms by 5%.

The user's satisfaction in this case was absolute, 100% of users gave a better assessment to the Web application that uses context information as input method, achieving an average rating of 8.83, compared to the 4.27 of the traditional web application.

6   Conclusions

The introduction of context information in mobile web applications can be used for multiple purposes, such as providing web applications with new functionalities. For example, by reading data from a sensor is possible to obtain information that the user doesn't know. The context information is also useful for creating applications of adaptive capacity and automatic configuration, context-sensitive searches, etc.

In this study we have used the context information for mobile web applications to get data directly from a dynamic physical environment and almost automatically, without requiring manual data entry from the user. The use of context information has been adapted to be inputted in mobile web applications with the objective of minimize the negative impact on user experience derived from the manual input on mobile devices with limited physical interfaces. The context aware web browser used to manage mobile web applications from most types of context information that can capture the current Smartphone and allows users to use of this data easily as entries in mobile web application.

Evaluations indicate that the use of data input mechanisms from the physical environment in mobile web applications can have considerable positive aspects for the user experience: reducing the time spent on data entry, reducing the number of display touches needed to interact with an application, decreasing the tendency to make mistakes and improving overall user satisfaction. While it is true that this approach is not applicable to all systems and mobile web applications as part of their application depends on the business logic, it has proven very efficient in some business logic. The demonstration presented in this research opens the discussion on the potential benefits to be gained and mobile applications that offer alternatives (based on context information) to the traditional methods of data entry on the web.

References

1. Chang, Y.F., Chen, C.S., Zhou, H.: Smart Phone for Mobile Commerce. Computer Standards & Interfaces 31(4), 740–747 (2009)
2. W3C Mobile Web Initiative (2012), http://www.w3.org/Mobile/
3. Kaasinen, E., Roto, V., Roloff, K., Väänänen-Vainio-Mattila, K., Vainio, T., Maehr, W., Joshi, D., Shrestha, S.: User Experience of Mobile Internet: Analysis and Recommendations. Intl. Journal of Mobile Human Computer Interaction 1(4), 4–23 (2009)
4. Holmes, J.: Microsoft Is that a Rich Web in Your Pocket? (2011), http://www.slideshare.net/joshholmes/is-that-a-rich-web-in-your-pocket
5. Lee, A.: Exploiting Context for Mobile User Experience. In: Position Papers for the 1st Workshop on Semantic Models for Adaptive Interactive Systems (SEMAIS 2010), pp. 1–4 (2010)
6. Schmidt, A., Aidoo, K.A., Takaluoma, A., Tuomela, U., Van Laerhoven, K., Van de Velde, W.: Advanced Interaction in Context. In: Gellersen, H.-W. (ed.) HUC 1999. LNCS, vol. 1707, pp. 89–101. Springer, Heidelberg (1999)

7. Koskela, T., Kostamo, N., Kassinen, O., Ohtonen, J., Ylianttila, M.: Towards Context-Aware Mobile Web 2.0 Service Architecture. In: 2007 International Conference on Mobile Ubiquitous Computing, Systems, Services and Technologies (UBICOMM 2007), pp. 41–48. IEEE (2007)
8. Chen, H., Finin, T., Joshi, A.: Semantic Web in the Context Broker Architecture. In: 2nd IEEE Annual Conference on Pervasive Computing and Communications (PerCom 2004), pp. 277–286 (2004)
9. Schilit, B., Adams, N., Want, R.: Context-Aware Computing Applications. In: 1st Workshop on Mobile Computing Systems and Applications (WMCSA 1994), pp. 85–90. IEEE (1994)
10. Abowd, G.D., Dey, A.K., Brown, P.J., Davies, N., Smith, M., Steggles, P.: Towards a Better Understanding of Context and Context-Awareness. In: Gellersen, H.-W. (ed.) HUC 1999. LNCS, vol. 1707, pp. 304–307. Springer, Heidelberg (1999)
11. Kim, N., Lee, H.S., Oh, K.J., Choi, J.Y.: Context-Aware Mobile Service for Routing the Fastest Subway Path. Expert Systems with Applications 36(2), 3319–3326 (2009)
12. Lahti, J., Palola, M., Korva, J., Westermann, U., Pentikousis, K., Pietarila, P.: A Mobile Phone-Based Context-Aware Video Management Application. In: Creutzburg, R., Takala, J.H., Chen, C.W. (eds.) Multimedia on Mobile Devices II. Proceedings of the SPIE, vol. 6074, pp. 204–215. International Society for Optics and Photonics (2006)
13. Popescu, A. (ed.): Google Inc.: W3C Geolocation API Specification (2012), http://dev.w3.org/geo/api/spec-source.html
14. Hsu, I.-C.: An Architecture of Mobile Web 2.0 Context-Aware Applications in Ubiquitous Web. Journal of Software 6(4), 705–715 (2011)
15 Pascual, J., Garcia, R., Sanjuan, O., Pelayo, B.C., Cueva, J.M.: Extensible Architecture for Context-Aware Mobile Web Applications. Expert Systems with Applications 39(10), 9686–9694 (2012)
16. Kaasinen, E., Roto, V., Roloff, K., Väänänen-Vainio-Mattila, K., Vainio, T., Maehr, W., Joshi, D., Shrestha, S.: User Experience of Mobile Internet: Analysis and Recommendations. International Journal of Mobile Human Computer Interaction 1(4), 4–23 (2009)
17. Xiao, Y., Tao, Y., Li, Q.: A New Mobile Web Presentation with Better User Experience. In: 2009 International Conference on Networks Security, Wireless Communications and Trusted Computing (NSWCTC 2009), vol. 1, pp. 137–141. IEEE (2009)
18. Hwang, Y., Kim, J., Seo, E.: Structure-Aware Web Transcoding for Mobile Devices. IEEE Internet Computing 7(5), 14–21 (2003)
19. Hwang, Y., Seo, E., Kim, J.: WebAlchemist A Structure-Aware Web Transcoding System for Mobile Devices. In: 2002 WWW Workshop on Mobile Search (2002)
20. Hemphill, C., Muthusamy, Y.: Developing Web-Based Speech Applications. In: 5th European Conference on Speech Communication and Technology (Eurospeech 1997), pp. 895–898 (1997)
21. Digalakis, V.V., Neumeyer, L.G., Perakakis, M.: Quantization of Cepstral Parameters for Speech Recognition over the World Wide Web. IEEE Journal on Selected Areas in Communications 17(1), 82–90 (1999)
22. W3C Voice Browsing (2012), http://www.w3.org/standards/webofdevices/voice
23. Bayer, S.: Embedding Speech in Web Interfaces. In: 4th International Conference on Spoken Language (ICSLP 1996), vol. 3, pp. 1684–1687 (1996)
24. Shopshavy (2012), http://shopsavvy.com/

Author Index

Printed in the United States
by Baker & Taylor Publisher Services